ROBERT V. KAIL   ANNE M. C. BARNFIELD

Children and Their Development

FOURTH CANADIAN EDITION

 Pearson

VICE PRESIDENT, EDITORIAL: Anne Williams
EXECUTIVE ACQUISITIONS EDITOR: Kimberley Veevers
MARKETING MANAGER: Darcey Pepper
CONTENT MANAGER: Madhu Ranadive
PROJECT MANAGER: Colleen Wormald/Christina Veeren
CONTENT DEVELOPER: Martina van de Velde

PRODUCTION SERVICES: Cenveo® Publisher Services
PERMISSIONS PROJECT MANAGER: Kathryn O'Handley
PHOTO PERMISSIONS RESEARCH: iEnergizerAptara®, Ltd.
TEXT PERMISSIONS RESEARCH: iEnergizerAptara®, Ltd.
COVER DESIGNER: Anthony Leung
COVER IMAGE: Rawpixel.com/Shutterstock

Pearson Canada Inc., 26 Prince Andrew Place, North York, Ontario M3C 2H4.

978-0-13-464656-5

1   17

Library and Archives Canada Cataloguing in Publication

Kail, Robert V., author
    Children and their development / Robert V. Kail, Purdue University,
Anne M.C. Barnfield, Brescia University College.—Fourth Canadian edition.

Includes bibliographical references and index.
ISBN 978-0-13-464656-5 (hardcover)

    1. Child development—Textbooks. 2. Textbooks. I. Barnfield, Anne,
author II. Title.

HQ767.9.K33 2018   305.231   C2017-906755-9

To Laura, Matt, and Ben
— Robert V. Kail

To my father and stepmother, Philip and
Christine Barnfield—educators
— Anne M. C. Barnfield

Brief Contents

Contents

List of Boxes

FOCUS ON RESEARCH

CULTURAL INFLUENCES

CHILDREN'S LIVES

SPOTLIGHT ON THEORIES

Preface

Like many professors-turned-textbook-authors, Robert Kail wrote this book because none of the texts available met the aims of the child-development classes that he taught. This, the fourth Canadian edition, does so from a Canadian perspective. In the next few paragraphs, we want to describe those aims and how this book is designed to achieve them.

Goal 1: Use effective pedagogy to promote students' learning. The focus on a student-friendly book begins with the structure of the chapters. Each chapter consists of three or four modules that provide a clear and well-defined organization to the chapter. Each module begins with a set of learning objectives and a vignette that introduces the topic to be covered. Special topics that are set off in other textbooks as feature boxes are fully integrated with the main text and identified by a distinctive icon. Every feature ends with at least one critical thinking question to encourage students' engagement with the material presented. Each module ends with several questions intended to help students check their understanding of the major ideas in the module.

The end of each chapter includes several additional study aids. Unifying Themes links the ideas in the chapter to a major developmental theme. See for Yourself suggests activities that allow students to observe firsthand topics in child development. Resources includes books and websites where students can learn more about child development. Key Terms is a list of all of the important boldfaced terms appearing in the chapter. The Summary is a concise, one-page review of the chapter. The Test Yourself questions further confirm and cement students' understanding of the chapter material.

These different pedagogical elements *do* work; students using previous editions frequently comment that the book is easy to read and presents complex topics in an understandable way.

Goal 2: Use fundamental developmental issues as a foundation for students' learning of research and theory in child development. Child-development courses sometimes overwhelm students because of the sheer number of topics and studies. In fact, today's child-development science is really propelled by a concern with a handful of fundamental developmental issues, such as the continuity of development and the roles of nature and nurture in development. In *Children and Their Development*, four of these foundational issues are introduced in Chapter 1, then reappear in subsequent chapters to scaffold students' understanding. As we mentioned already, the end of the chapter includes the Unifying Themes feature, in which the ideas from the chapter are used to illustrate one of the foundational themes. By reappearing throughout the text, the themes remind students of the core issues that drive child-development science.

Goal 3: Teach students that child-development science draws on many complementary research methods, each of which contributes uniquely to scientific progress. In Module 1.4, we portray child-development research as a dynamic process in which scientists make a series of decisions as they plan their work. In the process, they create a study that has both strengths and weaknesses. Each of the remaining chapters of the book contains a Focus on Research feature that illustrates this process by showing—in an easy-to-read, question-and-answer format—the different decisions that investigators made in designing a particular study. The results are shown, usually with an annotated figure, so that students can learn how to interpret graphs. The investigators' conclusions are described, and we end each Focus on Research feature by mentioning the kind of converging evidence that would strengthen the authors' conclusions. Thus, the research methods introduced in Chapter 1 reappear in every chapter, depicting research as a collaborative enterprise that depends on the contributions of many scientists using different methods.

Goal 4: Show students how findings from child-development research can improve children's lives. Child-development scientists and students alike want to know how the findings of research can be used to promote children's development. In Chapter 1 of *Children and Their Development*, we describe the different means by which researchers can use their work to improve children's lives. In the chapters that follow, these ideas come alive in the Children's Lives feature, which provides examples of research-based solutions to common problems in children's lives. From these features, students realize that child-development research really matters—that parents, teachers, and policymakers can use research to foster children's development.

New to the Fourth Canadian Edition

The fourth Canadian edition of *Children and Their Development* has improvements to the Canadian perspective, highlighting more work by Canadian researchers. More international research and information is also included. In updating this textbook, we have added many new citations and references to research published since 2014. Demographic information and statistics, such as birth rates have been revised, where new information exists. We have also added new content to every chapter. Of particular note:

Chapter 1 has some revision of descriptions of theories in child development; also, updated examples of different research methods with expanded information on, and examples of, field experiments.

Chapter 2 has updated information, including updates regarding access to IVF in Canada; a new Focus on Research feature on hereditary bases of peer relationships; extensively revised material on molecular genetics and its application; and new material about methylation as an epigenetic mechanism.

Chapter 3 has updated information on fetal behaviour and abilities; a revised and updated Spotlight on Theories feature, with Canadian information; new material on environmental pollutants, including some updates to the Focus on Research feature on links between environmental toxins and sex ratios; information on the Zika virus and its effects; additional information regarding prenatal development, especially sensory development; an updated section on the impact of cocaine, revised material on the impact of epidural analgesia; updated information on home versus hospital birth; additional information on prematurity and its long-term effects for the child; and updates on sudden infant death, now referred to as sudden unexpected infant death (SUID).

Chapter 4 includes revised material on sleep; revisions to the section on nutrition, including an updated section on ways to encourage young children to eat healthfully; additional information on Canadian Indigenous peoples in the Cultural Influences box; much-revised material on the impact of timing of maturation on boys' development; a new list of factors that lead to obesity, with additional information and updated statistics on obesity rates in Canada; updated Focus on Research feature on face processing, now utilizing Canadian research.

Chapter 5 has much revised coverage of face perception, noting Canadian research in this area; new coverage of attention, including information on recently described networks of attentional processes and their development and updates to the section on ADHD.

Chapter 6 includes information on Canadian research on Indigenous storytelling as a form of scaffolding; contains much-revised coverage of executive function and of naïve psychology (now called folk psychology); and a revised section on Theory of Mind in Autism, including important Canadian research in this area.

Chapter 7 includes updates on children's use of memory strategies; new material on the impact of children's misconceptions on their scientific thinking; and much-revised coverage of reading and of quantitative reasoning.

Chapter 8 has completely revised coverage of dynamic assessment (formerly, dynamic testing); updates to the Cultural Influences box, including information on Canadian Indigenous peoples; a new Focus on Research feature on making tests less threatening to counter stereotype threat; a new Spotlight on Theory feature on the nature of impaired reading comprehension; and much-reorganized material on gifted children.

Chapter 9 contains revised coverage of the role of sentence cues in word learning; updated information on cochlear implants; a new Focus on Research feature on why exposure to parents' speech increases children's vocabulary; and much-revised coverage on language acquisition in bilingual children.

Chapter 10 includes updates and new material on regulation of emotion; a much-revised Spotlight on Theories feature; much-revised information on temperament and its links to personality, including revisions to the Cultural Influences box; and a new Focus on Research feature on the long-term consequences of temperament.

Chapter 11 has reorganized coverage of self-recognition, self-awareness, and self-esteem—including new material on narcissism; revised information on identity formation and ethnic identity; and a revised section on prejudice that includes new material on the impact of discriminatory behaviour.

Chapter 12 contains new material on moral thinking as a core domain; a much-revised Cultural Influences feature; new material on the role of oxytocin in promoting social behaviour; an updated Spotlight on Theories feature; and much-revised coverage of victims of aggression, including new information on victimization and an effective anti-bullying program.

Chapter 13 has extensively revised coverage of gender-related differences including new information on differences in memory and in effortful control as well as depression in adolescents; and revised coverage of cognitive theories of gender identity, including additional material on gender schemata and effects of gender essentialism.

Chapter 14 contains new material on cultural and socioeconomic influences on parenting styles; additional material on intervention programs that teach parenting skills; updates to the feature on Grandmothers in Indigenous families; much-revised coverage of adopted children, including new material on open adoption; new material on children's play and friendships; new information on links between poverty, stress, and children's health; additions on the impact of political violence and homelessness on children's development; and revisions and updates to the sections on contributions to school success of programs for mentoring and teacher training.

Support Materials

Children and Their Development, Fourth Canadian Edition, is accompanied by a superb set of ancillary materials. They include the following:

MEDIA SUPPLEMENTS

- **MyVirtualChild.** MyVirtualChild is an interactive simulation that allows students to play the role of parent and raise their own virtual child. By making decisions about specific scenarios, students can raise their child from birth to age 18 and learn first-hand how their own decisions and other parenting actions affect their children over time. MyVirtualChild helps students think critically as they apply their course work to the practical experiences of raising a virtual child. You can access MyVirtualChild at www.myvirtualchild.com.

INSTRUCTOR SUPPLEMENTS

PEARSON
my test

MyTest: Pearson MyTest is a powerful assessment-generation program that helps instructors easily create and print quizzes, tests, exams, as well as homework or practice handouts. Questions and tests can all be authored online, allowing instructors ultimate flexibility and the ability to efficiently manage assessments at any time, from anywhere. MyTest for *Children and Their Development* contains over 2000 multiple-choice, true/false, and short-answer essay questions, which are also available in Microsoft Word format (see below).

The following supplements can be downloaded from a password-protected section of Pearson Education Canada's online catalogue (**www.pearsoncanada.ca/**). Navigate to your book's catalogue page to view a list of those supplements that are available. See your local sales representative for details and access.

Instructor's Resource Manual: Each chapter in the manual includes the following resources: Chapter Learning Objectives; Lecture Suggestions and Discussion Topics; Classroom Activities, Demonstrations, and Exercises; Out-of-Class Assignments and Projects; Lecture Notes; Multimedia Resources; Video Resources; and Handouts. Designed to make your lectures more effective and to save you preparation time, this extensive resource gathers together the most effective activities and strategies for teaching your developmental psychology course. The Instructor's Manual is in PDF format.

PowerPoint Presentations: Each chapter's PowerPoint presentation highlights the key points covered in the text.

Image Library: This set of images, illustrations, figures, and charts from the text is provided in electronic format for instructor use.

Test Item File: The test bank in Microsoft Word format contains over 2000 multiple-choice, true/false, and short-answer essay questions. The test bank is also available in MyTest format (see above).

Pearson Custom Library For enrollments of at least 25 students, you can create your own textbook by choosing the chapters that best suit your own course needs. To begin building your custom text, visit www.pearsoncustomlibrary.com. You may also work with a dedicated Pearson Custom editor to create your ideal text—publishing your own original content or mixing and matching Pearson content. Contact your local Pearson Representative to get started.

To the Student

In this book, we'll trace children's development from conception through adolescence. Given this goal, you may expect to find chapters devoted to early childhood, middle childhood, and the like. But this book is organized differently—around topics. Chapters 2 through 5 are devoted to the genetic and biological bases of human development, and the growth of perceptual and motor skills. Chapters 6 through 9 cover intellectual development—how children learn, think, reason, and solve problems. Chapters 10 through 14 concern social and emotional development—how children acquire the customs of their society and learn to play the social roles expected of them.

This organization reflects the fact that when scientists conduct research on children's development, they usually study how some specific aspect of how a child develops. For example, a researcher might study how memory changes as children grow or how friendship in childhood differs from that in adolescence. Thus, the organization of this book reflects the way researchers actually study child development.

ORGANIZATION OF CHAPTERS AND LEARNING AIDS

Each of the chapters (except Chapter 1) includes several modules that are listed at the beginning of each chapter. Each module begins with a set of learning objectives phrased as questions, a mini-outline listing the major subheadings of the module, and a brief vignette that introduces the topics to be covered in the module. The learning objectives, mini-outline, and vignette tell you what to expect in the module.

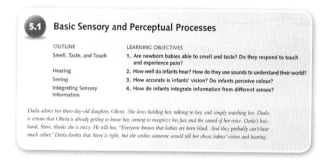

Each module in Chapters 2 through 14 includes at least one special feature that expands or highlights a topic. There are four different kinds of features; you can recognize each one by its distinctive icon:

Focus on Research provides details on the design and methods used in a particular research study. Closely examining specific studies demystifies research and shows that scientific work is a series of logical steps conducted by real people.

Cultural Influences shows how culture influences children and illustrates that developmental journeys are diverse. All children share the biological aspects of development, but their cultural contexts differ. This feature celebrates the developmental experiences of children from different backgrounds.

Children's Lives shows how research and theory can be applied to improve children's development. These practical solutions to everyday problems show the relevance of research and theory to real life, and show how results from research are used to create social policy that is designed to improve the lives of children and their families.

Spotlight on Theories examines an influential theory of development and shows how it has been tested in research.

Two other elements are designed to help you focus on the main points of the text. First, whenever a key term is introduced in the text, it appears in *Blue bold italic* like this, and the definition appears in **black boldface type.** This format should make key terms easier for you to find and learn. Second, summary tables appear periodically throughout the book, reviewing key ideas and providing a capsule account of each. For example, the following Summary Table shows the many study aids that we've included in the book.

SUMMARY TABLE

STUDY AIDS USED IN CHILDREN AND THEIR DEVELOPMENT, THIRD CANADIAN EDITION

Study Aid	Key Features
Module-opening material	Learning objectives, vignette, mini-outline
Special features	Focus on Research, Children's Lives, Cultural Influences, Spotlight on Theories, each with Critical Thinking questions
Design elements that promote learning	Boldface key terms defined in text, summary tables (like this one)
Check Your Learning	Recall, interpret, and apply questions
End-of-chapter material	Unifying Themes, See for Yourself, Resources, Key Terms, Summary, Self-test

Each module concludes with Check Your Learning questions to help you review the major ideas in that module. As you can see in the inset, there are three kinds of questions: recall, interpret, and apply.

 Check Your Learning

RECALL List the major parts of a nerve cell and the major regions of the cerebral cortex.

Describe evidence that shows the brain's plasticity.

INTERPRET Compare growth of the brain before birth with growth of the brain after birth.

APPLY How does the development of the brain, as described in this module, compare to the general pattern of physical growth described in Module 4.1?

If you can answer the questions in Check Your Learning correctly, you are on your way to mastering the material in the module. However, do not rely exclusively on Check Your Learning as you study for exams. The questions are designed to give you a quick check of your understanding, not a comprehensive assessment of your knowledge of the entire module.

At the very end of each chapter are several additional study aids. Unifying Themes links the contents of the chapter to the developmental themes introduced in Module 1.3. See for Yourself suggests some simple activities for exploring issues in child development on your own. Resources includes books and websites where you can learn more about children and their development. Key Terms is a list of all the important terms that appear in the chapter, along with the page where each term is defined. The Summary provides a concise review of the entire chapter, organized by module and the primary headings within the module. Finally, the Test Yourself questions further confirm and cement your understanding of the chapter material.

TERMINOLOGY

Every field has its own terminology, and child development is no exception. We use several terms to refer to different periods of infancy, childhood, and adolescence. Although these terms are familiar, we use each to refer to a specific range of ages:

Newborn	Birth to 1 month
Infant	1 month to 1 year
Toddler	1 to 2 years
Preschooler	2 to 6 years
School-age child	6 to 12 years
Adolescent	12 to 18 years
Adult	18 years and older

Sometimes for the sake of variety we use other terms that are less tied to specific ages, such as *babies, youngsters,* and *elementary-school children.* When we do, you will be able to tell from the context what groups are being described.

We also use very specific terminology in describing research findings from different cultural and ethnic groups. The appropriate terms to describe different cultural, racial, and ethnic groups change over time. For example, the terms *coloured people, Negroes, Black Canadians,* and *African Canadians* have all been used to describe Canadians who trace their ancestry to Africa. In this book, we use the term *African Canadian* because it emphasizes the unique cultural heritage of this group of people. Following this same line of reasoning, we use the terms *European Canadian* (instead of *Caucasian* or *white*), *Indigenous* (instead of *First Nations, Métis, Inuit, Indian* or *American Indian*), *Asian Canadian,* and *Latin American Canadian.*

These labels are not perfect. Sometimes they blur distinctions within ethnic groups. For example, the term *Hispanic Canadian* ignores differences between individuals who came to Canada from Puerto Rico, Mexico, and Guatemala; the term *Asian Canadian* blurs variations among people whose heritage is East Indian, Japanese, Chinese, or Korean. Whenever researchers identified the subgroups in their research sample, we use the more specific terms in describing results. When you see the more general terms, remember that conclusions may not apply to all subgroups within the group.

A Final Word

Robert Kail wrote the first American edition of this book to make child development come alive for his students at Purdue. Although we can't teach you directly, we hope this book sparks your interest in children and their development. Please let us know what you like and dislike about the book so that it can be improved in later editions. You can email me, Anne Barnfield, at abarnfie@uwo.ca— I'd love to hear from you.

Acknowledgments

For the Canadian editions of the book, I would like to thank those who helped with the original work. In addition, I would like to thank the following reviewers for their many helpful comments and suggestions:

Tina Bonnett, Fanshawe College
Leanna Closson, Saint Mary's University
Sandra Hessels, Huron University College at Western University
Alissa Pencer, Dalhousie University
Jill Singleton-Jackson, University of Windsor

I must also thank Ky Pruesse for the initial concept of the Canadian edition; Kimberley Veevers, Acquisitions Editor, who started the editing process; Martina van de Velde, who continued the process; and, for the fourth edition, Christina Vereen, Ruth Chernia, and Kritika Kaushik, who brought the book through production. I would also like to thank Annamarie Chalikakis for her invaluable assistance when this whole process began and Brescia students Kasha McEwen (with the first edition). Sileny Chamorro (for the second edition), and Zeena Wong (who saved me much time with this, fourth edition!) for their assistance in retrieving information and performing literature searches. My husband, Richard Van de Wetering, as ever, deserves special thanks for his patience and understanding.
—*Anne M. C. Barnfield*

About the Authors

Robert V. Kail is a Distinguished Professor of Psychological Sciences at Purdue University. His undergraduate degree is from Ohio Wesleyan University, and his PhD is from the University of Michigan. Kail is editor of *Child Development Perspectives* and the editor emeritus of *Psychological Science*. He received the McCandless Young Scientist Award from the American Psychological Association, was named the Distinguished Sesquicentennial Alumnus in Psychology by Ohio Wesleyan University, and is a fellow of the Association for Psychological Science. He has also written *Scientific Writing for Psychology: Lessons in Clarity and Style*. His research focuses on cognitive development during childhood and adolescence. Away from the office, he enjoys photography and working out. His website is **http://www2.psych.purdue.edu/~rk/home.html.**

Anne M. C. Barnfield is an Associate Professor of Psychology at Brescia University College. Her undergraduate degree is from the University of London, UK, and her PhD is from the University of Sussex, UK. Barnfield is a manuscript reviewer for the journals *Personality and Individual Differences*, *Perceptual and Motor Skills*, and the *Human-Animal Interaction Bulletin*, as well as an occasional book reviewer for *The Journal of Asian Martial Arts*. She is a member of the APA Human-Animal Interaction Division, the Society for the Teaching of Psychology, and the Canadian Society for Brain, Behaviour and Cognitive Science. Her research focuses on the beneficial influences of sport participation for children, particularly those with special needs, and applications of Equine Assisted Therapy, with a focus on anxiety disorders. Away from the office, she enjoys karate, archery, and horseback riding. The Brescia University College website is: **http://www.brescia.uwo.ca/.**

1 The Science of Child Development

Marzanna Syncerz/Fotolia

Setting the Stage

Foundational Theories of Child Development

Themes in Child-Development Research

Doing Child-Development Research

Beginning as a microscopic cell, every person takes a fascinating journey designed to lead to adulthood. This trip is filled with remarkably interesting and challenging events. In this text, we'll trace this journey as we learn about the science of child development, a multidisciplinary study of all aspects of human growth from conception to young adulthood. As an adult, you've already lived the years that are at the heart of this text. We hope you enjoy reviewing your own developmental path from the perspective of child-development research and that this perspective leads you to new insights into the developmental forces that have made you the person you are today.

Chapter 1 sets the stage for our study of child development. We begin, in **Module 1.1**, by looking at philosophical foundations for child development and the events that led to the creation of child development as a new science. In **Module 1.2**, we examine theories that are central to the science of child development. In **Module 1.3**, we explore themes that guide much of the research in child development. Finally, in **Module 1.4**, we learn about the methods scientists use to study children and their development.

1.1 Setting the Stage

OUTLINE

Historical Views of Children and Childhood

Origins of a New Science

LEARNING OBJECTIVES

1. What ideas did philosophers have about children and childhood?
2. How did the modern science of child development emerge?
3. How do child-development scientists use research findings to improve children's lives?

Kendra loves her 12-month-old son, Joshua, but she is eager to return to her job as a loan officer at a local bank. Kendra knows a woman in her neighbourhood who has cared for some of her friends' children, and they all think she is wonderful. But deep down, Kendra wishes she knew more about whether this type of care is really best for Joshua. She also wishes that her neighbour's daycare centre had a "stamp of approval" from someone who knows how to evaluate such facilities.

Kendra's question about the best way to care for her infant son is just the most recent in a long line of questions that she has had about Joshua since he was born. When Joshua was a newborn, Kendra wondered if he could recognize her face and her voice. As her son grows, she'll continue to have questions: Why is he so shy at preschool? Should he take classes for gifted children or would he be better off in regular classes? What can she do to be sure that he won't use drugs?

These questions—and hundreds more like them—touch issues and concerns that parents such as Kendra confront regularly as they do their best to rear their children. And parents are not the only ones asking these questions. Many professionals who deal with children—teachers, healthcare providers, and social workers, for example—often wonder what is best for children's development. Does children's self-esteem affect their success in school? Should we believe young children when they claim they have been abused? As well, government officials must decide what programs and laws provide the greatest benefit for children and their families. How does welfare reform affect families? Are teenagers less likely to have sex when they participate in abstinence-only programs?

So many questions, and all of them important! Fortunately, the field of child development, which traces physical, mental, social, and emotional development from conception to maturity, provides answers to many of them. To begin, let's look at the origins of child development as a science.

Historical Views of Children and Childhood

For thousands of years, philosophers have speculated on the fundamental nature of childhood and the conditions that foster a child's well-being. The Greek philosophers Plato (428–347 BCE) and Aristotle (384–322 BCE) believed that schools and parents had responsibility for teaching children the self-control that would make them effective citizens. But both philosophers, particularly Aristotle, also worried that too much self-discipline would stifle children's initiative and individuality, making them unfit to be leaders.

Plato and Aristotle also had ideas about knowledge and how it is acquired. Plato believed that experience could not be the source of knowledge because human senses are too fallible. He argued instead that children are born with innate knowledge of many concrete objects (such as animals and people), as well as with knowledge of abstractions (such as courage, love, and goodness). In Plato's view, children's sensory experiences simply trigger knowledge that they've had since birth. The first time a child sees a dog, her innate knowledge allows her to recognize it as such; no learning is necessary. In contrast, Aristotle denied the existence of innate knowledge, believing instead that knowledge is rooted in perceptual experience. Children acquire knowledge piece by piece, based on the information provided by their senses.

These contrasting views resurfaced during the Age of Enlightenment. The English philosopher John Locke (1632–1704) asserted that the human infant is a *tabula rasa*, or "blank slate," and claimed that experience moulds the infant, child, adolescent, and adult into a unique individual. According to Locke, parents should instruct, reward, and discipline young children, gradually relaxing their authority as children grow. In our opening vignette, Locke would have advised Kendra that childcare experiences will undoubtedly affect Joshua's development (although Locke would not specify how).

During the following century, Locke's view was challenged by the French philosopher Jean-Jacques Rousseau (1712–1778), who believed that newborns are endowed with an innate sense of justice and morality that unfolds naturally as the child grows. During this unfolding, children move through the same developmental stages that we recognize today—infancy, childhood, and adolescence. Rather than emphasizing parental discipline, Rousseau argued that parents should be responsive, and he encouraged them to be receptive to their children's needs, as he explained in his book *Émile*, written in 1762. Rousseau would emphasize the value of caregivers who are responsive to Joshua's needs.

Rousseau shared Plato's view that children begin their developmental journey well prepared with a stockpile of knowledge. Locke, like Aristotle two thousand years before, believed that children begin their journey packed lightly, picking up necessary knowledge along the way, through experience. These debates might have continued to be solely philosophical for millennia except for a landmark event: the emergence of child development as a science.

Origins of a New Science

The push toward child development as a science came in part from the significant role played by children themselves during the momentous transformation of the working environment in England known as the Industrial Revolution, which began in the mid-eighteenth century. For much of recorded history, as soon as children no longer needed constant care from adults—by about five to seven years of age—they were considered grown up and entered the world of work. Many children worked at home, in the fields, or were apprenticed to learn a trade. Beginning in the mid-1700s, England moved from a largely rural culture relying on agriculture to an urban-oriented society organized around factories, especially textile mills. Children moved with their families to cities and worked long hours in factories and in mines under horrendous conditions and for little pay (Postman, 1982). Accidents were common, and many children were maimed or killed. In textile mills, for example, the youngest children often had the hazardous job of picking up loose cotton from beneath huge power looms while the machines were in operation.

Reformers, appalled at these conditions, worked hard to enact legislation that would limit child labour and put more children in schools. These initiatives were the subject of political debates throughout much of the 1800s; after all, factory owners were among the most powerful people in Britain, and they adamantly opposed efforts to limit access to plentiful cheap labour. But the reformers ultimately carried the day and, in the process, made the well-being of children a national concern.

Another major event that set the stage for the new science of child development was the publication of Charles Darwin's theory of evolution. Darwin (1859) argued that individuals within a species differ; some individuals are better adapted to a particular environment, making them more likely to survive and to pass along their characteristics to future generations. Some scientists of the day noted similarities between Darwin's description of evolutionary change within species and the age-related changes in human behaviour. **This prompted many scientists, including Darwin himself, to write what became known as** *baby biographies*—**detailed, systematic observations of individual children.** The observations in the biographies were often subjective, and conclusions were sometimes reached on the basis of minimal evidence. Nevertheless, the systematic and extensive records in baby biographies paved the way for objective, analytic research.

Taking the lead in this new science at the dawn of the twentieth century was G. Stanley Hall (1844–1924), who generated theories of child development based on evolutionary theory and conducted studies to determine age trends in children's beliefs and feelings about a range of topics. Perhaps more importantly, Hall founded the first English-language scientific journal in which scientists could publish findings from child-development research. Hall also founded a child study institute at Clark University and was the first president of the American Psychological Association.

Meanwhile, in France, Alfred Binet (1857–1911) had begun to devise the first mental tests, which we'll examine in Module 8.2. In Austria, Sigmund Freud (1856–1939) startled the world by suggesting that the experiences of early childhood seemed to account for patterns of behaviour in adulthood. And American John B. Watson (1878–1958), the founder of behaviourism, began to write and lecture on the importance of reward and punishment for childrearing practices. (You'll learn more about Freud's and Watson's contributions in Module 1.2.)

Psychological research in Canada also dates from the late 1800s, when psychology was studied in departments of philosophy, a usual occurrence at that time. In 1920, the psychology department of the University of Toronto became the first to be independent of philosophy (Pols, 2002).

An important figure in the early study of psychology in Canada is James Mark Baldwin (1861–1934). Baldwin, an American and a graduate of Princeton, is known for

 QUESTION 1.1
Morgan is 18 months old. Her father believes she should have a very structured day, one that includes some physical activity, time spent reading and doing puzzles, and, finally, lots of reassuring hugs and kisses. Is Morgan's dad a believer in Rousseau's or Locke's view of childhood? *(Answer is on page 7.)*

his research at the University of Toronto, where he was appointed to the department of philosophy in 1889. There he set up the first psychology laboratory in Canada, which began research in 1891 (Hoff, 1992). Baldwin felt that a theoretical basis for experimentation was important and seems to have felt that baby biographies stifled theory, being too focused on observation (Harris, 1985). He himself performed experimental research, for example, on infant handedness, and tested proposals derived from his theories.

The Canadian Psychological Association (CPA) was founded in the late 1930s. The idea was initially proposed in 1938, during the American Association for the Advancement of Science (AAAS) meeting held in June of that year at the Château Laurier hotel in Ottawa. At that meeting, a group of Canadian psychologists met to discuss founding a specifically Canadian organization (Dzinas, 2000). Following this first meeting, a draft constitution was drawn up, and the CPA was founded in 1939 (Dzinas, 2000; Ferguson, 1992).

It was in 1933, however, that the emerging scientific forces in developmental psychology came together in a new interdisciplinary organization called the Society for Research in Child Development (SRCD). Its members included psychologists, physicians, educators, anthropologists, and biologists, all of whom were linked by a common interest in discovering the conditions that could promote children's welfare and foster their development (Parke, 2004). In the ensuing years, SRCD membership has grown to more than 5000 and is now the main professional organization for child-development researchers. SRCD, along with similar organizations devoted to child-development science (e.g., International Society for the Study of Behavioural Development, International Society on Infant Studies, Society for Research on Adolescence) promotes multidisciplinary research and encourages the application of research findings to improve children's lives.

Progress in developmental psychology was halted by World War II, when most child-development scientists in North America abandoned their research to assist the war effort (Sears, 1975)—for example, Canadian psychologists advised the Royal Air Force in England on training methods (English, 1992; Ferguson, 1992). Many female psychologists also became well known during this time, taking on leading roles in both military and non-military activities (Wright, 1992).

After the war, women became more prominent in the CPA, with some becoming directors on the governing board of the association (Wright, 1992). Psychology as a discipline grew, and by the 1950s and 1960s developmental psychology was thriving, marking the beginning of the modern era of child-development research.

More recently, a new branch of child-development research has emerged. *Applied developmental science* **uses developmental research to promote healthy development, particularly for vulnerable children and families** (Lerner, Fisher, & Giannino, 2006). Scientists with this research interest contribute to sound family policy in a number variety of ways (Shonkoff & Bales, 2011). Some ensure that the consideration of policy issues and options is based on factual knowledge derived from child-development research. For example, when government officials need to address problems affecting children, child-development experts provide useful information about children and their development (Fasig, 2002; Shonkoff & Bales, 2011). Others contribute by serving as advocates for children. Working with child advocacy groups, child-development researchers alert policymakers to children's needs and argue for family policy that addresses those needs. Still other child-development experts evaluate the impact of government policies on children and families (e.g., the effectiveness of provincial regulation of Children's Aid Societies). Finally, one of the best ways to sway policymakers is to create working programs. When researchers create a program that effectively combats problems affecting children or adolescents (e.g., sudden infant death syndrome or teenage pregnancy), this can become powerful ammunition for influencing policy (Huston, 2008).

Thus, from its origins more than 100 years ago, modern child-development science has become a mature discipline, generating a vast catalogue of knowledge from which exciting discoveries continue to emerge. Scientists actively use this knowledge to improve the lives of children, as we'll see in the Children's Lives features that appear throughout this text. The research that you'll encounter in this textbook is rooted in a set of developmental theories that provide the foundation of modern child-development research. These theories are the focus of the next module.

 ANSWER 1.1
His emphasis on structure suggests that he believes in the importance of children's experiences, which is a basic concept in Locke's view of childhood.

 Check Your Learning

RECALL What two events set the stage for the creation of child-development science?

Who were the leaders in the new field of child development before the formation of the Society for Research in Child Development?

INTERPRET Explain the similarities between Rousseau's and Plato's views of child development; how did their views differ from those shared by Locke and Aristotle?

APPLY Suppose a child-development researcher is an expert on the impact of nutrition on children's physical and emotional development. Describe several different ways in which the researcher might help inform public policy concerning children's nutrition.

 Foundational Theories of Child Development

OUTLINE

The Biological Perspective

The Psychodynamic Perspective

The Learning Perspective

The Cognitive-Developmental Perspective

The Contextual Perspective

LEARNING OBJECTIVES

1. What are the major tenets of the biological perspective?

2. How do psychodynamic theories account for development?

3. What is the focus of learning theories?

4. How do cognitive-developmental theories explain changes in children's thinking?

5. What are the main points of the contextual approach?

Will has just graduated from high school, first in his class. For his mother, Betty, this is a time to reflect on Will's past and ponder his future. Will has always been a happy, easygoing child and he has always been interested in learning. Betty wonders why he is so perpetually good-natured and so curious. If she knew the secret, she laughs, she could write a best-selling book and be a guest on daytime TV shows like Dr. Phil!

Before you read on, stop for a moment and think about Betty's question. How would you explain Will's interest in learning, his good nature, and his curiosity? Perhaps Betty has been a fantastic mother, doing all the right things at just the right time. Perhaps, year after year, his teachers quickly recognized Will's curiosity and encouraged it. Or was it simply Will's destiny to be this way? Each of these explanations is a very simple theory; each tries to explain Will's curiosity and good nature. In child-development research, theories are much more complicated, but their purpose is the same: to explain behaviour and development. **In child development science, a *theory* is an organized set of ideas that is designed to explain and make predictions about development.**

Theories lead to hypotheses that we can test in research; in the process, each hypothesis is confirmed or rejected. Think about the different explanations for Will's behaviour. Each one leads to a unique hypothesis. If, for example, teacher encouragement has caused Will to be curious, we hypothesize that he would no longer be curious if his teachers stop encouraging that curiosity. When the outcomes of research are as hypothesized, a theory gains support. When results run counter to the hypothesis, the theory is deemed incorrect and revised. Revised theories then provide the basis for new hypotheses, which lead to new research, and the cycle continues. With each step along the way, a theory comes closer to becoming a complete account. In the Spotlight on Theories features throughout this text we'll look at specific theories, the hypotheses derived from them, and the outcomes of the research that tests those hypotheses.

Over the history of child development as a science, many theories have guided research and thinking about children's development. The earliest developmental theories were useful in generating research, and findings from that research led child-development scientists to newer, improved, or different theories. In this module, we describe the earlier theories that provided the scientific foundation for modern ones, because the newer theories described later in this text are best understood in terms of their historical roots.

Some theories share assumptions and ideas about children and development. Grouped together, they form five major theoretical perspectives in child-development research: the biological, psychodynamic, learning, cognitive-developmental, and contextual perspectives. As you read about each perspective in the next few pages, think about how each one differs from the others in its view of development.

The Biological Perspective

According to the biological perspective, intellectual and personality development, as well as physical and motor development, are rooted in biology. One of the first biological theories—maturational theory—was proposed by Arnold Gesell (1880–1961). **According to *maturational theory,* child development reflects a specific and pre-arranged scheme or plan within the body.** In Gesell's view, development is simply a natural unfolding of a biological plan; experience matters little. Like Jean-Jacques Rousseau 200 years before him, Gesell encouraged parents to let their children develop naturally. Without interference from adults, Gesell claimed, behaviours such as speech, play, and reasoning would emerge spontaneously according to a predetermined developmental timetable.

Maturational theory was eventually discarded because it had little to say about the impact of environment on children's development. However, other biological theories give greater weight to experience. *Ethological theory* **views development from an evolutionary perspective.** In this theory, many behaviours are adaptive—they have survival value. For example, clinging, grasping, and crying are adaptive for infants because they elicit caregiving from adults. Ethological theorists assume that people inherit many of these adaptive behaviours.

So far, ethological theory seems like maturational theory, with a dash of evolution added. How does experience fit in? Ethologists believe that all animals are biologically programmed in such a way that some kinds of learning occur only at certain ages. **A** *critical period* **in development is the time when a specific type of learning can take place; before or after the critical period the same learning is difficult or even impossible.**

One of the best-known examples of a critical period comes from the work of Konrad Lorenz (1903–1989), an Austrian zoologist who noticed that newly hatched geese followed their mother about. He theorized that goslings are biologically programmed to follow the first moving object they see after hatching. **Usually this was the mother, so following her was the first step in** *imprinting,* **creating an emotional bond with the mother.** Lorenz tested his theory by showing that if he removed the mother immediately after the geese hatched and replaced it with another moving object, the goslings would follow that object and treat it as "Mother." As the photo shows, the replacement objects could even be humans and, in his early experiments, included Lorenz himself. The gosling had to see the moving object within about a day of hatching, however, or it would not imprint on the moving object. In other words, the critical period for imprinting lasts about a day; when goslings experience the moving object outside of the critical period, imprinting does not take place. Even though the underlying mechanism is biological, experience is essential for triggering the programmed, adaptive behaviour.

Ethological theory and maturational theory both highlight the biological bases of child development. Biological theorists remind us that children's behaviour is the product of a long evolutionary history. Consequently, a biological theorist would tell Betty that Will's good nature and his outstanding academic record are both largely products of his biological endowment—his heredity.

The Psychodynamic Perspective

FREUD'S THEORIES. The psychodynamic perspective is the oldest scientific perspective on child development, originating in the work of Sigmund Freud (1856–1939) in the late nineteenth and early twentieth centuries. Freud was a physician who specialized in diseases of the nervous system. Many of his patients were adults whose disorders seemed to have no obvious biological causes. As Freud listened to his patients describe their problems and their lives, he became convinced that early experiences establish patterns that endure throughout a person's life. **Using his patients' case histories, Freud created the first** *psychodynamic theory,* **which holds that development is largely determined by how well people resolve certain conflicts at different ages.**

The role of conflict is evident in Freud's descriptions of the three primary components of personality. **The** *id* **is a reservoir of primitive instincts and drives.** Present at birth, the id presses for immediate gratification of bodily needs and wants. A hungry baby crying illustrates the id in action.

Sigurgeir Sigurjonsson/Nordicphotos/ Alamy Stock Photo

Newly hatched goslings follow the first moving object that they see, treating it as "Mother," even when it's a human.

 QUESTION 1.2
Keunho and Young-shin are sisters who moved to Toronto from Korea when they were 15 and 10 years old, respectively. Although both of them have spoken English almost exclusively since their arrival in Canada, Keunho still speaks with a bit of an accent and occasionally makes grammatical errors; Young-shin's English is flawless—she speaks like a native. How could you explain Young-shin's greater skill in terms of a critical period? *(Answer is on page 19.)*

Sonya Etchison/Shutterstock

According to Freud's theory, the id would encourage the child on the right to grab the toy away from the other child, but the superego would remind her that doing so would be wrong.

The *ego,* is the practical, rational component of personality. The ego begins to emerge during the first year of life as infants learn that they cannot always have what they want. The ego tries to resolve conflicts that occur when the instinctive desires of the id encounter the obstacles of the real world. The ego often tries to channel the id's impulsive demands into more socially acceptable channels. For example, in the photo the child without the toy is obviously envious of the child who has the toy. According to Freud, the id would urge the child to grab the toy, but the ego would encourage the child to play with the peer and, in the process, get to play with the toy.

The third component of personality, the *superego,* is the "moral agent" in the child's personality. It emerges during the preschool years as children begin to internalize adult standards of right and wrong. If the peer in the previous example left the attractive toy unattended, the id might tell the other child to grab it and run, but the superego would remind the child that taking another's toy is wrong.

Freud also proposed stages of development. In his theory, Freud was really concentrating on personality development, but this is also an example of an early stage theory. Freud believed development was structured in psychosexual stages and that we all go through five stages of development, each named for a particular area of the body where attention is focused. In order, the stages are the oral, anal, phallic, latency (when drives are quiescent), and genital (the final, mature self). Freud believed that conflicts at any stage of development could lead to fixations, where mental energies are occupied in activities reminiscent of that stage.

Today scientists recognize many shortcomings in Freud's theory as a whole (e.g., some key ideas are too vague to be tested in research). Nevertheless, two of Freud's insights have had a lasting impact on child-development research and theory: first, his conclusion that early experiences can have enduring effects on children's development; second, his idea that children often experience conflict between what they want to do and what they know they should do.

ERIKSON'S PSYCHOSOCIAL THEORY. Erik Erikson (1902–1994), one of Freud's students, embraced Freud's idea of conflict but emphasized the psychological and social aspects of conflict rather than the biological and physical aspects. **In Erikson's *psychosocial theory,* development comprises a sequence of stages, each defined by a unique crisis or challenge.** Erikson also proposed that development could continue throughout life, including stages for during adulthood. The complete theory includes eight stages, as shown in Table 1-1. The name of each stage reflects the challenge that individuals face at a particular age. For example, the challenge for adolescents is to develop an identity. Adolescents who do not meet this challenge will not establish truly intimate relationships but will become overly dependent on their partners as a source of identity.

Whether we call them conflicts, challenges, or crises, the psychodynamic perspective emphasizes that the journey to adulthood is difficult because the path is strewn with obstacles. Outcomes of development reflect the manner and ease with which children surmount life's barriers. When children overcome early obstacles easily, they are better

TABLE 1-1

ERIKSON'S EIGHT STAGES OF PSYCHOSOCIAL DEVELOPMENT

Psychosocial Stage	Age	Challenges
Basic trust versus mistrust	Birth to 1 year	To develop a sense that the world is safe, "a good place"
Autonomy versus shame and doubt	1 to 3 years	To realize that one is an independent person who can make decisions
Initiative versus guilt	3 to 7 years	To develop a willingness to try new things and to handle failure
Industry versus inferiority	6 years to adolescence	To learn basic skills and to work with others
Identity versus identity confusion	Adolescence	To develop a lasting, integrated sense of self
Intimacy versus isolation	Young adulthood	To commit to another in a loving relationship
Generativity versus stagnation	Middle adulthood	To contribute to younger people through child-rearing, childcare, or other productive work
Integrity versus despair	Late life	To view one's life as satisfactory and worth living

able to handle the later ones. Returning to this module's opening vignette, a psychodynamic theorist would tell Betty that Will's cheerful disposition and his academic record suggest that he handled life's early obstacles well, which is a good sign for his future development.

The Learning Perspective

Learning theorists endorse John Locke's view that the infant's mind is a blank slate on which experience writes. John Watson (1878–1958) was the first theorist to apply this approach to child development, arguing that learning from experience determines what children will be.

EARLY LEARNING THEORIES. **Watson's research was based on the form of learning called** *classical conditioning,* **first described by Ivan Pavlov,** who showed that a previously neutral stimulus could become associated with a naturally occurring response and eventually come to elicit a similar response on its own. Watson applied classical conditioning procedures to humans, most famously in the conditioning of fear in children. Watson discovered that sudden, loud noise naturally elicited fear in infants. In experiments with an infant referred to as "Little Albert," Watson paired a white rat with a loud, unpleasant noise that startled Albert. After a few pairings of the rat with the noise, Albert began to show fear at the sight of the rat. Watson believed that this and other experiments showed the application of classical conditioning principles to human behaviour. Although later analyses of Watson's experiments with Little Albert have cast doubt on how clear-cut the findings were (e.g., Harris, 1979)—and his methods would certainly be viewed as unethical today—this experiment remains a classic example of early child-development research. Associating something with a natural response is only one way of learning, however, and other theorists expanded the field by developing different theories.

B.F. Skinner (1904–1990) furthered research on the learning perspective by proposing a different theory of learning. **Skinner studied** *operant conditioning,* **in which the consequences of a behaviour determine whether that behaviour is repeated.** Skinner showed that two kinds of consequences were especially influential. **A** *reinforcement* **is a consequence that increases the future likelihood of the behaviour that it follows.** Positive reinforcement consists of giving a reward—such as chocolate, gold stars, or paycheques—to increase the likelihood of a behaviour being repeated. If parents want to encourage their daughter to clean her room, they could use positive reinforcement by rewarding her with praise, food, or money whenever she completes the chore. Negative reinforcement consists of rewarding people by taking away unpleasant things. The same parents could use negative reinforcement by saying that whenever she cleans her room, the child wouldn't have to wash dishes or fold laundry.

A *punishment* **is a consequence that decreases the future likelihood of the behaviour that it follows.** Punishment suppresses a behaviour either by imposing something aversive or by withholding something pleasant. If the child fails to clean her room, the parents could punish her by making her do extra chores (adding something aversive) or by not allowing her to watch television (withholding a pleasant event). The use of punishment has drawbacks, however, the main one being that punishment does not identify the desired behaviour. Punishment only says "stop this," not "do that instead." Much research shows that reliance on punishment by parents, particularly physical punishment, produces poorer outcomes for child behaviour (e.g., MacKenzie, Nicklas, Waldfogel, & Brooks-Gunn, 2012; Straus, 2000).

People are often confused by the positive/negative and reinforcer/punisher distinctions when discussing operant conditioning outcomes. One simple way to remember them is to think of positive and negative as mathematical symbols—as in adding and subtracting. Adding something to a situation is positive, removing something from a situation is negative. A reinforcer is something to which people look forward; a punisher is to be avoided. With these distinctions in mind, think of the different possible combinations:

	Reinforcer	**Punisher**
POSITIVE	Parents reward child for cleaning up her room by giving her a cookie.	Parents punish child for not cleaning up her room by shouting at her.
NEGATIVE	Parental nagging to "go clean your room" stops when the child starts cleaning up.	Child is not allowed to watch television that evening because she did not clean her room.

Applied properly, reinforcement and punishment are indeed powerful influences on children. However children often learn without reinforcement or punishment. **Children may learn simply by watching those around them, which is known as** *imitation* **or** *observational learning.* For example, imitation occurs when one toddler throws a toy after seeing a peer do so, or when a school-age child offers to help an older adult carry groceries because she has seen her parents do the same, or, as in the photo on the left, when a son tries to shave like his father.

SOCIAL COGNITIVE THEORY. Perhaps imitation makes you think of "monkey-see, monkey-do," of simple mimicking. Early investigators certainly had this view, but

Throughout their development, children learn much from imitating the actions of others.

later research showed they were wrong. **Albert Bandura (1925–), originally from Alberta and now at Stanford University in the United States, developed much of the basis of the** *social cognitive theory* **of learning.** The "Bobo doll" study (Bandura, Ross, & Ross, 1963) is a classic example of both direct observational learning and the fact that observation does not always lead to simple imitation. In this study children watched an adult physically abuse a large clown doll, performing very specific actions, such as hitting the doll with other toys. The children were then led to the same playroom containing all the toys to which the adult had had access, including the Bobo doll. Many of the children performed the exact same behaviours, showing that after seeing an action, children could repeat it. Some did not spontaneously imitate the action, but all the children could do so, if asked to repeat actions or if given incentive, showing that they had acquired the behaviours.

It has also been shown that children are more likely to imitate a person if the person is perceived as popular, smart, or talented. In addition, they are more likely to imitate when the behaviour they see is rewarded than when it is punished. Findings such as these imply that imitation is more complex than sheer mimicry; children look to others for information about appropriate behaviour. When the behaviour of popular, smart peers is reinforced, imitating them makes sense.

When someone is as talented as Sidney Crosby, it makes sense for others to try to imitate him—and young children often do just that.

PostMedia News/ZUMAPRESS/Newscom

Bandura bases his social cognitive theory on this more complex view of reward, punishment, and imitation. Bandura calls his theory *cognitive* because he believes that children are actively trying to understand what goes on in their world; the theory is *social* because, along with reinforcement and punishment, what other people do is an important source of information about the world (Bandura, 2006, 2012).

Bandura also argues that experience gives children a sense of *self-efficacy*— **beliefs about their own abilities and talents.** Self-efficacy beliefs help determine when children will imitate others. A child who believes he is not athletic is unlikely to try imitating Sidney Crosby's hockey skills, despite the fact that Crosby is obviously talented and popular. But another youngster who does believe he is good at hockey *is* likely to imitate Crosby because he believes Crosby is talented, and so it makes sense to imitate him. Thus, whether children imitate others depends on who the other person is, on whether that person's behaviour is rewarded, and on the children's beliefs about their own talents.

Bandura's social cognitive theory is a far cry from Skinner's operant conditioning. The social cognitive child who actively interprets events replaces the operant conditioning child who responds mechanically to reinforcement and punishment. Nevertheless, Skinner, Bandura, and all learning theorists share the view that experience propels children along their developmental journeys. Returning to this module's opening scenario, all these researchers would tell Betty that she can thank experience for making Will both happy and academically successful.

The Cognitive-Developmental Perspective

The *cognitive-developmental perspective* **focuses on how children think and on how their thinking changes as they grow.** Jean Piaget (1896–1980) proposed the best known of the cognitive-developmental theories. He believed that children naturally try to make sense of their world. Throughout infancy, childhood, and adolescence, youngsters want to understand the workings of both the physical and the social world. For example, infants want to know about objects: What happens when I push this toy off the table? And babies want to know about people: Who is this person who feeds and cares for me?

PIAGET'S THEORY OF COGNITIVE DEVELOPMENT. Piaget argued that as children try to comprehend their surroundings they act like scientists, creating theories about the physical and social worlds. These theories are tested daily by experience, because they lead children to expect certain things to happen. As with real scientific theories, when the predicted events occur, a child's belief in her theory grows stronger. When the predicted events do not occur, the child revises her theory. For example, think about the baby in the photo. Her theory of objects like the rattle she's holding might include the idea that "If I let go, the rattle will fall to the floor." If she drops some other object—a plate or an article of clothing—she will find that it too falls to the floor and she can make the theory more general: Objects that are dropped fall to the floor.

Vanessa Davies/Dorling Kindersley, Ltd

In Piaget's theory, even infants have rudimentary theories about objects and their properties.

Piaget also believed that at a few critical points in development, children realize their theories have basic flaws. When this happens, children revise their theories radically. These changes are so fundamental that the revised theory is, in many respects, a brand new theory. Piaget claimed that radical revisions occur three times in development: once at about age two, a second time at about age seven, and a third time just before adolescence. These radical changes mean children go through four distinct stages in cognitive development. Each stage represents a fundamental change in how children understand and organize their environment, and each stage is characterized by more sophisticated types of reasoning. For example, the sensorimotor stage begins at birth and lasts until about age two. As the name implies, sensorimotor thinking is closely linked to the infant's sensory and motor skills. This stage and the three later stages are shown in Table 1-2.

According to Piaget, children's thinking becomes more sophisticated as they develop, reflecting the more sophisticated theories that they create. Returning to our opening scenario, Piaget would have little to say about Will's good nature. As for Will's academic success, Piaget would explain that all children naturally want to understand their worlds; Will is simply unusually skilled in this regard. In Module 6.1, we will further explore Piaget's contribution to our understanding of cognitive development and also examine more modern theories.

The Contextual Perspective

Most developmentalists agree that environment is an important force in development. Traditionally, however, most theories of child development have emphasized environmental forces that affect children directly. Examples of direct environmental influences

TABLE 1-2

PIAGET'S FOUR STAGES OF COGNITIVE DEVELOPMENT

Stage	Approximate Age	Characteristics
Sensorimotor	Birth to 2 years	Infant's knowledge of the world is based on senses and motor skills. By the end of the period, infant uses mental representations.
Preoperational	2 to 7 years	Child learns how to use symbols, such as words and numbers, to represent aspects of the world but relates to the world only through his or her own perspective.
Concrete operational	7 to 11 years	Child understands and applies logical operations to experiences, provided the experiences are focused on the here and now.
Formal operational	Adolescence and beyond	Adolescent or adult thinks abstractly, speculates on hypothetical situations, and reasons deductively about what may be possible.

are a parent praising a child, an older sibling teasing a younger one, and a nursery-school teacher discouraging girls from playing with trucks. These direct influences are important in children's lives, but in the contextual perspective they are simply one part of a much larger system in which each element of the system influences all other elements. This larger system includes parents and siblings, as well as important individuals outside of the family, such as extended family, friends, and teachers. The system also includes institutions such as schools, television, the workplace, and places of worship.

All these people and institutions fit together to form a *culture*—**the knowledge, attitudes, and behaviour associated with a group of people.** Culture can refer to a particular country or people (e.g., French culture), to a specific point in time (e.g., popular culture of the 1990s), or to a group of individuals who maintain specific, identifiable cultural traditions, such as an Indigenous family who participate in a sweet grass smudging ceremony. A culture provides the context in which a child develops, and it is thus an important source of influence on development throughout childhood and adolescence.

VYGOTSKY'S THEORY OF CONTEXTUAL DEVELOPMENT. One of the first theorists to emphasize cultural context in child development was Lev Vygotsky (1896–1934). Vygotsky, a Russian psychologist, focused on ways that adults convey the beliefs, customs, and skills of their culture to children. Vygotsky believed that because a fundamental aim of all societies is to enable children to acquire essential cultural values and skills, every aspect of a child's development must be considered against this backdrop. For example, most parents in Canada want their children to work hard in school and to be admitted to college or university. In the same way, Efe parents living in central Africa want their children to learn to gather food, build houses, and, as you can see in the photo on the next page, hunt; these skills are fundamental to the Efe because they are critical for survival in their environment. Vygotsky viewed development as an apprenticeship in which children develop while they work with skilled adults, including teachers and parents. In Module 6.2, we'll learn more about Vygotsky's distinctive contributions to our understanding of cognitive development.

Returning to our opening vignette, Vygotsky would agree with learning theorists in telling Betty that the environment has been pivotal in her son's amiable disposition

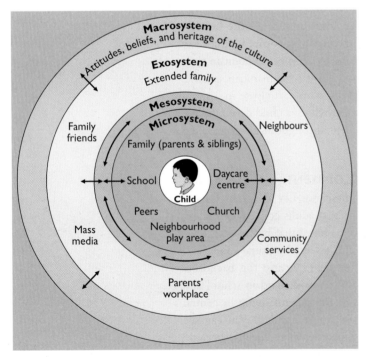

According to the contextual view, parents help children master the essential values and skills of their culture, such as learning how to hunt.

and his academic achievements. However, the contextual theorist would insist that "environment" means much more than the reinforcements, punishments, and observations that are central to learning theory. The contextual theorist would emphasize the manner in which Betty had conveyed the values of curiosity and of academic success to her son; Betty's membership in a cultural group that values doing well in school also contributed to Will's development.

As we think about families it is tempting to believe that parents' actions are what really matter—that through their behaviour, parents directly and indirectly determine their children's development. This view of parents as "all-powerful" was part of early psychological theories (e.g., Watson, 1925), but most theorists now view families from a contextual perspective. That is, families form a system of interacting elements, with parents and children influencing one another (Cox & Paley, 2003; Schermerhorn & Cummings, 2008), and families are part of a much larger system that includes extended family, friends, and teachers as well as institutions that influence development (e.g., schools).

BRONFENBRENNER'S THEORY OF ECOLOGICAL SYSTEMS. This system's view of children and families is exemplified in a theory proposed by Urie Bronfenbrenner (1995; Bronfenbrenner & Morris, 2006) that holds that the developing child is embedded in a series of complex and interactive systems. As Figure 1-1 shows, in *Ecological Systems Theory* **the environment is divided into five components: the microsystem, the mesosystem, the exosystem, the macrosystem, and the chronosystem.**

At any point in life, the *microsystem* **consists of the people and objects in an individual's immediate environment.** These are the people closest to a child, such as parents, siblings and other close family members. Some children have more than one microsystem; for example, a young child might have the microsystems of the family and of the daycare setting. As you can imagine, microsystems strongly influence development.

Microsystems themselves are connected to create the *mesosystem.* The mesosystem represents the fact that what happens in one microsystem is likely to influence what happens in others. Perhaps you have found that a stressful day at work or school can make you grouchy at home. This indicates that your mesosystem is alive and well; your microsystems of home and work are connected emotionally for you.

Figure 1-1 Bronfenbrenner's Ecological Systems Theory views the child as being embedded in a series of interacting systems.

The *exosystem* **refers to social settings that a person may not experience first-hand but that still influence development.** For example, a mother's work environment is part of her child's exosystem, because she may pay more attention to her child when her work is going well and less attention when she is under a great deal of work-related stress. Although the influence of the exosystem is at least second-hand, its effects on the developing child can be quite strong. Think about the woman in the photo below. She doesn't look as if she is having a good day at work; do you think she will do her best mothering when she gets home? Probably not, which means that her workplace has affected her child's development.

The broadest environmental context is the *macrosystem,* **the subcultures and cultures in which the microsystem, mesosystem, and exosystem are embedded.** A mother, her workplace, her child, and the child's school are part of a larger cultural setting, such as Chinese Canadians living in British Columbia or Italian Canadians living in large cities like Toronto and Montreal. Members of specific cultural sub-groups share a common identity, a common heritage, and common values.

Finally, these systems all change over time, in a dimension known as the *chronosystem.* This dimension reminds us that microsystem, mesosystem, exosystem, and macrosystem are not static but are always in flux. For example, the child's microsystem changes when an older sister leaves home to attend college, and the child's exosystem changes when a mother leaves an easy but low-paying job for a more challenging but higher paying job. And, of course, children themselves change over time, which often influences the way in which they are affected by the other elements in the system. For example, a family's move to a distant city may affect a school-age child more than a toddler because the older child must change schools and replace long-time friends (Adam, 2004).

According to a systems approach to parenting, a parent who has a frustrating day at work may be a less effective parent when she gets home.

When viewed as part of an interactive system like the one shown in Figure 1-1, parents still influence their children, both directly (for example, by encouraging them to study hard) and indirectly (for example, by being generous and kind to others). However, the influence is not exclusively from parent to children but is mutual: Children influence their parents, too. By their behaviours, attitudes, and interests, children affect how their parents behave toward them. When children resist discipline, for example, parents may become less willing to reason with them and more inclined to use force.

Even more subtle influences become apparent when families are viewed as systems of interacting elements. For example, fathers' behaviours can affect mother–child relationships. A demanding husband may leave his wife with little time, energy, or interest in helping her son with his homework. Or when siblings argue constantly, parents may become preoccupied with avoiding problems rather than encouraging their children's development.

These examples show that narrowly focusing on parents' impact on children misses the complexities of family life. But there is even more to the systems view. The family itself is embedded in other social systems, such as neighbourhoods, schools, and religious institutions (Johnson, 2012; Parke & Buriel, 1998); these other institutions can affect family dynamics. Sometimes they simplify child-rearing, as when neighbours are trusted friends and can help care for each other's children. Other times, however, they complicate child-rearing. Grandparents who live nearby can create friction within the family. Having a supportive relationship with a member of the community can aid a child, however, making up for deficiencies in family relationships caused by difficulties such as job loss or divorce.

Martin Guhn and Hillel Goelman of the University of British Columbia used systems theory to develop recommendations for research and practice in evaluating children's development, well-being, and school readiness. The proposed approach would take into account both individual variables, such as the child's health, and influences at the community level, such as socioeconomic variables (Guhn & Goelman, 2011). For example, social institutions in the community, such as recreation centres or organizations such as Big Brothers Big Sisters, are important because they can have a beneficial effect, ameliorating problems in other areas of a child's life (De Wit et al., 2006; Duerden & Witt, 2010).

Research by David De Wit (Centre for Addiction and Mental Health in London, Ontario) and colleagues from across Canada has shown that the Big Brothers Big Sisters programs alleviate emotional problems and anxieties and improve the social skills of children assigned to such programs. In fact, De Wit et al. (2006) found that the only problem with the program was the ethical one of keeping children in the control group waiting for assignment to a big brother or big sister.

At times, the impact of the larger systems is indirect, as when work schedules cause a parent to be away from home or when schools are forced to eliminate programs that benefit children. The various systems thus interact, and the situation is complex. Later in this book, in Chapter 14, we'll look at some of these issues in more detail.

THE BIG PICTURE. Comparing the basics of five major perspectives in just a few pages is like trying to see all the major sights of a large city in one day: It can be done, but it's demanding, and after a while everything blurs together. Relax. The Summary Table gives a capsule account of all five perspectives and their important theories.

SUMMARY TABLE

CHARACTERISTICS OF DEVELOPMENTAL PERSPECTIVES

Perspective	Key Assumptions	Illustrative Theories
Biological	Development is determined primarily by biological forces.	*Maturational theory*: emphasizes development as a natural unfolding of a biological plan
		Ethological theory: emphasizes that children's and parents' behaviour has adapted to meet specific environmental challenges
Psychodynamic	Development is determined primarily by how a child resolves conflicts at different ages.	*Freud's theory*: emphasizes the conflict between primitive biological forces and societal standards for right and wrong
		Erikson's theory: emphasizes the challenges posed by the formation of trust, autonomy, initiative, industry, and identity.
Learning	Development is determined primarily by a child's environment.	*Skinner's operant conditioning*: emphasizes the role of reinforcement and punishment.
		Bandura's social cognitive theory: emphasizes children's efforts to understand their world using reinforcement, punishment, and others' behaviour.
Cognitive-Developmental	Development reflects children's efforts to understand the world.	*Piaget's theory*: emphasizes the different stages of thinking that result from children's changing theories of the world.
Contextual	Development is influenced by both immediate and more distant environments, which typically influence each other.	*Vygotsky's theory*: emphasizes the role of parents (and other adults) in conveying culture to the next generation.
		Bronfenbrenner's theory: emphasizes the interaction of different aspects of the environment and their influence—direct or indirect—upon the child.

These perspectives are the basis for the contemporary theories that we introduce throughout this book. For example, Piaget's theory is the forerunner of modern explanations for infants' understanding of objects and for preschoolers' theory of mind (both described in Module 6.3). Similarly, Erikson's theory has contributed to work on mother-infant attachment (see Module 10.3) and formation of identity during adolescence (see Module 11.1).

The modern theories described throughout the text are derived from all five perspectives listed in the Summary Table. Why? Because no single perspective provides a truly complete explanation of all aspects of children's development. Theories from the cognitive-developmental perspective are useful for understanding how children's thinking changes as they grow older. In contrast, theories from the contextual and learning perspectives are particularly valuable in explaining how environmental forces such as parents, peers, schools, and culture influence children's development. By drawing on all the perspectives, we can better understand the different forces that contribute to children's development. Just as you can better appreciate a beautiful painting by examining it from different vantage points, child-development researchers often rely on multiple perspectives to understand why children develop as they do.

Another way to understand the forces that shape development is to consider several themes of development—themes that cut across different theoretical perspectives and specific research topics. We'll look at these themes in Module 1.3.

 ANSWER 1.2
Perhaps there is a critical period for language learning that ends when adolescence begins— that is, children learn to speak a language like a native if exposed to that language extensively in childhood but not if most of their exposure takes place later, in adolescence and young adulthood. (We'll learn more about such a critical period in Chapter 9.)

 ## Check Your Learning

RECALL Describe the different theories that typify the biological perspective on child development.

What are the main features of the contextual perspective on child development?

INTERPRET Explain the similarities and the differences between Erikson's and Piaget's stage theories of children's development.

APPLY Imagine that a friend complains that his one-year-old seems to cry a lot compared to other one-year-olds. How would theorists from each of the five perspectives listed in the table on page 18 explain his son's frequent crying?

 # 1.3 Themes in Child-Development Research

OUTLINE
Continuity of Development
Impact of Nature and Nurture
The Active Child
Links Between Different Domains of Development

LEARNING OBJECTIVES
1. How well can developmental outcomes be predicted from early life?
2. How do heredity and environment influence development?
3. What role do children have in their own development?
4. Is development in different domains connected?

Sanjay Gopal smiles broadly as he holds his newborn grandson for the first time. So many thoughts rush into his mind: What would Ranjeet experience growing up? Would the poor neighbourhood they live in prevent him from reaching his potential? Would the family genes for good health be passed on? How would Ranjeet's life growing up in Canada differ from Sanjay's own experiences growing up in India?

Like most grandparents, Sanjay wonders what the future holds for his grandson, and his questions actually reflect four basic themes in development that are the focus of this module. These themes will provide you with a foundation for understanding and organizing the many specific facts about child development that fill the rest of this book. To help you do this, at the end of Chapters 2 through 14, the Unifying Themes feature links the contents of the chapter to one of the themes.

Continuity of Development

This theme concerns the predictability of development. Do you believe that happy, cheerful five-year-olds remain outgoing and friendly throughout their lives? If you do, this shows that you believe development is a continuous process. According to this view, once a child starts down a particular developmental path, the child stays on that path throughout life. In other words, if Ranjeet is friendly and intelligent as a five-year-old, he will be friendly and intelligent at 15 and at 25. The other view is that development is not continuous. According to this view, Ranjeet might be friendly and intelligent as a 5-year-old, obnoxious and foolish at 15, and quiet but wise at 25. **Thus, the** *continuity-versus-discontinuity issue* **is really about the "relatedness" of development: Are early aspects of development consistently related to later aspects?**

In reality, neither of these views is accurate. Development is not perfectly predictable. A friendly, intelligent five-year-old does not guarantee a friendly, intelligent 15- or 25-year-old, but the chances of a friendly, intelligent adult are greater than if the child had been obnoxious and foolish. There are many ways to become a friendly and intelligent 15-year-old; being a friendly and intelligent five-year-old is not a required step, but it is probably the most direct route.

 QUESTION 1.3

As a child, Heather was painfully shy and withdrawn, but as an adult she is very outgoing, the life of many a party. What does Heather's life tell us about the continuity or discontinuity of shyness? *(Answer is on page 22.)*

Impact of Nature and Nurture

We want to introduce this theme with a story about author Robert Kail's sons. Ben, Kail's first son, was a delightful baby and toddler. He awoke each morning with a smile on his face, eager to start another fun-filled day. Ben was rarely upset; when he was, he was quickly consoled by being held or rocked. Kail presumed that his cheerful disposition must reflect fabulous parenting. Consequently, he was stunned when his second son, Matt, spent much of the first year of his life being fussy and cranky. He was easily irritated and hard to soothe. Why wasn't the all-star parenting that had been so effective with Ben working with Matt? The answer, of course, is that Ben's parenting wasn't the sole cause of his happiness. Kail thought environmental influences accounted for Ben's amiable disposition, but, in fact, biological influences also played an important role.

This anecdote illustrates the *nature–nurture issue*: **What roles do biology (nature) and environment (nurture) play in child development?** If Ranjeet is outgoing and friendly, is it due to his heredity or his experiences? Scientists once hoped to answer questions like this by identifying either heredity or environment as *the* cause. Their goal was to be able to say, for example, that intelligence was due to heredity or that personality was due to experience. Today we know that virtually no aspect of child development is due exclusively to either heredity or environment. Instead, development is always shaped by both: Nature and nurture interact (Sameroff, 2010). A major goal of child-development research is to understand how heredity and environment jointly determine children's development.

The Active Child

When Robert Kail teaches child development, he asks students their plans for when they have children. How will they rear them? What do they want their children to grow up to be? It's interesting to hear his students' responses. Many have big plans for their future children. It's just as interesting, though, to watch students who already have children roll their eyes in a "You don't have a clue" way at what the others say. The parent-students in class admit that they too once had grand designs about child-rearing. What they quickly learned, however, was that their children shaped the way in which they parented.

These two points of view illustrate the *active–passive child issue*: **Are children simply at the mercy of their environment (passive child) or do children actively influence their own development through their unique individual characteristics (active child)?** The passive view corresponds to Locke's description of the child as a blank slate on which experience writes; the active view corresponds to Rousseau's view of development as a natural unfolding that takes place within the child. Today, we know that experiences are indeed crucial, though not always in the way envisioned by Locke. Often, it's a child's interpretation of experiences that shapes her or his development. From birth, children like Ranjeet try to make sense of their world, and in the process, they help shape their own destinies.

This youngster's enjoyment makes it more likely that her parents will read to her in the future and shows that children can influence their own development.

A child's unique characteristics also may cause him or her to have some experiences but not others. Think about the child in the photo, who loves having her parents read her picture books. Her excitement is contagious and makes her parents eager to read to her. In contrast, if a child squirms or seems bored during reading, parents may be less likely to take the time to read to the child. In both cases, children's behaviour during reading influences whether and how often parents read to them in the future.

Many researchers now consider that all relationships are a two-way street: It is not just the parents or other adults who influence the child—the child has influence too. Thus, as in the example about reading, relationships are interactive and bi-directional. Susan Lollis and Leon Kuczynski of the University of Guelph, Ontario, explained this concept in a review article (Lollis & Kuczynski, 1997), where they noted that parent-child interactions need to be viewed in the context of the parent-child relationship precisely because of the bi-directionality of that relationship.

Auremar/Fotolia

Links Between Different Domains of Development

Child-development researchers usually focus on specific domains or areas of development, such as physical growth, cognition, language, personality, and social relationships. One researcher might study how children learn to speak grammatically; another might explore children's reasoning about moral issues. Of course, you should not think of each aspect of development as an independent entity, completely separate from the others. On the contrary, development in different domains is always intertwined. Cognitive and social development, for example, are not independent; advances in one area affects advances in the other. Ranjeet's cognitive growth (e.g., he becomes an excellent student) will influence his social development (e.g., he becomes friends with peers who share his enthusiasm for school).

Having introduced the themes, let's see them together once before we move on.

- *Continuity*: Early development is related to later development, but not perfectly.

- *Nature and nurture*: Development is always jointly influenced by heredity and environment.

- *Active children*: Children influence their own development.

- *Connections*: Development in different domains is connected.

Q&A ANSWER 1.3
In Heather's life, shyness has definitely been discontinuous. Even though Heather was shy early in life, she is not shy now.
· · · · · · · · · · · · · · · · · ·

Most child-development scientists would agree that these are important general themes in any child's development. However, just as lumber, bricks, pipe, and wiring can be used to assemble a variety of houses, these themes also show up in different ways in the major theories of child development. Think, for example, about the nature–nurture issue. Of the five perspectives, the biological perspective is at one extreme in emphasizing the impact of nature; at the other extreme, the learning and contextual perspectives emphasize nurture.

These perspectives also see different degrees of connectedness across different domains of development. Piaget's cognitive-developmental theory emphasizes connections: Because children strive to have an integrated theory to explain the world, cognitive and social growth are linked closely. In contrast, the learning perspective holds that the degree of connectedness depends entirely on the nature of environmental influences. Similar environmental influences in different domains of children's lives produce many connections; dissimilar environmental influences would produce few connections.

 Check Your Learning

RECALL Describe the difference between continuous development and discontinuous development.

Cite examples showing that development in different domains is connected.

INTERPRET Explain the difference between nature and nurture and how these forces are thought to affect children's development.

APPLY How might parents respond differently to an active child compared to a quiet child?

1.4 Doing Child-Development Research

OUTLINE

Measurement in Child-Development Research

General Designs for Research

Designs for Studying Age-Related Change

Ethical Responsibilities

Communicating Research Results

Child-Development Research and Family Policy

LEARNING OBJECTIVES

1. How do scientists measure topics of interest in children's development?
2. What general research designs are used in child-development research?
3. What designs are unique to the study of age-related change?
4. What ethical procedures must researchers follow?
5. How do researchers communicate results to other scientists?
6. How does child-development research influence family policy?

Leah and Joan are both mothers of 10-year-old boys. Their sons have many friends, but the basis for the friendships is not obvious to the mothers. Leah believes that opposites attract; children form friendships with peers who have interests and abilities that make up for things they lack. Joan doubts this; her son seems to seek out other boys who are near clones of himself in their interests and abilities.

Suppose Leah and Joan know you're taking a course in child development, so they ask you to settle their argument. You know, from what you've learned in Module 1.2, that Leah and Joan each have simple theories about children's friendships. Leah's theory is that complementary children are more often friends, whereas Joan's theory is that similar children are more often friends. You know that these theories should be tested with research, but how? Like all scientists, child-development researchers follow the scientific method, which involves several steps:

- Identify a question to be answered or a phenomenon to be understood.
- Form a hypothesis that is a tentative answer to the question or a tentative explanation of the phenomenon.
- Select a method for collecting data that can be used to evaluate the hypothesis.

In our vignette, Leah and Joan have already taken the first two steps: They want to know why children become friends, and each has a simple theory about this phenomenon, a theory that can be used to generate hypotheses. What remains is to find a method for collecting data, which is our focus for the rest of this module. How do child-development scientists select methods that provide evidence that is useful for testing hypotheses about child development?

When devising methods, child-development scientists make several important decisions. They need to decide how to measure the phenomenon of interest; how to design the study; how to ensure that the proposed research respects the rights of the participants; and, how to communicate their results to other researchers once the study is completed.

In naturalistic observation, researchers record children's spontaneous behaviour in natural environments, such as this school classroom.

Robertmandel138/Fotolia

Child-development researchers do not always stick to this same sequence of decisions. For example, researchers will always consider the rights of those taking part—the research participants—as they make each of the other decisions, perhaps even rejecting a procedure because it might violate those rights. Nevertheless, for simplicity, we will use this sequence to describe the steps of decision making in developmental research.

Measurement in Child-Development Research

Research usually begins by deciding how to measure the topic or behaviour of interest. For example, the first step toward answering Leah and Joan's question about friendship would be to decide how to measure friendship. Child-development researchers typically use one of four approaches: observing systematically, using tasks to sample behaviour, asking children for self-reports, or measuring physiological responses.

SYSTEMATIC OBSERVATION. As the name implies, *systematic observation* **involves watching children and carefully recording what they do or say.** Two forms of systematic observation are common. **In** *naturalistic observation,* **children are observed as they behave spontaneously in a real-life situation.** Of course, researchers can't keep track of everything that a child does. **Beforehand they must decide which** *variables*—**factors subject to change—to record.** Researchers studying friendship, for example, might decide to observe children in a school classroom like the one in the photo on the previous page. They would record where each child sits and who talks to whom, and they might check from a list certain behaviours such as "sharing."

Naturalistic observation is illustrated in research by Pepler, Craig, and Roberts (1998) from Toronto, who studied 6- to 12-year-olds' responses to their peers' prosocial and aggressive behaviour. These researchers used video cameras that overlooked a North York (Toronto), Ontario, school playground; for 20 minutes, the experimenter videotaped one child before moving on to the next child on the list. This procedure was repeated another day, providing researchers with a 40-minute record of each child's behaviour on the playground. From these videotapes, the experimenter first measured instances of prosocial behaviour (e.g., laughing with peers, friendly pats on the back) and antisocial behaviour (e.g., hitting, kicking, verbal aggression) then looked at what children did when they were the focus of prosocial or antisocial behaviour.

In *structured observation,* **the researcher creates a setting likely to elicit the behaviour of interest.** Structured observations are particularly useful for studying behaviours that are difficult to observe naturally because they are uncommon, or occur in private settings. For example, an investigator using natural observations to study children's responses to emergencies wouldn't make much progress because, by definition, emergencies don't occur at predetermined times and locations. However, using structured observation, an investigator might stage an emergency, perhaps by having a nearby adult cry for help, and then observing and recording children's responses. Similarly, naturalistic observation of interactions with friends is difficult because they often take place at home. However, children who are friends could be asked to come to the researcher's laboratory, which might be furnished with comfortable chairs and tables. They would be asked to perform some activity typical of friends, such as playing a game or deciding what movie to see. By observing friends' interactions in a setting like the one in the photo on the next page (perhaps through a one-way mirror), researchers could learn more about how friends interact.

A good example of structured observation comes from a study by Sturge-Apple, Davies, and Cummings (2010) of parenting strategies. These researchers asked a mother to join her six-year-old child in a room that contained many attractive toys. Mother and child were encouraged to play with the toys for five minutes, then the mother was told to encourage the child to help clean up the toys. The play and cleanup sessions were videotaped, and later the researchers used the tapes to measure parental behaviour, including, for example, the extent to which the mother used praise and approval to encourage her child to clean up. This procedure was repeated with other mothers and children as well. By creating a situation that would be moderately challenging for mothers—most six-year-olds would rather continue playing, not clean up!—Sturge-Apple et al. hoped to gain insights into parental behaviour.

Structured observation involves creating a situation—such as asking children to play a game—that is likely to lead to behaviours of interest, such as competition.

Structured observations allow researchers to observe behaviours that would otherwise be difficult to study, but investigators must be careful that the settings they create do not disturb the behaviour of interest. For instance, observing friends as they play a game in a mock family room has many artificial aspects to it: The friends are not in their own homes; they were told (in general terms) what to do; and they know they're being observed. Similarly, the moms in the study by Sturge-Apple et al. (2010) knew that they were being videotaped and may have wanted to display their very best parenting behaviour. Any or all of these factors may cause children to behave differently than they would in the real world.

Researchers must be careful that their method does not distort the behaviour they are observing. Think about what happens when you get out a camera: Some of your friends probably react by putting their hands in front of their faces and making excuses for *not* being photographed; others strike poses and pull faces, hoping that you *will* take their picture. The mere appearance of the camera has caused changes in, or *biased*, people's behaviour.

There are two main forms of bias in observational studies—observer bias and observer influence. *Observer bias* **occurs when the researcher tends to notice those behaviours that support the hypothesis and to discount those that do not, or interprets behaviours in such a way that they support the hypothesis.** A particular form of observer bias is *expectancy effect*, where the observer's expectations, influence their observations (Shaughnessy, Zechmeister, & Zechmeister, 2009). Researchers must guard against observer biases, which can be avoided, or at least diminished, by establishing firm behavioural definitions and observation guidelines prior to the observations.

Observer influence **is a form of participant bias, occurring when the participants change their behaviour because they are being observed**—just as your friends might react to your camera. This change in behaviour can be avoided by having observations disguised (e.g., by unobtrusively videotaping or by observing through a one-way mirror) or by habituating participants to the observer. *Habituation* **allows participants to get used to the researcher's presence.** In preparation for research with preschool children, for example, author Anne Barnfield went to the school for a few days to spend an hour or two in the classroom. After a while, the children no longer paid attention to her because they had habituated to her presence.

Andy Crawford/Dorling Kindersley, Ltd

Figure 1-2 Specific tasks, such as choosing a picture, may be used to sample behaviour.

SAMPLING BEHAVIOUR WITH TASKS. When investigators cannot observe a behaviour directly, one alternative is to create tasks that seem to sample the behaviour of interest. For example, to measure memory, investigators sometimes use a digit span task: Children listen as a sequence of numbers is presented aloud. After the last digit is presented, the children try to repeat the digits in the exact order in which they heard them. To measure children's ability to recognize different emotions, investigators sometimes use the task shown in Figure 1-2. The child has been asked to look at the facial expressions and point to the person who is happy.

Sampling behaviour with tasks is popular with child-development researchers because it is so convenient. A potential problem with this approach, however, is that the task may not accurately measure the behaviour of interest. For example, asking children to judge emotions from photographs may not be valid because it underestimates what children do in real life. Can you think of reasons why this might be the case? We mention several reasons on page 41.

SELF-REPORTS.   The third approach to measurement, using self-reports, is actually a special case of using tasks to measure children's behaviour. *Self-reports* **are simply children's own responses to questions about the topic of interest.** When questions are posed in written form, the report is a questionnaire; when questions are posed orally, the report is an interview. In either format, questions are created that probe various aspects of the topic of interest. For example, to examine the impact of similarity on friendship, you might tell research participants the following:

> Jacob and Dave have just met each other at school. Jacob likes to read and play the clarinet in the school orchestra and is not interested in sports; Dave likes to play games on his Xbox 360 and is a star on the soccer team. Do you think Jacob and Dave will become friends?

Children participating in the study would rate the odds that Jacob and Dave are likely to become friends.

A typical questionnaire is one used by Anne Barnfield and her colleagues in a study of psychological effects of therapeutic riding (TR) for special needs children (Carey, Murray, & Barnfield, 2013). The questionnaire was originally developed and validated by the American Camp Association, and it measured a number of constructs, requiring children to rate their own level of self-esteem, leadership skills, friendship skills, and positive values. Questionnaire items included statements such as "Other kids think I am fun to be around" or "I spend time helping others." Children indicated whether each statement was true of them, using a four-point scale that ranged from "strongly disagree" to "strongly agree."

Self-reports are useful because they can lead directly to information on the topic of interest. They are also relatively convenient, particularly when they can be administered to groups of children or adolescents. However, self-reports are not always valid measures of people's behaviour because their answers are sometimes inaccurate. Why? When asked about past events, people may not remember them accurately. For example, an adolescent asked about childhood friends may not remember those friendships well. **Also, answers** may be influenced by *response bias*—some responses may be more socially acceptable than others and participants, particularly children, are more likely to select those than socially unacceptable answers. For example, some children in the Carey et al. (2013) study may have been reluctant to admit that their self-perception was strongly influenced by their peer's approval. As long as investigators keep these weaknesses in mind, however, self-reports are a valuable tool for child-development research.

PHYSIOLOGICAL MEASURES. A final approach is less common but can be very powerful: measuring children's physiological responses. Heart rate, for example, often slows down when children are paying close attention to something interesting. Consequently, researchers often measure heart rate to determine a child's degree of attention. As another example, the hormone cortisol is often secreted in response to stress. By measuring cortisol levels in children's saliva, scientists can determine when children are experiencing stress (Koss et al., 2013).

As both of these examples suggest, physiological measures are usually specialized focusing on a particular aspect of a child's behaviour (attention and stress in the two examples). What's more, they are often used alongside other behaviourally oriented methods. A researcher studying stress might observe children, looking for overt signs of stress; ask parents to rate their children's stress; and also measure cortisol in children's saliva. If all three measures lead to the same conclusions about stress, the researcher can be much more confident about the conclusions.

Another important group of physiological measures includes those used to study brain activity. For centuries, philosophers and scientists could only guess about the role of the brain in thinking and feeling. Techniques developed during the past 25 years allow modern scientists to record many facets of brain functioning as children are performing specific tasks. We describe these methods in Module 4.3. For now, the important point is that child-development scientists are making great strides in identifying the brain regions associated with reasoning, memory, emotions, and other psychological functions.

The four approaches to measurement are presented in the Summary Table.

SUMMARY TABLE

WAYS OF MEASURING BEHAVIOUR IN CHILD-DEVELOPMENT RESEARCH

Method	Strength	Weakness
Systematic Observation		
Naturalistic observation	Captures children's behaviour in its natural setting	Difficult to use with behaviours that are rare or that typically occur in private settings
Structured observation	Can be used to study behaviours that are rare or that typically occur in private settings	May be invalid if the structured setting distorts the behaviour
Sampling Behaviour with Tasks	Convenient—can be used to study most behaviours	May be invalid if the task does not sample behaviour as it occurs naturally
Self-Reports (questionnaires and interviews)	Convenient—can be used to study most behaviours	May be invalid because children answers incorrectly due to forgetting or response bias
Physiological Measures	Can provide independent, converging evidence that can confirm behavioural measures	Are often specific to particular types of behaviours and, consequently, may not be available for all topics

Uppercut RF/Glow Images

If arguments like this one are more common among boys than girls, then that difference should be evident in observations of children's behaviour, as well as in other measures such as self-reports.

EVALUATING MEASURES. After researchers choose a method of measurement, they must show that it is both reliable and valid. **A measure is** *reliable* **if the results are consistent over time**. A measure of friendship, for example, would be reliable if it yields the same results about friendship each time it is administered. All measures used in child-development research must be shown to be reliable, or they cannot be used.

A measure is valid if it really measures what researchers think it measures. There are a number of sub-types of *validity*. For example, a measure of friendship is valid only if it can be shown to actually measure friendship (and not, say, popularity). Validity is often also established by showing that the measure in question is closely related to another measure known to be valid. We could confirm that a questionnaire measuring friendship is valid by showing that scores on the questionnaire are related to peers' and parents' measures of friendship.

Throughout this book, you'll come across many studies using these different methods. You'll also see that studies of the same topic or behaviour often use different methods. This is desirable because the approaches to measurement have different strengths and weaknesses; finding the same results regardless of the approach leads to particularly strong conclusions. Suppose, for example, that a researcher using self-reports claims that arguments like the one shown in the photo are more common in boys' friendships than in girls' friendships. It would be reassuring if other investigators have found the same result from systematic observation as well as from sampling behaviour with tasks.

Poco_bw/Fotolia

Much research is based on samples of children living in developed countries in North America and other parts of the world; those results may not generalize to children living in developing nations.

REPRESENTATIVE SAMPLING. Valid measures depend not only on the method of measurement, but also on the children who are tested. **Researchers are usually interested in broad groups of children called** *populations.* Examples of populations would be all Canadian seven-year-olds or all African Canadian adolescents. However, it would be extremely difficult for researchers to study every member of such large groups. **Virtually all studies include only a** *sample* **of children, a subset of the population.** Researchers must take care that their sample really represents the population of interest. An unrepresentative sample can lead to invalid research. For example, what would you think of a study of children's friendship if you learned that the sample consisted entirely of eight-year-olds whose friends were primarily preschool children? This sample of eight-year-olds would seem to be very unusual, and you would hesitate to generalize the results from this sample back to the population at large.

As you read on, you'll discover that much of the research we describe was conducted with samples of middle-class European, Canadian, and American youngsters. Are these samples representative of all children in North America? Of children like those in the photo who grow up in developing countries? Sometimes, but not always. Be careful not to assume that findings from this group necessarily apply to people in other groups (Jensen, 2012), especially for a multicultural nation like Canada.

General Designs for Research

Having formulated a hypothesis, identified variables, and selected a method to collect data on the topic or behaviour of interest, researchers must then choose and implement an overall conceptual approach called a *reliable research design*. Child-development researchers usually use one of two designs: correlational or experimental studies.

CORRELATIONAL STUDIES. In a *correlational study,* investigators look at relations between variables as they exist naturally in the world. In the simplest possible correlational study, a researcher measures two variables then sees how they are related. Imagine a researcher who wants to test the idea that smarter children have more friends. To test this claim, the researcher would measure two variables for each child: the number of friends the child has and the child's intelligence.

The results of a correlational study are usually expressed as a *correlation coefficient,* abbreviated as r, which stands for the direction and strength of a relation between two variables. Correlations can range from −1.0 to +1.0

- *When r equals 0, two variables are completely unrelated:* Children's intelligence is unrelated to the number of friends they have.

- *When r is greater than 0, scores are related positively:* Children who are smart tend to have more friends than children who are not as smart. That is, more intelligence is associated with having more friends.

- *When r is less than 0, scores are related, but inversely:* Children who are smart tend to have fewer friends than children who are not as smart. That is, more intelligence is associated with having fewer friends.

In interpreting a correlation coefficient, you need to consider both the sign *and* the size of the correlation. The sign indicates the *direction* of the relation between variables. A *positive correlation* means that larger values on one variable are associated with larger values on the second variable; a *negative correlation* means that larger values on one variable are associated with smaller values on a second variable. Sometimes people can become confused about the meaning of correlations and think that positive means a "good" correlation and negative a "bad" one. It helps to remember that the sign does not indicate any value judgment, it only shows direction. For example, if fewer hours watching television correlates with better grades in your psychology class, that is a negative correlation, but certainly not a bad thing! As an example of an experiment involving (in this case, positive) correlation, Belsky, Houts, and Pasco Fearon (2010) wondered whether the age at which girls entered puberty was related to the security of their emotional attachment to their mother during infancy (a topic that we'll examine in detail in Module 10.3). The investigators assessed security of mother-infant attachment when girls were 15 months old and used data from physical exams to determine when girls entered puberty. The correlation was .47, indicating that, in general, daughters with more secure attachment as infants tended to enter puberty at an older age.

The *strength* of a relation is measured by how much the correlation differs from 0, either positively or negatively. If the correlation between intelligence and number of friends was .75, the relation between these variables would be very strong: Knowing a child's intelligence, you could accurately predict how many friends the child has. If, instead, the correlation was .25, the link between intelligence and number of friends would be relatively weak: Although more intelligent children would have more friends on average, there would be many exceptions to this rule. Similarly, a correlation of −.75 would indicate a strong negative relation between intelligence and number of friends, but a correlation of −.25 would indicate a weak negative relation. Thus, in the study by Belsky et al. (2010) on links between attachment and onset of puberty, the correlation of .47 indicates a medium-sized relation between attachment security and age of onset of puberty. Many girls with secure attachment to their mother as infants entered puberty at a relatively older age, but not all of them; some girls with secure attachment started puberty at a relatively younger age.

The results of a correlational study tell whether variables are related, but this design does not address the question of cause and effect between the variables. A correlation can only show that two variables go along together; it does not necessarily imply a causal relation between them. Suppose a researcher finds that the correlation between intelligence and number of friends is .7. This means that children who are smarter have more friends than children who are not as smart. How would you interpret this correlation? Figure 1-3 shows that three interpretations are possible. Maybe being smart causes children to have more friends. Another interpretation is that having more friends causes children to be smarter. A third interpretation is that neither variable causes the other; instead, intelligence and number of friends are caused by a third variable that was not measured in the study. Perhaps parents who are warm and supportive tend to have children who are smart and who also have many friends. Any of these interpretations could be true. Cause and effect cannot be distinguished in a correlational study. When investigators want to track down causes, they must use a different design, an experimental study.

EXPERIMENTAL STUDIES. In an *experiment,* **an investigator systematically varies the factors thought to cause a particular behaviour. The factor that is varied is called the** *independent variable;* **the behaviour that is measured is called the** *dependent variable.* To remember the difference between the two types of variables, think of the independent variable as being *independent of* the participant, who has no choice; the dependent variable, or outcome, *depends upon* the group to which the individual is assigned. In an experiment, the investigator randomly assigns children

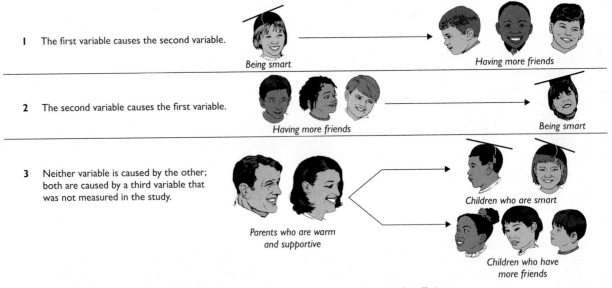

1   The first variable causes the second variable.

Being smart   *Having more friends*

2   The second variable causes the first variable.

Having more friends   *Being smart*

3   Neither variable is caused by the other; both are caused by a third variable that was not measured in the study.

Parents who are warm and supportive

Children who are smart

Children who have more friends

Figure 1-3 Three Interpretations of a Correlation Coefficient.

to different groups or conditions that are treated exactly alike except for the single factor that varies across groups (i.e., the independent variable). The dependent variable is then measured in all groups. Because children have been assigned to groups randomly, differences between the groups reflect the different treatment the children received in the experiment.

When results of experiments are calculated, they are subjected to more rigorous statistical analyses. **These** *inferential statistics* **allow one to draw conclusions.** What is actually tested is the likelihood that the null hypothesis is true. **The** *null hypothesis* **basically states that nothing that the experimenter did has had any effect on anything done as part of the experiment.** The statistical results are expressed in terms of probabilities. The convention in psychology is to consider a probability of less than or equal to .05 significance. In other words, the result is attributed to the experimental manipulation—the independent variable—and not to random chance 95 times in 100. This significance level is important because it shows the likelihood of correctly rejecting the null hypothesis and accepting the experimental hypothesis (APA, 2010). A greater degree or higher level of significance may be reported if such is found—for example, if the probability is found to be .01 (Shaughnessy, Zechmeister, & Zechmeister, 2009).

Suppose, for example, that an investigator hypothesizes that children share more with friends than with children they do not know. Figure 1-4 shows how the investigator might test this hypothesis. Based on random assignment, some Grade 5 children would be asked to come to the investigator's laboratory with a good friend. Other Grade 5 students would come to the laboratory site without a friend and would be paired with a child they don't know. The laboratory itself would be decorated to look like a family room in a house. The investigator would create a task in which one child is given an interesting object to play with—perhaps a Wii video game—but the other child receives nothing. The experimenter would explain the task to the children and then claim that she needs to leave the room briefly. Actually, the experimenter would go to a room with a one-way mirror and observe whether the child with the Wii offers to let the other child play.

This same scenario would be used with all pairs of children: The room and Wii would be the same, and the experimenter would always be away for the same amount of time. The circumstances would be held as constant as possible for all children, except that some children participate with friends while others do not. If children who participated with friends shared the Wii more often with the other child, the investigator could say with confidence that children are more likely to share with their friends than with children they don't know. Statistical analyses of the results can be conducted and conclusions about cause and effect are possible because there was a direct manipulation of an independent variable (participating with a friend or with an unknown child) under controlled conditions.

You can see the use of an experiment in a study by Buttelmann, Zmyj, Daum, & Carpenter (2013). Infants readily imitate other's actions. However, are infants selective in their imitation? For example, are they more likely to imitate an adult who seems to be a member of their cultural group? To answer this question,

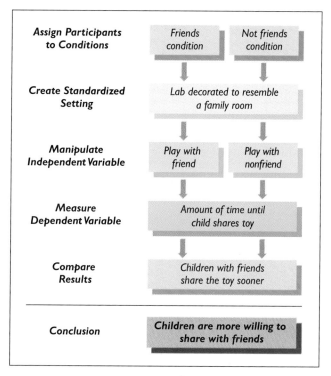

Figure 1-4 Setting up an experimental procedure to test a hypothesis.

Buttelmann and colleagues randomly assigned 14-month-olds to observe either an adult speaking in the infant's native language or an adult speaking in a foreign language. The adult told a few simple stories—either in the native or foreign language—then silently demonstrated some novel actions with an unfamiliar object (e.g., turning on an unfamiliar lamp-in-a-box by touching the side of the box with his head). Finally, infants were shown the unfamiliar objects (e.g., the lamp-in-a-box) and encouraged to play with it.

In this experiment, the independent variable was whether the infant observed an adult telling stories in a native or foreign language; the dependent variable was the extent to which infants imitated the adult by performing the novel action. In fact, infants were more likely to imitate the adult who spoke in a native language: 44 percent of the infants imitated the adult when he spoke in a native language, but only 31 percent did so when he spoke in a foreign language. Because infants were randomly assigned to conditions, Buttelmann et al. (2013) could conclude that the adult's language caused infants to be more likely to imitate.

Child-development researchers usually conduct experiments such as this in laboratory-like settings to control all the variables that might influence the outcome of the research. A shortcoming of laboratory work is that the behaviour of interest is not studied in its natural setting. Consequently, the results may be invalid because they are artificial—specific to the laboratory setting and not representative of the behaviour in the natural environment.

To avoid this limitation, researchers sometimes rely on a special type of experiment. **In a *field experiment*, the researcher manipulates independent variables in a natural setting so that the results are more likely to be representative of behaviour in real-world settings.** To illustrate a field experiment, let's return to the hypothesis that children share more with friends. We might conduct the research in a classroom where students must complete a group assignment. In collaboration with teachers, we place the children in groups of three: In some groups, all three children are good friends; in others, the three children are acquaintances but not friends. When the assignment is complete, the teacher gives each group leader many stickers and tells the leader to distribute them to group members based on how much each child contributed. We predict that leaders will share more (i.e., distribute the stickers more evenly) when group members are friends than when they are not.

A good example of a field experiment is a study by DeLoache and colleagues (2010), who wondered whether videos designed to promote vocabulary actually help babies learn words. DeLoache et al. (2010) assigned one-year-olds randomly to one of three conditions. In one, several times each week the infant and parent watched a commercial DVD designed to increase the infant's vocabulary. In a second condition, parents were simply told the 25 words featured in the DVD and encouraged to help their infants master them. In a third, control condition, infants saw no videos and parents weren't told the words. After four weeks, experimenters tested infants' knowledge of the 25 words in the DVD. Infants were shown two objects, one depicting a word shown in the video. The experimenter said the word and asked infants to point to the corresponding object.

In this experiment, the independent variable was the type of exposure to the words (via DVD, from parents, none) and the dependent variable was the number of times that infants pointed to the correct object upon hearing the word. Was the video useful? No. Infants who had watched the video knew the same number of words as infants in the control condition. And infants in both of these groups knew fewer words than infants whose parents had been encouraged to teach words. Because infants were randomly assigned to conditions, DeLoache and colleagues (2010) could conclude that the type of exposure to words caused differences in the number of words that infants learned.

Field experiments allow investigators to draw strong conclusions about cause and effect because they embed manipulation of an independent variable in a natural setting. However, field experiments are often impractical because of logistical problems. In most natural settings, children are supervised by adults (e.g., parents and teachers) who must be willing to become allies in the proposed research. Adults may not want to change their routines to fit a researcher's needs. In addition, researchers usually sacrifice some control in field experiments. In the study by DeLoache et al. (2010) of baby videos, for example, the investigators relied upon parents to show the videos as instructed and to provide honest reports of how often they watched the videos with their children. No doubt some parents complied with instructions better than others and some parents were more truthful in their reports of how often they watched videos.

Both the main research designs used by developmentalists—correlational and experimental—have strengths and weaknesses. No method is perfect. Consequently, no single investigation can definitely answer a question, and researchers rarely rely on one study or even one method to reach conclusions. Instead, they prefer to find converging evidence from as many different kinds of studies as possible. Suppose, for example, our hypothetical laboratory and field experiments showed that children did indeed share more readily with their friends. One way to be more confident of this conclusion would be to do correlational research, perhaps by observing children during lunch and measuring how often they share food with others.

Experimental and correlational research is *quantitative,* **meaning it adds together many pieces of data. Researchers may also use** *qualitative research,* **in which there is more in-depth study of individuals.** Sometimes information cannot be gained from running an experiment, and the researcher has to try a different methodology. For example, to understand children's thinking, a researcher could set up experiments to see what children could do, such as a Piagetian conservation of volume of liquid task as will be discussed in Chapter 6. But to find out how a child truly thinks or feels *about* something, the researcher might have to interview and discuss with the child, as is sometimes done in research on morality (see Chapter 12). Organizations such as the Canadian Psychological Association (CPA) are becoming more open to qualitative research methods that in the past were more typically associated with disciplines such as anthropology or sociology.

Designs for Studying Age-Related Change

Sometimes child-development research is directed at a single age group, such as Grade 5 children (as in the experiment on sharing between friends and nonfriends), memory in preschool-age children, or mother–infant relationships in one-year-olds. In these cases, after deciding how to measure the behaviour of interest and whether the study will be correlational or experimental, the investigator can skip directly to the last step and determine whether the study is ethical.

However, much research in child development concerns changes that occur as children develop. Consequently, in conjunction with the chosen general research design, investigators must also select a strategy for assessing age-related change. Three strategies are used to incorporate different age groups into experimental and correlational research: the longitudinal approach, the cross-sectional approach, and the longitudinal-sequential approach.

Longitudinal Study

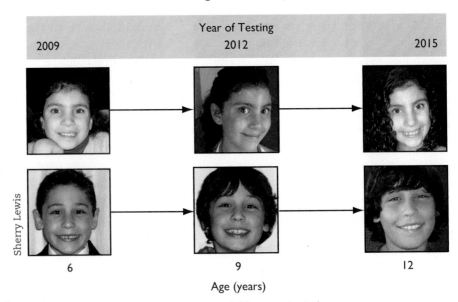

Figure 1-5 A longitudinal study—the same children are tested across a span of six years.

LONGITUDINAL DESIGN. In a *longitudinal design,* **the same individuals are observed or tested repeatedly at different points in their lives.** As the name implies, the longitudinal approach takes a lengthwise view of development and is the most direct way to watch growth occur. For example, as shown in Figure 1-5, children might be tested first at age 6 and then again at ages 9 and 12. There is no manipulation of variables between times; the researcher measures the influence of the independent variables over time (Bryman, Teevan, & Bell, 2012). The longitudinal approach is well suited to studying almost any aspect of development. More important, it is the only way to answer questions about the continuity or discontinuity of behaviour: Will characteristics such as aggression, dependency, or mistrust observed in infancy or early childhood persist into adulthood? Will a traumatic event, such as a child being abandoned by his or her parents, influence later social and intellectual development? Such questions can be explored only by testing children early in development and then retesting them later. For example, the study by Belsky et al. (2010) of parenting (described on page 29) was part of an ongoing longitudinal study of more than 1000 children born in the United States in 1991. In this study, children were tested repeatedly during childhood, adolescence, and young adulthood. A similar study has been started in Canada, called the National Longitudinal Survey of Children and Youth, which began in 1994–1995. Statistics Canada is collecting data every two years, with the study projected to last 25 years (Michaud, 2001; Bryman et al., 2012). Consequently, investigators will be able to see how children's experiences during their preschool years affect them as adolescents and young adults.

Usually the repeated testing of longitudinal studies extends over years, but not always. **In a special type of longitudinal design, called a *microgenetic study,* children are tested repeatedly over a span of days or weeks, typically with the aim of observing change directly as it occurs.** For example, researchers might test children every week, starting when they are 12 months old and continuing until 18 months.

Microgenetic studies are particularly useful when investigators have hypotheses about a specific period when developmental change should occur. In this case, researchers arrange to test children frequently before, during, and after this period, hoping to see change as it happens (e.g., Opfer & Siegler, 2007).

The longitudinal approach, however, has disadvantages that frequently offset its strengths. An obvious one is cost: The expense of merely keeping up with a large sample of people can be staggering. Other problems are not so obvious:

- **Practice effects:** When children are given the same test many times, they may become "test-wise." Improvement over time that is attributed to development may actually stem from practice with a particular test. Changing the test from one session to the next solves the practice problem but makes it difficult to compare responses to different tests.

- **Selective attrition:** Another problem is the constancy of the sample over the course of research. Some children may drop out because they move away. Others may simply lose interest and choose not to continue. These dropouts are often significantly different from their peers, which can distort the outcome. For example, a study might find that memory improves between ages 8 and 11. What has actually happened, however, is that 8-year-olds who found the testing too difficult quit the study, thereby raising the group average when children were tested as 11-year-olds.

- **Cohort effects: When children in a longitudinal study are observed over a period of several years, the developmental change may be particular to a specific generation of people known as a** *cohort.* For example, the longitudinal study we described earlier includes babies born in 1991 in the United States. The results of this study may be general (i.e., apply to infants born in 1950 as well as infants born in 2000), but they may reflect experiences that were unique to infants born in the early 1990s.

Because of these and other problems with the longitudinal method, child-development researchers also use cross-sectional studies.

CROSS-SECTIONAL DESIGN. In a *cross-sectional study*, **developmental changes are identified by testing children of different ages at one particular point in their development.** In other words, as shown in Figure 1-6, a researcher might chart the differences in some attribute between, say, ages 6, 9, and 12. For example, when Anne Barnfield (1999) studied age-related change in performance on a memory task, she tested groups of 4-, 10-, 16-, and 20-year-olds during the 1996–1997 school year. This was much faster than waiting six years for the 4-year-olds to become 10-year-olds, and then again for those 10-year-olds to turn 16, and then 20. It also avoided many of the problems associated with longitudinal studies, including practice effects and selective attrition. Cohort effects are still a problem, however: The results may apply to children who are 4-, 10-, and 16-years-old at the time of testing (1996 in the example) but not generalize to previous or future generations. And cross-sectional studies have a unique shortcoming: Because children are tested at only one point in their development, we learn nothing about the continuity of development. Consequently, we cannot tell whether an aggressive 6-year-old remains aggressive at ages 9 and 12, because the individual child would be tested at ages 6, 9, *or* 12, but not at all three ages.

Cross-Sectional Study

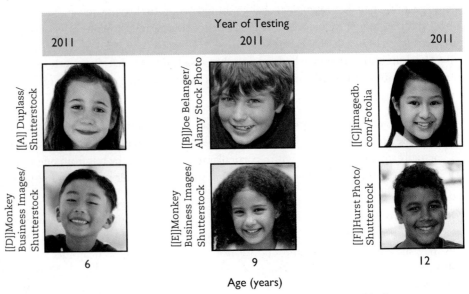

Figure 1-6 A cross-sectional study: children at different ages are tested in the same year.

LONGITUDINAL-SEQUENTIAL DESIGN. Because longitudinal and cross-sectional designs have weaknesses, investigators sometimes use a hybrid design: **A** *longitudinal-sequential study,* **includes sequences of samples, each studied longitudinally.** For example, researchers might start with 6- and 9-year-olds. As shown in Figure 1-7, each group is tested twice—at the beginning of the study and again three years later. As in a pure longitudinal study, the sequential

Longitudinal-Sequential Study

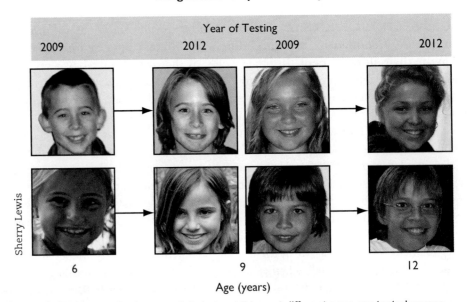

Figure 1-7 A longitudinal-sequential study: children at different ages are tested across several years.

design provides some information about continuity of development: Researchers can determine whether aggressive 6-year-olds become aggressive 9-year-olds and whether aggressive 9-year-olds become aggressive 12-year-olds. Of course, to determine whether aggressive 6-year-olds become aggressive 12-year-olds would require a full-blown longitudinal study.

Longitudinal-sequential studies allow researchers to determine whether their study is affected by practice effects or cohort effects: The key is to compare the results for the age common to both sequences (in the example in the figure, nine-year-olds). Practice and cohort effects tend to make scores different for the two groups of nine-year-olds, so if scores are the same, a researcher can be confident that practice and cohort effects are not a problem in the study.

Each of the three designs for studying development (longitudinal, cross-sectional, and longitudinal-sequential) can be combined with the two general research designs (observational and experimental), resulting in six prototypic designs. To illustrate the different possibilities, think back to our hypothetical laboratory experiment on children's sharing with friends and nonfriends (described on page 31). If we tested 7- and 11-year-olds with either friends or nonfriends, this would be a cross-sectional experimental study. If we observed 7-year-olds' spontaneous sharing at lunch and then observed the same children four years later, this would be a longitudinal-correlational study.

The different designs are summarized in the Summary Table. In this text, you'll read about studies using these various designs, but the two cross-sectional designs will show up more frequently than the other designs. Why? For most developmentalists, the ease of

SUMMARY TABLE

DESIGNS USED IN CHILD-DEVELOPMENT RESEARCH

Type of Design	Definition	Strengths	Weaknesses
GENERAL DESIGNS			
Correlational	Observe variables as they exist in the world and determine their relations	Behaviour is measured as it occurs naturally	Cannot determine cause and effect
Experimental	Manipulate independent and dependent variables	Control of variables allows conclusions about cause and effect	Work is often laboratory based, which can be artificial
DEVELOPMENTAL DESIGNS			
Longitudinal	One group of children is tested repeatedly as they develop	Only way to chart an individual's development and look at the continuity of behaviour over time	Expensive; participants drop out; repeated testing can distort performance
Cross-sectional	Children of different ages are tested at the same time	Convenient; solves most problems associated with longitudinal studies	Cannot study continuity of behaviour; cohort effects complicate interpretation of differences between groups
Longitudinal-sequential	Different groups of children are tested longitudinally	Provides information about continuity; researchers can determine the presence of practice and cohort effects	Provides less information about continuity than a full longitudinal study and is more time consuming than a cross-sectional study

cross-sectional studies compared to longitudinal studies more than compensates for the limitations of cross-sectional studies.

INTEGRATING FINDINGS FROM DIFFERENT STUDIES. Several times in this module, we have emphasized the value of conducting multiple studies on a topic using different methods. The advantage of this approach, of course, is that conclusions are most convincing when the results are the same regardless of method. In reality, though, findings are often inconsistent. Suppose, for example, that many researchers find that children often share with friends, some researchers find that children share occasionally with friends, and a few researchers find that children never share with friends. What results should we believe? What should we conclude? *Meta-analysis* **is a tool that allows researchers to synthesize the results of many studies to estimate relations between variables** (Cooper, Hedges, & Valentine, 2009). In conducting a meta-analysis, investigators find all studies published on a topic over a substantial period of time (e.g., 10 to 20 years), then record and analyze the results and important methodological variables.

The usefulness of meta-analysis is illustrated in a study by Juffer and van IJzendoorn (2007), who asked whether adopted children differ from nonadopted children in terms of self-esteem. They found 88 studies, published between 1970 and 2007, which included nearly 11 000 adopted persons. In each of the 88 studies, self-esteem was measured, often by asking participants to rate themselves on scales containing items like "I am a worthwhile person." Analyzing across the results of all 88 studies, Juffer and van IJzendoorn found that self-esteem did not differ in adopted and nonadopted individuals. This was true regardless of the age of the child when adopted, whether it was an international versus domestic adoption, or whether the child was adopted by parents of his or her own race versus parents of another race. Evidently, adoption has no impact on self-esteem; Juffer and van IJzendoorn argued that this outcome shows "adopted children's resilience to recover from severe deprivation within the context of the adoptive family" (2007, p. 1079).

Thus, meta-analysis is a particularly powerful tool because it allows scientists to determine whether a finding generalizes across many studies that use different methods. In addition, meta-analysis can reveal the impact of those different methods on results (e.g., whether self-reports suggest more sharing between friends than observational studies) and can also reveal gaps in research and failure of application. Jeanie Tse of McGill University in Montreal wanted to perform a meta-analysis on the effectiveness of day treatment programs for preschoolers with behaviour disorders (Tse, 2006). She searched the psychological literature from 1974 to 2003, looking for properly conducted trials of treatment programs aimed at children aged two to five. No such trials were found; no one had properly tested different methods of treatment for preschoolers. Tse concluded that such research needed to be done and that any research that would be done should be applied in clinical practice.

Ethical Responsibilities

Having selected a way of measuring the behaviour of interest and having chosen a research design, researchers must confront one very important remaining step: Determining whether their research is ethical—that it does not violate the rights of participating children and families. Of course, scientists must always consider the ethics of research with humans, but this is especially true for children, who are vulnerable and sensitive. Professional organizations such as the CPA and government agencies have codes of conduct that specify the rights of research participants and procedures to protect those participants. In recent years, ethical issues have been subject to more and more scrutiny, with a corresponding increase in required regulation and control. In 1998 three major governmental research agencies in Canada—the Canadian Institutes of Health Research (CIHR), the Natural Sciences and Engineering Research Council of Canada (NSERC), and the Social Sciences and Humanities Research Council of Canada (SSHRC)—published a comprehensive set of guidelines for research with humans in a document named Tri-Council Policy Statement: Ethical Conduct for Research Involving Humans. The Tri-Council guidelines set out expectations for conduct by researchers, and any government-funded institution must abide by these guidelines (CIHR, NSERC, & SSHRC, 2014). All research laboratories, colleges, and universities in Canada must have a Research Ethics Board (REB) that oversees research and judges whether the proposed research is allowed under ethical codes. The Tri-Council guidelines even specify the makeup of such a board. The following guidelines are included in all major ethics codes such as those of the CPA or Tri-Council:

- *Seek to do research that benefits humanity:* Research is often done to find information or to see how something comes about, but the researcher should not be acting out of idle curiosity. The researcher should have a goal in mind that either adds to human knowledge or directly assists people.

- *Minimize risks to research participants:* Use methods that have the least potential for harm or stress to research participants. During the research, monitor the procedures to avoid any unforeseen stress or harm.

- *Describe the research to potential participants so they can determine whether they wish to participate:* Prospective research participants should be told all details of the research so they can make an educated decision about participating, a process known as **obtaining** *informed consent.* Children are minors and are not legally capable of giving consent; consequently, as shown in the photograph, researchers must describe the study to parents and ask them for permission for their children to participate. Even then, the researcher must ask the child for her or his agreement to participate, sometimes referred to as *assent* (as distinct from true informed consent). Assent can be a difficult issue, however, as children are often reluctant to question authority figures and may believe that if their parents gave permission, they must take part in the study. Therefore, careful explanation is necessary to enable the child to give proper assent.

- *Avoid deception; if participants must be deceived, a thorough explanation of the true nature of the research must be provided as soon as possible:* Providing complete information about a study in advance can sometimes bias or distort participants' responses. Consequently, investigators sometimes provide only partial information or even mislead participants about the true purpose of the study. As soon as is feasible—typically just after the experiment—any false information must be corrected and the reasons for the deception must be provided.

Before children can participate in research, a parent or legal guardian must provide written consent.

Ryan McVay/Photodisc/Getty Images

- *Keep results anonymous or confidential:* Research results should be anonymous, which means that participants' data cannot be linked to their name. When anonymity is not possible, research results should be confidential, which means that only the investigator conducting the study knows the identities of the individuals.

- *Give a debriefing afterward:* As noted above, researchers should clearly explain the purposes of the experiment afterward. The participant is debriefed—given as full an explanation as possible—appropriate to their level of understanding. If deception was used or if any aspect could cause the participant discomfort, it must be explained and reactions dealt with before the participant goes home. Debriefing also allows the participant to find out more about the research and can help the researcher, since any misunderstanding by the participant (which might have affected performance) can be discovered (Shaughnessy, Zechmeister, & Zechmeister, 2009).

QUESTION 1.4

Ethan, a 10-year-old, was at school when a researcher asked if he wanted to earn $10 doing an experiment. The money sounded good to Ethan, so he participated. Despite the pay, Ethan left the experiment feeling upset because he overheard the experimenter telling his teacher how poorly Ethan had done. What are three ethical problems with this research? *(Answer is on page 43.)*

· · · · · · · · · · · · · · · · · ·

As part of observing these standards, and often discrete from them, the researcher must weigh the costs and benefits of the proposed research. Both the CPA and Tri-Council explicitly consider evaluating costs and benefits to the individual and to society to be important, as do many other organizations, for example, the American Psychological Association (APA, 2010).

Before researchers can conduct a study, they must convince their institution's REB that they have carefully addressed each of these ethical points. The REB must have at least five members; at least two members must understand the particular field of research, and at least one member must have knowledge of ethics (CIHR, NSERC, & SSHRC, 2014). If the REB objects to any aspects of the proposed study, the researcher must revise those aspects and present them anew for the REB's approval.

Much child-development research does not raise ethical red flags because the methods are harmless and avoid deception. Some methods, however, involve risk or deception; in these cases, REBs must balance the rights of children against the value of the research for contributing to knowledge and thereby improving children's lives. For example, in Module 10.3 we'll see that one tool for studying mother-infant relationships involves separating mothers and infants briefly then watching infants' responses. Many infants are upset when their mother leaves, and some are difficult to console when she returns. Obviously, this method is not pleasant for infants. But scientists have determined that it produces no lasting harm and therefore is suitable as long as parents receive a thorough description of the study beforehand and they consent to participate.

Communicating Research Results

When the study is complete and the data have been analyzed, researchers may write a report of their work. This report uses a standard format that usually includes four main sections: an introduction that describes the topic or question and the authors' hypotheses; a method section that describes the research design and the procedures used; a results section presenting findings, verified with statistical analyses; and a discussion section in which the authors explain the links between their results and their hypotheses. The APA has produced a book, *Publication Manual of the American Psychological Association,* that lays out all the necessary aspects of writing a research report and is now in its sixth edition (APA, 2010). Other organizations also use the APA manual, and even journals not produced by the APA often require APA format for publication.

Researchers submit their report to one of several scientific journals that specialize in child-development research, such as *Child Development, Developmental Psychology,* or the *Journal of Experimental Child Psychology.* The editor of the journal asks other scientists to evaluate the report, decide whether the work was well done, and whether the findings represent a substantial advance in scientific understanding of a topic. If the reviewing scientists recommend that the report be published, it will appear in the journal, where other child-development researchers can learn of the results.

These research reports are the basis for virtually all the information that we present in this book. As you've read through this first chapter, you've seen names in parentheses, followed by a date, like this:

(Durrant & Ensom, 2012).

This in-text citation indicates the person(s) who did the research and the year the research report was published. By looking in the References section at the end of this book, which is organized alphabetically by author, you can find the title of the article and the journal in which it was published. As with writing reports, references in psychology in North America are generally given as required by the APA publication manual.

Other formats of publication also exist, such as government publications like the Statistics Canada reports that you will sometimes see referenced in this text, as well as reports in more mainstream media. In recent years emphasis has been placed on wider distribution of knowledge—beyond the traditional journal article—to reach the general public. For example, a researcher who has performed a study with schoolchildren may provide an explanation of the study and its findings for a school newsletter.

Maybe all these different steps in research seem tedious and involved to you. For a child-development researcher, however, much of the excitement of doing research is planning a novel study that will provide useful information to other specialists. The Focus on Research feature that appears in each of the remaining chapters of this text is designed to convey both the creativity and the challenge of doing child-development research. Each feature focuses on a specific study. Some are studies published recently; others are classics that defined a new field of investigation or provided definitive results in some area. In each Focus feature, we trace the decisions that researchers made as they planned their study. In the process, you'll see the ingenuity of researchers as they pursue questions of child development. You'll also see that any individual study has limitations. Only when converging evidence from many studies—each using a unique combination of measurement methods and designs—points to the same conclusion can we feel confident about research results. Many scientists, practitioners, and elected officials are eager to use this knowledge to create policies that benefit children. We'll look at this connection between research and policy in the final part of this module.

Responses to question on page 26 about using photographs to measure children's understanding of emotions: Children's understanding of emotions depicted in photographs may be less accurate than in real life because (1) in real life, facial features are usually moving—not still, as in the photographs—and movement may be one of the clues that children naturally use to judge emotions; (2) in real life, facial expressions are often accompanied by sounds, and children may use both sight and sound to understand emotion; and (3) in real life, children most often judge facial expressions of people they know (parents, siblings, peers, teachers), and knowing the "usual" appearance of a face may help children determine emotions accurately.

Child-Development Research and Family Policy

WHY LINK RESEARCH TO POLICY?   Child-development researchers have long been interested in applying their work to improving children's lives. After all, it would make sense to use the knowledge gained from research to form standards and policies (Rutter, 2002). Links between child development and family policy have become much stronger in recent years. One reason for the stronger link is that families are changing in North America (Zigler, 1998). Researchers and parents alike have been concerned about the potential impact of changing family arrangements (NICHD Early Child Care Research Network, 2002).

Changes in family life raise questions that trouble child-development professionals, parents, and policymakers alike. For example, when parents divorce, who should receive custody of the children? When children like the one in the photo spend most days at a childcare facility, what are the effects? Many child-development researchers now participate actively in designing and implementing social policy concerning children and their families. In fact, a new orientation to child-development research has emerged. As noted earlier in this chapter, applied developmental science uses developmental research to promote healthy development. As the name implies, scientists with this orientation are interested in applied research that has direct implications for family policy. A current example concerns children and adolescents within justice systems. Assumptions that are not justified may be made about cognitive abilities and understanding, and developmentally appropriate interview techniques are required (e.g., Owen-Kostelnik, Reppucci, & Meyer, 2006). Research can assist in finding best practices in such situations and can guide policymaking.

WAYS TO INFLUENCE FAMILY POLICY.   Child-development researchers contribute to sound family policy through a number of distinct pathways (White, 1996): by building understanding of children, by serving as their advocates, and by evaluating health-promoting policies and programs. When government officials need to address problems affecting children, child-development experts can provide useful information (Fasig, 2002). Child-development researchers contribute to policymaking by ensuring that the general consideration of policy issues and options is based on factual knowledge derived from child-development research.

Picture Partners/Alamy Stock Photo

Many parents have to rely on other people to look after their children when they are at work.

In Canada, the situation is complicated by the fact that some aspects of policy are the constitutional responsibility of provincial governments and some are the responsibility of the federal government. The federal government mainly controls aspects such as economics and criminal justice; for example, the child tax credit is administered by the federal government. Provincial governments take responsibility for many other policies that may affect children, such as health or culture. For example, Children's Aid Societies (CAS) are provincially regulated. The noted sociologist Jane Jenson of the Université de Montréal proposed that Canada is moving to "an investing-in-children paradigm" (Jenson, 2004, p. 169), with policies resulting from advocacy for children. And both levels of government reportedly appear to view family policy as an important concern (e.g., Vail, 2002).

As we have seen from Ecological Systems Theory in Module 1.1, policies and programs—macrosystem influences—can affect families and children even though they are not the primary targets of the policy. In this case, child-development experts may be called upon to evaluate the policy. Existing theory and research in child development can indicate how policy features are likely to affect families and children, for example, the report prepared by Dr. Charles Pascal of OISE/University of Toronto for then-Premier of Ontario Dalton McGuinty on the implementation of early learning policy in Ontario (Pascal, 2009). By using existing findings to indicate the likely impact of policies and by providing reliable methods to measure impact, child-development researchers can help judge how families and children are affected by policies.

EMPHASIS ON POLICY IMPLICATIONS IMPROVES RESEARCH.

Emphasizing policy also improves research by making scientists take a broader perspective and use more sophisticated research designs. A focus on family policy forces researchers to consider a much broader perspective on child development than they might otherwise, often crossing traditional disciplinary lines between psychology, sociology, and economics (McCall & Groark, 2000).

A concern for family policy has also improved the methods used by researchers. In addition, child-development researchers and statisticians have devised more powerful correlational methods that permit some statements about causality (West, Biesanz, & Pitts, 2000). **A** *quasi-experimental design* **includes multiple groups that were not formed by random assignment.** For example, researchers might want to compare children's reading level at the end of a school year in two schools, one using a traditional reading curriculum and another using an innovative curriculum. Because children were not assigned randomly to the two schools, this is a quasi-experiment. Such methods allow researchers to account for possible differences and to use statistics to equate the groups of children at the beginning of the year, thereby making it easier to compare them at the end of the year and make conclusions about causality.

The message here should be clear: Closer links between child-development research and family policy produce better policy and better research. To emphasize this connection, many of the other chapters in this book have a feature called Children's Lives. Some of these features provide concrete examples of the close ties between research and policy.

 ANSWER 1.4
First, the experimenter apparently did not describe the study in detail to Ethan, but only mentioned the pay. Second, children can participate only with the written consent of a parent or legal guardian. Third, results are anonymous and not to be shared with others.

 # Check Your Learning

RECALL List the ethical responsibilities of scientists who do research with children.

What steps are involved in reporting the results of research to the scientific community?

INTERPRET Compare the strengths and weaknesses of different approaches to measurement in child-development research.

APPLY Suppose you wanted to determine the impact of divorce on children's academic achievement. What would be the merits of correlational versus experimental research on this topic? How would a longitudinal study differ from a cross-sectional study?

UNIFYING THEMES Connections

In this first Unifying Themes feature, we want to underscore the theme that *development in different domains is connected.* With the research methods introduced in Module 1.4 (and used in many of the studies described throughout the book), researchers often look at separate elements of children's development—memory, physical growth, or peer relations, for example. This strategy makes sense because the elements are easier to understand in isolation. But effective family policy reminds us that these elements are interconnected in real children. Physical, cognitive, social, and emotional development are linked: Change in one area almost always leads to change in another.

See for Yourself

Earlier in this chapter we noted that there are always ethical responsibilities in research, and especially so in research with children. For each of these See for Yourself sections, remember that you must take care to act in an ethical and responsible manner.

For example, here you are encouraged to ask parents about their childrearing methods. As would a responsible psychology researcher, you should do this sensitively and ethically. You should reassure parents of the confidentially of the discussion and should not write down anything that could identify the parents to whom you have spoken or their child(ren).

One good way to see how children influence their own development is to talk to parents who have more than one child. Ask them if they used the same child-rearing methods with each child or if they used different techniques with each. If they used different techniques, find out why. You should see that, although parents try to be consistent in a general philosophy for rearing their children, many of the specific parenting techniques will vary from one child to the next, reflecting the children's influence on the parents. See for yourself!

Resources

For more information about ...

the different theories described in Module 1.2, we recommend William C. Crain's *Theories of Development: Concepts and Applications* (2010), available from Pearson/ Prentice Hall, for its comprehensive account of each of the theoretical perspectives.

research in child development, visit the Society for Research in Child Development (SRCD) website at **www.srcd.org**.

research and family policy, visit the website of the Community-University Partnership for the Study of Children, Youth, and Families at **www.cup.ualberta.ca**.

Key Terms

active-passive child issue   21
applied developmental science   6
baby biographies   5
chronosystem   17
classical conditioning   11

cognitive-developmental
  perspective   14
cohort   35
continuity-versus-discontinuity
  issue   20
correlation coefficient   29

correlational study   29
critical period   9
cross-sectional study   35
culture   15
debriefing   40
dependent variable   30

Summary

1.1 Setting the Stage

1. Historical Views of Children and Childhood

Plato and Aristotle provided the first philosophical views of childhood. Their ideas were picked up in the seventeenth century. Locke emphasized the role of experience in children's lives, but Rousseau viewed development as a natural unfolding.

2. Origins of a New Science

Child development emerged as a science in the 19th century, reflecting reformers' concern for children's well-being and scientists' enthusiasm for Darwin's theory of evolution. Leaders in this new field were G. Stanley Hall (theories of child development), Binet (mental tests), Freud (role of early experience), and Watson (behaviourism).

1.2 Foundational Theories of Child Development

Theories provide explanations for development and hypotheses for research. Traditionally, five broad perspectives have guided researchers.

1. The Biological Perspective

According to this perspective, biological factors are critical for development. In maturational theory, child development reflects a natural unfolding of a prearranged biological plan. Ethological theory states that children's and parents' behaviour is often adaptive.

2. The Psychodynamic Perspective

Freud emphasized the roles of early experience and of conflict in children's development. Erikson proposed that psychosocial development consisted of eight universal stages, each characterized by a particular struggle.

3. The Learning Perspective

Operant conditioning is based on reinforcement, punishment, and environmental control of behaviour. Social learning theory proposes that people learn by observing others. Social cognitive theory emphasizes that children actively interpret what they see.

4. The Cognitive-Developmental Perspective

The cognitive-developmental perspective focuses on thought processes. Piaget proposed that children's thinking progresses through four stages.

5. The Contextual Perspective

Vygotsky emphasized the role of culture in children's development. He argued that skilled adults help children acquire the beliefs, customs, and skills of their culture. Bronfenbrenner proposed that the child should be considered as embedded within a series of interacting systems.

1.3 Themes in Child-Development Research

Four themes help unify the findings from child-development research that are presented throughout this book.

1. Continuity of Development
Development is not perfectly predictable; early development sets the stage for later development but does not fix it irrevocably.

2. Impact of Nature and Nurture
Heredity and environment are interactive forces that work together to chart the course of development.

3. The Active Child
Children constantly interpret their experiences and often influence the experiences they have according to their individual characteristics.

4. Links Between Different Domains of Development
Development in different domains of children's lives is always connected. Cognitive development affects social development and vice versa.

1.4 Doing Child-Development Research

1. Measurement in Child-Development Research
Research typically begins by determining how to measure the topic of interest. Systematic observation involves recording children's behaviour as it takes place, either in a natural environment or in a structured setting. Researchers sometimes create tasks to obtain samples of children's behaviour. In self-reports, children answer questions posed by the experimenter. Sometimes researchers also measure physiological responses (e.g., heart rate). Researchers must also obtain a sample that is representative of some larger population.

2. General Designs for Research
In correlational studies, investigators examine relations between variables as they occur naturally. In experimental studies, they manipulate an independent variable to determine the impact on a dependent variable. Field studies involve manipulation of independent variables in a natural setting. The best approach is to use both experimental and correlational studies to provide converging evidence.

3. Designs for Studying Age-Related Change
To study developmental change, some researchers use a longitudinal design in which the same children are observed repeatedly as they grow. A cross-sectional design involves testing children in different age groups. Meta-analysis is used to synthesize the results of different studies on the same topic.

4. Ethical Responsibilities
Experimenters must minimize the risks to potential research participants, describe the research so that potential participants can decide whether they want to participate, avoid deception, and keep results anonymous or confidential.

5. Communicating Research Results
Investigators write reports describing their findings and publish them in scientific journals. These publications form the foundation of scientific knowledge about child development.

6. Child-Development Research and Family Policy
Child-development researchers have become increasingly interested in applying the results of their work to family policy because of many changes in the Canadian family. Researchers help to shape family policy by providing useful knowledge about children and their development so that policies can be based on accurate information. They also contribute by evaluating the impact of programs on families and children, and by developing effective programs that can be implemented elsewhere. Focusing on public policy implications in turn improves research because researchers must take a broader perspective on children's development than they would otherwise.

Test Yourself

1. The view of a child's mind as a *tabula rasa* emphasizes the role of _____ in shaping a child's development.

2. _____ are detailed, systematic observations of individual children.

3. In maturational theory, development consists of _____.

4. Ethologists show that some behaviours can only be learned during a _____,

when organisms are biologically prepared for that learning.

5. Freud's psychodynamic theory emphasized the role of _____ in shaping later development.

6. In Erikson's psychosocial theory, development is driven by the need to resolve conflict between _____.

7. According to Jean Piaget, children of all ages create _____.

8. A systems view of families divides the environment into the microsystem, the mesosystem, the exosystem, the macrosystem, and the _____.

9. Finding that early development is related to later development is evidence for _____ in development.

10. According to the _____ of children, they are masters of their own destinies.

11. A potential shortcoming of structured observations is that _____.

12. In a _____, high scores on one variable are associated with high scores on a second variable.

13. A measure is _____ when it actually measures what it's supposed to measure.

14. In a(n) _____, a researcher manipulates an independent variable and measures its effect on a dependent variable.

15. The biggest advantage of longitudinal studies is that a researcher can _____.

Answers: (1) experience; (2) baby biographies; (3) the unfolding of a specific and prearranged scheme or plan within the body; (4) critical period; (5) early experiences; (6) a person's biological drives and society's standards of right; (7) theories that help them understand their worlds; (8) chronosystem; (9) continuity; (10) active view; (11) the artificial nature of the setting may distort the behaviour of interest; (12) positive correlation; (13) valid; (14) experimental study; (15) determine the extent to which behaviours at a younger age are related to behaviours at an older age.

2

Genetic Bases of Child Development

Monkey Business Images/Shutterstock

2.1

Mechanisms of Heredity

2.2

Heredity, Environment, and Development

Parents often hear it said about one of their children: "He (or she) comes by that naturally." The usual prompt for such a comment is that the child has just done something exactly as one of the parents did at the same age. Such remarks remind us that many behavioural characteristics are inherited from parents, just as physical characteristics such as height and hair colour are inherited.

In this chapter, we'll see how heredity influences children and their development. We'll start, in **Module 2.1**, by examining the basic mechanisms of heredity. Then, in **Module 2.2**, we'll see how heredity and environment work together to shape children's development.

2.1 Mechanisms of Heredity

OUTLINE

The Biology of Heredity

Single Gene Inheritance

Genetic Disorders

LEARNING OBJECTIVES

1. What are chromosomes and genes?

2. What are dominant and recessive traits? How are they inherited?

3. What disorders are inherited? Which are caused by too many or too few chromosomes?

Leslie and Glenn have decided to try to have a baby. They are thrilled at the thought of starting their own family, but also worried because Leslie's grandfather had sickle-cell disease and died when he was just 24 years old. Leslie is terrified that their baby could inherit the disease that killed her grandfather. Leslie and Glenn wish someone could reassure them that their baby will be okay.

How could we reassure Leslie and Glenn? To start with, we need to know more about sickle-cell disease. Red blood cells like the ones in the photo on the next page carry oxygen to and carbon dioxide from the body. When a person has sickle-cell disease, the red blood cells look like those in the second bottom photo on the next page—long and curved, like a sickle. These stiff, misshapen cells cannot pass through small capillaries, so oxygen cannot reach all parts of the body. The trapped sickle cells also block the passage of white blood cells, which are the body's natural defence against bacteria. Consequently, people with sickle-cell disease are often tired, may experience acute pain for hours or days, and are prone to infections. About 10 percent of people with the disease die by age 20 and 50 percent die by age 50 (Kumar et al., 2010).

Sickle-cell disease is inherited. Because Leslie's grandfather had the disorder, it apparently runs in her family. Would Leslie's baby inherit the disease? To answer this question, we need to examine the mechanisms of heredity.

Raise a cyber child and discover the world of parenthood at …

My Virtual Child …

The Biology of Heredity

The 5 millilitres or so of semen released into the vagina during an ejaculation contain between 200 million to 500 million sperm. Only a few hundred of these sperm actually complete the 15- to 20-centimetre journey to the fallopian tubes. If an egg is present, many sperm simultaneously begin to burrow their way through the cluster of nurturing cells that surround the egg. When a sperm like the one in the photo penetrates the cellular wall of the egg, chemical changes occur, immediately blocking out all other sperm. Eggs and sperm are called gametes. **Most cells of the body have a full set of 46 chromosomes—tiny structures in the nucleus that contain genetic material. The gametes each have**

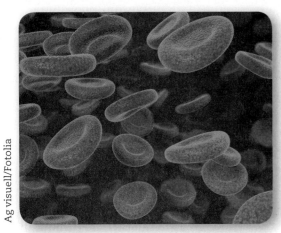

Ag visuell/Fotolia

Red blood cells carry oxygen throughout the body.

half that number—23 *chromosomes.* We can see the reason for this when we think about conception: When an egg and sperm combine at fertilization, the new individual will then have the full set of 46 chromosomes. Thus, when a sperm penetrates an egg, their chromosomes combine to produce 23 pairs of chromosomes. The development of a new human being is under way.

For most of history, the merging of sperm and egg took place only after sexual intercourse. This is no longer the case. Born in England in 1978, Louise Brown captured the world's attention as the first "test-tube baby," conceived in a laboratory dish instead of in her mother's body. Today, assisted reproductive technology is no longer experimental; it is used more than 160 000 times annually with American women, producing more than 60 000 babies (Centers for Disease Control and Prevention, 2013). In Canada, numbers are lower, with nearly 15 000 treatment cycles resulting in 24 percent live births per cycle, or approximately 3600 babies (Canadian Fertility and Andrology Society [CFAS], 2013a). Direct comparison may be difficult, however, as there have been efforts in Canada to reduce the number of multiple pregnancies (more than one baby) in assisted reproduction procedures (CFAS, 2013a). Many new techniques are available to couples who cannot conceive a child through sexual intercourse. **The best known of these,** *in vitro fertilization (IVF),* **involves mixing sperm and egg together in a laboratory dish and then placing a few of these fertilized eggs in the mother's uterus.** The photo shows this laboratory version of assisted conception, with the sperm in the dropper being placed in the dish containing the eggs. If the eggs are fertilized, in about 24 hours they are placed in the mother's uterus with the hope that they will become implanted in the uterine wall.

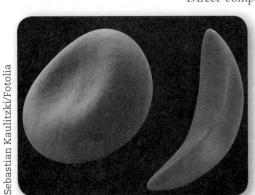

Sebastian Kaulitzki/Fotolia

Sickle-shaped blood cells associated with sickle-cell disease cannot pass through the body's smallest blood vessels.

The sperm and egg usually come from the prospective parents, but sometimes they are provided by donors. Occasionally the fertilized egg is placed in the uterus of a surrogate mother who carries the baby to term. Thus, a baby could have as many as five "parents": the man and woman who provide the sperm and egg, the surrogate mother who carries the baby, and the couple who rears the baby.

New reproductive techniques offer hope for couples who have long wanted a child, and studies of the first generation of children conceived through these techniques indicate that their social and emotional development is perfectly normal (Golombok, 2013). But there are difficulties as well. Only about one-third of attempts at in vitro fertilization succeed; many couples will thus go through more than one attempt at fertilization. What is more, when a woman becomes pregnant, she is more likely to have twins or triplets because often multiple eggs are transferred to increase the odds that at least one fertilized egg will implant in her uterus (although, as noted earlier, in Canada, clinics are working to reduce the numbers of such multiple pregnancies). The mother is also at greater risk for giving birth to a baby with low birth weight or birth defects. Finally, the procedure is expensive—the typical cost in the United States of a single cycle of treatment is between $10 000 and $15 000. The costs are similar in Canada, and vary by province. Although some procedures may be paid for by publicly funded health services (e.g., one IVF treatment per woman in her *lifetime* in Ontario; Ontario Ministry of Health and Long-Term Care, 2016), among the provinces only Quebec will fully fund infertility treatments (Canadian Fertility and Andrology Society, 2013b).

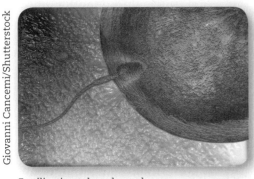

Giovanni Cancemi/Shutterstock

Fertilization takes place when a sperm penetrates an egg cell.

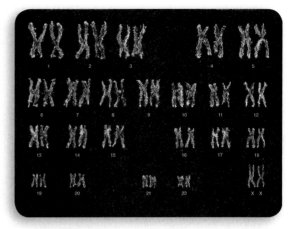

Monkey Business Images/Shutterstock

A dropper is being used to place sperm in the dish that contains egg cells.

Lawrence Lawry/Photographer's Choice RF/Getty Images

Humans have 23 pairs of chromosomes: 22 pairs of autosomes and one pair of sex chromosomes.

These problems emphasize that, although technology has increased the alternatives for infertile couples, pregnancy on demand is still well in the future.

Whatever the source of the egg and sperm, and wherever they meet, their merger is a momentous event: The resulting 23 pairs of chromosomes define a child's heredity—what he or she will do "naturally." For Leslie and Glenn, this moment also determines whether their child inherits sickle-cell disease.

To understand how heredity influences child development, let's begin by taking a closer look at chromosomes. The photo shows all 46 chromosomes, organized in pairs ranging from the largest to the smallest. **The first 22 pairs of chromosomes are called** *autosomes;* **the chromosomes in each pair are about the same size.** In the 23rd pair, however, the chromosome labelled X is much larger than the chromosome labelled Y. **The 23rd pair determines the sex of the child; hence, these two are known as the** *sex chromosomes.* An egg always contains an X 23rd chromosome, but a sperm contains either an X or a Y. When an X-carrying sperm fertilizes the egg, the 23rd pair is XX and the result is a girl. When a Y-carrying sperm fertilizes the egg, the 23rd pair is XY, and the result is a boy.

Each chromosome actually consists of one molecule of *deoxyribonucleic acid*—**or** *DNA.* The DNA molecule resembles a spiral staircase. As you can see in Figure 2-1, the rungs of the staircase carry the genetic code, which consists of pairs of nucleotide bases: Adenine is paired with thymine, and guanine is paired with cytosine. The order of the nucleotide pairs is the code that causes the cell to create specific amino acids, proteins, and enzymes—important biological building blocks. **Each group of nucleotide bases that provides a specific set of biochemical instructions is called a** *gene.* For example, three consecutive thymine nucleotides give the instruction to create the amino acid phenylalanine.

Figure 2-2 on page 52 summarizes these links between chromosomes, genes, and DNA. The figure shows that each cell contains chromosomes that carry genes made up of DNA.

A child's 46 chromosomes include about 25 000 genes (Pennisi, 2005). Chromosome 1 has the most genes (nearly 3000), and the Y chromosome has the fewest (just over 200). Most of these genes are the same in all people—fewer than one percent of genes cause differences between people (Human Genome Project, 2003). **The complete set of genes makes up a person's heredity and is known as the person's** *genotype.*

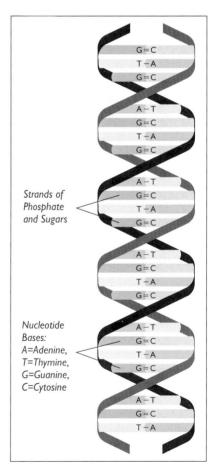

Strands of Phosphate and Sugars

Nucleotide Bases: A=Adenine, T=Thymine, G=Guanine, C=Cytosine

Figure 2-1 Pairs of nucleotide base carry the genetic code on a strand of DNA.

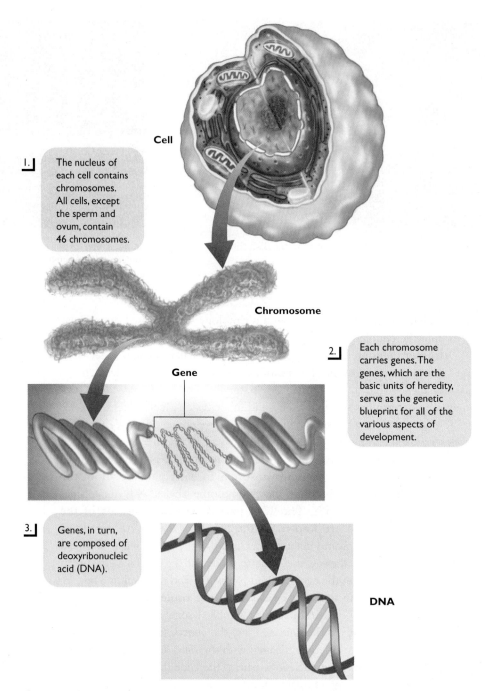

Cell

1. The nucleus of each cell contains chromosomes. All cells, except the sperm and ovum, contain 46 chromosomes.

Chromosome

2. Each chromosome carries genes. The genes, which are the basic units of heredity, serve as the genetic blueprint for all of the various aspects of development.

Gene

3. Genes, in turn, are composed of deoxyribonucleic acid (DNA).

DNA

Figure 2-2 Chromosomes, genes, and DNA within the cell.

Through biochemical instructions that are coded in DNA, genes regulate the development of all human characteristics and abilities. **Genetic instructions, in conjunction with environmental influences, produce a** *phenotype,* **an individual's physical, behavioural, and psychological features.**

In the rest of this module, we'll see the different ways that the instructions contained in genes produce different phenotypes.

Single Gene Inheritance

How do genetic instructions produce the misshapen red blood cells of sickle-cell disease? **Genes come in different forms that are known as** *alleles.* In the case of red blood cells, for example, one of two alleles can be present on chromosome 11. One allele has instructions for normal red blood cells; the other allele has instructions for sickle-shaped red blood cells. **Sometimes the alleles in the pair of chromosomes are the same, which makes them** *homozygous.* **Sometimes the alleles differ, which makes them** *heterozygous.* In Leslie's case, her baby could be homozygous, in which case it would have either two alleles for normal cells *or* two alleles for sickle-shaped cells. Alternatively, Leslie's baby might be heterozygous, which means that it would have one allele for normal cells and one for sickle-shaped cells.

How does a genotype produce a phenotype? The answer is simple if a person is homozygous. When both alleles are the same and therefore have chemical instructions for the same phenotype, that phenotype usually results. (We'll see some exceptions in Module 2.2.) If Leslie's baby had alleles for normal red blood cells on both of the chromosomes in its 11th pair, the baby would be almost guaranteed to have normal cells. If, instead, the baby had two alleles for sickle-shaped cells, her baby would almost certainly suffer from the disease.

When a person is heterozygous, the process is more complex. **Often one allele is** *dominant,* **which means that its chemical instructions are followed, whereas the instructions of the other, the** *recessive* **allele, are ignored.** In the case of sickle-cell disease, the allele for normal cells is dominant, and the allele for sickle-shaped cells is recessive. This is good news for Leslie: As long as either she or Glenn contribute the allele for normal red blood cells, her baby will not develop sickle-cell disease.

Figure 2-3 summarizes what we've learned about sickle-cell disease. The upper-case *A* denotes the allele for normal blood cells, and the lower-case *a* denotes the allele for sickle-shaped cells. In the diagram, Glenn's genotype is homozygous dominant because he's positive that no one in his family has had sickle-cell disease. From Leslie's family history, we see that she could be homozygous dominant or heterozygous; in the diagram, we've assumed the latter. You can see that Leslie and Glenn cannot have a baby with sickle-cell disease.

However, Leslie and Glenn's baby could be affected in another way. **Sometimes one allele does not dominate another completely, a situation known as** *incomplete dominance.* In incomplete dominance, the phenotype that results often falls between the phenotype associated with either allele. This is the case for the genes that control red blood cells. **Individuals with one dominant and one recessive allele have** *sickle-cell trait:* **In most situations they have no problems, but when they are seriously short of oxygen they suffer a temporary, relatively mild form of the disease.** Thus, sickle-cell trait is likely to appear when the person exercises vigorously, becomes dehydrated, or is at high altitudes (Fidler, 2012). Leslie and Glenn's baby will have sickle-cell trait if it inherits a recessive gene from Leslie and a dominant gene from Glenn, as shown in Figure 2-3.

One aspect of sickle-cell disease that we haven't considered so far is why this disorder primarily affects African Canadian children. The Cultural Influences feature addresses this point and, in the process, tells more about how heredity operates.

 QUESTION 2.1
If Glenn learns that he is heterozygous dominant for sickle-cell disease instead of homozyogus dominant, how would this affect the chance that he and Leslie would have a child with sickle-cell disease? *(Answer is on page 58.)*

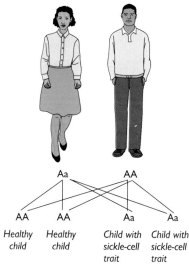

Aa		AA	
AA	AA	Aa	Aa
Healthy child	*Healthy child*	*Child with sickle-cell trait*	*Child with sickle-cell trait*

Figure 2-3 The potential allele pairings for Leslie and Glenn.

Cultural Influences

Why Do African Canadians Inherit Sickle-Cell Disease?

Sickle-cell disease affects about 1 in 400 African Canadian children. In contrast, virtually no children of European ancestry have the disorder. Why? Surprisingly, because the sickle-cell allele has a benefit: Individuals with this allele are more resistant to malaria, an infectious disease that is one of the leading causes of childhood death worldwide. Malaria is transmitted by mosquitoes, so it is most common in warm climates, including many parts of Africa. Africans with the sickle-cell allele are less likely to die from malaria than Africans who have alleles for normal blood cells. This means that the sickle-cell allele is more likely to get passed along to the next generation.

This explanation of sickle-cell disease has two implications. First, sickle-cell disease should be found in any group of people living where malaria is common. This can be seen in that sickle-cell disease can also affects some of those who trace their roots to malaria-prone regions of the Caribbean, Central America, and South America. Second, since malaria is exceedingly rare in Canada, the sickle-cell allele has no survival value to African Canadians. Accordingly, the sickle-cell allele should become less common in successive generations of African Canadians; research indicates that this is happening.

There is an important lesson here: An allele may have survival value in one environment but not in others. In more general terms, the impact of heredity depends on the environment. We'll explore this lesson in more detail in Module 2.2.

Critical Thinking Question: How best would you advise prospective parents whose child could suffer from a disorder like sickle cell disease?

The simple genetic mechanism responsible for sickle-cell disease, involving a single gene pair with one dominant allele and one recessive allele, is also responsible for many other common traits, as shown in Table 2-1. In each case, individuals with the recessive phenotype have two recessive alleles, one from each parent. Individuals with the dominant phenotype have at least one dominant allele.

Most of the traits listed in Table 2-1 are biological and medical phenotypes. These same patterns of inheritance can cause serious disorders, as we'll see in the next section.

Genetic Disorders

Genetics can derail development in two ways. First, some disorders are inherited—sickle-cell disease is an example of an inherited disorder. Second, sometimes eggs or sperm have more or fewer than the usual 23 chromosomes. In the next few pages, we'll see how inherited disorders and abnormal numbers of chromosomes can alter a child's development.

INHERITED DISORDERS. Sickle-cell disease is one of many disorders that are homozygous recessive; that is, it is triggered when a child inherits recessive alleles

---

TABLE 2-1

SOME COMMON PHENOTYPES ASSOCIATED WITH SINGLE PAIRS OF GENES

Dominant Phenotype	Recessive Phenotype
Curly hair	Straight hair
Full head of hair	Pattern baldness (men)
Dark hair	Blond hair
Thick lips	Thin lips
Cheek dimples	No dimples
Normal hearing	Some types of deafness
Normal vision	Nearsightedness
Farsightedness	Normal vision
Normal colour vision	Red-green colour blindness
Type A blood	Type O blood
Type B blood	Type O blood
Rh-positive blood	Rh-negative blood

Source: Based on McKusick, V.A. Mendelian Inheritance in Man. A Catalog of Human Genes and Genetic Disorders, Volume 3, 1995. The Johns Hopkins University Press.

---

from both parents. Table 2-2 lists four more disorders that are commonly inherited in this manner.

Relatively few serious disorders are caused by dominant alleles. Why? If the allele for the disorder is dominant, every person with at least one of these alleles will have the disorder. But individuals affected with these disorders typically do not live long enough

---

TABLE 2-2

COMMON DISORDERS ASSOCIATED WITH RECESSIVE ALLELES

Disorder	Frequency	Characteristics
Albinism	1 in 15 000 births	Tissues lack melanin; in the eye this causes visual problems and extreme sensitivity to light.
Cystic fibrosis	1 in 3000 births among those of European descent; less common in those of African and Asian descent	Excess mucus clogs respiratory and digestive tracts. Lung infections are common.
Phenylketonuria (PKU)	1 in 10 000 births	Phenylalanine, an amino acid, accumulates in the body and damages the nervous system, causing intellectual disability (intellectual developmental disorder).
Tay-Sachs disease	1 in 2500 births among Jews of European descent	The nervous system degenerates in infancy, causing deafness, blindness, intellectual disability, and, during the preschool years, death.

Source: Based on American Lung Association, 2007; Committee on Genetics, 1996; Hellekson, 2001; Online Mendelian Inheritance in Man, 2013; Thompson, 2007.

Hemophilia: Inheritance of a sex-linked disorder

		Mother (carrier) X X	
		X	X
Father **X Y**	X	X X normal girl	X X carrier girl
	Y	X Y normal son	X Y hemophiliac son

Figure 2-4 How a sex-linked disorder can be passed on.

to reproduce, so dominant alleles that produce fatal disorders soon vanish from the species. **An exception is** *Huntington's disease,* **a fatal disease characterized by progressive degeneration of the nervous system.** Huntington's disease is caused by a dominant allele found on chromosome 4. Individuals who inherit this disorder develop normally through childhood, adolescence, and young adulthood. However, during middle age, nerve cells begin to deteriorate; by this time many adults with Huntington's have already had children, many of whom will develop the disease themselves.

Some disorders are *sex-linked,* **where the gene causing the disorder is carried on one of the sex chromosomes. For example, in** *hemophilia,* **a disorder in which the blood does not clot easily and sufferers can bleed severely with even minor injury, the gene is carried on the X chromosome.** The disorder is most commonly expressed in males since males only have one X chromosome, so the risk is greater for male children, as shown in Figure 2-4. Females are generally only carriers of the disorder. As with the example of sickle-cell disease, the allele for hemophilia is recessive. Thus, a woman—with two X chromosomes—would be protected by the dominant allele but risks passing the disorder on to her sons.

Fortunately, most inherited disorders are rare. Phenylketonuria (PKU), for example, occurs once in every 10 000 births, and Huntington's disease occurs even less frequently. Nevertheless, adults who believe that these disorders run in their families want to know whether their children are likely to inherit the disorder. The Children's Lives feature shows how these couples can get help in deciding whether to have children.

More common than inherited diseases are disorders that are caused by the wrong number of chromosomes, as we'll see next.

ABNORMAL NUMBER OF CHROMOSOMES.
Sometimes individuals do not receive the normal complement of 46 chromosomes. If they are born with extra, missing, or damaged chromosomes, development is always disturbed. **The best example is** *Down syndrome,* **a genetic disorder that is caused by an extra 21st chromosome and that results in intellectual disability.**[1] Like the child in the photo, people with Down syndrome have almond-shaped eyes and a fold over the eyelid. The head, neck, and nose of a child with this disorder are usually smaller than normal. During the first

Denis Kuvaev/Shutterstock

Children with Down syndrome typically have upward-slanting eyes with a fold over the eyelid, a flattened facial profile, as well as a smaller than average nose and mouth.

[1] The scientific name is Trisomy 21, because a person with the disorder has three 21st chromosomes instead of two. But the common name is Down syndrome, reflecting the name of the English physician, John Langdon Down, who described the disorder in the 1860s.

several months, babies with Down syndrome seem to develop normally. Thereafter, though, their mental and behavioural development begins to lag behind that of the average child. For example, a child with Down syndrome might not sit up without help until about one year, not walk until two, or not talk until three—months or even years behind children without Down syndrome. By childhood, motor and mental development is substantially delayed.

Children's Lives

Genetic Counselling

Family planning is not easy for couples who fear that their children may inherit serious or even fatal disorders. The best advice is to seek the help of a genetic counsellor before the woman becomes pregnant. Working with the would-be parents, a genetic counsellor constructs a detailed family history that can be used to decide whether it's likely that either the man or the woman carries the allele for the disorder that concerns them.

According to the opening vignette, a family tree for Leslie and Glenn would confirm that Leslie is likely to carry the recessive allele for sickle-cell disease. The genetic counsellor would then take the next step, obtaining a sample of Leslie's cells (typically from her blood or saliva). The sample would be analyzed to determine whether the 11th chromosome carries the recessive allele for sickle-cell disease. If Leslie learns she is homozygous—has two dominant alleles for healthy blood cells—then she and Glenn can be assured their children will not inherit sickle-cell disease. If Leslie learns that she has one recessive allele, then she and Glenn will know they have a 50 percent risk of having a baby with sickle-cell trait. Tests can also be administered after a woman is pregnant to determine whether the child she is carrying has an inherited disorder. We'll learn about these tests in Chapter 3.

Critical Thinking Questions: What if parents could do more than just know whether their child might be at risk for a disorder such as sickle cell disease; what if parents could "genetically tailor" their child to their preferences, for example to be tall, to have superior intelligence, or to be good at sports? Would you do this for your own child? What would be the advantages/disadvantages for individuals, and for society as a whole?

Rearing a child with Down syndrome presents special challenges. During the preschool years, children with Down syndrome need special programs to prepare them for school. Educational achievement of children with Down syndrome is likely to be limited, and their average life expectancy is about 50 years (Coppus, 2013). Nevertheless, as we'll see in Chapter 8, many people with Down syndrome lead fulfilling lives.

What causes Down syndrome? Individuals with Down syndrome typically have an extra 21st chromosome that is usually provided by the egg (Vraneković et al., 2012). Why the mother provides two 21st chromosomes is unknown. However, the odds that a woman will bear a child with Down syndrome increase markedly as she gets older. For a woman in her late 20s, the risk of giving birth to a baby with Down syndrome

TABLE 2-3

COMMON DISORDERS ASSOCIATED WITH THE SEX CHROMOSOMES

Disorder	Sex Chromosomes	Frequency	Characteristics
Klinefelter's syndrome	XXY	1 in 500 to 1000 male births	Tall, small testicles, sterile, below-normal intelligence, passive
XYY complement	XYY	1 in 1000 male births	Tall, some cases apparently have below-normal intelligence
Turner's syndrome	X	1 in 2500 to 5000 female births	Short, limited development of secondary sex characteristics, problems perceiving spatial relations
XXX syndrome	XXX	1 in 500 to 1200 female births	Normal stature but delayed motor and language development

Source: Based on Milunsky, A. (2002). Your genetic destiny: Know your genes, secure your health, and save your life. Cambridge, MA: Perseus Publishing. Reprinted by permission of Aubrey Milunsky.

ANSWER 2.1
Glenn and Leslie would have a 25% chance of having a child with sickle-cell disease, a 50% chance of having a child with sickle-cell trait, and a 25% chance of having a child with neither sickle-cell disease nor sickle-cell trait.

is about 1 in 1000; for a woman in her early 40s, the risk is about 1 in 50. The increased risk may be because of the age of her eggs; a woman's eggs have been in her ovaries since her own prenatal development. Eggs may deteriorate over time as part of aging, or eggs may become damaged because an older woman has a longer history of exposure to hazards in the environment, such as X-rays.

An extra autosome (as in Down syndrome), a missing autosome, or a damaged autosome always has far-reaching consequences for development because the autosomes contain huge amounts of genetic material. Nearly half of all fertilized eggs abort spontaneously within two weeks of conception, primarily because of abnormal autosomes. Thus, most zygotes that would not develop normally are eliminated naturally (Moore, Persaud, & Torchia, 2012).

Abnormal sex chromosomes can also disrupt development. Table 2-3 lists four of the more frequent disorders associated with atypical numbers of X and Y chromosomes. Keep in mind that *frequent* is a relative term; although these disorders occur more frequently than PKU or Huntington's disease, the table shows that most are rare. Notice that no disorders consist solely of Y chromosomes. The presence of an X chromosome appears to be necessary for life.

These genetic disorders demonstrate the remarkable power of heredity. Nevertheless, to fully understand how heredity influences development, we need to consider the environment, which we'll do in Module 2.2.

Check Your Learning

RECALL Describe the difference between dominant and recessive alleles.

Distinguish genetic disorders that are inherited from those that involve abnormal numbers of chromosomes.

INTERPRET Why do relatively few genetic disorders involve dominant alleles?

APPLY Suppose that a friend of yours discovers that she may have the recessive allele for the disease cystic fibrosis. What advice would you give her?

Heredity, Environment, and Development

OUTLINE

Behavioural Genetics

Paths from Genes to Behaviour

LEARNING OBJECTIVES

1. What methods do scientists use to study the impact of heredity and environment on children's development?

2. How do heredity and environment work together to influence child development?

Sadie and Molly are fraternal twins. As babies, Sadie was calm and easily comforted, but Molly was "fussy" and hard to soothe. When they entered school, Sadie relished contact with other people and preferred play that involved others. Meanwhile, Molly was more withdrawn and was quite happy to play alone. Their grandparents wonder why these twins seem so different.

Why are Sadie and Molly so different despite having similar genes? To answer this question, we'll first look at the methods that child-development scientists use to study hereditary and environmental influences on children's development. Then we'll examine some basic principles that govern hereditary and environmental influences.

Behavioural Genetics

Behavioural genetics **is the branch of genetics that deals with inheritance of behavioural and psychological traits.** Behavioural genetics is complex, in part because behavioural and psychological phenotypes are complex. The traits controlled by single genes—such as those shown in Table 2-1—usually represent "either-or" phenotypes. That is, the genotypes are usually associated with two (or sometimes three) well-defined phenotypes. For example, a person either has normal colour vision or has red-green colour blindness; a person either has blood that clots normally, has sickle-cell trait, or has sickle-cell disease.

Most important behavioural and psychological characteristics are not either-or cases but represent an entire range of different outcomes. Take extroversion as an example. You probably know a few extremely outgoing individuals and a few intensely shy people, but most of your friends and acquaintances are somewhere in between. Classifying your friends would probably produce a distribution of individuals across a continuum, from extreme extroversion at one end to extreme introversion at the other.

Many behavioural and psychological characteristics, including intelligence and aspects of personality, are distributed in this fashion, with a few individuals at either end of the continuum and most near the middle. **Phenotypes distributed like this often reflect the combined activity of many separate genes, a pattern known as** *polygenic inheritance.* To see how many genes work together to produce a behavioural phenotype that spans a continuum, let's consider a hypothetical example. Suppose that four pairs of genes contribute to extroversion, that the allele

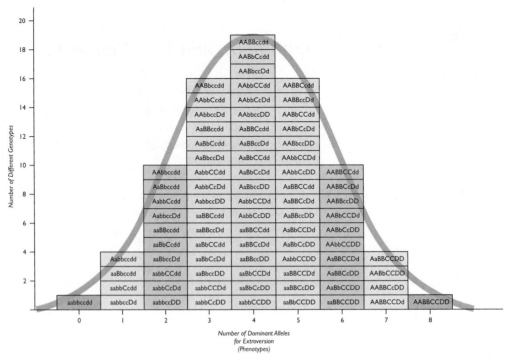

Figure 2-5 For simple polygenic inheritance the overall distribution of phenotypes produces a bell curve.

for extroversion is dominant, and that the total amount of extroversion is simply the total of the dominant alleles. If upper-case letters represent dominant alleles and lower-case letters represent the recessive alleles, the four gene pairs would be Aa, Bb, Cc, and Dd.

These four pairs of genes would produce 81 different genotypes and nine distinct phenotypes. For example, a person with the genotype AABBCCDD has eight alleles for extroversion (a party animal). A person with the genotype aabbccdd has no alleles for extroversion (a wallflower). All other genotypes involve some combinations of dominant and recessive alleles, so these genotypes are associated with phenotypes that represent intermediate levels of extroversion. Figure 2-5 shows that the most common outcome would be for people to inherit exactly four dominant and four recessive alleles: 19 of the 81 genotypes produce this pattern (e.g., AABbccDd, AaBbcCDd). A few extreme cases (very outgoing or very shy) coupled with many intermediate cases produce the familiar bell-shaped distribution that characterizes many behavioural and psychological traits.

Remember, this example is completely hypothetical. Extroversion is *not* based on the combined influence of four pairs of genes. But this example shows how several genes working together could produce a continuum of phenotypes. Something like our example is probably involved in the inheritance of numerous human behavioural traits, except that many more pairs of genes are involved and, of course, environment also influences phenotype (Plomin, DeFries, McClearn, & McGruffin, 2001).

METHODS OF BEHAVIOURAL GENETICS. If many behavioural phenotypes involve countless genes, how can we hope to unravel the influence of heredity?

Traditionally, behaviour geneticists have relied on statistical methods in which they compare groups of people known to differ in their genetic similarity. Twins, for example, provide important clues about the influence of heredity. **Identical twins are called** *monozygotic twins* **because they come from a single fertilized egg that splits in two.** Because identical twins come from the same fertilized egg, they have the same genes that control body structure, height, and facial features, which explains why identical twins like those in the photo look alike. **In contrast, fraternal or** *dizygotic twins* **come from two separate eggs fertilized by two separate sperm.** Genetically, fraternal twins are just like any other siblings; on average, about half their genes are the same. In twin studies, scientists compare identical and fraternal twins to measure the influence of heredity. If identical twins are more alike than fraternal twins, heredity is implicated.

Identical twins are called monozygotic twins because they came from a single fertilized egg that split in two and, consequently, they have identical genes.

An example will help illustrate the logic underlying comparisons of identical and fraternal twins. Suppose we want to determine whether extroversion is inherited. We would first measure extroversion in a large number of identical and fraternal twins. We might use a questionnaire with scores ranging from 0 to 100 (100 indicating maximal extroversion). Some of the hypothetical results are shown in Table 2-4.

Look first at the results for the fraternal twins. Most have similar scores for extroversion: The Aikman twins both have high scores, and the Herrod twins have low scores. On the other hand, the scores of the identical twins are even more alike, typically differing by no more than five points. This greater similarity between identical twins than between fraternal twins would be evidence that extroversion is inherited, just as the fact that identical twins look more alike than fraternal twins is evidence that facial appearance is inherited.

You can see the distinctive features of this approach in the Focus on Research feature, which describes a twin study that examined the influence of heredity on children's relationships with peers.

TABLE 2-4

SCORES FROM A HYPOTHETICAL TWIN STUDY ON A MEASURE OF EXTROVERSION

Fraternal Twins				Identical Twins			
Family	One	Other	Difference	Family	One	Other	Difference
Aikman	80	95	15	Bettis	100	95	5
Fernandez	70	50	20	Harbaugh	32	30	2
Herrod	10	35	25	Park	18	15	3
Stewart	25	5	20	Ramirez	55	60	5
Tomczak	40	65	25	Singh	70	62	8

Focus on Research

Hereditary Bases of Children's Peer Relationships

Who were the investigators, and what was the aim of the study? Children differ in the ease with which they get along with classmates and make friends. For some, interactions with peers are easy and rewarding; for others, peer interactions are troubled and painful. Michele Boivin and his colleagues from the Université de Montreal and Université de Laval—Mara Brendgen, Frank Vitaro, Ginette Dionne, Alain Girard, Daniel Pérusse and Richard Tremblay—wondered whether heredity contributed to children's success in peer relations; to find out, they conducted a twin study (Boivin et al., 2013).

How did the investigators measure the topic of interest? Children were shown photos of their classmates and asked to select the three classmates they enjoyed playing with the most and the three they liked playing with the least. A measure of children's success in peer relations was created by counting the number of times that each child was selected as a preferred playmate and subtracting the number of times that the child was selected as an unpreferred playmate. Larger scores on this measure reflect many choices as a preferred playmate and few as an unpreferred playmate.

Who were the children in the study? Initially, the sample included 198 pairs of identical twins and 276 pairs of fraternal twins, all in Grade 1. Three years later, peer relationships were measured again; this time 182 pairs of identical twins and 257 pairs of fraternal twins participated.

What was the design of the study? This study was correlational because Boivin and his colleagues examined similarity of children's peer relationships in identical and fraternal twins. The study was also longitudinal because peer relationships were assessed twice, once in Grade 1 and again in Grade 4.

Were there ethical concerns with the study? No. Parents provided consent for their children to participate and peer selections were kept confidential.

What were the results? The primary results are correlations for children's peer relationships. All the correlations are positive, a result indicating that when one twin had successful peer relations, the other often did as well. However, at both grades the correlation for identical twins is greater than the correlation for fraternal twins, indicating a much closer match in quality of peer relations for identical twins.

What did the investigators conclude? Because success in peer relations was more similar among identical twins than among fraternal twins, this suggests an important role for heredity in the ease with which children interact with their peers. Of course "success in interacting with peers" is not inherited directly. What's more likely is that children inherit certain tendencies—they're hyperactive or too aggressive—that are obstacles for successful peer interactions.

What converging evidence would strengthen these conclusions? First, although the peer selection task is a widely used and valid measure of the quality of children's peer interactions, it would be useful to determine whether these results would hold when peer interactions were observed directly. Second, the sample was not large enough to analyze the data separately for boys and girls. Such analyses, from larger samples, would be informative because boys and girls may interact differently with their peers (as we'll see in Chapters 13 and Chapter 15).

Critical Thinking Questions: If we know that one twin in, say, a kindergarten class, is unsociable, perhaps due to aggressive behaviours, should we then make interventions (such as teaching self-control) with both twins? Would it be fair to a child to assume possibility of aggression because his or her twin sibling was aggressive? On the other hand, would it be fair to peers to not intervene, knowing that a child has a propensity for aggression?

Adopted children are another important source of information about heredity. They are compared with their biological parents, who provide the child's genes, and their adoptive parents, who provide the child's environment. If an adopted child's behaviour resembles that of his or her biological parents, this shows the impact of heredity; if the adopted child's behaviour resembles his or her adoptive parents, this shows the influence of the environment.

If we wanted to use an adoption study to determine whether extroversion is inherited, we would measure extroversion in a large sample of adopted children, their biological mothers, and their adoptive mothers. (Why just mothers? Because obtaining data from biological fathers of adopted children is often difficult.) The results of this hypothetical study are shown in Table 2-5.

Overall, children's scores are similar to their biological mothers' scores: Extroverted children like Michael tend to have extroverted biological mothers; introverted children like Troy tend to have introverted biological mothers. In contrast, children's scores don't show any clear relation to their adoptive mothers' scores. For example, although Michael has the highest score and Troy has the lowest, their adoptive mothers have very similar scores. Children's greater similarity to biological than to adoptive parents would be evidence that extroversion is inherited, or at least that it has a strong genetic component.

Twin studies and adoption studies, which are described in the Summary Table, are powerful tools. They are not foolproof, however. A potential flaw in twin studies is that parents and others may treat identical twins more similarly than they treat fraternal twins. This would make identical twins more similar than fraternal twins in their experiences as well as in their genes. Adoption studies have their own Achilles heel. Adoption agencies sometimes try to place youngsters in homes like those of their biological parents. For example, if an agency believes that the biological parents are bright, the agency may try harder to have the child adopted by parents that the agency believes are bright. This can bias adoption studies because biological and adoptive parents end up being similar.

TABLE 2-5

SCORES FROM A HYPOTHETICAL ADOPTION STUDY ON A MEASURE OF EXTROVERSION

Child's Name	Child's Score	Biological Mother's Score	Adoptive Mother's Score
Anila	60	70	35
Jerome	45	50	25
Kerri	40	30	80
Michael	90	80	50
Troy	25	5	55

SUMMARY TABLE

PRIMARY RESEARCH METHODS FOR BEHAVIOURAL GENETICS

Method	Defined	Evidence for Heredity	Main Weakness
Twin study	Compares monozygotic and dizygotic twins	Monozygotic twins more alike than dizygotic twins	Others may treat monozygotic twins more similarly than they treat dizygotic twins.
Adoption study	Compare children with their biological and adoptive parents	Children more like biological parents than adoptive parents	Selective placement: Children's adoptive parents may resemble their biological parents.

The problems associated with twin and adoption studies are not insurmountable. Because twin and adoption studies have different flaws, if the two kinds of studies produce similar results on the influence of heredity, we can be confident of those results. In addition, behavioural geneticists are moving beyond traditional methods such as twin and adoption studies to connect behaviour to molecular genetics (Plomin, 2013). Today, researchers can obtain DNA by gathering cheek cells from inside a child's mouth. A solution containing the DNA is placed on a microarray—a "chip" about the size of a postage stamp—that contains thousands of known sequences of DNA. Every match between the child's DNA and the known sequences is recorded, creating a profile of the child's genotype. Researchers then look to see if the genotype is associated with behaviour phenotypes. For example, in one study 10 alleles were linked with children's skill in mathematics (Docherty et al., 2010).

This kind of molecular genetics research is challenging, in part because detecting the tiny effects of individual genes requires samples of thousands of children. But this research has the promise of linking individual genes to behaviour. And when used with traditional methods of behavioural genetics (e.g., adoption studies), the new methods promise much greater understanding of how genes influence behaviour and development (Plomin, 2013).

WHICH PSYCHOLOGICAL CHARACTERISTICS ARE AFFECTED BY HEREDITY?

Research reveals consistent genetic influence in many psychological areas, including personality, mental ability, psychological disorders, attitudes, and interests. One expert summarized this work by saying, "Nearly every … psychological phenotype (normal and abnormal) is significantly influenced by genetic factors" (Bouchard, 2004, p. 151). In the examples of twin and adoption studies, we've already seen the impact of heredity on peer relations and intelligence. You can see the range of genetic influence from a trio of twin studies, each involving young children:

- The number of letter sounds that children knew (e.g., "kuh" for k, which is an important prerequisite for learning to read) was correlated .68 for identical twins but .53 for fraternal twins (Taylor & Schatschneider, 2010).

- Scores on a measure of the ability to resist temptation—that is, obeying an instruction to not eat a tempting snack or touch an attractive gift—were correlated .38 for identical twins but .16 for fraternal twins (Gagne & Saudino, 2010).

- Scores on a measure of aggressive play with peers were correlated .55 for identical twins but .16 for fraternal twins (Brendgen et al., 2011).

Each of these studies shows the familiar signature of genetic influence: Be it knowing letter sounds, resisting temptation, or behaving aggressively toward peers, identical twins were more alike than were fraternal twins (i.e., larger correlations are found for identical twins than for fraternal twins).

We will look at the contributions of heredity (and environment) to children's development throughout this book. For now, keep in mind two conclusions from twin studies and adoption studies like those we've described so far. On the one hand, the impact of heredity on behavioural development is substantial and widespread. Heredity has a sizeable influence on such different aspects of development as intelligence and personality. On the other hand, heredity is never the sole determinant of behavioural development. If genes alone were responsible, then identical twins would have identical behavioural and psychological phenotypes. But we've seen that the correlations for identical twins fall short of the score of 1, which would indicate identical scores for identical twins. Correlations of .5 and .6 mean that identical twins' scores are not perfectly consistent. One twin may, for example, play very aggressively with peers but the other does not. These differences reflect the influence of the environment. In fact, as we saw in Chapter 1, scientists agree that virtually all psychological and behavioural phenotypes involve nature and nurture working together to shape development (LaFreniere & MacDonald, 2013).

Paths from Genes to Behaviour

How do genes work together to make, for example, some children brighter than others and some children more outgoing than others? That is, how does the information stored on strands of DNA influence a child's behavioural and psychological development? The specific paths from genes to behaviour are largely uncharted (Meaney, 2010), but in the next few pages we'll discover some of their general properties.

HEREDITY AND ENVIRONMENT INTERACT DYNAMICALLY THROUGHOUT DEVELOPMENT.   A traditional view is that heredity provides the clay of life and experience does the sculpting. In fact, genes and environments constantly interact throughout a child's development (LaFreniere & MacDonald, 2013; Meaney, 2010). To illustrate, the link between a genotype and a phenotype is often described as direct— given a certain genotype, a specific phenotype occurs, necessarily and automatically. Actually, the path from genotype to phenotype is massively more complicated and less direct than this. A more accurate description would be that a genotype leads to a phenotype but only if the environment "cooperates."

A good example of this is the disease phenylketonuria (PKU for short), which occurs only when children inherit a particular recessive gene on chromosome 12 from both parents (i.e., the child is homozygous recessive). Children with this genotype lack an enzyme that breaks down phenylalanine, an amino acid. Consequently, phenylalanine accumulates in the child's body, damaging the nervous system and leading to delayed mental development. Phenylalanine is abundant in many foods that most children eat regularly—meat, chicken, eggs, cheese—so the environment usually provides the input (phenylalanine) necessary for the phenotype (PKU) to emerge. However, in the middle of the twentieth century, the biochemical basis for PKU was discovered and now newborns are tested for the disorder. Infants who have the genotype for the disease are immediately placed on a diet that limits phenylalanine, and so the disease does not emerge; the nervous system of such a child develops normally. In more general terms, a genotype is expressed differently (no disease) when it is exposed to a different environment (one lacking phenylalanine). **The term** *reaction range* **refers to this effect—the range of phenotypes that the same genotype may produce in reaction to the environment where development takes place.**

The effect can work in the other direction, too, with the environment triggering genetic expression. That is, children's experiences can help to determine how and when genes are activated. For instance, teenage girls begin to menstruate at a younger age if they have had a stressful childhood (Belsky, Houts, & Fearon, 2010). The exact pathway of influence is unknown (though it probably involves the hormones that are triggered by stress and those that initiate ovulation), but this is a clear case in which the environment advances the expression of the genes that regulate the developmental clock (Ellis, 2004).

We've used a rare disease (PKU) and a once-in-a-lifetime event (onset of menstruation) to show intimate connections between nature and nurture in children's development. These examples may make it seem as if such connections are relatively rare, but nothing could be further from the truth. At a biological level, genes always operate in a cellular environment. There is constant interaction between genetic instructions and the nature of the immediate cellular environment, which can be influenced by a host of much broader environmental factors (e.g., hormones triggered by a child's experiences). **This continuous interplay between genes and multiple levels of the environment (from cells to culture) that drives development is known as** *epigenesis.* Returning to the analogy of sculpting clay, an epigenetic view of moulding would be that new and different forms of genetic clay are constantly being added to the sculpture, leading to resculpting by the environment, which causes more clay to be added, and the cycle continues. Hereditary clay and environmental sculpting are continuously interweaving and influencing each other.

Research in molecular genetics has begun to reveal ways in which experiences affect us. Sometimes experiences change the expression of DNA—the genetic code is preserved but some genes are "turned off." **This process is known as** *methylation* **because the chemical silencer is a methyl molecule** (van IJzendoorn, Bakermans-Kranenburg, & Ebstein, 2011). To illustrate, in one study bullying by peers was associated with increased methylation of a gene that has been linked to mood (Ouellet-Morin et al., 2013). In other words, an experience (bullying) led to changes in heredity (a gene linked to mood was "turned off").

Because of the epigenetic principle, you need to be wary when you read statements like "X percent of a trait is due to heredity." **In fact, behavioural geneticists often use correlations from twin and adoption studies to calculate a** *heritability coefficient,* **which estimates the extent to which differences between people reflect heredity.** For example, intelligence has a heritability coefficient of about .5, which means that about 50 percent of the differences in intelligence between people is due to heredity (Bouchard, 2004).

Why be cautious? One reason is that many people mistakenly interpret heritability coefficients to mean that 50 percent of an *individual's* intelligence is due to heredity; this is incorrect because heritability coefficients apply to groups of people, not to a single person.

A second reason for caution is that heritability coefficients apply only to a specific group of people living in a specific environment. They cannot be applied to other groups of people living in the same environment or to the same people living elsewhere. For example, a child's height is certainly influenced by heredity, but the value of a heritability coefficient depends on the environment. When children grow in an environment that has ample nutrition—allowing all children to grow to their full genetic potential—heritability coefficients will be large. But when some children receive inadequate nutrition, this aspect of their environment will limit their height and, in the process, reduce the heritability coefficient.

Similarly, the heritability coefficient for reading disability is greater for parents who are well educated than for parents who are not (Tucker-Drob, Briley, & Harden, 2013). Why? Well-educated parents more often provide the academically stimulating environment that fosters a child's reading; consequently, reading disability in this group usually reflects heredity. In contrast, less-educated parents less often provide the needed stimulation, and thus reading disability reflects a mixture of genetic and environmental influences.

This brings us back to the principle that began this section: "Heredity and environment interact dynamically throughout development." Both genes and the environment are powerful influences on development, but we can understand one only by considering the other, too. This is why it is essential to expand research beyond the middle-class, European Canadian or American youngster commonly studied by child-development scientists. Only by studying diverse groups of children can we really understand the many ways in which genes and the environment propel children through their developmental journeys (Tucker-Drob et al., 2013).

GENES CAN INFLUENCE THE KIND OF ENVIRONMENT TO WHICH A CHILD IS EXPOSED. In other words, nature can help to determine the kind of nurturing that a child receives (Scarr, 1992; Scarr & McCartney, 1983). A child's genotype can lead people to respond to the child in a specific way. For example, imagine a child who is bright and outgoing (both due, in part, to the child's genes). That child may receive plenty of attention and encouragement from teachers. In contrast, a child who is not as bright and is more withdrawn (again, due in part to heredity) may easily be overlooked by teachers. In addition, as children grow and are more independent, they actively seek environments related to their genetic makeup. Children who are bright (due in part to heredity) may actively seek peers, adults, and activities that strengthen their intellectual development. Similarly, children who are outgoing (due in part to heredity), like the one in the photo, actively seek the company of other people, particularly extroverts like themselves. **This process of deliberately seeking environments that fit one's heredity is called** *niche-picking*. Niche-picking is first seen in childhood and becomes more common as children get older and can control their environments. Through niche-picking, the environment amplifies genetic differences as, for example, bright children seek intellectually stimulating environments that make them even smarter and extroverted children seek socially stimulating environments that make them even more outgoing (Tucker-Drob et al., 2013).

Children who are outgoing often like to be with other people, and they deliberately seek them out, a phenomenon known as niche-picking.

Studio 8/Pearson Education Ltd

Niche-picking is a prime example of the interaction between nature, nurture, and development. Experiences determine which phenotypes emerge, and genotypes influence the nature of children's experiences. The story of Sadie and Molly also makes it clear that, to understand how genes influence development, we need to look carefully at how environments work, our next topic.

ENVIRONMENTAL INFLUENCES TYPICALLY MAKE CHILDREN WITHIN A FAMILY DIFFERENT.

One of the fruits of behavioural genetic research is a greater understanding of the manner in which environments influence children (Harden, 2014). Traditionally, scientists considered some environments beneficial for children and others detrimental. This view has been especially strong in regard to family environment. Some parenting practices are thought to be more effective than others, and parents who use these effective practices are believed to have children who are, on average, better off than children of parents who do not use these practices. This view leads to a simple prediction: Children within a family should be similar because they all receive the same type of effective (or ineffective) parenting. However, dozens of behavioural genetic studies show that, in reality, siblings are not very much alike in their cognitive and social development (Plomin & Spinath, 2004).

Does this mean that family environment is not important? No. **These findings point to the importance of** *nonshared environmental influences,* **the environmental forces that make siblings different from one another.** Although environmental forces are important, they usually affect each child in a unique way, thus making siblings different from one another. For example, parents may be more affectionate with one child than another; they may use more physical punishment with one child than another; or they may have higher academic expectations of one child than another. One teenager may have friends who like to drink, while his sibling's friends discourage drinking (e.g., Tarantino et al., 2014). All of these contrasting environmental influences tend to make siblings different, not alike. Environment is important, but as we describe its influence throughout this text, you must keep in mind that each child in a family experiences a unique environment.

Much of what we have said about genes, environment, and development is summarized in Figure 2-6. Parents are the source of children's genes and, at least for young children, the primary source of children's experiences. Children's genes also influence the experiences they have and the impact of those experiences. However, to capture the idea of nonshared environmental influences, we would need a separate diagram for each child, reflecting the fact that parents provide unique genes and a unique family environment for each of their offspring. And to capture the idea that genes are expressed across a child's lifetime, we would need to repeat the diagram for each child many times, emphasizing that heredity-environment influences at any given point are affected by prior heredity-environment exchanges.

Using this framework, we can speculate about why Sadie and Molly, the fraternal twins from the opening vignette, are so different. Perhaps their parents passed along more genes for sociability to Sadie than to Molly. During infancy, their parents included both girls in play groups with other babies. Perhaps Sadie found this exciting but Molly found it annoying and a bit stressful. Over time, possibly, their parents

QUESTION 2.2
Erik, 19, and Jason, 16, are brothers. Erik excels in school—he gets straight A's, is president of the math club, and enjoys tutoring younger children. Jason hates school, and his grades show it. How can nonshared environmental influences explain these differences? *(Answer is on page 69.)*

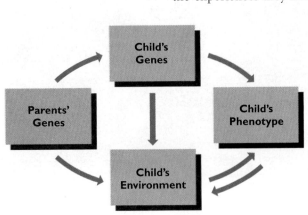

Figure 2-6 The interactions of genes, environment, and development.

unwittingly encouraged Sadie's relationships with her peers and worried less about Molly's peer relationships because she seemed to be perfectly content to look at books, colour, or play alone with puzzles. Apparently heredity gave Sadie a slighter larger dose of sociability, but experience ended up accentuating the difference between the sisters.

In a similar manner, throughout the rest of this book, we'll examine links between nature, nurture, and development. One of the best places to see the interaction of nature and nurture is during prenatal development. This is the topic of Chapter 3.

 ## Check Your Learning

RECALL What is polygenic inheritance and how does it explain behavioural phenotypes?

Describe the basic features, logic, and weaknesses of twin and adoption studies.

INTERPRET Explain how reaction range and niche-picking show the interaction between heredity and environment.

APPLY Leslie and Glenn, the couple from Module 2.1 who were concerned that their baby could have sickle-cell disease, are already charting their baby's life course. Leslie, who has always loved to sing, is confident that her baby will be a fantastic musician, and she easily imagines a regular routine of music lessons, rehearsals, and concerts. Glenn, a pilot, is just as confident that his child will share his love of flying; he is already planning trips the two of them can take together. Are Leslie's and Glenn's ideas more consistent with the active or passive views of children? What advice might you give to Leslie and Glenn about factors they are not taking into consideration?

 ANSWER 2.2

Here are three examples of nonshared environmental influences. First, as the older child, Erik's parents may have held him to higher academic standards, insisting that he do well in school; perhaps they relaxed their standards for Jason. Second, maybe Erik found a circle of friends who enjoyed school and encouraged one another to do well in school; Jason, on the other hand, may have found a group of friends who enjoyed hanging out at the mall instead of studying. Third, by the luck of the draw, Erik may have had a string of outstanding teachers who made school exciting, while Jason may have had an equal number of not-so-talented teachers who made school boring.

UNIFYING THEMES   Nature and Nurture

This entire chapter is devoted to a single theme: *Development is always jointly influenced by heredity and environment.* We have seen again and again how heredity and environment are essential ingredients in all developmental recipes, though not always in equal parts. In sickle-cell disease, an allele has survival value in malaria-prone environments, but not in environments where malaria has been eradicated. Children with genes for normal intelligence will develop below-average, average, or above-average intelligence depending on the environment in which they grow. Nature and nurture—development always depends on both.

See for Yourself

The Human Genome Project, completed in 2003, was designed to identify the exact location of all 25 000 human genes in human DNA and to determine the sequence of roughly 3 billion pairs of nucleotides like those shown in Figure 2-1. At www.genome.gov you can learn about the history of the project, about the health implications of the project, and about some of the ethical issues that are raised by mapping of the human genome. See for yourself!

Resources

For more information about . . .

human heredity, try Matt Ridley's *Genome: The Autobiography of a Species in 23 Chapters* (HarperCollins, 2000), which describes progress in genetics research by telling fascinating stories about the impact of chromosomes on intelligence, language, cancer, sex, and more.

children with Down syndrome, visit the Canadian Down Syndrome Society website at *www.cdss.ca.*

Key Terms

alleles   53

autosomes   51

behavioural genetics   59

chromosomes   50

deoxyribonucleic acid (DNA)   51

dizygotic (fraternal) twins   61

dominant   53

Down syndrome   56

epigenesis   66

gene   51

genotype   51

hemophilia   56

heritability coefficient   66

heterozygous   53

homozygous   53

Huntington's disease   56

incomplete dominance   53

in vitro fertilization   50

monozygotic (identical) twins   61

methylation   66

niche-picking   67

nonshared environmental influences   68

phenotype   52

polygenic inheritance   59

reaction range   66

recessive   53

sex chromosomes   51

sex-linked   56

sickle-cell trait   53

Summary

2.1 Mechanisms of Heredity

1. The Biology of Heredity

At conception, the 23 chromosomes in the sperm merge with the 23 chromosomes in the egg. The 46 chromosomes that result include 22 pairs of autosomes plus two sex chromosomes. Each chromosome is one molecule of DNA, which consists of nucleotides organized in a structure that resembles a spiral staircase. A section of DNA that provides specific biochemical instructions is called a *gene*. All of a person's genes make up a *genotype*; *phenotype* refers to the physical, behavioural, and psychological characteristics that develop when the genotype is exposed to a specific environment.

2. Single Gene Inheritance

Different forms of the same gene are called *alleles*. A person who inherits the same allele on a pair of chromosomes is homozygous; in this case, the biochemical instructions on the allele are followed. A person who inherits different alleles is heterozygous; in this case, the instructions of the dominant allele are followed, whereas those of the recessive allele are ignored. In incomplete dominance, the person is heterozygous, but the phenotype is midway between the dominant and recessive phenotypes.

3. Genetic Disorders

Most inherited disorders are carried by recessive alleles. Examples include sickle-cell disease, albinism, cystic fibrosis, phenylketonuria, and Tay-Sachs disease. Some disorders are sex-linked, such as hemophilia. Inherited disorders are rarely carried by dominant alleles because individuals with such a disorder usually don't live long enough to have children. An exception is Huntington's disease, which doesn't become symptomatic until middle age.

Most fertilized eggs that do not have 46 chromosomes are aborted spontaneously soon after conception. One exception occurs with Down syndrome, which is caused by an extra 21st chromosome. Individuals with Down syndrome have a distinctive appearance and are developmentally delayed. Disorders of the sex chromosomes, such as Klinefelter's syndrome, are more common because these chromosomes contain less genetic material.

2.2 Heredity, Environment, and Development

1. Behavioural Genetics

Behavioural and psychological phenotypes that reflect an underlying continuum (such as intelligence) often involve polygenic inheritance. In polygenic inheritance, the phenotype reflects the combined activity of many distinct genes. Polygenic inheritance has been examined traditionally by studying twins and adopted children, and more recently, through molecular genetics. These studies indicate some influence of heredity in three areas: intelligence, psychological disorders, and personality.

2. Paths from Genes to Behaviour

The impact of heredity on a child's development depends on the environment in which the genetic instructions are carried out, and these heredity-environment interactions occur throughout a child's life. A child's genotype can affect the kinds of experiences she has; children and adolescents often actively seek environments related to their genetic makeup. Environments affect siblings differently (nonshared environmental influence): Each child in a family experiences a unique environment.

Test Yourself

1. The human genotype consists of 22 pairs of _____ and one pair of sex chromosomes.

2. Each chromosome actually consists of one molecule of _____.

3. Inherited disorders are usually caused by _____ alleles.

4. Genetic counselling usually involves obtaining a detailed family history as well as _____.

5. When a child has extra, missing, or damaged chromosomes, the usual result is that _____.

6. Down syndrome is caused by _____.

7. _____ is the branch of genetics concerned with the inheritance of behavioural and psychological traits.

8. In _____, the phenotype reflects the combined influence of many pairs of genes.

9. When a fertilized egg splits in two, _____ result.

10. Twin studies are based on the assumption that _____.

11. In an adoption study, an inherited trait will cause adopted children to resemble their _____.

12. The main drawback to adoption studies is that _____.

13. _____ refers to the constant interaction across development between genes and multiple levels of the environment.

14. Niche-picking refers to the fact that children and adolescents _____.

15. _____ make children within a family different from each other.

Answers: (1) autosomes; (2) DNA; (3) recessive; (4) doing genetic testing; (5) development is disrupted; (6) an additional 21st chromosome; (7) Behavioural genetics; (8) polygenic inheritance; (9) monozygotic (identical) twins; (10) when heredity is involved, identical twins resemble each other; (11) biological parents; (12) agencies may place adoptees in environments like those of their biological parents; (13) Epigenesis; (14) end up being exposed to environments based on their genes; (15) Nonshared environmental influences.

3
Prenatal Development, Birth, and the Newborn

Tom Merton/OJO Images/Getty Images

From Conception to Birth

Influences on Prenatal Development

Happy Birthday!

The Newborn

If you ask parents to name some of the most memorable experiences of their lives, many mention events associated with pregnancy and childbirth. From the exciting news that a woman is pregnant through to the birth nine months later, the experience evokes awe and wonder. The events of pregnancy and birth provide the foundation on which all child development is built. In **Module 3.1**, we'll trace the events that occur during prenatal development transforming a sperm and egg into a living, breathing human being. In **Module 3.2**, we'll learn about a variety of developmental problems that can occur before birth. In **Module 3.3**, we'll turn to birth. We'll see what happens during labour and delivery and also consider some problems that can arise. In **Module 3.4**, we'll discover what newborn babies are generally like.

3.1 From Conception to Birth

OUTLINE

Period of the Zygote
(Weeks 1–2)

Period of the Embryo
(Weeks 3–8)

Period of the Fetus
(Weeks 9–38)

LEARNING OBJECTIVES

1. What happens to a fertilized egg during the first two weeks after conception?

2. When do body structures and internal organs emerge during prenatal development?

3. When do body systems begin to function well enough to support life?

Eun Jung has just learned that she is pregnant with her first child. Like many other parents-to-be, she and her husband, Kinam, are ecstatic. Soon however, they realize how little they know about "what happens when" during pregnancy. They are eager to visit the obstetrician to learn more about the typical timetable of events during pregnancy.

The changes that transform a fertilized egg into a newborn human make up *prenatal development.* Prenatal development takes an average of 38 weeks, which are divided into three stages: the period of the zygote, the period of the embryo, and the period of the fetus. Each period gets its name from the term used to describe the baby-to-be at that point in prenatal development.

In this module, we'll trace the major developments during each period. As we go, you'll learn the answer to the "what happens when" question that intrigues the parents-to-be.

Raise a cyber child and discover the world of parenthood at …

My Virtual Child . . .

Period of the Zygote (Weeks 1–2)

Figure 3-1 traces the major events of the first period of prenatal development, which begins with fertilization and lasts about two weeks. **It ends when the fertilized egg, called a** *zygote,* **implants itself in the wall of the uterus.** During these two weeks, the zygote grows rapidly through cell division and travels along the fallopian tube toward the uterus. Within hours, the zygote divides for the first time; after that, division occurs every 12 hours. Occasionally, the zygote separates into two clusters that then develop into identical twins. Fraternal twins, which are more common, are

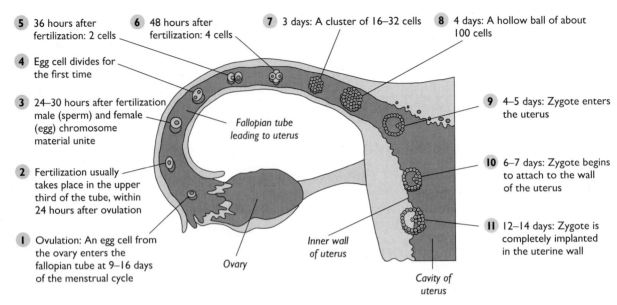

5 36 hours after fertilization: 2 cells

6 48 hours after fertilization: 4 cells

7 3 days: A cluster of 16–32 cells

8 4 days: A hollow ball of about 100 cells

4 Egg cell divides for the first time

3 24–30 hours after fertilization male (sperm) and female (egg) chromosome material unite

Fallopian tube leading to uterus

9 4–5 days: Zygote enters the uterus

2 Fertilization usually takes place in the upper third of the tube, within 24 hours after ovulation

10 6–7 days: Zygote begins to attach to the wall of the uterus

1 Ovulation: An egg cell from the ovary enters the fallopian tube at 9–16 days of the menstrual cycle

Inner wall of uterus

11 12–14 days: Zygote is completely implanted in the uterine wall

Ovary

Cavity of uterus

Figure 3-1 Development across the period of the zygote.

created when two eggs are released at the same time and each is fertilized by a different sperm cell.

While it is from the early division of the zygote that monozygotic twins arise, in rare cases the zygote may divide even more, giving rise to more identical individuals, such as triplets. The Dionne quintuplets, known as the "Dionne Quints"—five children born from one pregnancy—are a famous example of multiple monozygotes. In 1934, in Northern Ontario, five identical girls were born to the Dionne family through a natural pregnancy and childbirth, in a time before fertility drugs. Astoundingly, all five girls survived. This extremely rare occurrence made the Dionne children the focus of intense public interest, as described by Pierre Berton in his book *The Dionne Years: A Thirties Melodrama*. In the case of the Dionne quintuplets, the original fertilized zygote is believed to have split once, then each new zygote split, producing four potential individuals. A final splitting of one of the four zygotes resulted in a total of five (Berton, 1977). However many times a zygote splits, the resulting cell masses then continue to develop individually. **After about four days, the zygote comprises about 100 cells, resembles a hollow ball, and is called a** *blastocyst.*

By the end of the first week following conception, the zygote reaches the uterus. **The next step is** *implantation:* **The blastocyst burrows into the uterine wall and establishes connections with the mother's blood vessels.** Implantation takes about a week to complete and triggers hormonal changes that prevent menstruation, signaling to the woman that she is pregnant.

The implanted blastocyst, shown in the photograph, is less than a millimetre in diameter, yet its cells have already begun to differentiate. In Figure 3-2, which shows a cross-section of the blastocyst and the wall of the uterus, you can see different layers

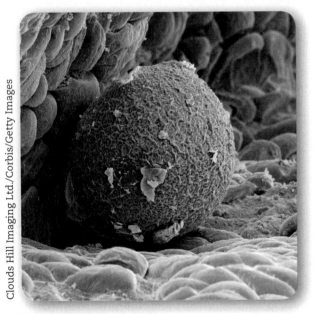

By the end of the period of the zygote, the fertilized egg has been implanted in the wall of the uterus and has begun to make connections with the mother's blood vessels.

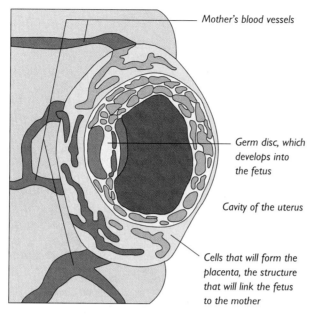

Mother's blood vessels

Germ disc, which develops into the fetus

Cavity of the uterus

Cells that will form the placenta, the structure that will link the fetus to the mother

Figure 3-2 Cross-section of blastocyst and uterine wall.

of cells. **A small cluster of cells near the centre of the blastocyst, the** *germ disc,* **eventually develops into a baby.** The other cells are destined to become structures that support, nourish, and protect the developing organism. **The layer of cells closest to the uterus becomes the** *placenta,* **a structure for exchanging nutrients and wastes between the mother and the developing organism.**

Implantation and differentiation of cells mark the end of the period of the zygote. Comfortably sheltered in the uterus, the blastocyst is well prepared for the remaining 36 weeks of the marvellous journey to birth.

Period of the Embryo (Weeks 3–8)

Once the blastocyst is completely embedded in the uterine wall, it is called an *embryo.* This new period typically begins the third week after conception and lasts until the end of the eighth week. During the period of the embryo, body structures and internal organs develop. At the beginning of the period, three layers form in the embryo. **The outer layer, or** *ectoderm,* **will become hair, the outer layer of skin, and the nervous system; the middle layer, or** *mesoderm,* **will form muscles, bones, and the circulatory system; the inner layer, or** *endoderm,* **will form the digestive system and the lungs.**

One dramatic way to see the changes that occur during the embryonic period is to compare a three-week-old embryo with an eight-week-old embryo. The three-week-old embryo shown in the photo is about two millimetres long. Cell specialization is under way, but the organism looks more like a salamander than a human being. Growth and specialization proceed so rapidly that the eight-week-old embryo shown in the photo on the next page looks very different: You can see an eye, the jaw, an arm, and a leg. The brain and the nervous system are also developing rapidly, and the heart has been beating for nearly a month. Most of

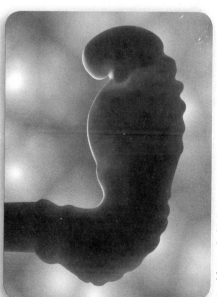

At three weeks after conception, the fertilized egg is about two millimetres long and resembles a salamander.

David Marchal/Alamy Stock Photo

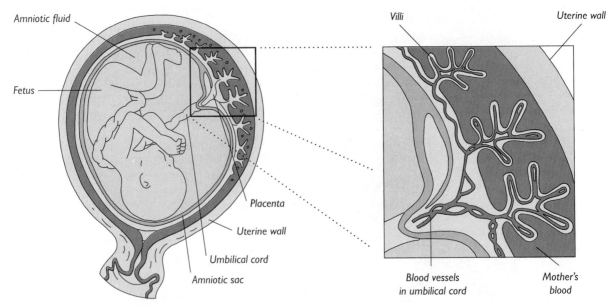

Figure 3-3 The embryonic/fetal environment within the uterus, and the position of villi in the uterine wall.

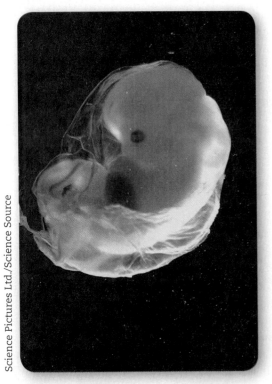

Science Pictures Ltd./Science Source

At eight weeks after conception, near the end of the period of the embryo, the fertilized egg is recognizable as a baby-to-be.

the organs found in a mature human are in place in some form. (The sex organs are a notable exception.) Yet, being only 2.5 centimetres long and weighing just a few grams, the embryo is much too small for the mother to feel its presence.

The embryo's environment is shown in Figure 3-3. **The embryo rests in an** *amniotic sac,* **which is filled with** *amniotic fluid* **that cushions the embryo and maintains a constant temperature.** The embryo is linked to the mother by two structures. **The** *umbilical cord* **houses blood vessels that join the embryo to the placenta.** In the placenta, the blood vessels from the umbilical cord run close to the mother's blood vessels but are not actually connected to them. **Instead, the blood flows through** *villi*—**finger-like projections from the umbilical blood vessels,** shown in Figure 3-3. As you can see, villi lie in close proximity to the mother's blood vessels and thus allow nutrients, oxygen, vitamins, and waste products to be exchanged between mother and embryo.

With body structures and internal organs in place by the end of the embryonic period, another major milestone passes in prenatal development. What still has to occur is for these structures and organs to begin working properly. This is accomplished in the final period of prenatal development, as we'll see in the next section.

Period of the Fetus (Weeks 9–38)

The final and longest phase of prenatal development, the *period of the fetus,* **extends from the ninth week after conception until birth.** During this period, the baby-to-be becomes much larger and its body systems begin to work. At the beginning of this period, the fetus weighs just a few grams. At about four months, the fetus weighs roughly 110 to 225 grams, enough for the mother to feel it move: Pregnant women often

Fetal Growth From 8 to 40 Weeks

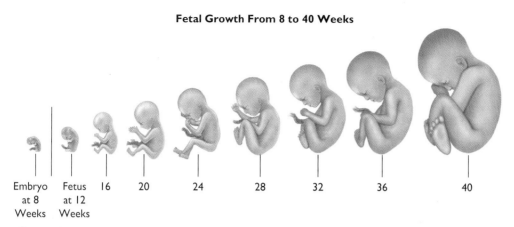

| Embryo at 8 Weeks | Fetus at 12 Weeks | 16 | 20 | 24 | 28 | 32 | 36 | 40 |

Figure 3-4 Increases in growth and development across the fetal period.

say the fetus's fluttering movements feel like popcorn popping or a goldfish swimming inside them! During the last five months of pregnancy, the fetus gains, on average, an additional three or four kilograms. Figure 3-4, which depicts the fetus at one-eighth of its actual size, shows these incredible increases in size.

During the fetal period, the finishing touches are put on the body systems that are essential to human life, such as the nervous, respiratory, and digestive systems. Some highlights of this period include the following:

- *At four weeks after conception*, a flat set of cells curls to form a tube. One end of the tube swells to form the brain; the rest forms the spinal cord. By the start of the fetal period, the brain has distinct structures and has begun to regulate body functions. **During the period of the fetus, all regions of the brain grow, particularly the** *cerebral cortex,* **the wrinkled surface of the brain that regulates many important human behaviours.**

- *Near the end of the embryonic period*, male embryos develop testes and female embryos develop ovaries. In the third month, the testes in a male fetus secrete a hormone that causes a set of cells to become a penis and scrotum; in a female fetus, this hormone is absent, so the same cells become a vagina and labia.

- *During the fifth and sixth months after conception*, eyebrows, eyelashes, and scalp hair emerge. **The skin thickens and is covered with a thick, greasy substance called** *vernix,* **which protects the fetus during its long bath in amniotic fluid.**

- *By about six months after conception*, fetuses vary in their usual heart rates and in how much their heart rate changes in response to physiological stress. In one study (DiPietro, Bornstein, Hahn, Costigan, & Achy-Brou, 2007), fetuses with greater heart rate variability were, as two-month-olds, more advanced in their motor, mental, and language development. Greater heart rate variability may be a sign that the nervous system is responding efficiently to environmental change (as long as the variability is not extreme).

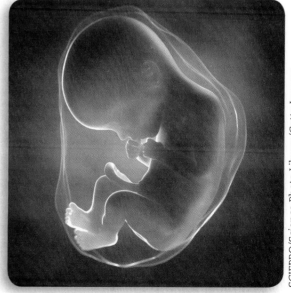

At 22 to 28 weeks after conception, the fetus has achieved the age of viability, meaning that it has a chance of surviving if born prematurely.

With these and other rapid changes, **by 22 to 28 weeks, most systems function well enough that a fetus born at this time has a chance to survive, which is why this age range is called the** *age of viability.* By this age, the fetus has a distinctly baby-like look, as you can see in the photo on the previous page. However, babies born this early have trouble breathing because their lungs are not yet mature. Also, they cannot regulate their body temperature very well because they lack the insulating layer of fat that appears in the eighth month after conception. With modern neonatal intensive care, infants born this early can survive, but they face other challenges, as described in Module 3.3.

Q&A   QUESTION 3.1

Julia is eight months pregnant and spends hours each day talking to her baby-to-be. Julia's husband considers this a waste of time, but Julia is convinced that her baby-to-be will benefit. What do you think? *(Answer is on* page 80.*)*

FETAL BEHAVIOUR.   During the fetal period, the fetus actually starts to behave (Joseph, 2000). The delicate movements that were barely noticeable at four months are now obvious. In fact, the fetus is a budding gymnast and kick-boxer rolled into one; it can punch or kick and turn somersaults. When active, the fetus moves about once a minute (DiPietro et al., 2004). However, these bursts of activity are followed by times when the fetus is still, as regular activity cycles emerge. Although movement is common in a healthy pregnancy, some fetuses are more active than others, and these differences predict infants' behaviour: An active fetus is more likely than an inactive fetus to be an unhappy, difficult baby (DiPietro et al., 1996b).

Another sign of growing behavioural maturity is that the fetus's senses work. The fetus can hear the mother's heart beating and can hear its mother speak and hear others speak to her (Lecanuet, Granier-Deferre, & Busnel, 1995). And there are tastes: As the fetus swallows amniotic fluid, it responds to different flavours in the fluid. Late in pregnancy enough light can pass through the abdominal wall for a fetus to see (Del Giudice, 2011).

The fetus can remember these sensory experiences. For example, the fetus responds distinctively (its heart rate changes) to a recording of its mother voice compared with recordings of an unfamiliar female's voice (Kisilevsky et al., 2009). And after birth, babies can remember events experienced in the uterus. Infants and children prefer foods that they tasted during prenatal development. In one study (Mennella, Jagnow, & Beauchamp, 2001), women drank carrot juice several days a week during the last month of pregnancy. When their infants were five and six months old, they preferred cereal flavoured with carrot juice. In another study (Hepper et al., 2013), eight- and nine-year-olds were more likely to prefer garlic-flavoured potatoes if their mothers had eaten garlic while pregnant.

In addition, infants recognize speech that they heard during prenatal development. In one study (DeCasper & Spence, 1986), newborns recognized *The Cat in the Hat* when their mother had read it daily for the last several weeks of pregnancy. In another study (Partanen et al., 2013), newborns recognized novel words presented during the fetal period of prenatal development. The ability of the fetuses in these studies to learn from experience shows that typical prenatal development leaves babies well prepared for life outside the uterus.

After reading findings like these, you may be tempted to buy products that claim to "teach" the fetus by providing auditory stimulation (e.g., rhythmic sounds, speech, music). Makers of these products claim that a fetus exposed to such stimulation will reach developmental milestones earlier and be better prepared for school. However, we suggest that you save your money. The learning shown in the studies described in the previous paragraph—such as recognizing voices—occurs quite rapidly after birth without prenatal "education." And some of the more sophisticated forms of learning that are claimed are probably impossible in utero, either because they require simultaneous visual stimulation (e.g., to pair voices with faces) or because they depend on brain development that takes place after birth.

The prenatal changes described in this module are summarized in the Summary Table. The milestones listed make it clear that prenatal development does a remarkable job of preparing the fetus for independent living as a newborn baby. But these astonishing prenatal changes can take place only when a mother provides a healthy environment for her baby-to-be. The Improving Children's Lives feature describes what pregnant women should do to provide the best foundation for prenatal development.

SUMMARY TABLE

CHANGES DURING PRENATAL DEVELOPMENT

Trimester	Period	Weeks	Size	Highlights
First	Zygote	1–2		Fertilized egg becomes a blastocyst that is implanted in the uterine wall.
	Embryo	3–4	A few mm	Period of rapid growth; most body parts including nervous system (brain and spinal cord), heart, and limbs are formed.
	Embryo	5–8	2.5 cm, a few grams	
	Fetus	9–12	7.5 cm, about 30 grams	Rapid growth continues, most body systems begin to function.
Second	Fetus	13–24	10–40 cm, 1 kg	Continued growth; fetus is now large enough for a woman to feel its movements, fetus is covered with vernix.
Third	Fetus	25–38	50 cm, 3–4 kg	Continued growth; body systems become mature in preparation for birth, layer of fat is acquired, reaches age of viability.

Improving Children's Lives

Five Steps Toward a Healthy Baby

1. *Visit a healthcare provider for regular prenatal checkups.* You should have monthly visits until you get close to your due date, when you will have a checkup every other week or maybe even weekly.

2. *Eat healthy foods.* Be sure your diet includes foods from each of the five major food groups (cereals, fruits, vegetables, dairy products, and meats and beans). Your healthcare provider may recommend that you supplement your diet with vitamins, minerals, and iron to be sure you are providing your unborn baby with all the nutrients it needs.

3. *Stop drinking alcohol and caffeinated beverages. Stop smoking.* Consult your healthcare provider before taking any over-the-counter medications or prescription drugs.

4. *Exercise throughout pregnancy* (in consultation with a healthcare provider). If you are physically fit, your body is better equipped to handle the needs of the baby.

5. *Get enough rest*, especially during the last two months of pregnancy. Also, attend childbirth education classes so that you will be prepared for labour, delivery, and your new baby.

For further information, see the Health Canada "Healthy Pregnancy" website, at www.hc-sc.gc.ca/hl-vs/preg-gros/index-eng.php, or the Public Health Agency of Canada's "Healthy Pregnancy Guide," available at www.phac-aspc.gc.ca/hp-gs/guide/index-eng.php.

As critically important as these steps are, they do not guarantee a healthy baby, unfortunately. In Module 3.2, we'll see how prenatal development can sometimes go awry.

 ANSWER 3.1
The fetus can hear Julia speaking, and these one-sided conversations probably help the fetus become familiar with Julia's voice. Other benefits are not obvious, however, because the fetus can't understand *what* she is saying.
. . . .

 ## Check Your Learning

RECALL Describe the three stages of prenatal development. What are the highlights of each?

What findings show that there is fetal behaviour?

INTERPRET Compare the events of prenatal development that precede the age of viability with those that follow it.

APPLY In the last few months before birth, the fetus has some basic perceptual and motor skills; a fetus can hear, see, taste, and move. What are the advantages of having these skills in place months before they are really needed?

3.2 Influences on Prenatal Development

OUTLINE

General Risk Factors

Teratogens: Diseases, Drugs, and Environmental Hazards

How Teratogens Influence Prenatal Development

Prenatal Diagnosis and Treatment

LEARNING OBJECTIVES

1. How is prenatal development influenced by a pregnant woman's nutrition, the stress she experiences while pregnant, and her age?

2. What is a teratogen, and what specific diseases, drugs, and environmental hazards can be teratogens?

3. How exactly do teratogens affect prenatal development, and what effects do they have on the continuing development of the child?

4. How can prenatal development be monitored? Can abnormal prenatal development be corrected?

Chloe is barely two months pregnant at her first prenatal checkup. As she waits for her appointment, she looks at the list of questions that she wants to ask her obstetrician: "I spend much of my workday talking on a cell phone. Is radiation from the phone harmful to my baby?" "When my husband and I get home from work, we drink a glass of wine to help unwind from the stress of the day. Is moderate drinking like this okay?" "I'm 38. I know older women more often give birth to babies with disabilities. Is there any way I can know if my baby will have disabilities?"

All of Chloe's questions concern potential harm to her baby-to-be. She worries about the safety of her cell phone, about her nightly glass of wine, and about her age. Chloe's concerns are well founded. Beginning with conception, environmental factors influence the course of prenatal development, and they are the focus of this module.

General Risk Factors

As the name implies, general risk factors can have widespread effects on prenatal development. Scientists have identified three general risk factors: nutrition, stress, and a mother's age.

NUTRITION. The mother is the developing child's sole source of nutrition, so a balanced diet that includes foods from each of the five major food groups is vital. Most pregnant women need to increase their intake of calories by about 10 to 20 percent to meet the needs of prenatal development. A woman should expect to gain between 11 and 16 kilograms during pregnancy, assuming that her weight was average before pregnancy. A woman who is underweight before becoming pregnant may gain as much as 18 kilograms; a woman who was overweight should gain at least 7 kilograms (Health Canada, 2010b). For a woman of average weight, about one-quarter of this gain reflects the increased weight of the uterus, the placenta, and the fluid in the amniotic sac; another quarter comes from increases in a woman's breasts and energy stores; yet another quarter comes from the increased volume of blood fluids and protein; the final quarter is the weight of the baby (Health Canada, 2012).

Food quantity is only part of the equation for a healthy pregnancy. *What* a pregnant woman eats is also very important. Proteins, vitamins, and minerals are all essential for prenatal development. For example, folic acid, one of the B vitamins, is important for the nervous system to develop properly (Goh & Koren, 2008). **When mothers do not consume adequate amounts of folic acid, their babies are at risk for** *spina bifida,* **a disorder in which the embryo's neural tube does not close properly during the first month of pregnancy.** Because the neural tube develops into the brain and spinal cord, improper closing results in permanent damage to the spinal cord and the nervous system.

Many children with spina bifida need crutches, braces, or wheelchairs. In Canada, since 1998, government policy has required that flour and pasta be fortified with folic acid, and even before this date, health campaigns encouraged women to consume folic acid-rich foods and folic acid supplements (Kadir & Economides, 2002). Over the past two decades, there has been a significant reduction in the incidence of neural tube defects such as spina bifida in Canada, particularly since the food fortification regulation was enacted. Studies by health researchers have shown that since fortification the Canadian incidence of neural tube defects has declined by about 50 percent (De Wals et al., 2008; Gucciardi, Pietrusiak, Reynolds, & Rouleau, 2002).

A longitudinal study in Europe, *The Dutch Famine Study*, has looked at effects of nutrition on development and across the lifespan. A famine in part of Holland during World War II led to strict food rationing in the winter of 1940. Physical and cognitive effects of extreme prenatal nutritional deprivation could be studied as a result of this "natural experiment" (Susser, Hoek, & Brown, 1998). Many people were unaffected by this event, but a significant number of those individuals who were conceived at the time of the famine have been found in adulthood to have neurodevelopmental abnormalities and an increased risk of disorders such as schizophrenia. More recently, inadequate intake of macronutrients (e.g., protein) and micronutrients (e.g., zinc, iron) during prenatal development has been shown to lead to problems in attention, memory, and intelligence (Monk, Georgieff, & Osterholm, 2013). Consequently, healthcare providers typically recommend that pregnant women supplement their diet with additional proteins, vitamins, and minerals.

STRESS. Does a pregnant woman's mood affect the zygote, embryo, or fetus in her uterus? Is a woman who is happy during pregnancy more likely to give birth to a happy baby? Is a pregnant woman like the harried office worker in the photo on the next page more likely to give birth to an irritable baby? **These questions address the impact on prenatal development of chronic** *stress,* **which refers to a person's physical and psychological responses to threatening or challenging situations.** Women who report greater anxiety during pregnancy more often give birth early or have babies who weigh less than average (Copper et al., 1996; Tegethoff, Greene, Olsen, Meyer, & Meinlschmidt, 2010). What's more, when women are anxious throughout pregnancy, their children are less able to pay attention as infants and more prone to behavioural problems as preschoolers (Huizink et al., 2002; O'Conner et al., 2002). Robert Coplan of Carleton University in Ottawa and colleagues examined associations between a mother's anxiety during and after pregnancy and infant temperament (Coplan, O'Neil, & Arbeau, 2005). Maternal anxiety both before and after birth was linked to greater infant distress reactions and difficulty in soothing the infant once distressed, thus giving evidence of an association between maternal anxiety and infant temperament. Coplan et al. (2005) also note that there may be a range of mechanisms—from biological (genetics) to behavioural (forms of learning)—underlying this link. Similar results emerged from studies of pregnant women exposed to disasters such as the September 11 attacks on the World Trade Center: Their children's physical and behavioural development was affected (Engel, Berkowitz, Wolff, & Yehuda, 2005; Laplante et al., 2004). Finally, the harmful effects of stress are not linked to anxiety in general but are specific to worries about pregnancy, particularly in the first few months (Davis & Sandman, 2010; DiPietro, Novak, Costigan, Atella, & Reusing, 2006).

Increased stress can harm prenatal development in several ways. First, when a pregnant woman experiences stress, her body secretes hormones that reduce the flow of oxygen to the fetus while simultaneously increasing its heart rate and activity level (Monk et al., 2000). Second, stress can weaken a pregnant woman's immune system, making her more susceptible to illness (Cohen & Williamson, 1991). This in turn can damage fetal development. Third, pregnant women under stress are more likely to smoke or drink alcohol and less likely to rest, exercise, and eat properly (DiPietro, 2004; Monk et al., 2013). Fourth, stress may produce epigenetic changes (described on page 66) in which genes that help children to regulate their behaviour are made less effective (Monk, Spicer, & Champagne, 2012). All these can endanger prenatal development.

We must emphasize that the results described here apply to women who experience *chronic* stress. Virtually all women sometimes become anxious or upset while pregnant. Such occasional, relatively mild anxiety is not thought to have any harmful consequences for prenatal development.

When pregnant women experience chronic stress, they're more likely to give birth early or have smaller babies, but this may be because women who are stressed are more likely to smoke or drink and less likely to rest, exercise, and eat properly.

MOTHER'S AGE. Traditionally, the 20s were thought to be the prime child-bearing years. Teenage women as well as women who were 30 or older were considered less fit for the rigours of pregnancy. Is being a 20-something really important for a successful pregnancy?

Let's answer this question separately for teenage and older women. Compared to women in their 20s, teenage mothers are more likely to have problems during pregnancy, labour, and delivery. This is largely because pregnant teenagers are more likely to be economically disadvantaged and not receive good prenatal care, often because they are unaware of the need. In countries without universal healthcare, many pregnant teens are not able to afford proper prenatal care even if they do understand its importance. Compared to women in their 20s, teenage girls are at greater risk of giving birth early and of having low-birth-weight babies (Khashan, Baker, & Kenny, 2010). Even when a teenager receives adequate prenatal care and gives birth to a healthy baby, all is not rosy. When early intervention occurs, and family, school and community offer support, then outcomes of teen pregnancy can be positive. Unfortunately, because such support is often lacking, generally children of teenage mothers do less well in school and may have behavioural problems (D'Onofrio et al., 2009; Fergusson & Woodward, 2000). If there is insufficient support, common problems of teenage motherhood—less education, poverty, and marital difficulties—can affect the child's later development (Moore & Brooks-Gunn, 2002). In the Spotlight on Theories feature, we'll see one explanation that child-development researchers have proposed for why these problems occur.

Spotlight on Theories

A Theory of the Risks Associated with Teenage Motherhood

BACKGROUND   Children born to teenage mothers typically don't fare very well. During childhood and adolescence, these children usually have lower scores on mental ability tests, get lower grades in school, and more often have behavioural problems (e.g., they're too aggressive). However, why teen motherhood leads to these outcomes remains poorly understood.

THE THEORY   It has been proposed (Jaffee, 2003) that teenage motherhood leads to harmful consequences through two distinct mechanisms. **One mechanism, called** *social influence,* **refers to events set in motion when a teenage girl gives birth, events that make it harder for her to provide a positive environment for her child's development.** For example, she may have to drop out of school, limiting her employment opportunities. Or other socio-economic deprivations and disadvantages may lead to having less time to spend on parenting, negatively affecting the child.

According to the second mechanism, called *social selection,* **some teenage girls are more likely than others to become pregnant, and the same factors that cause girls to become pregnant may put their children at risk.** Teenage girls with conduct disorder, for example—who often lie, break rules, and are aggressive—are more likely to get pregnant. The behaviours that define conduct disorder don't bode well for effective parenting.

Jaffee's original research looked at both these mechanisms. Here we'll focus on just one, the social influence mechanism.

Hypothesis: According to the social influence mechanism, measures of the initial child-rearing environment should predict outcomes for children born to teenage mothers. For example, if teenage motherhood results in less education and less income, these variables should predict children's outcomes.

Test: Jaffee (2003) evaluated both hypotheses in a 20-year longitudinal study conducted in New Zealand and found negative effects due to both social influence and social selection mechanisms. A similar study by Ellen Lipman, Katholiki Georgiades and Michael Boyle (2011) of McMaster University in Hamilton, Ontario, used the 1983 Ontario Child Health Study and its follow-up from 2001 to look at outcomes for children born to teen mothers. Lipman and colleagues investigated the associations between behaviours as young adults for those born to teenage mothers or to a former teen mother later in her life (i.e., those born when the women were teens compared to their later-born children). Measures such as educational achievement, mental health, life satisfaction, and personal income were evaluated for the two groups.

Lipman et al. (2011) found that being born to a teenage mother was associated with lower educational achievement, less life satisfaction, and lower personal income. Compared to children born when the mothers were over 21, the children of teen mothers showed poorer outcomes. Consistent with the social influence mechanism, at the time of giving birth teenage mothers were likely to be less educated and had lower incomes, and to be of lower socioeconomic status.

Conclusion: The adverse outcomes associated with teenage motherhood don't have a single explanation; however, the social influence mechanism can explain some important factors. Some of the adversity can be traced to cascading events brought on by giving birth as a teenager: Early motherhood typically limits education and income, hindering a mother's efforts to provide an environment that is conducive to a child's optimal development.

Application: Policymakers have created many social programs designed to encourage teenagers to delay child-bearing. Work such as that of Jaffe and of Lipman and colleagues suggests that policies are needed to limit the cascading harmful effects of child-bearing for those teens who do get pregnant (e.g., programs that allow them to complete their education without neglecting their children). There is also a need to help such girls learn the skills required to be an effective parent. As Lipman et al. (2011) noted, such interventions would be beneficial both immediately and in the longer term.

Critical Thinking Question: The programs suggested above deal with the person who is pregnant—the teenage girl—but what about the other person involved, the father of the baby? What programs might be set up for teenage boys to help prevent teen pregnancies?

Of course, some teenage mothers finish school, find good jobs, and have happy marriages; their children do well in school, both academically and socially. These success stories are more likely when teenage mothers live with a relative—typically the child's grandmother (Gordon, Chase-Lansdale, & Brooks-Gunn, 2004). However, teenage pregnancies with happy endings are definitely the exception: Life is a struggle for most teenage mothers and their children. Educating teenagers about the true consequences of teen pregnancy is crucial.

Are older women better suited for pregnancy? This is an important question because present-day Canadian women typically wait longer than ever to become pregnant. Completing an education and beginning a career often delay childbearing. In 2012, the average age of Canadian mothers at the time of their first child was 29.8 years, and the birthrate among women over 30 was nearly double what it was 1980 (Human Resources and Skills Development Canada, 2013; Statistics Canada, 2016a). Across Western Europe, mothers are also delaying childbirth, leading to the mean age at childbirth in Europe in 2009 being nearly 30 (European Commission: EuroStat, 2011).

Today we know that older women like the one in the photo on the following page have more difficulty getting pregnant and are less likely to have successful pregnancies. Women in their 20s are twice as fertile as women in their 30s (Dunson, Colombo, & Baird, 2002), and past 35 years of age, the risks of miscarriage and stillbirth increase rapidly. For example, among 40- to 45-year-olds, pregnancies are much more likely to result in miscarriage or in babies with low birth weight (Khalil et al., 2013). What's more, women in their 40s are more liable to give birth to babies with Down syndrome. However, as mothers, older women are effective. For example, they are just as able as younger women to provide the sort of sensitive, responsive caregiving that promotes a child's development (Bornstein, Putnick, Suwalsky, & Gini, 2006).

The number of older mothers is likely to increase because of advances in medical science. Modern reproductive technologies now make it possible for women to have babies at quite advanced ages and even after menopause, when the reproductive system naturally shuts down. The oldest mothers currently on record are women in their 60s (Associated Press, 2009; Reuters, 2007). The oldest Canadian mother is Ranjit Hayer (Coutts, 2007), who

Older women have more difficulty getting pregnant and are more likely to have miscarriages, but they are effective mothers.

gave birth at age 60. These were not natural conceptions, however: In such cases the egg came from a donor, and the mother had to be treated with hormones throughout pregnancy to mimic the natural physical state of a younger, pre-menopausal woman. This case has led to a discussion of the ethics of such situations: A woman may be desperate to have "her own baby," but does this justify the medical expenses and the risks to both mother and baby? And what about the life of a child born to a mother old enough to be his or her grandparent? The oldest woman (so far!) to give birth, an Indian woman named Daljinder Kaur, was 70 (Khoo, 2016). The previous record holder, a Spanish woman named Maria del Carmen Bousada, had twins at age 66 but then died at the age of 69, leaving her two boys motherless (Associated Press, 2009).

Although men can become parents later in life than women can naturally, they are not exempt from the effects of age. Research from Denmark suggests that paternal age may be linked to risks of congenital malformations. Zhu et al. (2005) compared the number and type of malformations found in children born to fathers aged from 20 to 50-plus years old. Although there was no overall difference in the number of malformations with fathers of different ages, some specific malformations or syndromes, including Down syndrome, were more common with older fathers. Zhu and colleagues speculated that this was due to mutations of the gametes in older men. Similar findings for Autism Spectrum Disorder (ASD) have been reported from Israel and from Iceland. The older the fathers the more likely they were to have offspring who suffered from ASD (Kong et al., 2012; Reichenberg et al., 2006), and this difference appears to be due to mutations in genes passed on by the father (Kong et al., 2012). As we noted in Chapter 2, gametes contain the genetic material—the chromosomes and genes—that give the instructions for development. So the age of the father as well as the mother can influence prenatal development.

In general, prenatal development is most likely to proceed normally when women are between the ages of 20 and 35, are healthy and eat well, get good health care, and lead lives that are free of chronic stress. But even in these optimal cases, prenatal development can be disrupted, as we'll see in the next section.

Teratogens: Diseases, Drugs, and Environmental Hazards

In the late 1950s, many pregnant women in Europe took thalidomide, a sedative prescribed to help reduce morning sickness. Samples of the drug came to Canada in 1959, and it became a licensed prescription drug here in 1962 (Picard, 2012). Soon, however, came reports that many of the women who had taken thalidomide were giving birth to babies with deformed arms, legs, hands, or fingers. **Thalidomide is a powerful *teratogen,* an agent that causes abnormal prenatal development.** Ultimately, more than 10 000 babies worldwide were harmed before thalidomide was withdrawn from the market (Kolberg, 1999; Picard, 2012). In 2012, a statue as a memorial to victims of thalidomide was set up in Germany, and an apology was issued by the head of the company that made the drug. A Canadian, Frances Oldham Kelsey, prevented a thalidomide disaster in the United States. In 1960, as a medical

Peathegee Inc/Brand X Pictures/Getty Images

officer of health for the U.S. Food and Drug Administration (FDA), Dr. Kelsey refused approval for thalidomide, citing a need for further research into the drug's effects. In 1962 Dr. Kelsey was given the U.S. President's Award for Distinguished Federal Civilian Service, and in 2015 received the Order of Canada in recognition of her work (NIH, n.d.; Peritz, 2015).

Prompted by the thalidomide catastrophe, scientists began to study teratogens extensively. Today we know a great deal about the three primary types of teratogens: diseases, drugs, and environmental hazards. Let's look at each.

DISEASES. Sometimes women become ill while pregnant. Most diseases, such as colds and many strains of flu, do not affect the developing organism. However, several bacterial and viral infections can be harmful and, in some cases, fatal to the embryo or fetus. Five of the most common of these infections are listed in Table 3-1.

Some diseases pass from the mother through the placenta to attack the embryo or fetus directly. They include cytomegalovirus (a type of herpes), rubella, and syphilis. Other diseases attack at birth: The virus is present in the lining of the birth canal, and the baby is infected during the birth process. Genital herpes is transmitted this way. AIDS is transmitted both ways—through the placenta and during passage through the birth canal. A more recent worry has been the spread of a dangerous form of Zika virus in South America and the Southern United States. Zika is transmitted via the bites of infected mosquitoes and, once in the mother's blood, can cross the placenta. Zika infection often results in what is called *microcephaly*—an abnormally small head. Recent research in Brazil has found that the virus affects brain development, with brain scans showing abnormalities of brain structure (de Olivera-Szejnfeld et al., 2016); thus even those apparently unaffected at birth might experience problems later. Professor Amir Attaran of the University of Ottawa was one of the authors of a letter to the World Health Organization (WHO) signed by nearly 200 bioethicists who called for the 2016 Olympic Games—held in Rio de Janiro, Brazil—to be cancelled because of the risk of spreading the virus (Attaran, Caplan, Gaffney, & Igel, 2016). Attaran et al. (2016) were worried that persons attending the Olympics could become infected and then carry the virus home to their own countries. The virus is unlikely to become established in Canada, however, because the mosquitoes that carry the virus cannot live here; the main risk to Canadians is from travel to Zika-affected areas.

Daniel Castelo Branco/Agencia o Dia/ Agencia Estado/Xinhua/Alamy Stock Photo

Although Zika's effects on adults tend to be mild, if a woman is infected with Zika during pregnancy, the virus can cause abnormal development of the fetus, primarily microcephaly.

TABLE 3-1

TERATOGENIC DISEASES AND THEIR CONSEQUENCES

Disease	Potential Consequences
AIDS	Frequent infections, neurological disorders, death
Cytomegalovirus	Deafness, blindness, abnormally small head, developmental disabilities
Genital herpes	Encephalitis, enlarged spleen, improper blood clotting
Rubella (German measles)	Developmental disabilities; damage to eyes, ears, and heart
Syphilis	Damage to the central nervous system, teeth, and bones

The only way to guarantee that such diseases do not harm prenatal development is for a woman not to contract the disease before or during her pregnancy. Medication may help the woman but will not prevent the disease from damaging the developing baby.

DRUGS.   Thalidomide illustrates the harm that drugs can cause during prenatal development. Table 3-2 lists other drugs that are known teratogens.

Notice that most of the drugs in the list are substances that you might use routinely: Accutane (used to treat acne), alcohol, aspirin, caffeine, and nicotine. Nevertheless, when consumed by pregnant women, they pose special dangers (Behnke & Eyler, 1993).

Cigarette smoking typifies the potential harm to the developing fetus from teratogenic drugs (Cornelius, Taylor, Geva, & Day, 1995; Espy et al., 2011). The nicotine in cigarette smoke constricts blood vessels and thus reduces the oxygen and nutrients that can reach the fetus through the placenta. Pregnant women who smoke are more likely to miscarry (abort the fetus spontaneously) and to bear children who are smaller than average at birth (Cnattingius, 2004; Ernst, Moolchan, & Robinson, 2001). Furthermore, as children develop they are also more likely to show signs of impaired attention, language, and cognitive skills, along with behavioural problems (Brennan, Grekin, Mortensen, & Mednick, 2002; Wakschlag et al., 2006).

When pregnant women drink large amounts of alcohol, their children often have fetal alcohol syndrome (FAS). Children with FAS tend to have a small head and a thin upper lip as well as delayed development.

Research by P.A. Fried and colleagues at Carleton University, Ottawa, has shown how detrimental prenatal exposure to smoking can be. Fried's research has looked at the effects of both cigarette smoking and marijuana use (Fried, 2002; Fried & Watkinson, 2001). Youth who were known to have been affected by either substance prenatally were tested with memory tasks and parts of the Wechsler Intelligence Scale for Children. Maternal smoking of either tobacco cigarettes or marijuana had negative effects. Those adolescents whose mothers smoked cigarettes showed memory deficits, and those whose mothers used marijuana had problems with attention (Fried & Watkinson, 2001). Longitudinal behavioural effects were also found among adolescents, with those whose mothers had smoked cigarettes or used marijuana more likely to do so themselves (Porath & Fried, 2005). Finally, even second-hand smoke harms the fetus: When pregnant women don't smoke but their environment is filled with tobacco smoke, their babies tend to be smaller at birth and to be born early (Meeker & Benedict, 2013). The extent of these harmful effects depends on degree of exposure—heavy smoking is more harmful than moderate smoking—and on the fetal genotype: Some children inherit genes that are more effective in defending them in utero against the toxins in cigarette smoke (Price, Grosser, Plomin, & Jaffee, 2010).

Rick's Photography/Shutterstock

TABLE 3-2

TERATOGENIC DRUGS AND THEIR CONSEQUENCES

Drug	Potential Consequences
Accutane	Abnormalities of the central nervous system, eyes, and ears
Alcohol	Fetal alcohol spectrum disorder, cognitive deficits, heart damage, retarded growth
Aspirin	Deficits in intelligence, attention, and motor skills
Caffeine	Lower birth weight, decreased muscle tone
Cocaine and heroin	Retarded growth, irritability in newborns
Marijuana	Lower birth weight, less motor control
Nicotine	Retarded growth, possible cognitive impairments

Even so, the message is clear and simple: Pregnant women shouldn't smoke, and they should avoid others who do.

Alcohol also carries serious risk. **Pregnant women who consume large quantities of alcoholic beverages may give birth to babies with** *fetal alcohol spectrum disorder (FASD).* The most extreme form, fetal alcohol syndrome (FAS), is most likely among pregnant women who are heavy recreational drinkers—that is, women who drink five or more ounces of alcohol a few times each week (May et al., 2013). Children with FAS usually grow more slowly than average and have heart problems and atypical facial features. Like the child in the photo on the previous page, youngsters with FAS often have a small head, a thin upper lip, a short nose, and widely spaced eyes.

FAS is the leading cause of developmental disabilities in North America. Approximately nine in every 1000 Canadian newborns suffer from FAS (Health Canada, 2006), and the percentage is disproportionately high in some communities. Among some Indigenous communities, incidence of FAS can be as high as 10 percent (Chudley, Conry, Cook, Loock, Rosales, & LeBlanc, 2005). Children with FAS have serious attentional, cognitive, and behavioural problems (e.g., Howell et al., 2006; Sokol, Delaney-Black, & Nordstrom, 2003), probably because exposure to alcohol prenatally causes neural impairments and actual brain damage (De Guio et al., 2014; Lebel at al., 2008). Catherine Lebel and colleagues at the University of Alberta have used MRI brain scans to map out the regions of the brain most affected. Figure 3-5 shows the brain regions where anomalies have been found in FASD children.

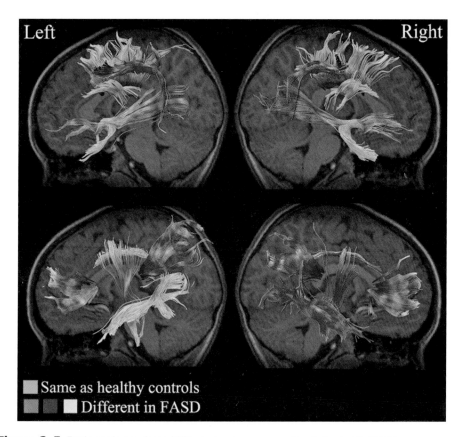

Figure 3-5 Brain regions where MRI scans show anomalies linked with FASD.

Republished with permission of John Wiley & Sons, Inc., from Alcoholism: Clinical and Experimental Research, Authors Catherine Lebel, Carmen Rasmussen, Katy Wyper, Lindsay Walker, Gail Andrew, Jerome Yager, Christian Beaulieu, Vol. 32 (10), 2008; permission conveyed through Copyright Clearance Center, Inc.

Does this mean that moderate drinking is safe? No. When women drink moderately throughout pregnancy, their children are often afflicted with partial fetal alcohol syndrome (p-FASD), which refers to children whose overall physical growth is normal but who have some facial abnormalities and impaired cognitive skills. Another less severe variant is alcohol-related neurodevelopmental disorder (ARND). Children with ARND are typical in appearance but have deficits in attention, memory, and intelligence (Loock et al., 2005; Pettoni, 2011).

It can be difficult to say for certain whether a child has been affected by alcohol. Learning difficulties, for example, can result from a variety of conditions. Diagnosis of FASD usually depends on a combination of discerning physical characteristics and testing for intellectual and behavioural deficits. A new test developed by Canadian researchers may make diagnosis simpler. James Reynolds and colleagues at Queen's University in Ontario have discovered that eye movements can be used to distinguish children suffering from FASD (Green et al., 2009; Green, Munoz, & Reynolds, 2005). Reynolds and colleagues developed a test that tracks eye movements; children with FASD show a specific pattern of eye movement not found in other conditions. If this test proves valid, it will allow reliable identification of children with FASD at a younger age than is now possible, allowing parents and doctors to put special programs in place to help these children earlier. Early recognition and testing allow for the use of the most appropriate intervention strategies (Mukherjee, Hollins, & Turk, 2006).

Is there any amount of drinking that is safe during pregnancy? Maybe, but that amount has yet to be determined. Gathering definitive data is complicated by two factors: First, researchers usually determine the amount a woman drinks by her own responses to interviews or questionnaires. If for some reason she does not accurately report her consumption, it is impossible to accurately estimate the amount of harm associated with drinking. Second, any safe level of consumption is probably not the same for all women. It is thus safest for all women to avoid drinking alcohol during pregnancy.

Factors such as those we have just discussed make it impossible to guarantee safe levels of alcohol or any of the other drugs listed in Table 3-2. The best policy, therefore, is for a pregnant woman to avoid drugs if at all possible (including over-the-counter, prescription, and illegal drugs) and to consult a healthcare professional before using essential drugs.

ENVIRONMENTAL HAZARDS.   As a by-product of life in an industrialized world, people are often exposed to toxins in the food they eat, fluids they drink, and air they breathe. Chemicals associated with industrial waste are the most common environmental teratogens, and the quantities involved are usually minute. However, just as with drugs, the amount of a chemical that might go unnoticed by an adult can cause serious damage to a developing fetus (Moore, 2003). Chemicals such as polychlorinated biphenyls (PCBs) or lead in the environment can have damaging effects, causing cognitive deficits or increased risk of disorders such as schizophrenia (Opler & Susser, 2005). Thus exposure to environmental pollutants generally can have negative effects on prenatal development. Table 3-3 lists five well-documented environmental teratogens.

You may be wondering about one ubiquitous feature of modern environments that doesn't appear in Table 3-3: cell phones. Is a pregnant woman's cell-phone usage hazardous to the health of her fetus? At this point, there's no definitive answer to that question. The radio frequency radiation that cell phones generate has sometimes been linked to health risks in adults (e.g., cancer), but the findings are very inconsistent (Verschaeve, 2009; Vijayalaxmi & Prihoda, 2012). There are few scientific studies of the impact of cell phones on prenatal development. In a study conducted in Denmark,

QUESTION 3.2
Sarah is 22 and pregnant for the first time. She smokes half a pack of cigarettes each day and has one bottle of light beer with dinner. Sarah can't believe that relatively small amounts of smoking and drinking could hurt the baby she's carrying. What would you say? (*Answer is on page 99.*)

TABLE 3-3

ENVIRONMENTAL TERATOGENS AND THEIR CONSEQUENCES

Hazard	Potential Consequences
Air pollutants*	Low birth weight, premature birth, lower test scores
Lead	Developmental disabilities
Mercury	Retarded growth, developmental disabilities, cerebral palsy
PCBs	Impaired memory and verbal skill
X-rays	Retarded growth, leukemia, developmental disabilities

Note: Air pollutants include carbon monoxide, ozone, lead, sulphur dioxide, and nitrous oxides.

cell-phone use during and after pregnancy was associated with increased risk for behaviour problems in childhood (Divan, Kheifets, Obel, & Olsen, 2008), but in a study conducted in the Netherlands, cell-phone use during pregnancy was unrelated to children's behavioural problems (Guxens et al., 2013). At this point, more research is needed to know whether radio frequency radiation from a pregnant woman's use of a cell phone is a health risk. We do know, of course, one way in which cell phones represent a huge health risk for pregnant women: Talking while driving is incredibly distracting and reduces a driver's performance to the level seen by people driving under the influence of alcohol (Strayer, Drews, & Crouch, 2006), increasing the odds of being in an accident by more than 50 percent (Asbridge, Brubacher, & Chan, 2013). So, while we wait for research to provide more information, the best advice for a pregnant woman would be to keep a cell phone at a distance when it's not being used and never use it while driving.

In the Focus on Research feature, we'll look at the effects of environmental teratogens in detail.

Focus On Research

Impact of Prenatal Exposure to Environmental Toxins on Sex Ratios

Who were the investigators, and what was the aim of the study? About 15 years ago, the number of male children born to mothers in the Aamjiwnaang First Nation was shown to be declining. Down from a stable 50:50 sex ratio, the proportion of males born decreased to about one-third. The Aamjiwnaang people live near Sarnia, Ontario, in an area of heavy industrial chemical production known as "Chemical Valley." Many petrochemical, polymer, and other industrial chemical plants are located in this region. Chemicals such as dioxins, hexachlorobenzene (HCB), and polychlorinated biphenyls (PCBs) are known to have negative effects on the body and may alter sex ratios. Like many industrial products, these chemicals have contaminated the local environment; high concentrations of the chemicals have been found in the air, water, and soil of the Aamjiwnaang people's land (Dhillon & Young, 2010; Luginaah, Smith, & Lockridge, 2010). The community was concerned, particularly regarding health issues and children's health (Luginaah et al., 2010), and cooperated with medical researchers in studying this issue. Constanze Mackenzie of the Faculty of Medicine at the University of Ottawa, Ada Lockridge of the Aamjiwnaang Environment Committee, and Margaret Keith of the Occupational Health Clinics for Ontario Workers in Sarnia-Lambton investigated whether the close proximity of the Aamjiwnaang to the chemical industries led to chemical exposure that might have affected sex ratios.

How did the investigators measure the topic of interest? Mackenzie, Lockridge, and Keith needed to compare live-birth sex ratios over recent years and see if they related to chemical contamination in the environment. To assess sex ratios, they looked at birth records from 1984 to 2003. Information on chemical exposure came from a large-scale health and environment survey being conducted by the Aamjiwnaang First Nation.

Who were the participants in the study? The sample records included all children who were born in the Aamjiwnaang First Nation from 1984 to 2003.

What was the design of the study? The study was correlational because the investigators were interested in the relation that existed naturally between two variables: exposure to environmental contaminants and sex ratio.

Were there ethical concerns with the study? No. The participants had been exposed to chemicals naturally, prior to the start of the study. (Obviously, it would not have been ethical for researchers to do an experiment that involved asking pregnant women to deliberately expose themselves to pollutants.) The investigators obtained permission from the Aamjiwnaang First Nation to use their birth and health records.

What were the results? Exposure to chemicals such as HCB, PCBs, and other contaminants affects sex ratios. From a proportion of 0.538 male births in 1984–1988 (0.512 is the expected rate for Canada), the ratio fell to 0.348 during 1999–2003. The researchers were unsure, however, exactly which of the numerous chemical pollutants (or combinations of chemicals) found in the area were responsible.

What did the investigators conclude? Prenatal exposure to chemical contamination affects sex ratios; specifically, lowering the number of boys born. This decline would have an ongoing effect on the sex balance in the community.

What converging evidence would strengthen these conclusions? The results show that chemicals affect sex ratio. More convincing would be longitudinal results showing that people in other regions who have been exposed to similar chemicals are also more likely to have daughters than sons. Some evidence is now coming out that shows that this may be so. Sex ratio imbalance is being found in some Inuit communities, and it has been proposed that this is due to high levels of chemical pollutants that have accumulated in the local food chain and thus ended up in the blood of pregnant women in Arctic villages (Arctic Monitoring and Assessment Programme, 2009).

Critical Thinking Question: Before reading on in this chapter, think: Given the research explained here, what additional advice would you give to pregnant women about their environments?

Environmental teratogens are treacherous because people are usually unaware of their presence in the environment. The women in the Mackenzie et al. (2005) study from the Focus on Research feature, for example, did not realize they were being exposed to chemicals in the environment (this may have been through food, water, or air). This invisible danger makes it more difficult for a pregnant woman to protect herself from environmental teratogens. Pregnant women need to be careful of the air they breathe and what they consume, for example, by making sure that all foods are cleaned thoroughly to rid them of insecticides. Convenience foods, which often contain chemical additives, should be avoided as much as possible, as well as air that's been contaminated by household products such as cleansers, paint strippers, and fertilizers. In situations where they might come into contact with potential teratogens (e.g., in cleaning products) women should switch to less potent chemicals, for example, using baking soda instead of more chemically laden cleansers. They should also wear protective gloves, aprons, and masks to reduce their contact with potential teratogens. Finally, because the number of environmental teratogens continues to increase, expectant mothers should check with their healthcare provider to learn if other materials should be avoided.

How Teratogens Influence Prenatal Development

By assembling all the evidence of harm caused by diseases, drugs, and environmental hazards, scientists have identified five important general principles about how teratogens usually work (Hogge, 1990; Jacobson & Jacobson, 2000; Vorhees & Mollnow, 1987).

1. *The impact of a teratogen depends on the genotype of the organism.* A substance may be harmful to one species but not to another. To determine the safety of thalidomide, researchers had tested the drug in pregnant rats and rabbits, whose offspring developed normal limbs. Yet when pregnant women took the same drug in comparable doses, many produced children with deformed limbs. Thalidomide was harmless to rats and rabbits but not to people. Moreover, some women who took thalidomide gave birth to babies with normal limbs, yet others who took comparable doses at the same time in their pregnancies gave birth to babies with deformities. Apparently, heredity makes some individuals more susceptible than others to a teratogen.

2. *The impact of teratogens changes over the course of prenatal development.* The timing of exposure to a teratogen is critical. Figure 3-6 shows how the consequences of teratogens differ for the periods of the zygote, embryo, and fetus. During the period of the zygote, exposure to teratogens usually results in spontaneous abortion of the fertilized egg. During the embryonic period, exposure produces major defects in body structure. For example, women who took thalidomide during the embryonic period had babies with ill-formed or missing limbs. Women who contract rubella during the embryonic period have babies with heart defects. During the fetal period, exposure to teratogens either produces minor defects in body structure or causes body systems to function improperly. For example, when women drink large (or even moderate) quantities of alcohol during the fetal period, the fetus develops fewer brain cells.

    Even within the different periods of prenatal development, developing body parts and systems are more vulnerable at certain times. The blue shading in Figure 3-6 indicates a time of maximum vulnerability; yellow shading indicates a time when the developing organism is less vulnerable. The heart, for example, is most sensitive to teratogens during the first two-thirds of the embryonic period. Exposure to teratogens before this time rarely produces heart damage; exposure after this time results in milder damage.

3. *Each teratogen affects a specific aspect (or aspects) of prenatal development.* In other words, teratogens do not harm all body systems; instead, damage is selective. If a pregnant

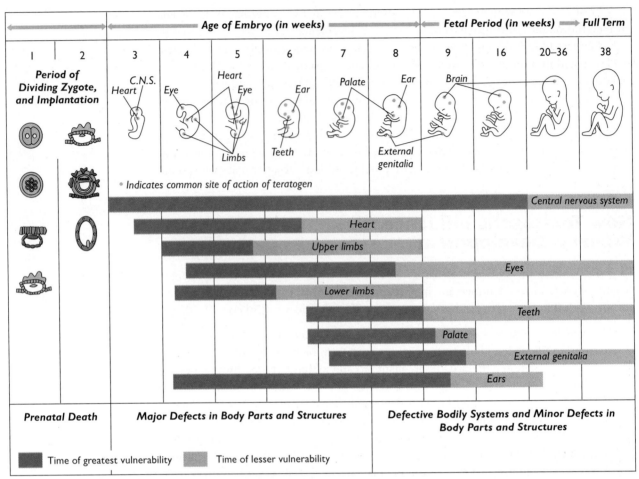

Figure 3-6 Consequences of exposure to teratogens at different stages of prenatal development.

woman contracts rubella, her baby may have problems with eyes, ears, and heart, but limbs will be normal. If a pregnant woman consumes PCB-contaminated fish, her baby typically will have normal body parts and normal motor skills but below average cognitive skills.

4. *The impact of teratogens depends on the dose.* Just as a single drop of oil won't pollute a lake, small doses of teratogens may not harm the fetus. In research on PCBs, for example, cognitive skills were affected only in those children who had the greatest prenatal exposure to these by-products. In general, the greater the exposure, the greater the risk for damage (Adams, 1999).

An implication of this principle is that researchers should be able to determine safe levels for a teratogen. In reality, this is very difficult to do because sensitivity to teratogens will not be the same for all people (and it's not practical to establish separate safe amounts for each person). Hence, the safest rule is zero exposure to teratogens.

5. *Damage from teratogens is not always evident at birth* but may appear later in life. In the case of malformed infant limbs or babies born addicted to cocaine, the effects of a teratogen are obvious immediately. A cocaine baby goes through withdrawal—shaking, crying, and being unable to sleep. Sometimes, however, the damage from a teratogen becomes evident only as the child develops. For example, between 1947

and 1971, many pregnant women in North America and Europe took the drug diethylstilbestrol (DES) to prevent miscarriages. Their babies appeared normal at birth, but as adults, females were more likely to have breast cancer or a rare cancer of the vagina and to have difficulty becoming pregnant themselves; sons of women who took DES may be less fertile and at risk for testicular cancer (National Cancer Institute, 2006). This is a case in which the impact of the teratogen is not evident until decades after birth.

THE REAL WORLD OF PRENATAL RISK. We have discussed risk factors individually, as if each were the only potential threat to prenatal development. In reality, many infants are exposed to multiple general risks and multiple teratogens. Pregnant women who drink alcohol often smoke (Baron et al., 2013). Pregnant women who are under stress often drink alcohol and may self-medicate with aspirin or other over-the-counter drugs. Many of these same women live in poverty, which means they may have inadequate nutrition and receive minimal medical care during pregnancy. When all the risks are combined, prenatal development is rarely optimal (Yumoto, Jacobson, & Jacobson, 2008).

This pattern explains why it is often challenging for child-development researchers to determine the harm associated with individual teratogens. Cocaine is a perfect example. You may remember stories in newspapers and magazines about "crack babies" and their developmental problems. Children exposed to cocaine during prenatal development suffer from a range of problems in physical growth, cognitive development, behavioural regulation, and psychopathology (e.g., Buckingham-Howes et al., 2013; Schuetze, Molnar, & Eiden, 2012). It has been argued, however, that many of the problems associated with cocaine may be partly the consequence of concurrent smoking and drinking during pregnancy and the inadequate parenting that these children receive (Bennett, Bendersky, & Lewis, 2008; Lambert & Bauer, 2012). Similarly, harmful effects attributed to smoking during pregnancy may also stem from the fact that pregnant women who smoke are more likely to be less educated and to have a history of psychological problems, including anti-social behaviour (D'Onofrio et al., 2010).

Of course, findings like these do not mean that pregnant women should feel free to light up (or, for that matter, to shoot up). Instead, they highlight the difficulties involved in determining the harm associated with a single risk factor (e.g., smoking) when it usually occurs alongside many other risk factors (e.g., inadequate parenting, continued exposure to smoke after birth).

From what we've said so far in this module, you may think that developing children have little chance of escaping harm. But most babies are born in good health. Of course, a good policy for pregnant women is to avoid diseases, drugs, and environmental hazards that are known teratogens. Doing so, coupled with thorough prenatal medical care and adequate nutrition, is the best recipe for normal prenatal development.

Prenatal Diagnosis and Treatment

"I really don't care whether I have a boy or girl, just as long as my baby's healthy." Legions of parents worldwide have felt this way, but until recently all they could do was hope for the best. Today, however, advances in technology give parents a much better idea of whether their baby is developing normally.

Even before a woman becomes pregnant, a couple may go for genetic counselling, described in Module 2.1. In genetic counselling, a counsellor constructs a family tree for each prospective parent to check for heritable disorders. If it turns out that one (or both) carries a disorder, further tests can determine that person's genotype. With this more detailed information, a genetic counsellor can discuss choices with prospective parents, who may choose to conceive naturally, taking their chances that the child will be healthy, or decide to use sperm or eggs from other people. Yet another choice would be to adopt a child.

After a woman becomes pregnant, how can we know if prenatal development is progressing normally? Traditionally, obstetricians gauged development by feeling the size and position of the fetus through a woman's abdomen. This technique is not very precise and, of course, could not be done at all until the fetus was large enough to feel. Today, however, new techniques have revolutionized our ability to monitor prenatal growth and development. **A standard part of prenatal care in Canada is the use of *ultrasound*, a procedure using sound waves to generate a picture of the fetus.** As the photo shows, an instrument about the size of a small hair dryer is rubbed over the woman's abdomen; an image is shown on a nearby TV monitor. The procedure is painless, and parents are thrilled to be able to see their babies and watch them move. The basic black-and-white picture ultrasound is still the most widely used form today, but exciting new forms of 3D and even 4D (three dimensional over time) ultrasound now exist. These techniques use ultrasound to produce a three-dimensional image of the developing baby and can allow examination of behaviours such as facial expressions as well as simple physical assessment of the fetus (Hata, Dai, & Marumo, 2010).

Ultrasound can be used as early as four or five weeks after conception; before this time the fetus is not large enough to generate an interpretable image. Ultrasound pictures are useful for determining the date of conception, which enables the physician to predict the due date more accurately. Ultrasound pictures are also valuable in showing the position of the fetus and placenta in the uterus, and they can be used to identify gross physical deformities such as abnormal growth of the head. As shown in the photo here, ultrasound can also help to detect twins or other multiple pregnancies. Finally, beginning at about 20 weeks after conception, ultrasound images can reveal the child's sex. Unfortunately, in some countries this has led to misuse of the technology for sex-selection of children. In some cultures, girls are viewed less favourably than boys, and a girl fetus may be aborted, particularly if it is a first child. Researchers from India report that both amniocentesis and ultrasound screening are being misused in this way (Tandon & Sharma, 2006). Thus the wide availability of ultrasound screening seems to have led to a subsequent sex imbalance in populations in recent years, which has led to governments stepping in to try to stop the practice of sex-selection. In China in 2015, the overall sex ratio at birth was 1.16 males to every female (United Nations, 2015); in other words, about six boys are born for every five girls. In one city, sex ratios were 165 boys per 100 girls, a finding that led to official policy to support girl babies and to stop medical institutions revealing the sex of the unborn child (Watts, 2007). In India, despite it being made illegal to use ultrasound for sex screening purposes, similar problems with sex balance and "missing girls" have led to the government setting up a Save

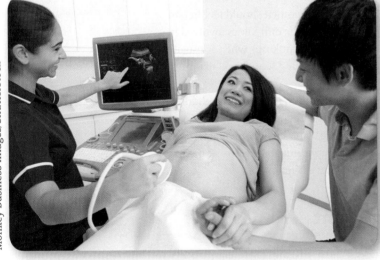

A standard part of prenatal care is ultrasound, in which sound waves are used to generate an image of the fetus that can be used to determine its position in the uterus.

Monkey Business Images/Shutterstock

the Girl Child campaign (Nolen, 2009). Because of such issues, even in some hospitals in Canada those performing an ultrasound will not tell parents the sex of the child. The Society of Obstetricians and Gynaecologists of Canada has published a policy statement arguing against such sex selection (Thiele & Leier, 2010). The ethics of this issue have even been debated in Parliament (Somerville, 2012).

When a genetic disorder is suspected, two other techniques are particularly valuable because they provide a sample of fetal cells that can be analyzed. **In** *amniocentesis,* **a needle is inserted through the mother's abdomen to obtain a sample of the amniotic fluid that surrounds the fetus.** Amniocentesis is typically performed at approximately 16 weeks after conception. As you can see in Figure 3-7, ultrasound is used to guide the needle into the uterus. The withdrawn fluid contains skin cells that can be grown in a laboratory dish and then analyzed to determine the genotype of the fetus.

In *chorionic villus sampling (CVS),* **a sample of tissue is obtained from the chorion (a part of the placenta) and analyzed.** Figure 3-8 shows a small tube being inserted through the vagina and into the uterus to collect a small plug of cells from the placenta. CVS is often preferable to amniocentesis because it can be done at about 10 to 12 weeks after conception, nearly four to six weeks earlier than amniocentesis. (Amniocentesis can't be performed until the amniotic sac is large enough to provide easy access to amniotic fluid.)

Results are returned from the lab in about two weeks following amniocentesis and in seven to ten days following CVS. (The wait is longer for amniocentesis because genetic material cannot be evaluated until enough cells have reproduced for analysis.) With samples obtained from either amniocentesis or CVS, about 200 different genetic disorders can now be detected. For example, for pregnant women in their late 30s or 40s, either

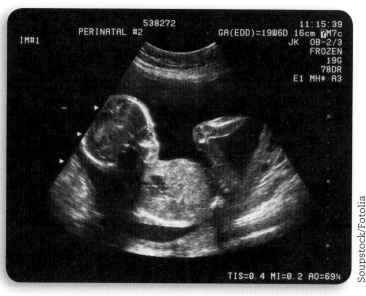

Soupstock/Fotolia

Ultrasound images can reveal the position of the fetus in the uterus and reveal the presence of multiple pregnancies.

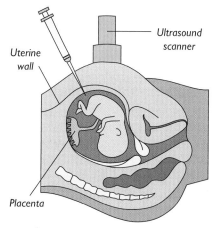

Figure 3-7 In amniocentesis a needle, guided by ultrasound, is inserted through the mother's abdomen to sample the amniotic fluid.

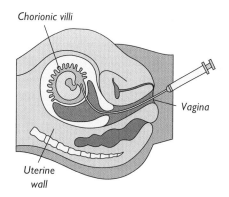

Figure 3-8 In chorionic villus sampling (CVS), a sample of tissue is obtained from the chorion.

SUMMARY TABLE

METHODS OF PRENATAL DIAGNOSIS

Procedure	Description	Primary Uses
Ultrasound	Sound waves used to generate an image of the fetus	Determine due date and position of fetus in uterus; check for physical deformities, multiple births, and child's sex
Amniocentesis	Sample of fetal cells are obtained from amniotic fluid	Screen for genetic disorders
Chorionic villus sampling (CVS)	Sample of tissue obtained from the chorion (part of the placenta)	Screen for genetic disorders

amniocentesis or CVS will often be used to determine whether the fetus has Down syndrome. These procedures are virtually error free, but they have a price: Miscarriages are slightly more likely after amniocentesis or CVS (Wilson, 2000). A woman must decide if the beneficial information gained from amniocentesis or CVS justifies the slight risk of a miscarriage. These procedures are summarized in the Summary Table.

Ultrasound, amniocentesis, and chorionic villus sampling have made it much easier to determine whether prenatal development is progressing normally. But what happens when it is not? Until recently, a woman's options were limited: She could continue the pregnancy or end it. But options are expanding. **A whole new field called** *fetal medicine* **is developing that focuses on treating prenatal problems before birth.** Many tools are now available to solve problems that are detected during pregnancy (Rodeck & Whittle, 2009). One approach is to treat disorders medically, by administering drugs or hormones to the fetus. For example, in fetal hypothyroidism, the fetal thyroid gland does not produce enough hormones, leading to retarded physical and mental development. This disorder can be treated by injecting the necessary hormones directly into the amniotic cavity, resulting in normal growth.

Another way to correct prenatal problems is fetal surgery (Warner, Altimier, & Crumbleholme, 2007). For example, spina bifida has been corrected with fetal surgery in the seventh or eighth month of pregnancy. Surgeons cut through the mother's abdominal wall to expose the fetus, then cut through the fetal abdominal wall; the spinal cord is repaired, and the fetus is returned to the uterus. When treated with prenatal surgery, infants with spina bifida are less likely to need a shunt to drain fluid from the brain and, as preschoolers, are more likely to be able to walk without support (Adzick, et al., 2011).

Fetal surgery has also been used to treat a disorder affecting identical twins in which one twin—the "donor"—pumps blood through its own and the other twin's circulatory system. The donor twin usually fails to grow. Surgery corrects the problem by sealing off the unnecessary blood vessels between the twins (Baschat, 2007). Another type of fetal surgery is performed to correct heart defects, as in a recent case widely reported in the media in Canada (e.g., Ubelacker, 2017). Doctors in the fetal medicine programs at Mount Sinai and Sick Kids hospitals in Toronto operated on a baby in utero to correct a heart abnormality that could have been fatal minutes after birth. The operation was a success, and the baby is now doing well. Fetal surgery holds great promise, but it is still highly experimental and therefore only considered as a last resort.

Yet another approach to treating prenatal problems is *genetic engineering*—**replacing defective genes with synthetic normal genes.** Take sickle-cell disease as an example.

Remember, from Module 2.1, that if a baby inherits the recessive allele for sickle-cell disease from both parents, the child has misshapen red blood cells that cannot pass though capillaries. In theory, it should be possible to take a sample of cells from the fetus, remove the recessive genes from the 11th pair of chromosomes, and replace them with the dominant genes. These "repaired" cells could then be injected into the fetus, where they would multiply and cause normal red blood cells to be produced (David & Rodeck, 2009). As with fetal surgery, however, translating idea into practice is challenging (O'Brien, 2013). Researchers are still studying these techniques with mice and sheep (Coutelle et al., 2005). There have been some successful applications of genetic engineering with older children; for example, treating inherited retinal degeneration (Maguire et al., 2009). Despite such advances, however, routine use of this method in fetal medicine is still years away.

 ANSWER 3.2
She's probably wrong. There are no known "safe" amounts of cigarette smoking or drinking. For example, her drinking might be enough to cause alcohol-related neurodevelopmental disorder.

> *Answers to Chloe's questions:* Return to Chloe's questions in the module-opening vignette (page 81) and answer them for her. If you're not certain, we'll help by giving you the pages in this module where the answers appear:
>
> - **Question about her cell phone—pages 90–91**
> - **Question about her nightly glass of wine—pages 89–90**
> - **Question about giving birth to a baby with developmental disabilities—pages 85–86**

 ## Check Your Learning

RECALL What are the important general factors that pose risks to prenatal development?

Describe the main techniques for prenatal diagnosis that are available today.

INTERPRET Explain how the impact of a teratogen changes over the course of prenatal development.

APPLY What would you say to a 45-year-old woman who is eager to become pregnant but is unsure about the possible risks associated with pregnancy at her age?

 # 3.3 Happy Birthday!

OUTLINE	LEARNING OBJECTIVES
Labour and Delivery	**1.** What are the stages in labour and delivery?
Approaches to Childbirth	**2.** What are "natural" ways of coping with the pain of childbirth? Is childbirth at home safe?
Adjusting to Parenthood	**3.** What are the effects of postpartum depression?
Birth Complications	**4.** What are some complications that can occur during birth?

Dominique is six months pregnant; soon she and her partner will begin childbirth classes at the local hospital. She is relieved that the classes are finally starting because this means that pregnancy is nearly over. But all the talk she has heard about "breathing exercises" and "coaching" sounds mysterious to her. Dominique wonders what's involved and how the classes will help her during labour and delivery.

As women near the end of pregnancy, they may find that sleeping and breathing become more difficult and that they tire more rapidly. Women generally look forward to birth, in some cases to relieve their discomfort and, of course, to see their baby. In this module, we'll see the different stages involved in birth, review various approaches to childbirth, and look at problems that can arise. We'll also look at childbirth classes like the one Dominique will be taking.

Labour and Delivery

In a typical pregnancy, a woman goes into labour about 38 weeks after conception, an event that's triggered by the flow of hormonal signals between the fetus, the mother, and the placenta (Smith et al., 2012). *Labour* is named appropriately, for it is the most intense, prolonged physical effort that humans experience. Labour is usually divided into the three stages shown in Figure 3-9 and in the Summary Table. The first stage begins when the muscles of the uterus start to contract. These contractions force amniotic fluid up against the cervix, the opening at the bottom of the uterus that is the entryway to the birth canal. The wavelike motion of the amniotic fluid with each contraction causes the cervix to gradually enlarge.

At the beginning of this stage, contractions are weak and spaced irregularly. The contractions gradually become stronger and more frequent. At the end of Stage 1, in the transition phase, contractions are intense and sometimes occur without interruption. Women report that the transition phase is the most painful part of labour. By the end of transition, the cervix is dilated about 10 centimetres in diameter.

Stage 1 typically lasts from 12 to 24 hours for the birth of a first child, and most of the time is spent in the relative tranquility of the early phase. Stage 1 is usually shorter for subsequent births, with three to eight hours being common. However, as the wide ranges suggest, these times are only rough approximations; the actual times vary greatly among women and are virtually impossible to predict.

When the cervix is fully enlarged, the second stage of labour begins. Most women feel a strong urge to push the baby out, using their abdominal muscles. This pushing, along with uterine contractions, propels the baby down the birth canal. **Soon the top of the baby's head appears, an event known as** *crowning.* In about an hour for first births and less for later births, the baby passes through the birth canal and emerges from the mother's body. **Most babies arrive head first, but a small percentage come out feet or bottom first, which is known as a** *breech presentation.*[1]

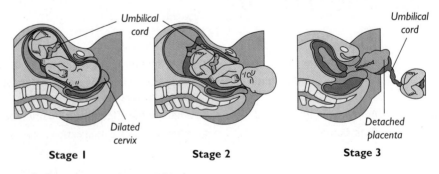

Figure 3-9 The Three Stages of Labour.

---

[1]The term is "breech" <u>not</u> "breach," as it refers to the baby coming out breeches (an old-fashioned form of short trousers) end first.

(Author Robert Kail was one of these rare bottom-first babies.) The baby's birth marks the end of the second stage of labour.

With the baby born, you might think that labour is over, but it's not. There is a third stage, in which the placenta (also called, appropriately, the *afterbirth*) is expelled from the uterus. This stage is quite brief, typically lasting 10 to 15 minutes.

The stages of labour are summarized in the following table.

SUMMARY TABLE

STAGES OF LABOUR

Stage	Duration	Primary Milestone
1	12–24 hours	Cervix enlarges to 10 cm
2	1 hour	Baby moves down the birth canal
3	10–15 minutes	Placenta is expelled

Approaches to Childbirth

Robert Kail notes that "when my mother went into labour (with me), she was admitted to a nearby hospital, where she soon was administered a general anaesthetic. My father went to a waiting room, where he and other fathers-to-be anxiously awaited news of their babies. Some time later my mother recovered from anaesthesia and learned that she had given birth to a healthy baby boy. My father, who had grown tired of waiting, had gone back to work, so he got the good news in a phone call."

These were standard hospital procedures in 1950, and virtually all North American babies were born this way. No longer. In the middle of the twentieth century, two European physicians—Grantly Dick-Read (1959) and Fernand Lamaze (1958)—criticized the traditional Western view in which labour and delivery had come to involve elaborate medical procedures that were often unnecessary and often left women afraid of giving birth. A pregnant woman's fear led her to be tense, thereby increasing the pain she experienced during labour. Physicians such as Lamaze argued for a more "natural" approach to childbirth, viewing labour and delivery as life events to be celebrated rather than medical procedures to be endured.

Today many varieties of prepared childbirth are available to pregnant women. Most share some fundamental beliefs. One is that birth is more likely to be problem-free and rewarding when mothers and fathers understand what is happening during pregnancy, labour, and delivery. Consequently, *prepared childbirth* means going to classes to learn basic facts about pregnancy and childbirth (like the material presented in this chapter).

A second common element is that natural methods of dealing with pain are emphasized over medication. Why? When a woman is anaesthetized, either with general anaesthesia or regional anaesthesia such as epidural analgesia, in which drugs are injected into the space below the spinal cord and only the lower body is numbed, she cannot use her abdominal muscles to help push the baby through the birth canal. These medications reduce the pain of childbirth but sometimes cause women to experience headaches or decreased blood pressure (American College of Obstetricians and Gynecologists, 2011a). Also, drugs that reduce the pain of childbirth cross the placenta and can affect the baby, for example, making the baby withdrawn or irritable for a time after the birth (Brazelton, Nugent, & Lester, 1987; Ransjoe-Arvidson et al., 2001). These effects are temporary, but they may give the new mother the impression that she has a difficult baby. It is best, therefore, to minimize the use of pain-relieving drugs during birth.

Relaxation is the key to reducing birth pain without drugs. Because pain often feels greater when a person is tense, pregnant women learn to relax during labour, through deep breathing or by visualizing a reassuring, pleasant scene or experience. Whenever they begin to experience pain during labour, they use these methods to relax.

A third common element of prepared childbirth is the involvement of a supportive adult, who may be the father-to-be, a relative, a close friend, or a trained birth assistant known as a doula (a *doula* **is a person familiar with childbirth who is not part of the medical staff but instead provides emotional and physical support throughout labour and delivery**). These people provide emotional support, act as advocates (communicating a woman's wishes to healthcare personnel), and help a woman use techniques for managing pain. When pregnant women are supported in this manner, their labour tends to be shorter, they use less medication, and they report greater satisfaction with childbirth (Hodnett, Gates, Hofmeyr, & Sakala, 2012).

Another basic premise of the trend toward natural childbirth is that birth need not always take place in a hospital. Nearly all babies in the United States are born in hospitals; only 1 percent are born at home (Martin et al., 2013). For Americans accustomed to hospital delivery, home delivery can seem like a risky proposition and some medical professionals remain skeptical (Declercq, 2012). Most Canadian babies are also born in hospital; however, home birth is a common practice in some European countries. In the Netherlands, for example, about one-third of all births take place at home (Wiegers, van der Zee, & Keirse, 1998). Advocates note that home delivery is less expensive and that most women are more relaxed during labour in their homes. Many women also enjoy the greater control they have over labour and birth in a home delivery. That said, women should consider birth at home only if they are healthy, their pregnancy has been problem free, labour and delivery are expected to be problem free, a trained healthcare professional is present to assist, and comprehensive medical care is readily available should the need arise (Wax, Pinette, & Cartin, 2010).

One of the healthcare professionals often involved in childbirth is the trained midwife. Midwives may provide care throughout pregnancy and for several weeks after the birth. Midwifery services are regulated in most, but not all, provinces of Canada (Canadian Institute for Health Information, 2004), which means that midwifery services may or may not be paid for by provincial health programs. Although midwives are generally associated with at-home births, the number of hospital births attended by midwives in Canada has been increasing over recent years. In Ontario, the number of hospital births attended by midwives increased sevenfold between 1994 and 2001 (Canadian Institute for Health Information, 2004). Among many Indigenous peoples, the midwife is regarded as an important member of the community, and

Monkey Business Images/Shutterstock

During childbirth preparation classes, pregnant women learn exercises to help them relax and reduce the pain associated with childbirth.

midwifery is esteemed as a source of traditional knowledge (National Aboriginal Health Organization, 2004). The importance of and respect accorded the midwife in Indigenous culture is reflected in the names for this profession. Indigenous languages use words such as "watch" or "care" in terms referring to midwives. Among the Nuu-chah-nulth (a people of British Columbia), the term for midwife translates as "she who can do everything" (National Aboriginal Health Organization, 2004, p. 24). Such terms acknowledge the midwives' expertise as noted by others in the community and the honour accorded them within these cultures.

In many countries around the world, including Canada, a midwife can deliver the baby.

Adjusting to Parenthood

For parents, the time immediately after a trouble-free birth is often full of excitement, pride, and joy—the much-anticipated baby is finally here! But it is also a time of adjustment for parents (and for siblings, as we'll see in Module 14.3). A woman experiences many physical changes after birth. Her breasts begin to produce milk, her uterus gradually becomes smaller, returning to its normal size in five or six weeks, and her levels of female hormones (e.g., estrogen) drop.

Parents must also adjust psychologically. They reorganize old routines, particularly those related to any previously born children, to fit the new arrival's sleep-wake cycle (which is described in Module 3.4). Sometimes, in the process, fathers feel left out as mothers devote most of their attention to the baby.

Researchers once believed that an important part of parents' adjustment involved forming an emotional bond to the infant. That is, the first few days of life were thought to be a critical period for close physical contact between parents and babies; without such contact, parents and babies would find it difficult to bond emotionally (Klaus & Kennell, 1976). Today, however, we know that such contact in the first few days after birth—although beneficial for babies and pleasurable for babies and parents alike—is not essential for normal development (Eyer, 1992). In Module 10.3, we'll learn what steps are essential to forge these emotional bonds and when they typically take place.

Becoming a parent can be a huge adjustment, so it's not surprising that roughly half of all new mothers find that their initial excitement gives way to irritation, resentment, and crying spells—the so-called "baby blues." These feelings usually last a week or two and probably reflect both the stress of caring for a new baby and the physiological changes that take place as a woman's body returns to a nonpregnant state (Brockington,1996).

For 10 to 15 percent of new mothers, however, irritability continues for months, and is often accompanied by feelings of low self-worth, disturbed sleep, poor appetite, and apathy—a condition known as *postpartum depression.* Postpartum depression does not strike randomly. Biology contributes: Changes in hormonal levels following birth place some women at risk for postpartum depression (O'Hara & McCabe, 2013). Experience also contributes: Women are more likely to experience postpartum depression when they were depressed before pregnancy, are coping with other life stresses (e.g., death of a loved one or moving to a new residence), did not plan to become pregnant, and/or lack other adults (e.g., the father) to support their adjustment to motherhood (Edwards et al., 2012; O'Hara, 2009).

QUESTION 3.3

Rosa gave birth a week ago. Once or twice a day, she has crying spells and usually gets angry at her husband even though he's been quite helpful to her and the baby. Do you think Rosa has postpartum depression? *(Answer is on* page 109.*)*

Women who suffer postpartum depression may be lethargic and emotionless and are not likely to mother warmly and enthusiastically. They typically do not touch and cuddle their new babies much or talk to them, and they are less effective in the common but essential tasks of feeding and sleep routines (Field, 2010). When postpartum depression persists over years, children's development is affected (Goodman et al., 2011). For example, antisocial behaviour is more common (Hay, Pawlby, Waters, Perra, & Sharp, 2010), and such effects are stronger when children have few opportunities to interact with nondepressed adults.

Thus, postpartum depression should not be taken lightly: If a mother's depression doesn't lift after a few weeks, she should seek help. Home visits by trained healthcare professionals can be valuable (O'Hara & McCabe, 2013). During these visits, these healthcare professionals show mothers better ways to cope with the many changes that accompany the new baby; they also provide emotional support by being caring, sensitive listeners; and, if necessary, they can refer the mother to other needed resources in the community. Finally, it's worth mentioning one simple way to reduce the risk of postpartum depression: breastfeeding. Mothers who breastfeed are less likely to become depressed, perhaps because breastfeeding releases hormones that are antidepressants (Gagliardi, 2005).

Birth Complications

Women who are healthy when they become pregnant usually have a normal pregnancy, labour, and delivery. When women are not healthy or don't receive adequate prenatal care, problems can surface during labour and delivery. (Of course, even healthy women have problems but not as often.) The more common birth complications are listed in Table 3-4.

Some of these complications, such as a prolapsed umbilical cord, are dangerous because they can disrupt the flow of blood through the umbilical cord. **If this flow of blood is disrupted, infants do not receive adequate oxygen, a condition known as** *hypoxia.* Hypoxia sometimes occurs during labour and delivery because the umbilical cord is pinched or squeezed shut, cutting off the flow of blood to the baby. Hypoxia is very serious because it can lead to developmental disabilities or death (Hogan, de Haan, Datta, & Kirkham, 2006).

To guard against hypoxia, fetal heart rate is monitored during labour, either by ultrasound or with a tiny electrode that is passed through the vagina and attached to the scalp of the fetus. An abrupt change in heart rate can be a sign that the fetus is not receiving

TABLE 3-4

COMMON BIRTH COMPLICATIONS

Complication	Features
Cephalopelvic disproportion	The infant's head is larger than the pelvis, making it impossible for the baby to pass through the birth canal.
Irregular position	In shoulder presentation, the baby is lying crosswise in the uterus and the shoulder appears first; in breech presentation, the buttocks appear first.
Pre-eclampsia	A pregnant woman has high blood pressure, protein in her urine, and swelling in her extremities (due to fluid retention).
Prolapsed umbilical cord	The umbilical cord precedes the baby through the birth canal and is squeezed shut, cutting off oxygen to the baby.

enough oxygen. If the heart rate does change suddenly, a healthcare professional will try to confirm whether the fetus is in distress, perhaps by measuring fetal heart rate with a stethoscope on the mother's abdomen.

When a fetus is in distress or when the fetus is in an irregular position or is too large to pass through the birth canal, a physician may decide to remove it from the mother's uterus surgically (American College of Obstetricians and Gynecologists, 2011b). **In a** *Caesarean section (or C-section)* **an incision is made in the abdomen to remove the baby from the uterus.** A C-section is riskier for mothers than a vaginal delivery because of increased bleeding and greater danger of infection. A C-section poses little risk for babies, although they are often briefly lethargic from the anaesthesia that the mother receives before the operation. Mother-infant interactions are much the same for babies delivered vaginally or by planned or unplanned C-sections (Durik, Hyde, & Clark, 2000).

Birth complications are not only hazardous for a newborn's health but can also have long-term effects. When babies experience many birth complications, they are at risk for possibly becoming aggressive or violent and for developing psychiatric disorders (e.g., de Haan et al., 2006; Fazel et al., 2012). This is particularly true for newborns with birth complications who later experience family adversity such as living in poverty. In one study (Arseneault, Tremblay, Boulerice, & Saucier, 2002), boys who had life-threatening birth complications such as umbilical cord prolapse or pre-eclampsia were more aggressive as 6-year-olds and more violent as 17-year-olds (e.g., they participated in gang fights or carried weapons). This was true, however, only when boys had also experienced family adversity such as limited income or the absence of a parent. This outcome underscores the importance of excellent healthcare throughout pregnancy and labour and the need for a supportive environment throughout childhood.

PREMATURITY AND LOW BIRTH WEIGHT. Normally, gestation takes 38 weeks from conception to birth. *Premature infants* **are born less than 37 weeks after conception** (Canadian Institute for Health Information [CIHI], 2009; World Health Organization, 2005). *Small-for-date,* **or small for gestational age (SGA; CIHI, 2009), infants are substantially smaller than would be expected based on the length of time since conception.** Sometimes these two complications coincide but not necessarily. Some, but not all, small-for-date infants are premature; conversely, some, but not all, premature infants are small-for-date. In other words, an infant can go the full nine-month term and be under the average 3.5 to 4 kilograms birth weight of newborns; the child is therefore small-for-date but not premature. Similarly, an infant born at seven months that weighs 1.36 kilograms (the average weight of a seven-month fetus) is only premature. But if the baby born after seven months weighs

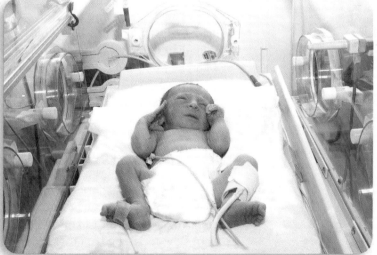

Small-for-date babies often survive, but typically their cognitive and motor development is delayed.

less than the average, it is both premature and small-for-date. About 8 percent of babies born in Canada are preterm, and another 8.5 percent are small-for-date (CIHI, 2012).

Of the two complications, prematurity is the less serious. Although survival rates differ from country to country, in modern industrialized nations, advances in medicine have increased survival rates for premature babies (e.g., Blennow et al., 2009; Larroque et al., 2008). Even for the extremely preterm (22 to 26 weeks gestation), most will survive if given appropriate neonatal intensive care (Blennow et al., 2009; Stephens, Tucker, & Vohr, 2010). The University of Iowa Children's Hospital keeps records on the smallest surviving premature babies in their "Tiniest Babies Registry." (Check out the website, given at the end of this chapter.) In the first year or so, premature infants often lag behind full-term infants in many facets of development, but by age two or three, differences vanish and most premature infants develop normally thereafter (Greenberg & Crnic, 1988). Research currently shows variable findings, though. A British research group analyzing data from six longitudinal studies reports that children born before gestational age of 34 weeks are more likely to have cognitive difficulties and learning problems in elementary school than full-term children (Wolpe, Johnson, Jaekel, & Gilmore, n.d.). A longitudinal study by researchers at McMaster University in Ontario, however, has found that even very premature babies with extremely low birth weight generally did well, with the proportion who graduate from high school not significantly different than that of the general population (Saigal et al., 2006).

Prospects are usually not so optimistic for small-for-date babies like the one shown in the photo on the previous page. These infants are most often born to women who smoked or drank alcohol frequently during pregnancy or who did not eat enough nutritious food (Chomitz, Cheung, & Lieberman, 1995). Babies that weigh less than 1500 grams at birth often do not survive; when they do, their cognitive and motor development are usually delayed (Kavsek & Bornstein, 2010). Small-for-date babies who weigh more than 1500 grams have better prospects if they receive appropriate care. Like the infant in the photo on the previous page, small-for-date babies are placed in special, sealed beds, where temperature and air quality are regulated carefully. These beds effectively isolate infants, depriving them of environmental stimulation. Consequently, they often receive auditory stimulation, such as a tape recording of soothing music or their mother's voice, or visual stimulation provided from a mobile placed over the bed. Infants also receive tactile stimulation—they are massaged several times daily. These forms of stimulation foster physical and cognitive development in small-for-date babies (Field & Diego, 2010).

The *kangaroo care* position, in which infants dressed only in a diaper are held against an adult's bare chest in a sling or blanket, has been popularized in Canadian neonatal units. Initially developed in South America, this form of care is used with premature and special care infants to give skin-to-skin contact and positive stimulation, even to babies in intensive care (e.g., Women's Hospital Manitoba, n.d.). These forms of stimulation foster physical and cognitive development in small-for-date babies (Field, Diego, & Hernandez-Reif, 2007; Ghavane et al., 2012; Zhang & Liu, 2012). Canadian research has shown that the kangaroo care position also reduces pain responses to the heel-prick used in hospitals to draw blood for testing (e.g., for PKU, as mentioned in Chapter 2) in full-term and even very premature babies (Johnston et al., 2008).

Special care for small-for-date babies should continue when infants leave the hospital for home. Consequently, interventions for such babies typically include training programs designed for parents of infants and young children. In these programs, parents learn how to respond appropriately to their child's behaviours. For example, they are taught the signs that a baby is in distress, over-stimulated, or ready to interact. Parents also learn games and activities to use to foster their child's development. In addition, children are enrolled in high-quality childcare centres where the curriculum is coordinated with the parent training. This sensitive care promotes development in low-birth-weight babies, sometimes allowing the babies to catch up to full-term infants in their cognitive development (Hill, Brooks-Gunn, & Waldfogel, 2003).

Long-term positive outcomes for these infants depend critically on the provision of a supportive and stimulating home environment. Unfortunately, not all at-risk babies have these optimal experiences. Many experience stress or disorder in their family life. In these cases, development is usually affected (Poehlmann et al., 2011). The importance of a supportive environment for at-risk babies was demonstrated dramatically in a longitudinal study of all children born in 1955 on the Hawaiian island of Kauai (Werner & Smith, 2001). At-risk newborns who grew up in stable homes were indistinguishable from children born without birth complications. ("Stable family environment" was defined as two supportive, mentally healthy parents present throughout childhood.) When at-risk newborns had an unstable family environment, because of divorce, parental alcoholism, or mental illness, for example, they lagged behind their peers in intellectual and social development.

The Hawaiian study underscores a point we have made several times in this chapter: Development is best when pregnant women receive good prenatal care and children live in a supportive environment. The Cultural Influences feature makes the same point in a different way, by looking at infant mortality around the world.

Cultural Influences

Infant Mortality

The term *infant mortality* refers to the number of infants out of 1000 births who die before their first birthday. The good news is that the global infant mortality rate has been gradually declining over the past few decades. The worldwide infant mortality rate decreased from 63 per 1000 in 1990 to 32 per 1000 in 2015 (WHO, 2017). Worldwide, about 45 percent of infant deaths occur neonatally (UNICEF, WHO, World Bank, & UN-DESA Population Division, 2015). Thus, preventing neonatal deaths would significantly reduce infant mortality. Simple interventions, such as improved sanitation, increased vaccination rates, and a greater focus on women's health, have already contributed to declines in infant and child (under five) mortality across the world (UNICEF, 2007). Canada ranks 161st out of 189 countries for under-five child mortality rates. As shown in Figure 3-10, in infant mortality, Japan has the lowest rate and, at the other end of the spectrum, Afghanistan has the highest, closely followed by Sierra Leone and Angola. War and conflict lead to disruptions in health care, basic services, and food security, all of which are important for infant and child survival globally (UNICEF, 2007). Living in a wealthy country with ample resources does not guarantee a low infant mortality rate, however.

In many respects, medical facilities in the United States are among the finest in the world. Why then do American babies fare so poorly compared to infants from other countries? As you can see in Figure 3-10, while Canada ranks with the top countries, doing as well as most European nations, the United States is near the bottom of the industrialized countries of the world (UNICEF, 2004). The difference is small in percentage terms, but if the United States were to reduce its infant mortality rate to the 4 percent that is in line with European countries, this would mean that 8000 American babies who now die annually before their first birthday would live.

This surprising statistic has led to commentary both in scientific journals (e.g., Kuehn, 2008) and in popular media articles, with titles like "America's lost children"

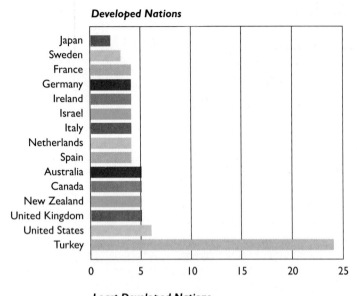

Developed Nations

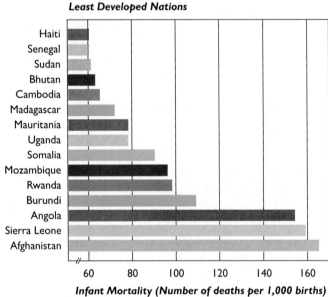

Least Developed Nations

Infant Mortality (Number of deaths per 1,000 births)

Figure 3-10 Infant mortality rates for different countries around the world.

(Adler, 2007). So why do so many infants living in one of the most advanced countries on Earth die before their first birthday?

Low birth weight is one reason so many American babies die. The United States has more babies with low birth weight than virtually all other industrialized countries, and we've already seen that low birth weight places an infant at risk. Low birth weight can usually be prevented when a pregnant woman gets regular prenatal care, but many pregnant women in the United States receive inadequate or no prenatal care because they have no health insurance (Cohen, Martinez, & Ward, 2010). Virtually all the countries that rank ahead of the United States—including Canada, with our universal healthcare system—provide complete prenatal care at little or no cost. Many of these countries also provide paid leaves of absence for pregnant women (OECD, 2006). Maternity leave is common in many European countries, and sometimes paternity leave is as well. In Canada, both are available. Exact figures depend on provincial legislation, but basic maternity leave entitles the mother to between 15 to 18 weeks of unpaid leave, depending on the province. The employer may pay a portion of salary, and employment insurance benefits may continue throughout the period of leave (Human Resources and Skills Development Canada, n.d.). Paternity leave is also variable. Parental leave, in which one or both parents may take time off work after the baby is born, is becoming more common in Canada. Parental leave may range from as few as 12 weeks to as many as 52 weeks (Human Resources and Skills Development Canada, n.d.).

Prenatal development is the foundation of all development, and only with regular prenatal check-ups can we know if this foundation is being laid properly. Pregnant women and the children they carry need this care, and countries must ensure that expectant mothers receive it. As well, time off work helps mothers and fathers care for their baby in the first weeks of life. In the least-developed countries, inadequate prenatal care is common and mothers often have inadequate nutrition. After birth, infants in these countries face the twin challenges of receiving adequate nutrition and avoiding disease. However, since 1990, improved prenatal care and improved health care and nutrition for infants have cut the global infant mortality rate significantly (UNICEF, 2007). With continued improvements in such care, the main challenges for infants worldwide will be bonding with parents, walking, and talking, not simply surviving.

Critical Thinking Question: If you were an advisor to the federal government's overseas aid program, what advice would you give for the best use of aid resources for underdeveloped nations?

Check Your Learning

RECALL What are the three stages of labour? What are the highlights of each stage?

Describe the main features of prepared approaches to childbirth.

INTERPRET Explain why some at-risk newborns develop normally but others do not.

APPLY Lynn is pregnant with her first child and would like to give birth at home. Her husband is dead set against the idea and claims that it is much too risky. What advice would you give them?

ANSWER 3.3
At this point, probably not. It's normal for women to feel sad and angry for a week or so after giving birth. But if Rosa's feelings persist for a few more weeks, then they may well be symptoms of postpartum depression.

3.4 The Newborn

OUTLINE	LEARNING OBJECTIVES
Assessing the Newborn	1. How do we determine if a baby is healthy and adjusting to life outside the uterus?
The Newborn's Reflexes	2. How do reflexes help newborns interact with the world?
Newborn States	3. What behavioural states are observable in newborns?
Perception and Learning in the Newborn	4. How well do newborns experience the world? Can they learn from experience?

Lisa and Matt, proud but exhausted new parents, are astonished at how their lives now revolve around 10-day-old Hannah's eating and sleeping. Lisa feels as if she is feeding Hannah around the clock. When Hannah naps, Lisa thinks of all the things she should do, but she usually naps herself because she is so tired. Matt wonders when Hannah will start sleeping through the night so that he and Lisa can finally get a good night's sleep themselves.

The newborn baby that thrills parents like Lisa and Matt may not be particularly good-looking, as the photo of Robert Kail's son Ben shows. It was taken when Ben was 20 seconds old. Like other newborns, Ben was covered with blood and vernix, the white-coloured "grease" that protects the fetus's skin during the many months of prenatal development. His head was temporarily distorted from coming through the birth canal; he had a potbelly; and he was bow-legged. Still, to his parents he was beautiful, and they were delighted he'd finally arrived.

What can newborns like Hannah and Ben do? We'll answer that question in this module and, as we do, learn when Lisa and Matt can expect to resume a full night's sleep.

Assessing the Newborn

Imagine that a mother has just asked you if her newborn baby is healthy. How would you decide? **The *Apgar score,* a measure devised by obstetrical anesthesiologist Virginia**

This newborn baby—Robert Kail's son Ben—is covered with vernix, has bowed legs, and his head is distorted from the journey down the birth canal.

Naypong/Shutterstock

Apgar, is used to evaluate a newborn baby's condition. Health professionals look for five vital signs: breathing, heartbeat, muscle tone, presence of reflexes (e.g., coughing), and skin tone. As you can see in Table 3-5, each of the five vital signs receives a score of zero, one, or two, with two being optimal.

The five scores are added together, with a score of seven or more indicating a baby in good physical condition. A score of four to six means the newborn will need special attention and care. A score of three or less signals a life-threatening situation that requires emergency medical care (Apgar, 1953).

The Apgar score provides a quick, approximate assessment of the newborn's status by focusing on the body systems needed to sustain life. For a comprehensive evaluation of the newborn's well-being, pediatricians and child-development specialists use the Neonatal Behavioral Assessment Scale, or NBAS (Brazelton & Nugent, 1995). The NBAS is used with newborns to two-month-olds to provide a detailed portrait of the baby's behavioural repertoire. The scale includes 28 behavioural items along with 18 items that test reflexes. The baby's performance is used to evaluate the functioning of four systems:

- **Autonomic.** The newborn's ability to control body functions such as breathing and temperature regulation
- **Motor.** The newborn's ability to control body movements and activity level
- **State.** The newborn's ability to maintain a state (e.g., staying alert or staying asleep)
- **Social.** The newborn's ability to interact with people

The NBAS is based on the view that newborns are remarkably competent individuals who are well prepared to interact with their environment. Reflecting this view, examiners go to great lengths to bring out a baby's best performance. They do everything possible to make a baby feel comfortable and secure during testing. And if the infant does not at first succeed on an item, the examiner provides some assistance (Alberts, 2005).

Not only is the NBAS useful to clinicians in evaluating the well-being of individual babies, but researchers have also found it a valuable tool. Sometimes performance on the NBAS is used as a dependent variable. For example, harm associated with teratogens has been shown by lower scores on the NBAS (e.g., Engel et al., 2009). Researchers also use scores on the NBAS to predict later development (e.g., Stjernqvist, 2009).

TABLE 3-5

FIVE SIGNS EVALUATED IN THE APGAR SCORE

Points	Activity	Pulse	Grimace (response to irritating stimulus)	Appearance (skin colour)	Respiration
2	Baby moves limbs actively	100 beats per minute or more	Baby cries intensely	Normal colour all over	Strong breathing and crying
1	Baby moves limbs slightly	Fewer than 100 beats per minute	Baby grimaces or cries	Normal colour except for extremities	Slow, irregular breathing
0	No moment; muscles flaccid	Not detectable	Baby does not respond	Baby is blue-grey, pale all over	No breathing

TABLE 3-6

SOME MAJOR REFLEXES FOUND IN NEWBORNS

Name	Response	Significance
Babinski	A baby's toes fan out when the sole of the foot is stroked from heel to toe.	Unknown
Blink	A baby's eyes close in response to bright light or loud noise.	Protects the eyes
Moro	A baby throws its arms out and then inward (as if embracing) in response to a loud noise or when its head falls.	May help a baby cling to its mother
Palmar	A baby grasps an object placed in the palm of its hand.	Precursor to voluntary grasping
Rooting	When a baby's cheek is stroked, it turns its head toward the stroking and opens its mouth.	Helps a baby find the nipple
Stepping	A baby who is held upright by an adult and is then moved forward begins to step rhythmically.	Precursor to voluntary walking
Sucking	A baby sucks when an object is placed in its mouth.	Permits feeding
Withdrawal	A baby withdraws its foot when the sole is pricked with a pin.	Protects a baby from unpleasant stimulation

The Newborn's Reflexes

As we've just seen, the NBAS was based on a view—shared widely by child-development researchers—that newborns are well prepared to begin interacting with their world. **An important part of this preparation is a rich set of *reflexes,* unlearned responses that are triggered by a specific form of stimulation.** Table 3-6 lists the many reflexes commonly found in newborns.

Some reflexes pave the way for newborns to get the nutrients they need to grow: Rooting and sucking ensure that the newborn is well prepared to begin a new diet of life-sustaining milk. Other reflexes protect the newborn from danger in the environment. The blink and withdrawal reflexes, for example, help newborns avoid unpleasant stimulation. Yet other reflexes serve as the foundation for larger, voluntary patterns of motor activity. For example, the stepping reflex looks like a precursor to walking.

Reflexes indicate whether the newborn's nervous system is working properly. For example, infants with damage to their sciatic nerve, which is found in the spinal cord, do not show the withdrawal reflex; infants who have problems with the lower part of the spine do not show the Babinski reflex. If these or other reflexes are weak or missing altogether, a thorough physical and behavioural assessment is called for (Falk & Bornstein, 2005).

Newborn States

Newborns spend most of their day alternating among four states (St. James-Roberts & Plewis, 1996; Wolff, 1987):

- *Alert inactivity.* The baby is calm and attentive, with eyes open; the baby appears to be deliberately inspecting the environment.
- *Waking activity.* The baby's eyes are open, but they seem unfocused; the baby moves arms or legs in bursts of uncoordinated motion.

- *Crying.* The baby cries vigorously, usually accompanying this with agitated but uncoordinated motion.
- *Sleeping.* The baby's eyes are closed and the baby drifts back and forth from periods of regular breathing and stillness to periods of irregular breathing and gentle arm and leg motion.

Researchers have been particularly interested in crying, because parents want to know why babies cry and how to calm them, and sleeping, because babies do spend so much time asleep!

CRYING.   Newborns spend two to three hours each day crying or on the verge of crying. If you've never spent much time around newborns, you might think that all crying is pretty much alike. In fact, babies cry for different reasons and cry differently for each one. Scientists and parents can identify three distinctive types of cries (Snow, 1998). **A *basic cry* starts softly then gradually becomes more intense and usually occurs when a baby is hungry or tired; a *mad cry* is a more intense version of a basic cry; and a *pain cry* begins with a sudden, long shriek, followed by a long pause and gasping crying.**

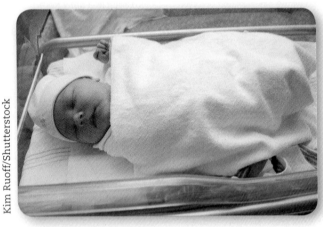

Swaddling is an effective way to soothe a baby who is upset.

Parents are naturally concerned when their baby cries, and if they cannot quiet a crying baby, their concern mounts and can easily give way to frustration and annoyance. It's no surprise, then, that parents develop little tricks for soothing their babies. Many Western parents lift a crying baby to the shoulder and walk or gently rock the baby. Sometimes they also sing lullabies, pat the baby's back, or give the baby a pacifier. Yet another method is to put a newborn into a car seat and go for a drive; Robert Kail remembers doing this as a last resort at 2 a.m., when his son Ben was 10 days old. After about the 12th time around the block, Ben finally stopped crying and fell asleep.

Another useful technique is *swaddling,* in which an infant is wrapped tightly in a blanket. Swaddling, shown in the photo, is used in many cultures around the world, including Turkey and Peru as well as countries in Asia. Swaddling provides warmth and tactile stimulation that usually works well to soothe a baby (Delaney, 2000).

Parents are sometimes reluctant to respond to their crying infant for fear of producing a baby who cries constantly. Yet they hear their baby's cry as a call for help that they shouldn't ignore. What to do? Should parents respond? "Yes" until their baby is about three months old. However, with older babies parents should consider why their infant is crying and the intensity of the crying (St. James-Roberts, 2007). When an older baby wakes during the night and cries quietly, a parent should wait a bit before responding, giving the baby a chance to calm herself. Of course, if parents hear a loud noise from an infant's bedroom followed by a mad cry, they should respond immediately. Parents need to remember that crying is actually the newborn's first attempt to communicate with others. They need to decide what the infant is trying to tell them and whether that warrants a quick response or whether they should let the baby soothe herself.

 QUESTION 3.4

When Marie's four-month-old son cries, she rushes to him immediately and does everything possible to console him. Is this a good idea? *(Answer is on* page 115.*)*

SLEEPING.   Crying may get parents' attention, but sleep is what newborns do more than anything else. They sleep 16 to 18 hours daily. The problem for tired parents Lisa and Matt from the vignette is that newborns sleep in naps taken around the clock. Newborns typically go through a cycle of wakefulness and sleep about every four hours. That is, they

Kim Ruoff/Shutterstock

will be awake for about an hour, sleep for three hours, then start the cycle anew. During the hour when newborns are awake, they regularly move between the different waking states several times. Cycles of alert inactivity, waking activity, and crying are common.

As babies grow older, the sleep-wake cycle gradually begins to correspond to the day-night cycle (St. James-Roberts & Plewis, 1996). There is a shift to more night-time sleep between six and 12 weeks of age. Most babies begin sleeping through the night at about three or four months, a major milestone for bleary-eyed parents like Lisa and Matt, and exposure to natural light could facilitate this.

By six months of age, most North American infants are sleeping in a crib in their own room. Although this practice seems "natural" to North American parents, in much of the rest of the world, children sleep with their parents throughout infancy and the preschool years. Such parent–child "co-sleeping" is commonly found in cultures where people define themselves less as independent individuals and more as part of a group. For parents in cultures that value such interdependence—including Egypt, Italy, Japan, and Korea, as well as the Maya in Guatemala and the Inuit in Canada—co-sleeping is an important step in forging parent-child bonds, just as sleeping alone is an important step toward independence in cultures that value self-reliance (Nelson, Schiefenhoevel, & Haimerl, 2000; Tan, 2009; Worthman & Brown, 2007).

How does co-sleeping work? Infants may sleep in a cradle placed next to their parents' bed or in a basket in their parents' bed. When they outgrow this arrangement, they sleep in the bed with their mother; depending on the culture, the father may sleep in the same bed (as shown in the photo on the right), in another bed in the same room, in another room, or in another house altogether!

You might think that co-sleeping would make children more dependent on their parents, but research provides no evidence of this (Barajas, Martin, Brooks-Gunn, & Hale, 2011; Okami, Weisner, & Olmstead, 2002). Plus, co-sleeping has the benefit of avoiding the lengthy, elaborate rituals that are often involved in getting youngsters to sleep in their own room alone. With co-sleeping, children and parents simply go to bed together, with few struggles.

While asleep, babies alternate between two types of sleep. **In** *rapid-eye-movement (REM) sleep,* **newborns move their arms and legs, they may grimace, and their eyes may move about beneath their eyelids.** Brain waves register fast activity, the heart beats more rapidly, and breathing is also more rapid. **In regular or** *non-REM sleep,* **breathing, heart rate, and brain activity are steady, and newborns lie quietly without the twitching associated with REM sleep.** REM sleep becomes less frequent as infants grow. By four months of age, only 40% of sleep is REM sleep. By the first birthday, REM sleep drops to about 33%, closer to the adult average of 20% (Lushington et al., 2013).

Co-sleeping, in which infants and young children sleep with their parents, is common in many countries around the world.

Vinicius Tupinamba/Shutterstock

The function of REM sleep is still debated. Older children and adults dream during REM sleep, and brain waves during REM sleep resemble those of an alert, awake person. Consequently, many scientists believe that REM sleep stimulates the brain in some way that helps foster growth in the nervous system (Halpern, MacLean, & Baumeister, 1995; Roffwarg, Muzio, & Dement, 1966).

SUDDEN UNEXPECTED INFANT DEATH. For many parents of young babies, sleep is sometimes a cause for concern. **In** *sudden unexpected infant death (SUID),* **a healthy**

baby dies suddenly, for no apparent reason. In fact, this problem was re-named from Sudden Infant Death Syndrome (SIDS) to SUID to acknowledge the difficulty of understanding cause (Centers for Disease Control—DC, 2016a). SIDS is now seen as one type of SUID. In 2009, 114 infant deaths were attributed to SUID (Statistics Canada, 2012e). There is good news, however, in that this number appears to be declining. The most recent Canadian statistics available are that in 2012 this figure was down to 51 (Statistics Canada, 2016b). Thus from 2009 to 2012 the number of SUIDs dropped significantly.

Scientists do not know the exact causes of SUID, but one idea is that two- to four-month-old infants are particularly vulnerable to SUID because many newborn reflexes are waning during these months, and thus infants may not respond effectively when breathing becomes difficult. For example, they may not reflexively move their heads away from a blanket or pillow that is smothering them (Lipsitt, 2003).

Researchers have also identified several risk factors associated with SUID (Carpenter et al., 2013; Sahni, Fifer, & Myers, 2007). Babies are more vulnerable if they were born prematurely or with low birth weight. They are also more vulnerable when their parents smoke. SUID is also more likely when a baby sleeps on its stomach (face down) than when it sleeps on its back (face up). Finally, SUID is more likely during winter, when babies sometimes become overheated from too many blankets and too heavy sleepwear (Carroll & Loughlin, 1994). Evidently, SUID infants, many of whom were born prematurely or with low birth weight, are less able to withstand physiological stresses and imbalances that are brought on by cigarette smoke, breathing that is SUID has accumulated, child advocates have called for action. The result is described in the Children's Lives feature.

Children's Lives

Back to Sleep!

In 1992, based on mounting evidence that SUID occurred more often when infants slept on their stomachs, the American Academy of Pediatrics (AAP) began advising parents to

Figure 3-11 Advertising poster for the Back to Sleep campaign.

Courtesy of the National Institute of Health.

put babies to sleep on their backs or sides. In 1999, a major SUID awareness program in Canada began. Health Canada, the Canadian Foundation for the Study of Infant Deaths, the Canadian Paediatric Society, and the Canadian Institute of Child Health joined forces to publicize the risk of SUID and to promote the Back to Sleep program as a way to encourage the safest sleeping practices. The Back to Sleep campaigns in the United States and Canada were widely promoted through brochures, posters like the one shown in Figure 3-11, and videos. Since the Back to Sleep campaign began, research shows that far more infants are now sleeping on their backs and that the incidence of SUID has dropped (Dwyer & Ponsonby, 2009). The message for all parents—particularly if their babies were premature or small-for-date—is to keep their babies away from smoke, to put them on their backs to sleep, and not to overdress them or wrap them too tightly in blankets.

Critical Thinking Question: The Children's Lives feature mentions some ways in which the Back to Sleep program has been promoted. How else might this message be distributed?

Perception and Learning in the Newborn

Do you believe it is important to talk to newborns and give them fuzzy little toys? Should their rooms be bright and colourful? If you do, then you probably believe two basic things about newborns: First, that newborns can have perceptual experiences—that they can see, smell, hear, taste, and feel. Second, that sensory experiences are somehow registered in the newborn through learning and memory, because unless experiences are registered, they cannot influence later behaviour. You'll be happy to know that research confirms your beliefs. All the basic perceptual systems are operating at some level at birth. The world outside the uterus can be seen, smelled, heard, tasted, and felt (Cohen & Cashon, 2003; Slater et al., 2010). Moreover, newborns have the capacity to learn and remember. And they can change their behaviour based on their experiences (Rovee-Collier & Barr, 2010).

We'll discuss these perceptual changes in more detail in Chapter 5, and we'll discuss learning and memory in Chapter 7. For now, the important point is that newborns are remarkably prepared to interact with the world. Adaptive reflexes coupled with perceptual and learning skills provide a solid foundation for the rest of child development.

 ## Check Your Learning

RECALL What are the different functions of reflexes?

Describe the four primary states of infant behaviour.

INTERPRET Compare the Apgar and the NBAS as measures of a newborn baby's well-being.

APPLY What would you recommend to parents of a two-month-old who are worried about SUIDS?

 ANSWER 3.4
Probably not. Marie needs to relax a bit. If her son is in danger, she'll recognize a pain cry or a mad cry. Otherwise, Marie should wait a moment before going to her son, to try to decide why he is crying and to give him a chance to calm himself.

UNIFYING THEMES Continuity

This chapter is a good opportunity to highlight the theme that *early development is related to later development, but not perfectly.* Remember the Hawaiian study (on page 107)? That study showed that outcomes for at-risk infants are not uniform. When at-risk infants grow up in a stable, supportive environment, they become quite typical children. But when they grow up in stressful environments, they lag intellectually and socially. Similarly, SUID is more likely to affect babies born prematurely and with low birth weight, yet not all of these babies die unexpectedly. When premature and low-birth-weight babies sleep on their backs, are not overheated, and do not inhale smoke, they are unlikely to have SUID. Traumatic events early in development, such as being born early or underweight, do not predetermine the rest of a child's life, but they do make some developmental paths easier to follow than others.

See for Yourself

Words can scarcely capture the miracle of a newborn baby. If you have never seen a newborn, you should. Arrange to visit the maternity ward of a local hospital—you may be allowed to visit a neonatal unit where babies are kept in incubators, though most babies born in Canadian hospitals now stay in the hospital room with their mother. You will be asked to comply with the hospital's rules and regulations for visitors, and remember to be ethical and responsible!

The babies you see in the hospital will no longer be covered with blood or vernix, but you may be able to see how the newborn's head is often distorted by its journey through the birth canal. As you watch the babies, look for reflexive behaviour and changes in states. Watch while a baby sucks its fingers. Find a baby who seems to be awake and alert, then note how long the baby stays this way. When alertness wanes, watch for the behaviours that replace it. Finally, observe how different newborns look and act. The wonderful variety and diversity found among human beings is already evident in those who are hours or days old. See for yourself!

Resources

For more information about …

 babies, try T. Berry Brazelton's *Infants and Mothers: Differences in Development* (Delacorte, 1994). This classic book written by the famous pediatrician and scientist traces the early development of three very different babies. In the process, it shows the wide range of patterns of development.

 prenatal development, visit the website of the Multi-Dimensional Human Embryo, which has images and animation depicting the fetus at various stages of prenatal development: **http://embryo.soad.umich.edu.**

 premature babies, look at The University of Iowa Children's Hospital "Tiniest Babies Registry," where records of smallest surviving premature babies are kept, including how each is doing now. See **http://webapps1.healthcare.uiowa.edu/tiniestbabies/getInfantList.aspx.**

Key Terms

age of viability   78
amniocentesis   97
amniotic fluid   76
amniotic sac   76
Apgar score   109
basic cry   112
blastocyst   74
breech presentation   100
Caesarean section
   (C-section)   105
cerebral cortex   77
chorionic villus sampling (CVS)   97
crowning   100
doula   102
ectoderm   75

embryo   75
endoderm   75
fetal alcohol spectrum disorder
   (FASD)   89
fetal medicine   98
genetic engineering   98
germ disc   75
hypoxia   104
implantation   74
infant mortality   107
kangaroo care   106
mad cry   112
mesoderm   75
non-REM (regular)
   sleep   113

pain cry   112
period of the fetus   76
placenta   75
postpartum depression   103
premature infants   105
prenatal development   73
rapid-eye-movement (REM) sleep
   (irregular sleep)   113
reflexes   111
small-for-date
   infants   105
social influence   84
social selection   84
spina bifida   82
stress   82

Summary

3.1 From Conception to Birth

1. Period of the Zygote (Weeks 1–2)

The first period of prenatal development lasts two weeks. It begins when the egg is fertilized by the sperm and ends when the fertilized egg has implanted in the wall of the uterus.

2. Period of the Embryo (Weeks 3–8)

The second period of prenatal development begins two weeks after conception and ends eight weeks after conception. This is a period when most major body structures are formed.

3. Period of the Fetus (Weeks 9–38)

The third period of prenatal development begins nine weeks after conception and lasts until birth. In this period, the fetus becomes much larger and body systems begin to function.

3.2 Influences on Prenatal Development

1. General Risk Factors

Prenatal development can be harmed if a pregnant woman does not provide adequate nutrition for the developing baby or experiences considerable stress herself. Teenagers often have problem pregnancies because they rarely receive adequate prenatal care. After age 35, women are less fertile and more likely to have problematic pregnancies, but they are still effective mothers.

2. Teratogens: Diseases, Drugs, and Environmental Hazards

Teratogens are agents that can cause abnormal prenatal development. Several diseases and drugs are teratogens. Environmental teratogens are particularly dangerous because a pregnant woman may not know when these substances are present.

3. How Teratogens Influence Prenatal Development

The effect of teratogens depends on the genotype of the unborn baby, on when during prenatal development the baby is exposed to the teratogen, and on the amount of exposure. The impact of a teratogen may not be evident until later in life.

4. Prenatal Diagnosis and Treatment

Ultrasound uses sound waves to generate a picture of the fetus that reveals the position of the fetus, its sex, and any gross physical deformities. When genetic disorders are suspected, amniocentesis or chorionic villus sampling (CVS) is used to determine the genotype of the fetus. Fetal medicine corrects problems of prenatal development medically, surgically, or through genetic engineering.

3.3 Happy Birthday!

1. Labour and Delivery

Labour consists of three stages. In Stage 1, the muscles of the uterus contract, causing the cervix to enlarge. In Stage 2, the baby moves through the birth canal. In Stage 3, the placenta is delivered.

2. Approaches to Childbirth

Prepared childbirth assumes that parents should understand what takes place during pregnancy and birth. In prepared childbirth, women learn to cope with pain through relaxation and the help of a supportive adult.

Although most Canadian babies are born in hospitals, home birth is safe when the mother is healthy, the delivery is expected to be trouble-free, and a healthcare professional is present.

3. Adjusting to Parenthood

Following the birth of a child, a woman's body changes physically. Both parents also adjust psychologically, and sometimes fathers feel left out. After giving birth, some women experience postpartum depression: They are irritable, have poor appetites and disturbed sleep, and are apathetic. Women who experience postpartum depression should seek treatment because it interferes with effective parenting.

4. Birth Complications

During labour and delivery, the flow of blood to the fetus can be disrupted, causing hypoxia, which is a lack of oxygen to the fetus. If the fetus is endangered, the doctor may do a Caesarean section, removing it from the uterus surgically. Babies with many birth complications are at risk for becoming aggressive and developing psychiatric disorders.

Premature babies develop more slowly at first but catch up in a few years. Small-for-date babies who weigh less than 1500 grams often do not develop normally; larger small-for-date babies fare well when their environment is stimulating and stress-free.

Infant mortality rates vary throughout the world and are usually lowest in industrialized nations. Infant mortality is relatively high in the United States compared to other industrialized nations, primarily because of low birth weight and inadequate prenatal care.

3.4 The Newborn

1. Assessing the Newborn

The Apgar score measures five vital signs to determine a newborn's physical well-being. The Neonatal Behavioral Assessment Scale provides a comprehensive evaluation of a baby's behavioural and physical status.

2. The Newborn's Reflexes

Some reflexes help infants adjust to life outside the uterus; some protect them; and some are the basis for later motor behaviour.

3. Newborn States

Newborns spend their days in one of four states: alert inactivity, waking activity, crying, and sleeping. A newborn's crying comprises a basic cry, a mad cry, and a pain cry.

Newborns spend approximately two-thirds of every day asleep and go through a complete sleep-wake cycle once every four hours or so. Newborns spend about half their time in REM sleep, characterized by active brain waves and frequent movements of the eyes and limbs. REM sleep may stimulate nervous system growth.

Some apparently healthy babies die unexpectedly – sudden unexpected infant death (SUID). Babies are vulnerable to SUID when they are premature, have low birth weight, sleep on their stomachs, are overheated, or are exposed to cigarette smoke. Encouraging parents to have babies sleep on their backs has reduced the number of SUID cases.

4. Perception and Learning in the Newborn

Newborns' perceptual and learning skills function reasonably well, allowing them to experience the world.

Test Yourself

1. The fertilized egg implants in the wall of the uterus during the period of the _____.

2. Differentiation of cells begins in the period of the _____.

3. The developing organism becomes much larger and its bodily systems begin to work during the period of the _____.

4. General risk factors during prenatal development include inadequate nutrition, stress, and _____.

5. Diseases, drugs, and _____ are common categories of teratogens.

6. Exposure to teratogens during the period of the fetus usually results in _____.

7. _____ is a procedure that generates an image of the fetus, which can be used to determine its sex and the existence of multiple pregnancies.

8. One way to check for genetic disorders in a fetus is amniocentesis; another is _____.

9. The first stage of labour is usually the longest, but the baby is born in the _____ stage.

10. Prepared childbirth emphasizes education, _____, and the presence of a supportive adult.

11. A woman who, following childbirth, experiences prolonged irritation, feelings of low-self worth, and disturbed sleep is probably suffering from _____.

12. At-risk infants often develop normally if _____.

13. _____ uses five vital signs to provide a quick, rough evaluation of a newborn's status.

14. Infants spend their day alternating between sleeping, crying, alert inactivity, and _____.

15. The national program to eliminate sudden infant death syndrome (SIDS) encourages _____.

Answers: (1) zygote; (2) embryo; (3) fetus; (4) maternal age; (5) environmental hazards; (6) minor defects in bodily structure or improperly functioning body systems; (7) Ultrasound; (8) chorionic villus sampling (CVS); (9) second; (10) relaxation; (11) postpartum depression; (12) they are exposed to a stable, supportive environment; (13) The Apgar score; (14) waking activity; (15) parents to place infants on their backs for sleeping.

4

Growth and Health

Renee Jansa/Fotolia

Physical Growth

Challenges to Healthy Growth

The Developing Nervous System

Humans take longer to become physically mature than any other animal. We spend about 20 percent of our lives—all of childhood and adolescence—growing physically. This slow journey to physical maturity is an interesting story in itself. But physical growth is just as important for its impact on other aspects of children's development, including cognition, social behaviour, and personality. As children grow physically, they become less dependent on others for care, they are treated differently by adults, and they come to view themselves as older and more mature. By knowing more about children's physical growth, you'll be better prepared to understand other aspects of development that we'll study in the rest of the book.

In this chapter, we'll learn how children grow physically. In **Module 4.1**, we'll look at different facets of physical growth and some of the reasons why people differ in their physical growth and stature. Then, in **Module 4.2**, we'll explore problems that can disrupt physical growth. In **Module 4.3**, we'll look at physical growth that's not so obvious—the development of the brain.

4.1 Physical Growth

OUTLINE

Features of Human Growth

Mechanisms of Physical Growth

The Adolescent Growth Spurt and Puberty

LEARNING OBJECTIVES

1. What are the important features of physical growth during childhood? How do they vary from child to child?
2. How do sleep and nutrition contribute to healthy growth?
3. What are the physical changes associated with puberty, and what are their consequences?

Pete has just had his 15th birthday, but as far as he is concerned, there is no reason to celebrate. Although most of his friends have grown about 15 centimetres in the past year or so, have a much larger penis and larger testicles, and have mounds of pubic hair, Pete looks just as he did when he was 10 years old. He is embarrassed by his appearance, particularly in the locker room, where he looks like a little boy among men. "Won't I ever change?" he wonders.

For parents and children alike, physical growth is a topic of great interest. Parents marvel at how quickly babies add kilos and centimetres; two-year-olds proudly proclaim, "I bigger now!" Many adolescents take great satisfaction in finally becoming taller than a parent; others, like Pete, suffer through their teenage years as they wait for the physical signs of maturity. Growth and health are affected by the availability of healthcare. In Canada, we are fortunate to have a free, universal healthcare system that provides pre- and postnatal care and child healthcare for all. In addition, sound advice abounds regarding the benefits of simple preventive measures such as good nutrition on children's well-being; for example, *Canada's Food Guide* (Health Canada, 2016) advises parents on how much of which foods to give their children for optimum health and growth. Sadly, as we will see elsewhere in this chapter, in some countries lack of access to healthcare and public health information affects the growth and health of children.

In this module, we'll examine some of the basic features of physical growth and variations in growth patterns. We'll also consider the mechanisms responsible for growth. Finally, we'll end the module by studying puberty—a phase of physical growth that is so special that it should be considered separately.

Raise a cyber child and discover the world of parenthood at …

My Virtual Child …

Features of Human Growth

DESCRIBING GROWTH.   Probably the most obvious way to measure physical growth is in terms of sheer size—height and weight. The growth charts in Figure 4-1 show the average changes in height and weight that take place as children grow from birth to age 20. Between birth and 2 years, for example, average height increases from about 48 to 80 centimetres; average weight increases from 3 to 10 kilograms. (A useful rule of thumb is that boys achieve half their adult height by 2 years, and girls by 18 months.)

What is not so obvious from growth charts is that increases in height and weight are not steady. Looking at the average increase in weight and height annually—as opposed to the average total weight and height for each year—gives quite a different picture of the pattern of physical growth. The graphs in Figure 4-2 show that growth is extraordinarily rapid during the first year, when the average baby grows about 25 centimetres and gains 7 kilograms. Growth is fairly steady through the preschool and elementary-school years— about 7.5 centimetres and 3 to 4 kilograms each year. In early adolescence, growth is rapid again. During this growth spurt, which corresponds to the peaks in the middle of the charts in Figure 4-2, teenagers typically grow 10 centimetres and gain 7 to 8 kilograms each year. After this spurt, which begins 1 to 2 years earlier in girls, growth again slows as children reach adulthood.

Growth follows two distinct trends: *cephalocaudal,* **literally "head to tail," and** *proximodistal,* **meaning from close in to farther out.** In other words, development proceeds in two main directions. One is a general neuronal maturation from head to foot, and the other is a maturation from the centre of the body to the extremities. Thus, control of gross (overall) muscular movement develops before finer control of the extremities—the hands and feet. Think about a skill such as catching a ball: A very young child will try to trap the ball with her arms, but an older child will be able to catch with the hands and grasp the ball (we will discuss the refinement of motor movement more in Module 5.3). Physical growth in the prenatal period and through childhood follows these two trends.

As children grow, their body parts develop at different rates: The head and trunk grow faster than the legs. Consequently, infants and young children are not simply scaled-down

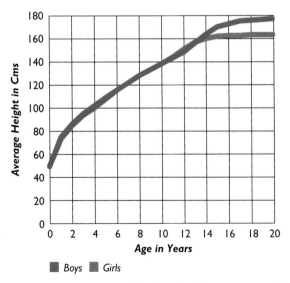
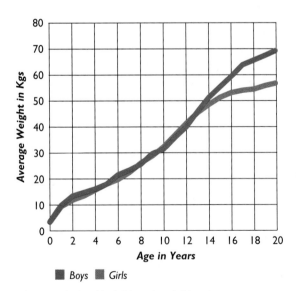

Figure 4-1 Growth charts for average changes in total height and weight across childhood.

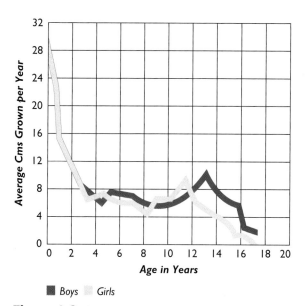

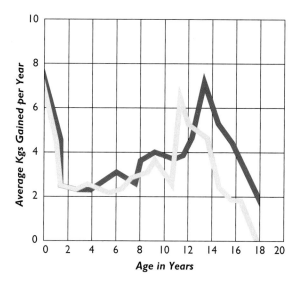

■ *Boys* ■ *Girls*

Figure 4-2 Growth charts for average yearly changes in height and weight.

versions of adults. As you can see in Figure 4-3, infants and toddlers have disproportionately large heads and trunks, making them look top-heavy compared to older children and adolescents. As growth of the hips, legs, and feet catches up later in childhood, bodies take on proportions that are more adult-like.

MUSCLE, FAT, AND BONES. Other important features of physical growth take place inside the body, with the development of muscle, fat, and bones. Virtually all of the body's muscle fibres are present at birth. During childhood, muscles become longer and thicker as individual fibres fuse together. This process accelerates during adolescence, particularly for boys.

A layer of fat appears under the skin near the end of the fetal period of prenatal development. Just as insulation in walls stabilizes the temperature inside a house, fat helps the fetus and infant regulate body temperature. Fat continues to accumulate rapidly during the first year after birth, producing the familiar chubby baby look. During the preschool years, children actually become leaner, but in the early elementary-school years, they begin to acquire more fat again. This happens gradually at first, then more rapidly during adolescence. The increase in fat in adolescence is more pronounced in girls than in boys.

Bone begins to form during prenatal development, starting as *cartilage,* a soft, flexible tissue. During the embryonic period, the centre of the tissue turns to bone. Then, shortly before birth, **the ends of the cartilage structures, known as** *epiphyses,* **turn to bone.** Now the structure is hard at each end and in the centre. Working from the centre, the cartilage turns to bone until finally the enlarging centre section reaches the epiphyses, ending skeletal growth.

If we combine the changes in muscle, fat, and bone with changes in body size and shape, we have a fairly complete picture of physical growth during childhood. What's missing? The central nervous system, which we cover separately in Module 4.3.

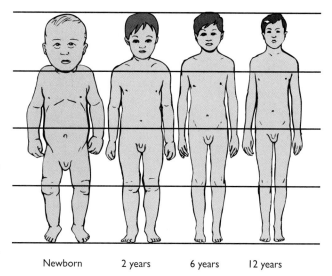

Newborn   2 years   6 years   12 years

Figure 4-3 Changes in bodily proportions across childhood.

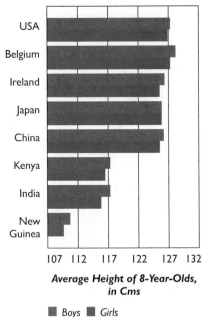

Average Height of 8-Year-Olds, in Cms

■ Boys ■ Girls

Figure 4-4 Average heights for boys and girls from different countries around the world.

VARIATIONS ON THE AVERAGE PROFILE. The picture of children's physical growth that we have described so far is a typical profile; there are important variations on this prototype. For example, in his article reporting a longitudinal study of height and body mass of players for the Montreal Canadiens, McGill University researcher David Montgomery noted that, in 1920, players for the hockey team averaged 1.75 metres in height. In 2003, the average height of Canadiens' players was 1.85 metres, a difference of a full 10 centimetres (Montgomery, 2006). The changing height of hockey players simply corresponds to changes in the Canadian population at large. Today, adults and children are taller and heavier than previous generations, largely due to improved health and nutrition. **Changes in physical development from one generation to the next are known as** *secular growth trends.* Secular trends have been quite large. A medieval knight's armour would fit today's 10- to 12-year-old boy; the average height of American sailors in the War of 1812 was 158 centimetres!

"Average" physical growth varies not only from one generation to the next, but also from one country to another. Figure 4-4 shows the average height of eight-year-old boys and girls in several countries around the world. Youngsters from the United States, Western European countries, Japan, and China are about the same height, approximately 125 centimetres. Children in Africa and India are shorter, averaging about 116 centimetres. And 8-year-olds in Polynesia are shorter still, averaging 109 centimetres.

We need to remember that "average" and "normal" are not the same—many children are much taller or shorter than average and perfectly normal, of course. For example, among North American eight-year-old boys, normal weights range from approximately 20 kilos to 34 kilos.[1] In other words, an extremely light but normal eight-year-old boy would weigh only slightly more than half as much as his extremely heavy but normal peer. What is "normal" can vary greatly, and this applies not only to height and other aspects of physical growth, but also to all aspects of development. Whenever a "typical" or "average" age is given for a developmental milestone, you should remember that the normal range for passing the milestone is much wider. Some children pass the milestone sooner than the stated age and some later, but all are normal.

We've seen that children's heights vary within a culture, across time, and between cultures. What accounts for these differences? To answer this question, we need to look at the mechanisms responsible for human growth.

Mechanisms of Physical Growth

Physical growth is easily taken for granted. Compared to other milestones of child development, like learning to read, physical growth seems to come so easily. Children, like the proverbial weeds, seem to sprout without any effort at all. In reality, physical growth is complicated. Of course, heredity is involved: As a general rule, two tall parents will have tall children; two short parents will have short children; and one tall parent and one short parent will have offspring of average height.

How are genetic instructions translated into actual growth? Sleep and nutrition are both involved.

---

[1]The Canadian Paediatric Society now uses internationally standardized growth charts developed by the World Health Organization in 2007 (WHO, 2013a; Dietitians of Canada and Canadian Pediatric Society, 2010).

SLEEP. In Module 3.4, we saw that infants spend more time asleep than awake. The amount of time that children spend asleep drops gradually, from roughly 11 hours at age 3, to 10 hours at age 7, and 9 hours at age 12 (Snell, Adam, & Duncan, 2007). **Sleep is essential for normal growth because about 80 percent of the hormone that stimulates growth—named, appropriately,** *growth hormone*—**is secreted while children and adolescents sleep** (Smock, 1999). Growth hormone is secreted by the pituitary gland in the brain; from the brain, growth hormone travels to the liver, where it triggers the release of another hormone, somatomedin, which causes muscles and bones to grow (Tanner, 1990).

Sleep also affects children's psychological development. When children are chronically sleepy—because they wake often during the night or don't sleep a consistent amount nightly—they are prone to behavioural problems such as depression and anxiety (El-Sheikh et al., 2013). What's more, when children do not get enough sleep, they do less well in school (Astill, van der Heijden, van IJzendoorn, & van Someren, 2012). When deprived of sleep, children are less able to control their own behaviour, and thus it is more difficult for them to complete school tasks. In addition, sleep is a time when new learning is consolidated with existing knowledge (Henderson, Weighall, Brown, & Gaskell, 2012), thus disrupted sleep can interfere with the consolidation of new information and skills presented during the school day.

Findings like these show that children benefit from a "good night's sleep." One way for parents to help children sleep better and longer is to have a regular bedtime routine that includes the same sequence of activities beginning at about the same time every night. When children follow a routine consistently, they find it easier to fall asleep and are more likely to get a restful night's sleep.

Sleep loss can be a particular problem for adolescents. On the one hand, adolescents often stay up later at night finishing ever-larger amounts of homework, spending time with friends, or working at a part-time job. On the other hand, adolescents often start school earlier than younger elementary-school students. The result is often a sleepy adolescent who struggles to stay awake during the school day (Carskadon, 2002). Many adolescents compound the problem by sacrificing sleep to study longer. This strategy often backfires: At school during the day after their late-night studying, teenagers often have trouble understanding material presented in class and do poorly on tests (Gillen-O'Neel, Huynh, & Fuligni, 2013). Thus, a good night's sleep is an important part of healthy academic and personal development for adolescents and children.

NUTRITION. The fuel for growth comes from the foods children eat and the liquids they drink. Nutrition is particularly important during infancy, when physical growth is so rapid. In a two-month-old, roughly 40 percent of the body's energy is devoted to growth. Because growth requires so much energy, young babies must consume about 50 calories per 0.5 kg of weight (compared with 15 to 20 calories per 0.5 kg for an adult).

Breastfeeding is the best way to ensure that babies get the nourishment they need. Human milk contains the proper amounts of carbohydrates, fats, protein, vitamins, and minerals for babies. Breastfeeding also has several other advantages compared to bottle-feeding (Dewey, 2001). First, breastfed babies are ill less often, because a mother's breast milk contains antibodies that kill bacteria and viruses; thus breastfed babies are at lower risk of gastrointestinal and respiratory infections (Duijts, Jaddoe, Hofman, & Moll, 2010). Second, breastfed babies are less prone to diarrhea and constipation. Third, breastfed babies typically make the transition to solid foods more easily, apparently because they are accustomed to changes in the taste of breast milk that reflect a mother's diet. Fourth, breast

QUESTION 4.1
Tanya is pregnant with her first child and wonders whether breastfeeding is really worthwhile. What advantages of breastfeeding would you mention to her? *(Answer is on page 135.)*

milk cannot be contaminated (as long as a nursing mother avoids certain drugs, such as cocaine); in contrast, contamination is often a significant problem when formula is used in developing countries to bottle-feed babies.

The many benefits of breastfeeding do not mean that bottle-feeding is harmful. Formula, when prepared in sanitary conditions, provides generally the same nutrients as human milk, but infants who have been formula-fed are more prone to developing allergies, and formula does not protect infants from disease. However, bottle-feeding does have advantages. A mother who cannot readily breastfeed can still enjoy the intimacy of feeding her baby, and other family members can participate in feeding. In fact, breast- and bottle-fed babies forge comparable emotional bonds with their mothers (Jansen, de Weerth, & Riksen-Walraven, 2008), so women in industrialized countries can choose either method and know that their babies' dietary and psychological needs are being met.

Experts recommend that children be breastfed until they are two years old and that they be introduced to solid food at six months (e.g., UNICEF, 2010; WHO 2017). The Canadian Paediatric Society issued a joint statement with Health Canada, Dietitians of Canada, and the Breastfeeding Committee for Canada, recommending that breastfeeding should be "exclusively for the first six months, and continued for up to two years or longer with appropriate complementary feeding" (Canadian Paediatric Society, 2014/2017, n.p.). In fact, in many developing countries mothers approximate these guidelines, breastfeeding their children up to two years of age (Arabi et al., 2012). But in the United States and other developed nations, such as Canada, roughly half of mothers stop breastfeeding by six months, in part because it is inconvenient when they return to full-time work (U.S. Centers for Disease Control, 2012).

Preschoolers grow more slowly than infants and toddlers, so they need to eat less per kilogram of weight than before. One rule of thumb is that preschoolers should consume about 90 calories per kilogram of body weight, which works out to be roughly 1500 to 1700 calories daily for many children in this age group.

More important than the sheer number of calories, however, is a balanced diet that includes all the major food groups. Table 4-1 shows a healthy diet that provides adequate calories and nutrients for preschool children. The servings listed in the table are definitely not a complete list of the foods that are good for young children; they are simply examples of healthy choices (and quantities) for children. Many, many other foods could have been listed, too. A healthy diet does not mean that children must eat the same foods over and over again.

TABLE 4-1

EATING TO MEET PRESCHOOLERS' NUTRITIONAL NEEDS

Group	Number of Servings	What Counts as a Serving?
Vegetables and Fruits	4	250 ml raw leafy vegetables, 125 ml fresh, frozen, or canned vegetables, 1 medium apple, 125 ml canned fruit
Grains	3	1 slice bread, 30 g cold cereal
Milk and alternatives	2	250 ml cup milk, 250 ml soy beverage, 50 g cheese
Meat and alternatives	1	75 g cooked lean meat, 30 ml peanut butter, 175 ml tofu

Source: Based on *Canada's Food Guide* (2016)—recommended servings for ages two to three.

A healthy diet not only draws on all four food groups, but also avoids too much sugar and too much fat—especially trans fats (Health Canada, 2016). For preschool children, no more than approximately 30 percent of the daily caloric intake should come from fat, which works out to be roughly 500 calories from fat. Unfortunately, too many preschool children, like the ones in the photo, become hooked on fast-food meals, which are notoriously high in fat. A Whopper burger, fries, and shake have nearly 600 calories from fat, 100 more than children should consume all day! Excessive fat intake can contribute to obesity (which we'll discuss later in this chapter), so parents should be cautious about their preschool children's fat intake (Whitaker, Wright, Pepe, Seidel, & Dietz, 1997).

Encouraging preschool children to eat healthy foods is tough for parents, because some preschoolers become notoriously picky eaters. Like the little girl in the photo, toddlers and preschool children often declare foods "yucky" that they once ate willingly. As an infant, author Robert Kail's daughter loved green beans. When she reached age two, and was better at recognizing and choosing foods for herself, she decided that green beans were awful and refused to eat them. Such finicky behaviour can be annoying, but it may also actually be adaptive for increasingly independent preschoolers. Because preschoolers don't know what is safe to eat and what isn't, choosing to eat only foods they find familiar protects them from potential harm (Aldridge, Dovey, & Halford, 2009).

Many North American children eat far too many fast-food meals, which are notoriously high in empty calories.

Parents should not be overly concerned about this finicky period. Although some children do eat less than before (in terms of calories per kilo), virtually all picky eaters get adequate food for growth. Nevertheless, several methods can be used to encourage youngsters to eat more healthfully:

- Reward children when they eat healthy foods; in one study (Cooke et al., 2011), when four- to six-year-olds received a sticker if they tasted a vegetable, consumption increased sixfold and persisted for three months after rewards were dropped.

- Show young children photos of same-age, same-sex peers who look happy when eating the target food; children are more likely to imitate such models (Frazier et al., 2012).

- Teach children about nutrition, emphasizing that different body functions require a diverse diet that includes a variety of nutrients; in one study (Gripshover & Markman, 2013), preschoolers taught these concepts from story books ate twice as many vegetables.

- At meals, offer children new foods one at a time and in small amounts; encourage but don't force children to eat new foods; and when children reject a new food, continue to offer it over several meals so that it will become familiar (American Academy of Pediatrics, 2008).

Beginning at about two years of age, many youngsters become picky eaters, rejecting food that they once ate willingly.

Collectively, these guidelines can help children receive the nutrition they need to grow.

The Adolescent Growth Spurt and Puberty

The biological start of adolescence is *puberty,* **which refers to the adolescent growth spurt and sexual maturation.** The adolescent growth spurt is easy to see in the graphs in Figures 4-1 and 4-2. Physical growth is slow during the elementary-school years: In an average year, a six- to ten-year-old girl or boy gains about 2.25 to 3 kilograms and grows 5 to 8 centimetres. During the peak of the adolescent growth spurt, though, a girl may gain as many as 9 kilograms in a year, and a boy, 11 kilograms (Tanner, 1970). This growth spurt lasts a few years.

Figure 4-2 also shows that girls typically begin their growth spurt about two years before boys do. That is, girls typically start the growth spurt at about age 11, reach their peak rate of growth at about 12, and achieve their mature stature at about age 15. In contrast, boys start the growth spurt at age 13, hit peak growth at 14, and reach mature stature at 17. This two-year difference in the growth spurt can lead to awkward social interactions between 11- and 12-year-old boys and girls because during those years, as the photo shows, girls are often taller and look more mature than boys.

During the growth spurt, bones become longer (which, of course, is why adolescents grow taller) and denser. Bone growth is accompanied by several other changes that differ for boys and girls. Muscle fibres become thicker and denser during adolescence, producing substantial increases in strength. However, muscle growth is much more pronounced in boys than in girls (Smoll & Schutz, 1990). Body fat also increases during adolescence, but much more rapidly in girls than boys. Finally, heart and lung capacities increase more in adolescent boys than in adolescent girls. Together, these changes help to explain why the typical adolescent boy has more strength, is quicker, and has greater endurance than the typical adolescent girl.

In the Children's Lives feature, you'll see how healthy bone growth in adolescence is also an essential defence against a disease that strikes during middle age.

Adolescents not only become taller and heavier, they also become mature sexually. **Sexual maturation includes changes in** *primary sex characteristics,* **which refers to organs that are directly involved in reproduction.** These organs include the ovaries, uterus, and vagina in girls and the scrotum, testes, and penis in boys. **Sexual maturation**

During the adolescent growth spurt, girls are often much taller than boys of the same age.

Andy Reynolds/Getty Images

Children's Lives

Preventing Osteoporosis

Osteoporosis **is a disease in which a person's bones become thin and brittle and, as a consequence, sometimes break.** Although osteoporosis can strike at any age, people over 50 are at greatest risk because bone tissue starts to break down more rapidly than new bone can be formed. About 1.8 million Canadians over 40 have osteoporosis, with women five times more likely than men to report having osteoporosis (Public Health Agency of Canada, 2015). More women than men suffer this form of bone loss because after menopause the ovaries no longer produce as much estrogen, which guards against bone deterioration.

Osteoporosis often has its roots in childhood and adolescence, when bones acquire nearly all their mass. For bones to develop properly, children and adolescents need to consume approximately 1300 milligrams of calcium daily. This is the equivalent of about 750 millilitres of milk, 15 grams of cheese, and 250 millilitres of spinach. In addition, children and adolescents should engage in weight-bearing exercise for 30 minutes daily, at least five days a week. Weight-bearing exercises strengthen bones by making them carry the body's weight. Walking briskly, running, playing tennis, climbing stairs, aerobic dancing, and cross-country skiing are all good forms of weight-bearing exercise. Swimming, cycling, and rowing do not require the bones to support body weight, so they are not good weight-bearing exercises (although, of course, they do benefit the heart, lungs, and muscles).

Unfortunately, many adolescents do not get enough calcium or exercise for healthy bone growth. Consequently, in 1998, the U.S. Centers for Disease Control and Prevention, the U.S. Department of Health and Human Services' Office on Women's Health, and the National Osteoporosis Foundation collaborated to create a national bone health campaign. Originally called Powerful Girls. Powerful Bones, the program was designed to encourage 9- to 12-year-old girls to consume more calcium and to exercise more often. Ads appeared in magazines and newspapers and on radio and TV to emphasize the importance of healthy bone growth. A website was created that includes information about bone health along with games that encourage adolescents to learn more about how diet and exercise contribute to healthy growth. In addition, the program established links with local communities, such as providing lesson plans and activities on bone health for teachers and school nurses. In 2008, the program was renamed Best Bones Forever and was extended to include 12- to 18-year-olds.

Similar programs are now running in Canada—for example, Go Girls! Originally sponsored by the Ontario Physical and Health Education Association (OPHEA) and now run by Big Brothers Big Sisters of Canada, the Go Girls! motto, shown in Figure 4-5, is "Healthy bodies, healthy minds." This program aims to get adolescent girls physically active and to provide information on healthy eating. Young women of university age (18 to 25) mentor younger girls, setting up exercise and sports activities as well as social events aimed at improving physical fitness, health knowledge, and self-esteem (Big Brothers Big Sisters of Canada, n.d.). Go Girls! information can be accessed via the Big Brothers Big Sisters of Canada website at **www.bigbrothersbigsisters.ca/**.

Programs such as those sponsored by the National Bone Health Campaign (NBHC) or Big Brothers Big Sisters are too new for us to know their effectiveness.

Big Brothers Big Sisters of Canada

Figure 4-5 The Go Girls program promotes active living and healthy eating, which help proper physical development.

(After all, the real test won't come for another 35 to 40 years, when the girls in the target audience reach the age when they will be at risk for osteoporosis.) However, the hope is that by communicating effectively with adolescents and their parents (emphasizing that healthy bones are an essential part of overall healthy, positive growth), adolescents will get more calcium and become more active physically, thereby forging the strong bones that are the best defence against osteoporosis.

Critical Thinking Questions: What might be a limitation of such programs? How could more girls be reached with such messages about the need for physical activity and healthy eating?

also includes changes in *secondary sex characteristics,* **which are physical signs of maturity that are not linked directly to the reproductive organs.** These include the growth of breasts and the widening of the pelvis in girls, the appearance of facial hair and the broadening of shoulders in boys, and the appearance of body hair and changes in voice and skin in both boys and girls.

Changes in primary and secondary sexual characteristics occur in a predictable sequence. For girls, puberty begins with the growth of the breasts and the growth spurt, followed by the appearance of pubic hair. *Menarche,* **the onset of menstruation, typically occurs at about age 13.** Data from the National Longitudinal Survey of Children and Youth shows that the mean age of menarche for girls in Canada is 12.72 years, although there is variation, with some girls maturing earlier and others later than this average age (Al-Sahab, Ardern, Hamadeh, & Tamim, 2010). Early menstrual cycles are usually irregular and without ovulation.

For boys, puberty usually commences with the growth of the testes and scrotum, followed by the appearance of pubic hair, the start of the growth spurt, and growth of the penis. **At about age 13, most boys reach** *spermarche,* **the first spontaneous ejaculation of sperm-laden fluid.** Initial ejaculations often contain relatively few sperm; only months or sometimes years later are there sufficient sperm to fertilize an egg (Dorn, Dahl, Woodward, & Biro, 2006).

The onset of sexual maturity is one of the first signs that an adolescent is on the threshold of adulthood. For girls, menarche is a definite sign of sexual maturation. In some cultures, menarche is seen as a private and even shameful event, whereas in others, it is a cause for celebration. From interviews with a cross-cultural sample of women, Ayse Uskul at York University in Toronto found that most European societies tend to view menarche as a time of self-consciousness and not something for general discussion. Other cultures, however, view menarche as a time of celebration and confirming of womanhood. In Zambia, a girl is given new clothes; in South India, a feast is held and gifts of jewellery are common (Uskul, 2004). As we'll see in the Cultural Influences feature, many cultures celebrate this transition.

MECHANISMS OF MATURATION. What causes the many physical changes that occur during puberty? The pituitary gland in the brain is the key player. As we mentioned on page 125, the pituitary helps to regulate physical development by releasing growth hormone. In addition, the pituitary regulates pubertal changes by signalling other glands to secrete hormones. During the early elementary-school years—long before any outward signs of puberty—the pituitary signals the adrenal glands to release androgens, initiating the biochemical changes that will produce body hair. A few years later in girls, the pituitary signals the ovaries to release estrogen, which causes the breasts to enlarge, the female genitals to mature, and fat to accumulate. In boys, the pituitary signals the testes to release the androgen testosterone, which causes the male genitals to mature and muscle mass to increase.

Cultural Influences

Adolescent Rites of Passage

Throughout much of history, many cultures have had special rituals or rites of passage that recognized adolescence as a unique phase in an individual's life. In ancient Japan, for example, a ceremony was performed for 12- and 14-year-old boys and girls in which they received adult clothing and adult hairstyles. Traditionally, as adolescents, indigenous Australian males walked alone in the wilderness, retracing their ancestors' paths.

Variants of these ceremonies that continue to this day include bar and bat mitzvah, which recognize that young Jewish adolescents are now responsible for their own actions, and quinceañera, which celebrates the coming of age of 15-year-old girls in many Spanish-speaking regions in North, Central, and South America. The Western Apache, who live in the southwest portion of the United States, also have a traditional ceremony to celebrate a girl's menarche (Basso, 1970). After a girl's first menstrual period, a group of older adults decides when the ceremony will be held and selects a sponsor—a woman of good character and wealth (she helps to pay for the ceremony) who is unrelated to the initiate. The ceremony itself begins at sunrise and lasts a few hours. The initiate dresses in ceremonial attire and dances or chants, sometimes accompanied by her sponsor or a medicine man. The intent of these actions is to transform the girl into Changing Woman, a heroic figure in Apache myth. With this transformation comes longevity and perpetual strength.

In the upper Fraser Valley of British Columbia, a Sts'ailes Indigenous girl wears her coming-of-age regalia.

Stefan Labbé

Many Indigenous peoples in Canada also hold such ceremonies. For example, the Nakwasda'xw of British Columbia have a traditional ceremony—Ixantsila—to mark a girl's coming of age at menarche. Over four days various rituals are performed, under the guidance of a trusted medicine woman. On the fourth day, there is a ceremony to mark the girl being now seen as a woman. You can see a short film of this ceremony at **www.ourworldlanguage.com/2015/11/ixantsila-ceremony-coming-of-age.html**.

Whenever and wherever ceremonies like this are performed, they serve many of the same functions. On the one hand, they are a signal to all in the community that the initiate is now an adult. On the other hand, these rituals tell the initiates themselves that their community now has adult-like expectations for them.

Critical Thinking Questions: How does our culture celebrate puberty or recognize adulthood? Can you think of any ceremonies or milestones that mark such changes in status for the average Canadian?

The timing of pubertal events is regulated, in part, by genetics (Cousminer et al., 2013). This is shown by the closer synchrony of pubertal events in identical twins than in fraternal twins: If one identical twin has body hair, odds are that the other twin will, too (Mustanski, Viken, Kaprio, Pulkkinen, & Rose, 2004). Genetic influence is also shown by the fact that a mother's age at menarche is related to her daughter's age at menarche (Belsky, Bakermans-Kranenburg, & van IJzendoorn, 2007). However, these genetic forces are strongly influenced by the environment, particularly by an adolescent's nutrition and health. In general, puberty occurs earlier in adolescents who are well nourished and healthy than in adolescents who are not (St. George, Williams, & Silva, 1994).

Three other findings underscore the importance of nutrition and health in the onset of puberty. Cross-cultural comparisons reveal that menarche occurs earlier in areas of the world where nutrition and healthcare are adequate. For example, menarche occurs an average of two to three years earlier in Western European and North American countries than in African countries. Also, within regions, socioeconomic status matters: Girls from affluent homes are more likely to receive adequate nutrition and healthcare, and consequently reach menarche earlier (Steinberg, 1999). Finally, girls from developing countries who are adopted into affluent homes experience puberty earlier than peers in their home countries (Teilmann et al., 2006).

Historical data point to the same conclusion concerning the importance of nutrition and healthcare. In many industrialized countries around the world, the average age of menarche has declined steadily over the past 150 years. For example, in Europe, the average age of menarche was 17 in 1840, compared to about 13 today (Cole, 2000; Nebesio & Hirsch Pescovitz, 2005; Roche, 1979). This drop reflects improvements in general health and better healthcare over this period (Ellis, 2004). In these countries, age of menarche is no longer dropping, which suggests that with adequate nutrition, the biological lower limit for menarche is, on average, about 13 years (Cole, 2000).

You may remember, from Chapter 1, that the social environment also influences the onset of puberty, at least for girls. Menarche occurs at younger ages in girls who experience chronic stress or who are depressed (James, Ellis, Schlomer, & Garber, 2012). Other stresses within the family may also have an effect on menarche; for example, Belsky et al. (2010) discovered that girls have their first menstrual period at a younger age when their mothers used harsh punishment with them as preschoolers and young children.

The exact nature of these links is not known, but many explanations focus on the circumstances that would trigger the release of hormones that regulate menarche. One proposal is that when young girls experience chronic socioemotional stress—their family life is harsh and they lack warm, supportive parents—the hormones elicited by this stress may help to activate those that in turn trigger menarche. This mechanism would even have an evolutionary advantage: If events of a girl's life suggest that her future reproductive success is uncertain—as indicated by chronic socioemotional stress—then it may be adaptive to reproduce as soon as possible instead of waiting until later when she would be more mature and better able to care for her offspring. That is, the evolutionary gamble in this case might favour "lower quality" offspring now over "higher quality" offspring later (Ellis, 2004).

A different account, one that emphasizes the role of fathers, is described in the Spotlight on Theories feature.

These and other theories are being actively studied today. Where scientists agree, however, is that onset of menarche is *not* just under genetic and biological control; social and emotional factors also contribute.

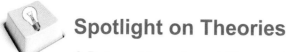

Spotlight on Theories

A Paternal Investment Theory of Girls' Pubertal Timing

BACKGROUND Environmental factors can cause adolescent girls to enter puberty earlier. Some scientists believe that stress is the main factor in an adolescent girl's life that may cause her to mature early, but other scientists continue to look for factors that influence the onset of puberty in girls.

THE THEORY Bruce J. Ellis (Ellis & Essex, 2007; Ellis et al., 2003) has proposed a paternal investment theory that emphasizes the role of fathers in determining timing of puberty. This theory is rooted in an evolutionary perspective that links timing of puberty—and in the process, timing of reproduction—to the resources (defined broadly) in the child's environment. When an environment is predictable and rich in resources, delayed reproduction is adaptive because this allows an adolescent girl to complete her own physical, cognitive, and socioemotional development, with the end result that she is a better parent. In contrast, when an environment is unstable and has few resources, it may be adaptive to mature and reproduce early rather than risk the possibility that reproduction may be impossible later.

According to Ellis, when a girl's childhood experiences indicate that paternal investment is common and of high quality, this may delay timing of maturation. But when those experiences indicate that paternal investment is uncommon and often of low quality, this may trigger early maturation. Delaying puberty is adaptive when high-quality fathers are plentiful, because it allows the girl to mature herself; but accelerating puberty is adaptive when high-quality fathers are rare, because it allows a girl to be mature sexually should a high-quality father become available, and because it means that her mother is likely to be available to help with child care.[2]

Hypothesis: If a girl's childhood experiences with paternal investment influence the timing of maturation, then the quantity and quality of a girl's experiences with her own father should predict the age when she enters puberty. Girls who have infrequent or negative interactions with their fathers should enter puberty earlier than girls who have frequent or positive interactions with their fathers because infrequent or negative experiences would indicate that the environment has few high-quality fathers.

Test: Tither and Ellis (2008) studied two groups of biological sisters. In one group the father was absent due to divorce or separation; in the other, families were intact. Tither and Ellis measured the quality of the father's parenting and the age when daughters experienced menarche.

Two main findings support the theory. First, younger sisters had experienced a longer absence of the father—greater disruption—than older sisters and thus should have experienced menarche earlier. They did, beginning to menstruate at an earlier age than both their older sisters and younger sisters from intact families. Second, this effect was most pronounced in daughters whose fathers were psychologically distant or had mental health problems. These girls experienced a double dose of ineffective fathering: He was usually absent and did more harm than good when he was present.

Conclusion: As predicted, pubertal timing was influenced by the quantity and quality of father-daughter interactions. Puberty was earlier when father-daughter interactions

[2]These are not conscious mechanisms: Young girls are not thinking to themselves, "The men around here are losers, so I might as well get on with it." Instead, neural pathways that are sensitive to the presence of caring men may act to suppress the hormonal paths that trigger puberty.

were uncommon or negative, which, according to Ellis, indicates that the environment contained relatively few high-quality fathers.

Application: We saw in Module 3.2 that teenage moms and their children usually travel a rocky road; it's always best if adolescent girls delay child-bearing until they are older. Paternal investment theory suggests that one way to reduce teen pregnancy is to encourage fathers to have more frequent and more positive interactions with their daughters. This will help delay the onset of puberty, reducing the odds that she will become pregnant as a teenager and helping in other ways as well, as we'll see on pages 363–364. Of course, a father's investment in his daughters (as well as his sons) has benefits that extend far beyond physical maturation, as we'll see throughout the book.

Critical Thinking Question: What other sociocultural influences might be at work here?

As teenagers enter puberty, they become very concerned with their appearance.

PSYCHOLOGICAL IMPACT OF PUBERTY. Of course, teenagers are well aware of the changes taking place in their bodies. Not surprisingly, some of these changes affect their psychological development. For example, compared to children and adults, adolescents are much more concerned about their overall appearance. Like the girl in the photo, many teenagers look in the mirror regularly, checking for signs of additional physical change. Generally, girls worry more than boys about appearance and are more likely to be dissatisfied with their appearance (Vander Wal & Thelen, 2000). Girls are particularly likely to be unhappy with their appearance when appearance is a frequent topic of conversation with friends, leading girls to spend more time comparing their own appearance with that of their peers. Peers, however, have relatively little influence on boys' satisfaction with their appearance; instead, boys are unhappy with their appearance when they expect to have an idealized strong, muscular body but don't (Carlson Jones, 2004).

In addition, adolescents are affected by the timing of maturation: Many children begin puberty years before or after the norm. An early-maturing boy might begin puberty at age 11, whereas a late-maturing boy might start at 15 or 16. An early-maturing girl might start puberty at 9, a late-maturing girl at 14 or 15.

Maturing early or late has psychological consequences that differ for boys and girls. Several longitudinal studies show that early maturation can be harmful for girls. Girls who mature early often lack self-confidence, are less popular, are more likely to be depressed and to have behaviour problems, and are more likely to smoke and drink (Mendle, Turkheimer, & Emery, 2007; Schelleman-Offermans, Knibbe, & Kuntsche, 2013). Part of the problem is that early maturation may lead girls to relationships with older boys and these girls are ill prepared to cope with the demands of these relationships (Stattin, Kerr, & Skoog, 2011). In turn, this can result in life-changing effects on early-maturing girls who are pressured into sex and become mothers while still teenagers: as adults, they typically have less prestigious, lower-paying jobs (Mendle et al., 2007). The good news here is that the harmful effects of early maturation can be offset by other factors: When early-maturing girls have warm, supportive parents, for example, they are less likely to suffer the harmful consequences of early maturation (Ge, Brody, Conger, Simons, & Murry, 2002).

Westend61 GmbH/Alamy Stock Photo

Maturing early can be harmful for boys, too. Early-maturing boys are at risk for psychological disorders such as depression; they are also more prone to substance abuse and to inappropriately early sexual activity (Mendle & Ferrero, 2012). Being physically advanced for their age may cause early-maturing boys to have problems with their peers who have not yet matured (leading to depression) and cause them to spend more time with older boys (exposing them to risky behaviour). However, the effects of early maturation are weaker for boys than they are for girls (Graber, 2013).

For boys and girls, maturing late poses few risks. Late-maturing girls fare well; late-maturing boys are at somewhat greater risk for depression (Mendle & Ferrero, 2012). But otherwise Pete, the late-maturing boy in the opening vignette, has nothing to worry about. When he finally matures, others will treat him like an adult and the few extra years of being treated like a child will not be harmful (Weichold & Silbereisen, 2005).

Because children enter puberty at different ages, early-maturing children often tower over their late-maturing agemates.

 Check Your Learning

RECALL Summarize the mechanisms of physical growth.

What is puberty and how does it differ for boys and girls?

INTERPRET Why is sleep important for healthy growth and development?

APPLY The onset of puberty would seem to be due entirely to biology. In fact, the child's environment influences the onset of puberty. Summarize the ways in which biology and experience interact to trigger the onset of puberty.

 ANSWER 4.1
You could tell her that breastfed babies tend to be healthier, get diarrhea less often, and make the transition to solid foods more easily. You could also mention that it's almost impossible to contaminate breast milk.

 4.2 **Challenges to Healthy Growth**

OUTLINE
Malnutrition
Eating Disorders: Anorexia and Bulimia
Obesity
Disease
Accidents

LEARNING OBJECTIVES
1. What is malnutrition? What are its consequences? What is the solution to malnutrition?
2. How do nature and nurture lead some adolescent girls to diet excessively?
3. Why do some children become obese? How can they lose weight permanently?
4. How do diseases and accidents threaten children's development?

Ricardo, age 12, has been overweight for most of his life. He dislikes the playground games that entertain most of his classmates during recess, preferring to stay indoors. He has relatively few friends and is not particularly happy with his lot in life. Many times Ricardo has lost weight by dieting, but he's always regained it quickly. His parents know that being overweight is a health hazard, and they wonder if there is anything that will help their son.

Compared to many childhood tasks, physical growth seems easy. To paraphrase a famous line from the movie *Field of Dreams*, "If you feed them, they will grow." Of course, it's not this simple, in part because many children face obstacles on the path of healthy physical growth, some of which concern nutrition. Growth requires enormous reserves of energy, and many children do not eat enough food to provide this energy. Other children and adolescents eat too much. Other problems include disease and accidents, which affect millions of children worldwide. We'll look at these problems in this module, and as we do, we'll learn some of the reasons Ricardo is overweight and what he can do about it.

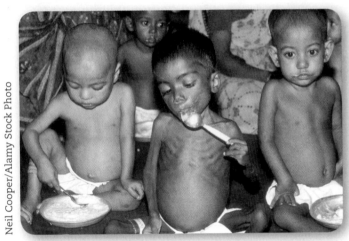

Malnutrition is acute in developing countries, where one child in three is malnourished.

Neil Cooper/Alamy Stock Photo

Malnutrition

An adequate diet is only a dream to many of the world's children. **Worldwide, about one in three children under age five suffers from *malnutrition*, as indicated by being small for their age** (UNICEF-WHO-The World Bank, 2012). Many, like the children in the photo, are from developing countries, but malnutrition is regrettably common in industrialized countries, too. Many Canadian children growing up homeless and in poverty are malnourished. According to the Campaign 2000 Let's Make Poverty History 2012 report on child poverty in Canada, 979 000 children in Canada—almost one in seven—lives in poverty (Campaign 2000, 2012). Many of these children go to bed hungry, and although children are only 22 percent of the population, 37 percent of food bank users in 2008 were children (Campaign 2000, 2009).

Malnourishment is especially damaging during infancy because growth is so rapid during these years. By the school-age years, children with a history of infant malnutrition often have difficulty maintaining attention in school; they are easily distracted. Malnutrition during rapid periods of growth apparently damages the brain, affecting a child's intelligence and ability to pay attention and learn (Benton, 2010; Morgane et al., 1993; Nyaradi, Li, Hickling, Foster, & Oddy, 2013).

Malnutrition would seem to have a simple cure—an adequate diet. But the solution is more complex than that. Malnourished children are frequently listless and inactive, behaviours that are useful because they conserve energy. At the same time, when children are routinely unresponsive and lethargic, parents may provide fewer and fewer experiences that foster their children's development. For example, parents who start out reading to their children at night may stop because their malnourished children seem uninterested and inattentive. The result is a self-perpetuating cycle in which malnourished children are forsaken by parents, who feel that nothing they do gets a response so they quit trying. A biological influence—lethargy stemming from insufficient nourishment—causes a profound change in the experiences—parental teaching—that shape a child's development (Worobey, 2005).

To break the vicious cycle, children need more than an improved diet; their parents must also be taught how to foster their children's development. Programs that combine dietary supplements with parent training offer promise in treating malnutrition (Engle & Huffman, 2010; Nahar et al., 2012). Children in these programs often catch up with their peers in physical and intellectual growth, showing that the best way to treat malnutrition is by addressing both biological and sociocultural factors (Super, Herrera, & Mora, 1990). The international Let's Make Poverty History campaign encourages governments to do just that, for example, by allocating social spending for programs for families with young children, and providing secure, affordable housing (Campaign 2000, 2009, 2012).

SHORT-TERM HUNGER. Breakfast should provide about one-fourth of a child's daily calories, yet many children—in both developed and developing countries—do not eat breakfast (Grantham-McGregor, Ani, & Gernald, 2001). When children eat a nutritious breakfast regularly, they're often more successful in school (Adolphus, Lawton, & Dye, 2013).

One strategy to attack this problem is to provide free and reduced-price meals for children at school. Lunch programs are the most common, but breakfast and dinner are sometimes available, too. These programs have a tremendous positive impact on children. Because the children are better fed, they are absent from school less often and their achievement scores improve (Grantham-McGregor et al., 2001).

Eating Disorders: Anorexia and Bulimia

In 2010, French model and actress Isabelle Caro died of respiratory disease, just months after turning 26. Near her death she weighed less than 34 kilos; Caro suffered from an eating disorder: *anorexia nervosa* **is a disorder marked by a persistent refusal to eat and an irrational fear of being overweight.** Individuals with anorexia nervosa have a grossly distorted image of their own body. Like the girl in the photo, they claim to be overweight despite being painfully thin (Wilson, Heffernan, & Black, 1996). Anorexia is a serious disorder that can damage the heart, brain, or kidneys, sometimes causing death. A related eating disorder is bulimia nervosa. **Individuals with** *bulimia nervosa* **alternate between binge eating, when they eat uncontrollably, and purging—through self-induced vomiting or with laxatives.** The frequency of binge eating varies remarkably among people with bulimia nervosa, from a few times a week to more than 30 times a week. What is common to all individuals with bulimia is the feeling that they cannot stop eating (Mizes, Scott, & Tonya, 1995).

Adolescent girls with anorexia nervosa believe that they are overweight, and they refuse to eat.

Anorexia and bulimia are alike in many respects. Both disorders mostly affect females. Although eating disorders emerge primarily in adolescence (Wang & Brownell, 2005), concern has arisen since the 1990s over the younger ages at which eating disorders seem to be starting (e.g., Hill & Oliver, 1992). What's more, many of the same factors put girls at risk for both eating disorders. A meta-analysis (Jacobi et al., 2004) of studies of individuals with eating disorders indicated that heredity puts some girls at risk, and molecular genetic studies have implicated genes that regulate both anxiety and food intake (Klump & Culbert, 2007). Several psychosocial factors also put people at risk for eating disorders. When children have a history of eating problems, such as being a picky eater or being diagnosed with pica (eating nonfood objects such as chalk, paper, or dirt) they're at greater risk for anorexia and bulimia during adolescence. Teenagers who have negative self-esteem or mood or anxiety disorders are also at risk (Hutchinson, Rapee, & Taylor, 2010). However, the most important risk factors for adolescents are being overly concerned about their body and weight and having a history of dieting (George & Franko, 2010). Teenage girls are at risk when they frequently watch TV shows that emphasize attractive, thin characters, and when their friends frequently talk about weight and diet constantly in order to stay thin (Grabe, Hyde, & Ward, 2008; Rancourt et al., 2013). The meta-analysis by Jacobi et al. (2004) also identified some risk factors that are unique to anorexia and bulimia. For example, overprotective parenting is associated with anorexia but not bulimia. In contrast, obesity in childhood is associated with bulimia but not anorexia.

Although eating disorders are more common in girls, boys make up about 10 percent of diagnosed cases of such eating disorders. Because boys with these eating disorders are far less common, researchers have conducted much less research on boys. However, some of the known risk factors are childhood obesity, low self-esteem, pressure from parents and peers to lose weight, and participating in sports that emphasize being lean (Dominé, Berchtold, Akré, Michaud, & Suris, 2009; Ricciardelli & McCabe, 2004; Shoemaker & Furman, 2009). A different form of eating disorder that is more commonly associated with boys is body dysmorphic disorder. **In *body dysmorphic disorder* individuals are not satisfied with their body shape or the shape of a particular part of the body, and perceived muscularity is often the focus.** This disorder is mostly found in young athletes and boys concerned with a "masculine" physique. Those suffering from the disorder will see themselves as "weak" or insufficiently muscular and will adopt very specific diet and exercise regimens to attempt to improve muscle mass and definition (Cafri, van den Berg, & Thompson, 2006; Raudenbush & Meyer, 2003). Male high-school athletes may see leanness as vitally important to a positive body image (MacKinnon et al., 2003; Cafri et al., 2006). Fixations on leanness or muscular definition can lead to obsessive concern over body fat, causing reduced food intake and thus also supporting a form of anorexia.

Fortunately, programs exist that can help protect young people from eating disorders (Stice & Shaw, 2004). The most effective programs are designed for at-risk youth, for example, for those who already say they are unhappy with their body. The best programs are interactive—they allow youth to become involved and learn new skills, such as ways to resist social pressure to be thin. They also work to change critical attitudes (e.g., ideals regarding thinness) and critical behaviours (e.g., dieting and overeating). At-risk adolescents who participate in these programs are helped; they are more satisfied with their appearance and less likely to diet or overeat (Stice, South, & Shaw, 2012). Treatment is available for those teens affected by eating disorders. Like prevention programs, treatment typically focuses on modifying key attitudes and behaviours (Puhl & Brownell, 2005).

Obesity

Ricardo, the boy in the module-opening vignette, is overweight; he is very heavy for his height. **The technical definition for being overweight is based on the *body mass index (BMI),* which is an adjusted ratio of weight to height.** Children and adolescents who are in the upper 5% (very heavy for their height) are defined as being overweight. In recent decades, prevalence of obesity has been on the rise in Canada, with 18% of adults now categorized as obese, and this statistic is projected to continue to increase (Twells, Gregory, Reddigan, & Midodzi, 2014). Obese children are likely to become obese adults. According to the Canadian Community Health Measures Surveys (CCHS) of 2009 to 2011, and Statistics Canada's *Health Reports*, about one-third of Canadian children and adolescents are overweight (Roberts, Shields, de Groh, Aziz, & Gilbert, 2012). The most recent CCHS surveys showed that 20% of those age 5 to 17 years were overweight, and 12% were obese (Roberts et al., 2012). Other research has confirmed the prevalence of obesity in Canadian children and, as with adult obesity, figures do seem to be rising. The risk of being overweight or obese is now seen as early as age 2 (He & Sutton, 2004).

Similar findings exist for the United States. In 2001, the U.S. Surgeon General announced that childhood obesity in the United States had reached epidemic proportions.

In the past 25 to 30 years, the number of overweight children in the United States has doubled and the number of overweight adolescents has tripled, so that today roughly one child or adolescent out of six in America is overweight (U.S. Department of Health and Human Services, 2010). The Canadian government also used the term "epidemic" in 2005, when it published a report called *The Obesity Epidemic in Canada* (Starky, 2005). These findings are important not only for current health but also because being overweight in adolescence is predictive of obesity in adulthood (Tremblay, Morrison, & Tremblay, 2006).

Given the health risks associated with obesity, it is unfortunate that many parents and children seem to underestimate their own weight and think themselves a normal weight when in fact they are overweight or even obese. Katerina Maximova and her colleagues from Quebec hospitals and universities found that overweight children and adolescents were likely to misperceive their own weight. Misperception was most common for those in environments where others (e.g., parents and school friends) were also overweight (Maximova et al., 2008). It seems that a heavyweight comparison group caused the children to see themselves as "average" rather than as overweight, a troubling finding given that about one-quarter of young Canadians are overweight. This can lead to unhealthy lifestyles, because those who do not consider their weight to be a health risk do not pay attention to health information and do not alter their lifestyle to a more healthy one (Maximova et al., 2008).

Overweight youngsters like the boy in the photo are often unpopular, have low self-esteem, and do poorly in school (Gable, Krull, & Chang, 2012; Puhl & Latner, 2007). Furthermore, throughout life they are at risk for many medical problems, including high blood pressure and diabetes, because the vast majority of overweight children and adolescents become overweight adults (Tremblay et al., 2006; U.S. Department of Health and Human Services, 2010).

No single factor causes children to become obese. Instead, several factors contribute, including the following:

Imagestate Media Partners Limited-Impact Photos/Alamy Stock Photo

- Heredity—Obesity runs in families, showing that genes contribute, perhaps by causing some people to overeat, to be sedentary, or to be less able to convert fat to fuel (Cheung & Mao, 2012).

- Parents—Many parents urge children to "clean their plates" even when the children are no longer hungry, and other parents routinely use food to comfort children who are upset; these practices cause children to rely on external cues to eat instead of eating only when they're hungry (Coelho, Jansen, Roefs, & Nederkoom, 2009; Wansink & Sobal, 2007).

- Sedentary lifestyle—Children are more prone to obesity when they are physically inactive, such as watching television instead of playing outdoors (Tremblay et al., 2011).

- Too little sleep—Children and adolescents who do not sleep enough tend to gain weight, perhaps because being awake longer affords them more opportunities to eat, by increasing their feelings of hunger or by making them too tired to exercise (Magee & Hale, 2012).

Individually these factors may not lead to obesity. But collectively they may put children on the path to obesity: A child is at greater risk if he or she is genetically prone to overeat, is sedentary, and is chronically sleepy. To understand childhood obesity, we need to consider all of these risk factors as well as the amount and quality of food that's available in the child's environment (Harrison et al., 2011).

Childhood obesity has reached epidemic proportions in North America and in other parts of the world.

Obese youth can lose weight. The most effective weight-loss programs focus on changing children's eating habits and encouraging them to become more active. Children set goals for eating and exercise; parents help them set realistic goals, reward them for progress, and monitor their own eating and exercising. When programs incorporate these features, obese children do lose weight (Oude Luttikhuis et al., 2009; West, Sanders, Cleghorn, & Davies, 2010). However, even after losing weight, many children participating in these programs remain overweight. Consequently, it is best to avoid overweight and obesity in the first place by encouraging children to eat healthfully and to be active physically.

Unfortunately, many youngsters in Canada are still not getting enough physical activity. Statistics on participation in physical education (PE) in Ontario high schools show a decline in participation in PE in recent years. From 1999 to 2005, the overall percentage of high-school students enrolled in PE declined 10 percent, from 70.3 to 60.3 percent (Faulkner et al., 2007). Programs are starting to be put in place, however, to encourage physical activity, particularly in schools. For example, in response to findings that over half of British Columbia's 12- to 19-year-olds were insufficiently active, the province created the *Action Schools! BC* program (Action Schools! BC, n.d). This initiative aims to promote active, healthy living in youngsters by incorporating physical activity and advice about healthy eating at school and to promote extracurricular activities. Though some argue that school-based programs do not change BMI (Harris et al., 2009), the main point of such initiatives is to make healthy lifestyle habits a long-term outcome. Our government is trying to combat obesity in Canada in this way, in previous years by offering tax credits and subsidies for enrolment in sports programs (Madore, 2007) as well as providing health information such as *Canada's Food Guide*. In addition, the Federal Government updated the *Canadian Physical Activity Guidelines* to try to give clear advice on how much activity is needed for healthy development. (You may have seen the advertisements on TV, in which parents are encouraged to get children more physically active.) The current Canadian Society for Exercise Physiology (CSEP) guidelines are that both children (5- to 11-year-olds) and youth (12- to 17-year-olds) "should accumulate at least 60 minutes of moderate- to vigorous-intensity physical activity daily" (CSEP, 2011, n.p.). Unfortunately, young Canadians are not meeting these targets for activity levels. A subsequent analysis by the organization Active Healthy Kids Canada gave the country an F on a "report card" for children's physical activity levels as only seven percent were meeting the government's daily guidelines. There was some good news, however, in that 44 percent of Canadian children were physically active for 60 minutes three days a week, and many children do participate in some activity with school PE, active play, or organized activities and sports (Active Healthy Kids Canada, 2012).

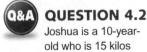

Q&A QUESTION 4.2
Joshua is a 10-year-old who is 15 kilos overweight. What can he and his parents do to help him lose weight? (*Answer is on page 142.*)

Disease

Around the world, nearly eight million children die before their fifth birthday; countries in Africa account for more than half of these childhood deaths (World Health Organization, 2013b). These are staggering numbers—a yearly death rate that is roughly equivalent to the entire population of Ontario or to six times the number of *all* deaths of under-fives in Canada. Five conditions are the leading killers of young children worldwide: pneumonia, diarrhea, measles, malaria, and malnutrition (World Health Organization, 2012). The majority of these deaths can be prevented with proven, cost-effective treatments. For example, diarrhea kills by dehydrating youngsters, yet death can be averted if children promptly drink water that contains salt and potassium.

As part of a vigorous effort to prevent childhood illness, for the past two decades the World Health Organization (WHO) has worked to vaccinate children worldwide. Because of these efforts, vaccination rates have skyrocketed in many developing countries. WHO also has joined with the United Nations Children's Fund (UNICEF) to create the Integrated Management of Childhood Illness (IMCI) program to combat the five childhood killers mentioned earlier: pneumonia, diarrhea, measles, malaria, and malnutrition (World Health Organization, 2004). Because many children who are ill have symptoms related to two or more of these five conditions, IMCI uses an integrated strategy that focuses on the overall health of the child. One component of IMCI is training healthcare professionals to become more skilled in dealing with childhood illnesses. A second component is improving healthcare systems so that they are better able to respond to childhood illness (e.g., ensuring that required medicines are available). A third component involves changing family and community practices to make them more conducive to healthy growth. For example, to protect children from mosquitoes that carry malaria, children are encouraged to sleep under netting, as the baby in the photo is doing. IMCI has been adopted in more than 60 countries and is playing a pivotal role in improving children's health worldwide (Bhutta et al., 2010; Victora, Adam, Bruce, & Evans, 2006).

One way to protect young children from disease is to adopt practices that foster healthy growth, such as having them sleep under netting that protects them from mosquitoes that carry malaria.

Accidents

In North America, most infant deaths are due to medical conditions associated with birth defects or low birth weight. From age one on, however, children are more likely to die from accidents than from any other single cause (Canadian Red Cross, 2013, 2014; Ontario Ministry of Transportation, 2012). Motor vehicle accidents are the most common cause of accidental death in children. Some accidents occur as a result of vehicle collisions with child pedestrians, although safety measures such as pedestrian crossings and use of crossing guards near schools, for example, reduce collision risk (Rothman, McArthur, To, Buliung, & Howard, 2014). Most accidental deaths occur when children are passengers in vehicles, and many of these deaths could have been prevented had the children and adolescents been wearing seatbelts, or the infants and children been restrained properly in an approved infant car seat like the one shown in the photo. In fact, the federal government's Motor Vehicle Safety Act requires such car seats in Canada, as well as booster seats for children who no longer fit in an infant car seat but are still too small for a regular seatbelt. In addition, drivers are responsible by law for making sure that everyone under the age of 16 is properly buckled up (Ontario Ministry of Transportation, 2012). Without such restraints, children and adolescents typically suffer massive head injuries when thrown through the windshield or onto the road in a car accident. In Canada, motor vehicle crashes are the most likely cause of death and injury, including brain trauma, for youths aged 15 to 24 years (MacDonald, Yanchar, & Hébert, 2007).

One simple way to protect infants, toddlers, and young children is to insist that they be restrained in an approved seat when riding in a car.

Infants and toddlers also drown, die from burns, or suffocate. Often these deaths happen because young children are supervised inadequately (Morrongiello & Schell, 2010;

Children sometimes have accidents because parents overestimate their children's abilities, allowing them to do such potentially dangerous activities as ride bikes on unsafe streets.

Petrass & Blitvich, 2013). All too common, for example, are reports of young children who wander away and jump or fall into a swimming pool that lacks protective fencing—and then drown. Parents need to remember that children are often eager to explore their environs, yet they are unable to recognize many hazards. Parents must keep a protective eye on their young children at all times. With older children, parents should not overestimate their children's cognitive and motor skills, since some accidents happen because parents have too much confidence in these skills. For example, parents may allow their child, like the children in the photo to ride to school in a bike lane adjacent to fast-moving vehicles—even though the child may not always pay attention—or negotiate traffic when they may not always recognize when there is not enough time to cross a busy street safely (Morrongiello, Klemencic, & Corbett, 2008; Stevens, Plumert, Cremer, & Kearney, 2013).[3]

Motor vehicle accidents remain the leading cause of death of adolescents. The difference, of course, is that adolescents are no longer passengers but are driving. Sadly, far too many adolescents are killed because they drive too fast, drive while drunk or texting, or drive without wearing a seatbelt (U.S. Centers for Disease Control and Prevention, 2012). Roughly 36 percent of teenagers who die each year do so as a result of a car crash, and 60 percent of those teens were not wearing a seatbelt (Traffic Injury Research Foundation [TIRF], 2005). Another TIRF report noted that in 2012 about a third (34.5 percent) of deaths in car accidents for 16- to 19-year-olds in Canada were alcohol-related (TIRF, 2015).

In the United States, accident statistics for adolescents are significantly influenced by the availability of guns. Among teenage boys in the United States, firearms represent a leading cause of death, and firearms are responsible for the deaths of more 15- to 19-year-old African American youths than any other single cause (Federal Interagency Forum on Child and Family Statistics, 2013). In Canada, guns are less readily available, particularly handguns. Still, firearms are a major cause of death even here. More male youths die from firearms injuries "than from cancer, or from falls, fires and drownings combined" (Canadian Paediatric Society [CPS], 2005, n.p.). Thus the CPS recommends that firearms not be kept in homes where children and teens live (CPS, 2005).

Although the term *accident* implies that the event happened by chance and no one was to blame, most accidents involving children and adolescents can be foreseen and either prevented or steps taken to reduce injury. In the case of automobile accidents, for example, simply wearing a seat belt enhances safety immensely. Accidents involving firearms can be reduced by making guns less accessible to children and adolescents (e.g., locking away guns and ammunition). School- and community-based safety programs represent a cost-effective way to reduce childhood accidents (Nilsen, 2007; Schwebel, Davis, & O'Neal, 2012). Children can learn safe ways of walking or riding their bikes to school and then be allowed to practise these skills, supervised by an adult. With programs such as these, children readily learn behaviours that foster safety.

Q&A ANSWER 4.2
Joshua and his parents need to work together to create a healthier lifestyle that changes his eating habits and encourages him to be more active. By agreeing on realistic goals (e.g., losing 3 kilos in a month or playing for 30 minutes outdoors each day) and using rewards, they can help Joshua achieve his goals. Also, Joshua himself must learn to record what and how much he eats and how much he exercises.

· · · · · · · · · · · · · · · · · · ·

[3]As a 10-year-old, Robert Kail's son Matt crashed his new bike into the back of a parked car because he was too busy watching the gears shift. Fortunately, Matt escaped with just a few scrapes—but the incident illustrates how easily a childish lapse in concentration can lead to a cycling accident.

Check Your Learning

RECALL Summarize the factors that put adolescent girls at risk for anorexia nervosa and for bulimia nervosa.

What are the leading causes of death for toddlers and preschool children? For adolescents?

INTERPRET Distinguish the biological factors that contribute to obesity from environmental factors.

APPLY How does malnutrition show the impact that children can have on their own development?

4.3 The Developing Nervous System

OUTLINE	LEARNING OBJECTIVES
Organization of the Mature Brain	1. What are the parts of a nerve cell? How is the brain organized?
The Developing Brain	2. When is the brain formed in prenatal development? When do different regions of the brain begin to function?

While crossing the street, 10-year-old Martin was struck by a passing car. He was in a coma for a week but then gradually became more alert, and now he seems to be aware of his surroundings. Needless to say, Martin's mother is grateful that he survived the accident, but she wonders what the future holds for her son.

The physical changes that we see as children grow are impressive, but even more awe-inspiring are the changes we cannot see—those involving the brain and the nervous system. An infant's feelings of hunger, a child's laugh, and an adolescent's efforts to learn algebra all reflect the functioning brain and the rest of the nervous system. All the information that children learn, including language and other cognitive skills, is stored in the brain.

How does the brain accomplish these many tasks? How is the brain affected by an injury like the one that Martin suffered? To begin to answer these questions, let's look at how the brain is organized in adults.

Organization of the Mature Brain

The basic unit of the brain and the rest of the nervous system is the *neuron,* **a cell that specializes in receiving and transmitting information.** Neurons come in many different shapes, as you can see in the different photos on the next page. Figure 4-6 makes it easier to understand the basic parts found in all neurons. **The** *cell body* **at the centre of the neuron contains the basic biological machinery that keeps the neuron alive. The receiving end of the neuron, the** *dendrite,* **looks like a tree with many**

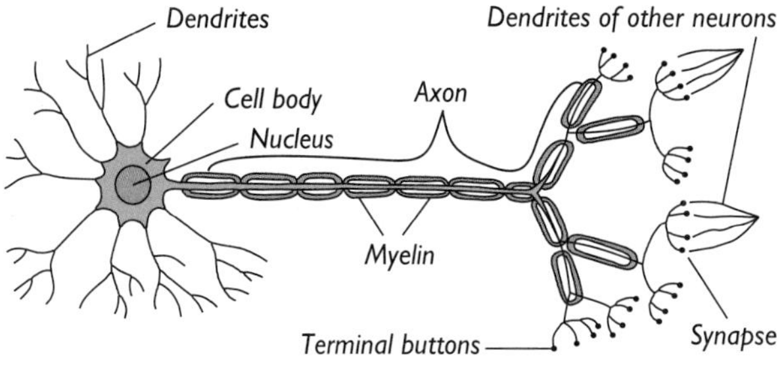

Figure 4-6 The basic structure of a neuron.

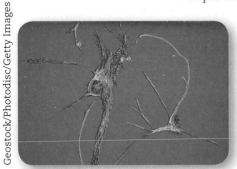

Figure 4-7 labels: Frontal cortex, Motor cortex, Left Hemisphere, Right Hemisphere, Sensory cortex, Visual cortex, Auditory cortex

Figure 4-7 Regions of the cerebral cortex.

Geostock/Photodisc/Getty Images

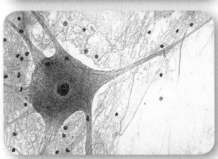

Ed Reschke

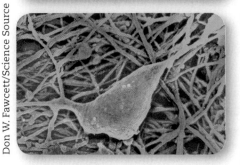

Don W. Fawcett/Science Source

Neurons come in many shapes, but they all have the same function—transmitting information.

branches. The highly branched dendrite allows one neuron to receive input from many thousands of other neurons (Morgan & Gibson, 1991). **The tube-like structure at the other end of the cell body is the** *axon,* **which sends information to other neurons. The axon is wrapped in** *myelin,* **a fatty sheath that allows it to transmit information more rapidly.** The boost in neural speed from myelin is like the difference between driving and flying: from about 2 metres per second to 15 metres per second. **At the end of the axon are small knobs called** *terminal buttons,* **which release** *neurotransmitters,* **chemicals that carry information to nearby neurons.** Finally, you can see that the terminal buttons of one axon do not actually touch the dendrites of other neurons. **The gap between one neuron and the next is a** *synapse.* Neurotransmitters cross synapses to carry information between neurons.

Take 50 to 100 billion neurons like these and you have the beginnings of a human brain. An adult's brain weighs a little less than 1.5 kilograms and easily fits into your hands. **The wrinkled surface of the brain is the** *cerebral cortex;* **made up of about 10 billion neurons; the cortex regulates many of the functions that we think of as distinctly human. The cortex consists of left and right halves, called** *hemispheres* **that are linked by millions of axons in a thick bundle called the** *corpus callosum.* The characteristics that you value most—your engaging personality, your way with words, your uncanny knack for reading others—are all controlled by specific regions of the cortex, many of which are shown in Figure 4-7.

Your personality and your ability to make and carry out plans are largely functions of an area at the front of your cortex called, appropriately, the *frontal cortex.* For most people, the ability to produce and understand language, to reason, and to compute is largely due to neurons in the cortex of the left hemisphere. Also, for most people, artistic and musical abilities, perception of spatial relationships, and the ability to recognize faces and emotions mainly come from neurons in the right hemisphere.

Now that we know a bit about the organization of the mature brain, let's look at how the brain develops and begins to function.

The Developing Brain

Scientists who study brain development are guided by several key questions: How and when do brain structures develop? When do different brain regions begin to function? Why do brain regions take on different functions? In this section, we'll see how research has answered each question.

EMERGING BRAIN STRUCTURES. We know from Module 3.1 that the beginnings of the brain can be traced to the period of the zygote. **At roughly three weeks after conception, a group of cells form a flat structure known as the** *neural plate.* At four weeks, the neural plate folds to form a tube that ultimately becomes the brain and spinal cord. When the ends of the tube fuse shut, neurons are produced in one small region of the neural tube. Production of neurons begins about 10 weeks after conception, and by 28 weeks the developing brain has virtually all the neurons it will ever have. During these weeks, neurons form at the incredible rate of more than 4000 per second (Kolb, 1989).

From the neuron-manufacturing site in the neural tube, neurons migrate to their final positions in the brain. The brain is built in stages, beginning with the innermost layers. Neurons in the deepest layer are positioned first, followed by neurons in the second layer, and so on. This layering process continues until all six layers of the mature brain are in place, which occurs about seven months after conception (Rakic, 1995). As you can see in Figure 4-8, the nerve cells move to the top by wrapping themselves around supporting cells, just as a snake might climb a pole.

In the fourth month of prenatal development, axons begin to acquire myelin—the fatty wrap that speeds up neural transmission. This process continues through infancy and into childhood and adolescence (Paus, 2010). Neurons that carry sensory information are the first to acquire myelin; neurons in the cortex are among the last, with cortical myelination continuing through adolescence into the late teens and even early 20s (Whitaker, et al., 2016). The effect of more myelin can be seen in improved coordination and reaction times. The older the infant and, later, the child, the more rapid and coordinated are his or her reactions. (We'll talk more about this phenomenon when we discuss fine-motor skills in Module 5.3.)

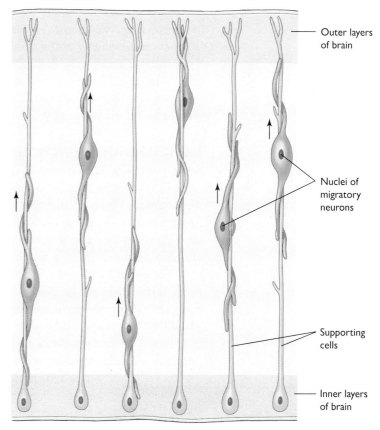

Figure 4-8 Just like a snake might climb a pole, neurons migrate to their final location in the brain by wrapping themselves around supporting cells.

In the months after birth, the brain grows rapidly. Axons and dendrites grow longer, and, like a maturing tree, dendrites quickly sprout new limbs. As the number of dendrites increases, so does the number of synapses, reaching a peak number at about the first birthday. This rapid neural growth is shown in Figure 4-9. **Soon after, synapses begin to disappear gradually in a phenomenon known as** *synaptic pruning.* Thus, beginning

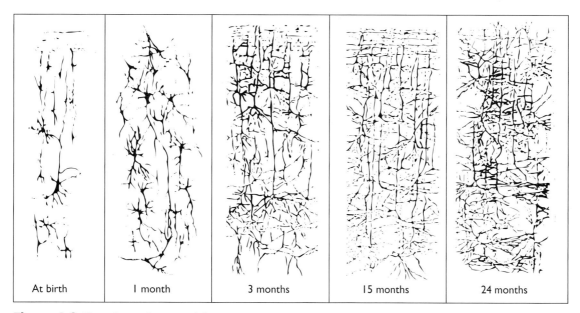

Figure 4-9 Neural growth across infancy.

in infancy and continuing into early adolescence, the brain goes through its own version of "downsizing," weeding out unnecessary connections between neurons. This pruning depends on the activity of the neural circuits: synapses that are active are preserved, but those that aren't active are eliminated (Webb, Monk, & Nelson, 2001). Pruning is completed first for brain regions associated with sensory and motor functions. Regions associated with basic language and spatial skills are completed next, followed by regions associated with attention and planning (Casey, Tottenham, Liston, & Durston, 2005).

STRUCTURE AND FUNCTION.   Because the mature brain is specialized, with different psychological functions localized in particular regions, developmental researchers have had a keen interest in determining the origins and time course of the brain's specialization. For many years, the only clues to specialization came from children who had suffered brain injury. The logic here was to link the location of the injury to the impairment that results: If a region of the brain regulates a particular function (e.g., understanding speech), then damage to that region should impair the function.

Fortunately, relatively few children suffer brain injury. But this meant that scientists needed other methods to study brain development. **One of them,** *electroencephalography (EEG),* **involves measuring the brain's electrical activity from electrodes placed on the scalp,** as shown in the photo. If a region of the brain regulates a function, then the region should show distinctive patterns of electrical activity while a child is using that function. **A newer technique,** *functional magnetic resonance imaging (fMRI),*

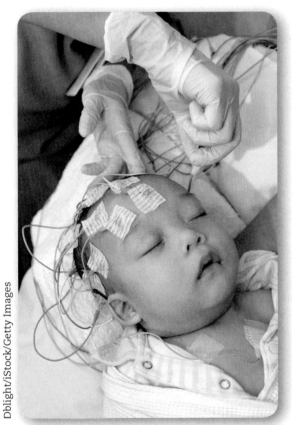

One way to study brain functioning is to record the brain's electrical activity using electrodes placed on a child's scalp.

Dblight/iStock/Getty Images

uses magnetic fields to track the flow of blood in the brain. With this method, shown in the photo on page 147, the research participant's brain is surrounded by an incredibly powerful magnet that can track blood flow in the brain as participants perform different cognitive tasks (Casey et al., 2005). The logic here is that active brain regions need more oxygen, which increases blood flow to those regions.

None of these methods is perfect; each has drawbacks. For example, fMRI is used sparingly because it's expensive, and participants must lie still for several minutes at a time. Despite these limitations, the combined outcome of research using these different approaches has identified some general principles that describe the brain's specialization as children develop.

1. Specialization occurs early in development. You may remember from an introductory psychology course that certain areas of the brain are specialized for certain functions; many of these regions are already specialized very early in infancy. For example, early specialization of the frontal cortex is shown by the finding that damage to this region in infancy results in impaired decision making and abnormal emotional responses (Anderson, Damasio, Tranel, & Damasio, 2001). Similarly, EEG studies show that a newborn infant's left hemisphere generates more electrical activity in response to speech than does the right hemisphere (Molfese & Burger-Judisch, 1991). Thus, by the time a child is born, the cortex of the left hemisphere is already specialized for language processing. As we'll see in Chapter 9, this specialization allows language to develop rapidly during infancy. Finally, studies of children with prenatal brain damage indicate that, by infancy, the right hemisphere is specialized for understanding certain kinds of spatial relations (Stiles, Reilly, Paul, & Moses, 2005).

Of course, this early specialization does not mean that the brain is functionally mature. During the remainder of childhood and into adulthood, these and other regions of the brain continue to become more specialized. Mapping of the brain using multiple MRI scans is leading to an understanding of how brain structures develop and change with age (e.g., Brown et al., 2012).

2. Specialization takes two specific forms. First, with development, the brain regions that are active during cognitive processing become more focused and less diffuse—an analogy would be to a thunderstorm that covers a huge region versus one that concentrates the same power in a much smaller region (Durston et al., 2006). Second, the kinds of stimuli that trigger brain activity shift from being general to being specific (Johnson, Grossman, & Cohen Kadosh, 2009). Processing of face-like stimuli by the brain shows both trends: It becomes focused in a particular area (the fusiform gyrus) and becomes tuned narrowly to faces (Cohen Kadosh, K., Johnson, Dick, Cohen Kadosh, R., & Blakemore, 2013; Scherf, Behrmann, Humphreys, & Luna, 2007). These forms of specialization are evident in the Focus on Research feature.

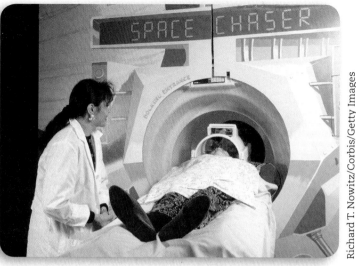

Richard T. Nowitz/Corbis/Getty Images

In fMRI, a powerful magnet tracks the flow of blood to different brain regions and shows parts of the brain that are active as the subject performs different tasks.

Focus On Research

Brain Specialization for Processing of Emotional Expressions

Who were the investigators, and what was the aim of the study? In the mature brain, a part of the limbic system called the amygdala is known to be important in the processing of emotional and motivational stimuli and seems to be important for social-emotion processing. The amygdala is involved in both recognition and processing of such stimuli, including recognition of emotions in other people's facial expressions. For example, imaging studies show that this region is particularly active when individuals detect the presence of a face and must distinguish the emotion being expressed. Rebecca Todd and her colleagues at the University of Toronto—Jennifer Evans, Drew Morris, Marc Lewis and Margot Taylor (2011)—wanted to know whether this brain region was equally involved in processing of facial expression by children and young adults. The researchers were also looking at effect of salience—importance to the person—of faces, using photos of familiar (participant's mothers) and unfamiliar faces (other women), but for simplicity, we'll just look at the emotion (happy/angry) face aspect of the study here.

How did the investigators measure the topic of interest? Todd and her colleagues (Todd et al., 2011) showed participants photographs of emotionally expressive faces while lying in an fMRI scanner like the one shown on this page.

Who were the participants in the study? The researchers tested 3.5- to 8.5-year-olds, and 18- to 33-year-olds. The "child" group was subsequently sub-divided into younger children (three-and-a-half to six years) and older children (six-and-a-half to nine years old)

What was the design of the study? This study was experimental because Todd and her colleagues (Todd et al., 2011) were interested in the impact of the type of stimulus—happy

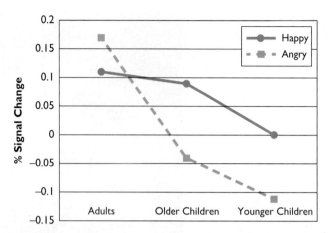

Figure 4-10 Age Group by Expression interaction: Both older (about 7 years) and younger children (about 5 years) showed significantly greater activation for happy than angry faces.

Republished with permission of Oxford University Press, from The Changing Face of Emotion: Age-related Patterns of Amygdala Activation to Salient Faces, R.M.Todd, J.W. Evans, D. Morris, M.D. Lewis, & M.J. Taylor, Vol 6 (1), 2011; permission conveyed through Copyright Clearance Center, Inc.

versus angry faces—on brain activity. The study was cross-sectional because it included three groups (younger children older children and adults), each tested once.

Were there ethical concerns with the study? No. The behavioural task was harmless—simply looking at photographs. Generally fMRI is very safe. However, researchers routinely check to see whether prospective participants might have metal in their bodies (e.g., a pacemaker, or hearing aid, or an object from an accident such as a bullet), which is a hazard because of the powerful magnets that are built into scanners. The researchers described these potential risks to participants (and, for children to their parents), then obtained written consent.

What were the results? Figure 4-10 shows the magnitude of activation in the amygdala for all three age groups, for happy and for angry faces. Notice that children show substantially greater recognition for happy than for angry faces (Figure 4-11); this effect was reversed for adults.

What did the investigators conclude? Activation of the amygdala in response to facial expression of emotion develops over childhood, and while in childhood there is a preferential recognition of happy faces, this reverses by adulthood. Thus, as Todd and her colleagues note, "Preferential amygdala processing of specific emotions changes over the lifespan" (2011, p. 21).

What converging evidence would strengthen these conclusions? An obvious way to provide converging evidence would be to use electroencephalography (described on page 146) to record electrical activity in the brain as children, adolescents, and adults looked at photos of faces. The Todd et al. (2011) findings would be supported if a differentiated pattern of electrical activity—greater activity in response to happy faces in children, but to angry faces in adults—was found.

Thus, the study by Todd et al. (2011) shows specificity of emotional processing: Face processing shows initial preference for happy faces (shown by the increased activity in response to happy faces in children) but later becomes tuned to more negative facial expressions (shown by more activity in response to angry faces in adults).

Critical Thinking Questions: What are some limitations of this research? And how might these limitations be resolved?

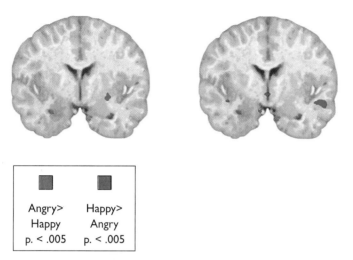

Figure 4-11 Contrast between angry and happy faces in the group of 14 adults revealing greater activation for angry than happy faces at a threshold.

Republished with permission of Oxford University Press, from The Changing Face of Emotion: Age-related Patterns of Amygdala Activation to Salient Faces in *Soc Cogn Affect Neurosci,* Rebecca M. Todd, corresponding author Jennifer W. Evans, Drew Morris, Marc D. Lewis, and Margot J. Taylor, Vol. 6 © 2010; permission conveyed through Copyright Clearance Center, Inc.

3. Different brain systems specialize at different rates. Think of a new housing development involving construction of many multistory homes. In each house, the first floor is completed before higher floors, but some houses are finished before others are even started. In this same way, brain regions involving basic sensory and perceptual processes specialize well before those regions necessary for higher-order processes (Fox, Levitt, & Nelson, 2010). Similarly, some brain systems that are sensitive to reward reach maturity in adolescence, but the systems responsible for self-control aren't fully specialized until adulthood (Casey & Caudle, 2013; Galván, 2013).[4]

4. Successful specialization requires stimulation from the environment. To return to the analogy of the brain as a house, the newborn's brain is perhaps best conceived as a partially finished, partially furnished house: A general organizational framework is present, with preliminary neural pathways designed to perform certain functions. The left hemisphere has some language pathways, and the frontal cortex has some emotion-related pathways. However, completing the typical organization of the mature brain requires input from the environment (Greenough & Black, 1992). **In this case, environmental input influences** *experience-expectant growth:* **Over the course of evolution, human infants have typically been exposed to some forms of stimulation that are used to**

The region of the brain that controls the fingers of the left hand is probably well developed in this skilled cellist.

Vadim Ponomarenko/Shutterstock

[4]This may be one reason why adolescents engage in such risky behaviour (e.g., drinking while driving, having unprotected sex): The brain centres associated with self-control are immature relative to those associated with reward (Somerville & Casey, 2010).

adjust brain wiring, strengthening some circuits and eliminating others. For example, under normal conditions, healthy human infants experience moving visual patterns (e.g., faces) and varied sounds (e.g., voices). Just as a newly planted seed depends on a water-filled environment for growth, a developing brain depends on environmental stimulation to fine-tune circuits for vision, hearing, and other systems (Black, 2003).

Of course, experiences later in life also sculpt the brain (and we'll see this in several later chapters). *Experience-dependent growth* **denotes changes in the brain that are not linked to specific points in development and that vary across individuals and across cultures.** Experience-dependent growth is illustrated by a preschool child's learning of a classmate's name, an elementary-school child's discovery of a shortcut home from school, and an adolescent's mastery of the functions of a new cell phone. In each case, brain circuits are modified in response to an individual's experiences. With today's technology, we can't see these daily changes in the brain. But when they accumulate over many years—as when individuals acquire expertise in a skill—brain changes can be detected. For example, skilled cellists like the one in the photo have extensive brain regions devoted to controlling the fingers of the left hand as they are positioned on the strings (Elbert et al., 1995). Similarly, years of driving a taxicab produces changes in the hippocampus, a region of the brain implicated in navigation and way-finding (Maguire, Woollett, & Spiers, 2006).

5. The immature brain's lack of specialization confers a benefit: greater plasticity. Just as the structures in a housing development follow a plan that specifies the location of each house and its design, brain development usually follows a predictable course that reflects epigenetic interactions (page 66) between the genetic code and required environmental input. Sometimes, however, the normal course is disrupted. A person may experience events harmful to the brain (e.g., injured in an accident) or may be deprived of some essential ingredients of successful "brain building" (e.g., necessary experiences).

Research that examines the consequences of these atypical experiences shows that the brain has some plasticity. Remember Martin, the child in the vignette whose brain was damaged when he was struck by a car? His language skills were impaired after the accident. This was not surprising, because the left hemisphere of Martin's brain had absorbed most of the force of the collision. But within several months, Martin had completely recovered his language skills. Apparently, other neurons took over language-related processing from the damaged neurons. This recovery of function is not uncommon—particularly for young children—and shows that the brain is plastic. In other words, young children often recover more skills after brain injury than older children and adults, apparently because functions are more easily reassigned in the young brain (Kolb & Teskey, 2012; Demir, Levine, & Goldin-Meadow, 2010).

There are, however, limits to plasticity. These are shown by studies of Romanian children who were abandoned soon after birth and lived for months—sometimes years—in orphanages where care was appalling: Infants and toddlers were provided food and shelter but few toys, minimal speech with caregivers, and no personal relationships with caregivers. Following adoption by families in the United Kingdom, these children progressed rapidly in their cognitive development but did not catch up to the normal course of development; what's more, cognitive deficits were greater for children who had stayed longer in the orphanages (Rutter et al., 2010). Experiences later in these children's development could not compensate for the extreme deprivation in infancy, showing that the brain is not completely plastic. Now that we understand that these issues exist, we must be

Q&A **QUESTION 4.3**
Ashley was distraught when her two-year-old daughter fell down a full flight of steps and hit her head against a concrete wall, leading to a trip to the emergency room. What could you say to reassure Ashley about her daughter's prognosis? *(Answer is on page 151.)*

even more vigilant about providing sufficient, appropriate experiences to young children. Subsequent research in Romania has shown that providing early enrichment for disadvantaged children is crucial in aiding optimal brain development (Bick, Zhu, Stamoulis, Fox, Zanah, & Nelson, 2015; Sheridan, Fox, Zeanah, McLaughlin, & Nelson, 2012). Assistance in the early years, before age five, is essential to overcome potential negative effects of an impoverished environment and to improve overall cognitive, social, and emotional development (Almas et al., 2012; Boyce, Sokolowski, & Robinson, 2012).

BRAIN-BASED EDUCATION?   Greater understanding of brain development and the impact of experience has led many scientists, educators, and parents to hope that this knowledge could lead to improved education. After all, if the brain is the organ of learning and the goal of school is to promote students' learning, then knowledge of brain development should yield better ways to teach. Many have jumped on the "brain-based education" bandwagon, and it is true that research on brain development is providing valuable insights into some very specific academic skills, such as the nature of children's reading problems (Szücks & Goswami, 2007). However, there is reason to be cautious about redesigning an entire curriculum based on our current understanding of brain development. Many critics point out that although our current understanding of such development may lead to a handful of very general statements about the conditions that foster children's learning, we still know too little to devise full-fledged curricula that are "brain-friendly" (Sylvan & Christodoulou, 2010). As Kurt Fischer, director of Harvard's Mind, Brain, and Education Program, and his colleague Mary Helen Immordino-Yang (2008, p. xviii) put it,

> Unfortunately, most of what is called "brain-based education" has no grounding at all in brain or cognitive science. . . . In typical claims for brain-based education, beliefs about learning and schooling are restated in the language of brain science, but there is no brain research on which those restatements are based.

Still, there is reason to be optimistic that coming decades will provide the foundation needed for a curriculum based on a solid understanding of the emerging brain (Fischer & Immordino-Yang, 2008).

 ANSWER 4.3
You could explain that young children often recover from brain injury more easily than older children and adults do. So, unless her daughter has suffered extensive damage to the brain, she should be all right.

 # Check Your Learning

RECALL List the major parts of a nerve cell and the major regions of the cerebral cortex.

Describe evidence that shows the brain's plasticity.

INTERPRET Compare growth of the brain before birth with growth of the brain after birth.

APPLY How does the development of the brain, as described in this module, compare to the general pattern of physical growth described in Module 4.1?

UNIFYING THEMES Connections

This chapter is an excellent opportunity to highlight the theme that *development in different domains is connected.* Consider the impact of the timing of puberty. Whether a child matures early or late affects social development (early-maturing girls are often less popular. Or consider the impact of malnutrition. Malnourished youngsters are often listless, which affects how their parents interact with them (the parents are less likely to provide stimulating experiences). Less stimulation, in turn, slows the children's intellectual development. Physical, cognitive, social, and personality development are linked: Change in one area generally leads to change of some kind in the others.

See for Yourself

Children love playgrounds. Unfortunately, hundreds of thousands of North American children are injured on playgrounds annually. The Canadian Paediatric Society's Injury Prevention Committee estimates that in Canada 29 000 children require emergency treatment for playground injuries each year (Canadian Paediatric Society, 2012). Some of these accidents could have been prevented had parents (or other adults) been present or paying closer attention to the children at play. Go to a local playground and watch children as they play. Remember to be an ethical observer—you are there simply to watch, not be intrusive or to interfere. Notice how many children unknowingly put themselves at risk as they play. Also notice how well the children's play is monitored by adults. See for yourself!

Resources

For more information about . . .

ways to help children and adolescents stay physically fit, try Kenneth H. Cooper's (1999) *Fit Kids,* published by Broadman & Holman, which describes a program of diet and exercise developed by the originator of the concept of aerobic fitness.

children's nutrition, visit the website of Canada's Food Guide: **www.healthcanada.gc.ca/foodguide**

playground safety, visit the Canadian Paediatric Society's website: **www.cps.ca**

Key Terms

anorexia nervosa   137
axon   144
body dysmorphic disorder   138
body mass index (BMI)   138
bulimia nervosa   137
cell body   143
cephalocaudal   122

cerebral cortex   144
corpus callosum   144
dendrite   143
electroencephalography (EEG)   146
epiphyses   123
experience-dependent growth   150
experience-expectant growth   149

frontal cortex   144
functional magnetic resonance imaging (fMRI)   146
growth hormone   125
hemispheres   144
malnutrition   136
menarche   130

Summary

4.1 Physical Growth

1. Features of Human Growth

Physical growth is particularly rapid during infancy, slows during the elementary-school years, and then accelerates again during adolescence. Physical growth refers not only to height and weight but also to development of muscle, fat, and bones.

Children are taller today than in previous generations. Average heights vary around the world, and within any culture there is considerable variation in the normal range of height.

2. Mechanisms of Physical Growth

Physical growth depends on sleep, in part because most growth hormone is secreted while children sleep. Nutrition is also important, particularly during periods of rapid growth, such as infancy and adolescence. Breastfeeding provides babies with all the nutrients they need and has other advantages. Many children and adolescents do not get adequate nutrients because of poor diets.

3. The Adolescent Growth Spurt and Puberty

Puberty includes the adolescent growth spurt as well as sexual maturation. Girls typically begin the growth spurt earlier than boys, who acquire more muscle, less fat, and greater heart and lung capacities. Sexual maturation, which includes primary and secondary sex characteristics, occurs in predictable sequences for boys and girls.

Pubertal changes occur when the pituitary gland signals the adrenal gland, ovaries, and testes to secrete hormones that initiate physical changes. The timing of puberty is influenced greatly by health, nutrition, and social environment.

Pubertal change affects adolescents' psychological functioning. Teens become concerned about their appearance. Early maturation tends to be harmful for girls because it may cause them to engage in age-inappropriate behaviour. Timing of maturation seems to be less of an issue for boys.

4.2 Challenges to Healthy Growth

1. Malnutrition

Malnutrition is a global problem—including in North America—that is particularly harmful during infancy, when growth is rapid. Malnutrition can cause brain damage, affecting children's intelligence and their ability to pay attention. Treating malnutrition requires improving children's diet and training their parents to provide stimulating environments.

2. Eating Disorders: Anorexia Nervosa and Bulimia Nervosa

Anorexia nervosa and bulimia nervosa are eating disorders that typically affect adolescent girls and are characterized by an irrational fear of being overweight. Several factors contribute to these disorders, including heredity, a childhood history of eating problems and, during adolescence, negative self-esteem and a preoccupation with one's body and weight. These eating disorders are far less common in boys, although body dysmorphic disorder is more likely in boys than girls. Risk factors for eating disorders in boys include childhood obesity, low self-esteem, social pressure to lose weight, and participation in certain sports. Treatment and prevention programs for eating disorders emphasize changing adolescents' views of thinness or body shape and changing their eating-related behaviours.

3. Obesity

Many obese children and adolescents are unpopular, have low self-esteem, and are at risk for medical disorders. Obesity reflects heredity, influences of parents, and a sedentary lifestyle. In effective programs for treating obesity in youth, children are encouraged to change their eating habits and to become more active; their parents help them set realistic goals and monitor their daily progress.

4. Disease
Millions of children around the world die annually from pneumonia, diarrhea, measles, malaria, and malnutrition. Integrated Management of Childhood Illness (IMCI) is a new, integrated approach designed to promote children's health.

5. Accidents
In North America, children and adolescents are more likely to die from accidents than any other single cause. Many of these fatalities involve motor vehicles and could be prevented if passengers were restrained properly. Older children and adolescents are sometimes involved in accidents because parents overestimate their children's abilities.

4.3 The Developing Nervous System

1. Organization of the Mature Brain
Nerve cells, called neurons, are composed of a cell body, a dendrite, and an axon. The mature brain consists of billions of neurons organized into nearly identical left and right hemispheres connected by the corpus callosum. The frontal cortex is associated with personality and goal-directed behaviour, the cortex in the left hemisphere with language, and the cortex in the right hemisphere with nonverbal processes.

2. The Developing Brain
Brain structure begins in prenatal development, when neurons form at an incredible rate. After birth, neurons in the central nervous system become wrapped in myelin, allowing them to transmit information more rapidly. Throughout childhood, unused synapses disappear gradually through a process of pruning.

Brain specialization is evident in infancy; further specialization involves more focused brain areas and narrowing of stimuli that trigger brain activity. Different systems specialize at different rates. Specialization depends upon stimulation from the environment. The relative lack of specialization in the immature brain makes it better able to recover from injury.

Test Yourself

1. Physical growth is particularly rapid during infancy and _____.

2. Sleep is essential for normal growth because this is when most _____ is secreted.

3. Breastfeeding has many advantages for infants, including protecting from disease (through the mother's antibodies), reducing cases of diarrhea and constipation, easing the transition to solid foods, and _____.

4. The role of the environment in triggering puberty is shown by cross-national comparisons, by historical data, and by the impact of _____ on the onset of puberty in girls.

5. Maturing early often has harmful consequences for _____.

6. To break the vicious cycle of malnutrition, children need an improved diet and _____.

7. Adolescents afflicted with _____ alternate between binge eating and purging themselves.

8. One reason why obese children overeat is that they pay more attention to _____ cues to eating.

9. Integrated Management of Childhood Illness attempts to combat childhood diseases by improving skills of healthcare professionals, improving healthcare systems so that they are more responsive to childhood diseases, and _____.

10. _____ are the leading cause of death for North American adolescents.

11. The _____ is the part of the neuron that contains the biological machinery that keeps it alive.

12. During prenatal development and continuing into childhood and adolescence, axons of nerve cells acquire myelin, a fatty wrap that allows neurons to _____.

13. With development, brain systems become more specialized, in that the smaller brain regions become activated and _____ .

14. In _____ growth, a developing brain depends upon environmental stimulation to fine-tune neural circuits.

15. A developing brain is more plastic than a mature brain, which means that following injury a developing brain _____ .

Answers: (1) adolescence; (2) growth hormone; (3) avoiding contamination, which can be a significant problem with bottle-feeding in developing countries; (4) the social environment (in particular, a stressful environment); (5) girls; (6) parental education that teaches parents how to foster their children's development; (7) bulimia nervosa; (8) external; (9) changing family and community practices to prevent illness (e.g., having children sleep under mosquito netting); (10) Motor-vehicle accidents; (11) cell body; (12) transmit information more rapidly; (13) more specific stimuli trigger brain activity; (14) experience-expectant; (15) is more likely to recover.

5 Perceptual and Motor Development

Gorilla/Shutterstock

 5.1

Basic Sensory and Perceptual Processes

 5.2

Complex Perceptual and Attentional Processes

 5.3

Motor Development

When author Robert Kail's daughter was a toddler, her afternoon naps often came at a time when her older brother needed to practise his drums. Her parents closed her bedroom door, but the thumping of the drums was still pretty loud. The first few times this happened, the little girl would startle when the drumming began, then soon fall back to sleep. After a few days, though, she hardly stirred at all when the drumming began. This behaviour illustrates perception in action: Our senses are assaulted with stimulation, but much of it is ignored. *Sensory and perceptual processes* **are the means by which people receive, select, modify, and organize stimulation from the world.** Sensory and perceptual processes are the first step in the complex process that eventually results in "knowing." We'll begin studying perceptual development in **Module 5.1** by looking at the origins of sensory processes in infancy. In **Module 5.2**, we'll see how more complex perceptual and attentional processes develop in childhood.

Perceptual processes are closely linked to *motor skills*—**coordinated movements of the muscles and limbs.** Perception often guides a child's movement, as when vision is used to avoid obstacles. In turn, a child's movement in the environment provides enormous variety in perceptual stimulation. In **Module 5.3**, we'll see how improvements in motor skills enhance children's ability to explore, understand, and enjoy the world.

5.1 Basic Sensory and Perceptual Processes

OUTLINE	LEARNING OBJECTIVES
Smell, Taste, and Touch	**1.** Are newborn babies able to smell and taste? Do they respond to touch and experience pain?
Hearing	**2.** How well do infants hear? How do they use sounds to understand their world?
Seeing	**3.** How accurate is infants' vision? Do infants perceive colour?
Integrating Sensory Information	**4.** How do infants integrate information from different senses?

Darla adores her three-day-old daughter, Olivia. She loves holding her, talking to her, and simply watching her. Darla is certain that Olivia is already getting to know her, coming to recognize her face and the sound of her voice. Darla's husband, Steve, thinks she is crazy. He tells her, "Everyone knows that babies are born blind. And they probably can't hear much either." Darla doubts that Steve is right, but she wishes someone would tell her about babies' vision and hearing.

Darla's questions are really about her newborn daughter's sensory and perceptual skills. To help Darla understand, we need to remember that humans have different kinds of sense organs, each receptive to a unique kind of physical energy. The retina at the back of the eye, for example, is sensitive to some types of electromagnetic energy, and sight is the result. The eardrum detects changes in air pressure, and hearing is the result. Cells at the top of the nasal passage detect airborne molecules, and smell is the result. In each case, the sense organ translates the physical stimulation into nerve impulses that are sent to the brain.

The senses begin to function early in life, which is why this module is devoted entirely to infancy, but how can we know what an infant senses? Because infants cannot

Raise a cyber child and discover the world of parenthood at …

My **Virtual** Child …

tell us what they smell, hear, or see, researchers have had to devise other ways to find out. For instance, an investigator presents two stimuli to a baby, such as a high-pitched tone and a low-pitched tone, or a sweet-tasting substance and a sour-tasting substance. Then the investigator records the baby's responses, such as heart rate, facial expression, or eye movements. If the baby consistently responds differently to the two stimuli (e.g., she looks in the direction of one tone, but not the other), the baby must be distinguishing between them.

Another approach is based on the fact that infants usually prefer novel stimuli to familiar stimuli. **When a novel stimulus is presented, babies pay much attention, but they pay less attention as it becomes more familiar, a phenomenon known as** *habituation.* Researchers use habituation to study perception by repeatedly presenting a stimulus such as a low-pitched tone until an infant barely responds. Then they present a second stimulus, such as a higher-pitched tone. If the infant responds strongly, then researchers conclude that the baby can distinguish the two stimuli.

In this module, you'll learn what these techniques have revealed about infants' sensory and perceptual processes. These processes are interesting in their own right; you'll see that an infant's senses are astonishingly powerful. They are also important to study because in order for us to understand a child's complicated thoughts and feelings, we first need to know how infants take in information from the world around them.

Smell, Taste, and Touch

Newborns have a keen sense of smell; they respond positively to pleasant smells and negatively to unpleasant smells (Mennella & Beauchamp, 1997). They have a relaxed, contented-looking facial expression when they smell honey or chocolate, but they frown, grimace, or turn away when they smell rotten eggs or ammonia. Young babies can also recognize familiar odours. Newborns will look in the direction of a pad that is saturated with their own amniotic fluid. They will also turn toward a pad saturated with the odour of their mother's breast milk or her perfume (Porter & Winburg, 1999; Schaal, Soussignan, & Marlier, 2002).

Newborns also have a highly developed sense of taste. They readily differentiate salty, sour, bitter, and sweet tastes (Schwartz, Issanchou, & Nicklaus, 2009). Most infants prefer sweet and salty substances—they react to these by smiling, sucking, and licking their lips (Beauchamp & Mennella, 2011). In contrast, you can probably guess what the toddler in the photo has tasted! This grimace is a typical response when infants are fed bitter or sour substances (Kaijura, Cowart, & Beauchamp, 1992). Infants are also sensitive to changes in the taste of breast milk, which reflects a mother's diet. Infants will nurse more after their mother has consumed a sweet-tasting substance such as vanilla (Mennella & Beauchamp, 1996).

Newborns are also sensitive to touch. As we described in Module 3.4, many areas of the newborn's body respond reflexively when touched. Touching an infant's cheek, mouth, hand, or foot produces reflexive movements, documenting that infants perceive touch. What's more, babies' behaviour in response to apparent pain-provoking stimuli suggests that they experience pain (Warnock & Sandrin, 2004). For example, look at the baby in the photo on the next page, who is receiving an inoculation. He has opened his mouth to cry and, although we cannot hear him, the sound of his cry is probably the unique pattern associated with pain. The pain cry begins suddenly, is high-pitched, and is not easily soothed.

Infants and toddlers do not like bitter or sour tastes!

This baby is also agitated; his heart rate has jumped, and he is moving his hands, arms, and legs. All together, these signs strongly suggest that babies experience pain (Craig, Whitfield, Grunau, Linton, & Hadjistarropoulos, 1993; Goubet, Clifton, & Shah, 2001). There is some suggestion that quite simple measures can reduce pain sensation in babies, however. Siobhan Gormally and colleagues at McGill University, Montreal, investigated the effects of contact and sweet tastes on the pain responses of newborns. When newborns are given a "heel-stick procedure" in which a pinprick-type puncture is made in the heel to obtain a few drops of blood for testing, they often cry and show distress at this presumably painful stimulus. Gormally et al. (2001) investigated the effects of holding a baby and of giving a taste of sucrose at the moment of receiving the heel-stick procedure. Two- to three-day-old infants were tested, and both the holding and the sucrose taste were found to have a soothing effect, with a combination of both being the most effective. The researchers proposed that such simple caregiving behaviours could be a useful method for reducing pain experienced by young infants (Gormally et al., 2001).

Perceptual skills are extraordinarily useful to newborns and young babies. Smell and touch help them recognize their mothers and make it much easier for them to learn to eat. Early development of smell, taste, and touch prepare newborns and young babies to learn about the world.

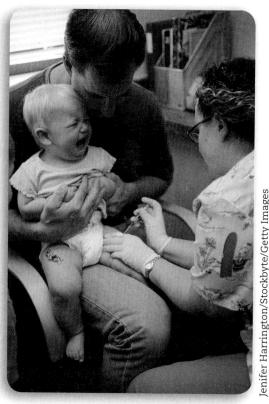

An infant's response to an inoculation—a distinctive facial expression coupled with a distinctive cry—clearly suggests that the baby feels pain.

Hearing

We know from Module 3.1 that a fetus can hear at seven or eight months. As you would expect from these results, newborns typically respond to sounds in their surroundings. If a parent is quiet but then coughs, an infant may startle, blink his eyes, and move his arms or legs. These responses may seem natural, but they do indeed indicate that infants are sensitive to sound.

Not surprisingly, infants do not hear as well as adults. *Auditory threshold* **refers to the quietest sound that a person can hear.** An adult's auditory threshold is fairly easy to measure: A tone is presented, and the adult simply tells when he or she hears it. Because infants can't tell us what they hear, researchers have devised a number of clever techniques to measure infants' auditory thresholds (Saffran, Werker, & Werner, 2006). For example, in one method, the infant is seated on a parent's lap. Both parent and baby wear headphones, as does an observer seated in another room, watching the baby through an observation window. An experimenter periodically presents tones over the baby's headphones; neither the observer nor the parent knows when tones are to be presented (and they can't hear the tones through their headphones). On each trial, the observer simply judges whether the baby responds in any fashion, such as by turning her head or altering her facial expression or activity level. Afterward, the experimenter determines how well the observer's judgments match the trials: If a baby can hear the tone, the observer should have noted a response only when a tone was presented.

This type of testing reveals that, overall, adults can hear better than infants; adults can hear some quiet sounds that infants can't (Saffran et al., 2006). More important, this testing shows that infants hear sounds best that have pitches in the range of human speech—neither very high- nor very low-pitched. Infants can differentiate vowels from consonant sounds, and by four and a half months, they can recognize their own names (Jusczyk, 1995; Mandel, Jusczyk, & Pisoni, 1995). In Module 9.1, we'll learn more about infants' remarkable skill at hearing language sounds.

Jenifer Harrington/Stockbyte/Getty Images

QUESTION 5.1
Tiffany is worried
that her 12-month-
old daughter may be
hearing impaired.
What symptoms would
suggest that she has
cause for concern? If
these symptoms are
present, what should
she do? *(Answer is on
page 164.)*

Infants also distinguish different musical sounds. They can distinguish different melodies, and they prefer melodies that sound pleasant over those that sound unpleasant or dissonant (Trainor & Heinmiller, 1998). And infants are sensitive to the rhythmic structure of music. After infants have heard a simple sequence of notes, they can tell the difference between a new sequence that fits the original versus one that does not (Hannon & Trehub, 2005). This early sensitivity to music is remarkable but perhaps not so surprising when you consider the importance of music to human culture.

Thus, by the middle of the first year, most infants respond to much of the information provided by sound. However, not all infants are able to do so, which is the topic of the Children's Lives feature.

Children's Lives

Hearing Impairment in Infancy

Some infants are born with limited hearing; others are born deaf (exact figures are hard to determine; but one figure given is that about 4 in 1000 babies per year are born deaf or hard of hearing (Ontario Ministry of Children and Youth Services, 2016), and all babies are equally susceptible. Heredity is the leading cause of hearing impairment in newborns. After birth, the leading cause is meningitis, an inflammation of the membranes surrounding the brain and spinal cord.

What are signs of hearing impairment that a parent should watch for? Obviously, parents should be concerned if a young baby never responds to sudden, loud sounds. They should also be concerned if their baby has repeated ear infections. Provincial governments give advice for parents. For example, the Ontario Ministry of Children and Youth Services has a checklist for parents to monitor responses to sound. According to the Ministry, parents should be concerned if their baby is not startled by sudden, loud sounds by six months of age, does not respond to his or her own name by nine months, and does not begin to imitate speech sounds and use simple words by 12 months (Ontario Ministry of Children and Youth Services, 2016).

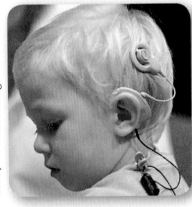

Children with hearing impairment may benefit from a cochlear implant, a device that converts speech signals into electrical impulses that can stimulate nerve cells.

Gene J. Puskar/AP Images

If parents notice these problems, their baby should be examined by a physician, who will check for ear problems, and an audiologist, who will measure the infant's hearing. Parents should never delay checking for possible hearing impairment. The earlier the problem is detected, the more likely the baby can be helped (Smith, Quittner, Osberger, & Miyamoto, 1998).

If testing reveals that a baby has impaired hearing, several treatments are possible, depending on the degree of hearing loss. Some children with partial hearing benefit from mechanical devices. Hearing aids help some children, but others—like the child in the photo—benefit from a cochlear implant, an electronic device placed in the ear that converts speech into electric signals that stimulate nerve cells in the inner ear. Training in lip-reading helps others.

Children with hearing loss can also learn to communicate with sign language. Over time, policies about hearing loss have changed. At one time, learning speech, even for the deaf, was attempted. It is now known that it is mastering language (either oral language or sign language) that is important and that by communicating effectively a child's cognitive and social development will be normal. The key is to recognize impairment promptly.

Critical Thinking Question: How might audiologists or speech-language pathologists work with psychologists in cases of infant hearing impairment?

Seeing

Babies spend much of their waking time looking around, sometimes scanning their environment broadly and sometimes seemingly focusing on nearby objects. But what do infants actually see? Is their visual world a sea of grey blobs? Or do they see the world essentially as adults do? Actually, neither is the case, but, as you'll see, the second is closer to the truth.

From birth, babies respond to light and can track moving objects with their eyes. But what is the clarity of their vision, and how can we measure it? *Visual acuity* **is defined as the smallest pattern that can be distinguished dependably.** No doubt you've had your visual acuity measured by trying to read rows of progressively smaller letters or numbers from a chart. The same basic logic is used in tests of infants' visual acuity, which are based on two premises. First, most infants will look at patterned stimuli instead of plain, nonpatterned stimuli. For example, if we were to show the two stimuli in Figure 5-1 to infants, most would look longer at the striped pattern than at the grey pattern. Second, as we make the lines narrower (along with the spaces between them), there comes a point at which the black and white stripes become so fine that they simply blend together and appear grey, just like the all-grey pattern.

Figure 5-1 Visual acuity test of grey compared to wide stripes.

To estimate an infant's visual acuity, then, we pair the grey square with squares that have different widths of stripes, like those in Figure 5-2: When infants look at the two stimuli equally, it indicates that they are no longer able to distinguish the stripes of the patterned stimulus. By measuring the width of the stripes and their distance from an infant's eye, we can estimate acuity (detecting thinner stripes indicates better acuity). Measurements of this sort indicate that newborns and one-month-olds see at six metres what normal adults see at 60 to 120 metres. Infants' acuity improves rapidly and, by the first birthday, is essentially the same as that of a normal adult (Kellman & Arterberry, 2006).

Figure 5-2 Visual acuity test of grey compared to narrower stripes.

Infants begin to see the world not only with greater acuity during the first year but also in colour. How do we perceive colour? The wavelength of light is the source of colour perception. Figure 5-3 shows that lights we see as red have a relatively long wavelength, whereas violet, at the other end of the colour spectrum, has a much shorter wavelength. **We detect wavelength—and therefore colour—with specialized neurons called** *cones* **that are in the retina of the eye.** Some cones are particularly sensitive to short-wavelength light (blues and violets); others are sensitive to medium-wavelength light (greens and yellows); and still others are sensitive to long-wavelength light (reds and oranges). These different kinds of cones are linked in complex circuits of neurons in the eye and in the brain, and this neural circuitry allows us to see the world in colour.

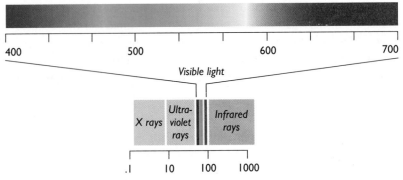

400   500   600   700

Visible light

| X rays | Ultra-violet rays | Infrared rays |

.1   10   100   1000

Wavelength of Light in Nanometres (billionths of a metre)

Figure 5-3 Light wavelengths: the visible spectrum and its position within the electromagnetic spectrum.

These circuits gradually begin to function in the first few months after birth. Newborns and young babies can perceive few colours, but by three months the three kinds of cones and their associated circuits are working and infants are able to see the full range of colours (Kellman & Arterberry, 2006). In fact, by three to four months, infants' colour perception seems similar to that of adults (Adams & Courage, 1995; Franklin, Pilling, & Davies, 2005). In particular, infants, like adults, tend to see categories of colour. For example, if a yellow light's wavelength is gradually increased, the infant will suddenly perceive it as a shade of red rather than a shade of yellow (Dannemiller, 1998). And by three months, infants prefer red and blue over other colours (Zemach, Chang, & Teller, 2007).

The ability to perceive colour, along with rapidly improving visual acuity, gives infants great skill in making sense of their visual experiences. As we'll see in the next section, what makes this growing visual skill even more powerful is that around the same time infants also start to connect information obtained from different senses.

Integrating Sensory Information

So far, we have discussed infants' sensory systems separately, but most infant experiences are better described as "multimedia events." A nursing mother like the one in the photo provides visual and taste cues to her baby. A rattle stimulates vision, hearing, and touch. In fact, much stimulation is not specific to one sense but spans multiple senses. Temporal information, such as duration or tempo, can be conveyed by sight or sound. For example, you can detect the rhythm of a person clapping by seeing the hands meet or by hearing the sound of hands striking. Similarly, the texture of a surface—whether it's rough or smooth, for example—can be detected by sight or by feel.

Infants readily perceive many of these relations. For example, infants can visually recognize an object that they have only touched previously (Sann & Streri, 2007). Similarly, babies can detect relations between information presented visually and auditorily; they look longer when an object's motion apparently matches its sound (it makes higher-pitched sounds as it rises and lower-pitched sounds as it falls) than when it doesn't (Walker et al., 2010). They also can link the temporal properties of visual and auditory stimulation, such

A mother who breastfeeds provides her baby with a multimedia event: the baby sees, smells, hears, feels, and tastes her!

as duration and rhythm (Lewkowicz, 2000a). Finally, they even link their own body movement to their perceptions of musical rhythm, "feeling the beat" (Gerry, Faux, & Trainor, 2010).

Traditionally, coordinating information from different senses (e.g., vision with hearing, vision with touch) was thought to be demanding for infants. However, recent thinking challenges this view. One idea is that cross-modal perception is actually easier for infants, because in infancy regions in the brain devoted to sensory processing are not yet specialized. For example, some regions in an adult's brain respond only to visual stimuli; those same regions in an infant's brain respond to visual *and* auditory input (Spector & Maurer, 2009; Wagner & Dobkins, 2011).

Another explanation of infants' ability to integrate information from different senses is described in the Spotlight on Theories feature.

Spotlight on Theories

The Theory of Intersensory Redundancy

BACKGROUND Traditionally, coordinating information from different senses (e.g., vision with hearing, vision with touch) was said to be challenging for infants and, consequently, one that should emerge later, only after infants first master perceptual processes in each sense separately. In this view, a baby might perceive a favourite teddy bear's appearance, feel, and smell but would only gradually integrate these perceptions.

THE THEORY However, Lorraine Bahrick and Robert Lickliter (2002, 2012) have proposed a different view. **They note that certain information, such as duration, rate, and intensity is *amodal,* in that it can be presented in different senses.** For example, when a mother claps her hands in time to music, the sounds of the claps, as well as the appearance of the hands coming together and moving apart, provide clues to the tempo of the music.

In Bahrick and Lickliter's *intersensory redundancy theory,* **the infant's perceptual system is particularly attuned to amodal information that is presented to multiple sensory modes.** That is, perception is best—particularly for young infants—when information is presented redundantly to multiple senses. When an infant sees and hears the mother clapping (visual, auditory information), she focuses on the information conveyed to both senses and pays less attention to information that is available in only one sense, such as the colour of the mother's nail polish or the sounds of her humming along with the tune. Or the infant can learn that the mother's lips are chapped from seeing the flaking skin and by feeling the roughness as the mother kisses her. According to intersensory redundancy theory, it's as if infants follow the rule "Any information that's presented to multiple senses must be important, so pay attention to it!"

Hypothesis: If infants are particularly attentive to information presented redundantly to multiple senses, then they should notice changes in amodal information *at a younger age* when the information is presented to multiple senses than when the information is presented to a single sense. In other words, if the mother claps slowly and then quickly, infants should detect this change at a younger age when they see and hear the clapping than when they only see her or only hear her.

Test: Flom and Bahrick (2007) studied infants' ability to detect differences in an adult's emotional expression—whether she was happy, angry, or sad. In the multimodal condition, infants watched a video of a woman who appeared to be talking directly to them. Her facial expression and tone of voice conveyed one of the three emotions. After several trials, infants saw a new video depicting the same woman expressing a different emotion. At four months of age infants looked longer at the new video, showing that they detected the change in the woman's emotional expression. However, when the experiment was repeated but with the soundtrack turned off—so that emotional information was conveyed by vision alone—infants did not detect the difference in emotional expression until they were seven months old.

Conclusion: This result supports the hypothesis. Infants detected a change in emotional expression at a younger age (four months) when it was presented in multiple sensory modes than when it was presented in a single mode (seven months).

Application: The theory of intersensory redundancy says that infants learn best when information is presented simultaneously to multiple senses. Parents can use this principle to help babies learn. Language learning is a good example. Of course, talking to babies is beneficial (a topic we explore in depth in Chapter 9). But talking face to face with babies is best because then they see the visual cues that distinguish language sounds. When Mom says, "Oooh" her lips form a tight circle; when she says, "Ahhhh" her mouth is open wide. By talking face to face, Mom is presenting information about sounds redundantly—auditorily and visually—making it easier for her infant to distinguish these sounds (Burnham & Dodd, 2004).

Critical Thinking Question: Why might "intersensory redundancy" have arisen? What is the advantage for the infant?

 ANSWER 5.1
By 12 months of age, Tiffany's daughter should be looking in the direction of sounds (and should have been doing so for several months), should respond to her name, and should make some speech-like sounds of her own. If she doesn't do these things, Tiffany should take her daughter to see a pediatrician and to an audiologist right away.

Integrating information from different senses underscores the theme that has dominated this module: Infants' sensory and perceptual skills are impressive. Olivia, Darla's newborn daughter from the opening vignette, can definitely smell, taste, and feel pain. She can distinguish sounds; her vision is a little blurry but will improve rapidly, and soon she will see the full range of colours; and she makes connections between sights and sounds and between her other senses. Of course, over the coming year, Olivia's perceptual skills will become more finely tuned. She will become particularly adept at identifying stimuli that are common in her environment (Scott, Pascalis, & Nelson, 2007). But for now, Olivia, like most infants, is well prepared to make sense of her environment.

✓ Check Your Learning

RECALL Summarize what's known about infants' ability to smell, taste, and touch.

Describe the important developmental milestones in vision during infancy.

INTERPRET Compare the impact of nature and nurture on the development of infants' sensory and perceptual skills.

APPLY Perceptual skills are quite refined at birth and mature very rapidly. What evolutionary purposes are served by this rapid development?

5.2 Complex Perceptual and Attentional Processes

OUTLINE

Perceiving Objects

Attention

Attention Deficit Hyperactivity Disorder

LEARNING OBJECTIVES

1. How do infants perceive objects?

2. What are the components of attention? How do they develop?

3. What is attention deficit hyperactivity disorder? How does it affect children's development?

Soon after Stephen entered Grade 1, his teacher remarked that he sometimes seemed out of control. He was easily distracted, often moving aimlessly from one activity to another. He also seemed to be impulsive and had difficulty waiting his turn. This behaviour continued in Grade 2, and he began to fall behind in reading and arithmetic. His classmates were annoyed by his behaviour and began to avoid him. His parents wonder whether Stephen just has lots of energy or whether he has a problem.

Where we draw the dividing line between "basic" and "complex" perceptual processes is quite arbitrary. As you'll see, Module 5.2 is a logical extension of the information presented in Module 5.1. We'll begin by looking at how we perceive objects. We'll also look at the processes of attention and some children who have attentional problems. By the end of the module, you'll understand why Stephen behaves as he does.

Perceiving Objects

When you look at the pattern in the photo what do you see? You probably recognize it as part of a human eyeball, even though all that is physically present in the photograph are many different coloured dots. In this case, perception actually creates an object from sensory stimulation. That is, our perceptual processes determine that certain features go together to form objects. This is particularly challenging because we often see only parts of objects—nearby objects often obscure parts of more distant objects. Nevertheless, in the photo on page 166, we recognize that the orange is a distinct object even though it is partially hidden by the apple.

A newborn's perception of objects is limited, but develops rapidly in the first few months after birth (Johnson, 2001). By four months, infants use a number of cues to determine which elements go together to form objects. One important cue is motion: Elements that move together are usually part of the same object (Kellman & Banks, 1998). For example, in Figure 5-4, a pencil appears to be moving back and forth behind a coloured square. If the square were removed, you would be surprised to see a pair of pencil stubs, as shown on the right side of the diagram. The common movement of the pencil eraser and pencil point lead us to believe that they are part of the same pencil.

Young infants, too, are surprised by demonstrations like this. If they see a display like the moving pencils, they will then look very briefly at a whole pencil, apparently because they expected it. In contrast, if after seeing the moving pencil they are shown the two pencil stubs, they look much longer, as if trying to figure out

Perceptual processes allow us to interpret this pattern of lines, textures, and colours as an eyeball.

Robnroll/Shutterstock

QUESTION 5.2
When six-month-old
Sebastian watches
his mother type on
a keyboard, how
does he know that
her fingers and the
keyboard are not sim-
ply one big unusual
object? *(Answer is
on page 174.)*

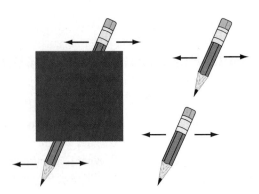

Figure 5-4 When two objects move together we can perceive them as parts of the same object.

Nigel Monckton/Fotolia

Many cues tell us that these are multiple objects, not one unusually shaped object: The objects differ in colour, the apples have a slightly different texture than the orange, and the apples in the foreground partially block the orange in the background.

what happened (Amso & Johnson, 2006; Kellman & Spelke, 1983; Eizenman & Bertenthal, 1998). Babies use common motion to identify objects and, given the right conditions, newborns do, too (Valenza & Bulf, 2011).

Motion is one clue to object unity, but infants use others too, including, colour, texture, and aligned edges. As you can see in Figure 5-5, infants more often group features together (i.e., believe they are part of the same object) when they're the same colour, have the same texture, and when their edges are aligned (Johnson, 2001).

PERCEPTUAL CONSTANCIES. A challenge for infants is recognizing that an object is the same even though it may look different. For example, when a mother moves away from her baby, the image that she casts on the retinas of her baby's eyes gets smaller. Do babies have a nightmare that their mother's head is shrinking as she moves away? No. **Early on, infants master *size constancy;* that is, the realization that an object's actual size remains the same despite changes in the size of its retinal image.**

How do we know that infants have a rudimentary sense of size constancy? Suppose we let an infant look at an unfamiliar teddy bear. Then we show the infant the same bear, at a different distance, paired with a larger replica of the bear. If infants lack size constancy, the two bears will be seen as equally novel and babies should respond to each similarly. If, instead, babies have size constancy, they will recognize the first bear as familiar, the larger bear as novel, and be more likely to respond to the novel bear. In fact, by four or five months, babies treat the bear that they have seen twice and at different distances—and, therefore, with different retinal images—as familiar (Granrud, 1986). This outcome is possible only if infants have size constancy. Thus, infants do not believe that mothers (and other people or objects) constantly change size as they move closer or farther away (Kellman & Arterberry, 2006).

Size is just one of several perceptual constancies. Others are brightness and colour constancy, as well as shape constancy, shown in Figure 5-6. All these constancies are achieved, at least in rudimentary form, by four months (Aslin, 1987; Dannemiller,

1998). Consequently, even young infants are not confused, thinking that the world is filled with many very similar-looking but different objects. Instead, they can tell that an object is the same, even though it may look different. Mom is still Mom, whether she is nearby or far away and whether she is clearly visible outdoors or barely visible in a dimly lit room.

DEPTH. In addition to knowing *what* an object is, babies need to know *where* it is. Determining left and right as well as high and low is relatively easy because these dimensions (horizontal, vertical) can be represented directly on the retina's flat surface. Distance or depth is more complicated because this dimension is not represented directly on the retina. Instead, many different cues are used to estimate distance or depth.

At what age can infants perceive depth? Eleanor Gibson and Richard Walk (1960) addressed this question in a classic experiment that used a specially designed apparatus. **The *visual cliff* is a glass-covered platform; on one side, a pattern appears directly under the glass, but on the other, it appears several feet below the glass.** Consequently, one side looks shallow but the other appears to have a steep drop-off, like a cliff. As you can see in the photo on the following page, in the experiment the baby is placed on the platform and the mother coaxes her infant to come to her. Most babies willingly crawl to their mothers when she stands on the shallow side of the platform. But virtually all babies refuse to cross the deep side, even when the mother calls the infant by name and tries to lure him or her with an attractive toy. Clearly, infants can perceive depth by the time they are old enough to crawl.

What about babies who cannot yet crawl? When babies as young as one and a half months are placed on the deep side of the platform, their heartbeat slows down. Heart rate often decelerates when something interesting is noted, so this would suggest that one-and-a-half-month-olds notice that the deep side is different. At seven months, the infants' heart rate accelerates, a sign of fear. Thus, although young babies can detect a difference between the shallow and deep sides of the visual cliff, only older, crawling babies are actually afraid of the deep side (Campos et al., 1978). It seems that fear of the apparent drop is related to the amount of experience an infant has in crawling. In crawling and walking as they explore new environments, infants appear to learn through experience (Adolph, 2000).

How do infants infer depth on the visual cliff and elsewhere? They use several kinds of cues. **Among the first are *kinetic cues*, in which motion is used to estimate depth.** *Visual expansion* **refers to the fact that as an object moves closer, it fills an ever greater proportion of the retina.** Visual expansion is the reason why we flinch when someone unexpectedly tosses a pop can toward us; it is what allows a batter to estimate when a baseball will arrive over the plate.

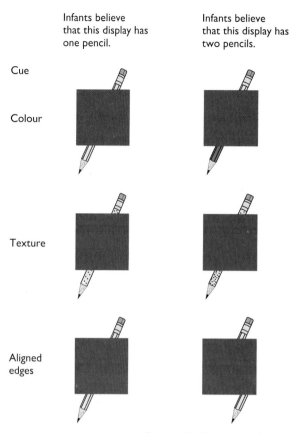

Figure 5-5 Infants are more likely to believe items are part of the same object when they share features, such as colour or texture.

Shape Constancy: Even though the door appears to change shape as it opens, we know that it really remains a rectangle.

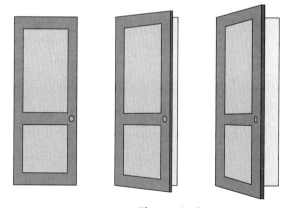

Figure 5-6 Shape Constancy: Even though the door appears to change shape as it opens, we know that it really remains a rectangle.

Mark Richards/PhotoEdit

Infants avoid the "deep" side of the visual cliff, indicating that they perceive depth.

Goce risteski/Fotolia

Texture gradient: **The texture of objects changes from coarse but distinct for nearby objects to finer and less distinct for distant objects.** In the photo, we judge the distinct flowers to be close and the blurred ones, distant.

Another cue, *motion parallax,* **refers to the fact that nearby moving objects move across our visual field faster than those at a distance.** Motion parallax is in action when you look out the side window of a moving car: Trees next to the road move rapidly across the visual field, but mountains in the distance move much more slowly. Babies use these cues in the first weeks after birth; for example, one-month-olds blink if a moving object looks as if it's going to hit them in the face (Nuñez & Yonas, 1994).

Yet another cue becomes important at about four months of age: *Retinal disparity* **is based on the fact that the left and right eyes often see slightly different versions of the same scene.** When objects are distant, the images appear in very similar positions on the retina; when objects are near, the images appear in much different positions. Thus, greater disparity in positions of the image on the retina signals that an object is close. At about four months, infants use retinal disparity as a depth cue, correctly inferring that objects are nearby when disparity is great (Kellman & Arterberry, 2006).

By seven months, infants use several cues for depth that depend on the arrangement of objects in the environment (e.g., Hemker, Granrud, Yonas, & Kavsek, 2010). **These are sometimes called** *pictorial cues* **because they are the same cues that artists use to convey depth in drawings and paintings.**

So far in this module, we've seen that young babies use simple relations between stimuli in order to infer an object, recognize that objects are the same despite changes in appearance, and use many cues to infer depth. Another aspect to consider is the influence of developing motor skills.

THE IMPACT OF MOTOR-SKILL DEVELOPMENT ON PERCEPTUAL SKILLS.   A common theme in the past few pages is that infants develop powerful perceptual skills over their first year. This change reflects an epigenetic plan in which genetic instructions unfold in the context of a stimulating environment. Essential to this plan are the infant's own emerging motor skills. That is, as we mentioned at the beginning of this chapter, as infants' motor skills improve, they experience their environment differently and literally see their world in new and more sophisticated ways.

One example of the impact of motor skills comes from infants' growing ability to hold and manipulate objects. As we'll see in Module 5.3, four-month-olds can hold a toy with their fingers, but not until a few months later do infants become skilled at holding a toy, turning it to see its appearance on different sides and stroking it with a finger to discover its texture. These improved motor skills allow children to learn more about the properties of objects, transforming how they perceive objects: Infants who can explore objects are more likely to understand the three-dimensional nature of objects and to

Interposition: **Nearby objects partially obscure more distant objects.** The glasses obscure the bottle, so we decide the glasses are closer (and use this same cue to decide that the right glass is nearer than the left glass).

Linear perspective: **Parallel lines come together at a single point in the distance.** Thus, we use the space between the lines as a cue to the distance and, consequently, decide that the train in the photo is far away because the parallel tracks appear to grow close together.

Relative size: **Nearby objects look substantially larger than objects seen in the distance.** Knowing that the runners are all really about the same size, we judge the ones that look smaller to be farther away.

notice the details of an object's appearance, such as its colour (Baumgartner & Oakes, 2013; Schwarzer et al., 2013).

Another example makes use of a familiar phenomenon: When you drive down a tree-lined road, the trees rapidly move from ahead of you to behind you. Having spent many hours in a car, you interpret the changing appearance of the trees as a cue that you are moving. For this same reason, when you are sitting in an airliner parked at a gate and another airliner at an adjacent gate backs out, you feel as if you are moving forward. This experience can be simulated by placing people in rooms in which the side walls and ceiling can move forward or backward. If the walls move from front to back, those seated in the middle of the room feel as if they are moving forward and they often lean back to compensate. Infants who can move themselves by creeping or crawling, do the same, but infants who can't move themselves do not (Uchiyama et al., 2008). Only after gaining the experience of propelling themselves through the environment can infants interpret front-to-back movement to mean that they are moving forward. Thus, just as an art-appreciation course allows you to see the Mona Lisa from a different perspective, infants' emerging abilities to move themselves and to manipulate objects create bold new perceptual experiences.

This same theme—perceptual skills change rapidly during infancy—is apparent in the next section, which focuses on how infants perceive faces.

PERCEIVING FACES. Babies depend on other people to care for them, so it's not surprising that young babies are attuned to human faces. For example, Canadian research has shown that newborns prefer faces with normal features over faces in which features are scrambled (Easterbrook, Kisilevsky, Muir, & Laplante, 1999), and upright faces over inverted faces (Mondloch et al., 1999). Infants also seem to prefer attractive faces over unattractive faces (Slater et al., 2000). Findings like these lead some scientists to claim that babies are innately attracted to moving stimuli that are face-like (e.g., consist of three high-contrast blobs close together). In other words, newborns' face perception may be reflexive, based on primitive circuits in the brain. At about two or three months of age, different circuits in the brain's cortex begin to control infants' looking at faces, allowing infants to learn about faces and to distinguish different faces (Morton & Johnson, 1991).

Through the first few months after birth, infants have a general prototype for a face—one that includes human and nonhuman faces (Pascalis, de Haan, & Nelson, 2002). However, over the first year infants fine-tune their prototype of a face so that it reflects faces that are familiar in their environments (Pascalis et al., 2014). For example, three-month-olds prefer to look at faces from their own race, but they can recognize faces from other races (and other species). In contrast, six-month-olds often fail to recognize faces of individuals from other, unfamiliar races (Anzures et al., 2013). Apparently, older infants' greater familiarity with faces of their own race leads to a more precise configuration of faces, one that includes faces of familiar racial and ethnic groups. This interpretation is supported by the finding that individuals born in Asia but adopted as infants by European parents recognize European faces better than Asian faces (Sangrigoli et al., 2005). What's more, if older infants receive extensive experience with other-race faces, they can learn to recognize them (Anzures et al., 2012).

These changes in face-recognition skill show the role of experience in fine-tuning infants' perception, a theme that will emerge again in the early phases of language learning (Module 9.1). And these improved facial-recognition skills are adaptive because they provide the basis for social relationships that infants form during the rest of the first year, which we'll examine in Module 10.3.

Focus On Research

Early Visual Experiencing and Face Processing

Who were the investigators, and what was the aim of the study? Over the first year, infants rapidly become more skilled at recognizing faces, presumably as they are exposed to an ever-larger number of faces and are able to fine-tune their face-recognition processes. If this argument is correct, infants need such early visual experience or they might lose the ability to perform some aspects of processing of information about facial features. Thus, lack of experience could lead to deficits in facial recognition. Testing this hypothesis was the aim of a study by Canadian researchers Richard Le Grand, Catherine J. Mondloch, Daphne Maurer, and Henry P. Brent (2001).

How did the investigators measure the topic of interest? Le Grand and colleagues wanted to determine whether being deprived of normal visual input from birth for several months resulted in deficits in processing of facial feature information. Consequently, they had children who had had cataracts removed as infants view photos of a human face with the features altered either by moving the relative spacing of the eyes and mouth or by replacing the eyes and mouth with those from another photo. Two sets of photos were produced, one pair where the configuration of the face (space between features) was altered and one pair where the features themselves were altered (replaced by those from another picture), as shown in Figure 5-7. The experimenters recorded participants' ability to distinguish between the two faces—altered and original—in the pairs of photos.

Who were the participants in the study? The study included 14 patients, 9 to 14 years old, who all had had surgery as babies to remove congenital cataracts. The participants had been born with dense, central cataracts—which allowed discrimination of light and dark but not any patterned visual stimulation. The cataracts were removed between 62 and 187 days after birth (on average about four months). The participants' abilities to discriminate between the two types of manipulated face photographs were tested and compared to the abilities of a control group with no known visual impairments.

What was the design of the study? This study was experimental. The independent variable was the type of face (configural or featural). The dependent variable was the participants' ability to discriminate between the two faces in each pair of photos.

Were there ethical concerns with the study? No. There was no obvious harm associated with looking at pictures of faces.

What were the results? In each pair of faces, if participants could tell both kinds of sets (featural and configural) apart, then this would show that early visual experience was not necessary for facial recognition. If there were any problems in discriminating between the two sets of photos, this would indicate the type of facial recognition affected by lack of early visual experience. The researchers found that the cataract patients could discriminate between the featural photos—those with different eyes and mouths—but not between the configural photos—those with different spatial positioning of the features.

What did the investigators conclude? Le Grand et al. (2001) concluded that their findings "indicate that visual experience during the first few months of life is necessary for the normal development of expert face processing" (p. 890). That is, from experience, infants finely tune their face-processing systems to recognize both the features and the relative spacing of those features of human faces.

What converging evidence would strengthen these conclusions? These findings show that the face-processing systems of congenital cataract patients do not work as well for configural as for featural processing of human faces. The investigators proposed that the neural structure of the brain underlying face processing requires full experience with faces for its proper development. In addition, use of brain-mapping methods would be beneficial (described on pages 146–147) to determine if the brain regions associated with face recognition change as face-processing systems become more finely adjusted across the first year of life.

Critical Thinking Questions:

1. If brain mapping were done to look at brain regions involved in face processing, which brain regions would likely be found to be active?

2. What about other sensory processing—how might experience be important for hearing, or for sense of touch, for instance?

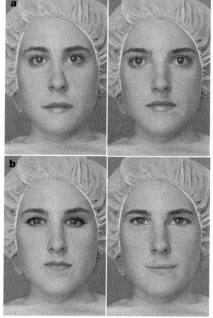

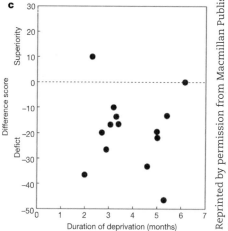

Reprinted by permission from Macmillan Publishers Ltd.: Nature; Neuroperception: Early Visual Experience and Face Processing, Vol. 410, © 2001, advance online publication, doi:10.1038/35073749.

Figure 5-7 Le Grand et al. (2001) had participants in their study view the pairs of faces. Participants were asked whether the faces were the same or different. If participants could distinguish between the first pair of faces, they had intact configural processing; if they could tell the second pair apart they had retained featural processing ability.

Attention

Have you ever been in a class where you knew you should be listening and taking notes, but the lecture was just so boring that you started noticing other things—the construction going on outside or an attractive person seated nearby? After a while, maybe you reminded yourself to "pay attention!" We get distracted because our perceptual systems are marvelously powerful. They provide us with far more information at any one time than we could possible interpret.

Attention **refers to processes that allow people to control input from the environment and regulate behaviour.** Scientists distinguish three networks of attentional processes, each with unique functions and neural circuitry (Posner et al., 2012). The orienting network is associated with selection—it determines which stimuli will be processed further and which will be ignored. This network is well developed in infancy and is what drives, for example, an infant to turn his or her head toward a flashing light. The alerting network keeps a child's attentional processes prepared, ready to detect and respond to incoming stimuli. This network is also well developed in infancy and is illustrated by a baby who, hearing a parent's footsteps in a nearby room, looks at a doorway in anticipation of parent's arrival.

The executive network is responsible for monitoring thoughts, feelings, and responses as well as resolving conflicts that may occur. This is the most complex element of attention and the slowest to develop. For example, when one-year-olds play with a new toy, they may be easily distracted by a program on a nearby TV: The toy and the TV program compete for attention, and because the executive network is immature, the infant cannot ignore the TV to focus on the toy (Ruff & Capozzoli, 2003).

Experimental research shows the extended development of the executive network. For example, in one task there are left and right buttons and a left- or right-facing arrow is shown to indicate which button to press. When a conflict is introduced—by adding a smaller arrow pointing in the opposite direction of the large arrow—preschool children respond more slowly and less accurately; the executive network is less able to help them resolve the conflicting directions indicated by the large and small arrows (Posner & Rothbart, 2007). Similarly, when children learn to sort pictures according to one rule (e.g., sort by colour) and then are asked to sort them again using a different rule (e.g., now sort by shape), preschool children often return to sorting by the old rule, even though they can describe the new rule perfectly! They are less able to ignore the conflict generated by the old rule, which causes them to sort some cards by colour even when they know the new rule says to sort by shape (Zelazo et al., 2013).

Because the executive network has such a broad reach and develops so slowly, it is a crucial force in children's development, influencing their physical health, mental health, and success in school (Diamond, 2013). We'll learn more about the structure of the executive network and its link to school success in Module 6.2. And in Module 10.2 we'll see that differences in this network represent a key component of children's temperament.

Gianni Muratore/Alamy Stock Photo

Attentional processes allow infants (and older children) to ignore stimuli that aren't important.

In the meantime, teachers and parents *can* help young children pay attention better. For example, *Tools of the Mind* is a curriculum for preschool and kindergarten children that uses pretend play to improve the attentional processes of the executive network (Diamond & Lee, 2011). Pretend play may seem like a surprising way to improve attention, but staying "in character" while pretending teaches children to inhibit inappropriate "out of character" behaviour. And it encourages thinking flexibly as children respond to their playmates' improvisation. Teachers also contribute by providing visual reminders of the need to pay attention, such as showing a drawing of an ear to remind children to listen.

Parents can also help promote their children's attentional skills. In one study (Neville et al., 2013), parents and their preschool children attended an after-school program that included activities designed to improve children's attention. For example, in one task children were taught how to colour carefully while being distracted by a nearby peer who was playing with a balloon. Parents were taught ways to support their children's attention. After children participated in this program, their attention improved (e.g., attending to a specified event while ignoring a distracting event).

Techniques like these improve children's attention and can be particularly useful with children who have the attentional problems—described in the next section.

Attention Deficit Hyperactivity Disorder

Children with attention deficit hyperactivity disorder—ADHD for short—have special problems when it comes to paying attention. Roughly 3 to 7 percent of all school-age children are diagnosed with ADHD; boys outnumber girls by a ratio of four to one (Goldstein, 2011). Stephen, the child in the module-opening vignette, exhibits three symptoms at the heart of ADHD (American Psychiatric Association, 2004):

- *Hyperactivity:* Children with ADHD are unusually energetic, fidgety, and unable to keep still, especially in situations like school classrooms where they need to limit their activity.

- *Inattention:* Youngsters with ADHD skip from one task to another. They do not pay attention in class and seem unable to concentrate on schoolwork.

- *Impulsivity:* Children with ADHD often act before thinking; they may run into a street before looking for traffic, or interrupt others who are speaking.

Not all children with ADHD show all these symptoms to the same degree. Some children with ADHD are hyperactive and either impulsive; others are primarily inattentive (Frick & Nigg, 2012) Children with ADHD often have problems with conduct, academic performance, and getting along with their peers (Murray-Close et al., 2010; Stevens & Ward-Estes, 2006). Many children who are diagnosed with ADHD will have problems related to overactivity, inattention, and impulsivity as adolescents and young adults (Barbaresi et al., 2013; Biederman, Petty, Evans, Small, & Faraone, 2010).

Over the years, ADHD has been linked to TV, food allergies, and sugar, but research does not consistently implicate any of these as causes (e.g., Wolraich et al., 1994). Instead, scientists believe that genes put some children at risk for ADHD by affecting the alerting

Hyperactivity is one of three main symptoms of ADHD; the others are inattention and impulsivity.

Ranplett/Vetta/Getty Images

and executive networks of attention and the brain structures that support those networks (Gizer & Waldman, 2012; Johnson et al., 2008). But environmental factors also contribute. For example, prenatal exposure to alcohol and other drugs can place children at risk for ADHD (Milberger et al., 1997).

Because ADHD affects academic and social success throughout childhood and adolescence, researchers have worked hard to find effective treatments. By the mid 1980s, it had become clear that ADHD could be treated. For example, children with ADHD often respond well to stimulant drugs such as Ritalin. It may seem odd that stimulants are given to children who are already overactive, but these drugs stimulate the parts of the brain that normally inhibit hyperactive and impulsive behaviour. Thus, stimulants actually have a calming influence on many youngsters with ADHD, allowing them to focus their attention (Barkley, 2004). Drug therapy was not the only approach: Psychosocial treatments also worked and were designed to improve children's cognitive and social skills, and often included home-based intervention and intensive summer programs (Richters et al., 1995). For example, children can be taught to remind themselves to read instructions before starting assignments. And they can be reinforced by others for inhibiting impulsive and hyperactive behavior (Lee et al., 2012; Webster-Stratton, Reid, & Beauchaine, 2011). ADHD is not all "bad"; a student who had worked in a daycare gave Anne Barnfield a list of "Thirty good things about kids with ADHD" that a parent had provided. The list included such positives as "good conversationalist," "inquisitive," and "optimistic."

Longitudinal studies of effects of different types of treatments have shown that there is no "quick fix" for ADHD (e.g., Molina et al., 2009). Instead, ADHD is perhaps better considered a chronic condition, like diabetes or asthma, one that requires ongoing monitoring and treatment (Hazell, 2009).

Q&A ANSWER 5.2
Her hands and fingers move together, independently of the keyboard, and her hands and fingers have a common colour and texture that differs from those of the keyboard.
. . . .

✓ Check Your Learning

RECALL Describe the cues that babies use to infer depth.

What are the main symptoms of ADHD?

INTERPRET Describe evidence showing that early experience with faces fine-tunes the infant's perception of faces.

APPLY What happens to children with ADHD when they become adolescents and young adults? How does this address the issue of continuity of development?

5.3 Motor Development

OUTLINE	LEARNING OBJECTIVES
Locomotion	1. What are the component skills involved in learning to walk, and at what age do infants typically master them?
Fine-Motor Skills	2. How do infants learn to coordinate the use of their hands? When and why do most children begin to prefer to use one hand?
Physical Fitness	3. Are children physically fit? Do they benefit from participating in sports?

Nancy is 14 months old and a world-class crawler. Using hands and knees, she gets nearly anywhere she wants to go. Nancy does not walk and seems to have no interest in learning how. Her dad wonders whether he should be doing something to help Nancy progress beyond crawling. And deep down, he worries that perhaps he should have provided more exercise or training for Nancy when she was younger.

The photos on the next page share a common theme. Each depicts an activity involving *motor skills*—coordinated movements of the muscles and limbs. Infants face two challenges involving motor skills. **They must learn** *locomotion*—**that is, to move about in the world.** Newborns are relatively immobile, but infants soon learn to crawl, stand, and walk. Learning to move through the environment upright leaves the arms and hands free, which allows infants to grasp and manipulate objects. **Infants must learn the** *fine-motor skills* **associated with grasping, holding, and manipulating objects.** In the case of feeding, for example, infants progress from being fed by others to holding a bottle, to feeding themselves with their fingers, to eating with a spoon.

Although demanding, locomotion and fine-motor skills are worth mastering because of their benefits. Being able to move around and to grasp gives children access to an enormous amount of information about their environment. They can explore objects that look interesting, and they can keep themselves close to their parents. Improved motor skills promote children's cognitive and social development, not to mention making a child's life more interesting!

In this module, we'll see how children acquire locomotor and fine-motor skills. As we do, we'll find out whether Nancy's dad needs to worry about her lack of interest in walking.

Locomotion

In little more than a year, advances in posture and locomotion change the newborn from a stationary being into an upright, standing individual who walks through the

2tun/Fotolia

Dusan Kostic/Fotolia

Motor skills involve coordinating movements of muscles and limbs.

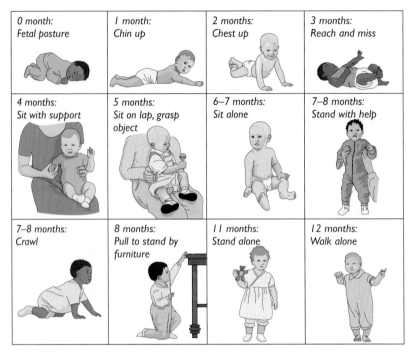

Figure 5-8 Ages by which most infants achieve important milestones in motor development.

environment. Figure 5-8 shows some of the important milestones in motor development and the age by which most infants achieve them. The Infant Developmental Milestones Study is a longitudinal study that, as its name suggests, tracks ages at which motor achievements are reached. Dr. Warren Eaton of the University of Manitoba and colleagues are collecting data on the ages at which babies and infants in Canada reach developmental milestones. By about four months, most babies can sit upright with support. By six or seven months, they can sit without support, and by seven or eight months, they can stand if they hold onto an object for support. A typical 11-month-old can stand alone briefly and walk with assistance. **Youngsters at this age are called** *toddlers,* **after the toddling manner of early walking.** Of course, not all children walk at exactly the same age. Some walk before their first birthday; others, like Nancy, the world-class crawler in the module-opening vignette, take their first steps as late as 17 or 18 months. By 24 months, most children can climb steps, walk backwards, and kick a ball.

Researchers once thought these developmental milestones reflected maturation (e.g., McGraw, 1935). Walking, for example, was thought to emerge naturally when the necessary muscles and neural circuits matured. Today, however, locomotion—and, in fact, all motor development—is viewed from a new perspective. **According to** *dynamic systems theory,* **motor development involves many distinct skills that are organized and reorganized over time to meet the demands of specific tasks.** For example, walking includes maintaining balance, moving limbs, perceiving the environment, and having a reason to move. Only by understanding each of these skills and how they are combined to allow movement in a specific situation can we understand walking (Spencer, Perone, & Buss, 2011).

As Kail and Zollner (2005) note, in Canada in the past, devices known as "baby walkers" were popular. An infant who could not yet walk but was able to sit without support would be placed in the walker. Baby walkers were thought to be harmless, fun exercise for the baby, but significant safety issues soon became apparent. Young infants could move the walkers but had no real control over them. In numerous cases, young infants took themselves over the edges of staircases and suffered serious falls. One student in a Brescia child development class stated that her earliest memory was of pushing herself in a baby walker down a flight of steps and her view of the concrete wall apparently rushing to meet her! Although initially thought to be useful in aiding development of loco-motion, baby walkers proved to do more harm than good. When a voluntary restriction on sales of baby walkers by manufacturers failed to end their use, Health Canada issued an outright ban on the devices (Health Canada, 2004).

In the remainder of this section, we'll see how learning to walk reflects the maturity and coalescence of many component skills.

POSTURE AND BALANCE.   The ability to maintain an upright posture is funda-mental to walking. But upright posture is virtually impossible for young infants because the shape of their body makes them top-heavy. Consequently, as soon as a young infant starts to lose her balance, she tumbles over. Only with growth of the legs and muscles can infants maintain an upright posture (Thelen, Ulrich, & Jensen, 1989).

Once infants can stand upright, they must continuously adjust their posture to avoid falling down (Metcalfe et al., 2005). By a few months after birth, infants begin to use visual cues and an inner-ear mechanism to adjust their posture. To show the use of visual cues for balance, researchers had babies sit in a room with striped walls that moved. When adults sit in such a room, they perceive themselves as moving (not the walls) and adjust their posture accordingly; so do infants, which shows that they use vision to maintain upright posture (Bertenthal & Clifton, 1998).

Balance is not, however, something that infants master just once. Instead, infants must relearn balancing for sitting, crawling, walking, and other postures. Why? The body rotates around different points in each posture (e.g., the wrists for crawling versus the ankles for walking), and different muscle groups are used to generate compensating motions when infants begin to lose their balance. Consequently, it's hardly surprising that infants who easily maintain their balance while sitting topple over time after time when crawling. Infants must recalibrate the balance system as they take on each new posture, just as basketball players recalibrate their muscle movements when they move from dunking to shooting a three-pointer (Adolph, 2000, 2002).

STEPPING.   Another essential element of walking is moving the legs alternately, repeatedly transferring the weight of the body from one foot to the other. Children don't step spontaneously until approximately 10 months because they must be able to stand upright to step.

Can younger children step if they are held upright? Thelen and Ulrich (1991) devised a clever procedure to answer this question. Infants were placed on a treadmill and held upright by an adult. When the belt on the treadmill started to move, infants could respond in one of several ways. They could simply let both legs be dragged rearward by the belt. Or they could let their legs be dragged briefly, then move them forward together in a hopping motion. Many six- and seven-month-olds demonstrated the mature pat-tern of alternating steps on each leg that is shown in the photo on the next page. Even more amazing is that when the treadmill was equipped with separate belts for each leg that moved at different speeds, babies adjusted, stepping more rapidly on the faster belt. Apparently, the alternate stepping motion that is essential for walking is evident long before infants walk independently. Walking unassisted is not possible, though, until other component skills are mastered.

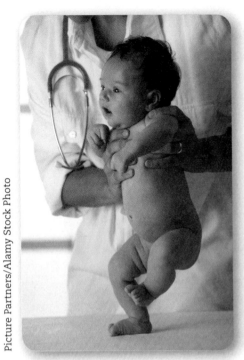

Newborns step reflexively when they are held upright and moved forward.

Picture Partners/Alamy Stock Photo

ENVIRONMENTAL CUES. Many infants learn to walk in the relative security of flat, uncluttered floors at home. But they soon discover that the environment offers a variety of surfaces, some more conducive to walking than others. Infants use cues in the environment to judge whether a surface is suitable for walking. For example, they are more likely to cross a bridge when it's wide and has a rigid handrail than when it is narrow and has a wobbly handrail (Berger, Adolph, & Lobo, 2005; Kretch & Adolph, 2013a). And when walking down stairs, if a step is too large to descend safely, novice walkers often continue (and fall) but older, experienced walkers either stop or slide down on their backs; only experienced walkers recognize the cues that signal steps that are safe for walking (Kretch & Adolph, 2013b). If they cannot decide whether a surface is safe, they depend on an adult's advice (Tamis-LeMonda et al., 2008). Results like these show that infants use perceptual cues to decide whether a surface is safe for walking.

COORDINATING SKILLS. Dynamic systems theory emphasizes that learning to walk demands orchestration of many individual skills. Each component skill must first be mastered alone and then integrated with the other skills (Werner, 1948). **That is, mastery of intricate motions requires both** *differentiation*—**mastery of component skills; and their** *integration*—**combining them in proper sequence into a coherent, working whole.** In the case of walking, not until 9 to 15 months do children master the component skills so that they can be coordinated to allow independent, unsupported walking.

Mastering individual skills and coordinating them well does not happen overnight. Instead, it takes time and repeated practice. Novice walkers take nearly 1500 steps per hour, covering about one-third of a kilometre, and falling more than 30 times; infants obviously get lots of natural practice (along with feedback from falls) as they master walking (Adolph et al., 2012). Similarly, we'll see in the Cultural Influences feature that some cultures include customs that help children learn to walk.

Cultural Influences

Cultural Practices that Influence Motor Development

In Europe and North America, most infants can typically walk without help near their first birthday. But infants in other cultures often begin to walk (and reach other milestones illustrated on page 176) at an earlier age because childcare customs allow children to practise their emerging motor skills. For example, in some traditional African cultures, infants sit and walk at younger ages. Why? Infants are commonly carried by their parents in the piggyback style shown in the photo on the next page, which helps develop muscles in the infants' trunk and legs.

Some cultures even take a further step. They believe that practice is essential for motor skills to develop normally, so parents (or siblings) provide daily training sessions. For example, the Kipsigis of Kenya help children learn to sit by having them sit while propped up (Super, 1981). And among the West Indians of Jamaica, mothers have an elaborate exercise routine that allows babies to practise walking (Hopkins & Westra, 1988). Not surprisingly, infants with these opportunities learn to sit and walk earlier, findings that are confirmed by experimental work in which some parents participate in activities that let babies practise controlling their bodies (Lobo & Galloway, 2012).

You may be surprised that some cultures do just the opposite— they have practices that discourage motor development. The Ache, an indigenous group in Paraguay, protect infants and toddlers from harm by carrying them constantly (Kaplan & Dove, 1987). In Chinese cities, parents often allow their children to crawl only on a bed surrounded by pillows, in part because they don't want their children crawling on a dirty floor (Campos et al., 2000). In both cases, infants reach motor milestones a few months later than the ages illustrated on page 176.

Even European and North American infants are crawling at older ages today than they did in previous generations (Dewey et al., 1998; Lung & Shu, 2011). This generational difference reflects the effectiveness of the Back to Sleep campaign described on page 114. Because today's babies spend less time on their tummies, they have fewer opportunities to discover that they can propel themselves by creeping, which would otherwise prepare them for crawling.

Thus, cultural practices can accelerate or delay the early stages of motor development, depending on the nature of practice that infants and toddlers receive (Adolph & Robinson, 2013). In the long run, however, the age of mastering various motor milestones is not critical for children's development. All healthy children learn to walk, and whether this happens a few months before or after the "typical" ages shown on page 176 has no bearing on children's later development (Lung & Shu, 2011).

Morane/Fotolia

In many African cultures, infants are routinely carried piggyback style, which strengthens the infant's legs, allowing them to walk at a younger age.

Critical Thinking Questions: This section in the textbook describes some cultural practices that may foster or hinder walking, e.g., carrying an infant on the caregiver's back or allowing crawling only on a bed. What other culturally specific childcare customs can you think of, and how might these affect infant's motor development? Are there any customs that are specific to your cultural background that you could share with classmates?

BEYOND WALKING. If you can recall the feeling of freedom that accompanied your first driver's licence, you can imagine how the world expands for infants and toddlers as they learn to move independently. The first tentative steps are followed by others that are more skilled. With more experience, infants take longer, straighter steps. Like adults, they begin to swing their arms, rotating the left arm forward as the right leg moves, then repeating with the right arm and left leg (Ledebt, 2000; Ledebt, van Wieringen, & Savelsbergh, 2004). Children's growing skill is evident in their running and hopping. Most two-year-olds have a hurried walk instead of a true run; they move their legs stiffly (rather than bending them at the knees) and are not airborne, as is the case when running. By five or six years, children run easily, quickly changing directions or speed. Infants use their new walking skills to get distant objects—a favourite toy that's in a different room of the house—and carry them to share with other people (Karasik, Tamis-Lemonda, & Adolph, 2011). In the next section, we'll see how infants' fine-motor skills allow them to grasp objects.

Fine-Motor Skills

A major accomplishment in infancy is skilled use of the hands (Bertenthal & Clifton, 1998). Newborns have little apparent control of their hands, but one-year-olds are extraordinarily talented.

A typical four-month-old grasps an object with fingers alone.

REACHING AND GRASPING. At about four months, infants can successfully reach for objects (Bertenthal & Clifton, 1998). These early reaches often look clumsy—and for a good reason. When infants reach, their arms and hands don't move directly and smoothly to the desired object (as do those of older children and adults). Instead, the infant's hand moves like a ship under the direction of an unskilled navigator. It moves a short distance, slows, then moves again in a slightly different direction, a process that is repeated until the hand finally contacts the object (McCarty & Ashmead, 1999). As infants grow, their reaches have fewer movements, though they are still not as continuous and smooth as those of older children and adults (Berthier, 1996).

Reaching requires that an infant move the hand to the location of a desired object. Grasping poses a different challenge: Now the infant must coordinate movements of individual fingers in order to grab an object. Grasping, too, becomes more efficient during infancy. Most four-month-olds use just their fingers to hold objects.

Like the baby in the photo, they wrap an object tightly with their fingers alone. Not until seven or eight months do most infants use their thumbs to hold objects (Siddiqui, 1995). At about this age, infants begin to position their hands to make it easier to grasp an object. In trying to grasp a long thin rod, for example, infants place their fingers perpendicular to the rod, which is the best position for grasping (Wentworth, Benson, & Haith, 2000). And they reach more slowly for smaller objects that require a more precise grip (Berthier & Carrico, 2010). However, not until their first birthday do babies make multiple adjustments when reaching for objects (Schum, Jovanovic, & Schwarzer, 2011).

Infants' growing control of each hand is accompanied by greater coordination of the two hands. Although four-month-olds use both hands, their motions are not coordinated; rather, each hand seems to have a mind of its own. Infants may hold a toy motionless in one hand while shaking a rattle in the other. At roughly five to six months, infants can coordinate the motions of their hands so that each hand performs different actions that serve a common goal. So a child might, for example, hold a toy animal in one hand and pet it with the other (Karniol, 1989). These skills continue to improve after a child's first birthday: one-year-olds reach for most objects with one hand; by two years, they reach with one or two hands, as appropriate, depending on the size of the object (van Hof, van der Kamp, & Savelsbergh, 2002).

Oksana Kuzmina/Shutterstock

These many changes in reaching and grasping are well illustrated as infants learn to feed themselves. At about six months, they are often given "finger foods" (e.g., sliced bananas). Infants can easily pick up such foods, but getting them into the mouth is another story. The hand grasping the food may be raised to the cheek, then moved to the edge of the lips, and finally shoved into the mouth. Mission accomplished—but only with many detours along the way! But eye-hand coordination improves rapidly, so before long, foods that vary in size, shape, and texture reach the mouth directly.

At about the first birthday, youngsters are usually ready to try eating with a spoon. At first, they simply play with the spoon, dipping it in and out of a dish filled with food or sucking on it empty. With a little help, they learn to fill the spoon with food and place it in the mouth, though the motion is awkward because they do not rotate the wrist. Instead, most one-year-olds fill a spoon by placing it directly over a dish and lowering it until the bowl of the spoon is full. Then, they raise the spoon to the mouth, all the while keeping the wrist rigid. In contrast, two-year-olds rotate the hand at the wrist while scooping food from a dish and placing the spoon in the mouth—the same motion that adults use.

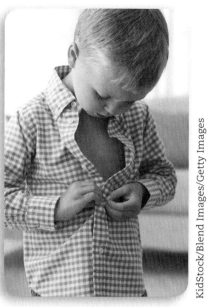

By age five, fine-motor skills are developed to the point that most youngsters can dress themselves.

After infancy, fine-motor skills progress rapidly. Preschool children become much more dexterous, able to make many precise and delicate movements with their hands and fingers. Greater fine-motor skill means that preschool children can begin to care for themselves eating and dressing without a parent's help. For example, a two- or three-year-old can put on some simple clothing and use zippers but not buttons; by three or four years, children can fasten buttons and take off their clothes when going to the bathroom; like the child in the photo, most five-year-olds can dress and undress themselves, except for tying shoes, which children typically master at about age six.

In each of these actions, the same principles of dynamic systems theory apply as seen in our previous discussion of locomotion. Complex acts involve many component movements. Each must be performed correctly and in the proper sequence. Development involves first mastering the separate elements and then assembling them to form a smoothly functioning whole. Eating finger food, for example, requires grasping food, moving the hand to the mouth, then releasing the food. As the demands of tasks change and as children develop, the same skills are often reassembled to form a different sequence of movements.

HANDEDNESS. When young babies reach for objects, they do not seem to prefer one hand over the other; they use their left and right hands interchangeably. They may shake a rattle with their left hand and moments later pick up blocks with their right. By the first birthday, most youngsters are emergent right-handers. Like the toddler in the bottom photo, they use the left hand to steady the toy while the right hand manipulates the object. This early preference for one hand becomes stronger and more consistent during the preschool years and is well established by kindergarten (Marschik et al., 2008; Nelson, Campbell, & Michel, 2013).

Most toddlers use their left hand to hold an object steady and their right hand to explore the object.

What determines whether children become left- or right-handed? Some scientists believe that a gene biases children toward right-handedness (Corballis, Badzakova-Trajkova, & Häberling, 2012). Consistent with this idea, identical twins are more likely than fraternal twins to have the same handedness—both are right-handed or both are left-handed (Medland et al., 2009). But experience also contributes to handedness. Modern industrial cultures favour right-handedness. School desks, scissors, and can openers, for example, are designed for right-handed people and can be used by left-handers only with difficulty. Special left-handed versions of such items can be purchased in certain stores, and right-handers using such items can see how difficult the world can be for left-handers. Co-author Anne Barnfield's stepmother is left-handed, and Anne's father once cut himself trying to use a special left-handed cutter simply to slice a tomato! Left-handed people have to deal with such problems on a daily basis. In North America, elementary-school teachers used to urge left-handed children to use their right hands. As this practice has diminished in the past 50 years, the percentage of left-handed children has risen steadily (Provins, 1997). Thus, handedness is influenced by both heredity and environment.

Physical Fitness

The use of motor skills—that is, being active physically—has many benefits for children. It promotes growth of muscles and bone, cardiovascular health, and cognitive processes (Best, 2010; Biddle & Asare, 2011; Hillman, Buck, Themanson, Pontifex, & Castelli 2009) and can help to establish a lifelong pattern of exercise (Perkins, Jacobs, Barber, & Eccles, 2004). Individuals who exercise regularly—30 minutes at least 3 times a week—reduce their risk for obesity, cancer, heart disease, and diabetes, as well as psychological disorders including depression and anxiety (Tomson, Pangrazi, Friedman, & Hutchison, 2003). Running, vigorous walking, swimming, aerobic dancing, biking, and cross-country skiing are all examples of activities that can provide this level of intensity.

How fit are children and adolescents? The Canadian Fitness and Lifestyle Research Institute (CFLRI) is engaged in an ongoing study using pedometers to objectively measure children's physical activity levels. In 2005, the CFLRI started collecting data for the nationwide Canadian Physical Activity Levels Among Youth (CAN PLAY) Study. This ongoing study assesses physical activity of Canadian children and young people by annually collecting data on basic activity levels, measured in numbers of steps taken. General findings of the study are that children who participate in organized sports

Q&A **QUESTION 5.3**
Jenny and Ian are both left-handed, and they fully expected their son, Tyler, to prefer his left hand, too. But he's eight months old already and seems to use both hands to grasp toys and other objects. Should Jenny and Ian give up their dream of being the three left-handed musketeers? *(Answer is on page 184.)*

Amy Myers/Fotolia

Participating in sports can enhance children's physical, motor, cognitive, and social development.

SolStock/iStock/Getty Images

When adult coaches emphasize skill development and having fun, children maintain interest and are less likely to quit sports.

are more physically active, and children with more active parents tend to be more active themselves (CFLRI, 2011). Studies of Canadian social trends bear out the latter finding—the rate of children's sport involvement in Canada is strongly influenced by activity and involvement of parents (Kremarik, 2000; Clark, 2008). Other research has looked at actual fitness tests and found that when children are tested against objective criteria, their actual level of fitness is low. In studies that include a full battery of fitness tests, such as a 1500-metre run, pull-ups and sit-ups, fewer than half the children usually meet standards for fitness on all tasks (Morrow, Martin, Welk, Zhu, & Meredith, 2010). You'll remember from Module 4.2 that government agencies have stated that obesity has reached epidemic proportions among North American children and adolescents (Starky, 2005; U.S. Department of Health and Human Services, 2010).

Many factors contribute to current low levels of fitness. In most schools, physical education classes are held only once or twice a week and are usually not required of high-school students (Johnston, Delva, & O'Malley, 2007). Even when students are in these classes, they spend nearly half the time standing around instead of exercising (Lowry, Wechsler, Kann, & Collins, 2001; Parcel et al., 1989). Television and other sedentary leisure-time activities may contribute too. Children who watch TV often tend to be less fit physically (Lobelo, Dowda, Pfeiffer, & Pate, 2009), but the nature of this relationship remains poorly understood: Children who watch TV or use computers a lot may have fewer opportunities to exercise, but it may be that children who are in poor physical condition choose sedentary activities over exercise.

Many experts believe that schools should offer physical education more frequently each week, and many suggest that physical education classes should offer a range of activities in which all children can participate and that can be the foundation for a lifelong program of fitness (National Association for Sport and Physical Fitness, 2004). Thus, instead of emphasizing team sports such as touch football, physical education classes should emphasize activities like running, walking, racquet sports, and swimming; these can be done throughout adolescence and adulthood and either alone or with another person. Canadian schools are beginning to integrate such programs, as with the *Action Schools!* B.C. initiative mentioned in Chapter 4. Families can encourage fitness, too. Instead of spending an afternoon watching TV and eating popcorn, they can go biking together. Or families can play exergames, which are digital games like *Dance Dance Revolution* that combine video gaming with exercise; playing these regularly enhances physical fitness (Staiano & Calvert, 2011).

PARTICIPATING IN SPORTS. Many children and adolescents get exercise by participating in team sports, including baseball, softball, basketball, and soccer. Although rates of participation have declined slightly over the past two decades, about half of all Canadian children take part in some form of organized sport (Clark, 2008). Obviously, when children, like the girls in the photo on page 182, play sports, they get exercise and improve their motor skills, but there are other benefits too. Sports can enhance participants' self-esteem and can help them to learn initiative (Bowker, 2006; Eime, Young, Harvey, Charity, & Payne, 2013). Sports can also give children a chance to learn important social skills, such as how to work effectively as part of a group, often in complementary roles. Sport participation may also have beneficial effects on mental health for adolescents. Lynne Armstrong and Ian Manion from the University of Ottawa surveyed suicidal thinking in rural youth. They found that engagement in structured extracurricular activities such as sports teams had beneficial effects for adolescent mental health, giving feelings of competency and decreasing suicidal ideation (Armstrong & Manion, 2006). Finally, playing sports allows children to use their emerging cognitive skills as they devise new playing strategies or modify the rules of a game.

The potential benefits of participation in sports also depend on the adults who are involved. When adult coaches encourage their players and emphasize skill development, children usually enjoy playing and often improve their skills and increase their self-esteem (Coatsworth & Conroy, 2009; Smith & Smoll, 1997). In contrast, when coaches emphasize winning over skill development and criticize or punish players for bad plays, children lose interest and stop playing (Bailey & Rasmussen, 1996; Smith & Smoll, 1996). When adolescents find sports too stressful, they often get "burned out": they lose interest and quit (Raedeke & Smith, 2004). As long as adults promote positive, achievement-oriented values and value ethical behaviour, sport can even influence moral development (Lee, Whitehead, Ntoumanis, & Hatzigeorgiadis, 2008). Many youth sports organizations provide guidelines for players, coaches, and parents so that children will enjoy participating. The Canadian Soccer Association has developed guidelines for fair play with codes for players, coaches, and parents—setting out for each group the principles by which they should abide, in order to foster fairness in play and in practice (ThinkFirst Foundation of Canada, n.d.). The Coaching Association of Canada (CAC) encourages parents to look for positive coaching principles in those leading their children's sports. According to the CAC, a good coach is a good communicator who understands children's minds and who tailors instructions appropriately (LeBlanc, 1996). When coaches (and parents) follow such principles, players almost certainly have fun and continue to play the sport. Everyone involved needs to remember that children play games for recreation, which means they should have fun!

Q&A ANSWER 5.3
No. At eight months of age, it is too early for Tyler to show a consistent preference for one hand. They need to wait; by 13 to 15 months, they should have a much better idea whether Tyler will be left-handed.

✓ Check Your Learning

RECALL Describe the skills that infants must master to be able to walk.

How do fine-motor skills improve with age?

INTERPRET What are the pros and cons of children and adolescents participating in organized sports?

APPLY Describe how participation in sports illustrates connection between motor, cognitive, and social development.

UNIFYING THEMES Active Children

Each module in this chapter touched on the theme that *children influence their own development*. That is, repeatedly we saw that infants are extremely well equipped to interpret and explore their environments themselves. In Module 5.1, we saw that most sensory systems function quite well in the first year, providing infants with accurate raw data to interpret. In Module 5.2, we learned that attentional skills originate in infancy; through habituation, infants ignore some stimuli and attend to others. Finally, in Module 5.3, we discovered that locomotor and fine-motor skills improve rapidly in infancy; by the first birthday, infants can move independently and handle objects skillfully. Collectively, these accomplishments prepare infants extraordinarily well to explore their world and make sense of it.

See for Yourself

To see the origins of attention, you need a baby and a small bell. A one- to five-month-old is probably best because babies at this age can't move around on their own, so they won't wander away. As always, be ethical: Gain the parent or guardian's permission first, and consider the child's assent (mentioned in Chapter 1). A baby cannot speak, but any sign of distress should be taken as dissent on the part of the child and you should stop the task. While the infant is awake, place her on her back. Then move behind the baby's head (out of sight) and ring the bell a few times. You don't need to ring the bell loudly—a moderate volume will do. You should see the orienting response described on page 172: The baby will open her eyes wide and perhaps try to turn in the direction of the sound. Every two or three minutes, ring the bell again. You should see the baby respond less intensely each time until, finally, she ignores the bell completely. Attention in action! See for yourself!

Resources

For more information about ...

infant development in general, try Slater, Lewis, Anzures, and Lee's *Introduction to Infant Development-Canadian Edition* (Oxford University Press, 2011). It has chapters on perceptual development and motor development that examine similar issues to the information given here, but in a bit more depth.

the Infant Developmental Milestones Study, visit the study website at the University of Manitoba: **http://home .cc.umanitoba.ca/~eaton/infant-developmental-milestones.htm.**

ADHD, visit this website, maintained by the U.S. National Institute of Mental Health: **www.nimh.nih.gov/ health/topics/attention-deficit-hyperactivity-disorder-adhd/index .shtml.**

Or this site, maintained by Mental Health Canada:

www.mentalhealthcanada.com/ConditionsandDisordersDetail .asp?lang=e&category=60.

Key Terms

Summary

5.1 Basic Sensory and Perceptual Processes

1. Smell, Taste, and Touch

Newborns are able to smell and can recognize their mother's odour; they can also taste, preferring sweet substances and responding negatively to bitter and sour tastes. Infants respond to touch. Judging from their responses to painful stimuli, which are similar to those of older children, we know they experience pain.

2. Hearing

Babies can hear, although they are less sensitive to higher- and lower-pitched sounds than are adults. Babies can distinguish different sounds (both from language and music).

3. Seeing

A newborn's visual acuity is relatively poor, but one-year-olds can see as well as adults with normal vision. Colour vision develops as different sets of cones begin to function; by three or four months of age, children can see colour as well as adults can.

4. Integrating Sensory Information

Infants begin to integrate information from different senses (e.g., sight and sound, sight and touch). Infants are often particularly attentive to information presented redundantly to multiple senses.

5.2 Complex Perceptual and Attentional Processes

1. Perceiving Objects

Infants use motion, colour, texture, and edges to distinguish objects. By about four months, infants have begun to master size, brightness, shape, and colour constancy. Infants first perceive depth by means of kinetic cues, including visual expansion and motion parallax. Later, they use retinal disparity and pictorial cues (linear perspective, texture gradient, relative size, interposition) to judge depth. Infants perceive faces early in the first year. Experience leads infants to fine-tune their facial template so that it resembles the faces they see most often.

2. Attention

Attention includes the orienting and alerting networks, which function well in infancy, and the executive network, which develops more slowly. Teachers and parents can teach young children strategies for paying attention more effectively.

3. Attention Deficit Hyperactivity Disorder

Children with ADHD are typically hyperactive, inattentive, and impulsive. They sometimes have conduct problems and do poorly in school. The most effective approach to ADHD appears to be a combination of medication with psychosocial treatment.

5.3 Motor Development

1. Locomotion

Infants progress through a sequence of motor milestones during the first year, culminating in walking a few months after the first birthday. Like most motor skills, learning to walk involves differentiation of individual skills, such as maintaining balance and stepping on alternate legs, and then integrating these skills into a coherent whole. This differentiation and integration of skills is central to the dynamic systems theory of motor development. Experience can accelerate specific motor skills.

2. Fine-Motor Skills

Infants first use only one hand at a time, then both hands independently, then both hands in common actions, and finally both hands in different actions with a common purpose.

Most people are right-handed, a preference that emerges after the first birthday and becomes well established during the preschool years. Handedness is influenced by heredity and environment.

3. Physical Fitness

Although children report spending much time being physically active, in fact, fewer than half of North American school children meet all standards for physical fitness. Part of the explanation for the lack of fitness is inadequate physical education in school. Screen time may also contribute. Experts recommend that physical education in schools be more frequent and more oriented toward developing patterns of lifetime exercise. Families can become more active, thereby encouraging children's fitness.

Participating in sports can promote motor, cognitive, and social development. Adult coaches can often help children to improve their skills, but they sometimes overemphasize competition. Children sometimes quit playing when coaches emphasize winning over skill development.

Test Yourself

1. Newborns prefer _____tasting substances.

2. Infants can best hear sounds pitched _____.

3. If an infant does not respond to his or her name by _____months, this may be a sign of hearing impairment.

4. By three or four months of age, infants' colour perception is similar to that of adults, including the fact that infants see the spectrum as representing different _____of colour.

5. According to _____, infants are particularly sensitive to amodal information that is presented in more than one sensory system simultaneously.

6. Infants use many cues to object unity, including common motion, colour, _____, and aligned edges.

7. Infants use kinetic cues to judge depth, including visual expansion and _____.

8. Between three and nine months of age, face processing becomes _____.

9. When infants encounter an unfamiliar stimulus, they often show a(n) _____in which they startle, they stare at the stimulus, and their heart rate changes.

10. The three defining symptoms of attention deficit hyperactivity disorder include hyperactivity, inattention, and _____.

11. Maintaining an upright posture is particularly challenging for infants because their body _____.

12. _____refers to breaking down a complex motor skill into its component parts.

13. Four-month-olds use both hands to explore an object, but the two hands _____.

14. By their _____birthday, most children show a preference for one hand over the other (and for most of them, it is the right hand).

15. Children and adolescents often drop out of organized sports when _____.

Answers: (1) sweet; (2) in the range of human voices; (3) eight or nine; (4) categories; (5) intersensory redundancy theory; (6) texture; (7) motion parallax; (8) more finely tuned; (9) orienting response; (10) impulsivity; (11) shape makes them top-heavy; (12) Differentiation; (13) are not well coordinated; each acts as if it has a mind of its own; (14) first; (15) coaches emphasize winning over skill development and participation.

6

Theories of Cognitive Development

Contrastwerkstatt/Fotolia

Setting the Stage: Piaget's Theory

Modern Theories of Cognitive Development

Understanding in Core Domains

On the TV show *Family Guy*, Stewie is a one-year-old who can't stand his mother (Stewie: "Hey, mother, I come bearing a gift. I'll give you a hint. It's in my diaper and it's not a toaster.") and hopes to dominate the world. Much of the humour, of course, turns on the idea that babies are capable of sophisticated thinking—they just can't express it. Of course, few adults would really attribute such advanced thinking skills to a baby. But what thoughts *do* lurk in the mind of an infant who is not yet speaking? And how do an infant's fledgling thoughts blossom into the powerful reasoning skills that older children, adolescents, and adults use daily? In other words, how does thinking change as children develop, and why do these changes take place?

For many years, the best answers to these questions came from the theory proposed by Jean Piaget that was mentioned in **Module 1.2**, which we'll look at in more detail in **Module 6.1**. In **Module 6.2**, we'll examine some of the modern theories that guide today's research on children's thinking. In **Module 6.3**, we'll see how children acquire knowledge of objects, living things, and people.

6.1 Setting the Stage: Piaget's Theory

OUTLINE

Basic Principles of Piaget's Theory

Stages of Cognitive Development

Piaget's Contributions to Child Development

LEARNING OBJECTIVES

1. What are the basic principles of Piaget's theory of cognitive development?

2. How does thinking change as children move through Piaget's four stages of development?

3. What are the lasting contributions of Piaget's theory? What are some of its shortcomings?

When Ethan, an energetic two-and-a-half-year-old, saw a monarch butterfly for the first time, his mother, Kat, told him, "Butterfly, butterfly; that's a butterfly, Ethan." A few minutes later, a zebra swallowtail landed on a nearby bush, and Ethan shouted in excitement, "Butterfly, Mama, butterfly!" A bit later, a moth flew out of another bush; with even greater excitement in his voice, Ethan shouted, "Butterfly, Mama, more butterfly!" As Kat was telling Ethan, "No, honey, that's a moth, not a butterfly," she marvelled at how rapidly Ethan seemed to grasp new concepts with so little direction from her. How was this possible?

For much of the twentieth century, scientists would have answered Kat's question by referring to Jean Piaget's theory. Piaget was trained as a biologist, but he developed a keen interest in epistemology, the branch of philosophy dealing with the nature and origins of knowledge. He decided to investigate the origins of knowledge not as philosophers had—through discussion and debate—but by doing experiments with children.

Because Piaget's theory led the way to all modern theories of cognitive development, it's a good introduction to the study of children's thinking. We'll first consider some basic principles of the theory and how they explain why Ethan understands as quickly as he does. Then we'll look at Piaget's stages of development, and end the module by examining the enduring contributions of Piaget's work to child-development science.

Raise a cyber child and discover the world of parenthood at...

My **Virtual** Child

Basic Principles of Piaget's Theory

Piaget believed that children are naturally curious. Children want to make sense out of their experiences and, in the process, construct their understanding of the world. For Piaget, children at all ages are like scientists in that they create theories about how the world works. Of course, children's theories are often incomplete and sometimes incorrect. Nevertheless, theories are valuable to the child because they make the world seem more predictable.

In using their theories to make sense of what's going on around them, children often have new experiences that are readily understood within the context of these theories. **According to Piaget,** *assimilation* **occurs when new experiences are readily incorporated into a child's existing theories.** Imagine an infant like the one in the photo, who knows that the family dog barks and often licks her face. When she has the same experience at a relative's house, this makes sense because it fits her simple theory of dogs. Thus, understanding the novel dog's behaviour represents assimilation. But sometimes theories are incomplete or incorrect, causing children to have unexpected experiences. **For Piaget,** *accommodation* **occurs when a child's theories are modified based on experience.** The baby with a theory of dogs is surprised the first time she encounters a cat—it resembles a dog but meows instead of barking and rubs up against her instead of licking. Revising her theory to include this new kind of animal illustrates accommodation.

This infant's "theory of dogs" includes the facts that dogs are friendly and like licking people's faces.

Assimilation and accommodation are illustrated in the vignette at the beginning of the module. Piaget would say that when Kat named the monarch butterfly for Ethan, he formed a simple theory, something like "butterflies are bugs with big wings." The second butterfly differed in colour but was still a bug with big wings, so it was readily assimilated into Ethan's new theory of butterflies. However, when Ethan referred to the moth as a butterfly, Kat corrected him. Presumably, Ethan was then forced to accommodate this new experience. The result was that he changed his theory of butterflies to make it more precise; the new theory might be something like "butterflies are bugs with thin bodies and big, colourful wings." He also created a new theory, something like "a moth is a bug with a bigger body and plain wings."

In this example, assimilation and accommodation involve ideas, but these processes begin much earlier, in a young baby's actions. For example, a baby who can grasp a ball soon discovers that she can grasp blocks, rattles, and other small objects; extending grasping to new objects illustrates assimilation. When she discovers that some objects cannot be grasped unless she uses two hands, this illustrates accommodation: Her revised "theory of grasping" now distinguishes objects that can be grasped with one hand from those that require two hands.

Assimilation and accommodation are usually in balance, or equilibrium. That is, children find they can readily assimilate most experiences into their existing theories, but occasionally they need to accommodate their theories to adjust to new experiences. This balance between assimilation and accommodation is illustrated both by the baby's theories of small animals and by Ethan's understanding of butterflies.

Periodically, however, the balance is upset and a state of disequilibrium results. Children discover that their current theories are not adequate because they are spending much more time accommodating than assimilating. **When disequilibrium occurs, children** reorganize their theories to return to a state of equilibrium, a process that Piaget called *equilibration*. To restore the balance, current but now-outmoded ways of thinking are replaced by a qualitatively different, more advanced theory.

In Piaget's theory, cognitive development driven by equilibration results in the formation of mental structures called *schemas* **(or** *schemata*)**.** Piaget used the term "schema" to refer to thought—to cognitive structures (Piaget & Inhelder, 1969). Schemas are not static—they do not stay the same once formed but are active, continually changing, and developing. The integration of these mental structures allows organization of information into a coherent whole. As Piaget himself put it: "Every schema is thus coordinated with all the other schemata … [in] a system of mutual implications and interconnected meanings" (1952, p. 7).

Returning to the metaphor of the child as a scientist, sometimes scientists find that a theory contains critical flaws. When this occurs, they can't simply revise; they must create a new theory that draws upon the older theory but is fundamentally different. For example, when the astronomer Copernicus realized that the Earth-centred theory of the solar system was wrong, he retained the concept of a central object but proposed that it was the Sun, a fundamental change in the theory. In much the same way, children periodically reach a point when their current theories seem to be wrong much of the time, so they abandon these theories in favour of more advanced ways of thinking about their physical and social worlds.

According to Piaget, these revolutionary changes in thought occur three times over the life span, at approximately two, seven, and 11 years of age. This divides cognitive development into four stages: the *sensorimotor stage* (birth to age two, encompassing infancy); the *preoperational stage* (age two to six, encompassing preschool and early elementary school); the *concrete operational stage* (age seven to 11, encompassing middle and late elementary school); and the *formal operational stage* (age 11 and up, encompassing adolescence and adulthood).

Piaget held that all children go through all four stages and in exactly this sequence. For example, sensorimotor thinking should always lead to preoperational thinking; a child cannot "skip" preoperational thinking and move directly from sensorimotor to concrete operational thought. However, the ages listed are only approximate: Some youngsters were thought to move through the stages more rapidly than others, depending on their ability and their experience. In the next section, we'll look more closely at each stage.

Stages of Cognitive Development

Just as you can recognize a McDonald's restaurant by the golden arches and Nike shoes by the "swoosh," each of Piaget's stages is marked by a distinctive way of thinking about and understanding the world. In the next few pages, we'll learn about these unique trademarks or characteristics of Piaget's stages.

THE SENSORIMOTOR STAGE.   We know from Chapter 5 that infants' perceptual and motor skills improve quickly. Piaget proposed that these rapidly changing perceptual and motor skills in the first two years of life form a distinct phase in human development: **The** *sensorimotor stage* **spans birth to two years old, a period during which the infant progresses from simple reflex actions to symbolic processing.** In the twenty-four months of this stage, infants' thinking progresses remarkably along three important fronts.

ADAPTING TO AND EXPLORING THE ENVIRONMENT.   Newborns respond reflexively to many stimuli, but between one and four months reflexes are first modified by experience. An infant may inadvertently touch his lips with his thumb, which leads to

Between four and eight months, infants eagerly explore new objects.

Oksana Kuzmina/Fotolia

sucking and the pleasing sensations associated with sucking. Later, the infant tries to recreate these sensations by guiding his thumb to his mouth. Sucking no longer occurs only reflexively when a mother places a nipple at the infant's mouth; instead, the infant can initiate sucking by himself.

Between four and eight months, the infant shows greater interest in the world, paying far more attention to objects. For example, the infant shown in the photo accidentally shook a new rattle. Hearing the interesting noise, the infant grasped the rattle again, tried to shake it, and expressed great pleasure at the sound that resulted. This sequence was repeated several times.

At about eight months of age infants reach a watershed: the onset of deliberate, intentional behaviour. For the first time, the "means" and "ends" of activities are distinct. If, for example, a father places his hand in front of a toy, an infant will move the father's hand to be able to play with the toy. "Moving the hand" is the means to achieve the goal of "grasping the toy." Using one action as a means to achieve an end is the first indication of purposeful, goal-directed behaviour during infancy.

Beginning at about 12 months, infants become active experimenters. An infant may deliberately shake different objects, trying to discover which ones produce sounds, or may decide to drop different objects to see what happens. As a result, the infant discovers that stuffed animals land quietly, whereas bigger toys often make a more satisfying "clunk" when they hit the ground. These actions represent a significant extension of intentional behaviour. Now babies repeat actions with different objects solely for the purpose of seeing what happens.

UNDERSTANDING OBJECTS.   The world is filled with animate objects, such as dogs, spiders, and college students, as well as inanimate objects, such as cheeseburgers, socks, and this text. But they all share a fundamental property—they exist independently of our actions and thoughts concerning them. Much as we may dislike spiders, they still exist when we close our eyes or wish they would go away. **Understanding that objects exist independently is called** *object permanence.* Piaget made the astonishing claim that infants lacked this understanding for much of the first year. That is, he proposed that an infant's understanding of objects could be summarized as "out of sight, out of mind." For infants, objects are ephemeral, existing when in sight and no longer existing when out of sight.

The photo illustrates the sort of research that led Piaget to conclude that infants have little understanding of objects. If a tempting object such as an attractive toy is placed in front of a four- to eight-month-old, the infant will probably reach for and grasp the object. If, however, the object is then hidden by a barrier, as in the photo, or covered with a cloth, the infant will neither reach nor search. Instead, like the baby in the photo, the infant seems to have lost all interest in the object, as if the now hidden object no longer exists. To paraphrase the familiar saying: "Out of sight, out of existence!"

According to Piaget, children under eight months old have a limited understanding of objects: They believe that when objects are out of sight, they no longer exist.

Doug Goodman/Science Source

At about eight months, infants search for an object that an experimenter has covered with a cloth. In fact, many eight- to 12-month-olds love to play this game—an adult covers the object and the infant sweeps away the cover, laughing and smiling all the while! But, despite this accomplishment, Piaget believed that their understanding of object permanence is incomplete. At this age, when infants see an object hidden under one container several times, then see it hidden under a second container, they usually look for the toy under the first container. This mistake is known as the "A-not-B error" (because babies reach for an object at the first location, A, not the second location, B), and Piaget claimed that it shows infants' limited understanding of objects: Infants do not distinguish the object from the actions they use to locate it, such as reaching for a particular container. According to Piaget, infants do not have full understanding of object permanence until about 18 months.

Richard Mittleman/Alamy Stock Photo

USING SYMBOLS.   By 18 months, most infants have begun to talk and gesture, evidence of the emerging capacity to use symbols. Words and gestures are symbols that stand for something else. When the infant in the photo waves, this is just as effective and symbolic as saying "Goodbye" to bid farewell. Children also begin to engage in pretend play, another use of symbols. A 20-month-old may move her hand back and forth in front of her mouth, pretending to brush her teeth.

In just two years, the infant progresses from reflexive responding to actively exploring the world, understanding objects, and using symbols. These achievements are remarkable and set the stage for preoperational thinking, which we'll examine next.

By 18 months, most toddlers will use simple gestures, which is evidence of their emerging ability to use symbols.

THE PREOPERATIONAL STAGE.   With the power of symbols, the child crosses the hurdle into preoperational thinking. **The** *preoperational stage,* **which spans ages two to seven, is marked by the child's use of symbols to represent objects and events.** Throughout this period, preschool children gradually become proficient at using common symbols such as words, gestures, graphs, maps, and models. Although preschool children's ability to use symbols represents a huge advance over sensorimotor thinking, their thinking remains quite limited compared to that of school-age children. Why? To answer this question, we need to look at some important characteristics of thought during the preoperational stage.

Preoperational children typically believe that others see the world—both literally and figuratively—exactly as they do. *Egocentrism* **refers to young children's difficulty in seeing the world from another's viewpoint.** When youngsters stubbornly cling to their own way, they are not simply being contrary. Rather, preoperational children do not comprehend that other people have different ideas and feelings.

Suppose, for example, you ask the preschooler in Figure 6-1 to select the image that shows how the objects on the table look to you. Most select the drawing on the far left, which shows how the objects look to the child, rather than the drawing on the far right—the correct choice. Preoperational youngsters evidently suppose that the mountains are seen the same way by all; they presume that theirs is the only view, rather than one of many conceivable views (Piaget & Inhelder, 1956).

Egocentrism sometimes leads preoperational youngsters to attribute their own thoughts and feelings to others. **Preoperational children sometimes credit inanimate objects with life and lifelike properties, a phenomenon known as** *animism* (Piaget, 1929). A three-and-a-half-year-old known to author Robert Kail (RK) illustrated preoperational animism in a conversation she had with Kail one rainy day:

Christine:	The sun is sad today.
RK:	Why?
Christine:	Because it's cloudy. He can't shine. And he can't see me!

Figure 6-1 A perspective-taking task, in which preoperational children respond egocentrically.

RK:	What about your trike. Is it happy?
Christine:	No. He's sad, too.
RK:	Why is that?
Christine:	'Cause I can't ride him. And because he's all alone in the garage.

Caught up in her egocentrism, Christine believes that objects like the sun and her tricycle think and feel as she does.

Children in the preoperational stage also have the psychological equivalent of tunnel vision: They often concentrate on one aspect of a problem but ignore other equally relevant aspects. *Centration* **is Piaget's term for this narrowly focused thought that characterizes preoperational youngsters.** Piaget demonstrated centration in his experiments involving conservation, which tested when children realize that important characteristics of objects (or sets of objects) stay the same despite changes in their physical appearance.

A typical conservation problem, involving conservation of liquid quantity, is shown in the photos below. Children are shown identical glasses filled with the same amount of juice. After children agree that the two glasses have the same amount, juice is poured from one glass into a taller, thinner glass. The juice looks different in the tall, thin glass—it rises higher—but of course the amount is unchanged. Nevertheless, a preoperational child typically claims that the tall, thin glass has more juice than the original glass. (And, if the juice is poured into a wider glass, they believe it has less.)

What is happening here? According to Piaget, preoperational children centre on the level of the juice in the glass. If the juice is higher after it is poured, preoperational children believe that there must be more juice now than before. Because preoperational thinking is centred, these youngsters ignore the fact that the change in the level of the juice is always accompanied by a change in the diameter of the glass.

Centration and egocentrism are major limits to preoperational children's thinking, but these are overcome in the next stage, the concrete operational stage.

THE CONCRETE OPERATIONAL STAGE. During the early elementary-school years, children enter a new stage of cognitive development that is distinctly more adult-like and much less child-like. **In the** *concrete operational stage,* **which spans ages**

Spencer Grant/Science Source

In the conservation task, preparational children believe that the tall, thin glass has more liquid, an error reflecting the centred thought that is common in children at this stage.

seven to 11, children begin to use mental operations to solve problems and to reason. What are the mental operations that are so essential to concrete operational thinking? *Mental operations* **are strategies and rules that make thinking more systematic and more powerful.** Some mental operations apply to numbers. For example, addition, subtraction, multiplication, and division are familiar arithmetic operations that concrete operational children use. Other mental operations apply to categories of objects. For example, classes can be added (mothers + fathers = parents) and subtracted (parents − mothers = fathers). Still other mental operations apply to spatial relations among objects. For example, if point A is near both points B and C, then points B and C must be close to each other also.

Another important property of mental operations is that they can be reversed. Each operation has an inverse that can "undo" or reverse the effect of an operation. If you start with five and add three, you get eight; by subtracting three from eight, you reverse your steps and return to five. For Piaget, reversibility of this sort applied to all mental operations. Concrete operational children are able to reverse their thinking in a way that preoperational youngsters cannot. In fact, reversible mental operations are part of why concrete operational children pass the conservation task shown in the photos on page 194: Concrete operational thinkers understand that if the transformation were reversed (in this case, the juice was poured back into the original container), the objects would be identical.

Concrete operational thinking is much more powerful than preoperational thinking. Remember that preoperational children are egocentric (believing that others see the world as they do) and centred in their thinking; neither of these limitations applies to children in the concrete operational stage. But concrete operational thinking has its own shortcomings. As the name implies, concrete operational thinking is limited to the tangible and real, to the here and now. The concrete operational youngster takes "an earthbound, concrete, practical-minded sort of problem-solving approach, one that persistently fixates on the perceptible and inferable reality right there in front of him" (Flavell, 1985, p. 98). That is, thinking abstractly and hypothetically is beyond the ability of concrete operational thinkers.

THE FORMAL OPERATIONAL STAGE. In the *formal operational stage,* **which extends from roughly age 11 into adulthood, children and adolescents apply mental operations to abstract entities; they think hypothetically and reason deductively.** Freed from the concrete and the real, adolescents explore the possible—what might be and what could be.

Unlike reality-oriented concrete operational children, formal operational thinkers understand that reality is not the only possibility. They can envision alternative realities and examine their consequences. For example, ask a concrete operational child, "What would happen if gravity meant that objects floated up?" or "What would happen if men gave birth?" and you're likely to get a confused or even irritated look and comments like, "It doesn't—they fall" or "They don't—women have babies." Reality is the foundation of concrete operational thinking. In contrast, formal operational adolescents use hypothetical reasoning to probe the implications of fundamental changes in physical or biological laws.

Formal operations also allow adolescents to take a more sophisticated approach to problem solving. Formal operational thinkers can solve problems by creating hypotheses (sets of possibilities) and testing them. Piaget (Inhelder & Piaget, 1958) showed this aspect of adolescent thinking by presenting children and adolescents with several flasks, each containing what appeared to be the same clear liquid. They were told that one

QUESTION 6.1
When three-year-old Jamila talks on the phone, she often replies to questions by nodding her head. Jamila's dad has explained that her listeners can't see her—that she needs to say "Yes" or "No." But Jamila invariably returns to head nodding. How would Jean Piaget explain this behaviour to Jamila's dad? *(Answer is on page 199.)*

Curve/Vetta/Getty Images

Children in the concrete operational stage often solve problems by "plunging right in" instead of thinking hypothetically to come up with a well-defined set of solutions to a problem.

combination of the clear liquids would produce a blue liquid and were asked to determine the necessary combination.

A typical concrete operational youngster, like the ones in the photo, plunges right in, mixing liquids from different flasks haphazardly. In contrast, formal operational adolescents understand that the key is setting up the problem in abstract, hypothetical terms. The problem is not really about pouring liquids but about forming hypotheses about different combinations of liquids and testing them systematically. A teenager might mix liquid from the first flask with liquids from each of the other flasks. If none of these combinations produces a blue liquid, he or she might mix the liquid in the second flask with each of the remaining liquids. A formal operational thinker would continue in this manner until he or she found the critical pair that produces the blue liquid.

Because adolescents' thinking is not concerned solely with reality, they are also better able to reason logically from premises and draw appropriate conclusions. **The ability to draw appropriate conclusions from facts is known as** *deductive reasoning.* Suppose we tell a person the following two premises:

1. If you hit a glass with a hammer, the glass will break.
2. Mary hit a glass with a hammer.

The correct conclusion, following the two premises, is that "the glass broke," a conclusion that formal operational adolescents will reach. Concrete operational youngsters, too, will sometimes reach this conclusion but based on their experience and not because the conclusion is logically necessary. To see the difference, imagine that the two facts are now as follows:

1. If you hit a glass with a feather, the glass will break.
2. Mary hit a glass with a feather.

The conclusion "the glass broke" follows from these two statements just as logically as it did from the first pair. In this instance, however, the conclusion is counterfactual—it goes against what experience tells us is really true. Concrete operational 10-year-olds resist reaching conclusions that are counter to known facts; they reach conclusions based on their knowledge of the world. In contrast, formal operational 15-year-olds often reach counterfactual conclusions. They understand that these problems are about abstract entities that need not correspond to real-world relations.

Hypothetical reasoning and deductive reasoning are powerful tools for formal operational thinkers. In fact, we can characterize this power by paraphrasing the quotation about concrete operational thinking that appears on page 195: "Formal operational youth take an abstract, hypothetical approach to problem solving; they are not constrained by the reality that is staring them in the face but are open to different possibilities and alternatives." The ability to ponder different alternatives makes possible the experimentation with lifestyles and values that occurs in adolescence, topics we'll encounter on several occasions later in this text.

With the achievement of formal operations, qualitative change in cognitive development is over in Piaget's theory. Adolescents and adults acquire more knowledge as they grow older, but in Piaget's view their fundamental way of thinking remains unchanged. Table 6-1 summarizes Piaget's description of cognitive changes between birth and adulthood.

TABLE 6-1

PIAGET'S FOUR STAGES OF COGNITIVE DEVELOPMENT

Stage	Approximate Age	Characteristics
Sensorimotor	Birth to 2 years	Infants' knowledge of the world is based on senses and motor skills. By the end of the period, infants use mental representations and understand object permanence.
Preoperational	2 to 6 years	Children learn how to use symbols such as words and numbers to represent aspects of the world, but they relate to the world only through their own perspective. Thinking is centred.
Concrete operational	7 to 11 years	Children understand and apply logical operations to experiences, provided they are focused on the here and now.
Formal operational	Adolescence and beyond	Adolescents or adults think abstractly, speculate on hypothetical situations, and reason deductively about what may be possible.

Piaget's Contributions to Child Development

Piaget's theory dominated child-development research and theory for much of the twentieth century. As one expert phrased it, "Many of Piaget's contributions have become so much a part of the way we view cognitive development nowadays that they are virtually invisible" (Flavell, 1996, p. 202). Three of these contributions are worth emphasizing (Brainerd, 1996; Siegler & Ellis, 1996):

- *The study of cognitive development itself*. Before Piaget, child-development scientists paid little attention to cognitive development. Piaget showed why cognitive processes are central to development and offered some methods that could be used to study them.

- *A new view of children.* **Piaget emphasized** *constructivism,* **the view that children are active participants in their own development who systematically construct ever more sophisticated understandings of their worlds.** This view now pervades thinking about children (so much so that it's one of the themes in this book), but it began with Piaget.

- *Fascinating, often counterintuitive discoveries.* One reason why Piaget's work attracted so much attention is that many of the findings were completely unexpected and became puzzles that child-development researchers couldn't resist trying to solve. For example, researchers have tested thousands of youngsters trying to understand the "A-not-B" error (page 193) and why children fail the conservation task (page 194). In the words of one expert, "Piaget had the greenest thumb ever for unearthing fascinating and significant developmental progressions" (Flavell, 1996, p. 202).

 ### Children's Lives

Teaching Practices That Foster Cognitive Growth: Educational Applications of Piaget's Theory

Piaget's contributions extend beyond research. In fact, his view of cognitive development has some straightforward implications for teaching practices that promote cognitive growth:

- *Facilitate rather than direct children's learning.* Cognitive growth occurs as children construct their own understanding of the world, so the teacher's role is to create environments where children can discover for themselves how the world works. A teacher shouldn't simply try to tell children how addition and subtraction are complementary but instead should provide children with materials that allow them to discover the complementarity themselves.

- *Recognize individual differences when teaching.* Cognitive skills develop at different rates in different children. Consequently, instruction geared to an entire class is often boring for some students and much too challenging for others. *Instruction is most effective when it is tailored to individual students.* For some students in a classroom, the goal of instruction about addition may be to master basic facts; for others, it may be to learn about properties such as commutativity and associativity.

- *Be sensitive to children's readiness to learn.* Children profit from experience only when they can interpret this experience with their current cognitive structures. It follows then that *the best teaching experiences are slightly ahead of the children's current level of thinking.* As a youngster begins to master basic addition, the teacher should not jump right to subtraction, but rather first go to slightly more difficult addition problems.

- *Emphasize exploration and interaction.* Cognitive growth can be particularly rapid when children discover inconsistencies and errors in their own thinking (Legare, Gelman, & Wellman, 2010). *Teachers should therefore encourage children to look at the consistency of their thinking but then let children take the lead in sorting out the inconsistencies.* If a child is making mistakes in borrowing on subtraction problems, a teacher shouldn't correct the error directly but should encourage the child to look at a large number of these errors to discover what he or she is doing wrong.

WEAKNESSES OF PIAGET'S THEORY.   Although Piaget's contributions to child development are legendary, some elements of his theory have held up better than others (Miller, 2011; Newcombe, 2013; Siegler & Alibali, 2005).

- *Piaget's theory underestimates cognitive competence in infants and young children and overestimates cognitive competence in adolescents.* In Piaget's theory, cognitive development is steady in early childhood but not particularly rapid. In contrast, a main theme of modern child-development science is that of the extraordinarily competent infant and toddler. By using more sensitive tasks than Piaget's, modern investigators have shown that infants and toddlers are vastly more capable than expected based on Piaget's theory. For example, we'll see in Module 6.3 that infants have much greater understanding of objects than Piaget believed. Paradoxically, however, Piaget *overestimated* cognitive skill in adolescents, who often fail to reason according to formal operational principles and revert to less sophisticated reasoning. For example, we'll see in Module 7.2 that adolescents often let their beliefs bias their reasoning.

- *Piaget's theory is vague concerning processes and mechanisms of change.* Many of the key components of the theory, such as accommodation and assimilation, turned out to be too vague to test scientifically. Consequently, scientists abandoned them in favour of other cognitive processes that could be evaluated more readily and provide more convincing accounts of children's thinking.

- *Piaget's stage model does not account for variability in children's performance.* In Piaget's view, each stage of intellectual development has unique characteristics that leave their mark on everything a child does. Preoperational thinking is defined by egocentrism and centration; formal operational thinking is defined by abstract and hypothetical reasoning. Consequently, children's performance on different tasks should be very consistent. In fact, children's thinking falls far short of this consistency. A child's thinking may be sophisticated in some domains but naïve in others (Siegler, 1981). This inconsistency does not support Piaget's view that children's thinking should always reflect the distinctive imprint of their current stage of cognitive development. In other words, cognitive development is not as stage-like as Piaget believed.

- *Piaget's theory undervalues the influence of the sociocultural environment on cognitive development.* Returning to the metaphor of the child as scientist, Piaget describes the child as a lone scientist, constantly trying to figure out by herself how her theory coordinates with data and experience. In reality, a child's effort to understand her world is a far more social enterprise than Piaget described. Her growing understanding of the world is profoundly influenced by interactions with family members, peers, and teachers, and takes place against the backdrop of cultural values. Piaget's theory did not neglect these social and cultural forces entirely, but they are not prominent in the theory.

Because of the criticisms of Piaget's theory, many researchers have taken several different paths in studying cognitive development. In the next module, we'll look at three different approaches that are linked to Piaget's work.

 ANSWER 6.1
Piaget would reassure Jamila's dad that her behaviour is perfectly normal. Preschoolers usually believe that others see the world as they do, a phenomenon that Piaget called "egocentrism." In this case, because Jamila knows that she is nodding her head, she believes that others must know it, too.

 Check Your Learning

RECALL What are the stages of cognitive development in Piaget's theory? What are the defining characteristics of each?

Summarize the main shortcomings of Piaget's account of cognitive development.

INTERPRET Piaget championed the view that children participate actively in their own development. How do the sensorimotor child's contributions differ from those of the formal operational child?

APPLY Based on what you know about Piaget's theory, what would his position have been on the continuity-discontinuity issue, the argument about whether early aspects of development are related to later aspects?

 6.2 **Modern Theories of Cognitive Development**

OUTLINE

The Sociocultural Perspective: Vygotsky's Theory

Information Processing

Core-Knowledge Theories

LEARNING OBJECTIVES

1. In Vygotsky's sociocultural theory, how do adults and other people contribute to children's cognitive development?

2. According to information-processing psychologists, how does thinking change with development?

3. What naïve theories do children hold about physics, psychology, and biology?

Victoria, a four-year-old, loves solving jigsaw puzzles with her dad. She does the easy ones by herself. But she often has trouble with the harder ones, so her dad helps—he orients pieces correctly and reminds Victoria to look for edge pieces. Victoria may do 10 or 12 puzzles before she loses interest; then she delights in telling her mom, in great detail, about all the puzzles she solved. After these marathon puzzle sessions, Victoria's dad is often surprised that a child who is so sophisticated in her language skills struggles with the harder jigsaw puzzles.

Many theories have built on the foundation of Piaget's pioneering work. In this module, we'll look at three different theoretical approaches, each designed to take research in cognitive development beyond Piaget's theory. As we do, you'll learn more about Victoria's cognitive and language skills.

The Sociocultural Perspective: Vygotsky's Theory

Child-development scientists often refer to child development as a journey that can proceed along many different paths. As we've seen, in Piaget's theory, children make the journey alone as they interact with the physical world. Other people (and culture in general) certainly influence the direction that children take, but the child is seen as a solitary adventurer-explorer boldly forging ahead.

In contrast, according to the *sociocultural perspective,* **children are products of their culture**: Children's cognitive development is brought about not only by social interaction, but it is inseparable from the cultural contexts in which children live. Cultural contexts organize cognitive development in several ways. First, culture often defines which cognitive activities are valued: In Western cultures youngsters are expected to learn to read but not to navigate using the stars (Gauvain & Munroe, 2012). Second, culture provides tools that shape the way children think (Gauvain & Munroe, 2009). The cognitive skills that children use to solve arithmetic problems, for example, depend on whether their culture provides an abacus, like the one in the photograph, or paper and pencil or a handheld calculator. Third, higher-level cultural practices help children to organize their knowledge and communicate it to others. For instance, in most North American schools, students are expected to think and work alone rather than collaborate (Matusov, Bell, & Rogoff, 2002). Thus, "culture penetrates human intellectual functioning and its development at many levels, and it does so through many organized individual and social practices" (Gauvain, 1998, p. 189).

One of the original—and still influential—sociocultural theories was proposed by Lev Vygotsky (1896–1934), the Russian psychologist described in Chapter 1. Vygotsky saw development as an apprenticeship in which children advance when they collaborate with others who are more skilled. Child development, according to Vygotsky (1978), is never a solitary journey. Instead, children always travel with others and usually progress most rapidly when they walk hand in hand with an expert partner. Of particular importance is attaining use of language, because then the child can engage in dialogues about culturally important tasks with the more experienced partner.

Isaiah Love/Fotolia

Sociocultural theories emphasize that cultures influence cognitive development by the tools that are available to support children's thinking, such as an abacus.

To Vygotsky and other sociocultural theorists, the social nature of cognitive development is captured in the concept of *intersubjectivity,* **which refers to mutual, shared understanding among participants in an activity.** When Victoria and her father solve puzzles together, they share an understanding of the goals of their activity and of their roles in solving the puzzles. This shared understanding allows Victoria and her dad to work together in complementary fashion on the puzzles. **Such interactions typify** *guided participation,* **in which cognitive growth results from children's involvement in structured activities with others who are more skilled than they.** Through guided participation, children learn from others how to connect new experiences and new skills with what they already know (Rogoff, 2003). Guided participation is shown when a child learns a new video game from a peer or an adolescent learns a new karate move from a partner.

Vygotsky died of tuberculosis when he was only 37 years old, so he never had the opportunity to formulate a complete theory of cognitive development like that of Piaget. Nevertheless, his ideas are influential because they fill some gaps in Piaget's account of cognitive development. Three of Vygotsky's most important contributions are the concepts of zone of proximal development, scaffolding, and private speech.

THE ZONE OF PROXIMAL DEVELOPMENT. Angela likes helping her 11-year-old son with his math homework, particularly when it includes word problems. Her son does most of the work, but Angela often gives him hints. For example, she might help him decide what arithmetic operations are required. When Angela's son tries to solve these problems by himself, he rarely succeeds. **The difference between what Angela's son can do with assistance and what he can do alone defines the** *zone of proximal development.* That is, the zone refers to the difference between the level of performance a child can achieve when working independently and the higher level of performance that is possible when working under the guidance of more skilled adults or peers (Daniels, 2011; Wertsch & Tulviste, 1992).

Think, for example, about a preschooler who is asked to clean her bedroom. She doesn't know where to begin. By structuring the task for the child—"Start by putting away your books, then your toys; then put your dirty clothes in the hamper"—an adult can help the child accomplish what she cannot do by herself. Similarly, the zone of proximal development explains why Victoria, in the module-opening vignette, solves difficult jigsaw puzzles with a bit of help from her dad. Just as training wheels help children learn to ride a bike by allowing them to concentrate on other aspects of bicycling, collaborators help children perform effectively by providing structure, hints, and reminders.

The idea of a zone of proximal development follows naturally from Vygotsky's basic premise that cognition develops first in a social setting and only gradually comes under the child's independent control. Understanding how the shift from social to individual learning occurs brings us to the second of Vygotsky's key contributions.

Experienced teachers often provide much direct instruction as children first encounter a task and then provide less instruction as children "catch on."

SCAFFOLDING. Have you ever had the good fortune to work with a master teacher, one who seemed to know exactly when to say the right thing to help you over an obstacle but otherwise let you work uninterrupted? *Scaffolding* **refers to a teaching style that matches the amount of assistance to the learner's needs.** Early in learning a new task, when a child knows little, teachers, like the one in the photo on the previous page, provide a lot of direct instruction. But as the child begins to catch on to the task, the teacher provides less instruction and only occasional reminders (Gauvain, 2001). The distinguished developmental psychologist Mary Wright, who founded a research preschool in the psychology department at the then University of Western Ontario, noted that teachers need to scaffold (rather than do the task for the child) as a necessary component to the child's learning to perform a task alone. Wright gave a simple example: When the children prepared to go outside in the winter, the preschool teachers did not dress the children in their snowsuits; they provided assistance. "The teacher helps the children, *never* [do] the children help the teacher. It is the children's job" to get ready themselves (Wright, 1983, p. 60). So the teacher might give help by getting a zipper started, but the child then does the zipping. Eventually, the child learns to align the ends of the zipper herself and to perform the complete process. Thus, in scaffolding, as the child becomes capable of doing more of the task herself, the amount of assistance decreases until eventually she performs the task completely.

We saw earlier how a parent helping a preschooler clean her room must provide detailed structure. As the child does the task more often, the parent needs to provide less structure. Similarly, when high-school students first try to do proofs in geometry, the teacher must lead them through each step; as the students begin to understand how proofs are done and can do more on their own, the teacher gradually provides less help.

Do parents worldwide scaffold their children's learning? If so, do they use similar methods? The Cultural Influences feature answers these questions.

Cultural Influences

How Do Parents in Different Cultures Scaffold Their Children's Learning?

Cross-cultural research by Barbara Rogoff and her colleagues (1993) suggests that parents and other adults in many cultures scaffold learning, but they do it in different ways. These researchers studied parents and one- to two-year-olds in four different settings: a medium-sized U.S. city, a small tribal village in India, a large city in Turkey, and a town in the highlands of Guatemala. In one part of the study, parents tried to get their toddlers to operate a novel toy (e.g., a wooden doll that danced when a string was pulled). No ground rules or guidelines concerning teaching were given; parents were free to be as direct or uninvolved as they wished.

What did parents do? In all four cultural settings, the vast majority attempted to scaffold their children's learning, either by dividing a difficult task into easier subtasks or by doing parts of the task themselves, particularly the more complicated parts. However, as the graphs in Figure 6-2 show, parents in different cultures scaffold in different ways. Turkish parents give the most verbal instruction and use some gestures (pointing, nodding, and shrugging). U.S. parents also use these methods but to slightly lesser degrees. Turkish and U.S. parents almost never touch (such as nudging a child's elbow) or gaze (use eye contact, such as winking or staring). Indian parents seem to use roughly equal amounts of speech, gesture, and touch or gaze to scaffold. Guatemalan parents also use all three techniques and, overall, Guatemalan parents provide the most scaffolding of the four cultures.

An interesting example from Canada comes from the work of Anne McKeough and her colleagues at the University of Calgary, who have investigated traditional storytelling as a basis for learning in Indigenous communities. While many cultures use narrative as a method of teaching, this form of transmission of culturally relevant knowledge is especially important to Indigenous people. Working with Indigenous peoples, McKeough et al. (2008) developed a "Story Teaching Programme," using lessons based on legends and stories of the Stoney/Nakota people and books written by Indigenous authors. McKeough et al. (2008) demonstrated that the scaffolding provided by adult storytelling—cognitive scaffolding, mnemonics (including graphics), and so on—increased children's literacy.

Evidently, parents worldwide try to simplify learning tasks for their children, but the methods that they use to scaffold learning vary across cultures.

Critical Thinking Questions: What might be the "best" ways in which to scaffold children's learning? How would these ways work for different kinds of tasks?

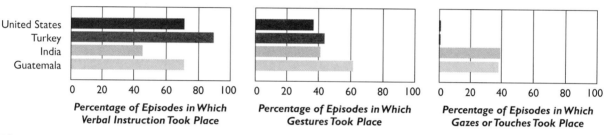

Figure 6-2 Different levels of scaffolding method use across cultures.
Based on Rogoff, B., Mistry, J., Goncu, A. & Mosier, C. (1993). Guided participation in cultural activity by toddlers and caregivers. *Monographs of the Society for Research in Child Development*, 58, Serial No. 236.

The defining characteristic of scaffolding—giving help but not more than is needed—clearly promotes learning (Cole, 2006). Youngsters do not learn readily when they are constantly told what to do or when they are simply left to struggle through a problem unaided. However, when teachers collaborate with them—allowing children to take on more and more of a task as they master its different elements—they learn more effectively (Murphy & Messer, 2000). Scaffolding is an important technique for transferring skills from others to the child, both in formal settings, such as schools, and in informal settings, such as the home or playground (Bernier, Carlson, & Whipple, 2010).

PRIVATE SPEECH. The little boy in the photo is talking to himself as he plays. **This behaviour demonstrates** *private speech,* **comments not directed to others but intended to help children regulate their own behaviour.** Vygotsky viewed private speech as an intermediate step toward self-regulation of cognitive skills (Fernyhough, 2010). At first, children's behaviour is regulated by speech directed at them by other people. When youngsters first try to control their own behaviour and thoughts without others present, they instruct themselves by speaking aloud. **Finally, as children gain ever greater skill, private speech becomes** *inner speech,* **Vygotsky's term for thought.** Thus, Vygotsky theorized that children's language use during tasks was not (as Piaget thought) egocentric and nonsocial but was in fact communicative—communicating with the self.

Young children often talk to themselves as they perform difficult tasks; this helps them control their own behaviour.

If children use private speech to help control their behaviour, then we should see children using it more often on difficult tasks than on easy tasks and more often after a mistake than after a correct response. These predictions are generally supported in research (Berk, 1992, 2003) that documents the power of language in helping children learn to control their own behaviour and thinking. Research by Robert Duncan from the University of Waterloo and Michael Pratt from Wilfrid Laurier University provides further support for Vygotsky's view of private speech. Duncan and Pratt (1997) videotaped preschool-aged children working on different tasks, such as a paper-folding craft. Tasks were either easy or difficult, and some of the tasks were repeated across three testing sessions. Children tried easy tasks and hard tasks, some of which became familiar to them with practice. Analysis of speech from the videotapes showed more private speech when children were working on new or difficult tasks and a decline in private speech with easier and more familiar tasks, thus supporting Vygotsky's theory (Duncan & Pratt, 1997). This work has been supported by more recent research from the UK, in which private speech was found to be used in this way across time, with different tasks, and in different contexts (Lidstone, Meins, & Fernyhough, 2011).

Vygotsky's view of cognitive development as an apprenticeship—collaboration between expert and novice—complements the Piagetian view of cognitive development described in Module 6.1. Also, like Piaget's theory, Vygotsky's perspective has several implications for helping children learn. We have already seen that a good teacher's main mission is to scaffold student's learning, not direct it. In other words, teachers should provide an environment that will allow students to learn on their own. This involves finding a middle ground: Students learn little when teachers provide too much instruction (e.g., "Here's how you do it and here's the right answer") or too little instruction ("Try to figure it out yourself"). Instead, a teacher needs to determine a child's current knowledge and provide the experience—in the form of a suggestion, question, or activity—that propels the child to more sophisticated understanding (Polman, 2004; Scrimsher & Tudge, 2003).

Perhaps even more important is Vygotsky's emphasis on learning as a cooperative activity in which students work together. Sometimes this collaboration takes the form of peer tutoring, in which students teach each other. Tutors often acquire a richer and deeper understanding of the topic they teach; tutees benefit, too, in part because teaching is one-on-one but also because tutees are more willing to tell a peer when an explanation is not clear. Another form of cooperative learning involves groups of students working together on projects (e.g., a group presentation) or to achieve common goals (e.g., deciding rules for a classroom). These activities help students to take responsibility for a project and to become good team players. Students also learn how to consider different viewpoints and how to resolve conflicts. Cooperative learning has benefits for students: They do learn—achievement scores increase (Rohrbeck, Ginsburg-Block, Fantuzzo, & Miller, 2003)—and cooperative learning improves students' self-concepts—students feel more competent, and they learn social skills such as how to negotiate, build consensus, and resolve conflicts (Ginsburg-Block, Rohrbeck, & Fantuzzo, 2006).

Information-Processing Theories

In Module 6.1, we saw that one criticism of Piaget's theory is that the mechanisms of change—accommodation, assimilation, and equilibration—were vague and difficult to study scientifically. Consequently, identifying mechanisms of growth has been a priority of child-development scientists, and in the 1960s, researchers first began to use computer systems as analogies to explain how thinking develops. **Just as computers consist of**

hardware and software that the computer runs, *information-processing theory* **proposes that human cognition consists of mental hardware and mental software.**
Figure 6-3 shows how information-processing psychologists use the computer analogy to examine human cognition. The mental hardware has three components: sensory memory, working memory, and long-term memory.

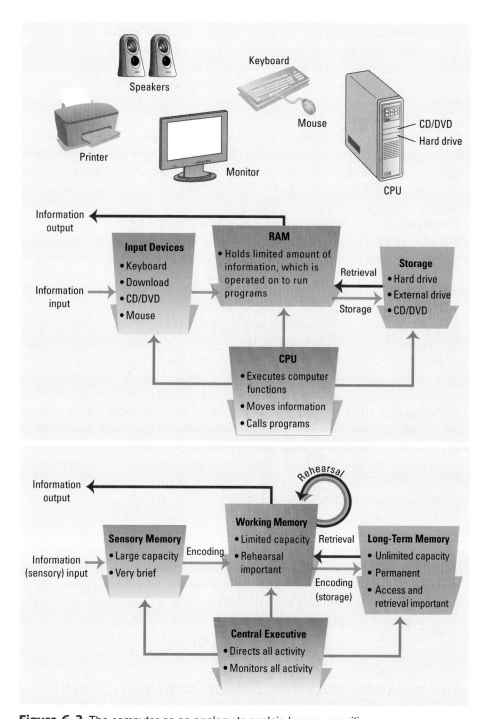

Figure 6-3 The computer as an analogy to explain human cognition.

Source: JOAN LITTLEFIELD; COOK, GREG. CHILD DEVELOPMENT: PRINCIPLES AND PERSPECTIVES, 2nd Edition © 2009. Reprinted and Electronically reproduced by permission of Pearson Education, Inc., Upper Saddle River, New Jersey

Sensory memory **is where information is held very briefly in raw, unanalyzed form (no longer than a few seconds).** For example, look at your hand as you clench your fist, rapidly open your hand (to extend your fingers), and then rapidly re-clench your fist. If you watch carefully, you can see an image of your fingers that lasts for a moment after you re-clench your hand. What you are seeing is an image stored in sensory memory.

Working memory **is the site of ongoing cognitive activity.** In a personal computer, RAM (random access memory) holds the software that we're using and stores data used by the software. In much the same way, working memory includes both ongoing cognitive processes and the information that they require (Baddeley, 2012). For example, as you read these sentences, part of working memory is allocated to the cognitive processes responsible for determining the meanings of individual words; working memory also briefly stores the results of these analyses while they are used by other cognitive processes to give meaning to sentences.

Long-term memory **is a limitless, permanent storehouse of knowledge of the world.** Long-term memory is like a computer's hard drive, a fairly permanent storehouse of programs and data. It includes facts (e.g., Terry Fox attempted to run across Canada), personal events (e.g., "I moved to Quebec in July 2014"), and skills (e.g., how to play the cello).

Information in long-term memory is rarely forgotten, though it is sometimes hard to access. For example, do you remember the name of the Canadian author, feminist, and social activist who was a member of the Famous Five group of women who petitioned for women to be recognized as "persons"? If her name doesn't come to mind, look at this list:

Thatcher   Wynne   McClung   Wollstonecraft

Now do you know the answer? (If not, it appears before the Summary Table on page 210.) Just as books are sometimes misplaced in a library, you sometimes cannot find a fact in long-term memory. Given a list of names, though, you can go directly to the location in long-term memory associated with each name and determine which one is the famed social activist.

Coordinating all these activities is the *central executive* **(also called** *executive functioning*)**, which refers to the executive network of attention described in Module 5.2 and resembles a computer's operating system** (e.g., Windows 10 or Linux). Executive function includes three related components: inhibiting inappropriate thoughts and actions; shifting from one action, thought, or task to another; and updating the contents of working memory (Bull & Lee, 2014).

When children are thinking—be it reading, finding their way to a friend's house, or deciding what to eat for dessert—the system in Figure 6-3 is involved, usually in conjunction with specialized strategies that are designed for particular tasks. Reading, for example, calls upon strategies for identifying sounds associated with specific letters; way-finding calls upon strategies for recognizing familiar landmarks as a way to verify that you are on course. Thus, in the information-processing view, thinking involves the general system shown in Figure 6-3, implementing specialized strategies in the same way that a computer system runs specialized software (e.g., word-processing software, graphing software) to accomplish different tasks.

HOW INFORMATION PROCESSING CHANGES WITH DEVELOPMENT.   For Piaget, accommodation, assimilation, and equilibration are behind the steady age-related march to ever-more sophisticated thinking. Information-processing psychologists have their own ideas of mechanisms that drive cognitive development (Halford & Andrews, 2011; Siegler & Alibali, 2005). Let's look at some of them.

BETTER STRATEGIES. Older children usually use better strategies to solve problems (Bjorklund, 2012). That is, as children develop, they use strategies that are faster, more accurate, and easier. For example, trying to find a parent in a crowded auditorium, a younger child might search each row, looking carefully at every person; an older child might remember that the parent is wearing a purple sweater and only look at people in purple. Both children will probably find the parent, but the older child's approach is more efficient. Thus, as children get older and more knowledgeable, their mental software becomes more sophisticated and more powerful, just as the current version of PowerPoint is vastly more capable than PowerPoint 1.0 (which ran only in black and white when it was released in 1987).

How do children learn more effective strategies? Of course, parents and teachers often help: By structuring children's actions and providing hints, adults demonstrate new strategies and how best to use them. However, youngsters also learn new strategies by watching and working with more skilled children (Tudge, Winterhoff, & Hogan, 1996). For example, children and adolescents watch others play video games to learn good game strategies. Children also discover new strategies on their own (Tsubota & Chen, 2012). For example, when Robert Kail's daughter was five, he watched her match words with their antonyms in a language workbook. The pages always had an equal number of words and antonyms, so she quickly learned to connect the last word with the one remaining antonym, without thinking about the meaning of either.

MORE EFFECTIVE EXECUTIVE FUNCTIONING. The components of executive functioning improve steadily during childhood. As children develop, they are better able to inhibit inappropriate thoughts or actions. For example, an older child would be better able to ignore classmates whispering nearby and listen to her teacher's directions. Similarly, with development, children become more flexible at shifting from one task to another. To illustrate, older children are better able to move smoothly from practising arithmetic facts to writing a short story. Finally, updating also improves with age: An older girl who is playing basketball is better able to update the game's score after each team makes a basket (Diamond, 2013). These age-related improvements in executive functioning fuel many cognitive-development changes, including improved reasoning and mastery of academic skills (Bull & Lee, 2014; Richland & Burchinal, 2013).

INCREASED AUTOMATIC PROCESSING. Think back to when you were learning a new skill, like how to type. At first, you had to think about every single step in the process. If you were asked to type "child," you probably started by trying to remember the location of "c" on the keyboard and then deciding which finger to use to reach that key. You had to repeat this process for each of the remaining four letters. But as your skill grew, each step became easier until you could type "child" without even thinking about it; your fingers seem to move automatically to the right keys, in the right sequence. **Cognitive activities that require virtually no effort are known as** *automatic processes.*

To understand how automatic processes affect developmental change, we need to return to working memory. In the early phases of learning a skill, each individual step (like finding "c" on the keyboard) must be stored in working memory. Because there are so many steps, an unmastered skill can easily occupy much of the capacity of working memory. In contrast, when a skill has been mastered, individual steps are no longer stored in working memory, which means that more capacity is available for other activities.

As children and adolescents acquire greater skill at new tasks such as typing, some aspects of the task are performed automatically, which means they require no effort.

Jupiterimages/Stockbyte/Getty Images

QUESTION 6.2
Sixteen-year-old Quinn has just completed driver's ed, and he loves to get behind the wheel. For the most part, his parents are okay with his performance, but they absolutely refuse to let him listen to the radio while he's driving. Quinn thinks this is a stupid rule. Do you? *(Answer is on page 210.)*

Compared to adolescents and adults, children have limited experience in most tasks, so they perform few processes automatically. Instead, their processing requires substantial working memory capacity. As children gain experience, however, some processes become automatic, freeing working memory capacity for other processes (Rubinstein, Henik, Berger, & Shahar-Shalev, 2002). Thus, when faced with complex tasks involving many processes, older children are more likely to succeed because they can perform some of the processes automatically. In contrast, younger children must think about all or most of the processes, taxing or even exceeding the capacity of their working memory.

INCREASED SPEED OF PROCESSING. As children develop, they complete most mental processes at an ever-faster rate (Cerella & Hale, 1994). Improved speed is obvious when we measure how fast children of different ages respond on tasks. Across a wide range of cognitive tasks, such as deciding which of two numbers is greater, naming a pictured object, and searching memory, four- and five-year-olds are generally one-third as fast as adults, whereas eight- and nine-year-olds are one-half as fast as adults (Kail et al., 2013).

Age differences in processing speed are critical when a specified number of actions must be completed in a fixed period of time. For example, perhaps you've had the unfortunate experience of trying to understand a professor who lectures at warp speed. The instructor's speech was so rapid that your cognitive processes couldn't keep up, which meant that you didn't get much out of the lecture. The problem is even more serious for children, who process information much more slowly than adults.

The four types of developmental change shown in the Summary Table represent powerful mechanisms driving cognitive development during childhood and adolescence. These mechanisms produce steady age-related increases in cognitive skill. In contrast to Piaget's theory, according to this theory there are no abrupt or qualitative changes that create distinct cognitive stages.

Finally, what would information-processing researchers say about Victoria, from the module-opening vignette? They would probably want to explain why she finds some puzzles harder than others. Using the list of developmental mechanisms that we have

SUMMARY TABLE

TYPES OF DEVELOPMENTAL CHANGE IN INFORMATION PROCESSING

Type of Developmental Change	Defined	Example
Better strategies	Older children use faster, more accurate, and easier strategies.	Younger children may "sound out" a word's spelling, but older children simply retrieve it from memory.
More effective executive functioning	Older children are more skilled at inhibiting, shifting, and updating.	Asked by a teacher to format assignments in a new way (e.g., write their name in a different location on the page), older children are more successful in adapting to the new format.
Increased automatic processing	Older children execute more processes automatically (without using working memory).	Asked to get ready for bed, an older child goes through all the tasks (e.g., brushes teeth, puts on pajamas) while thinking about other things, but a younger child focuses on each task, as well as what to do next.
Increased speed of processing	Older children can execute mental processes more rapidly than younger children.	Shown a picture of a dog, older children can retrieve the name "dog" from memory more rapidly.

examined in the previous few pages, they would note that complex puzzles may require more sophisticated strategies that are too demanding for her limited working-memory capacity. However, as she does more and more puzzles with her dad, some parts of these complex strategies are likely to become automated, making it easier for Victoria to use them.

Core Knowledge Theories

Imagine a 12-year-old (1) trying to download apps for her new iPad, (2) wondering why her dad is grouchy today, and (3) taking her pet dog for a walk. According to Piaget, and most information-processing theorists, in each case, the same basic mechanisms of thinking are at work, even though the contents of the child's thinking ranges from objects to people to pets. In this view, different types of knowledge are like different kinds of cars—they come in countless numbers of makes, models, and colours, but deep down they are alike—they all have an engine, four wheels, doors, windows, and so on.

In contrast to this view, *core-knowledge theories* **propose distinctive domains of knowledge, some of which are acquired very early in life** (Newcombe, 2013; Spelke & Kinzler, 2007). In this view, knowledge is more like the broader class of vehicles: Much knowledge is general, represented by the large number of cars. But distinct, specialized forms of knowledge also exist, represented by buses, trucks, and motorcycles. Returning to our hypothetical 12-year-old, core-knowledge theorists would claim that her thinking about objects, people, and pets might reflect fundamentally different ways of thinking.

Core-knowledge theories were created, in part, to account for the fact that most children acquire some kinds of knowledge relatively easily and early in life. For example, think about learning language (a native language, not a second language) versus learning calculus. Most children learn to talk—in fact, the *inability* to talk is a sign of atypical development—and they do so with little apparent effort. (When was the last time you heard a three-year-old complaining that learning to talk was just *too* hard?) Calculus, in comparison, is mastered by relatively few, usually only after hours of hard work solving problem after problem.

According to core-knowledge theorists, some forms of knowledge are so important for human survival that specialized systems have evolved that simplify learning of those forms of knowledge. In the case of language, for example, spoken communication has been so essential throughout human history that mental structures evolved to simplify language learning. Other evolutionarily important domains of knowledge include knowledge of objects and simple understanding of people.

The nature of these mental structures, or *modules*, is very much a matter of debate. Some core-knowledge theorists believe they are like the math or graphics co-processor on a computer: They're pre-wired to analyze one kind of data very efficiently (numbers and images, respectively, for the computer) but nothing else. The language module, for example, would be sensitive to speech sounds and would be pre-wired to derive grammatical rules from sequences of words. Another view of these specialized mental structures borrows from Piaget's metaphor of the child as a scientist who creates informal theories of the world. However, core-knowledge theorists believe that children's theories are focused on core domains, rather than being all-encompassing as Piaget proposed. Also, in creating their theories, children don't start from scratch; instead, a few innate principles provide the starting point. For example, infants' early theories of objects seem to be rooted in a few key principles such as the principle of cohesion, the idea that objects move as connected wholes (Spelke & Kinzler, 2007). Both of these ideas of mental structures may be right: That is, some forms of knowledge may be better described as modular, but others are more consistent with the child-as-scientist view.

What are the domains of knowledge that have these specialized mental structures? Language was the first core domain identified by scientists; there is so much to learn about children's mastery of language that we've devoted an entire chapter to it (Chapter 9). In addition, many child-development researchers agree that young children rapidly acquire knowledge of objects, people, and living things and they create informal or naïve theories of physics, psychology, and biology. Like language, acquiring knowledge in each of these domains has been central to human existence: Naïve physics allows children to predict where and how objects will move in the environment; naïve psychology makes for more successful interactions with others; and naïve biology is important in avoiding predators and in maintaining health.

Finally, if core-knowledge theorists were asked to comment on Victoria (from the module-opening vignette), they would emphasize the contrast between her sophisticated language skills and her relatively undeveloped puzzle-solving skill. Language represents an evolutionarily important domain, so Victoria's precocity here is not surprising; doing jigsaw puzzles is not a specialized domain with evolutionary significance, which explains her relative lack of skill in that task.

We'll see how knowledge in core domains changes with development in Module 6.3. For now, the Summary Table reviews the defining features of the three theories we've explored in Module 6.2.

As you think about the three theoretical perspectives listed in the Summary Table, keep in mind that each goes beyond Piaget's theory in a unique direction. The sociocultural approach expands the focus of cognitive development research from a solitary child to one who is surrounded by people and the culture they represent; the information-processing perspective expands the focus of developmental mechanisms from accommodation and assimilation to executive functioning, processing speed, and other mechanisms derived from mental hardware and mental software; core-knowledge theories expand the focus to recognize distinct domains of evolutionarily significant knowledge. Thus, these three perspectives provide complementary, not competing, accounts of cognitive development.

Response to question on page 206: Nellie McClung was the famous political and social activist who, along with four others (Henrietta Muir Edwards, Louise McKinney, Emily Murphy, and Irene Parlby), fought and won the Persons Case in 1929.

Q&A ANSWER 6.2

Though Quinn may not like the rule, it's probably a good one. Beginning drivers like Quinn are told to keep the music turned off because listening would consume working memory capacity that is needed for driving. However, with more experience behind the wheel, many driving skills will become automatic, freeing capacity that can be used to listen to the radio. Patience, Quinn, your time will come!

SUMMARY TABLE

CHARACTERISTICS OF MODERN THEORIES OF COGNITIVE DEVELOPMENT

Approach	Characteristics
Vygotsky's sociocultural theory	Views cognitive development as a sociocultural enterprise; experts use scaffolding to help a novice acquire knowledge; children use private speech to regulate their own thinking.
Information-processing theories	Based on the computer metaphor; view cognitive change in terms of better strategies, increased capacity of working memory, more effective inhibitory and executive processing, more automatic processing, and faster processing speed.
Core-knowledge theories	View cognitive development as an innate capability to easily acquire knowledge in such specialized domains of evolutionary importance such as language, knowledge of objects, and understanding of people.

Check Your Learning

RECALL What three concepts are fundamental to Vygotsky's sociocultural theory?

What specialized domains of knowledge have been identified by core-knowledge theorists?

INTERPRET Do the developmental mechanisms in the information-processing perspective emphasize nature, nurture, or both? How?

APPLY How might an information-processing theorist explain sociocultural influences on cognitive development (e.g., scaffolding)?

6.3 Understanding in Core Domains

OUTLINE

Understanding Objects and Their Properties

Understanding Living Things

Understanding People

LEARNING OBJECTIVES

1. What do infants understand about the nature of objects?
2. When and how do young children distinguish between living and nonliving things?
3. How do young children acquire a theory of mind?

Amy, a reporter for a magazine that reviews products, is assigned to do a story on different kinds of "sippy cups"— plastic cups with a lid and spout that are spill-proof and so are perfect for babies who are learning to use a cup. Amy brought home 12 different sippy cups and used each one for a day with her 14-month-old son. She discovered that some definitely worked better than others, but what amazed her is that after the first day, her son always knew what to do with the cup. Despite differences in colour, size, and the shape of the spout, he apparently recognized each one as a sippy cup because he immediately lifted each new style to his mouth and started drinking. Amy wondered how he could do this.

The world is filled with endless varieties of "stuff," including sippy cups, cats, and basketball players. Recognizing different instances of the same kind of thing—that is, being able to categorize—is an essential skill for young children. By knowing that an object belongs to a category, we learn some of its properties, including what it can do and where we're likely to find it. Amy's son, for example, quickly learned the essentials of a sippy cup; later he recognized each different cup as being a member of the general category of sippy cups and knew exactly what to do with them. If he couldn't categorize, every experience would be novel—upon seeing yet another slightly different sippy cup, he would need to figure out what to do with it as if it were a totally new object.

How do infants form categories? Important clues come from perceptual features and their organization. A sippy cup, for example, consists of a cylinder with a spout at one end. After infants have learned these features and how they are related, they can recognize sippy cups regardless of their colour or size (Quinn, 2004, 2011). Similarly, they can learn the features that distinguish, for example, dogs from cats, or flowers from chairs. One popular view is that infants' first categories denote groups of objects with many similar perceptual features—the "dog" category includes four-legged animals with a distinctive snout, the "tree" category includes large bark-covered objects with limbs (Rakison & Yermolayeva, 2010).

Perceptual features aren't the only basis for children's categories. Functions are also important. When two objects look different but perform the same function (e.g., make the same sound when shaken), children judge them to be in the same category. Similarly, when adults label objects that look different with the same word, young children believe that the objects are in the same category (Gelman & Meyer, 2011).

Children's earliest categories are often formed at a basic level, where category members look similar or have similar functions. Examples would be trees, flowers, dogs, birds, cars, and chairs. Children also learn that trees and flowers are part of the more general category of plants, and they learn that dogs and birds are part of the more general category of animals (Mareschal & Tan, 2007). At the same time, children learn that their first categories can also be subdivided; for example, they recognize that flowers include the subcategories of rose, tulip, and daisy.

In the remainder of this module, we'll see how infants and older children use these categorization skills to carve the world into domains and create theories within those domains. We'll consider infants' knowledge of objects, living things, and people.

Understanding Objects and Their Properties

As adults, we know much about objects and their properties. For example, we know that if we place a coffee cup on a table, it will remain there unless moved by another person; it will not move by itself or simply disappear. And we don't release a coffee cup in mid-air because we know that an unsupported object will fall. Young children's understanding of these properties has long interested child-development researchers, in part because Piaget claimed that understanding of objects develops slowly, taking many months to become complete. However, other investigators have used clever procedures to show that babies understand objects much earlier than Piaget claimed. Renée Baillargeon (1987, 1994), for example, assessed *object permanence* using a procedure in which infants first saw a silver screen that appeared to be rotating back and forth. When they were familiar with this display, one of two new displays was shown In the realistic event, a red box appeared in a position behind the screen, making it impossible for the screen to rotate as far back as it had previously. Instead, the screen rotated until it made contact with the box, then rotated forward. In the unrealistic event, shown in Figure 6-4, the box appeared, but the screen continued to rotate as before. The screen rotated back until it was flat, then rotated forward, again revealing the box. The illusion was possible because the box was mounted on a movable platform that allowed the box to drop out of the way of the moving screen. However, from the infant's perspective, it appeared as if the box vanished behind the screen, only to reappear.

The disappearance and reappearance of the box violates the idea that objects exist permanently. Consequently, an infant who understands the permanence of objects should find the unrealistic event a truly novel stimulus and look at it longer than the realistic event. Baillargeon found that four-and-a-half-month-olds consistently looked longer at the unrealistic event than the realistic event. Infants apparently thought that the unrealistic event was novel, just as we are surprised when an object vanishes from under a magician's scarf. Evidently, then, infants have some understanding of object permanence early in the first year of life.

Of course, understanding that objects exist independently is just a start; objects have other important properties and infants know many of them (Baillargeon, Lie, Gertner, & Wu, 2011). By about six months, infants are surprised when an object that is released in

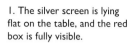

1. The silver screen is lying flat on the table, and the red box is fully visible.

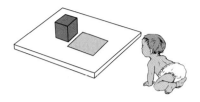

2. The silver screen has begun to rotate, but the red box is largely visible.

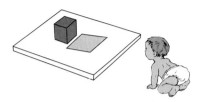

3. The silver screen is now vertical, blocking the red box.

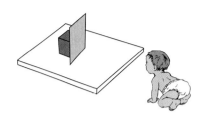

4. The silver screen continues to rotate, blocking the red box, which has started to drop through the trap door.

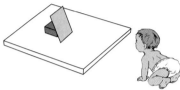

5. The silver screen is completely flat, apparently having "rotated through" the red box, which is actually now under the table.

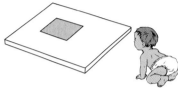

6. The silver screen is rotating back toward the infant but still blocks the red box.

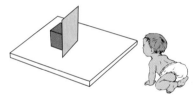

7. The silver screen is again flat and the box fully visible to the infant.

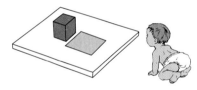

Figure 6-4 Baillargeon's experiment, showing possible/impossible events with a physical object, tests object permanence in young infants.

mid-air doesn't fall, when an object remains stationary after being hit, or when an object passes through another solid object (Luo, Kaufman, & Baillargeon, 2009). At this age, infants are surprised when a tall object is completely hidden when placed behind a shorter object, apparently because it violates their expectations about concealment (Walden, Kim, McCoy, & Karrass, 2007; Wang & Baillargeon, 2005). Finally, infants distinguish properties of liquids and solids: In experiments with a blue liquid and an identical looking but solid, blue resin block, young infants expecting an apparent liquid to flow showed surprise at seeing the resin block slide, and vice versa (Hespos, Ferry, & Rips, 2009).

These amazing demonstrations attest to the fact that the infant is indeed an accomplished naïve physicist (Baillargeon, 2004). Of course, the infant's theories are far from complete; physical properties can be understood at many different levels (Hood, Carey, & Prosada, 2000). Using gravity as an example, infants can expect that unsupported objects will fall, elementary-school children know that such objects fall due to gravity, and physics students know that the force of gravity equals the mass of an object times the acceleration caused by gravity. Obviously, infants do not understand objects at the level of physics students. And some properties of objects aren't learned until after infancy. For example, not until the preschool years do children understand ownership—that people can acquire objects by receiving them as gifts, by buying them, or by creating them (Nancekivell, Van de Vondervoort, & Friedman, 2013). The important point is that infants rapidly create a reasonably accurate theory of some basic properties of objects, a theory that helps them to expect that objects such as toys will act in predictable ways.

QUESTION 6.3
One afternoon, 15-month-old Brandon and six-month-old Justin see a dragonfly for the first time as it flies around in the backyard, hunting mosquitoes. Are either Brandon or Justin likely to conclude that a dragonfly is a living thing? *(Answer is on page 221.)*

Understanding Living Things

Another fundamental aspect of understanding is making the distinction between living and nonliving things. Adults know that living things, for example, are made of cells, inherit properties from parents, and move spontaneously. Knowledge of living things begins in infancy, when babies first distinguish animate objects (e.g., people, insects, other animals) from inanimate objects (e.g., rocks, plants, furniture, tools). Motion is critical in early understanding of the difference between animate and inanimate objects; that is, infants and toddlers use motion to identify animate objects. By 12 to 15 months, children have determined that animate objects are self-propelled, can move in irregular paths, and act to achieve goals (Biro & Leslie, 2007; Opfer & Gelman, 2011; Rakison & Hahn, 2004).

By the preschool years, children's naïve theories of biology have come to include many of the specific properties associated with living things (Wellman & Gelman, 1998). Many four-year-olds' theories of biology include the following elements:

- *Movement:* Children understand that animals can move themselves but inanimate objects can only be moved by other objects or by people. Shown the events in Figure 6-5—an animal and a toy car hopping across a table in exactly the same manner—preschoolers claim that only the animal can really move itself (Gelman & Gottfried, 1996).

- *Growth:* Children understand that, from their first appearance, animals get bigger and physically more complex but that inanimate objects do not. They believe, for

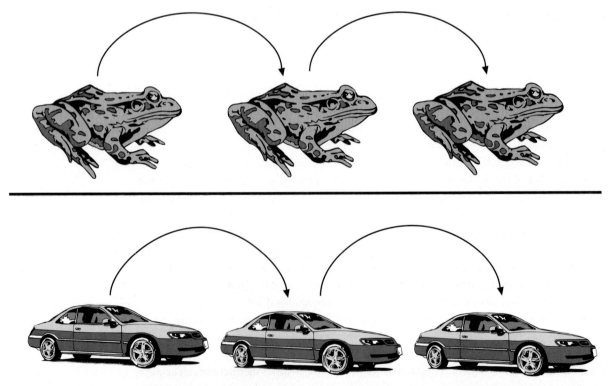

Figure 6-5 Preschoolers understand that even though two objects may move in a similar manner, only the animal is alive.

example, that sea otters and termites become larger as time goes by but that tea kettles and teddy bears do not (Margett & Witherington, 2011; Rosengren, Gelman, Kalish, & McCormick, 1991).

- *Internal parts:* Children know that the insides of animate objects contain different materials than the insides of inanimate objects. Preschool children judge that blood and bones are more likely to be inside an animate object but that cotton and metal are more likely to be inside an inanimate object (Simons & Keil, 1995).

- *Inheritance:* Children realize that only living things have offspring that resemble their parents. Asked to explain why a dog is pink, preschoolers believe that some biological characteristic of the parents probably made the dog pink; asked to explain why a phone is pink, preschoolers rely on mechanical causes (e.g., a worker used a machine), not biological ones (Diesendruck et al., 2013; Weissman & Kalish, 1999).

- *Illness:* Preschoolers believe that permanent illnesses, such as colour blindness or food allergies, are more likely to be inherited from parents but that temporary illnesses, such as a sore throat or a runny nose, are more likely to be transmitted through contact with other people (Raman & Gelman, 2005). They also understand that people can become ill when they eat contaminated food (Legare, Wellman, & Gelman, 2009).

- *Healing:* Children understand that, when injured, animate things heal by regrowth, whereas inanimate things must be fixed by humans. Preschoolers know that hair will grow back when cut from a child's head but must be repaired by a person when cut from a doll's head (Backscheider, Shatz, & Gelman, 1993).

Ken Ilio/Moment/Getty Images

Young children's thinking about living things is often teleological: Children believe that objects and parts of objects were created with a purpose in mind. For example, a fish has smooth skin so that it won't cut other fish swimming next to it.

By four years of age, children's understanding of living things is so sophisticated that children aren't fooled by lifelike robots: four-year-olds know that robots are machines that (a) do not eat or grow and (b) are made by people and can break (Jipson & Gelman, 2007). Nevertheless, preschoolers believe that robots represent a special kind of machine because youngsters attribute human-like traits (e.g., being friendly) to robots (Kahn, Gary, & Shen, 2013).

A fundamental part of young children's theory of living things is a commitment to *teleological explanations*—**children believe that livings things and parts of living things exist for a purpose.** A child like the one in photo above may say that fish have smooth skin so that they won't cut other fish that swim alongside them (Kelemen, 2003). Similarly, a child may explain that lions exist so that people can see them in a zoo. One view is that teleological explanations are based on children's knowledge that objects such as tools and machines are usually made with a purpose in mind. Children may follow a similar logic in thinking that living things (and their parts) were designed with a specific purpose in mind (Kelemen & DiYanni, 2005). And this teleological thinking has echoes of animistic thinking described on page 193: Children attribute their own intentions and goals to other living objects.

Young children's theories of living things are also rooted in *essentialism*—**children believe that all living things have an essence that can't be seen but gives a living thing its identity.** All birds share an underlying "bird-ness" that distinguishes them from dogs, which, of course, share an underlying "dog-ness." And bird-ness is what allows birds to fly and sing (Gelman, 2003). Young children's essentialism explains why four-year-olds believe that a baby kangaroo adopted by goats will still hop and have a pouch and why they believe that a watermelon seed planted in a cornfield will produce watermelons (Solomon & Zaitchik, 2012). The baby kangaroo and the watermelon seed have kangaroo-ness and watermelon-ness that cause properties of kangaroos and watermelons to emerge in maturity.

Most children in Western cultures, however, do not have well-defined ideas about what is the essence of any creature. They believe that such essences are inside an animal, because they think that removing an animal's inside parts changes the animal's identity: For example, a dog that has blood and bones removed is no longer a dog (Gelman & Wellman, 1991). But their ideas about essences are limited to a vague notion of "inside parts" located near the centre of the body (Newman & Keil, 2008). However, preschool children living in an Indigenous community in Wisconsin—the Menominee—have more refined ideas. Blood relations matter a great deal in this community because, for example, regulations regarding school funding and hunting are based in part on the number of "full-blooded" Menominee living in the community. Preschool Menominee children believe that a baby cow raised by pigs would grow up to look and act like a cow, which is the usual essentialist response. But, when told that a baby cow received a complete blood transfusion from its adoptive pig parent, now preschool children believed that the cow would grow up to be a pig. For Menominee preschoolers, blood is the essence of cow-ness or pig-ness (Waxman, Medin, & Ross, 2007).

Where do children get this knowledge of living things? Some of it comes just by watching animals, which children love to do. But parents also contribute: When reading books about animals to preschoolers, they frequently mention the properties that distinguish animals, including self-initiated motion (e.g., "The seal is jumping in the water") and psychological properties (e.g., "The bear is really mad!"). Such talk helps to highlight important characteristics of animals for youngsters (Gelman, Coley, Rosengren, Hartman, & Pappas, 1998).

Of course, although preschoolers' naïve theories of biology are complex, their theories aren't complete. Preschoolers don't know, for instance, that genes are the biological basis for inheritance (Springer & Keil, 1991). And, although preschoolers know that plants grow and heal, they nevertheless do not consider plants to be living things. It's not until seven or eight years of age that children routinely decide that plants are alive. Preschoolers' reluctance to call plants living things may stem from their belief in goal-directed motion as a key property of living things: This is not easy to see in plants, but when five-year-olds are told that plants move in goal-directed ways—for example, tree roots turn toward a source of water or a Venus flytrap closes its leaves to trap an insect—they decide that plants are alive after all (Opfer & Siegler, 2004).

Despite these limits, children's naïve theories of biology, when joined with their naïve theories of physics, provide powerful tools for making sense of their world and for understanding new experiences.

Understanding People

The last of the three fundamental theories concerns *folk psychology,* **which refers to our informal beliefs about other people and their behaviour.** Think back to the last time you wanted to figure out why someone—a friend, lover, coworker, sibling, or parent—acted as he or she did. Why did your friend go to a movie with someone else instead of going to a concert with you? Why did your brother say nothing about your brand new coat? In common situations like this, adults are often amateur psychologists, explaining people's actions in terms of their desires or goals (Carlson, Koenig, & Harms, 2013). Your friend went to the movie because she was angry with you for not lending her your car; your brother didn't comment on your coat because he was preoccupied. Just as naïve physics allows us to predict how objects act, and naïve biology allows us to understand living things, naïve psychology allows us to predict or understand how people act.

A cornerstone of folk psychology is the idea that people's behaviour is often intentional-designed to achieve a goal (Woodward, 2009). Imagine a father who says, "Where are the crackers?" in front of his one-year-old daughter, then begins opening kitchen cabinets, moving some objects to look behind them. Finding the box of crackers, he says, "Here they are!" An infant who understands intentionality would realize how her father's actions—searching, moving objects—was related to the goal—finding the crackers.

Many clever experiments have revealed that one-year-olds do indeed have this understanding of intentionality. One of them is described in the Focus on Research feature.

Focus On Research

Understanding Others' Intentions

Who were the investigators, and what was the aim of the study? Kara Olineck and Diane Poulin-Dubois of Concordia University, Montreal (2009) investigated infants' understanding of intention with a series of attention and imitation tasks. The overall aim of the study was to examine understanding of intention and how different aspects of such understanding might be interrelated. Thus, in their study, Olineck and Poulin-Dubois ran a series of four tests. For simplicity we will look at only one of these tests here—a behaviour re-enactment task based on earlier research by Meltzoff (1995) and Bellagamba, Camaioni, and Colonnesi (2006).

How did the investigators measure the topic of interest? Olineck and Poulin-Dubois had 14-month-olds watch an experimenter perform an action but fail to achieve an apparent goal. The experimenter, for example, looked as if she wanted to pull apart a two-piece wooden toy, but acted as though her hand slipped off in the action of pulling. In another example she went to drop a string of beads into a cylinder but instead missed the opening so that the beads fell onto the table.

Who were the children in the study? For the behavioural re-enactment task, the participants were 20 14-month-olds.

What was the design of the study? The study was experimental. The independent variable was the demonstration by the experimenter. The dependent variable was the number of target actions correctly reproduced.

Were there ethical concerns with the study? No. The children watched simple actions being performed and apparently found the stimuli used attractive. Their parents had granted consent for the children to participate.

What were the results? When the infants were given the same objects, they typically imitated the experimenter's intended action—pulling the toy apart or placing the beads in the cylinder—not what she really did. Infants' interpretations emphasized what the actions were intended to accomplish, not the actions per se.

What did the investigators conclude? Olineck and Poulin-Dubois (2009) concluded that 14-month-old children could distinguish the intention behind an action by another person. The infants showed that they could understand the difference between intended and accidental actions.

What converging evidence would strengthen these conclusions? To be fair, we should note that Olineck and Poulin-Dubois were running some of the research that would provide converging evidence in the other parts of their study. The other tasks used in this research, such as visual attention tasks and selective action imitation tasks, supported the findings of the behavioural re-enactment task. With some tasks done at 10 months and others (such as the one focused on here) at 14 months, the researchers noted that their findings "provide the first evidence that there is developmental continuity in infants' understanding of intentional action" (Olineck & Poulin-Dubois, 2009, p. 404). Further converging evidence would be provided if other researchers could replicate the finding of developmental continuity in infants' understanding of others' intentions.

Critical Thinking Question: What would we expect the "developmental continuity" of understanding of intention to be? That is, what do you think the "timeline" for this would be?

Many studies yield results like this one, in which infants are able to identify the goal from the adult's actions (e.g., Sommerville & Woodward, 2005; Southgate & Csibra, 2009). What's more, the regions of the brain that control goal-related motions (e.g., grasping a cup) often become active in the infant's brain before the adult achieves a goal, as if the infant knows what goal the adult has in mind (e.g., Southgate et al., 2010).

From this early understanding of intentionality, young children's naïve psychology expands rapidly. **Between ages two and five, children develop a *theory of mind,* a naïve understanding of the relations between mind and behaviour.** One of the leading researchers on theory of mind, Henry Wellman (2002, 2011, 2012), believes that children's theory of mind moves through several phases during the preschool years. In the earliest phase, preschoolers understand that people can have different desires: One child might want raisins for a snack whereas another child wants crackers. In the next phase, children know that people can have different beliefs: In trying to find a missing shoe, one child might believe that the shoe is in the kitchen and another child believes that it's in the car. In the third phase, children understand that different experiences can lead to different states of knowledge: A child who has seen a toy hidden in a drawer knows what's in the now-closed drawer, but a child who did not see the toy hidden does not.

The next phase represents a fundamental shift in children's theory of mind: Children understand that behaviour is based on a person's beliefs about events and situations, *even when those beliefs are wrong.* Children's understanding of the influence of such false beliefs is revealed in tasks such as the one shown in Figure 6-6 on page 218. Anne knows that the marble has been moved to the box, but Sally believes that the marble is still in the basket. Not until four years of age do most children correctly say that Sally will look for the marble in the basket (acting on her false belief); four-year-olds understand that Sally's behaviour is based on her beliefs, even though her belief is wrong (Frye, 1993).

In the final phase, children understand that people may feel one emotion but show another. For example, a child who is disappointed by a birthday present smiles anyway because she doesn't want her parents to know how she really feels.

This general developmental pattern is evident in many cultures around the world. Tara Callaghan of St. Francis Xavier University in Nova Scotia and a group of colleagues from several countries (2005) tested understanding of false beliefs in preschool children from five cultural settings: Canada, India, Peru, Samoa, and Thailand. In all five settings, the majority of three-year-olds made the false-belief error, at four years about half made the error, and by five years almost no children did (Callaghan et al., 2005; Liu, Wellman, Tardif, & Sabbagh, 2008). Thus, children's theory of mind becomes more sophisticated over the preschool years, and this general progression is found for children around the world (Wellman, 2012).

So we can see that at about four years of age, there is a fundamental change in children's understanding of the centrality of beliefs in a person's thinking about the world. Children now "realize that people not only have thoughts and beliefs, but also that thoughts and beliefs are crucial to explaining why people do things; that is, actors' pursuits of their desires are inevitably shaped by their beliefs about the world" (Bartsch & Wellman, 1995, p. 144).

The early phases of children's theory of mind seem clear. How this happens is very much a matter of debate, however. One of the first explanations for the development of a theory of mind suggested that it is based on an innate, specialized module coming online in the preschool years that automatically recognizes behaviours associated with different mental states such as wanting, pretending, and believing. This view was prompted, in part, by the finding that children with autism, a disorder in which individuals are uninterested in other people and have limited social skills, lag behind typically developing children in understanding false belief (Peterson, Wellman, & Slaughter, 2012). As we'll see in the Children's Lives feature, although autistic children definitely find false-belief tasks to be challenging, the proper interpretation of that result is very much debated.

Figure 6-6 The Sally–Anne task false-belief task: Where will Sally look for her marble?

Children's Lives

Theory of Mind in Autism

Autism is the most serious of a family of disorders known as Autism Spectrum Disorders (ASD). Individuals with ASD acquire language later than usual and their speech often echoes what others say to them. They sometimes become intensely interested in objects (e.g., making the same actions with a toy over and over), sometimes to the exclusion of everything else. They often seem uninterested in other people, and when they do interact, those exchanges are often awkward, as if the individuals with ASD are not following the rules that govern social interactions. Symptoms usually emerge early in life, typically by 18 to 24 months of age. As many as one in every 68 U.S. children is diagnosed with ASD, and ASD is about four-and-a-half times more common in boys than girls (CDC, 2016b). Rates are assumed to be similar in Canada (e.g., Autism Speaks Canada, 2016). ASD is heritable, and many studies point to atypical brain functioning, perhaps due to abnormal levels of neurotransmitters (NINDS, 2009).

Important research on biological aspects of autism is being done in Canada, at Queen's University in Kingston, Ontario. Mark Sabbagh and his colleagues in the Department of Psychology at Queens's are investigating possible underlying brain mechanisms. There is some evidence for biological mechanisms in that theory-of-mind abilities are similar in parents and their children, pointing to heritable aspects as ASDs. The researchers do note, however, that "it is difficult to tease apart the mechanisms of genetics and socialization" (Sabbagh, & Seamans, 2008, p. 359). Sabbagh's work has shown that the developmental roots of ASD may relate to specific brain circuits, which if functioning atypically may affect social and cognitive abilities in those with ASD (e.g., Sabbagh, 2004). Thus, different development of certain pathways in the brain may underlie the deficits in social-cognitive understanding seen in those with ASD.

As mentioned, children with ASD grasp false belief very slowly, and this performance leads some researchers to conclude that the absence of a theory of mind—sometimes called "mindblindness" (Baron-Cohen, 2005)—is the defining characteristic of ASD (Tager-Flusberg, 2007). Other scientists are not convinced. Although no one doubts that autistic children find false-belief tasks puzzling, some scientists say that mindblindness is a by-product of other deficits and not the cause of the symptoms associated with ASD. One idea is that ASD reflects problems in executive function (described on page 206): According to this view, autistic children's social interactions are impaired because they are relatively unable to plan, to inhibit irrelevant actions, and to shift smoothly between actions (Pellicano, 2013). Another idea emphasizes a focused processing style that is common in ASD. For example, children with ASD find hidden objects faster than typically developing children do (Chen et al., 2012), but this emphasis on perceptual details usually comes at the expense of maintaining a coherent overall picture. Consequently, in social interactions, children with ASD may focus on one facet of another person's behaviour (e.g., her gestures) but ignore other verbal and nonverbal cues (e.g., speech, facial expressions, body language) that collectively promote fluid interactions. Research to evaluate these claims is still ongoing; it's likely that the answers will indicate that multiple factors contribute to ASD.

ASD cannot be cured. However, therapy can be used to improve language and social skills in children with autism. In addition, medications can be used to treat some of the symptoms, such as to reduce repetitive behaviour (Leekam, Prior, & Uljarevic, 2011). When ASD is diagnosed early and autistic children grow up in supportive, responsive environments and receive appropriate treatments, they can lead satisfying and productive lives.

The theory-of-mind module that some suspect is missing in autistic children is thought to emerge during the preschool years in typical development. But, just as the role for this module has been challenged in autism, not everyone is convinced that it drives theory of mind in typical development. Some evidence points to a role for executive function in the onset of theory of mind: Children's scores on tasks designed to measure executive function predict their scores on false-belief tasks (e.g., Lackner, Sabbagh, Hallinan, Liu, & Holden, 2012). Other evidence emphasizes the contribution of language, which develops rapidly during the same years that theory of mind emerges (as we'll see in Chapter 9). Some scientists believe that children's language skills contribute to growth of theory of mind, perhaps reflecting the benefit of an expanding vocabulary that includes verbs describing mental states, such as "think," "know," "believe" (Pascual, Aguardo, Sotillo, & Masdeu 2008). Or the benefits may reflect children's mastery of grammatical forms that can be used to describe a setting in which a person knows that another person has a false belief (Farrant, Maybery, & Fletcher, 2012).

A different view is that a child's theory of mind emerges from interactions with other people, interactions that provide children with insights into different mental states (Dunn & Brophy, 2005; McAlister & Peterson, 2013). Through conversations with parents and older siblings that focus on other people's mental states, children learn facts of mental life, and this helps children to see that others often have different perspectives than they do. In other words, when children frequently participate in conversations that focus on other people's moods, their feelings, and their intentions, they learn that people's behaviour is based on their beliefs, regardless of the accuracy of those beliefs.

Critical Thinking Questions: Therapy can be used to help children with ASD improve social and language skills. What sort of therapeutic interventions do you think would be most helpful for such children? What are the best ways such therapies could be offered?

Probably through some combination of these forces, preschool children attain a theory of mind. After these years, their naïve psychology moves beyond theory of mind and embraces an ever-expanding range of psychological phenomena. For example, at about age 10, children know that psychological states such as being nervous or frustrated can produce physical states such as vomiting or headache (Notaro, Gelman, & Zimmerman, 2001). For now, the important point is that children's folk psychology flourishes in the preschool years, allowing them to see that other people's behaviour is not unpredictable but follows regular patterns. When this understanding is joined with their theories of naïve biology and naïve physics, young children have extensive knowledge of both the physical and social worlds, knowledge that they can use to function successfully in those worlds.

 ANSWER 6.3
By 12 to 15 months old, toddlers know that living things are self-propelled, move along irregular paths, and act to achieve goals. They saw evidence of these latter two (movement along an irregular path to achieve a goal), so it is likely that Brandon—but not Justin—is old enough to decide the dragonfly is alive.

 # Check Your Learning

RECALL Summarize the evidence indicating that Piaget underestimated infants' understanding of object permanence.

What properties of living things are featured in young children's theories of biology?

INTERPRET A typical one-year-old's understanding of objects exceeds her understanding of people. Why might this be the case?

APPLY What do you think would happen if you conducted a meta-analysis on studies of infants' understanding of objects? Would the pattern of age-related change in understanding objects be much the same around the world?

UNIFYING THEMES   Active Children

This chapter emphasizes that *children influence their own development*. This idea is the cornerstone of both Piaget's theory and of the core-knowledge account of development. Beginning in infancy and continuing through childhood and adolescence, children are constantly trying to make sense of what goes on around them. Experiences provide intellectual food for children to digest. Parents, teachers, and peers are important in cognitive development, not so much for what they teach directly as for the guidance and challenges they provide. Thus, throughout the developmental journey the child is a busy navigator, trying to understand the routes available and trying to decide among them.

See for Yourself

The best way to see some of the developmental changes that Piaget described is to test some children with the same tasks that Piaget used. Remember your ethical responsibilities, particularly regarding permission from parents/guardians beforehand and child assent and dissent during the testing. The conservation task described on page 194 is a good one to use because it is simple to set up, and children usually enjoy it. Get some glasses and coloured liquids, then ask a three- or four-year-old and a seven- or eight-year-old to confirm that the two quantities are the same. Then pour one liquid into another container as shown on page 194 and ask children if the quantities are still the same. Ask them to explain their answers. The differences between three- and seven-year-olds' answers are truly remarkable. See for yourself!

Resources

For more information about …

further analyses of some of the major experiments included in this chapter, read Slater and Quinn's *Developmental Psychology: Revisiting the classic studies* (published by Sage, 2012), an edited volume in which experts in different areas of developmental psychology discuss classic studies, such as Piaget's work or the Sally–Anne study on theory of mind, and their influence on current thinking about development.

Piaget's life, his theory, and his research (as well as related research on cognitive development), visit the website of the Jean Piaget Society: **www.piaget.org**.

Key Terms

accommodation 190	concrete operational stage 194	essentialism 215
animism 193	constructivism 197	executive functioning 206
assimilation 190	core-knowledge theories 209	folk psychology 216
automatic processes 207	deductive reasoning 196	formal operational stage 195
central executive 206	egocentrism 193	guided participation 201
centration 194	equilibration 191	information-processing theory 205

Summary

6.1 Setting the Stage: Piaget's Theory

1. Basic Principles of Piaget's Theory

In Piaget's view, children construct theories that reflect their understanding of the world. Children's theories are constantly changing based on their experiences. In assimilation, experiences are readily incorporated into existing theories. In accommodation, experiences cause theories to be modified to encompass new information.

When accommodation becomes much more frequent than assimilation, it is a sign that children's theories are inadequate, so children reorganize them. This reorganization produces four different stages of mental development from infancy through adulthood. All individuals go through all four phases, but not necessarily at the same rate.

2. Stages of Cognitive Development

The first two years of life constitute Piaget's sensorimotor stage. Over these two years, infants adapt to and explore their environment, understand objects, and begin to use symbols.

From ages two to seven, children are in Piaget's preoperational stage. Although now capable of using symbols, their thinking is limited by egocentrism, the inability to see the world from another's point of view. Preoperational children also are centred in their thinking, focusing narrowly on particular parts of a problem.

Between ages seven and 11, children begin to use and can reverse mental operations to solve perspective-taking and conservation problems. The main limit to thinking at this stage is that it is focused on the concrete and real.

With the onset of formal operational thinking, adolescents can think hypothetically and reason abstractly. In deductive reasoning, they understand that conclusions are based on logic, not experience.

3. Piaget's Contributions to Child Development

Piaget's enduring contributions include emphasizing the importance of cognitive processes in development, viewing children as active participants in their own development, and discovering many counterintuitive developmental phenomena. The theory's weaknesses include poorly defined mechanisms of change and an inability to account for variability in children's performance.

6.2 Modern Theories of Cognitive Development

1. The Sociocultural Perspective: Vygotsky's Theory

Vygotsky believed that cognition develops first in a social setting and only gradually comes under the child's independent control. The difference between what children can do with assistance and what they can do alone defines the zone of proximal development.

Control of cognitive skills is most readily transferred from others to the child through scaffolding, a teaching style that allows children to take on more and more of a task as they master its different components.

2. Information-Processing Theories

According to the information-processing approach, cognition involves a general-purpose information-processing system that includes a central executive along with sensory, working, and long-term memories. Any specific cognitive activity involves this system plus specialized "software" that is specific to the task at hand.

Information-processing psychologists believe that cognitive development reflects more effective strategies, more effective executive processing (inhibiting, shifting, updating), more frequent automatic processing, and increased speed of processing.

3. Core-Knowledge Theories

According to core-knowledge theories, there are distinct domains of knowledge (e.g., language, understanding objects) that are acquired by infants, toddlers, and preschoolers. These domains have typically evolved because they are essential for human survival. Some theorists believe these domains of knowledge are rooted in pre-wired systems; others use Piaget's metaphor of child-as-scientist and describe them as specialized theories.

6.3 Understanding in Core Domains

1. Understanding Objects and Their Properties

Infants understand that objects exist independently. They also know that objects move along continuous paths and do not move through other objects.

2. Understanding Living Things

Infants and toddlers use motion to distinguish animate from inanimate objects. By the preschool years children know that living things move themselves, grow bigger and physically more complex, have different internal parts than objects, resemble their parents, inherit some diseases from parents but contract other diseases from contact with others, and heal when injured. Preschoolers' thinking about living things is often marked by teleological explanations and essentialism.

3. Understanding People

By age one, infants recognize that people perform many acts intentionally, with a goal in mind. During the preschool years, children's theory of mind becomes progressively more sophisticated. One landmark is the understanding that people's behaviour is based on beliefs about events and situations, even when those beliefs are wrong. Contributing to children's acquisition of a theory of mind are a specialized cognitive module, basic psychological processes such as language, and social interactions that allow children to experience different mental states.

Test Yourself

1. Piaget's theory is built around the metaphor of children as _____.

2. In Piaget's theory, _____ is illustrated by a breastfed baby who changes the way that she sucks to get milk from a bottle.

3. The accomplishments of the sensorimotor stage include adapting to and exploring the environment, understanding objects, and _____.

4. A defining feature of children in the _____ stage of development is that they are often egocentric; that is, they are unable to take the perspective of other people.

5. During the _____ stage, thinking is rule-oriented and logical but limited to the tangible and real.

6. Piaget underestimated the ability of _____ but overestimated the ability of adolescents.

7. The _____ refers to the difference between what children can accomplish alone and what they can do with assistance.

8. According to Vygotsky, young children often rely on _____ to help them regulate their own behaviour.

9. In information-processing theories, the _____ is like a computer's operating system in coordinating the flow of information through the system.

10. According to the information-processing account, cognitive development reflects several age-related changes, including better strategies, increased capacity of working memory, more automatic processing, and _____.

11. _____ propose that specialized processing systems evolved to simplify learning of certain kinds of knowledge, such as language.

12. Research on infants' understanding of objects suggests that babies have _____ understanding than Piaget suggested.

13. Infants and toddlers rely upon _____ to identify animate objects.

14. Preschoolers' beliefs about living things are rooted in teleology (living things exist for a reason) and _____.

15. By age four, children have a reasonably sophisticated _____, understanding, for example, that people will act on their beliefs even when those beliefs are false.

Answers: (1) scientists; (2) accommodation; (3) using symbols; (4) preoperational; (5) concrete operational; (6) infants; (7) zone of proximal development; (8) private speech; (9) central executive; (10) faster speed of processing; (11) Core-knowledge theories; (12) greater; (13) self-propelled motion; (14) essentialism—the idea that living things have a hidden "essence" that defines them; (15) theory of mind.

7 Cognitive Processes and Academic Skills

Val Lawless/Shutterstock

Memory

Problem Solving

Academic Skills

Electronic Media

One day, author Robert Kail spent a morning in a Grade 1 classroom watching six- and seven-year-olds learn to read, to spell simple words, and to do simple addition problems. He then spent the afternoon in a Grade 5 classroom. Like the younger students, these 10- and 11-year-olds devoted much of their time to the traditional three Rs, but with much more complicated material. They were reading books with hundreds of pages, writing two-page essays, and solving problems that involved multiplication and division.

This remarkable transformation over the course of just a few years is possible in part because of profound changes in how children think as they mature. We'll examine these changes in **Module 7.1**, where we'll see how memory expands as children grow, and also in **Module 7.2**, where we'll consider children's and adolescents' problem-solving skills. In **Module 7.3**, we'll take a closer look at academic skills, tracing children's evolving mastery of reading, writing, and mathematics. Finally, in **Module 7.4** we'll look at the influence of electronic media on children's development.

7.1 Memory

OUTLINE

Origins of Memory

Strategies for Remembering

Knowledge and Memory

LEARNING OBJECTIVES

1. How well do infants remember?

2. How do strategies help children to remember?

3. How does children's knowledge influence what they remember?

One afternoon, four-year-old Cheryl came home sobbing and reported that Mr. Johnson, a neighbour and long-time family friend, had taken down her pants and touched her "private parts." Her mother was shocked. Mr. Johnson had always seemed an honest, decent man, which made her wonder if Cheryl's imagination had simply run wild. Yet, at times, he did seem a bit peculiar, so her daughter's claim had a ring of truth.

Regrettably, episodes like this do occur in Canada today. When child abuse is suspected and the child is the sole eyewitness, the child often testifies during prosecution of the alleged abuser. But can preschool children like Cheryl be trusted to recall events accurately on the witness stand? To answer this question, we need to understand more about how memory develops. We'll start by examining the origins of memory in infancy, then see what factors contribute to its development in childhood and adolescence.

Raise a cyber child and discover the world of parenthood at . . .

My Virtual Child

Origins of Memory

The roots of memory are laid down soon after birth (Bauer, Larkina, & Deocampo, 2011). Young babies remember events for days or even weeks at a time. Among the studies that opened our eyes to the ability of infants to remember were those conducted by Rovee-Collier (1997, 1999). The method used in her studies is shown in the photo on page 228. A ribbon from a mobile is attached to a two- or three-month-old's leg; within a few minutes, babies learn to kick to make the mobile move. When Rovee-Collier brought the mobile to the infant's homes several days or a few weeks later, babies would still kick to make the mobile move. If Rovee-Collier waited several weeks to return, most of the

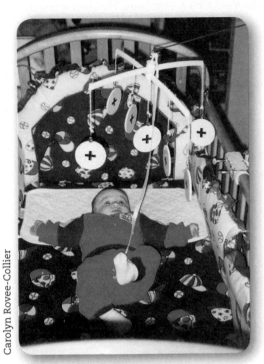

Carolyn Rovee-Collier

Infants rapidly learn that kicking moves a mobile; days later, babies will kick immediately, showing that they remember the connection between their action and the mobile's movement.

Based on Rovee-Collier, C. (1999). The development of infant memory. *Current Directions in Psychological Science, 8,* 80–85.

babies forgot that kicking moved the mobile. When that happened, she gave them a reminder—she moved the mobile herself without attaching the ribbon to the infant's foot. Then she would return the next day, hook up the apparatus, and the babies would kick to move the mobile.

Rovee-Collier's experiments show that three important features of memory exist as early as two and three months of age: (1) An event from the past is remembered; (2) over time, the event can no longer be recalled; and (3) a cue can serve to dredge up a forgotten memory.

From these humble origins, memory improves rapidly in older infants and toddlers. Youngsters can recall more of what they experience and remember it longer (Bauer & Leventon, 2013; Bauer & Lukowski, 2010). When shown novel actions with toys and later asked to imitate what they saw, toddlers can remember more than infants, and remember the actions for longer periods (Bauer, San Souci, & Pathman, 2010). For example, if shown how to make a rattle by first placing a wooden block inside a container and then putting a lid on the container, toddlers are more likely than infants to remember the necessary sequence of steps. In addition, memory is more flexible in older infants and toddlers: They are able to remember past events even when the context associated with those events has changed (Bauer et al., 2010).

Figure 7-1 shows the remarkable increase in the length of time that children can remember the connection between actions (kicking, pushing) and consequences (movements of mobile or train)—from a week or less in young babies to more than three months for one-and-a-half-year-olds. Young children may even have better autobiographical memory (memory of their own past) than previously believed. Carole Peterson of Memorial University, Newfoundland, in a literature review of the research on children's long-term autobiographical memory, came to the conclusion that while some studies show a decline in memory with delay, other studies show remarkably good recall of life events by children after even a number of years (Peterson, 2012).

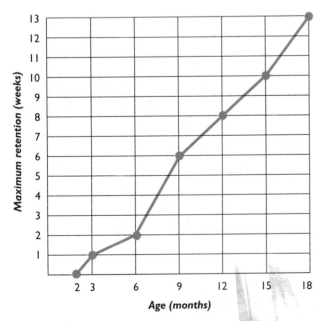

Figure 7-1 Change with age in length of time children can remember.

BRAIN DEVELOPMENT AND MEMORY. These improvements in memory can be traced, in part, to growth in the brain regions that support memory (Bauer et al., 2010). The brain structures primarily responsible for the initial storage of information, such as the hippocampus, develop during the first year. However, the structures responsible for retrieving these stored memories-the frontal cortex, for example-develop much later, into the second year. In addition, part of the hippocampus is not mature until about 20 to 24 months. Thus, development of memory during the first two years reflects growth in these two different brain regions.

Once youngsters begin to talk, we can study their memory skills using most of the same methods we use with older children and adults. Research using these methods has linked age-related improvement in memory to two factors (Pressley & Hilden, 2006). First, as children grow, they use more effective strategies for remembering. Second, children's growing factual knowledge of the world allows them to organize information more completely and, therefore, to remember better. We'll look at each of these factors in the next few pages.

Strategies for Remembering

When you study for exams, you may outline chapters in a text or highlight important passages; when you have several errands to complete, you create a list; and when you misplace your cell phone, you may think back to where you know you had it last. **Each of these actions is a** *memory strategy,* **an action to promote remembering.** Children begin to use memory strategies early. Preschool children look at or touch objects that they have been told to remember (DeLoache, 1984). Looking and touching are not very effective strategies, but they tell us that preschoolers understand that they should be doing *something* to try to remember; remembering doesn't happen automatically! During the elementary-school years, children begin to use more effective strategies (Schwenck, Bjorklund, & Schneider, 2009). **For example, seven- and eight-year-olds use** *rehearsal,* **a strategy of repeating information that must be remembered.** A child wanting to call a new friend will rehearse the phone number from the time she hears it until she places the call.

As children get older, they learn other memory strategies. **One is** *organization:* **structuring material to be remembered so that related information is placed together.** For example, a Grade 7 student trying to remember the provinces and territories of Canada might organize them geographically (e.g., the Prairie provinces—Alberta, Saskatchewan, and Manitoba grouped together; or the far north—Yukon, Northwest Territories, and Nunavut) or chronologically (e.g., Ontario, Quebec, New Brunswick, and Nova Scotia were the original provinces).

Another strategy is *elaboration*—**embellishing information to be remembered to make it more memorable.** To see elaboration in action, imagine a child who can never remember if the second syllable of "rehearsal" is spelled *her* (as it sounds) or *hear*. The child could remember the correct spelling by reminding herself that "rehearsal" is like *re-hearing*. Thus, imaging herself re-hearing a sound would make it easier to remember the spelling of "rehearsal." Elaboration may be both verbal and visual. In a study of Canadian elementary-school students, Teena Willougby and her colleagues showed that children may use either organization or elaboration, although there were age differences for imagery. In this study, verbal elaboration was encouraged by asking "why" questions about the material. Visual elaboration involved constructing visual images relating to the material to be remembered. While all children were successful at using verbal elaboration, younger children had more difficulty with visual elaboration. Children in Grade 2 could not use imagery strategies without assistance, but by Grade 6, imagery strategies were comparable to those of adults (Willoughby, Porter, Belsito, & Yearsley, 1999). And as children grow, they are also more likely to use external aids to memory—such as taking notes or writing down information on calendars so that, like the girl in the photo shown here, they will not forget future events (Eskritt & Lee, 2002; Eskritt & McLeod, 2008).

One strategy that assists working memory is to group information into "chunks." *Chunking* **is the process of organizing related items into one meaningful group.** This improves working memory capacity, or memory span, as it allows for more items to be held concurrently. The normal working memory capacity is approximately seven items

School-age children often use external aids to help them remember, such as writing down events on a calendar.

Weekend Images Inc./Getty Images

playing

(e.g., Miller, 1956). The items can be simply single letters or numbers, or they could be a group, as in a group of letters in a word. Even very young children may be capable of this use of such concepts to increase memory capacity. Given cues to help them group arrays of items, 14-month-old infants show more effective use of memory (Feigenson & Halberda, 2008). A network, or structure, of concepts also assists in remembering; such a structure can lead to multiple pathways for possible recall—a strategy noted over a century ago by American psychologist William James (James, 1981/1890).

METACOGNITION.   Just as there is not much value to a filled toolbox if you do not know how to use the tools, memory strategies are not much good unless children know when to use them. For example, rehearsal is a good strategy for remembering phone numbers but a poor one for remembering the Charter of Rights and Freedoms or the plot of *Hamlet*. During the elementary-school years and adolescence, children gradually learn to identify different kinds of memory problems and the memory strategies most appropriate to each. For example, when reading a textbook or watching a television newscast, outlining and writing a summary are good strategies because they identify the main points and organize them. Children gradually become more skilled at selecting appropriate strategies, but even high-school students do not always use effective learning strategies when they could (Grammer et al., 2011; Pressley & Hilden, 2006).

After children choose a memory strategy, they need to monitor its effectiveness. For example, by self-testing—asking themselves questions about the material—children can determine whether the strategy is helping them learn. If it's not, they need to begin anew, re-analyzing the memory task to select a better approach. If the strategy is working, they should determine the portion of the material they have not yet mastered and concentrate their efforts there. Monitoring improves gradually with age. Even preschool children can distinguish what they know from what they don't (Ghetti, Hembacher, & Coughlin, 2013), but older children and adolescents do so more accurately (Bjorklund, 2005).

Diagnosing memory problems accurately and monitoring the effectiveness of memory strategies are two important elements of *metamemory,* **which refers to a child's informal understanding of memory.** As children develop, they learn more about how memory operates and devise intuitive theories of memory that represent an outgrowth of the theory of mind described in Module 6.3 (Lockl & Schneider, 2007). For example, children learn that memory is fallible (i.e., that they sometimes forget!) and that some types of memory tasks are easier than others (e.g., remembering the main idea of Hamlet's soliloquy is simpler than remembering it word for word). This growing knowledge of memory helps children to use memory strategies more effectively, just as an experienced carpenter's accumulated knowledge of wood indicates when to use nails, screws, or glue to join two boards (Ghetti & Lee, 2011).

Children's growing understanding of memory is paralleled by a growing understanding of all cognitive processes. **Such knowledge and awareness of cognitive processes is called** *metacognitive knowledge.* Metacognitive knowledge increases rapidly during the elementary-school years: Children come to know much about perception, attention, intentions, knowledge, and thinking (Flavell, 2000; McCormick, 2003). For example, school-age children know that sometimes they deliberately direct their attention—as in searching for a parent's face in a crowd. But they also know that sometimes events capture their attention—as in an unexpected clap of thunder (Parault & Schwanenflugel, 2000).

One of the most important features of children's metacognitive knowledge is their understanding of the connections among goals, strategies, monitoring, and outcomes. As shown in Figure 7-2, children come to realize that on a broad spectrum of tasks—as

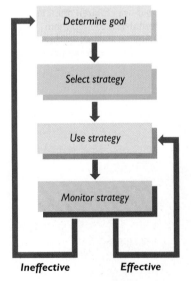

Figure 7-2 The flow of connections between goals, strategies, and monitoring.

diverse as learning words in a spelling list, learning to spike a volleyball, or learning to get along with an overly talkative classmate seated nearby—they need to regulate their learning by understanding the goal and selecting a means to achieve that goal. Then they determine whether the chosen method is working. **Effective** *cognitive self-regulation—* **that is, skill at identifying goals, selecting effective strategies, and monitoring accurately—is a characteristic of successful students** (Usher & Pajares, 2009; Zimmerman, 2001). A student may decide that writing each spelling word twice before a test is a good way to get all the words right. When the student gets only 70 percent correct on the first test, he switches to a new strategy (e.g., writing each word four times, plus writing its definition), showing the adaptive nature of cognitive processes in self-regulated learners. General self-regulation can also be beneficial to learning. Another way to think of self-regulation is to consider it as being able to be calm, alert, and focused. A child in this state will be better able to take in information and to utilize it appropriately. Dr. Stuart Shanker of York University in Toronto is an authority on this aspect of self-regulation and is noted for applying it to schooling, working with school boards to bring this concept into the classroom (Education Canada, 2016; Shanker, 2014).

Some students do not master these learning strategies spontaneously, but they might acquire them when teachers emphasize them in class (Grammer, Coffman, & Ornstein, 2013; Ornstein et al., 2010). In addition, several programs teach students strategies for studying more effectively (Pressley, 2002). For example, teachers explain and demonstrate several basic strategies that promote greater reading comprehension, including first selecting a goal for reading, making a mental picture of what is going on in the text, periodically predicting what will happen next, and summarizing aloud what has happened so far. Children practise these strategies separately and as part of a reading "toolkit." Empowered with reading strategies like these, students' understanding of text is deeper and they typically obtain higher scores on standardized tests of reading comprehension (Pressley & Hilden, 2006).

Strategies, metamemory, and metacognition are essential for effective learning and remembering, but as you'll see in the next few pages, knowledge is also an aid to memory (Schneider, 2011).

Knowledge and Memory

To see how knowledge influences memory, let's look at a study in which 10-year-olds and adults tried to remember sequences of numbers (Chi, 1978). As shown in Figure 7-3, adults remembered more numbers than children. Next, participants tried to remember the positions of objects in a matrix. This time, 10-year-olds' recall was much better than that of adults.

What was responsible for this surprising outcome? Actually, the objects were chess pieces on a chessboard positioned as they would be in actual games. The adults were novice players but the children were experts. For the adults, who lacked knowledge of chess, the patterns seemed arbitrary. The children, in contrast, had prior knowledge that allowed them to organize and give meaning to the patterns, and thus could recognize and then recall the whole configuration instead of many isolated pieces. The children could organize the material into chunks, but it was as if the adults were seeing this meaningless pattern:

cbcmtvcaanhl

whereas the children were seeing this:

cbc mtv caa nhl

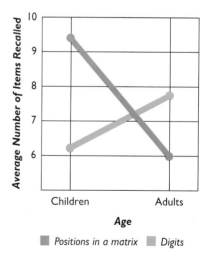

Positions in a matrix *Digits*

Figure 7-3 How knowledge influences memory: experience and age effects.

Data from Chi, M. T. H. (1978). Knowledge structures and memory development. In R. Siegler (Ed.), *Children's thinking: What develops?* Hillsdale, NJ: Erlbaum.

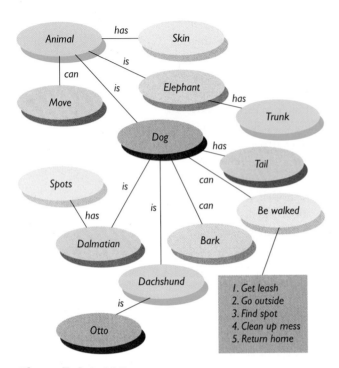

Figure 7-4 A child's knowledge network for animals.

Usually, of course, the knowledge that allows a child to organize information and give it meaning increases gradually with age (Schneider & Bjorklund, 1998). Researchers often depict knowledge as a network like the one in Figure 7-4, which shows part of a 13-year-old's knowledge of animals. The entries in the network are linked by different types of associations. Some of the links denote membership in categories (a Dalmatian is a dog), and others denote properties (an elephant has a trunk). **Still others denote a** *script,* **a memory structure used to describe the sequence in which events occur.** The list of events in "walking the dog" is a script.

A network diagram like this for a younger child would have fewer entries and fewer and weaker connecting links. Consequently, the youngster would not be able to organize information as extensively, making remembering more difficult than for an older child.

Nevertheless, the knowledge that young children have is organized, and this turns out to be a powerful asset. In the case of events that fit scripts, for example, they need not try to remember each individual activity; instead, they simply remember the script. When the preschoolers in the photo want to tell their dad about baking cookies, they can simply retrieve the "baking cookies" script and use it to organize their recall. Knowledge, however, can distort memory. If a specific experience does not match a child's knowledge (e.g., it differs from a script), the experience is sometimes forgotten or distorted so that it conforms to their existing knowledge (Farrar & Boyer-Pennington, 1999; Williams & Davidson, 2009). For example, when told a story about a female helicopter pilot, many youngsters will remember the pilot as a man because their knowledge network specifies that pilots are men.

Because older children often have more knowledge than younger children, they are sometimes more prone to memory distortions than younger children (Brainerd, Reyna, & Ceci, 2008). In the Spotlight on Theories feature, we'll see one theory that accounts for this surprising finding.

Thus, although children's growing knowledge usually helps them to remember, sometimes it can interfere with accurate memory. In the next section, we'll look at another link between knowledge and memory—children's memory of their own lives.

AUTOBIOGRAPHICAL MEMORY. Do you remember the name of your teacher in Grade 4 or where your high school graduation was held? In answering these questions, you searched memory, just as you would search memory to answer questions such as "What is the capital of France?" and "Who invented the snowmobile?" However, answers to questions about France and snowmobiles are based on general knowledge that you have not experienced personally; in contrast, answers to questions about your Grade 4 teacher and your high school graduation are based on knowledge unique to your own life. *Autobiographical memory* **refers to people's memory of the significant events and experiences of their own lives.**

Highly familiar activities, such as baking cookies, are often stored in memory as scripts that denote the events in the activity and the sequence in which they occur.

Corbis Super RF/Alamy Stock Photo

Spotlight on Theories

Fuzzy Trace Theory

BACKGROUND   Children's knowledge of the world usually helps them remember, but sometimes it leads to inaccurate or distorted memory. Such memory errors, although common for children and adolescents, are still poorly understood.

THE THEORY   **According to the** *fuzzy trace theory,* **developed by Charles J. Brainerd and Valerie Reyna (2005, 2013), most experiences can be stored in memory exactly (verbatim) or in terms of their basic meaning (gist).** A 10-year-old who reads an invitation to a birthday party may store the information in memory as "the party starts at 7:30 P.M." (verbatim) or as "the party is after dinner" (gist). A 14-year-old who gets a mark on a science test may store it as "I got 75 percent correct" (verbatim) or "I got an average mark" (gist).

Throughout development, children store information in memory in both verbatim and gist formats. Young children are biased toward verbatim memory traces; during childhood and adolescence, a bias toward gist traces emerges. That is, older children and adolescents typically represent experiences and information in terms of gist, instead of verbatim. (The theory gets its name from its emphasis on gist memory traces that are vague or fuzzy.)

Hypothesis: Some memory errors depend on gist processing. If older children and adolescents are biased to gist processing, they should be more prone to those errors than are younger children. For example, a common error occurs when people are asked to remember related words such as "rest," "awake," "bed," "snooze," "blanket," "snore," and "dream." Typically, about three-fourths of adults will claim to have seen the word "sleep" even though it was not presented. Because older children, adolescents, and adults extract the gist of the meanings of these words ("they're about sleep"), they should be more susceptible to the illusion than younger children, who more often store words verbatim.

Test: Brainerd, Holliday, Reyna, Yang, & Toglia (2010) presented words to 7- and 11-year-olds and adults. As in the previous example, many words in the list were highly associated with a critical word, which was not presented. Later, another list of words was presented, including some that were part of the first list and some that were not. Participants were asked to recognize the words that were part of the first list. Not surprisingly, word recognition increased substantially with age: adults recognized 88% of the words, compared with 76% for 11-year-olds and 71% for 7-year-olds. More interesting is how frequently children and adolescents "recognized" the critical word that had not actually been presented: Adults did so 60% of the time, compared with 40% for 11-year-olds and 22% for 7-year-olds.

Conclusion: False memories—in this case "recognizing" a word that was never presented—were less common in young children than in older children and adults. This result is consistent with fuzzy trace theory, in which these memory errors are a consequence of the greater tendency for older children and adults to remember the gist of what they have experienced. Fuzzy trace theory is also supported by the finding that when children are encouraged to abstract the gist of the words in the list—to look for similar meanings—they respond like adults in "recognizing" the critical word.

Application: Siblings sometimes argue about past events—who did or said something in the past. For example:

older child: "I took the trash out last night just like I always do."

younger child: "Nuh-uh. You were too busy. So I did it."

Listening to these arguments, it is tempting for parents to side with the older child, assuming that older children usually remember past events more accurately. That's not a bad assumption, but the paradox is that the same processes that enhance older children's remembering also make them more prone to certain kinds of memory errors. Consequently, parents need to be cautious and be certain that the situation is not one in which an older child's memory is likely to be inaccurate, an illusion caused by the older child's greater reliance on gist processing. In the example here, the older child's memory of what happened may actually be based on his well-established script of what he usually does in the evening.

Critical Thinking Questions: In this feature the example of an older child forgetting the one time he did not do his chores is used. What other examples might occur when using gist processing—the "fuzzy trace"—might cause errors in recall?

Autobiographical memory is important because it helps people construct a personal life history. In addition, autobiographical memory allows us to relate our experiences to others, creating socially shared memories (Bauer, 2006).

Autobiographical memory originates in the preschool years. According to one influential theory (Nelson & Fivush, 2004), autobiographic memory emerges gradually, as children acquire different skills. Infants and toddlers have the basic memory skills that allow them to remember past events. Layered on top of these memory skills during the preschool years are language skills and a child's sense of self. Language allows children to become conversational partners. After infants begin to talk, parents often converse with them about past and future events—particularly about personal experiences in the child's past and future. Parents may talk about what the child did today at daycare or remind the child about what she will be doing this weekend. In conversations like these, parents teach their children the important features of events and how events are organized (Fivush, Reese, & Haden, 2006). Children's autobiographical memories are richer when parents talk about past events in detail and, specifically, when they encourage children to expand their description of past events by, for instance, using open-ended questions (e.g., "Where did Mommy go last night?"). When parents use this conversational style with their preschool children, they have earlier memories of their childhood when they reach young adolescence (Jack, MacDonald, Reese, & Hayne, 2009).

The richness of parent-child conversations also helps to explain a cultural difference in autobiographical memory. Compared to adults living in East Asia, Europeans and North Americans typically remember more events from their early years and remember those events in more detail (Ross & Wang, 2010). This difference in early memories can be traced to cultural differences in parent-child conversational styles: The elaborative style is less common among Asian parents, which means that Asian youngsters have fewer opportunities for the conversations about past events that foster autobiographical memory

(Kulkofsky, Wang, & Koh, 2009; Schröder et al., 2013). Similarly, parent–child conversations explain why women's autobiographical memories tend to be richer—more vivid, more emotion-laden, and more elaborate—than men's emotional memories: Parents use the elaborative conversational style more often with daughters than with sons (Grysman & Hudson, 2013).

An emergent sense of self also contributes to autobiographical memory. We describe sense of self in detail in Module 11.1, but the key idea is that one- and two-year-olds rapidly acquire a sense that they exist independently in space and time. An emerging sense of self thus provides coherence and continuity to children's experience. Children realize that the self who went to the park a few days ago is the same self who is now at a birthday party and the same self who will read a book with Dad before bedtime. The self provides a personal timeline that anchors a child's recall of the past (and anticipation of the future). Thus, a sense of self, language skills that allow children to converse with parents about past and future, and basic memory skills all contribute to the emergence of autobiographical memory in preschool children.

Infantile amnesia is the inability to remember events from early in life, such as the birth of a younger sibling.

Older children, adolescents, and adults remember few events from their lives that occurred before autobiographical memory is in place. *Infantile amnesia* **refers to the inability to remember events from one's early life.** Adults and school-age children recall nothing from the first two years of life and relatively little from the preschool years (Hayne & Jack, 2011). For example, when the two-year-old in the photo is older, he won't remember his brother's birth (Peterson & Rideout, 1998; Quas et al., 1999).[1] But there's a good chance the older boy will remember his brother's second—and certainly his third—birthday.

Many of the same factors that forge an autobiographical memory contribute to infantile amnesia (Hayne & Jack, 2011). For example, once children learn to talk (beginning at about 12 to 15 months), they tend to rely on language to represent their past (Nelson, 1993). Consequently, their earlier, prelingual experiences may be difficult to retrieve from memory, just as after you reorganize your bedroom you may have trouble finding things (Simcock & Hayne, 2002). In addition, it appears that memories do not consolidate as well (i.e., are not laid down as strongly) in childhood as in adulthood and so are more likely to degrade or be lost (Bauer & Larkina, 2014). Some theorists also argue that, because infants and toddlers have no sense of self, they lack the autobiographical timeline that is used to organize experiences later in life (Howe & Courage, 1997).

Thus personal experiences from the earliest years usually cannot be recalled because of inadequate language or inadequate sense of self (Hayne & Jack, 2011). Beginning in the preschool years, however, autobiographical memory provides a cohesive framework for remembering life's significant events. Unfortunately, some children's autobiographical

---

[1]Perhaps you are not convinced because you vividly recall significant events that occurred when you were two years old, such as the birth of a sibling, a move to a different home, or the death of a close friend or relative. In reality, you are probably not remembering the actual event. Instead, we can almost guarantee that you are remembering others' retelling of these events and your role in them, not the events themselves. Events like these are often socially shared memories, and that is the basis for your memory.

Ted Foxx/Alamy Stock Photo

When trying to remember past events, young children sometimes "remember" what others suggest might have happened in the past, particularly when the suggestion comes from a person in authority.

memories include memories of abuse. Can these memories be trusted? We'll see in the next section.

EYEWITNESS TESTIMONY.   Remember Cheryl, the four-year-old in the module-opening vignette who claimed that a neighbour had touched her "private parts"? If Cheryl's comments lead to a police investigation, Cheryl's testimony will be critical. Can her recall of events be trusted, however? This question is difficult to answer. In legal proceedings, children are often interviewed repeatedly, sometimes as many as 10 to 15 times—with interviewers sometimes asking leading questions or making suggestive remarks. Over the course of repeated questioning, the child may confuse what actually happened with what others suggest may have happened. As you'll see in the Focus on Research feature, preschoolers are particularly prone to confusion of this sort (Ceci & Bruck, 1995, 1998).

Perhaps you are skeptical of findings like these. Surely it must be possible to tell when a young child is describing events that never happened. In fact, although law enforcement officials and child protection workers believe they can usually tell whether children are telling the truth, professionals often cannot distinguish true and false reports (Klemfuss & Ceci, 2012). This problem is compounded because repeated questioning of child witnesses may result in deliberate or unintentional memory distortion. According to Welder (2000), in Canada, "on average, children are questioned 11 times prior to testifying in court" (p. 166). Thus to elicit accurate recall, the questioning of children has to be done in a sensitive and nonleading manner. Analysis of videotapes of actual interviews reveals that even trained investigators often ask children leading questions and make suggestive comments (Lamb, Sternberg,

Focus On Research

Do Stereotypes and Suggestions Influence Preschoolers' Reports?

QUESTION 7.1
When Courtney was 12-months-old, she fell on the sidewalk and went to the emergency room for stitches in her chin. Now she is a mother and enjoys telling her children how brave she was at the hospital. What about this story doesn't ring true? *(Answer is on page 240.)*

Who were the investigators, and what was the aim of the study? During legal proceedings, children are often interviewed repeatedly. In the process, interviewers sometimes suggest that certain events took place. Cheryl might be asked, "When Mr. Johnson touched your private parts, was anyone else around?"—a question implying that Mr. Johnson definitely touched Cheryl. Furthermore, interviewers may suggest to children that the accused is a "bad" person, which may make suggestions of abuse more plausible to children. Michelle D. Leichtman and Stephen J. Ceci (1995) wanted to know if repeated questioning and hints about an adult's nature would influence preschool children's recall of events.

How did the investigators measure the topic of interest? Leichtman and Ceci had a man named Sam Stone briefly visit classes of three- and four-year-olds and five- and six-year-olds at a daycare centre. During his visit, Sam greeted the teacher, who introduced him to the class. Sam mentioned that the story being read by the teacher was one of his favourites; then he waved goodbye and left the room.

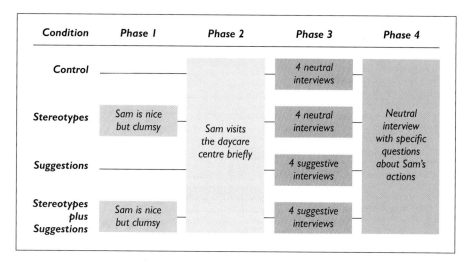

Figure 7-5 Four conditions and timeline of the Sam Stone study.

Leichtman and Ceci created four different conditions, shown in Figure 7-5, which differed in what children were told before and after Sam's visit. Children in the control condition were interviewed after the visit, every week for four weeks. In these interviews, youngsters were simply asked to describe Sam's visit.

The *stereotype* condition differed from the *control* condition in one way: Three times prior to Sam's visit, teachers described Sam as a nice but clumsy man, thereby implying that children should expect Sam to be clumsy. The *suggestions* condition also differed from the control condition: During each of the four weekly interviews that followed Sam's visit, the interviewer made misleading suggestions that Sam had ripped a book and soiled a teddy bear, such as "Remember when Sam Stone ripped the book? Did he rip it on purpose or by accident?" (p. 577). Of course, he had done neither. In the fourth condition, *stereotypes plus suggestions*, teachers told children about Sam's clumsiness before the visit and interviewers made misleading suggestions afterward.

Finally, 10 weeks after Sam had visited the classroom, a different interviewer, one not present during Sam's visit or the previous interviews, asked children several questions about what had happened when Sam visited, including whether Sam had ripped a book or soiled a teddy bear.

Who were the children in the study? A total of 176 preschool children participated. Half were three- and four-year-olds, and half were five- and six-year-olds.

What was the design of the study? This study was experimental. There were three independent variables: (1) the age of the child, (2) whether the child was told before Sam's visit that he was clumsy, and (3) whether the child received misleading suggestions after Sam's visit. The dependent variable was the child's answer to the interviewers' misleading questions. That is, Leichtman and Ceci counted the percentage of times that children said they had actually seen Sam rip a book or soil the teddy bear, events that never happened. The study was also cross-sectional because it included a group of younger children (three- and four-year-olds) and a group of older children (five- and six-year-olds).

Were there ethical concerns with the study? No. Sam's visit, the teachers' comments about Sam beforehand, and the interviews afterward posed no special risks to children.

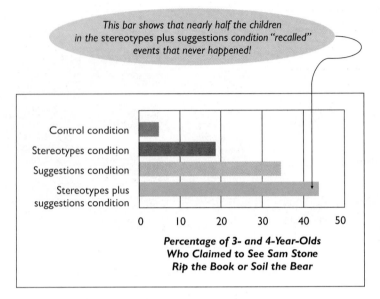

Figure 7-6 Influence of suggestion on children's recall of events.

Based on Leichtman, M. D., & Ceci, S. L. (1995). *The effects of stereotypes and suggestions on preschoolers' reports.* Developmental Psychology, 31, 568–578.

What were the results? Children's answers to the misleading questions are shown in Figure 7-6. For simplicity, we have shown only the data for three- and four-year-olds. The data for five- and six-year-olds were similar but the effects were smaller—that is, the older children were less suggestible than the younger children. Almost no children in the control condition claimed to have seen Sam rip a book or soil a teddy bear. However, some children in the stereotyped condition claimed to have seen Sam rip a book or soil a teddy bear, and more than one-third of the children in the suggestions condition claimed he did one or the other. When stereotypes and suggestions were combined, almost half the children said they had seen events that never took place. Although the five- and six-year-olds described events much more accurately, even 15 percent of these youngsters claimed to have seen Sam rip a book or soil a bear.

What did the investigators conclude? Leichtman and Ceci believe that whether preschoolers are suggestible depends entirely on how their memory for events is probed. The results from their control condition suggest that without stereotypes and suggestions, preschoolers are unlikely to report events that never happened. However, when adults suggest that a person is likely to behave in a particular way and later imply that some events actually did happen, many preschoolers will go along. Based on their results, it is probable that, since Cheryl's report was spontaneous and not elicited by repeated questions, it is trustworthy.

What converging evidence would strengthen these conclusions? Falsely claiming that a visitor ripped a book is a far cry from testifying falsely in a case of child abuse. You can think of many ways in which the target events differ: Abuse involves the child directly, is very embarrassing to the child, and is extraordinarily stressful; observing the torn book is none of these. Consequently, it would be valuable to determine whether young children are equally suggestible when remembering incidents of abuse. Of course, designing an experiment of this sort would be unethical; we can't expose children directly to abuse, nor can we suggest to them that others have been abused. A compromise is to study children's memory for the events of a physical exam by a healthcare professional. These exams involve the child's body and are often mildly embarrassing and mildly stressful. Research such as this can demonstrate whether young children are suggestible in settings that more closely resemble actual child abuse, yet it still preserves the rights of children as research participants.

Critical Thinking Question: Given the problems with accuracy of eyewitness testimony and the ways in which children's memories can be influenced by adult questioning, how would you train police officers to deal with child witnesses? In other words, if you were to design a training program or workshop for your provincial police force or the R.C.M.P., what are the main issues you would focus on?

& Esplin, 2000). For example, in one famous case in which a preschool teacher named Kelly was accused of sexually abusing children in her class, the children were asked the following leading questions (among many, many others):

Do you think that Kelly was not good when she was hurting you all?

When did Kelly say these words: "Piss," "shit," "sugar"?

When Kelly kissed you, did she ever put her tongue in your mouth?

(Bruck & Ceci, 1995)

Each of the questions is misleading by implying that something happened when actually it might not have. When, as in the situation in the photo on page 236, the questioner is an adult in a position of authority, children often believe that what is suggested by the adult actually happened (Candel, Hayne, Strange, & Prevoo, 2009; Ceci & Bruck, 1998).

Children's memories can also be tainted simply by overhearing others—adults or peers—describe events. When, for example, some children in a class experience an event (e.g., a class field trip or a special class visitor), they often talk about the event with classmates who weren't there; later, these absent classmates readily describe what happened and often insist they were actually there (Principe & Ceci, 2002; Principe & Schindewolf, 2012).

Preschool children are particularly suggestible. Why? One idea is that they are less able than older children and adults to know the source of information that they remember (Poole & Lindsay, 1995). For example, a father recalling his daughter's piano recitals will know the source of many of his memories: Some are from personal experience (he attended the recital); some he recorded; and some are based on his daughter's descriptions. Preschool children are not particularly skilled at such source monitoring. When recalling past events, preschoolers become confused about who did or said what and, when confused in this manner, they frequently assume that they must have experienced something personally. Consequently, when preschool children are asked leading questions (e.g., "When the man touched you, did it hurt?"), this information is also stored in memory but without the source. Because preschool children are not skilled at monitoring sources, they have trouble distinguishing what they actually experienced from what interviewers imply that they experienced (Ghetti, 2008).

Although preschoolers are easily misled, they can provide reliable testimony. Guidelines for interviewers have been derived from research, with the aim of improving the reliability of child witnesses (Ceci & Bruck, 1995, 1998; Gordon, Baker-Ward, & Ornstein,

2001). Most of these protocols make similar recommendations regarding "best practices" for interviewing children. Specifically, interviewers should

- interview children as soon as possible after the event in question.

- encourage children to tell the truth, to feel free to say "I don't know" to questions, and to correct interviewers when they say something that is incorrect.

- start by asking children to describe the event in their own words ("Tell me what happened after school …") and follow up with open-ended questions ("Can you tell me more about what happened while you were walking home?") and minimize the use of specific questions (because they may suggest to children events that did not happen).

- allow children to understand and feel comfortable in the interview format by beginning with a neutral event (e.g., a birthday party or holiday celebration) before moving to the event of interest.

- ask questions that consider alternate explanations of the event (i.e., explanations that do not involve abuse).

ANSWER 7.1
Due to infantile amnesia, it's not very likely that Courtney is remembering her actual experience in the emergency room. Instead, her recall of these events is based on what she remembers others saying about what happened that day. She has heard these stories so many times that she can easily imagine seeing herself in emerg as a 12-month-old.

Following these guidelines fosters the conditions under which children are likely to recall the past more accurately and thereby be better witnesses (Hershkowitz, Lamb, Orbach, Katz, & Horowitz, 2012; Poole & Bruck, 2012). Canadian researcher Laura Melnyk of King's University College at the University of Western Ontario and her colleagues have proposed policy recommendations for interviewing children who give testimony (e.g., Melnyk, Crossman, & Scullin, 2007; London, Bruck, Poole & Melnyk, 2011). In addition to ideas similar to those listed above, the recommendations of Melnyk and colleagues include using a structured interview format. Having a structured interview prevents use of coercive techniques (in part because it provides a framework for the interview), increases rapport with the child, and increases the reliability of the information that is obtained. In recent years, various reforms have been enacted to protect child witnesses in Canada—the stressors involved in court cases are being recognized and special provisions are being made for children, especially in abuse cases. Amendments to the Criminal Code of Canada regarding testimony by children and other vulnerable persons were enacted in 2006, opening the way to the development of strategies such as videotaped testimony, that is, testifying by closed-circuit television (CCTV) from a different room (Bala, Paetsch, Bertrand, & Thomas, 2011). Policy changes like these show how research findings can be a stable foundation for public policy.

 Check Your Learning

RECALL Describe how children use strategies to help them remember.

Summarize the processes that give rise to autobiographical memory in toddlers.

INTERPRET Distinguish the situations in which gist-processing of experience is advantageous (i.e., it leads to better memory) from those in which it is not.

APPLY Describe how research on children's eyewitness testimony illustrates connections among emotional, cognitive, and social development.

7.2 Problem Solving

OUTLINE

Developmental Trends in Solving Problems

Features of Children's and Adolescents' Problem Solving

Scientific Problem Solving

LEARNING OBJECTIVES

1. Do older children and adolescents typically solve problems better than younger children?

2. What factors contribute to the success of children and adolescents in solving problems?

3. Can children and adolescents reason scientifically?

Brad, age 12, wanted to go to a hobby shop on New Year's Day. His mother, Terri, doubted that the store was open on a holiday, so she asked Brad to call first. Moments later, Brad returned and said, "Let's go!" When they arrived at the hobby shop, it was closed. Annoyed, Terri snapped, "I thought you called!" Brad answered, "I did. They didn't answer, so I figured they were too busy to come to the phone." Later that day, Brad's three-year-old sister grabbed an open can of pop from the kitchen counter, looked at Terri, and said, "This isn't yours 'cause there's no lipstick." Terri thought her daughter's inference was sophisticated, particularly when compared to her son's illogical reasoning earlier in the day.

According to Piaget's theory, reasoning and problem solving become progressively more sophisticated as children develop. Piaget believed that young children's reasoning (reflected in the term "preoperational thought") was particularly limited and that adolescents' reasoning (reflected in the term "formal operational thought") was quite powerful. But research has since shown that this account was wrong in two ways. First, it underestimated young children who, like Brad's sister, often astonish us with the inferences they draw. Second, it overestimated adolescents who, like Brad, frequently frustrate us with their flawed logic.

In this module, we'll trace the growth of problem-solving skills in childhood and adolescence. We'll see that young children do indeed solve problems with far greater skill than predicted by Piaget but that, throughout development, many factors limit the success with which children, adolescents, and adults solve problems.

Developmental Trends in Solving Problems

Solving problems is as much a part of children's daily lives as eating and sleeping. Think about some of the following common examples:

- After dinner, a child tries to figure out how to finish homework and watch his favourite TV program.

- A child wants to get her bike out of the garage, where it is trapped behind the car and the lawnmower.

- A teenager wants to come up with a way to avoid raking the leaves.

In each case, there is a well-defined goal (e.g., riding the bike, avoiding a chore), and the child is deciding how to achieve it.

As a general rule, as children get older, they solve problems like these more often and solve them more effectively. Of course, this doesn't mean that younger children

Anton Novožilov/Shutterstock

Even infants can solve some problems effectively, for example, by pulling on a string to bring a toy within reach.

are always inept at solving problems. In fact, research has produced many instances in which young children solve problems successfully. For example, when asked what they could do if they went to the beach but forgot to bring lunch, most four- and five-year-olds suggest plausible, effective solutions such as buying lunch at the concession building (Hudson, Shapiro, & Sosa, 1995). What's more, even infants can solve simple problems (Barrett, Davis, & Needham, 2007). If an attractive toy is placed out of reach, infants like the baby in the photo will use other means to bring the toy to them, such as pulling on a string, or if the toy is on a cloth, pulling the cloth. Both are simple but wonderfully effective methods of achieving the goal of playing with an interesting toy (Willatts, 1999).

Also, as Brad's behaviour in the vignette reveals, adolescents are not always skilled problem solvers. Their problem solving is often inefficient, haphazard, or just plain wrong. For example, think about the following problem:

Imagine that you want to enter one of two raffles. The first one advertises, "50 tickets, 5 winners, so you have a 10 percent chance of winning!" The second advertises, "500 tickets, 40 winners, so you have an 8 percent chance of winning!" Which raffle would you enter?

Many adolescents choose to enter the second raffle—even though they've just read that the odds of winning are less (8 percent versus 10 percent)—apparently because they see that there are 40 winning tickets, not just 5 (Kokis et al., 2002). In the process, of course, they ignore the fact that the second raffle has 460 losing tickets compared to only 45 in the first raffle!

Thus, research confirms what we saw in the vignette with Brad and his sister: Although children tend to become more effective problem solvers as they get older, even young children sometimes show remarkable problem-solving skills, and adolescents can be error prone. In the next section, we'll look at some of the elements that govern children's success in solving problems.

Features of Children's and Adolescents' Problem Solving

Because problem solving is such an important skill, child-development scientists have been eager to reveal the circumstances that promote children's problem solving. The results of this work are described in the next few pages, organized around important themes that characterize children's problem solving.

YOUNG CHILDREN SOMETIMES FAIL TO SOLVE PROBLEMS BECAUSE THEY DON'T ENCODE ALL THE IMPORTANT INFORMATION IN A PROBLEM.

When solving a problem, people construct a mental representation that includes the important features of a problem. *Encoding processes* **transform the information in a problem into a mental representation.** When the problem is to get the bike that's trapped in the back of the garage, for example, encoding creates a representation that includes the goal (get the bike) as well as other critical elements of the problem (e.g., the location of the obstacles).

Quite often children's representations of problems are incorrect or incomplete. They fail to encode problem features (or they encode them incorrectly), making it unlikely that they will solve problems. On conservation of liquid problems like the one shown on page 194, young children's representations often include the heights of the containers but not their diameters. Or when shown mathematical equivalence problems such as "6 + 2 = 5 + _____" they often mistakenly encode the problem as "6 + 2 + 5 = _____" (McNeil, 2014).

When young children's representations lack these key features, it's not surprising that they fail to solve problems. As children grow, their encodings are more likely to be complete, perhaps due to increases in the capacity of working memory and because of greater knowledge of the world (as we'll see in the next section). But even adults' representations are often incomplete. To illustrate, think about what appears on the heads side of a loonie. It's a bust of the Queen, but is it facing left or right? Some words appear also, but what are they? Is there a date? Where? Your representation of the loonie is far from complete, because you have encoded only the features that are essential for using it in solving real problems involving cash (i.e., it is gold coloured and features a likeness of the Queen's head). Now get out a real loonie and check your recall!

YOUNG CHILDREN SOMETIMES FAIL TO SOLVE PROBLEMS BECAUSE THEY DON'T PLAN AHEAD. Solving problems, particularly complex ones, often requires planning ahead. For example, the goal of getting ready for school requires planning, because it involves coordinating a number of tasks—get dressed, eat breakfast, brush teeth, find backpack—that must be completed under time pressure. Faced with problems like this, young children rarely come up with an effective plan. Why? Several factors contribute (Ellis & Siegler, 1997; McCormack, 2011):

- Young children often believe—unrealistically—that they can solve a problem by boldly forging ahead without an explicit plan. Like many people who hate to read the directions that come with new toys or games, young children often find it difficult to resist the urge "let's get moving" in favour of "let's figure this out."

- Planning is hard work, and if young children find that their plans often fail, they may see little point in investing the effort.

- Young children may expect parents and other adults to solve complex problems for them.

These factors don't mean that young children never plan or can't plan. For example, when four-year-olds are asked to solve mazes and are urged to avoid "dead ends" in the maze, they typically pause before drawing and look ahead to find a solution (Gardner & Rogoff, 1990). Thus, young children can plan, if they're asked to and the problem is not too complex. Many problems, however, make it difficult or even pointless for young children to plan.

SUCCESSFUL PROBLEM SOLVING TYPICALLY DEPENDS UPON KNOWL- EDGE SPECIFIC TO THE PROBLEM AS WELL AS GENERAL PRO- CESSES. Solving a problem often requires that children know some critical facts. For example during the elementary-school years, children become much more adept at solving arithmetic word problems such as this one: "Joe has two candy bars; then Jessica gives him four more. How many candy bars does Joe have in all?" This improvement comes about as children master their basic arithmetic facts and as they learn how to map different types of word problems onto arithmetic problems (Kail & Hall, 1999). Because older children usually have more of the knowledge relevant to solving a problem, they are more successful.

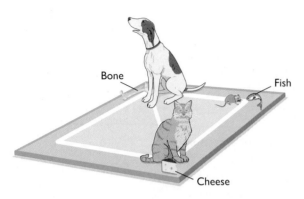

Figure 7-7 A problem requiring children to perform counter-intuitive actions to achieve a goal.

Effective problem solving depends on more than problem-specific knowledge. Children often use generic strategies—ones not specific to particular tasks or problems—to find a solution. **An example is** *means-ends analysis,* **in which a person determines the difference between the current and desired situations, and then does something to reduce the difference.** If no single action leads directly to the goal, then the person establishes a subgoal, one that moves the person closer to the goal. To illustrate, think of a nine-year-old who has pangs of hunger while reading in her bedroom—her goal is getting something to eat. There's no food in her bedroom, so "go to the kitchen" becomes a subgoal and, once there, she can achieve her main goal. Likewise, the baby on page 242 used means-ends analysis in pulling the string toward himself to achieve the main goal of grabbing the toy.

Even preschool children use means-ends analyses to solve problems. For example, a two-and-a-half-year-old who wants a favourite book that is out of reach on a shelf will find a chair to stand on. The chair is the means to achieve the subgoal of "getting within reach of the book." Means-end analyses work for young children mainly when used on simple problems in which the difference between the current and desired situations can be achieved in a few moves. Younger children tend to struggle with more complex problems, however, as is evident in their efforts to solve the dog-cat-mouse problem shown in Figure 7-7. Three animals and their favourite foods are placed on corners and the child is asked to move the animals along the paths, one at a time, until each animal is paired with its favourite food. But, two animals cannot share the same corner, and all animals must be placed in corners. Moving the cat to the empty corner would achieve part of that goal, and that's what most children do. In contrast, they rarely move an animal away from its favourite food (even though that's often required temporarily), because that is a "bad move" according to means-end analyses (Klahr, 1985). We can see that younger children have difficulty with problems that require generating many subgoals and keeping track of these while en route to the overall goal (DeLoache, Miller, & Pierroutsakos, 1998; McCormack, 2011).

CHILDREN AND ADOLESCENTS USE A VARIETY OF STRATEGIES TO SOLVE PROBLEMS.

In Piaget's view, children and adolescents solve problems in fundamentally different ways: Eight-year-olds, for example, consistently do so using concrete operational logic, but 13-year-olds do so using formal operational logic. The modern view, introduced in Module 6.2, differs: Children and adolescents call upon several strategies to solve problems. For example, while playing board games in which a roll of the dice determines how many spaces to move, young children use many strategies to determine the number of moves from the dice (Bjorklund & Rosenblum, 2002). If the dice show 5 and 2, sometimes a child counts aloud "1, 2, 3, 4, 5, 6, 7," and then moves 7 spaces; sometimes the child simply counts "5, 6, 7" and moves; and other times the child glances briefly at the dice, then moves, as if she recalled the sum from memory.

Much the same thing happens, of course, when older children or adolescents learn a new game or a new skill. Initially, they try many different ways to solve a problem. As they gain experience solving a particular type of problem, they learn the easiest, most effective strategy and use it as often as possible (Siegler, 2000).

This general approach is captured in Siegler's (1996, 2007) overlapping waves model. According to Siegler (1996), children use multiple strategies to solve problems,

Q&A QUESTION 7.2
Ten-year-old Kayla awakes to see the season's first snowfall. She can hardly wait to get outside, but then she remembers that her sled is hanging on a hook in the garage, beyond her reach. Use means-ends analysis to show how she could achieve her goal of sledding. *(Answer is on page 248.)*

and over time they tend to use strategies that are faster, more accurate, and take less effort. The model is illustrated in Figure 7-8, which shows how often different hypothetical strategies are used, based on a person's age. Strategy A, for example, is very common among young children but becomes less common with age; Strategy E shows just the opposite profile, becoming more common with age. The vertical lines make it easy to see how often various strategies are used at different ages. Among seven-year-olds, Strategy A is most common, followed by B and D; in contrast, among 14-year-olds, Strategy D is most common, followed by C and E. Thus, children and adolescents are alike in choosing from a well-stocked toolkit to solve problems; they differ in that adolescents typically have a more sophisticated set of tools.

Some theorists go further and imagine that the problem-solving toolkit includes two general kinds of tools (Klaczynski, 2004; Stanovich, Toplak, & West, 2008). **Sometimes children and adolescents solve problems using** *heuristics*—**that is, rules of thumb that do not guarantee a solution but are useful in solving a range of problems.** Heuristics tend to be fast and require little effort. Sometimes children solve problems analytically—depending on the nature of the problem, they may compute an answer mathematically or use logical rules.

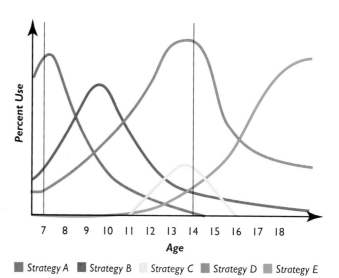

Figure 7-8 Siegler's overlapping waves model of strategy use.

Based on Siegler, R. S. (1996). *Emerging minds: The process of change in children's thinking.* New York, NY: Oxford University Press.

To see the difference between heuristic and analytic solutions, think about the following problem:

> Erica wants to go to a baseball game to try to catch a fly ball. She calls the main office and learns that almost all fly balls have been caught in section 43. Just before she chooses her seats, she learns that her friend Jimmy caught two fly balls last week sitting in section 10. Which section is most likely to give Erica the best chance to catch a fly ball? (Kokis et al., 2002, p. 34)

The heuristic solution relies on personal experience: When in doubt, imitate other people who have been successful. In this case, that means sitting where the friend sat. The analytic solution, in contrast, involves relying upon the statistical information that, historically, the odds of catching a fly ball are greatest in section 43. Adolescents are more likely than children to solve problems like this one analytically, but some children solve them analytically and some adolescents rely on the heuristic approach (Kokis et al., 2002). In fact, this is a general pattern: Heuristic and analytic solutions are both used throughout childhood and adolescence, but use of analytic solutions becomes more frequent as children develop (Furlan, Agnoli, & Reyna, 2013; Kail, 2013).

COLLABORATION OFTEN ENHANCES CHILDREN'S PROBLEM SOLVING.

In research, children typically solve problems by themselves, but in everyday life, they often collaborate with parents, siblings, and peers. This collaboration is usually beneficial when the partner is a parent, older child, or more knowledgeable peer. As we saw in Module 6.2, parents and older children often scaffold children's efforts to solve problems, providing structure and direction that allow younger children to accomplish more than they could alone. In laboratory studies, for example, parents often tailor help to the child's needs, watching quietly when children are making headway but giving words of encouragement and hints when their children are puzzled or confused (Rogoff, 1998).

Oleg Mikhaylov/Shutterstock

Collaborative problem solving is often ineffective with young children because they lack the cognitive and social skills needed to work together.

Collaboration with peers is sometimes but not always productive, and the settings that are conducive to effective peer collaboration remain something of a mystery to children (Siegler & Alibali, 2005). On the one hand, collaboration involving young children like the ones shown in the photo often fails simply because preschool children lack many of the social and linguistic skills needed to work as part of a team. Peer collaboration is also often unproductive when problems are so difficult that neither child has a clue about how to proceed. On the other hand, peer collaboration works when both children are invested in solving the problem and when they share responsibility for doing so.

Despite its virtues, collaboration does not come easily to children attending schools in the United States, Canada, and Europe, where they are exposed to instruction that emphasizes an individual student's participation and achievement. In contrast, in some schools in the rest of the world—for example, in Mexico and Japan—students are taught to support their classmates, to learn from and build on their ideas and suggestions, and to view classmates as resources. In this setting, collaboration comes naturally to children (Chavajay, 2008; Silva, Correa-Chávez, & Rogoff, 2010).

Scientific Problem Solving

In Chapter 6, we saw that many child-development researchers rely on the child-as-scientist metaphor, in which experiences provide the "data" from which children construct theories that capture their understanding of the material and social world. These theories are usually described as informal because they lack the rigour of real scientific theories and because children and adolescents rarely conduct true experiments designed to test their theories. However, when it comes to the skills associated with real scientific reasoning, children and even adolescents typically have some conspicuous faults (Kuhn, 2012):

- ***Children and adolescents often have misconceptions about scientific phenomena that interfere with their scientific thinking.*** In other words, through experience with the physical and social worlds, children and adolescents construct mental models that help them to understand those worlds, even though the models are often wrong. For example, six-year-olds often believe that the earth is stationary but that the sun and moon move up and down (Klahr, Zimmerman, & Jirout, 2011). Similarly, young children often believe that energy is a property of people or living things, not all physical systems or objects (Nordine, Krajcik, & Fortus, 2011). Unlearning these flawed conceptions is often a necessary first step in children's and adolescents' scientific thinking (Klahr et al., 2011).

- ***Children and adolescents often devise experiments in which variables are*** *confounded—* ***they are combined instead of evaluated independently—so that the results are ambiguous.*** For example, if asked to determine how the size of a car's engine, wheels, and tailfins affect its speed, children often manipulate more than one variable at a time. They compare a car with a large engine, large wheels, and large tailfins to a car with a small engine, small wheels, and small tailfins. Not until adulthood do individuals commonly devise experiments in which one variable is manipulated (e.g., size of the wheels) and the rest are held constant, which allows clear conclusions regarding cause and effect (Schauble, 1996).

- ***Children and adolescents often reach conclusions prematurely, basing them on too little evidence.*** That is, instead of conducting all of the experiments necessary to isolate the impact of variables, children and adolescents typically conduct a subset of the experiments and then reach conclusions prematurely (Zimmerman, 2007). In the previous example about determining a car's speed, children rarely do enough experimentation to provide conclusive evidence about each variable. They might run experiments showing that a car runs fast with a large engine and slower with large tailfins, but they might also assume that wheel size has no effect without actually doing the critical experiments (Kuhn, Garcia-Mila, Zohar, & Andersen, 1995).

These findings suggest that children and adolescents have limited scientific skills. Other findings, however, indicate that young children do have some rudimentary scientific skills. For example, children can sometimes identify the kind of evidence that would support a hypothesis. If trying to determine whether an animal has a good sense of smell, six- to eight-year-olds know that it's better to conduct an experiment that uses a weak-smelling food than a strong-smelling food. And if trying to decide whether a mouse that is running loose in a house is large or small, they know that it is better to place a piece of food in a box that has a small opening rather than in one with a large opening (Sodian, Zaitchik, & Carey, 1991). In these studies, young children are not designing complete experiments on their own; instead, they are simply evaluating part of an experiment that someone else has planned, which may explain their improved skill (DeLoache, Miller, & Pierroutsakos, 1998).

It is also clear that even young children can be trained to think more scientifically. For example, elementary-school children can be trained to understand the need to avoid confounded experiments by manipulating one variable at a time. Such training is straightforward—by showing both confounded and unconfounded experiments, then illustrating

ANSWER 7.2
Main goal: Go sledding. Subgoal 1: Get sled. Fact: Sled is on hook in garage, out of reach. Subgoal 2: Get parent to reach sled. Fact: Mom gone to work, Dad is asleep. Subgoal 3: Wake Dad.

the difficulty in drawing clear conclusions from confounded experiments—and results in long-lasting improvements in children's understanding of well-designed experiments (Lorch et al., 2010).

Thus, the general developmental trend for scientific reasoning resembles the one we saw previously for general problem solving: Overall, children's skill improves steadily as they grow, but young children are sometimes amazingly skilled, while older children and adolescents are sometimes surprisingly inept (Kuhn, 2011). In the next module, we'll see whether children's academic skills (reading, writing, arithmetic) develop in a similar manner.

Check Your Learning

RECALL Describe findings that counter the general belief that children are more successful at solving problems as they get older.

Summarize the reasons why young children often fail to solve problems.

INTERPRET Compare the widely embraced metaphor of children-as-scientists with the outcomes from research on actual scientific reasoning by children and adolescents.

APPLY Based on what you know about children's success at solving problems collaboratively, would you recommend that children and adolescents work together on homework?

7.3 Academic Skills

OUTLINE
Reading
Writing
Knowing and Using Numbers

LEARNING OBJECTIVES
1. What are the components of skilled reading?
2. As children develop, how does their writing improve?
3. When do children understand and use quantitative skills?

When Jasmine, a bubbly three-year-old, is asked how old she will be on her next birthday, she proudly says, "Four!" while holding up five fingers. Asked to count four objects, whether they are candies, toys, or socks, Jasmine almost always says, "1, 2, 6, 7 . . . SEVEN!" Jasmine's older brothers find all this very funny, but her mother thinks that, notwithstanding the obvious mistakes, Jasmine's behaviour shows that she knows a lot about numbers and counting. But what, exactly, does Jasmine understand? That question has her mother stumped!

Children and adolescents use their cognitive skills to accomplish many tasks in a variety of settings. Among the most important of these, however, are the school-related tasks of learning to read, write, and do math. Child-development researchers have studied these domains extensively, as you'll see in this module, which examines the traditional three Rs. We'll start with reading, then examine writing, and end with numbers, where you'll learn why Jasmine counts as she does.

Reading

Try reading the following sentence:

АндреΩ достал билеты на концерт.

Unless you can read Russian, you probably didn't make much headway, did you? Now try this one:

Snore secretary green plastic sleep trucks.

You probably read these words quite easily, but did you get anything more out of this sentence than the one in Russian? These examples show two important processes involved in skilled reading. *Word recognition* **is the process of identifying a unique pattern of letters.** Without knowing Russian, your word recognition was not successful in the first sentence. You did not know that билеты means "tickets" or that концерт means "concert." What's more, because you could not recognize individual words, you had no idea of the meaning of this sentence. *Comprehension* **is the process of extracting meaning from a sequence of words.** In the second sentence, your word recognition was perfect, but comprehension was still impossible because the words were presented in a random sequence. These examples remind us just how difficult learning to read can be.

In the next few pages, we'll look at how children read. We'll start with the skills that children must have if they are to learn to read, and then move to word recognition and comprehension.

FOUNDATIONS OF READING SKILL. Reading involves extracting meaning from print, and children have much to learn to do this successfully. Children need to know that reading is done with words made of letters, not with pictures or scribbles, that words on a page are separated by spaces, and that in English words are read from left to right. And, of course, they need to know the names of individual letters. These skills improve gradually over the preschool years, particularly when children are frequently involved in literacy-related activities such as reading with an adult, playing with magnetic letters, or trying to print simple words. Not surprisingly, children who know more about letters and word forms learn to read more easily than their peers who know less (Levy, Gong, Hessels, Evans, & Jared, 2006; Treiman & Kessler, 2003).

A second essential skill is sensitivity to language sounds. **The ability to hear the distinctive sounds of letters is a skill known as** *phonological awareness.* English words consist of syllables, and a syllable is made up of a vowel that is usually but not always accompanied by consonants. For example, *dust* is a one-syllable word that includes the initial consonant *d* the vowel *u* and the final consonant cluster *st*. Phonological awareness is shown when children can decompose words in this manner by, for example, correctly answering "What's the first sound in dust?" or "Dust without the *d* sounds like what?" Phonological awareness is strongly related to success in learning to read: Children who can readily distinguish language sounds learn to read more readily than children who do not (Melby-Lervåg, Lyster, & Hulme, 2012). In fact, as we'll see in Module 8.3, insensitivity to language sounds is one of the core features of reading disability.

Learning to read in English is particularly challenging because English is often inconsistent in the way that letters are pronounced (e.g., compare the sound of *a* in "bat," "far," "rake," and "was") and the way that sounds are spelled (e.g., the long *e* sound is the same in each of these spellings: "team," "feet," "piece," "lady," "receive," "magazine").[2] In contrast, many other languages—Greek, Finnish, German, Italian, Spanish, Dutch— are far more consistent, which simplifies the mapping of sounds to letters. In Italian, for example, most letters are pronounced in the same way; reading a word like *domani* (tomorrow) is simple because beginning readers just move from left to right, converting each letter to sound, using simple rules: *d*, *m*, and *n* are pronounced as in English, *o* as in "cold," *a* as in "car," and *i* as in "see" (Barca, Ellis, & Burani, 2007). Even though children learn to read more rapidly in languages where letter-sound rules are more consistent, pho- nological awareness remains the single best predictor of reading success in many languages (Caravolas et al., 2012; Ziegler et al., 2010).

If phonological skill is so essential for learning to read, how can we help children master language sounds? The Children's Lives feature describes one easy way.

Storybook reading like that described in this feature is an informal way that parents can foster prereading skills. The benefits are not limited to the first steps in learning to read; rather, they persist into the middle elementary-school years and are just as useful for children learning to read other languages than their own (Chow et al., 2008; Sénéchal & LeFevre, 2002).

When preschool teachers use storybook reading to talk about reading-related skills, their students typically read better in elementary school. For example, in one study (Piasta, Justice, McGinty, & Kaderavek, 2012), preschool teachers in one condition read

Children's Lives

Rhyme Is Sublime Because Sounds Abound

The Cat in the Hat and *Green Eggs and Ham* are two books in the famous Dr. Seuss series. You may remember these stories for their zany plots and extensive use of rhyme. When parents frequently read rhymes—not just Dr. Seuss, but also Mother Goose and other nursery rhymes—their children become more aware of word sounds. Rhyming passages ("Is Spot hot? No, he's not!") draw children's attention to the different sounds that make up words. The more parents read rhymes to their children, the greater their children's phonological awareness, which makes learning to read much easier (Bradley & Bryant, 1983; Ehri et al., 2001).

So the message is clear. Read to children—the more, the better. As the photo here shows, children love it when adults read to them, and learn- ing more about word sounds is icing on the cake!

Critical Thinking Question: Reading rhyming books like those by "Dr. Seuss" aid in developing phonological awareness. In what other ways could parents foster this skill?

Gareth Boden/Pearson Education Ltd.

Picture-book reading is mutually enjoyable for parent and child and can promote children's prereading skills.

---

[2]The famous British playwright George Bernard Shaw ridiculed English spelling by writing "fish" as *ghoti*, with *gh* as in "laugh," *o* as in "women," and *ti* as in "motion"!

a different book to their students every week. In another condition, teachers read a book but added comments about print (e.g., "Here are the cat's words. She says, 'I'm thirsty!'"), about letters (e.g., "This is a C."), and about words (e.g., "This word is cat."). When their teachers pointed to reading-related features of the storybooks, children read more skillfully in first grade (Piasta et al., 2012).

RECOGNIZING WORDS. At the very beginning of reading, children sometimes learn to read a few words "by sight," but they have no understanding of the links between printed letters and the word's sound. **The first step in true reading is** *decoding,* **identifying individual words by sounding out the letters in them.** Beginning readers, like the boy in the photo below, often say the sounds associated with each letter and then blend the sounds to produce a recognizable word. After a word has been sounded out a few times, it becomes a known word that can be read by retrieving it directly from long-term memory. That is, children decode words by recognizing familiar patterns of letters and syllables (Nunes, Bryant, & Barros, 2012).

Thus from their very first efforts to read, most children use direct retrieval for a few words. From that point on, the general strategy is to try retrieval first and, if that fails, to sound out the word or ask a more skilled reader for help (Siegler, 1986). For example, when Robert Kail's daughter Laura was just beginning to read, she knew "the," "Laura," and several one-syllable words that ended in *at*, such as "bat," "cat," and "fat." Shown a sentence like

Laura saw the fat cat run

she would say, "Laura s-s-s … ah-h … wuh … saw the fat cat er-r-r … uh-h-h n-n-n … run." Familiar words were retrieved rapidly, but the unfamiliar ones were slowly sounded out. With more reading experience, children sound out fewer words and retrieve more (Siegler, 1986). In other words, by sounding out novel words, children store information about words in long-term memory that is required for direct retrieval (Cunningham, Perry, Stanovich, & Share, 2002; Share, 2008).

EDUCATIONAL IMPLICATIONS FOR TEACHING READING. Teaching young children to read is probably the most important instructional goal for most Canadian elementary schools. Historically, teachers have used one of three methods to teach reading (Rayner et al., 2001, 2002). The oldest method is teaching phonics. For hundreds of years, Canadian children have learned to read by first focusing on letter names and then their typical sounds, and then moving on to syllables and words. Young children might be taught that *b* sounds like "buh" and that *e* sounds like "eeee," so that putting them together makes "buh-eee … be."

Learning all the letters and their associated sounds can be tedious and can perhaps discourage children from their efforts to learn to read. Consequently, teachers have looked to other methods. In the whole-word method, children are taught to recognize whole words on sight, usually beginning with a small number (50 to 100) of very familiar words, which are repeated over and over to help children learn their appearance (e.g., "run, spot, run!"). In the whole-language method, which has been quite popular in North America for about 30 years, learning to read is thought

Beginning readers rely heavily on sounding out to recognize words, but even beginning readers retrieve some words from memory.

Ikat Photography/Pearson Education Ltd.

to occur naturally as a by-product of immersing the child in language-related activities such as following print as a teacher reads aloud or writing their own stories, inventing their own spellings as necessary (e.g., "Hr neak wz sor"). Teaching phonics is discouraged in the whole-language method.

Although each of these methods has some strengths, research clearly shows that phonics instruction is essential (Rayner et al., 2001, 2002). Children are far more likely to become successful readers when they are taught letter-sound correspondences, and this is particularly true for children at risk for reading failure. The mapping of sounds onto letters, which is the basis of all alphabet-based languages such as English and German, is not something that most children master naturally and incidentally; most children need to be taught letter-sound relations explicitly.

Of course, mindless drilling of letter-sound combinations can be deathly boring. But flash cards and drills are not the only way to master this knowledge; children can acquire it in the context of language games and activities that they enjoy. Teaching children to read some words visually is a good practice, as is embedding reading instruction in other activities that encourage language literacy. However, these practices should be designed to complement phonics instruction, not replace it (Rayner et al., 2001, 2002). Opinion now seems to be settling into a "middle way" view of instruction, which sees phonics as important, but also sees contextual cues as a secondary mechanism (Martin-Chang, Ouellette, & Madden, 2014). Sandra Lyn Martin-Chang from Concordia University, Montreal, and her colleagues from other Canadian universities, propose that the context provided by words embedded in sentences can serve as a self-teaching mechanism, with children able to read more unknown words when these are presented in context than when presented in isolation (Martin-Chang, Levy, & O'Neil, 2006).

COMPREHENSION. As children become more skilled at decoding words, reading begins to have a lot in common with understanding speech. The means by which people understand a sequence of words is much the same whether the source of words is printed text or speech or, for that matter, Braille or sign language (Oakhill & Cain, 2004). As we saw at the beginning of this module, however, decoding words accurately does not guarantee that children will understand what they've read. This phenomenon is captured in the Simple View of Reading model in which reading comprehension is viewed as the product of two general processes: word decoding and language comprehension (Gough & Tunmer, 1986). Children can't comprehend what they read when either a word cannot be decoded or it is decoded but not recognized as a familiar word. Thus, skilled reading depends on accurate decoding coupled with understanding the meaning of the decoded word.

As children gain more reading experience, they better comprehend what they read. Several factors contribute to this improved comprehension (Siegler & Alibali, 2005):

- *Children's language skills improve, which allows them to understand words that they've decoded*: As children's vocabulary expands, they are more likely to recognize words that they have decoded. For example, a Grade 1 student with good decoding skills might be able to decode "prosper" but not understand it; by Grade 5 or 6, children's larger vocabulary means that they could decode and understand "prosper." In addition, older children know more about grammatical structure of sentences, knowledge that helps them comprehend the meaning of an entire sentence (Muter et al., 2004; Oakhill & Cain, 2012).

- *Children become more skilled at recognizing words, allowing more working memory capacity to be devoted to comprehension* (Zinar, 2000). When children struggle to recognize individual words, they often cannot link them to derive the meaning of a passage. In contrast, when children recognize words effortlessly, they can focus their efforts on deriving meaning from the whole sentence.

- *Working memory capacity increases, which means that older and better readers can store more of a sentence in memory as they try to identify the propositions it contains* (De Beni & Palladino, 2000; Nation, Adams, Bowyer-Crane, & Snowling, 1999). This extra capacity is handy when readers move from sentences like "Kevin hit the ball" to "In the bottom of the ninth, with the bases loaded and the Cardinals down 7–4, Kevin put a line drive into the left-field bleachers, his fourth home run of the series."

- *Children acquire more general knowledge of their physical, social, and psychological worlds, which allows them to understand more of what they read* (Ferreol-Barbey, Piolate, & Roussey, 2000; Graesser, Singer, & Trabasso, 1994). For example, even if a six-year-old could recognize all of the words in the longer sentence about Kevin's home run, the child would not fully comprehend the meaning of the passage because he or she lacks the necessary knowledge of baseball.

- *With experience, children better monitor their comprehension.* When readers don't grasp the meaning of a passage because it is difficult or confusing, they read it again (Baker, 1994; Baker & Brown, 1984). Try this sentence (adapted from Carpenter & Daneman, 1981): "The Midwest State Fishing Contest would draw fishermen from all around the region, including some of the best bass guitarists in Michigan." When you first encountered "bass guitarists" you probably interpreted "bass" as a fish. This didn't make much sense, so you reread the phrase to determine that "bass" refers to a type of guitar. Older readers are better able to realize that their understanding is not complete and take corrective action.

- *With experience, children use more appropriate reading strategies.* The goal of reading and the nature of the text dictate how you read. When reading a popular or romance novel, for example, do you often skip sentences (or perhaps paragraphs or entire pages) to get to the "good parts"? This approach makes sense for casual reading but not for reading textbooks, recipes, or how-to manuals. Reading a textbook requires attention to both the overall organization and the relationship of details to that organization. Older, more experienced readers are better able to select a reading strategy that suits the material being read; in contrast, younger, less-skilled readers less often adjust their reading to fit the material (Brown, Pressley, Van Meter, & Schuder, 1996; Cain, 1999).

Collectively, greater language and word recognition skills, greater working memory capacity, greater world knowledge, greater monitoring skill, and use of more appropriate reading strategies allow older and more experienced readers to get more meaning from what they read. In the next part of this module, you'll see how child-development researchers use similar ideas to explain children's developing ability to write.

Writing

Though few of us end up being a Dionne Brand, a Margaret Atwood, or a Yann Martel, most adults do write, both at home and at work. Learning to write begins early but takes years. Before children enter school, they know some of the essentials of writing. For example, four- and five-year-olds often know that writing involves placing letters on a page to communicate an idea (McGee & Richgels, 2004). But skilled writing develops very gradually because it is a complex activity that requires coordinating cognitive and language skills to produce coherent text.

Developmental improvements in children's writing can be traced to a number of factors (Adams, Treiman, & Pressley, 1998; Siegler & Alibali, 2005).

GREATER KNOWLEDGE AND ACCESS TO KNOWLEDGE ABOUT TOPICS.

Writing is about telling something to others. With age, children have more to tell as they gain more knowledge about the world and incorporate this knowledge into their writing (Benton et al., 1995). For example, asked to write about a mayoral election, children are apt to describe it as being like a popularity contest; in contrast, adolescents more often describe it in terms of political issues that are both subtle and complex. Of course, students are sometimes asked to write about topics quite unfamiliar to them. In this case, older children's and adolescents' writing is usually better because they are more adept at finding useful reference material and incorporating it into their writing.

GREATER UNDERSTANDING OF HOW TO ORGANIZE WRITING.

One difficult aspect of writing is organization—arranging all the necessary information in a manner that readers find clear and interesting. In fact, children and young adolescents organize their writing differently than older adolescents and adults (Bereiter & Scardamalia, 1987). **Young writers often use a** *knowledge-telling strategy,* **writing down information on the topic as they retrieve it from memory.** For example, asked to write about the day's events at school, a Grade 2 student wrote:

> It is a rainy day. We hope the sun will shine. We got new spelling books. We had our pictures taken. We sang Happy Birthday to Barbara. (Waters, 1980, p. 155)

The story has no obvious structure. The first two sentences are about the weather, but the last three deal with completely independent topics. Apparently, the writer simply described each event as it came to mind.

During adolescence, writers begin to use a *knowledge-transforming strategy*, **deciding what information to include and how best to organize it for the point they wish to convey to their reader.** This approach involves considering the purpose of writing (e.g., to inform, to persuade, to entertain) and the information needed to achieve this purpose. It also involves considering the needs, interests, and knowledge of the anticipated audience.

Asked to describe the day's events, most older adolescents can select from among genres in creating a piece of writing, depending on their purpose for writing and the intended audience. An essay written to entertain peers about humorous events at school, for example, would differ from a persuasive one written to convince parents about problems with the required course load (Midgette, Haria, & MacArthur, 2008). And both of these essays would differ from one written to inform an exchange student about a typical day in a Canadian high school. In other words, although children's knowledge-telling strategy gets words on paper, the more mature knowledge-transforming strategy produces a more cohesive text for the reader.

GREATER EASE IN DEALING WITH THE MECHANICAL REQUIREMENTS OF WRITING.

Soon after Robert Kail earned his pilot's licence, he took his son Matt for a flight. A few days later, Matt wrote the following story for his Grade 2 weekly writing assignment:

> This weekend I got to ride in a one-propellered plane. But this time my dad was alone. He has his licence now. It was a long ride. But I fell asleep after five minutes. But when we landed I woke up. My dad said, "You missed a good ride." My dad said, "You even missed the jets!" But I had fun.

Matt spent more than an hour writing this story, and the original (now hanging in Kail's office) is filled with erasures where he corrected misspelled words, ill-formed letters, and incorrect punctuation. Had Matt simply described the flight aloud (instead of writing it), his task would have been much easier. In oral language, he could ignore capitalization, punctuation, spelling, and printing of individual letters. These many mechanical aspects of writing can be a burden for all writers, but particularly for young writers.

In fact, research shows that when youngsters like the one in the photo are absorbed by the task of printing letters correctly, the quality of their writing usually suffers. As children master printed and cursive letters, they can pay more attention to other aspects of writing (Medwell & Wray, 2014; Olinghouse, 2008). Similarly, correct spelling and good sentence structure are particularly hard for younger writers; as they learn to spell and to generate clear sentences, they write more easily and more effectively (Graham, Berninger, Abbott, Abbott, & Whitaker, 1997; McCutchen, Covill, Hoyne, & Mildes, 1994).

Young children often find writing difficult because of the difficulty they experience in printing letters properly, spelling words accurately, and using correct punctuation.

GREATER SKILL IN REVISING. Few authors get it down right the first time. Instead, they revise and revise, then revise some more. Unfortunately, young writers often don't revise at all—the first draft is usually the final draft. To make matters worse, when young writers revise, the changes do not necessarily improve their writing (Fitzgerald, 1987). Effective revision requires the ability to detect problems and know how to correct them (Baker & Brown, 1984; Beal, 1996). As children develop, they are better able to find problems with their writing and to know how to correct them (Limpo, Alves, & Fidalgo, 2014), particularly when the topic is familiar to them and when more time passes between the initial writing and the revising (Chanquoy, 2001; McCutchen, Francis, & Kerr, 1997).

These past few paragraphs make it clear why good writing is so gradual in developing: Many different skills are involved, and each is complicated in its own right. Word-processing software makes writing easier by handling some of these skills (e.g., checking spelling, simplifying revision), and research indicates that writing improves when people use word processing software (Clements, 1995; Rogers & Graham, 2008). Fortunately, students *can* be taught to write better. When instruction focuses on the building blocks of effective writing—strategies for planning, drafting, and revising text—students' writing improves substantially (Graham & Perin, 2007; Tracy, Reid, & Graham, 2009).

Of course, mastering the full set of writing skills is a huge challenge, one that spans childhood, adolescence, and adulthood. Much the same could be said for mastering quantitative skills, as we'll see in the next section.

Knowing and Using Numbers

Basic number skills originate in infancy, long before babies learn names of numbers. Many babies experience daily variation in quantity. They play with two blocks and see that another baby has three; they watch as a father sorts laundry and finds two black socks but only one blue sock; and they eat one hot dog for lunch while an older brother eats three.

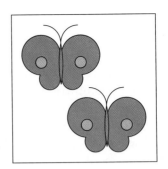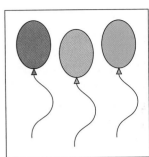

Figure 7-9 Simple pictures used in experiments to test babies' understanding of number.

From these experiences, babies apparently come to appreciate that quantity or amount is one of the ways in which objects in the world can differ. This conclusion is based on research in which babies are tested with sequences of pictures like those shown in Figure 7-9. The actual objects in the pictures differ, as do their size, colour, and position in the picture. Notice, however, that the first three pictures each show two things: two flowers, two cats, two butterflies. When the first of these pictures is shown, infants look at it for several seconds. But, as more pictures of "two things" are presented, infants habituate (become familiar with them; see Module 5.1): They glance at the picture briefly, then look away. But if a picture of a single object or, like the last drawing in the figure, a picture of three objects is then shown, infants again look for several seconds, their interest apparently renewed. Because the only systematic change is the number of objects depicted in the picture, we know that babies can distinguish stimuli on the basis of number. Typically, five-month-olds can distinguish two objects from three and, less often, three objects from four (Cordes & Brannon, 2009; Wynn, 1996).

How do infants distinguish differences in quantity? Older children might count, but of course infants have not yet learned names of numbers. Instead, the process is probably more perceptual in nature. Research shows that by six months, infants can distinguish one object from two and two objects from three. However, when sets include four or more objects, infants distinguish them only when one set is at least twice as large as the other. In other words, infants cannot distinguish four objects from six objects but they can distinguish six from twelve (Cantrell & Smith, 2013; Opfer & Siegler, 2012). One idea is that infants use different systems to represent numbers: One is used for sets of one to three objects and is precise; the other is used for larger sets and estimates numbers approximately. Supporting this distinction, different regions in the infant's brain are activated when small and large sets of objects are shown (Hyde & Spelke, 2011). Other evidence to support this concept of basic perception of small quantity has come from observations of a hunter-gatherer people living in the Amazon jungle. Members of the Pirahã tribe seem to recognize only the numbers "one," "two," and then "many" (Gordon, 2004, 2010). No other number names exist in the Pirahã language, and their performance on number tasks resembles that of infants faced with representations of small numbers. These findings have led to the proposal that an innate capacity exists to recognize numbers of objects up to three (Gordon, 2004), but beyond the number three number concepts appear to be more dependent upon approximation and, later, learning.

As well as distinguishing basic quantities, young babies can do simple addition and subtraction—*very* simple. In experiments using the method shown in Figure 7-10 on page 257, infants view a stage with one toy mouse. A screen then comes up to hide the

Sequence of events I+I=I or 2

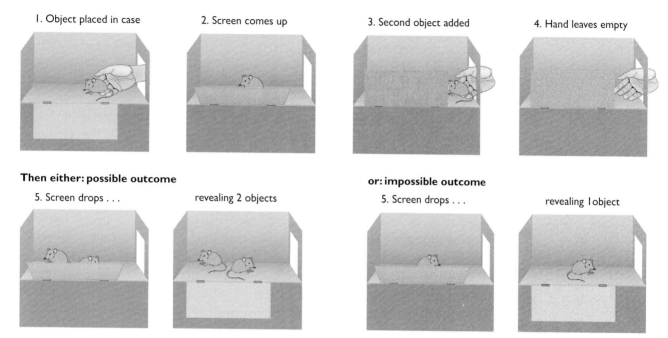

1. Object placed in case   2. Screen comes up   3. Second object added   4. Hand leaves empty

Then either: possible outcome

5. Screen drops . . .   revealing 2 objects

or: impossible outcome

5. Screen drops . . .   revealing I object

Figure 7-10 Experimental set-up to investigate babies' understanding of addition.

mouse and a hand appears with a second mouse, which is placed behind the screen. When the screen is removed and reveals only one mouse, five-month-olds look longer than when two mice are revealed. Apparently, five-month-olds expect that one mouse plus another mouse should equal two mice, and they look longer when this expectancy is violated (Wynn, 1992). And when the stage first has two mice, one of which is removed, infants are surprised when the screen is removed and two mice are still on the stage. These experiments only work with very small numbers, indicating that the means by which infants add and subtract are very simple and probably unlike the processes that older children use (Mix, Huttenlocher, & Levine, 2002).

Finally, scientists have shown that infants can compare quantities. One way to relate two quantities is their ratio, and, amazingly, six-month-olds are sensitive to ratio (McCrink & Wynn, 2007). Shown stimuli that feature two blue circles for every yellow circle (e.g., 8 blue, 4 yellow; 30 blue, 15 yellow), infants look longer when they are next shown stimuli that have a ratio of four blue circles to every yellow circle (e.g., 36 blue, 9 yellow). Infants are also aware of the larger of two quantities. If 10-month-olds watch an adult place two crackers in one container but three crackers in a second container, the infants usually reach for the container with more crackers (Feigenson, Carey, & Hauser, 2002).

Carmen Rasmussen and Jeffrey Bisanz at the University of Alberta propose that working memory, mentioned earlier as important for problem solving, is a significant factor in early numerical calculation skills. In their study, Rasmussen and Bisanz (2005) found that for preschoolers, visual-spatial memory and mental models were important. For Grade 1 children (who were, on average, only 20 months older), verbal problem solving and phonological memory were more important. Preschool children thus convert information from basic visual representation into a more complex symbolic representation, aided by increased ability for verbal representation.

Overall, then, there appears to be evidence for both small number apprehension and recognition of differences between larger numbers. How this works is subject to debate, however. Feigenson and her colleagues have argued for two "core systems" of numbers, one representing small numbers precisely (such as one versus three crackers) and one that represents larger numbers but more approximately (as with the sets of dots; e.g., Feigenson, Dehaene, & Spelke, 2004). Adding to the story, from research using scalp electrodes to measure brain-wave patterns, Izard, Dehaene-Lambertz, and Dehaene (2008) believe that there are separate brain pathways for recognizing objects' *identities* and the *number* of the objects. University of Western Ontario researcher Daniel Ansari, who has done work on fMRI mapping of infants' number sense (e.g., Ansari, Garcia, Luca, Hamon, & Dhital, 2005) proposed that—like most things in our lives—there is a combination of biological and environmental factors at work in number representation. Ansari (2008) concludes that "basic representations and competencies that are thought to have a long evolutionary history interact with development, learning and enculturation to enable the use of culturally invented mental tools such as abstract numerical symbols" (p. 289). This learning to use symbols is the topic of our next section.

LEARNING TO COUNT. Names of numbers are not among most babies' first words, but by two years, youngsters know some number words and have begun to count. Usually, their counting is full of mistakes. In Jasmine's counting sequence that was described in the vignette—"1, 2, 6, 7"—she skips 3, 4, and 5. But research has shown that if we ignore her mistakes momentarily, the counting sequence reveals that she does understand a great deal. Gelman and Meck (1986) simply placed several objects in front of a child and asked, "How many?" By analyzing children's answers to many of these questions, they discovered that by age three, most children have mastered three basic principles of counting, at least when it comes to counting up to five objects.

- *One-to-one principle:* **There must be one and only one number name for each object that is counted.** A child who counts three objects as "1, 2, a" understands this principle because the number of number words matches the number of objects to be counted.

- *Stable-order principle:* **Number names must be counted in the same order.** A child who counts in the same sequence—for example, consistently counting four objects as "1, 2, 4, 5"—shows understanding of this principle.

- *Cardinality principle:* **The last number name differs from the previous ones in a counting sequence by denoting the number of objects.** Typically, three-year-olds reveal their understanding of this principle by repeating the last number name, often with emphasis: "1, 2, 4, 8 … EIGHT!"

During the preschool years, children master these basic principles and apply them to ever larger sets of objects. By age five, most youngsters apply these counting principles to as many as nine objects. And children are more likely to master counting principles when parents mention numbers in their speech, such as counting objects with their children or simply saying the number of objects present (Gunderson & Levine, 2011). (To see if you understand the counting principles, go back to Jasmine's counting in the vignette and decide which principles she has mastered; the answer is given before Check Your Learning on page 264.)

Of course, children's understanding of these principles does not mean that they always count accurately. On the contrary, children can apply all these principles consistently while counting incorrectly. They must master the conventional sequence of the number names and the counting principles to learn to count accurately. Learning the number names beyond nine is easier because the counting words can be generated based on rules for combining decade number names (10, 20, 30, 40) with unit names (1, 2, 3, 4). Later, similar rules are used for 100s, 1000s, and so on. By age four, most youngsters know the numbers to 20, and some can count to 99 (Siegler & Robinson, 1982).

Despite these number rules, learning to count beyond 10 is more complicated in English than in other languages. For example, *eleven* and *twelve* are completely irregular names, following no rules. Also, the remaining "teen" number names differ from the numbers in the 20s, 30s, and the rest in that the decade number name comes after the unit (thir*teen*, four*teen*) rather than before (*twenty*-three, *thirty*-four). Also, some decade names only loosely correspond to the unit names on which they are based: *twenty*, *thirty*, and *fifty* resemble *two*, *three*, and *five* but are not the same.

In contrast, the Chinese, Japanese, and Korean number systems are almost perfectly regular. *Eleven* and *twelve* are expressed as *ten-one* and *ten-two*. There are no special names for the decades: *Two-ten* and *two-ten-one* are the names for 20 and 21. These simplified number names help explain why youngsters growing up in Asian countries count more accurately than North American preschool children of the same age (Miller, Smith, Zhu, & Zhang, 1995). What's more, the direct correspondence between the number names and the base-ten system makes it easier for Asian youngsters to learn some mathematical concepts. For example, if a child has ten blocks, then gets six more, a North American five-year-old will carefully count the additional blocks to determine that he now has sixteen. In contrast, a Chinese five-year-old will not count but quickly say "16" because she understands that in the base-ten system, 10 + 6 = 16 (Ho & Fuson, 1998).

By the time children are ready to begin school, their grasp of arithmetic concepts has progressed considerably. For example, they implicitly understand that addition is commutative (e.g., 4 + 2 = 2 + 4). Shown one bear that receives four candies, then three more, as well as a second bear that receives three candies then four more, five-year-olds believe that the two bears have the same number of candies (Canobi, Reeve, & Pattison, 2002). But some of their understanding is distorted, such as their grasp of the number line. If five-year-olds are shown a line with 0 and 100 at the ends, then asked to place marks corresponding to 2, 8, 16, 46, and 81 on the line, they will usually produce something like Figure 7-11 (Booth & Siegler, 2006; Siegler & Mu, 2008). Preschool children's representation of the numbers is skewed, with much larger gaps between the digits 1 through 10 and much smaller gaps between the digits 10 through 100.

Figure 7-11 A typical preschooler's representation of number on a number line from 0 to 100.

Young children use many strategies to solve simple arithmetic problems, including counting on their fingers.

James Peragine/Shutterstock

ADDING AND SUBTRACTING. By four or five years of age, most children have encountered arithmetic problems that involve simple addition or subtraction. A four-year-old might put two green beans on her plate, then watch in dismay as her dad gives her four more. Now she wonders, "How many do I have in all?" Like the child in the photo, many youngsters solve this sort of problem by counting. They first count out four fingers on one hand, then count out two more on the other. Finally, they count all six fingers on both hands. To subtract, they do the same procedure in reverse (Siegler & Jenkins, 1989; Siegler & Shrager, 1984).

Youngsters soon abandon this approach for a slightly more efficient method. Instead of counting the fingers on the first hand, they simultaneously extend the number of fingers on the first hand corresponding to the larger of the two numbers to be added. Next, they count out the smaller number with fingers on the second hand. Finally, they count all of the fingers to determine the sum (Groen & Resnick, 1977).

After children begin to receive formal arithmetic instruction in Grade 1, addition problems are solved less frequently by counting aloud or by counting fingers (Jordan, Kaplan, Ramineni, & Locuniak, 2009). Instead, children add and subtract by counting mentally. That is, children act as if they are counting silently, beginning with the larger number, and adding on. By age eight or nine, children have learned the addition tables so well that sums of the single-digit integers (from 0 to 9) are facts that are simply retrieved from memory (Ashcraft, 1982).

These counting strategies do *not* occur in a rigid developmental sequence. Instead, as we mentioned in describing the overlapping waves model (see page 245), individual children use many different strategies for addition, depending on the problem. Children usually begin by trying to retrieve an answer from memory. If they are not reasonably confident that the retrieved answer is correct, then they resort to counting aloud or on fingers (Siegler, 1996). Retrieval is most likely for problems with small addends (e.g., 1 + 2, 2 + 4) because these problems are presented frequently in textbooks and by teachers. Consequently, the sum is highly associated with the problem, which makes the child confident that the retrieved answer is correct. In contrast, problems with larger addends, such as 9 + 8, are presented less often. The result is a weaker link between the addends and the sum and, consequently, a greater chance that children need to determine an answer by resorting to a backup strategy such as counting.

Arithmetic skills continue to improve as children move through elementary school. They become more proficient in addition and subtraction, learn multiplication and division, and in high school and college move on to the more sophisticated mathematical concepts involved in algebra, geometry, trigonometry, and calculus (De Brauwer & Fias, 2009). Of course, these math skills and concepts come more easily to some children than others. By the time they enter kindergarten, children differ substantially in their math skill. One factor that's associated with early math skill is the approximate number system described on page 256: preschoolers with better math skills have a more finely tuned approximate number system. In other words, they approximate quantities more precisely (Bonny & Lourenco, 2013; Fuhs & McNeil, 2013). However, other findings suggest that knowing numbers (e.g., pointing to "6" when an experimenter says, "six") may be the most important prerequisite for success in mastering arithmetic (Göbel, Watson, Lervåg, & Hulme, 2014), just as knowing letters and their sounds is a prerequisite for success in learning to read.

Similarly, research has identified several factors that predict those elementary-school children who will succeed in math during middle school and high school. Some are specific to math, such as mastery of arithmetic and understanding of fundamental math concepts (e.g., fractions, the number line), but others are more general, such as working memory and processing speed (Geary, 2011; Siegler et al., 2012). In short, children are successful in math when they can draw on a solid base of math skills and knowledge as well as powerful cognitive skills.

QUESTION 7.3
Barb enjoys asking her six-year-old daughter, Erin, to solve simple arithmetic problems, such as 4 + 2 and 3 + 1. Erin likes solving these problems, but Barb finds it puzzling that Erin may solve a problem by counting on her fingers one day and by saying the answer aloud on the next day. Is Erin's behaviour unusual? *(Answer is on page 264.)*

Estimated average scores and confidence intervals for countries and provinces: Science

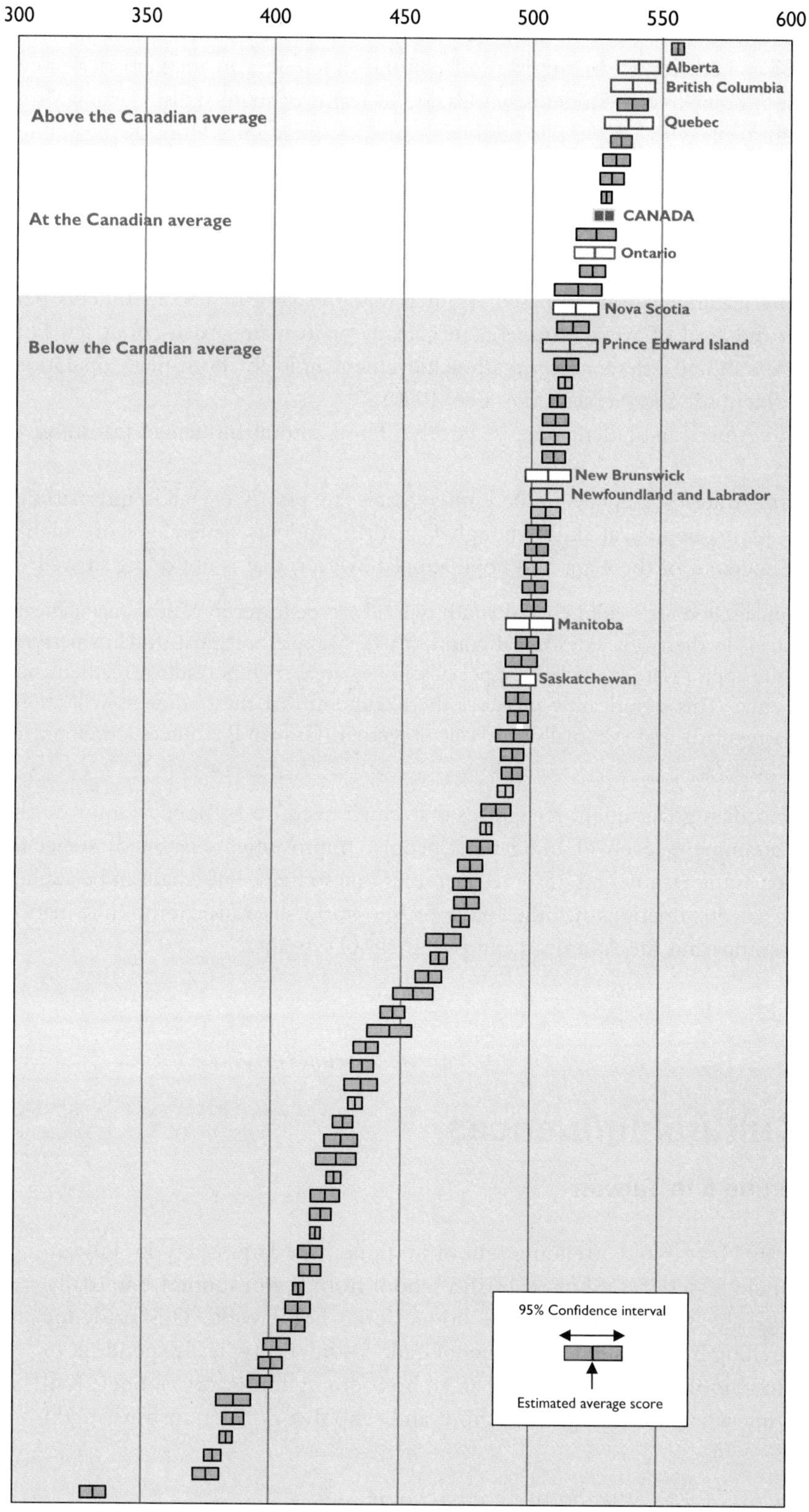

Countries and provinces	Average	S.E.
Singapore	556	(1.2)
Alberta	541	(4.0)
British Columbia	539	(4.3)
Japan	538	(3.0)
Quebec	537	(4.7)
Estonia	534	(2.1)
Chinese Taipei	532	(2.7)
Finland	531	(2.4)
Macao-China	529	(1.1)
CANADA	528	(2.1)
Vietnam	525	(3.9)
Ontario	524	(3.9)
Hong Kong-China	523	(2.5)
BSJG-China	518	(4.6)
Nova Scotia	517	(4.5)
Korea	516	(3.1)
Prince Edward Island	515	(5.4)
New Zealand	513	(2.4)
Slovenia	513	(1.3)
Australia	510	(1.5)
United Kingdom	509	(2.6)
Germany	509	(2.7)
The Netherlands	509	(2.3)
New Brunswick	506	(4.5)
Newfoundland and Labrador	506	(3.2)
Switzerland	506	(2.9)
Ireland	503	(2.4)
Belgium	502	(2.3)
Denmark	502	(2.4)
Poland	501	(2.5)
Portugal	501	(2.4)
Manitoba	499	(4.7)
Norway	498	(2.3)
United States	496	(3.2)
Saskatchewan	496	(3.1)
Austria	495	(2.4)
France	495	(2.1)
Sweden	493	(3.6)
Czech Republic	493	(2.3)
Spain	493	(2.1)
Latvia	490	(1.6)
Russian Federation	487	(2.9)
Luxembourg	483	(1.1)
Italy	481	(2.5)
Hungary	477	(2.4)
Lithuania	475	(2.7)
Croatia	475	(2.5)
Iceland	473	(1.7)
Israel	467	(3.4)
Malta	465	(1.6)
Slovak Republic	461	(2.6)
Greece	455	(3.9)
Chile	447	(2.4)
Bulgaria	446	(4.4)
United Arab Emirates	437	(2.4)
Uruguay	435	(2.2)
Romania	435	(3.2)
Cyprus	433	(1.4)
Moldova	428	(2.0)
Albania	427	(3.3)
Turkey	425	(3.9)
Trinidad and Tobago	425	(1.4)
Thailand	421	(2.8)
Costa Rica	420	(2.1)
Qatar	418	(1.0)
Colombia	416	(2.4)
Mexico	416	(2.1)
Montenegro	411	(1.0)
Georgia	411	(2.4)
Jordan	409	(2.7)
Indonesia	403	(2.6)
Brazil	401	(2.3)
Peru	397	(2.4)
Lebanon	386	(3.4)
Tunisia	386	(2.1)
Republic of Macedonia	384	(1.2)
Kosovo	378	(1.7)
Algeria	376	(2.6)
Dominican Republic	332	(2.6)

Note: OECD countries appear in italics. The OECD average was 493, with a standard error of 0.4. The results of Argentina, Kazakhstan, and Malaysia are excluded because of insufficient coverage to ensure comparability (see Appendix B.1.2 for these results). See Appendix B.3.1 for further comparisons between provinces and participating countries. Results for the province of Quebec in this table should be treated with caution because of a possible non-response bias (see Appendix A for further details).

Figure 7-12 Estimated average scores and confidence intervals for provinces and countries: Mathematics.

Note: The OECD average is 494 with a standard error of 0.5.

Source: O'Grady, Deussing, Scerbina, Fung, & Muhe, *Measuring Up: Canadian Results of the OECD PISA Study,* Council of Ministers of Education, Canada, 2016.

COMPARING NORTH AMERICAN STUDENTS WITH STUDENTS IN OTHER COUNTRIES.   Let's return to the issue of cultural differences in mathematical competence. When compared to students worldwide in terms of math skills, Canadian students do quite well, with only a few countries, such as Singapore, Hong Kong-China, and Japan performing significantly better (OECD, 2016; O'Grady, Deussing, Scerbina, Fung, & Muhe, 2016). Unfortunately, students in the United States don't fare as well. For example, Figure 7-12 shows the math results from a major international comparison (O'Grady et al., 2016). Canada does well, but U.S. students have lower scores than those in many leading nations. Phrased another way, the very best U.S. students perform only at the level of average students in Canada or in many Asian countries. Furthermore, the cultural differences in math achievement hold for both math operations and math problem solving (Stevenson & Lee, 1990).

Why do American students rate so poorly? The Cultural Influences feature gives some answers.

In North America, students in the United States fare poorly overall in international comparisons of mathematical skills, though Canadian students generally score highly. There is one segment of the Canadian population, however, that is not doing so well:

> Aboriginal school-age children and youth typically score lower in educational achievement than do their non-Aboriginal counterparts. Many Aboriginal students perform below the appropriate grade level, especially in key areas such as reading, mathematics, and science. This significantly increases the likelihood that these students will attend school irregularly and eventually drop out altogether (Human Resources Development Canada, 2002).

The Canadian government recognizes that much needs to be done to improve the educational attainment levels of Indigenous people. Improvements targeted at specific situations such as the remoteness of some reserves is one strategy, but what can be applied generally? What do situations in other parts of the world show us? Some information comes from comparing the American and Asian school systems.

Cultural Influences

Grade 5 in Taiwan

Shin-ying is an 11-year-old attending school in Taipei, the largest city in Taiwan. Like most Grade 5 students, Shin-ying is in school from 8 a.m. until 4 p.m. daily. Most evenings, she spends two to three hours doing homework. This academic routine is gruelling by U.S. standards, where Grade 5 students typically spend six to seven hours in school each day and less than an hour doing homework. Robert Kail asked Shin-ying what she thought of school and schoolwork. Her answers might surprise you.

RK: Why do you go to school?

SHIN-YING: I like what we study.

RK: Any other reasons?

SHIN-YING: The things that I learn in school are useful.

RK: What about homework? Why do you do it?

SHIN-YING: My teacher and my parents think it's important. And I like doing it.

RK: Do you think that you would do nearly as well in school if you didn't work so hard?

SHIN-YING: Oh no. The best students are always the ones who work the hardest.

Schoolwork is the focal point of Shin-ying's life. While many schoolchildren in the United States are unhappy when schoolwork intrudes on time for play and television, Shin-ying is enthusiastic about school and school-related activities.

Shin-ying is not unusual among Chinese elementary-school students. Many of her comments illustrate findings that emerge from detailed analyses of classrooms, teachers, students, and parents in studies comparing students in Japan, Taiwan, and the United States (Ni, Chiu, & Cheng, 2010; Pomerantz, Ng, Cheung, & Qu, 2014; Stevenson & Lee, 1990; Stigler, Gallimore, & Hiebert, 2000):

- *Time in school and how it is used.* By Grade 5, students in Japan and Taiwan spend 50 percent more time in school than American students do. More of this time is devoted to academic activities than in the United States, and instruction in Asian schools is often better organized and more challenging.

- *Time spent in homework and attitudes toward it.* Students in Taiwan and Japan spend more time on homework and value homework more than American students.

- *Parents' attitudes.* American parents are more often satisfied with their children's performance in school; in contrast, Japanese and Taiwanese parents set much higher standards for their children.

- *Parents' beliefs about effort and ability.* Japanese and Taiwanese parents believe more strongly than American parents that effort, not native ability, is the key factor in school success.

Thus, students in Japan and Taiwan excel because they spend more time both in and out of school on academic tasks. Furthermore, their parents and teachers set loftier scholastic goals and believe that students can attain these goals with hard work. Japanese classrooms even post a motto describing ideal students—*gambaru kodomo*—those who strive the hardest.

Parents underscore the importance of schoolwork in many ways to their children. For example, even though homes and apartments in Japan and China are very small by North American standards, Asian youngsters, like the child in the photo, typically have a desk in a quiet area where they can study undisturbed (Stevenson & Lee, 1990). For Japanese and Taiwanese teachers and parents, academic excellence is paramount, and it shows in their children's success.

Many Asian schoolchildren have a quiet area at home where they can study undisturbed.

Koide Tomoya/a.collectionRF/Getty Images

Critical Thinking Question: As noted in Module 7.3, Canadian students generally score quite well in cross-national comparisons of school ability, with the exception of Indigenous children. How might provincial/territorial and federal governments go about improving the situation for these schoolchildren?

EDUCATIONAL IMPLICATIONS OF CROSS-CULTURAL FINDINGS ON ACADEMIC ACHIEVEMENT.
What can Americans learn from other countries' educational systems? Experts (Stevenson & Stigler, 1992; Tucker, 2011) suggest several ways American schools could be improved:

- Improve teachers' training by allowing them to work closely with older, more experienced teachers, and give them more free time to prepare lessons and correct students' work.

- Organize instruction around sound principles of learning, such as providing multiple examples of concepts and giving students adequate opportunities to practise newly acquired skills.

- Create curricula that emphasize problem solving and critical thinking.

- Set higher standards for children, who need to spend more time and effort in school-related activities in order to achieve those standards.

Changing teaching practices and attitudes toward achievement would begin to reduce the gap between American students and students in other industrialized countries, particularly Asian countries. Some of these suggestions could also be applied to the problem in Canada of the disparity between educational achievements of Indigenous and non-Indigenous children. Ignoring these educational discrepancies will mean an increasingly undereducated workforce and citizenry in a more complex world.

Response to question about Jasmine's counting on page 258: Since Jasmine uses four number names to count four objects ("1, 2, 6, 7 … SEVEN!"), she understands the one-to-one principle. The four number names are always used in the same order, so she grasps the stable-order principle. And, finally, she repeats the last number name with emphasis, so she understands the cardinality principle.

Q&A ANSWER 7.3
No. In many domains, including simple arithmetic, children use multiple strategies. They will solve a problem one way (e.g., counting on their fingers) and when asked the problem again, solve it a different way (e.g., retrieving the answer from memory).

✓ Check Your Learning

RECALL What are some of the prerequisite skills that children must master to learn to read?

Summarize the differences between education in China and education in the United States.

INTERPRET Compare the mathematical skills that are mastered before children enter school with those that they master after beginning school.

APPLY Review the research on pages 252–253 regarding factors associated with skilled reading comprehension. Which of these factors—if any—might also contribute to skilled writing?

7.4 Electronic Media

OUTLINE

Television

Computers

LEARNING OBJECTIVES

1. How does watching television affect children's attitudes and behaviour?
2. How does TV viewing influence children's cognitive development?
3. How do children use computers at home and in school?

Whenever Bill visits his granddaughter, Harmony, he is struck by the amount of time Harmony spends watching television. Many of the programs she watches are worthwhile. Nevertheless, Bill wonders if such a steady diet of TV watching might somehow be harmful. Images pop on and off the screen so rapidly that Bill wonders how Harmony will ever learn to pay attention, particularly in other settings that aren't as rich in visual stimulation.

In generations past, children learned their culture's values from parents, teachers, religious leaders, and print media. These sources of cultural knowledge are still with us, but they coexist with new technologies that do not always portray parents' values; these include streaming TV, video game players, tablets, smartphones, and the internet. As Huesmann (2007) explains:

> ... radio, television (TV), movies, video games, cell phones, and computer networks have assumed central roles in our children's daily lives. For better or worse the mass media are having an enormous impact on our children's values, beliefs and behaviours. (p. S6)

More forces than ever before can influence children's development. Two of these technologies—television and computers—are the focus of this module. As we look at their influence, we'll see if Bill's concern for his granddaughter is well founded.

Television

Canadian communications theorist Marshall McLuhan once said "The medium is the message"—but is it? Some critics argue that the medium itself—independent of the contents of programs—has several harmful effects on viewers, particularly children (Huston & Wright, 1998). The following are among the criticisms:

- Because TV programs consist of many brief segments presented in rapid succession, children who watch a lot of TV develop short attention spans and have difficulty concentrating in school.

- Because TV provides ready-made, simple-to-interpret images, children who watch a lot of TV become passive, lazy thinkers and become less creative.

- Children who spend a lot of time watching TV spend less time in more productive and valuable activities, such as reading, participating in sports, and playing with friends.

QUESTION 7.4
Brent is a six-year-old boy who loves to read. His parents are thinking about limiting his TV viewing because they're afraid it will cut into the time he spends reading. Do research findings suggest that Brent's parents are on the right track? *(Answer is on page 267.)*
· · · · · · · · · · · · · · · · · ·

In fact, as stated, none of these criticisms is consistently supported by research. The first criticism—TV watching reduces attention span—is the easiest to dismiss. Research repeatedly shows that increased TV viewing does not lead to reduced attention, greater impulsivity, reduced task persistence, or increased activity levels (Huston & Wright, 1998; Foster & Watkins, 2010). The *content* of TV programs, however, can influence these dimensions of children's behaviour—for example, children who watch impulsive models behave more impulsively themselves—but TV per se does not harm children's ability to pay attention. Bill, the grandfather in the opening vignette, need not worry that the amount of his granddaughter's TV viewing will limit her ability to pay attention later in life.

As for the criticism that TV viewing fosters lazy thinking and stifles creativity, the evidence is mixed. On the one hand, some educational programs depict people being creative and encourage children to pretend; when children watch these programs frequently, they're often more creative. On the other hand, when children often watch programs that are action oriented, they may be less creative. The content and pacing of these often do not provide viewers with the time to reflect that is essential for creativity (Calvert & Valkenburg, 2013)

Finally, according to the last criticism, TV viewing replaces other socially more desirable activities: The simple-minded view is that every hour of TV viewing replaces an hour of some more valuable activity such as reading or doing homework. To illustrate the problems with this view, let's look at reading. The correlation between time spent watching TV and reading tends to be negative—heavy TV viewers read less (Ennemoser & Schneider, 2007; Schmidt & Vandewater, 2008). But we need to be cautious in interpreting this correlation (see Figure 1-3 on page 30). The easy interpretation is that watching a lot of TV causes children to read less. However, an alternate interpretation is also plausible: Children who are poor readers (and thus are unlikely to spend much time reading) end up watching a lot of TV. For youngsters who read poorly, an hour spent watching TV replaces some activity, but not an hour that would have been spent reading (Huston & Wright, 1998).

Research does reveal one way in which the medium itself is harmful. In many homes, the TV is on constantly—from morning until bedtime—even though no one is explicitly watching a specific program. In this case, TV is often a powerful distraction. Young children will make frequent, brief glances at the TV, enough to disrupt the quality of their play. Similarly, during parent-child interaction, parents will steal quick looks at the TV, which reduces the quantity and quality of parent-child interactions (Kirkorian, Pempek, Murphy, Schmidt, & Anderson, 2009; Setliff & Courage, 2011).

When we move past the medium per se and consider the content of programmes, TV does substantially affect children's cognitive development, as you'll see in the next section.

INFLUENCE ON COGNITION.   Big Bird, Bert, Ernie, and other members of the cast of *Sesame Street*, have been helping to educate preschool children for almost 50 years. Today, mothers and fathers who watched *Sesame Street* as preschoolers are watching with their own youngsters. Remarkably, the time preschool children spend watching *Sesame Street* predicts their grades in high school and the amount of time they spend reading as adolescents (Anderson, Huston, Schmitt, Linebarger, & Wright, 2001).

Sesame Street has been joined by programs designed to teach young children about language and reading skills (*Martha Speaks, Super Why!, Word Girl*) and programs that teach basic science and math concepts (*Curious George, Cyberchase, Sid the Science Kid, The Dinosaur Train*). Programs like these (and older programs, such as *Electric Company, 3-2-1 Contact,* and *Square One TV*) show that the power of TV can be harnessed to help children learn important academic skills (Ennemoser & Schneider, 2007).

The Canadian Pediatric Society (CPS) recently published a position statement on young children's screen time—time spent with any screen, from televisions to smartphones—and what should be best practice (Digital Health Task Force, 2017). Children under five were the focus of the report because of the important development that occurs during this period and because early interactions can influence later behaviours and attitudes, setting routines and habits. While the CPS did note potential benefits from good quality, educational programs, as just outlined, there are also risks associated with indiscriminate screen exposure. Ways to minimize such risks were outlined in the statement. The CPS's recommendations for children under five years old are grouped under four main principles, the four Ms: Minimize screen time, Mitigate risks, be Mindful about screen time, and Model healthy screen use (Digital Health Task Force, 2017). If parents and other family members follow these recommendations, appropriate screen time can result and harmful effects will be much reduced.

Computers

COMPUTERS IN THE CLASSROOM. New technologies soon find themselves in the classroom. Personal computers are no exception; virtually all North American schools now use personal computers to aid instruction. Computers serve many functions in the classroom (Roschelle, Pea, Hoadley, Gordin, & Means, 2000). One function is that of instructor: As shown in the photo, children use computers to learn reading, spelling, arithmetic, science, and social studies. Computers allow instructions to be individualized and interactive. Students proceed at their own pace, receiving feedback and help when necessary (Hurts, 2008; LeVasseur, Macaruso, & Shankweiler, 2008; Roschelle et al., 2000). Computers are also a valuable medium for experiential learning. Simulation programs allow students to explore the world in ways that would be impossible or dangerous otherwise. For instance, students can change the law of gravity or see what happens to a city when no taxes are imposed. Finally, computers can help students achieve traditional academic goals (Steelman, 1994). A graphics program can allow students who are less talented artistically to produce beautiful illustrations. A word-processing program can relieve much of the drudgery associated with revising, thereby encouraging better writing.

Overall, then, computers are like television in that the technology per se does not necessarily influence children's development. However, the way the technology is used—for example, playing violent computer games versus using word-processing software to help revise a short story—can affect children positively or negatively, depending on the use and content.

Q&A ANSWER 7.4
Probably not. Children who read well and enjoy reading will find time to read. Research suggests that, for these youngsters, TV viewing will not replace time spent reading. Frankly, a better strategy would be to limit *what* he watches on TV, not how much he watches.

Bill Aron/PhotoEdit

Computerized instruction can be extremely useful because it allows instruction to be individualized and interactive, which allows students to work at their own pace and receive personalized feedback.

 ## Check Your Learning

RECALL Summarize research that has examined the impact on children of TV as a medium.

What are the primary ways in which computers are used in schools?

INTERPRET Compare and contrast the ways in which TV viewing and being online might affect children's development.

APPLY What if you had the authority to write new regulations for children's TV programs? What shows would you encourage? What shows would you want to limit?

UNIFYING THEMES   Active Children

This chapter highlights the theme that *children influence their own development.* Japanese and Chinese elementary-school children typically like studying (an attitude fostered by their parents), and this makes them quite willing to do homework for two or three hours nightly. This in turn contributes to their high levels of scholastic achievement. American schoolchildren usually detest homework and do as little of it as possible, which contributes to their relatively lower level of scholastic achievement (as noted by measures such as the OECD's PISA study mentioned earlier in this chapter). Thus, children's attitudes help to determine how they behave, which determines how much they will achieve over the course of childhood and adolescence.

See for Yourself

Create several small sets of objects that vary in number. You might have two nickels, three candies, four buttons, five pencils, six erasers, seven paper clips, and so on. Place each set of objects on a paper plate. Then find some preschool children; four- and five-year-olds would be ideal. As usual, gain parental permission to do this exercise, and check for the child's assent. Put a plate in front of each child and ask, "How many?" Then watch to see what the child does. If possible, tape-record the children's counting so that you can analyze it later. If this is impossible, try to write down exactly what each child says as he or she counts. Note that any recordings or notes taken should be rendered anonymous and your specific findings kept confidential. Later, go back through your notes and determine whether the children followed the counting principles described on page 258. You should see that children, particularly younger ones, more often follow the principles while counting small sets of objects than larger sets. See for yourself!

Resources

For more information about . . .

self-regulation in schools, see the MEHRIT Centre's webpage at https://self-reg.ca/.

cultural differences in scholastic achievement, try Harold W. Stevenson and James W. Stigler's *The Learning Gap* (Summit Books, 1992), which describes research comparing schooling in the United States and in Asia.

tips and exercises to help develop better study skills, visit websites such as the Academic Success Resources page of York University's Learning Skills Services department: www.yorku.ca/cds/lss/skillbuilding.html.

Key Terms

autobiographical memory   232
cardinality principle   258
chunking   229
cognitive self-regulation   231
comprehension   249
confounded   247
decoding   251
elaboration   229
encoding processes   242

fuzzy trace theory   233
heuristics   245
infantile amnesia   235
knowledge-telling strategy   254
knowledge-transforming
   strategy   254
means-end analysis   244
memory strategies   229
metacognitive knowledge   230

metamemory   230
one-to-one principle   258
organization   229
phonological awareness   249
rehearsal   229
script   232
stable-order principle   258
word recognition   249

Summary

7.1 Memory

1. Origins of Memory
Rovee-Collier's studies of kicking show that infants can remember, forget, and be reminded of events that occurred in the past.

2. Strategies for Remembering
Beginning in the preschool years, children use strategies to help them remember. With age, children use more powerful strategies, such as rehearsal and outlining. Using memory strategies successfully depends first on analyzing the goal of a memory task, and second on monitoring the effectiveness of the chosen strategy. Analyzing goals and monitoring are two important elements of metamemory, which is a child's informal understanding of how memory operates.

3. Knowledge and Memory
A child's knowledge of the world can be used to organize information that needs to be remembered. When several events occur in a specific order, they are remembered as a single script. Knowledge improves memory for children and adolescents, although older individuals often reap more benefit because they have more knowledge. Knowledge can also distort memory by causing children and adolescents to forget information that does not conform to their knowledge, or to remember events that are part of their knowledge but that did not actually take place.

Autobiographical memory refers to a person's memory about his or her own life. Autobiographical memory emerges in the early preschool years, often prompted by parents' asking children about past events. Infantile amnesia—children's and adults' inability to remember events from early in life—may reflect the absence of language or sense of self.

Young children's memory in court cases is often inaccurate because children are questioned repeatedly, which makes it hard for them to distinguish what actually occurred from what adults suggest may have occurred. Children's testimony is more reliable if children are interviewed promptly, if they're encouraged to tell the truth, if they're first asked to explain what happened in their own words, and if interviewers ask questions that test alternate accounts of what happened.

7.2 Problem Solving

1. Development Trends in Solving Problems
As a general rule, as children develop they solve problems more often and solve them more effectively. However, exceptions to the rule are not uncommon: Young children sometimes solve problems successfully, while adolescents sometimes fail.

2. Features of Children's and Adolescents' Problem Solving
Young children sometimes fail to solve problems because they do not plan ahead and because they do not encode all the necessary information in a problem. Successful problem solving typically depends on knowledge specific to the problem, along with general processes; involves the use of a

variety of strategies; and is enhanced by collaborating with an adult or older child.

3. Scientific Problem Solving

Although the child-as-scientist metaphor is popular, in fact, children's and adolescents' scientific reasoning often has many shortcomings: Children and adolescents often have misconceptions that interfere with real scientific understanding; they tend to design confounded experiments; they reach conclusions prematurely based on inadequate evidence; and they have difficulty integrating theory and data.

7.3 Academic Skills

1. Reading

Reading encompasses a number of component skills. Prereading skills include knowing letters and the sounds associated with them. Word recognition is the process of identifying a word. Beginning readers more often accomplish this by sounding out words; advanced readers more often retrieve a word from long-term memory. Comprehension, the act of extracting meaning from text, improves with age because of several factors: Working memory capacity increases; readers gain more world knowledge; and readers are better able to monitor what they read and to match their reading strategies to the goals of the reading task.

2. Writing

As children develop, their writing improves, reflecting several factors: They know more about the world, and so they have more to say; they use more effective ways of organizing their writing; they master the mechanics (e.g., handwriting, spelling) of writing; and they become more skilled at revising their writing.

3. Knowing and Using Numbers

Infants can distinguish quantities, probably by means of basic perceptual processes. Children begin to count by about age two, and by three years of age, most children have mastered the one-to-one, stable-order, and cardinality principles, at least when counting small sets of objects. Counting is how children first add, but it is replaced by more effective strategies such as retrieving sums directly from memory.

In mathematics, American students lag behind students in most other industrialized nations, chiefly because of cultural differences in the time spent on schoolwork and homework and in parents' attitudes towards school, effort, and ability. A problem for Canada is the disparity between Indigenous and non-Indigenous students' educational achievements.

7.4 Electronic Media

1. Television

Many popular criticisms about TV as a medium (e.g., that it shortens children's attention span) are not well supported by research. However, the content of TV programs can affect children. Youngsters who frequently watch prosocial TV become more skilled socially, and preschoolers who watch *Sesame Street* improve their academic skills and adjust more readily to school.

2. Computers

At home, children use computers to play games (and are influenced by the content of the games they play) and to access the internet. Computers are used in school as tutors, to provide experiential learning, and as a multipurpose tool to achieve traditional academic goals.

Some video games are designed to be educational, but many used for entertainment are very violent. Playing violent games does seem to have negative effects on the user, and parents should be wary of allowing teens to spend much time playing such games.

Test Yourself

1. Important features of memory are evident in young infants: They can remember past events, but with the passage of time some events are no longer recalled, although _____ can help to retrieve a forgotten memory.

2. Diagnosing memory problems and monitoring the effectiveness of memory strategies are two important elements of _____.

3. According to fuzzy trace theory, older children and adolescents are more prone to memory errors because they tend to remember _____.

4. Autobiographical memory develops early as children acquire basic memory skills, language, and _____.

5. Young children often fail to solve problems because they don't encode all the information that is necessary and because _____.

6. Children and adolescents both rely on heuristic and analytic solutions, but _____ solutions are more common among adolescents.

7. When children try to reason scientifically, they often devise confounded experiments, frequently reach conclusions prematurely, and have difficulty _____.

8. In many languages, _____ is the best predictor of a child's success in learning to read.

9. _____ instruction is an essential part of programs designed to teach children to read.

10. When young children write, they often rely upon a _____ strategy.

11. Infants can distinguish different quantities because _____.

12. By three years, children have mastered the _____, stable-order, and cardinality principles of counting (for small sets of objects).

13. Two reasons why students in Asian countries often excel in math achievement are that their parents set higher standards and their parents believe that _____.

14. Watching _____ programs on television can help young children in their interactions with others.

15. Computers can be useful in schools by providing opportunities for _____.

Answers: (1) a cue; (2) metamemory; (3) gist (not verbatim); (4) a sense of self; (5) they do not plan ahead; (6) analytic; (7) integrating theory and data; (8) phonological awareness; (9) Phonics; (10) knowledge-telling; (11) the perceptual system is sensitive to quantity; (12) one-to-one; (13) hard work, not innate ability, is the key to achievement; (14) prosocial; (15) experiential learning.

8 Intelligence and Individual Differences in Cognition

David Handley/Dorling Kindersley, Ltd.

What Is Intelligence?

**Features of
IQ Scores**

**Special Children,
Special Needs**

Have you ever taken a standardized test in your student career? An achievement or aptitude test during elementary or high school? Starting in 1996, Ontario introduced province-wide testing for students in Grades 3, 6, 9, and 10 (Education Quality and Accountability Office, 2013). Ontario's tests assess students "in relation to the expected standard of achievement, rather than in comparison to other students" (Desbiens, 2011, n.p.). The Education Quality and Accountability Office (EQAO) testing is intended for comparison of the provinces on literacy and numeracy, and for ranking of schools, rather than for ranking the children themselves. In the United States, standardized testing is more common; for example, high-school students usually take the Scholastic Aptitude Test (SAT) to enter post-secondary education. Psychological testing began in schools early in the twentieth century and continues to be an integral part of education in the twenty-first century, particularly in the United States, where such testing was first popularized.

Of all standardized tests, none attract more attention and generate more controversy than tests designed to measure intelligence. Intelligence tests have been hailed by some as one of psychology's greatest contributions to society—and cursed by others. Intelligence tests and what they measure are the focus of Chapter 8. We'll start in **Module 8.1** by looking at different definitions of intelligence. In **Module 8.2**, we'll see how intelligence tests work and examine some factors that influence test scores. In **Module 8.3**, we'll look at special children—youngsters whose intelligence sets them apart from their peers.

8.1 What is Intelligence?

OUTLINE	LEARNING OBJECTIVES
Psychometric Theories	1. What is the psychometric view of the nature of intelligence?
Gardner's Theory of Multiple Intelligences	2. How does Gardner's theory of multiple intelligences differ from the psychometric approach?
Sternberg's Theory of Successful Intelligence	3. What are the components of Sternberg's theory of successful intelligence?

Diana is an eager Grade 4 teacher who loves history. Consequently, every year she's frustrated when she teaches a unit on the War of 1812. Although she's passionate about the subject, her enthusiasm is not contagious. Instead, her students' eyes glaze over and she can see young minds drifting off—and they never seem to grasp the historical significance of this war. Diana wishes there were a different way to teach this unit, one that would engage her students more effectively.

Before you read further, how would you define "intelligence"? If you are typical of most North Americans, your definition probably includes the ability to reason logically, connect ideas, and solve real problems. You might mention "verbal ability," meaning the ability to speak clearly and articulately. You might also mention "social competence," referring, for example, to an interest in the world at large and an ability to admit when you have made a mistake (Sternberg & Kaufman, 1998).

As you'll see in this module, many of these ideas about intelligence are included in psychological theories of intelligence. We'll begin by considering the oldest theories of intelligence, those associated with the psychometric tradition. Then we'll look at two newer approaches and, along the way, get some insights into ways that Diana could make the War of 1812 come alive for her class.

Raise a cyber child and discover the world of parenthood at. . .

My Virtual Child

Psychometric Theories

Psychometricians **are psychologists who specialize in measuring psychological characteristics such as intelligence and personality.** When psychometricians want to research a particular question, they usually begin by administering a large number of tests to many individuals. Then they look for patterns in performance across the different tests. The basic logic underlying this technique is similar to the logic a hunter uses to decide whether some dark blobs in a jungle river are three separate rotting logs or a single alligator (Cattell, 1965). If the blobs move together, the hunter decides they are part of the same structure—an alligator. If they do not move together, they are three different structures—three logs. Similarly, if changes in performance on one psychological test are accompanied by changes in performance on a second test—that is, if the scores move together—then the tests appear to measure the same attribute or factor.

For example, suppose you believe that intelligence is broad and general. In other words, you believe that some people are smart regardless of the situation, task, or problem, whereas others are not so smart. According to this view, children's performance should be consistent across tasks. Smart children should always receive high scores, and less smart youngsters should always get lower scores. In fact, more than 100 years ago, Charles Spearman (1904) reported findings supporting the idea that a general factor for intelligence, or *g*, is responsible for performance on all mental tests.

Other researchers, however, have found that intelligence consists of distinct abilities. For example, Thurstone and Thurstone (1941) analyzed performance on a wide range of tasks and identified seven distinct patterns, each reflecting a unique ability: perceptual speed, word comprehension, word fluency, space, number, memory, and induction. Thurstone and Thurstone also acknowledged a general factor that operated in all tasks, but they emphasized that the specific factors were more useful in assessing and understanding intellectual ability.

These conflicting findings have led many psychometric theorists to propose hierarchical theories of intelligence that include both general and specific components (Deary, 2012). John Carroll (1993, 1996), for example, proposed a hierarchical theory with three levels, shown in Figure 8-1. At the top of the hierarchy is *g*, general intelligence. In the middle level are eight broad categories of intellectual skill. For example, *fluid intelligence* **refers to the ability to perceive relations among stimuli.** Each of the abilities in the

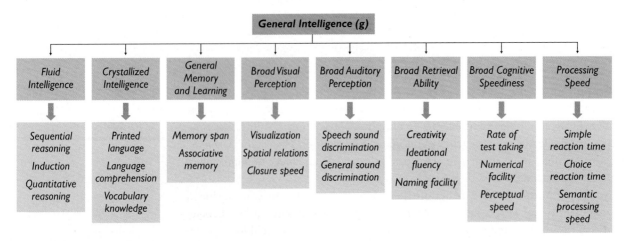

Figure 8-1 Carroll's hierarchical theory of intelligence.

Source: Based on Carroll, J. B. (1993). *Human Cognitive Abilities: A Survey of Factor-Analytic Studies.* New York: Cambridge University Press.

second level is further divided into the skills listed in the bottom and most specific level. *Crystallized intelligence,* **for example, comprises a person's culturally influenced accumulated knowledge and skills, including understanding printed language, comprehending language, and knowing vocabulary.**

Carroll's hierarchical theory is a compromise between the two views of intelligence—general versus distinct abilities. But some critics still find it unsatisfactory because it ignores the research and theory on cognitive development described in Chapters 6 and 7. These critics believe we need to look beyond the psychometric approach to understand intelligence. In the remainder of this module, then, we'll look at two newer theories that have done just this.

Gardner's Theory of Multiple Intelligences

Only recently have child-development researchers viewed intelligence from the perspective of modern theories of cognition and cognitive development. These new theories present a much broader theory of intelligence and how it develops. Among the most ambitious is Howard Gardner's (1983, 1999, 2002, 2006) theory of multiple intelligences. Rather than using test scores as the basis for his theory, Gardner drew on research in child development, studies of brain-damaged persons, and studies of exceptionally talented people. Using these resources, Gardner identified seven distinct intelligences when he first proposed the theory in 1983. In subsequent work, Gardner (1999, 2002) identified two additional intelligences; the complete list is shown in Table 8-1.

The first three intelligences in this list—linguistic intelligence, logical-mathematical intelligence, and spatial intelligence—are included in psychometric theories of intelligence. The last six intelligences are not: Musical, bodily-kinesthetic, interpersonal, intrapersonal, naturalistic, and existential intelligences are unique to Gardner's theory. According to Gardner, Laura St. John's beautiful playing on the cello, Penny Oleksiak's Olympic swimming, and former Governor General Michaëlle Jean's grace and charm in dealing with people are all features of intelligence that are totally ignored in traditional theories.

TABLE 8-1

NINE INTELLIGENCES IN GARDNER'S THEORY OF MULTIPLE INTELLIGENCES

Type of Intelligence	Definition
Linguistic	Knowing the meanings of words, having the ability to use words to understand new ideas, and using language to convey ideas to others
Logical-mathematical	Understanding relations that exist among objects, actions, and ideas, as well as the logical or mathematical operations that can be performed on them
Spatial	Perceiving objects accurately and imagining in the "mind's eye" the appearance of an object before and after it has been transformed
Musical	Comprehending and producing sounds varying in pitch, rhythm, and emotional tone
Bodily-kinesthetic	Using one's body in highly differentiated ways, as dancers, craftspeople, and athletes do
Interpersonal	Identifying different feelings, moods, motivations, and intentions in others
Intrapersonal	Understanding one's emotions and knowing one's strengths and weaknesses
Naturalistic	Understanding the natural world, distinguishing natural objects from artifacts, grouping and labelling natural phenomena
Existential	Considering "ultimate" issues, such as the purpose of life and the nature of death

Source: Gardner, 1983, 1999, 2002.

How did Gardner arrive at these nine distinct intelligences? First, each has a unique developmental history. Linguistic intelligence, for example, develops much earlier than the other eight. Second, each intelligence is regulated by distinct regions of the brain, as shown by studies of brain-damaged persons. Spatial intelligence, for example, is regulated by particular regions in the brain's right hemisphere. Third, each has special cases of talented individuals. The field of music, for example, is well known for individuals showing incredible talent at an early age. Claudio Arrau, one of the twentieth century's greatest pianists, could read musical notes before he could read words; Yo-Yo Ma, the famed cellist, performed in concert for President John F. Kennedy at seven years of age.

Prompted by Gardner's theory, researchers have begun to look at other nontraditional aspects of intelligence. **Probably the best known is** *emotional intelligence (EI),* **which is the ability to use one's own and others' emotions effectively for solving problems and living happily.** Emotional intelligence made headlines in 1995 because of a bestselling book, *Emotional Intelligence,* in which the author, Daniel Goleman (1995), argued that "emotions [are] at the center of aptitudes for living" (p. xiii). One major model of emotional intelligence (Salovey & Grewal, 2005; Mayer, Salovey, & Caruso, 2008) includes several distinct facets, including perceiving emotions accurately (e.g., recognizing a happy face), understanding emotions (e.g., distinguishing happiness from ecstasy), and regulating emotions (e.g., hiding one's disappointment). People who are emotionally intelligent tend to have more satisfying interpersonal relationships, have greater self-esteem, and be more effective in the workplace (Joseph & Newman, 2010; Farh, Seo, & Tesluk, 2012).

Most of the research on emotional intelligence has been done with adults, in large part because Goleman (1998; Goleman, Bayatzis, & McKee, 2002) argued that EI can be the key to a successful career. Child-development researchers have studied emotion but usually from a developmental angle—they have wanted to know how emotions change with age. (We'll look at that research in Module 10.1.) Research on children's EI has become more prominent in recent years, however, and some of this research has been done in Canada. James Parker of Trent University in Peterborough, Ontario, has collaborated with colleagues from across Canada and in the United States to expand the study of EI in younger age groups (e.g., Parker et al., 2005).

IMPLICATIONS FOR EDUCATION. The theory of multiple intelligences has important implications for education. Gardner (1993, 1995) believes that schools should foster all intelligences, rather than just the traditional linguistic and logical-mathematical intelligences, and that teachers should capitalize on the strongest intelligences of individual children. That is, teachers need to know a child's profile of intelligence—the child's strengths and weaknesses—and gear instruction to the strengths (Chen & Gardner, 2005). For example, Diana, the Grade 4 teacher in the opening vignette, could help some of her students understand the War of 1812 by studying the music of that period (musical intelligence). Other students might benefit by an emphasis on maps that show the movement of armies in battle (spatial intelligence). Still others might profit from focusing on the experiences of Indigenous people living in Canada and America during that period (interpersonal intelligence).

These guidelines do not mean that teachers should gear instruction solely to a child's strongest intelligence, pigeonholing youngsters as numerical learners or spatial learners. Instead, whether the topic is Canada's Confederation or Shakespeare's *Hamlet,* instruction should try to engage as many different intelligences as possible (Gardner, 1999, 2002). The typical result is a much richer understanding of the topic by all students.

Some schools have enthusiastically embraced Gardner's ideas (Gardner, 1993). Are these schools better than those that have not? Educators in schools using the theory think so; they cite evidence that their students benefit in many ways (Kornhaber, Fierros, & Veenema, 2004), although some critics are not yet convinced (Waterhouse, 2006). In fact, a general criticism is that the theory has relatively little empirical support (Kaufman, Kaufman, & Plucker, 2013). Nevertheless, there is no doubt that Gardner's work has helped liberate researchers from narrow psychometric-based views of intelligence.

A comparably broad but different view of intelligence comes from another new theory that we'll look at in the next section.

Sternberg's Theory of Successful Intelligence

Robert Sternberg has studied intelligence for more than 35 years. He began by asking how adults solve problems on intelligence tests. Over the years, his work led to a comprehensive theory of intelligence. Sternberg (1999) defines successful intelligence as the skillful use of one's abilities to achieve one's personal goals. Goals can be short-term (getting an A on a test, heating a snack in the microwave, or winning the 100-metre hurdles) or longer term (having a successful career and a happy family life). Achieving these goals by using one's skills defines successful intelligence.

In achieving personal goals, people use three different kinds of abilities. *Analytic ability* **involves analyzing problems and generating different solutions.** Suppose a teenager wants to download songs to her iPod but cannot do so. Analytic intelligence is shown when she considers possible causes of the problem—maybe the iPod is broken or maybe the software to download songs wasn't installed correctly. Analytic intelligence also involves thinking of different solutions: She could surf the internet for clues about what is wrong or ask a sibling for help.

Creative ability **involves dealing flexibly with novel situations and problems.** Returning to our teenager, suppose that she discovers her iPod is broken just as she is ready to leave on a day-long car trip. Lacking the time (and money) to buy a new player, she might show creative intelligence in dealing successfully with a novel goal: finding another enjoyable activity to do to pass the time on the long drive.

Finally, *practical ability* **involves knowing what solution or plan will actually work.** In principle, problems can often be solved in various ways, but in reality only one solution may be practical. Our teenager may realize that surfing the net for a way to fix the iPod is the only real choice, because her parents would not approve of many of the songs she likes if they learned about them while helping her, and she doesn't want her sibling to know that she is downloading those songs.

Like the theory of multiple intelligences, the theory of successful intelligence suggests that students learn best when instruction is geared to their strength. A child with strong analytic ability, for example, may find algebra simpler when the course emphasizes analyses and evaluation; a child with strong practical ability may be at his best when the material is organized around practical applications. Thus, the theory of successful intelligence shows how instruction can be matched to students' strongest abilities, enhancing students' prospects for mastering the material (Grigorenko, Jarvin, & Sternberg, 2002).

A key element of Sternberg's theory is that successful intelligence is revealed in people's pursuit of goals. Of course, these goals vary from one person to the next and, just as importantly, often vary even more in different cultural, ethnic, or racial groups. This makes it tricky—at best—to compare intelligence and intelligence test scores for individuals from different groups, as we'll see in the Cultural Influences feature.

 QUESTION 8.1
Kathryn is convinced that her daughter is really smart because she has a huge vocabulary for her age. Would a psychometrician, Howard Gardner, and Robert Sternberg agree with Kathryn's opinion? *(Answer is on page 279.)*

Cultural Influences

How Culture Defines What Is Intelligent

In Brazil, many school-age boys sell candy and fruit on the streets, yet they often cannot identify the numbers on money.

In Brazil, many elementary-school-age boys, like the one in the top photo, sell candy and fruit to bus passengers and pedestrians. These children often cannot identify the numbers on paper money, yet they know how to purchase their goods from wholesale stores, make change for customers, and keep track of their sales (Saxe, 1988).

Adolescents who live on Pacific Ocean islands near New Guinea learn to sail boats, like the one in the bottom photo, hundreds of miles across open seas to get from one small island to the next. They have no formal training in mathematics, yet they use a complex navigational system based on the positions of stars and estimates of the boat's speed (Hutchins, 1983).

In Northern Ontario, the Oji-Cree peoples value respect for others and the acquisition of traditional skills. Children are allowed great freedom to learn from the environment. Children in this culture grow up learning to be self-sufficient and independent, at the same time caring for others and the natural world (Berry & Bennett, 1992).

If either the Brazilian vendors or the island navigators were given the tests that measure intelligence in Canadian students, they would fare poorly. And they probably couldn't download music to an iPod. The Oji-Cree would consider taking time over a task more important than arriving at a quick conclusion. Does this mean that these children are less intelligent than average Canadian children? Of course not. The specific skills and goals that are important to Canadian and American conceptions of successful intelligence, and that are assessed on many intelligence tests, are less valued in these other cultures. And, by the same token, most bright Canadian non-Indigenous children would be lost trying to navigate a boat in the open sea or fail at survival in the Far North. Each culture defines what it means to be intelligent, and the specialized computing skills of vendors, navigators, and hunters are just as intelligent in their cultural settings as other skills are in mainstream Canadian and American culture (Sternberg & Kaufman, 1998).

Critical Thinking Questions: What other examples of culturally specific "intelligent" behaviours can you think of? How would the average Canadian fare?

Adolescents living on islands in the Pacific Ocean near New Guinea navigate small boats across hundreds of miles of open water, yet they have no formal training in mathematics.

As with Gardner's theory, researchers are still evaluating Sternberg's theory. As you can see in the table below, which summarizes the different approaches, theorists are still debating the question of what intelligence *is*. But, however it is defined, the fact remains that individuals differ substantially in intellectual ability, and numerous tests have been devised to measure these differences. The construction, properties, and limits of these tests are the focus of the next module.

SUMMARY TABLE

FEATURES OF MAJOR APPROACHES TO INTELLIGENCE

Approach	Distinguishing Features
Psychometric	Intelligence is a hierarchy of general and specific skills.
Gardner's theory of multiple intelligences	Nine distinct intelligences exist: linguistic, logical-mathematical, spatial musical, bodily-kinesthetic, interpersonal, intrapersonal, naturalistic, and existential.
Sternberg's theory of successful intelligence	Successful intelligence is defined as the use of analytic, creative, and practical abilities to pursue personal goals.

 Check Your Learning

RECALL Describe the psychometric perspective on intelligence.

Summarize the main features of Sternberg's theory of successful intelligence.

INTERPRET Compare and contrast the major approaches to intelligence on the extent to which they make connections between different aspects of development. That is, to what extent does each perspective emphasize cognitive processes versus integrating physical, cognitive, social, and emotional processes?

APPLY On page 276, we mentioned activities that would allow Diana, the Grade 4 teacher, to take advantage of musical, spatial, and interpersonal intelligences to help engage more of her students in a unit on the War of 1812. Think of activities that would allow her to engage Gardner's remaining intelligences in her teaching.

 ANSWER 8.1
All three would agree that verbal ability is one part of intelligence. The psychometrician and Howard Gardner would both tell Kathryn that intelligence includes other skills (although they would not mention the same ones). Sternberg, however, would emphasize that it's the application of verbal skill in the context of analytic, creative, and practical abilities that really matters.

 8.2 Features of IQ Scores

OUTLINE	LEARNING OBJECTIVES
Binet and the Development of Intelligence Testing	**1.** Why were intelligence tests devised initially? What are modern tests like?
What do IQ Scores Predict?	**2.** What do tests predict? How does dynamic testing differ from traditional testing?
Hereditary and Environmental Factors	**3.** What are the roles of heredity and environment in determining intelligence?
Impact of Ethnicity and Socioeconomic Status	**4.** How do ethnicity and socioeconomic status influence intelligence test scores?

Charlene, an African Canadian Grade 3 student, received a score of 75 on an intelligence test administered by a school psychologist. Based on the test score, the psychologist believes that Charlene is a child with cognitive developmental delay and should receive special education. Charlene's parents are indignant; they believe that the tests are biased against African Canadians and that the score is meaningless.

European and North American schools faced significant changes at the beginning of the twentieth century. In the United States, between 1890 and 1915, school enrolment nearly doubled as great numbers of immigrants arrived and as reforms restricted child labour and emphasized education (Chapman, 1988). Increased enrolment in the education systems of the Western world meant that teachers suddenly had more students who did not learn as readily as the "select few" who had populated their classes previously. How to deal with these "less capable" children was one of the pressing issues of the day (Giordano, 2005). In this module, you'll see how intelligence tests were devised initially to address a changed school population and how such tests became particularly popular in the United States. Then we'll look at a simple question: "How well do modern tests work?" Finally, we'll examine how race, ethnicity, social class, environment, and heredity influence intelligence, and we'll learn how to interpret Charlene's test score.

Binet and the Development of Intelligence Testing

With the rise of formal education and the corresponding increase in numbers of school children, several problems faced educators at the beginning of the twentieth century. Among them was how to identify which children would most benefit from schooling and which would be likely to have difficulties. In 1904, the minister of public instruction in France asked two noted psychologists, Alfred Binet and Theophile Simon, to formulate a way to identify children who were likely to succeed in school. Binet and Simon's approach was to select simple tasks that French children of different ages ought to be able to do, such as naming colours, counting backwards, and remembering numbers in order. Based on preliminary testing, Binet and Simon determined problems that typical three-year-olds could solve, that typical four-year-olds could solve, and so on. **Binet and Simon introduced the concept of** *mental age (MA),* which referred to the difficulty of the problems that children could solve correctly. A child who solved problems that the average seven-year-old could pass would have an MA of seven.

Binet and Simon used mental age to distinguish "bright" from "dull" children. A bright child would have the MA of an older child; for example, a six-year-old with an MA of nine was considered bright. A dull child would have the MA of a younger child, for example, a six-year-old with an MA of four. Binet and Simon confirmed that bright children did better in school than dull children. It should be noted that Binet and Simon did not intend their test to be used to "label" children. Rather, their purpose was to assess level of ability to help the child be placed appropriately in school to best further his or her education. We would remind you here that you should be careful about use of any IQ test results: These two- or three-digit numbers do not define the person—regardless of what the free tests on the internet might imply!

THE STANFORD-BINET. When the Binet-Simon test was introduced in the United States, Lewis Terman, of Stanford University, revised Binet and Simon's test to fit the norms of the American population and published a version known as the Stanford-Binet in 1916. **Terman described performance as an** *intelligence quotient, or IQ,* **which was simply the ratio of mental age to chronological age (CA), multiplied by 100**:

$$IQ = MA/CA \times 100$$

At any age, children who are perfectly average will have an IQ of 100 because their mental age equals their chronological age. Figure 8-2 shows the typical distribution of test scores in the population. Roughly two-thirds of children taking a test will have IQ scores between 85 and 115 and 95 percent will have scores between 70 and 130.

The IQ score can also be used to compare intelligence in children of different ages. A four-year-old with an MA of 5 has an IQ of 125 (5/4 × 100), the same as an eight-year-old with an MA of 10 (10/8 × 100).

IQ scores are no longer computed simply by the MA/CA formula. Instead, children's IQ scores are determined by comparing their test performance to that of others their age. When children perform at the average for their age, their IQ is 100. Children who perform above the average have IQs greater than 100; children who perform below the average have IQs less than 100. Nevertheless, the concept of IQ as the ratio of MA to CA helped popularize the Stanford-Binet test.

By the 1920s, the Stanford-Binet had been joined by many other intelligence tests. Educators enthusiastically embraced the tests as an efficient and objective way to assess a student's chances of succeeding in school (Chapman, 1988). Nearly 100 years later, the Stanford-Binet remains a popular test; the latest version was revised in 2003. Like the earlier versions, the modern Stanford-Binet consists of various cognitive and motor tasks, ranging from the extremely easy to the extremely difficult. The test may be administered to individuals ranging in age from approximately two years to adulthood, but the test items used depend on the child's age. For example, preschool children may be asked to name pictures of familiar objects, string beads, answer questions about everyday life, or fold paper into shapes. Older individuals may be asked to define vocabulary words, solve an abstract problem, or decipher an unfamiliar code. Based on a person's performance, a total IQ score is calculated, along with scores measuring five specific cognitive factors: fluid reasoning, knowledge, quantitative reasoning, visual-spatial processing, and working memory

As mentioned at the beginning of this module, although testing is used in Canada, it is particularly popular in the United States. In part, this may be due to the original uses of the tests, which included screening the large numbers of immigrants to that country in the early 1900s. The argument has been made that the rise of psychology as a profession in the United States was closely linked with the advent of measures of individual differences, especially intelligence, while in Canada, psychology did not really become prominent until after World War II (Marks, 1976). Also proposed is the idea that intelligence testing is more closely linked to public policy in the United States than in other countries (Ramey & Landesman-Ramey, 2000) and that there is a particular relationship between the construct of intelligence and the culture in the United States (Serpell, 2000). In fact, one expert has argued that "IQ is the most important predictor of an individual's ultimate position within American society" (Brody, 1992). Students are thus given standardized tests much more often in the U.S. than here in Canada.

Another test used frequently with six- to 16-year-olds is the Wechsler Intelligence Scale for Children-V, or WISC-V for short. The substantially revised WISC-V includes subtests for five cognitive domains, such as verbal and performance skills; some example test items are shown in Figure 8-3. Based on their performance, children receive an overall IQ score as well as scores for verbal comprehension, visual-spatial reasoning, fluid reasoning, working memory, and processing speed. This test has been normed for the Canadian population and is now available as the *Wechsler Intelligence Scale for Children®-Fifth Edition:*

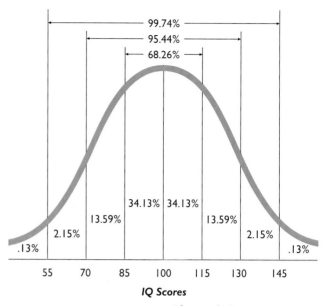

Figure 8-2 The typical distribution of IQ test scores in the population.

An advantage of an individual intelligence test is that the examiner can be sure that the child is attentive and not anxious during testing.

Canadian (WISC®-V CDN). This test is more likely to be used for assessment of children in Canada than other forms, such as the Stanford–Binet, which is more widely used in the United States.

The Stanford–Binet and the WISC-V are alike in that they are administered to one person at a time. Other tests can be administered to groups of individuals, with the advantage of providing information about many individuals quickly and inexpensively, typically without the need of trained psychologists. But individual testing like that shown in the photo optimizes the motivation and attention of the child; it also provides an opportunity for a sensitive examiner to assess factors that may influence test performance. The examiner may notice that the child is relaxed and that test performance is therefore a reasonable sample of the individual's talents. Or the examiner may observe that child is so anxious that she cannot do her best. Such determinations are not possible with group tests. Consequently, most psychologists prefer individualized tests of intelligence over group tests.

INFANT TESTS.   The Stanford–Binet and the WISC-V cannot be used to test intelligence in infants. For this purpose, many psychologists

Verbal Scale	*Information: The child is asked questions that tap his or her factual knowledge of the world.* 1. How many wings does a bird have? 2. What is steam made of?
	Comprehension: The child is asked questions that measure his or her judgment and common sense. 1. What should you do if you see someone forget his book when he leaves a restaurant? 2. What is the advantage of keeping money in a bank?
	Similarities: The child is asked to describe how words are related. 1. In what way are a lion and a tiger alike? 2. In what way are a saw and a hammer alike?
Performance Scale	*Picture arrangement: Pictures are shown and the child is asked to place them in order to tell a story.*  
	Picture completion: The child is asked to identify the part that is missing from the picture.

Figure 8-3 Items Like Those Appearing on Different Subtests of the WISC-V.

use the Bayley Scales of Infant Development (Bayley, 1970, 1993, 2006). Designed for use with one- to 42-month-olds, the Bayley Scales consist of five scales: cognitive, language, motor, social-emotional, and adaptive behaviour. To illustrate, the motor scale assesses an infant's control of its body, its coordination, and its ability to manipulate objects. For example, six-month-olds should turn their head toward an object that the examiner drops on the floor, 12-month-olds should imitate the examiner's actions, and 16-month-olds should build a tower from three blocks.

STABILITY OF IQ SCORES. If intelligence is a stable property of a child, then scores obtained at younger ages should predict IQ scores at older ages. In other words, smart babies should become smart elementary-school students, who should become smart adults. In fact, scores from infant intelligence tests generally are not related to IQ scores obtained later in childhood, adolescence, or adulthood (McCall, 1993). Not until 18 or 24 months of age do infant IQ scores predict later IQ scores (Kopp & McCall, 1982). Why? Infant tests measure different abilities than do tests administered to children and adolescents: Infant tests place more emphasis on sensorimotor skills and less on tasks involving cognitive processes such as language, thinking, and problem solving.

According to this reasoning, a measure of infant cognitive processing might yield more accurate predictions of later IQ. In fact, estimates of infants' information-processing do predict later IQ more effectively than do scores from the Bayley. For example, measures of infants' memory are related to IQ scores during middle childhood and adolescence (Bornstein, Hahn, & Wolke, 2013; Rose, Feldman, Jankowski, & Van Rossem, 2012). In other words, babies who process information more efficiently and more accurately grow up to be smarter children and adolescents.

If scores on the Bayley Scales do not predict later IQs, why are these tests used at all? The answer is that they are important diagnostic tools: Researchers and healthcare professionals use scores from the Bayley Scales to determine whether development is progressing normally. That is, low scores on these tests are often a signal that a child may be at risk for problems later (Luttikhuizen dos Santos, de Kieviet, Königs, van Elburg, & Oosterlaan, 2013).

Although infant test scores do not reliably predict IQ later in life, scores obtained in childhood do. For example, the correlation between IQ scores at six years of age and adult IQ scores is about .7 (Brody, 1992; Kaufman & Lichtenberger, 2002). This is a relatively large correlation and shows that IQ scores are reasonably stable during childhood and adolescence. Nevertheless, during these years, many children's IQ scores will fluctuate between 10 and 20 points (McCall, 1993; Weinert & Hany, 2003).

 QUESTION 8.2
Amanda's 12-month-old son completed an intelligence test and received a slightly below-average score. Amanda is distraught because she is afraid her son's score means that he will struggle in school. What advice would you give Amanda? *(Answer is on page 293.)*

Features of IQ Scores

IQ scores are quite powerful predictors of developmental outcomes. Of course, since IQ tests were devised to predict school success, it is not surprising that they do this quite well. IQ scores predict school grades, scores on achievement tests, and number of years of education; the correlations are usually between .5 and .7 (Brody, 1992; Geary, 2005).

These correlations are far from perfect, which reminds us that some youngsters with high test scores do not excel in school and others with low test scores manage to get good grades. In fact, some researchers find that self-discipline predicts grades in school even better than IQ scores do (Duckworth & Carlson, 2013). In general, however, tests do a reasonable job of predicting school success.

Not only do intelligence scores predict success in school, they predict occupational success also (Deary, 2012). Individuals with higher IQ scores are more likely to hold high-paying, high-prestige positions within medicine, law, and engineering (Oswald & Hough, 2012; Schmidt & Hunter, 2004). Among scientists with equal education, those with higher IQ scores hold more patents and have more articles published in scientific journals (Park, Lubinski, & Benbow, 2008). Some of the linkage between IQ and occupational success occurs because these professions require more education, and we have already seen that IQ scores predict educational success. Even within a profession—where all individuals have the same amount of education—IQ scores predict job performance and earnings, particularly for more complex jobs (Henderson, 2010; Schmidt & Hunter, 2004). If, for example, two teenagers have summer jobs running tests in a biology lab, the smarter of the two will probably learn the procedures more rapidly and, once learned, conduct them more accurately and efficiently.

Finally, intelligence scores even predict longevity: Individuals with greater IQ scores tend to live longer, in part because they are less likely to smoke, they drink less alcohol, they stay active physically, and they eat more healthfully (Deary, 2012).

IMPROVING PREDICTIONS WITH DYNAMIC TESTING. Traditional tests of intelligence, such as the Stanford-Binet and the WISC-V, measure knowledge and skills that a child has accumulated up to the time of testing. These tests do not directly measure a child's potential for future learning; instead, the usual assumption is that children who have learned more in the past will probably learn more in the future. Critics argue that tests would be more valid if they directly assessed a child's potential for future learning.

Dynamic assessment **measures a child's learning potential by having the child learn something new in the presence of the examiner and with the examiner's help.** Dynamic assessment differs from traditional testing in several ways (Tzuriel, 2013). First, the goal of traditional testing is to predict children's performance relative to their peers; the goal of dynamic assessment is diagnosis, revealing a child's strengths and weaknesses as a learner. Second, traditional testing follows a standardized format that focuses on a child's unaided performance; dynamic assessment is interactive and, drawing on Vygotsky's ideas of the zone of proximal development and scaffolding (discussed in Module 6.2), focuses on the kind of guidance and feedback that children need to succeed (Sternberg & Grigorenko, 2002). Third, traditional testing focuses on the child's average performance across a variety of items; dynamic assessment focuses on a child's peak performance—identifying the circumstances in which children learn best.

Dynamic assessment is most valuable for children who have difficulties learning in school, such as children with intellectual disabilities (described on pages 295–296). These children often receive low scores on traditional intelligence tests, scores that provide few insights into the child's abilities. In other words, IQ scores document that these children are less skilled than typically developing children, but they don't pinpoint the skills that children do have or the conditions that promote children's use of their skills. This information is provided by dynamic assessment and estimates a child's learning potential more accurately than traditional tests do (Tzuriel, 2013).

Hereditary and Environmental Factors

In a typical Canadian or American elementary school, several Grade 1 students will have IQ scores greater than 120 and a similar number will have IQ scores in the low 80s. What accounts for the 40-point difference in these youngsters' scores? Heredity plays an important role (Bouchard, 2009), as does experience (Bronfenbrenner & Morris, 2006).

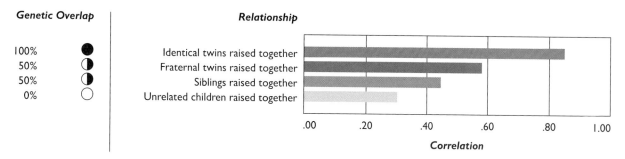

Figure 8-4 Influence of heredity: correlation of genetic relatedness and IQ scores.
Based on Plomin, R., & Petrill, S. A. (1997). *Genetics and intelligence: What's new* Intelligence, 24, 53–77.

Some of the evidence for hereditary factors is shown in Figure 8-4. If genes influence intelligence, then siblings' test scores should be more alike as siblings become more similar genetically (Plomin & Petrill, 1997). In other words, because identical twins are identical genetically, they should have virtually identical test scores (a correlation of 1). Fraternal twins have about 50 percent of their genes in common, just like nontwin siblings of the same biological parents. Consequently their test scores should be (a) less similar than scores for identical twins, (b) similar to scores of other siblings who have the same biological parents, and (c) more similar than scores of children and their adopted siblings. You can see in the graph of Figure 8-4 that each of these predictions is supported.

Further evidence for heredity in intelligence comes from an analysis of 11 000 twin pairs in a form of meta-analysis of information from six studies across four countries. Researchers combined data from Australia, The Netherlands, the United States, and the United Kingdom. This study was interesting in that only those from the top 15 percent of the IQ distribution were studied. It was found that for *high* intelligence, genes did explain about half of the variance in IQ; that is, of the differences in intelligence between twins, at least half was due to genetic factors (Haworth et al., 2009).

Studies of adopted children also suggest the impact of heredity on IQ: If heredity helps determine IQ, then children's IQs should be more like those of their biological parents than of their adoptive parents. In fact, throughout childhood and adolescence, the correlation between children's IQ and their biological parents' IQ is greater than the correlation between children's IQ and their adoptive parents' IQ. What's more, as adopted children get older, their test scores increasingly resemble those of their biological parents (Plomin & Petrill, 1997). These results are evidence for the greater impact of heredity on IQ as a child grows.

Do these results mean that heredity is the sole determinant of intelligence? No. Three areas of research show the importance of environment on intelligence. The first is research on characteristics of families and homes. If intelligence were solely due to heredity, environment should have little or no impact on children's intelligence. In fact, children tend to have greater IQ scores when the family environment is intellectually stimulating—when parents talk frequently to the children, when they provide their children with cognitive challenging materials such as puzzles and

Children who achieve high scores on intelligence tests often come from homes that are well organized and include many age-appropriate books and toys that can stimulate a child's intellectual growth.

Tomsickova Tatyana/Shutterstock

books, and when they expose children to stimulating experiences outside the home, such as visits to museums (Nisbett et al., 2012).

The impact of the environment on intelligence is also implied by a dramatic rise in IQ test scores during the twentieth century (Flynn & Weiss, 2007). For example, scores on the WISC-III increased by nearly 10 points over a 25-year period (Flynn, 1999). The change may reflect industrialization, which requires a more intelligent workforce and brings about better schools, smaller families, and more stimulating leisure-time activities (Nisbett et al., 2012). Regardless of the exact causes of increased IQ scores, the increase per se shows the impact of changing environmental conditions on intelligence.

The importance of a stimulating environment for intelligence is also demonstrated by intervention programs that prepare economically disadvantaged children for school. Without preschool, children from low-income families often enter kindergarten or Grade 1 lacking key readiness skills for academic success, which means they rapidly fall behind their peers who have these skills. Consequently, providing preschool experiences for children from poor families has long been a part of U.S. federal policies to eliminate poverty. The Children's Lives feature traces the beginnings of these programs.

Children's Lives

Providing Children with a Head Start for School

For more than 50 years, the Head Start program in the United States has been helping foster the development of preschool children from low-income families. This program's origins can be traced to two forces. First, in the early 1960s, child-development researchers argued that environmental influences on children's development were much stronger than had been estimated previously. An influential review (Hunt, 1961) of the impact of experience on intelligence concluded that children's intellectual development could reach unprecedented heights when scientists identified optimal environmental influences. In addition, a novel program in Tennessee directed by Susan Gray (Gray & Klaus, 1965) gave credibility to the argument by showing that a summer program coupled with weekly home visits throughout the school year could raise intelligence and language in preschool children living in poverty. These findings suggested that claims of boosting children's intelligence were not simply pipe dreams.

The second force was a political one. When American President Lyndon Johnson launched the War on Poverty in 1964, the Office of Economic Opportunity (OEO) was the command centre. Sargent Shriver, the OEO's first director, found himself with a huge budget surplus. Most of the War on Poverty programs targeted adults, and because many of these programs were politically unpopular, Shriver was reluctant to spend more money on them. Shriver realized that no programs were aimed specifically at children and that such programs would be much less controversial politically. Critics might try to argue that poor adults "deserve their fate" because they are lazy or irresponsible, but such arguments are not very convincing when applied to young children. What's more, Shriver was personally familiar with the potential impact of programs targeted at young children through his experience as president of the Chicago School Board and his wife's work on the President's Panel on Mental Retardation (Zigler & Muenchow, 1992).

Shriver envisioned a program that would better prepare poor children for Grade 1. He convened a planning committee, including professionals from medicine, social work, education, and psychology, that devised a comprehensive program that would meet the health and educational needs of young children by involving professionals and parents. Head Start began in May 1965, and by that summer, half a million American youngsters were enrolled. The program now enrolls nearly a million American children living in poverty and has, since its inception in 1965, met the needs of more than 33 million children (Administration for Children and Families, 2015).

Critical Thinking Question: The feature notes that Head Start programs help children to be better prepared for school. In what other ways would such a program be beneficial?

How effectively do intervention programs like these programs meet the needs of preschool youngsters? Head Start takes different forms in different communities, which makes it difficult to make blanket statements about the overall effectiveness of the program. However, high-quality Head Start programs *are* effective overall. When children such as those in the photo below attend good Head Start programs, they are healthier and do better in school (Ludwig & Phillips, 2007; Protzko, Aronson, & Blair, 2013). For example, Head Start graduates are less likely to repeat a grade level or to be placed in special education classes, and they are more likely to graduate from high school.

Canada's Aboriginal Head Start (AHS) program is based on the American example and was started in 1995 (Stairs, Bernhard, & Aboriginal Colleagues,[1] 2002). An expansion in 1998 led to the Aboriginal Head Start on Reserve (AHSOR) program, which supports Indigenous children from birth to six years of age, and their families, who live on-reserve (Health Canada, 2011a). As Stairs et al. (2002) note, the AHS used the basic concepts of the American Head Start program but adapted the idea to focus on the goals and cultures of Indigenous Canadians. The main purpose of AHS/AHSOR is to foster education along with "positive Aboriginal self-identity and empowerment" (Stairs et al., 2002, p. 310). Testing, as we will discuss shortly, is often based on a particular sociocultural viewpoint. The same is true for education, which can be marginalizing for those who do not come from the majority culture. One example given by Stairs et al. (2002) is that *collectivity,* **the interdependence of the members of the community, is a much more important aspect of life for Indigenous cultures than for mainstream Canadian culture.** Thus in an AHS program, the need for support of the family and community, as well as the child, is recognized as important for academic success. The AHS program aims to foster "Aboriginal solutions for Aboriginal children" (AHS, 2008). Local needs and goals are considered, with involvement of parents, community groups and local leaders (Health Canada, 2010a, 2011a). The more holistic approach to learning taken by Aboriginal cultures is also included and has positive benefits for literacy (George, 2003) and education generally (Nguyen, 2011). AHS and AHSOR engage and involve indigenous cultures to promote positive growth in their children.

High-quality Head Start programs are effective: Graduates are less likely to repeat a grade in school and are more likely to graduate from high school.

Bob Ebbesen/Alamy Stock Photo

---

[1]Stairs and Bernhard (2002) could not give specific names of all their Aboriginal colleagues as co-authors; however, they did want to acknowledge input from their "Aboriginal colleague friends" (p. 325).

Interventions such as Head Start work. A meta-analysis by Geoffrey Nelson and Anne Weshues of Wilfrid Laurier University and Jennifer MacLeod from the Wellington-Dufferin-Guelph Health Unit showed that such programs were indeed effective and that cognitive benefits extended through elementary school. Nelson, Weshues, and MacLeod (2003) concluded that, although effects were greatest during the preschool years, cognitive effects were still noticeable through Grade 8, and social-emotional effects were noted into high school. What's more, as adults, those who experienced such interventions were more likely to have graduated from post-secondary education and more likely to be working full time (Campbell et al., 2012).

Of course, massive intervention over many years is expensive, but so are the economic consequences of poverty, unemployment, and their by-products. In fact, economic analyses show that, in the long term, these programs more than pay for themselves in the form of increased earnings (and tax revenues) for participating children and in lowered costs associated with the criminal justice system (Bartik, Gormley, & Adelstein, 2012; Reynolds, Temple, White, Ou, & Robertson 2011). Programs such as AHS show that the repetitive cycle of school failure and education can be broken. In the process, they show that intelligence is fostered by a stimulating and responsive environment.

Impact of Ethnicity and Socioeconomic Status

Ethnic groups differ in their average scores on many intelligence tests. People of Asian ancestry tend to have the highest scores, followed by those with European, then Hispanic, and lastly African ancestry (Hunt & Carlson, 2007). A great deal of argument has taken place over the meaning of these findings, however. When J. Phillipe Rushton of the University of Western Ontario (UWO) first published his work in this field, an uproar ensued because Rushton interpreted his findings of racially based IQ differences as due to heritable—genetically based—traits. A number of psychologists, including some of Rushton's colleagues at UWO, wrote articles that countered his research, pointing out issues of flawed reasoning and methodology, as well as challenging his conclusions (e.g., Cain & Vanderwolf, 1990; Zuckerman & Brody, 1988). Some researchers now argue that the concept of "race" is redundant (e.g., Cooper, Kaufman, & Ward, 2003), at least as far as variability in traits is concerned (Mountain & Risch, 2004). Despite this last assertion, the debate has continued (e.g., Dickens & Flynn, 2006; Rushton & Jensen, 2006). The scoring gaps have become smaller since the 1960s, however, and reflect, in part, group differences in socioeconomic status (Nisbett et al., 2012; Rindermann & Thompson, 2013). Children from economically advantaged homes tend to have higher test scores than children from economically disadvantaged homes, and European Canadian and Asian Canadian families are more likely to be economically advantaged, whereas Latin American Canadian and African Canadian families are more likely to be economically disadvantaged. When researchers who are making comparisons of children's IQ take socioeconomic status into account, group differences in IQ test scores are significantly reduced: "Adjustments for economic and social differences in the lives of black and white children all but eliminate differences in the IQ scores between these groups" (Brooks-Gunn, Klebanov, & Duncan, 1996, p. 396). Nevertheless, when children of comparable socioeconomic status are compared, group differences in IQ test scores are reduced but not eliminated (Magnuson & Duncan, 2006). Let's look at four explanations for the observed differences in nonadjusted IQ scores.

A ROLE FOR GENETICS?   On pages 284–285, you learned that heredity helps determine a child's intelligence: Smart parents tend to beget smart children. Does this also mean that group differences in IQ scores reflect genetic differences? No. Most researchers agree that there is no evidence that some ethnic groups have more "smart genes" than others. Instead, they believe that the environment is largely responsible for these differences (Nisbett et al., 2012).

A popular analogy (Lewontin, 1976) demonstrates the thinking here. Imagine two kinds of corn: Each kind produces both short and tall plants, and height is known to be due to heredity. If one kind of corn grows in a good soil—with plenty of water and nutrients—the mature plants will reach their genetically determined heights; some short, some tall. If the other kind of corn grows in poor soil, few of the plants will reach their full height, and overall the plants of this kind will be much shorter. Thus, even though height is quite heritable for each type of corn, the difference in height between the two groups is due solely to the quality of the environment. Similarly, though IQ scores may be quite heritable for different groups, limited exposure to stimulating environments may mean that one group ends up with lower IQ scores overall, just like the group of plants growing up in poor soil.

EXPERIENCE WITH TEST CONTENTS. Some critics contend that differences in test scores reflect bias in the tests themselves. One major example is that test items reflect the cultural heritage of the test creators, most of whom were economically advantaged Americans of European ancestry, and so tests are biased against economically disadvantaged children from other groups (Champion, 2003). Critics thus point to test items like this one:

A conductor is to an orchestra as a teacher is to what?

book   school   class   eraser

Children whose background includes exposure to orchestras are more likely to answer this question correctly than children who lack this exposure. Thus one problem with the use of tests is that a test may be biased toward members of the sociocultural group that initially developed the test (e.g., Anastasi, 1976). One of the questions on an early intelligence test developed in the United States was

Crisco is a a) medicine b) disinfectant c) toothpaste d) food product

Perhaps you know the answer to that question is *d) food product,* but what about this one?

Marmite is a a) medicine b) disinfectant c) toothpaste d) food product

The answer is also *d),* but did you know that? Co-author Anne Barnfield is originally from England, where the spread called Marmite is commonly eaten, but Crisco is not sold. She uses this example in classes to show students how culture-specific questions can influence scores on tests. If all the questions on an immigration test had been like the first example, one of your textbook authors might never have been allowed into Canada!

Clinical psychologist Jacques Gouws, working in Cambridge and Hamilton, Ontario, noted particular problems of administration of all types of psychometric tests with immigrants to Canada. As Gouws (2003) pointed out in an article in *Psychology Ontario,* it is not sufficient to simply have an interpreter translate a test into a person's first language. In addition to the culture-specific aspects just discussed, even word meanings can change in translation, making the test no longer valid. All test items and scales must be truly equivalent to give a fair version of a test to a person from a different cultural background.

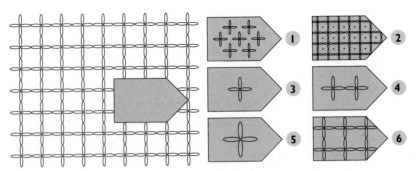

Figure 8-5 A sample item from Raven's Progressive Matrices test.

Similar advice comes from European research. Stobart (2005), from the University of London, U.K., investigated fairness of assessment in multicultural societies and proposed that "fairness is fundamentally a sociocultural, rather than a technical, issue" (p. 275). He notes that it is obviously unfair to test children on items or information that they have not had equal opportunity to learn. And researchers from the University of Amsterdam concluded that standard tests such as IQ tests were unfair to those whose background was not that of the dominant culture (Craig & Beishuizen, 2002). Traditional psychometric tests have come to be viewed as biased in favour of the main group in any society, particularly if that group originally developed the tests. Thus the administration of tests can be unfair when cultural differences exist.

The problem of bias led to the development of *culture-fair intelligence tests,* **which include test items based on experiences common to many cultures.** An example is Raven's Progressive Matrices, which consist solely of items like the one shown in Figure 8-5. Examinees are asked to select the piece that would complete the design correctly (*6,* in this case). Although items like this are thought to reduce the impact of specific experience, ethnic group differences still remain in performance on so-called culture-fair intelligence tests (Anastasi, 1988; Herrnstein & Murray, 1994). Apparently, familiarity with test-related items per se is not the key factor responsible for group differences in performance.

STEREOTYPE THREAT.   When people know that they belong to a group that is said to lack skill in a domain, they become anxious when performing in that domain for fear of confirming the stereotype, and they often do poorly as a result. **This self-fulfilling prophecy, in which knowledge of stereotypes leads to anxiety and reduced performance consistent with the original stereotype, is called** *stereotype threat.* One example from research at the University of British Columbia is the effect of stereotype threat on women's performance in mathematics. When young women read a passage that implied that genetics was responsible for lower performance in mathematics by females, they scored worse on math tests than those who had read a passage proposing environmental causes of sex differences in this ability (Dar-Nimrod & Heine, 2006). Applied to intelligence, the argument is that children of African ancestry experience stereotype threat when they take intelligence tests, which contributes to their lower scores (Steele, 1997; Steele & Aronson, 1995). For example, imagine two 10-year-olds taking an intelligence test for admission to a special program for gifted children. The European Canadian child worries that if he fails the test, he won't be admitted to the program. The African Canadian child has the same fears but also worries that if he does poorly it will confirm the stereotype that African Canadian children don't get good scores on IQ tests. Such effects have been found in comparisons of children from different racial backgrounds in the United States (Suzuki & Aronson, 2005), where we have noted there is greater interest in IQ testing and also a greater racial divide than in "multicultural" Canada. It does appear, though, that generally, children from minority groups often get low scores on intelligence tests because they worry about stereotypes and are wary in testing situations.

Stereotype threat seems to exert influence by multiple effects on cognitive processes, for example, affecting working memory, or attention (Jamieson & Harkins, 2007; McConnell, Beilock, Jellison, Rydell, & Carr, 2004). It seems that performance can be influenced in different ways, but it is always affected negatively. One way to combat the effect of stereotype threat is to give people positive examples. Reading or writing a passage that boosts self-worth of members of a certain group has been shown to reduce gaps in achievement by improving scores (Cohen, Garcia, Apfel, & Master, 2006). And stereotype threat has been shown to be reduced (and performance improved) when African American students experience self-affirmation—they remind themselves of values that are important to them and why (Sherman et al., 2013). As the Focus on Research feature shows, stereotype threat is also reduced when children are told that a test is an opportunity to learn new things, not a measure of ability.

Focus On Research

Making Tests Less Threatening

Who were the investigators, and what was the aim of the study? Stereotype threat works when people fear that their performance will confirm a stereotype. Consequently, one way to reduce threat should be to convince people that the task they're performing is unrelated to the stereotype. This was the approach used by Adam Alter and his colleagues (2010) to reduce stereotype threat.

How did the investigators measure the topic of interest? All participants completed 10 problems from a standardized math test. Half the participants were told that the problems measured their math ability; half were told that solving challenging math problems would help them do well in school. In addition, half the participants were asked to report their race before solving the problems, a manipulation designed to put the students at greater risk for stereotype threat; half provided this information after solving the problems, when it could not affect their performance.

Who were the participants in the study? The study included 49 African American students in Grades 4 to 6.

What was the design of the study? This study was experimental. The independent variables included the framing of the math problems (as a measure of math ability or as a challenge that would help them do well in school) and when students reported their race (before or after solving the math problems). The dependent variable was the number of math problems solved correctly. Although the study included students in Grades 4 to 6, the investigators did not examine age-related differences; consequently, the study was neither cross-sectional nor longitudinal.

Were there ethical concerns with the study? No. Parents provided consent for their children to participate. The math problems were common ones, taken from a test used by the school to assess students' progress. Finally, to counter any lingering effects of stereotype threat, all students were told that they had done well on the test.

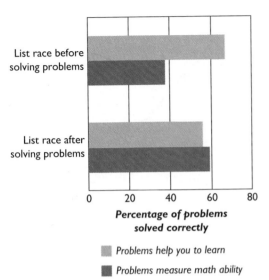

Figure 8-6 The average number of problems that students solved in the four conditions.

Based on Alter, A. L., Aronson, J., Darley, J. M., Rodriguez, C., & Ruble, D. N. (2010). *Rising to the threat: Reducing stereotype threat by reframing the threat as a challenge.* Journal of Experimental Social Psychology, 46, 166–171.

What were the results? Figure 8-6 shows the average number of problems that students solved in the four conditions. You can see that students solved the fewest problems when they provided their race before solving the problems and when the problems were portrayed as a measure of ability, an outcome that shows the impact of stereotype threat. In contrast, when stereotype threat could not operate—because the problems were portrayed as a challenging way for students to improve their learning or because race was not salient (it had not been mentioned prior to solving the problems)—students solved more problems.

What did the investigators conclude? Alter and his colleagues concluded that "reframing a threatening task as a challenge eradicated the negative effects of stereotype threat. . . . [P]articipants who were reminded that they belonged to a marginalized group performed more poorly than their peers on an academic test, except when the test was framed as a challenge. This manipulation was subtle and inexpensive, which suggests that it might be a useful stereotype threat-management intervention" (Alter et al., 2010, p. 170).

What converging evidence would strengthen these conclusions? The results show that reframing math problems helps African American students avoid stereotype threat. It would be valuable to determine other kinds of reframing that may reduce or eliminate stereotype threat and see how well reframing works with other groups who experience stereotype threat (e.g., females and math problems).

Critical Thinking Question: What strategies might help school-age children overcome stereotype threat?

TEST-TAKING SKILLS. The impact of experience and cultural values can extend beyond particular items to a child's familiarity with the entire testing situation. Tests underestimate a child's intelligence if, for example, the child's culture encourages children to solve problems in collaboration with others and discourages them from excelling as individuals. In some cultures, children may feel it is inappropriate to answer certain questions or to speak out to an adult examiner—for example, in some Canadian Indigenous cultures (Stairs et al., 2002). If behaviour during a test is being assessed, cultural differences may also influence results. Anne Barnfield was told by an Indigenous Canadian student at Brescia University College that, in the student's culture, it was considered rude for a child to look an adult—an elder—in the face when speaking. Children in this Indigenous community would look down when speaking with an adult. This behaviour contrasts with the European Canadian practice of looking directly at a person when conversing. The Indigenous child could be seen as evasive by an examiner, when, in fact, the child is simply doing what in her culture is polite.

Socioeconomic status can also affect responses. Because they are wary of questions posed by unfamiliar adults, many economically disadvantaged children often answer test questions by saying, "I don't know." Obviously, this strategy guarantees an artificially low test score. When these children are given extra time to feel at ease with the examiner, they respond less often with "I don't know," and their test scores improve considerably (Zigler & Finn-Stevenson, 1992).

CONCLUSION: INTERPRETING TEST SCORES. If all tests reflect cultural influences, at least to some degree, how should we interpret test scores? Remember that tests assess successful adaptation to a particular cultural context: They predict success in a school environment, which usually espouses middle-class values. Regardless of ethnic group—African Canadian, Chinese Canadian, or European Canadian—a child with a high test score is more likely to have the intellectual skills needed for academic work based on middle-class values (Hunt & Carlson, 2007). A child with a low test score, like Charlene in the module-opening vignette, apparently lacks those skills. Does a low score mean Charlene is destined to fail in school? No. It simply means that, based on her current skills, she is unlikely to do well. Improving Charlene's skills will improve her school performance.

We want to end this module by emphasizing a crucial point: By focusing on groups of people, it is easy to overlook the fact that the average difference in IQ scores between various ethnic groups is relatively small compared to the entire range of scores for these groups (Sternberg, Grigorenko, & Kidd, 2005). You can easily find youngsters with high IQ scores from all ethnic groups, just as you can find youngsters with low IQ scores from all groups. In the next module, we'll look at children at the extremes of ability. Also, as we note at the end of this chapter, all development, including intelligence is influenced by both heredity and environment. Simplistic interpretations of IQ scores must be avoided. In fact, Binet himself feared that his practical device for helping place children in school could be used for "labelling" individuals. We should interpret test scores with caution and remember the many ways of conceptualizing intelligence and the many influences at work in its development.

 ANSWER 8.2
Tell her to relax. Scores on intelligence tests for infants are not related to scores taken on tests in childhood or adolescence, so the lower-than-average score has virtually no predictive value.

 ## Check Your Learning

RECALL What are modern intelligence tests like? How well do they work?

Describe the reasons that ethnic groups differ in their average scores on intelligence tests.

INTERPRET Explain the evidence that shows the roles of heredity and environment on intelligence.

APPLY Suppose that a local government official proposes to end all funding for preschool programs for disadvantaged children. Write a letter to this official in which you describe the value of these programs.

 ## Special Children, Special Needs

OUTLINE
Gifted and Creative Children
Children with Disability

LEARNING OBJECTIVES
1. **What are the characteristics of gifted and creative children?**
2. **What are the different forms of intellectual disability?**

Sanjit, a Grade 2 student, takes two separate intelligence tests, and both times he has above-average scores. Nevertheless, Sanjit absolutely cannot read. Letters and words are as mysterious to him as ancient Egyptian hieroglyphs would be to the average Canadian university student. His parents take him to an ophthalmologist, who determines that Sanjit's vision is 20–20; nothing is wrong with his eyes. What is wrong?

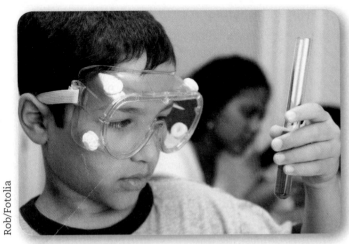

Rob/Fotolia

Traditional definitions of giftedness emphasized test scores; modern definitions emphasize exceptional talent in a variety of areas, beginning with academic areas but also including the arts.

Throughout history, societies have recognized children with limited mental abilities as well as those with extraordinary talents. Today, we know a great deal about the extremes of human talents. We'll begin this module with a look at gifted and creative children. Then we'll look at children with disabilities and discover why Sanjit can't read.

Gifted and Creative Children

In many respects Bernie, is an ordinary middle-class 12-year-old: He is the goalie on his soccer team, takes piano lessons on Saturday mornings, sings in his church youth choir, and likes to go rollerblading. However, when it comes to intelligence and academic prowess, Bernie leaves the ranks of the ordinary. He received a score of 175 on an intelligence test and is taking a college calculus course. Bernie is *gifted,* **a term that traditionally has referred to individuals with scores of 130 or greater on intelligence tests** (Horowitz & O'Brien, 1986).

Because giftedness was traditionally defined in terms of IQ scores, exceptional ability is often associated primarily with academic skill. Modern definitions of giftedness are broader and include exceptional talent in an assortment of areas, including art, music, creative writing, and dance (Subotnik, Olszewski-Kubilius, & Worrell, 2011; Winner, 2000). In many Canadian cities, schools may specialize in one of these areas— for example, St. Mary's Choir School for music or the Lester B. Pearson School for the Arts in London, Ontario.

Whether the field is music or math, though, exceptionally talented children have several characteristics in common (Subotnik et al., 2011). First, their ability is substantially above average; being smart is necessary but not sufficient for being gifted. Second, gifted children are passionate about their subject and have a powerful desire to master it.

Third, gifted children are creative in their thinking, coming up with novel thoughts and actions. **Creativity is associated with** *divergent thinking,* **where the aim is not a single correct answer (often there isn't one) but fresh and unusual lines of thought** (Callahan, 2000). For example, creativity is shown when children respond in different, innovative ways to a common stimulus, as shown in Figure 8-7, a page filled with circles. The child is asked to draw as many different pictures as they can; both the number of responses and the originality of the responses are used to measure creativity.

Fourth, exceptional talent must be nurtured. Without encouragement and support from parents and stimulating and challenging mentors, a youngster's talents will wither. Talented children need a curriculum that is challenging and complex; they need teachers who know how to foster talent; and they need like-minded peers who stimulate their interests (Subotnik et al., 2011). With this support, gifted children's achievement can be remarkable. In a 25-year

Figure 8-7 An example of a measure of creativity: The more numerous, and more divergent, the pictures the higher the level of creativity.

longitudinal study, gifted teens were, as adults, extraordinarily successful in school and in their careers (Kell, Lubinski, & Benbow, 2013). In Canada, intelligence tests may be used for screening for giftedness. For example, Betty Reiter's (2004) research with elementary-school children in Alberta examined use of a WISC-III short form for this purpose. In Ontario, children with exceptionalities, including giftedness, can be placed on an Individual Education Plan (IEP), which is a special education program tailored to the child's particular needs and abilities (Ontario Ministry of Education, 2000, 2004).

Gifted and creative children represent one extreme of human ability. At the other extreme are youngsters with disability, the topic of the next section.

Children with Disability

"Little David," so named because his father was also named David, was the oldest of four children. He learned to sit only days before his first birthday; he began to walk at two; and he said his first words as a three-year-old. By age five, David was far behind his age-mates developmentally. David had Down syndrome, a disorder (described in Module 2.1) that is caused by an extra twenty-first chromosome.

CHILDREN WITH INTELLECTUAL DISABILITY. Down syndrome is an example of a condition that leads to *intellectual disability,* **which refers to substantial limitations in intellectual ability, as well as problems adapting to an environment, with both emerging before 18 years of age.** Limited intellectual skill often is defined as a score of 70 or less on an intelligence test such as the Stanford–Binet. Adaptive behaviour includes conceptual skills important for successful adaptation in daily living (e.g., literacy, understanding money and time), social skills (e.g., interpersonal skill), and practical skills (e.g., personal grooming, occupational skills). Adaptive behaviour is usually evaluated from interviews with a parent or other caregiver. Only individuals who are under the age of 18, who have problems adapting in these areas, and who have IQ scores of 70 or less are considered to have an intellectual disability (AAIDD Ad Hoc Committee on Terminology and Classification, 2010).[2]

Modern explanations pinpoint four factors that place individuals at risk for intellectual disability:

- *Biomedical factors*, including chromosomal disorders, malnutrition, and traumatic brain injury
- *Social factors*, such as poverty and impaired parent-child interactions
- *Behavioural factors*, such as child neglect or domestic violence
- *Educational factors*, including impaired parenting and inadequate special education services

No individual factor in this list *necessarily* leads to intellectual disability. Instead, the risk for intellectual disability grows as more of these are present (AAIDD Ad Hoc Committee on Terminology and Classification, 2010). For example, the risk for intellectual disability is great for a child with Down syndrome whose parents live in poverty and cannot take advantage of special education services.

As you can imagine, the many factors that can lead to intellectual disability mean that the term encompasses an enormous variety of individuals. One way to describe this variation is in terms of the kind and amount of support that is needed. At one extreme,

[2]What we now call "intellectual disability" was long known as mental retardation, and you may still see use of that term in some contexts, e.g., in law in the United States. However, intellectual disability is the preferred term because it better reflects the condition not as a deficit in the person but as a poor "fit between the person's capacities and the context in which the person is to function" (AAIDD Ad Hoc Committee on Terminology and Classification, 2010, p. 13).

QUESTION 8.3
Ryan's eight-year-old daughter has been diagnosed with a reading disability. Ryan is concerned that this is just a politically correct way of saying that his daughter is stupid. Is he right? *(Answer is on page 298.)*

some people have so few skills that they must be supervised constantly. Consequently, they usually live in institutions for persons with intellectual disability, where they can sometimes be taught self-help skills such as dressing, feeding, and toileting (Reid, Wilson, & Faw, 1991). At the other extreme are individuals who go to school and master many academic skills, but not as quickly as a typical child does. They often work and many marry. With comprehensive training programs that focus on vocational and social skills, they are often productive citizens and satisfied human beings (Ellis & Rusch, 1991).

CHILDREN WITH LEARNING DISABILITY.   A key element of the definition of intellectual disability is substantially below-average intelligence. In contrast, by definition children with learning disability have average intelligence. That is, **children with** *learning disability* **(a) have difficulty mastering an academic subject, (b) have normal intelligence, and (c) are not suffering from other conditions that could explain poor performance, such as sensory impairment or inadequate instruction.**

About 5 percent of all school-age children in North America are classified as learning disabled. In Canada, in 2006, just over 120 000 children between age five and 14 were classified as learning disabled (Brennan, 2009). The number of distinct disabilities and the degree of overlap among them are still debated (Torgesen, 2004). However, most scientists agree that three disabilities are particularly common (Hulme & Snowling, 2009): **difficulties in reading individual words, sometimes known as** *developmental dyslexia;* **difficulties in understanding words that have been read successfully, which is called** *impaired reading comprehension;* **and, finally, difficulties in mathematics, which is termed** *mathematical learning disability or developmental dyscalculia.*

Youngsters with reading disability often struggle to distinguish different letter sounds.

Understanding learning disabilities is complicated because each type has its own causes (Landerl, Fussenegger, Moll, & Willburger, 2009) and thus requires its own treatment. For example, developmental dyslexia is the most common type of learning disability. (It's so common that sometimes it's just referred to as reading disability.) Many children with this disorder have problems in phonological awareness (described in Module 7.3), which refers to understanding and using the sounds in written and oral language. For children with developmental dyslexia—like Sanjit (in the vignette that opened this module) or the boy in the photograph on the this page—distinguishing *bis* from *bep* or *bis* from *dis* is very difficult; apparently the sounds all sound very similar (Ziegler et al., 2010).

Children with developmental dyslexia typically benefit from two kinds of instruction: training in phonological awareness—experiences that help them to identify subtle but important differences in language sounds—as well as explicit instruction on the connections between letters and their sounds. With intensive instruction of this sort, youngsters with developmental dyslexia can read much more effectively (Hulme & Snowling, 2009).

Children with impaired reading comprehension have no trouble reading individual words, but they understand far less of what they read. Asked to read sentences such as "The man rode the bus to go to work" or "The dog chased the cat through the woods," they do so easily but find it difficult to answer questions about what they have read (e.g., What did the man ride? Where did the man go?). In the Spotlight on Theories feature, we'll see why these children often struggle with meaning.

Britt Erlanson/The Image Bank/ Getty Images

Spotlight on Theories

Impaired Reading Comprehension Is Impaired Language Comprehension

BACKGROUND   In Module 7.3 we saw that reading involves decoding individual words as well as comprehending sentences or larger passages. In developmental dyslexia, children read individual words inaccurately and slowly; in impaired reading comprehension, they recognize individual words normally but have trouble making sense of what they've read.

THE THEORY   Margaret Snowling, Charles Hulme, and their colleagues (e.g., Clarke, Truelove, Hulme, & Snowling, 2014; Snowling & Hulme, 2012) use the Simple Model of Reading to explain impaired reading comprehension. In this model, decoding processes convert printed words into speech; then language comprehension skills are used to understand decoded words. Specifically, reading comprehension is supported by children's knowledge of word meanings (vocabulary) and their knowledge of grammar. In Snowling and Hulme's theory, both kinds of knowledge are limited in children with impaired reading comprehension. For example, in reading *The girl could not predict the winner*, children with impaired reading comprehension may read *predict* accurately but not understand the sentence because they don't know the meaning of *predict*. Similarly, with *The teacher was hit by the ball* these children may misunderstand the sentence—thinking it's about a teacher hitting a ball—because they lack knowledge of passive voice.

Hypothesis: Snowling and Hulme's theory leads to two predictions. On the one hand, because children with impaired reading comprehension decode words skillfully, they should succeed on tasks measuring the phonological skills essential for decoding words. On the other hand, they should be less successful on tasks that measure their knowledge of word meanings and grammar.

Test: Nation, Cocksey, Taylor, and Bishop (2010) conducted a longitudinal study in which children's reading, language, and phonological skills were tested several times between five and eight years of age. At age eight, Nation and her colleagues identified 15 children with impaired reading comprehension—children whose word reading skills were age appropriate but whose reading comprehension skills were limited. They matched these children with 15 average readers who had comparable word reading skills along with age-appropriate reading comprehension.

Next, the researchers compared the two groups in terms of their phonological and language skills, beginning at age five (before children had been taught how to read). On the one hand, the groups were similar in their phonological skills (e.g., both groups were able to say what *dish* would sound like without the *d*). On the other hand, children with impaired reading comprehension knew the meaning of fewer words and understood less grammar (e.g., they were likely to say that a drawing of a teacher hitting a ball matched *The teacher was hit by the ball*).

Conclusion: As predicted by Snowling and Hulme's account, children with impaired reading comprehension have intact phonological skills but limited knowledge of word meanings and grammar. In other words, impaired reading comprehension is really less about problems with reading per se and more about impaired language. When children have limited vocabulary and gaps in their knowledge of grammar, they comprehend less of what they hear and read.

Application: Snowling and Hulme's theory has a straightforward implication: If we improve language skills in children with impaired reading comprehension, their reading comprehension should improve. In fact such training (e.g., increasing children's vocabulary) produces substantial gains in children's reading comprehension, sometimes to the point that children who were once impaired read at an age-appropriate level (Clarke, Snowling, Truelove, & Hulme, 2010). This research shows an effective way to treat impaired reading comprehension and also shows the practical value of a good theory.

Critical Thinking Question: What specific teaching strategies might help school-age children to overcome impaired reading comprehension?

A third common form of learning disability is mathematical disability. Roughly 5 to 10 percent of young children struggle with arithmetic instruction from the very beginning. These youngsters progress slowly in their efforts to learn to count, to add, and to subtract; many are also diagnosed with reading disability. As they move into Grade 2 and 3 (and beyond), these children often use inefficient methods for computing solutions—for example, still using their fingers in Grade 3 to solve problems such as $9 + 7$ (Geary, 2010; Jordan, 2007).

We know far less about mathematical learning disability, largely because mathematics engages a broader set of skills than reading (which really involves just two broad classes: decoding and comprehension). Some scientists propose that the heart of the problem is that the approximate number system (described on page 256) provides less precise estimates of quantities for children with mathematical learning disability (Geary, 2013). Another possibility is that youngsters with mathematical disability are impaired in counting and retrieving arithmetic facts from memory (Hulme & Snowling, 2009). Still others suggest that mathematical disability reflects problems in the basic cognitive processes that are used in doing arithmetic, such as working memory and processing speed (Geary, Hoard, Byrd-Craven, Nugent, & Numtee, 2007).

Q&A **ANSWER 8.3**
No. Part of the definition of learning disability is normal intelligence; children with learning disability have a specific, well-defined disability in conjunction with normal intelligence.

Because mathematical disability is so poorly understood, effective interventions have just begun. For example, children at risk for mathematical learning disability benefit from intensive practice designed to increase their knowledge and understanding of numbers (Fuchs et al., 2013). As we learn more about the core problems that define mathematical disability, researchers and educators should be able to fine-tune instruction for these children. When that happens, children with mathematical disability, like children with developmental dyslexia and impaired reading comprehension, will be able to develop their full intellectual potential.

✓ Check Your Learning

RECALL Summarize the different factors that put children at risk for intellectual disability.

How is learning disability defined? What are the different types of learning disability?

INTERPRET Compare and contrast traditional and modern definitions of giftedness.

APPLY How might Jean Piaget, Howard Gardner, and Robert Sternberg define intellectual disability?

UNIFYING THEMES Nature and Nurture

In this chapter, we want to underscore the theme that *development is always jointly influenced by heredity and environment*. In no other area of child development is this theme as important, because the implications for social policy are so profound. If intelligence were completely determined by heredity, for example, intervention programs would be a waste of time and tax dollars, because no amount of experience would change nature's prescription for intelligence. But we've seen several times in this chapter that neither heredity nor environment is all-powerful when it comes to intelligence. Studies of twins, for example, remind us that heredity clearly has substantial impact on IQ scores. Identical twins' IQs are consistently more alike than are fraternal twins' IQs, a result that documents heredity's influence on intelligence. Yet, at the same time, intervention studies such as Head Start in the United States and the AHS program in Canada show that intelligence is malleable. Children's intelligence can be enhanced by stimulating environments and community support.

Thus, heredity imposes some limits on how a child's intelligence develops, but the limits are fairly modest. We can nurture all children's intelligence considerably if we are willing to invest the time and effort.

See for Yourself

We've seen that the definition of intelligence differs across cultural settings. See how parents define intelligence by asking them to rate the importance of four common aspects of intelligence:

- Problem-solving skill (thinking before acting, seeing different sides to a problem)
- Verbal skill (speaking clearly, having a large vocabulary)
- Creative skill (asking many questions, trying new things)
- Social skill (playing and working well with other people, respecting and caring for others)

Be ethical: Maintain confidentiality, and reassure parents that there are no "right" or "wrong" answers—you just want to see what people think. Ask parents to rate the importance of each element on a 6-point scale, where 1 means extremely unimportant to intelligence and 6 means extremely important. Try to ask parents from different ethnic groups; then compare your results with other students' results to see if parents' views of intelligence are similar or different and if cultural background affects parents' definitions. See for yourself!

Resources

For more information about . . .

the lives of brilliant and creative people, read Howard Gardner's *Creating Minds* (Basic Books, 1993), which illustrates each different intelligence in Gardner's theory by tracing its development in the life of an extraordinary person, including Albert Einstein, Martha Graham, and Pablo Picasso.

learning disabilities, visit the website of the Learning Disabilities Association of Canada: **www.ldac-acta.ca.**

Key Terms

analytic ability   277
collectivity   287
creative ability   277
crystallized intelligence   275
culture-fair intelligence tests   290
developmental dyslexia   296
divergent thinking   294
dynamic assessment   284

emotional intelligence (EI)   276
fluid intelligence   274
gifted   294
impaired reading
   comprehension   296
intellectual disability   295
intelligence quotient (IQ)   280
learning disability   296

mathematical learning disability
   (developmental dyscalculia)   296
mental age (MA)   280
practical ability   277
psychometricians   274
stereotype threat   290

Summary

8.1 What Is Intelligence?

1. Psychometric Theories

Psychometric approaches to intelligence include theories that describe intelligence as a general factor as well as theories that include specific factors. Hierarchical theories include both general intelligence and various specific skills, such as verbal and spatial ability.

2. Gardner's Theory of Multiple Intelligences

Gardner's theory of multiple intelligences proposes nine distinct intelligences. Three are found in psychometric theories (linguistic, logical-mathematical, and spatial intelligence), but six are new (musical, bodily-kinesthetic, interpersonal, intrapersonal, naturalistic, and existential intelligence). Gardner's theory has stimulated research on nontraditional forms of intelligence, such as emotional intelligence. The theory also has implications for education, suggesting, for example, that schools should adjust teaching to each child's unique intellectual strengths.

3. Sternberg's Theory of Successful Intelligence

According to Robert Sternberg, intelligence is defined as the use of abilities to achieve short- and long-term goals and it depends upon three abilities: analytic ability to analyze problems and generate solutions, creative ability to deal adaptively with novel situations, and practical ability to know what solutions will work.

8.2 Features of IQ Scores

1. Binet and the Development of Intelligence Testing

Binet created the first intelligence test to identify students who would have difficulty in school. Using this work, Terman created the Stanford-Binet, which introduced the concept of the intelligence quotient (IQ). Another widely used test, the WISC-V, provides IQs based on verbal and performance subtests. Infant tests, such as the Bayley Scales, typically assess mental and motor development.

Scores on infant intelligence tests do not predict adult IQ scores, but infant information-processing predicts childhood IQs, and preschool IQ scores predict adult IQs.

2. Features of IQ Scores

Intelligence tests are reasonably valid measures of achievement in school. They also predict people's performance in the workplace.

Dynamic assessments measure children's potential for future learning and complement traditional tests, which emphasize knowledge acquired prior to testing.

3. Hereditary and Environmental Factors

Evidence for the impact of heredity on IQ comes from the findings that (a) siblings' IQ scores are more alike when siblings are more similar genetically, and (b) adopted children's IQ scores are more like their biological parents' test scores than their adoptive parents' scores. Evidence for the impact of the environment comes from findings on the impact of home environments, historical change, and effects of intervention programs on IQ scores.

4. Impact of Ethnicity and Socioeconomic Status

Ethnic groups differ in their average scores on IQ tests. This difference is not due to genetics or to familiarity with specific test items but rather to children's familiarity and comfort with the testing situation. Nevertheless, IQ scores remain valid predictors of school success because middle-class experience is often a prerequisite for school success.

8.3 Special Children, Special Needs

1. Gifted and Creative Children

Traditionally, gifted children have been those with high scores on IQ tests. Modern definitions of giftedness are broader and include exceptional talent in, for example, the arts. Gifted children are substantially above average in ability, passionate about their subject, and creative. Their talent needs to be nurtured by challenging and supportive environments. Gifted children are usually socially mature and emotionally stable.

Creativity is associated with divergent thinking—that is, thinking in novel and unusual directions. Tests of divergent thinking can predict which children are most likely to be creative when they are older. Creativity can be fostered by experiences that encourage children to think flexibly and explore alternatives.

2. Children with Disability

Individuals with intellectual disability have IQ scores of 70 or lower and problems in adaptive behaviour. Biomedical, social, behavioural, and educational factors place individuals at risk for intellectual disability.

Children with a learning disability have normal intelligence but have difficulty mastering specific academic subjects. Common variants include developmental dyslexia (difficulty decoding individual words), impaired reading comprehension (problems understanding what one has read), and mathematical learning disability. The most common is reading disability, which often can be traced to inadequate understanding and use of language sounds. When such language-related skills are taught, children's reading improves.

Test Yourself

1. The psychometric approach to intelligence relies upon _____.

2. _____ theories of intelligence measure both *g* (general intelligence) and specific components, such as fluid intelligence.

3. In formulating his theory of multiple intelligences, Gardner drew upon _____, studies of brain-damaged persons, and studies of persons with exceptional talent.

4. Linguistic, logical-mathematical, and _____ intelligences are included in psychometric theories as well as in Gardner's theory of multiple intelligences.

5. Sternberg's theory of successful intelligence includes _____, creative, and practical abilities.

6. Infant IQ tests do not predict childhood IQ accurately, but are still valuable because _____.

7. Dynamic assessments of intelligence _____.

8. IQ scores predict success in school as well as predicting _____.

9. Evidence for the impact of heredity on IQ comes from studies of twins (in which identical twins had more similar scores than fraternal twins) and from _____.

10. The role of the environment on intelligence is revealed by research linking home environments to intelligence, _____, and the impact of intervention programs.

11. Ethnic group differences have been linked to _____.

12. Intelligence is associated with convergent thinking, whereas creativity is associated with _____ thinking.

13. Intellectual disability is defined by limited intellectual ability and _____, both of which emerge before age 18.

14. Children with _____ have normal intelligence and sensory functioning yet have difficulty mastering an academic subject.

15. Common learning disabilities include developmental dyslexia, _____, and mathematical learning disability (developmental dyscalculia).

Answers: (1) performance on intelligence tests; (2) Hierarchical; (3) child-development research; (4) spatial; (5) analytic; (6) they can be used to determine whether development is progressing normally; (7) measure a child's learning potential; (8) occupational success; (9) adopted children (adoptees' scores resembled the scores of their biological parents, not their adoptive parents); (10) increases in IQ scores during the latter part of the 20th century; (11) stereotype threat; (12) divergent; (13) problems adapting to the environment; (14) learning disability; (15) impaired reading comprehension.

9 Language and Communication

Contrastwerkstatt/Fotolia

9.1

The Road to Speech

9.2

Learning the Meanings of Words

9.3

Speaking in Sentences

9.4

Using Language to Communicate

9.5

Sign Language and Gestural Communication

Toni Morrison, a contemporary African American writer who won the Nobel Prize for Literature in 1993, said, "We die. That may be the meaning of life. But we do language. That may be the measure of our lives." Language is indeed a remarkable human tool. Language allows us to express thoughts and feelings to others and to preserve our ideas and learn from the past.

Given the complexities of language, it's truly amazing that most children master it rapidly and easily. That mastery is the focus of this chapter, which examines five aspects of language. We'll begin, in **Module 9.1**, by looking at the first steps in acquiring language: learning about speech sounds. **Module 9.2** looks at how children learn to speak and how they learn new words thereafter. In **Module 9.3**, we'll examine children's early sentences and the rules that children follow in creating them. In **Module 9.4**, we'll learn how children use language to communicate with others. Finally, in **Module 9.5**, we'll see what gestures and signed languages tell us about language and its development.

9.1 The Road to Speech

OUTLINE	LEARNING OBJECTIVES
Elements of Language	1. What are the basic sounds of speech, and how well can infants distinguish them?
Perceiving Speech	2. How does infant-directed speech help children learn about language?
First Steps to Speech	3. What is babbling, and how does it become more complex in older infants?

As a seven-month-old, Chelsea began to make her first word-like sounds, saying "dah" and "nuh." Several weeks later, she began to repeat these syllables, saying "dah-dah" and "nuh-nuh." Now at 11 months, her speech resembles sentences with stressed words: "dah-NUH-bah-BAH!" Chelsea's parents are astonished that her sentences could sound so much like real speech yet still be absolutely meaningless!

From birth, infants make sounds—they laugh, cry and, like Chelsea, produce sounds that resemble speech. Yet for most of their first year, infants do not talk. This contrast raises two important questions about infants as nonspeaking creatures. First, can babies who are unable to speak understand any of the speech that is directed at them? Second, how do infants like Chelsea progress from crying to more effective methods of oral communication, such as speech? We'll answer both questions in this module, but let's begin by considering exactly what we mean by *language*.

Raise a cyber child and discover the world of parenthood at. . .

My Virtual Child

Elements of Language

When you think of language, what comes to mind? English, perhaps? Or maybe German, Spanish, Korean, or Zulu? What about American Sign Language (ASL) or Langue des Signes du Québécoise (LSQ)? **Defined broadly, *language* is a system that relates sounds (or gestures) to meaning.** Language differs from simple communication in four main ways:

• It has arbitrary units and is therefore symbolic.

• It is structured and meaningful.

- It shows displacement—one can communicate about events distant in time and space, not just here and now.
- It is characterized by generativity—you can produce an infinite number of utterances from a language's vocabulary, provided that you follow the structure.

Think about a child saying, "Yesterday at the park a dog frightened me." The words themselves are arbitrary; they only have meaning because meaning has been assigned to those sounds. You know what happened: There was a dog that scared the child. The event happened yesterday, in another place and time. And the child may never have spoken those words in that order before today. This is completely different from the dog snarling at the child. The dog was communicating—showing its feelings—but only for that moment in that situation.

Languages are expressed in many forms—through speech, writing, and gesture. Furthermore, languages consist of different subsystems. Spoken languages usually involve five distinct but interrelated elements:

- *Phonology* **refers to the sounds of a language.** About 200 different sounds are used in all known spoken languages; all the different words in English are constructed from about 45 of them.
- *Morphology* **refers to rules of meaning within the language.** The smallest unit of meaning in a language is called a "morpheme." Morphemes are meaningful combinations of phonemes. Some words are single morphemes, for example "car" or "dog." These are examples of "free morphemes," those that stand alone. Other morphemes are called "bound morphemes"; examples are the *-s* for plurals or the *-ing* suffix. These bound morphemes change the meaning of a word: Dog becomes dogs, and run becomes running.
- *Semantics* **denotes the study of words and their meaning.** *Webster's Third New International Dictionary* includes roughly a half million words, and a typical college-educated English speaker has a vocabulary of about 150 000 words.
- *Syntax* **refers to rules that specify how words are combined to form sentences.** For example, one simple rule specifies that, in English, a noun is followed by a verb (e.g., dog barks, ball rolls) in a sentence.
- *Pragmatics* **refers to the communicative functions of language and the rules that lead to effective communication.** For example, rules for effective communication specify that speakers should be clear and their comments relevant to the topic of conversation.

Learning language involves mastering each of these elements. Children must learn to hear the differences in speech sounds and how to produce them; they must learn the meaning of words and rules for combining them in sentences; and they must learn appropriate and effective ways to talk with others. In the remainder of this module (and the rest of this chapter), we'll see how children come to understand language and use it themselves.

Perceiving Speech

We learned in Module 5.1 that even newborn infants hear remarkably well. Newborns also prefer to listen to speech over comparably complex nonspeech sounds (Vouloumanos Hauser, Werker, & Martin, 2010). Vouloumanos and Werker (2004), studying Canadian infants from English-speaking families, showed that infants ranging in age from two to seven months listened longer to speech sounds than to otherwise similar, nonspeech, sounds. But can babies distinguish speech sounds? To answer this question, we first need to know more about the elements of speech. **The basic building blocks of language are *phonemes,* unique sounds that can be joined to create words.** Phonemes include consonant sounds such as the sound of *t* in "toe" and "tap," and vowel sounds such as the sound of *e* in "get" and "bed." Infants can distinguish most of these sounds, many of them by as early as one month after birth (Aslin, Jusczyk, & Pisoni, 1998).

Figure 9-1 A procedure to investigate infants' distinction of phonemes.

How do we know that infants can distinguish different vowels and consonants? Researchers have devised a number of clever techniques to determine if babies respond differently to distinct sounds. One approach is illustrated in Figure 9-1. A rubber nipple is connected to a computer so that sucking causes the computer to play a sound out of a loudspeaker. In just a few minutes, one-month-olds learn the relation between their sucking and the sound: They suck rapidly to hear nothing more than the sound of *p* as in "pin," "pet," and "pat" (pronounced "puh").

After a few more minutes, infants seem to tire of this repetitive sound and suck less often, which represents the habituation phenomenon described in Module 5.1. But if the computer presents a new sound, such as the sound of *b* in "bed," "bat," or "bird" (pronounced "buh"), babies begin sucking rapidly again. Evidently, they recognize that the sound of *b* is different from *p* because they suck more often to hear the new sound (Jusczyk, 1995).

THE IMPACT OF LANGUAGE EXPOSURE.   Not all languages use the same set of phonemes; a distinction that is important in one language may be ignored in another. For example, unlike English, French and Polish differentiate between nasal and non-nasal vowels. To hear the difference, say the word "rod." Now repeat it holding your nose. The subtle difference between the two sounds illustrates a non-nasal vowel (the first version of "rod") and a nasal one (the second).

Because an infant might be exposed to any of the world's languages, it would be adaptive for young infants to be able to perceive a wide range of phonemes. In fact, research shows that infants can distinguish phonemes that are not used in their native language. For example, Japanese does not distinguish the consonant sound of *r* in "rip" from the sound of *l* in "lip," and Japanese adults trying to learn English have great difficulty distinguishing these sounds. At about six to eight months, infants in both Japanese- and English-speaking environments can distinguish these sounds equally well. However, by 10 to 12 months, perception of *r* and *l* improves for North American infants—presumably because they hear these sounds frequently—but declines for Japanese babies (Kuhl et al., 2006).

Janet Werker at the University of British Columbia (UBC) is renowned for her research on infant speech perception. Much of the research of Werker and her colleagues has focused on phonemic distinction and how this ability develops and changes. An early study by Werker (1989) showed that the ability to distinguish phonemes not used in the native language declines across the first year of life, as just described. The study also outlined theoretical perspectives on how this might be happening. Initially, recognition of all phonemes is useful; the infant has the ability to learn any language that the adults around it speak. But being able to recognize any language phonemes could be useful for learning other languages, so why do we lose such a skill, and in so short a time? In this two-phase study, Werker first showed that infants of six to eight months who came from English-speaking families were able to discriminate between two phonemes from the Hindi language just as well as Hindi-speaking adults could. English-speaking adults could not detect the Hindi phonemic difference, which is not used in the English language. Then, to investigate the timing of the loss of this ability, Werker compared abilities to distinguish phonemic contrasts from a Indigenous Canadian language of British Columbia (Nthlakapmx, or "Thompson"), Hindi, and English. Infants were tested at three points across the first year of life—six to eight months, eight to 10 months, and 12 months of age. The major finding of this part of the research was that the ability to discriminate non-native language phonemic distinctions declines across the first year of life. Most of the youngest infants could make the discrimination, but for children from English-speaking families, the ability decreased with age: Nearly all six- to eight-month-olds could make the phonemic distinctions for the other two languages, but only half of eight- to 10-month olds had the ability, which was effectively lost by 12 months of age.

So why might the ability to make phonemic distinctions be lost? As with many aspects of human development, it is probably a combination of both innate and environmental factors. In this case, it would appear to be a combination of sound sensitivity interacting with environmental experience. The decline in phonemic recognition seems to be due to a perceptual reorganization to match the native language (Carroll, 1999; Werker, 1989). The infant needs continuing experience with the different language phonemes to maintain the ability to perceive and thus to discriminate those phonemes (Werker, 1989). Any innate language acquisition ability depends on environmental support, and at the same time, environment can have an effect only if mechanisms are influenced by it (Hoff, 2006). Newborns apparently are biologically capable of hearing the entire range of phonemes in all languages worldwide. As babies grow and are more exposed to a particular language, however, they notice only the linguistic distinctions that are meaningful in their own language (Werker, Yeung, & Yoshida, 2012). Thus, specializing in one language apparently comes at the cost of making it more difficult to recognize sounds in other languages (Best, 1995). More recent research has provided further support for Werker's proposal that a phonemic perceptual reorganization takes place across the first year of life, with findings that although it is not impossible to make distinctions later on, after 10 months of age it does become much more difficult (Burns, Yoshida, Hill, & Werker, 2007; Yoshida, Pons, Maye, & Werker, 2010). This pattern of greater specialization in speech perception is reminiscent of the profile for face perception described in Module 5.2. With greater exposure to human faces, babies develop a more refined notion of a human face, just as they develop a more refined notion of the sounds (or signs) that are important in their native language (Pascalis et al., 2014).

IDENTIFYING WORDS.   Of course, hearing individual phonemes is only the first step in perceiving speech. One of the biggest challenges for infants is identifying recurring patterns of sounds—words. Imagine, for example, an infant overhearing this conversation between a parent and an older sibling:

sibling:	Jerry got a new *bike*.
parent:	Was his old *bike* broken?
sibling:	No. He'd saved his allowance to buy a new mountain *bike*.

An infant listening to this conversation hears *bike* three times. Can the infant learn from this experience? Yes. When seven- to eight-month-olds hear a word repeatedly in different sentences, they later pay more attention to this word than to words they haven't heard previously. Evidently, seven- and eight-month-olds can listen to sentences and recognize the sound patterns that they hear repeatedly (Houston & Juscyzk, 2003; Saffran, Aslin, & Newport, 1996). Also, by six months of age, infants pay more attention to content words (e.g., nouns, verbs) than to function words (e.g., articles, prepositions) and they look at the correct parent when they hear "mommy" or "daddy" (Shi & Werker, 2001; Tincoff & Jusczyk, 1999).

In normal conversation, there are no silent gaps between words, so how do infants distinguish individual words? Stress is one important clue. English contains many one-syllable words that are stressed and many two-syllable words that have a stressed syllable followed by an unstressed syllable (e.g., "*dough*nut," "*tooth*paste," "*bas*ket"). Infants pay more attention to stressed syllables than unstressed syllables, which is a good strategy for identifying the beginnings of words (Bortfeld & Morgan, 2010; Thiessen & Saffran, 2003). And infants learn words more readily when they appear at the beginning and ends of sentences, probably because the brief pause between sentences makes it easier to identify first and last words (Seidl & Johnson, 2006).

Another useful method is statistical. Infants notice syllables that go together frequently (Jusczyk, 2002). For example, in many studies, eight-month-olds heard the following sounds, which consisted of four three-syllable artificial words said over and over in a random order.

<u>pa bi ku</u> <u>go la tu</u> <u>da ro pi</u> <u>ti bu do</u> <u>da ro pi</u> <u>go la tu</u> <u>pa bi ku</u> <u>da ro pi</u>

We've underlined the words and inserted gaps between them so that you can see them more easily, but in the actual studies there were no breaks at all, just a steady flow of syllables for three minutes. Later, infants listened to these words less than to new words that were novel combinations of the same syllables. They had detected *pa bi ku, go la tu, da ro pi,* and *ti bu do* as familiar patterns and listened to them less than to words like *tu da ro,* a new word made up from syllables they had already heard (Aslin & Newport, 2012; Ngon et al., 2013).

Yet another way that infants identify words is through their emerging knowledge of how sounds are used in their native language. For example, think about these two pairs of sounds: *s* followed by *t* and *s* followed by *d*. In English, both pairs of sounds are quite common at the end of one word and the beginning of the next: "bu*s t*akes," "ki*ss t*ook"; "thi*s d*og," "pa*ss d*irectly." However, *s* and *t* occur frequently within words, too ("*st*op," "li*st*," "pe*st*," "*st*ink"), but *s* and *d* do not. Consequently, when *d* follows an *s*, it probably starts a new word. In fact, nine-month-olds follow rules like this one because when they hear novel words embedded in continuous speech, they are more likely to identify the novel word when the final sound in the preceding word occurs infrequently with the first sound of the novel word (Mattys & Jusczyk, 2001).

Another strategy that infants use is to rely on familiar function words, such as the articles "a" and "the," to break up the speech stream. These words are very common in adults' speech; by six months most infants recognize them and use them to determine the onset of a new word (Shi, 2014). For example, for infants familiar with "a," the sequence like *aballabataglove* becomes "a ball," "a bat," "a glove" The new words are isolated by the familiar ones.

Thus infants use many powerful tools to identify words in speech. Of course, they do not yet understand the meanings of these words; at this point, they simply recognize a word as a distinct configuration of sounds. Nevertheless, these early perceptual skills are important because infants who are more skilled at detecting speech sounds know more words as toddlers, and overall their language is more advanced at four to six years of age (Newman, Ratner, Jusczyk, Jusczyk, & Dow, 2006).

Parents and other adults often help infants master language sounds by talking in a distinctive style. **In *infant-directed speech,* adults speak slowly and with exaggerated changes in pitch and loudness.** If you could hear the mother in the photo talking to

When parents talk to babies, they often use infant-directed speech, which is slower and more varied in pitch and volume than adult-directed speech.

her baby, you would notice that she alternates between speaking softly and loudly and between high and low pitches and that her speech seems very expressive emotionally (Liu, Tsao, & Kuhl, 2007; Trainor, Austin, & Desjardins, 2000). (Infant-directed speech is also known as "motherese," because this form of speaking was first noted in mothers, although it is now known that most caregivers talk this way to infants.)

Infant-directed speech attracts infants' attention (Lewkowicz, 2000b), perhaps because its slower pace and accentuated changes provide infants with increasingly more salient language clues (Cristia, 2010). For example, infants can segment words more effectively when they hear them in infant-directed speech (Thiessen, Hill, & Saffran, 2005). In addition, infant-directed speech includes especially good examples of vowels (Kuhl et al., 1997), which may help infants learn to distinguish these sounds. And when talking to infants, speaking clearly is a good idea. In one study (Liu, Kuhl, & Tsao, 2003), infants who could best distinguish speech sounds had mothers who spoke most clearly.

Within different languages, different stress patterns are also used as part of speech. It appears that babies are capable of distinguishing the stress patterns within their native language as phonemic distinctions, and they "tune in" to the patterns used in the language that is being spoken by the people around them. This has been referred to as "phonetic category learning" (Werker et al., 2007). A comparative study by researchers at the University of British Columbia and at Communication Science Laboratories in Kyoto, Japan, showed that English-speaking Canadian parents and Japanese parents used exaggerated forms of phonetic distinctions made in their respective languages when using infant-directed speech to teach infants new words (Werker et al., 2007). Cues present in the infant-directed speech are thought to help the infant distinguish differently stressed vowel sounds (e.g., forms of *e* and *i* sounds) that are used in the native language. (Interestingly, as noted later in this text's discussion of temperament, the Japanese babies were quieter and more compliant, sitting still for the duration of the study. Canadian babies were much fussier, and twice as many were needed to gain the same amount of data for comparisons!)

Infant-directed speech, then, helps infants perceive the sounds that are fundamental to their language. Unfortunately, some babies cannot hear speech sounds because they are deaf. How can these infants best learn language? The Children's Lives feature addresses this question.

QUESTION 9.1

Kristin spends hours talking to her infant son. Her husband enjoys spending time with his wife and son but wishes Kristin would stop using "baby talk" with their son and just talk in her regular voice. The sing-song pattern drives him crazy, and he can't believe that it's any good for their son. Is he right? *(Answer is on page 310.)*

Children's Lives

Are Cochlear Implants Effective for Young Children?

About one child out of 1000 is born deaf or has profound hearing loss before mastering language. Of these youngsters, about 10 percent are born to deaf parents. In these cases, the child's deafness is usually detected early, and parents communicate with their children using sign language. Deaf infants and toddlers seem to master sign language in much the same way and at about the same pace that hearing children master spoken language. For example, deaf 10-month-olds often babble in signs: They produce sequences of signs that are meaningless but resemble the tempo and duration of real signs.

The remaining 90 percent of deaf infants and toddlers have parents with usual hearing abilities. Communicating with signs is not really an option for these children because their parents don't know sign language. Consequently, the usual recommendation for deaf children of hearing parents is to master spoken language, sometimes through methods that emphasize lip reading and speech therapy, and sometimes using these methods along with signs and gestures. Unfortunately, with any of these methods, deaf children rarely master spoken language. Their ability to produce and comprehend spoken language falls years behind their peers with normal language (Hoff, 2014).

Since the mid-1990s, however, deaf children have had a new option. As described on page 160, the *cochlear implant* **is a device that picks up speech sounds and converts them to electrical impulses that stimulate nerve cells in the ear.** Cochlear implants are a tremendous benefit for people who lose their hearing after they master language. Adults with cochlear implants can converse readily with hearing speakers, and some can converse on the phone (which is difficult otherwise because they cannot lip read and because telephone lines sometimes distort speech sounds).

The potential benefit of cochlear implants for young children is a more controversial issue, as there is also a sociocultural aspect to the use of such devices. Many of those who consider themselves Deaf (note the capitalization)—those who communicate with sign language and self-identify as part of a specific culture—regard cochlear implants as an imposition upon the child. Deaf culture sees the surgical insertion of cochlear implants as an attempt to "fix" people who are fine as they are. Many Deaf in Canada would prefer teaching deaf children sign language, the language of the Deaf culture, as their primary form of communication (Cochlear War, n.d.; Lane & Grodin, 1997).

Cochlear implants have been found to promote language acquisition in deaf children, however. When children deaf from birth receive cochlear implants, their spoken language skills end up substantially better than those of children who do not have cochlear implants. In fact, after receiving cochlear implants, many deaf children acquire spoken language at roughly the same rate as children with normal hearing (Svirsky, Robbins, Kirk, Pisoni, & Miyamoto, 2000; Wie, Falkenberg, Tvete, & Tomblin, 2007). Does this give any benefit over other methods of ameliorating hearing loss, though? A research team from the University of Calgary, University of Ottawa, and Ottawa hospitals compared outcomes for children using hearing aids versus cochlear implants and found that while both groups of children developed good language skills, those with hearing aids outscored those with implants on some measures (Fitzpatrick et al., 2012).

Thus, while cochlear implants can help some children, other children benefit less from the implants, an outcome that has led researchers to try to identify the keys to success for this procedure. Age of implantation matters, as does the extent of the child's hearing loss. Cochlear implants are more successful with children who are younger and who have some residual hearing. The quality of the child's language environment also contributes: Children with cochlear implants learn language more rapidly when their parents provide a stimulating language environment, particularly when they frequently talk about what the child is looking at or doing (Cruz et al., 2013). Thus, a cochlear implant is an effective tool that can enhance language in children who are deaf, particularly when children receive implants when they are young. However, it is not a cure; following implantation, parents need to provide a particularly rich language experience for their children to master language.

Critical Thinking Questions: What do you think of the arguments for and against cochlear implants for young children? Are the implants a good thing, or form of social engineering?

First Steps to Speech

As any new parent can testify, newborns and young babies make many sounds—they cry, burp, and sneeze. However, language-based sounds do not appear immediately. **At two months, infants begin to produce vowel-like sounds, such as "oooooo" or "ahhhhhh," a phenomenon known as** *cooing*. Sometimes infants become quite excited as they coo, perhaps reflecting the joy of simply playing with sounds.

After cooing comes *babbling,* **speech-like sound that has no meaning.** A typical six-month-old might say "dah" or "bah," utterances that sound like a single syllable consisting of a consonant and a vowel. Over the next few months, babbling becomes more elaborate as babies apparently experiment with more complex speech sounds. Older infants sometimes repeat a sound as in "bahbahbah" and begin to combine different sounds, "dahmahbah" (Hoff, 2009).

Babbling is not just mindless playing with sounds—it is a precursor to real speech. We know this, in part, from video records of people's mouths while speaking. When adults speak, their mouth is open somewhat wider on the right side than on the left side, reflecting the left hemisphere's control of language and muscle movements on the body's right side (Graves & Landis, 1990). Infants do the same when they babble, but not when making non-babbling sounds, which suggests that babbling is fundamentally linguistic (Holowka & Petitto, 2002). And, as mentioned on page 308, even babies learning sign language "babble" with their hands.

Other evidence for the linguistic nature of babbling comes from studies of developmental change in babbling: At roughly eight to 11 months of age, infants' babbling sounds more like real speech because infants like Chelsea (in the vignette) stress some syllables, and they vary the pitch of their speech (Snow, 2006). For example, in declarative sentences in English, pitch first rises then falls toward the end of the sentence. In questions, however, the pitch is level then rises toward the end of the question. **This pattern of rising or falling pitch is known as** *intonation.* Older babies' babbling reflects these patterns: Babies who are brought up by English-speaking parents have both the declarative and question patterns of intonation in their babbling. Babies exposed to a language with different patterns of intonation, such as Japanese or French, reflect their language's intonation in their babbling (Levitt & Utman, 1992).

The appearance of intonation in babbling indicates a strong link between perception and production of speech: Infants' babbling is influenced by the characteristics of the speech that they hear (Goldstein & Schwade, 2008). Beginning in the middle of the first year, infants try to reproduce the sounds of language that others use in trying to communicate with them (or, in the case of Deaf infants with Deaf parents, the signs that others use). Hearing the word "dog," an infant may first say "dod," then "gog" before finally saying "dog" correctly. In the same way that beginning typists gradually link movements of their fingers with particular keys, through babbling, infants learn to use their lips, tongue, and teeth to produce specific sounds, gradually making sounds that approximate real words (Poulson, Kymissis, Reeve, Andreatos, & Reeve, 1991).

The ability to produce sound, coupled with the one-year-old's advanced ability to perceive speech sounds, sets the stage for the infant's first true words. In Module 9.2, we'll see how this happens.

 ANSWER 9.1

No, he's wrong. Infant-directed speech helps babies to learn language, in part because changes in pitch attract an infant's attention and because the slower pace and accentuated changes help infants to detect differences in speech sounds. But we'll agree with Kristin's husband that infant-directed speech can become grating after a while!

✓ Check Your Learning

RECALL How do infants distinguish words in the speech they hear?

What evidence indicates that babbling is a precursor to speech?

INTERPRET Compare the developmental milestones during infancy for perceiving speech and those for producing speech.

APPLY Suppose that a three-month-old baby born in Romania was adopted by a Swedish couple. How would the change in language environment affect the baby's language learning?

9.2 Learning the Meanings of Words

OUTLINE	LEARNING OBJECTIVES
Understanding Words as Symbols	**1. How do children make the transition from babbling to talking?**
Fast Mapping Meanings to Words	**2. What rules do children follow to learn new words?**
Individual Differences in Word Learning	**3. What different styles of language learning do young children use?**
Encouraging Word Learning	**4. What conditions foster children's learning of new words?**
Beyond Words: Other Symbols	**5. How does children's understanding of symbols progress beyond language?**

Sebastien is 20 months old and loves to talk. What amazes his parents is how quickly he learns new words. For example, the day his parents brought home a new computer, Sebastien watched as they set it up. The next day, he spontaneously pointed to the computer and said, "puter." This happens all the time—Sebastien hears a word once or twice then uses it correctly himself. Sebastien's parents wonder how he does this, particularly because learning vocabulary in a foreign language is so difficult for them!

At about their first birthday, most youngsters say their first words. In many languages, those words are similar (Nelson, 1973; Tardif et al., 2008) and include terms for mother and father, greetings ("Hi," "Bye-bye"), as well as foods and toys ("juice," "ball"). Words such as these tend to be those for which children already have sensorimotor concepts—as in Piaget's theory, outlined in Chapter 6. Researchers from McMaster University in Hamilton have noted that language acquisition is aided by sensorimotor features of words, and they propose that this is why nouns like "dog" are more often found in children's early vocabularies (Howell, Jankowicz, & Becker, 2005). By age two, most youngsters have a vocabulary of a few hundred words, and by age six, a typical child's vocabulary includes over 10 000 words (Bloom, 1998).

Like Sebastien, most children learn new words with extraordinary ease and speed. How do they do it? We'll answer that question in this module.

Understanding Words as Symbols

When author Robert Kail's daughter, Laura, was nine months old, she sometimes babbled "bay-bay." A few months later, she still said "bay-bay" but with an important difference. As a nine-month-old, "bay-bay" was simply an interesting set of sounds that that had no special meaning to her. As a 13-month-old, however, "bay-bay" was her way of saying "baby." What had happened between nine and 13 months? Laura had begun to understand that speech is more than just entertaining sound. She realized that sounds form words that refer to objects, actions, and properties. Put another way, Laura recognized that words are symbols, entities that stand for other entities. She had already formed concepts such as "round, bouncy things" and "furry things that bark" and "little humans that adults carry" based on her own experiences. With the insight that speech sounds can denote these concepts, she began to match sound patterns (words) and concepts (Reich, 1986).

Babies begin to gesture at about the same time that they say their first words; both accomplishments show that infants are mastering symbols.

If this argument is correct, we should find that children use symbols in other areas, not just in language: They do. Gestures are symbols, and like the baby in the photo, infants begin to gesture shortly before their first birthday (Goodwyn & Acredolo, 1993). Young children may open and close their hands to request an object or wave "bye-bye" when leaving. Infants' vocabularies of gestures and spoken words expand at about the same rate, consistent with the idea that words and gestures reflect the infant's emerging understanding of symbols (Caselli, Rinald, Stefanini, & Volterra, 2012). In these cases, gestures and words convey a message equally well.

What's more, gestures sometimes pave the way for language. Before knowing an object's name, infants often point to it or pick it up for a listener, as if saying, "I want this!" or "What's this?" In one study, 50 percent of all objects were first referred to by gesture and, about three months later, by word (Iverson & Goldin-Meadow, 2005). Given this connection between early gestures and first spoken words, it is not surprising that toddlers who are more advanced in their use of gesture tend to have, as preschoolers, more complex spoken language (Rowe, Raudenbush, & Goldin-Meadow, 2012).

Fast Mapping Meanings to Words

Once children have the insight that a word can symbolize an object or action, their vocabularies grow, though slowly at first. A typical 15-month-old, for example, may learn two to three new words each week. **However, at about 18 months, many children experience a *naming explosion* during which they learn new words—particularly names of objects—much more rapidly than before.** Children subsequently learn 10 or more new words each week (Fenson et al., 1994; McMurray, 2007).

This rapid rate of word learning is astonishing when we realize that most words have many plausible but incorrect referents. To illustrate, imagine what's going through the mind of the child in the photo on the next page. The mother has just pointed out of the window to a flower, saying, "Flower. That is a flower. See the flower." To the mother (and you), this all seems crystal clear and incredibly straight-forward. But what might a child learn from this episode? Perhaps the correct referent for "flower," but a youngster could just as reasonably conclude that "flower" refers to the petals, to the colour of the flower, or to the mother's actions in pointing to the flower.

Surprisingly, though, most youngsters learn the proper meanings of simple words in just a few presenta-tions. **Children's ability to connect new words to their meanings so rapidly that they cannot be considering all possible meanings for the new word is called** *fast mapping.* How can young children learn new words so rap-idly? Researchers believe that many distinct factors contrib-ute to young children's rapid word learning (Hollich, Hirsh-Pasek, & Golinkoff, 2000).

When a parent points to an object and says a word, babies could possibly link the name to the object, to a property of the object (e.g., colour), or to the act of pointing. In fact, babies consistently interpret the word as the object's name, an assumption that allows them to learn words more rapidly.

JOINT ATTENTION.   Parents encourage word learning by carefully watching what interests their children. When toddlers touch or look at an object, parents often label it for them. When a youngster points to a banana, a parent may say, "Banana, that's a banana." Such labelling in the context of joint attention promotes word learning, par-ticularly when infants and toddlers participate actively, directing their parents' attention (Beuker, Rommelse, Donders, & Buitelaar, 2013).

Of course, to take advantage of this help, infants must be able to tell when parents are labelling instead of just conversing. In fact, when adults label an unfamiliar object, young children are much more likely to assume that the label is the object's name when adults show signs that they are referring to the object, either by looking or pointing at it while labelling (Liebal, Behne, Carpenter, & Tomasello, 2009; Nurmsoo & Bloom, 2008). Young children also consider an adult's credibility as a source: If an adult seems uncertain or has given incorrect names for words in the past, preschoolers are less likely to pick up words from them (Birch, Akmal, & Frampton, 2010; Corriveau, Kinzler, & Harris, 2013). Thus, beginning in the toddler years, parents and children work together to create conditions that foster word learning: Parents label objects, and youngsters rely on adults' behaviour to interpret the words they hear. Finally, although joint attention helps children to learn words, it is not required: Children learn new words when those words are used in ongoing conversation and when they overhear others use novel words (Shneidman & Goldin-Meadow, 2012).

CONSTRAINTS ON WORD NAMES.   Joint attention simplifies word learning for children, but the problem remains: How does a toddler know that "banana" refers to the object she's touching, as opposed to her activity (touching) or to the object's colour? Young children follow several simple rules that constrain their inferences about a word's meaning

These rules have been revealed with methods illustrated in a study by Au and Glusman (1990). Preschoolers were shown a monkey-like stuffed animal with pink horns and the researcher called it a "mido." Mido was then repeated several times, always refer-ring to the stuffed animal with pink horns. Later, these youngsters were asked to find a "theri" in a set of stuffed animals that included several midos. Never having heard of a theri, what did the children do? They never picked a mido; instead, they selected other stuffed animals. Knowing that "mido" referred to monkey-like animals with pink horns, they decided that "theri" had to refer to another stuffed animal.

Apparently, children were following this simple but effective rule for learning new words:

- *If an unfamiliar word is heard in the presence of objects that already have names and objects that do not, the word refers to one of the objects that does not have a name.*

Researchers have discovered several other simple rules that help children match words with the correct referent (Hoff, 2009; Woodward & Markman, 1998):

- *A name refers to a whole object,* not its parts or its relation to other objects, and refers not just to this particular object but to all objects of the same type (Hollich, Golinkoff, & Hirsh-Pasek, 2007). For example, when a grandparent points to a stuffed animal on a shelf and says "dinosaur," children conclude that "dinosaur" refers to the entire dinosaur, not just its ears or its nose, not to the fact that the dinosaur is on a shelf, and not to this specific dinosaur but to all dinosaur-like objects.

- *If an object already has a name* and another name is presented, the new name denotes a subcategory of the original name. If the child who knows the meaning of the word "dinosaur" sees his brother point to another dinosaur and hears his brother say "T-Rex," the child will conclude that T-Rex is a special type of dinosaur.

- *Given many similar category members,* a word applied consistently to only one of them is a proper noun. If a child who knows "dinosaur" sees that one of a group of dinosaurs is always called "Dino," the child will conclude that Dino is the name of that dinosaur.

Rules like these make it possible for children like Sebastien, the child in the vignette, to learn words rapidly because they reduce the number of possible referents. The child in the photo on page 313 follows these rules to decide that "flower" refers to the entire object, not its parts or the action of pointing to it.

SENTENCE CUES. Children hear many unfamiliar words embedded in sentences containing words they already know. The other words and the overall sentence structure can be helpful clues to a word's meaning (Yuan & Fisher, 2009). For example, when a parent describes the event in the photo using familiar words but an unfamiliar verb, children often infer that the verb refers to the action performed by the subject of the sentence (Arunachalam, Escovar, Hansen, & Waxman, 2013). When the youngsters hear, "The man is juggling," they will infer that "juggling" refers to the man's actions with the balls because they already know "man" and because *-ing* refers to ongoing actions. Similarly, toddlers know that *a* and *the* often precede nouns, and that *he, she,* and *they* precede verbs. Thus, they will conclude that "a boz" refers to an object but "she boz" refers to an action (Cauvet et al., 2014).

COGNITIVE FACTORS. The naming explosion coincides with a time of rapid cognitive growth, and children's increased cognitive skill helps them to learn new words. As children's thinking becomes more sophisticated and, in particular, as they start to have goals and intentions, language becomes a means to express those goals and to achieve them (Bloom & Tinker, 2001). In addition, young children's improving attentional and perceptual skills also promote word learning. In the Spotlight on Theories feature, we'll see how children's attention to shape (e.g., balls are round; pencils are slender rods) helps them learn new words.

Topham/The Image Works

Children in the photo already know "man" and "bats"; consequently, when they hear "The man is juggling the bats" they decide that juggling refers to the man's actions with the bats.

Spotlight on Theories

A Shape-Bias Theory of Word Learning

BACKGROUND   Many developmental scientists believe that young children could master a complex task like word learning only by using built-in, language-specific mechanisms (e.g., fast-mapping rules such as "unfamiliar words refer to objects that don't have names"). However, not all scientists agree that specialized processes are required; they argue that word learning can be accomplished by applying basic processes of attention and learning.

THE THEORY   Linda B. Smith (2000; 2009) argues that shape plays a central role in learning words. Infants and young children spontaneously pay attention to an object's shape, and they use this bias to learn new words. In Smith's theory, children first associate names with a single object: "Ball" is associated with a specific tennis ball, and "cup" is associated with a favourite sippy cup. As children encounter new balls and new cups, however, they hear the same words applied to similarly shaped objects and reach the conclusion that balls are round and cups are cylinders with handles. With further experience, children derive an even more general rule: Objects that have the same shape have the same name. From this, children realize that paying attention to shape is an easy way to learn names.

Hypothesis: If bias to attend to shape helps children learn words as names, then the age at which children first show the shape bias should coincide with a jump in the number of names that children learn. In other words, as soon as children realize that similarly shaped objects have the same name, they should start learning names much more rapidly.

Test: Gershkoff-Stowe and Smith (2004) conducted a longitudinal study in which parents kept detailed records of their toddlers' word learning for several months. In addition, toddlers were tested every three weeks. They were shown a multicoloured U-shaped wooden object and told it was a "dax." Then they were shown several objects, some of which were also U-shaped but differed in colour and material (e.g., a blue U-shaped sponge). Other objects were the same colour (i.e., multicoloured) or the same material (i.e., wood) but not U-shaped. Children were then asked to give all the "dax" to the experimenter.

The crucial findings concern the age at which shape bias emerges and the age of the beginning of the naming explosion. Gershkoff-Stowe and Smith defined the onset of shape bias as the first session in which toddlers gave both U-shaped objects—but no others—to the experimenter. The onset of the naming explosion was defined as the first week in which toddlers learned 10 or more new words. These two ages were highly correlated, with $r = .85$, indicating a tight link between onset of shape bias and the naming explosion.

Conclusion: As predicted, once toddlers showed a shape bias—that is, they realized that a name applies to objects that have the same shape but not to objects of the same colour or made of the same material—they then used this knowledge to learn new words faster. This result supports Smith's theory and the general idea that word learning may not require specialized mechanisms.

Application: If shape bias helps children learn words, can we teach this bias and foster word learning? The answer is yes. Smith and colleagues (Smith, Jones, Landau, Gershkoff-Stowe, & Samuelson, 2002) had toddlers and an experimenter play with four pairs of novel objects; each pair of objects had the same name and the same shape but differed in colour and material. A "dax" was still a U-shaped object; a "zup" referred to an elliptical-shaped object with a slot in one end. During play, the experimenter named each object 10 times. When children played with objects in this way, they learned the names of real words rapidly. From playing with "dax" and "zup," toddlers apparently learned that paying attention to shape is a good way to learn object names. Likewise, by systematically showing toddlers that the same name applies to many similarly shaped objects (e.g., book, crayon, comb, spoon), parents can teach youngsters the value of paying attention to shape to learn word names.

Critical Thinking Question: In the feature, the nonsense words in the experiments described were used to refer to very specific, shaped objects. At the end, it is noted that caregivers could use the same procedures with "real life" objects to encourage children in recognition and naming. How could this teaching of object names be used to a caregiver's advantage?

DEVELOPMENTAL CHANGE IN WORD LEARNING. Some of the word-learning tools described in the past few pages are particularly important at different ages (Hirsh-Pasek & Golinkoff, 2008). Before 18 months, infants learn words relatively slowly—often just one new word each day. At this age, children rely heavily on simple attentional processes (e.g., the shape bias) to learn new words. But by 24 months, most children are learning many new words daily. This faster learning reflects children's greater use of language cues (e.g., constraints on names) and a speaker's social cues. At any age, infants and toddlers rely on a mixture of word-learning tools, but with age, they gradually move away from attentional cues to language and social cues.

NAMING ERRORS. These many ways of learning new words are not perfect; initial mappings of words onto meanings are often only partially correct (Hoff & Naigles, 2002). **A common mistake is *underextension*, defining a word too narrowly.** Using the word "car" to refer only to the family car and "ball" to refer only to one favourite toy ball are examples of underextension. **Between one and three years, children sometimes make the opposite error, *overextension*, defining a word too broadly.** Children may use "car" to also refer to buses and trucks or use "doggie" to refer to all four-legged animals.

The overextension error occurs more frequently when children are producing words than when they are comprehending words. Two-year-old Jason may say "doggie" to refer to a goat but nevertheless correctly point to a picture of a goat when asked. Because overextension is more common in word production, it may actually reflect another fast-mapping rule that children follow: "If you can't remember the name for an object, say the name of a related object" (Naigles & Gelman, 1995).

Both underextension and overextension disappear gradually as youngsters refine meanings for words with more exposure to language.

Individual Differences in Word Learning

The naming explosion typically occurs at about 18 months of age, but, as with many developmental milestones, the timing of this event varies widely for individual children. Some youngsters have a naming explosion as early as 14 months, but for others it may be as late as 22 months (Goldfield & Reznick, 1990). Another way to make this point is to look at variation in the size of children's vocabulary at a specific age. At 18 months, for example, an average child's vocabulary would have about 75 words, but a child in the 90th percentile would know nearly 250 words, and a child in the 10th percentile fewer than 25 words (Fenson et al., 1994).

The range in vocabulary size for a typical 18-month-old is huge—from 25 to 250 words! What can account for this difference? Heredity contributes: Twin studies find that vocabulary size is more similar in identical twins than in fraternal twins (Dionne, Dale, Boivin, & Plomin, 2003). The heritability difference for vocabulary size is fairly small, however, indicating a relatively minor role for genetics.

More important are two other factors. One is *phonological memory,* **the ability to remember speech sounds briefly.** Phonological memory is often measured by saying a nonsense word to children—"ballop" or "glistering"—and asking them to repeat it immediately. Children's skill in recalling such words is strongly related to the size of their vocabulary (Gathercole et al., 1992; Leclercq & Majerus, 2010). Children who have difficulty remembering speech sounds accurately find word learning particularly challenging, which is not surprising since word learning involves associating meaning with an unfamiliar sequence of speech sounds.

However, the single most important factor in growth of vocabulary is the child's language environment. Children have larger vocabularies when they are exposed to a lot of high-quality language. The more words children hear, the better (Hurtado, Marchman, & Fernald, 2008). Specifically, children learn more words when their parents' speech is rich in different words and is grammatically sophisticated (Huttenlocher et al., 2010; Rowe, 2012) and when parents respond promptly and appropriately to their children's talk (Tamis-Lemonda & Bornstein, 2002).

Why does an environment filled with speech help children learn new words? One obvious mechanism is that such an environment provides children with many examples of words to learn. But, as we'll see in the Focus on Research feature, exposure to ample speech promotes vocabulary in another, less direct manner.

 QUESTION 9.2
Gavin and Mitch are both 16 months old. Gavin's vocabulary includes about 14 words, but Mitch's has about 150 words—more than 10 times as many as Gavin. What factors contribute to this difference? *(Answer is on page 324.)*

 Focus on Research

Why Does Exposure to Parents' Speech Increase Children's Vocabulary?

Who were the investigators, and what was the aim of the study? Many studies have shown that toddlers learn more when their home environment is rich in language. We know little about the specific ways in which such language-rich environments foster word learning. Adriana Weisleder and Anne Fernald (2013) conducted a study to test the hypothesis that abundant exposure to language hones a child's language-processing skills, making it easier for the child to learn new words.

How did the investigators measure the topic of interest? Weisleder and Fernald measured the child's language environment by having the child wear a small audio recorder that recorded all the speech that a child heard in a day. Weisleder and Fernald measured language processing by showing children pairs of pictures of familiar objects (e.g., dog, shoe), followed by the name of one of the pictures. They measured the percentage of time that children looked at the picture that matched the name. Finally, parents completed a standard vocabulary checklist, indicating the words that their child used and understood.

Who were the children in the study? Weisleder and Fernald tested 29 toddlers.

What was the design of the study? This study was correlational: Weisleder and Fernald were interested in links between children's language environment, their language-processing efficiency, and the size of their vocabulary. The study was longitudinal: the child's language environment and language-processing efficiency was assessed when children were 19 months old; vocabulary was assessed when children were 24 months old.

Were there ethical concerns with the study? No. The tasks posed no danger to the infants or to their parents. Parents provided consent for their participation and for their child's participation.

What were the results? One striking finding was the variation in children's language environments. At one extreme were parents who directed more than 12 000 words to their child in a 10-hour day; at the other extreme were parents who directed only 670 words to their child. Overall, the amount of child-directed speech was correlated .44 with children's language-processing efficiency at 19 months and .57 with their vocabulary at 24 months. In other words, greater exposure to language was associated with more efficient language processing and a larger vocabulary. In addition, processing efficiency at 19 months was correlated .53 with vocabulary at 24 months. Using advanced statistics, Weisleder and Fernald showed that exposure to more child-directed speech led to more efficient language processing, which, in turn, yielded larger vocabularies.

What did the investigators conclude? The findings support the hypothesis that language-processing efficiency links a language-rich environment with larger vocabularies. In the words of Weisleder and Fernald,

> a critical step in the path from early language experience to later vocabulary knowledge is the influence of language exposure on infants' speech-processing skill. . . . Infants who hear more talk have more opportunities to interpret language and to exercise skills that are vital to word learning, such as segmenting speech and accessing lexical representations. (p. 2149)

What converging evidence would strengthen these conclusions? Weisleder and Fernald used only a single measure of language-processing efficiency; it would be useful to extend the work with other measures of this construct. In addition, to determine the long-lasting effects of language-processing efficiency on children's word learning, it would be valuable to test the children again when they're older.

Critical Thinking Question: Given the above findings, what can parents best do to help their babies learn new words?

WORD LEARNING STYLES. Size of vocabulary is not the only way in which young children differ in their word learning. As youngsters expand their vocabulary, they often adopt a distinctive style of learning language (Bates, Bretherton, & Snyder, 1988; Nelson, 1973). **Some children have a** *referential style;* **their vocabularies mainly consist of words that name objects, people, or actions.** For example, Caitlin, a referential child, had 42 name words in her 50-word vocabulary but only two words for social interactions or questions. **Other children have an** *expressive* *style;* **their vocabularies include some names but also many social phrases that are used like a single word, such as "go away," "what'd you want?" and "I want it."** A typical expressive child, Candace, had a more balanced vocabulary: 22 name words and 13 for social interactions and questions.

Referential and expressive styles represent end points on a continuum; most children are somewhere in between. For children with referential emphasis, language is primarily an intellectual tool—a means of learning and talking about objects (Masur, 1995). In contrast, for children with expressive emphasis, language is more of a social tool—a way of enhancing interactions with others. Of course, both of these functions—intellectual and social—are important functions of language, which explains why most children blend the referential and expressive styles of learning language.

Encouraging Word Learning

How can parents and other adults help children learn words? For children to expand their vocabularies, they need to hear others speak. Not surprisingly, then, children learn words more rapidly if their parents speak to them frequently (Huttenlocher, Haight, Bryk, Seltzer, & Lyons, 1991; Roberts, Burchinal, & Durham, 1999). Of course, sheer quantity of parental speech is not all that matters. Parents can foster word learning by naming objects that are the focus of a child's attention (Dunham, Dunham, & Curwin, 1993). Parents can name different products on store shelves as they point to them. During a walk, parents can label the objects—birds, plants, vehicles—that the child sees.

Parents and caregivers can also help children learn words by reading with them. Reading together is fun for parents and children alike, and it provides opportunities for children to learn new words (Song et al., 2012). However, the way that parents read makes a difference. When parents carefully describe pictures as they read, preschoolers' vocabularies increase (Reese & Cox, 1999). Asking children questions also helps (Sénéchal, Thomas, & Monker, 1995). When an adult reads a sentence (e.g., "Arthur is *angling*"), then asks a question (e.g., "What is Arthur doing?"), a child must match the new word (angling) with the pictured activity (in this case, fishing) and say the word aloud. When parents read without questioning, children can ignore words they don't understand. Questioning forces children to identify meanings of new words and practice saying them.

Parents remain an important influence on school-age children's vocabulary development: Children learn words when exposed to a parent's advanced vocabulary, particularly in the context of instructive and helpful interactions (Weizman & Snow, 2001). Reading is another great way to learn new words. Written material—books, magazines, newspapers, textbooks—almost always contains more unfamiliar words than conversational language, so reading is rich in opportunities to expand vocabulary (Hayes, 1988). Not surprisingly, children who read frequently tend to have larger vocabularies than children who read less often (Allen, Cipielewski, & Stanovich, 1992).

Czanner/Fotolia

Although North American babies typically spend more than an hour every day watching video, they learn little language from such exposure.

IMPACT OF VIDEO.   Television has been a regular part of North American children's lives since the 1950s, but video has assumed an even larger role with the ready availability of inexpensive DVD players and child-oriented DVDs. A typical preschool child in North America spends more than two hours each day watching video, and infants like the one in the photo on the previous page spend more than an hour watching (Linebarger & Vaala, 2010). We learned some things about the impact of electronic media in Module 7.4; here, the issue is the influence of such media in helping children to learn new words.

For preschool children, viewing video can help word learning, under some circumstances. For example, preschool children who regularly watch *Sesame Street* usually have larger vocabularies than preschoolers who watch *Sesame Street* only occasionally (Wright et al., 2001). Other programs that promote word learning are those that tell a story (e.g., *Thomas the Tank Engine*) as well as programs like *Blue's Clues* and *Dora the Explorer*, which directly ask questions of the viewer. The benefits of these programs are greatest when preschoolers watch them with adults, in part because the video contents become the focus of joint attention, as described on page 313. In contrast, most cartoons have no benefit for language learning (Linebarger & Vaala, 2010).

What about videos claiming that they promote word learning in infants? Most of the evidence suggests that before 18 months of age, infant-oriented video series (e.g., Baby Einstein, Brainy Baby) are not effective in promoting infants' word learning (Linebarger & Vaala, 2010). The field experiment by DeLoache et al. (2010), described in Chapter 1, also reported this sort of negative evidence. One reason is that these videos are "poorly designed, insufficient to support language processing, and developmentally inappropriate" (Linebarger & Vaala, 2010, p. 184). Another reason stems from a phenomenon that we'll consider in detail at the end of this module: 12- to 18-month-olds have limited understanding of relationships between real objects and their depictions in photographs and video. In other words, they have difficulty relating what they see in the video to those objects and actions as experienced in their own lives.

Research on video and parents' influence points to a simple but powerful conclusion: Children are most likely to learn new words when they participate in activities that force them to understand the meanings of new words and use those new words (O'Doherty et al., 2011). Is learning new words (and other aspects of language) more difficult for children learning two languages? The Cultural Influences feature has the answer.

Cultural Influences

Growing up Bilingual

According to government statistics, Canada is becoming a more multilingual society. The 2011 census reports that more than 200 languages are named as "mother tongue" by members of the Canadian population (Statistics Canada, 2012g). Growing numbers of immigrants who come from countries where neither French nor English is the native language has led to an increase in linguistic diversity in Canada in recent years. In 2011, nearly seven million Canadians had a mother tongue other than English or French; Canada's two official languages are widely spoken, however, with 98 percent of the population able to speak either English or French (Statistics Canada, 2012g). Other languages spoken include Punjabi (now the most common non-official language–mother tongue), Chinese, European languages, languages from Asia and the Middle East, and Atikamekw—a Canadian Indigenous language— most often spoken at home (Statistics Canada, 2012f). Thus many Canadian school children come from homes where English is not the primary language. These youngsters usually speak

English and another language, such as Chinese, like the children in the photo.

Across Canada, 17.5 percent of the population is French-English bilingual, able to hold a conversation in both official languages (Statistics Canada 2012g), and about half of the children in the world live in multilingual environments (Hoff, 2006). Of course, a wide variety of language environments exist—bilingualism is simply the one that has been most studied. What can studies of bilingualism tell us? Is learning two languages easier or harder than learning just one language? For much of the 20th century, the general view was that bilingualism harmed children's development. One child psychology text published roughly 60 years ago reported that being raised in a bilingual environment would compromise children's language development (Thompson, 1952). Today, we know this conclusion is wrong because it was based on studies of poor, immigrant children's scores on intelligence tests. In retrospect, the immigrant children's test scores had more to do with their poverty and unfamiliarity with a new culture than with their bilingualism.

Bilingual children learn language at about the same rate as monolingual children and often have a more sophisticated understanding of the underlying symbolic nature of language.

Fancy/Veer/Corbis/Getty Images

In fact, modern studies lead to a different picture. True, when one- and two-year-olds learn two languages simultaneously, they often progress somewhat slowly at first. Christopher Fennell from the University of Ottawa, working with Krista Byers-Heinlein and Janet Werker at the University of British Columbia, has shown that bilingual infants tend to mix words from the two languages and are less skilled at using language-specific sounds to guide word learning (Fennell, Byers-Heinlein, & Werker, 2007). Fennell et al. (2007) proposed that perhaps the increased demands of learning two languages at the same time means that the infants cannot distinguish such differences at first. Soon, however, they separate the languages, and bilingual children reach most language milestones at about the same age as monolingual children (Pettito et al., 2001). When each language is considered separately, bilingual children often have somewhat smaller vocabularies than monolingual children (Umbel, Pearson, Fernandez, & Oller, 1992). However, since bilingual youngsters often know words in one language but not the other, their total vocabulary (i.e., words known in both languages plus words known in either language but not both) is greater than that of monolingual children (Hoff, Core, Rumiche, Señor, & Parra, 2012). Work by Ellen Bialystok of York University and her colleagues has shown that, in addition, bilingual children surpass monolingual children in other language skills. Bilingual preschoolers are more likely to understand that the printed form of a word is unrelated to the meaning of the word (Bialystok, 1997; Bialystok, Shenfield, & Codd, 2000). For example, bilingual preschoolers are less likely to believe that words denoting large objects (e.g., "bus") are longer than words denoting small objects (e.g., "bug"). Bilingual children also better understand that words are simply arbitrary symbols. Bilingual youngsters, for instance, are more likely than monolingual children to understand that, as long as all English speakers agreed, then "dog" could refer to cats and "cat" could refer to dogs (Bialystok, 1988; Campbell & Sais, 1995).

In addition, bilingual children often are more skilled at switching back and forth between tasks and often are better able to inhibit inappropriate responses (Bialystok & Martin, 2004; Carlson & Meltzoff, 2008). If asked to sort cards first by colour, then by shape, children often sort by the first rule: Instead of sorting by shape, they revert to sorting by colour (the first rule). Bilingual children are less prone to this sort of mistake, perhaps because they must routinely inhibit relevant words while speaking, listening, or reading. For example, when shown a photo of a dog and asked, "What's this?" preschoolers bilingual in French and English must respond "dog" while suppressing "*chien.*"

Apparently, such experience makes bilingual children generally better at inhibiting competing responses, and this occurs regardless of culture (Bialystok & Viswanathan, 2009). As Bialystok herself noted in a review paper, bilingualism's effect "is a striking example of how ordinary experiences accumulate to modify cognitive networks and cognitive abilities" (Bialystok, 2011, p. 233).

Canada has two official languages, and many children speak at least one of these by the time they attend school. Canadians generally view their country as multicultural, whereas Americans see their country as a "melting pot." Many children in the United States cannot speak English by the time they should begin school, and how to teach these children has prompted much debate. One view is that all Americans should speak English, and so all teaching should be in English. Another view is that children learn more effectively in their native tongue, and so all teaching should be done in that language. Much of the American debate over the proper language of instruction is political, reflecting a desire for a society with a universal cultural heritage and language rather than a society with pluralistic heritages and languages.

An additional consideration for Canada is that many immigrant families arrive already speaking one language—their native language. **People living in Canada who speak a language other than one of the two official languages are referred to as** *allophones.* Of course, a child whose family immigrates to Canada may also know either English or French and thus be bilingual upon arrival in Canada. Such children may then pick up the second official language, giving them additional linguistic capabilities. Children who are Deaf or Hard of Hearing (DHH) make up a small subgroup of immigrants. These children face particular challenges, and some may have no language exposure at all before coming to Canada. Current advice in Ontario, particularly for older children, is to teach ASL rather than speech, as signed language appears to be more readily acquired once the optimum age for language acquisition has passed (Kokai, 2003).

Ignoring the political aspects, research shows that the best method of schooling for immigrant children uses the child's native language *and* the local language—for example, English (Padilla et al., 1991; Wong-Fillmore, Ammon, McLaughlin, & Ammon, 1985). Initially, children receive basic English-language teaching while they are taught other subjects in their native language. Gradually, more instruction is in English, in step with children's growing proficiency in the second language. When instruction is in children's native language and English, they are most likely to master academic content and literacy skills in both languages (Farver, Lonigan, & Eppe, 2009).

French immersion schooling presents a similar situation. Anglophone children initially begin learning school subjects in English and French, with gradually more instruction in French until all schooling is in that language. In Canada, bilingualism is apparent in everyday life, so even if a child is not in immersion schooling, incidental exposure to the other official language is present in everything from television shows (entertainment as well as educational programming) to the backs of cereal boxes. (One author of this text learned the French word for "peanut" from the peanut butter jar!) Although minimal input such as simply overhearing a language spoken occasionally is not sufficient to learn that language (Hoff, 2006), the constant exposure to bilingual materials can help those learning French or English in other ways to improve or to maintain competency. Many children also attend schools in which still other languages are taught, for example the Edmonton public school system's Mandarin language program (Harding, 2006). Other children may attend an additional school on Saturdays or in the evenings to learn a language from their family background, for example, Hebrew. Knowing more than one language, and particularly French-English bilingualism in Canada, is considered important for many work environments that will be encountered later in life. As noted in this section, knowing more than one language has many advantages for children, particularly metalinguistic understanding—knowing that language is something in and of itself, and that words are symbolic representations.

Critical Thinking Questions: Many children in provinces outside Quebec go to French immersion schools, and often children attend extra language schooling (e.g., Hebrew school or Chinese language lessons) in addition to regular schooling. At what age do you think children should start such schooling to best acquire an additional language, to become bilingual or even multi-lingual? Why?

Beyond Words: Other Symbols

To end this module, let's return to the topic that began it—symbols. Words are indeed powerful and immensely useful symbols. As children grow, however, they learn other symbol systems. Pictures, for example, are symbols that represent something else. The link between a picture and what it represents is often very clear. Wallet photos, for instance, are easily recognized as representations of familiar people (at least to the wallet's owner). But the seemingly transparent connection between photographs and the object photographed actually poses a problem for young children—photos are not the actual object but simply a representation of it. Young children must learn that shaking a picture of a rattle will not make a noise and that inverting a picture of a glass of juice will not cause it to spill. In fact, if shown realistic photos of familiar toys, nine-month-olds often try to grasp the toy in the photo, much as they would grasp the real object. By 18 months, toddlers rarely do this, indicating that toddlers understand that photos are representations of objects, not the objects themselves (Troseth, Pierroutsakos, & DeLoache, 2004).

Deaf children acquire understanding of symbolic representations, too. They learn that particular gestures or hand shapes refer to objects, people, or concepts. Sign languages are real languages, although this fact was not really understood until research undertaken in the 1960s showed that sign languages such as ASL, widely used throughout both Canada and the United States, fulfilled all the characteristics of true language (e.g., Bellugi & Klima, 1978). A particular sign can be imitative of the object or action, or may be quite abstract. The important aspect is that the child learns that the symbol represents something (more on this subject in Module 9.5).

A scale model is another kind of symbolic representation. A scale model of the solar system helps students understand the relative distances of planets from the sun; a scale model of a college campus shows the location of campus landmarks to new students; and a scale model of an airplane allows aeronautical engineers to measure how air flows over a wing. Scale models are useful because they are realistic looking—simply smaller versions of the real thing. Nevertheless, young children do not understand the relation between scale models and the objects they represent: The ability to use scale models develops early in the preschool years. To illustrate, if young children watch an adult hide a toy in a full-size room, then try to find the toy in a scale model of the room that contains all the principal features of the full-scale room (e.g., carpet, window, furniture), three-year-olds find the hidden toy readily, but two-and-a-half-year-olds do not (DeLoache, 1995).

Why is this task so easy for three-year-olds and so difficult for two-and-a-half-year-olds? Do the younger children simply forget the location of the toy by the time they look at the scale model of the room? No. If returned to the full-size room, they easily find the hidden toy. Judy DeLoache and her colleagues believe that a two-and-a-half-year-old's "attention to a scale model as an interesting and attractive object makes it difficult for them

Judy DeLoache

In a study that examined children's understanding of scale models as symbols, Judy DeLoache and her colleagues convinced two-and-a-half-year-olds that this oscilloscope could shrink the doll and other objects.

to simultaneously think about its relation to something else" (DeLoache, Miller, & Rosengren, 1997, p. 308). In other words, young children are drawn to the model as a real object and therefore find it hard to think about the model as a symbol of the full-size room.

If this argument is correct, two-and-a-half-year-olds should be more successful using the model if they don't have to think of it as a symbol for the full-size room. DeLoache and her colleagues tested this hypothesis in what is Robert Kail's favourite study of all time. To test this argument about symbolism, DeLoache and colleagues (2010) created a condition designed to eliminate the need for children to think of the model as both an object and as a symbol. Children saw the oscilloscope shown in the photograph, which was described as a shrinking machine. They saw a toy doll—Terry the Troll—placed in front of the oscilloscope; then the experimenter and child left the room briefly while a tape recorder played sounds that were described as sounds "the machine makes when it's shrinking something." When experimenter and child returned, Terry had shrunk from eight inches to two inches. Next, Terry was hidden in the full-size room, the experimenter aimed the "shrinking machine" at the full-size room, then experimenter and child left the room. While the tape recorder played shrinking sounds, research assistants quickly removed everything from the full-size room and substituted the model. Then experimenter and child returned, and the child was asked to find Terry.

Children rarely found the toy when tested with the usual instructions, but they usually did in the "shrinking machine" condition. Apparently, two-and-a-half-year-olds find it very difficult to think of the model as an object and as a symbol, and consequently cannot find the hidden toy, even though the model is an exact replica of the full-size room. In contrast, when children can think of the model as the room, but much smaller, they readily find the toy.

A map is more demanding for children because it is only a two-dimensional (flat) representation of objects in the world. Nevertheless, by four years of age, children can use simple maps to find objects (Shusterman, Lee, & Spelke, 2008; Spelke, Gilmore, & McCarthy, 2011). What is more, this skill emerges when children have no exposure to maps: In a study conducted in isolated villages in South America where there were no maps, rulers, or schools, children used simple maps as capably as North American children (Dehaene, Izard, Pica, & Spelke, 2006).

Of course, after children have mastered scale models and maps, a host of other symbolic forms await them, including graphs and musical notation. But children take their first steps toward lifelong access to symbols as infants, when they master words and gestures.

 ANSWER 9.2
The two main factors are phonological memory and the boys' language environments. It's likely that Mitch has a better phonological memory—he can remember speech sounds more accurately and longer—and that he gets exposed to more speech and more sophisticated speech.

✓ Check Your Learning

RECALL What factors help children learn new words so rapidly?

Summarize some of the ways in which children's vocabularies differ quantitatively and qualitatively.

INTERPRET Explain why a child's first words are best viewed as a breakthrough in children's understanding of symbols.

APPLY Suppose you have been asked to write a brochure for first-time parents about ways they can foster word learning in their toddlers. What would you write?

9.3 Speaking in Sentences

OUTLINE

From Two-Word Speech to Complex Sentences

How Do Children Acquire Grammar?

LEARNING OBJECTIVES

1. How do children progress from speaking single words to creating complicated sentences?

2. How do children acquire the grammar of their native language?

Jaime's daughter, Luisa, is a curious two-and-a-half-year-old who bombards her father with questions. Jaime enjoys Luisa's questioning, but he is bothered by the way she phrases her questions. Luisa says, "What you are doing?" and "Why not she sleep?" Obviously, Jaime doesn't talk this way, so he wonders where Luisa learned to ask questions like this. Is it normal, or is it a symptom of some type of language disorder?

Not long after children begin to talk, they start combining words to form simple sentences. These simple sentences are the first step in a new area of language learning—mastering *syntax*, a language's rules for combining words to create sentences. We'll begin this module by tracing the stages in children's acquisition of syntax and, along the way, see that Luisa's way of asking questions is quite normal for youngsters learning English. Then we'll examine different factors that influence children's mastery of syntax.

From Two-Word Speech to Complex Sentences

At about one-and-a-half years of age, children begin to combine individual words to create two-word sentences, like "more juice," "gimme cookie," "truck go," "my truck," "Mommy go," "Daddy bike." **Researchers call this kind of talk** *telegraphic speech* **because, like telegrams of days gone by, it consists only of words directly relevant to meaning.** Before text messages and email, people sent urgent messages by telegraph, and the cost was based on the number of words. Consequently, telegrams were brief and to the point, containing only the important nouns, verbs, adjectives, and adverbs, much like children's two-word speech.

In their two-word speech, children follow rules to express different meanings. For example, the sentences "truck go" and "Daddy eat" are both about agents—people or objects that do something and the actions they perform. Here the rule is "agent + action." In contrast, "my truck" is about a possessor and a possession; the rule for creating these sentences is "possessor + possession."

When children are in the two-word stage, they use several basic rules to express meaning (Brown, 1973). For example, *Daddy eat* and *Mommy fall* illustrate the rule agent + action; *gimme juice* and *push truck* illustrate the rule action + object. Regardless of the language they learn, children's two-word sentences follow a common set of rules that are very useful in describing ideas concerning people and objects, their actions, and their properties (Tager-Flusberg, 1993).

BEYOND TELEGRAPHIC SPEECH. Beginning at about the second birthday, children move to three-word and even longer sentences. For example, at one-and-a-half years of age, Robert Kail's daughter Laura would say, "gimme juice" or "bye-bye

This is a wug.

*Now there is another one.
There are two of them.
There are two_____.*

Figure 9-2 A simple demonstration of application of general grammatical rules.

Reprinted by permission of Jean Berko Gleason.

QUESTION 9.3
Describing a vacation, three-year-old Kelly said, "I sleeped in a tent!" What feature of grammatical development does her comment illustrate? *(Answer is on page 332.)*

Mom." As a two-and-a-half-year-old, she had progressed to "When I finish my ice cream, I'll take a shower, okay?" and "Don't turn the light out—I can't see better!" **Children's longer sentences are filled with** *grammatical morphemes,* **words or endings of words (such as** *-ing***,** *-ed***, or** *-s***) that make a sentence grammatical.** To illustrate, a one-and-a-half-year-old might say, "kick ball," but a three-year-old would be more likely to say, "I am kicking the ball." Compared to the one-and-a-half-year-old's telegraphic speech, the three-year-old has added several elements, including a pronoun, "I," to serve as the subject of the sentence; the auxiliary verb "am"; *-ing* to the verb "kick"; and an article, "the," before "ball." Each of these grammatical morphemes makes the older child's sentence slightly more meaningful and much more grammatical.

How do children learn all of these subtle nuances of grammar? Conceivably, a child might learn that the word "kicking" describes kicking that is ongoing and that "kicked" describes kicking that occurred in the past. Later, the child might learn that "raining" describes current weather and "rained" describes past weather. But learning different tenses for individual verbs—one by one—would be remarkably slow. More effective would be to learn the general rules that verb + *-ing* denotes an ongoing activity and verb + *-ed* denotes a past activity. In fact, this is what children do: They learn general rules about grammatical morphemes. For example, suppose you show preschoolers pictures of nonsense objects like the ones in Figure 9-2 and label it: "This is a wug." Then you show pictures of two of the objects while saying, "Now there is another one. There are two of them. There are two . . ." Preschoolers usually say, "wugs" (Berko, 1958). Because *wug* is a novel word, children can answer correctly only by applying the rule of adding *-s* to indicate plural.

Sometimes, of course, applying the general rule can lead to very creative communication. As a three-year-old, Kail's daughter would say, "unvelcro it," meaning detach the Velcro tape. She had never heard unvelcro, but she created this word from the rule that *un-* + verb means to reverse or stop the action of a verb. Creating such novel words is, in fact, evidence that children learn grammar by applying rules, not learning individual words.

Additional evidence that children master grammar by learning rules comes from preschoolers' *over-regularization,* **applying rules to words that are exceptions to the rule.** Youngsters learning English may incorrectly add an *-s* instead of using an irregular plural, saying, for example, "two mans" instead of "two men" or "two foots" instead of "two feet." With the past tense, children may add *-ed* instead of using an irregular past tense—"I goed" instead of "I went" or "she runned" instead of "she ran" (Maratsos, 2000; Marcus et al., 1992). Children apparently know the general rule but not all the words that are exceptions.

The rules governing grammatical morphemes range from fairly simple to very complex. The rule for plurals—to add *-s*—is simple to apply and, as you might expect, is one of the first grammatical morphemes that children master. Adding *-ing* to denote ongoing action is also simple, and it too is mastered early. More complex forms, such as the various forms of the verb "to be," are mastered later; but, remarkably, by the end of the preschool years, children typically have mastered most of the rules that govern grammatical morphemes.

At the same time that preschoolers are mastering grammatical morphemes, they extend their speech beyond the subject-verb-object construction that is basic in English. You can see these changes in the way children ask questions. Children's questions during two-word speech are marked by intonation alone. Soon after a child can declare, "My ball," he can also ask "My ball?" Children quickly discover *wh* words (i.e., who, what, when, where, why), but they don't use them correctly. Like Luisa, the two-and-a-half-year-old in the module-opening vignette, many youngsters merely attach the *wh* word to the beginning of a sentence without changing the rest of the sentence: "What he eating?" "What we see?" But by three or three-and-a-half years of age, youngsters insert the required auxiliary verb before the subject, creating "What is he eating?" or "What will we see?" (deVilliers & deVilliers, 1985; Rowland, Pine, Lieven, & Theakston, 2005).

Between ages three and six, children also learn to use negation ("That isn't a butterfly") and embedded sentences ("Jennifer thinks that Bill took the book"). They begin to comprehend passive voice ("The ball was kicked by the girl") as opposed to the active voice ("The girl kicked the ball"), although full understanding of this form continues into the elementary-school years (Hoff, 2014). The basic grammar concepts can vary between languages, for example, a subject-verb-object structure as in English, or a subject-object-verb word order as in Japanese (Carroll, 1999). Although errors in bilingual children's language use tend to show confusion, or "cross-linguistic transfer" (Nicoladis, 2006) between the grammatical structures of the two languages, by the time the majority of children enter kindergarten, they use most of the grammatical forms of their native language with great skill.

How Do Children Acquire Grammar?

How do children master the fundamentals of grammar at such a young age? Theorists have proposed several answers to this question.

THE BEHAVIOURIST ANSWER.   The simplest explanation for learning grammar is that children imitate the grammatical forms they hear. In fact, B.F. Skinner (1957) and other learning theorists once claimed that all aspects of language—sounds, words, grammar, and communication—are learned through imitation and reinforcement (Moerk, 2000; Whitehurst & Vasta, 1975). Critics were quick to point to some flaws in the learning explanation of grammar, however. One problem is that most of children's sentences are novel, which is difficult to explain in terms of simple imitation of adults' speech. For example, when young children create questions by inserting a *wh* word at the beginning of a sentence ("What she doing?"), who are they imitating?

Also troublesome for the learning view is that, even when children imitate adult sentences, they do not imitate adult grammar. In simply trying to repeat "I am drawing a picture," young children will say "I draw picture." And parents rarely reinforce their young children's speech based on its grammatical correctness; instead they respond based on its meaning, even when it is grammatically incorrect. Furthermore, linguists, particularly Noam Chomsky (1957, 1995), have argued that grammatical rules are far too complex for toddlers and preschoolers to infer them solely on the basis of speech that they hear.

THE NATIVIST ANSWER.   Beginning with Chomsky (1957), linguists proposed that children are born with mechanisms that simplify the task of learning grammar (Slobin, 1985). According to this view, children are born with neural circuits in the brain that allow them to infer the grammar of the language that they hear. That is, grammar itself is not built into the child's nervous system, but processes that guide the learning of grammar are. For example, **according to** *semantic bootstrapping theory,* **children are born knowing that nouns usually refer to people or objects and that verbs are actions; they use this knowledge to infer grammatical rules.**[1] Hearing sentences

[1]The name for this theory comes from the phrase "Pull yourself up by your bootstraps," which means improving your situation by your own efforts. The phrase is from an eighteenth-century fantasy tale about a baron who falls in a deep hole and escapes by pulling up on his bootstraps.

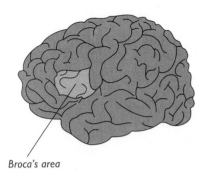

Broca's area

Figure 9-3 The region of the left frontal cortex active in combination of words into meaningful sentences: Broca's area.

such as "Billy drinks," "Susan sleeps," and "Jen reads," children infer that noun + verb makes a grammatical sentence in English (Pinker, 1989). Consistent with this idea, by two years of age, English-speaking children know that a typical transitive sentence (e.g., "the bunny ate the carrot") includes an agent (the subject), an action (the transitive verb), and a patient (the object of the action). Told that "the pig is dorping the cow," two-year-olds match this with a video of a pig performing an action on a cow (Gertner, Fischer, & Eisengart, 2006).

This proposal that inborn mechanisms help children learn grammar might not be as intuitively appealing as imitation, but many findings indirectly support this view:

1. Specific regions of the brain are known to be involved in language processing. If children are born with a "grammar-learning processor," it should be possible to locate a specific region or regions of the brain that are involved in learning grammar. In fact, you may remember from Module 4.3 that for most people, the left hemisphere of the brain plays a critical role in understanding language. Some functions of language have been located even more precisely. For example, the area in blue in Figure 9-3 is Broca's area—a region in the left frontal cortex that is necessary for combining words into meaningful sentences. French researchers have found that the same brain areas that process speech in adults are activated by speech sounds at three months of age—functioning well before any speech production (Dehaene-Lambertz, Dehaene, & Hertz-Pannier, 2002). By two years of age, specific regions of the left hemisphere are activated when sentences break simple grammatical rules, such as a noun appearing when a verb would be expected (Bernal, Dehaene-Lambertz, Millotte, & Christophe, 2010). The fact that specific areas in the brain, such as Broca's area, have well-defined functions for language makes it plausible that children have specialized neural circuits that help them learn grammar.

Chimps can be taught very simple grammatical rules, but only after massive training that is unlike the experiences of toddlers and preschoolers.

2. Only humans learn grammar readily. If grammar is learned solely through imitation and reinforcement, then it should be possible to teach rudimentary grammar to nonhumans. If, instead, learning grammar depends on specialized neural mechanisms that are unique to humans, then efforts to teach grammar to nonhumans should fail. This prediction has been tested many times by trying to teach grammar to chimpanzees, the species closest to humans on the evolutionary ladder. For example, chimps like the one in the photo have been taught to communicate using gestures taken from sign language. Other chimps have been taught using plastic chips to stand for words. The result? Chimps master a handful of grammatical rules governing two-word speech but only with massive effort that is completely unlike the preschool child's learning of grammar, and the resulting language is unlike children's grammar in many ways (Hoff, 2014). For example, one chimp, Nim, gradually used longer sentences but only because he repeated himself (e.g., "eat Nim eat Nim"), not because he expressed more complicated ideas. Because numerous efforts to teach grammar to chimps have failed, this suggests that children rely on some type of mechanism specific to humans to master grammar.

3. Children develop linguistic communication with little or no formal input. Studies of "home sign" among deaf people seem to support the concept of an innate basis for language. A deaf child will spontaneously produce gestural communication very similar in structure to a hearing child's verbal language (e.g., Goldin-Meadow, 1999; Goldin-Meadow & Mylander, 1984). An entire national sign language called Idioma de

Signos Nicaraguense developed in this way in Nicaragua. Deaf children brought together in special schools developed basic communication into a signed language with its own grammar (Senghas & Coppola, 2001; Senghas, Kita, & Özyürek, 2004). Several other similar, spontaneously developed languages exist, such as the Al-Sayyid Bedouin Sign Language (ABSL), and are now being studied by psychologists and linguists for what they can tell us about language development (Erad, 2005). Another source of evidence comes from study of languages developed in linguistically diverse, island communities (Bickerton, 1984, 1990). Initially, when people of different linguistic backgrounds come together they may develop a "basic" form of communication called a *pidgin,* a rudimentary language that allows people to get along; for example, to greet a neighbour or buy food at the market (Baptista, 2005). The children of pidgin speakers, however, then develop and use a more complete form of language, called a *creole.* Nativists believe that the children of pidgin speakers spontaneously generate true languages—creoles—because of their innate linguistic mechanisms.

4. There is a critical period for learning language. The period from birth to about 12 years is a critical period for acquiring language generally and mastering grammar particularly. If children do not acquire language in this period, they will never truly master language later. Canadian research has shown that this period is critical for any form of language experience, whether spoken or signed. Studying language learning in deaf people with varying amounts of early sign or spoken language exposure, Mayberry, Lock, and Kazmi (2002) showed that the ability to learn languages is determined by early experience with language, in whatever form.

Evidence of a critical period for language also comes from studies of feral and isolated children. Feral children are those found living in the wild, such as Victor, "the wild boy of Aveyron" (Itard, 1801, 1806/1962). Victor was found living like an animal in the woods near Aveyron in France in 1799. Although his hearing was normal, Victor could not speak. A local physician, Jean Marc Gaspard Itard, worked with Victor for several years, trying to teach him social behaviours and language. Victor learned to speak only a few words and to show that he knew the meanings of a few more, but seemed to have little true understanding of language. Victor was approximately 16 when he was found—and so was beyond the critical period for language when Itard's instruction commenced (Carroll, 1999). In one appalling instance illustrating the effects of isolation, a baby girl named Genie was restrained by a harness during the day and a straightjacket-like device at night. No one was permitted to talk to Genie, and she was beaten when she made any noise. When Genie was discovered, at age 13, she did not speak at all. After several years of language training, her mastery of grammar remained limited, resembling the telegraphic speech of a two-year-old (Curtiss, 1989; Rymer, 1993).

Further evidence for a critical period for learning language comes from studies of individuals learning second languages. Individuals master the grammar of a foreign language at the level of a native speaker only if they are exposed to the language prior to adolescence (Newport, 1991). How can one period of time be so much more influential for language than others? Why can't missed language experiences be made up after age 12? A critical period for language answers these questions. That is, just as females ovulate for only a limited portion of their lifespan, the neural mechanisms involved in learning grammar may function only during infancy and childhood.

5. The development of grammar is tied to the development of vocabulary. The mastery of grammar is closely related to vocabulary growth, in a way that suggests both are part of a common, emerging language system (Dixon & Marchman, 2007). One idea, for example, is that as children learn words, they learn not only a word's meaning, but also about the kinds of sentences in which a word appears and its position in those sentences. They learn the meaning of the word "teacher" and that "teacher" can appear as the actor and object in transitive sentences. Grammar then emerges naturally as children learn more and more words.

Two fascinating findings document this tight link between growth of vocabulary and emergence of grammar. First, in bilingual (English-Spanish) children, growth of vocabulary and grammar were found to be related within each language, but not across languages (Conboy & Thal, 2006). In other words, children's English vocabulary predicted the complexity of their English sentences (but not their Spanish sentences), while their Spanish vocabulary predicted the complexity of their Spanish sentences (but not their English sentences). It appears that in each language children need a "critical mass" of words before grammar can emerge. Second, children who are adopted by adults who speak another language (typically through an international adoption) represent a valuable natural experiment. Most children are adopted as infants, toddlers, or preschoolers, which means they differ considerably in the cognitive skills they can use to learn grammar. Nevertheless, the size of children's vocabulary, not their age, predicts the complexity of their grammar (Snedeker, Geren, & Shafto, 2007). That is, if a three-year-old and a seven-year-old each know 400 words, their grammar will be comparable, despite the age difference. This tight coupling of vocabulary and grammar in adopted and bilingual children fits with the idea that development of vocabulary and grammar is regulated by a common, language-specific system.

Although these findings are consistent with the idea that children have innate grammar-learning mechanisms, they do *not* prove the existence of such mechanisms. Consequently, scientists have continued to look for other explanations.

THE COGNITIVE ANSWER.   Not all researchers believe that children must have specialized mechanisms to learn grammar. Some theorists (e.g., Braine, 1992) believe that children learn grammar through powerful cognitive skills that help them rapidly detect regularities in their environments, including patterns in the speech they hear. According to this approach, it is as if children establish a huge Excel spreadsheet that has all the speech they have heard in one column and the context in which they heard it in a second column; periodically, infants scan the columns looking for recurring patterns (Maratsos, 1998). For example, children might be confused the first time they hear -*s* added to the end of a familiar noun. However, as the database expands to include many instances of familiar nouns with an added -*s*, children discover that -*s* is always added to a noun when there are multiple instances of the object. Thus, they create the rule: noun + -*s* = plural. With this view, children learn language by searching for regularities across many examples that are stored in memory, not through an inborn grammar-learning device (Bannard & Matthews, 2008). Scientists who subscribe to this view argue that infants' impressive ability to extract regularities in the speech sounds that they hear (described on page 326) would work just as effectively to extract regularities in sentence structure (Kidd, 2012).

THE SOCIAL-INTERACTION ANSWER.   This approach is eclectic, drawing on each of the views we've considered so far. From the behaviourist approach, it takes an emphasis on the environment; from the nativist approach, that language learning is distinct; and from the cognitive view, that children have powerful cognitive skills they can use to master language. The unique contribution of this perspective is in emphasizing that children master language generally and grammar specifically in the context of social interactions (Bloom & Tinker, 2001). That is, much language learning takes place in the context of interactions between children and adults, with both parties eager for better communication. Children have an ever-expanding repertoire of ideas and intentions that they wish to convey to others, and caring adults want to understand their children, so both parties work to improve language skills as a means toward better communication. Thus, improved communication provides an incentive for children to master language and for adults to help them.

You can see the nature of these interactions in the following example, in which a child wants a cookie (after Hulit & Howard, 2002, pp. 37–38). Like the child in the photo, a nine-month-old who wants a cookie might point to it while looking at the mother. In turn, the mother gives the cookie, saying, "Here's the cookie." By age two, a child might say, "Gimme cookie, please?" with the mother responding, "Yes, I'll give you the cookie." At nine months and at two years, the child's desire to have the cookie motivates communication (pointing at nine months, spoken language at two years) and gives the mother opportunities to demonstrate more advanced forms of language.

None of these accounts, summarized in the Summary Table, provides a comprehensive account of how grammar is mastered. Many scientists believe the final explanation will include contributions from the linguistic, cognitive, and social-interaction accounts. That is, children's learning of grammar will be explained in terms of some mechanisms specific to learning grammar, children actively seeking to identify regularities in their environment, and from linguistically rich interactions between children and adults (MacWhinney, 1998).

According to the social-interaction account of language learning, children are eager to master grammar because it allows them to communicate their wishes and needs more effectively.

SUMMARY TABLE

DIFFERENT APPROACHES TO EXPLAINING CHILDREN'S ACQUISITION OF GRAMMAR

Approach	Children are Thought to Master Grammar . . .
Behaviourist	by imitating speech they hear.
Linguistic	with inborn mechanisms that allow children to infer the grammatical rules of their native language.
Cognitive	using powerful cognitive mechanisms that allow children to find recurring patterns in the speech they hear.
Social Interaction	in the context of social interactions with adults, in which both parties want improved communication.

Of course, many parents do not care much about theories of language, but they do want to know how they can help their children master grammar and other aspects of language. Adults eager to promote children's language development can follow a few guidelines:

1. *Talk with children frequently and treat them as partners in conversation*; try talking with children interactively, not directively.

PhotoAlto/Sandro Di Carlo Darsa/Getty Images.

2. *Use a child's speech to show new language forms.* Expand a child's remark to introduce new vocabulary or new grammatical forms. Rephrase an ungrammatical remark to show the correct grammar.

3. *Encourage children to go beyond minimal use of language* by having them answer in phrases and sentences, not single words. Have them replace vague words such as *stuff* or *somebody* with more descriptive ones.

4. *Listen.* This guideline has two parts. First, because children often talk slowly, it is tempting for adults to complete their sentences for them. Don't. Let children express themselves. Second, pay attention to what children are saying and respond appropriately. Let children learn that language works.

5. *Make language fun.* Use books, rhymes, songs, jokes, and foreign words to increase a child's interest in learning language.

Of course, as children's language improves during the preschool years, others can understand it more readily, which means that children become better at communicating. These emerging communication skills are described in the next module.

ANSWER 9.3
Saying "sleeped" instead of "slept" shows that Kelly knows the rule about adding *-ed* to a verb to make it the past tense. It also shows that children overgeneralize such rules—using them with verbs to which they don't apply.

 Check Your Learning

RECALL Describe the major milestones that mark children's progress from two-word speech to complex sentences.

What are the main accounts of how children master grammar?

INTERPRET How do the various explanations of grammatical development differ in their view of the child's role in mastering grammar?

APPLY How might the cognitive processes described in Chapter 7 help children learn grammar?

 9.4   Using Language to Communicate

OUTLINE
Taking Turns
Speaking Effectively
Listening Well

LEARNING OBJECTIVES
1. When and how do children learn to take turns in conversation?
2. What are the skills required to be an effective speaker?
3. What is involved in becoming a good listener?

Marla and Kitty, both nine-year-olds, usually are good friends, but right now they are boiling mad at each other. Marla was going to the store with her dad to buy some new markers. Kitty found out and gave Marla money to buy some markers for her, too. Marla returned with the markers, but they were not the kind that Kitty liked, so she was angry. Marla was angry because she did not think Kitty should be mad; after all, it was Kitty's fault for not telling her what kind to buy. Meanwhile, Marla's dad hopes they come to some understanding soon and stop all the shouting.

Imagining these girls arguing is an excellent way to learn what is needed for effective communication. Both talk at the same time; their remarks are rambling and incoherent; and neither bothers to listen to the other. For effective oral communication, these girls need to follow a few simple guidelines:

- People should take turns, alternating as speaker and listener.
- A speaker's remarks should relate to the topic and be understandable to the listener.
- A listener should pay attention and let the speaker know if his or her remarks don't make sense.

Complete mastery of these guidelines is a lifelong pursuit; after all, even adults often miscommunicate with one another because they do not observe one or more of these rules. However, in this module, we'll trace the development of effective communication skills and, along the way, discover why young children like Marla and Kitty sometimes fail to communicate.

Taking Turns

Many parents begin to encourage "turn-taking" long before infants say their first words. Parents such as the mother in the photo often structure a conversation around a baby's early sounds, even when those sounds lack any obvious communicative intent (Field & Widmayer, 1982):

parent:	Can you see the bird?
infant (cooing):	ooooh
parent:	It is a pretty bird.
infant:	ooooh
parent:	You're right. It's a cardinal.

Soon after one-year-olds begin to speak, parents encourage their youngsters to participate in conversational turn-taking. To help children along, parents often carry both sides of a conversation to demonstrate how the roles of speaker and listener alternate (Shatz, 1983):

| **parent (to infant):** | What's Amy eating? |
| **parent (illustrating reply):** | She's eating a cookie. |

Parents and other caregivers often work hard to allow infants and toddlers to "fit in" to a conversation. That is, caregivers scaffold youngsters' attempts to converse, making it more likely that children will succeed. Such early conversations between caregivers and infants are not universal, however. In some non-Western cultures, preverbal infants are not considered appropriate conversational partners, so adults do not talk to them. Only after infants are older do others begin to converse with them (Hoff, 2009).

When parents speak with young babies, they often alternate the roles of speaker and listener, showing conversational turn-taking.

ArtFamily/Fotolia

By age two, spontaneous turn-taking is common in conversations between youngsters and adults (Barton & Tomasello, 1991). By age three, children have progressed to the point that if a listener fails to reply promptly, the child will repeat a remark to elicit a response (Garvey & Berninger, 1981). A three-year-old might say, "Hi, Paul" to an older sibling who is busy reading. If Paul does not answer in a few seconds, the three-year-old might say, "Hi, Paul" again. When Paul remains unresponsive, the three-year-old is likely to shout, "PAUL!"—showing that, by this age, children understand the rule that a comment deserves a response. Preschool children seem to interpret the lack of a response as, "I guess you didn't hear me, so I'll say it again, louder!"

Speaking Effectively

When do children first try to initiate communication with others? In fact, what appear to be the first deliberate attempts to communicate typically emerge at 10 months (Golinkoff, 1993). Infants at this age may touch or point to an object while simultaneously looking at another person. They continue this behaviour until the person acknowledges them. It is as if the child is saying, "This is an awesome toy! I want you to see it, too."

Beginning at 10 months, an infant may point, touch, or make noises to get an adult to do something. In line with Piaget's theory of cognitive development, the infant becomes more purposive in behaviour. An infant, like the one in the photo, who wants something that is out of reach may make noises while pointing to the object. The noises capture an adult's attention, and the pointing indicates what the baby wants (Tomasello, Carpenter, & Liszkowski, 2007). The communication may be a bit primitive by adult standards, but it works for babies! And mothers typically translate their baby's pointing into words, so that gesturing paves the wave for learning words (Goldin-Meadow, Mylander, & Franklin, 2007).

After the first birthday, children begin to use speech to communicate and often initiate conversations with adults (Bloom, Margulis, Tinker, & Fujita, 1996). Toddlers' first conversations are about themselves, but their conversational scope expands rapidly to include objects in the environment (e.g., toys, food). Later, conversations begin to include more abstract notions, such as hypothetical objects and past or future events (Foster, 1986).

Of course, young children are not always skilled conversational partners. At times their communications are confusing, leaving a listener to wonder, "What was that all about?" Saying something clearly is often difficult because clarity can be judged only by considering the listener's age, experience, and knowledge of the topic, along with the context of the conversation. For example, think about the simple request, "Please hand me the Phillips-head screwdriver." This message may be clear to older listeners familiar with different types of screwdrivers, but it won't mean much to younger listeners who think all screwdrivers are alike. And, if the toolbox is filled with Phillips-head screwdrivers of assorted sizes, the message won't be clear even to a knowledgeable listener.

Constructing clear messages is a fine art, but, amazingly, by the preschool years, youngsters begin to adjust their messages to match the listener and the context. In a classic study (Shatz & Gelman, 1973), four-year-olds explained how a toy worked, once to a two-year-old and once to an adult. The four-year-olds talked more overall to adults than to two-year-olds, and used longer sentences with adult listeners than with two-year-old listeners. Also, when speaking with two-year-olds, children used simpler grammar and more attention-getting words, such as *see, look, watch,* and *hey.* Here, for example, is how one four-year-old child explained the toy to her two different

Even before children can speak, they make gestures to communicate with others.

Maya Barnes Johansen/The Image Works

Q&A   **QUESTION 9.4**
Shauna's older brother asked, "Where's your locker this year?" Shauna replied, "Next to Mrs. Rathert's room." When Shauna's grandmother, who lived in another city, asked the same question, Shauna's reply was much longer: "After you go in the front door, you turn left and go down a long hall until you get to some stairs. Then . . ." What feature of effective communication is shown in Shauna's two answers to the same question? *(Answer is on page 337.)*

listeners (the toy is a garage with drivers and trucks that carry marbles to a dumping station):

| TO ADULT LISTENER: | You're supposed to put one of these persons in, see? Then one goes with the other little girl. And then the little boy. He's the little boy and he drives. And then they back up. . . . And then the little girl falls out and then it goes backwards. |
| TO TWO-YEAR-OLD LISTENER: | Watch, Perry. Watch this. He's back in here. Now he drives up. Look, Perry. Look here, Perry. Those are marbles, Perry. Put the men in here. Now I'll do it. (Shatz & Gelman, 1973, p. 13) |

These findings show that preschoolers are already sensitive to characteristics of the listener in formulating a clear message. Subsequent findings also show that children consider the listener and setting in devising clear messages:

- *Preschool children give more elaborate messages to listeners* who lack critical information than to listeners who have the information (Nadig & Sedivy, 2002; O'Neill, 1996). For example, a child describing where to find a toy will give more detailed directions to a listener whose eyes were covered when the toy was hidden. Also, if a word's meaning might be ambiguous in the context of the conversation (e.g., bat as an animal versus a piece of sporting equipment), young children sometimes gesture to indicate the meaning (Kidd & Holler, 2009). And if a listener wants to complete a task without help, five-year-olds sometimes provide helpful information but conceal their intent to help, so that the listener thinks she has completed the task without assistance (Grosse, Scott-Phillips, & Tomasello, 2013).

- *School-age children speak differently to adults and peers.* They are more likely to speak politely with adults and be more demanding with peers (Anderson, 2000; Warren-Leubecker & Bohannon, 1989). A child might ask a parent, "May I have one of your cookies?" but say to a peer, "Give me one of your cookies."

- **In the United States, some African Americans speak** *African American English,* **a variant of standard U.S. English that has slightly different grammatical rules.** For example, "He be tired" in African American English is synonymous with "He usually is tired" in standard English. Many African American children learn both African American English and standard English, and they switch back and forth, using standard English more often in school and when talking with European Americans but using African American English more often at home and when talking with African American peers (Warren & McCloskey, 1993).

All these findings show that school-age children (and sometimes preschoolers) are well on their way to understanding the factors that must be considered in creating clear messages. From a surprisingly young age, children express themselves to others and adjust their conversations to fit listeners. Are young children equally adept at listening? We'll find out in the next section.

Listening Well

To listen well, a person must continuously decide whether a speaker's remarks make sense. If they do, then a listener needs to reply appropriately, typically by extending the conversation with another remark that is on topic. Otherwise, the listener needs to provide feedback that the speaker was confusing (e.g., "I don't get what you mean").

Few toddlers master these fundamental conversational skills. Their replies are more likely to be unrelated to the topic than related to it (Bloom, Rocissano, & Hood, 1976). Asked "Where's the sock?" a one-and-a-half-year-old might say something like "I'm hungry!" By three years of age, children are more adept at continuing conversations by making remarks that relate to the topic being discussed.

By four years of age, children sometimes realize that a message is vague or confusing (Nilsen & Graham, 2012), but they often don't ask speakers to clarify their intent. Instead, young listeners often assume that they know what the speaker had in mind (Beal & Belgrad, 1990).

Because young children's remarks often contain ambiguities, and because as listeners they often do not detect ambiguities, young children often miscommunicate, just like Marla and Kitty in the opening vignette. Kitty probably didn't communicate exactly what kind of markers she wanted, and Marla didn't understand that the directions were unclear. Throughout the elementary-school years, youngsters gradually master the many skills involved in determining whether a message is consistent and clear (Ackerman, 1993).

Sometimes messages are confusing because they conflict with what a listener thinks is true. For example, suppose a child is told that the family cat, which always stays indoors, has run away. Even preschoolers are more likely to believe such a message when told by a parent than by a classmate because they know the parent is better informed about this particular topic (Robinson, Champion, & Mitchell, 1999). By seven or eight years of age, children can be skeptical listeners—taking what a speaker says with a grain of salt—when, for example, a speaker has a vested interest in a topic. When a child announces to an entire class that her birthday party is going to be the "best one all year," school-age children believe her less than if they heard the information from an independent, third party (Mills & Keil, 2005).

Sometimes listeners must go beyond the words to understand the real meaning of a message. Metaphor is one example. When parents tell their teenagers, "Your bedroom is a junkyard," the remark is not to be taken literally but highlights the fact that the bedroom is a mess and filled with things that could be thrown away. Understanding nonliteral meanings of messages develops slowly (e.g., Dews et al., 1996). In the case of metaphor, young children easily understand simple metaphors in which the nonliteral meaning is based on references to concrete objects and their properties. For example, a parent might say to a five-year-old, "You're a fish," referring to how well the child swims and enjoys the water, and the child will likely understand.

More complex metaphors require that children make connections based on abstract relations. For example, in Shakespeare's *Romeo and Juliet*, Romeo proclaims that "Juliet is the sun." You might interpret this line to mean that Juliet is the centre of Romeo's universe or that without Juliet, Romeo will die. The first interpretation depends on your knowledge of astronomy; the second, on your knowledge of biology. Younger children lack this sort of knowledge to comprehend metaphors, so they try to interpret them literally. Only when children gain the necessary content knowledge do they understand metaphors based on abstract relations (Franquart-Declercq & Gineste, 2001).

Sarcasm is another form of communication that is not to be interpreted literally. When a soccer player misses the ball entirely and a teammate says, "Nice kick," the literal meaning of the remark is the opposite of the intended meaning. Like understanding of metaphor, understanding of sarcasm develops gradually (Creusere, 1999). When people emphasize their sarcasm by speaking in mocking or overly enthusiastic tones, school-age children can detect their meaning. However, if sarcasm must be detected solely from the context—by realizing that the comment is the opposite of what would be expected—only adolescents and adults are likely to understand the real meaning of the remark (Capelli, Nakagawa, & Madden, 1990).

Further research has shown that children's understanding of subtleties such as the difference between sarcasm and irony also develops across childhood. Melanie Glenwright of the University of Manitoba and Penny Pexman of the University of Calgary have investigated children's understanding of verbal sarcasm and irony (Glenwright & Pexman, 2010). Nine- to ten-year-olds and five- to six-year-olds were tested to see whether they could distinguish between the two types of remarks. After a puppet show where characters made sarcastic remarks (remarks aimed at a person) or ironic remarks (which are more aimed at objects), all children showed that they understood that such remarks were not meant to be taken literally. The nine- to 10-year-olds could make basic distinctions between the two types of remarks (although they still had some trouble explaining the difference), but the five- to six-year-olds could not, showing that understanding of the difference between the two types of remark develops gradually across childhood.

This discussion of listening skills completes our catalogue of the important accomplishments that take place in communication during childhood. As children enter kindergarten, they have mastered many of the fundamental rules of communication, and as they grow older, they acquire even greater proficiency.

 ANSWER 9.4
Shauna has changed her description to reflect her listener's knowledge. Her description is more elaborate for her grandmother (who is unfamiliar with her school) than for her brother (who knows it well).

 Check Your Learning

RECALL What findings illustrate that preschool children are sometimes effective speakers?

Summarize children's understanding of messages that are not meant to be taken literally.

INTERPRET What are the strengths and weaknesses of infants as communicators?

APPLY In Chapter 6, we saw that Piaget characterized preschool children as egocentric. Are the findings described in this module consistent with Piaget's view?

 9.5 **Signed Language and Gestural Communication**

OUTLINE	LEARNING OBJECTIVES
Using Gestures to Communicate	1. When and how do gestures count as communication?
Signed Language	2. How do signed languages operate?
Evidence for Language Development	3. What do signed languages tell us about language development?

A friend has given Jen a "baby sign" kit to use with Jen's six-month-old daughter, Michaela. Although the box for the kit proclaims that it "will let you talk to your baby before words!" Jen is confused. How can sign language come before words? Will it really do any good?

In several places throughout this chapter, we have noted evidence from studies of signed languages that support theories of language development. Now we will take a closer look at forms of communication that do not require speech.

Using Gestures to Communicate

We all use gestures to communicate—a shake of the head for "No," a wave of the hand to signal "Goodbye." And as noted earlier, babies will point at objects they want or to draw an adult's attention to something. People will use gestures on their own (e.g., thumbs up for "okay") and also gesture while speaking (Goldin-Meadow, 1999). These basic movements allow us to communicate to others. However, while gestures are *communication*, they are not *language*. Remember the criteria for language that we noted at the beginning of this chapter? Just as with the snarling dog, a head shake to indicate "No" does not fulfill the criteria for language—it cannot communicate more than the minimum of intention in the here and now.

As with other aspects of language, the desire to communicate is probably innate, but which gestures mean what has to be learned from those around us. Even Victor, the wild boy of Aveyron, mentioned earlier, used gestures to communicate (Carroll, 1999). Cultural differences in gestures show that specific gesture use is learned. In European countries, a handshake on meeting is customary. In Japan, people bow on meeting to indicate respect. These forms of communication are socially prescribed and learned as one grows up in a particular culture. In one country in Africa, a social situation has changed the use of a particular gesture. In 2003, during elections in Zimbabwe, people stopped waving to one another with an open hand (the usual hi there or goodbye wave) because an open hand was the symbol of one of the opposition parties, and waving in the usual manner could lead to reprisals from the ruling party for giving a political signal. Mothers began teaching children to wave bye-bye with a closed fist instead (Nolen, 2003). Gestures thus have meaning in the same way that words have meaning—because all speakers of a language agree on that meaning. The word "dog" indicates a certain animal, and so does *chien*; the words refer to the same animal, and speakers of English and of French all agree on the words' meanings. Shaking a fist at someone indicates anger to most Canadians, while waving a fist now means "Goodbye" to most Zimbabweans.

Signed Language

Sign languages such as American Sign Language (ASL) or Langue des Signes du Québec (LSQ) *are* true languages (e.g., Goldin-Meadow, 1999); the criteria for defining a language can be applied to sign languages. Although sign language has existed for centuries, it was not until the 1960s that researchers definitively showed that signed languages were languages (Bellugi & Klima, 1978). Until that time, it had been assumed that signed languages were simply a collection of mime and imitative gestures. Signs such as that shown in Figure 9-4 are part of a language, however. Let's look at how one sign language, ASL, fulfills the criteria for language:

1. It has arbitrary units and is therefore symbolic. A sign may imitate the thing that it represents—ASL has a high degree of *iconicity*, with the sign resembling the thing that it means (Carroll, 1999)—but many signs are arbitrary representations.

2. ASL is structured and meaningful. Although ASL does not follow the same grammatical structure as English, neither do many other languages in the world. English uses a subject-verb-object construction (SVO), and while ASL may do so, often the subject or object must come first. For example, in English one says "The cat ran up the tree." In ASL, this is signed as "Tree, cat, run up, finish" (with the "finish" modifier showing that the event happened in the past). Partly this reflects ASL's origins in France, and the influence of French language structure, but also, since ASL is a visuospatial language, the object has to be "placed" first so that the other signs then apply to it.

3. ASL shows displacement. ASL can be used to communicate about events distant in time and space. It is as easy to sign "Yesterday I went to the gym" or "Tomorrow I have Psych class" in ASL as it is to say this in a spoken language.

4. There is generativity. A signer can combine signs in any number of ways, provided that the basic linguistic structure of the sign language is followed. The grammatical structure of a signed language differs, with movement features often changing meaning or tense, but correct grammar exists for signed language just as with spoken language.

Learning sign language seems to proceed in the same way as learning speech, and the types of mistakes made in ASL and English are remarkably similar, even as one gains experience. Bellugi and colleagues have shown that, just as speakers make "slips of the tongue," signers make "slips of the hand" (Newkirk, Klima, Pedersen, & Bellugi, 1980; Emmorey, 2002). That these errors occur in similar ways for two quite different language systems (Carroll, 1999) suggests that language is a property of the human mind.

Figure 9-4 Gestural communication—the boy and the adult converse using ASL.

Evidence for Language Development

Evidence from studies of signed languages supports the construct of language as having a cognitive basis but at the same time being influenced by environment. Although most deaf children have hearing parents, some have Deaf parents (remember that capitalization of "Deaf" denotes a socio-cultural group). With the different situations that arise, we can study how language is—or is not—acquired in the presence or absence of linguistic input. As noted in several places in this chapter, research on such situations has provided supporting evidence for different aspects of language development.

One interesting type of sign users are Children of Deaf Adults (CODA). These children can hear, but their parents cannot; the children speak, but the parents use sign language to communicate. CODA children thus often grow up bilingual in a spoken and a signed language. Any child of Deaf parents grows up in an environment where sign language is present from birth, and infants learning sign language go through the same stages of language development as those of speech—they will babble in sign, produce one gesture, move to the two-gesture combination stage, and so on. A collaborative Canadian-U.S. study by Pettito et al. (2004) found that, as with Deaf infants, hearing babies learning sign language babble in sign. The study also showed that hand movements associated with language could be reliably differentiated from nonlinguistic hand movements. The similarity between sign babbling and speech babbling development allowed the researchers to conclude that babbling was thus a specific, linguistic activity.

In Module 9.3, we discussed the arguments in favour of the innateness of languages, and for a critical period for language development. We noted that some evidence for these concepts comes from studies of children who are deaf and their linguistic experience early in life. Working at McGill University, Rachel Mayberry and her colleagues

 QUESTION 9.5
Your hearing neighbours, who do not know sign language, have an infant, Rachael, who is deaf. While babysitting little Rachael, you notice that she regularly lifts her hand to her mouth when she is hungry. Can this gesture be considered language? *(Answer is on page 340.)*

compared language development in deaf and hearing people. It was found that those with some language experience in infancy, whether sign or speech, have higher levels of language proficiency (Mayberry, Lock, & Kazmi, 2002). Apparently infant language learning occurs in the same way for all those with early linguistic input, regardless of the *form* of that input (Lieberman, Borovsky, Hatrak, & Mayberry, 2015). Further support for the critical-period hypothesis comes from the case study of a boy who was deaf from birth and who had no sign language experience (Grimshawe, Adlestein, Bryden & McKinnon, 1995). The boy, "E.M.," was given hearing aids at age 15. Before that time, he had no language experience because he could not hear and had had no contact with the Deaf community. As with Genie, the isolated child, E.M. learned some verbal language but had great difficulty with grammatical structures.

Signing seems to be acquired earlier than speech in infants. It appears that this is because the large movements required by signs are easier and that infants are more likely producing gestures than referent signs (Carroll, 1999). Despite this qualification, however, signing with babies has become popular, with hearing parents of hearing babies attempting to foster early communication with ASL using "baby sign." (A friend of Anne Barnfield's tried ASL with her second child and swears that it made communicating with her infant son much simpler than with her daughter, her first child.) This popularity has even led to classes to teach parents sign language for babies. Such classes could be useful, and certainly get parents interacting with babies, but we should be cautious about expecting too much. What we can be sure of is that all healthy children, given exposure to linguistic input, will develop language and develop it in the same way.

 ANSWER 9.5

Although the gesture may be imitative (of eating), if Rachael regularly uses the same gesture in the same way to refer to one specific need, the gesture could be considered linguistic. Using the gesture to note that you, not she, may be hungry, or pairing it with a shake of the head to indicate not hungry, would provide further evidence of linguistic use. The infant may be beginning to develop a "home sign" language.

 Check Your Learning

RECALL Why is a gesture communication but not necessarily language?

Summarize evidence from studies of ASL that points to the necessity of linguistic input in infancy.

INTERPRET What are the main arguments for an innate aspect to language, and what are the arguments for the influence of environment?

APPLY Would you advise a parent to try to teach a baby sign language? Why or why not?

UNIFYING THEMES Connections

This chapter provides an appropriate opportunity to stress the theme that *development in different domains is connected*: Language has important connections to biological, cognitive, and social development. A link to biological development would be children's mastery of grammar: In ways that we don't yet fully understand, children seem to be endowed with a mechanism that smoothes the path to mastering grammar. A link to cognitive development would be children's first words: Speaking words (or signing for languages like ASL) reflects the cognitive insight that speech sounds (or signs) are symbols. A link to social development would be the communication skills that enable children to interact with peers and adults.

See for Yourself

Berko's (1958) "wugs" task is fun to try with preschool children. Obtain consent from parents and try this for yourself with some young children. Remember, as always, your ethical responsibilities and the children's right to dissent. Photocopy the drawing on page 326 and show it to a preschooler, repeating the instructions that appear on that page. You should find that the child quite predictably says, "two wugs." Create some pictures of your own to examine other grammatical morphemes, such as adding -ing to denote ongoing activity or adding -ed to indicate past tense. See for yourself!

Resources

For more information about . . .

how children master language in the first three years of life, read Roberta M. Golinkoff and Kathy Hirsch-Pasek's *How Babies Talk: The Magic and Mystery of Language in the First Three Years of Life* (Dutton/Penguin, 1999).

American Sign Language (ASL), visit the American Sign Language browser, http://commtechlab.msu.edu/sites/aslweb/browser.htm.

Key Terms

African American English 335
allophone 322
babbling 310
cochlear implant 309
cooing 310
creole 329
expressive style 319
fast mapping 313
grammatical morphemes 326

infant-directed speech 307
intonation 310
language 303
morphology 304
naming explosion 312
overextension 316
over-regularization 326
phonemes 305
phonological memory 317

phonology 304
pidgin 329
pragmatics 304
referential style 318
semantic bootstrapping theory 327
semantics 304
syntax 304
telegraphic speech 325
underextension 316

Summary

9.1 The Road to Speech

1. Elements of Language

Language includes five distinct elements: phonology (sounds), morphology (rules of meaning), semantics (word meaning), syntax (rules for language structure), and pragmatics (rules for communication).

2. Perceiving Speech

Phonemes are the basic units of sound that make up words. Infants can hear phonemes soon after birth. They can even hear phonemes that are not used in their native language, but this ability is lost by the first birthday. Before they speak, infants can recognize words, apparently by noticing stress and syllables that go together. Infants prefer infant-directed speech—adult speech that is directed at infants, is slower, and has greater variation in pitch—because it provides them with additional language clues.

3. First Steps to Speech

Newborns are limited to crying to communicate, but at about three months of age babies begin to coo. Babbling soon follows and consists of a single syllable; over several months, babbling includes longer syllables and intonation.

9.2 Learning the Meanings of Words

1. Understanding Words as Symbols

Children's first words represent a cognitive accomplishment that is not specific to language. Instead, the onset of language is due to a child's ability to interpret and use symbols. Consistent with this view are parallel developments in the use of gestures and in the use of signs for those learning signed languages.

2. Fast Mapping Meanings to Words

Most children learn the meanings of words too rapidly for them to be considering all plausible meanings systematically. Instead, children use a number of fast-mapping rules to determine probable meanings of new words. Joint attention, constraints, sentence cues, and cognitive skills all help children learn words. The rules do not always lead to the correct meaning. An underextension denotes a child's meaning that is narrower than an adult's meaning; an overextension denotes a child's meaning that is broader.

3. Individual Differences in Word Learning

Individual children differ in vocabulary size; these differences are attributable to phonological memory and the quality of the child's language environment. Some youngsters use a referential word-learning style that emphasizes words as names and views language as an intellectual tool. Other children use an expressive style that emphasizes phrases and views language as a social tool.

4. Encouraging Word Learning

Children's word learning is fostered by experience, including being read to, watching television, and, for school-age children, reading to themselves. The key ingredient is making children think about the meanings of new words.

5. Beyond Words: Other Symbols

As children learn language, they also learn about other symbol systems. The understanding of signed languages by Deaf children parallels the understanding of words as symbols by the hearing. By 18 months, toddlers understand that photos are representations of other objects; by three years, children understand that a scale model is a representation of an identical but larger object. Preschoolers can use simple maps.

9.3 Speaking in Sentences

1. From Two-Word Speech to Complex Sentences

Not long after their first birthday, children produce two-word sentences that are based on simple rules for expressing ideas or needs. These sentences are sometimes called "telegraphic" because they use the fewest possible words to convey meaning. Moving from two-word to more complex sentences involves adding grammatical morphemes. Children first master grammatical morphemes that express simple relations, then those that denote complex relations.

As children acquire grammatical morphemes, they also extend their speech to other sentence forms, such as questions, and later to more complex constructions, such as passive sentences.

2. How Do Children Acquire Grammar?

Behaviourists proposed that children acquire grammar through imitation, but that explanation is incorrect. Today's explanations come from three perspectives. The nativist perspective emphasizes inborn mechanisms that allow children to infer the grammatical rules of their native language; the cognitive perspective emphasizes cognitive processes that allow children to find recurring patterns in the speech they hear; and the social-interaction perspective emphasizes social interactions with adults in which both parties want improved communication.

9.4 Using Language to Communicate

1. Taking Turns

Parents encourage turn-taking even before infants talk and later demonstrate both the speaker and listener roles for their children. By age three, children spontaneously take turns and prompt one another to speak.

2. Speaking Effectively

Before they can speak, infants use gestures and noises to communicate. During the preschool years, children gradually become more skilled at constructing clear messages, in part by adjusting their speech to fit their listeners' needs. They also begin to monitor their listeners' comprehension, repeating messages if necessary.

3. Listening Well

Toddlers are not good conversationalists because their remarks do not relate to the topic. Preschoolers are unlikely to identify ambiguities in another's speech. Also, they sometimes have difficulty understanding messages that are not meant to be taken literally, such as metaphor and sarcasm.

9.5 Signed Language and Gestural Communication

1. Using Gestures to Communicate

Gestures are used every day to communicate in a simple way, but they lack the criteria for language. Specific gestures are influenced by culture and learned as one grows up in a particular society, and their meanings rely on agreement by members of that society.

2. Signed Language

Signed languages are more than simple gestures or mimicking since they fulfill all the criteria for true language. Similarity in developmental learning and in mistakes made in signed and spoken languages imply that language is a property of the human mind.

3. Evidence for Language Development

Different situations that arise with hearing, deaf, and Deaf people allow comparisons of language development. Both sign and speech develop in similar ways and show a similar requirement for early exposure to language to develop, whatever the modality.

Test Yourself

1. Newborns can hear a wide range of language sounds, but by the first birthday infants readily distinguish only those sounds _____.

2. To pick out individual words from a steady stream of speech, infants use _____, knowledge of what phonemes sound good together and where they appear in words, and familiar function words.

3. In _____, adults speak slowly and with exaggerated changes in pitch and loudness.

4. During the first year, babbling becomes progressively more language-like, and at about 8 to 11 months sounds like real speech because _____.

5. A child's first word probably reflects the child's mastery of symbols because _____.

6. At about 18 months children experience a _____: They start to learn new words much more rapidly than before.

7. _____ and the child's language environment contribute to individual differences in the size of children's vocabulary.

8. There are many ways that parents can help infants to learn new words (e.g., reading books to them), but _____ is not one of them.

9. The benefits of bilingualism include greater understanding of the symbolic nature of language and _____.

10. In the telegraphic speech that is common among one-and-a-half-year-olds, children _____.

11. Overregularizations in children's speech (e.g., "I goed to the store") show that children master grammar by _____.

12. The development of grammar includes contributions from language-specific processes, cognitive skills, and _____.

13. An example of preschoolers' communicative skill is that when talking with younger children, four-year-olds _____.

14. Simple gestures can be _____ but not language.

15. Similarities in development of signed languages and speech give evidence for _____ of language.

Answers: (1) that are meaningful in their own language; (2) stress cues; (3) infant-directed speech; (4) it mimics the intonation patterns of the infant's native language; (5) children begin to use other symbols, such as gestures, at about the same time that they start to speak; (6) naming explosion; (7) Phonological memory; (8) showing them infant-oriented language videos; (9) greater skill at task-switching and inhibiting inappropriate responses; (10) include only words that are directly relevant to meaning; (11) learning rules; (12) social interaction; (13) use simpler grammar and more attention-getting words; (14) communication; (15) innateness.

10

Emotional Development

Echo/Juice Images/Getty Images

 10.1

Emerging Emotions

 10.2

Temperament

 10.3

Attachment

If you're a fan of *Star Trek*, you know that Mr. Spock shows little emotion because he is half Vulcan, and people from the planet Vulcan do not express emotions. Few of us would like to live an emotionless life like Mr. Spock because feelings enrich our lives. As partial testimony to their importance, the English language has more than 500 words that refer to emotions (Averill, 1980). Joy, happiness, satisfaction, and yes, anger, guilt, and humiliation are just a few of the feelings that give life meaning.

In this chapter, we'll see how emotions emerge and how they affect development. In **Module 10.1**, we'll discuss when children first express different emotions and recognize emotions in others. In **Module 10.2**, we'll see that children have different behavioural styles and that these styles are rooted, in part, in emotions. Finally, in **Module 10.3**, we'll examine the infant's first emotional relationship, the one that develops with the primary caregiver.

 10.1 **Emerging Emotions**

OUTLINE	LEARNING OBJECTIVES
The Function of Emotions	**1.** Why do people "feel"? Why do they have emotions?
Experiencing and Expressing Emotions	**2.** At what ages do children begin to experience and express different emotions?
Recognizing and Using Others' Emotions	**3.** When do children begin to understand other people's emotions? How do they use this information to guide their own behaviour?
Regulating Emotions	**4.** When do children show evidence of regulating emotion, and why is this an important skill?

Nicole was ecstatic that she was finally going to see her seven-month-old nephew, Claude. She rushed into the house and, seeing Claude playing on the floor with blocks, swept him up in a big hug. After a brief, puzzled look, Claude burst into angry tears and began thrashing around, as if saying to Nicole, "Who are you? What do you want? Put me down! Now!" Nicole quickly handed Claude to his mother, who was surprised by her baby's outburst and even more surprised that he continued to sob while she rocked him.

This vignette illustrates three common emotions. Nicole's initial joy, Claude's anger, and his mother's surprise are familiar to all of us. In this module, we'll begin by discussing *why* people have feelings at all. Then we'll look at when children first express emotions, how children come to understand emotions in others, and, finally, how children regulate their emotions. As we do, we'll learn why Claude reacted to Nicole as he did, and how Nicole could have prevented Claude's outburst.

Raise a cyber child and discover the world of parenthood at …

My Virtual Child

The Function of Emotions

Why do people feel emotions? Wouldn't life be simpler if people were emotionless like computers or residents of Mr. Spock's Vulcan? No, probably not. Think, for example, about activities that most adults find pleasurable: a good meal, sex, holding their children, and accomplishing a difficult but important task. These activities were and remain essential to the continuity of humans as a species, so it's not surprising that we find them pleasant (Gaulin & McBurney, 2001).

Modern theories emphasize the functional value of emotion. According to the functional approach, emotions are useful because they help people adapt to their environment (Boiger & Mesquita, 2012; Shariff & Tracy, 2011). Take fear, as an example. Most of us would rather not be afraid, but there are instances in which feeling fearful is very adaptive. Imagine you are walking alone, late at night, in a poorly lighted section of campus. You become frightened and, as a consequence, are particularly attentive to sounds that might signal the presence of threat, and you probably walk quickly to a safer location. Thus, fear is adaptive because it organizes your behaviour around an important goal—avoiding danger (Tooby & Cosmides, 2008).

Similarly, other emotions are adaptive. Happiness, for example, is adaptive in contributing to stronger interpersonal relationships: When someone is happy with another person, they smile, and this often causes the other person to feel happy too, strengthening the relationship (Izard & Ackerman, 2000). Disgust is adaptive in keeping people away from substances that might make them ill: When we find that the milk in a glass is sour, we experience disgust and push the glass away (Oaten, Stevenson, & Case, 2009). Thus, in the functional approach, most emotions developed over the course of human history to meet unique life challenges and help humans to survive.

Experiencing and Expressing Emotions

DEVELOPMENT OF BASIC EMOTIONS. The three emotions in the opening vignette—happiness, anger, and surprise—are considered "basic emotions," as are the emotions of interest, disgust, sadness, and fear (Draghi-Lorenz, Reddy, & Costall, 2001). *Basic emotions* **are experienced by people everywhere, and each consists of three elements: a subjective feeling, a physiological change, and an overt behaviour** (Izard, 2007). For example, suppose you wake to the sound of a thunderstorm and then discover your roommate has left for class with your umbrella. Subjectively, you might feel a jolt of anger; physiologically, your heart would beat faster; and behaviourally, you would probably be scowling.

Social smiles emerge at two to three months of age and seem to express an infant's happiness at interacting with others.

Using facial expressions and other overt behaviours, scientists have traced the growth of basic emotions in infants. Many scientists believe that young babies simply experience broad positive and broad negative emotional states (Camras & Fatani, 2008). These broad emotional categories differentiate rapidly and by approximately six months of age, infants are thought to experience all basic emotions (Lewis, 2008). The onset of happiness, for example, is evident in a baby's smiles. In the first month, infants may smile while asleep or when touched softly. The meaning of these smiles isn't clear; they may just represent a reflexive response to bodily states. However, an important change occurs at about two to three months of age. *Social smiles* **first appear: Infants smile when they see another person.** As with the baby in the photo, the social smile seems to reflect the infant's pleasure in simple interactions with others. When smiling, they sometimes coo (the early form of vocalization described in Module 9.1) and they may move their arms and legs to express excitement.

Anger is one of the first negative emotions to emerge from generalized distress, and it typically does so between four and six months. Infants become angry, for example, if a favourite food or toy is taken away (Sullivan & Lewis, 2003). Reflecting their growing understanding of goal-directed behaviour (see Module 6.1), infants also become angry when their attempts to achieve a goal are frustrated (Braungart-Rieker, Hill-Soderlund, & Karrass, 2010). For example, if a parent restrains an infant trying to pick up a toy, the guaranteed result is a very angry baby.

Like anger, fear emerges later in the first year. **At about six months of age, infants become wary in the presence of an unfamiliar adult, a reaction known as** *stranger wariness.* When a stranger approaches, a six-month-old typically looks away and begins to fuss (Mangelsdorf, Shapiro, & Marzolf, 1995). The baby in the photo is showing the signs of stranger wariness. The grandmother has picked him up without giving him a chance to warm up to her, and the outcome is as predictable as it was with Claude, the baby in the vignette who was frightened by his aunt: He cries, looks frightened, and reaches with arms outstretched in the direction of someone familiar.

Fear of strangers increases over the first two years, but how wary an infant feels around strangers depends on a number of factors (Brooker et al., 2013; Thompson & Limber, 1991). First, infants tend to be less fearful of strangers when the environment is familiar, and more fearful when it is not. Infants are less afraid of strangers whom they see at home than strangers they see when visiting someone for the first time. Second, the amount of anxiety depends on the stranger's behaviour. Instead of rushing to greet or pick up the baby, as Nicole did in the vignette, a stranger should talk with other adults and, in a while, perhaps offer the baby a toy (Mangelsdorf, 1992). If the situation is handled this way, many infants will soon become curious about the stranger instead of afraid.

Wariness of strangers is adaptive because it emerges at the same time that children begin to master creeping and crawling (described in Module 5.3). Like Curious George, the monkey in a famous series of children's books, babies are inquisitive and want to use their new locomotor skills to explore their worlds. Being wary of strangers provides a natural restraint against the tendency to wander away from familiar caregivers. However, as youngsters learn to interpret facial expressions and recognize when a person is friendly, their wariness of strangers declines.

Of the negative emotions, we know the least about disgust. Preschool children may respond with disgust at the odour of feces or at being asked to touch a maggot or being asked to eat a piece of candy that is resting on the bottom of a brand-new potty seat (Widen & Russell, 2013). Parents likely play an important role in helping children to identify disgusting stimuli: Mothers respond quite vigorously to disgust-eliciting stimuli when in the presence of their children. They might say, "That's revolting!" while moving away from the stimulus (Stevenson, Oaten, Case, Repacholi, & Wagland, 2010). This early sensitivity to disgust is useful because many of the cues that elicit disgust are also signals of potential harm: Disgusting stimuli such as feces, vomit, and maggots can all transmit disease.

EMERGENCE OF COMPLEX EMOTIONS. In addition to basic emotions such as happiness and anger, people feel complex emotions such as pride, shame, guilt, and embarrassment. **Sometimes known as the** *self-conscious emotions,* **these emotions involve feelings of success when standards or expectations are met, and feelings of failure when they are not.** These emotions do not surface until 18 to 24 months of age because they depend on the child's having some understanding of the self, which typically occurs between 15 and 18 months. Children feel guilty, for example, when they've done something they know they should not have done (Kochanska, Gross, Lin, & Nichols, 2002). A child who breaks a toy thinks, "You told me to be careful, but I wasn't!" A child may show embarrassment at being asked to "perform"

By six months of age, infants are wary of strangers and often become upset when they encounter people they don't know, particularly when strangers rush to greet or hold them.

Photospower/iStock/Getty Images

Myrleen Fergueson Cate/PhotoEdit

By 18 to 24 months of age, children start to experience complex emotions, including pride in accomplishing a difficult task.

SUMMARY TABLE			
INFANTS' EXPRESSION OF EMOTIONS			
Type	**Defined**	**Emerge**	**Examples**
Basic	Experienced by people worldwide; include a subjective feeling, a physiological response, and an overt behaviour	Birth to nine months	Happiness, anger, fear
Complex (self-conscious)	Responses to meeting or failing to meet expectations or standards	18 to 24 months	Pride, guilt, embarrassment

for grandparents by burying his face in his hands. However, children feel pride when they accomplish a challenging task for the first time. The toddler in the photo is probably thinking something like, "I've never done this before, but this time I did it—all by myself!" Thus, children's growing understanding of themselves (which we discuss in detail in Module 11.1) allows them to experience complex emotions like pride and guilt (Lewis, 2000).

The features of basic and complex emotions are summarized in the accompanying Summary Table.

LATER DEVELOPMENTS. As children grow, their catalogue of emotions continues to expand. For example, think about regret and relief, emotions that adults experience when they compare their actions with alternatives. Imagine, for example, that you are cramming for a test and decide that you have time to review your lecture notes but not re-read the text. If the test questions turned out to be based largely on the lectures, you feel a sense of relief because your decision led to a positive outcome compared to "what might have been." If, however, the test questions cover only the text, you feel regret because your decision led to a terrible outcome: "If only I had re-read the text!" In fact, some five- and six-year-olds experience regret and relief, and by nine years of age, most children experience both emotions appropriately (Van Duijvenvoorde, Huizenga, & Jansen, 2014).

In addition to adding emotions to their repertoire, older children experience basic and complex emotions in response to different situations or events. In the case of complex emotions, cognitive growth means that elementary-school children experience shame and guilt in situations where they would not have when they were younger (Reimer, 1996). For example, unlike preschool children, many school-age children would be ashamed if they neglected to defend a classmate who had been wrongly accused of something.

Fear is another emotion that can be elicited in different ways, depending on a child's age. Many preschool children are afraid of the dark and of imaginary creatures. These fears typically diminish during the elementary-school years as children grow cognitively and better understand the difference between appearance and reality. Replacing these fears are concerns about school, health, and personal harm (Silverman, La Greca, & Wasserstein, 1995). Such worries are common and not cause for concern in most children. In some youngsters, however, they become so extreme that they overwhelm the child (Chorpita & Barlow, 1998). For example, a seven-year-old's worries about school would not be unusual unless her concern grew to the point that she refused to go to school. Many youngsters plead, argue, and fight with their parents daily over going to school. Understanding the reasons for such school refusal behaviour is essential because, not surprisingly,

QUESTION 10.1
Katrina often expresses her joy, anger, and fear but has yet to show pride, guilt, or embarrassment. Based on this profile, how old do you think Katrina is? *(Answer is on page 353.)*

refusing to go to school puts children on a path that leads to academic failure and leaves them with few options in the workplace. School refusal behaviour sometimes reflects a child's desire to avoid school-related situations that are frightening (e.g., taking a test, speaking in front of a class, meeting new people). School refusal is sometimes an effort to get attention from parents and sometimes reflects a child's desire to pursue enjoyable activities, such as playing video games, instead of aversive ones, such as doing schoolwork (Kearney, 2007).

Once valid external threats such as bullying have been ruled out, parents might consider getting help from a therapist. Fortunately, school refusal behaviour can be treated effectively, typically with a combination of behavioural and cognitive strategies (Pina, Zerr, Gonzales, & Ortiz, 2009). The former include gradual exposure to fear-provoking school situations, techniques for relaxing when confronting these situations, and reinforcement for attending school. The latter include providing children with strategies for coping with their anxiety and helping them reinterpret school situations (e.g., realize that teachers are not picking on them). In addition, parents can be trained to establish effective morning routines and reward school attendance (Kearney, Haight, Gauger, & Schafer, 2011). With use of these techniques, school refusal becomes much less common. In one meta-analysis (Pina et al., 2009), school attendance increased from 30 percent before treatment to 75 percent after. What's more, children's other school-related fears were much reduced.

CULTURAL DIFFERENCES IN EMOTIONAL EXPRESSION. Children worldwide express many of the same basic and complex emotions. However, cultures differ in the extent to which emotional expression is encouraged (Hess & Kirouac, 2000). In many Asian countries, for example, outward displays of emotion are discouraged in favour of emotional restraint. Consistent with these differences, in one study (Camras et al., 1998), European American 11-month-olds cried and smiled more often than Chinese 11-month-olds. In another study (Camras, Chen, Bakeman, Norris, & Cain 2006), American preschoolers were more likely than Chinese preschoolers to smile at funny pictures and to express disgust after smelling a cotton swab dipped in vinegar.

Cultures also differ in the events that trigger emotions, particularly complex emotions. Situations that evoke pride in one culture may evoke embarrassment or shame in another. For example, North American elementary-school children often show pride in personal achievement, such as getting the highest mark on a test or winning a spelling bee. In contrast, Asian elementary-school children are embarrassed by a public display of individual achievement but show great pride when their entire class is honoured for an achievement (Furukawa, Tangney, & Higashibara, 2012; Lewis, Takai-Kawakami, Kawakami, & Sullivan 2010).

Expression of anger also varies around the world. Imagine that one child has just completed a detailed drawing when a classmate spills a drink on it, ruining it completely. Most North American children would respond with anger. In contrast, children growing up in Asian countries that practise Buddhism (e.g., Mongolia, Thailand, Nepal) rarely respond with anger because this goes against the Buddhist tenet to extend loving kindness to all people, even those whose actions hurt others (Cole, Tamang, & Shrestha, 2006).

Thus culture can influence when and how much children express emotion. Of course, expressing emotion is only part of the developmental story. Children must also learn to recognize others' emotions, which is our next topic.

Children living in Canada, the United States, and Europe often express great pride in personal achievement.

Hill Street Studios/Tetra Images/Alamy Stock Photo

Recognizing and Using Others' Emotions

Imagine that you are broke and plan to borrow $20 from your roommate when she returns from class. Shortly, she storms into your apartment, slams the door, and throws her backpack on the floor. Immediately, you change your plans, realizing that now is hardly a good time to ask for a loan. This example reminds us that, just as it is adaptive to be able to express emotions, it is also adaptive to be able to recognize others' emotions and sometimes change our behaviour as a consequence.

When can infants first identify emotions in others? Perhaps as early as four months of age and definitely by six months, infants begin to distinguish facial expressions associated with different emotions. They can, for example, distinguish a happy, smiling face from a sad, frowning face (Bornstein & Arterberry, 2003; Montague & Walker-Andrews, 2001) and when they hear happy-sounding voices, they tend to look at happy faces, not ones that appear frustrated or angry (Vaillant-Molina, Bahrick, & Flom, 2013). In addition, fearful, happy, and neutral faces elicit different patterns of electrical activity in the infant's brain (Leppanen, Moulson, Vogel-Farley, & Nelson, 2007), which also shows the ability to differentiate facial expressions of emotion. What's more, like adults, infants are biased toward negative emotions (Vaish, Woodward, & Grossmann, 2008); they attend more rapidly to faces depicting negative emotions (e.g., anger) and pay attention to them longer than emotionless or happy faces (LoBue & DeLoache, 2010; Peltola et al., 2008).

Also like adults, infants use others' emotions to direct their behaviour. **Infants in an unfamiliar or ambiguous environment often look at their caregiver, as if searching for cues to help them interpret the situation, a phenomenon known as** *social referencing.* If a parent looks afraid when shown a novel object, 12-month-olds are less likely to play with the toy than if a parent looks happy (Repacholi, 1998). Infants' use of their parents' cues is precise. If two unfamiliar toys are shown to a parent who expresses disgust at one toy but not the other, 12-month-olds will avoid the toy that elicited the disgust but not the other toy (Moses, Baldwin, Rosicky, & Tidball, 2001). And if 12-month-olds encounter an unfamiliar toy in a laboratory setting where one adult seems familiar with the toy but another adult does not, infants will look at the knowledgeable adult's expression to decide whether to play with the toy (Stenberg, 2012). By 18 months of age, children's understanding is even more sophisticated: When one adult demonstrates an unfamiliar toy and a second adult comments, in an angry tone, "That's really annoying! That's so irritating!" 18-month-olds play less with the toy compared to when the second adult makes neutral remarks in a mild manner. These youngsters apparently decided that it was not such a good idea to play with the toy if it might upset the second adult again (Repacholi & Meltzoff, 2007; Repacholi, Meltzoff, & Olsen, 2008). Thus the research on social referencing shows that infants are remarkably skilled in using their other people's emotions to help them direct their own behaviour. From these beginnings, expressions of emotion are recognized with steadily greater skill throughout childhood and into adolescence.

UNDERSTANDING EMOTIONS.   As their cognitive skills grow, children begin to understand *why* people feel as they do. By kindergarten, for example, children know that undesirable or unpleasant events often make a person feel angry or sad (Lagattuta, 2014). Children even know that they more often feel sad when they think about the undesirable event itself (e.g., a broken toy or a friend who moves away), but feel angry when they think about the person who caused the undesirable event (e.g., the person who broke the toy or the friend's parents who wanted to live in another city). Kindergarten children also understand that a child who is feeling sad or angry may do less well on school tasks like spelling or math (Amsterlaw, Lagattuta, & Meltzoff, 2009) and that people worry when faced with the possibility that an unpleasant event may recur (Lagattuta, 2014).

During the elementary-school years, children begin to comprehend that people sometimes experience "mixed feelings." They understand that some situations may lead people, for example, to feel happy and sad at the same time (Larsen, To, & Fireman, 2007). The increased ability to see multiple, differing emotions coincides with the freedom from the centred thinking that characterizes the concrete operational stage (Module 6.1).

As children develop, they also begin to learn *display rules,* **culturally specific standards for appropriate expressions of emotion in a particular setting or with a particular person or persons.** Adults know, for example, that expressing sadness is appropriate at funerals but expressing joy is not. Preschool children's understanding of display rules is shown by the fact that they control their anger more when provoked by peers they like than when provoked by peers they do not like (Fabes et al., 1996). Also, school-age children and adolescents are more willing to express anger than sadness and, like the child in the photo, more willing to express both anger and sadness to parents than to peers (Zeman & Garber, 1996; Zeman & Shipman, 1997). These display rules vary across culture: Compared with children growing up in Asian cultures, children living in Western cultures are encouraged to express their emotions more (Novin, Rieffe, Banerjee, Miers, & Cheung, 2011).

What experiences contribute to children's understanding of emotions? Parents and children frequently talk about past emotions and why people felt as they did; this is particularly true for negative emotions such as fear and anger (Lagattuta & Wellman, 2002). Not surprisingly, children learn about emotions by hearing parents talk about feelings, explaining how they differ and the situations that elicit them (Brown & Dunn, 1996; Kucirkova & Tompkins, 2014). Also, a positive, rewarding relationship with parents and siblings is related to children's understanding of emotions (Brown & Dunn, 1996; Thompson, Laible, & Ontai, 2003). The nature of this connection is still a mystery. One possibility is that within positive parent-child and sibling relationships, people express a fuller range of emotions (and do so more often) and are more willing to talk about why they feel as they do, providing children more opportunities to learn about emotions.

Children's growing understanding of emotions in others contributes in turn to a growing ability to help others. They are more likely to recognize the emotions that signal a person's need. Better understanding of emotions in others also contributes to children's growing ability to play easily with peers because they can see the impact of their behaviour on others. We'll cover empathy and social interaction in detail later in the text; for now, the important point is that recognizing emotions in others is an important prerequisite for successful, satisfying interactions. Another element of successful interactions is regulating emotions, our next topic.

As children develop, they learn their culture's rules for expressing emotions. For example, many children living in North America might cry in private or with parents but would avoid crying in public, particularly when with their peers.

Jupiterimages/Creatas/Getty Images

Regulating Emotions

Think of a time when you were *really* angry at a good friend. Did you shout at the friend? Did you try to discuss matters calmly? Or did you ignore the situation altogether? Shouting is a direct expression of anger, but calm conversation and overlooking a situation are deliberate attempts to regulate emotion. People often regulate emotions: We routinely try to suppress fear (e.g., we know there is no real need to be afraid of the dark), anger (e.g., we really don't want to let a friend know just how upset we are), and joy (e.g., we don't want to seem like we're gloating about our good fortune).

As these examples illustrate, regulating emotions skillfully depends on cognitive processes such as those described in Chapters 6 through 9 (Zelazo & Cunningham, 2007). Attention is an important part of emotion regulation: We can control emotions such as fear by diverting attention to other less emotional stimuli, thoughts, or feelings (Rothbart & Sheese, 2007). We can also use strategies to reappraise the meaning of an event (or of feelings or thoughts), so that it provokes less emotion (John & Gross, 2007). For example, a soccer player nervous about taking a penalty kick can reinterpret her state of physiological arousal as being "pumped up" instead of being "scared to death."

Because cognitive processes are essential for emotional regulation, the research described in Chapters 6 through 9 would lead us to expect that successful regulation develops gradually through childhood and adolescence and that at any age some children will be more skilled than others are at regulating emotions (Thompson, Lewis, & Calkins, 2008). In fact, both patterns are evident in research. Emotion regulation clearly begins in infancy. By four to six months of age, infants use simple strategies to regulate their emotions (Buss & Goldsmith, 1998; Rothbart & Rueda, 2005). When something frightens or confuses an infant—for example, the appearance of a stranger, or a mother who suddenly stops responding—he or she often looks away (just as older children and even adults might turn away or close their eyes to block out disturbing stimuli). Frightened infants also move closer to a parent, another effective way of helping to control their fear (Parritz, 1996). Of course, because infants and toddlers have limited ability to regulate their emotions, parents and other caregivers often help: As we saw in Module 3.4, holding, rocking, and talking softly are effective in soothing an infant who is upset (Jahromi, Putnam, & Stifter, 2004).

As children develop, they regulate their own emotions and rely less on others. For example, if preschool children are asked to wait to open a present until their mother finishes a task, they may entertain themselves (e.g., making faces in a mirror) to control their frustration at having to wait (Roben, Cole, & Armstrong, 2013). School-age children and adolescents are even more skilled at regulating emotions, in part because they can rely on cognitive strategies. For example, a child might reduce his disappointment at not receiving a much-anticipated and hoped-for gift by telling himself that he didn't really want the gift in the first place. Older children and adolescents become skilled at matching the strategies for regulating emotion to the particular setting (Zimmer-Gembeck & Skinner, 2011). For example, when faced with emotional situations that are unavoidable, such as going to the dentist to have a cavity filled, children adjust to the situation (e.g., by thinking of the positive consequences of treating the tooth) instead of trying to avoid it

Some children regulate their emotions better than others, and those who do not, will tend to have problems interacting with peers and have adjustment problems (Olson, Lopez-Duran, Lunkenheimer, Chang, & Sameroff, 2011; Zalewski, Lengua, Wilson, Trancik, & Bazinet, 2011). When children cannot control their anger, worry, or sadness, they often have difficulty resolving the conflicts that inevitably surface in peer relationships (Fabes et al., 1999). For example, when children argue over which game to play or which movie to watch, their unregulated anger can interfere with finding a mutually satisfying solution. Thus, ineffective regulation of emotions leads to more frequent conflicts with peers and, consequently, less satisfying peer relationships and less adaptive adjustment to school (Eisenberg et al., 2001; Olson, Sameroff, Kerr, Lopez, & Wellman, 2005).

In this module, we've seen how children express, recognize, and regulate emotions; in the next module, we'll discover that emotion is an important feature of children's temperament.

 # Check Your Learning

RECALL Describe biological and cultural contributions to children's expression of emotion.

How do infants and children regulate their emotions? What are the consequences when children cannot regulate their emotions well?

INTERPRET Distinguish basic emotions from complex (self-conscious) emotions.

APPLY Cite similarities between developmental change in infants' expression and regulation of emotion, and developmental change in infants' comprehension and expression of speech (described in Module 9.1).

 # 10.2 Temperament

OUTLINE	LEARNING OBJECTIVES
What Is Temperament?	**1.** What are the different features of temperament?
Hereditary and Environmental Contributions to Temperament	**2.** How do heredity and environment influence temperament?
Stability of Temperament	**3.** How stable is a child's temperament across childhood?
Temperament and Other Aspects of Development	**4.** What are the consequences of different temperaments?

Soon after Yoshimi arrived in Canada from Japan to begin graduate studies, she enrolled her five-month-old son in daycare. She was struck by the fact that, compared to her son, the European Canadian babies in the daycare centre were "wimps" (slang she had learned from North American television). The other babies cried often and with minimal provocation. Yoshimi wondered whether her son was unusually tough or whether he was just a typical Japanese baby.

When you were observing young babies—perhaps as part of the See for Yourself feature in Chapter 3— were some of them like Yoshimi's, quiet most of the time, while others cried often and impatiently? Maybe you saw some infants who responded warmly to strangers and others who seemed very shy. **Such behavioural styles, which are fairly stable across situations and are biologically based, make up an infant's** *temperament.* For example, all babies become upset occasionally and cry. However, some, like Yoshimi's son, recover quickly, while others are hard to console. These differences in emotion and style of behaviour are evident in the first few weeks after birth and are important throughout life.

We'll begin this module by looking at different ways that scientists define temperament.

What Is Temperament?

Q&A **QUESTION 10.2**
Ten-month-old Nina is usually cheerful, enjoys going on outings with her dad, and sleeps soundly every night. How would Thomas and Chess describe Nina's temperament? *(Answer is on page 360.)*

Alexander Thomas and Stella Chess (Thomas, Chess, & Birch, 1968; Thomas & Chess, 1977) pioneered the study of temperament with the New York Longitudinal Study, which traced the lives of 141 individuals from infancy through adulthood. Thomas and Chess interviewed parents about their babies and had individuals unfamiliar with the children observe them at home. From these interviews and observations, Thomas and Chess suggested that infants' behaviour varies along nine temperamental dimensions. One dimension was *activity*, which referred to an infant's typical level of motor activity. A second was *persistence*, which referred to the amount of time that an infant devoted to an activity, particularly when obstacles were present.

Using all nine dimensions, Thomas and Chess identified three patterns of temperament. Most common were "easy" babies, who were usually happy and cheerful, tended to adjust well to new situations, and had regular routines for eating, sleeping, and toileting. A second, less common group were "difficult" babies, who tended to be unhappy, were irregular in their eating and sleeping, and often responded intensely to unfamiliar situations. Another less common group was made up of "slow-to-warm-up" babies. Like difficult babies, slow-to-warm-up babies were often unhappy; but unlike difficult babies, slow-to-warm-up babies were not upset by unfamiliar situations.

The New York Longitudinal Study launched research on infant temperament, but today's researchers no longer emphasize creating different categories of infants, such as "easy" or "slow-to-warm-up." Instead, researchers want to determine the different dimensions that underlie temperament. One modern approach to temperament is described in the Spotlight on Theories feature.

Spotlight on Theories

A Theory of the Structure of Temperament in Infancy

BACKGROUND Most scientists agree that *temperament* refers to biologically based differences in infants' and children's emotional reactivity and emotional self-regulation. However, scientists disagree on the number and nature of the dimensions that make up temperament

THE THEORY Mary K. Rothbart (2011) has devised a theory of temperament that includes three different dimensions:

- *Surgency/extraversion* **refers to the extent to which a child is generally happy, active, vocal, and regularly seeks interesting stimulation.**

- *Negative affect* **refers to the extent to which a child is angry, fearful, frustrated, shy, and not easily soothed.**

- *Effortful control* **refers to the extent to which a child can focus attention, is not readily distracted, and can inhibit responses.**

These dimensions of temperament are evident in infancy, continue into childhood, and are related to dimensions of personality that are found in adolescence and adulthood. However, the dimensions are not independent: Infants who are high on effortful control tend to be high on surgency/extraversion and low on negative affect. In other words, babies who can control their attention and inhibit responses tend to be happy and active but not angry or fearful.

Hypothesis: If temperament is biologically based and includes the three dimensions of Rothbart's theory, then those dimensions of temperament should be observed in children around the world. That is, cross-cultural studies of temperament should consistently reveal the dimensions of surgency/extraversion, negative affect, and effortful control.

Test: Many scientists have examined the structure of temperament in young children growing up in different countries around the world. In most of the studies, parents of young children completed questionnaires measuring their children's temperament. For example, the Infant Behaviour Questionnaire (IBQ-R) assesses different dimensions of Rothbart's theory of temperament. The items "When given a new toy, how often did the baby get very excited about getting it?" and "When put into the bath water, how often did the baby splash or kick?" both measure the surgency/extraversion dimension; "When frustrated with something, how often did the baby calm down within five minutes?" measures the negative-affect dimension. For each item, parents rated how often the behaviour had been observed in the past seven days, using a scale that ranged from "never" to "always."

Parents' responses are evaluated with factor analysis, a method that looks for patterns in parents' responses. To illustrate, the surgency/extraversion dimension would be supported if parents who judged that their infants were always excited about a new toy also said that their babies always splashed or kicked during a bath (because both items are thought to measure surgency/extraversion). In fact, factor analyses revealed that three temperamental dimensions—surgency/extraversion, negative affect, and effortful control— are evident in responses of parents from Belgium, China, Japan, the Netherlands, and the United States (Casalin, Luyten, Vliegen, & Meurs 2012; Sleddens, Kremers, Candel, De Vries, & Thijs 2011). That is, the three basic dimensions of temperament emerge when parents worldwide describe their children.

Conclusion: As predicted, the structure of temperament was the same in many cultures. This supports Rothbart's claim that the dimensions of her theory of temperament are biologically rooted and, consequently, should be evident regardless of the specific environment or culture in which a child develops.

Application: An important theme of temperament research is that children's development proceeds best when their temperament fits well with the environment in which they grow up. That is, because temperament is rooted in biological factors, parents should accept their baby's unique temperamental characteristics and adjust their parenting accordingly. For example, babies who are quiet and shy clearly benefit when parents actively stimulate them (e.g., by describing and explaining). But these same activities are actually counterproductive with active, outgoing babies who would rather explore the world on their own (Miceli, Whitman, Borkowsky, Braungart-Riekder, & Mitchell, 1998). Thus, Rothbart's theory, and other research on temperament, reminds us that parent-child interactions represent a two-way street in which interactions are most successful when both parties—child and parent—adjust to the needs of the other.

Critical Thinking Questions: Rothbart's theory that temperament includes three different dimensions seems to be upheld by the research. As we know by now, however, behaviour is formed by a combination of both heredity and environmental factors. In what ways would environmental influences be important? At the end of the feature, parents stimulating or not stimulating a baby (depending on the baby's temperament) is given as an example. What other different factors could interact with the temperament dimensions proposed by Rothbart, and how?

Big Cheese Photo/SuperStock

The hereditary contribution to temperament is shown by the fact that twins are typically similar in their level of activity.

Hereditary and Environmental Contributions to Temperament

Most theories agree that temperament reflects both heredity and experience (Caspi, Roberts, & Shiner, 2005). The influence of heredity is shown in twin studies: Identical twins are more alike in most aspects of temperament than fraternal twins (Goldsmith, Pollak, & Davidson, 2008). In other words, if one identical twin is temperamentally active, the other usually is too—like the youngsters in the photo (Saudino, 2012). However, the impact of heredity also depends on the temperamental dimension and the child's age. For example, negative affect is more influenced by heredity than the other dimensions, and temperament in childhood is more influenced by heredity than is temperament in infancy (Wachs & Bates, 2001).

The environment also contributes to children's temperament in at least three different ways. First, temperament can be affected directly by parents' behaviour; for example, infants are less emotional when parents are responsive (Hane & Fox, 2006; Leerkes, Blankson, & O'Brien, 2009). Second, the environment can amplify the genetic effects of temperament through the mechanisms described in Module 2.2; for example, infants with high levels of negative affect are more likely to elicit harsh parenting (Saudino & Wang, 2012). Third, temperament may make some children particularly susceptible to environmental influences—either beneficial or harmful (van IJzendoorn & Bakermans-Kranenburg, 2012). Several studies have focused on the DRD4 gene, which is linked to brain systems that regulate attention, motivation and reward, and novelty-seeking in adults. Children with a specific variant of the DRD4 gene are particularly susceptible to the quality of the environment: They are more likely to benefit from positive environments, such as high-quality daycare, and more likely to be harmed by negative environments, such as prenatal stress (Bakermans-Kranenburg & van IJzendoorn, 2011; Belsky & Pluess, 2013; Zohsel et al., 2014).

DRD4 is *not* a temperament gene, but it is linked to behaviours that make up temperament (e.g., novelty seeking, fearlessness). Consequently, these findings suggest that temperament may make some children particularly sensitive to environmental influences. It's as if some children are sailboats with small rudders, so that wind—representing environmental influence—can easily change their developmental course; other children have temperamentally larger rudders, and they are less affected by these environmental winds.

Heredity and experience may also explain why Yoshimi, the Japanese mother in the opening vignette, has such a hardy son. The Cultural Influences feature tells the story.

Cultural Influences

Why Is Yoshimi's Son so Tough?

If you've ever watched an infant getting an injection, you know the inevitable response. After the syringe is removed, the infant's eyes open wide and then the baby begins to cry, as if saying, "Wow, that hurt!" Infants differ in how intensely they cry and in how readily they are soothed, reflecting differences in the emotionality dimension of temperament, but virtually all European Canadian babies cry.

It is easy to suppose that crying is a universal response to the pain from the inoculation, but it is not. In such stressful situations, compared with European Canadian infants,

Japanese and Chinese infants resemble Yoshimi's son: They are less likely to become upset and they are soothed more readily (Kagan et al., 1994; Lewis, Ramsay, & Kawakami, 1993). What's more, Japanese and Chinese babies smile and laugh less often and are more inhibited (Chen, Wang, & DeSouza, 2006; Gartstein, Slobodskaya, Zylicz, Gosztyla, & Nakagawa, 2010).

Why are Asian infants less emotional than their European Canadian counterparts? Heredity may be involved, but we cannot overlook experience. Compared to European Canadian mothers, Japanese mothers spend more time in close physical contact with their babies, constantly and gently soothing them; this may reduce the tendency to respond emotionally.

Critical Thinking Questions: Why *is* Yoshimi's son "tough"? This issue is mentioned in the feature, but expand upon the basic answer. In what ways might caregiver–child interaction be different and how could these differences support differential child behaviours between cultures? Do you know of any other cultural differences that could be examined or discussed?

Stability of Temperament

Do calm, easygoing babies grow up to be calm, easygoing children, adolescents, and adults? Are difficult, irritable infants destined to grow up to be cranky, whiny children? In fact, temperament is moderately stable throughout infancy, but becomes more stable in the preschool years (Shiner & Caspi, 2012). For example, when inhibited toddlers are adults, they respond more strongly to unfamiliar stimuli (Schwartz, Wright, Shin, Kagan, & Rauch, 2003). Thus Sam, an inhibited three-year-old, is more likely to be shy as a 12-year-old than Dave, an outgoing three-year-old. However, it's not necessarily Sam's destiny to be shy as a 12-year-old. Instead, some youngsters are naturally predisposed to be sociable, emotional, or active; others *can* act in these ways, too, but only if the behaviours are nurtured by parents and others.

In many respects, temperament resembles personality, so it's not surprising that many child-development researchers have speculated about potential connections between the two. One view suggests both direct and indirect links between temperament and personality (Shiner & Caspi, 2012). The direct link is that temperamental dimensions provide a well-defined path to personality traits. For example, extroversion is a personality trait that refers to a person's warmth, gregariousness, and activity level. Extroverted individuals tend to be affectionate, prefer the company of others, and like being active; introverted people tend to be more reserved, enjoy solitude, and prefer a more sedate pace (Costa & McRae, 2001). Extroversion looks like a blend of the temperamental dimensions of positive affect and activity level, and inhibited children are more likely as adults to be introverted than extroverted (Caspi et al., 2005).

The indirect link is that a child's temperament helps to shape environmental influences, and these experiences can determine the course of personality development

Temperament is moderately stable throughout infancy; for example, babies who as newborns cry when they experience stress tend, as five-month-olds, to cry when they experience stress from being restrained.

Herjua/Shutterstock

(Shiner & Caspi, 2012). Outgoing Dave may befriend children who are outgoing like himself; experiences with these children will encourage his dispositional tendency to be gregarious and lead him to be extroverted as an adolescent and adult. In many respects, temperament resembles personality, but remember that temperament changes as children develop, depending on their experiences. An inhibited child who finds herself in a school group with children with similar interests may "open up" and become much more outgoing over time; her early inhibited temperament is not related to her later outgoing personality. Thus, we should not expect children's temperament to be consistently related to their personality as adults.

In the next section, we'll see some of the connections between temperament and other aspects of development.

Temperament and Other Aspects of Development

In their New York Longitudinal Study, Thomas and Chess discovered that about two-thirds of the preschoolers with difficult temperaments had developed behavioural problems by the time they entered school. In contrast, fewer than one-fifth of the children with easy temperaments had behavioural problems (Thomas et al., 1968). Later studies have documented this link between a difficult temperament—youngsters who anger easily and have relatively little control—and later behaviour problems, both in the United States and China (Gartstein, Putnam, & Rothbart, 2012; Zhou, Lengua, & Wang, 2009). However, difficult temperament does not necessarily lead to adjustment problems: Children with difficult temperaments can fare well when parents are warm, supportive, and respect their children's autonomy (Stright, Gallagher, & Kelley, 2008).

Other scientists have followed the lead of the New York Longitudinal Study in looking for links between temperament and outcomes of development, and they have found that temperament is an important influence on development. Consider these examples:

- Persistent children are likely to succeed in school, whereas active and distractible children are less likely to succeed (Eisenberg, Duckworth, Spinrad, & Valiente, 2014; Martin, Olejnik, & Gaddis, 1994).

- Shy, inhibited children often have difficulty interacting with their peers and often do not cope effectively with problems (Eisenberg, Shepard, Fabes, Murphy, & Guthrie, 1998; Young, Fox, & Zahn-Waxler, 1999).

- Anxious, fearful children are more likely to comply with a parent's rules and requests, even when the parent is not present (Kochanska et al., 2007).

- Children who are frequently angry or fearful are more prone to depression (Lengua, 2006).

- Children who are capable of greater effortful control as three- and four-year-olds have higher scores on measures of working memory (Wolfe & Bell, 2007) and, as school-age children, are less likely to be diagnosed with ADHD (Martel & Nigg, 2006).

- Children who are uninhibited and lack self-regulation are prone to alcohol-, drug-, and gambling-related problems as adults (Slutske, Moffitt, Poulton, & Caspi, 2012; Zucker, Heitzeg, & Nigg, 2011).

The Focus on Research feature shows that temperament in childhood is also related to an array of outcomes in adolescence and adulthood.

Focus on Research

Temperament Influences Outcomes in Adolescence and Adulthood

Who were the investigators, and what was the aim of the study? Many studies show that when children regulate their emotions and behaviour ineffectively, they often encounter developmental problems. However, much of the research consists of cross-sectional studies or longitudinal studies that cover just a few years. And much of the work focuses on a single problem area. Terrie Moffitt and her colleagues (2011) hoped to determine whether self-regulation in childhood was related to a range of important developmental outcomes in adolescence and adulthood.

How did the investigators measure the topic of interest? The research was based on data obtained as part of the Dunedin Multidisciplinary Health and Development Study (DMHDS), a longitudinal study that has followed the lives of more than 1000 children in New Zealand. A group of researchers from several countries—New Zealand, the United States, England, and Canada—looked at outcomes from the DMHDS study. Between three and 11 years of age, self-regulation was assessed from ratings provided by parents, teachers, trained observers, and the children themselves. For example, everyone rated whether the child had difficulty completing tasks. The researchers also measured children's IQ and their family's socioeconomic status.

As adolescents, participants were asked if they smoked, had dropped out of school, or had become parents. As adults, participants had a physical exam and were interviewed about their mental health and substance use. Also, their criminal activity was determined from a computer search of court records.

Who were the children in the study? The Dunedin study began with 1037 infants and most have been tested repeatedly through their adult years. (The study is ongoing and the participants are now in their early 40s.)

What was the design of the study? This study was correlational because Moffitt and her colleagues were interested in the relation that existed naturally between self-regulation during childhood and outcomes in adolescence and adulthood. The study was longitudinal because participants have been tested throughout childhood, adolescence, and adulthood.

Were there ethical concerns with the study? No. The measures are straightforward and without obvious risk. When participants were children, their parents provided consent; as adults, they provided their own consent.

What were the results? The graph in Figure 10-1 shows links between self-regulation in childhood and outcomes in adolescence and adulthood. The findings are expressed as the relative likelihood of an outcome for children who are skilled and less skilled in their self-regulation (defined as being at the 70th and 30th percentile of self-regulation, respectively). If children skilled and less skilled in self-regulation were equally likely to have risky outcomes, the ratio would be 1.0. However, in each case the ratio is greater than 1, indicating that the outcomes were more likely for children who were less skilled in self-regulation. To take an extreme example, children less skilled in self-regulation were more than twice as likely to drop out

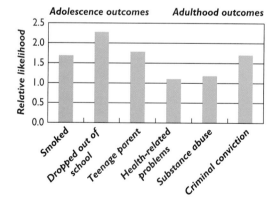

Figure 10-1

Based on Moffitt, T.E., Arseneault, L., Belsky, D., Dickson, N., Hancox, R.J., Harrington, H., et al. (2011). A gradient of childhood self-control predicts health, wealth, and public safety. *Proceedings of the National Academy of Sciences*, 108, 2693–2698.

of school. Similarly, they were more likely to smoke and more likely to become parents; as adults, they were more likely to have health-related problems, to have problems with substance abuse, and to be convicted of a crime.

What did the investigators conclude? When children are temperamentally unable to regulate their emotions and behaviour skillfully, they are at risk for developmental paths that lead to an array of undesirable outcomes. Moffitt et al. (2011) write, "Our findings imply that innovative policies that put self-control center stage might reduce . . . costs that now heavily burden citizens and governments" (p. 2697).

What converging evidence would strengthen these conclusions? In many ways the Dunedin study is a model of best practices in developmental science. Of course, one problem that plagues any longitudinal study is the possibility of cohort effects—the results may be specific to this particular cohort of people born in New Zealand in the early 1970s and not apply more generally. For example, as the participants entered young adulthood, New Zealand experienced a severe recession, an event that meant few jobs were available at a time when participants were eager to join the workforce. Might that unique experience affect the study's findings? The only way to know for sure is to conduct other longitudinal work in which young adults don't experience an economic recession.

Critical Thinking Questions: It would appear, then, that temperament has a life-long influence, with greater self-regulation linked to more positive life outcomes. What advice do you think caregivers should be given about fostering self-regulation in children? What about teachers, interacting with children in schools?

Although these findings underscore the fact that temperament is an important force in children's development, temperament rarely is the sole determining factor. Instead, the influence of temperament often depends on the environment in which children develop. To illustrate, let's consider the link between temperament and behaviour problems. Infants and toddlers who temperamentally resist control—those who are difficult to manage, who are often unresponsive, and who are sometimes impulsive—tend to be prone to behaviour problems, particularly aggression, when they are older. However, more careful analysis shows that resistant temperament leads to behaviour problems primarily when mothers do not exert much control over their children. Among mothers who do exert control—those who prohibit, warn, and scold their children when necessary—resistant temperament is not linked to behaviour problems (Bates, Pettit, Dodge, & Ridge, 1998).

 ANSWER 10.2
Thomas and Chess would say that she's a prototypical "easy" baby: She's happy; she adjusts well to new situations (shown by how much she enjoys going to new places with her dad); and she has a regular routine for sleeping.

Similarly, young adolescents are more likely to drink, smoke, and use drugs when they experience many life stressors (e.g., when someone in the family has a serious accident or illness, when a parent loses a job, or when parents and the child are frequently in conflict) and when their parents themselves smoke and drink. But this is less true for young adolescents with temperaments marked by positive affect (Wills, Sandy, Yaeger, & Shinar, 2001). That is, young adolescents who are temperamentally cheerful apparently are less affected by life stressors, apparently because they don't see the stressors as that threatening, consequently are less likely to drink, smoke, or use drugs.

This research reminds us that emotion is a fundamental element of temperament. In the next module, we'll look at emotion from yet another perspective—that of the emotional relationship formed between an infant and its primary caregiver.

 **Check Your Learning**

RECALL How is temperament influenced by heredity and environment?

Summarize the influence of temperament on other aspects of development.

INTERPRET Compare and contrast the Thomas and Chess approach to temperament with Rothbart's theory of temperament.

APPLY Based on what you know about the stability of temperament, what would you say to a parent who is worried that her 15-month-old seems shy and inhibited?

10.3 **Attachment**

OUTLINE

The Growth of Attachment

The Quality of Attachment

LEARNING OBJECTIVES

1. How does an attachment relationship develop between an infant and the primary caregiver?
2. What different types of attachment relationships are there? What are the consequences of different types of relationships?

Ever since Samantha was a newborn, Karen and Dick looked forward to going to their favourite restaurant on Friday night. They enjoyed the break from childcare responsibilities, and liked being able to talk without interruptions. But recently they've had a problem: When they leave her with a sitter, eight-month-old Sam gets a frightened look on her face and usually begins to cry hysterically. Karen and Dick wonder if Sam's behaviour is normal and if their Friday night dinners are coming to an end.

The social-emotional relationship that develops between an infant and a parent (usually, but not necessarily, the mother) is special. This is a baby's first social-emotional relationship, so scientists and parents alike believe it should be satisfying and trouble-free to set the stage for later relationships. In this module, we'll look at the steps involved in creating the baby's first emotional relationship. Along the way, we'll see why eight-month-old Sam has begun to cry when Karen and Dick leave her with a sitter.

The Growth of Attachment

Today's parents are encouraged to shower their babies with hugs and kisses; the more affection young children receive, the better! This advice may seem obvious, but actually it is a relatively recent recommendation, dating from the middle of the 20th century. It emerged, in part, from observations of European children whose parents were killed during World War II. Despite being well fed and receiving necessary healthcare, the children's development was far from normal: their mental development was slow, and they often seemed withdrawn and listless (Bowlby, 1953; Spitz, 1965). Some scientists claimed that these problems came about because the children lived in institutions (e.g., orphanages and refugee camps) where they could not form a close social-emotional bond with adults.

Soon after, studies of monkeys that were reared in isolation confirmed this idea. Although the monkeys received excellent physical care, they stayed huddled in a corner of their cages, clutching themselves and rocking constantly; when placed with other monkeys, they avoided them as much as they could (Harlow & Harlow, 1965). Clearly, in the absence of regular social interactions with caring adults, normal development is thrown way off course.

In explaining the essential ingredients of these early social relationships, most modern accounts take an evolutionary perspective. **According to** *evolutionary psychology,* **many human behaviours represent successful adaptation to the environment.** That is, over human history, some behaviours have made it more likely that people will reproduce and pass on their genes to following generations. For example, we take it for granted that most people enjoy being with other people. But evolutionary psychologists argue that our social nature is a product of evolution: For early humans, being in a group offered protection from predators and made it easier to locate food. Thus early humans who were social were more likely than their asocial peers to live long enough to reproduce, passing on their social orientation to their offspring (Gaulin & McBurney, 2001). Over many, many generations, "being social" had such a survival advantage that nearly all people are socially oriented (though in varying amounts, as we know from research on temperament in Module 10.2).

Blend Images - KidStock/Brand X Pictures/ Getty Images

When an infant has formed an attachment with a caregiver, that person becomes a secure, stable emotional base for the infant.

Applied to child development, evolutionary psychology highlights the adaptive value of children's behaviour at different points in development (Bjorklund & Jordan, 2013). For example, think about the time and energy that parents invest in childrearing. Without such effort, infants and young children would die before they were sexually mature, which means that a parent's genes could not be passed along to grandchildren (Geary, 2002). Here too, although parenting just seems "natural," it really represents an adaptation to the problem of guaranteeing that one's helpless offspring can survive until they are sexually mature.

An evolutionary perspective of early human relationships comes from John Bowlby (1969, 1991). **According to Bowlby, children who form an** *attachment* **to an adult—that is, an enduring social-emotional relationship—are more likely to survive.** This person is usually the mother but need not be; the key is a strong emotional relationship with a responsive, caring person. Attachments can form with fathers, grandparents, or someone else. Bowlby described four phases in the growth of attachment:

- *Preattachment* (birth to six to eight weeks). During prenatal development and soon after birth, infants rapidly learn to recognize their mothers by smell and sound, which sets the stage for forging an attachment relationship (Hofer, 2006). In addition, evolution has endowed infants with many behaviours that elicit caregiving from an adult. When babies cry, smile, or gaze intently at a caregiver's face, the caregiver will usually smile back or hold the baby. The infant's behaviours and the responses they evoke in adults create an interactive system that is the first step in the formation of attachment relationships.

- *Attachment in the making* (six to eight weeks to six to eight months). During these months, babies begin to behave differently in the presence of familiar caregivers and unfamiliar adults. Babies now smile and laugh more often with the primary caregiver; when babies are upset, they are more easily consoled by the primary caregiver. Babies are gradually identifying the primary caregiver as the person they can depend on when they are anxious or distressed.

- *True attachment* (six to eight months to 18 months). By approximately seven or eight months, most infants have singled out the attachment figure—usually the mother—as a special individual. The attachment figure is now the infant's stable social-emotional base. For example, a seven-month-old like the one in the photo on the previous page will explore a novel environment but periodically look toward his or her mother, as if seeking reassurance that all is well. The behaviour suggests that the infant trusts the mother, and it indicates that the attachment relationship has been established. In addition, this behaviour reflects important cognitive growth: It means that the infant has a mental representation of the mother, an understanding that she will be there to meet the infant's needs (Lewis, Koroshegi, Douglas, & Kampe, 1997). This is why infants like eight-month-old Sam from the earlier vignette are distressed when they are separated from the attachment figure: They have lost their secure base.

- *Reciprocal relationships* (18 months on). Infants' growing cognitive and language skills and their accumulated experience with their primary caregiver make infants better able to act as true partners in the attachment relationship. They often take the initiative in interactions and negotiate with parents ("Please read me another story!"). They begin to understand their caregivers' feelings and goals, and sometimes use this knowledge to guide their own behaviour (e.g., social referencing, described on page 350). They also cope with separation more effectively because they can anticipate that caregivers will return.

THE ROLE OF FATHERS. Attachment typically first develops between infants and their mothers because mothers are usually the primary caregivers of North American infants. Babies soon become attached to fathers, too, even though fathers in developed nations spend less time in caregiving tasks (e.g., feeding or bathing a child) than mothers do (Lamb & Lewis, 2010). Statistics Canada gives overall census figures for men and women for childcare and household duties: In 2010, women spent an average of about 2 hours a day on household duties, compared to around 1.5 hours for men (Marshall, 2012). When it comes to childcare, however, there is a greater difference, certainly in Canada, with the most recent figures showing that women spend 50.1 hours and men spend 24.4 hours per week on unpaid childcare (Statistics Canada, 2015a). Over the past 50 years, childcare has shifted somewhat from being viewed as "women's work" to a responsibility that can be shared equally by mothers and fathers, but women are still far more likely to be involved in direct care of infants and toddlers than fathers (Lindsay, 2008; Parke, 2002; Statistics Canada, 2015a). Instead, fathers typically spend more time playing with their babies than taking care of them, and even their style of play differs. Physical play like that shown in the photo is the norm for fathers, whereas mothers spend more time reading and talking to babies, showing them toys, and playing games like patty cake (Paquette, 2004). Infants often

Fathers spend much of their time with babies playing with them (instead of taking care of them) and tend to play with them more vigorously and physically than mothers do.

Kichigin19/Fotolia

prefer to play with fathers but rely on mothers when they are distressed (Field, 1990). These differences between mothers' and fathers' behaviours have become smaller, however, as men and women have come to share responsibilities for childcare and breadwinning (Lamb & Lewis, 2010).

The Quality of Attachment

Attachment between infant and mother usually occurs by eight or nine months of age, but the attachment can take on different forms. Mary Ainsworth (1978, 1993) pioneered the study of attachment relationships using a procedure that has come to be known as the Strange Situation. You can see in Figure 10-2 that the Strange Situation involves a series of episodes, each about three minutes long. The mother and infant enter an unfamiliar room filled with interesting toys. The mother leaves briefly, then mother and baby are reunited. Meanwhile, the experimenter observes the baby, recording its responses. It is the whole pattern of behaviours throughout the Strange Situation that is important. Reaction to both separation and reunion give important information about the nature of the infant–caregiver relationship.

Based on how the infant reacts, researchers identify four different types of attachment relationships (Ainsworth, 1993; Thompson, 2006). One is a secure attachment, and three are insecure attachments (avoidant, resistant, disorganized):

- *Secure attachment:* **The baby may or may not cry when the mother leaves, but when she returns, the baby wants to be with her; if the baby has been crying, it stops.** Babies in this group seem to be saying, "I missed you terribly, but now that you're back, I'm okay." Approximately 60 to 65 percent of North American babies have secure attachment relationships.

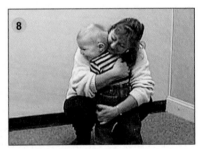

① Shows the experimental room to mother and infant, then leaves the room.

② Infant is allowed to explore the playroom for three minutes; mother watches but does not participate.

③ A stranger enters the room and remains silent for one minute, then talks to the baby for a minute, and then approaches the baby. Mother leaves unobtrusively.

④ The stranger does not play with the baby but attempts to comfort it if necessary.

⑤ After three minutes, the mother returns, greets, and consoles the baby.

⑥ When the baby has returned to play, the mother leaves again, this time saying "bye-bye" as she leaves.

⑦ Stranger attempts to calm and play with the baby.

⑧ After three minutes, the mother returns and the stranger leaves.

Figure 10-2 Steps in the "Strange Situation."

- *Avoidant attachment:* **The baby is not visibly upset when the mother leaves and, when she returns, may ignore her by looking or turning away.** Infants with an avoidant attachment look as if they're saying, "You left me again. I always have to take care of myself!" About 20 percent of North American infants have avoidant attachment relationships, which is one of the three forms of insecure attachment.

- *Resistant attachment:* **The baby is upset when the mother leaves, remains upset or even angry when she returns, and is difficult to console.** Like the baby in the photo, these babies seem to be telling the mother, "Why do you do this? I need you desperately and yet you just leave me without warning. I get so angry when you're like this." About 10 to 15 percent of North American babies have this resistant attachment relationship, which is another form of insecure attachment.

- *Disorganized (disoriented) attachment:* **The baby seems confused when the mother leaves, and when she returns, seems not to really understand what's happening.** The baby often has a dazed look on its face as if wondering, "What's going on here? I want you to be here, but you left and now you're back. I don't know whether to laugh or cry!" About 5 to 10 percent of North American babies have this disorganized attachment relationship, the last of the three kinds of insecure attachment.

Infants with a resistant attachment are upset or angry with Mom when they're reunited with her following a separation.

Kris Ubach and Quim Roser/Cultura/Getty Images

The Strange Situation has long been the gold standard for studying attachment, but investigators use other methods to complement the Strange Situation. One of them, the Attachment Q-Set, can be used with young children as well as infants and toddlers. In this method, trained observers watch mothers and children interact at home; then the observer rates the interaction on many attachment-related behaviours (e.g., "Child greets mother with a big smile when she enters the room"). The ratings are totalled to provide a measure of the security of the child's attachment. Scores obtained with the Q-set converge with assessments derived from the Strange Situation (van IJzeendorn, Vereijken, Bakermans-Kranenburg, & Riksen-Walraven, 2004).

PATTERNS OF ATTACHMENT WORLDWIDE Worldwide, secure attachment is the most common form: In most countries, roughly 55 to 70 percent of infants are classified as being securely attached. However, the percentage of infants in the different categories of insecure attachment differs substantially across cultures (van IJzendoorn & Sagi-Schwartz, 2008; van IJzendoorn, Schuengel, & Bakermans-Kranenburg, 1999). For example, in Japan, resistant attachment (in which the infant wants to be picked up at reunion but squirms as if to avoid the mother's hugs) is much more common than avoidant attachment (in which the infant does not wish to be picked up at all following reunion). The reverse pattern has been found in Germany (Van IJzendoorn & Sagi-Schwartz, A. (2008).

These differences may reflect cultural variations in the impact of parents' expectations about infant behaviour on infants' responses in the Strange Situation. German parents, for example, are more likely to encourage independence, which may explain why avoidant attachment is more common in German infants. In contrast, Japanese parents see the mother–child relationship as particularly interdependent, and Japanese mothers spend much time holding their infants closely (Rothbaum, Weisz, Pott, Miyake, & Morelli,

2000). This may explain why Japanese infants rarely avoid their mothers during reunion after separation.

These cultural variations in frequency of different types of insecure attachment should not overshadow the substantial cultural consistency in the prevalence of secure attachment. Evolutionary psychologists would argue that this prevalence must mean that secure attachment is adaptive relative to the other forms. In the next section, we'll see that this is true.

CONSEQUENCES OF QUALITY OF ATTACHMENT. Erikson, Bowlby, and other theorists (Waters & Cummings, 2000) believe that attachment, as the first social relationship, provides the basis for all of an infant's later social relationships. In this view, infants who experience the trust and compassion of a secure attachment should develop into preschool children who interact confidently and successfully with their peers. In contrast, infants who do not experience a successful, satisfying first relationship should be more prone to problems in their social interactions as preschoolers.

Many findings are consistent with these predictions. Children with secure attachment relationships have higher-quality friendships and fewer conflicts in their friendships than children with insecure attachment relationships (McElwain, Booth-LaForce, & Wu, 2011). What's more, secure attachment in infancy is associated with more stable and higher-quality romantic relationships in adolescence and young adulthood (Collins, Welsh, & Furman, 2009; Englund et al., 2011). Finally, research consistently links insecure attachment to behaviour problems involving anxiety, anger, and aggressive behaviour (Kerns & Brumariu, 2014; Madigan et al., 2013). Researchers from the Univertisté de Québec à Montréal and Univeristé de Montréal have found that insecure attachment, particularly disorganized attachment, was linked with increased risk of such behaviour problems in the elementary-school years (Moss, Cyr, Bureau, Tarabulsy, & Dubois-Comtois, 2005); Moss, Smolla, Guerra, Mazzarello, Chayer, & Berthiaume, 2006).

The conclusion seems inescapable: As they grow, infants who have secure attachment relationships tend to have satisfying social interactions, but infants with disorganized attachment do not. Why? One explanation focuses on the lasting impact of this first social relationship. Secure attachment evidently leads infants to see the world positively and to trust other humans, characteristics that lead to more skilled social interactions later in childhood adolescence, and adulthood (Dykas & Cassidy, 2011). Another view does not discount the impact of this early relationship, but adds another wrinkle: Theorists who emphasize continuity of caregiving argue that parents who establish secure attachments with infants tend to be warm, supportive, and skilled at parenting throughout their child's development (McElwain et al., 2011; Thompson, 2006). Thus, it is continuous exposure to high-quality parenting that promotes secure attachment in infancy and positive social relationships in childhood and adolescence. These accounts are not mutually exclusive: A successful first relationship and continued warm parenting likely work together to foster children's development.

A key ingredient in creating a secure mother-infant attachment is for the mother to respond appropriately and predictably to her infant's needs.

FACTORS DETERMINING QUALITY OF ATTACHMENT. Because secure attachment is so important to a child's later development, researchers have tried to identify the factors involved. Undoubtedly the most important is the interaction between primary caregivers and babies. A secure attachment is most likely when caregivers respond to infants predictably and appropriately (De Wolff & van IJzendoorn, 1997; Tomlinson, Cooper, & Murray, 2005). For example, the mother in the photo on the previous page recognized that her baby was upset, responded promptly, and is soothing baby. The mother's behaviour evidently conveys that social interactions are predictable and satisfying, and apparently this behaviour instills in infants the trust and confidence that are the hallmarks of secure attachment.

Why does predictable and responsive caregiving promote secure attachment relationships? To answer this question, think about your own friendships and romantic relationships. These relationships are usually most satisfying when we believe we can trust the other people and depend on them in times of need. The same formula seems to hold for infants. **Infants develop an** *internal working model,* **a set of expectations about caregivers' availability and responsiveness generally and in times of stress.** When caregivers are dependable and caring, babies come to trust them, knowing they can be relied upon for comfort. That is, babies develop an internal working model in which they believe their caregivers are concerned about their needs and will try to meet those needs (Huth-Bocks, Levendosky, Bogat, & von Eye, 2004; Thompson, 2000).

In a particularly clever demonstration of infants' working models of attachment (Johnson et al., 2010), infants were shown animated videos depicting a large ellipse (mother) paired with a small ellipse (child). The video began with the mother and child ellipses together; then the mother moved away from the child, who began to cry. On some trials, the mother ellipse returned to the child ellipse; on other trials, she continued to move away. Securely attached infants looked longer at the trials depicting an unresponsive mother, but insecurely attached infants looked longer at the trials when the mother returned. Evidently, each group has a working model of how parents respond—securely attached infants expect parents to respond but insecurely attached infants do not—and they look longer at the trials that violated their expectations of maternal behaviour.

Not all caregivers react to babies in the reliable and reassuring manner that fosters secure attachment. Some respond intermittently or only after the infant has cried long and hard. And when these caregivers finally respond, they are sometimes annoyed by the infant's demands and may misinterpret the infant's intent. Over time, these babies tend to see social relationships as inconsistent and often frustrating, conditions that do little to foster trust and confidence.

Why are some caregivers more responsive (and thus more likely to foster secure attachment) than others? According to modern attachment theory (e.g., Cassidy, 1994), adults have internal working models of the attachment relationship with their own parents or caregivers, and these working models guide interactions with their own infants. When questioned about attachment relationships with the Adult Attachment Interview (George, Kaplan, & Main, 1985; Bakermans-Kranenburg & van IJzendoorn, 2009), adults can be classified into one of three groups, one corresponding to the secure attachment of childhood and the other two corresponding to insecure attachments:

- *Secure adults* **describe childhood experiences objectively and value the impact of their caregiver-child relationship on their development.**

- *Dismissive adults* **sometimes deny the value of childhood experiences and sometimes are unable to recall those experiences precisely, yet they often idealize their caregivers.**

- *Preoccupied adults* **describe childhood experiences emotionally and often express anger or confusion regarding relationships with their caregivers.**

According to attachment theory, only adults with autonomous attachment representations are likely to provide the sensitive caregiving that promotes secure attachment relationships. In fact, many studies show that caregivers' secure attachment representations are associated with sensitive caregiving, and, in turn, with secure attachment in their infants (Mills-Koonce et al., 2011; Pederson, Gleason, Moran, & Bento, 1998; Tarabulsy et al., 2005). Furthermore, as we mentioned earlier, infants with secure attachment relations often become young adults with secure attachment representations, completing the circle. Research on adolescents' reactions to meeting new peers has shown that attachment representations are predictive of behaviour in such social interactions (Feeney, Cassidy, & Ramos-Marcuse, 2008). Elaine Scharfe of Trent University has done some interesting research on how representations of attachment are affected in university students who experience the major transitions of coming to and graduating from university (Scharfe & Cole, 2006). From Scharfe & Cole's (2006) study, it seems that patterns of attachment are moderately stable—that is, they are not unchangeable, but once formed, attachment representations tend to influence relationships in one's life.

In recent years, the longitudinal study of attachment has become a major field of research. As noted above, there are different styles of caregiver-infant interactions, depending on how the adult views their own childhood attachment relationship. Davila and Sargent (2003) proposed that it is not the actual relationship that is important, but how people as adults viewed those events. Someone who interpreted an event as being negative would have a different view of their own attachment relationship than one who experienced the same event but did not assign much importance to the event. Work by Canadian researchers from Guelph and Western universities supports this view that is the person's own understanding of their attachment relationship that is important. If a parent has a realistic view of his or her own attachment relationship, rather than, say, not acknowledging that there may have been problems, the parent tends to have a positive attachment relationship with their own child (Bailey, Redden, Pederson, & Moran, 2016). Thus, self-awareness seems to be an important factor in intergenerational attachment.

Further support for such ideas comes from a major study of how parenting practices continue across generations within a family (Belsky, Jaffee, Sligo, Woodward, & Silva, 2005). As with the longitudinal study that was the subject of this chapter's Focus on Research feature (Moffitt et al., 2011), this was part of the DMHDS research in New Zealand. In this study, parents who themselves had been studied as young children were videotaped as they interacted with their own three-year-old children. The main finding was that a person's own childhood parenting experiences can influence how they then act as a parent themselves, and supportive parenting practices can be passed on as much as harsh ones. If this is the case, it would be worth adding information about intergenerational transmission of parenting styles to classes for expectant or new parents.

Fortunately, it appears that training can help mothers respond more effectively to their baby's needs (Bakermans-Kranenburg, van IJzendoorn, & Juffer, 2003; Dozier, Zeanah, & Bernard, 2013). Mothers can be taught how to interact more sensitively, affectionately, and responsively, paving the way for secure attachment and the lifelong benefits associated with a positive internal working model of interpersonal relationships

WORK, ATTACHMENT, AND CHILDCARE. Since the 1970s, more women in the workforce and more single-parent households have made childcare a fact of life for many Canadian families. We describe childcare in detail in Module 14.3, but here we want to focus on one specific aspect: What happens to primary caregiver-infant attachment when other people care for the infant much of the time? Parents and policymakers alike have been concerned about the impact of such care. Is there, for example, a maximum amount of time per week that infants should spend in care outside the home? Is there a minimum age below which infants should not be placed in care outside the home? The Children's Lives feature describes work that has attempted to answer these and other questions about the impact of early childcare on children's development.

QUESTION 10.3
Marie is the mother of a three-month-old. She is eager to return to her job as a civil engineer, but she worries that she may harm her baby by going back to work so soon. What could you say to reassure her? *(Answer is on page 370.)*

Children's Lives

Determining Guidelines for Childcare for Infants and Toddlers

Because so many North American families need childcare for their infants and toddlers, a comprehensive study of early childcare was required to provide parents and policymakers with appropriate guidelines. This is a subject of fairly recent interest, which seems to have first been undertaken in the United States. There the task fell to the U.S. National Institute of Child Health and Human Development, which began the Early Child Care Study in 1991. Researchers recruited 1364 mothers and their newborns from 12 U.S. cities. Both mothers and children have been tested repeatedly (and the testing continues because the study is ongoing). In Canada, a similar study, the Transition to Child Care Study, was begun in 1992 (McKim, Cramer, Stuart, & O'Connor, 1999). The Canadian study recruited families from the Ottawa-Carleton area of Ontario. This study was smaller than the American one at about one-tenth the size; data was gathered from 189 families with young children (McKim et al., 1999).

From the outset, one of the concerns was the impact of early childcare on mother-infant attachment, but the results so far show no overall effects of childcare experience on mother-infant attachment, for either the American or Canadian studies (McKim et al, 1999; NICHD Early Child Care Research Network, 1997, 2001). In both studies, the findings showed that a secure mother-infant attachment was just as likely, regardless of the quality of childcare, the amount of time the child spent in care, the age when the child began care, how frequently the parents changed childcare arrangements, and the type of childcare (e.g., at a childcare centre or in the home with a nonrelative).

However, when the effects of childcare were considered along with characteristics of mothers, an important pattern was detected: Children with less sensitive mothers, and especially those children who were also in extensive out-of-home care, showed less secure relationships (McKim et al., 1999). Similar findings were reported in the U.S. study, where at 15 and 36 months of age, insecure attachments were more common when less sensitive mothering was combined with low quality or large amounts of childcare (NICHD Early Child Care Research Network, 1997, 2001). As the investigators put it, "Poor quality, unstable, or more than minimal amounts of childcare apparently added to the risks already inherent in poor mothering, so that the combined effects were worse than those of low maternal sensitivity and responsiveness alone" (1997, p. 877). These conclusions are particularly convincing because the same pattern of results was found in Israel in a large-scale study of childcare and attachment also modelled after the NICHD Early Child Care study (Sagi, Koren-Karie, Gini, Ziv, & Joels, 2002).

These results provide clear guidelines for parents and other primary caregivers. The essential ingredient for secure attachment is high-quality parenting. With such parenting,

ANSWER 10.3
Tell her that the findings of the Transition to Child Care Study make it clear that as long as Marie provides high-quality parenting—she responds appropriately and predictably to her baby's needs—she and her baby should have a secure attachment even if the baby is in daycare full time.

a secure attachment is likely regardless of a child's experience in childcare. Of course, parents should still look for high-quality childcare, and we'll explore this topic in detail in Module 14.3.

Critical Thinking Question: Before going on to Module 14.3, think about what you would consider the important aspects of childcare; what would you look for in childcare provision?

 ## Check Your Learning

RECALL Describe the evolutionary perspective on adult-infant attachment.

What are the different forms of caregiver-infant attachment? What are the consequences of these different forms?

INTERPRET Compare the infant's contributions to the formation of caregiver-infant attachment with the adult's contributions.

APPLY Based on what you know about the normal developmental timetable for the formation of caregiver-infant attachment, what would seem to be the optimal age range for children to be adopted?

UNIFYING THEMES Active Children

Temperament is one of the best examples in this book of the theme that *children influence their own development*. Temperament helps determine how caregivers and other adults and peers respond to children. Parents and peers, for example, usually respond positively to temperamentally easy children. Parents find it more straightforward to establish a secure attachment with an easy child than with a difficult child. Peers get along better with easy children than with shy, inhibited children. Children's temperament alone does not dictate the direction of their development, but it makes some directions much easier to follow than others.

See for Yourself

Arrange to visit a local daycare centre where you can unobtrusively observe preschoolers for several days. Be sure that you comply with any of the centre's regulations—some may require a police check, referred to as "vulnerable sector screening," for example—as well as the standard ethical principles for observations. As you watch the children, see if you can detect the temperamental differences that are described in Module 10.2. Can you identify an emotional child, an active child, and a social child? Also, notice how adults respond to the children. Notice whether the same behaviours lead to different responses from adults, depending on the child's temperament. See for yourself!

Resources

For more information about . . .

children's temperament, read *Educating the Human Brain* (American Psychological Association, 2006) by Michael I. Posner and Mary K. Rothbart. The authors use research on temperament to illustrate how genes and experience shape the brain's development.

attachment, visit the website of a group of prominent attachment researchers at **www.johnbowlby.com**.

Key Terms

attachment 362
avoidant attachment 365
basic emotions 346
dismissive adults 367
disorganized (disoriented)
   attachment 365
display rules 351

effortful control 354
evolutionary psychology 362
internal working model 367
negative affect 354
preoccupied adults 367
resistant attachment 365
secure adults 367

secure attachment 364
self-conscious emotions 347
social referencing 350
social smiles 346
stranger wariness 347
surgency/extraversion 354
temperament 353

Summary

10.1 Emerging Emotions

1. The Function of Emotions

Modern theories emphasize the functional value of emotion. Emotions such as fear, happiness, and disgust are valuable because they help people adapt, by keeping them away from danger and strengthening social relationships.

2. Experiencing and Expressing Emotions

Basic emotions, which include happiness, anger, and fear emerge in the first year. Fear first appears in infancy as stranger wariness. Complex (self conscious) emotions have an evaluative component and include guilt, embarrassment, and pride. These emotions appear between 18 and 24 months and require more sophisticated cognitive skills than basic emotions like happiness and fear. Cultures differ in the rules for expressing emotions and the situations that elicit particular emotions.

3. Recognizing and Using Others' Emotions

By six months, infants have begun to recognize the emotions associated with different facial expressions. They use this information to help them evaluate unfamiliar situations. Beyond infancy, children understand the causes and consequences of different emotions, that people can feel multiple emotions simultaneously, and the rules for displaying emotions appropriately.

4. Regulating Emotions

Infants use simple strategies to regulate emotions such as fear. As children grow, they become better skilled at regulating their emotions. Children who do not regulate emotions well tend to have problems interacting with others.

10.2 Temperament

1. What Is Temperament?

Temperament refers to biologically based, stable patterns of behaviour that are evident soon after birth. The New York Longitudinal Study suggested three main categories of temperament, but most modern theories focus on dimensions of temperament. According to Rothbart's theory, temperament includes three main dimensions: surgency/extraversion, negative affect, and effortful control.

2. Hereditary and Environmental Contributions to Temperament

The major theories agree that both heredity and environment contribute to temperament. Twin studies show that heredity affects temperament, more in childhood than in infancy. The environment influences temperament through parents' behaviour and by amplifying effects of genes. And temperament makes some children more susceptible to environmental influences.

3. Stability of Temperament

Temperament is somewhat stable in infancy and becomes more stable beginning in the preschool years. Temperament in childhood is somewhat related to personality in adulthood.

4. Temperament and Other Aspects of Development

Many investigators have shown that temperament is related to other aspects of development. Difficult babies are more likely to have behavioural problems by the time they are old enough to attend school. Persistent children are more successful in school; shy children sometimes have problems with peers; anxious children are more compliant with parents; and angry or fearful children are prone to depression. However, the impact of temperament always depends on the environment in which children develop.

10.3 Attachment

1. The Growth of Attachment

Attachment is an enduring social-emotional relationship between infant and caregiver. Bowlby's theory of attachment is rooted in evolutionary psychology and describes four stages in the development of attachment: preattachment, attachment in the making, true attachment, and reciprocal relationships.

2. The Quality of Attachment

Research with the Strange Situation, in which infant and caregiver are separated briefly, reveals four primary forms of attachment. Most common is a secure attachment, in which infants have complete trust in the caregiver. Less common are three types of insecure attachment relationships that lack this trust. In avoidant relationships, infants deal with the lack of trust by ignoring the caregiver; in resistant relationships, infants often seem angry with the caregiver; in disorganized (disoriented) relationships, infants seem to not understand the caregiver's absence.

Children who have had secure attachment relationships during infancy often interact with their peers more readily and more skillfully. Secure attachment is most likely to occur when caregivers respond sensitively and consistently to the infants' needs. Adults who value their relationship with their own parents/primary caregivers are most likely to use the sensitive caregiving that promotes secure attachments with their own infants.

Test Yourself

1. Modern approaches to emotion emphasize the _____ of emotions in helping people to adapt to their environment.

2. _____ are experienced by people worldwide and consist of a subjective feeling, a physiological change, and an overt behaviour.

3. Complex emotions (sometimes called self-conscious emotions) develop between 18 and 24 months of age because they depend on the child having _____.

4. In _____, infants look to a parent to help them interpret an unfamiliar or ambiguous environment.

5. Compared to younger children's emotion regulation, older children and adolescents rely on themselves, not parents, to regulate emotions; more often rely on mental strategies to regulate emotions; and _____.

6. In the New York Longitudinal Study, most babies were happy and cheerful; they were called _____ babies.

7. Rothbart's theory of temperament includes three dimensions: surgency/extraversion, negative affect, and _____.

8. Temperament is _____ from infancy through adulthood.

9. Inhibited children are more likely as adults to have an _____ personality.

10. When young children with difficult temperaments grow up, they are prone to _____.

11. Modern theories view attachment from an evolutionary perspective and emphasize the _____.

12. Young infants are interested in people and can identify their mothers, but not until _____ months of age do infants identify a single attachment figure who provides a stable social-emotional base.

13. In the Strange Situation, infants with _____ attachment are not upset when the caregiver leaves and ignore their caregiver when she or he returns.

14. Around the world, _____ attachment is the most common form.

15. The most important factor in determining a secure attachment is _____.

Answers: (1) functional value; (2) Basic emotions; (3) some understanding of himself or herself; (4) social referencing; (5) match regulation strategies more accurately to the setting; (6) easy; (7) effortful control; (8) relatively stable; (9) introverted; (10) behavioural problems; (11) survival value of a strong social-emotional relationship between caregiver and child; (12) 6 to 8; (13) avoidant; (14) secure; (15) caregivers responding predictably and appropriately to the baby.

11

Understanding Self and Others

Pikselstock/Shutterstock

 11.1

Who Am I?
Self-Concept

 11.2

Self-Esteem

 11.3

Understanding Others

More than a century ago, G. Stanley Hall, an influential American developmental psychologist, wrote that adolescence was "strewn with wreckage of mind, body and morals" (Hall, 1904, p. xiv). Judging by today's movies and media, Hall's view persists: When teens aren't presented as runaways, drug addicts, and shoplifters, they're moody and withdrawn or manic. But how accurate is this picture? What does current research show about adolescence and the process of developing independence and identity?

In **Module 11.1**, we'll look at the mechanisms that give rise to a person's identity, and we'll see whether adolescent "storm and stress" is a necessary step in achieving an identity. Of course, people are often happier with some aspects of themselves than with others. These evaluative aspects of identity are the focus of **Module 11.2**. Finally, in **Module 11.3**, we'll look at how we develop an understanding of others, because as we learn more about ourselves we learn more about other people too.

 ## 11.1 Who Am I? Self-Concept

OUTLINE
Origins of Self-Recognition
The Evolving Self-Concept
The Search for Identity

LEARNING OBJECTIVES
1. When do infants first acquire a sense of self?
2. How does self-concept become more elaborate as children grow?
3. How do adolescents achieve an identity?

Dea was born in Seoul of Korean parents but was adopted by a Dutch couple in southern Ontario when she was three months old. Growing up, she has always considered herself a Canadian. Now in high school, however, Dea realizes that others see her as an Asian Canadian, a possible identity that she has never much thought about. She wonders, "Who am I really? Canadian? Dutch Canadian? Asian Canadian?"

Like Dea, do you sometimes wonder who you are? **Answers to "Who am I?" reflect a person's** *self-concept,* **which refers to the attitudes, behaviours, and values that a person believes make him or her a unique individual.** One answer to "Who am I?"—from a 15-year-old—shows just how complex a person's self-concept can be:

> I'm smart, shy, quiet, and self-conscious, except when I'm around my friends. Then I can be loud and sometimes obnoxious! I'd like to be more outgoing all the time, but that's not me. And I wish that I was more responsible, like at school. But then I'd be a real nerd, and who wants that?

As an adult, your answer is probably even more complex. How did you acquire this complex self-concept? We'll answer that question in this module, beginning with the origins of an infant's sense of self. Later, we'll see how identity becomes elaborated after infancy and see how individuals like Dea develop an ethnic identity.

Raise a cyber child and discover the world of parenthood at …

My Virtual Child

Origins of Self-Recognition

What is the starting point for self-concept? Following the lead of the nineteenth-century philosopher and psychologist William James, modern researchers believe that the foundation of self-concept is the child's awareness that he or she exists. At some point early in life, children must realize that they exist independently of other people and objects in the environment, and that their existence continues over time.

A rudimentary form of this awareness emerges in infancy. From watching their arms and legs as they move, infants become aware of their bodies. They realize that a moving hand is their hand; it belongs to them. Youngsters usually reach the next landmark in self-awareness at about 18 to 24 months; this development is revealed in studies in which a mother places a red mark on her infant's nose; she does this surreptitiously, while wiping the baby's face. Then the infant is placed in front of a mirror. Many one-year-olds touch the red mark on the mirror, showing that they notice the mark on the face in the mirror. At about 15 months of age, however, an important change occurs: Many babies see the red mark in the mirror, then reach up and touch *their own* noses. By age two, most children do this (Bullock & Lütkenhaus, 1990; Lewis, 1997). When these older toddlers notice the red mark in the mirror, they understand that the funny-looking nose in the mirror is their own.

Although even very young babies enjoy looking at that "thing" in the mirror, it is not until about 15 months of age that babies realize *they* are the thing in the mirror—one of the first signs of an emerging sense of self.

This pattern of age-related change is found among infants living in communities that have no mirrors (or other reflective surfaces), which shows that toddlers' behaviour is not due to their growing understanding of mirrors (Kärtner, Keller, Chaudhary, & Yovsi, 2012; Priel & deSchonen, 1986). However, self-awareness on the mirror task emerges at a younger age in Western cultures that view people as autonomous. In other words, young children become aware that they are independent beings when their cultures emphasize that independent nature (Kärtner et al., 2012).

We don't need to rely solely on the mirror task to know that self-awareness emerges between 18 and 24 months of age. During this same period, toddlers look more at photographs of themselves than at photos of other children. They also refer to themselves by name or with a personal pronoun, such as "I" or "me," and sometimes they know their age and their gender. These changes, which often occur together, suggest that self-awareness is well established in most children by age two (Lewis & Ramsay, 2004; Kärtner et al., 2012).

During the preschool years, children begin to recognize continuity in the self over time; the "I" in the present is linked to the "I" in the past (Lazardis, 2013). Awareness of a self that is extended in time is fostered by conversations with parents about the past and the future. Through such conversations, a three-year-old celebrating a birthday understands that she's an older version of the same person who had a birthday a year previously (Koh & Wang, 2012). And during the elementary school years, children can project themselves into the future, anticipating what the present "I" may be like in years to come (Bohn & Berntsen, 2013).

Once self-awareness is established, children begin to acquire a self-concept. That is, once children fully understand that they exist and that they have a unique mental life, they begin to wonder who they are. They want to define themselves. In the next section, we'll see how this self-concept becomes more complex as children develop.

Pauline Breijer/Shutterstock

The Evolving Self-Concept

Before you go any further, return to the teenager's description on page 375. It relies heavily on psychological traits. The first sentence alone includes eight adjectives referring to these traits: smart, shy, quiet, self-conscious, loud, obnoxious, outgoing, and responsible. How do children develop such a complex view of themselves? For toddlers and preschoolers, self-concept is much simpler. Asked to describe themselves, preschoolers are likely to mention physical characteristics ("I have blue eyes"), their preferences ("I like cookies"), their possessions ("I have trucks"), and their competencies ("I can count to 50").

These features all share a focus on attributes of children that are observable and concrete (Harter, 2006). They also emphasize personal characteristics that are (relatively) unchanging across time and setting. All preschool children mention such characteristics, but they dominate European American preschoolers' descriptions of themselves. In contrast, in many Asian cultures, the self is defined, to a much greater extent, by children's social relationships. For example, in describing themselves, Chinese preschoolers are more likely than European American preschoolers to say, "I love my mommy" or "I play with Qi at school," showing that the self is embedded in relationships with others (Wang, 2006).

At about five to seven years of age, children's self-descriptions begin to change (Harter, 2005). Children are more likely to mention emotions ("Sometimes I get angry"). They are also more likely to mention the social groups to which they belong ("I'm on a soccer team"). Finally, in contrast to preschool children, who simply mention their competencies, elementary-school children describe their level of skill in relation to their peers ("I'm the best speller in my whole class").

Self-concepts change again as children enter adolescence (Harter, 2006). They now include attitudes ("I love algebra") and personality traits ("I'm usually a very happy person"). Adolescents also begin to make religious and political beliefs part of their self-concept ("I'm a Catholic" or "I'm a Conservative"). Another change is that adolescents' self-concepts often vary with the setting. A teenager might say, "I'm really shy around people that I don't know, but I let loose when I'm with my friends and family."

Yet another change is that adolescents' self-concepts are often future oriented: Adolescents often describe themselves in terms of what they will be when they reach adulthood (Harter, 2005; Steinberg at al., 2009). These descriptions may include occupational goals ("I'm going to be an English teacher"), educational plans ("I plan to go to a community college to learn about computers"), or social roles ("I want to get married as soon as I finish high school").

The gradual elaboration of self-concept from the preschool years to adolescence is outlined in the Summary Table. Two general changes are evident: First, self-concept becomes richer as children grow; adolescents simply know much more about themselves than do preschoolers. Second, the type of knowledge that children have of themselves changes. Preschoolers' understanding is linked to the concrete, the real, and the here and now. Adolescents' understanding, in contrast, is more abstract and more psychological and sees the self as evolving over time. The change in children's knowledge of themselves should not surprise you because it is exactly the type of change that Piaget described. Concrete-operational children's focus on the real and tangible extends to their thoughts about themselves, just as formal-operational adolescents' focus on the abstract and hypothetical applies to their thoughts about themselves.

Adolescence is also a time of increasing self-reflection. Adolescents look for an identity to integrate the many different and sometimes conflicting elements of the self (Marcia, 1991). We'll look at this search for identity in detail in the next section.

DEVELOPMENTAL CHANGES IN SELF-CONCEPT

Preschoolers	School-Age Children	Adolescents
Possessions	Emotions	Attitudes
Physical characteristics	Social groups	Personality traits
Preferences	Comparisons with peers	Beliefs vary with the setting
Competencies		Future oriented

I like cars and trucks.

I'm the best goalie in my class.

I'm quiet and shy at school.

The Search for Identity

Erik Erikson (1968) believed that adolescents struggle to achieve an identity that will allow them to participate in the adult world. How do they accomplish this? To learn more about possible identities, adolescents use the hypothetical reasoning skills of the formal operational stage to experiment with different selves. Adolescents' advanced cognitive skills allow them to imagine themselves in different roles.

Much of the testing and experimentation is career oriented. Some adolescents, like the ones shown in the photo, may envision themselves as rock stars; others may imagine being a professional athlete, an overseas aid worker, or a best-selling novelist. Other testing is romance oriented. Teens may fall in love and imagine living with the loved one. Still other explorations involve religious and political beliefs (Harre, 2007; Lopez, Huynh, & Fuligni, 2011). Teens give different identities a trial run just as you might test drive different cars before selecting one. By fantasizing about their future, adolescents begin to discover who they will be.

The self-absorption that marks the teenage search for identity is referred to as *adolescent egocentrism* (Elkind, 1978; Schwartz, Maynard, & Uzelac, 2008). Unlike preschoolers, adolescents know that others have different perspectives on the world. At the same time, many adolescents wrongly believe that they are the focus of others' thinking and attention. A teen who drops her books, like the one in the photo on next page, may imagine that all her friends are thinking only about how sloppy she is. **Many adolescents feel that they are, in effect, actors whose performance is being watched constantly by their peers, a phenomenon known as the** *imaginary audience.*

Adolescent self-absorption is also demonstrated by the *personal fable,* **teenagers' tendency to believe that their experiences and feelings are unique,**

As part of their search for an identity, adolescents often try on different roles, such as trying to imagine what life might be like as a rock star.

that no one has ever felt or thought as they do. Whether it is the excitement of first love, the despair of a broken relationship, or the confusion of planning for the future, adolescents often believe they are the first to experience these feelings and that no one else could possibly understand the power of their emotions (Elkind & Bowen, 1979). **Adolescents' belief in their uniqueness also contributes to an** *illusion of invulnerability*—**the belief that misfortune happens only to others.** They think they can have sex without becoming pregnant or drive recklessly without being in an auto accident. Those misfortunes, they believe, happen only to others.

Adolescent egocentrism, imaginary audiences, personal fables, and the illusion of invulnerability become less common as adolescents make progress toward achieving an identity. What exactly is involved in achieving an identity? James E. Marcia, Professor Emeritus at Simon Fraser University in B.C., has investigated the formation of identity. Marcia has proposed that, in dealing with the identity crisis, most adolescents experience different phases or *statuses*, though not necessarily in the following order (Marcia, 1980, 1991):

Adolescents often believe that others are constantly watching them, a phenomenon known as *imaginary audience*; consequently, they're often upset or embarrassed when they make obvious mistakes or blunders, such as spilling food or drink, or dropping things.

- *Diffusion:* **Individuals in this status are confused or overwhelmed by the task of achieving an identity and are doing little to achieve one.**

- *Foreclosure:* **Individuals in this status have an identity determined largely by adults rather than from personal exploration of alternatives.**

- *Moratorium:* **Individuals in this status are still examining different alternatives and have yet to find a satisfactory identity.**

- *Achievement:* **Individuals in this status have explored alternatives and have deliberately chosen a specific identity.**

Unlike Piaget's stages, these four phases do not necessarily occur in sequence. Most young adolescents are in a state of diffusion or foreclosure. The common element in these phases is that teens are not exploring alternative identities. They are avoiding the crisis altogether or have resolved it by taking on an identity suggested by parents or other adults. As individuals move beyond adolescence and into young adulthood and have more opportunity to explore alternative identities, diffusion and foreclosure become less common and achievement and moratorium become more common (Meeus, van de Schoot, Keijsers, Schwartz, & Branje 2010). During late adolescence and young adulthood, however, people may alternate between moratorium and achievement statuses: For example, having explored a range of occupations and selected one provisionally, older adolescents explore the chosen occupation in depth, and if it doesn't feel right—a good fit to them, worthy of a deep commitment—they reconsider their choice and re-enter the moratorium status (Luyckx et al., 2013).

Typically, young people do not reach the achievement status for all aspects of identity at the same time (Goossens, 2001; Kroger & Green, 1996). Some adolescents may reach the achievement status for occupation before achieving it for religion and politics. Others reach the achievement status for religion before other domains. Evidently, few youth achieve a sense of identity all at once; instead, the crisis of identity is first resolved in some areas and then in others.

QUESTION 11.1

Jenny thinks she might like to be an engineer, but she also enjoys dance. To help decide what path would be best for her, Jenny has taken a battery of interest inventories, and her guidance counsellor has suggested universities where she could pursue both engineering and dance. Which of the four statuses best describes Jenny, at least as far as a possible occupation is concerned? *(Answer is on page 386.)*

What circumstances help adolescents to achieve identity? Parents are influential (Marcia, 1980, 1983). When parents encourage discussion and recognize their children's autonomy, the children are more likely to reach the achievement status. Apparently, these youth feel encouraged to undertake the personal experimentation that leads to identity. In contrast, when parents set rules with little justification and enforce them without explanation, children are more likely to remain in the foreclosure status. These teens are discouraged from experimenting personally; instead, their parents simply tell them what identity to adopt. Overall, adolescents are most likely to establish a well-defined identity in a family atmosphere where parents encourage children to explore alternatives on their own but do not pressure them or provide explicit direction (Koepke & Denissen, 2012; Smits, Soenens, Vansteenkiste, Luyckx, & Goossens, 2010).

Beyond parents, peers are also influential. When adolescents have close friends whom they trust, they feel more secure exploring alternatives (Doumen et al., 2012). The broader social context also contributes (Bosma & Kunnen, 2001). Exploration takes time and access to resources; neither may be readily available to adolescents living in poverty (e.g., they can't explore because they have to drop out of school to support themselves and their family). Finally, through their personality, adolescents themselves may affect the ease with which they achieve an identity. Individuals who are more open to experience and are more agreeable (friendly, generous, helpful) are more likely to achieve an identity (Crocetti, Rubini, Luyckx, & Meeus, 2008; Klimstra et al., 2013).

ETHNIC IDENTITY. For many adolescents growing up in North America today, achieving an identity is even more challenging because they are members of ethnic minority groups. The Cultural Influences feature describes one example.

Cultural Influences

Dea's Ethnic Identity

Dea, the adolescent in the opening vignette, belongs to the approximately one-fifth of adolescents and young adults living in Canada who are members of ethnic minority groups (Statistics Canada, 2011a), a proportion projected to rise steadily over the next few decades (Malenfant, Lebel, & Martel, 2010). These groups include African Canadians, Asian Canadians, Latin American Canadians, and Canada's Indigenous people. **Such individuals typically develop an** *ethnic identity:* **They feel a part of their ethnic group and learn the special customs and traditions of their group's culture and heritage** (Phinney, 2005).

An ethnic identity seems to be achieved in three phases. Initially, adolescents have not examined their ethnic roots; they are just not interested. For youngsters in this phase, ethnic identity is not yet an important personal issue.

Part of the search for an ethnic identity involves learning cultural traditions, such as learning how to prepare foods associated with one's ethnic group.

In the second phase, adolescents begin to explore the personal impact of their ethnic heritage. Curiosity and questioning are characteristic of this stage, for instance, wanting to know about their culture and how it differs from others. Part of this phase involves learning cultural traditions; for example, many adolescents learn to prepare ethnic food.

In the third phase, individuals achieve a distinct ethnic self-concept. Once in this phase, an Asian Canadian adolescent like Dea might explain her ethnic identification as that she had been born in Korea and was thus Korean, but she is now in Canada with other people from different cultures and also considers herself to be Canadian.

To see if you understand the differences between these stages of ethnic identity, reread the vignette on page 375 about Dea and decide which stage applies to her. The answer appears on page 386, just before Check Your Learning.

Critical Thinking Questions: How can parents and other adults help children with ethnic identity? What could adults do to help children understand and develop their own ethnic identities?

Older adolescents are more likely than younger ones to have achieved an ethnic identity because they are more likely to have had opportunities to explore their cultural heritage (French, Seidman, Allen, & Aber, 2006). As adolescents explore their ethnic identity, they often change the way they refer to themselves. For example, a Canadian teen whose parents were born in Vietnam might refer to herself at different times as Vietnamese, Vietnamese Canadian, or Asian Canadian, in no particular order (Fuligni, Kiang, Witkow, & Baldelomar, 2008).

As is true for identity formation in general, parents matter. Adolescents are most likely to achieve an ethnic self-concept when their parents encourage them to learn about their cultural heritage and prepare them for possible discrimination. For example, African American adolescents have a more advanced ethnic identity when their mothers tell them about Black history and racism (McHale et al., 2006; Seaton, Yip, Morgan-Lopez, & Sellers, 2012). Similarly, Latino teens have a more advanced ethnic identity when their parents emphasize the importance of knowing their cultural heritage and routinely highlight that heritage by, for example, displaying cultural artifacts in the home (Umaña-Taylor & Guimond, 2010).

Do adolescents benefit from a strong ethnic identity? Yes. Adolescents who have achieved an ethnic identity tend to have higher self-esteem and find their interactions with family and friends more satisfying (Mandara, Gaylord-Harden, Richard, & Ragsdale, 2009; Rivas-Drake et al., 2014). They are also happier and worry less (Kiang, Yip, Gonzales-Backen, Witkow, & Fuligni, 2006). In addition, adolescents with a strong ethnic identity are less affected by discrimination—they maintain their self-worth after experiencing racial or ethnic discrimination (Neblett, Rivas-Drake, & Umaña-Taylor, 2012; Tynes, Umaña-Taylor, Rose, Lin, & Anderson, 2012).

Some individuals achieve a well-defined ethnic self-concept and at the same time identify strongly with the mainstream culture. In Canada, for example, many Chinese Canadians embrace both Chinese and Canadian culture; in England, many South Asians identify with both Indian and British cultures. We need to remember, however, that racial and ethnic groups living in North America are diverse. Ancestry can be African, Asian, Hispanic, European, or Indigenous, and these cultures and heritages differ. We should expect, then, that the nature and consequences of a strong ethnic self-concept would differ across these and other ethnic groups (Phinney, 2005).

Even within any particular group, the nature and consequences of ethnic identity can change over successive generations (Cuellar, Nyberg, Maldonado, & Roberts, 1997). As successive generations become more assimilated into mainstream culture, they may identify less strongly with ethnic culture (Marks, Patton, & García Coll, 2011). When parents maintain strong feelings of ethnic identity that their children do not share, problems sometimes develop, as immigrant parents cling to the "old ways" while their children embrace the new culture. For example, in one study of Chinese immigrants to Canada by Catherine Costigan and Daphné Dokis from the University of Victoria in British Columbia, children were less interested in school and had more conflicts with parents when they strongly identified with Canada but their parents did not (Costigan & Dokis, 2006). Similar results have been found for Chinese immigrants to the United States (Kim, Chen, Wang, Shen, & Orozco-Lapray, 2013): When children identified with the United States but their parents did not, parents were less supportive of their children, which caused them to do less well in school. In another study (Schofield, Parke, Kim, & Coltrane, 2008), Mexican American children had more conflicts with parents and more behavioural problems when they identified themselves as "Anglo" and their parents identified themselves as Mexican.

When people first come to a new country, they are faced with many changes and must learn to adapt in order to live in different sociocultural surroundings. We will look at research into how immigrant youth adapt to coming to a new country in the Focus on Research feature.

Focus On Research

Identity and Acculturation of Immigrant Youth

Who were the investigators, and what was the aim of the study? When young people immigrate, they move to a new country with a different culture. How do young people adapt when they settle in a different country with different social and cultural norms? John W. Berry of Queen's University in Kingston, Ontario, worked with an international group of researchers from Canada, the United States, Norway, and the Netherlands, in a major study of immigrant youth and their adaptation to new countries (Berry, Phinney, Sam, & Vedder, 2006). **This study focused on** *acculturation,* **the process of integrating into and adopting the customs of a different culture.** This extensive study examined the ways in which immigrant youth between the ages of 13 and 18 adapted, and how well they dealt with adaptation. The young immigrants were compared to representative samples of youngsters of the same age from each of the 13 countries studied.

How did the investigators measure the topic of interest? The young participants completed a comprehensive, structured questionnaire. Sets of questions measured acculturation, cultural identity (both ethnic and national), language proficiency and use, contact with peers from within the ethnic group and from the wider society, family relationships, perception of discrimination, and psychological and sociocultural adaptation.

Who were the children in the study? The study involved about 8000 adolescents: over 5000 immigrant youth and just over 2600 "national youth." Ages ranged from 13 to 18 years, with an average age of 15. There were roughly equal numbers of boys and girls in the samples.

What was the design of the study? This study used a complex form of correlational analysis called factor analysis (mentioned in Module 10.2), which looks at whether certain variables group together. Berry and colleagues were interested in finding clusters of responses that would show measures of common aspects of adaptation.

Were there ethical concerns with the study? No. The youths were told that filling out the questionnaire was voluntary and all responses were anonymous.

What were the results? Four "acculturation profiles" were found, from most to least well integrated, along with two forms of adaptation, psychological and sociocultural. Those most acculturated were also the best adapted both psychologically and socioculturally.

What did the investigators conclude? Berry et al. (2006) advised that, while acculturation was helpful, immigrant youth should not lose their heritage. Integration should be encouraged along with links to the wider society. At the same time, however, immigrants should maintain their own culture. The larger society should aid new immigrants in this and support both acculturation and maintenance of ethnocultural identity. The outcome of this research study seems to show that all countries should work toward the multicultural ideal endorsed in Canada: acceptance of diversity and promotion of equity regardless of one's origins.

What converging evidence would strengthen these conclusions? A longitudinal study would allow follow-up and would see whether those best acculturated continued to be the best adapted. More in-depth research to investigate the differing acculturation and adaptation profiles, and to see whether these held up when examined by different methodologies, would strengthen the researchers' conclusions. Although not strictly a follow-up, more recent research by Berry and colleagues does seem to support the idea that acculturation and integration, while maintaining ties to a person's heritage, lead to greater life satisfaction and better mental health and well-being (e.g., Berry & Hou, 2016).

Critical Thinking Questions: (i) Here we look at government policy again. What can/should provincial/territorial and federal governments do to help new Canadians integrate into society but also retain their cultural heritage? (ii) Have you come to Canada from a different country, or do you have a different cultural background from that of "mainstream" Canada? What were your experiences and how do you feel about acculturation?

Finally, let's think about adolescents for whom an ethnic identity is a particular challenge—those whose parents come from different racial or ethnic groups. Identity in biracial adolescents can be quite fluid. Some biracial adolescents first identify themselves as monoracial, then embrace a biracial identity; others shift in the opposite direction, converging on a single racial identity; still others shift from one racial identity to another (Doyle & Kao, 2007). Collectively, youth with shifting racial identities tend to have lower self-esteem than those with a consistent biracial identity (Csizmadia, Brunsma, & Cooney, 2012; Hitlin, Brown, & Elder, 2006).

In 2002, Canada's ethnic diversity was assessed when the Department of Canadian Heritage and Statistics Canada collaborated to conduct an Ethnic Diversity Survey (Statistics Canada, 2003a, n.p.). This survey was a form of census that examined ethnocultural backgrounds of non-Aboriginal Canadians. Nearly half of respondents reported British, French, or Canadian ancestry, and another one-fifth reported European ancestry other than British or French. Thirteen percent of the population reported non-European descent, and 22 percent said that they were of mixed ethnic heritage or that they did not know their ethnic background. As the Statistics Canada report on the diversity survey notes, "Canada is a multicultural society whose ethnic makeup has been shaped over time by different waves of immigrants and their descendants, as well as by the Aboriginal peoples of the country" (Statistics Canada, 2003a). An additional finding was that "Canadian" identity increased with generations in Canada, as subsequent generations integrated into the mainstream culture. As you have seen in the Focus on Research feature, however, Canadian society allows for both acculturation and maintenance of ethnic identity—probably the healthiest model.

STORM AND STRESS.   According to many novelists and filmmakers, the search for identity that we have described in the past few pages is inherently a struggle, a time of storm and stress for adolescents. Although this view may make for best-selling novels and hit movies, in reality, the rebellious teen is vastly overstated. Adolescents generally enjoy happy and satisfying relationships with their parents (Steinberg, 2001). Most teens love their parents and feel loved by them. And they embrace many of their parents' values and look to parents for advice.

Cross-cultural research provides further evidence that for most teens, adolescence is not a time of turmoil and conflict. Offer, Ostrov, Howard, and Atkinson (1988) interviewed adolescents from 10 countries and found that most adolescents were moving confidently and happily toward adulthood. As Figure 11-1 shows, most adolescents around the world reported that they were usually happy, and few avoided their homes.

The Offer et al. (1988) work is more than a quarter-century old, but newer studies paint much the same picture. In one study of Arab adolescents living in Israel (Azaiza, 2005), 82 percent of adolescents said they felt wanted by their family and 89 percent reported that they appreciated their family. In another study (Güngör & Bornstein, 2010), adolescents in Turkey and Belgium rated their mothers as being very supportive, endorsing items such as "My mother supports me in dealing with problems" and "My mother talks to me in a comforting way." These findings are consistent with the older studies and undercut the myth of adolescence as necessarily being a time when adolescent storms rain on parent–child relationships.

Of course, parent–child relations *do* change during adolescence. As teens become more independent, their relationships with their parents become more egalitarian. Parents must adjust to their children's growing sense of autonomy by treating them more like equals (Laursen & Collins, 1994). This growing independence means that teens spend less time with their parents, are less affectionate toward them, and argue more often with them about matters of style, taste, and freedom (Shanahan, McHale, Crouter, & Osgood, 2007; Stanik, Riina, & McHale, 2013). Although adolescents do have more disagreements with parents, these disputes are usually relatively mild—bickering, not all-out shouting matches—and usually concern an adolescent's personal choices (e.g., hairstyle, clothing), autonomy, and responsibilities (Chen-Gaddini, 2012; Ehrlich, Dykas, & Cassidy, 2012). These changes are natural by-products of an evolving parent–child relationship in which the "child" is nearly a fully independent young adult (Steinberg & Silk, 2002).

Before you think that this portrait of parent–child relationships in adolescence is too good to be true, we want to add two cautionary notes. First, conflicts between parents and their adolescent children are often very distressing for parents, who may read far more into these conflicts than their teenagers do (Steinberg, 2001). Parents sometimes fear that arguments over attire or household chores may reflect much more fundamental disagreements about values: A mother may interpret her son's refusal to clean his room as a rejection of values concerning the need for order and cleanliness, when the son simply doesn't want to waste time cleaning a room that he knows will become a mess again in a matter of days. Second, for a minority of families—roughly 25 percent—parent–child conflicts in

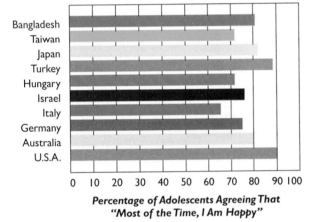

Percentage of Adolescents Agreeing That "Most of the Time, I Am Happy"

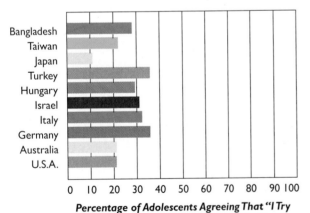

Percentage of Adolescents Agreeing That "I Try to Stay Away from Home Most of the Time"

Figure 11-1 Results of cross-cultural research into adolescents' views of family and home life.

Source: Based on Offer, D., Ostrov, E., Howard, K. I., & Atkinson, R. (1988). *The teenage world: Adolescents' self-image in ten countries*. New York: Plenum.

adolescence are more serious and are associated with behaviour problems in adolescents (Ehrlich et al., 2012). These more harmful conflicts are more common among adolescents who don't regulate their emotions well (Eisenberg et al., 2008), and they often predate adolescence; even as children, these adolescents were prone to conflict with their parents (Steeger & Gondoli, 2013; Steinberg, 2001).

DEPRESSION. The challenges of adolescence can lead some youth to become depressed (Fried, 2005). Depressed individuals have pervasive feelings of sadness, are irritable, have low self-esteem, sleep poorly, and are unable to concentrate. According to the Canadian Mental Health Association (2016), about 5 percent of males and 12 percent of females aged 12 to 19 have experienced a major depressive episode. Adolescent girls are more often affected than boys, probably because social challenges in adolescence are often greater for girls than boys (Center for Behavioral Health Statistics and Quality, 2012; Hammen & Rudolph, 2003).

Depression is often triggered when adolescents experience a serious loss, disappointment, or failure, such as the death of a loved one or when a much-anticipated date turns out to be a fiasco (Schneiders et al., 2006). Of course, many adolescents and adults experience negative events like these, but most do not become depressed. Why? One contributing factor is temperament: Children who are less able to regulate their emotions are, as adolescents, more prone to depression (Karevold, Røysamb, Ystrom, & Mathiesen, 2009). Another factor is a belief system in which adolescents see themselves in an extremely negative light. Depression-prone adolescents are, for example, more likely to blame themselves for failure (Gregory et al., 2007). Thus, after the disappointing date, a depression-prone teen is likely to think, "I acted like a fool," instead of placing blame elsewhere by thinking "Gee, he was a real jerk!"

Parents and families can also put an adolescent at risk for depression. Not surprisingly, adolescents more often become depressed when their parents are emotionally distant and uninvolved, when their parents are contemptuous and cruel, or when family life is stressful due to economic disadvantage or marital conflict (Karevold et al., 2009; Schwartz et al., 2012; Yap, Allen, & Ladouceur, 2008). And when parents rely on punitive discipline—hitting and shouting—adolescents often resort to the negative attributions (e.g., blaming themselves) that can lead to depression (Lau, Rijsdijk, Gregory, McGuffin, & Eley, 2007).

Heredity also plays a role, putting some adolescents at greater risk for depression (Haeffel et al., 2008; Lau, Belli, Gregory, Napolitano, & Eley, 2012). Neurotransmitters may be the underlying mechanism. Some adolescents may feel depressed because lower levels of neurotransmitters make it difficult for them to experience happiness, joy, and other pleasurable emotions (Kaufman & Charney, 2003).

To treat depression, some adolescents take antidepressant drugs designed to correct the imbalance in neurotransmitters. However, drug treatment has no lasting effects—it works only while people are taking the drugs—and it has been linked to increased risk of suicide (Vitiello & Swedo, 2004). Consequently, psychotherapy is a better choice for treating depressed adolescents. One common approach emphasizes cognitive and social skills; that is, adolescents learn how to have rewarding social interactions and to interpret them appropriately (Hollon, Haman, & Brown, 2002). These treatments *are* effective (Weisz, McCarty, & Valeri, 2006)—and depressed adolescents do need help. Left untreated, depression can interfere with performance in school and social relationships and may also lead to recurring depression in adulthood (Nevid, Rathus, & Greene, 2003; Rudolph, Ladd, & Dinella, 2007). Also effective are prevention programs, which can substantially reduce the number of depressive episodes in high-risk youth (Stice, Shaw, Bohon, Martin, & Rohde, 2009).

ANSWER 11.1
Jenny appears to be in the moratorium status because she is actively exploring different alternatives.

Response to question on page 381 about Dea's ethnic identity: Dea, the Dutch Asian Canadian high-school student, doesn't know how to integrate the Korean heritage of her biological parents with the Dutch Canadian culture in which she was reared. This would put her in the second phase of acquiring an ethnic identity. On the one hand, she is examining her ethnic roots, which means she has progressed beyond the initial stage. On the other hand, she has not yet integrated her Asian and European roots, and so has not reached the third and final phase.

Check Your Learning

RECALL What evidence indicates that sense of self emerges during the second year of life? What contributes to the emergence of a sense of self?

Describe research that undermines the view of adolescence as a period of "storm and stress."

INTERPRET Compare and contrast the three stages in the achievement of an ethnic identity with Piaget's description of the concrete and formal operational stages of cognitive development.

APPLY The Abadi family has just immigrated to Canada from Syria. The mother and father want their two children to grow up appreciating their Syrian heritage, but they worry that a strong ethnic identity may not be good for their children. What advice would you give Mr. and Mrs. Abadi about the impact of ethnic identity on children's development?

11.2   Self-Esteem

OUTLINE	LEARNING OBJECTIVES
Developmental Change in Self-Esteem	**1.** How does self-esteem change as children develop?
Variations in Self-Esteem Associated with Ethnicity and Culture	**2.** How does self-esteem vary depending on ethnicity and culture?
Sources of Self-Esteem	**3.** What factors influence the development of self-esteem?
Low Self-Esteem: Cause or Consequence?	**4.** Is children's development affected by low self-esteem?

Throughout elementary school, Amanda was happy with herself—she knew she was smart, reasonably popular, and reasonably attractive. But since she entered Grade 9, she's worried that she's no longer so smart, popular, and attractive. Her growing self-doubt is obvious to her mom, who wonders whether Amanda should see a mental-health professional.

Amanda's mom is concerned about her daughter's *self-esteem,* **which refers to a person's judgment and feelings about his or her own worth.** Children with high self-esteem judge themselves favourably and feel positive about themselves. In contrast, children with low self-esteem judge themselves negatively, are unhappy with themselves, and often would rather be someone else. In this module, we'll see how self-esteem is measured, how it changes as children develop, what forces shape it, and whether Amanda's mom should be concerned.

Developmental Change in Self-Esteem

Think about your own self-esteem. Do you think you have high self-esteem or low self-esteem? To help you answer this question, read each of these sentences and decide how well each applies to you:

> I'm very good at schoolwork.
> I find it very easy to make friends.
> I do very well at all kinds of different sports.
> I'm happy with the way I look.

If you agreed strongly with each of these statements, you definitely have high self-esteem.

When children and adolescents respond to these sentences, their responses reveal two important developmental changes in self-esteem: change in the structure of self-esteem and change in overall levels of self-esteem.

STRUCTURE OF SELF-ESTEEM.

By four or five years of age, which is the earliest we can measure self-esteem, children have a differentiated view of themselves. They can distinguish overall self-esteem as well as self-esteem in specific domains (Marsh, Ellis, & Craven, 2002). This structure should seem familiar because it is like intelligence: In Module 8.1, we saw that hierarchical theories of intelligence begin with a general intelligence that is divided into more specific abilities, such as verbal ability and spatial ability. In the case of self-esteem, overall self-esteem is at the top of the hierarchy, with self-esteem in more specialized areas underneath (Harter, 2006). In the elementary-school years, four specialized areas stand out:

- *Scholastic competence:* How competent or smart the child feels in doing schoolwork.
- *Athletic competence:* How competent the child feels at sports and games requiring physical skill or athletic ability.
- *Social competence:* How competent the child feels in relationships with parents and peers.
- *Physical appearance:* How good-looking the child feels and how much the child likes his or her physical characteristics, such as height, weight, face, and hair.

During the elementary-school years, children's academic self-concepts become particularly well defined (Marsh & Craven, 2006; Marsh & Yeung, 1997). As children accumulate successes and failures in school, they form beliefs about their ability in different content areas (e.g., English, math, science), and these beliefs contribute to their overall academic self-concept. A child who believes that she is skilled at English and math but not so skilled in science will probably have a positive academic self-concept overall. But a child who believes he is untalented in most academic areas will have a negative academic self-concept.

During adolescence, other domains of self-esteem are added, including job competence, close friendships, and romantic appeal. What's more, the social component of self-esteem becomes particularly well differentiated. Adolescents distinguish self-worth in many different social relationships. A teenager may, for example, feel very positive about her relationships with her parents but believe that she's unsuccessful in romantic relationships. Another teen may feel loved and valued by his parents but think that co-workers at his part-time job can't stand him (Harter, Waters, & Whitesell, 1998).

Children's overall self-worth is not simply the average of their self-worth in specialized areas. Instead, self-esteem in some domains contributes more than others. Research, such as that by Jennifer Shapka of the University of British Columbia and her colleagues, has shown that for many children and adolescents, self-esteem concerning appearance has the biggest influence on overall self-esteem (e.g., Shapka & Keating, 2005). Thus, Allison, whose self-worth in the academic, athletic, and social domains is just average, has high self-esteem overall because she believes that she is very good looking. In contrast, although Colleen has high self-esteem in academics and athletics, her overall self-esteem is only average because she considers herself relatively unattractive.

Between the late preschool years and adolescence, self-esteem therefore becomes more complex as older children and adolescents identify distinct domains of self-worth. This growing complexity is not surprising—it reflects the older child's and adolescent's greater cognitive skill and the more extensive social world of older children and adolescents.

CHANGES IN LEVEL OF SELF-ESTEEM.   At what age is self-esteem greatest? The answer may surprise you: It is during the preschool years. Most preschool children have very positive views of themselves across many different domains (Marsh, Ellis, & Craven, 2002). This outcome isn't surprising if you think back to Piaget's description of the preoperational period (Module 6.1). Preschool children are egocentric; they have difficulty taking another person's viewpoint. Unable to see themselves as others do, preschoolers blissfully believe that they are extremely competent in all domains.

Children's self-esteem is often influenced by comparisons with peers; a child who discovers that he's not a very fast runner may lose athletic self-esteem.

As children progress through the elementary-school years, self-esteem usually drops somewhat. Why? In reality, of course, all children are *not* above average. During the elementary-school years, children begin to compare themselves with peers (Ruble, Boggiano, Feldman, & Loebl, 1980). When they do, they discover that they are not necessarily the best readers or the fastest runners. They may realize that they are only average readers. Or like someone who is lagging behind in a race, they come to understand that they are among the slowest runners in the class. This realization means that children's self-esteem usually drops somewhat during the elementary school years.

By the end of the elementary school years, children's self-esteem has usually stabilized (Harter, Whitesell, & Kowalski, 1992) as children learn their place in the "pecking order" of different domains and adjust their self-esteem accordingly. However, self-esteem sometimes drops when children move from elementary school to high school (Twenge & Campbell, 2001). Apparently, when students from different elementary schools enter the same high school, they know where they stand compared to their old elementary-school classmates but not compared to students from other elementary schools. Consequently, peer comparisons begin anew, and self-esteem often suffers temporarily. As a new school becomes familiar and students gradually adjust to the new pecking order, however, self-esteem again increases. Thus, Amanda, the girl in the module-opening vignette, is showing the classic profile, and there's no reason for her mom to worry: Amanda will soon find herself again and self-doubt will wane.

 QUESTION 11.2
During the summer, Karina moved with her family to a new city, where she will begin high school. What will probably happen to Karina's self-esteem as she enters her new school? *(Answer is on page* 392*).*

Sonya Etchison/Fotolia

Variations in Self-Esteem Associated with Ethnicity and Culture

The developmental changes in structure and average levels of self-esteem that we've just described are not universals. Instead, ethnicity and culture each influence these developmental trends, producing important variations. For example, growth of self-worth among U.S. children and adolescents varies depending on their ethnicity. Compared to European American children, African Americans and Hispanic Americans have lower self-esteem during most of the elementary-school years. However, in adolescence the gap narrows for Hispanic Americans and actually reverses for African American adolescents, who have greater self-esteem than their European American peers (Gray-Little & Hafdahl, 2000; Herman, 2004; Twenge & Crocker, 2002). In contrast, Asian American children have greater self-esteem than European American children during the elementary school years, but less self-esteem during middle school and high school (Twenge & Crocker, 2002; Witherspoon, Schotland, Way, & Hughes, 2009).

Scientists don't fully understand why these changes take place. The differences involving Hispanic American and African American children may involve ethnic identity. Beginning in early adolescence, many African American and Hispanic American teens take pride in belonging to a distinct social and cultural group, and this raises their sense of self-worth (Gray-Little & Hafdahl, 2000; Umaña-Taylor, Diversi, & Fine, 2002).

The differences for Asian Americans may reflect their cultural heritage. Children from Asian countries (e.g., China, Japan, Korea) tend to have lower self-esteem than children from North America and Europe, and the difference increases in adolescence (Harter, 2012). Part of this difference is that Asian cultures emphasize modesty to a greater extent than Western cultures; as Asian youngsters internalize this cultural standard, they are reluctant to proclaim extremely positive feelings of self-worth (Cai, Brown, Deng, & Oakes, 2007). But that's not the whole story. Asian adolescents are also more willing to admit their weaknesses (Hamamura, Heine, & Paulhus, 2008). Consequently, although Western adolescents often emphasize areas of strength but ignore weaknesses when estimating overall self-esteem (e.g., as with the example of Allison mentioned on page 388), Asian adolescents' global self-esteem is lower because it reflects strengths *and* weaknesses. Finally, the social-comparison process that fuels self-worth in Western countries is far less common in Asian cultures. Children in Western cultures compare themselves with others in their group and feel good about themselves when they come out on top. In contrast, Asian children and adolescents see themselves as integral parts of their social groups and eschew social comparisons because they can undermine group harmony (Falbo, Poston, Triscari, & Zhang, 1997).

Sadly, at any age and in any domain, it is easy to find children who do not view themselves very positively. Some children are ambivalent about their self-worth; others actually feel negative about themselves. In one study (Cole, 1991), roughly 25 percent of nine- and ten-year-olds had negative self-esteem in at least three domains. Why do these children have so little self-worth compared to their peers? We'll answer this question in the next section.

Sources of Self-Esteem

Why do some children feel so positively about themselves while others feel so negatively? Research indicates two important sources of children's self-esteem. One is based on children's actual competence in domains that are important to them. Children's self-worth is greater when they are skilled in areas that matter to them. In other words, children's interests, abilities, and self-concept are coupled. Children tend to like domains in which they do well, and their self-concepts reflect this (Denissen, Zarret, & Eccles, 2007). Mark, who likes math and gets good grades in math, has a positive math self-concept: "I'm good at math and do well when I have to learn something new in math. And I'd probably like a job that involves math." Heredity contributes, indirectly. Genes help to make some children smarter, more sociable, more attractive, and more skilled athletically. Consequently, such children are more likely to have greater self-worth because they are competent in so many domains. In other words, genes lead to greater competence, which fosters greater self-worth (Harter, 2012; Neiss, Sedikides, & Stevenson, 2006).

Children's and adolescents' self-worth is also affected by how others view them, particularly people who are important to them. Parents matter, of course, even to adolescents. Children are more likely to view themselves positively when their parents are affectionate toward them and involved with them (Behnke, Plunkett, Sands, & Bámaca-Colbert, 2011; Ojanen & Perry, 2007). Around the world, children have higher self-esteem when families live in harmony and parents nurture their children (Scott, Scott, & McCabe, 1991). A father who routinely hugs his daughter and gladly takes her to piano lessons is saying to her, "You are important to me." When children hear this regularly from parents, they evidently internalize the message and come to see themselves positively.

However, work by Dweck and colleagues has shown that parents and teachers should be cautious as to the kind of praise that they give to children (e.g., Kamins & Dweck, 1999; Mueller & Dweck, 1998). Adults may think that praise aids self-esteem, but constant praise, such as being told "You're great" or "You're so smart," can cause a decrease in self-worth and performance. When adults use inflated praise—

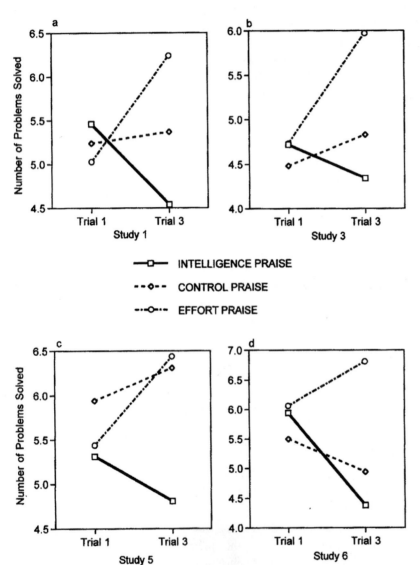

Figure 11-2 Mueller and Dweck (1988) found that type of praise can influence effort on tasks.

Mueller, C.M., & Dweck, C.S. (1998). Praise for intelligence can undermine children's motivation and performance. *Journal of Personality and Social Psychology*, 75(1), 33–52.

for example, saying, "You played that song amazingly well!" when their playing was mediocre—this causes children with low self-esteem to shy away from challenges, because they're afraid they won't succeed (Brummelman, Thomaes, Orobio de Casto, Overbeek, & Bushman, 2014). And type of praise can influence persistence: Mueller and Dweck (1998) found that simply changing phrasing from "You must be smart at these problems" to "You must have worked hard at these problems" (p. 36) led to dramatic differences in children's persistence after an apparent setback, as shown in Figure 11-2. General praise for ability can lead the child to choose easy options or to not try hard for fear of failure.

Praise that focuses on effort encourages the child to try hard, even if the task seems difficult.

Parental discipline also is related to self-esteem. Children with higher self-esteem generally have parents who have reasonable expectations for their children and are willing to discuss rules and discipline with their children (Awong, Grusec, & Sorenson, 2008; Laible & Carlo, 2004). Parents who fail to set rules are, in effect, telling their children that they don't care—they don't value them enough to go to the trouble of creating rules and enforcing them. In much the same way, parents who refuse to discuss discipline with their children are saying, "Your opinions don't matter to me." Not surprisingly, when children internalize these messages, the result is lower overall self-worth.

Peers' views are important, too. Children's and particularly adolescents' self-worth is greater when they believe that their peers think highly of them (Harter, 2012). Lauren's self-worth increases, for example, when she hears that Paula, Matt, and Michael think she's the smartest kid in Grade 8. Conversely, self-esteem drops when peers provide negative feedback, especially when those peers are popular themselves (Thomas et al., 2010).

Thus children's and adolescents' self-worth depends on their being competent at something they value and on being valued by people who are important to them. By encouraging children to find their special talents and by being genuinely interested in their progress, parents and teachers can enhance the self-esteem of all students.

Low Self-Esteem: Cause or Consequence?

Having low self-esteem is associated with many developmental problems (Baumeister, Campbell, Krueger, & Vohs, 2003). Children with low self-esteem are:

- More likely to have problems with peers (Parker, Low, Walker, & Gamm, 2005; Rubin, Coplan, & Bowker, 2009)
- More prone to psychological disorders such as depression (Boden, Fergusson, & Horwood, 2008; Orth, Robins, Widaman, & Conger, 2014)
- More likely to be involved in bullying and aggressive behaviour (Donnellan, Trzesniewski, Robins, Moffitt, & Caspi, 2005; Trzesniewski et al., 2006)
- More likely to do poorly in school (Marsh & Yeung, 1997).

These outcomes provide an excellent opportunity to remember the difficulty in identifying causal forces from correlational studies. Does low self-esteem cause children to have few friends, because peers want to avoid them? Or do poor peer relations cause children to have low self-esteem? Either claim is plausible, and longitudinal studies can help to distinguish them. For example, in research looking at the link between self-esteem and depression, the typical outcome is that low self-esteem measured early in development predicts depression later in development. However, depression detected early in development predicts low self-esteem later in development weakly or not at all (Sowislo & Orth, 2013; van Tuijl et al., 2014). In other words, a 13-year-old with low self-esteem is at risk to become a depressed 16-year-old, but a depressed 13-year-old is at little risk to become a 16-year-old with low self-esteem.

What sometimes happens is that low self-esteem contributes to the outcome but is also caused by the outcome. For example, the claim that "low self-esteem leads to poor peer relations" is supported by findings that, over the course of a school year, children with low social self-esteem often withdraw from peer interactions and, by year's end, are more likely to be left out of social activities and to have few or no friends. But the claim that "poor peer relations reduces social self-worth" is also supported, this time by findings that children who have few friends at the beginning of a school year (but adequate social self-worth) tend to withdraw socially, and by year's end their self-worth has dropped (Caldwell, Rudolph, Troop-Gordon, & Kim, 2004). Thus, poor peer relations reduce self-esteem in the peer context and disrupt future peer interactions, causing social self-worth to drop even more, making children even less likely to have good peer relations—the cycle goes on and on (Rubin et al., 2009). Of course, the same kind of cycle can increase children's self-worth: Success in social relationships can breed positive self-worth, which breeds more success.

Understanding this complex cause-effect-cause pattern is important in deciding how to help children with low self-esteem. Some children benefit directly from therapy that increases their self-esteem. Others, however, who need to change their own behaviour also benefit from learning how to improve their social skills (a topic that we discuss again in Modules 12.4 and 14.2). And, we need to remember that all children have some talents that can be nurtured. Taking the time to recognize each child creates the feelings of "being special" that promote self-esteem.

But we want to end this module on a cautionary note: Too much self-esteem is potentially as big a problem as too little self-esteem. *Narcissistic* **children and adolescents have a grandiose view of themselves, believe themselves to be better than others, and yet relish attention and compliments from others.**[*] Narcissistic children are prone to aggression—their overly positive view of themselves leads them to feel entitled to be aggressive when they don't get their way or believe that others are making fun of them. And they're prone to depression when they notice that their inflated self-worth is at odds with reality (Pauletti, Menon, Menon, Tobin, & Perry, 2012). Given these findings, it's unfortunate that we know little about the factors that lead children and adolescents to become narcissistic. One idea is that children are at risk when they crave parents' attention and their parents are warm but manipulative (Thomaes, Brummelman, Reijntjes, & Bushman, 2013).

Thus far in this chapter, we've focused on children's growing understanding of themselves. In the next module, we'll look at parallel changes that occur in children's understanding of other people.

ANSWER 11.2
Karina's self-esteem is likely to drop, at least temporarily, because she won't know where she stands in comparison to her new classmates (e.g., whether she still is one of the smartest kids, one of the best basketball players, and so on). After she has discovered where she fits in, her self-esteem will increase.

....

✔ Check Your Learning

RECALL What are the salient features of self-esteem during the elementary-school years?

Summarize the ways in which self-esteem changes during childhood and adolescence.

INTERPRET Explain the forces that lead some children to have high self-esteem but others to have low self-esteem.

APPLY Suppose you attended a presentation for parents of younger high-school students, in which a counsellor emphasized the importance of children having high self-esteem. The counsellor asserts that when children have low self-esteem, they do poorly in school and don't get along well with their peers. Would you agree or disagree with the counsellor's claims? Why?

---

[*]Narcissism gets its name from Narcissus, a mythological figure who fell in love with his reflection in a pool.

11.3 Understanding Others

OUTLINE

Describing Others

Understanding What Others Think

Prejudice

LEARNING OBJECTIVES

1. As children develop, how do they describe others differently?

2. How does understanding of others' thinking change as children develop?

3. When do children develop prejudice toward others?

When 12-year-old Ian agreed to babysit his five-year-old brother, Kyle, his mother reminded him to keep Kyle out of the basement because Kyle's birthday presents were there, unwrapped. But as soon as their mother left, Kyle wanted to go to the basement to ride his tricycle. When Ian told him no, Kyle burst into angry tears and shouted, "I'm gonna tell Mom you were mean to me!" Ian wished he could explain to Kyle, but he knew that would just cause more trouble!

We know from Modules 11.1 and 11.2 that Ian, as a young adolescent, has a growing understanding of himself. This vignette suggests that his understanding of other people is also growing. He understands why Kyle is angry, and he also knows that if he gives in to Kyle, his mother will be angry when she returns. Children's growing understanding of others is the focus of this module. We'll begin by looking at how children describe others, then examine their understanding of how others think. We'll also see how children's recognition of different social groups can lead to prejudices.

Describing Others

As children develop, their self-descriptions become richer, more abstract, and more psychological. These same changes occur in children's descriptions of others. Children begin by describing other people in terms of concrete features, such as behaviour and appearance, and progress to describing them in terms of abstract traits (Livesley & Bromley, 1973). For instance, when asked to describe a girl that she liked a lot, seven-year-old Tamsen said,

> Vanessa is short. She has black hair and brown eyes. She uses a wheelchair because she can't walk. She's in my class. She has dolls just like mine. She likes to sing and read.

Tamsen's description of Vanessa is probably not too different from the way she would have described herself: The emphasis is on concrete characteristics, such as Vanessa's appearance, possessions, and preferences. Contrast this with the following description, which Tamsen gave as a 10-year-old:

> Kate lives in my apartment building. She is a very good reader and is also good at math and science. She's nice to everyone in our class. And she's very funny. Sometimes her jokes make me laugh so-o-o hard! She takes piano lessons and likes to play soccer.

Tamsen's account still includes concrete features, such as where Kate lives and what she likes to do. However, psychological traits are also evident: Tamsen describes Kate as nice and funny. By age 10, children move beyond the purely concrete and observable in describing others. During adolescence, descriptions become even more complex, as you can see in the following, from Tamsen as a 16-year-old:

> Jeannie is very understanding. Whenever someone is upset, she's there to give a helping hand. Yet in private, Jeannie can be so sarcastic. She can say some really nasty things about people. But I know she'd never say that stuff if she thought people would hear it because she wouldn't want to hurt their feelings.

This description is more abstract: Tamsen now focuses on psychological traits like understanding and concern for others' feelings. It's also more integrated: Tamsen tries to explain how Jeannie can be both understanding and sarcastic. Although she began, as a seven-year-old, by emphasizing concrete characteristics, as a 16-year-old, she tries to integrate traits to form a cohesive picture.

More recent work also supports the trend to more abstract and richer psychological descriptions of others, but indicates that young children's understanding of other people is more sophisticated than is suggested by their verbal descriptions of people they know (Heyman, 2009). Indeed, modern work indicates that four- and five-year-olds have begun to think about other people in terms of psychological traits such as being smart, friendly, helpful, and shy. They can use behavioural examples to infer an underlying trait: Told about a child who won't share cookies or won't allow another child to play with a toy, four- and five-year-olds accurately describe the child as selfish. In addition, given information about a trait, they correctly predict future behaviour: Told about a child who is shy, they believe that the child will not volunteer to help a puppeteer and will be quiet at a meal with many relatives (Liu, Gelman, & Wellman, 2007).

One idiosyncrasy of young children's descriptions of others is they see others "through rose-coloured glasses"—that is, until about 10 years of age, children have a bias to look for positive traits, not negative traits, in others. Young children are willing to believe that someone is smart (or friendly or helpful) based on relatively little evidence (and based on inconsistent evidence), but require much more evidence (and more consistent evidence) to decided that someone is mean or stupid. This bias may simply be an extension of children's positive evaluations of themselves—recall from page 388 that self-esteem is greatest in preschoolers and declines gradually during the elementary-school years (Boseovski, 2010).

Understanding What Others Think

One trademark of the preschool child's thinking is difficulty in seeing the world from another's point of view. Piaget's term for this was *egocentrism*, and it was a defining characteristic of his preoperational stage of development (see Module 6.1). In much the same way, preschool children's communication is often ineffective because they don't consider the listener's perspective when they talk (see Module 9.4). As children move beyond the preschool years, though, they realize that others see the world differently, both literally and figuratively. For example, in the module-opening vignette, 12-year-old Ian knows why his little brother, Kyle, is angry: Kyle thinks that Ian is being bossy and mean. Ian understands that Kyle doesn't know there is a good reason why he can't go to the basement.

Sophisticated understanding of how others think is achieved gradually throughout childhood and adolescence. Robert Selman (1980, 1981) has proposed a theory of how understanding others' thinking—or *perspective taking*—occurs. Selman's theory is based on two of Piaget's key assumptions, namely, that understanding others occurs in stages and that movement from one stage to the next is based on cognitive development. Table 11-1 shows Selman's five stages of perspective taking.

TABLE 11-1

SELMAN'S STAGES OF PERSPECTIVE TAKING

Stage	Approximate Ages	Description
Undifferentiated	3–6 years	Children know that self and others can have different thoughts and feelings, but they often confuse the two.
Social-informational	4–9 years	Children know that perspectives differ because people have access to different information.
Self-reflective	7–12 years	Children can step into another's shoes and view themselves as others do; they know that others can do the same.
Third person	10–15 years	Children and adolescents can step outside the immediate situation to see how they and another person are viewed by a third person.
Societal	14 years to adult	Adolescents realize that a third person's perspective is influenced by broader personal, social, and cultural contexts.

To see the progression from stage to stage, imagine two boys arguing about what to do after school. One wants to go to a playground, and the other wants to watch TV. If the boys were five-year-olds (undifferentiated stage), neither would really understand why the other wants to do something different. Their reasoning is simple: "If I want to go to the playground, you should too!"

During the early elementary-school years (social-informational stage), each child understands that the other wants to do something different, and they explain their differing views in terms of the other person lacking essential information. Their thinking is along the lines, "I know that you want to watch TV, but if you knew what I knew, you'd want to go to the playground." By the late elementary-school years (self-reflective stage), the boys would understand that each wants to do something different and they could "step into the other's shoes" to understand why: "I know you want to go to the playground because you haven't been there all week."

In early adolescence (third-person stage), the boys could step even farther apart and imagine how another person (e.g., a parent or teacher) could view the disagreement. Finally, in late adolescence (societal stage), the boys (now young men, really) can remove themselves even further and appreciate, for example, that many people would think it's silly to watch TV on a beautiful sunny day.

As predicted by Selman's theory, research shows that, as children get older, their reasoning moves through each stage, in sequence. In addition, children at more advanced cognitive levels tend to be at more advanced stages in perspective taking (Gurucharri & Selman, 1982; Krebs & Gillmore, 1982). However, many scientists are not convinced that more sophisticated perspective taking occurs in such a stage-like fashion; they believe that it improves steadily throughout childhood and adolescence (just as cognitive development is now seen to be more continuous than Piaget's theory predicted).

Some investigators have linked improved perspective taking to the developing theory of mind, described in Module 6.3 (Chandler & Carpendale, 1998). The traditional false-belief task, for example, reveals children's understanding that another person's actions are often based on their beliefs, even when those beliefs are wrong. As an illustration, suppose children hear the following story:

 QUESTION 11.3
Gracie can hardly wait for her cousin Andrew to arrive for a week-long visit. Gracie knows Andrew will want to go swimming right away because Gracie loves to swim. Based on this example, what stage of perspective taking is Gracie in? About how old is she? *(Answer is on page 400.)*

Lindsay and Angela are in the park and see some kids playing softball. Lindsay wants to play, so she runs home for her glove. Angela waits at the park for her, but while Lindsay's away, the kids decided it's too hot for softball and leave to get some ice cream.

Children understand false belief if they say that Lindsay will return to the ball field (acting on her false belief that the kids are still playing ball). But we can add a new wrinkle to the story.

As the kids are leaving the park, one of them thinks that Lindsay might like to join them for ice cream, so she calls Lindsay and tells her the plan.

Now children are asked, "Where does Angela think Lindsay thinks the kids are?" Children understand second-order belief if they say that Angela thinks that Lindsay will go to the ball field. **This sort of "he thinks that she thinks . . ." reasoning is known as** *recursive thinking.* It emerges at about five or six years of age and improves steadily during the elementary-school years, due to the combined effects of increased language skill and greater executive functioning (Miller, 2009).

One of the benefits of a developing appreciation of others' thoughts and viewpoints is that it allows children to get along better with their peers. That is, children who can readily take another's perspective are typically well liked by their peers (Banerjee, Wattling, & Caputi, 2011; FitzGerald & White, 2003). Of course, mere understanding does not guarantee good social behaviour; sometimes children who understand what another child is thinking take advantage of that child. In general, though, greater understanding of others seems to promote positive interactions, a topic that we'll discuss further in Chapter 12 on moral understanding and behaviour.

Prejudice

Around the world, many adults are prejudiced against individuals solely based on their membership in a social group (e.g., a racial, ethnic, or religious group). Preferring one's group over others is first observed in two- to four-year-olds, becomes stronger in five- to seven-year-olds, and remains strong thereafter (Raabe & Beelmann, 2011). By the preschool years, most children can distinguish males from females and can identify people from different ethnic groups (Nesdale, 2001). **Once children learn their membership in a specific group, they can show** *prejudice,* **a negative view of others based on their membership in a specific group.** After children learn their membership in a specific group, they typically have an enhanced view of their own group. That is, preschool and kindergarten children attribute to their own group many positive traits, such as being friendly and smart, and few negative traits, such as being mean (Bigler, Jones, & Lobliner, 1997; Patterson & Bigler, 2006).

Negative views of other groups form more slowly, beginning in the elementary-school years (Buttelmann & Böhm, 2014). In young children, negative views typically do not involve overt hostility; it is simply that other groups "come up short" when compared to one's own group (Aboud, 2003). However, when children believe that children from other groups dislike them or think they are better, then children's views of other groups become more negative (Nesdale, Maass, Durkin, & Griffiths, 2005).

As children move into the elementary-school years, prejudice usually declines somewhat. Evidence comes from studies such as one done with schoolchildren in Montreal, Quebec, that showed that children's views became more flexible and prejudice declined with increasing age from kindergarten through to Grade 6 (Powlishta et al., 1994). Cognitive development explains the decline. Preschool and kindergarten children usually view people in social groups as being much more homogeneous than they really are. As children grow, they begin to understand that people in social groups are heterogeneous—they know that individual European Canadians, girls, and obese children, for example, are not all alike. As children realize that social groups consist of all kinds of different people, prejudice lessens.

As children move into the elementary-school years, their knowledge of racial stereotypes and prejudices increases steadily; by 10 or 11 years of age, most children are aware of broadly held racial stereotypes (Pauker, Ambady, & Apfelbaum, 2010). During these years, prejudice declines some, in part because children learn norms that discourage openly favouring their own group over others (Apfelbaum, Pauker, Ambady, Sommers, & Norton, 2008). But implicit bias remains—many children automatically associate their group with positive features and associate other groups with bad features (Baron & Banaji, 2006).

During early adolescence, prejudice often increases again. This resurgence apparently reflects two different processes (Black-Gutman & Hickson, 1996; Teichman, 2001). One is experiential: Exposed to the prejudices of those around them, children and adolescents internalize some of these views (Castelli, Zogmaister, & Tomelleri, 2009). A second process concerns adolescents' identity. In the search for identity (described on pages 378–380), adolescents' preferences for their own groups often intensifies (Rutland, Killen, & Abrams, 2010). Thus, greater prejudice in older children and adolescents reflects both a more positive view of their own group as well as a more negative view of other groups. Bob, a 14-year-old European Canadian growing up in Saskatchewan, becomes more prejudiced because he views his own European Canadian heritage more positively and acquires from his parents and peers prejudicial attitudes toward Indigenous people.

Identifying *how* children form actual prejudices is challenging because ethical concerns limit us to correlational studies. In the Spotlight on Theories feature, we'll look at one approach in which bias and prejudice are viewed as a natural by-product of children's efforts to understand their social worlds.

Spotlight on Theories

Developmental Intergroup Theory

BACKGROUND   Bias and prejudice emerge early in development and are found in children worldwide. And, although we've mostly discussed racial bias in this module, children rapidly develop other biases as well, such as gender bias (the topic of Chapter 13). Why are bias and prejudice so prevalent, and why do they develop so early?

THE THEORY   Rebecca Bigler and Lynn Liben (2007) believe that bias and prejudice emerge naturally out of children's efforts to understand their social world. You'll recall from Module 6.3 that young children actively categorize animate and inanimate objects as part of their effort to understand the world around them. As children's social horizons expand beyond their parents to include peers, they continue to categorize, trying to decide how different groups of people "go together." That is, they look for obvious clues that could be used to distinguish people. They use perceptually salient features (e.g., race, gender, age), as well as verbal labels that adults may apply to different groups (e.g., "Girls go to lunch first, then the boys").

After children have identified the salient features that define peers in their environment, they begin to classify people whom they encounter along these dimensions. Jacob is now seen as a white boy; Kalika is now seen as a Black girl. Finally, children seek to learn more about each of the groups that they have defined. As they do this, their thinking is guided by essentialism, the belief that individuals who belong to the same group share internal, unseen similarities (i.e., essences). In addition, they are biased toward their own group and generate more favourable characterizations of them.

Hypothesis: The first step in forming bias is detecting features in a setting that distinguishes groups of people. Consequently, making a person-related feature more salient in an environment should make it more likely that this feature will contribute to bias. In other words, if teachers insisted that all left-handed children wear gloves on their left hand and right-handed children wear gloves on their right hand, this would make handedness a salient feature of people in the environment and should lead children to favour same-handed peers.

Test: Patterson and Bigler (2006) tested three- to five-year-olds attending daycare. The children were assigned to a "red group" or a "blue group" and wore red or blue T-shirts every day. In classrooms in the experimental group, teachers used the colour names to refer to children (e.g., "Good morning Blues!") and to organize the classroom (e.g., they created lines of Reds and Blues to leave the classroom). In classrooms in the control group, children wore coloured T-shirts, but teachers never referred to them or used colour names in any way.

After three weeks, children's perceptions and preferences were measured. As predicted, when teachers made colour an important feature of the social world, children developed bias toward their own group. For example, children in these classrooms (a) believed that a new student would want to join their group, (b) said that they were happier than students in the other group, and (c) expressed greater liking for children in their own group and played with those children more often. In the control classrooms—where teachers did not mention clothing colour—children developed none of these biases.

Conclusion: As predicted, children developed bias in favour of their designated colour group when teachers made that colour salient in the daycare environment. This finding supports the general view that bias and prejudice are a natural by-product of children's efforts to determine the features in an environment that distinguish different groups.

Application: Because children are eager to know more about their social worlds and they categorize so skillfully, they easily notice features that signal group differences. This means that parents in particular and society in general face a huge challenge in reducing or eliminating bias. Parents can encourage their children to interact in multiracial groups of boys and girls, so that neither race nor gender is as salient for children. Institutions can have comparable policies. For example, teachers can be very careful to avoid use of gender labels in their classrooms (just as they avoid racial labels).

Unfortunately, the best efforts along these lines might reduce bias, but are unlikely to eliminate it. Hence, it is important to know about ways to deal with bias after it has formed. We'll look at this next.

Critical Thinking Question: As the feature notes, bias exists. Before reading on in this chapter, think of two or three ways in which adults can try to eliminate (or at least reduce) bias.

The research described in the Spotlight on Theories feature shows that children develop biases when social groups are salient in their environment. Other work shows that the mere presence of different groups is often sufficient to generate bias. For example, if researchers ask children to join a group that's marked by the colour of a shirt or a distinctive badge, young children prefer their group, attribute more positive features to their group, and ascribe negative behaviours (e.g., being stingy) to children of other groups (Dunham, Baron, & Carey, 2011; Schug, Shusterman, Barth, & Patalano, 2013). Even toddlers prefer their own group: They more often imitate adults who speak their native language and prefer puppets who are kind to others and who like the same foods that the children like (Buttelmann, Zmyj, Daum, & Carpenter, 2013; Hamlin, Mahajan, Liberman, & Wynn, 2013).

Of course, children differ in the extent of their prejudice. Children and adolescents are more prejudiced when they are exposed to prejudices in their parents and other influential individuals (Castelli et al., 2009; Degner & Dalege, 2013). Contact with other groups also matters: Even modest amounts of interactions with other groups can reduce or eliminate bias (Raabe & Beelmann, 2011).

What can parents, teachers, and other adults do to reduce or eliminate children's biases? One way is to encourage contacts between children from different groups (Aboud et al., 2012; White, Abu-Rayya, & Weitzel, 2014). However, contact alone usually accomplishes little. Intergroup contact is most effective in reducing prejudice when:

- the participating groups of children are equal in status;
- the contact between groups involves pursuing common goals (instead of competing) and encourages children to think of groups as part of a larger common group; and
- parents and teachers support the goal of reducing prejudice (Cameron, Rutland, Brown, & Douch, 2006; Killen & McGlothlin, 2005).

To illustrate, adults might have children from different groups work together on a class project, as shown in the photo. In sports, the common task might be mastering a new skill. By working together, Gary starts to realize that Vic acts, thinks, and feels as he does simply because he is Vic, not because he is an Italian Canadian.

Another useful approach is to ask children to play different roles (Davidson & Davidson, 1994; Tynes, 2007). They can be asked to imagine that, because of their race, ethnic background, or sex, they have been insulted verbally or not allowed to participate in special activities. A child might be asked to imagine that she cannot go to a private swimming club because she's African Canadian or that she wasn't invited to a party because she is Chinese. Afterwards, children reflect on how they felt when prejudice and discrimination were directed at them. And they are asked to think about what would be fair—what should be done in situations like these?

From such experiences, children and adolescents discover for themselves that a person's membership in a social group tells us very little about that person. They learn, instead, that all children are different, each a unique mix of experiences, skills, and values.

One way to reduce children's prejudice is to have children from different groups work together toward a common goal, such as completing a school assignment.

Wavebreak Media Ltd./Corbis

Increasing interaction between children of different racial groups was one of the consequences of the U.S. Supreme Court's decision in *Brown v. Board of Education of Topeka* (347 U.S. 483), a case that shows how child-development research influenced social policy.

In 1950, African American and white children in most states in the United States attended separate schools. Segregated schooling had been the law in America for more than 100 years, bolstered by several Supreme Court decisions. In the fall of 1950, the chapter of the National Association for the Advancement of Colored People (NAACP) in Topeka, Kansas, decided to test the constitutionality of the law. Thirteen African American parents, including Oliver Brown, attempted to enroll their children in white-only schools; when they were turned away, the NAACP sued the Topeka Board of Education.

A key element in the NAACP's case was that separate schools were inherently harmful to African American children because such schools apparently legitimized the children's second-class status. To support this claim, the NAACP legal team relied on testimony from Dr. Kenneth B. Clark. In previous work, Clark (1945; Clark & Clark, 1940) had shown that African American children typically thought that white dolls were "nice" but that brown dolls were "bad." He found the same results with African American children attending segregated Topeka schools, leading him to testify that

> these children . . . like other human beings who are subjected to an obviously inferior status in the society in which they live, have been definitely harmed in the development of their personalities . . . .

In May 1954, the Supreme Court in the United States rendered the landmark decision ruling that segregated schools were unconstitutional. After the Brown decision, Clark continued his work on civil rights and worked on behalf of African American youth. For his lifelong effort to inform public policy on African American children and their families, in 1987 he received the Gold Medal for Life Achievement in Psychology in the Public Interest from the American Psychological Foundation; he died in 2005.

Clark's work is a compelling demonstration of the manner in which child-development research can have far-reaching implications for policy—in this case, helping to eliminate racially segregated schools in the United States. The integrated schools that resulted have helped to reduce prejudice by providing children with opportunities to learn about peers from other ethnic and racial groups.

A similar finding comes from recent research into religious divisions and effects of school type on self-esteem in Northern Ireland (McClenahan, Irwing, Stringer, Giles, & Wilson, 2003; McKeown, Stringer, & Cairns, 2016). In Northern Ireland, a general social divide exists along religious lines—Protestant and Catholic—and schools tend to be segregated by religion. General feelings of mistrust still exist between members of the religious groups (McAloney, Stringer, & Mallett, 2013). Attempts have been made to overcome divisions by implementing integrated schools where teachers, staff, and pupils come equally from both sides of the religious divide. McClenahan et al. (2003) used Harter's Self Perception Profile for Children (SPPC), a measure of self-worth in children (Harter, 1985, 1988), to examine whether the type of school the students were enrolled in affected self-esteem. These studies showed that students from the Roman Catholic religious minority tended to have lower self-esteem when in segregated schools, with lower feelings of social acceptance and global self-worth, "reflecting the stereotypes of the majority/minority categorizations of Protestants and Catholics within Northern Ireland" (McClenahan et al., 2003, p. 517). Catholic children in the integrated schools, however, saw themselves more positively, and showed higher academic self-esteem (scholastic competence). Even within integrated schools, however, children may self-segregate, for example, by sitting only with members of the same religious group. It has been suggested that schools could help improve inter-group relations by use of classroom seating plans and class activities that encourage inter-group interactions (McKeown, Stringer & Cairns, 2016). As with the American schools, contact with members of "other" groups is important to reduce prejudice. And it does seem that the increased inter-group contact and lack of negative labelling based on religious denomination allows the children in integrated schools to view themselves more positively (McClenahan et al., 2003).

Thus, whether the perceived difference is skin colour, religion, or some other aspect of the self, reducing labelling and increasing positive interactions allow children to see one another just as people, and reduce prejudice.

Dr. Kenneth B. Clark's research on prejudice was influential in the United States Supreme Court's ruling that segregated schools in the United States are unconstitutional.

 ANSWER 11.3
Gracie is confusing what she wants to do ("I love to swim and can't wait to go!") with what Andrew wants to do (which she doesn't know). This would put her in Selman's undifferentiated stage because she is confusing her thoughts with Andrew's. And this means she's probably between three and six years old.
. . . .

Robert Maass/Corbis/Getty Images

Check Your Learning

RECALL Describe the different stages in Selman's theory of perspective taking. Summarize developmental change in prejudice.

INTERPRET Compare developmental change in children's descriptions of others with developmental change in children's self-concept (described in Modules 11.1 and 11.2).

APPLY Based on what you've learned in this module, what can parents and teachers do to discourage prejudice in children?

UNIFYING THEMES Nature and Nurture

This chapter is a good occasion to feature the theme that *development is always jointly influenced by heredity and environment*. The emergence of self-awareness between 15 and 24 months is primarily due to biological forces. Regardless of circumstances, children become self-aware between the ages one and two. However, elaborating self-awareness into a specific self-concept depends largely on a child's experiences at home and in school. The specific direction that children take in establishing an identity is strongly influenced by those around them, particularly their parents and teachers.

See for Yourself

The mirror recognition task, described on page 376, is great fun to do, and you'll be astonished by the rapid change in children's responses between one and two years of age. For this task, you simply need a mirror, some tissue, blush, and a few co-operative parents of 12- to 18-month-olds. Remember, ethically you need to get parental permission first! Have the parents play with their toddler near the mirror and, in the process, wipe the toddler's nose with a tissue that has blush on it. Then see how the toddler responds to the nose that is now red. Some 12-month-olds will do nothing; others will touch the red nose in the mirror. When 15- to 18-month-olds see themselves, though, they should stop, get a curious expression on their faces, and then reach up to touch their own noses. See for yourself!

Resources

For more information about . . .

adolescent search for identity, read Erik Erikson's *Gandhi* (Norton, 1969), a Pulitzer Prize-winning book in which Erikson shows how the adolescent search for identity influenced the development of this great leader of India.

deciding on a career or finding a job that's right for you, visit a website maintained by the Government of Canada's department *Service Canada* at **www.service canada.gc.ca/eng/lifeevents/job.shtml**.

Key Terms

acculturation 382
achievement 379
adolescent egocentrism 378
diffusion 379
ethnic identity 380

foreclosure 379
illusion of invulnerability 379
imaginary audience 378
moratorium 379
narcissism 392

personal fable 378
prejudice 396
recursive thinking 396
self-concept 375
self-esteem 386

Summary

11.1 Who Am I? Self-Concept

1. Origins of Self-Recognition

At about 15 months, infants begin to recognize themselves in the mirror, one of the first signs of self-recognition. They also begin to prefer to look at pictures of themselves, to refer to themselves by name and with personal pronouns, and sometimes to know their age and gender. Evidently, by two years of age, most children have the rudiments of self-awareness.

2. The Evolving Self-Concept

Preschoolers often define themselves in terms of observable characteristics such as possessions, physical characteristics, preferences, and competencies. During the elementary-school years, self-concept begins to include emotions, a child's membership in social groups, and comparisons with peers. During adolescence, self-concept includes attitudes, personality traits, beliefs, and future plans. In general, adolescents' self-concepts are more abstract, more psychological, and more future oriented than self-concepts in younger children.

3. The Search for Identity

The search for identity typically involves four statuses. Diffusion and foreclosure are more common in early adolescence; moratorium and achievement are more common in late adolescence and young adulthood. Adolescents are most likely to achieve an identity when parents encourage discussion and recognize their autonomy; they are least likely to achieve an identity when parents set rules and enforce them without explanation.

Adolescents from ethnic groups often progress through three phases in acquiring an ethnic identity: initial disinterest, exploration, and identity achievement. Achieving an ethnic identity usually results in higher self-esteem.

Contrary to myth, adolescence is not usually a period of storm and stress. Most adolescents love their parents,

feel loved by them, rely on them for advice, and adopt their values. The parent-child relationship becomes more egalitarian during the adolescent years, reflecting adolescents' growing independence. A small number of adolescents become depressed, often because their explanations of their own behaviour are flawed.

11.2 Self-Esteem

1. Developmental Change in Self-Esteem

Self-esteem becomes more differentiated in older children and adolescents as they evaluate themselves on more aspects of self-esteem, including different types of academic skills. Global self-esteem is very high during the preschool years but declines in the elementary-school years as children start to compare themselves to peers. Self-esteem also declines temporarily when children make school transitions.

2. Variations in Self-Esteem Associated with Ethnicity and Culture

Ethnicity and culture each influence important variations on the developmental changes in structure and average levels of self-esteem. African American and Hispanic American children have lower self-esteem in childhood but self-esteem increases in adolescence. Children from Asian countries tend to have lower self-esteem than children from North America and Europe, reflecting internalization of a cultural standard of modesty, ready admission of weaknesses, and less frequent comparison with peers.

3. Sources of Self-Esteem

Children's self-esteem is greater when parents are affectionate and involved with them and when parents set rules and discuss disciplinary action. Self-esteem also depends on peer comparisons. Self-esteem is usually greater when children know that others view them positively.

4. Low Self-Esteem: Cause or Consequence?

When children have low self-esteem, they are more likely to have poor peer relations, suffer psychological disorders such as depression, be involved in antisocial activities, and do poorly in school. Therapy and improved social skills can enhance children's self-esteem. Narcissistic children have an inflated view of their self-worth and are often too aggressive.

11.3 Understanding Others

1. Describing Others

Children's descriptions of others change in much the same way that their descriptions of themselves change. During the early elementary-school years, descriptions emphasize concrete characteristics. In the late elementary-school years, they emphasize personality traits. In adolescence, they emphasize an integrated picture of a person. Children use their descriptions to predict others' behaviours.

2. Understanding What Others Think

According to Selman's perspective-taking theory, children's understanding of how others think progresses through five stages. In the first, the undifferentiated stage, children often confuse their own and another's view. In the last, the societal stage, adolescents take a third person's perspective and understand that this perspective is influenced by context.

3. Prejudice

Prejudice emerges in the preschool years, soon after children recognize different social groups. Prejudice declines during childhood but often increases in older children and adolescents. Prejudice, which emerges in the preschool years and becomes stronger in the elementary-school years, is a common byproduct of children's efforts to categorize social groups. Prejudiced thinking can lead to discriminatory behaviour. The best way to reduce prejudice is with additional exposure to individuals from other social groups, and by educating children about the negatives of prejudice and racism.

Test Yourself

1. When a 12-month-old with a mark on her face looks into a mirror, she'll probably _____.

2. _____ define themselves in terms of their physical characteristics, possessions, and preferences.

3. An emphasis on the future is unique to self-concept during _____.

4. In the _____ status, individuals have not explored alternatives but have an identity determined largely by adults.

5. Adolescents are more likely to achieve an ethnic identity when _____.

6. Adolescence is not a period of storm and stress for most families, but it can be for adolescents who _____.

7. During the elementary-school years, domains of self-esteem include scholastic competence, _____, social competence, and physical appearance.

8. Self-esteem is greatest during _____.

9. When children and adolescents from minority groups experience discriminatory behaviour, they are _____.

10. Children with high self-esteem often have parents whose disciplinary practices are characterized by _____.

11. Children with low self-esteem _____.

12. Young children's descriptions of others are unusual in that they _____.

13. Children who are more skilled in taking the perspective of others typically _____.

14. Prejudice typically increases in adolescence because teens internalize some prejudiced views of those around them and _____.

15. Contact between diverse groups of children can reduce prejudice when the groups have equal status, the contact involves pursuit of mutual goals, and _____.

Answers: (1) touch the mark in the mirror; (2) Preschool children; (3) adolescence; (4) foreclosure; (5) their parents encourage them to learn about their heritage and prepare them for discrimination; (6) don't regulate their emotions well; (7) athletic competence; (8) the preschool years; (9) less at risk if they have a well-developed ethnic identity; (10) rules and reasonable expectations, paired with a willingness to discuss discipline; (11) are more likely to be involved in antisocial behaviour; (12) consistently look for good things in others, not bad things; (13) get along better with peers; (14) their search for identity leads them to have a more positive view of their own group; (15) parents and other adults support the goal of reducing prejudice.

12

Moral Understanding and Behaviour

Juice Images Ltd./Getty Images

Self-Control

Reasoning about Moral Issues

Helping Others

Aggression

Imagine entering a nursery filled with two-day-olds. Some are asleep; some are crying; others are simply lying quietly. However, the nurse tells you that the newborns include Nelson Mandela, Mother Teresa, Adolf Hitler, Mohandas Gandhi, and Martin Luther King, Jr. Although seemingly identical now, four of the newborns will rank among the twentieth century's greatest figures, and one will be guilty of unspeakable horrors. Why? What determines whether children act morally or immorally? Whether they care about others or take from others? Whether they become "good Samaritans" or follow a path of evil? The four modules in this chapter provide some answers to these questions. In **Module 12.1**, we'll see how children learn to control their behaviour. In **Module 12.2**, we'll look at how children and adolescents reason about moral issues, and in **Module 12.3**, we'll look at factors that encourage children to be kind to others. Finally, in **Module 12.4**, we'll see why children act aggressively toward others.

12.1 Self-Control

OUTLINE

Beginnings of Self-Control

Influences on Self-Control

Improving Children's Self-Control

LEARNING OBJECTIVES

1. When does self-control begin, and how does it change as children develop?
2. What factors influence children's ability to maintain self-control?
3. What strategies can children use to improve their self-control?

Shirley returned from a long day at work tired but eager to celebrate her son Ryan's fourth birthday. Her excitement quickly turned to dismay when she discovered that Ryan had taken a huge bite of icing from the birthday cake while the babysitter fixed lunch. Before she had left for work that morning, Shirley had explicitly told Ryan not to touch the cake. Why couldn't Ryan wait? Why did he give in to temptation? What could Shirley do to help Ryan control himself better in the future?

In this vignette, Shirley wishes that her son had greater *self-control,* **the ability to control one's behaviour and to inhibit impulsive responding to temptations.** A child who obeys a parent's request that she not touch a nicely wrapped present is showing self-control, as is an adolescent who studies for an exam instead of going to the mall with his friends, knowing that tomorrow he can enjoy the mall *and* a good mark on his exam.

Self-control is one of the first steps toward moral behaviour because children must learn that they cannot constantly do whatever tempts them at the moment. Instead, society has rules for behaviour in certain situations, and children must learn to restrain themselves.

In this module, we'll first see how self-control initially emerges. Then we'll learn some of the factors that determine how well children control themselves. Finally, we'll look at strategies that children use to improve their self-control.

Raise a cyber child and discover the world of parenting at ...

My Virtual Child

Beginnings of Self-Control

Self-control emerges in infancy and gradually improves during the preschool years (Kopp, 1997; Li-Grining, 2007). A rough chronology looks like this:

- At about their first birthday, infants become aware that people impose demands on them and they must react accordingly. Infants learn that they are not entirely free

QUESTION 12.1
Two-year-old Amanda spilled a cup filled with juice, just after she'd been asked to leave it on the counter. Amanda's dad thinks she should be disciplined for disobeying a direct instruction; her mom thinks Amanda is too young to control herself. How would you advise Amanda's parents? *(Answer is on page 408.)*

to behave as they wish; instead, others set limits on what they can do. These limits reflect both concern for their safety ("Don't touch! It's hot") as well as early social-ization efforts ("Don't grab Ravisha's toy").

- At about two years of age, toddlers have internalized some of the controls imposed by others and are capable of some self-control in their parents' absence. For example, although the boy on the right in the photo looks as if he wants to play with the toy that the other toddler has, so far he has inhibited his desire to grab the toy, perhaps because he remembers that his parents have told him not to take things from others.

- At about three years of age, children become capable of self-regulation; they can devise ways to control their own behaviour. To return to the example of a play-mate's interesting toy, children might tell themselves that they really don't want to play with it, or they might turn to another activity that removes the temptation to grab the toy.

Although preschoolers are able to regulate impulsive behaviour somewhat, they still have much to learn, and control is achieved only gradually throughout the elementary-school years. One way to chart this development is with studies of delay of gratification, in which children are offered the choice of a relatively small reward immediately or a much larger reward if they wait. In one study (Steelandt, Thierry, Broihanne, & Dufour, 2012), nearly all four-year-olds waited four minutes for a larger cookie, but relatively few two-year-olds did. In another study (Rotenberg & Mayer, 1990), children and adolescents were offered the choice of a small piece of candy immediately or an entire bag of chips if they waited one day. About one-third of the six- to eight-year-olds in the study opted to wait for the chips. In contrast, half of the 9- to 11-year-olds and nearly all of the 12- to 15-year-olds waited a day for the chips. Thus, although self-control may be evident in tod-dlers, mastery occurs gradually throughout child-hood, probably reflecting maturation of circuitry in the brain's frontal cortex that is critical for inhibiting behaviour (Berkman, Graham, & Fisher, 2012).

By two years of age, many children have enough self-control that they can resist the temptation to take an interesting toy away from another child.

Even more remarkable are the results from longitudinal studies on the long-term consistency of self-control. These studies find that preschoolers' self-control predicts out-comes in adolescence and young adulthood. In Module 10.2, we saw that children who are less able to control themselves are, as teenagers, more likely to drop out of school, to smoke, and to become parents (Moffitt et al., 2011; Moffitt, Poulton, & Caspi, 2013). In addition, preschoolers who show the greatest self-control are, as adolescents, more atten-tive, have higher SAT scores, and are less likely to experiment with drugs and alcohol; as young adults, they are better educated, have higher self-esteem have better cognitive control, and are less likely to be overweight (Mischel et al., 2011; Schlam, Wilson, Shoda, Mischel, & Ayduk, 2013).

Obviously, individuals differ in their ability to resist temptation, and this character-istic is remarkably stable over time. But why are some children and adults better able than others to exert self-control? As you'll see in the next section of this module, parents and children's temperament both contribute to children's self-control.

Dm909/Moment Open/Getty Images

Influences on Self-Control

Parents like Shirley are disappointed and upset when their children lack self-control. What can parents do? Research consistently links greater self-control with a disciplinary style in which parents are warm and loving but establish well-defined limits on what behaviour is acceptable (Feldman & Klein, 2003; Vazsonyi & Huang, 2010). Self-control is enhanced when parents discuss disciplinary issues with their children instead of simply asserting their power as parents (e.g., "You'll do it because I say so"). When Shirley disciplines Ryan, she should remind him of the clear behavioural standard (not touching the cake), explain her disappointment ("Now nobody else will see how pretty your cake was!"), and suggest ways that he could resist similar temptations in the future. This parental discipline style is called *inductive reasoning*—**inducing the child to reason, to think for him or herself about the situation.** As we will see, inductive reasoning is the form of discipline more likely to lead to moral development.

Research also shows that children's self-control is usually *lower* when parents are very strict with them (Donovan, Leavitt, & Walsh, 2000; Feldman & Wentzel, 1990). By constantly directing their children to do one thing but not another, parents do not give them either the opportunity or the incentive to internalize control (Kochanska, Coy, & Murray, 2001). Joan Grusec from the University of Toronto and Jaqueline Goodnow of Macquarie University in Sydney, Australia, reviewed the research on parental discipline techniques and how these affected children's internalization of values. Grusec and Goodnow (1994) concluded that use of the discipline technique of inductive reasoning, compared to other forms of discipline, made a difference in whether children internalized moral values (Grusec & Goodnow, 1994). We will look at development and understanding of values later in this chapter, in Module 12.2, but we mention this research here as it shows how self-control in the moral domain is affected by parents' strictness. Very strict parents actually hinder their children's internalization of controls and standards; the child is more reliant on external control and less able to exercise self-control.

Parents are not the only important influence on children's self-control; remember, from Module 10.2, that temperament also matters. One dimension of temperament is effortful control, which describes a child's ability to focus attention, to ignore distraction, and to inhibit inappropriate responses. Thus, some children are simply temperamentally better suited to maintaining self-control and regulating their behaviour (Stifter, Cipriano, Conway, & Kelleher, 2009).

Even culture might play a role in development of self-control. Xinyin Chen (then at the University of Western Ontario) and colleagues compared compliance to parental requests in Chinese and Canadian toddlers (Chen et al., 2003). As part of a larger study on children's social and emotional development, Chen and his colleagues were investigating how regulation of behaviour shifts from external (usually parental) control to internal self-control. In this particular study, Chen et al. (2003) compared Chinese and Canadian two-year-olds on compliance and cooperation with adults (an experimenter and a parent). Chinese toddlers were more likely to be willingly compliant and less likely to protest than Canadian children. The researchers suggest that because cooperation and self-restraint are more highly valued in Chinese society than in North America, children may internalize these behaviours more readily and earlier in China. In further research, Chen and French (2008) noted that the values different societies place on behavioural control affect peer relationships and conflict management. Despite cross-cultural differences in timing and degree, however, Canadian parents still do want their children to learn self-control: "Nevertheless, parents in North America expect increasing voluntary self-control from their children with age and . . . help them to gradually learn voluntary control by using sensitive and inductive parenting strategies" (Chen et al., 2003, p. 435).

Of course, regardless of their temperament or culture, children are not perfectly consistent in their self-control. Children who are able to resist temptation on one occasion may give in the next time. Why do children show self-control on some tasks but not on others? As we'll see in the next section, the answer lies in children's plans for resisting temptation.

One way to resist the temptation of desirable objects is to think about something else or do something else, such as singing.

Duane Osborne/Corbis/Getty Images

Improving Children's Self-Control

Imagine it's one of the first nice days of spring. You have two major exams that you should study for, but it's so-o-o-o tempting to spend the entire day with your friends, sitting in the sun. What do you do to resist this temptation and stick to studying? You might remind yourself that these exams are very important. You might also move to a windowless room to keep your mind off the tempting weather. Stated more generally, effective ways to resist temptation include reminding yourself of the importance of long-term goals over short-term temptations and reducing the attraction of the tempting event or circumstance.

During the preschool years, some youngsters begin to use both of these methods spontaneously. In an experiment by Mischel and Ebbesen (1970), three- to five-year-olds were asked to sit alone in a room for 15 minutes. If they waited the entire time, they would receive a desirable reward. Children could call the experimenter back to the room at any time by a prearranged signal; in this case, they would receive a much less desirable reward.

Some children, of course, were better able than others to wait the full 15 minutes. How did they do it? Some children talked to themselves: "I've gotta wait to get the best prize!" As Vygotsky described (Module 6.2), these youngsters were using private speech to control their own behaviour. Others sang. Still others invented games. All were effective techniques for enduring 15 boring minutes to receive a desired prize.

Later studies show that children are far better able to delay gratification when they have a concrete way of handling tempting situations (Mischel & Ayduk, 2004; Peake, Hebl, & Mischel, 2002). Effective plans include (a) reminders to avoid looking at the tempting object; (b) reminders of rules against touching a tempting object; and (c) activities designed to divert attention from the tempting object, such as playing with other objects. Overall then, how children think about tempting objects or outcomes makes all the difference. Even preschoolers can achieve self-control by making plans that include appropriate self-instruction. For example, in the vignette, Shirley could have helped Ryan make a plan to resist temptation. She might have told him, "When you feel like you want to eat some cake, tell yourself, 'No cake until Mom gets home,' and go play in your bedroom." Children can improve their self-control with the programs described in Module 5.2 for training executive function (Berkman et al., 2012).

As children learn to regulate their own behaviour, they also begin to learn about moral rules—cultural rights and wrongs—that are described in the next module.

 ANSWER 12.1
All other things being equal, Amanda's dad is probably right. A typical two-year-old should be able to control himself or herself when the standard is clear and reasonable, which it seems to be in this case.

Check Your Learning

RECALL Describe the three phases in the emergence of self-control during infancy and the preschool years.

How does temperament influence a child's self-control?

INTERPRET What does longitudinal research on preschool children's ability to delay gratification tell us about the continuity of development?

APPLY Shirley described the birthday cake episode to her own mother, who replied, "It's simple, my dear. You're the parent. He's the kid. You're the boss. Tell him what to do." What would you say to Shirley's mom?

 **12.2 Reasoning about Moral Issues**

OUTLINE	LEARNING OBJECTIVES
Piaget's Views	1. How does reasoning about moral issues change during childhood and adolescence?
Kohlberg's Theory	2. How do concern for justice and caring for other people contribute to moral reasoning?
Beyond Kohlberg's Theory	3. What factors help promote more sophisticated reasoning about moral issues?
Promoting Moral Reasoning	4. How can youth be encouraged to reason at more advanced levels?

Howard, the least popular boy in Grade 8, had been wrongly accused of stealing a Grade 6 student's iPad. Min-shen, another Grade 8 student, knew that Howard was innocent, but said nothing to the school's principal for fear of what his friends would say about siding with Howard. A few days later, when Min-shen's father heard about the incident, he was upset that his son apparently had so little "moral fibre." Why hadn't Min-shen acted in the face of an injustice?

On one of the days when author Robert Kail was writing for this module, his local paper had two articles about youth from the area. One article was about a 14-year-girl who was badly burned while saving her younger brothers from a fire in their apartment. Her mother said she wasn't surprised by her daughter's actions because she had always been an extraordinarily caring person. The other article was about two 17-year-old boys who had beaten an elderly man to death. They had only planned to steal his wallet, but when he insulted them and tried to punch them, they became enraged.

Reading articles like these, you can't help but question why some people act in ways that earn our deepest respect and admiration, whereas others earn our utter contempt as well as our pity. At a more mundane level, we wonder why Min-shen didn't tell the principal the truth about the theft. In this module, we'll begin our exploration of moral understanding and behaviour by looking at children's thinking about moral issues: How do children judge what is "good" and what is "bad"? Let's start by looking at Jean Piaget's ideas about the development of moral reasoning.

Piaget's Views

Robert Kail remembers playing Chutes and Ladders (Snakes and Ladders) with his son Matt when Matt was about six years of age. This board game allows you to advance rapidly when you land on a space that has a ladder but sends you backward if you land on a chute. To speed up the game, Kail suggested to Matt that they be allowed to advance if they landed on a chute as well as a ladder: "I reminded him that he liked to climb slides at playgrounds, so my suggestion had some logic to it. Matt would have none of this. He told me, 'It's a rule that you have to go backward when you land on a chute. You can't go forward. The people who made Chutes and Ladders say so. Just read the instructions, Daddy.' I tried again to persuade him (because, in my humble opinion, Chutes and Ladders gives new meaning to "bored" games), but he was adamant."

Matt's inflexibility, which is typical of six-year-olds, can be explained by Piaget's theory of moral development, which includes three stages (Piaget, 1962). In the first stage, which lasts from age two years to about four, children have no well-defined ideas about morality—they are *premoral* **having not yet developed moral sensibility.** But beginning at about five years and continuing through age seven, **children are in a stage of** *moral realism;* **they believe that rules are created by wise adults and therefore must be followed and cannot be changed.** This morality is referred to as *heteronomous morality*—**absolute rules handed down by another.** Another characteristic of the stage of moral realism is that children believe in *immanent justice*—**the idea that breaking a rule always leads to punishment.** Suppose Matt Kail had been forced to use his father's new rules for Chutes and Ladders and that the next day he had tripped on his way to school, scraping his knee. Believing in immanent justice, he would have seen the scraped knee as the inevitable consequence of breaking the rule the previous day.

At about age eight to 10, children progress to the stage of *moral relativism,* **or the understanding that rules are created by people to help them get along. These children are now considered to have** *autonomous morality,* **which is morality based more on free will.** Children progress to this more advanced level of moral reasoning, in part, because advances in cognitive development allow them to understand the reasons for rules. They also begin to pay more attention to consequences of actions and intentions; for example, is breaking something or causing damage to something an accident, or is it deliberate? Children in the heteronomous stage of morality tend to focus on amount of damage caused, while those in the autonomous stage will consider intentions as well as consequences. Furthermore, from interactions with their peers, children come to understand the need for rules and how they are created. For example, as the boys in the photograph decide where to ride their skateboards, they might follow a rule that everybody can suggest some place and then they'll vote. The boys understand that this rule isn't absolute; they follow it because it's reasonably fair and, by using this rule, they spend more time skating and less time arguing.

Children in the stage of moral relativism also understand that because people agree to set rules in the first place, they can also change them if they see the need. If the skateboarding boys decided another rule would be fairer and would help them get along better, they could adopt the new rule.

Some of Piaget's ideas about moral reasoning have stood the test of time better than others. For example, later research has shown that children's early moral reasoning

By eight years of age, children understand that people create rules to get along; for example, these boys may follow the rule that they'll vote to decide where to ride their skateboards.

Uwe Krejci/Digital Vision/Getty Images

does not consider adult authority final and absolute. Instead, preschool children believe adults' authority is limited. Preschoolers believe that pushing a child or damaging another child's possession is wrong, even when an adult says that it's okay (Tisak, 1993). A lasting contribution of Piaget's work, however, is the idea that moral reasoning progresses through a sequence of stages, driven by cognitive development and interactions with peers. Piaget's idea that moral reasoning progresses through a sequence of stages set the stage for a prominent theory of moral development proposed by Lawrence Kohlberg that is the focus of the next section.

Kohlberg's Theory

To begin, we'd like to tell you a story about Heidi, a star player on a soccer team that Robert Kail coached several years ago. Heidi was terribly upset because the team was undefeated and scheduled to play in a weekend tournament to determine the league champion, but on Sunday of this same weekend, a Habitat for Humanity house was to be dedicated to her grandfather, who had died a few months previously. If Heidi skipped the tournament game, her friends on the team would be upset; if she skipped the dedication, her family would be disappointed. Heidi couldn't do both and didn't know what to do.

Dilemmas like Heidi's were the starting point for Kohlberg's theory. That is, he created moral dilemmas in which any action involved some undesirable consequences, and he asked children, adolescents, and adults what they would do in the situation. Kohlberg was not interested in the decision per se; instead he focused on the reasoning used to justify a decision. Why should Heidi go to the tournament? Why should she go to the dedication?[1]

Kohlberg's best-known moral dilemma is about Heinz, whose wife is dying:

> In Europe, a woman was near death from cancer. One drug might save her, a form of radium that a druggist in the same town had recently discovered. The druggist was charging $2000, 10 times what the drug cost him to make. The sick woman's husband, Heinz, went to everyone he knew to borrow the money, but he could only get together about half of what it cost. He told the druggist that his wife was dying and asked him to sell it cheaper or let him pay later. But the druggist said, "No." The husband got desperate and broke into the man's store to steal the drug for his wife (Kohlberg, 1969, p. 379).

Although more hangs in the balance for Heinz than for Heidi, both face moral dilemmas in that the alternative courses of action have desirable and undesirable features.

Kohlberg analyzed children's, adolescents', and adults' responses to a large number of dilemmas and identified three levels of moral reasoning, each divided into two stages. Across the six stages, the basis for moral reasoning shifts. In the earliest stages, moral reasoning is based on external forces such as the promise of reward or the threat of punishment. At the most advanced levels, moral reasoning is based on a personal, internal moral code and is unaffected by others' views or society's expectations. You can clearly see this gradual shift in the three levels:

- *Preconventional level:* **For most children, many adolescents, and some adults, moral reasoning is controlled almost solely by obedience to authority and by rewards and punishments.**

    Stage 1: Obedience orientation. People believe that adults know what is right and wrong. Consequently, a person should do what adults say is right to avoid being

---

[1] As it turned out, Heidi didn't have to resolve the dilemma. The team lost its tournament game on Saturday, so she could go to the dedication on Sunday.

punished. A person at this stage might argue that Heinz should not steal the drug because it is against the law (which was made by adults).

Stage 2: Instrumental orientation. People look out for their own needs. They often are nice to others because they expect the favour to be returned in the future. A person at this stage might say it was all right for Heinz to steal the drug because his wife might do something nice for him in return (that is, she might reward him).

- *Conventional level:* **For most adolescents and adults, moral decision making is based on social norms—what is expected by others.**

Stage 3: Interpersonal norms. Adolescents and adults believe that they should act according to others' expectations. The aim is to win the approval of others by behaving as a "good person" would behave. An adolescent or adult at this stage might argue that Heinz should not steal the drug because then others would see him as an honest citizen who obeys the law.

Stage 4: Social system morality. Adolescents and adults believe that social roles, expectations, and laws exist to maintain order within society and to promote the good of all people. An adolescent or adult in this stage might reason that Heinz should steal the drug because a husband is obligated to do all that he possibly can to save his wife's life. Or, a person in this stage might reason that Heinz should not steal the drug because stealing is against the law and society must prohibit theft.

- *Postconventional level:* **For some adults, typically those older than 25, moral decisions are based on personal, moral principles.**

Stage 5: Social contract orientation. Adults agree that members of cultural groups adhere to a "social contract" because a common set of expectations and laws benefits all group members. However, if these expectations and laws no longer promote the welfare of individuals, they become invalid. Consequently, an adult in this stage might reason that Heinz should steal the drug because social rules about property rights are no longer benefiting individuals' welfare.

Stage 6: Universal ethical principles. Abstract principles like justice, compassion, and equality form the basis of a personal moral code that may sometimes conflict with society's expectations and laws. An adult at this stage might argue that Heinz should steal the drug because life is paramount and preserving life takes precedence over all other rights.

The Summary Table puts all the stages together, providing a quick review of Kohlberg's theory.

SUMMARY TABLE

STAGES IN KOHLBERG'S THEORY OF MORAL DEVELOPMENT

Preconventional Level: Punishment and Reward

Stage 1: Obedience to authority

Stage 2: Nice behaviour in exchange for future favours

Conventional Level: Social Norms

Stage 3: Live up to others' expectations

Stage 4: Follow rules to maintain social order

Postconventional Level: Moral Codes

Stage 5: Adhere to a social contract when it is valid

Stage 6: Personal morality based on abstract principles

SUPPORT FOR KOHLBERG'S THEORY. Kohlberg proposed that individuals move through the six stages in the order listed and in only that order. Consequently, older and more sophisticated thinkers should be more advanced in their moral development, and indeed they usually are (Stewart & Pascual-Leone, 1992). Stages 1 and 2 are common among children and young adolescents, whereas Stages 3 and 4 are common among older adolescents and adults. In addition, longitudinal studies show that individuals progress through each stage in sequence, and virtually no individuals skip stages (Colby, Kohlberg, Gibbs, & Lieberman, 1983). Longitudinal studies also show that, over time, individuals become more advanced in their level of moral reasoning or remain at the same level. Research, such as that of Lawrence Walker from the University of British Columbia, has shown that people do not regress to a lower level (Walker & Taylor, 1991). In Walker and Taylor's (1991) longitudinal study, moral reasoning of children from Grades 1, 4, 7, and 10 was followed over a two-year period. Although the amount of increase showed individual variability, the majority of the children showed definite increase in moral reasoning ability (Walker & Taylor, 1991).

Further support for Kohlberg's theory comes from research on the link between moral reasoning and moral behaviour. Less advanced moral reasoning reflects the influence of external forces such as rewards and social norms, whereas more advanced reasoning is based on a personal moral code. Therefore, individuals at the preconventional and conventional levels would act morally when external forces so demand, but otherwise they might not. In contrast, individuals at the postconventional level, where reasoning is based on personal principles, should be compelled to moral action even when external forces might not favour this.

Consistent with this claim, adolescents who defend their principles in difficult situations tend to be more advanced in Kohlberg's stages (Gibbs et al., 1986). For example, students like those in the photograph who protest social conditions tend to have higher moral reasoning scores. This explains why Min-shen, the boy in the vignette, said nothing. Speaking out on behalf of the unpopular student is unlikely to lead to reward and violates social norms against "squealing" on friends. Consequently, a Grade 6 student—who is probably in the preconventional or conventional level of moral reasoning—would likely let the unpopular student be punished unfairly.

On some other features, Kohlberg's theory does not fare as well. One is that moral reasoning is not as consistent as would be expected from the theory. Teenagers reasoning at the conventional level should always base their moral decisions on others' expectations, but such consistency is not the norm. Moral reasoning by teenagers may be advanced for some problems but much less sophisticated for others (Krebs & Denton, 2005).

Another concern is Kohlberg's claim that his sequence of stages is universal: All people in all cultures should progress through the six-stage sequence. Indeed, children and adolescents in cultures worldwide do seem to reason about moral dilemmas at Stages 2 or 3, just like North American children and adolescents (Gibbs, Basinger, Grime, & Snarey, 2007). But, beyond the earliest stages, moral reasoning in other cultures is often not described well by Kohlberg's theory. Many critics note that Kohlberg's emphasis on individual rights and justice reflects traditional American culture and Judeo-Christian theology. Not all

QUESTION 12.2
When Paige was told the Heinz dilemma, she replied, "He should steal the drug. Everyone would understand why he did it. And if he just let his wife die, his family and friends would think he's a terrible husband. They would never speak to him again." Which of Kohlberg's stages best describes Paige's thinking? About how old is she? *(Answer is on page 419.)*

Students who show moral courage by participating in protest movements typically have more advanced moral reasoning.

Jim West/Alamy Stock Photo

cultures and religions share this emphasis; consequently, moral reasoning might be based on different values in other cultures (Turiel, 2006). For example, the Hindu religion emphasizes duty and responsibility to others, not individual rights and justice (Simpson, 1974). Consistent with this emphasis, when Hindu children and adults respond to moral dilemmas, they favour solutions that provide care for others, even when individual rights or justice may suffer (Miller & Bersoff, 1992). For example, Hindu children and adults sometimes condone theft if it's the best way to meet one's responsibilities to care for others. Thus, the bases of moral reasoning are not universal as Kohlberg claimed; instead, they reflect cultural values.

Beyond Kohlberg's Theory

Kohlberg's theory triggered modern research on moral development but no longer dominates the field. Now many complementary perspectives help complete our picture of the development of moral thinking.

GILLIGAN'S ETHIC OF CARING.   Carol Gilligan (1982; Gilligan & Attanucci, 1988) argued that Kohlberg's emphasis on justice applies more to males than to females, whose reasoning about moral issues is often rooted in concern for others. According to Gilligan, this "ethic of care" leads females to put a priority on fulfilling obligations to other people, and those obligations guide their moral decision making.

In Gilligan's theory, the most advanced level of moral reasoning is based on the understanding that caring is the cornerstone of all human relationships, ranging from parent-child relationships to the relationship that exists between a homeless person and a volunteer at a shelter.

Like Kohlberg, Gilligan believes that moral reasoning becomes qualitatively more sophisticated as individuals develop, progressing through a number of distinct stages. However, Gilligan emphasizes care (helping people in need) instead of justice (treating people fairly).

Research yields little evidence supporting Gilligan's claim that females and males differ in the bases of their moral reasoning. In a comprehensive meta-analysis (Jaffee & Hyde, 2000), males tended to get slightly higher scores on problems that emphasized justice, whereas females tended to get slightly higher scores on problems that emphasized caring. But the differences were small and do not indicate that female's moral reasoning is predominated by a concern with care or that males' moral reasoning is predominated by a concern with justice. Even though males and females do not differ as expected, Gilligan's theory is important in emphasizing that moral reasoning is broader than Kohlberg claimed: Most people think about moral issues in terms of *both* justice and caring, depending upon the nature of the moral dilemma and the context (Turiel, 2006).

DEVELOPMENT OF DOMAINS OF SOCIAL JUDGMENT.   Another approach notes that moral judgments (whether based on justice or care) represent just one of several important domains in which children and adults make social judgments (Smetana, 2006; Turiel, 1998). To illustrate the domains, think about the following preschool children:

- Brian, who often kicks or pushes his younger brother when their mom isn't looking
- Kathryn, who never puts her toys away when she's done playing with them
- Brad, who likes to wear his underpants inside out

Although each child's behaviour is in some sense "wrong," only the first child's behaviour—kicking and pushing—represents a moral transgression because Brian's actions can harm another person. **In contrast,** *social conventions* **are arbitrary standards of behaviour agreed to by a cultural group to facilitate interactions within the group.** Thus, social convention says that we can eat French fries but not green beans with our fingers and that children like Kathryn should clean up after themselves. **Finally, the** *personal domain* **pertains to choices concerning one's body (e.g., what to eat and wear) and choices of friends or activities.** Decisions here are not right or wrong but instead are seen as personal preferences left up to the individual (Smetana, 2002). Thus, Brad's decision to wear his underpants inside out is unusual but not wrong.

During the preschool years, children begin to differentiate these domains (Lagattuta, Nucci, & Bosacki, 2010; Turiel, 1998; Yau, Smetana, & Metzger, 2009). For example, they believe that breaking a moral rule is more serious and should be punished more severely than breaking a social convention. And preschool children believe that moral rules apply regardless of the situation (e.g., it's never okay to hit other children) and cannot be overruled by adults. In contrast, preschoolers claim that social conventions are established by adults, which means they can be changed (e.g., it's okay for a school to say that students should address teachers by their first names). Finally, even preschoolers believe that the personal domain is just that: one where the individual should choose and not have the choices dictated by others.

Moral rules are common across cultures, but by definition, social conventions are not. The Cultural Influences feature shows how a social convention governing the same behaviour—polite lying—takes different forms in Western and Asian cultures.

Cultural Influences

Lies, White Lies, and Blue Lies

Preschool children claim that lying is wrong—telling a lie to hide one's transgressions is violating a moral rule. Older children have a more nuanced view and claim that "polite lying" is justified if it helps the welfare of others or would prevent an injustice. In other words, school-age children have mastered their culture's view that polite lies are social conventions designed to protect others (Lee, 2013).

Nevertheless, the circumstances that justify polite lying vary with culture. White lies are common in Western culture: Children often lie to protect another person. When asked by an experimenter if they like an undesirable gift (e.g., a bar of soap), most school-age children say "yes." Such white lies are more common as children develop, and the usual justification is that it would be rude to tell the truth; the white lie makes a person happy, which is more important than telling the truth (Popliger, Talwar, & Crossman, 2011).

In contrast, in China polite lying is more likely to take the form of a "blue lie," one that helps the group and, in the process, hurts an individual. If a classmate who sings poorly wants to join the choir, Chinese children believe that lying to the child ("Sorry but there are no spaces left in the choir") is acceptable because it protects the quality of the choir; North American children believe that lying to the choir ("My friend sings really well") is acceptable because it makes the friend happy (Fu, Xu, Cameron, Herman,

& Lee, 2007). These cultural standards for polite lying reflect more general differences between Asian and Western cultures in their emphasis on the group and the individual (e.g., recall, from Module 10.1, that Asian children take pride in group achievement but North American children take pride in individual achievement). And they show that social conventions vary in predictable ways across cultures.

Critical Thinking Questions: The feature on cultural influences and social judgment mentions that the same domains of social judgment are seen worldwide but that the actions that make up the domains can be different. Is this important? What do you think about the norms of different cultures for social judgments? Is one culture's way right or wrong, better or worse?

How do children come to understand the different domains of morality, social convention, and personal autonomy? The Cultural Influences feature shows that children's understanding of these different domains is shaped, in part, by their experiences. Parents' responses to different kinds of transgressions also play a role (Turiel, 1998). When a child breaks a moral rule, adults talk about the impact of the act on the victim and how that person could be hurt. In contrast, when a child violates a social convention, adults more often talk about the need to follow rules and to obey parents, teachers, and other people in authority. Finally, conversations in the personal domain are different: Here adults typically do not specify a "right" or "wrong" choice but instead encourage children to make their own choices (Nucci & Weber, 1995).

Thus, from the viewpoint of domains of social judgment, moral reasoning is part of a much larger developmental accomplishment: Children understand that there are different domains of social decision making, each with unique rules of authority and sanctions for misbehaviour. By the preschool years, children have made remarkable progress in understanding the distinction among the moral, social-conventional, and personal domains. This progress continues throughout development, with distinctions being made between moral and social values. Prencipe and Helwig (2002) conducted research in Toronto with schoolchildren aged 8, 10, and 13, and 21-year-old university students. This study showed that the capacity to reason about moral values, and the distinctions made between types of values, increased with age. Thus, ways of understanding and level of understanding improve with development across childhood and into early adulthood

ORIGINS OF MORAL REASONING IN INFANCY   Research on domains of social judgment shows that by three years of age, children understand that moral rules are special—they can't be changed and they apply broadly (Smetana et al., 2012). Other research suggests that moral reasoning may begin at even younger ages: 19-month-olds expect resources to be divided evenly (Sloane, Baillargeon, & Premack, 2012), and 6- to 10-month-olds prefer helpful actors over those who hinder others (Hamlin, Wynn, & Bloom, 2007).

Findings like these have led some scientists to propose an evolutionary basis to moral judgments (Hamlin, 2014; Tomasello & Vaish, 2013). The gist of the argument is that a sense of morality evolved to allow early humans to live together in groups: Because people are often selfish, a moral sense evolved to allow them to cooperate with others, sometimes sacrificing their own interests for those of the group.

According to this account, an innate moral sense would include three essential components: (1) moral goodness—feeling concern for other people and helping them in time of need; (2) moral evaluation—identifying and disliking group members who do not cooperate; and (3) moral retribution—punishing group members whose behaviour undermines the group. Consistent with the theory, each of these components has been observed in infants: They are concerned when others are upset; they favour people who help and dislike those who don't; and they punish uncooperative individuals by denying them rewards (Davidov, Zahn-Waxler, Roth-Hanania, & Knafo, 2013; Hamlin, 2013). Although this work on infants' moral reasoning is just beginning, many scientists believe that moral reasoning may represent another core domain such as those described in Module 6.2, one that evolved because it was a form of knowledge essential for humans to survive in groups.

THE ROLE OF EMOTIONS.   So far we've considered moral development primarily in cognitive terms: as a rational decision-making process in which children deliberately evaluate the virtues of different actions. Yet moral decision making is often quite emotional (e.g., in the module-opening vignette, Min-shen actually became quite upset as he debated whether to tell the principal who had stolen the iPad) and activates emotional centres in the brain (Greene, 2007). Consequently, scientists have begun to study the interplay of cognition and emotion in shaping the development of moral judgments (Nucci & Gingo, 2011).

One idea is that emotional responses to events provide the raw data that allow children to create different categories of morally relevant concepts (Arsenio, Gold, & Adams, 2006). For example, even preschool children know that a boy would feel sad if someone stole his dessert or took his turn on a swing. And they know that a girl would feel happy if she helped a peer who dropped a stack of papers or if she shared her lunch with a friend who forgot hers. Repeated experience with these kinds of events leads children to form scripts about the emotional consequences of different actions, and children then create categories of events that lead to similar emotional outcomes. Thus exposure to a number of similar experiences leads to formation of categories. For example, one script in which a child becomes sad after a theft or another script in which a child becomes sad following unprovoked aggression may lead children to create a concept of unfair victimization.

Thus, children's emotional response to social-moral events is an important step in creating different categories of moral concepts. In Modules 12.3 and 12.4, we'll see that the nature of children's emotional responses to social interactions predicts whether they act prosocially or act aggressively.

Promoting Moral Reasoning

Whether morality is based on justice or care, most cultures and most parents want to encourage adolescents to think carefully about moral issues. What can be done to help adolescents develop more mature forms of moral reasoning? Research by Walker (1980) at the Ontario Institute for Studies in Education at the University of Toronto showed that sometimes simply being exposed to more advanced moral reasoning is sufficient to promote developmental change. Provided that the children were beginning entry into the formal operations level of cognition, they could advance in moral reasoning. Thus, adolescents might notice, for example, that older friends do not wait to be rewarded to help others. Or a teenager may notice that respected peers take courageous positions regardless of the social consequences. Such experiences apparently cause adolescents to re-evaluate their reasoning on moral issues and propel them toward more sophisticated thinking.

Discussion can be particularly effective in revealing shortcomings in moral reasoning (Berkowitz, Sherblom, Bier, & Battistich, 2006). When people reason about moral issues with others whose reasoning is at a higher level, the usual result is that the reasoning of individuals at lower levels improves. Canadian research has shown that this is particularly true when the conversational partner with the more sophisticated reasoning makes an effort to understand the other's view, by requesting clarification or paraphrasing what the other child is saying (Walker, Hennig, & Krettenauer, 2000). Incorporating morality into the school curriculum also helps foster understanding morality. Katherine Covell and Brian Howe at the Children's Rights Centre of Cape Breton University, Nova Scotia, developed a curriculum designed to teach children their rights and responsibilities as laid out in the United Nations Convention on the Rights of the Child. This curriculum was taught as part of Grade 8 health or social studies classes in Nova Scotia schools over a six-month period. At the end of the six months, children were assessed on factors such as self-esteem, acceptance of others, and understating of rights. As Covell and Howe (2001) noted in their article reporting this study, titled "Moral education through the 3Rs: rights, respect and responsibility," those who had explicitly been taught about human rights and discussed this in class showed higher levels of self-esteem, perceived teachers and peers as more supportive, and had increased respect for the rights of others. Thus, teaching and modelling respect and moral values in schools seems to increase positive moral values (Covell & Howe, 2001). More recent research further supports these findings and extends the age range at which the "Rights, Respect, and Responsibility (RRR)" (Covell, Howe, & McNeil, 2008) curriculum has been found to be effective in children as young as five years old. Use of the RRR curriculum is now widespread and is also being used in the UK (Covell & Howe, 2009, 2011). As the researchers noted in a report for the county of Hampshire in England, "RRR is now widely seen as a world leader in programs of children's human rights education" (Covell & Howe, 2011, p. 2).

Several times in this chapter we have noted research on moral reasoning by Lawrence Walker from the University of British Columbia. Working with M. Kyle Matsuba, Walker studied youth who were considered to be "moral exemplars," who had been "nominated for their extraordinary moral commitment to the social organizations where they volunteered or worked" (Matsuba & Walker 2005, p. 275). Such youth were found to be especially aware of issues such as the suffering of others and to be more advanced morally (Matsuba & Walker, 2004). Further research by Walker and colleagues has shown that moral exemplars also show a specific personality pattern that includes caring and willingness to moral action (e.g., Dunlop, Walker, & Matsuba, 2012). People who might be considered moral exemplars are Craig Keilburger, Severn Cullis-Suzuki, and Bilaal Rajan. In 1995, when he was 12 years old, Keilburger read an article in the *Toronto Star* newspaper about the murder of a child labourer who had become an activist for the rights of other such exploited children. The murdered boy, Iqbal Masih, was the same age as Craig, 12. Keilburger found out that there were many child labourers in the world who were forced into work. He immediately set about doing something about this situation and founded an organization called Free the Children (now called WE). Initially comprising a group of school friends, the organization has become an international educational and advocacy network. Craig and his brother Marc co-founded the Free the Children international charity and Me for We, a social business enterprise. Craig Keilburger has been nominated three times for the Nobel Peace Prize (Free the Children, n.d.).

Like Craig Keilburger, Severn Cullis-Suzuki was inspired to action by a specific example of injustice. The Cullis-Suzuki family has always tried to respect nature and other peoples (Severn's father is renowned environmentalist David Suzuki). In a talk given at Brescia University College (March 8, 2007) Cullis-Suzuki recounted how, when she was in Grade 5, her family visited an Aboriginal family living in the Amazon region where clear-cutting was destroying the rain forests. Cullis-Suzuki returned from this trip and told her friends about the destruction of the rainforests. She then started the Environmental Children's Organization (ECO), and in 1992, at the age of 12, she was invited to give a speech to world leaders at the Earth Summit in Rio de Janeiro, Brazil.

Hearing of the problems of others in the world also started Bilaal Rajan of Toronto in philanthropy. When he was only four years old, Rajan heard about children suffering as a result of an earthquake in India. He began fundraising to send money to help the earthquake victims. Rajan went on to found the Hands for Help organization, write books, and speak publicly, and in 2005 was made UNICEF National Child Representative for Canada (bilaalrajan.com, n.d.).

Not everyone is a Rajan, a Cullis-Suzuki, or a Keilburger, but we would obviously like our children and adolescents to behave morally. Fortunately, it does appear that basic moral reasoning in young people can be encouraged. In fact, Bilaal Rajan's personal webpage promotes his book *Making Change: Tips from an Underage Achiever* to parents as a way of inspiring their children to act for social change.

Adolescents' moral reasoning (and moral behaviour) is also influenced by their involvement in religion. Adolescents who are more involved in religion have greater concern for others and place more emphasis on helping them (Youniss, McLellan, & Yates, 1999). An obvious explanation for this link is that religion provides moral beliefs and guidelines for adolescents. But participation in religion can promote moral reasoning in a second, less direct way. Involvement in a religious community—typically through youth groups associated with a church, synagogue, or mosque—connects teens to an extended network of caring peers and adults. From interacting with individuals in this network, earning their trust, and sharing their values, adolescents gain a sense of responsibility to and concern for others (King & Furrow, 2004).

In this module, we've seen how moral reasoning changes as children develop and that children's emotional response to social-moral events is an important step in creating different categories of moral concepts. In Modules 12.3 and 12.4, we'll see that the nature of children's emotional responses to social interactions predicts whether they act prosocially or act aggressively.

 ANSWER 12.2
Paige's thinking conforms to Kohlberg's Stage 3, in which morality is based on living up to others' expectations. That is, Paige believes that Heinz should steal the drug because he needs to act as others expect a husband should act. Stage 3 reasoning is common in older adolescents and young adults, so Paige is probably at least 15 years old.

 Check Your Learning

RECALL Summarize research that supports and refutes Kohlberg's theory of moral reasoning.

What are the different domains of social judgment? What do young children understand about each of them?

Describe ways to foster children's moral reasoning.

INTERPRET How do Piaget's stages of moral realism and moral relativism fit with Kohlberg's six stages?

APPLY Imagine that you were the father of Min-shen, the boy in the vignette who did not stand up for the boy who was wrongly accused of stealing the iPad. Based on the research described in this module, what might you do to try to advance Min-shen's level of moral reasoning?

12.3   Helping Others

OUTLINE	LEARNING OBJECTIVES
Development of Prosocial Behaviour	1. At what age do children begin to act prosocially? How does prosocial behaviour change with age?
Skills Underlying Prosocial Behaviour	2. What skills do children need to behave prosocially?
Situational Influences	3. What situations influence children's prosocial behaviour?
The Contribution of Heredity	4. How does heredity contribute to children's prosocial behaviour?
Socializing Prosocial Behaviour	5. How can parents encourage their children to act prosocially?

Six-year-old Juan got his finger trapped in the DVD player when he tried to remove a disc. While he cried and cried, his three-year-old brother, Antony, and his two-year-old sister, Carla, watched but did not help. Later, when their mother had soothed Juan and saw that his finger was not injured, she worried about her younger children's reactions. In the face of their brother's obvious distress, why had Antony and Carla done nothing?

Most parents, most teachers, and most religions try to teach children to act in cooperative, helping, giving ways—at least most of the time and in most situations. **Actions that benefit others are known as** *prosocial behaviour.* Of course, cooperation often "works" because individuals gain more than they would by not cooperating. *Altruism* **is prosocial behaviour that helps another with no expectation of direct benefit to the helper.** Altruism is driven by feelings of responsibility for other people. Two youngsters pooling their funds to buy a candy bar to share demonstrates cooperative behaviour. One youngster giving half her lunch to a friend who forgot his own lunch demonstrates altruism.

Many scientists believe that humans are biologically predisposed to be helpful, to share, to cooperate, and to be concerned for others (Hastings, Zahn-Waxler, & McShane, 2006; Wilson, 2000). Why has prosocial behaviour evolved over time? The best explanation has nothing to do with lofty moral principles. Instead the reason is much more pragmatic: People who frequently help others are more likely to receive help themselves, and this increases the chance that they will pass along their genes to future generations.

But, as the story of Juan and his siblings shows, children (and adults, for that matter) are not always helpful or cooperative. In this module, you'll learn how prosocial behaviour changes with age and discover some factors that promote prosocial behaviour.

Development of Prosocial Behaviour

Simple acts of altruism can be seen by 18 months of age. When toddlers and preschoolers see other people who are obviously hurt or upset, they appear concerned. Their sympathetic nervous system is activated, which is a common by-product of experiencing distressing or threatening events (Hepach, Vaish, & Tomasello, 2012). Like the child in the photo on the next page. They try to comfort the person by hugging him or patting him (Zahn-Waxler, Radke-Yarrow, Wagner, & Chapman, 1992). Apparently, at this early age, children recognize signs of distress. And if an adult is in obvious need of help—a teacher accidentally drops markers on a floor—most 18-month-olds spontaneously help get the markers (Warneken & Tomasello, 2006).

During the toddler and preschool years, children gradually begin to understand others' needs and learn more appropriate altruistic responses (van der Mark, van IJzendoorn, & Bakermans-Kranenburg, 2002). When three-year-old Alexis sees her father trying, unsuccessfully, to get her mother's attention, she may poke her mom to get her attention and then point to her father (Beier, Over, & Carpenter, 2014). These early attempts at altruistic behaviour often are limited because young children's knowledge of what they can do to help is modest. As youngsters acquire more strategies to help others, their preferred strategies become more adult-like (Eisenberg, Fabes, & Spinrad, 2006).

Thus, as a general rule, intentions to act prosocially increase with age, as do children's strategies for helping. Of course, not all children respond to the needs of others, either in toddlerhood or at later ages. Some children attach greater priority to looking out for their own interests. What makes some children more likely than others to help? We'll answer this question in the next section.

Even toddlers recognize when others are upset and try to comfort them.

Skills Underlying Prosocial Behaviour

Think back to an occasion when you helped someone. How did you know that the person needed help? Why did you decide to help? Although you didn't realize it at the time, your decision to help was probably based on several skills:

- *Perspective taking.* In Module 6.1, you learned about Piaget's concept of egocentrism, the preoperational youngster's inability to see things from another's point of view. Egocentrism limits children's ability to share or help because they simply do not realize the need for prosocial behaviour. They have only one perspective—their own. For example, young children might not help someone carrying many packages because they cannot envision that carrying lots of bulky things is a burden. Older children, however, can take the perspective of others, so they recognize the burden and are more inclined to help. Janet Strayer from Simon Fraser University in British Columbia and William Roberts from University College of the Cariboo studied the relation of parents' behaviours such as empathy and warmth to children's expressions of such emotional factors. Parents and children's empathy correlated, and this study gave evidence that, in general, the better children understand the thoughts and feelings of other people, the more willing they are to share and help others (Strayer & Roberts, 2004). Thus being able to take another's perspective increases likelihood of prosocial behaviours (Vaish, Carpenter, & Tomasello, 2009).

- *Empathy.* **The ability to experience another person's emotions is called** *empathy*. Children who deeply feel another person's fear, disappointment, sorrow, or loneliness are more inclined to help that person than are children who do not feel these emotions (Eisenberg et al., 2006; Malti & Krettenauer, 2013). In other words, youngsters like the one in the photo on the next page, who is obviously distressed by what he is seeing, are most likely to help others.

- *Moral reasoning.* In Module 12.2, you learned that reward and punishment influence young children's moral reasoning, whereas a concern for moral principles characterizes adolescents' and adults' moral decision making. Therefore, as you would expect, prosocial behaviour in young children is usually determined by the chance of reward or punishment. It also follows that, as children mature and begin to make moral decisions on the basis of fairness and justice, they become more

Juanmonino/E+/Getty Images

Children who are empathic—who understand how others feel—are more likely to help others in need.

prosocial. Consistent with this idea, Eisenberg, Zhou, and Koller (2001) found that Brazilian 13- to 16-year-olds were more likely to act prosocially when their moral reasoning was more advanced (e.g., based on internalized moral standards).

In sum, children and adolescents who help others tend to be better able to take another's viewpoint, to feel another's emotions, and to act on the basis of principles rather than rewards, punishments, or social norms. For example, a 15-year-old who spontaneously lends his favourite video game to a friend does so because he sees that the friend would like to play the game, he feels the friend's disappointment at not owning the game, and he believes that friends should share with each other.

Of course, perspective taking, empathy, and moral reasoning skills do not guarantee that children always act altruistically. Even when children have the skills needed to act altruistically, they may not because of the particular situation, as we'll see in the next section.

Situational Influences

Kind children occasionally disappoint us by being cruel, and children who are usually stingy sometimes surprise us by their generosity. Why? The setting helps determine whether children act altruistically or not.

- *Feelings of responsibility.* Children act altruistically when they feel responsible to the person in need. They are more likely to help siblings and friends than strangers, simply because they feel a direct responsibility to people that they know well (Costin & Jones, 1992). And they are more likely to help when prompted with photos showing two people who appear to be friends (Over & Carpenter, 2009). In other words, a simple reminder of the importance of friendship (or affiliation with others) can be enough to elicit helping.

- *Feelings of competence.* Children act altruistically when they feel that they have the skills necessary to help the person in need. Suppose, for example, that a child is growing more and more upset because she can't figure out how to work a computer game. A classmate who knows little about computer games is not likely to help because he doesn't know what to do to help. By helping, he could end up looking foolish (Peterson, 1983).

- *Mood.* Children act altruistically when they are happy or feeling successful but not when they are sad or feeling as if they have failed (Wentzel, Filisetti, & Looney, 2007). In other words, a preschooler who has just spent an exciting morning as the "leader" in nursery school is more inclined to share treats with siblings than is a preschooler who was punished by the teacher (Eisenberg, 2000).

- *Cost of altruism.* Children act altruistically when it entails few or modest sacrifices. A preschooler who has received a snack that she doesn't particularly like is more inclined to share it than is a child who has received her very favourite snack (Eisenberg & Shell, 1986).

When, then, are children most likely to help? When they feel responsible to the person in need, have the skills that are needed, are happy, or do not think they have to give up a lot by helping. When are children least likely to help? When they feel neither responsible for nor capable of helping, are in a bad mood, or believe that helping will entail a large personal sacrifice.

Using these guidelines, how do you explain why Antony and Carla, the children in the vignette, watched idly as their older brother cried? Hint: The last two factors—mood and cost—are not likely to be involved but, the first two may explain Antony and Carla's failure to help their older brother. Our explanation appears on page 425, just before Check Your Learning.

So far, we've seen that altruistic behaviour is determined by children's skills (such as perspective taking) and by characteristics of situations (such as whether children feel competent to help in a particular situation). Whether children are altruistic is also determined by genetics and by socialization, the topic of the remaining two sections in this module.

The Contribution of Heredity

As we mentioned on page 420, many scientists believe that prosocial behaviour represents an evolutionary adaptation: People who help others are more likely to be helped themselves and thus are more likely to survive and have offspring. According to this argument, we should expect to find evidence for heritability of prosocial behaviour, and in fact that's the case: Twin studies consistently find that identical twins are more alike in their prosocial behaviour than are fraternal twins (Gregory, Light-Häusermann, Rijsdijk, & Eley, 2009).

One likely path of genetic influence involves oxytocin, a hormone that influences many social behaviours (e.g., nurturance, empathy, affiliation, and cooperation) and that has been linked to a few specific genes. In this explanation of prosociality, it is proposed that some children may inherit oxytocin-promoting genes that facilitate such behaviour (Carter, 2014; Keltner, Kogan, Piff, & Saturn 2014).

Genes may also affect prosocial behaviour indirectly, by their influence on temperament. For example, children who are temperamentally less able to regulate their emotions (in part because of heredity) may help less often because they are so upset by another's distress that taking action is impossible (Eisenberg et al., 2007). Another temperamental influence may be via inhibition (shyness). Children who are temperamentally shy are often reluctant to help others, particularly people they don't know well (Young, Fox, & Zahn-Waxler, 1999). Even though these children realize that others need help and are upset by another person's apparent distress, shy children's reticence means that these feelings do not translate into action. Thus, in both cases, the children are aware that others need help, but, in the first instance, they are too upset themselves to figure out how to help, and in the second instance they know how to help but are too inhibited to follow through.

Socializing Prosocial Behaviour

In her talk at Brescia University College (mentioned in Module 12.2), Severn Cullis-Suzuki said that her promotion of environmental issues was particularly influenced by her parents, Tara Cullis and David Suzuki, and by the ways of the Haida Gwaii, the Aboriginal people of her home province of British Columbia. Severn's prosocial behaviour started in childhood, at home. How do parents foster altruism in their children? Several factors contribute:

- *Modelling.* When children see adults helping and caring for others, they often imitate such prosocial behaviour (Eisenberg et al., 2006). Parents who report frequent feelings of warmth and concern for others tend to have children who experience stronger feelings of empathy. When a mother is helpful and responsive, her children often imitate her by being cooperative, helpful, sharing, and less critical of others.

Q&A **QUESTION 12.3**
Paula worries that her son Elliot is too selfish and wishes that he were more caring and compassionate. As a parent, what could Paula do to encourage Elliot to be more concerned about others' welfare? *(Answer is on page 425.)*

In a particularly powerful demonstration of the impact of parental modelling, people who had risked their lives during World War II to protect Jews from the Nazis often reported their parents' emphasis on caring for all people (Oliner & Oliner, 1988).

- *Disciplinary practices.* Children behave prosocially more often when their parents are warm and supportive, set guidelines, and provide feedback; in contrast, prosocial behaviour is less common when parenting is harsh, threatening, and includes frequent physical punishment (Eisenberg & Fabes, 1998; Knight & Carlo, 2012; Moreno, Klute, & Robinson, 2008). Particularly important is parents' use of reasoning as a disciplinary tactic, with the goal of helping children see how their actions affect others. For example, after four-year-old Annie grabbed some crayons from a playmate, her father told Annie, "You shouldn't just grab things away from people. It makes them angry and unhappy. Ask first, and if they say 'no,' then you mustn't take them." As we noted in the earlier discussion of self-control and internalization of values (Module 12.1), inductive reasoning promotes internalization of such factors. Annie's father is thus helping her to understand why it is wrong to grab things, so that she can see this for herself and control herself in future interactions.

- *Opportunities to behave prosocially.* You need to practise to improve motor skills and the same is true of prosocial behaviours—children and adolescents are more likely to act prosocially when they are routinely given the opportunity to help and cooperate with others. At home, children can help with household tasks such as cleaning and setting the table. Adolescents can be encouraged to participate in community service, such as working at a food bank or, like the teenager in the photo, helping older adults. Experiences like these help to sensitize children and adolescents to the needs of others and allow them to enjoy the satisfaction of helping (Grusec, Goodnow, & Cohen, 1996; McLellan & Youniss, 2003).

Thus, many factors, summarized in the following Summary Table, contribute to children's prosocial behaviour. Combining all these ingredients, we can describe the development of children's altruistic behaviour this way: As children get older, their perspective

Myrleen Pearson/PhotoEdit

After children and adolescents have had the opportunity to help others, they often continue to be helpful because they better understand the needs of others.

SUMMARY TABLE

FACTORS CONTRIBUTING TO CHILDREN'S PROSOCIAL BEHAVIOUR

General Category	Types of Influence	Children are more likely to help when . . .
Skills	Perspective taking	they can take another person's point of view.
	Empathy	they feel another person's emotions.
	Moral reasoning	they base moral decisions on fairness.
Situational influences	Feelings of responsibility	they feel responsible to the person in need.
	Feelings of competence	they feel competent to help.
	Mood	they are in a good mood.
	Cost of altruism	the cost of prosocial behaviour is small.
Heredity	Temperament	they can control their emotions and are not shy.
Parents' influence	Modelling	parents behave prosocially.
	Discipline	parents reason with them.
	Opportunities	they practise helping at home and elsewhere.

taking and empathic skills develop, which enables them to see and feel another's needs. Nonetheless, children are never invariably altruistic (or, fortunately, invariably nonaltruistic) because properties of situations dictate altruistic behaviour too.

As parents and other adults try to encourage children's prosocial behaviour, one of the biggest obstacles is aggressive behaviour, which is common throughout childhood and adolescence. In the next module, we'll look at some of the forces that contribute to children's aggression.

> *Answer to question on page 423 about why Antony and Carla didn't help their brother:* Here are two explanations: First, neither Antony nor Carla may have felt sufficiently responsible to help because (a) with two children who could help, each child's feeling of individual responsibility is reduced, and (b) younger children are less likely to feel responsible for an older brother. Second, both children probably have been told not to use the DVD player by themselves. Consequently, they do not feel competent to help because they don't know how it works or what they should do to help Juan remove his finger.

 ANSWER 12.3
First, Paula can be sure to model the same behaviour that she'd like to encourage in her son—she needs to show compassion herself. Second, when disciplining Elliot, Paula should try to reason with him, emphasizing how his behaviour makes others feel. Third, Paula can ask Elliot to help around the house and suggest that he do some volunteer activity in the community.

 Check Your Learning

RECALL Describe developmental change in prosocial behaviour.
What are the situations in which children are most likely to help others?

INTERPRET Why must a full account of children's prosocial behaviour include an emphasis on skills (e.g., empathy) as well as situations (e.g., those in which a child feels responsible)?

APPLY Helping with household chores and voluntary community service often increase children's prosocial behaviour. Of the skills underlying prosocial behaviour (pages 421–422), which do you think are most affected by children's experience with helping at home and elsewhere?

 12.4 **Aggression**

OUTLINE	LEARNING OBJECTIVES
Change and Stability	**1.** When does aggressive behaviour first emerge? How stable is aggression across childhood, adolescence, and adulthood?
Roots of Aggressive Behaviour	**2.** How do families, television, and the child's own thoughts contribute to aggression?
Victims of Aggression	**3.** Why are some children victims of aggression?

Every day, seven-year-old Reza follows the same routine when he gets home from school: He watches one action-adventure cartoon on TV after another until it's time for dinner. Reza's mother is disturbed by her son's constant TV viewing, particularly because of the amount of violence in the shows that he likes. Her husband tells her to stop worrying: "Let him watch what he wants to. It won't hurt him and, besides, it keeps him out of your hair."

If you think back to your years in elementary school, you can probably remember a class bully—a child who was always teasing classmates and picking fights. **Such acts typify** *aggression,* **which is behaviour meant to harm others.** Aggressiveness is not the same as assertiveness, even though laypeople often use these words interchangeably. You've probably heard praise for an "aggressive businessperson" or a ballplayer who was "aggressive at running the bases." Psychologists and other behavioural scientists, however, would call these behaviours "assertive." Assertive behaviours are goal-directed actions to further the legitimate interests of individuals or the groups they represent, while respecting the rights of other persons. In contrast, aggressive behaviour—which can be physical or verbal—is intended to harm, damage, or injure, and is carried out without regard for the rights of others.

In this module, we will examine aggressive behaviour in children and see how it changes with age. Then we'll examine some causes of children's aggression, and, in the process, learn more about the impact of Reza's TV watching on his behaviour.

Change and Stability

By the time infants turn one, most have mastered the motor skills needed for simple aggression—grabbing and pushing—and many youngsters use these skills to get what they want (e.g., taking a toy from a peer, Hay et al., 2011). **In such** *instrumental aggression,* **a child uses aggression to achieve an explicit goal.** Instrumental aggression would include acts such as shoving another child in order to get to the head of the lunch line or, as shown in the photo on this page, grabbing a toy away from another child. By the start of the elementary-school years, another form of aggression emerges (Coie, Dodge, Terry, & Wright, 1991). *Hostile aggression* **is unprovoked; apparently its sole goal is to intimidate, harass, or humiliate another child.** Hostile aggression is illustrated by a child who spontaneously says to another, "You're stupid!" and then kicks the other child. **Yet another common type of aggression is** *reactive aggression,* **in which one child's behaviour leads to another child's aggression.** Reactive aggression is demonstrated by a child who loses a game and then punches the child who won, or when the child not chosen for the starring role in a play kicks the child who was selected.

In instrumental aggression, children use force to achieve a goal, such as taking a toy from another child.

Instrumental, hostile, and reactive aggression are most likely to be expressed physically by younger children. As children get older, they more often use language to express their aggression (Dodge, Coie, & Tremblay, 2006). **A particularly common form of verbal aggression is** *relational aggression,* **in which children try to hurt others by undermining their social relationships.** In relational aggression, which is more typical of girls than boys, children try to hurt others by telling friends to avoid a particular classmate, by spreading malicious gossip, or by making remarks meant to hurt others (Côté, Vaillancourt, Barker, Nagin, & Tremblay, 2007; Crick, Ostrov, Appleyard, Jansen, & Casas, 2004). Relational aggression is more common than physical aggression in schools, and can be extremely hurtful; it has been described as "covert psychological warfare" (Brendtro, 2001, p. 47). Two true stories from Robert Kail's child-development students portray relational aggression. After a heated argument in Grade 2, a student's former friend wrote "Erin is a big jerk" in block letters on the sidewalk where everyone walking to school would see the message. In another incident, a student named Beth related that, after she'd beaten a classmate in the Grade 5 spelling bee, that classmate's friends formed the "I hate Beth" club. Sadly, such behaviour is not infrequent here in Canada, although incidence has decreased in recent years. A recent Centre for Addiction and Mental Health (CAMH) report on an ongoing survey of Ontario students in Grades 7 to 12 noted this decline, with 33% of students reporting having been bullied in 2003, dropping to 24% in 2015 (Boak, Hamilton, Adlaf, Henderson, & Mann, 2016). Girls were more likely to be bullied than boys, with 28% of girls reporting being victimized at school, compared to 20% of boys (Boak et al., 2016).

STABILITY OF AGGRESSION OVER TIME. Forms of aggression change with development, but individual children's tendencies to behave aggressively are stable over time, particularly for children who are highly aggressive at a young age (Kjeldsen, Janson, Stoolmiller, Torgersen, & Mathiesen, 2014). Each of the following longitudinal studies shows that many aggressive young children grow up to be adolescents and adults who are aggressive, sometimes violent, and often commit crimes:

- In a study of more than 250 infants and toddlers growing up in Wales (Hay et al., 2014), six-month-olds who tried to bite or strike other people were as three-year-olds more likely to kick or hit peers to obtain toys.

- In a study of more than 900 Canadian girls from schools across Quebec (Coté, Zoccolillo, Tremblay, Nagin, & Vitaro, 2001), six-year-olds who had been rated by their teachers as frequently disrupting class (e.g., they were disobedient or they bullied classmates) were four to five times more likely to be diagnosed as teenagers with conduct disorder, a disorder in which individuals are chronically aggressive, destroy property, and lie or steal. And research by Coté and colleagues from Université de Montréal and McGill University has shown that specific behavioural profiles exist for both boys and girls at risk of developing conduct disorder as adolescents (Coté, Tremblay, Nagin, Zoccolillo, & Vitaro, 2002a, 2002b).

- In a study involving more than 200 German preschool children (Asendorpf, Denissen, & van Aken, 2008), those children who were judged by teachers to be most aggressive were, as young adults, 12 times more likely than the least aggressive children to have been charged for criminal activity.

Violent behaviour in adulthood is not the only long-term outcome of childhood aggression; poor adjustment to high school (e.g., dropping out, or failing a grade) and unemployment are others (Asendorpf, et al., 2008; Ladd, 2003). In one study, aggressive eight-year-olds tended to do poorly later in high school, leaving them few options for work as young adults and putting them at risk for problem drinking. By their early thirties, many of those who were highly aggressive children have limited education and low-status jobs; others are chronically unemployed (Alatupa et al., 2013; Kokko & Pulkkinen, 2000).

Findings from these and similar studies show that aggression is *not* simply a case of playful pushing and shoving that children will outgrow. On the contrary, a small minority of children who are highly aggressive develop into young adults who create havoc in society. What causes children to behave aggressively? Let's look at some of the roots of aggressive behaviour.

Roots of Aggressive Behaviour

Psychologists once believed that aggression was caused by frustration. The idea was that when children or adults were blocked from achieving a goal, they became frustrated and acted aggressively, often against the interfering person or object. Today, however, scientists look to many other causes, including biological factors, the family, the child's community and culture, and the child's own thoughts.

BIOLOGICAL CONTRIBUTIONS.   *Born to be Bad* is the title of at least two movies, two CDs (one by George Thorogood and one by Joan Jett), and three books. Implicit in this popular title is the idea that, from birth, some individuals follow a developmental track that leads to destructive, violent, or criminal behaviour. In other words, the claim is that biology sets the stage for people to be aggressive long before experience can affect development.

Is there any truth to this idea? In fact, biology and heredity do contribute to aggressive and violent behaviour. In twin studies, identical twins are usually more alike in their levels of physical aggression than are fraternal twins (Brendgen, Vitaro, Boivin, Dionne, & Perusse, 2006; Lacourse et al., 2014). There is also evidence from behavioural genetics research that there may be a biological basis for some types of aggression. A group of researchers from the United Kingdom, United States, and New Zealand, led by Avshalom Caspi, found certain genotypes may predispose individuals to antisocial behaviour (Caspi et al., 2002), and another group of researchers from universities in Quebec found significant effects of genes, at least for physical aggression (Brendgen, Boivin, Vitaro, Girard, Dionne, & Pérusse, 2008; Brendgen, Boivin, Vitaro, Bukowski, et al., 2008). But these studies do not tell us that aggression per se is inherited; instead they indicate that some children inherit factors that place them at risk for aggressive or violent behaviour. Temperament seems to be one such factor: Youngsters who are temperamentally difficult, overly emotional, or inattentive are, for example, more likely to be aggressive (Joussemet et al., 2008; Xu, Farver, & Zhang, 2009). Hormones represent another factor: Higher levels of the hormone testosterone may be associated with greater aggression and stronger responses to provocation (Carré, McCormick, & Hariri, 2011). Finally, some children may have a deficit in the neurotransmitters that inhibit aggressive behaviour (Van Goozen, Fairchild, Snoek, & Harold, 2007).

None of these factors—temperament, testosterone, or neurotransmitters—*causes* a child to be aggressive. They do however make aggressive behaviour more likely. For instance, children who are emotional and easily irritated may be disliked by their peers and be in frequent conflict with them, opening the door for aggressive responses. Thus, biological factors place children at risk for aggression but, as Brendgen and colleagues further research shows, environment is also important (e.g., Brendgen et al., 2008). Thus, to understand which children actually become aggressive, we need to look at interactions between inherited factors and children's experiences (Brendgen, 2012; Moffitt, 2005).

IMPACT OF THE FAMILY.   Although few parents deliberately teach their children to harm others, early family experiences are a prime training ground for learning patterns of aggression. Parents' approach to discipline is crucial. When parents use physical punishment or threats to discipline their children, the hidden message to children is that physical force works as a means of controlling others. A parent like the one in the photo on page 429 is saying, in effect, "The best way to get people to do what you want is to hurt them" (Lee, Altschul, & Gershoff, 2013; Gershoff, 2013). Mireille Joussemet of the Université de Montréal and colleagues from McGill University studied development of children's physical aggression from age six to 12. Although a number of factors were identified as influencing aggressive behaviour, the greatest risk factor for high levels of physical aggression in children was controlling parenting (Joussemet et al., 2008). Strong or aggressive parental responses are not essential in making a child aggressive. Neglect in infancy also can lead to aggression in childhood (Kotch et al., 2008), and when parents are coercive, unresponsive, and emotionally uninvested, their children are more likely to be aggressive (Blatt-Eisengart, Drabick, Monahan, & Steinberg, 2009; Rubin, Bukowski, & Parker, 2006). Some parents frequently threaten to withhold their love, express disappointment, and are overly possessive with their children, behaviours that represent the sort of social and emotional manipulation that defines relational aggression. Consequently, it's not surprising that children who experience heavy doses of such parenting are more likely to be relationally aggressive (Kuppens, Laurent, Heyvaert, & Onghena, 2013).

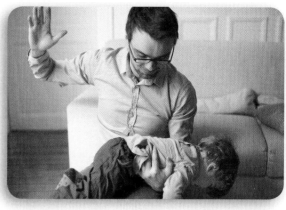

When parents use physical punishment often, their children are more likely to become aggressive.

In many families with aggressive children, a vicious circle seems to develop (Keijsers, Loeber, Branje, & Meeus, 2011). Compared to families with nonaggressive children, both aggressive children and their parents are more likely to respond to neutral behaviour with aggression. What's more, after an aggressive exchange has begun, both parents and children are likely to escalate the exchange, rather than break it off. Once a child has been labelled aggressive by parents and others, that child is more likely to be accused of aggression and to be singled out for punishment, even when the child has been behaving entirely appropriately on the occasion in question (Patterson, 2008). The "aggressive" child will be accused of all things that go wrong—from missing cookies to broken appliances—and other children's misbehaviours will be ignored.

Another aspect of parental behaviour that has been linked to aggression is *monitoring,* **which refers to parents' knowledge of where their children are, what they're doing, and whom they're with.** When parents do not monitor their children's behaviour, the children are more frequently aggressive (Patterson, 2008; Vieno, Nation, Pastore, & Santinello, 2009). Of course, monitoring requires children's cooperation to a certain extent, and children who are chronically aggressive often do not cooperate (e.g., teenagers not answering their cell phones when they see that a parent is calling), in part because they see monitoring as intrusive (Racz & McMahon, 2011).

So far we've seen that children's aggression is linked to parents' use of physical punishment and to their lack of monitoring. To this list we need to add another critical aspect of family life: the presence of conflict. When parents constantly argue and fight, their children are much more likely to be aggressive (Cummings, Schermerhorn, Davies, Goeke-Morey, & Cummings, 2006; Narayan, Englund, & Egeland, 2013). Children have "ringside seats" for many of these confrontations, and thus, they can see firsthand how parents use verbal and physical aggression against each other. Sadly, children often come to believe that these patterns of interacting represent "natural" ways of solving problems within a family (Graham-Bermann & Brescoll, 2000).

INFLUENCE OF COMMUNITY AND CULTURE. Parents are hardly alone in giving important lessons about aggression. Other influential voices in children's lives deliver powerful messages about aggressive behaviour.

- *Television and video games.* Most TV programs targeted at children contain acts of physical aggression (Wilson et al., 2002), and the average North American youngster will see several *thousand* murders on TV before reaching adolescence

(Waters, 1993). (If you find these numbers hard to believe, try the activities described in "See for Yourself" at the end of this chapter.) What does research tell us about this steady diet of televised mayhem and violence? Will Reza, the avid cartoon watcher in the vignette at the beginning of the module, become more aggressive? Or is his TV watching simply fun, as his father believes? In fact, longitudinal and cross-cultural studies have consistently found that children exposed to media violence tend to behave more aggressively and often grow up to be aggressive and violent adults. Canadian researchers from Queen's University, Kingston, Ontario, were three of the seven authors of a major study entitled "Television Viewing and Forms of Bullying among Adolescents from Eight Countries" (Kuntsche et al., 2006). The researchers found that both verbal and physical aggression resulted from frequent television viewing, though physical actions varied by country. Over 4000 Canadian children were among the participants in this study, and Canada has nothing to boast about—Canadian children were just as likely as those from other countries to call names, spread rumours, or kick and push others. The link to television viewing holds true even when confounding variables such as parents' education and family income are controlled for (Fuld et al., 2009; Kuntsche et al., 2006). What's more, playing violent video games seems to lead to aggressive violent behaviour in much the same way that watching violent TV does (Anderson et al., 2003; Willoughby, Adachi, & Good, 2012), particularly when children play habitually and identify with aggressive game characters (Konijn, Nije Bijvank, & Bushman, 2007). Playing violent video games also leads players to see targets of aggression as less human, making aggression against them more acceptable (Greitemeyer & McLatchie, 2011). In short, Reza's father is clearly wrong: Frequent exposure to media violence does make children more aggressive.

• **Peers.** Aggressive children often befriend other aggressive children, and the outcome is hardly surprising: Aggressive friends support and encourage each other's aggressive behaviour (Banny, Heilbron, Ames, & Prinstein, 2011; Powers, Bierman, & The Conduct Problems Prevention Research Group, 2013). Just as friends drawn together by a mutual interest in music enjoy listening to CDs together, friends whose common bond is their aggressive behaviour enjoy teaming up to attack their peers; they often "share" targets of aggression (Card & Hodges, 2006). Aggressive adolescents often join gangs, which has a catalytic effect on aggressive and violent behaviour. That is, even though adolescents who join gangs are already aggressive, their membership in a gang leads to more frequent and more violent antisocial behaviour (Thornberry, Krohn, Lizotte, Smith, & Tobin, 2003).

• **Failure in school.** Aggressive children are often uninterested in school, and their grades reflect this lack of interest. One interpretation of this finding is that aggressive children's behaviour interferes with their learning. Instead of spending time on school tasks such as learning to add, aggressive youngsters are busy creating mayhem or being undisciplined; in the process, they create conflicted relationships with their teachers—another impediment to school success (Stipek & Miles, 2008). Another interpretation is that children who have difficulty learning in school become frustrated and unhappy, and they express their frustration by aggressing against their peers.

Both views may be right (Masten et al., 2005; Miles & Stipek, 2006). School failure may breed aggressive behaviour, and aggressive behaviour, in turn, leads to school failure. In other words, this may be a vicious circle in which the starting point can be either aggressive behaviour or school failure. Once started, the other soon follows and the cycle grows. A five-year-old boy who kicks and pushes classmates is struggling to learn to read. His failure breeds even greater anger and aggression toward his classmates, which causes him to fall further behind academically. Over time, he becomes more aggressive and more of a failure in school (Masten et al., 2005).

- *Poverty.* Aggressive and antisocial behaviour is more common among children living in poverty than among children who are economically advantaged (Williams, Conger, & Blozis, 2007). Some of the impact of poverty can be explained by factors that we've already considered. For example, living in poverty is extremely stressful for parents and often leads to the very parental behaviours that promote aggression—harsh discipline and lax monitoring (Shaw & Shelleby, 2014). Poverty contributes to violent behaviour in another manner, by helping to create a culture of violence.

- *Culture of violence.* Violent crime is far more common in poverty-stricken neighbourhoods, and exposure to such violence fosters aggressive behaviour in adolescents. This can be a particular issue in places where weapons such guns are more readily available. For example, in a group of Chicago adolescents, those living in poverty were more likely to be exposed to firearm violence (e.g., seeing someone shot) and, as they got older, were more likely to be aggressive and violent themselves (Bingenheimer, Brennan, & Earls, 2005). Similarly, individuals living in the South and West regions of the United States often endorse a "culture of honour" that endorses aggressive and violent behaviour to defend one's honour, family, and property (Hayes & Lee, 2005). In such states, adolescents are more likely to report carrying firearms to school, and school shootings such as those at Columbine High School are more common, even after controlling for numerous relevant variables (Brown, Osterman, & Barnes, 2009). Finally, on a much smaller scale, elementary-school classrooms that contain many aggressive children often create a climate that sanctions aggression, and aggressive behaviour is contagious, spreading from one child to the next (Powers et al., 2013). In other words, just as frequent exposure within a family to physical punishment and marital conflict leads children to believe that aggression is a natural way to solve problems, exposure in the classroom or at the community level to violence and pro-aggression attitudes leads adolescents to condone aggressive and violent behaviour.

COGNITIVE PROCESSES. The perceptual and cognitive skills described in Chapters 6 through 8 also play a role in aggression. One general factor is executive functioning, described on page 206. Children who are less skilled in inhibiting, shifting, and updating behaviours and thoughts are prone to aggressive behaviour (Ellis, Weiss, & Lochman, 2009; McQuade, Murray-Close, Shoulberg, & Hoza, 2013; Schoemaker et al., 2013).

Cognitive processes contribute to aggression in another way, too: Aggressive youth often respond aggressively because they are not skilled at interpreting other people's intentions, and, without a clear interpretation in mind, they respond aggressively by default (Dodge, Bates, & Pettit, 1990). Far too often they think, "I don't know what you're up to, and when in doubt, attack." In the Spotlight on Theories feature we'll learn more about a theory of cognitive processing that helps to reveal how aggressive children think about other people.

Spotlight on Theories

Social-Information-Processing Theory and Children's Aggressive Behaviour

BACKGROUND   Genetics, parents, TV, peers, and poverty all contribute to make some children prone to aggression. What these influences have in common is that they lead some children to see the world as a hostile place in which they must be wary of other people. But precisely characterizing the aggressive child's hostile view has been a challenge.

THE THEORY   To explain how children perceive, interpret, and respond to people, Nicki R. Crick and Kenneth Dodge (1994; Dodge & Crick, 1990; Fontaine & Dodge, 2006) formulated an information-processing model of children's thinking, which is shown in Figure 12-1. According to the model, responding to a social stimulus involves several steps. First, children selectively attend to certain features of the social stimulus but do not attend to others. Second, children try to interpret the features that they have processed; that is, they try to give meaning to the social stimulus. Third, children evaluate their goals for the situation. Fourth, children retrieve from memory a behavioural response that is

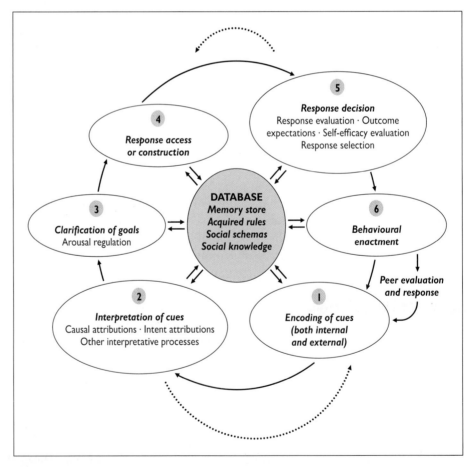

Figure 12-1 The faulty processing of information proposed by social-information-processing theory as occurring in aggressive children.

Based on Crick, N. R., & Dodge, K. A. (1994). A review and reformulation of social information-processing mechanisms in children's social adjustment. *Psychological Bulletin*, 115, 74–101.

associated with the interpretation and goals of the situation. Fifth, children evaluate this response to determine if it is appropriate. Sixth, the child proceeds with the behaviour.

Applied to aggressive children, the theory says that aggressive children's processing is biased and restricted in many of the steps in the diagram and that this flawed information processing is part of what leads these children to be more aggressive: They systematically misperceive people's actions (Crick & Werner, 1998; Egan, Monson, & Perry, 1998).

Hypothesis: According to social-information-processing theory, aggressive children's processing of social information (e.g., people) is biased in each of the stages depicted in Figure 12-1. In the fourth and fifth stages of processing—accessing response options and evaluating them—this bias leads to the hypothesis that aggressive children should respond hostilely when this interpretation is not warranted. For example, when an aggressive child picks up a book from a desk and another child says, "That's my book" in a nonprovocative manner, aggressive children are expected to be more likely to respond in a hostile way (e.g., "I was just looking at it. I didn't know it was yours. No need to jump all over me.") than in a neutral way (e.g., "Okay, I was wondering whose it was.").

Test: Fontaine, Yang, Dodge, Pettit, and Bates (2009) evaluated this hypothesis by asking adolescents to watch videos in which one person's action (e.g., picking up a book) leads to another person's neutral response (e.g., "That's my book"). Then the videos showed hostile and nonhostile responses; adolescents in the study were asked how easily they might act in these ways and how they might feel in doing so. Aggressive adolescents more often endorsed the hostile response but less aggressive adolescents tended to endorse the nonhostile response.

Conclusion: When confronted with situations in which a person's actions are not clear, aggressive children and adolescents often respond in a hostile manner by default. In other words, aggressive children view the world through suspicious eyes, as if others are always "out to get them," and consequently they respond to many neutral interactions with unwarranted hostility and anger.

Application: If aggressive children are unskilled at interpreting and responding to others' actions, would training in these skills improve their social behaviour? The answer seems to be "yes." When children are taught more sophisticated social-cognitive skills—including better strategies for resolving conflicts—they become better able to recognize other people's emotions, to interpret others' intentions, and to deal with peer-related problems without aggressing. Collectively, these improved social skills mean that children are less prone to antisocial behaviours such as aggression (Dodge, Godwin, & The Conduct Problems Prevention Research Group, 2013).

Debra Pepler of York University in Toronto and her colleagues have performed research into bullying in Canadian schools. In one study by Pepler et al. (2006), the forms of relationships involved in bullying were examined. Questionnaires on bullying were administered to both elementary- and high-school students. From analysis of the completed questionnaires, it was discovered that aggression was used in bullying to gain power over others. Bullying was also seen as a pattern of interaction: As Pepler et al. (2006) noted, "In our research program on bullying, we have come to understand bullying as a relationship problem" (p. 382). Similar to Dodge and colleagues, Pepler et al. (2006) propose the use of intervention programs, particularly for adolescents, to counteract such behaviour patterns.

Critical Thinking Question: According to social-information-processing theory, an aggressive child's interpretation of the world is flawed, leading to aggression as a primary social response. As mentioned in the feature, training seems to help reduce aggressive responding. What additional measures or forms of training can you think of that would help children prone to aggression to respond more appropriately to social stimuli?

MULTIPLE, CASCADING RISKS. Obviously, many factors contribute to make some children and adolescents more prone to aggressive and sometimes violent behaviour. When risk factors mount up in children's lives, they are at ever-greater risk for aggressive behaviour (Greenberg et al., 1999). What's more, many of the factors operate in a cascading fashion, such that later risk factors build on prior factors (Vaillancourt, Brittain, McDougall, & Duku, 2013): Poverty or maternal depression can lead to harsh, ineffective parenting. In turn, this leads children to be unprepared for school (both academically and socially), which leads to school failure and conduct problems. These difficulties cause some parents to become less active and less invested in parenting, which means that they monitor their children less often, allowing them to associate with deviant, aggressive peers (Dodge, Greenberg, & Malone, 2008).

Thus, the developmental journey that leads to a violent, aggressive, antisocial adolescent starts in early childhood but gains momentum along the way. Consequently, efforts to prevent children from taking this path must begin early, be maintained over childhood, and target both children and their parents. An example of a successful intervention program is Fast Track (Bierman et al., 2013; Conduct Problems Prevention Research Group, 2011), which is designed to teach academic and social skills to elementary-school children as well as life and vocational skills to adolescents. In addition, parents are taught skills for effective child rearing and, later, how to stay involved with their children and to monitor their behaviour. At Grade 12—two years after the program had ended—aggressive and destructive behaviour among children who were at highest risk in kindergarten was cut in half compared to similar high-risk children assigned to a control condition.

A specific intervention program to reduce aggression may not be necessary, however. For the average child, sport participation may have similar benefits. Although there are conflicting arguments—with organized sports viewed as "character building" and yet also as providing examples of aggression (Cox, Qui, & Li, 1993; Weiss & Smith, 2002)—it does appear that sports can have beneficial effects in control of aggression. As mentioned at the start of this module, a distinction exists between assertive and aggressive behaviour: It is fine to be assertive on the ice to get the puck, but slashing with a stick is aggression (and could be hostile or instrumental, depending on the situation).

Unfortunately, hockey also provides an example of negative social influences: *Socialized aggression* **is aggression that is expected within a situation**—for example, a hockey fight. This form of aggression "is socially sanctioned by the public" (Deardorff, 2000, p. 218) and even expected. Children might then be at risk of learning negative behaviours, but they do not look only to sports personalities as role models. As we have seen, they are also strongly influenced by the other adults in their lives. Parents and coaches can act as positive role models for children and foster a sense of fair play. Thus, research shows "that sport might build character, but only under the right conditions" (Bredemeier and Shields, 2006, p. 1). If aggressive behaviour is not permitted and not socially sanctioned, and if coaches promote moral reasoning, sports can have positive behavioural effects (Barnfield, 2003; Bredemeier & Shields, 2006). Even participation in martial arts (e.g., karate, judo, or tae kwon do), a form of training that one might think would lead to aggression, actually has the opposite effect, largely due to the positive examples from instructors and the practice of self-discipline that these arts encourage (Barnfield, 2003; Zivin et al, 2001). Studies with children and adolescents have shown that traditional martial arts training acts to reduce violence and aggression and to increase self-regulation and prosocial behaviours (Lakes & Hoyt, 2004; Zivin et al, 2001). Martial arts training also has been shown to be effective as part of bullying-prevention programs (e.g., Twemlow et al., 2008).

As we will see in the Focus on Research feature, participation in martial arts has multiple benefits.

Focus On Research

Benefits of Martial Arts Participation for Children

Who were the investigators, and what was the aim of the study? Francoise Boudreau, Ralph Folman, and Burt Konzak (1995) wanted to examine the psychological and physical changes that might take place from participation in martial arts. They wanted to determine if karate would have beneficial effects on schoolchildren's fitness and on behaviours such as self-control and self-esteem.

How did the investigators measure the topic of interest? Boudreau and colleagues had parents of school-aged children who were enrolled in a karate program fill out questionnaires. The children were designated as either beginners (those just starting the program) or nonbeginners (those who had already been participating in karate before the study). Parents of both beginners and nonbeginners were asked about their expectations of karate training, and the parents of nonbeginners answered additional questions regarding changes in their children's health, behaviours, and attitudes since starting karate. The parents were surveyed about perceived changes in their child on a variety of measures, for example, "What impact do you believe karate training has had on your child since he/she first began?" and "Have you observed any changes in your child's 'physical health' which you would attribute to the karate training?" Questions were asked to assess aspects such as behaviour at home and at school, any academic improvements, any improvements in self-discipline and self-confidence, and whether the child was getting into fights.

Who were the children in the study? Boudreau et al. (1995) obtained information from parents of 174 children between the ages of six and 16. The children attended karate clubs that were all part of the Toronto Academy of Karate in Toronto, Ontario.

What was the design of the study? This study was correlational because the researchers were interested in relations that existed between karate participation and children's attitudes and behaviours.

Were there ethical concerns with the study? No. The parents could choose whether or not to fill in the questionnaires, and the children had already been enrolled in the karate classes and were freely participating in the training.

What were the results? The data were divided into two categories: physical and psychological. Expectations of parents for both beginner and nonbeginner groups were similar. For those children who were already participants in karate, outcomes could be measured, and both physical and psychological benefits were reported by parents. Physically, children showed increased fitness, decreased absences from school, and fewer visits to doctors. Physical activity can also have psychological benefits, and specific benefits found in this study were increased self-esteem and self-confidence, with greater assertiveness and better interpersonal relations. Boys particularly improved on interpersonal relations and girls on self-esteem and assertiveness. Other benefits noted were academic improvement, awareness of potential, and greater sense of commitment.

What did the investigators conclude? Karate training had multiple benefits, both physical and psychological, for school-aged children. Self-control was increased, and aggression decreased, by participation in this activity. Boudreau and colleagues also speculated that karate may have an effect on socialization of girls and boys in that it may "fill in the gaps in our traditional gender socialization, compensating for lack of self-confidence in girls and the lack of sensitivity often perceived among boys" (Boudreau et al. 1995, p. 59).

What converging evidence would strengthen these conclusions? Boudreau et al. (1995) assessed children with questionnaires distributed to parents. A useful next step would be to complement the results from those parental observations with an experimental study where groups of children were assigned to either martial arts training or other activities. Another logical extension would be to perform a longitudinal study, gathering parental observations, or testing children, annually as they get older.

Critical Thinking Question: The feature mentions benefits of martial arts participation, and how longitudinal, follow-up studies could be useful. What sort of studies could be run and what "natural" studies may exist?

Victims of Aggression

Every aggressive act is directed at someone. Most schoolchildren are the targets of an occasional aggressive act—a shove or kick to gain a desired toy, or a stinging insult by someone trying to save face. However, a small percentage of children are chronic targets of bullying—ongoing, verbal, relational, or physical aggression. In both Europe and North America, 10 to 25 percent of elementary-school children and adolescents are chronic victims of physical attacks, name calling, backstabbing, and similar aggressive acts (Juvonen & Graham, 2014). Margaret Atwood (1988) provides an example of such victimization in her novel *Cat's Eye*. As a child, Elaine is continually harassed by girls at her school:

> On the window ledge beside mine, Cordelia and Grace and Carol are sitting, jammed in together, whispering and giggling. I have to sit on a window ledge by myself because they aren't speaking to me. It's something I said wrong, but I don't know what it is because they won't tell me (p. 123).

Later, in high school, Elaine discovers how to be this way herself:

> I have such a mean mouth that I become known for it. I don't use it unless provoked, but then I open my mean mouth and short, devastating comments come out of it. . . . I know where the weak spots are (p. 251).

In these episodes, Elaine is the victim of verbal bullying and then becomes capable of such bullying herself. Victimization by physical force also occurs frequently. Think of a child who is beaten up daily on the playground. Other children are chronic targets of relational aggression: Think of children who are constantly the subject of rumours spread by their classmates (Crick, Casas, & Nelson, 2002). *Cyberbullying,* **which is electronic bullying in which victims are harassed via cell phones or the internet,** is an especially modern form of bullying and rumour-mongering. Qing Li of the University of Calgary noted that the increase in use of cell phones and widespread internet access had given rise to a new format for the bully (Li, 2005). Li found that one quarter of students had been victims of this "bullying via electronic communication tools" (2005, p. 178). Thus, young people may be targets of both "traditional" and electronic forms of bullying (Raskauskas & Stoltz, 2007). Recent figures are that about 20 percent of high school students report being the victim of cyberbullying, and girls are much more likely to be the victims, with 26 percent of girls being attacked in this way and 14 percent of boys (Boak et al., 2016). As one CAMH report noted, the level of cyberbullying is particularly troubling because technology now allows bullying to come into the home, reaching beyond the school setting (CAMH, 2012). Continued ridicule by peers can be overwhelming (Brendtro, 2001) and the inability to escape persecution that comes with cyberbullying can have terrible effects on victims, even leading to suicide. In response to such issues, in April 2013, the Nova Scotia government appointed Debra Pepler to lead a review investigating schools' policies and procedures around cyberbullying (Alphonso, 2013). The resulting report, by Pepler and co-author Penny Milton, was published June 14, 2013. In the report Pepler and Milton make 13 recommendations, including a call for stronger anti-bullying policies in schools.

As you can imagine, being tormented daily by their peers is hard on children. Research consistently shows that children who are chronic victims of aggression are often lonely, anxious, and depressed; they dislike school and their peers; and they have low self-esteem (Ladd & Ladd, 1998; Rudolph, Troop-Gordon, & Flynn, 2009). As adults, they're prone to poor health and unsatisfying social relationships (Wolke, Copeland, Angold, & Costello, 2013). Unfortunately, the same children tend to remain victims of bullying long-term. This is particularly true for girls, probably because of their being victims more of relational aggression (Wolke, Woods, & Samara, 2009). Ironically, the impact of bullying is reduced when children see others being bullied, apparently because they feel that they're not being singled out for harassment (Nishina & Juvonen, 2005). Although most children are happier when no longer victimized, the harmful effects linger for some: They are still lonely and sad despite not having been victims for one or two years (Kochenderfer-Ladd & Wardrop, 2001).

Why do some children suffer the sad fate of being victims? Some victims are actually aggressive themselves (van Lier et al., 2012; Veenstra et al., 2005). These youngsters often overreact, are restless, and are easily irritated. Their aggressive peers soon learn that these children are easily baited. A group of children will, for example, insult or ridicule such a child, knowing that he or she will probably start a fight even though outnumbered. Other victims tend to be withdrawn, submissive, and have low self-esteem. They are unwilling or unable to defend themselves from their peers' aggression, and so they are usually referred to as "passive victims" (Guerra, Williams, & Sadek, 2011; Ladd & Ladd, 1998; Salmivalli & Isaacs, 2005). When attacked, like the child in the photo, they show obvious signs of distress and usually give in to their attackers, thereby rewarding the aggressive behaviour. Thus, both aggressive and withdrawn–submissive children end up as victims; this pattern holds for children in China as well as for children in North America (Schwartz, Chang, & Farver, 2001).

Debra Pepler (whom we mentioned earlier at the end of the Spotlight on Theories feature), together with researchers Wendy Craig and Julie Blais from Queen's University in Kingston, Ontario, investigated children's responses to bullying and what strategies might work to reduce the bullying. Craig, Pepler, and Blais (2007) surveyed over 1800 Canadian children and youth, ranging in age from 4 to 19, through an online survey posted on bullying.org. The survey asked questions about how the children were bullied and what they had tried to do to deal with the situation. The results of the survey were in line with earlier research: Boys were more likely to be victims of physical aggression and girls of verbal or social aggression. Interestingly, girls were also more likely to be victims of cyberbullying. It seemed that education campaigns or information about bullying had little effect on victimized children's attempts to stop bullying, but rather it was their own needs to be assertive, and to stop something unpleasant that was affecting their lives that caused them to act. Many of the respondents in the study said that they did nothing, however, largely because of the difficulty of "standing up to" someone seen as a powerful opponent. Actions taken were not necessarily effective, such as ignoring the bullying

QUESTION 12.4
Brandon is constantly picked on by other kids at his school: The girls tease him and the boys often start fights with him. What could he and his parents do to improve his peer relations? *(Answer is on page 438.)*

When children give in to aggressive children, they often become chronic victims of aggression.

Jennie Woodcock/Reflections Photolibrary/ Corbis Documentary/Getty Images

or reacting with aggression towards the bully. The results of their survey led Craig et al. (2007) to call for adult support for victims of bullying to prevent passive acceptance of this abuse. They also noted that "it is important to provide children and youth with strategies that are effective" (p. 474), such as being assertive. Adult support and assistance in learning effective antibullying strategies are important for children and youth to enable them to respond to bullying in a way that has positive effects.

Thus, rather than letting children cope alone with victimization (using strategies that may or may not work), a better approach is to teach victimized children ways of dealing with aggression that are more effective than either overreacting or withdrawing passively (e.g., don't lash out when you're insulted, don't show that you're afraid when you're threatened). In addition, increasing self-esteem can help. When attacked, children with low self-esteem may think, "I'm worthless and have to put up with this because I have no choice." Increasing children's self-esteem makes them less tolerant of personal attacks (Egan & Perry, 1998). Finally, the best solution is to prevent bullying and victimization altogether; an effective way to do this is to create a school climate in which bullying is not condoned and victims are supported by their peers (Kärnä et al., 2011). A program to do just this was devised in Finland, and has now become a model for how to deal with bullying in schools.

Beginning in the 1990s, Finland became concerned about the prevalence of bullying in Finnish schools. Consequently, the Ministry of Education asked Dr. Christina Salmivalli, an expert on bullying from the University of Turku, to create a school-based antibullying program. The result was KiVa, which comes from the Finnish words for "against bullying" *kiusaamista vastaan*. The heart of the program is creating a classroom climate in which bullying is not tolerated. Through lessons and discussions about respect for others, role playing (e.g., playing the part of the victim), and computer games, children who witness bullying are empowered to act, supporting victims and reporting bullying to teachers. In addition, teachers learn strategies for dealing with cases of bullying. For example, they help a bully think about ways to change his or her aggressive behaviour and they provide support for victims (Rubin, 2012). The KiVa program is effective—bullying and victimization are reduced in schools where it has been implemented (Kärnä et al., 2013). Because of its success, KiVa has been adopted in nearly 3000 schools in Finland as well as in schools in Japan, Sweden, the Netherlands, the United Kingdom, and the United States (Rubin, 2012). KiVa's success shows how research on factors that drive bullying can be used create effective programs to eliminate it.

Throughout this module, we've seen the harm caused by aggression: Victims are hurt, and children who are chronically aggressive often lead problem-filled lives. Yet the research described in this module has also identified many of the roots of aggressive behaviour and it has suggested how children can learn other, more constructive ways to interact with peers.

 ANSWER 12.4
In the short term, Brandon should try to look and act as if the teasing and fighting doesn't bother him; in the longer term, one of the best things he can do is to make more friends in his class.
....

 Check Your Learning

RECALL Describe the different forms of aggression and the ages when they typically appear.

Summarize the primary phases of decision making in Crick and Dodge's information-processing model and the biases that are found in aggressive children's decision making.

INTERPRET Compare the impact of nature and nurture on children's aggressive behaviour.

APPLY Suppose that a group of elementary-school teachers wanted to know how to reduce the amount of aggressive behaviour in their classrooms. What advice would you give them?

UNIFYING THEMES   Continuity

This chapter has some nice illustrations of the theme that *early development is related to later development but not perfectly.* For example, we learned on page 408 that preschoolers who were best able to delay gratification were, as adolescents, less likely to yield to temptation and to be distractible. Yet the relation was not perfect: Many preschoolers who quickly gave into temptation became adolescents who were not distractible. This same theme is evident in the results of longitudinal studies of aggressive children (page 427). Many of these children commit serious crimes as adults, but not all do. Behaving aggressively in childhood definitely increases the odds of adult criminal activity, but it does not guarantee it.

See for Yourself

This assignment may seem like a dream come true—you are being required to watch TV. Pick an evening when you can watch network television programming from 8 p.m. until 10 p.m. (prime time). Your job is to count each instance of (a) physical force by one person against another and (b) threats of harm to compel another to act against his or her will. Select one network randomly and watch the program for 10 minutes. Then turn to another network and watch that program for 10 minutes. Continue changing the channels every 10 minutes until the two hours are over. Of course, it won't be easy to follow the plots of all these programs, but you will end up with a wider sample of programming this way. Repeat this procedure on a Saturday morning when you can watch two hours of children's cartoons (not *South Park!*).

Now simply divide the total number of aggressive acts by four to estimate the amount of aggression per hour. Then multiply this figure by 11 688 to estimate the number of aggressive acts seen by an average adolescent by age 19. (Why 11 688? Two hours of daily TV viewing—a very conservative number—multiplied by 365 days and 16 years.) Then ponder the possible results of that very large number. If your parents told you nearly 12 000 times that stealing was okay, would you be more likely to steal? Probably. Then what are the consequences of massive exposure to the televised message, "Solve conflicts with aggression"? See for yourself!

Resources

For more information about . . .

why some people are altruistic, read Samuel P. Oliner's *Do Unto Others: Extraordinary Acts of Ordinary People* (Westview Press, 2003). The author, a sociologist, uses stories of ordinary people—a hospice volunteer and a firefighter, among others—to identify the factors that lead people to acts of compassion and moral courage.

children's aggression, visit the website of Leave Out ViolencE (LOVE), a major Canadian nonprofit anti-violence organization, at www.leaveoutviolence.org.

cyberbullying, visit the website of PREVNet, a Canadian site with information on research on, and prevention of, cyberbullying: www.prevnet.ca.

Key Terms

Summary

12.1 Self-Control

1. Beginnings of Self-Control
At one year, infants are first aware that others impose demands on them; by three years, youngsters can devise plans to regulate their behaviour. During the school-age years, children become better able to control their behaviour.

Children differ in their self-control, but individuals are fairly consistent over time: Preschoolers who have good self-control tend to become adolescents and adults with good self-control.

2. Factors Influencing Self-Control
Children who have the best self-control tend to have parents who are loving, set limits, and discuss discipline with them. When parents are overly strict, their children have less self-control, not more. Temperament also influences children's self-control. Some children are temperamentally better suited to focus attention and to inhibit responses.

3. Strategies to Improve Children's Self-Control
Children are better able to regulate their own behaviour when they have plans to help them remember the importance of the goal and something to distract them from tempting objects.

12.2 Reasoning about Moral Issues

1. Piaget's Views
Piaget theorized that five- to seven-year-olds are in a stage of moral realism. They believe that rules are created by wise adults; therefore, rules must be followed and cannot be changed. At about eight years, children enter a stage of moral relativism, believing that rules are created by people to help them get along.

2. Kohlberg's Theory
Kohlberg proposed that moral reasoning includes preconventional, conventional, and postconventional levels. Moral reasoning is first based on rewards and punishments, and later on personal moral codes. As predicted by Kohlberg's theory, people progress through the stages in sequence and do not regress, and morally advanced reasoning is associated with more frequent moral behaviour. However, few people attain the most advanced levels, and cultures differ in the bases for moral reasoning.

3. Beyond Kohlberg's Theory
Gilligan proposed that females' moral reasoning is based on caring and responsibility for others, not justice. Research does not support consistent sex differences but has found that males and females both consider caring as well as justice in their moral judgments, depending on the situation.

During the preschool years, children differentiate moral rules, social conventions, and personal choices. They believe, for example, that social conventions can be changed, but moral rules cannot. And they understand that breaking a moral rule produces a harsher punishment than breaking a social convention. Some scientists believe that infants have an innate moral sense because they feel concern for others and dislike group members who do not cooperate. Children's emotional responses to events may help them form categories of morally relevant concepts.

4. Promoting Moral Reasoning
Many factors can promote more sophisticated moral reasoning, including observing others reason at more advanced levels and discussing moral issues with peers, teachers, and parents.

12.3 Helping Others

1. Development of Prosocial Behaviour
Even toddlers know when others are upset, and they try to offer comfort. As children grow older, they more often see the need to act prosocially and are more likely to have the skills to do so.

2. Skills Underlying Prosocial Behaviour
Children are more likely to behave prosocially when they are able to take others' perspectives, are empathic, and have more advanced moral reasoning.

3. Situational Influences
Children's prosocial behaviour is often influenced by situational characteristics. Children more often behave prosocially when they feel that they should and can help, when they are in a good mood, and when they believe that they have little to lose by helping.

4. The Contribution of Heredity

Genes influence prosocial behaviour via oxytocin, a hormone that is linked to social behaviours, and through temperament: Some children are unlikely to help because they are too shy or they become too upset themselves (because they can't control their emotions).

5. Socializing Prosocial Behaviour

Parenting approaches that promote prosocial behaviour include modelling prosocial behaviour, using reasoning in discipline, and giving children frequent opportunities inside and outside the home to use their prosocial skills.

12.4 Aggression

1. Change and Stability

Typical forms of aggression in young children include instrumental, hostile, and reactive aggression. As children grow older, physical aggression decreases and relational aggression becomes more common. Overall levels of aggression are fairly stable, which means that very aggressive young children often become involved in violent and criminal activities as adolescents and adults.

2. Roots of Aggressive Behaviour

Children's aggressive behaviour has many sources: genetics, harsh parenting, viewing violence on TV and in other media, aggressive peers, school failure, living in poverty, and biased interpretation of people's behaviour. Sport participation can be beneficial in reducing inappropriate aggression, provided that appropriate behaviour is modelled.

3. Victims of Aggression

Children who are chronic targets of aggression are often lonely and anxious. Some victims of aggression tend to overreact when provoked; others tend to withdraw and submit. Victimization can be overcome by increasing children's social skills and self-esteem. Bullying and can be reduced by KiVa, a school-based program that creates a classroom climate in which bullying is not tolerated.

Test Yourself

1. The first step in the development of self-control occurs when infants _____.

2. Children's self-control is affected by parents' discipline and by a child's _____.

3. Self-control can be improved by reminding children of the need to avoid temptation and by _____.

4. According to Piaget, until about eight years of age children are in a stage of moral realism in which they believe that _____.

5. At the _____ level in Kohlberg's theory, people believe that moral decision making is based on social norms (i.e., how others expect them to behave).

6. Gilligan argued that Kohlberg's theory places too much emphasis on justice in moral decision making and ignores the role of _____.

7. Domains of social judgment include moral transgressions, _____, and the personal domain.

8. Emotions may influence children's moral development by _____.

9. Skills necessary for prosocial behaviour include perspective taking, _____, and moral reasoning.

10. Aspects of a situation that influence helping include _____, feelings of competence, a child's mood, and the cost of altruism.

11. Parents foster altruistic behaviour by modelling it for children to see, by _____, and by providing children with the opportunity to behaviour prosocially.

12. In _____ aggression, children use aggression to achieve their goals.

13. Children are more likely to behave aggressively when their parents use physical punishment frequently, _____, and are in frequent conflict with each other.

14. Cultural influences on aggression include the media, peers, experiences in school, _____, and a culture of violence.

15. According to the social-information-processing framework, aggressive children are biased _____.

Answers: (1) become aware that others impose demands on them and they must react accordingly; (2) temperament; (3) activities that divert attention from temptation; (4) rules are created by wise adults and must be followed and cannot be changed; (5) conventional; (6) caring for others; (7) social conventions; (8) helping children create different categories of morally relevant concepts; (9) empathy; (10) a child's feelings of responsibility; (11) their disciplinary practices; (12) instrumental; (13) don't monitor their children's behaviour; (14) poverty; (15) to interpret actions in terms of aggressive intent and to respond aggressively by default.

13 Gender and Development

B2M Productions/Photographer's Choice RF/Getty Images

 13.1
Gender Stereotypes

 13.2
Differences Related
to Gender

 13.3
Gender Identity

 13.4
Gender Roles
in Transition

You barely have the phone to your ear before your brother-in-law shouts, "Camille had the baby!" "A boy or a girl?" you ask. Why are people so interested in a baby's sex? The answer is that being a boy or girl is not simply a biological distinction. **Instead, *boy* and *girl* are associated with distinct *social roles* that are cultural guidelines for people's behaviour. Starting in infancy, children learn about *gender roles*—behaviours considered appropriate for males and females.** As youngsters learn these roles, they begin to identify with one of these groups. **Children forge a *gender identity*—the perception of the self as either male or female.**

In this chapter, we will see how children acquire a gender role and a gender identity. We'll begin in **Module 13.1** by considering cultural stereotypes of males and females. In **Module 13.2**, we will examine actual psychological differences between boys and girls. In **Module 13.3**, we'll focus on how children usually come to identify with one sex. Finally, in **Module 13.4**, we'll discuss recent changes in gender roles. Throughout this chapter, we'll use the term *sex* to refer to aspects of females and males that are clearly biological (such as differences in anatomy) and the term *gender* to refer to all other characteristics that relate to femaleness and maleness. The definition on the Canadian Institutes of Health Research website is:

> *Gender* refers to the socially constructed roles, behaviours, expressions, and identities of girls, women, boys, men, and gender diverse people. It influences how people perceive themselves and each other, how they act and interact, and the distribution of power and resources in society. Gender is usually conceptualized as a binary (girl/woman and boy/man), yet there is considerable diversity in how individuals and groups understand, experience, and express it. (CIHR, 2016, n.p.)

 Gender Stereotypes

OUTLINE

How Do We View Men and Women?

Learning Gender Stereotypes

LEARNING OBJECTIVES

1. What are gender stereotypes, and how do they differ for males and females?

2. How do gender stereotypes influence behaviour? When do children learn their culture's stereotypes for males and females?

When Nancy was seven months pregnant, her 11-year-old son, Clark, announced that he really wanted a brother—not a sister. Clark explained, "A sister would drive me crazy. Girls never make up their minds about stuff, and they get all worked up over nothin'." "Where did Clark get these ideas?" Nancy wondered. "Is this typical for 11-year-olds?"

All cultures have *gender stereotypes*—beliefs about how males and females differ in personality traits, interests, and behaviours. Of course, because stereotypes are beliefs, they may or may not be true. In this module, we'll look at the features associated with gender stereotypes and discover when children like Clark learn about gender stereotypes.

Raise a cyber child and discover the world of parenthood at …

My Virtual Child

How Do We View Men and Women?

"Alex is active, independent, competitive, and aggressive." As you were reading this sentence, you probably assumed that Alex was a male. Why? Although Alex is a common name for both males and females, the adjectives used to describe Alex are more commonly associated with men than with women. In fact, most adults associate different traits with men and women, and these views have changed very little since the 1960s (Ruble, Martin, & Berenbaum, 2006). Men are said to be independent, competitive, aggressive, outgoing, ambitious, self-confident, and dominant. **These male-associated traits are called** *instrumental* **because they describe individuals who act on the world and influence it.** In contrast, women are said to be emotional, kind, creative, considerate, gentle, excitable, and aware of others' feelings. **Female-associated traits are called** *expressive,* **because they describe emotional functioning and individuals who value interpersonal relationships.**

Are these views shared by adults worldwide? John Williams and Deborah Best (1990) addressed these questions in an ambitious project involving 300 traits and participants in 30 countries. Figure 13-1 presents the results for just four traits and seven countries. You can see that each trait shows considerable cultural variation. For example, most Canadian and virtually all American participants consider men aggressive, but only a slight majority of Nigerian participants do. Thus North American views of men and women are not shared worldwide. In fact, what is notable about the research results is that Americans' gender stereotypes are more extreme than those in any other country listed. Keep this in mind as you think about what men and women can and cannot do and what they should and should not do. Your ideas about gender are shaped by your culture's beliefs, which are not held universally.

Understanding our tendency to stereotype gender behaviour is important because stereotypes are very limiting (Smith & Mackie, 2000). If we have stereotyped views, we expect males to act in particular ways and females to act in other ways, and we respond to

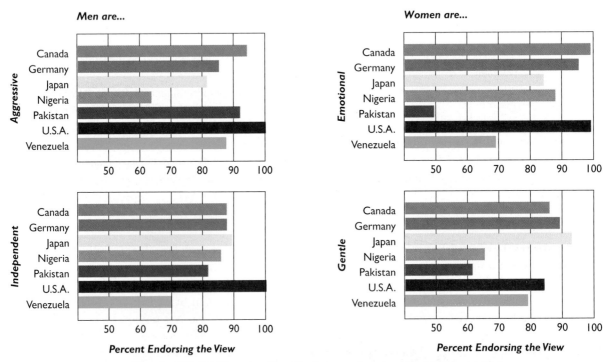

Figure 13-1 Different nationalities' views of personality traits by gender.

Data from Williams, J. E., & Best, D. L. (1990). *Measuring sex stereotypes: A thirty-nation study* (rev. ed.). Newbury Park, CA: Sage.

males and females solely on the basis of gender, not as individuals. For example, do you assume the youngster in the photo is a girl based on the child's taste in toys? Assuming the child is a girl would probably lead you to think she plays more quietly and is more easily frightened than if you assume the child is a boy (Karraker, Vogel, & Lake, 1995). Making stereotyped assumptions about gender leads to a whole host of inferences about behaviour and personality that may not be true.

When do children begin to learn their culture's stereotypes for males and females? We'll answer this question in the next section.

Learning Gender Stereotypes

Children do not live in a gender-neutral world for long. In a number of studies, Diane Poulin-Dubois of Concordia University, Montreal, and colleagues have investigated young children's knowledge of gender stereotypes. For example, although 12-month-old boys and girls look equally at gender-stereotyped toys, 18-month-olds do not: Girls look longer at pictures of dolls than at pictures of trucks, but boys look longer at pictures of trucks (Serbin, Poulin-Dubois, Colburne, Sen, & Eichstedt, 2001). However, when it comes to gender-stereotyped activities rather than objects, it may take a little longer for children to note apparent differences. In another study, toddlers at 18 months of age did not spend any longer looking at videos of women or men performing counter-stereotypic activities than when the actors performed gender-stereotypic or gender-neutral actions. At two years of age, however, infants do look longer at men performing "female" activities (such as putting on lipstick) and at women performing "male" actions (such as shaving), indicating that they see this as unusual (Hill & Flom, 2007). Poulin-Dubois and colleagues' work also shows that children as young as two years of age can demonstrate knowledge of gender-stereotyping of activities, such as shaving or vacuuming (Poulin-Dubois, Serbin, Eichstedt, Sen, & Beissel, 2002). By four years of age, children's knowledge of gender-stereotyped activities is extensive: They believe that girls play hopscotch but that boys play football; girls help bake cookies but boys take out the garbage; and women feed babies but men chop wood (Gelman, Taylor, & Nguyen, 2004). And they have begun to learn about behaviours and traits that are stereotypically masculine or feminine. Preschoolers believe that boys are more often aggressive physically but girls tend to be aggressive verbally (Giles & Heyman, 2005).

During the elementary-school years, children expand their knowledge of gender-stereotyped traits and behaviours. They learn stereotypes about personality traits—boys are tough and girls are gentle—and about academic subjects—math is for boys and reading is for girls (Cvencek, Meltzoff, & Greenwald, 2011; Heyman & Legare, 2004).

During the elementary-school years, children also learn that the traits and occupations associated with males tend to earn more money and have higher social status than those associated with females (Weisgram, Bigler, & Liben, 2010). Children apparently learn a simple rule—something like "Jobs for men are more prestigious than jobs for women"—because children learning unfamiliar jobs (e.g., a chandler makes candles) rate these occupations as more prestigious if they are illustrated with men rather than with women (Liben, Bigler, & Krogh, 2001). That this stereotyped valuing of jobs by sex is socially based can be seen when a particular profession is valued differently in different countries. In Russia most doctors are female, and being a doctor is not seen as a high-status job in that country, in fact quite the opposite (Halpern, 2012). This view of the physician has existed for some time in Russia, as

Gender stereotypes lead us to assume that this child is a girl simply because the child is playing with a doll.

QUESTION 13.1
Abigail believes that girls are gentler than boys, that boys are stronger than girls, but that boys and girls are equally talkative and confident. With these stereotypes, how old is Abigail likely to be? *(Answer is on page 446.)*

described by the Canadian author Farley Mowat (1970) in his book *The Siberians:* "In 1966, eighty-four per cent of Soviet doctors were women" (p. 267), and this was seen as largely due to a view of women being more suited to this "caring" profession. This stands in strong contrast to the Western view of "scientific" medicine, with the doctor stereotypically male and medicine viewed as a prestigious occupation.

As children develop, they also begin to understand that gender stereotypes do not always apply; older children are more willing than younger children to ignore stereotypes when judging other children. For example, told about a boy who likes to play with girls and pretend to iron, preschoolers think he would still want to play with masculine toys. By the middle elementary-school years, however, children realize that this boy's interests are not stereotypic, and he would rather play with stereotypically feminine toys (Blakemore, 2003).

Thus, although older children are more familiar with gender stereotypes, they see these stereotypes as general guidelines for behaviour that are not necessarily binding for all boys and girls (Banse, Gawronski, Rebetez, Gutt, & Morton, 2010; Conry-Murray & Turiel, 2012). In fact, older children consider gender stereotypes less binding than many social conventions and moral rules (Levy, Taylor, & Gelman, 1995; Serbin, Powlishta, & Gulko, 1993). This change is due to cognitive growth: As we saw in Module 11.3, in the context of views of different racial and ethnic groups, older children's cognitive development allows them to understand that stereotypes are generalizations that do not necessarily apply to all people (Bigler & Liben, 1992). Further investigation of such concepts has shown that while physical properties of being male or female generally are judged as stable by all age groups, across childhood and adolescence there is a steady increase in flexibility of view regarding behavioural properties of others (Taylor, Rhodes, & Gelman, 2009). Increased age is not the only factor leading to more flexible views of stereotypes. Girls tend to be more flexible about stereotypes (Ruble & Martin, 1998), perhaps because they see that male-stereotyped traits are more attractive and have more status than female-stereotyped traits. Social class also contributes. Adolescents and young adults (but not children) from middle-class homes tend to have more flexible ideas about gender than individuals from lower-class homes (e.g., Serbin, Powlishta, & Gulko, 1993). This difference may be due to education: Better-educated middle-class parents may impart less rigid views of gender to their children.

At this point, perhaps you're wondering whether there's any truth to gender stereotypes. For example, are boys really more dominant than girls? Are girls really more excitable than boys? For answers to these questions, let's go to Module 13.2.

 ANSWER 13.1
She is probably about five years old. (A more conservative estimate would be to say that she is in the early elementary-school years.) The logic behind this estimate is that she has learned some of the typical stereotypes of boys and girls (e.g., that girls are gentler than boys) but has yet to learn others (e.g., that boys are more confident than girls).

✓ Check Your Learning

RECALL How do older children's gender stereotypes differ from those of younger children?

What groups of children tend to have more flexible views of gender stereotypes?

INTERPRET Compare and contrast instrumental traits with expressive traits.

APPLY How might Piaget have explained older children's more flexible views of gender stereotypes?

13.2 Differences Related to Gender

OUTLINE

Differences in Physical Development and Behaviour

Differences in Intellectual Abilities and Achievement

Differences in Personality and Social Behaviour

Frank Talk about Gender Differences

LEARNING OBJECTIVES

1. How do boys and girls differ in physical development, intellectual abilities, and social behaviour? What factors are responsible for these gender differences?

2. What are the implications of these gender differences for boys' and girls' development?

The high-school student council was discussing a proposal to hold the prom in an expensive hotel in a nearby big city. Maggie thought this was a truly terrible idea, but most of the group seemed to like the plan, so she decided not to say anything. Just as she decided to keep quiet, her friend Charles announced that he was going to vote against the proposal and, as he described his reasons, Maggie realized that they were exactly the ones that she'd thought of but hadn't voiced.

Maggie and Charles both thought the proposal was flawed, but only Charles expressed those concerns. Why? We'll answer that question in this module as we explore gender-related differences in different domains of development. This territory was first charted in *The Psychology of Sex Differences* by Eleanor Maccoby and Carol Jacklin published in 1974, that summarized results from approximately 1500 research studies. Maccoby and Jacklin, concluded that gender differences had been established in only four areas: Girls have greater verbal ability, whereas boys have greater mathematical and visual-spatial ability, and boys are more aggressive than girls. Just as important, Maccoby and Jacklin did *not* find evidence to support popular ideas that girls are more social and suggestible than boys, have lower self-esteem, are less analytic in thinking, and lack achievement motivation.

Some critics challenged Maccoby and Jacklin on the grounds that they had included some weak studies and defined behaviours in ways that other researchers might not (Block, 1976). The debate stimulated more research; some of this research applied new statistical techniques that allowed for finer analysis, such as meta-analysis. Many developmentalists now believe that gender differences are more extensive than Maccoby and Jacklin suggested, but their book remains a classic because its comprehensiveness provided an excellent starting point for further research.

In the remainder of this module, we'll see what we've discovered about gender differences since Maccoby and Jacklin's classic analysis. We'll focus on differences in physical development, cognitive processes, and social behaviour.

Differences in Physical Development and Behaviour

Of course, differences in the reproductive system are what differentiate boys and girls, along with differences in secondary sex characteristics, such as lower voices and facial hair in boys and breast development and wider hips in girls. Boys are usually larger and stronger than girls, which means that they often physically outperform girls. You can see the difference at high school track meets: Boys usually run faster, jump higher, and throw objects farther and more accurately. And, as Figure 13-2 shows, boys throw and jump farther than girls long before high school. However, on tasks that involve fine-motor coordination, such as tracing and drawing, girls do better than boys (Thomas & French, 1985).

Some of the gender differences in gross-motor skills that require strength reflect the fact that as children approach and enter puberty, girls' bodies have proportionately more fat and less muscle than boys' bodies. This difference explains why, for example, boys can hang from a bar using their arms and hands much longer than girls can. However, for other gross-motor skills, such as running, throwing, and catching, body composition is much less important (Smoll & Schutz, 1990). In these cases, children's experience is crucial. Many girls and their parents believe that sports and physical fitness are less valuable for girls than boys. Consequently, girls spend less time in sports and fitness-related activities than boys, depriving them of opportunities to practise, which is essential for developing motor skills (Eccles & Harold, 1991). During recess, elementary-school girls are more often found swinging, jumping rope, or perhaps talking quietly in a group; in contrast, boys are playing football or shooting baskets. Socialization may contribute to this difference as much as physique, however. Consistent with this argument, gender differences in throwing are much smaller among Australian Aborigines, a group that traditionally expected girls to be able to throw during hunting (Thomas, Alderson, Thomas, Campbell, & Elliot, 2010).

As infants, boys are more active than girls, and this difference increases during childhood (Alexander & Wilcox, 2012; Saudino, 2009). For example, in a classroom, boys are more likely than girls to have a hard time sitting still. On playgrounds such as those in the photos on page 449 boys more often play vigorously, and girls more

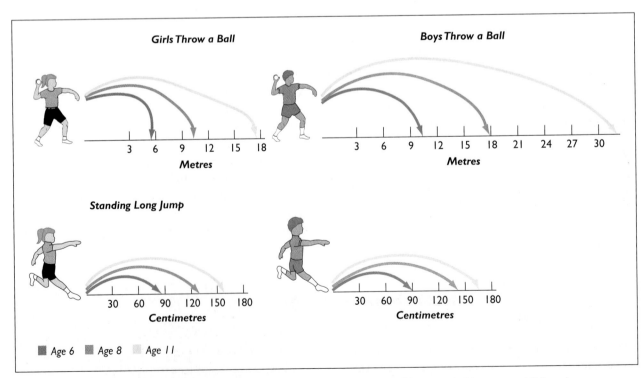

Figure 13-2 Comparative physical abilities of boys and girls across childhood.

often play quietly. Recall from Module 5.2 that boys are three times more likely than girls to be diagnosed with attention deficit hyperactivity disorder (Goldstein, 2011).

Girls tend to be healthier than boys. Female embryos are more likely than male embryos to survive prenatal development. This trend continues after birth: Infant boys are more prone to birth complications, and throughout life, boys are more prone to many diseases and dysfunctions (Jacklin, 1989). Adolescent boys and young men are more likely to engage in unhealthy, risk-taking behaviours, including drinking alcohol, reckless driving, and irresponsible sexual activity (Byrnes, Miller, & Schafer, 1999; Granie, 2009). Finally, as the brain matures in adolescence, girls' brains tend to have more cell bodies and dendrites (which form connections between neurons) while boys' brains have more glial cells (which provide nutrients and oxygen, and destroy pathogens) and more myelinated axons (Nisbett et al., 2012).

To summarize, boys tend to be bigger, stronger, and more active; girls tend to have better fine-motor coordination and to be healthier. In the next section, which concerns intellectual skills, you'll again see that gender differences vary from one skill to the next.

Differences in Intellectual Abilities and Achievement

Of the four gender-based differences discovered by Maccoby and Jacklin (1974), three concern intellectual skills: Girls tend to have greater verbal skill; boys tend to have greater mathematical and visual-spatial skill. Since Maccoby and Jacklin's work, we have learned much about the nature of gender differences in these areas.

VERBAL ABILITY.   Girls have larger vocabularies than boys and are more talkative (Feldman et al., 2000; Leaper & Smith, 2004). During elementary and high school, girls read, write, and spell better than boys; and this difference is found in virtually all industrialized countries (Miller & Halpern, 2014). Finally, more boys are diagnosed with language-related problems such as reading disability or specific language impairment (Wicks-Nelson & Israel, 2006; Halpern, 2012).

Why are girls more verbally talented than boys? Part of the explanation may lie in biological forces. The left hemisphere of the brain, which is central to language (see Module 4.3), may mature more rapidly in girls than in boys (Diamond, Johnson, Young, & Singh, 1983), although research findings on this "lateralization" explanation are mixed (Ullman, Miranda, & Travers, 2008). Some studies find that brain regions

Boys tend to be physically more active than girls, a difference that is evident when you watch children on a playground.

involved in reading differ for boys and girls (Burman, Minas, Bolger, & Booth, 2013) in a manner that suggests more efficient language processing in girls' brains. However, the findings are inconsistent (Eliot, 2013; Wallentin, 2009). Currently, the brain's contribution to sex differences in reading remains a puzzle. Evidence is more consistent regarding the role of experience. For example, during the toddler years, mothers talk more to daughters than to sons (Fivush, Brotman, Buckner, & Goodman, 2000), and by the elementary-school years, reading is often stereotyped as an activity for girls (Plante, de la Sablonnière, Aronson, & Théorêt, 2013), which may make girls more willing than boys to invest time and effort in mastering verbal skills such as reading. Finally, teachers contribute; they expect girls to read better than boys, and by an amount that exceeds the actual difference (Ready & Wright, 2011).

SPATIAL ABILITY. In Module 8.1, you saw that spatial ability is a component of most models of intelligence. **One aspect of spatial ability is *mental rotation,* the ability to imagine how an object will look after it has been moved in space.** The items in Figure 13-3 test mental rotation: The task is to determine which of the figures labelled A through E are rotated versions of the figure in the box on the left. (The correct answers are C and D.) During childhood and adolescence, boys tend to have better mental-rotation skill than girls (Govier & Salisbury, 2000; Voyer, Voyer, & Bryden, 1995). Even as infants, boys are more likely than girls to recognize stimuli that have been rotated in space (Alexander & Wilcox, 2012). However, on some other spatial tasks, such as mental rotation in two dimensions, sex differences are smaller, and on other spatial tasks, they vanish (Miller & Halpern, 2014).

Another aspect of spatial ability is *spatial memory,* **the ability to remember the position of objects in the environment**—a skill in which females excel (e.g., Eals & Silverman, 1994). Irwin Silverman and his colleagues at York University in Toronto have contributed to research into this aspect of spatial ability (the use of a test that they developed is described in the Focus on Research feature). Spatial ability also involves determining relations between objects in space while ignoring distracting information. For example, which of the tilted bottles of water in Figure 13-4 has the waterline drawn correctly? In an upright bottle, the waterline is at right angles to the sides of the bottle, but selecting the correct answer for the tilted bottle (A, in this case) requires that you ignore the conflicting perceptual information provided by the sides of the bottle. From adolescence on, boys are more accurate than girls on these kinds of tasks (Voyer, Voyer, & Bryden, 1995), although explicit training in such spatial skills has been shown to reduce gender differences (Halpern, 2012; Tzuriel & Egozi, 2010).

A number of studies have looked at difference in boys' and girls' use of spatial strategies; one of these is described in the Focus on Research feature.

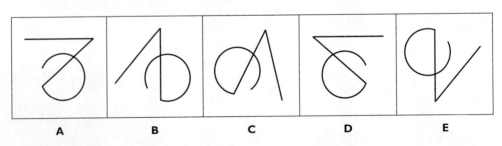

Figure 13-3 An example of a mental rotation task: Which of the figures A through E is a rotated version of the figure at the left?

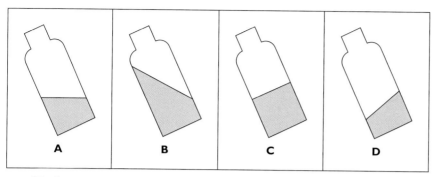

Figure 13-4 A spatial relations task: On which tilted bottle is the waterline drawn correctly?

 ## Focus On Research

Development of Sex Differences in Spatial Ability

Who were the investigators, and what was the aim of the study? We now know that males have an advantage in some spatial abilities, such as mental rotations, and that females surpass males in others, such as recall of object location. Questions exist, however, as to *why* such differences exist: Do males and females have separate abilities, and if so, what kind? Irwin Silverman of York University, Toronto, and Jean Choi from the University of Lethbridge, Alberta, conducted a study to investigate this issue (Silverman & Choi, 2006).

How did the investigators measure the topic of interest? Silverman and Choi used a set of three tasks: a map test of route learning, an "object array" test of spatial memory that was devised by Silverman & Eals (1992; shown in Figure 13-5), and the waterline task depicted in Figure 13-4. With the object array task, participants were asked to look at the array for one minute. A second array was then presented; the same set of drawings but with some in exchanged positions within the array. Participants circled any objects they thought were in the same position, and crossed through those they believed had been moved.

Who were the participants in the study? The study was an analysis of data from a set of studies with schoolchildren. The data was grouped for children aged 9 to 11, 12 to 14, and 15 to 17 years old.

What was the design of the study? This study was quasi-experimental because Silverman and Choi were interested in different scores on tests, compared by age group and by sex. (The study was *quasi*-experimental because age and sex could not be randomly assigned.) The study was cross-sectional because it included 9- to 11-year-olds, 12- to 14-year-olds, and 15- to 17-year-olds, and each participant was tested once.

Were there ethical concerns with the study? No. The tasks were similar to memory games found in puzzle books or computer games. Parents of children gave permission, and assent to participation was obtained from the children involved.

What were the results? As with previous research, a male-female difference was found with the different tasks. Girls tended to use landmarks more in the map task, while boys tended to use distance and direction more. Girls scored better on object location memory from the spatial array test and boys slightly better in the waterline task.

Figure 13-5 The Silverman and Eals object array task.

Republished with permission of Elsevier Inc. – Health Sciences Division, from *Sex Differences in Remembering the Locations of Objects in an Array: Location-Shifts Versus Location-Exchanges, Evolution and Human Behavior,* Thomas W. James and Doreen Kimura, Vol. 18, © Elsevier Science Inc., 1997; permission conveyed through Copyright Clearance Center, Inc.

What did the investigators conclude? Silverman and Choi (2006) concluded that there is "dual mechanism" for spatial navigation: Euclidian (direction and distance), which males tend to use, and topographical (placement and landmark use), used more by females. They propose that these evolved as separate mechanisms and that preferential usage emerges at about the same age in boys and girls.

What converging evidence would strengthen these conclusions? Silverman and Choi (2006) argued that the results of their study provided evidence for the theory that different strategies are the result of evolved mechanisms due to different skills used by ancestral humans: men as hunters and women as gatherers. There is some controversy over such explanations, however, as you will see in other parts of this module.

A longitudinal study in which children were given explicit training in spatial skills might further our understanding—if training eliminated the slight sex differences emerging across childhood, then environmental causes might be more important. If even training in such skills did not change the results, then biological factors would more likely be the explanation.

Critical Thinking Questions: (i) Before reading on in this chapter, speculate about what might be the causes of the sex differences found by research such as that of Silverman and Choi (2006)? (ii) How might these possible causes be investigated further?

An analysis by Silverman and Choi, with Michael Peters of the University of Guelph in Ontario (2007) of data from a worldwide internet study showed that, across 40 countries, men tended to do better at spatial rotations and women at spatial location memory. Explanations for such gender differences in spatial ability abound. Some explanations for gender differences in mental rotation and other spatial abilities emphasize biology. It has been argued that spatial skill was essential for successful hunting—in navigation and in calculating trajectories for weapons—and may represent an evolutionary adaptation for males (Halpern et al., 2007; Silverman, Choi, & Peters, 2007). As we have noted earlier, however, whilst biology seems to play a part, experience certainly contributes to gender differences in spatial skills too. For example, boys are more likely than girls to participate in activities that foster spatial skill, such as estimating the trajectory of an object moving through space (e.g., a baseball), using two-dimensional plans to assemble an object such as a scale model (Baenninger & Newcombe, 1995), or, like the boy in the photo, playing video games that involve visual-perceptual skills (Okagaki & Frensch, 1994; Terlecki & Newcombe, 2005). As well, parents may provide richer stimulation for sons on tasks that foster spatial skill. In one study (Levine, Ratliff, Huttenlocher, & Cannon, 2012), parents provided sons with more challenging puzzles and used more spatial language while solving the puzzles, referring to the shape, location, and orientation of puzzle pieces). Among children from lower-socioeconomic-status homes, however, boys and girls have comparable spatial skills (Levine, Vasilyeva, Lourenco, Newcombe, & Huttenlocher, 2005), which suggests that some experience associated with middle-class living is critical for the sex differences to emerge. This last point fits with the finding that training in different spatial skills has been shown to reduce gender differences (Halpern, 2012; Tzuriel & Egozi, 2010).

Each of these possible explanations of gender differences in spatial ability is supported by some studies, but not by others. Other factors may also influence test results. For example, some researchers propose that females are reluctant to guess at answers on spatial tasks, which may reduce their scores; a factor analytic study by Daniel Voyer and Kristen Saunders of the University of New Brunswick seems to support this explanation (Voyer & Saunders, 2004). Of course the explanations are not necessarily mutually exclusive. Biological and experiential forces may contribute to gender differences in spatial ability, just as both contribute to gender differences in verbal ability. In fact, further research by Voyer and colleagues has shown that participation in childhood activities with spatial aspects, such as sports or playing certain video games, predicts spatial ability in adulthood "over and above the influence of gender" (Doyle, Voyer, & Cherney, 2012, p. 112). Thus parents and others can foster verbal and spatial abilities in boys and girls because each is influenced considerably by experience, training, and practice (Doyle et al., 2012; Newcombe, 2002; Uttal et al., 2013).

Chlorophylle/Fotolia

Playing video games can enhance a child's spatial skill; the fact that boys play video games more often than girls may contribute to a gender difference in spatial skill.

MATHEMATICS. On standardized tests of math achievement, during the elementary-school years, girls usually get higher scores than boys. For tests administered during high school and college, boys used to get higher scores, but that difference has diminished substantially over the past 25 years; now boys have a negligible advantage (Lindberg, Hyde, Petersen, & Linn, 2010). This change apparently reflects efforts to encourage girls to pursue mathematics generally and to take more math courses specifically. For example, American boys and girls are now equally likely to take calculus courses in high school (National Science Foundation, 2008). And, as we'll see in the Cultural Influences feature, cross-cultural comparisons also point to an important role for cultural expectations in explaining gender differences in mathematics.

Cultural Influences

A Cross-Cultural Look at Gender Differences in Math

Several math achievement tests are administered internationally, and the results provide useful insights into the forces that drive gender differences in math. For example, the Program for International Student Assessment (PISA) is administered in more than 60 countries, with thousands of high-school students in each country taking tests measuring math, reading, and science abilities (Organisation for Economic Co-operation and Development, 2010). In many countries, there are small differences favouring boys (e.g., France, Germany). However, in some countries (e.g., Republic of Korea, the Slovak Republic), boys have substantially greater scores. And in Iceland, girls have the advantage (Else-Quest, Hyde, & Linn, 2010).

Why does the pattern vary so much? One view is that it reflects cultural differences in math-related career opportunities for men and women. When girls (and their parents and their teachers) see math as a means to achieve success, they are interested in math and take math courses. In contrast, if girls see math-related careers as "for boys only," they have little reason to invest time and energy in mastering math. This line of thinking leads to a straightforward prediction: In countries where women have much the same access to education, occupations, and political power as men, gender differences in math should be negligible. In contrast, where women are limited to traditionally feminine-stereotypic occupations that do not require math skills, gender differences in math should remain. Exactly this pattern is found in international comparisons of PISA math data (Else-Quest et al., 2010). For example, educational and professional opportunities are substantial in Iceland (where girls excel in math) but not in the Republic of Korea (where test results favour boys). In other words, these cross-cultural comparisons seem to suggest that "girls will perform at the same level as their male classmates when they are encouraged to succeed, are given the necessary educational tools, and have visible female role models excelling in mathematics" (Else-Quest et al., 2010, p. 125).

Critical Thinking Question: Given that cross-cultural comparisons imply that "girls will perform at the same level as their male classmates when they are encouraged to succeed, are given the necessary educational tools, and have visible female role models excelling in mathematics" (Else-Quest et al., 2010, p. 125), what interventions should we implement in Canada to help girls perform as well as boys?

Educators have worked hard to reduce gender stereotypes associated with math (Secada, Fennema, & Adajian, 1995), and findings like these show that such efforts are effective. A number of events and programs now exist to encourage girls to consider studying mathematics and engineering. One of the largest is GoEngGirl/GÉNIales, les filles, a coordinated event at schools of engineering across the province of Ontario (Ontario Network of Women in Engineering; ONWiE, 2015). On a Saturday in the fall, university engineering faculties organize speakers and demonstrations for day-long programs and open houses for girls in Grades 7 to 10. Other provinces and individual universities host similar events, for example, Memorial University's Faculty of Engineering Girl Quest and the University of Victoria's Women in Engineering and Computer Science festivals. In Alberta, an online social network called Cyber-mentor (www.cybermentor.ca) links girls aged 11 to 18 with women scientists and engineers. The aim of these initiatives is to get girls to think about science, mathematics, computing, and engineering as possible educational and career choices and not to see these as "boys' interests." These kinds of programs should have positive effects, since research has shown that exposure to counter-stereotypic models can overcome beliefs based on gender stereotypes. Exposure to women in leadership roles, including female faculty members, tends to mitigate effects of gender stereotyping (e.g., Dasgupta & Asgari, 2004).

Thus although gender differences in math continue in some places, efforts to encourage girls to succeed in this subject are having an effect and gender gaps in math and science have narrowed substantially. As noted in the Cultural Influences feature, comparisons from PISA results have shown that there is a slight gender difference in math and science scores overall, but in seven provinces there are no significant differences between males and females (Knighton, Brochu, & Gluszynski, 2010).

MEMORY. According to Maccoby and Jacklin (1974), verbal, spatial, and math abilities were domains in which boys and girls differed. One other domain has been added to the list by subsequent research: memory. Compared with boys and men, girls and women often remember the identity of objects as well as their location more accurately (Miller & Halpern, 2014; Voyer, Postma, Brake, & Imperato-McGinley, 2007). For example, if shown photos of faces, girls remember those faces more accurately than boys do (Herlitz & Lovén, 2013). In addition, when describing past events, a trip to a museum, a special visitor at school), girls tend to provide more elaborate and more emotion-filled descriptions (Grysman & Hudson, 2013).

Because these gender-related differences in memory have been documented only recently, they're not well understood. One suggestion is that they may be consequences of gender differences in other domains. For example, girls' advantage in language and recognizing emotions (described on pages 444 and 449) may allow them to construct more elaborate representations of stimuli and events, representations that are more resistant to forgetting. Another possibility links the differences in memory to the hippocampus, a brain structure that's critical for memory and is larger in girls than in boys (Lenroot & Giedd, 2010)

Differences in Personality and Social Behaviour

Are there differences in personality and social behaviour between boys and girls? In the 1970s, Maccoby and Jacklin (1974) found convincing evidence of only one gender difference in this realm: Boys were more aggressive than girls. In this section, we'll see what researchers have discovered in the ensuing four decades.

 QUESTION 13.2
Brianna is the mother of fraternal twins, a boy and a girl, who are just starting elementary school. She is determined that both of her children will excel in reading and math. Are Brianna's goals realistic? *(Answer is on page 460.)*

AGGRESSIVE BEHAVIOUR. No one doubts Maccoby and Jacklin's conclusion that boys are more physically aggressive than girls. As mentioned in Module 12.4, and as you can see in the photo, the gender difference in physical aggression is readily observed. Raymond Baillargeon of the Université de Montréal and colleagues from a number of other universities studied children enrolled in the Quebec Longitudinal Study of Child Development and found that as early as 17 months of age, there was a definite difference between boys and girls in physical aggression. Only 1 percent of girls, but 5 percent of boys, showed frequent physical aggression (Baillargeon et al., 2007). No matter how you look at it, boys are more aggressive than girls (Baillargeon et al., 2007; Card, Stucky, Sawalani, & Little, 2008). Of course, some qualifications apply. Boys are not always aggressive. They are, for example, more likely to be physically aggressive toward other boys than toward girls (Maccoby & Jacklin, 1980). Boys may try to beat up other boys, but, as a general rule, they do not try to beat up girls. And when they are provoked, girls can be physically aggressive, too (Bettencourt & Miller, 1996).

Physical aggression is far more common among boys than among girls.

Tudor Photography/Pearson Education, Inc.

Because boys and men are more aggressive in virtually all cultures and because males in nonhuman species are also more aggressive, scientists are convinced that biology contributes heavily to this gender difference. **Aggressive behaviour has been linked to** *androgens,* **hormones secreted by the testes.** Androgens do not lead to aggression directly. Instead, androgens make it more likely that boys will be aggressive by making them more excitable or easily angered and by making boys stronger (Archer, 2006; Dodge, Coie, & Lynam, 2006; Hay, 2007).

Even though hormones are involved, we cannot ignore experience. The media are filled with aggressive male models—from Vin Diesel to hockey "enforcers"—who are rewarded for their behaviour. What's more, parents are more likely to use physical punishment with sons than with daughters and are more tolerant of aggressive behaviour in sons than in daughters (Condry & Ross, 1985; Martin & Ross, 2005). In a study of sibling aggression, Jacqueline Martin and Hildy Ross of the University of Waterloo, Ontario, found that parents were more likely to prevent aggression by and directed toward girls but more tolerant of mild aggression by boys. Boys were generally more likely to be physically aggressive, and parents' tolerance of such aggression might socialize boys into its use (Martin & Ross, 2005). As we saw in Module 12.4, these are just the sorts of experiences that can precipitate a vicious cycle of increasing aggression, and this cycle is much more common for boys than girls. Although biology may make boys more prone to aggression, experience encourages boys rather than girls to express their aggression physically. Even animal studies have shown that experience is an important factor. Sapolsky & Share (2004) reported an instance of learning nonaggressive forms of interaction by wild baboons living in Kenya, Africa. Baboons live in groups (troops) with a hierarchical structure dominated by males and organized by the use of aggression. Several troops of baboons were under longitudinal observation. In one troop, all the dominant and thus most aggressive males died after a tuberculosis outbreak. The remaining less aggressive males and the females carried on living in the same area. This particularly unaggressive baboon troop survived, and the more relaxed behaviour pattern was transmitted to new animals that joined the group. Adolescent males typically leave the troop in which they are born and move to live with another group. Ten years after the disease incident, no males from the original troop remained, and many new males had migrated in, yet the peaceful culture persisted. (In comparison, the other baboon troops in the same region showed typical aggression patterns.) Although the researchers could not be certain of the cause, it did seem that the incoming young males learned that aggression was not necessary. As Sapolsky & Share (2004) noted, "If aggressive behaviour in baboons does have a cultural rather than a biological foundation, perhaps there's hope for us as well" (p. 418).

However, in humans, different types of aggressive behaviours do exist, and although boys' aggression may be more obvious because of its physical nature, girls can be aggressive, too (Ostrov & Godleski, 2010). In Module 12.4, we saw that girls rely on relational aggression in which they try to hurt others by damaging their relationships with peers (Crick & Grotpeter, 1995). They may call other children names, make fun of them, spread rumours about them, or—just as bad—pointedly ignore them. Boys are aggressive in this manner, too, but it's less obvious because physical aggression is so common and so noticeable in boys (Archer, 2004).

EMOTIONAL SENSITIVITY. According to the stereotypes listed on page 444, girls are better able to express their emotions and interpret others' emotions. In fact, this is a gender difference supported by research. For example, throughout infancy, childhood, and adolescence, girls identify facial expressions (e.g., a happy face versus a sad face) more accurately than boys do (Alexander & Wilcox, 2012; Thompson & Voyer, 2014). In addition, girls are more likely to express happiness and sadness, while boys are more likely to express anger (Chaplin & Aldao, 2013). Finally, for the complex (self-conscious) emotions described on pages 347–348, adolescent girls report experiencing shame and guilt more often than boys do (Else-Quest, Higgins, Allison, & Morton, 2012).

Most developmentalists believe that the gender difference in emotional sensitivity reflects both nature and nurture. On the nature side, regions of the brain's temporal lobe that play a leading role in processing emotional expression develop more rapidly in girls than in boys (McClure, 2000). On the nurture side, one idea is that because boys are more active and less able to regulate their behaviour, parents discourage sons from expressing emotions as a way of promoting self-regulation. In contrast, parents encourage daughters to express emotions because this is consistent with gender roles in which females are expected to be nurturing and supportive (Brody & Hall, 2008).

SOCIAL INFLUENCE. Another gender stereotype is that females are more easily influenced by others—that is, they are more persuadable. In fact, young girls are more likely than young boys to comply with an adult's request, and they are more likely to seek an adult's help (Jacklin & Maccoby, 1978)—a finding of Chen et al. (2003) for girls in both China and Canada in the cross-cultural study mentioned in Module 12.1. Girls and women are also influenced more than boys and men by persuasive messages and others' behaviour, especially when they are under group pressure (Becker, 1986; Eagly, Karau, & Makhijani, 1995). However, these gender differences may stem from the fact that females value group harmony more than boys and thus seem to give in to others (Miller, Danaher, & Forbes, 1986; Strough & Berg, 2000). For instance, at a meeting such as the one described in the module-opening vignette, girls are just as likely as boys to recognize the flaws in a bad idea, but girls are more willing to go along simply because they do not want the group to start arguing.

EFFORTFUL CONTROL. During story time in a preschool classroom, many children sit quietly, listening to the teacher read. However, if there's one child fidgeting or pestering a nearby child, the odds are that it's a boy. Consistent with this example, girls are more skilled at effortful control; compared with boys, they are better able to regulate their behaviour, to inhibit inappropriate responding, and to focus their attention (Else-Quest, Hyde, Goldsmith, & Van Hulle, 2006; Gagné, Miller, & Goldsmith, 2013). In addition, boys are far more likely to be diagnosed with attentional disorders such as ADHD (Hyde, 2014).

Earlier we saw that effortful control and ADHD have biological bases; these may contribute to gender-related differences. The average girl is more likely than the average boy to be biologically programmed to have better self-control, but the environment can amplify these differences. For example, when parents discover that their two-year-old son refuses to sit still in quiet settings (e.g., an older sibling's orchestra concert), they may stop taking him, depriving him of the opportunity to learn to control his behaviour

DEPRESSION.   Depression, a disorder in which individuals are chronically sad and irritable and have low self-esteem, is rare in childhood but becomes much more common in adolescence, particularly among teenage girls (Avenevoli & Steinberg, 2001). Data such as that from the Canadian Community Health Survey (CCHS) show that for Canada prevalence rates for depression in adolescence are around 5 to 6 percent for males and 10 to 12 percent for females (Afifi, Enns, Cox, & Martens, 2005; Canadian Mental Health Association, 2016). During adolescence, girls are more likely than boys to report negative events, such as fights with friends, and they report being more upset by these events than boys (Flook, 2011). Such episodes can lead some teens—especially girls—to be depressed (Mezulis, Salk, Hyde, Priess-Groben, & Simonson, 2014)

Tetra Images/Brand X Pictures/Getty Images

During adolescence, girls are more likely to suffer from depression than boys.

Several factors converge to make teenage girls more prone to depression. First, they experience more frequent stressors such as dissatisfaction with their appearance after pubertal change or conflict with close friends (Hankin, Mermelstein, & Roesch, 2007). Second, girls like the one in the photo at the left are more apt to interpret these negative life events in harmful terms, emphasizing social-emotional consequences to a far greater extent than boys do. For example, if a teenage girl were to fail a major exam, she would be more likely than a boy to interpret this event harshly, thinking, "I'm so stupid; my friends won't want to be with me if they know I'm this dumb." Third, much more than boys, girls are prone to ruminate about their problems; thinking about them over and over and talking about them with friends (Cox, Mezulis, & Hyde, 2010; Rood, Roelofs, Bögels, Nolen-Hoeksema, & Schouten, 2009). Fourth, hormonal changes at puberty may make teenage girls particularly vulnerable to interpersonal stressors (Martel, 2013).

Frank Talk about Gender Differences

The gender differences we've discussed in this module are summarized in the Summary Table. What should we make of these differences?

First, it's essential to remember that the gender differences described in this module represent differences in the *average scores* for boys and girls—differences that are relatively small. For example, Figure 13-6 shows the distribution of scores on a hypothetical reading test. As we would expect, overall, girls do better than boys.

SUMMARY TABLE

SEX DIFFERENCES IN PHYSICAL AND BEHAVIOURAL DEVELOPMENT

General Area	Specific Domain	Nature of Difference
Physical Development		
	Motor skills	Boys excel at tasks that require strength, but girls do better on tasks that require fine-motor coordination.
	Activity	Beginning in infancy, boys are more active than girls.
	Health	From conception through adulthood, girls are healthier.
Intellectual Abilities		
	Verbal ability	Girls have larger vocabularies; they also read, write, and spell better, and are less likely to have language-related impairments.
	Spatial ability	Boys are better on mental-rotation tasks and in determining relations between objects in space, but girls have better spatial location memory.
	Mathematics	Boys get higher scores on standardized tests, but primarily in countries where girls have limited educational and career opportunities.
Personality and Social Behaviour		
	Aggression	Boys are more aggressive physically; girls rely more on relational aggression.
	Emotional sensitivity	Girls are better able to identify and express emotions.
	Social influence	Because girls value group harmony more than boys do, girls are more susceptible to others' influence.
	Effortful control	Girls are better able to regulate their behaviour, to inhibit inappropriate responding, and to focus their attention; boys are more likely to be diagnosed with ADHD.
	Depression	Beginning in adolescence, girls are more prone to depression than boys.

However, the distributions of girls' and boys' scores overlap substantially. The area shaded in yellow shows the large percentage of boys who have higher reading scores than the average girl, and the area shaded in red shows the large percentage of girls who have lower reading scores than the average boy. The diagram makes it obvious that a difference in average scores does *not* mean that girls read well and boys read poorly.

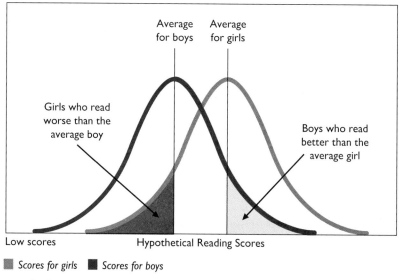

Figure 13-6 Distribution of scores on a hypothetical test: comparison of boys' and girls' scores.

Consequently, a boy who wants to become a writer should not be deterred because of small differences in average scores for boys and girls. Of course, we could draw similar diagrams in the other domains in which boys and girls differ and come to the same conclusion. The vast majority of gender differences are small—a majority corresponding to correlations of 0.20 or less—which means that boys' and girls' scores overlap considerably (Hyde, 2014).

Second, think about the huge number of abilities, behaviours, and traits that have not been considered in this module. Boys and girls do not differ in many, many aspects of cognition, personality, and social behaviour, a point that is easily lost when focusing on gender differences. In reality, a list of ways that boys and girls are similar is much longer than a list of differences (Hyde, 2014). In cognitive processing, memory, and understanding people—to name just a few areas—boys and girls are much more alike than different. If development is a journey, both boys and girls have many choices as they travel; few, if any, routes have signs that say "for girls only" or "for boys only."

In this module, we've focused on the behaviours and skills in which boys and girls differ; in the next module we'll see how children acquire a gender identity, a sense of "being a boy" or "being a girl."

ANSWER 13.2

Yes, her son and daughter may both excel in math. If the typical pattern of gender differences holds, however, her daughter may become the better reader.

✓ Check Your Learning

RECALL What were the primary gender differences that Maccoby and Jacklin described in their 1974 book?

Summarize features of personality and social behaviour in which boys and girls differ.

INTERPRET How do nature and nurture contribute to gender differences in intellectual abilities and achievement?

APPLY Based on what you know about differences between boys and girls in intellectual abilities and social behaviour, how might this module differ in the 40th edition of this book, published in 2106?

13.3 Gender Identity

OUTLINE

The Socializing Influences of People and the Media

Cognitive Theories of Gender Identity

Biological Influences

LEARNING OBJECTIVES

1. How do parents, peers, and the media influence children's learning of gender roles?

2. How do cognitive theories explain children's learning of gender roles?

3. How does biology influence children's learning of gender roles?

Taryn, who has just turned four, knows that she's a girl but is convinced that she'll grow up to be a man. Taryn plays almost exclusively with boys, and her favourite toys are trucks and cars. Taryn tells her parents that when she's bigger, she'll grow a beard and be a daddy. Taryn's father is confident that his daughter's ideas are a natural part of a preschooler's limited understanding of gender, but her mother wonders if they have neglected some important aspect of Taryn's upbringing.

According to the old saying, "Boys will be boys and girls will be girls," but how do boys become boys and girls become girls when it comes to gender roles? That is, how do children acquire their culture's roles for males and females? And how do children develop a sense of identity as a male or a female? We'll answer these questions in this module and, as we do, learn whether Taryn's wish to grow up to be a man is typical for youngsters her age.

The Socializing Influences of People and the Media

General opinion holds that parents and other adults—teachers and television characters, for example—directly shape children's behaviour regarding the roles associated with their sex. Boys are rewarded for boyish behaviour and punished for girlish behaviour.

This concept does have a theoretical basis: According to social cognitive theorists such as Albert Bandura (1977, 1986; Bandura & Bussey, 2004), and Walter Mischel (1970), children learn gender roles in much the same way they learn other social behaviours—by watching the world around them and learning the outcomes of actions. Thus, children learn what their culture considers appropriate behaviour for males and females by simply watching how others around them act. How well does research support social cognitive theory? Let's look first at research done with parents.

PARENTS.   An extensive meta-analysis of 172 studies involving 27 836 children by Hugh Lytton and David Romney of the University of Calgary, Alberta (Lytton & Romney, 1991), found that parents often treat sons and daughters similarly: Parents interact equally with sons and daughters, are equally warm to both, and encourage both sons and daughters to achieve and be independent. However, in behaviour related to gender roles, parents respond differently to sons and daughters (Lytton & Romney, 1991). Activities such as playing with dolls, dressing up, or helping an adult are encouraged more often in daughters than in sons; rough-and-tumble play and playing with blocks are encouraged more in sons than in daughters. Parents react more positively toward their children when the child is playing with toys seen as typical for their sex than when playing with toys seen as typical of the other sex (Berenbaum, Martin, Hanish, Briggs, & Fabes, 2008), and parents tolerate mild aggression more in sons than in daughters (Martin & Ross, 2005). Research from Concordia University in Quebec has shown that for prosocial behaviours—such as sharing or being friendly—mothers tend to influence both girls and boys to display more gender-stereotypic actions, while fathers influence boys to express more "masculine" prosocial behaviours (Hastings, McShane, Parker, & Ladha, 2007). It has also been found that following the birth of a child (especially a firstborn), parents tend to become more traditional in their attitudes regarding gender (Katz-Wise, Priess, & Hyde, 2010).

Fathers are more likely than mothers to treat sons and daughters differently. More than mothers, fathers such as the one in the photo often encourage gender-related play. Fathers also push their sons more but accept dependence in their daughters (Snow, Jacklin, & Maccoby, 1983). A father, for example, may urge his frightened young son to jump off the diving board ("Be a man!") but not be so insistent with his daughter ("That's okay, honey"). Apparently, mothers are more likely to respond

Fathers are more likely than mothers to treat their children in a stereotyped manner.

Stockbyte/Getty Images

based on their knowledge of the individual child's needs, but fathers respond based on gender stereotypes. A mother responds to her son knowing that he is smart but unsure of himself; a father may respond because of what he thinks boys should be like.

Of course, adults differ in their views on the relative rights and roles of males and females. Some have very traditional views, believing, for example, that men should be hired preferentially for some jobs and that it is more important for sons than daughters to attend college or university. Others have more gender-neutral views, believing, for example, that women should have the same business and professional opportunities as men, and that daughters should have the same educational opportunities as sons. It would be surprising if parents did not convey these attitudes to their children, and indeed they do (Crouter, Whiteman, McHale, & Osgood, 2007). A meta-analysis of 48 studies, including more than 10 000 pairs of parents and children, showed that children's gender-related interests, attitudes, and self-concepts are more traditional when their parents have traditional views and more gender-neutral when their parents have nontraditional views (Tenenbaum & Leaper, 2002).

A small but growing group of children are those with gay and lesbian parents. Initially, concerns were expressed about gender role development in children with homosexual parents—that not having one male and one female parent would have negative effects on children. Most research in this field has been of gender-role behaviour of children of lesbian parents, although some has looked at gay fathers. A recent longitudinal study tracking children of lesbian couples participating in the U.S. Longitudinal Lesbian Family Study indicated that adolescents who did and did not have male role models were comparable on gender role traits and in psychological well-being (Bos, Goldberg, Van Gelderen, & Gartrell, 2010). Overall, having two parents is generally better than one (in part simply because two people can give more time to children than one, possibly stressed, parent), but the gender of those parents seems to be irrelevant (Biblarz & Stacey, 2010).

TEACHERS.   After parents, teachers may be the most influential adults in children's lives. Many teachers help to differentiate gender roles by making gender salient in the classroom. In elementary schools, students may be told to form separate lines for boys and girls. Or teachers may praise the girls as a group for being quiet during a video, while criticizing the boys for laughing (Thorne, 1993). In addition, teachers spend more time interacting with boys than girls. Teachers call on boys more frequently, praise them more for their schoolwork, and spend more time scolding them for disruptive classroom behaviour (Good & Brophy, 1996). By using sex as a basis for differentiating children and by giving boys more attention, teachers foster gender-role learning (Ruble, Martin, & Berenbaum, 2006). Unfortunately, such research shows that teachers and sports coaches do not even know that they are doing this. Anne Barnfield had a student who performed an observational research study for a class project. The student watched her older brother teach a children's karate class. The study showed that the young male instructors for that class used terms like "sweetie" when instructing girls and "buddy" for boys. Girls tended to be praised for good form, boys for aggressiveness. None of the instructors knew that they were doing this until they saw the results of the student's observations, and were astonished that they were unaware of behaving in this way.

PEERS.   By the age of three, most children's play shows the impact of gender stereotypes—boys prefer blocks and trucks, whereas girls prefer tea sets and dolls—and youngsters are critical of peers who engage in cross-gender play (Aspenlieder,

Buchanan, McDougall, & Sippola, 2009). This is particularly true of boys who like stereotypically feminine toys or activities. Boys who play with dolls and girls (such as the one in the photo) who play with trucks will both be ignored, teased, or ridiculed by their peers, but a boy will receive harsher treatment than a girl (Levy, Taylor, & Gelman, 1995). Once children learn rules about gender-typical play, they often harshly punish peers who violate those rules.

Preschool children often tease their peers who engage in cross-gender play.

Peers influence gender roles in another way, too. During the preschool years, children begin to prefer playing with same-sex peers (Halim, Ruble, Tamis-Lemonda, & Shrout, 2013). Little boys play together with cars, and little girls play together with dolls. Segregation of playmates by sex occurs spontaneously and children often resist playing with members of the other sex, even in gender-neutral activities such as playing tag or colouring (Maccoby, 1990, 1998). This preference increases during childhood, reaching a peak in preadolescence. By age 10 or 11, the vast majority of peer activity is with same-sex children, and most of this involves sex-typed play: Boys are playing sports or playing with cars or action figures; girls are doing artwork or playing with pets or dolls (McHale, Kim, Whiteman, & Crouter, 2004). Then the tide begins to turn, but even in adulthood, time spent at work and at leisure is quite commonly segregated by gender (Hartup, 1983).

Why do boys and girls seem so attracted to same-sex play partners? One reason is self-selection by sex. Boys and girls want to play with others like themselves and after they know their sex, they pick others on that basis (Martin et al., 2013). Also, boys and girls differ in their styles of play. Boys usually prefer rough-and-tumble play and generally are more competitive and dominating in their interactions. In contrast, when girls play, they are usually more cooperative, prosocial, and conversation oriented (Martin, Fabes, Hanish, Leonard, & Dinella, 2011; Rose & Rudolph, 2006). Generally, boys do not enjoy the way that girls play, and girls are averse to boys' style of play (Maccoby, 1990, 1998).

Third, when girls and boys play together, girls do not readily influence boys. **Girls' interactions with one another are typically** *enabling*—**their actions and remarks tend to support others and sustain the interaction.** When drawing together, one girl might say to another, "Cool picture" or "What do you want to do now?" **In contrast, boy's interactions are often** *constricting*—**one partner tries to emerge as the victor by threatening or contradicting the other, by exaggerating, and so on.** In the same drawing task, one boy might say to another, "My picture's better" or "Drawing is stupid—let's watch TV." When these styles are brought together, girls find that their enabling style is ineffective with boys. The same subtle overtures that work with other girls have no impact on boys. Boys ignore girls' polite suggestions about what to do and ignore girls' efforts to resolve conflicts with discussion (Rose & Rudolph, 2006).

Some theorists believe that these contrasting styles may have an evolutionary basis (Geary, Byrd-Craven, Hoard, Vigil, & Numtee, 2003). Boys' concerns about dominating others may stem from a concern with establishing one's rank among a group of males because those males at the upper ranks have better access to mates and better access to resources needed for offspring. Girls' concerns about affiliation may be a by-product of

 QUESTION 13.3
Rick has encouraged his four-year-old son to play with the five-year-old girl who lives next door, but his son will have none of it—he refuses every time. Rick thinks that his son is being unreasonable and stubborn. Do you agree? *(Answer is on page 468.)*

the fact that women traditionally left their own communities (and relatives) to live in a husband's community. Having no relatives nearby enhanced the value of a close friend, which placed a premium on the affiliative behaviours that lead to and maintain friendships.

Regardless of the exact cause, early segregation of playmates by style of play means that boys learn primarily from boys and girls from girls. Over time, such social segregation by sex reinforces gender differences in play. Martin and Fabes (2001), for example, conducted a longitudinal study of same-sex play in preschool and kindergarten children. When young boys spent most of their time playing with other boys at the beginning of the school year, their play was more active and more aggressive by the end of the year. In contrast, when young girls spent most of their time playing with other girls at the beginning of the school year, their play was less active and less aggressive by the end of the year. Boys and girls who spent more time playing with other-sex children didn't show these changes. Thus, young boys and girls teach each other gender-appropriate play. As they do, this helps solidify a youngster's emerging sense of membership in a particular gender group and sharpens the contrast between genders.

TELEVISION.   Another source of influence on gender-role learning is television. For decades, males and females have been depicted on TV in stereotypical ways. Women tend to be cast in romantic or family roles; they are depicted as emotional, passive, and weak. Men are more often cast in leadership or professional roles and are depicted as rational, active, and strong (Leaper, Breed, Hoffman, & Perlman, 2002; Smith, Choueiti, Prescott, & Pieper, 2012). As you can imagine, children who watch a lot of TV end up with more stereotyped views of males and females. For example, Kimball (1986) studied gender role stereotypes in a small Canadian town that could not receive TV programs until a transmitter was installed in 1974. Children's views of personality traits, behaviours, occupations, and peer relations were measured before and after TV was introduced. Boys' views became more stereotyped on all four dimensions. For example, in their more stereotyped views of occupations, boys now believed that girls could be teachers and cooks, whereas boys could be physicians and judges. Girls' views became more stereotyped only for traits and peer relations. After TV was introduced, girls believed that boasting and swearing were characteristic of boys and that sharing and helping were characteristic of girls. Findings like these indicate that TV viewing causes children to adopt many of the stereotypes that dominate television programming (Oppliger, 2007; Signorielli & Lears, 1992).

Let's now return to our original question: How well does research support the social learning explanation of gender roles? Studies of parents, teachers, and peers show that children learn much about gender roles simply by observing males and females, but simple observation of real-life models or television characters cannot be the entire explanation. After all, young boys traditionally have far more opportunities to observe their mother's behaviour than their father's but are more likely to imitate their father's actions than their mother's. Thus, an important element in learning about gender is identifying with one gender and then actively seeking out activities that are seen as typical for that gender. This aspect of gender role learning is the focus of cognitive theories, which we'll examine in the next section.

Cognitive Theories of Gender Identity

One of the first descriptions of children's understanding of gender was proposed by Lawrence Kohlberg (1966; Kohlberg & Ullian, 1974), the same theorist who described moral development as a sequence of stages (pages 411–413). In Kohlberg's account, toddlers know that they are either boys or girls and label themselves accordingly. During the preschool years, children begin to understand that gender is stable; boys become men and girls become women. Yet at this age, they believe that a girl who wears her hair like a boy will become a boy and that a boy who plays with dolls will become a girl. Not until about five or six years of age do children come to understand that maleness and femaleness do not change over situations or according to personal wishes. They understand that a child's sex is unaffected by the clothing that a child wears or the toys that a child likes.

Taryn, the four-year-old in the opening vignette, is in the first stage: She knows that she's a girl. However, she does not yet understand that gender is stable and consistent.

As soon as children understand that gender is stable, they begin learning about gender-typical behaviour. Explaining how that learning takes place is the aim of a theory that is the focus of the "Spotlight on Theories" feature.

Spotlight on Theories

Gender Schema Theory

BACKGROUND   Preschool children learn gender roles rapidly. The environment, of course, provides many clues about typical roles for males and females. The question is: How do children use these clues to learn about the behaviours and characteristics typically associated with their sex?

THE THEORY   A theory proposed by Carol Martin (Martin & Ruble, 2004; Martin et al., 1999), illustrated in Figure 13-7, addresses how children learn about gender. **In** *gender schema theory,* **children first decide whether an object, activity, or behaviour is considered female or male, then they use this information to decide whether they should learn more about the object, activity, or behaviour.** That is, once children know their gender, they pay attention primarily to experiences and events that are gender appropriate (Martin & Halverson, 1987; Zosuls, Ruble, & Tamis-Lemonda, 2014). According to gender schema theory, a preschool boy who is watching a group

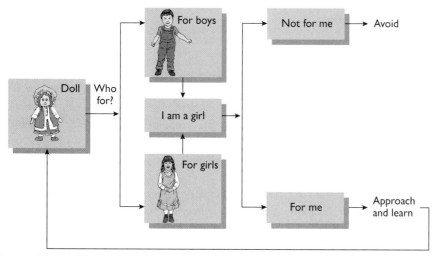

Figure 13-7 A diagrammatic representation of gender-schema theory.

of girls playing in sand will decide that playing in sand is for girls and that, because he is a boy, playing in sand is not for him. Seeing a group of older boys playing football, he will decide that football is for boys, and because he is a boy, football is acceptable and he should learn more about it.

Hypothesis: According to gender schema theory, children first establish gender identity and then begin actively learning about gender roles. Consequently, children who have established a gender identity should know much about gender roles, but children who have not established a gender identity should know little about gender roles.

Test: Zosuls et al. (2009) recorded children's language development from 10 to 21 months, looking for occasions when children referred to themselves as a boy or as a girl. In addition, at 17 and 21 months, children were observed as they played with several gender-stereotypic toys (truck, doll) and gender-neutral toys (telephone, miniature people). The investigators found that children who referred to themselves by gender played more often with gender-stereotypic toys. In other words, Beth, who has referred to herself as a girl, plays with dolls but not with trucks. In contrast, James, who has never referred to himself as a boy, plays with dolls and trucks equally.

Conclusion: As predicted, children's understanding that they are a boy (or girl) is the catalyst for learning about gender roles. As Martin and Ruble put it, "Children are gender detectives who search for cues about gender—who should or should not engage in a particular activity, who can play with whom, and why girls and boys are different" (2004, p. 67).

Application: After children understand gender, it is as if they see the world through special glasses that allow only gender-typical activities to be in focus (Liben & Bigler, 2002). Parents who do not want their children limited to traditional views of gender and to traditional gender roles might be tempted to encourage children to see things from a more neutral perspective. Once a child has acquired gender identity, however, acquiring a neutral perspective is probably easier said than done. A better strategy might be to expose children to many counter-stereotyped examples. By showing girls women who fly planes, work in construction, or manage companies, and by showing boys men who are nurses, preschool teachers, or dental hygienists, children can learn a much broader definition of what it means to be male or female.

Critical Thinking Question: How does culture influence what is seen as a "male" or "female" role?

Gender schema theory shows that *male* and *female* become much more salient in children's worlds after they understand gender. Consistent with this theory, Robert Kail remembers vividly taking his four-year-old daughter Laura to watch his son Ben play football. Kail wondered if Laura would become so bored and restless that they would need to leave. Wrong. Laura immediately discovered the cheerleaders (all girls) and insisted they sit right in front of them. Throughout the game (and the rest of the season), Laura's eyes were riveted to the cheerleaders' every move, and at home, she would imitate their routines. According to gender schema theory, four-year-old Laura knew that cheerleading was for girls and that because she was a girl, she needed to learn everything about it.[1]

[1]But during the elementary-school years she abandoned cheerleading for soccer and basketball.

After children have gender identity, they begin to use gender labels to evaluate toys and activities. Shown an unfamiliar toy and told that children of a specific sex *really* like this toy, young children like the toy much more if they believe others of their sex do, too (Shutts, Banaji, & Spelke, 2010). By school age, children know that gender roles are flexible, wearing pants doesn't make a girl into boy, wearing nail polish doesn't make a boy into a girl), and that masculine roles often have more status. Consequently, elementary-school girls realize that by being a tomboy they can have some of the status associated with being a boy without jeopardizing their identity as a girl (Halim, Ruble, & Amodio, 2011). There are still social pressures on girls that reduce their motivation to take up counter-stereotypic activities, however, and even those who identify as tomboys still tend to hold to overall gender stereotypes (Martin & Dinella, 2012).

As with gender-label influences on young children's toy choices, it appears that high-school girls' gender schemata can be altered to exclude math. A longitudinal study by Helen Watt and colleagues looked at gender differences in high school students' motivation toward mathematics and their career aspirations, in the United States, Australia, and Canada. Despite girls and boys achieving similar grades in mathematics (as noted in Module 13.2), this study found that girls tend to opt out of advanced math courses in the upper years of high school, which then limits occupational and further education options (Watt et al., 2012). In turn this has a limiting effect on studies and careers in the sciences, leading to computing and engineering being more male-dominated and biology and health subjects more female-dominated. In an evaluation of adolescents' views of science and science careers, based on PISA data, Sikora and Pokropek (2012) proposed that "gender essentialism," a societal view of males as "better" at certain tasks, led to stereotypic views of careers, and that it was this cultural influence that shaped students' career plans (Sikora & Pokropek, 2012). Thus despite girls and boys showing equal levels of achievement while at school, there emerges a gender-segregation in science-oriented further education and careers (Sikora & Pokropek, 2012; Watt et al., 2012).

A selective viewing of the world explains a great deal about children's learning of gender roles, but, as we'll see in the next section, there is a final important element that needs to be considered.

Biological Influences

Most child-development researchers agree that biology contributes to gender roles and gender identity. At one extreme, evolutionary developmental psychology proposes that men and women performed vastly different roles for much of human history: Women were more invested in child-rearing, and men were more invested in providing important resources (e.g., food, protection) for their offspring (Geary, 2002). In adapting to these roles, different traits and behaviours evolved for men and women. For example, men became more aggressive because that behaviour was adaptive in helping them ward off predators. Others argue against placing too much emphasis on such a perspective, particularly when, as a form of "after the fact" analysis, it is used to support current stereotypes (Halpern, 2000, 2012).

If gender roles are based in part on our evolutionary heritage, then behavioural genetic research should show the impact of heredity on gender-role learning. Indeed, twin studies show a substantial impact on gender-role learning (Iervolino, Hines, Golombok, Rust, & Plomin, 2005). If one identical twin strongly prefers sex-typical toys and activities, the other one usually does, too. Fraternal twins are also similar in their preference for sex-typical toys and activities, but not to the same extent as identical twins.

Twin studies point to a biological basis for gender role learning but do not tell us what factors are responsible. Some scientists believe that the sex hormones are important; consistent with this idea, for both boys and girls, exposure to testosterone during prenatal development leads to greater interest in masculine sex-typed activities during the elementary-school years (Constantinescu & Hines, 2012). This link is particularly evident in studies of children with *congenital adrenal hyperplasia* (CAH), **a genetic disorder in which, beginning in prenatal development, the adrenal glands secrete large amounts of androgen.** During childhood and adolescence, girls with CAH prefer masculine activities (such as playing with cars instead of dolls) and male playmates to a much greater extent than girls not exposed to these amounts of androgen, despite strong encouragement from parents to play with feminine toys (Miller & Halpern, 2014; Pasterski et al., 2005). Apparently, the androgen affects the prenatal development of brain regions critical for masculine and feminine gender role behaviour.

In a review article on sex differences in cognition, Doreen Kimura at Simon Fraser University in British Columbia stated that "sex hormones are a major influence in the organization, and perhaps the maintenance, of cognitive sex differences" (Kimura, 2004, p. 51). Kimura has favoured a biological, hormonal, and even brain-structure difference to explain these variations (Kimura, 2004); others would prefer a more socially based explanation. As McCarthy and Arnold wrote, "The study of sex differences in the brain has a long, rich history and remains a vibrant and controversial topic …" (McCarthy & Arnold, 2008, p. 15). Although some still dispute the absolute nature of sex differences in mental abilities, it is perhaps better to consider, as Diane Halpern has said, that "differences are not deficiencies" (Halpern, 2012, p. 4), and "[g]irls and boys, and women and men, are both similar and different—it is a false dichotomy to ask if they are similar *or* different" (Halpern, 2005, p. 136).

Perhaps the biopsychosocial model (Halpern, 2012) best explains gender differences. In other words, the most accurate conclusion to draw is that biology, the socializing influence of people and media, and the child's own efforts to understand gender-typical behaviour all contribute to gender roles and differences. Recognizing the interactive nature of these influences on gender learning also enables us to better understand how gender roles are changing today, which is the focus of the last module.

 ANSWER 13.3
No. Worldwide, boys rarely pick girls as play partners, and they resist when urged to do so by others. Rick's son is simply acting as most boys his age would; most girls would do the same if the tables were turned.

 Check Your Learning

RECALL Describe the forces of socialization that contribute to a child's development of gender identity.

Describe cognitive theories of gender identity.

INTERPRET How does children's acquisition of gender identity compare with growth in self-concept, described in Module 11.1?

APPLY The popular view is that children learn gender roles from adults (and society at large). But children are active participants in gender-role learning. Describe how children influence learning of gender roles.

13.4 Gender Roles in Transition

OUTLINE

Emerging Gender Roles

Beyond Traditional Gender Roles

LEARNING OBJECTIVES

1. What is androgyny, and how is it related to traditional conceptions of masculinity and femininity?

2. Can parents rear gender-neutral children?

Meda and Perry want their six-year-old daughter, Hope, to pick activities, friends, and ultimately a career based on her interests and abilities rather than on her gender. They have done their best to encourage gender-neutral values and behaviour. Both are therefore astonished that Hope seems to be totally indistinguishable from other six-year-olds reared by conventional parents. Hope's close friends are all girls. When Hope is with her friends, they play house or play with dolls. What seems to be going wrong with Meda and Perry's plans for a gender-neutral girl?

Gender roles are not etched in stone; they change with the times. In Canada, the range of acceptable roles for girls and boys and women and men has never been greater than today. For example, some fathers, such as the man in the photo, stay home to be the primary caregivers for children, and some women work full-time as sole support for the family. What is the impact of these changes on children? In this module, we'll answer this question by looking at new gender roles and at efforts by parents like Meda and Perry to rear gender-neutral children.

Gender roles continue to evolve, and the range of acceptable roles for men and women continues to expand.

Jürgen Fälchle/Fotolia

Emerging Gender Roles

Traditionally, masculinity and femininity were seen as ends of a continuum: Children possessing many traits associated with males were considered highly masculine, and those possessing many traits associated with females were considered highly feminine. A newer view of gender roles is based on the independent dimensions of instrumentality and expressiveness that were described in Module 13.1. In this view, traditional males are rated high on instrumentality but low on expressiveness, whereas traditional females are low on instrumentality but high on expressiveness. This approach recognizes that other combinations of traits are possible. *Androgynous* **people are rated high on both the instrumental and expressive dimensions.** (The term *androgyny* originates from the Greek words for "male"—*andro,* and "female"—*gyn.*) In other words, androgynous individuals can be both independent and emotional, self-confident and considerate, ambitious and creative.

Many theorists (e.g., Bem, 1996) argue that the ability to react with both instrumental and expressive behaviours is psychologically healthier than reacting primarily with one or the other. In fact, androgynous children often are better adjusted than children whose gender roles are highly stereotyped (DiDonato & Berenbaum, 2011; Norlander, Erixon, & Archer, 2000). However, the benefits of androgyny are greater for girls than for boys. Androgynous girls have higher self-esteem than expressive girls and are more likely to express their thoughts and feelings

Girls benefit from an androgynous gender role that combines the independence and self-confidence of the instrumental dimension with the emotional and considerate aspects of the expressive dimension.

publicly (Harter, Waters, & Whitesell, 1998). For example, a girl such as the one in the photo, who is independent and ambitious as well as considerate and creative, is more likely to feel positive about herself than a girl who embodies only the expressive traits traditionally associated with females.

Evidently, a balance of expressiveness and instrumentality may be especially adaptive across life's many tasks. Being independent and confident has benefits at home and at work, but so does being kind and considerate. As we'll see in the next section, however, teaching children to adopt nontraditional views of gender is challenging.

Beyond Traditional Gender Roles

Many researchers (e.g., Hyde, 2014) believe gender is overemphasized to children. They argue that adults often group children by gender unnecessarily. Consider, for example, a minister who rewards perfect church attendance with blue pencils for boys and pink pencils for girls. Children's gender is irrelevant to the reason for the reward, yet distinguishing boys and girls makes gender seem important and increases children's gender stereotypes (Bigler, 1995).

Many developmentalists believe that gender should be linked strictly to reproductive function instead of, as it is now, to traits, behaviours, and abilities. Is this possible? Children certainly can learn less stereotyped views of gender. School-age children can be taught that whether a person is well-suited for a job depends on the person's skills and interests, not the person's sex (Bigler & Liben, 1990). In addition, children can be taught how to identify gender prejudice and how to respond to sexist remarks (Brinkman, Jedinak, Rosen, & Zimmerman, 2011; Lamb, Bigler, Liben, & Green, 2009; Pahlke, Bigler, & Martin, 2014). Adults can help children to think this way, and more and more now do so. For example, the Girls LEAD summer camps at Brescia University College (discussed in Module 14.2) aim to do just this—to help young girls develop self-confidence and to encourage them to think themselves capable of taking on any occupation.

Accomplishing change over the long term in a natural setting may be more complicated, based on some results of the Family Lifestyles Project (Weisner & Wilson-Mitchell, 1990; Weisner, Garnier, & Loucky, 1994). This research examined families in which the parents were members of the 1960s and 1970s counterculture and were deeply committed to rearing their children without traditional gender stereotypes. In these families, men and women shared the household, financial, and childcare tasks.

The Family Lifestyles Project indicates that parents like Meda and Perry in this module's opening vignette can influence some aspects of gender stereotyping more readily than others. The children studied in the Family Lifestyles Project had few stereotypes about occupations: They agreed that girls could be national leaders and drive trucks and that boys could be nurses and secretaries. They also had fewer stereotyped attitudes about the use of objects: Boys and girls were equally likely to use an iron, a shovel, hammer

 QUESTION 13.4

Ms. Bower has her Grade 2 class form two lines—one for boys and one for girls—before they walk to the cafeteria for lunch. What do you think of this practice? *(Answer is on page 471.)*

and nails, and needle and thread. Nevertheless, children in these families tended to have same-sex friends, and they liked gender-stereotyped activities: The boys enjoyed physical play, and the girls enjoyed drawing and reading.

In the twenty-first century, both men and women are often employed outside the home, and both men and women care for children (Eagly & Wood, 2013). Some argue that the cultural changes of the past few decades cannot erase hundreds of thousands of years of evolutionary history (Geary, 2002) and that we should not be surprised that boys and girls play differently, that girls tend to be more supportive in their interactions with others, and that boys are usually more aggressive physically. Social learning theorists, however, would point out that learning can change behaviour. The Children's Lives feature suggests ways children can be helped to go beyond traditional gender roles and learn the best from both roles.

Children's Lives

Encouraging Valuable Traits, not Gender Traits

Parents and other adults can encourage children to learn the best from both of the traditional gender roles. Being independent, confident, caring, and considerate are valuable traits for all people, not just for boys or girls. Here are some guidelines to help achieve these aims:

- Since children learn gender roles from those around them, parents should be sure that they themselves are not gender bound. Mothers and fathers can mow lawns, make repairs, and work outside the home. Mothers and fathers can prepare meals, do laundry, and care for the young. This *does* make a difference: Robert Kail has always done most of the laundry in his house, and his daughter, at five, was astonished when Kail told her that in most homes mothers do the laundry.

- Parents should not base decisions about children's toys, activities, and chores on the child's sex. They should decide whether a toy, activity, or chore is appropriate for the child as an individual (based on age, abilities, and interests), rather than because the child is a boy or girl.

- Forces outside the home, such as the media and teachers, often work against parents who want their children to go beyond traditional gender roles. It is neither feasible nor wise to shelter children from these influences, but parents can encourage them to think critically about others' gender-based decisions. When band teachers insist that boys play trumpets and trombones while girls play clarinets and flutes, parents should ask children whether this makes sense. When a TV program shows a man coming to aid the stereotypical damsel in distress, parents should ask the child why the woman simply did not get herself out of her predicament.

By following these guidelines, adults can help children to develop all their talents, not just those that fit traditional views associated with males and females.

Critical Thinking Question: What other ways does society encourage gender-stereotypical traits, and how could these be countered?

 ANSWER 13.4
Forming two lines may be a good idea, but there is no reason why one should be for boys and the other for girls. After all, boys and girls are going to the same place, for the same reason. Segregating boys and girls needlessly, as in this case, simply makes gender seem more important than it really is.

Check Your Learning

RECALL What characteristics make up androgyny?

What elements of gender stereotyping seem fairly easy to change? What elements seem more resistant to change?

INTERPRET Why might girls benefit more than boys from an androgynous gender role?

APPLY What advice would you give to a mother who wants her daughter to grow up to be gender-free in her attitudes, beliefs, and aspirations?

UNIFYING THEMES Connections

Research on gender illustrates the theme that *development in different domains is connected*. Think about how children learn gender roles. According to conventional wisdom, children acquire masculine or feminine traits and behaviours through socialization by parents and other knowledgeable or authoritative persons in the child's culture. This process is important, but we have seen that learning gender roles is not simply a social phenomenon: Cognitive processes are essential. Children don't really begin to learn about gender roles until they understand that gender is stable; when

they do, gender-schema theory shows how children use this information to decide which experiences are relevant to them. Biology apparently contributes too, although we still do not really understand how. As Money and Ehrhardt proposed back in 1972 in the first edition of their book on gender, *Man and Woman, Boy and Girl*, nature *versus* nurture is an outmoded argument—we should be looking at interactions of biology and social environment. Biology, cognition, and social forces all shape the unique gender role that individual boys or girls play.

See for Yourself

To see that older children know more about gender stereotypes and understand that stereotypes are not binding, you will need to create some simple stories that illustrate stereotyped traits. We suggest that you use "independent," "confident," "appreciative," and "gentle." Each story should include two to three sentences that describe a child. Be sure that your stories contain no other clues that would hint that the child in the story is a boy or a girl. For example, this story illustrates "independent":

I know a child who likes to do things without help from adults. This child likes to do homework without help and enjoys travelling alone to visit cousins who live in another city.

After gaining appropriate permission, read your stories to some 11- and 12-year-olds. After you've read each story,

ask, "Is this child a boy, a girl, or could it be either?" Record the reply and then ask, "Would most people think that the child is a boy, or would most think that the child is a girl?"

In the first question, you're measuring children's understanding that gender stereotypes are flexible. You should find that children answer with "either one" about half of the time, indicating that they believe in some, but not total, flexibility in gender stereotypes. In the second question, you're measuring children's awareness of gender stereotypes. You should find that most children always answer the second question stereotypically; that people would identify the independent and confident children as boys and the appreciative and gentle children as girls. See for yourself!

Resources

For more information about …

sex/gender differences, try Diane Halpern's work *Sex Differences in Cognitive Abilities* – 4th edition (Psychology Press, 2012), which examines in detail many of the concepts and theories introduced in this chapter.

how to increase the impact of women on technology, visit the website of the Ontario Network of Women in Engineering (ONWiE) to get more information on the

"GoEngGirl/GÉNIales, les filles" program, www.onwie.ca/programs/go-eng-girl. Also, the Ontario Society of Professional Engineers (OSPE) has a women's mentoring site, see www.ospe.on.ca/engineering-professional-success.

Canada's only all women's university, see the Brescia University College website at www.brescia.uwo.ca.

Key Terms

androgens   456
androgynous   469
congenital adrenal hyperplasia
   (CAH)   468
constricting   463

enabling   463
expressive   444
gender identity   443
gender roles   443
gender schema theory   465

gender stereotypes   443
instrumental   444
mental rotation   450
social roles   443
spatial memory   450

Summary

13.1 Gender Stereotypes

1. How Do We View Men and Women?
Instrumental traits describe individuals who are acting on the world and are usually associated with males. Expressive traits describe individuals who value interpersonal relationships and are usually associated with females.

2. Learning Gender Stereotypes
By age four, children have substantial knowledge of gender-stereotyped activities; during the elementary-school years they come to know gender-stereotyped traits and behaviours. Older children also understand that traits and occupations associated with males have higher social status and that stereotypes are not necessarily binding.

13.2 Differences Related to Gender

In *The Psychology of Sex Differences*, published in 1974, Eleanor Maccoby and Carol Jacklin concluded that males and females differed in only four areas—verbal ability, spatial ability, math achievement, and aggression. Subsequent investigators have used their work as the starting point for analyzing gender differences.

1. Differences in Physical Development
Boys tend to be bigger, stronger, and more active than girls; girls tend to have better fine-motor coordination and to be healthier.

2. Differences in Intellectual Abilities and Achievement
Girls excel in verbal skills, whereas boys excel in spatial ability. Boys once had an advantage in math achievement, but the gap is now negligible because girls have more exposure to women who pursue math-relevant careers. Girls remember objects and their locations more accurately than boys do. Differences in intellectual abilities reflect both hereditary and environmental factors.

3. Differences in Personality and Social Behaviour
Boys are more aggressive physically than girls, and biology probably contributes heavily to this difference. Girls usually express their aggression by trying to damage other children's relations with peers. Girls are more sensitive to others' feelings and are more influenced by others; both differences are probably due to experience. Girls are more skilled in effortful control but in adolescence are more prone to depression than are adolescent boys.

4. Frank Talk about Gender Differences

Most gender differences are fairly small, which means that abilities for boys and girls overlap considerably. Also, despite the emphasis on gender differences, boys and girls are quite similar in many aspects of cognition, personality, and social behaviour.

13.3 Gender Identity

1. The Socializing Influences of People and the Media

Parents treat sons and daughters similarly, except in gender-related behaviour. Fathers may be particularly important in teaching about gender because they are more likely to treat sons and daughters differently. Teachers foster gender role learning by making gender salient.

By the preschool years, peers discourage cross-gender play by ridiculing peers who engage in this form of play. Peers also influence gender roles because children play almost exclusively with same-sex peers.

Television depicts men and women in a stereotyped fashion, and children who watch a lot of television are likely to have very stereotyped views of men and women.

2. Cognitive Theories of Gender Identity

Children gradually learn that gender is constant over time and cannot be changed according to personal wishes. After children understand that gender is constant, they begin to learn gender-typical behaviour. According to gender schema theory, children learn about gender by paying attention to behaviours of members of their own sex and ignoring behaviours of members of the other sex.

3. Biological Influences

The idea that biology influences some aspects of gender roles is supported by research on females exposed to male hormones during prenatal development.

13.4 Gender Roles in Transition

1. Androgyny and Emerging Gender Roles

Androgynous individuals embody both instrumental and expressive traits. Androgynous girls have higher self-esteem than traditional girls and are more likely to express themselves publicly; androgynous boys have about the same level of self-esteem as traditional boys.

2. Gender Neutrality: Beyond Traditional Gender Roles

Training studies show that children can learn less stereotyped views of gender, but studies of parents trying to rear gender-neutral children suggest that many stereotyped behaviours can be resistant to change.

Test Yourself

1. Instrumental traits, which are often associated with males, describe people who act on the world; _____ traits, which tend to be associated with females, describe people who value interpersonal relationships.

2. During the _____ years, children's knowledge of gender stereotypes expands to include personality traits.

3. By the middle elementary-school years, children know more gender stereotypes, but they also see stereotypes as _____.

4. Physically, boys tend to be stronger and more active; girls tend to have better fine-motor coordination and _____.

5. In the intellectual domain, boys often have greater spatial ability, but girls tend to have greater _____.

6. Girls do as well as boys in math in cultures where _____.

7. When boys are aggressive, it is usually physical; in contrast, the most common form of aggression with girls is _____.

8. In the domains of personality and social behaviour, girls are more sensitive emotionally, are _____, and are more prone to depression.

9. Although boys and girls differ in their average scores in several domains, it is also true that their scores _____.

10. _____ often respond to sons and daughters based on gender stereotypes, not based on knowledge of the individual child's needs.

11. Teachers contribute to gender-role learning by making gender salient in the classroom; peers contribute by _____.

12. Play is usually segregated by sex, in part because girls do not enjoy boys' rough-and-tumble play and because girls _____.

13. According to gender-schema theory, children first decide whether an object, activity, or behaviour is considered_____.

14. Girls exposed to large amounts of male hormones prefer masculine activities and _____.

15. Interventions designed to influence children's gender stereotypes show that it is fairly easy to change children's views of occupations but that children usually have same-sex friends and prefer _____.

Answers: (1) expressive; (2) elementary-school; (3) more flexible and not as obligatory; (4) to be healthier; (5) verbal ability; (6) males and females have comparable access to education, occupations, and political power; (7) relational; (8) more easily influenced by others (in part because they value group harmony); (9) overlap considerably; (10) Fathers; (11) being critical of peers who engage in gender-inappropriate play; (12) have an enabling style of play that is often ineffective with boys; (13) appropriate for males or females; (14) male playmates; (15) gender-stereotypic activities.

14

Social Influences

Oliveromg/Shutterstock

**Parenting and
Family Relationships**

**Peer Relationships
and Influences**

Influences of Society

Human beings are social animals—we live together with others of our kind. What are human society's influences upon a growing child? And how does the child influence those around him or her? In this chapter, we will look at social influences at three main levels: family, peers, and social institutions.

Family: What comes to mind when you think of family? Television gives us one answer: From *The Simpsons* to *Modern Family*, the North American family is often portrayed as having a mother, father, and their children. In reality, of course, Canadian families are as diverse as the people in them. Some families consist of a single parent and an only child, some consist of two same-sex partners and their children, and others include two parents, many children, and grandparents or other relatives. Canada's multicultural society gives us a number of additional factors to consider. As Kwak and Berry (2006) note, for Canada, "[I]t is inaccurate to talk about the family structure without considering various differences including culture of origin, immigration history, and socioeconomic background" (p. 286).

A common goal of families is nurturing children and helping them become full-fledged adult members of their culture and society. To learn how these goals are achieved, we'll begin, in **Module 14.1**, by looking at relationships within the family and see how families are changing in the 21st century. Then, in **Module 14.2**, we'll look at relationships with peers. Finally, in **Module 14.3**, we'll look at wider society—at the institutions that have an influence on children's lives.

14.1 Parenting and Family Relationships

OUTLINE

The Family as a System

Styles of Parenting

Parental Behaviour

Influences of the Marital System

Children's Contributions

The Impact of Divorce

Blended Families

The Role of Grandparents

Children of Gay and Lesbian Parents

Firstborn, Laterborn, and Only Children

Qualities of Sibling Relationships

Maltreatment and Its Consequences

Causes of Maltreatment

Preventing Maltreatment

LEARNING OBJECTIVES

1. How do parenting styles and parent behaviours affect children's development?

2. How do children help determine how parents rear them?

3. What are the effects upon children of different kinds of families?

4. How do sibling relationships change as children grow? What determines how well siblings get along?

5. What happens when parent-child relationships go awry?

Tanya and Sheila, both Grade 8 students, wanted to go to a Justin Bieber concert with two boys from their school. When Tanya asked if she could go, her mom said, "No way!" Tanya responded defiantly, "Why not?" In return, her mother exploded, "Because I say so. That's why. Stop pestering me." Sheila wasn't allowed to go either. When she asked why, her mom explained, saying, "I just think you're still too young to be dating. I don't mind your going to the concert. If you want to go just with Tanya, that would be fine. What do you think of that?"

Raise a cyber child and discover the world of parenthood at . . .

My **Virtual** Child

The vignette illustrates what we all know well from personal experience—parents go about childrearing in many different ways and children's responses can influence parents' behaviours. In this module, you'll learn about the different approaches parents take in raising children, and how children can affect parents; let's begin by thinking about parents as an important element in the family system.

The Family as a System

Families are rare in the animal kingdom. Only human beings and a handful of other species form family-like units. Why? Compared to the young in other species, children develop slowly. Because children are unable to care for themselves for many years, the family structure evolved as a way to protect and nurture young children during their development (Bjorklund, Yunger, & Pellegrini, 2002). Of course, modern families serve many other functions as well—they're economic units, and they provide emotional support—but childrearing remains the most salient and probably the most important family function.

As we saw in Module 1.2, in the systems view of families, parents and children influence each other, and parent-child relations are influenced by other individuals and institutions. In the remainder of this module, we'll describe parents' influences on children and then see how children affect their parents' behaviour.

Styles of Parenting

Parenting can be described in terms of general dimensions that are like personality traits in that they represent stable aspects of parental behaviour that remain across different situations, creating a characteristic manner or style in which parents interact with their children (Holden & Miller, 1999). When parenting is viewed in this way, two general dimensions of parental behaviour emerge. One is the degree of warmth and responsiveness that parents show their children. At one end of the spectrum are parents who are openly warm and affectionate with their children. They are involved with them, respond to their emotional needs, and spend considerable time with them. At the other end of the spectrum are parents who are relatively uninvolved with their children and, sometimes, even hostile toward them. These parents often seem more focused on their own needs and interests than those of their children. Warm parents enjoy hearing their children describe the day's activities; uninvolved or hostile parents are not interested, considering it a waste of their time. Warm parents know when their children are upset and try to comfort them; uninvolved or hostile parents pay little attention to their children's emotional states and invest little effort in comforting them when they are upset. As you might expect, children benefit from warm and responsive parenting (Pettit, Bates, & Dodge, 1997; Zhou et al., 2002).

A second general dimension of parental behaviour involves control, which comes in two forms (Grusec, 2011). Psychological control refers to parents' efforts to manipulate their children's emotional states by, for example, withdrawing their love or making children feel guilty. Behavioural control refers to parents' efforts to set rules for their children and to impose limits on what children can and cannot do. Some parents are dictatorial: They try to regulate every facet of their children's lives, like a puppeteer controlling a marionette. At the other extreme are parents who exert little or no control over their children: Their children do whatever they want without asking parents first or worrying about their parents' response. What is best for children is an intermediate amount of control in which parents set reasonable standards for their children's behaviour, expect their children to meet them, and monitor their children's behaviour (i.e., they usually know where their children are, what they are doing, and with whom). When parents have reasonable expectations for their children and keep tabs on their activity—for example, a mother knows that her 12-year-old is staying after school for choir practice, then going to the library—their children tend to be better adjusted (Kilgore, Snyder, & Lentz, 2000).

When the dimensions of warmth and control are combined, the result is four prototypic styles of parenting, as shown in Figure 14-1 (Baumrind, 1975, 1991).

- *Authoritarian parenting* **combines high control with little warmth.** These parents lay down the rules and expect them to be followed without discussion. Hard work, respect, and obedience are what authoritarian parents wish to cultivate in their children. There is little give-and-take between parent and child because authoritarian parents do not consider children's needs or wishes. This style is illustrated by Tanya's mother in the opening vignette, who feels no obligation whatsoever to explain her decisions.

- *Authoritative parenting* **combines a fair degree of parental control with being warm and responsive to children.** Authoritative parents explain rules and encourage discussion. This style is exemplified by Sheila's mother in the opening vignette. She explained why she did not want Sheila going to the concert and encouraged her daughter to discuss the issue with her.

- *Permissive parenting* **offers warmth and caring but little parental control.** These parents generally accept their children's behaviour and punish them infrequently. A permissive parent would readily agree to Tanya or Sheila's request to go to the concert, simply because it is something the child wants to do.

- *Uninvolved parenting* **provides neither warmth nor control.** Uninvolved parents provide for their children's basic physical and emotional needs but little else. These parents try to minimize the amount of time spent with their children and avoid becoming emotionally involved with them. Returning to the vignette, if Tanya or Sheila had uninvolved parents, they might have simply gone to the concert without asking, knowing that their parents would not care and would rather not be bothered.

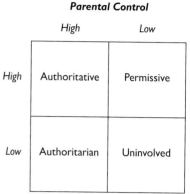

Figure 14-1 Interaction between the dimensions of warmth and control results in four parenting styles.

Research consistently shows that authoritative parenting is best for most children most of the time. Children with authoritative parents tend to be responsible, self-reliant, and friendly, and achieve higher marks in school (Amato & Fowler, 2002; Simons & Conger, 2007). A longitudinal study by Michael Pratt and colleagues from Wilfrid Laurier University in Waterloo, Ontario, found that an authoritative parenting style also fosters prosocial behaviour and moral values in adolescents, particularly in males (Pratt, Hunsberger, Pancer, & Alisat, 2003). Children with authoritarian parents, however, are often unhappy, have low self-esteem, and are often aggressive (e.g., Braza et al., 2014; Silk, Morris, Kanaya, & Sternberg, 2003; Zhou et al., 2008). Finally, children with permissive parents are often impulsive and have little self-control, while children with uninvolved parents often do poorly in school and are aggressive (Aunola, Stattin, & Nurmi, 2000; Driscoll, Russell, & Crockett, 2008).

It appears that parenting style is an important factor in the effectiveness of the family as a whole, too. Research by Allan McFarlane from McMaster University, Hamilton, Ontario, and his colleagues has shown that parental style is the most important influence on children's well-being when it was measured at adolescence. McFarlane, Bellissimo, and Norman (1995) surveyed 800 Grade 10 students in Hamilton schools on a number of variables, including depression, mother's and father's parenting style, behaviours, and family structure. Adolescent well-being, particularly lower depression ratings, was significantly linked to positive parenting styles. The authors concluded that parenting style had a strong influence on both adolescent well-being and a positive family environment (McFarlane et al., 1995). A more recent Canadian study, by researchers from McGill and Queen's universities further supports this link, with findings that family meals together, with good parent-adolescent communication, are associated with positive mental health in adolescence (Elgar, Craig, & Trites, 2013). Overall, then, the findings are that children typically thrive on a parental style that combines control, warmth, and affection.

VARIATIONS ASSOCIATED WITH CULTURE AND SOCIOECONOMIC STATUS. The general aim of childrearing—helping children become contributing members of their cultures—is much the same worldwide (Whiting & Child, 1953), and warmth and control are universal aspects of parents' behaviour. But views about the "proper" amount of warmth and the "proper" amount of control vary across cultures. European Canadians want their children to be happy and self-reliant individuals, and they believe these goals are best achieved when parents are warm and exert moderate control (Goodnow, 1992). In many countries, however, individualism is less important than cooperation and collaboration (Wang, Pomerantz, & Chen, 2007). In China, for example, emotional restraint and obedience are seen as the keys to family harmony (Chao, 2001). Consequently, parents in China often rely on an authoritarian style in which they are infrequently affectionate and expect their children to obey them without question (Lin & Fu, 1990; Zhou et al., 2008).

Another common pattern worldwide is for parents to be warm and controlling (Deater-Deckard et al., 2011). For example, Latino culture typically places greater emphasis on strong family ties and respecting the roles of all family members, particularly adults; these values lead parents to be more protective of their children and to set more rules for them (Halgunseth, Ispa, & Rudy, 2006). Thus, cultural values help specify culturally appropriate ways for parents to interact with their offspring.

Not only do parental styles vary *across* cultures, they vary *within* cultures, depending on parents' socioeconomic status. In North America, parents with lower socioeconomic status tend to be more controlling and more punitive—characteristics associated with the authoritarian parenting style—than are parents with higher socioeconomic status (Hoff-Ginsberg & Tardif, 1995). This difference may reflect educational differences that help to define socioeconomic status. Parents with higher socioeconomic status are, by and large, better educated and, consequently, often see development as a more complex process that requires the more nuanced and child-friendly approach that marks authoritative parenting (Skinner, 1985). Another contributing factor derives from an additional variable that defines socioeconomic status: income (Melby, Conger, Fang, Wickrama, & Conger, 2008). Because of their limited financial resources, parents with lower socioeconomic status often lead more stressful lives (e.g., they wonder whether they'll have enough money at the end of the month for groceries) and are far more likely to live in neighbourhoods where violence, drugs, and crime are commonplace. Thus, parents with lower socioeconomic status may be too stressed to invest the energy needed for authoritative parenting, and the authoritarian approach—with its emphasis on the child's immediate compliance—may actually protect children growing up in dangerous neighbourhoods (Parke & Buriel, 1998; Smetana, 2011).

These different styles are critical for understanding parenting, but there is more to effective childrearing, as we'll see in the next section.

Parental Behaviour

A *style* is a broad characterization of how parents typically behave. For example, if a parent is described as using an authoritarian style, you immediately have a sense of that parent's typical ways of interacting with his or her children. Nevertheless, the price for such a general description is that it tells us little about how parents behave in specific situations and how these parental behaviours influence children's development. Put another way, what specific behaviours can parents use to influence their children? Researchers who study parents name three: direct instruction, modelling, and feedback.

DIRECT INSTRUCTION. Parents often tell their children what to do, but simply playing the role of drill sergeant—"Clean your room!" "Turn off the TV!"—is not very effective. **A better approach is** *direct instruction,* **telling a child what to do, when, and why.** Instead of just shouting "Share your candy with your brother!" a parent should explain when and why it is important to share with a sibling.

In addition, just as coaches help athletes master sports skills, parents can help their youngsters master social and emotional skills. Parents can explain links between emotions and behaviour—"Caitlin is sad because you broke her crayon" (Gottman, Katz, & Hooven, 1996). They can also teach how to deal with difficult social situations—"When you ask Lindsey if she can sleep over, do it privately so you won't hurt Kaycee's or Hannah's feelings" (Mize & Pettit, 1997). In general, children who get this sort of parental "coaching" tend to be more socially skilled and, not surprisingly, get along better with their peers. (We'll have more to say about this in Module 14.2.)

By watching others (observational learning), children can learn behaviours that are expected (and may be rewarded) as well as behaviours that are considered inappropriate (and may lead to punishment).

LEARNING BY OBSERVING. Children learn a great deal from parents simply by watching them. For example, in Module 12.4, we saw that youngsters often learn how to interact with others by watching how their parents interact. *Observational learning* **can also produce** *counterimitation*—**learning what should not be done.** If an older brother like the one in the photo has been mean to a classmate and the father punishes him, the younger brother may learn to be friendly instead of mean.

Observational learning also likely contributes to intergenerational continuity of parenting behaviour from one generation to the next. For example, when parents use harsh physical punishment to discipline their children, these children tend to do the same when they are parents themselves (Bailey et al., 2009).

FEEDBACK. By giving feedback to their children, parents indicate whether a behaviour is appropriate and should continue or is inappropriate and should stop. Feedback comes in two general forms, which were explained in Chapter 1 when we discussed learning theories. *Reinforcement* **is any action that increases the recurrence of the response (behaviour) that it follows.** Parents may use praise to reinforce a child's studying or give a reward for completing household chores. *Punishment* **is any action that discourages the reoccurrence of the response (behaviour) that it follows.** Parents may forbid children to watch television when they get poor marks in school or may make children go to bed early for neglecting household chores.

QUESTION 14.1
When 10-year-old Dylan's family got a puppy, he agreed to walk it every day after school. But now when his mom asks him to do this, he gets angry because he'd rather watch TV. They argue for about 15 minutes, then Dylan's mom gives up and walks the dog herself—and Dylan goes back to watching TV. Analyze this situation. What could Dylan's mom do to prevent these regular arguments? *(Answer is on page 487.)*

Of course, parents have been rewarding and punishing their children for centuries, so what do psychologists know that parents do not know already? The most surprising discovery is that **parents often unwittingly reinforce the very behaviours they want to discourage, a situation called the** *negative reinforcement trap* (Patterson, 1980). This situation occurs in three steps, most often between a mother and her son. In the first step, the mother tells her son to do something he does not want to do. She might tell him to clean up his room, to come inside when he is outdoors playing with friends, or to study instead of watching television. In the next step, the son responds with some behaviour that most parents find intolerable: He argues, complains, or whines—not just briefly, but for an extended period. In the last step, the mother gives in—saying that the son does not need to do as she told him initially—simply to get the son to stop the behaviour that is so intolerable.

The feedback to the son is that arguing (or complaining or whining) works; the mother rewards that behaviour by withdrawing the request or command that the son did not like. That is, although we usually think a behaviour is strengthened when it is followed by the presentation of something that is valued, behaviour is also strengthened when it is followed by removing something that is disliked—basic negative reinforcement, in behaviouristic terms. As mentioned in Module 1.2, remember that in operant conditioning, reinforcement always leads to an increase in behaviour. The "negative" in negative reinforcement refers to taking away; it is not a value judgment. Thus, removing the unpleasant stimulus (the mother's nagging to clean up, for example) increases the likelihood of the behaviour (the son's noncompliance) reoccurring in a similar situation.

As for punishment, research shows that it works best when

- it is administered directly after the undesired behaviour occurs, rather than hours later;
- an undesired behaviour always leads to punishment, rather than usually or occasionally;
- it is accompanied by an explanation of why the child was punished and how punishment can be avoided in the future; and
- the child has a warm, affectionate relationship with the person administering the punishment.

At the same time, research reveals some serious drawbacks to punishment. One is that the impact of punishment is temporary, if children do not learn new behaviours to replace those that were punished. For example, denying TV to brothers who are fighting stops the undesirable behaviour, but fighting is likely to recur unless the boys learn new ways of solving their disputes.

A second drawback is that punishment can have undesirable side effects. Children become upset as they are being punished, which means they often miss the feedback that punishment is meant to convey. A child denied TV for misbehaving may become angry over the punishment itself and ignore why he is being punished.

Spanking illustrates the problems with punishment. As we saw in Module 12.4, physical punishment often leads children to behave aggressively; this has been found to be true in a range of countries that differ in their general approval of physical punishment (Gershoff et al., 2010). Although used by many parents around the world, spanking is ineffective in getting children to comply with parents and often leads them to be aggressive (Gershoff, 2013). And harsher forms of physical punishment are associated with a range of negative outcomes, including mental health problems, impaired parent-child relationships, and delayed cognitive development (Berlin et al., 2009; Gershoff & Bitensky, 2007). Because physical punishment is so harmful to children, many countries around the world (e.g., Costa Rica, the Netherlands, New Zealand, Spain) have banned it altogether (Global Initiative to End All Corporal Punishment of Children, 2011). Spanking also can lead to excessive use of physical punishment, which is the subject of the Maltreatment section later in this module.

One method combines the best features of punishment while avoiding its short-comings. **In** *time out,* **a child who misbehaves must briefly sit alone in a quiet, unstimulating location.** Some parents have children sit alone in a bathroom; others have children sit alone in a room, or in a corner, as shown in the photo. Time out is punishing because it interrupts the child's ongoing activity and isolates the child from other family members, toys, books, and, generally, all forms of rewarding stimulation.

The period is sufficiently brief—usually just a few minutes—for a parent to use the method consistently. During time out, both parent and child typically calm down. Then, when time out is over, a parent can talk with the child and explain why the punished behaviour is objectionable and what the child should do instead. Reasoning like this—even with preschool children—is effective because it emphasizes why a parent punished initially and how punishment can be avoided in the future.

You may have heard of time out, but what about "time in"? This is an alternative method in which the child is not isolated, but given attention focused on the problem behaviour. Time out can be seen by some young children as simply a form of punishment (Blaxall, 2008). **In** *time in* **the adult talks with the child immediately, to help them understand the situation and their own feelings.** This concept is gaining ground in Early Childhood Education (ECE) settings as a more positive alternative to the traditional time out.

Time out, in which children are isolated socially, is a particularly effective form of punishment.

These techniques can be taught to parents. Many meta-analyses document the effectiveness of programs that teach parenting skills (e.g., using positive reinforcement and using nonphysical punishment consistently), that promote good communication within families, and that make parents feel confident in their ability to be good parents. These kinds of intervention programs make parents feel more satisfied with their parenting, lead them to parent more effectively, and reduce children's behaviour problems (Brotman et al., 2011; Sanders & Kirby, 2014).

Thus, parents can influence children by direct instruction, by modelling behaviour that they value and not modelling what they do not want their children to learn, by giving feedback, and by adhering to the positive forms of the parenting styles that we examined in the first section of this module. In the next section, we'll explore a final, less direct way in which parents influence their children's development.

Influences of the Marital System

When Derek returns from shopping with chips and a six-pack of beer instead of diapers and baby food, Anita explodes in anger. "How could you? I used the last diaper an hour ago!" Huddled in the corner of the kitchen, their son Randy watches yet another episode in the daily soap opera that features Derek and Anita.

Although Derek and Anita are not arguing about Randy—in fact, they are so wrapped up in their conflict that they forget he is in the room—it is hard to conceive that a child would emerge unscathed from such constant parental conflict. Indeed, research shows that chronic parental conflict is harmful for children: When parents are constantly in conflict, children and adolescents often become anxious, withdrawn, and aggressive, and are more prone to chronic diseases and to be abusive in their own romantic relationships (Miller & Chen, 2010; Narayan, Englund, & Egeland, 2013; Rhoades, 2008). Parental conflict affects children's development through three distinct mechanisms. First, seeing parents fight jeopardizes a child's feeling that the family is stable and secure, making a child feel anxious, frightened, and sad. (Cummings, George, McCoy, & Davies, 2012; Davies, Cicchetti, & Martin, 2012). Second, chronic conflict between parents often spills over into the parent-child relationship. A wife who finds herself frequently arguing with and confronting her husband may adopt a similarly ineffective style in interacting with her children (Cox, Paley, & Harter, 2001). Third, when parents invest time and energy fighting with each other, they are often too tired or too preoccupied to invest themselves in high-quality parenting (Katz & Woodlin, 2002).

Of course, all marriages experience conflict at some point. Does this mean that all children bear at least some scars? Not necessarily. Many parents resolve conflicts in a manner that is constructive instead of destructive. To see this, suppose that one parent believes their child should attend a summer camp but the other parent believes it is too expensive and not worth it because the child attended the previous summer. Instead of shouting and name-calling (e.g., "You're always so cheap!") some parents seek mutually acceptable solutions: The child could attend the camp if she earns money to cover part of the cost, or the child could attend a different, less expensive camp. When families like the one in the photo routinely resolve disagreements this way, children actually respond *positively* to conflict, apparently because it shows that their family is cohesive and able to withstand life's problems (Goeke-Moray, Cummings, Harold, & Shelton, 2003). Youth exposed to this sort of constructive approach rely on it when solving conflicts in their peer and romantic relationships (Miga, Gdula, & Allen, 2012).

When parents resolve conflicts constructively, their children respond positively to conflict.

The extent of and resolution of conflict are obvious ways in which the parental system affects children, but they are not the only way. Many mothers and fathers form an effective parental team, working together in a coordinated and complementary fashion toward goals that they share for their child's development. For example, Mom and Dad may agree that their daughter is academically inclined and athletically skilled and that she should excel in both domains. Consequently, they are quite happy to help her achieve these goals. Mom gives her basketball tips, and Dad edits her school essays.

Not all parents work together well, however. Sometimes they do not agree on goals: One parent values sports over schoolwork, while the other reverses these priorities. Sometimes parents actively compete for their child's attention: Mom may want to take the child shopping, but Dad wants to take her to a ball game. Finally, parents sometimes act as gatekeepers, limiting one another's participation in parenting. Mom may feel that infant care is solely her area and may not allow Dad to participate. Dad may claim all school-related tasks and discourage Mom from getting involved.

These many examples show that, just as a doubles tennis team will not win many matches when each player ignores his or her partner, parenting is far less effective when parents try to "go it alone" instead of working together, collaborating as co-parents to

Jupiterimages/Stockbyte/Getty Images

achieve goals that they share, using methods that they both accept. Lack of teamwork, competition, and gatekeeping can lead to problems, causing children, for example, to become withdrawn and less likely to behave prosocially (McHale, Laurette, Talbot, & Pourquette, 2002; Scrimgeour, Blandon, Stifter, & Buss, 2013).

So far we've seen that to understand parents' impact on children's development, we need to consider the nature of the marital/partner relationship as well as parenting style and specific parenting behaviours (e.g., parents' use of feedback). In addition, forces outside the family can influence parenting and children's development. To illustrate, let's consider work-related influences. One such influence is a parent's job security: Children and adolescents lose self-esteem and find it difficult to concentrate in school when their parents become unemployed or, for that matter, when they simply worry that their parents might become unemployed (Barling, Zacharatos, & Hepburn, 1999; Kalil & Ziol-Guest, 2005).

Another well-known factor is work-related stress. Not surprisingly, when men and women lead stressful lives at work, they parent less effectively. Sometimes frazzled parents withdraw from family interactions. Over time, this gives the appearance that the parent is detached and disinterested, which makes children anxious and upset. And sometimes work-stressed parents are less accepting and less tolerant, leading to conflicts with their children (Crouter & Bumpus, 2001; Maggi et al., 2008).

Thus, a person's work life can profoundly affect children and adolescents by changing the parenting they experience. In Module 14.3, we'll look at another system-level influence on children: the neighbourhood where children live. For now, another way to view family systems in action is by switching perspectives and seeing how children affect parenting behaviour.

Children's Contributions

We emphasized earlier that the family is a dynamic, interactive system in which parents and children influence each other. In fact, children begin at birth to influence the way their parents treat them. Let's look at two characteristics of children that influence how parents treat them.

AGE. Parenting changes as children grow. The same parenting that is marvellously effective with infants and toddlers is inappropriate for adolescents. These age-related changes in parenting are evident in the two basic dimensions of parental behaviour—warmth and control. Warmth is beneficial throughout development—toddlers and teens alike enjoy knowing that others care about them. But the manifestation of parental affection changes, becoming more reserved as children develop. The enthusiastic hugging and kissing that delights toddlers embarrasses adolescents (Shanahan, McHale, Crouter, & Osgood, 2007).

Parental control also changes as children develop (Maccoby, 1984; Vazsonyi, Hibbert, & Snider, 2003). As children develop cognitively and are better able to make their own decisions, parents gradually relinquish control and expect children to assume more responsibility for themselves. And as children enter adolescence, they believe that parents have less authority to make decisions for them, especially in the personal domain (Darling, Cumsille, & Martínez, 2008). As noted, parents do gradually relinquish control—though sometimes not as rapidly as adolescents want them to—and increases in decision-making autonomy are associated with greater adolescent well-being (Qin, Pomerantz, & Wang, 2009; Wray-Lake, Crouter, & McHale, 2010).

TEMPERAMENT AND BEHAVIOUR. A child's temperament can have a powerful effect on parental behaviour (Brody & Ge, 2001). To illustrate the reciprocal influence of parents and children, imagine two preschoolers with different temperaments as they respond to a parent's authoritative style. The first child has an "easy" temperament, complying readily with parental requests and responding well to family discussions about parental expectations. These parent-child relations are a textbook example of successful authoritative parenting. But suppose, like the child in the photo, the second child has a "difficult" temperament and complies reluctantly and sometimes not at all. Over time, the parent becomes more controlling and less affectionate. The child in turn complies even less in the future, leading the parent to adopt an authoritarian parenting style (Bates et al., 1998; Paulussen-Hoogeboom, Stams, Hermanns, & Peetsma, 2007).

An example of the impact of children's behaviour on parents is that, when children respond to parents defiantly, their parents often resort to harsher forms of punishment.

As this example illustrates, parenting behaviours and styles often evolve as a consequence of the child's behaviour. With a moderately active young child who is eager to please adults, a parent may discover that a modest amount of control is adequate. But for a very active child who is not as eager to please, a parent may need to be more controlling and directive (Brody & Ge, 2001; Hastings & Rubin, 1999). Influence is reciprocal: Children's behaviour helps determine how parents treat them, and the resulting parental behaviour influences children's behaviour, which in turn causes parents to again change their behaviour (Choe, Olson, & Sameroff, 2013; Schermerhorn, Chow, & Cummings, 2010).

As time goes by, these reciprocal influences lead many families to adopt routine ways of interacting with each other. Some families end up functioning smoothly: Parents and children cooperate, anticipate each other's needs, and are generally happy. Unfortunately, other families do not do so well: Disagreements are common; parents spend much time trying unsuccessfully to control their children's defiant behaviour; and everyone is often angry and upset (Belsky, Woodworth, & Crnic, 1996; Kochanska, 1997). Still others are characterized by disengagement: Parents withdraw from each other and are not available to their children (Sturge-Apple, Davies, & Cummings, 2010). Over the long term, such troubled families do not fare well, so it's important that these negative reciprocal influences are dealt with early, as they arise (Carrere & Gottman, 1999; Christensen & Heavey, 1999).

The Impact of Divorce

The Canadian family has been changing steadily since the middle of the 20th century. First, people are older when they marry. In 1950, about half of all women in their early 20s were married, but by 2002, the figure was only 11%. In the early 1980s, average age on first marriage in Canada was 25.9 for women and 28.5 for men. In 2000, these figures were 31.7 and 34.3, respectively (Statistics Canada, 2004b). Second, families are smaller, having decreased from an average of four people in 1961 to three across the 2000s (Statistics Canada 2012a). In 1961, 16% of families—or one-sixth—consisted of six or more people; by 2001, this number was down to 2.6% (Statistics Canada, 2004b). Over the past 50 years, family structure in North America has changed. In Canada, the particular trends were to smaller families and more diverse families (Statistics Canada 2012b).

One example is that the increased divorce rate since the 1960s and the higher percentage of babies born to single mothers mean that more children are growing up in single-parent families (Children's Defense Fund, 2010; Statistics Canada, 2012b). In 2011, about 16% of Canadian families were single-parent families (Statistics Canada, 2012b). The most recent Canadian census included stepfamilies as a category for the first time; the census results showed that in 2011 just under 13% of Canadian families were stepfamilies (Statistics Canada, 2012c).

Because of these and other societal changes, today the family takes on many different forms in Canada and in other industrialized nations. Here we'll look at several of these forms and see how children develop within them. As we do, we'll look at the impact of divorce and the impact of marital conflict.

The parents of many Canadian youngsters divorce. The most recent figure available[1] is that in Canada, just over one-third (about 71 000) of marriages end in divorce every year (Statistics Canada, 2009c). According to all theories of child development, divorce is distressing for children because it involves conflict between parents and usually separation from one of them. Do the disruptions, conflict, and stress associated with divorce affect children? Of course they do. Having answered this easy question, many more difficult questions remain: Are *all* aspects of children's lives affected equally by divorce? *How* does divorce influence development? Why is divorce more stressful for some children than others?

WHAT ASPECTS OF CHILDREN'S LIVES ARE AFFECTED BY DIVORCE?

Hundreds of studies have been conducted on divorce, involving tens of thousands of preschool through college-age children. Comprehensive meta-analyses of this research reveal that in school achievement, conduct, adjustment, self-concept, and parent-child relations, children whose parents had divorced fared poorly compared to children from intact families (Amato, 2001; Amato & Keith, 1991; Lansford, 2009). However, the effects of divorce dropped from the 1970s to 1980s, perhaps because as divorce became more frequent in the 1980s, it became more familiar and less frightening. The effects of divorce increased again in the 1990s, perhaps reflecting a widening gap in income between single- and two-parent families (Amato, 2001).

When children of divorced parents become adults, the effects of divorce persist. As adults, children of divorce are more likely to experience conflict in their own marriages, to have negative attitudes toward marriage, and to become divorced themselves. They also report less satisfaction with life and are more likely to become depressed (Hetherington & Kelly, 2002; Segrin, Taylor, & Altman, 2005). These findings do not mean that children of divorce are destined to have unhappy, conflict-ridden marriages that inevitably lead to divorce, but children of divorce are at greater risk for such an outcome.

The first year following a divorce is often difficult for parents and children alike. But beginning in the second year, most children begin to adjust to their new circumstances (Hetherington & Kelly, 2002). Children adjust to divorce more readily if their divorced parents cooperate with each other, especially on disciplinary matters (Buchanan & Heiges, 2001). **In *joint custody*, both parents retain legal custody of the children.** Children benefit from joint custody if their parents get along well (Bauserman, 2002). Unfortunately, relatively few divorced couples get along well enough for joint custody to succeed; most divorced couples fight or simply ignore each other (Amato, Kane, & James, 2011).

ANSWER 14.1
This is a classic negative reinforcement trap: (1) Mom asks her son to do something, (2) he refuses and argues endlessly, and (3) Mom gives in to end the argument, thereby reinforcing the argumentative behaviour. Dylan's mom has a couple of alternatives. She could remind Dylan of the original agreement and hold fast to the rule that he can't watch TV until he's walked the dog. Maybe this rule isn't a good one any longer, however, for reasons that neither Dylan nor his mom could anticipate when they got the puppy. Then she and Dylan should talk about the agreement and find another way in which he can shoulder part of the responsibility of puppy care.

---

[1] Statistics Canada no longer updates this statistic, stating on its website "Note: 2008 is the last year for which Statistics Canada will provide information about divorces. The information will remain on the website, and it will not be updated" (Statistics Canada, 2016a).

When joint custody is not an option, mothers have traditionally been awarded custody; when this happens, children benefit when fathers remain involved in parenting (Fabricius & Luecken, 2007). In recent years, fathers have increasingly often been given custody, especially of sons. This practice coincides with findings that children often adjust better when they live with the same-sex parent: Boys often fare better with fathers and girls fare better with mothers (McLanahan, 1999). One reason boys are often better off with their fathers is that boys are likely to become involved in negative reinforcement traps (described earlier in this Module) with their mothers. Another explanation is that both boys and girls may forge stronger emotional relationships with same-sex parents than with other-sex parents (Zimiles & Lee, 1991). Analyzing available research for Statistics Canada, Bali Ram and Feng Hou of Ottawa concluded that some of the ideas about differential effects of divorce on boys and girls were largely myth. Boys and girls do react differently in some ways, however, with boys showing more externalized aggression and girls appearing more resilient to the stresses of family breakup, possibly due to the mother-daughter relationship (Ram & Hou, 2005). Others have argued, however, that this gender difference does not mean that girls are better at coping with parental divorce but that they present different problems. For example, girls tend more to depression (Adam & Chase-Lansdale, 2002; Hetherington, Bridges, & Insabella, 1998). It may be that a boy's "acting out" with aggression is obvious to see but a girl's "internalizing" of problems is simply less obvious. We should note that, though the overall risk of emotional and behavioural problems increases for those whose parents divorce, the majority of individuals are not at risk for long-term negative effects (Chase-Lansdale, Cherlin, & Kiernan, 1995).

HOW DOES DIVORCE INFLUENCE DEVELOPMENT?   Divorce usually results in several changes in family life that affect children (Amato & Keith, 1991). First, the absence of one parent means that children lose a role model, a source of parental help and emotional support, and a supervisor. For instance, a single parent may have to choose between helping one child complete an important paper or watching another child perform in a school play. Since she can't do both, one child will miss out.

Second, single-parent families often experience economic hardship, which creates stress and often means that activities once taken for granted are no longer available (Lansford, 2009). A single parent may no longer be able to afford books for pleasure reading, music lessons, or other activities that promote child development. Moreover, when a single parent worries about having enough money for food and rent, she has less energy and effort to devote to parenting.

Third, as we saw earlier in this module, conflict between parents is extremely distressing to children and adolescents (Leon, 2003), particularly for children who are emotionally insecure (Davies & Cummings, 1998). In fact, many of the problems ascribed to divorce are really caused by marital conflict occurring before the divorce (Amato, 2010; Shaw, Winslow, & Flanagan, 1999). Children whose parents are married but fight constantly often show many of the same effects associated with divorce (Katz & Woodin, 2002).

WHICH CHILDREN ARE MOST AFFECTED BY DIVORCE? WHY?   Some children are more affected by divorce than others. For example, children who are temperamentally more emotional tend to be more affected by divorce (Lengua, Sandler, West, Wolchick, & Curran, 1999). What's more, divorce is more harmful when it occurs during childhood and adolescence than during the preschool or college years (Amato & Keith, 1991), and the consequences differ for children and adolescents. Following divorce, children more often become anxious or develop behavioural problems, but adolescents more often do worse in school (Lansford et al., 2006).

Some children suffer more from divorce because of their tendency to interpret events negatively. We know from Module 12.4 that two children often have differing interpretations of exactly the same social event. Suppose, for example, that a father forgets to take a child on a promised outing. One child might believe that an emergency prevented the father from taking the child. A second child might believe that the father did not really want to spend time with the child in the first place and will never make similar plans again. Children who—like the second child—tend to interpret life events negatively are more likely to have behavioural problems following divorce (Mazur, Wolchick, Virdin, Sandler, & West, 1999).

Finally, children's efforts to cope with divorce-related stress can influence the impact of divorce. When children actively cope with their parents' divorce—either by trying to solve a problem or by trying to make it feel less threatening—they gain confidence in their ability to control future events in their lives. These efforts protect children from behavioural disorders such as anxiety or depression (Sandler, Tein, Mehta, Wolchick, & Ayers, 2000).

Just as children can reduce the harm from divorce by being active problem-solvers, parents can make divorce easier on their children. As we noted earlier, positive parenting styles can be more important than family constellation. Divorce causes major changes that are very stressful in children's lives, but there are a number of ways parents can make divorce less stressful for their children. Parents should

- explain together to children why they are divorcing and what their children can expect to happen;
- reassure children that they will always love them and will always be their parents; parents must back up these words with actions by remaining involved in their children's lives, despite the increased difficulty of doing so; and
- expect that their children will sometimes be angry or sad about the divorce; encourage children to discuss these feelings with them.

Parents should not

- compete with each other for their children's love and attention; children adjust to divorce best when they maintain good relationships with both parents;
- take out their anger with each other on their children;
- criticize their ex-spouse in front of the children; or
- ask children to mediate disputes; parents should work out problems without putting the children in the middle.

Following all these rules all the time is not easy. After all, divorce is stressful and painful for adults, too. But parents owe it to their children to try to follow these rules to minimize the disruptive effects of their divorce on their children's development.

Blended Families

Following divorce, most children live in a single-parent household for about five years. However, like the adults in the photo on the next page, more than two-thirds of men and women eventually remarry (Sweeney, 2010). **The resulting unit, consisting of a biological parent, stepparent, and children, is known as a** *blended family.* (Other terms for this family configuration are "remarried family" and "reconstituted family.")

Because mothers are more often granted custody of children, the most common form of blended family is a mother, her children, and a stepfather. Most stepfathers do

As divorce became more common in the 20th century, so did blended families, in which children live with a stepparent and sometimes with stepsiblings.

not participate actively in childrearing; they often seem reluctant to become involved (Clarke-Stewart & Bretano, 2005). Overall, becoming part of a blended family does not cause adjustment problems for children (Ryan & Claessens, 2013). Indeed, children typically benefit from the presence of a stepfather, particularly when he is warm and involved (King, 2006). Preadolescent girls, however, do not adjust readily to their mother's remarriage, apparently because it disrupts the intimate relationship they have established with her (Visher, Visher, & Pasley, 2003).

Adjusting to life in a blended family is more difficult when a stepfather brings his own biological children. In such families, parents sometimes favour their biological children over their stepchildren, being more involved with and warmer toward their biological children. Such preferential treatment almost always leads to conflict and unhappiness (Dunn & Davies, 2001; Sweeney, 2010). When the mother and stepfather argue, children usually side with their biological parents (Dunn, O'Connor, & Cheng, 2005).

The best strategy for stepfathers is to be interested in their new stepchildren but to avoid encroaching on established relationships. Newly remarried mothers must be careful that their enthusiasm for their new spouse does not come at the expense of time and affection for their children. And both parents and children need to have realistic expectations. The blended family can be successful and beneficial for children and adolescents, but it takes effort because of the complicated relationships, conflicting loyalties, and jealousies that usually exist (Sweeney, 2010; White & Gilbreth, 2001).

Over time, children adjust to the blended family. If the marriage is happy, most children profit from the presence of two caring adults. Nevertheless, when compared to children from intact families, children in blended families do less well in school and experience more symptoms of depression (Halpern-Meekin & Tach, 2008). Unfortunately, second marriages are slightly more likely than first marriages to end in divorce, particularly when stepchildren are involved (Teachman, 2008). This means that many children relive the trauma of divorce. Fortunately, effective programs are available to help members of blended families adjust to their new roles (Bullard et al., 2010). These emphasize effective co-parenting (described on pages 484–485) and, in particular, ways of dealing with the challenging behaviours children often display with stepparents. Such programs result in fewer problems with children and greater marital satisfaction.

The Role of Grandparents

With people living longer, three-generation families—child, parents, and grandparents—are becoming the norm in many industrialized nations. Although only about 5 percent of Canadian families have at least one grandparent living with other generations of family members (Statistics Canada, 2012a), most Canadian children see their grandparents at least once a month, more often if they live nearby. A small number of children in Canada, about 0.5 percent of all children, live in what are called "skip generation" families, meaning a family "with one or more grandparents where no parents were present" (Statistics Canada, 2012a, n.p.).

Grandmothers, especially maternal grandmothers, are usually more involved with grandchildren than grandfathers, and it has been suggested that this may be an evolutionary adaptation (Pollet, Netle, & Nelissen, 2007). That is, for most of human history, the onset of menopause has coincided, approximately, with the birth of grandchildren. Genetically speaking, middle-aged women may be more valuable in caring for their grandchildren—making sure that they survive to bear further children—than in bearing additional children of their own (Coall & Hartwig, 2011).

What roles do grandparents play in children's lives? One analysis suggests five specific styles of grandparenting (Mueller & Elder, 2003):

- *Influential grandparents* **are very close to their grandchildren, are very involved in their grandchildren's lives, and frequently perform parental roles, including discipline.**

- *Supportive grandparents* **are similar to influential grandparents—close and involved with grandchildren—but do not take on parental roles.**

- *Authority-oriented grandparents* **provide discipline for their grandchildren but otherwise are not particularly active in their grandchildren's lives.**

- *Passive grandparents* **are caught up in their grandchildren's development but not with the intensity of influential or supportive grandparents; they do not assume parental roles.**

- *Detached grandparents* **are uninvolved with their grandchildren.**

The first two grandparental roles—influential and supportive—are those in which grandparents are most involved with their grandchildren. Several factors determine whether grandparents assume these involved roles. Some factors are practical: Grandparents are more involved when they live near their grandchildren and when they have few rather than many grandchildren. Other factors concern grandparents' relationships with their children and their own grandparents: Grandparents are more concerned when their own children (i.e., the grandchildren's parents) encourage such involvement and when they knew their own maternal grandparent. Finally, the influential and supportive roles are more often taken by maternal grandparents than by paternal grandparents (Mueller & Elder, 2003). Obviously, no single factor determines the extent to which a grandparent takes an active role in a grandchild's development.

Not surprisingly, children and adolescents benefit from close ties with their grandparents. For example, children experience fewer emotional problems and are more prosocial when their grandparents are actively involved in childrearing (Attar-Schwartz, Tan, Buchanan, Fluri, & Griggs, 2009; Barnett, Scaramella, Neppl, Ontai, & Conger, 2010). Strong grandparent–grandchild relationships are particularly valuable when children and adolescents experience stress, such as that associated with divorce (Henderson, Hayslip, Sanders, & Louden, 2009): Strong relationships with grandparents are associated with better adjustment by children.

Grandparents are especially active in the lives of immigrant and minority children, often taking on parental roles (Hernandez, 2004; Minkler & Fuller-Thomson, 2005). The Cultural Influences feature describes the important role of grandmothers in Indigenous Peoples' family life.

By acting as surrogate parents, grandparents can affect their grandchildren's lives directly. However, grandparents also affect their grandchildren indirectly, through intergenerational transmission of parental attitudes and practices. For example, if parents are affectionate with their children, when these children become parents themselves, they will tend to be affectionate with their own children. In other words, the grandparents' affectionate behaviour results in their grandchildren experiencing affectionate care. In fact, the New Zealand longitudinal study by Belsky et al. (2005) on parenting style and

 QUESTION 14.2

Ollie, a four-year-old, sees his grandparents several times a week. They take him to preschool on Monday and Wednesday and try to do something special, such as getting an ice cream cone, each week. And they don't hesitate to remind him to say "please" and "thank you" and to wait his turn. What grandparental role best describes Ollie's grandparents? *(Answer is on page 494.)*

Cultural Influences

Grandmothers in Indigenous Families

Historically, in many Indigenous cultures grandparents were often involved in child-care and were integral members of families (Thompson, Cameron, & Fuller-Thomson, 2013). Although both grandmothers and grandfathers were held in great respect, the grandmother had a special place. Today, grandmothers are very often engaged in childcare and childrearing, both in the long and short term (Fuller-Thomson, 2005; Schweitzer, 1999). In Indigenous cultures, grandmothers are seen as powerful and nurturing. Often it is the grandmother who cares for the children, and it is she particularly who tells them the stories and teaches them skills that pass on their culture. In their description of a Métis women's circle, Leclair, Nicholson, and Hartley (2003) write of the contribution of their Elder: "Her contribution to the Circle includes sharing her cultural knowledge and her . . . experience" (p. 60). The extent of the grandmother's involvement depends on family circumstances and opportunities for involvement, but it is quite common for children to visit with their grandmother, particularly the maternal grandmother, for periods of time (Schweitzer, 1999). These arrangements are flexible, responding to changing needs: children may visit the grandmother, or she may stay with the family, or they may live separately and keep in touch (Thompson et al., 2013).

Indigenous grandmothers frequently adopt the role of influential grandparent (defined earlier in this module). When the daughter is a teenage mother, the grandmother may be the child's primary caregiver, an arrangement that benefits both the adolescent mother and the child. Freed from the obligations of childrearing, the adolescent mother is able to improve her situation by, for example, finishing school. The child benefits because grandmothers are often more effective mothers than teenage mothers: Grandmothers are less punitive and, like the grandmother in the photo, are very responsive to their grandchildren (Fuller-Thomson, 2005). The grandmother can also benefit, especially as she ages, from the assistance of the younger persons living with her (Schweitzer, 1999).

Traditionally in Indigenous cultures, women were leaders as much as men, and the wise older woman, a sort of "collective grandmother," was an important figure: "the women . . . were the leaders of our families, clans, communities and Nations" (Maracle, 2003, p. 73). Thus, although men might have formal leadership positions, women were often the ones with power. In this culture, women and men have particular, complementary duties. Women are seen as people with certain responsibilities, especially to the land, and childrearing is not necessarily their primary responsibility. For example, one woman was an important social activist for her people, and this role was regarded as a major responsibility. This woman's mother, the grandmother, cared for the social activist's children so that the activist could spend her time as an advocate for her people. The children did not feel deprived but rather grew up feeling proud that this strong woman leader came from their family (L. Sunseri, personal communication, April 17, 2007).

Even when grandmothers are not living in the house, children benefit when their mothers receive social and emotional support from grandmothers and other relatives.

Indigenous grandmothers often play an active role in rearing their grandchildren, which benefits the grandchildren.

Thus, grandmothers and other relatives can ease the burden of childrearing and benefit grandchildren by involving them in cultural activities and skills. Not surprisingly, children benefit from the added warmth, support, and guidance of an extended family.

Critical Thinking Questions: In what other ways do members of the extended family (aunts, uncles, cousins, and so on) have an influence on children? Are there cultural differences in the expectations about the influence of such family members?

attachment, noted in Module 10.3, showed just this outcome. Thus, it is important to think about the indirect as well as the direct influences that grandparents have on their grandchildren (Smith & Drew, 2002).

Children of Gay and Lesbian Parents

Many youngsters in North America have a gay or lesbian parent. In most of these situations, children were born in a heterosexual marriage that ended in divorce when one parent revealed his or her homosexuality. Less frequently, but becoming more common, children are born to single lesbians or to lesbian couples who have children through artificial insemination or adoption. In Canada, census figures revealed that, in 2009, approximately 1 percent of people identified themselves as homosexual (Statistics Canada, 2011b). With the passing of Bill C-38—a bill to legalize same-sex marriage—in 2005, Canada became the third country in the world (after the Netherlands and Belgium) to offer same-sex couples such recognition. Of course, many same-sex couples and their children were living as families before the legalization of same-sex unions, just as many heterosexual couples live together without marrying. However, same-sex partners can now marry in Canada, and following Bill C-38 many did so, formally establishing yet another form of family. The number of same-sex couples in Canada is increasing, though this is still a small percentage of the population at 0.8 percent of all couples (Statistics Canada, 2012b). As Fiona Nelson of the University of Calgary has noted, social services and family programs need to recognize these new varieties of families and their specialized needs (Nelson, 1999).

As parents, gay and lesbian couples are more similar to heterosexual couples than they are different, although lesbian and gay couples more often share child-rearing tasks evenly (Farr & Patterson, 2013). There is no indication that gay and lesbian parents are less effective parents than heterosexual parents. In fact, some evidence suggests that lesbian and gay couples may be especially warm and responsive to children's needs (Golombok et al., 2014).

Children reared by gay and lesbian parents seem to develop much like children reared by heterosexual couples (Golombok et al., 2003; Patterson, 2006). In fact, in research that directly pits the impact on children of family structure (heterosexual parents versus lesbian or gay parents) against family process variables (e.g., parental stress, parental discipline), process variables predict children's outcomes but family structure does not (Farr, Forssell, & Patterson, 2010; Golombok et al., 2014). For example, preschool boys and girls apparently identify with their own sex and acquire the usual accompaniment of gender-based preferences, interests, activities, and friends. As adolescents, most are heterosexual, although there is some evidence that daughters of lesbian mothers may be somewhat more likely to explore same-sex relationships (Gartrell, Bos, & Goldberg, 2011; Wainwright, Russell, & Patterson, 2004). In other respects—such as self-concept, social

Q&A **ANSWER 14.2**

Ollie's grandparents are best described as influential, because they're very involved in his life and because they take on parental tasks, including discipline.

skill, moral reasoning, and intelligence—children of lesbian mothers resemble children of heterosexual parents (Farr & Patterson, 2013; Patterson, 2006; Wainwright & Patterson, 2008). And, as is the case with heterosexual parents, children benefit from close relationships with warm, caring gay and lesbian parents (Farr et al., 2010; Wainwright & Patterson, 2008).

Research on children reared by gay and lesbian couples, along with findings concerning Indigenous grandmothers, reminds us that "good parenting" can assume many different forms. These research results also challenge the conventional wisdom that a two-parent family with mother and father both present *necessarily* provides the best circumstances for development. Multiple adults *are* important—that is evident from research on the impact of divorce on children—but *who* the adults are seems to matter less than what they do. Children benefit from good parenting skills, whether it is a mother and father, grandparents, or two women or two men doing the parenting.

Firstborn, Laterborn, and Only Children

For most of a year, all firstborn children are only children. Some children remain "onlies" forever, but most get brothers and sisters, particularly when firstborns are outgoing and smart (Jokela, 2010). Some firstborns are joined by many siblings in rapid succession; others are joined by just a single brother or sister. As the family acquires these new members, parent–child relationships become more complex (McHale, Updegraff, & Whiteman, 2013). Parents can no longer focus on a single child but must adjust to the needs of multiple children. Just as important, siblings influence each other's development, not just during childhood but throughout life. To understand sibling influence, let's look at differences among firstborns, laterborns, and only children.

Firstborn children are often "guinea pigs" for most parents, who have lots of enthusiasm but little practical experience rearing children. Parents typically have high expectations for their firstborns and are more affectionate more controlling, and more demanding with them (Furman & Lanthier, 2002). As more children arrive, parents become more adept at their roles, having learned "the tricks of the parent trade" with earlier children. With laterborn children, parents have more realistic expectations and are more relaxed in their discipline (e.g., Baskett, 1985).

The different approaches that parents take with their firstborns and laterborns help explain differences that are commonly observed between these children. Firstborn children generally have higher scores on intelligence tests and are more likely to go to university. They are also more willing to conform to parents' and adults' requests. Laterborn children, perhaps because they are less concerned about pleasing parents and adults but need to get along with older siblings, are more popular with their peers and more innovative (Beck, Burnet, & Vosper, 2006; Bjerkedal, Kristensen, Skjeret, & Brevik, 2007).

Blend Images/Shutterstock

Contrary to folklore, only children are not selfish and egotistical; instead, they tend to do well in school and often are leaders.

And what about only children? There is a popular view that parents such as the ones in the photo dote on the following page on onlies, with the result that the children are selfish and egotistical. Is the folklore correct? The answer is "No." Only children are more likely to succeed in school than other children and to have higher levels of intelligence and self-esteem, but don't differ in popularity, adjustment, and personality (Falbo & Polit, 1986; Falbo, 2012).

This research has important implications for China, where only children are the norm due to government efforts to limit family size. The Children's Lives feature tells the story.

Children's Lives

Assessing the Consequences of China's One-Child Policy

With more than a billion citizens, the People's Republic of China has the largest population of any country in the world. In the middle of the 20th century, Chinese leaders recognized that a large, rapidly growing population was a serious obstacle to economic growth and improvements in the standard of living. Consequently, the Chinese government implemented several programs to limit family size, and from 1979 to 2016 had a policy of one child per family. The policy was promoted with billboards, like the one in the photo, advertising the benefits of having only one child. Parents were encouraged to use contraceptives and, more importantly, one-child families received many economic benefits such as cash bonuses, better healthcare and childcare, and more desirable housing. As of January 1, 2016, the Chinese government abolished the one-child only policy, now allowing two children per family.

The one-child policy was effective in reducing the birth rate in China, and now social scientists are evaluating the outcomes of this policy on children and their families. For example, traditionally the Chinese have valued well-behaved children who get along well with others. Would the only children in today's China be less cooperative and more self-centred than previous generations of Chinese youngsters? Despite some newspaper stories of "Little Emperors"—demanding only children spoiled by being doted on by four grandparents and two parents (e.g., Jiaojiao, 2005)—the answer seems to be "No" (Hesketh, Zhou, & Wang, 2015). Many studies have compared only and non-only children in China; most comparisons find no differences. One of the few differences is that Chinese only children, like Western only children, are more successful in school (Falbo, 2012; Liu, Lin, & Chen, 2010).

As Chinese only children enter adulthood, a new concern will be care of the elderly. Traditionally, children have been responsible for their aging parents. This task becomes more demanding—financially and psychologically—when it cannot be shared with other siblings. Consequently, the Chinese government now encourages older parents and their adult children to sign a Family Support Agreement, which is a voluntary contract specifying the kinds and amounts of support that children will provide for their aging parents (Chou, 2011).

Critical Thinking Question: It is not only in China that families are now smaller. Around the world, fertility rates are declining, particularly in more developed countries. How might this affect us here in Canada?

Jeremy Sutton-Hibbert/Alamy Stock Photo

From 1979 to 2016, the Chinese government had a policy encouraging parents to have only one child. This policy was amended in 2016 to allow two children per family.

ADOPTED CHILDREN.   It is difficult to find official national statistics on adoptions within Canada. In an article from 1994 by Michael Sobol and Kerry Daly of the University of Guelph, the total number of domestic (within-Canada adoptions) was put at a little under 3000 in 1990, almost half the number of a decade previously. (Statistics Canada reports data by province and territory, rather than an overall figure.) In North America, the majority of adoptive parents are middle-class and of European descent and, until the 1960s, so were adopted children. However, improved birth control and legalized abortion in the late 1960s, and increasing acceptance of young mothers keeping their babies meant that hardly any European Canadian infants were relinquished for adoption, reflected in the drop in numbers noted by Sobol and Daly (1994). Consequently, beginning in the 1960s, parents began to adopt children of other races, as shown in the photo, and children from other countries. Figures for Canada show that over the past decade, international adoptions have remained fairly steady, at approximately 2000 per year (Statistics Canada, 2016b). At the same time, parents began to adopt children with special needs such as chronic medical problems or exposure to maltreatment (Brodzinsky & Pinderhughes, 2002; Gunnar, Bruce, & Grotevant, 2000).

Adopted children often experience adversity before being adopted. For example, children adopted from foster care have often experienced maltreatment that led them to be placed in foster care; many children adopted internationally were abandoned and lived in institutions prior to adoption. These circumstances aren't optimal for children's development, so it's not surprising that adopted children are at risk for many problems, including antisocial and aggressive behaviour, depression and anxiety, and learning problems (Grotevant & McDermott, 2014). However, outcomes are quite varied. Most adopted

children develop within the typical range. Problems are most likely when children are adopted after infancy and when their care before adoption was poor (e.g., they were institutionalized or lived in a series of foster homes). For example, the fall of the Ceauşescu regime in Romania in 1989 revealed hundreds of thousands of children living in orphanages under incredibly primitive conditions. Beginning in the 1990s, many of these children were adopted internationally. Some have shown remarkable catch-up growth, but many show multiple impairments, such as delayed cognitive development and disorders of attachment (Kreppner et al, 2007).

Thus, although adoption per se is not a fundamental developmental challenge for most children, quality of life before adoption certainly places some adopted children at risk. It is important to remember, however, that most adopted children fare well when they receive excellent care after adoption (Grotevant & McDermott, 2014). **Today, many adoptees and their parents wonder whether to have contact with the child's birth families, which is known as an** *open adoption.* Traditionally this practice was discouraged because of fear that it might lead children to be confused about their "real" parents. But such confusion does not surface in research: Youth who experience open adoptions are as well-adjusted as those who experience closed adoptions. Furthermore, youth in open adoptions have a deeper, more consistent identity as an adoptee, in part because open adoptions prompt conversations with parents about the nature of adoption (Grotevant, McRoy, Wrobel, & Ayers-Lopez, 2013).

In discussing firstborn, laterborn, only, and adopted children, we have not yet considered relationships that exist between siblings. These relationships can be powerful forces on development, as we'll see in the next section.

Beginning in the 1960s, interracial adoption became very common in North America.

Pascal Le Segretain/staff/Getty Images Entertainment/Getty Images

Qualities of Sibling Relationships

From the very beginning, sibling relationships are complicated. Expectant parents typically are excited by the prospect of another child, and their enthusiasm is contagious. Their children, too, eagerly await the arrival of the newest family member. However, the baby's arrival prompts varied responses. Some children are distressed, sad, and less responsive to parents, responses that are more common with younger children (Volling, 2012). Parents can minimize their older children's distress by remaining attentive to their needs (Howe & Ross, 1990).

Many older siblings enjoy helping their parents take care of newborns. Older children play with the baby, console it, feed it, or change its diapers. In middle-class Western families, such caregiving often occurs in the context of play, with parents nearby. In some cultures, however, children—particularly girls like the one in the photo—play an important role in providing care for their younger siblings (Zukow-Goldring, 2002).

As the infant grows, interactions between siblings become more frequent and more complicated. For example, toddlers tend to talk more to parents than to older siblings. But, by the time the younger sibling is four years old, the situation is reversed. Now young siblings talk more to older siblings than to their mother (Brown & Dunn, 1992). Older siblings become a source of care and comfort for younger siblings who are distressed or upset (Kim, McHale, Crouter, & Osgood, 2007; Gass, Jenkins, & Dunn, 2007), and older siblings serve as teachers for their younger siblings, teaching them to play games or how to cook simple foods (Maynard, 2002). Finally, when older children do well in school and are popular with peers, younger siblings often follow suit (Brody, Kim, Murry, & Brown, 2003).

As time goes by, some siblings grow close, becoming best friends in ways that nonsiblings can never be. Other siblings constantly argue, compete, and simply do not get along with each other. The basic pattern of sibling interaction seems to be established early in development and remains fairly stable (Kramer, 2010). In general, siblings who get along as preschoolers continue to get along as young adolescents, but siblings who quarrel as preschoolers often quarrel as young adolescents (Dunn, Slomkowski, & Beardsall, 1994).

Why are some sibling relationships filled with love and respect, but others are dominated by jealousy and resentment? What factors contribute to the quality of sibling relationships? First, children's sex and temperament matter. Sibling relations are more likely to be warm and harmonious between siblings of the same sex than between siblings of the opposite sex (Dunn & Kendrick, 1981) and when neither sibling is temperamentally emotional (Brody, Stoneman, & McCoy, 1994). Age is also important: Sibling relationships generally improve as the younger child approaches adolescence because siblings begin to perceive one another as equals (Kim et al., 2007; McHale et al., 2013).

Parents contribute to the quality of sibling relationships, both directly and indirectly (Brody, 1998). The direct influence stems from parents' treatment. Siblings more often get along when they believe that parents have no "favourites" but treat all siblings fairly (McGuire & Shanahan, 2010). When parents lavishly praise one child's accomplishments while ignoring another's, children notice the difference and their sibling relationship suffers (Updegraff, Thayer, Whiteman, Denning, & McHale, 2005).

This doesn't mean that parents must treat all their children the same. Children understand that parents treat their kids differently—based on their age or personal needs. Only when differential treatment is not justified do sibling relationships deteriorate (Kowal &

In many developing countries, older siblings are actively involved in caring for their younger siblings.

Jamie Marshall/Tribaleye Images/Alamy Stock Photo

QUESTION 14.3

Calvin, age eight, and his younger sister, Hope, argue over just about everything and constantly compete for their parents' attention. Teenage sisters Hilary and Elizabeth love doing everything together and enjoy sharing clothes and secrets about their teen romances. Why might Calvin and Hope get along so poorly but Elizabeth and Hillary get along so well? *(Answer is on page 499).*

Kramer, 1997). In fact, during adolescence, siblings get along better when each has a unique, well-defined relationship with parents (Feinberg, McHale, Crouter, & Cumsille, 2003).

The indirect influence of parents on sibling relationships stems from the quality of the parents' relationship with each other: A warm, harmonious relationship between parents fosters positive sibling relationships. Conflict between parents is associated with conflict between siblings, although intense marital conflict sometimes leads siblings to become closer, as they support each other emotionally (McHale et al., 2013).

One practical implication of these findings is that in their pursuit of family harmony (what many parents call "peace and quiet"), parents can influence some of the factors affecting sibling relationships but not others. Parents can help reduce friction between siblings by being equally affectionate, responsive, and caring with all of their children and by caring for one another. And they can encourage the sorts of behaviours that promote positive sibling relationships, including being engaged in mutually enjoyable activities, being supportive of each other, and appreciating their shared experiences (Kramer, 2010). At the same time, some dissension is natural in families, especially those with young boys and girls: Children's different interests lead to arguments, like the one in the photo. Faced with common simple conflicts—Who decides which TV show to watch? Who gets to eat the last cookie? Who gets to hold the new puppy?—a three-year-old brother and a five-year-old sister *will* argue because they lack the social and cognitive skills that allow them to find mutually satisfying compromises.

When siblings do fight—particularly young children—parents should intervene. When parents explain one sibling's behaviour to another (e.g., "He covered his eyes because he was scared"), siblings have more positive interactions (Kojima, 2000). And by helping their children settle differences, parents show children more sophisticated ways to negoti-

Preschool children often argue because they lack the social skills to settle disagreements in a mutually beneficial manner.

ate; later, children often try to use these techniques themselves instead of fighting (McHale et al., 2013). Research by Avigail Ram and Hildy Ross of the University of Waterloo supports this view. Ram and Ross (2001) had pairs of siblings divide up a set of six toys between them. Mostly the children used negotiation to resolve disputes, although conflict could arise. Even in conflict situations, however, "the children did not revert to extremely hostile moves" (Ram & Ross, 2001, p. 1720). Parents especially need to intervene when conflicts do escalate to the point that siblings are acting aggressively, yelling or swearing, or making denigrating comments. Obviously, parents need to protect their children from each other in the immediate situation. More importantly, though, if left unchecked, over time such conflicts can lead to behaviour problems (Garcia, Shaw, Winslow, & Yaggi, 2000).

Fortunately, parents can be shown how to mediate siblings' disputes. Smith and Ross (2007) administered brief training—90 minutes—in which parents were shown how to have children (1) identify points of agreement and disagreement, (2) discuss what they want to achieve (i.e., their goals for the situation), and (3) think of ways to resolve their dispute. After parents know how to mediate, siblings are better able to resolve conflicts successfully, and in doing so, they are more likely to talk calmly (instead of arguing), listen, apologize, and explain their actions. Thus, parents need not listen to their children argue endlessly; instead, they can show them social and problem-solving skills that will help them solve their conflicts successfully.

Maltreatment and Its Consequences

Maltreatment comes in many forms (Cicchetti & Toth, 2006). The two that often come to mind first are physical abuse involving assault that leads to injuries, and sexual abuse

Andrew Lam/Shutterstock

involving fondling, intercourse, or other sexual behaviours. Another form of maltreatment is neglect—not giving children adequate food, clothing, or medical care. Children can also be harmed by psychological abuse—ridicule, rejection, and humiliation (Wicks-Nelson & Israel, 2006).

The frequency of these various forms of child maltreatment is difficult to estimate because so many cases go unreported. In 2001, the Public Health Agency of Canada launched the Canadian Incidence Study of Reported Child Abuse and Neglect (CIS). The most recent cycle of this study for which there is a report available occurred in 2008, and the results show that the estimated incidence of child maltreatment in Canada increased to about 19 per 1000 children in 2003, up from about 9 per 1000 in 1998 (Public Health Agency of Canada, 2010). This statistic is not as bad as it might seem, however, given that it is believed that the increase reflects improved reporting of incidences of maltreatment, rather than an absolute increase in abuse. Data from 2008 show a slight drop in incidence, at about 16 per 1000 children. According to the CIS 2010 report, 34% of the cases involved neglect, another 34% involved exposure to domestic violence, 20% involved physical abuse, 9% involved emotional maltreatment, and 3% involved sexual abuse. Here we'll begin by looking at the consequences of maltreatment, then look at some causes, and, finally, examine ways to prevent maltreatment.

You probably aren't surprised to learn that the prognosis for youngsters exposed to maltreatment is not very good. Some, of course, suffer permanent physical damage. Even when there is no lasting physical damage, children's social and emotional development is often disrupted. They tend to have poor relationships with peers, often because they are too aggressive (Alink et al., 2012; Appleyard, Yang, & Runyan, 2010). Their cognitive development and academic performance are also disturbed. Abused youngsters typically get lower marks in school, score lower on standardized achievement tests, and are more frequently retained in a grade rather than promoted. Also, school-related behaviour problems such as being disruptive in class are common, in part because maltreated children are often socially unskilled, do not regulate their emotions well, and don't recognize others' emotions accurately (Burack et al., 2006; Kim-Spoon, Cicchetti, & Rogosch, 2013; Luke & Banerjee, 2013).

Harriet MacMillan of McMaster University and her colleagues have found that psychological and emotional abuse have extensive negative effects. A report for the American Academy of Pediatrics, co-authored by MacMillan, stated that these forms of abuse "may be the most challenging and prevalent forms of child abuse" (Hibbard, Barlow, MacMillan & the Committee on Child Abuse and Neglect and American Academy of Child and Adolescent Psychiatry Child Maltreatment and Violence Committee, 2012, p. 372). Abuse of any kind often leads children and adolescents to become depressed (Appleyard et al., 2010; Harkness, Lumley, & Truss, 2008). Adults who were abused as children often experience emotional problems such as depression or anxiety, are more prone to think about or attempt suicide, and are more likely to abuse spouses and their own children (Malinosky-Rummell & Hansen, 1993). In short, when children are maltreated, the effects are usually widespread and long lasting.

RESILIENCE. Although the overall picture is bleak, some children are remarkably resilient to the effects of abuse. In other words, in a group of children and adolescents who have been abused, many will show some (or all) of the consequences that we've just described. But for a handful, the impact of abuse is much reduced. Why are some children protected from the damaging effects of abuse but others are vulnerable?

One factor that protects children is their *ego-resilience,* **which denotes children's ability to respond adaptively and resourcefully to new situations.** The effects of abuse tend to be smaller when children are flexible in responding to novel and challenging

ANSWER 14.3
There are two obvious reasons why Elizabeth and Hilary get along better than Calvin and Hope. First, they are both girls, and same-sex sibs tend to have better relationships. Second, they are both adolescents and sibling relationships tend to improve during these years.

QUESTION 14.4
Kevin has never physically abused his 10-year-old son Alex, but he constantly torments Alex emotionally. For example, when Alex got an F on a spelling test, Kevin screamed, "I skipped the hockey game just to help you, but you still flunked. You're such a dummy." When Alex began to cry, Kevin taunted, "Look at Alex, crying like a baby." These interactions occur nearly every day. What are the likely effects of such repeated episodes of emotional abuse? *(Answer is on page 505.)*

social situations (Flores, Cicchetti, & Rogosch, 2005). Another protective factor is being engaged in school. When maltreated children are cognitively engaged in school—that is, they pay attention, complete tasks, and are well organized—they are less prone to antisocial and aggressive behaviour (Pears, Kim, Fisher, & Yoerger, 2013).

Of course, even better than reducing the impact of maltreatment would be to prevent it altogether. To do that, we need to know more about the causes of maltreatment, our next topic.

Causes of Maltreatment

Why would a parent abuse a child? Maybe you think parents would have to be severely disturbed to harm their own flesh and blood. Not really. The vast majority of abusing parents are not suffering from any specific mental or psychological disorder (Wolfe, 1985). Instead, a host of factors put some children at risk for abuse and protect others; the number and combination of factors determine if the child is a likely target for abuse (Cicchetti & Toth, 2006). Let's look at three of the most important factors: cultural context and community, the parents, and the children themselves.

CULTURE AND COMMUNITY.   The most general category of contributing factors has to do with cultural values and the social conditions of the community in which parents rear their children. For example, a culture's view of physical punishment may contribute to child maltreatment. Many countries in Europe and Asia have strong cultural prohibitions against physical punishment. It simply isn't done and would be viewed in much the same way we would view Canadian parents who punished their children by not feeding them for a few days. In many countries, including Austria, Croatia, Germany, Israel, and Sweden, spanking is against the law. But the scene in the photo on the next page, a father using physical punishment with his child, is more common in Canada. Unlike in Sweden, in Canada, spanking children is still legal. Section 43 of the Canadian Criminal Code allows physical discipline with use of force against a child, provided the force is what would be considered reasonable (Justice Canada, n.d.). Challenges to this section of the Criminal Code led to some qualification of what is considered "reasonable" (e.g., no hitting a child under the age of two, no use of belts or other instruments), but the section has been upheld (Durrant, 2006; Ontario Association of Children's Aid Societies, 2000). Spanking also has a certain amount of public support; one newspaper poll found that 42 percent of Canadians "believe spanking is beneficial to a child's development" (Logan, 2007, p. L3), while 37 percent do not support this view. This figure is of interest given that countries that do not condone physical punishment tend to have lower rates of child maltreatment (OECD, 2013) and that most physical abuse in Canada "takes place in a punitive context" (Durrant, 2006, p. 2). We noted earlier that spanking seems ineffective as a punishment, and the mounting evidence that any form of physical punishment has long-term negative effects has led to psychological and medical professional organizations taking a stand against its use. The *Canadian Medical Association Journal* (*CMAJ*) published an overview of 20 years of research that concluded that there is no valid reason for use of physical punishment and that its use is often detrimental to children (Durrant & Ensom, 2012). Another study by researchers from Manitoba and Ontario, using data from almost 35 000 adults in the United States, found that physical punishment in childhood (including hitting, grabbing, or spanking) was linked to later mental disorders such as mood disorders, anxiety, phobias, and drug and alcohol abuse (Affi, Mota, Dasiewicz, MacMillan, & Sareen, 2012). Although some parents still believe that physical punishment has its uses, it would appear that, as proposed in a *CMAJ* editorial, regardless of the moral aspect (i.e., is it right or wrong?) the research evidence shows that physical punishment of children is simply ineffective and in fact often actively harmful (Fletcher, 2012). As Dr. John Fletcher of the *CMAJ* noted, the time has come change our societal attitudes, and to teach parents to use "[p]ositive parenting, not physical punishment" (Fletcher, 2012, p. 1339).

In addition to cultural values, the communities in which children live can put them at risk for maltreatment and abuse. Living in poverty is one important risk factor: Maltreatment is more common in families living in poverty, in part because lack of money increases the stress of daily life (Duncan & Brooks-Gunn, 2000). When parents are worrying about whether they can buy groceries or pay the rent, they are more likely to punish

Child abuse is more common in countries that condone use of physical punishment.

their children physically instead of making the extra effort to reason with them. Similarly, abuse is more common among military families when a soldier is deployed in a combat zone (Gibbs, Martin, Kupper, & Johnson, 2007). In this case, maltreatment may be rooted in stress stemming from concern over the absent parent and temporary single parenthood.

A second risk factor is social isolation: Abuse is more likely when families are socially isolated from other relatives or neighbours, because isolation deprives children of adults who could protect them and deprives parents of social support that would help them cope with life stresses (Coulton, Crampton, Irwin, Spilsbury, & Korbin, 2007).

Cultural values and community factors clearly contribute to child abuse, but they are only part of the puzzle. After all, although maltreatment is more common among families living in poverty, it does not occur in a majority of these families, and it does occur in middle-class families too. Consequently, we need to look for additional factors to explain why abuse occurs in some families but not others.

PARENTS.   Faced with the same cultural values and living conditions, why do only a handful of parents abuse or mistreat their children? Which characteristics increase the odds that a parent will abuse his or her children? Child-development researchers have identified several important factors (Berlin, Appleyard & Dodge, 2011; Bugental & Happaney, 2004). First, parents who maltreat their children often were maltreated themselves, which may lead them to believe that abuse is simply part of childhood. This does not mean that abused children inevitably become abusing parents—only about one-third do—but a history of child abuse clearly places adults at risk for mistreating their own children (Berlin et al., 2011; Cicchetti & Toth, 2006). Second, parents who mistreat their children often use ineffective parenting techniques (e.g., inconsistent discipline), have such unrealistic expectations that their children can never meet them, and often believe that they are powerless to control their children. For example, when abusive parents do not get along with their children, they often consider this due to factors out of their control, such as children having a difficult temperament or being tired that day; they are less likely to think that their own behaviour contributed to unpleasant interactions. Third, in families where abuse occurs, the couple's interactions are often unpredictable, unsupportive, and unsatisfying for both parents. In other words, mistreatment of children is simply one symptom of family dysfunction. This marital discord makes life more stressful and makes it more difficult for parents to invest effort in childrearing.

CHILDREN'S CONTRIBUTIONS. To place the last few pieces in the puzzle, we must look at the abused children themselves. Our discussion of reciprocal influence between parents and children earlier in this module should remind you that children may inadvertently, through their behaviour, bring on their own abuse (Sidebotham, Heron, & ALSPAC Study Team, 2003). In fact, infants and preschoolers are abused more often than older children. Why? Because they are easier targets of abuse and they are less able to regulate aversive behaviours that elicit abuse. You've probably heard stories about a parent who shakes a baby to death because the baby wouldn't stop crying. Because younger children are more likely to cry or whine excessively—behaviours that irritate all parents sooner or later—they are more likely to be the targets of abuse.

For much the same reason, children who are chronically ill or who suffer disabilities like those described in Module 8.3 are more often abused (Govindshenoy & Spencer, 2007; Sherrod, O'Connor, Vietze, & Altemeier, 1984). When children are sick, they are more likely to cry and whine, annoying their parents. Also, when children are sick or disabled, they need extra care, which can mean additional expense. By increasing the level of stress in a family, sick children can inadvertently become the targets of abuse.

Stepchildren form another group at risk for abuse (Archer, 2013). Just as Cinderella's stepmother doted on her biological children but abused Cinderella, so stepchildren are more prone to be victims of abuse and neglect than are biological children. Adults are less invested emotionally in their stepchildren, and this lack of emotional investment leaves stepchildren more vulnerable.

Obviously, in all of these instances, children are *not* at fault and do not deserve the abuse. Nevertheless, normal infant or child behaviour can provoke anger and maltreatment from some parents.

Thus, many factors, summarized in the Summary Table, contribute to child maltreatment. Any single factor will usually not result in abuse; maltreatment is more likely when risk factors start to add up.

Preventing Maltreatment

The complexity of child abuse dashes any hopes for a simple solution (Kelly, 2011). Because maltreatment is more apt to occur when several contributing factors are present, eradicating child maltreatment would entail a massive effort. North American attitudes toward

SUMMARY TABLE	
FACTORS THAT CONTRIBUTE TO CHILD ABUSE	
General Category	**Specific Factor**
Cultural and community contributions	Abuse is more common in cultures that tolerate physical punishment.
	Abuse is more common when families live in poverty because of the stress associated with inadequate income.
	Abuse is more common when families are socially isolated because parents lack social supports.
Parents' contributions	Parents who abuse their children were often maltreated themselves as children.
	Parents who abuse their children often have poor parenting skills (e.g., unrealistic expectations, inappropriate punishment).
Children's contributions	Young children are more likely to be abused because they cannot yet regulate their behaviour.
	Sick children are more likely to be abused because their behaviour while ill is often perceived as aversive.
	Stepchildren are more likely to be abused because stepparents are less invested in their stepchildren.

"acceptable" levels of punishment and poverty would have to change. North American children will be abused as long as physical punishment is considered acceptable, and as long as poverty-stricken families live in chronic stress from simply trying to provide food and shelter. Parents also need counselling and training in parenting skills. Abuse will continue as long as parents remain ignorant of effective methods of parenting and discipline.

It would be naïve to expect all of these changes to occur overnight. However, by focusing on some of the more manageable factors, the risk of maltreatment can be reduced. Social supports help. When parents know they can turn to other helpful adults for advice and reassurance, they better manage the stresses of childrearing that might otherwise lead to abuse. Families also can be taught more effective ways of coping with situations that might otherwise trigger abuse (Wicks-Nelson & Israel, 2006). Through role-playing sessions, parents can learn the benefits of authoritative parenting and effective ways of using feedback and modelling (described earlier in this module) to regulate children's behaviour.

Providing social supports and teaching effective parenting are typically done when maltreatment and abuse have already occurred. Of course, preventing maltreatment in the first place is more desirable and more cost-effective. For prevention, one useful tool is familiar: early childhood intervention programs. Maltreatment and abuse can be cut in half when families participate for two or more years in intervention programs that include preschool education along with family support activities aimed at encouraging parents to become more involved in their children's education (Reynolds & Robertson, 2003). When parents participate in these programs, they become more committed to their children's education. This leads their children to be more successful in school, reducing a source of stress and enhancing parents' confidence in their child-rearing skills, and reducing the risks of maltreatment in the process.

Another successful approach focuses specifically on parenting skills in families where children are at risk for maltreatment. In one program (Bugental & Schwartz, 2009), mothers of infants at risk for abuse (due to medical problems at birth) participated in an extensive training program in which they learned to identify likely causes of problems associated with recurring problems encountered while caring for their babies (e.g., problems associated with feeding, sleeping, crying). They were then given help in devising methods to deal with those problems and in monitoring the effectiveness of the methods. When mothers participated in the program, they were less likely to use harsh punishment (a known risk factor for child maltreatment), and their children were less likely to suffer injuries at home (a common measure of parental neglect).

So, education of parents can begin even at the very start of the child's life, when the baby is born. This type of intervention is the subject of the Focus on Research feature.

Focus on Research

Education of Parents to Prevent Child Abuse

Who were the investigators, and what was the aim of the study? Given that many parents who harm their children do not set out intending to do so, it would make sense to educate parents about situations that might put them at risk of abusing their children. Shaken baby syndrome is a specific set of injuries that occur after a baby is shaken. Any injuries to the brain are a serious matter, and those caused by shaking can even lead to death of the infant. Ronald Barr and colleagues from the Centre for Community Child Health Care and the Child and Family Research Institute at the University of British Columbia and from the BC Children's Hospital in Vancouver, investigated whether educational materials could change caregiver behaviours that can contribute to shaken baby syndrome.

How did the investigators measure the topic of interest? Mothers of newborns were asked to keep a diary about their baby's behaviour across one day, and maternal knowledge about crying behaviour and effects of shaking were measured with a questionnaire. Half of the mothers were given educational materials, developed by the National Centre on Shaken Baby Syndrome, which explained "the Period of PURPLE." Each letter in the word PURPLE stands for an aspect of infant crying that frustrates caregivers and places the baby at risk of negative caregiver actions: P for Peak pattern, U for Unexpected, R for Resistance to soothing, P for a Pain-like look on the baby's face, L for Long bout of crying, and E for late afternoon and Evening timing. The materials explained these aspects of infant crying, acknowledged that they can be frustrating, and gave guidelines for dealing with a crying infant. Mothers received either the educational materials or a control package of general information on infant safety. Brochures and DVDs with the two types of information were given to mothers within two weeks of giving birth. All mothers in the study completed the Baby's Day diary at five weeks postpartum and the questionnaire at eight weeks.

Who were the participants in the study? Mothers of healthy, full-term infants were contacted at hospitals in Vancouver, B.C., about participating in the study. Over 1200 agreed to participate and were randomly assigned to either the Period of PURPLE educational materials group or the control group.

What was the design of the study? The overall design was experimental. The independent variable was the materials assigned to the mother. The dependent variable was the change in mother's knowledge about infant crying behaviour and about recommended responses to inconsolable crying.

Were there ethical concerns with the study? No, there were no ethical concerns with the study. Mothers were not being asked to do anything differently at home.

What were the results? Knowledge about infant crying and about possible behaviours, such as walking away when frustrated, were higher in mothers who had received the Period of PURPLE materials. The mothers in this group were also more likely to share such knowledge with others; useful, in that this might be passed on then to fathers also (only mothers were taking part in the study). Mother's knowledge of the dangers of shaking was high in both groups and did not differ significantly after the study.

What did the investigators conclude? Barr et al. (2009) noted that although their study was not designed to show whether educational materials would reduce incidence of shaken baby syndrome, they could conclude that the research results, at least, showed some caregiver behaviours could be changed. Changing caregiver behaviours could then result in reduction of incidence of shaken baby syndrome.

What converging evidence would strengthen these conclusions? The researchers concluded that materials given to parents around the time of the birth of their baby could increase parental knowledge and change behaviours. Furthering this kind of education could lead to a reduction in incidence of shaken baby syndrome. Now that this has been shown to be possible, larger scale studies could be run, and the Period of PURPLE materials become part of regular clinical practice. Outcomes could be measured longitudinally and statistics examined to see if the number of infants injured by shaking becomes reduced.

Critical Thinking Question: It would seem that the Period of PURPLE materials should be given out to all new parents or caregivers of babies. In what other ways might this information be propagated?

There are also effective programs targeting parents of older children who are at risk for maltreatment. One program, Parent-Child Interaction Therapy, focuses on (1) helping parents to build warm and positive relationships with their children, and (2) developing reasonable expectations for their children and using more effective disciplinary practices. When parents of at-risk children participate in this program, they report less stress, their behaviour with their children becomes more positive (more praise and fewer commands) and, critically, suspected abuse is less (Thomas & Zimmer-Gimbeck, 2011, 2012).

As we end this module, we need to remember that most parents who have mistreated their children deserve compassion, rather than censure. In most cases, parents and children are attached to each other; maltreatment is a consequence of ignorance and burden, not malice.

 Check Your Learning

RECALL Describe the factors that lead to child abuse.

How can we prevent child abuse?

INTERPRET How does child abuse demonstrate, in an unfortunate way, that children are sometimes active contributors to their own development?

APPLY Suppose that you read a letter to the editor of your local paper in which the author claims that parents who abuse their children are mentally ill. If you were to write a reply, what would you say?

 ANSWER 14.4

If this emotional abuse continues, virtually every aspect of Alex's psychological development is likely to be harmed. Alex will do poorly in school; his social and emotional development will be impaired; he won't get along well with peers; and he will be at risk for psychological disorders such as depression.

 14.2 Peer Relationships and Influences

OUTLINE	LEARNING OBJECTIVES
Development of Peer Interactions	**1. When do children first begin to interact with each other, and how do these interactions change during infancy, childhood, and adolescence?**
Friendship	**2. Why do children become friends, and what are the benefits of friendship?**
Romantic Relationships	**3. When do romantic relationships emerge in adolescence?**
Groups	**4. What are the important features and influences of groups in childhood and adolescence?**
Popularity and Rejection	**5. What are the causes and consequences of popularity and rejection?**

For six months, 17-year-old Gretchen has been dating Jeff, an 18-year-old. They have had sex several times, each time without contraception. Gretchen has suggested to Jeff that he buy some condoms, but he doesn't want to because someone might see him at the drugstore, and that would be too embarrassing. She has not pressed the issue because, although she never mentions it to Jeff, Gretchen sometimes thinks that getting pregnant would be cool: Then she and Jeff could move into their own apartment and begin a family.

Many of the major developmental theorists—including Freud, Erikson, Piaget, and Vygotsky—believed that children's development is strongly shaped by their interactions and relationships with peers. Whether with classmates, a small circle of friends, or in a romantic relationship like Gretchen's, children's and adolescents' interactions with peers are important developmental events.

In this module, we'll trace the development of peer interactions. Then we'll look at friendship and romantic relationships, where we'll better understand why Gretchen and Jeff are having unprotected sex. Finally, we'll consider children's membership in groups, including their social status within those groups.

Development of Peer Interactions

Peer interactions begin surprisingly early in infancy. Two six-month-olds will look, smile, and point at one another. Over the next few months, infants laugh and babble when with other infants (Rubin, Bukowski, & Parker, 2006).

Beginning at about the first birthday and continuing through the preschool years, peer relations rapidly become more complex. In a classic early study, Parten (1932) identified a developmental sequence in which children first play alone or watch others play, then progress to more elaborate forms of play, with each child having a well-defined role. Today, researchers no longer share Parten's view that children move through each stage of play in a rigid sequence, but the different forms of play that she distinguished are useful nonetheless.

The first type of social play to appear—soon after the first birthday—is *parallel play,* **in which youngsters play alone but maintain a keen interest in what other children are doing.** For example, each child in the photo on this page has his own toy but is watching the other boy play, too. During parallel play, exchanges between youngsters begin to occur. When one talks or smiles, the other usually responds (Howes, Unger, & Seidner, 1990).

Beginning at roughly 15 to 18 months of age, toddlers no longer just watch one another at play. **In** *associative play,* **youngsters engage in similar activities, talk or smile at one another, and offer each other toys.** Play is now truly interactive (Howes & Matheson, 1992). An example of simple social play would be two 20-month-olds pushing toy cars along the floor, making car sounds, and periodically trading cars.

Toward the second birthday, *cooperative play* **begins: Now children organize their play around a distinct theme and take on special roles based on the theme.** For example, children may play hide-and-seek and alternate roles of hider and finder, or they may have a tea party and alternate being the host and guest. By the time children are three and a half to four years old, parallel play is much less common, and cooperative play is the norm. Cooperative play typically involves peers of the same sex, a preference that increases until, by age six, youngsters choose same-sex playmates about two-thirds of the time (LaFreniere, Strayer, & Gauthier, 1984). When play with a member of the opposite sex does occur, it tends to be as part of a mixed-sex peer group (Fabes, Martin, & Hanish, 2003).

MAKE-BELIEVE. During the preschool years, cooperative play often takes the form of make-believe. Preschoolers have telephone conversations with imaginary partners or pretend to drink imaginary juice. In early phases of make-believe, children rely on realistic props to support their play. While pretending to drink, younger preschoolers use a real cup; while pretending to drive a car, they use a toy steering wheel. In later phases of make-believe, children no longer need realistic props; instead, they can imagine that a block

In parallel play, children play alone but pay close attention to what other nearby children are doing as they play.

Radius Images/Getty Images

is the cup or, that a paper plate is the steering wheel. Of course, this gradual movement toward more abstract make-believe is possible because of cognitive growth that occurs during the preschool years (Striano, Tomasello, & Rochat, 2001).

Although make-believe is a particularly striking feature of preschoolers' play, it emerges earlier. By 16 to 18 months of age, toddlers have an inkling of the difference between pretend play and reality. If toddlers see an adult who pretends to fill two glasses with water and then drinks from one of the glasses, they will pretend to drink from the other glass (Bosco, Friedman, & Leslie, 2006).

Of course, the first time that a parent pretends must be puzzling for toddlers. They probably wonder why mom is drinking from an empty glass or eating cereal from an empty bowl. But mothers help toddlers make sense out of this behaviour: When mothers pretend, they typically look directly at the child and grin, as if to say, "This is just for fun—it's not real!" And toddlers return the smile, as if responding, "I get it! We're playing!" (Nishida & Lillard, 2007). When children are older, they usually tell play partners that they want to pretend ("Let's pretend"), then describe those aspects of reality that are being changed ("I'll be the pilot and this is my plane," referring to the couch). It is as if children mutually agree to enter a parallel universe where just a few properties are changed (Rakoczy, 2008; Skolnick Weisberg & Bloom, 2009).

As you might suspect, culture influences the development of make-believe. In some cultures (e.g., India, Peru) parents do not routinely engage in pretend play with their children. Without such parental support, children don't begin pretend play until they're older (Callaghan et al., 2011). In addition, the contents of pretend play reflect the values important in a child's culture (Gosso, Morais, & Otta, 2007). For example, adventure and fantasy are favourite themes for European American youngsters, but family roles and everyday activities are favourites of Korean American children. Thus, cultural values influence both the emergence and the content of make-believe (Farver & Shin, 1997).

When preschool children engage in make-believe, they often use props to support their play; props used by younger preschoolers are usually very concrete, while those used by older preschoolers can be more abstract.

Make-believe play is not only entertaining for children, it also promotes cognitive development. Children who spend much time in make-believe play tend to be more advanced in language, memory, and executive functioning (Bergen & Mauer, 2000; Lillard et al., 2013). They also tend to have a more sophisticated understanding of other people's thoughts, beliefs, and feelings (Lindsey & Colwell, 2003).

Yet another benefit of make-believe is that it allows children to explore topics that frighten them. Children who are afraid of the dark may reassure a doll who is also afraid of the dark. By explaining to the doll why she shouldn't be afraid, children come to understand and regulate their own fear of darkness. Or children may pretend that a doll has misbehaved and must be punished, which allows them to experience the parent's anger and the doll's guilt. Make-believe allows children to explore other emotions, too, including joy and affection (Gottman, 1986; Lillard et al., 2013).

For many preschool children, make-believe play involves imaginary companions. Imaginary companions were once thought to be fairly rare, but many preschoolers, particularly firstborn and only children, report having imaginary companions (Taylor, Carlson, Maring, Gerow, & Charley, 2004). Children can usually describe what their imaginary playmates look and sound like (Tahiroglu, Mannering, & Taylor, 2011). Having an imaginary companion is associated with many *positive* social characteristics (Davis, Meins, & Fernyhough, 2011; Gleason & Hohmann, 2006; Roby & Kidd, 2008); compared with preschool children who lack imaginary friends, preschoolers with imaginary friends tend to be more sociable, have more real friends, and have greater self-knowledge than other preschoolers. Among older children who are at risk for developing behaviour problems, an imaginary companion promotes better adjustment during adolescence (Taylor, Hulette, & Dishion, 2010).

SOLITARY PLAY. At times throughout the preschool years, many children prefer to play alone. Should parents be worried? Usually, no. Solitary play comes in many forms and most are normal—even healthy. Bronwen Lloyd and Nina Howe of Concordia University used a creativity test and tests such as the picture completion test of the WISC-R to examine forms of thinking in preschool-aged children. Lloyd and Howe's (2003) research showed that active solitary play correlated positively with divergent thinking—a more creative, unconventional form of thinking. Spending free playtime alone colouring, solving puzzles, or assembling space ships with plastic building blocks is not a sign of maladjustment and may be beneficial to children's thinking. Many youngsters enjoy solitary activities and at other times choose very social play (Coplan & Ooi, 2014).

However, some forms of solitary play *are* signs that children are uneasy interacting with others (Coplan, Gavinski-Molina, Lagace-Seguin, & Wichmann, 2001; Harrist, Zaia, Bates, Dodge, & Petitt, 1997; Lloyd & Howe, 2003). One type of unhealthy solitary play is wandering aimlessly. Sometimes children go from one preschool activity centre to the next, as if trying to decide what to do. But really they just keep wandering, never settling into play with others or into constructive solitary play. Another unhealthy type of solitary play is hovering: A child stands near peers who are playing, watching them play but not participating. Over time, these behaviours do not bode well for youngsters (Coplan & Armer, 2007), so it is best for these youngsters to see a professional who can help them overcome their reticence in social situations.

PARENTAL INFLUENCE. Parents get involved in their preschool children's play in several ways (Parke & O'Neill, 2000):

- *Playmate.* Many parents enjoy the role of playmate (and many parents deserve an Oscar for their performances). They use the opportunity to scaffold their children's play (see Module 6.2), often raising it to more sophisticated levels (Tamis-LeMonda & Bornstein, 1996). For example, if a toddler is stacking toy plates, a parent might help the child stack the plates (play at the same level) or might pretend to wash each plate (play at a more advanced level). When parents demonstrate the reciprocal, cooperative nature of play, their children's play with peers is more successful (Lindsey, Cremeens, & Caldera, 2010).

- *Social director.* It takes two to interact, and young children rely on parents to create opportunities for social interactions. Many parents of young children arrange visits with peers, enrol children in activities (e.g., preschool programs), and take children to settings that attract young children (e.g., parks, swimming pools). All this effort is worth it: Children whose parents provide them with frequent opportunities for peer interaction tend to get along better with their peers (Ladd & Pettit, 2002).

- *Coach.* Successful interactions are based on a host of skills, including how to initiate an interaction, make joint decisions, and resolve conflicts. When parents help their children acquire these skills, children tend to be more competent socially and to be more accepted by their peers (Grusec, 2011; Mounts, 2011). For example, when mothers emphasize how targets of relational aggression feel, their children are less likely to resort to relational aggression (Werner, Eaton, Lyle, Tseng, & Holst, 2014). But there's a catch: The coaching must be constructive for children to benefit. Parent-coaches sometimes make suggestions that are misguided. Bad coaching is worse than none at all, as it harms children's peer relations (Russell & Finnie, 1990).

• *Mediator.* When young children play, they often disagree, argue, and sometimes fight. As shown in the photo, children play more cooperatively and longer when parents are present to help iron out conflicts (Mize, Pettit, & Brown, 1995). When young children cannot agree on what to play, a parent can negotiate a mutually acceptable activity. When both youngsters want to play with the same toy, a parent can arrange for them to share. Here, too, parents scaffold their preschoolers' play, smoothing the interaction by providing some of the social skills that preschoolers lack.

In addition to these direct influences on children's play, parents influence children's play indirectly via the quality of the parent–child attachment relationship. Recall from Module 10.3 that peer relationships in childhood and adolescence are most successful when the children, as infants, had a secure attachment relationship with their mother (Bascoe, Davies, Sturge-Apple, & Cummings, 2009; Brown & Bakken, 2011). A child's relationship with his or her parents is the internal working model for all future social relationships. When the parent–child relationship is of high quality and emotionally satisfying, children are encouraged to form relationships with other people. Another possibility is that a secure attachment relationship with the mother makes an infant feel more confident about exploring the environment, which in turn provides more opportunities to interact with peers. These two views are not mutually exclusive; both may contribute to the relative ease with which securely attached children interact with their peers (Hartup, 1992).

PEER RELATIONS AFTER PRESCHOOL. When children attend elementary school, the context of peer relations changes dramatically (Rubin, Bukowksi, & Parker, 2006). Not only does the sheer number of peers increase, but children are also exposed to a far more diverse set of peers than before. In addition, children find themselves interacting with peers in situations that range from reasonably structured with much adult supervision (e.g., a classroom) to largely unstructured with minimal adult supervision (e.g., a playground during recess).

An obvious change in children's peer relations during the elementary-school years is that, due to more experience with peers as well as cognitive and language development, children get along better than when they were younger. They become more skilled at initiating and maintaining interactions. And they use more sophisticated methods such as negotiation to resolve conflicts (Laursen, Finkelstein, & Betts, 2001).

What do school-age children do when they're together? In one study, Lynne Zarbatany of the University of Western Ontario and colleagues (Zarbatany, Hartmann, & Rankin, 1990) asked Canadian students in Grades 5 and 6 how they spent their time with peers. The students in the study indicated how often they participated with peers in each of 29 different activities. The results,

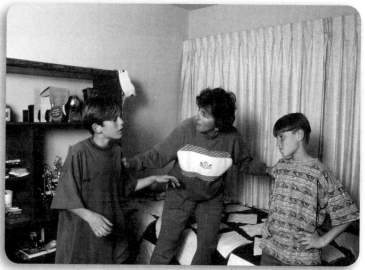

One way in which parents facilitate their children's play is by taking on the role of mediator—parents help resolve the disputes that inevitably develop when young children play.

shown in Figure 14-2, are not too surprising. The most common activities with peers are simple—just being together and talking (Larson, 2001; Zarbatany et al., 1990). This is true of high-school students as well: They spend more time talking and hanging out with friends than in watching videos, doing homework, or participating in school activities (Nelson & Gastic, 2009).

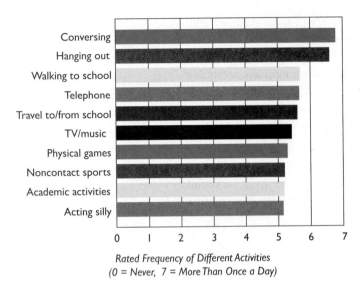

Conversing
Hanging out
Walking to school
Telephone
Travel to/from school
TV/music
Physical games
Noncontact sports
Academic activities
Acting silly

*Rated Frequency of Different Activities
(0 = Never, 7 = More Than Once a Day)*

Figure 14-2 Time spent in different activities by elementary-school children.

Based on Zarbatany, L., Hartmann, D. P., & Rankin, D. B. (1990). The psychological functions of preadolescent peer activities. *Child Development, 61,* 1067–1080.

Figure 14-2 also highlights another important feature of peer relations during the elementary-school years: children reported that they played physical games a few times each week, which reflects, in part, the emergence of a special type of play in school-age children. **In *rough-and-tumble play,* children playfully chase, punch, kick, shove, fight, and wrestle with peers.** Notice the word "play" in this definition: Unlike aggression, where the intention is to do harm, rough-and-tumble play is for fun. When children are involved in rough-and-tumble play, they are usually smiling and sometimes laughing (Pellis & Pellis, 2007). When parents or teachers intervene, the youngsters usually explain that there's no problem, they're just playing. Rough-and-tumble play is more common among boys than girls, and girls' rough-and-tumble play tends to emphasize running and chasing over wrestling and fighting.

As children move into adolescence, three features of their peer relationships loom large. Friendships become more intimate, youth have their first romantic relationships, and groups take on greater significance. These changes are so important that we'll consider each one separately. Let's start with friendship.

Friendship

Over time, even young children develop special relationships with certain peers. *Friendship* **is a voluntary relationship between two people that involves mutual liking.** By age four or five years, most children claim to have a "best friend." If you ask them how they can tell a child is their best friend, their response will probably resemble five-year-old Katelyn's:

INTERVIEWER:	Why is Heidi your best friend?
KATELYN:	Because she plays with me. And she's nice to me.
INTERVIEWER:	Are there any other reasons?
KATELYN:	Yeah, Heidi lets me play with her dolls.

Thus, the key elements of friendship for preschool and younger elementary-school children are that children like each other and enjoy playing together.

As children develop, their friendships become more complex. For older elementary-school children (eight to 11 years of age), mutual liking and shared activities are joined by features that are more psychological in nature, such as trust and assistance. At this age, children expect that they can depend on their friends—their friends will be nice to them, will keep their promises, and won't say mean things about them to others. And they expect friends to step forward in times of need. A friend should readily help with homework or willingly share a snack.

Adolescence adds another layer of complexity to friendships. Mutual liking, common interests, and trust remain. In fact, trust becomes even more important in adolescent friendships. New to adolescence is intimacy. Friends now confide in one another, sharing personal thoughts and feelings. Teenagers will reveal their excitement over a new romance or disappointment at not being cast in a school musical. Intimacy is more common in friendships among girls, who are more likely than boys to have one exclusive "best friend" (Markovits, Benenson, & Dolenszky, 2001). Because intimacy is at the core of their friendships, girls are also more likely to be concerned about the faithfulness of their friends and worry about being rejected (Benenson & Christakos, 2003; MacEvoy & Asher, 2012; Poulin & Chan, 2010).

The emergence of intimacy in adolescent friendships means that friends also come to be seen as sources of social and emotional support. Elementary-school children generally rely on close family members—parents, siblings, and grandparents—as primary sources of support when they need help or are upset; adolescents turn to close friends instead. Because adolescent friends share intimate thoughts and feelings, they can provide support during emotional or stressful periods (del Valle, Bravo, & Lopez, 2010; Levitt, Guacci-Franco, & Levitt, 1993).

Hand in hand with the emphasis on intimacy is loyalty. Having confided in friends, adolescents expect friends to stick with them through good and bad times. If a friend is disloyal, adolescents are afraid that they may be humiliated because their intimate thoughts and feelings will become known to a much broader circle of people (Berndt & Perry, 1990).

WHO BECOME FRIENDS?   In childhood and adolescence, most friends are like those in the photo: alike in age, sex, and race (Hamm, 2000; Mehta & Strough, 2009). Because friends are supposed to treat each other as equals, friendships are rare between an older, more experienced child and a younger, less experienced child. Because children typically play with same-sex peers (see Module 13.3), boys and girls rarely become close friends.

Although children's friendships are overwhelmingly with members of their own sex, a few children have friendships with other-sex children. Children with same- *and* other-sex friendships tend to be very well adjusted, whereas children with only other-sex friendships tend to be unpopular and less competent academically and socially, and to have lower self-esteem. Apparently, children with both same- *and* other-sex friends are so socially skilled and popular that both boys and girls are eager to be their friends. In contrast, children with only other-sex friendships are socially unskilled, unpopular youngsters who are rejected by their same-sex peers and form friendships with other-sex children as a last resort (Bukowski, Sippola, & Hoza, 1999).

Other-sex friendships are more common among teenagers (Arndorfer & Stormshak, 2008). By mid-adolescence, boys make up about 33 percent of girls' friends, but only 20 percent of boys' friends are girls. Boys benefit more from these other-sex friendships: Female friends provide more help and support to boys than male friends provide to girls (Poulin & Pedersen, 2007; Sears, Graham, & Campbell, 2009).

Friendships are more common between children and adolescents who are similar in race or ethnicity. In a study of effects of ethnicity on friendship, Barry Schneider and Kristopher Dixon (University of Ottawa), working with Stephen Udvari (University of Toronto), looked at quality of friendships of Grade 7 students in Montreal and Toronto (Schneider, Dixon, & Udvari, 2007). They found that friendships tended to be more common between children and adolescents from the same race or ethnic group than between those from different groups. Friendships among children of different groups are more common, however, in schools where classes are smaller (Hallinan & Teixeira, 1987) and when a child's school and neighbourhood are ethnically diverse (Quillian & Campbell, 2003). Such cross-group friendships are valuable: Children from majority groups typically form

Friends are typically alike in age, sex, race, and attitudes.

Q&A **QUESTION 14.5**

If Heidi is still Katelyn's best friend in high school, how would Katelyn's description of their friendship differ from the description she gave as a five-year-old? *(Answer is on page 520.)*

Thomas Cockrem/Alamy Stock Photo

more positive attitudes toward a minority group following a friendship with a youth from that group (Feddes, Noack, & Rutland, 2009). And children in cross-group friendships are less often targets of relational aggression (Kawabata & Crick, 2011).

Although same-race friendships are more common, research from McGill University in Quebec (Aboud, Mendelson, & Purdy, 2003) has shown that if a good interethnic friendship is formed, the same kinds of positive factors are found within the friendship as with same-ethnicity friendship. Aboud et al. (2003) studied aspects of friendship such as reliability and loyalty. Students attending a multi-ethnic elementary school in Montreal were surveyed about their friends, and friendships were assessed with the McGill Friendship questionnaire. Although children were found to have more same- than cross-race friends, all friendships were very similar in quality, with interethnic friendships providing "as much reliable alliance, help, and emotional security as same-race [friendships]" (Aboud et al., 2003, p. 171).

Research in Toronto schools has shown that, for adolescents, interethnic friendships were common where the opportunity exists to form such friendships. The authors of the Toronto school study noted that "The relative lack of ethnocentricity in students' friendships . . . may be due to the fact that the current study took place in one of the most culturally diverse cities in the world" (Smith & Schneider, 2000, p. 247).

Of course, friends are usually alike not only in age, sex, and race. They tend to be alike in popularity. Highly popular youth befriend popular peers and avoid friendships with less popular peers (Dijkstra, Cillessen, & Borch, 2013). In addition, friends have similar attitudes toward school, recreation, drug use, and plans for the future (Hamm, 2000; Newcomb & Bagwell, 1995). Children and adolescents befriend others who are similar to themselves, and as time passes, friends become more similar in their attitudes and values (Popp, Laursen, Kerr, Stattin, & Burk, 2008; Van Zalk et al., 2010). This does not mean that they become identical, however. As part of their research on twins, Philippe Rushton and Trudy Bonds of the University of Western Ontario found that friends are not photocopies of each other; friends are less similar, for example, than spouses or dizygotic twins (Rushton & Bonds, 2005).

QUALITY AND CONSEQUENCES OF FRIENDSHIP. You probably remember some childhood friendships that were long lasting and satisfying, whereas others rapidly wore thin and soon dissolved. What accounts for these differences in the quality and longevity of friendships? Sometimes friendships are brief because children have the skills to create friendships—they know funny stories, they kid around, they know good gossip—but lack the skills to sustain those friendships—they cannot keep secrets, are too bossy, or are too emotional (Blair et al., 2014; Jiao, 1999; Parker & Seal, 1996). Sometimes friendships end because, when conflicts arise, children are more concerned about their own interests and are unwilling to compromise or negotiate (Glick & Rose, 2011; Rose & Asher, 1999). And sometimes friendships dissolve when children discover that their needs and interests aren't as similar as they initially thought (Ellis & Zarbatany, 2007; Poulin & Boivin, 2000).

Considering that friendships disintegrate for many reasons, you're probably reminded that truly good friends are to be treasured. In fact, researchers consistently find that children benefit from having good friends. Compared to children who lack friends, children with good friends have higher self-esteem, are less likely to be lonely and depressed, and more often act prosocially—sharing and cooperating with others (Burk & Laursen, 2005; Hartup & Stevens, 1999). Children with good friends cope better with stressful experiences, such as doing poorly on an exam or being rejected by peers (Adams, Santo, & Bukowski, 2011; McDonald, Bowker, Rubin, Laursen, & Duchene,

2010), and they're less likely to be victimized by peers (Schwartz, Dodge, Pettit, Bates, & The Conduct Problems Prevention Research Group, 2000). The benefits of friendship are also long lasting. Children who have friends have greater self-worth as young adults (Bagwell, Newcomb, & Bukowski, 1998). Thus, for many adolescents, friends are important resources. Children learn from their friends and turn to them for support in times of stress.

Although children and adolescents benefit from their friends' support, there can be costs as well. **Sometimes friends spend much of their time together discussing each other's personal problems, which is known as** *co-rumination.* Girls do this more than boys (consistent with the fact that intimacy is more important to girls' friendships). Such co-rumination strengthens girls' friendships but also puts them at risk for greater depression and anxiety. In other words, when Avanti and Mishra spend day after day talking about problems with their parents and their schoolwork, they grow closer but also more troubled (Brendgen, Lamarche, Wanner, & Vitaro, 2010; Schwartz-Mette & Rose, 2012).

We thus need to recognize that not all friendships are beneficial for children and adolescents (Bagwell, 2004). Another example comes from research on friendship stability. Wendy Ellis and Lynne Zarbatany from the University of Western Ontario looked at the roles of aggression and victimization in maintaining or dissolving children's friendships. Ellis and Zarbatany (2007) gave elementary-school children in Grades 5 through 8 a questionnaire designed to assess the children's networks of friendships. This questionnaire was then repeated three months later to look at changes in friendships over time. Victimized children had few friends and seemed to have difficulty in forming friendships. Interestingly, befriending a victimized peer had negative social consequences for girls but not for boys, and these consequences tended to lead to breakdown of such friendships in girls. Aggressive children who were friends with nonaggressive peers tended to have difficulty keeping friends, as friendships dissolved due to the aggressive child's negative behaviours (Ellis & Zarbatany, 2007). Although Ellis and Zarbatany did not find any particular stability in friendships that were simply aggressive in general, relational aggression did maintain friendships. These friendships continued because children in such relationships were isolated from other peers, and they found it difficult to break off a friendship with the aggressive child, who might retaliate. There are other ways in which such friendships can be hazardous (Bagwell, 2004). For example, when aggressive children are friends, they often encourage each other's aggressive behaviour (Dishion, Poulin, & Burraston, 2001; Piehler & Dishion, 2007). Similarly, when teens engage in risky behaviour (e.g., they drink, smoke, or have sex), they often encourage each other's risky behaviour (Bot, Engels, Knibbe, & Meeus, 2005; Henry et al., 2007).

Finally, it is important to note that many youth are involved in relationships that are just the opposite of friendships. Mutual antipathies are characterized by shared dislike for each other, including some in which the feelings are quite intense (e.g., "I hate you!") as well as those in which the feelings are milder (e.g., children simply avoid each other). About one-third of North American children and adolescents have mutual antipathic relationships; those who do are more likely to be aggressive and withdrawn (Card, 2010). These relationships sometimes reflect dissimilarities between children (Nangle et al., 2004). Tom, who enjoys school, likes to read, and plans to go to Simon Fraser University, loathes Barry, who thinks that school is stupid, listens to his iPod constantly, and plans to quit high school to become a rock star; Barry feels the same way about Tom. Sometimes antipathies emerge from the wreckage of a broken friendship (Casper & Card, 2010). For example, when Kerri shares Rachel's intimate secrets with the rest of their group, Rachel retaliates by doing the same with Kerri's secrets; their friendship dissolves and they quickly develop an antipathic relationship. Finally, sometimes antipathies emerge as a way for highly popular children and adolescents to distance themselves from less popular peers (Berger & Dijkstra, 2013).

Romantic Relationships

The social landscape adds a distinctive landmark in adolescence: romantic relationships. Such relationships are uncommon during elementary school, but friendships can progress to romantic relationships in older children and adolescents. Jennifer Connolly, Wendy Craig, Adele Goldberg, and Debra Pepler of York and Queen's Universities surveyed children in Grades 5 through 8 (ages ranged from 9 to about 15) about romantic relationships. Twenty percent of those youngsters, "the early adolescent peer group" (Connolly, Craig, Goldberg, & Pepler, 2004) were in a current romantic relationship, and 24 percent had at least once been involved in such a relationship. A similar U.S. study reported that by high school roughly two-thirds of American adolescents had had a romantic relationship within the previous one and a half years, and most had been involved in a romance lasting nearly a year (Carver, Joyner, & Udry, 2003).

Cultural factors influence romantic relationships, however. European Canadian parents tend to encourage independence in their teenagers more than traditional Asian Canadian parents, who emphasize family ties and loyalty to parents. Romantic relationships are a sign of independence and usually result in less time spent with family, which may explain why Asian Canadian adolescents reported less interest in romantic relationships in the Connolly et al. (2004) study.

Romantic relationships build on friendships. Like friends, romantic partners tend to be similar in popularity and physical attractiveness. And a best friendship serves both as a prototype for and a source of support during ups and downs of close relationships (Collins, Welsh, & Furman, 2009). What's more, romantic relationships change over time in ways that resemble changes in friendship: Romantic relationships offer younger adolescents companionship (similar to that provided by a best friend) and an outlet for sexual exploration. Intimacy, trust, and support become important features of romantic relationships for older adolescents like those in the photo (Shulman & Kipnis, 2001).

When older adolescents are romantically involved, they believe that trust and support are an important part of their relationship.

It is tempting to dismiss teen romances as nothing more than "puppy love," but they are often developmentally significant (Collins et al., 2009). On one hand, adolescents involved in a romantic relationship are often more self-confident and have higher self-esteem (Harter, 2006); on the other hand, they report more emotional upheaval and conflict (Joyner & Udry, 2000). In addition, early dating with many different partners is associated with a host of problems in adolescence (e.g., drug use, lower grades) and with less satisfying romantic relationships in adulthood (Collins, 2003; Zimmer-Gembeck, Siebenbruner, & Collins, 2001).

SEXUAL BEHAVIOUR. Sexual exploration is an important feature of romantic relationships for younger adolescents. The 2009/10 Canadian Community Health Survey (CCHS) report has estimates that 30 percent of 15- to 17-year-olds and 68 percent of 18- to19-year-olds had already experienced sexual intercourse at least once (Statistics Canada, 2015b). No single factor predicts adolescent sexual behaviour. Instead, adolescents are more likely to be sexually active when they acquire (from parents, peers, and media) permissive attitudes toward sex, when their parents don't monitor their behaviour, when they are more physically mature, and when they drink alcohol regularly (Belsky et al., 2010; Hipwell, Keenan, Loeber, & Battista, 2010; Zimmer-Gembeck & Helfand, 2008). What's more, adolescents exposed to harsh environments (e.g., living in poverty) start having sex at younger ages, but adolescents with better executive functioning start when older (Carlson, Mendle, & Harden, 2014; Khurana et al., 2012).

The sexual behaviour of adolescents is a cause for concern because of the risk of teenage pregnancy. In Canada, statistics show a pregnancy rate of 28 per 1000 among girls aged 15 to 19 (Mckay, 2012). With an abortion rate of about 15 per 1000, this means approximately 13 births per 1000 teenaged girls. This is a substantial decline since the mid-1990s, when figures were in the mid- to high 40s per 1000 (Langille, 2007; McKay, 2012). The Canadian figures are at about the midpoint of those for other Western industrialized countries. Teen pregnancies are highest in the United States, with 57 pregnancies per 1000 15- to 19-year-olds (Sedgh, Finer, Bankole, Eilers, & Singh, 2015). In Canada, teen pregnancy rates vary by province. In 2010 Nunavut had the highest rates, followed by the Yukon and Manitoba. Prince Edward Island and Ontario have the lowest teen pregnancy rates (McKay, 2012).

As we saw in Module 3.2, teenage mothers and their children usually face bleak futures, but why do so many teens become pregnant? The answer is simple: Sexually active teenagers often fail to use birth control consistently or correctly (Guttmacher Institute, 2013). Several factors contribute to this failure (Gordon, 1996; Langille, 2007). First, many adolescents are ignorant of basic facts of conception and many believe that they are invulnerable—that only others become pregnant. Second, some teenagers do not know where to obtain contraceptives, and others, like Jeff in the module-opening vignette, are too embarrassed to buy them (Ralph & Brindis, 2010). Still others don't know how to use contraceptives. Third, becoming pregnant is appealing to some adolescent girls, like Gretchen from the vignette (Phipps, Rosengard, Weitzen, Meers, & Billinkoff, 2008). They think having a child is a way to break away from parents, gain status as an independent-living adult, and have "someone to love them."

The best way to reduce adolescent risky sexual behaviour and teen pregnancy is with comprehensive sex education programs (Kirby & Laris, 2009). These programs teach the biological aspects of sex and emphasize responsible sexual behaviour or abstinence from premarital sex altogether. They also include discussions about the pressure to become sexually involved and about ways to respond to this pressure. A key element is that in role-playing sessions students practise strategies for refusing to have sex. Youth who participate in programs like these are less likely to have intercourse; when they do have intercourse, they are more likely to use contraceptives. In contrast, there is little evidence that programs focusing solely on abstinence are effective in reducing sexual activity or encouraging contraceptive use—some versions may work, but many do not (Kirby, 2002).

SEXUAL ORIENTATION. For most adolescents, sexual behaviour involves members of the opposite sex. However, in early and mid-adolescence, roughly 15 percent of teens experience a period of sexual questioning, during which they sometimes report emotional and sexual attraction to members of their own sex (Carver, Egan, & Perry, 2004). For most adolescents, these experiences are simply a part of the larger process of role experimentation common to adolescence. However, like the teens in the photo, about 5 percent of teenage boys and girls identify their sexual orientation as gay or lesbian (Rotherman-Borus & Langabeer, 2001).

About 5 percent of adolescents find themselves attracted to members of their own sex and identify themselves as gay or lesbian.

Franckreporter/iStock/Getty Images

The roots of attraction to members of the same sex are poorly understood. The exact factors probably differ from one person to the next, but many scientists today believe that biology plays an important role (Lalumière, Blanchard, & Zucker, 2000). Some evidence suggests that heredity and hormones influence sexual orientation (Bailey, Dunne, & Martin, 2000). Genes and hormones may lead some boys to feel "different" during early adolescence, and these feelings lead to an interest in gender-atypical activities and, later, attraction to other males. The path to same-sex attraction is less predictable for females. Attraction to other females usually does not emerge until mid- or late adolescence and, in some cases, not until middle or old age. What's more, for many lesbian women, same-sex attraction grows out of deep feelings for a particular woman that, over time, extends to other females (Diamond, 2007).

Although the origins of sexual orientation are not yet well understood, it is clear that gay and lesbian individuals face many challenges. Their family and peer relationships are often disrupted, (Pearson & Wilkinson, 2013) and they endure verbal and physical attacks (Duncan & Hatzenbuehler, 2014). Given these problems, it is not surprising that gay and lesbian youth often experience mental health problems including depression and anxiety (Burton, Marshal, & Chisolm, 2014). In recent years, social changes have helped gay and lesbian youth respond more effectively to these challenges, including more (and more visible) role models and more centres for gay and lesbian youth. These resources are making it easier for gay and lesbian youth to understand their sexual orientation and to cope with the many other demands of adolescence; most end up being as well adjusted as heterosexual youth (Saewyc, 2011).

In concluding this section, we need to recognize that sexual behaviour and sexuality are enormously complicated and emotionally charged issues, even for adults. Adults who deal with adolescents need to recognize this complexity and help provide teenagers with skills for dealing with the issues involved in their emerging sexuality.

Groups

During adolescence, groups become an important feature of social life. Two types of groups are particularly common during adolescence. **A** *clique* **consists of four to six individuals who are good friends and, consequently, tend to be similar in age, sex, race, and interests.** Members of a clique spend time together and often dress, talk, and act alike. Cliques are often part of a larger group, too. **A** *crowd* **is a larger mixed-sex group of older children or adolescents who have similar values and attitudes and are known by a common label.** Maybe you remember some of the different crowds from your own youth? Jocks, preppies, burnouts, nerds, and brains—adolescents use these or similar terms to refer to crowds of older children or adolescents (Brown & Klute, 2003). Ethnic minority youth typically belong to such crowds, but some belong to ethnically based crowds instead (Brown, Herman, Hamm, & Heck, 2008).

Some crowds have more status than others. For example, students in many high schools claim that the jocks are the most prestigious crowd, whereas the burnouts are among the least prestigious. Self-esteem in older children and adolescents often reflects the status of their crowd. During the school years, youth from high-status crowds tend to have greater self-esteem than those from low-status crowds (Sussman, Pokhrel, Ashmore, & Brown, 2007). Some crowds typically dislike others. Crowds that support adult values, such as jocks and preppies, are less prone to psychological disorders, such as depression, than youth in crowds that don't support these values, such as burnouts (Doornwaard, Branje, Meeus, & ter Bogt, 2012).

Why do some students become nerds while others join the burnouts? Adolescents' interests and abilities matter, obviously. Academically inclined students who enjoy school gravitate to the brain or nerd crowds, while athletically talented teens become part of the jock crowd (Prinstein & LaGreca, 2004). Adolescents' crowds also reveal parents' influence. When parents practise authoritative parenting—they are warm but controlling—their children become involved with crowds that endorse adult standards of behaviour (for example, normals, jocks, brains). When parents' style is neglectful or permissive, their children are less likely to identify with adult standards of behaviour and instead join crowds like druggies that disavow adult standards (Brown, Mounts, Lamborn, & Steinberg, 1993).

GROUP STRUCTURE. Groups—whether in school, at a summer camp, or anywhere else—typically have a well-defined structure. **Most groups have a *dominance hierarchy*, with a leader to whom all other members of the group defer.** Other members know their position in the hierarchy—they yield to members who are above them in the hierarchy and assert themselves over members who are below them. A dominance hierarchy is useful in reducing conflict and allocating resources within groups because every member knows his or her place.

What determines where members stand in the hierarchy? With children, especially boys, physical power is often the basis for the dominance hierarchy. The leader is usually the most physically intimidating child (Hawley, 1999). Among girls and older boys, leaders have high self-esteem, good relationships with peers, and skills useful to the group. At a summer camp, for example, the leaders most often are the children with the greatest camping experience. Among Girl Guides or Girl Scouts, girls chosen to be patrol leaders tend to be bright and goal-oriented and to have new ideas (Edwards, 1994). These characteristics are appropriate because the primary function of patrol leaders is to help plan activities for the entire troop. Similarly, in a study of classroom discussion groups, the children who became leaders had good ideas and were outgoing (Li et al., 2007). Thus in these groups leadership based on key skills is effective because it gives the greatest influence to those with the skills most important to group functioning.

PEER PRESSURE. Groups establish *norms*—standards of behaviour that apply to all group members—and groups may pressure members to conform to these norms. Such peer pressure is often characterized as an irresistible, harmful force. The stereotype is that teenagers exert enormous pressure on each other to behave antisocially. In reality, peer pressure is neither all-powerful nor always evil. For example, most adolescents resist peer pressure to behave in ways that are clearly antisocial, such as stealing (Cook, Buehler, & Henson, 2009), and such resistance increases from mid to late adolescence (Steinberg & Monahan, 2007).

Peer pressure can be positive, too. Peers often urge one another to work hard in school; to participate in school activities, such as trying out for a play or working on the yearbook; or to become involved in community action projects such as Habitat for Humanity (Kindermann, 2007; Molloy, Gest, & Rulison, 2011). Some groups now work on positive peer pressure specifically for girls, an example being the Girls Leadership, Education, and Development (Girls LEAD) camps run at Brescia University College in Southern Ontario. These summer camps are run by women undergraduate students like the one in the photo on the next page and aim to provide positive role models and foster positive peer pressure among younger girls. Even today in Canada, young girls may be told by agemates "You can't because you're a girl" or fear censure from peers for acting in nonstereotypical ways. At a Girls LEAD camp, young campers

At camps such as Girls LEAD, young women aim to provide positive role models and foster positive peer pressure among girls.

are told they can do anything they want to and are encouraged to support one another in that belief. One young camper from the Grade 3 and 4 session said, "Sometimes people say that girls can't do stuff like math or science, but we proved them wrong." The Girls LEAD philosophy has been so successful that the camps have expanded to cater to girls from elementary through high school age groups. In 2010 Girls LEAD went international, with camps in the Caribbean, the first of these in Barbados.

Of course, peer influence is common throughout the life span. As we saw in Module 1.1, children and adults often imitate their peers' behaviour, particularly when the peer has high status and the behaviour is rewarded. But adolescents might be particularly susceptible to peer influence because they are forging an identity (Module 11.1), and matching the behaviour of a valued peer group might help to foster that identity. If Jordan sees that popular kids smoke, and part of her emerging identity is that she's in the popular group, she might start smoking too (Brechwald & Prinstein, 2011).

Peer pressure is not all-powerful. Instead, peer influence is stronger when (1) youth are younger and more socially anxious; (2) peers have high status; (3) peers are friends; and (4) standards for appropriate behaviour are not clear-cut, as in the case of tastes in music or clothing, or standards for smoking and drinking (Allen et al., 2012; Brechwald & Prinstein, 2011). Thus, when 14-year-old Doug's best friend (who is one of the most popular kids in school) gets his hair cut like Justin Beiber, Doug may do the same because he is young, the peer is popular and his friend, and there are no fixed standards for hair style. But when an unpopular girl that 18-year-old Kelly barely knows suggests to her that they go to the mall and shoplift some earrings, Kelly resists because she is older, the peer is unpopular and not a friend, and norms about shoplifting are clear.

Popularity and Rejection

Eileen is definitely the most popular child in her class. Other youngsters always want to play with her and sit near her at lunch or on the school bus. In contrast, Jay is the least popular child in the class. When he tries to join a game, the others quit. Students in the class dislike Jay as much as they like Eileen.

Popular and rejected children like Eileen and Jay can be found in every classroom and neighbourhood. In fact, studies of popularity by Shelley Hymel from the University of British Columbia and colleagues (Hymel, Vaillancourt, McDougall, & Renshaw, 2004) reveal that most children can be placed in one of five categories:

- *Popular children* are liked by many classmates.

- *Rejected children* are disliked by many classmates.

- *Controversial children* are both liked and disliked by classmates.

- *Average children* are liked and disliked by some classmates but without the intensity found for popular, rejected, or controversial children.

- *Neglected children* are ignored by classmates.

Of these categories, we know most about popular and rejected children. Each of these categories actually includes two subtypes. Most popular children are skilled academically and socially. They are good students who are usually friendly, cooperative, and helpful. They are more skillful at communicating and regulating themselves as well as better at integrating themselves into an ongoing conversation or play session—they "fit in" instead of "barging in" (Graziano, Keane, & Calkins, 2007; Kam et al., 2011). Marie-Hélène Véronneau and colleagues from the Université de Montréal have found that social success and academic success go together in middle childhood (Véronneau et al., 2010). A smaller group of popular children includes physically aggressive boys who pick fights with peers and relationally aggressive girls who, like the Plastics in the film *Mean Girls*, thrive on manipulating social relationships. Although these youth are not particularly friendly, their antisocial behaviour nevertheless apparently has a certain appeal to peers (Kuryluk, Cohen, & Audley-Piotrowski, 2011; Xie, Li, Boucher, Hutchins, & Cairns, 2006).

Are these avenues to popularity specific to North American children, or do they apply more generally? In many cultures around the world, including Canada, European countries, Israel, and China (e.g., Casiglia, Coco, & Zappulla, 1998; Chung-Hall & Chen, 2010), popular children seem to know how to get along with others. Sometimes, however, popular children have other characteristics that are unique to their cultural setting. In Israel, for example, popular children are more likely to be direct and assertive than in other countries (Krispin, Sternberg, & Lamb, 1992). Historically, in China shy children were often popular because their restrained behaviour was taken as a sign of social maturity. However economic reforms in China during the past 25 years have resulted in greater emphasis on taking initiative and being assertive. Consequently, shy children living in urban areas that have experienced economic reform are now rejected by peers, but they remain popular in more traditional rural areas (Chen, Wang, & Cao, 2011). Evidently, good social skills are at the core of popularity in most countries, but other features may also be important, reflecting culturally specific values.

As for rejected children, many are overly aggressive, hyperactive, socially unskilled, and unable to regulate their emotions. These children are usually much more hostile than popular-aggressive children and seem to view aggression as an end (which peers dislike) instead of using aggression as a means toward other ends (which peers may not actually like but grudgingly respect; Prinstein & Cillessen, 2003). Other rejected children are shy, withdrawn, timid, and, not surprisingly, lonely (Coplan et al., 2013; Rubin, Coplan, & Bowker, 2009).

CONSEQUENCES OF REJECTION. No one enjoys being rejected. Not surprisingly, peer rejection is a major obstacle in children's development. Over time, rejected youngsters become less involved in classroom activities; they end up feeling lonely and disliking school (Ladd, Herald-Brown, & Reiser, 2008; Sturaro, van Lier, Cuijpers, & Koot, 2011). Repeated peer rejection in childhood can also have serious long-term consequences (Ladd, 2006; Rubin et al., 2009). Rejected youngsters are more

Many rejected children are aggressive, and some learn this style of interaction from watching their parents in conflict.

Imtmphoto/Fotolia

likely than youngsters in the other categories to drop out of school, commit juvenile offences, and suffer from psychopathology.

CAUSES OF REJECTION.   Peer rejection can be traced, at least in part, to parental influence (Ladd, 1998). Children see how their parents respond to different social situations and often imitate these responses later. Parents who are friendly and cooperative with others demonstrate effective social skills. Parents who are belligerent and combative demonstrate much less effective social skills. In particular, when parents typically respond to interpersonal conflict like the couple in the photo on the previous page—with intimidation or aggression—their children may imitate them. This hampers their development of social skills and makes them less popular in the long run (Keane, Brown, & Crenshaw, 1990).

Parents' disciplinary practices also affect their children's social skill and popularity. Inconsistent discipline—punishing a child for misbehaving one day and ignoring the same behaviour the next—is associated with antisocial and aggressive behaviour, paving the way to rejection (Dishion, 1990). Consistent punishment that is linked with parental love and affection is more likely to promote social skill and, in the process, popularity (Dekovic & Janssens, 1992).

In sum, parenting can lead to an aggressive interpersonal style in a child, which in turn leads to peer rejection. The implication, then, is that by teaching youngsters (and their parents) more effective ways of interacting with others, we can make rejection less likely. With improved social skills, rejected children would not need to resort to antisocial behaviours. Rejected children (and other types of unpopular children) can be taught how to initiate interaction, communicate clearly, and be friendly. They can also be discouraged from behaviours that peers dislike, such as whining and fighting. This training is very similar to the training given aggressive adolescents, who are typically unpopular (see Module 12.4). Training of this sort does work. Rejected children can learn skills that lead to peer acceptance and thereby avoid the long-term harm associated with being rejected (LaGreca, 1993; Mize & Ladd, 1990).

Throughout this module, we've seen that peers affect children's development in many ways—for example, through different forms of play, through friendships, and through participation in social groups. In the next module, we'll look at the wider social influences on children's development, starting with childcare and after-school activities.

ANSWER 14.5

As a teenager, Katelyn's description of Heidi would focus more on intimacy. She might say, "I can tell Heidi stuff—special stuff, like secrets—that I wouldn't tell anyone else. And I know she'll keep my secrets." And Katelyn might mention that Heidi is loyal—willing to stand by her when other kids are teasing her.

✔ Check Your Learning

RECALL Describe the factors that seem to contribute to an adolescent's or young adult's sexual orientation.

How and when are teenagers most susceptible to peer pressure?

INTERPRET How might developmental change in peer interactions during infancy and the preschool years be explained by Piaget's stages of cognitive development, described in Module 6.1?

APPLY On page 518 you met Jay, who is the least popular child in his class. Jay's mom is worried about her son's lack of popularity and wants to know what she can do to help her son. Jay's dad thinks that Jay's mom is upset over nothing—he argues that, like fame, popularity is fleeting, and that Jay will turn out okay in the end. What advice would you give to Jay's parents?

14.3 Influences of Society

OUTLINE

Childcare and After-School Activities

Part-Time Employment

Neighbourhoods

School

LEARNING OBJECTIVES

1. How are children affected by nonparental childcare?

2. What is the impact of part-time employment on children's development?

3. How are children influenced by their neighbourhoods?

4. What are the hallmarks of effective schools and effective teachers?

When 15-year-old Aaron announced that he wanted an after-school job at the local supermarket, his mother was delighted, believing that he would learn much from the experience. Five months later, she had her doubts. Aaron had lost interest in school, and they argued constantly about how he spent his money.

So far in this chapter, we've seen the potent influence of families and of peers on children's development. Yet there are other noteworthy influences on children and their development—cultural institutions where children spend much of their lives. In this module, we'll look at four such institutions: childcare, the workplace, neighbourhoods, and school. As we do, we'll see whether part-time jobs like Aaron's help or harm youth.

Childcare and After School Activities

Each day, roughly half—at 46%—of Canadian children age five and under spend time in nonparental childcare (Sinha, 2014), a phenomenon linked to more dual-earner couples and to more single-parent households in Canada in the 21st century. In 2011, the most common forms of childcare were (1) care outside the child's home by a nonrelative (not in daycare), (2) care in a daycare centre, and (3) and private arrangements of care at home or outside the home, for example, by a relative (Sinha, 2014). The patterns varied across provinces, with parents in Quebec at 58% most likely to use childcare and those in Manitoba least, at 34%.

Many parents have misgivings about their children spending so much time in the care of others. Should parents worry? Does nonparental care harm children? Before turning to research for answers to these questions, let's put them in historical and cross-cultural perspective. Although nonmaternal care of children is often portrayed as unnatural—and therefore potentially harmful—for much of history and in many cultures, most children have been cared for by someone other than the mother, at least some of the time (Lamb, 1999; Leinaweaver, 2014). When viewed from the larger perspectives of history and other cultures, there is nothing "natural" or "traditional" about mothers having nearly exclusive responsibility for childcare. And there are even cross-cultural differences in beliefs about this responsibility, as we noted in the Cultural Influences section in Module 14.2. Nevertheless, in Canada (and many other industrialized countries) since World War II, the cultural ideal has been that children are better off when cared for at home by their mothers. Vail (2002) found that, while Canadians were more likely to agree than were residents of other industrialized nations that women with preschool-aged children should be able to work, ambivalent attitudes still exist toward mothers working and using childcare. Does research support the cultural ideal of the stay-at-home mother? In answering this question, most researchers worried about the impact of childcare on mother-infant attachment. As we saw in Module 10.3, the Canadian Transition to Childcare study showed, however, that attachment security was affected by childcare only when less sensitive mothers had their infants in low-quality childcare (McKim et al., 1999).

The most important factor in understanding the impact of childcare is the quality of care that children receive: Better care is linked to better outcomes. Children thrive when childcare has a relatively small number of children per caregiver (e.g., three infants or toddlers per caregiver) and the caregivers are well-trained, responsive, provide age-appropriate stimulating activities, and communicate well with parents (American Academy of Pediatrics, 2011). For example, when children receive high-quality childcare, their cognitive and language development is more advanced (Li, Farkas, Duncan, Burchinal, & Vandell, 2013). What's more, such care seems to be particularly beneficial for children from low-income families: High-quality childcare improves their school readiness, which translates into more success after they enter school (Dearing, McCartney, & Taylor, 2009). Thus, working parents can enrol their infants and preschoolers in high-quality daycare programs with no fear of harmful consequences.

Sometimes parents must rely on multiple sources of care, such as a family member for two days and centre care for three days. And sometimes parents switch caregivers. As you might imagine, multiple low-quality caregivers are detrimental to children, as are constantly changing childcare arrangements (Morrissey, 2009). However, multiple childcare providers can be beneficial when this is a stable arrangement and when each provider is of high quality (Tran & Weinraub, 2006).

When children enter elementary school, childcare becomes easier for working parents. However, many children still need care after school. Historically, after-school programs have focused on recreation: Children played games and sports, did arts and crafts, or participated in musical or dramatic productions. Recently, however, many after-school programs have focused more on academics. Children attending such programs often show modest improvements in school achievement, particularly when they attend higher quality programs (Vandell, Pierce, & Dadisman, 2005).

In addition, many children and adolescents participate in structured activities after school. The most common activities are sports, school clubs, and community service or religious organizations (Fredricks & Eccles, 2006; Larson, Hansen, & Moneta, 2006). As a general rule, children and adolescents benefit from participating. They are often more successful in school, are better adjusted, and are less likely to have behavioural problems (Beal & Crockett, 2010; Feldman Farb & Matjasko, 2012).

Many students participate in a number of activities, and such diverse participation is beneficial. Students who participate in multiple school activities tend to be better adjusted, more successful in school, less prone to drug use, and more involved in their communities (Feldman Farb & Matjasko, 2012; Fredricks & Eccles, 2006). This may surprise you in light of media reports that North American youth—particularly affluent youth—are stressed out because they're overscheduled after school. Research suggests, however, that most teenagers are not distressed by a busy after-school schedule; most children participate in activities because they enjoy them, not because they are pressured into them by achievement-oriented parents (Luthar, Shoum, & Brown, 2006).

Finally, many school-age children and adolescents care for themselves after school at least once a week (Mahoney & Parente, 2009). **Children who care for themselves are sometimes called *latchkey children*, a term that originated more than 200 years ago to describe children who raised a door latch to enter their own homes.** Some latchkey children, like the child in the photo on the next page, stay at home alone (sometimes with parental supervision in absentia via phone calls and text messages). Others may stay at friends' homes, where adults are sometimes present, or they may be unsupervised in public places such as shopping malls.

The popular perception is that latchkey children are a frightened, endangered lot. Research suggests that self-care can be risky under certain circumstances. Youth who care for themselves can get into trouble—abuse alcohol and drugs, become aggressive, and begin to fail in school—when they spend their after-school hours away from home, unsupervised, and live in neighbourhoods plagued by high crime rates. When these circumstances do not apply, older children and adolescents can care for themselves successfully (Mahoney & Parente, 2009).

Parents need to consider several factors when deciding whether they can leave their child home alone (Child Welfare Information Gateway, 2013). At the top of the list is the child's age—many experts recommend that children are not capable of self-care until they're 12, but others say that some eight-year-olds can care for themselves briefly (an hour to an hour and a half) during the day. In Canada the legal minimum age for leaving a child at home alone varies by province and territory, between 10 and 12 years (Canada Safety Council, n.d.). More important than age is the child's maturity: Is the child responsible? Does the child make good decisions on his or her own? Parents should also consider the child's attitudes and feelings about being left alone: Is the child anxious about being alone in the house? Finally, it's important for parents to consider their neighbourhood: Is it safe? Are there trusted neighbours whom the child can turn to if necessary?

If questions like these can be answered "Yes," then self-care will probably work. It is important that children be prepared for self-care. They need to know after-school routines (e.g., acceptable ways of getting home from school and how to check in with a parent), rules for their own behaviour after school (e.g., acceptable and unacceptable activities), guidelines on how to handle emergencies, and emergency phone numbers (Canada Safety Council, n.d.; Child Welfare Information Gateway, 2013).

Many North American children care for themselves after school, an arrangement that can be safe, depending on the child's age, the child's maturity, the neighbourhood, and the rules established for the child.

Squirmy1/iStock/Getty Images

Fortunately, employers have begun to realize that convenient, high-quality childcare makes for better employees and that the availability of excellent childcare helps attract and retain a skilled labour force. Cities help by modifying their zoning codes so that new shopping complexes and office buildings must include childcare facilities, such as those in the photo. With effort, organization, and help from the community and business, high-quality childcare can be available to all families.

Part-Time Employment

The teen in the photo on the next page is engaged in a North American adolescent ritual—the part-time job. Using data from Statistics Canada surveys, it can be calculated that in 2011, just over 50 percent of Canadians aged 15 to 24 had some form of paid employment (Statistics Canada, 2012d). Many adults praise teens for working, believing that early exposure to the workplace teaches self-discipline, self-confidence, and important job skills (Snedeker, 1982). Part-time work, however, can be harmful for many adolescents for several reasons:

Because many employees—particularly mothers who work full-time outside of the home—want high-quality childcare available, many companies now provide such care on site.

Arousa/Fotolia

Jim West/Alamy Stock Photo

Many North American adolescents hold part-time jobs; these can be beneficial but not when adolescents work more than 15 to 20 hours weekly.

1. **School performance suffers.** When students work more than approximately 20 hours per week, they become less engaged in school and are less likely to be successful in post-secondary education (Bachman, Staff, O'Malley, & Freedman-Doan, 2013; Monahan, Lee, & Steinberg, 2011). Many high-school students apparently do not have the foresight and self-discipline necessary to consistently meet the combined demands of work and school.

2. **Mental health and behavioural problems are more likely.** Adolescents who work more than 20 hours a week are more likely to experience anxiety and depression, and their self-esteem often suffers. Many adolescents find themselves in jobs that are repetitive and boring but stressful, and such conditions undermine self-esteem and breed anxiety. Extensive part-time work frequently leads to substance abuse and problem behaviour (e.g., antisocial behaviour, including theft), especially for younger teens who attend school sporadically (Monahan et al., 2011; Monahan, Steinberg, & Cauffman, 2013).

Why employment is associated with all of these problems is not clear. Perhaps employed adolescents turn to drugs to help them cope with the anxiety and depression brought on by work. Arguments with parents may become more common because anxious, depressed adolescents are more prone to argue or because wage-earning adolescents may believe that their freedom should match their income. Whatever the exact mechanism, extensive part-time work is clearly detrimental to the mental health of most adolescents.

3. **Affluence is misleading.** Adults sometimes argue that work is good for teenagers because it teaches them "the value of a dollar," but the typical teenage pattern is to earn and spend. Working adolescents spend most of their earnings on themselves—to buy clothing, snack foods, or cosmetics and to pay for entertainment. Few working teens set aside much of their income for future goals, such as a university education, or use it to contribute to their family's expenses (Shanahan, Elder, Burchinal, & Conger, 1996a, 1996b). Because parents customarily pay for many of the essential expenses associated with truly independent living—rent, utilities, and groceries, for example—working adolescents often have a vastly higher percentage of their income available for discretionary spending than working adults. Thus, the part-time work experience provides many teens with unrealistic expectations about how income can be allocated (Darling, Reeder, McGee, & Williams, 2006; Zhang, Cartmill, & Ferrence, 2008).

The message that emerges repeatedly from research on part-time employment is hardly encouraging. Like Aaron, the teenage boy in the vignette, many adolescents who work long hours at part-time jobs do not benefit from the experience. Instead, they do worse in school, are more likely to have behavioural problems, and learn how to spend money rather than how to manage it. These effects are similar for adolescents from different ethnic groups (Steinberg & Dornbusch, 1991) and are comparable for boys and girls (Bachman & Schulenberg, 1993). Ironically, though, there is a long-term benefit. Young adults who had a stressful part-time job as an adolescent are better able to cope with stressful adult jobs (Mortimer & Staff, 2004).

Does this mean that teenagers who are still in school should never work part time? Not necessarily. Part-time employment *can* be a good experience, depending on the circumstances. One key is the number of hours of work: Most students could easily work five hours weekly without harm, and many could work 10 hours weekly. Also important is the type of job. When adolescents have jobs that allow them to use existing skills (e.g., computing), acquire new skills, and receive effective mentoring, self-esteem is enhanced, and they learn from their work experience (Staff & Schulenberg, 2010; Vazsonyi & Snider, 2008). Yet another factor is the link between work and school. Teens often benefit from apprenticeships or internships that are explicitly linked to school so that work experiences complement classroom experiences (Symonds, Schwartz, & Ferguson, 2011). A final factor is how teens spend their earnings. When they save their money or use it to pay for clothes and school expenses, relations with their parents often improve and teens learn to balance saving and spending (Marsh & Kleitman, 2005; Shanahan et al., 1996b).

By these criteria, who is likely to show the harmful effects of part-time work? A teen who spends 30 hours a week bagging groceries and spends most of it on CDs or videos. And who is likely to benefit from part-time work? A teen who likes to tinker with cars, who spends Saturdays working in a repair shop, and sets aside some of his earnings for university.

Finally, summer jobs typically do not involve conflict between work and school. Consequently, many of the harmful effects associated with part-time employment during the school year do not hold for summer employment. In fact, such employment sometimes enhances adolescents' self-esteem, especially when they save part of their income for future plans (Marsh, 1991).

Neighbourhoods

For years, Mr. Rogers welcomed preschool children into a neighbourhood that was safe and nurturing. Not all children are so fortunate, however; their neighbourhoods are neither safe nor nurturing. Do these differences in neighbourhoods affect children's lives? We'll answer this question in the next few pages.

Before we consider how neighbourhoods affect children, we need to decide what constitutes a neighbourhood. Sometimes researchers define neighbourhoods in terms of school districts or other government boundaries, but Statistics Canada defines neighbourhoods in terms of census tracts (CT). These are defined as 2500 to 8000 people living in a homogeneous, geographically compact area (Statistics Canada, 2005). Using census-tract information, researchers have identified two features of neighbourhoods that are particularly useful when it comes to understanding children's development: *socioeconomic status*, reflecting the income and education of the residents, and *stability*, typically defined as the percentage of residents who have lived in the neighbourhood for several years (Leventhal & Brooks-Gunn, 2003).

Of course, defining neighbourhoods in terms of these features of census tracts is not perfect; this approach ignores some potentially important features of neighbourhoods. For example, it doesn't consider safety per se and doesn't measure the presence of institutions such as a church, temple, or school that can provide focus and vitality to a neighbourhood. The advantage of census tracts is that they are defined in a standard way across Canada, and mountains of data concerning census tracts are available to researchers.

Do neighbourhoods matter? Yes. All other things being equal, children benefit from living in a neighbourhood where most of the adults are well-educated and economically advantaged. These benefits are seen for both school achievement and psychological adjustment. Michael Boyle, Katholiki Georgiades, and Yvonne Racine of McMaster University, with Cameron Mustard from the University of Toronto, performed

 QUESTION 14.6
Nick is a 16-year-old who would love to have a career in the entertainment industry—TV, movies, or maybe in music. For now, he works two nights a week (about eight hours total) as an usher at a local movie theatre. At his parents' request, one-third of his take-home pay goes into a university fund. Is this part-time job likely to be harmful to Nick? *(Answer is on page 532.)*

a longitudinal study that looked at neighbourhood and family influences on children's educational attainment (Boyle, Georgiades, Racine, & Mustard, 2007). Children four to 16 years of age were first assessed in 1983 and followed up in 2001 as part of the Ontario Child Health Study. Neighbourhood and family effects interact, of course, but simply neighbourhood alone, as measured by "neighbourhood affluence," was found to have an influence on the lives of the children studied. In other words, when children live in economically advantaged neighbourhoods, they tend to do better in school and are somewhat less likely to have behavioural and emotional problems (Ackerman & Brown, 2006; Boyle, Georgiades, Racine, & Mustard, 2007).

Researchers agree that neighbourhoods per se do not influence children's behaviour. Instead, as we would expect from the contextual model of parenting (described in Module 14.1), the impact of neighbourhoods is indirect, transmitted through people (mainly parents and peers) and other social institutions. Several pathways of influence are possible (Leventhal & Brooks-Gunn, 2000). One pathway concerns the availability of institutional resources. Economically advantaged neighbourhoods more often have the kinds of resources that enhance children's development: libraries, museums, quality daycare, and good schools to foster children's cognitive development; medical services to provide for children's physical and mental health; and opportunities for adolescents to find work. In economically advantaged neighbourhoods that tend to have these resources, children are more likely to have experiences that lead to school success, good health, and the ability to find part-time jobs as teenagers. In contrast, in economically disadvantaged neighbourhoods that frequently lack these resources, children are often prepared inadequately for school, receive little medical care, and are unable to find jobs as teenagers, so they turn to delinquent or criminal behaviour.

A second way in which economically advantaged neighbourhoods have influence is that they are more likely to be stable and are more cohesive and close-knit, which means residents take a greater interest in neighbourhood goings-on, including those of children and adolescents (Chung & Steinberg, 2006; Odgers et al., 2009). Suppose, for example, adults see the two boys in the photo fighting in the park. In a cohesive neighbourhood, adults are more likely to intervene (e.g., break up the fight and scold the children for fighting) because they are committed to its residents; in a less cohesive neighbourhood, adults might ignore the children because they don't want the hassle of getting involved. Thus, in cohesive neighbourhoods, residents more often monitor the activities of neighbourhood children, making it more difficult for children to get into trouble.

Yet another link between poverty and children's development reflects the fact that when children live in poverty, their home life can often

Greenland/Shutterstock

People living in poorer neighbourhoods are less likely to know their neighbours and, consequently, are less likely to get involved in their neighbours' lives; for example, when children are fighting, adults may be reluctant to stop the fight because they don't know the children.

be described as chaotic (Chen, Cohen, & Miller, 2010). Their residence is often crowded and noisy, and their lives are often relatively unstructured and unpredictable. For example, children may not have a set time for doing homework, or even a place to do it. Living in such chaos often engenders a sense of helplessness. Children feel as if they have little control over their own lives and these feelings of helplessness are often associated with mental health problems and school failure (Bradley & Corwyn, 2007; Evans, Gonnella, Marcynyszyn, Gentile, & Salpekar, 2005). In addition, when children experience chronic poverty, as adults they're often less healthy because constant exposure to poverty-related stress overwhelms the developing child's physiological systems that battle stress (Evans & Kim, 2013; Hostinar & Gunnar, 2013). This effect begins very early. When a mother responds physiologically to stress, her baby does too (Waters, West, & Mendes, 2014).

Finally, neighbourhoods affect children through their impact on parenting behaviour. One account of this link is the focus of the Spotlight on Theories feature.

Spotlight on Theories

The Family Economic Stress Model

BACKGROUND   The harmful effects of poverty on children have been known for decades, but only recently have researchers attempted to understand the many different ways in which poverty harms children. Among the most difficult to understand is the way in which poverty causes children to receive less effective parenting.

THE THEORY   Adults living in chronic poverty often experience a great deal of stress from constantly worrying about whether they will have enough money to buy food or to pay rent. Rand Conger and Glen Elder (1994) proposed the family economic stress model (FESM) to explain how such poverty-induced stress could affect children's development. According to FESM, economic hardship results in a series of consequences:

1. Parents find that their income is not adequate to meet their needs.
2. This economic pressure affects parents' mental health, causing some to become depressed.
3. Once depressed, the quality of the marital relationship declines.
4. This results in less effective parenting (parents are not as warm with their children, praise them less frequently, and, instead are often angry and impatient with them).
5. Because children receive less effective parenting, behavioural problems are common (e.g., children become anxious or angry).

Thus, in FESM, poverty harms children's development because parents struggling to make ends meet become depressed and parent less effectively.

Hypothesis: When parents' economic situation changes for the worse—for example, one or both parents lose a job and can't find a comparable new job—this should start the cascade of consequences described in the FESM: Diminished income causes economic stress, which leads to depression, which leads to marital conflict and ineffective parenting, which finally disrupts children's development.

Test: Solantaus, Leinonen, and Punamäki (2004) provided a novel evaluation of this hypothesis by looking at families in Finland in the early 1990s, when that country experienced a deep economic decline that compared to the Great Depression in Canada and the United States in the 1930s. They took advantage of the fact that a large cross-section of Finnish families had been studied in the late 1980s, before the onset of the recession. Children and their families were then studied again in 1994, when the economic recession was at its peak. Solantaus and colleagues obtained measures of all the key constructs in FESM: family economic hardship, parental mental health, quality of marital interaction, parenting quality, and children's mental health. All were measured with questionnaires, which were completed by parents, children, and the children's teachers. Each of the links in FESM were supported: (1) Families who experienced more economic pressure reported more mental health problems; (2) parents who had more mental health problems reported that their marriages were less satisfying; (3) a less-satisfying marriage was associated with lower-quality parenting; and (4) lower quality parenting was associated with more frequent mental health problems in children.

Conclusion: Solantaus and colleagues found the outcomes predicted from FESM: Economic hardship triggered a sequence of events that ultimately harmed children's mental health. As they phrased it, "[The family] is a relationship unit, but it is also an economic unit. . . . This means that economic and relationship issues are intertwined, making the relationships vulnerable when the economy collapses" (Solantaus et al., 2004, p. 425).

Application: Based on these findings, we can add "improving children's mental health" to the long list of reasons to eliminate poverty. Until that happens, these findings and the FESM remind us of the difficulties of parenting effectively while living in poverty. Families living in poverty often need immediate help (e.g., services for parents and children who have mental health problems) as they pursue their longer term goal of leaving poverty.

Critical Thinking Question: What issues facing families today would be important inputs to the FESM?

Chronic poverty is particularly hard for parents because they usually have few social supports to help them cope with stress. When adults living in economically advantaged neighbourhoods find life so stressful that they need help, they can turn to neighbours or healthcare professionals. In contrast, adults living in poverty are less likely to turn to either a neighbour (because they don't know anyone well enough due to instability in the neighbourhood) or a healthcare professional (because one is not available nearby). Adults living in chronic poverty thus experience both more stress and, at the same time, fewer resources to cope with stress—which contributes to less effective parenting.

Thus children growing up in economically disadvantaged neighbourhoods typically have access to fewer institutional resources, are monitored less often by neighbours, often lead chaotic lives, and experience less effective parenting brought on by chronic stress. At the same time, research suggests that an effective way to invest in poverty-ridden neighbourhoods is by providing additional institutional resources (Huston et al., 2005). When neighbourhoods have good childcare and schools, many opportunities for recreation, and effective healthcare, children benefit directly. They also benefit indirectly because when parents feel less stress, they parent more effectively, and residents are less likely to move when there is more neighbourhood cohesiveness. There is some suggestion that boosting family income—either by providing cash supplements or increasing tax credits—increases children's achievement (Duncan & Magnuson, 2012). In a study of data from the Canadian National Longitudinal Survey of children and Youth, however, Dooley and Stewart (2007) cautioned that, while improved income does result in better child outcomes, only supplementing income as a way to improve the lives of children may be too simplistic, and that "early childhood education programs directed toward populations at high risk of developmental disadvantage may provide a better use of public funds" (Dooley & Stewart, 2007, p. 159).

Neighbourhoods—be they advantaged or disadvantaged—are usually relatively stable institutions where change occurs gradually, over months or years. Sometimes, however, neighbourhoods or entire communities are affected by disasters (e.g., floods, earthquakes, industrial accidents). In the United States, roughly one child in seven will experience some sort of disaster during childhood or adolescence (Becker-Blease, Turner, & Finkelhor, 2010). Not surprisingly, exposure to disasters is traumatic for children; mental health problems such as depression are frequent following exposure to disasters and risks typically increase with the degree of exposure (Masten & Narayan, 2012).

Other children experience upheaval because their neighbourhoods are the site of political violence. Children living in such neighbourhoods are more anxious, more depressed, and more aggressive, often because political violence undermines the children's view that their neighbourhood is safe and stable (Cummings, Goeke-Morey, Merrilees, Taylor, & Shirlow, 2014). Still other children lack neighbourhoods altogether; they're homeless or often moving from one temporary residence to another. Not surprisingly, children living in these conditions are often less successful in school and are at risk for behavioural problems (Masten et al., 2014).

However, as we've seen several times before, children and adolescents respond differently to adversity. Youth cope better with a disaster-related adversity when they are not also trying to deal with other family- or school-related stressors, and when they are better able to regulate their emotions and behaviour, and, in the case of political violence, when they identify strongly with their ethnic group (Cummings et al., 2014; Kithakye, Morris, Terranova, & Myers, 2010; Kronenberg et al., 2010; Masten et al., 2014). However, for children who do not cope well with this adversity, cognitive-behavioural treatment can help modify their disaster-related thinking and teach them ways to cope with stress-related feelings (LaGreca & Silverman, 2009). Following a disaster, all children are helped when familiar institutions are restored as soon as possible. Foremost among these is schools (Masten & Osofsky, 2010), which are the focus of the next (and last!) section.

Exposure to disasters such as the Fort McMurray wildfire is very stressful for youth, particularly when they are younger, dealing with other stresses in their lives, and do not regulate their emotions well.

Codie McLachlan/The Canadian Press

School

Around age four or five, most Canadian children head off to kindergarten, starting an educational journey that lasts 13 years for most and more than 17 years for some. How do schools influence children's development? There are as many answers to this question as there are types of schools in Canada—government-run public schools, separate systems such as Catholic schools in some provinces, and private schools that charge tuition. Although all must conform to basic ministry of education guidelines, schools differ on many dimensions, including their emphasis on academic goals and parent involvement. Teachers also differ in many ways, such as how they run their classrooms and how they teach. These and other variables affect how much students learn, as you'll see in the next few pages. Let's begin with school-based influences.

SCHOOL-BASED INFLUENCES ON STUDENT ACHIEVEMENT. Laurier High School, located in the centre of Toronto, has an enrolment of 2500 students in Grades 9 to 12. Opened in 1936, the building shows its age. The rooms are drafty, the desks are decorated with generations of graffiti, and new technology means an updated photocopier. Nevertheless, attendance at Laurier is good, most students graduate, and many continue their education at colleges and universities. Southport High School, located in a different Toronto neighbourhood, has about the same enrolment as Laurier High and the building is about the same age. Yet truancy is commonplace at Southport, where fewer than half the students graduate and almost none go to college or university.

These schools are hypothetical, but they accurately portray Canadian education. Some schools are much more successful than others, regardless of whether success is defined in terms of the percentage of students who are literate, graduate, or go to college or university. Why are some schools successful and not others? Researchers (DuBois, Portillo, Rhodes, Silverthorn, & Valentine, 2011; El Nokali, Bachman, & Votruba-Drzal, 2010; Good & Brophy, 2008; Pianta, 2007) have identified a number of factors linked with successful schools:

- *Staff and students alike understand that academic excellence is the primary goal, and standards are set accordingly.* The school day emphasizes instruction, and students are recognized publicly for their academic accomplishments.

- *The school climate is safe and nurturing.* Students know that they can devote their energy to learning (instead of worrying about being harmed in school), and they know the staff truly wants to see them succeed.

- *Parents are involved.* In some cases, parental involvement may be through formal arrangements, such as parent–teacher organizations, or it may be informal. Parents may spend some time each week in school grading papers or, like the parents in the photo, tutoring a child. Such involvement signals to both teachers and students that parents are committed to students' success.

- *Mentoring programs allow children and adolescents to learn from nonparental adults.* When youth come under the guidance of adults who have similar interests to theirs and who are supported in their advocacy and teaching roles, youth do better in school and improve their self-esteem as well as their peer relationships; these effects are often largest for children and adolescents at risk

- *Progress of students, teachers, and programs is monitored.* One way to know if schools are succeeding is by measuring performance. Students, teachers, and programs may be evaluated regularly, using objective measures that reflect academic goals.

In schools that follow these guidelines, students usually succeed. In schools where the guidelines are ignored, students more often fail. Of course, on a daily basis, individual teachers have the most potential for impact. Let's see how teachers can influence their students' achievement.

JackF/Fotolia

Successful schools encourage parents to become involved; for example, they may encourage parents to tutor students.

TEACHER-BASED INFLUENCES. Take a moment to recall your teachers in elementary school and high school. Some you probably remember fondly because they were enthusiastic and innovative and they made learning fun. You may remember others with bitterness; they seemed to have lost their love of teaching and children, making class unbearable. Your experience tells you that some teachers are better than others, but what exactly makes a good teacher? Personality and enthusiasm are not the key elements. Although you may enjoy warm and eager teachers, research (Good & Brophy, 2008; Gregory, Allen, Mikami, Hafen, & Pianta, 2014; Pianta, 2007; Walberg, 1995) shows that several other factors are critical when it comes to students' achievement. Students tend to learn the most when teachers:

- *Manage the classroom effectively so they can devote most of their time to instruction.* When teachers spend a lot of time disciplining students, or when students do not move smoothly from one class activity to the next, instructional time is wasted, and students tend to learn less.

- *Believe they are responsible for their students' learning and that their students will learn when taught well.* When students don't understand a new topic, these teachers repeat the original instruction (in case the student missed something) or create new instruction (in case the student heard everything but just didn't understand). These teachers keep trying because they feel at fault if students don't learn.

- *Pay careful attention to pacing.* They present material slowly enough that students can understand a new concept, but not so slowly that students get bored.

- *Emphasize mastery of topics.* Teachers should introduce a topic, then give students many opportunities to understand, practise, and apply the topic. Just as you'd find it hard to go directly from driver's education to driving a race car, students more often achieve when they grasp a new topic thoroughly and then gradually move on to other, more advanced topics.

- *Teach actively.* The best teachers don't just talk or give students an endless stream of worksheets. Instead, they demonstrate topics concretely or have hands-on demonstrations for students. They also have students participate in class activities and encourage students to interact, generating ideas and solving problems together.

- *Value tutoring.* Good teachers work with students individually or in small groups so they can gear their instruction to each student's level and check each student's understanding. They also encourage peer tutoring, in which more-capable students tutor less-capable students. Children who are tutored by peers do learn, and so do the tutors, evidently because teaching helps tutors organize their knowledge.

- *Teach children techniques for monitoring and managing their own learning.* Students are more likely to achieve when they are taught how to recognize the aims of school tasks and know effective strategies for achieving those aims (such as those described on pages 230–231).

- *Have access to resources that allow them to improve their teaching.* When teachers work directly with an expert teacher who provides feedback about their current teaching and offers evidence-based methods to improve it, their students fare better

So what makes for effective schools and teachers? No single element is crucial. Instead, many factors contribute to make some schools and teachers remarkably effective. Some of the essential ingredients include parents who are involved, teachers who care deeply about their students' learning and manage classrooms well, and a school that is safe, nurturing, and emphasizes achievement.

Of course, many schools are not very successful. However, as parents, teachers, and concerned citizens, we need to resist the idea that any single solution can cure a school's ills. As we have seen throughout this text, the outcome of development—in this case, academic achievement—is determined by many factors, including environmental forces (e.g., parents and teachers) as well as the contributions of children themselves. To foster academic success, we need to consider all these factors, not focus narrowly on only one or two.

Finally, as we consider the features of effective schools and effective teachers, it is important to remember that children's skills when they enter school are powerful

ANSWER 14.6
Probably not. He's not working enough for the job to interfere too much with school. Plus, he is interested in working in the entertainment industry, so there's some benefit to learning the business "from the ground up." Finally, he is saving a substantial amount of his pay, which means he's less likely to experience misleading affluence.

predictors of their achievement in school. Longitudinal studies clearly show that kindergarten children who know letters, some words, numbers, and simple quantitative concepts are on the path to success in school; this is true regardless of a child's socioeconomic status or ethnicity (Duncan et al., 2007; Marks & García Coll, 2007). Of course, as we've seen repeatedly, continuity across development is not perfect: Some five-year-olds who don't know their numbers will get As in calculus in high school, but they're the exception, not the rule. Consequently, it is crucial for children to begin kindergarten with a solid foundation of pre-reading and pre-arithmetic skills.

On a more general note, understanding why and how children succeed in school (and in other domains of life) is indeed a challenging puzzle, but scientists are making remarkable progress in solving the child-development puzzle. As we end the book, we hope you've enjoyed learning about their discoveries. Thank you for reading.

 Check Your Learning

RECALL What is known about the impact of part-time employment on adolescents? Summarize the ways in which poverty can influence children's development.

INTERPRET Compare and contrast the ways in which schools (as institutions) affect children's learning with the ways in which teachers affect children's learning.

APPLY Imagine that you're a parent who has taken a new job, which means that your 10-year-old daughter would need to care for herself at home from after school until about 6 p.m. What would you do to decide whether she's capable of such self-care? If you decided that she is capable, what would you do to prepare her?

UNIFYING THEMES Continuity

In this last chapter of the book, we want to emphasize the theme that while they are influenced by those around them, *children influence their own development*. This may seem to be an unusual chapter in which to emphasize this theme because, after all, we usually think of how parents influence their children. Several times in this chapter, however, we've seen that parenting is determined, in part, by children themselves. We saw that parents change their behaviour as their children grow older. Parents also adjust their behaviour depending on how their children respond to previous efforts to discipline. And in discussing causes of child maltreatment, we discovered that younger and sick children often unwittingly place themselves at risk for abuse because of their behaviour. Constant whining and

crying is trying for all parents and prompts a few to harm their children.

Of course, parents do influence their children's development in many important ways. But effective parenting recognizes that there is no all-purpose formula that works for all children or even, for that matter, for all children in one family. Instead, parents must tailor their childrearing behaviour to each child, recognizing the child's unique needs, strengths, and weaknesses.

Finally, we want to remind you that early development is related to later development, but not perfectly. Children who are rejected by their peers are, over time, more likely to do poorly in school, have lower self-esteem, and have behavioural problems. Of course, not all rejected children suffer this fate. Some do well in school, have high self-esteem, and avoid behavioural problems. Positive outcomes are more likely to occur when children learn effective skills for interacting with others. As we've seen many times in previous chapters, early experiences often point children toward a particular developmental path, but later experiences can cause them to change course

See for Yourself

Many students find it hard to believe that parents actually use the different styles described in Module 14.1. To observe how parents differ in their warmth and control, visit a place where parents and children interact together; shopping malls and fast-food restaurants are two good examples. As with the "See for Yourself" exercise from Chapter 4, remember to be an ethical observer and do not be intrusive or interfering. Observe parents and children and think about the parents' levels of warmth (responsive to the child's needs versus uninterested) and degree of control (relatively controlling versus uncontrolling). As you observe, decide whether parents are using feedback and modelling effectively. You should observe an astonishing variety of parental behaviour, some effective and some not. See for yourself!

Resources

For more information about . . .

divorce, try Mavis Hetherington and John Kelly's *For Better or Worse: Divorce Reconsidered* (W. W. Norton, 2003), in which the authors—one, the world's foremost authority on divorce, and the other a professional writer—trace the findings from a 30-year study to explain how divorce affects families. They also provide many practical suggestions for dealing with problems associated with divorce.

how to deal with all of the different problems, large and small, that come up in rearing children, visit the *Today's Parent* website at **www.today sparent.com**.

why some children and families are able to overcome poverty, read *Managing to Make it: Urban Families and Adolescent Success* (University of Chicago Press, 2000), by Frank F. Furstenberg, Thomas D. Cook, Jacquelynne Eccles, Glen H. Elder Jr., and Arnold Sameroff, which chronicles the way in which some parents living in poverty help to shield their children from dangers associated with living in poverty and, instead, direct them toward positive outcomes.

the impact of childcare on children's development, visit the website of The Childcare Resource and Research Unit of the University of Toronto **www.childcare canada.org**.

Key Terms

associative play   506
authoritarian parenting   479
authoritative parenting   479
authority-oriented grandparents   491
blended family   489
clique   516
cooperative play   506
co-rumination   513
counterimitation   481
crowd   516
detached grandparents   491

direct instruction   481
dominance hierarchy   517
ego-resilience   499
friendship   510
influential grandparents   491
joint custody   487
latchkey children   522
negative reinforcement trap   482
observational learning   481
open adoption   496
passive grandparents   491

parallel play   506
permissive parenting   479
punishment   481
reinforcement   481
rough-and-tumble play   510
supportive grandparents   491
time in   483
time out   483
uninvolved parenting   479

Summary

14.1 Parenting and Family Relationships

1. The Family as a System

According to the systems approach, the family is an evolutionary adaptation that consists of interacting elements; parents and children influence each other. The family itself is embedded in a context of interconnected systems that range from those in the child's immediate environment to the overall cultures and subcultures in which all the other systems are embedded.

2. Styles of Parenting

One dimension of parenting is the degree of parental warmth. Children clearly benefit from warm, caring parents. Another dimension is control. Effective parental control involves setting appropriate standards and enforcing them consistently. Combining warmth and control yields four parental styles: (1) Authoritarian parents are controlling but uninvolved; (2) authoritative parents are controlling but responsive to their children; (3) permissive parents are loving but exert little control; and (4) uninvolved parents are neither warm nor controlling. Authoritative parenting is usually best for children.

Childrearing is influenced by culture and family configuration; for example, compared to North American parents, Chinese parents tend to be more controlling and less affectionate. Parents living in poverty often rely more heavily on authoritarian parenting.

3. Parental Behaviour

Parents influence development by direct instruction and coaching. In addition, parents serve as models for their children, who sometimes imitate parents' behaviour directly and sometimes in ways that are the opposite of what they've seen (counterimitation).

Parents also use feedback to influence children's behaviour. Sometimes parents fall into the negative reinforcement trap, inadvertently reinforcing behaviours that they want to discourage. Punishment is effective when it is prompt, consistent, accompanied by an explanation, and delivered by a person with whom the child has a warm relationship. Time out is one useful form of punishment.

4. Influences of the Marital System

Chronic conflict is harmful to children, but children can actually benefit when their parents solve problems constructively. Not all parents work well together, because they disagree in childrearing goals or methods.

5. Children's Contributions

Parenting is influenced by characteristics of children themselves, such as their age and temperament.

6. Impact of Divorce on Children

Divorce harms children in many ways, ranging from school achievement to adjustment. The impact of divorce stems from less supervision of children, economic hardship, and parental conflict.

7. Blended Families

The blended family can be successful and beneficial for children and adolescents, but it takes effort because of the complicated relationships, conflicting loyalties, and jealousies that usually exist. When a mother remarries, daughters sometimes have difficulty adjusting, because the new stepfather encroaches on an intimate mother–daughter relationship. Best strategies include avoiding preferential treatment of biological children, showing warmth and caring to all family members, and maintaining a harmonious marital relationship.

8. The Role of Grandparents

Grandparents play many different roles with their grandchildren; the influential and supportive roles are two in which grandparents are particularly active in rearing grandchildren. In Indigenous families, grandmothers often care for their grandchildren for some of the time, an arrangement that benefits children. Grandparents also influence their grandchildren indirectly through the way they reared the child's parents.

9. Children of Gay and Lesbian Parents

Research on gay and lesbian parents suggests that they are more similar to heterosexual parents than different, and that their children develop much like children reared by heterosexual couples.

10. Firstborn, Laterborn, and Only Children

Firstborn children often are more intelligent and more likely to go to college, but laterborn children are more popular and more innovative. Only children are comparable to children with siblings on most dimensions. Some adopted children have problems, primarily if they were adopted at an older age and their quality of care before being adopted was poor.

11. Qualities of Sibling Relationships

The birth of a sibling can be stressful for older children, particularly when parents ignore their older child's needs. Siblings get along better when they are of the same sex, believe that parents treat them fairly, enter adolescence, and have parents who get along well.

12. Maltreatment and its Consequences

Children who are maltreated sometimes suffer permanent physical damage. Their peer relationships are often poor, and they tend to lag in cognitive development and academic performance.

13. Causes of Maltreatment

A culture's views on violence, poverty, and social isolation can foster child maltreatment. Parents who abuse their children are often unhappy, socially unskilled individuals. Younger, unhealthy children are more likely to be targets of maltreatment, as are stepchildren. Resilient children, especially those aided by other adults, can overcome negative parenting to have a good outcome in life.

14. Preventing Maltreatment

Prevention programs often focus on providing families with new ways of coping with problems, and on providing parents with resources to help them cope with stress.

14.2 Peer Relationships and Influences

1. Friendships

Children's first real social interactions, at about 12 to 15 months of age, take the form of parallel play, in which infants play alone while watching each other. At about two years of age, cooperative play organized around a theme becomes common. Make-believe play is also common and, in addition to being fun, promotes cognitive development and lets children examine frightening topics. Most solitary play is harmless. Parents foster children's play by acting as skilled playmates, serving as social director for their children, coaching social skills, and mediating disputes. Beyond preschool, peer relations improve and emphasize talking and being together, as well as rough-and-tumble play.

Friendships among preschoolers are based on common interests and getting along well. As children grow, loyalty, trust, and intimacy become more important features in their friendships. Friends are usually similar in age, sex, race, and attitudes. Children with friends are more skilled socially and better adjusted.

2. Romantic Relationships

For younger adolescents, romantic relationships offer companionship and the possibility of sexual exploration; for older adolescents, they provide trust and support. Pregnancy occurs because many adolescents engage in unprotected sex. Comprehensive sex education is effective in reducing teenage sexual activity. Adolescents often wonder about their sexual orientation, but only a small percentage report having homosexual experiences.

3. Groups

Older children and adolescents often form cliques—small groups of like-minded individuals that become part of a crowd. Members of higher status crowds often have higher self-esteem. Most groups have a dominance hierarchy, a well-defined structure with a leader at the top. Physical power often determines the dominance hierarchy, particularly among younger boys. With older children and adolescents, dominance hierarchies are more often based on skills that are important to group functioning.

Peers are particularly influential when standards of behaviour are unclear, such as for taste in music or clothing or concerning drinking.

Many popular children are socially skilled; they generally share, cooperate, and help others. Other popular children use aggression to achieve social goals. Some children are rejected by their peers because they are too aggressive; others are rejected for being shy. Both groups of rejected children are often unsuccessful in school and have behavioural problems.

14.3 Influences of Society

1. Childcare and After-School Activities

Many Canadian children are cared for by a father or other relative, in a daycare provider's home, or in a daycare centre. When children attend high-quality childcare, this fosters their cognitive and socioemotional development. After-school programs and structured activities are often beneficial, too. Children can care for themselves after school if they are mature enough, live in a safe neighbourhood, and are supervised in some way by an adult.

2. Part-time Employment

Adolescents who are employed for much more than 20 hours per week during the school year typically do poorly in school, often have lowered self-esteem and increased anxiety, and have problems interacting with others. Employed adolescents save relatively little of their income. Instead, they spend most of it on themselves, which can give misleading expectations about how to allocate income. Part-time employment can be beneficial if adolescents work relatively few hours, if the work allows them to use existing skills or acquire new ones, and if teens save some of their earnings. Summer employment can also be beneficial.

3. Neighbourhoods

Children are more likely to thrive when they grow up in a neighbourhood that is economically advantaged and stable. These neighbourhoods are better for children because more institutional resources (e.g., schools) are available, because residents are more likely to monitor neighbourhood children's behaviour, because home life is predictable, and because parents are not living in chronic stress associated with poverty.

4. School

Schools influence students' achievement in many ways. Students are most likely to achieve when their school emphasizes academic excellence, has a safe and nurturing environment, monitors pupils' and teachers' progress, and encourages parents to be involved.

Students achieve at higher levels when their teachers manage classrooms effectively, take responsibility for their students' learning, teach mastery of material, pace material well, value tutoring, and show children how to monitor their own learning.

Test Yourself

1. The two major dimensions of parental behaviour are warmth and _____.

2. In a _____, parents inadvertently reinforce the behaviours that they hope to discourage.

3. Two features of children that influence how parents treat them are age and _____.

4. Divorce influences children by forcing the loss of a role model and source of parental help, by creating economic hardship, and by _____.

5. Children usually benefit when a mother remarries; the exception is that _____.

6. According to an evolutionary perspective, grandparenting evolved because _____.

7. When children reared by gay and lesbian parents are compared to children reared by heterosexual parents, the usual result is that _____.

8. Adopted children are more likely to experience developmental problems when they are adopted at an older age and when _____.

9. Siblings get along best when they're of the same sex, when neither is emotional, when parents treat siblings fairly, and when parents _____.

10. The impact of maltreatment is less when children can respond adaptively to new situations and when they _____.

11. Factors that contribute to child maltreatment include community values, ineffective parenting, and _____.

12. Make-believe play is fun, promotes children's cognitive development, and helps them _____.

13. Parents are often involved in their children's play, taking on roles as _____, social director, coach, and mediator.

14. The best way to reduce adolescent sexual behaviour and teen pregnancy is with _____.

15. Peer pressure is strongest when youth are younger, peers have high status and are friends, and _____.

16. Some popular children are friendly, cooperative, and helpful; a smaller number tend to be _____.

17. Youth can care for themselves after school except when they _____ and live in unsafe neighbourhoods.

18. Part-time work can be a good experience for teens when they work relatively few hours, _____, and they save their money or use it to pay for clothes and school expenses.

19. Disadvantaged neighbourhoods affected children indirectly, in that fewer resources such as libraries are available, _____, and home life tends to be more chaotic.

20. In effective schools, academic excellence is the main goal, _____, parents are involved, and progress is monitored.

Answers: (1) control; (2) negative reinforcement trap; (3) temperament; (4) causing the distress produced by parental conflict; (5) sometimes preadolescent girls don't adjust well because the stepfather's presence interferes with a close mother–daughter relationship; (6) it was more valuable for middle-aged women to care for their grandchildren than to produce more children of their own; (7) both groups of children seem to develop similarly and both benefit from close relationships with warm, caring parents; (8) their care before adoption was poor; (9) have a warm, harmonious relationship with little conflict; (10) are more engaged in school; (11) children themselves (e.g., being ill or being a stepchild); (12) explore topics that frighten them; (13) playmate; (14) comprehensive sex education programs; (15) standards for appropriate behaviour are unclear (e.g., tastes in music or clothing, standards for smoking and drinking); (16) aggressive (physically aggressive for boys, relationally aggressive for girls); (17) spend their after-school time away from home, unsupervised; (18) the job allows them to acquire useful new skills; (19) neighbourhoods tend to be less cohesive, so that residents take less interest in neighbourhood events and people; (20) the school climate is safe and nurturing.

Glossary

A

accommodation According to Piaget, the modification of existing schemas based on new experiences.

acculturation The process of integrating into and adopting the customs of a different culture.

achievement status The identity status in Marcia's theory in which adolescents have explored alternative identities and are now secure in their chosen identities.

active-passive child issue The issue of whether children are simply at the mercy of the environment (passive child) or actively influence their own development through their own unique individual characteristics (active child).

adolescent egocentrism The self-absorption that is characteristic of teenagers as they search for identity.

African American English (AAE) A dialect of standard English spoken by some African Americans that has slightly different grammatical rules than standard English.

age of viability The age at which a fetus can survive because most of its bodily systems function adequately, typically at seven months after conception.

aggression Behaviour meant to harm others.

allele A variation of a specific gene.

allophones People living in Canada who speak a language other than one of the official languages of Canada. (This term is used particularly in Quebec, as well as in other parts of Canada.)

altruism Prosocial behaviour, such as helping and sharing, in which the helping individual does not expect to benefit directly from his or her behaviour.

amniocentesis A prenatal diagnostic technique that involves withdrawing a sample of amniotic fluid through the abdomen using a syringe.

amniotic fluid Fluid in the amnion that cushions the embryo and maintains a constant temperature.

amniotic sac An inner sac in which the developing child rests.

amodal Information such as duration, rate, or intensity that is not restricted to a single mode of presentation and can be presented in different senses.

analytic ability In Robert Sternberg's theory of intelligence, the ability to analyze problems and generate different solutions.

androgens Hormones secreted by the testes that influence aggressive behaviour.

androgynous Having a combination of gender role traits that includes both instrumental and expressive behaviours.

animism A phenomenon common in preschool children in which they attribute life and lifelike properties to inanimate objects.

anorexia nervosa A persistent refusal to eat accompanied by an irrational fear of being overweight.

Apgar score A measure used to evaluate a newborn's condition, based on breathing, heart rate, muscle tone, presence of reflexes, and skin tone.

applied developmental science A scientific discipline that uses child-development research to promote healthy development, particularly for vulnerable children and families.

assimilation According to Piaget, the incorporation of new information into existing schemas.

associative play A form of play in which toddlers engage in similar activities, talk or smile at one another, and offer each other toys.

attachment The affectionate, reciprocal relationship that is formed at about six or seven months of age between an infant and his or her primary caregiver, usually the mother.

attention Processes that determine which information will be processed further by an individual.

attributions An individual's personal explanation for success or failure.

auditory threshold The quietest sound that a person can hear.

authoritarian parenting A style of parenting that combines high levels of control and low levels of warmth toward children.

authoritative parenting A style of parenting that combines a moderate degree of control with warmth and responsiveness toward children.

authority-oriented grandparents Grandparents who provide discipline for their grandchildren but otherwise are not particularly active in their grandchildren's lives.

autobiographical memory A person's memory of the significant events and experiences of his or her own life.

automatic processes Cognitive activities that require virtually no effort.

autonomous morality A more advanced level of moral reasoning wherein morality is based on free will.

autosomes The first 22 pairs of chromosomes.

avoidant attachment A relationship in which infants turn away from their mothers when they are reunited following a brief separation.

axon A slender, elongated structure that emerges from the cell body and transmits information to other neurons.

B

babbling Speech-like sounds that consist of vowel–consonant combinations.

baby biographies Detailed, systematic observations of individual children, often by famous scientists, that helped pave the way for objective research on children.

basic cry A cry that starts softly and gradually becomes more intense; often heard when babies are hungry or tired.

basic emotions Emotions that are experienced by people worldwide and that consist of a subjective feeling, a physiological change, and an overt behaviour. Examples include happiness, anger, and fear.

behavioural genetics The branch of genetics that deals with inheritance of behavioural and psychological traits.

blastocyst The fertilized egg four days after conception, which consists of about 100 cells and resembles a hollow ball.

blended family A family consisting of a biological parent, a stepparent, and children.

body dysmorphic disorder A disorder in which the individual is not satisfied with his/her body shape or the shape of a particular part of the body, often focusing on perceived muscularity.

body mass index (BMI) An adjusted ratio of weight to height used to define overweight.

breech presentation A birth in which the baby's feet or bottom are delivered before the head.

bulimia nervosa An eating disorder in which individuals alternate between bingeing (eating uncontrollably) and purging through self-induced vomiting or with laxatives.

C

Caesarean section (C-section) A surgical procedure in which an incision is made in the mother's abdomen to remove the baby from her uterus.

cardinality principle The counting principle in which the last number name denotes the number of objects being counted.

cell body The centre of the neuron that keeps the neuron alive.

central executive The component of the information-processing system, analogous to a computer's operating system, that coordinates the activities of the system.

centration Narrowly focused thinking characteristic of Piaget's preoperational stage.

cephalocaudal Literally "head to tail"; a development pattern in which maturation occurs from the head down.

cerebral cortex The wrinkled surface of the brain that regulates many functions that are distinctly human.

chorionic villus sampling (CVS) A prenatal diagnostic technique that involves taking a sample of tissue from the chorion.

chromosomes Thread-like structures in the nucleus of the cell that contain genetic material.

chronosystem In Bronfenbrenner's systems view, the idea that the microsystem, mesosystem, exosystem, and macrosystem are not static but change over time.

chunking The process of organizing related items into one meaningful group, thus improving working memory capacity.

classical conditioning First described by Ivan Pavlov, who showed that a previously neutral stimulus could become associated with a naturally occurring response and eventually come to elicit a similar response on its own.

clique Small groups of friends who are similar in age, sex, race, and interests.

cochlear implant A device that picks up speech sounds and converts them to electrical impulses that stimulate nerve cells in the ear.

code switching When children switch back and forth between languages, or variations of a language, depending on the situation, e.g., African American English and standard English.

cognitive-developmental perspective An approach to development that focuses on how children think and on how their thinking changes over time.

cognitive self-regulation The ability to identify goals, select effective strategies, and monitor accurately; a characteristic of successful students.

cohort A specific generation or group of people (e.g., a class or school grade) undergoing the same experiences at the same time.

collectivity The concept that interdependence of the members of the community is important.

comprehension The process of extracting meaning from a sequence of words.

concrete operational stage The third of Piaget's stages, from 7 to 11 years of age, in which children first use mental operations to solve problems and to reason.

cones Specialized neurons in the back of the eye that detect wavelength of light and, therefore, colour.

confounded As applied to the design of experiments, an error in which variables are combined instead of evaluated independently, making the results of the experiment ambiguous.

congenital adrenal hyperplasia (CAH) A genetic disorder in which girls are masculinized because the adrenal glands secrete large amounts of androgen during prenatal development.

constricting An interaction style common among boys in which one child tries to emerge as the victor by threatening or contradicting the others, by exaggerating, and so on.

constructivism The view, associated with Piaget, that children are active participants in their own development who systematically construct ever more sophisticated understandings of their worlds.

construct validity When a test measures the theoretical construct it is supposed to be measuring.

continuity-versus-discontinuity issue An issue concerned with whether a developmental phenomenon follows a smooth progression throughout the life span or a series of abrupt shifts.

conventional level The second level of reasoning in Kohlberg's theory, where moral reasoning is based on society's norms.

cooing Early vowel-like sounds that babies produce.

cooperative play Play that is organized around a theme, with each child taking on a different role; begins at about two years of age.

core-knowledge theories The view that infants are born with rudimentary knowledge of the world that is elaborated upon based on children's experiences.

corpus callosum A thick bundle of neurons that connects the two cerebral hemispheres.

correlation coefficient A statistic that reveals the strength and direction of the relation between two variables.

correlational study A research design in which investigators look at relations between variables as they exist naturally in the world.

co-rumination Conversations with friends that focus on each other's personal problems; thought to contribute to depression in adolescent girls.

counterimitation A type of observational learning in which the child observes and learns what should *not* be done.

creative ability In Robert Sternberg's theory of intelligence, the ability to deal adaptively with novel situations and problems.

creole A full language seemingly spontaneously developed by children of pidgin speakers.

critical period A time in development when a specific type of learning can take place; before or after the critical period, the same learning is difficult or even impossible.

cross-sectional study A research design in which people of different ages are compared at the same point in time.

crowd A large group that includes many cliques with similar attitudes and values.

crowning The appearance of the top of the baby's head during labour.

crystallization The first phase in Super's theory of career development, in which adolescents use their emerging identities for ideas about careers.

crystallized intelligence A person's culturally influenced accumulated knowledge and skills, including understanding printed language, comprehending language, and knowing vocabulary.

culture The knowledge, attitudes, and behaviour associated with a group of people.

culture-fair intelligence tests Tests designed to reduce the impact of different experiences by including items based on experiences common to many cultures.

cyberbullying Electronic bullying in which victims are harassed via cell phones or the internet.

D

debriefing An explanation by the researcher of the purposes of the experiment after its completion. The participant is given as full an explanation as possible, in wording appropriate to his or her level of understanding.

decoding The ability to identify individual words.

deductive reasoning Drawing conclusions from facts; characteristic of formal operational thought.

deferred imitation Imitation that involves repetition of behaviour seen at another time and place. The behaviour is not immediately copied; imitation occurs later.

dendrite The end of the neuron that receives information; it looks like a tree with many branches.

deoxyribonucleic acid (DNA) A molecule composed of four nucleotide bases; DNA is the biochemical basis of heredity.

dependent variable The behaviour that is observed after other variables are manipulated.

depression A disorder characterized by pervasive feelings of sadness, irritability, and low self-esteem.

detached grandparents Grandparents who are uninvolved with their grandchildren.

developmental dyslexia Difficulties in reading individual words.

differentiation (motion) Distinguishing and mastering individual skills.

diffusion status The identity status in Marcia's theory in which adolescents do not have an identity and are doing nothing to achieve one.

direct instruction A parental behaviour in which adults try to influence their children's behaviour by telling them what to do, when, and why.

dismissive adults (attachment representation) A representation of parent–child relations in which adults describe childhood experiences in very general terms and often idealize their parents.

disorganized (disoriented) attachment A relationship in which infants don't seem to understand what's happening when they are separated and later reunited with their mothers.

display rules Culturally specific standards for appropriate expressions of emotion in a particular setting or with a particular person or people.

divergent thinking Thinking in novel and unusual directions.

dizygotic (fraternal) twins Twins that are the result of the fertilization of two separate eggs by two sperm.

dominance hierarchy An ordering of individuals within a group in which group members with lower status defer to those with greater status.

dominant The form of an allele whose chemical instructions are followed.

doula A person familiar with childbirth who provides emotional and physical support throughout labour and delivery.

Down syndrome A disorder caused by an extra chromosome, in which individuals are mentally retarded and have a distinctive appearance.

dynamic systems theory A theory that views development as involving many distinct skills that are organized and reorganized over time to meet demands of specific tasks.

dynamic assessment An approach to intelligence testing that measures a child's learning potential by having the child learn something new in the presence of the examiner and with the examiner's help.

E

Ecological Systems Theory A theory in which the environment is divided into five components: the microsystem, the mesosystem, the exosystem, the macrosystem, and the chronosystem.

ectoderm The outer layer of the embryo, which becomes the hair, outer layer of skin, and nervous system.

effortful control The extent to which a child can focus attention, is not readily distracted, and can inhibit responses.

ego According to Freud, the rational component of the personality that develops during the first few years of life.

egocentrism Difficulty in seeing the world from another's point of view; typical of children in Piaget's preoperational stage.

ego-resilience Children's ability to respond adaptively and resourcefully to new situations.

elaboration A memory strategy in which information is embellished to make it more memorable.

electroencephalogram (EEG) A record pattern of brain waves obtained from electrodes placed on the scalp.

embryo The name given to the developing baby once the zygote is completely embedded in the uterine wall.

emotional intelligence (EI) The ability to use one's own and others' emotions effectively for solving problems and living happily.

empathy Fully understanding, even experiencing, another person's feelings.

enabling An interaction style common among girls in which children's actions and remarks tend to support others and to sustain the interaction.

encoding processes The cognitive processes that transform the information in a problem into a mental representation.

endoderm The inner layer of the embryo, which becomes the lungs and the digestive system.

epigenesis The continuous interplay between genes and multiple levels of the environment (from cells to culture).

epiphyses The growth area near the end of a bone; formed before the centre is formed.

equilibration According to Piaget, the process by which children reorganize their schemas and, in the process, move to the next developmental stage.

essentialism The belief, common among young children, that all living things have an underlying essence that can't be seen but that gives a living thing its identity.

ethnic identity The feeling that one is part of an ethnic group; understanding special customs and traditions of the group's culture and heritage.

ethological theory A theory in which development is seen from an evolutionary perspective and behaviours are examined for their survival value.

evolutionary psychology The theoretical view that many human behaviours represent successful adaptation to the environment.

executive functioning A mechanism of growth that includes inhibitory processes, planning, and cognitive flexibility.

exosystem According to Bronfenbrenner, social settings that influence one's development even though one does not experience them firsthand.

experience-dependent growth Changes in the brain caused by experiences that are not linked to specific ages and that vary across individuals and across cultures.

experience-expectant growth Changes in the brain from environmental influences that typically occur at specified points in development and for all children.

experiment A systematic way of manipulating factors that a researcher thinks cause a particular behaviour.

expressive style A style of language learning that describes children whose vocabularies include many social phrases that are used like one word.

expressive traits Psychological characteristics that describe a person who is focused on emotions and interpersonal relationships.

F

familial mental retardation A form of mental retardation that does not involve biological damage but represents the low end of the normal distribution of intelligence.

fast mapping The fact that children make connections between new words and referents so quickly that they can't be considering all possible meanings.

fetal alcohol syndrome (FAS) A disorder affecting babies whose mothers consumed large amounts of alcohol while they were pregnant.

fetal medicine The branch of medicine that deals with treating prenatal problems.

field experiment A type of experiment in which the researcher manipulates independent variables in a natural setting so that the results are more likely to be representative of behaviour in real-world settings.

fine-motor skills Motor skills associated with grasping, holding, and manipulating objects.

fluid intelligence The ability to perceive relations among stimuli; problem-solving and abstract reasoning ability that is not dependent on specific knowledge.

folk psychology Our informal beliefs about other people and their behaviour.

foreclosure status The identity status in Marcia's theory in which adolescents have an identity that was chosen based on advice from adults rather than one that was a result of personal exploration of alternatives.

formal operational stage The fourth of Piaget's stages, from roughly age 11 into adulthood, in which children and adolescents can apply mental operations to abstract entities, allowing them to think hypothetically and reason deductively.

friendship A voluntary relationship between two people involving mutual liking.

frontal cortex A brain region that regulates personality and goal-directed behaviour.

functional magnetic resonance imaging (fMRI) A technique for measuring brain activity that uses magnetic fields to track the flow of blood in the brain.

fuzzy trace theory A theory proposed by Brainerd and Reyna in which experiences can be stored in memory verbatim or in terms of their basic meaning (gist).

G

gender identity The perception of oneself as either male or female.

gender role Culturally prescribed behaviours considered appropriate for males and females.

gender schema theory A theory that children learn gender roles by first deciding if an object, activity, or behaviour is considered female or male, then using this information to decide whether they should learn more about the object, activity, or behaviour.

gender stereotypes Beliefs and images about males and females that are not necessarily true.

gene A group of nucleotide bases that provide a specific set of biochemical instructions.

genetic engineering A branch of fetal medicine in which defective genes are replaced with synthetic normal genes.

genotype A person's hereditary makeup.

germ disc A small cluster of cells near the centre of the zygote that develops into the baby.

gifted Traditionally, individuals with intelligence test scores of at least 130.

grammar A language's rules for combining words to create sentences.

grammatical morphemes Words or endings of words that make a sentence grammatical.

growth hormone A hormone, secreted by the pituitary gland during sleep, that regulates growth by triggering the release of other hormones that cause muscles and bones to grow.

guided participation According to Vygotsky, structured interactions between a child and another more knowledgeable person; these are thought to promote cognitive growth.

H

habituation Becoming unresponsive to a stimulus that is presented repeatedly.

hemispheres The right and left halves of the cortex.

hemophilia A disorder in which the blood does not clot easily and sufferers can bleed severely from even minor injury.

heritability coefficient An estimate of the extent to which differences between people reflect heredity.

heteronomous morality A belief in absolute rules handed down by another that are therefore rules that must be followed and cannot be changed.

heterozygous The condition in which the alleles for hereditary characteristics differ from each other.

heuristics Rules of thumb that are handy for solving problems but that do not guarantee a solution.

homozygous The condition in which the alleles for hereditary characteristics are the same.

hostile aggression A form of unprovoked aggression, the aim of which seems to be intimidation, harassment, or humiliation of another.

Huntington's disease A type of dementia caused by a dominant allele; characterized by degeneration of the nervous system.

hypoxia Lack of oxygen during delivery, typically because the umbilical cord becomes pinched or tangled during delivery.

I

id According to Freud, the element of personality that desires immediate gratification of bodily wants and needs; present at birth.

illusion of invulnerability The belief, common among adolescents, that misfortune only happens to others.

imaginary audience Adolescents' feelings that their behaviour is constantly being watched by their peers.

imitation Copying observed behaviours.

immanent justice A characteristic of the stage of moral realism in which children believe that breaking a rule always leads to punishment.

impaired reading comprehension Difficulties in understanding words that have been read successfully.

implantation The process in which the zygote burrows into the uterine wall and establishes connections with a woman's blood vessels.

implementation The third phase in Super's theory of career development, in which individuals enter the workforce.

imprinting Learning that occurs during a critical period soon after birth or hatching, as demonstrated by chicks creating an emotional bond with the first moving object they see.

incomplete dominance The situation in which one allele does not dominate another completely.

independent variable The factor that is manipulated by the researcher in an experiment.

inductive reasoning A parental discipline strategy of inducing the child to reason, to think for him or herself about a situation.

infant-directed speech Speech that adults use with babies that is slow and loud and has exaggerated changes in pitch.

infant mortality The number of infants out of 1000 births who die before their first birthday.

infantile amnesia The inability to remember events from early in one's life.

inferential statistics A powerful form of statistics that allows one to draw conclusions and to speculate about causation.

influential grandparents Grandparents who are very close to their grandchildren, are very involved in their lives, and frequently perform parental roles, including discipline.

information-processing theory A view that human cognition consists of mental hardware and mental software.

informed consent A person's decision to participate in research after having been told enough about the research to make an educated decision; children are not legally capable of giving informed consent.

inhibitory processes Processes that prevent task-irrelevant information from entering working memory.

inner speech Vygotsky's term for thought.

instrumental aggression Aggression used to achieve an explicit goal.

instrumental traits Psychological characteristics that describe a person who acts on and influences the world.

integration Linking individual motions into a coherent, coordinated whole.

intellectual disability A disorder formerly known as mental retardation in which, before 18 years of age, individuals have substantially below-average intelligence and problems adapting to an environment.

intelligence quotient (IQ) Initially a ratio of mental age to chronological age multiplied by 100; now determined by population test score comparisons.

internal working model An infant's understanding of how responsive and dependable his or her mother is; thought to influence close relationships throughout the child's life.

interposition A perceptual cue to depth based on the fact that nearby objects partially obscure more distant objects.

intersensory redundancy theory A situation in which information is presented simultaneously to different sensory modes, such as rhythm.

intersubjectivity According to Vygotsky, mutual, shared understanding among people who are participating in an activity together.

intonation A pattern of rising and falling pitch in speech or babbling that often indicates whether the utterance is a statement, question, or command.

in vitro fertilization The technique of fertilizing eggs with sperm in a Petri dish and then transferring several of the fertilized eggs to the mother's uterus, where they might implant in the lining of the uterine wall.

J

joint custody When both parents retain legal custody of their children following a divorce.

K

kangaroo care A carrying position in which infants dressed only in a diaper are held against an adult's bare chest in a sling or blanket; used with premature and special care infants to give skin-to-skin contact and positive stimulation.

kinetic cues Visual cues in which motion is used to estimate depth.

knowledge-telling strategy A strategy for writing, often used by younger writers, in which information is written in sequence as it is retrieved from memory.

knowledge-transforming strategy A strategy for writing, often used by older writers, in which they decide what information to include and how best to organize it for the point they wish to convey to their reader.

L

language Any rule-based system for expressing ideas.

latchkey children Children who care for themselves after school.

learning disability The condition in which a child with normal intelligence has difficulty mastering at least one academic subject.

linear perspective A cue to depth perception based on the fact that parallel lines come together at a single point in the distance.

locomotion The ability to move around in the world.

longitudinal design A research design in which a single cohort is studied over multiple times of measurement.

longitudinal-sequential study A particular form of longitudinal design that includes sequences of samples, each studied longitudinally.

long-term memory A permanent storehouse that has unlimited capacity for memories.

M

macrosystem According to Bronfenbrenner, the cultural and subcultural settings in which the microsystem, mesosystem, and exosystem are embedded.

mad cry A more intense version of a basic cry.

malnutrition Inadequate nutrition that causes one to be small for one's age.

mathematical learning disability (developmental dyscalculia) Difficulties in mathematics.

maturational theory The view that child development reflects a specific and prearranged scheme or plan within the body.

means-end analysis A problem-solving heuristic in which people determine the difference between the current and desired situations, then do something to reduce the difference.

memory strategies Activities that improve remembering.

menarche The onset of menstruation.

mental age (MA) In intelligence testing, a measure of children's performance corresponding to the chronological age of those whose performance equals the child's.

mental operations Cognitive actions that can be performed on objects or ideas.

mental retardation A disorder in which, before 18 years of age, individuals have substantially below-average intelligence and problems adapting to an environment.

mental rotation One aspect of spatial ability involving the ability to imagine how an object will look after it has been moved in space.

mesoderm The middle layer of the embryo, which will become the muscles, bones, and circulatory system.

mesosystem According to Bronfenbrenner, the interrelations between different aspects of the microsystem.

meta-analysis A tool that allows researchers to synthesize the results of many studies to estimate relations between variables.

metacognitive knowledge A person's knowledge and awareness of cognitive processes.

metamemory A person's informal understanding of memory; includes the ability to diagnose memory problems accurately and to monitor the effectiveness of memory strategies.

methylation A process by which experience changes the expression of DNA—the genetic code is preserved, but a gene is silenced by a methyl molecule.

microgenetic study A special type of longitudinal study in which children are tested repeatedly over a span of days or weeks, with the aim of observing change directly as it occurs.

microsystem According to Bronfenbrenner, the people and objects that are present in one's immediate environment.

monitoring As applied to parent–child relations, parents' knowledge of where their children are, what they're doing, and who they are with.

monozygotic (identical) twins Twins that result when a single fertilized egg splits to form two new individuals.

moral realism A stage described by Piaget that begins at about five years of age and continues through age seven in which children believe that rules are created by wise adults and therefore must be followed and cannot be changed.

moral relativism A stage described by Piaget that begins at about age eight in which children understand that rules are created by people to help them get along.

moratorium status The identity status in Marcia's theory in which adolescents are still examining different alternatives and have yet to find a satisfactory identity.

morphology The rules of meaning within a language.

motion parallax A visual cue wherein the fact that nearby moving objects move across our visual field faster than those at a distance gives information about depth and distance.

motor skills Coordinated movements of the muscles and limbs.

myelin A fatty sheath that surrounds neurons in the central nervous system and allows them to transmit information more rapidly.

N

naming explosion A period, beginning at about age 18 months, in which children learn new words very rapidly.

naturalistic observation A method of observation in which children are observed as they behave spontaneously in a real-life situation.

nature–nurture issue An issue concerning the manner in which genetic and environmental factors influence development.

negative affect A dimension of temperament that refers to the extent to which a child is angry, fearful, frustrated, shy, and not easily soothed.

negative correlation A relation between two variables in which larger values on one variable are associated with smaller values on a second variable.

negative reinforcement trap A situation in which parents often unwittingly reinforce the very behaviours they want to discourage; particularly likely between mothers and sons.

neural plate A flat group of cells present in prenatal development that becomes the brain and spinal cord.

neuron A cell that is the basic unit of the brain and nervous system; specializes in receiving and transmitting information.

neurotransmitters Chemicals released by terminal buttons that carry information to nearby neurons.

niche-picking The process of deliberately seeking environments that are compatible with one's genetic makeup.

non-REM (regular) sleep Sleep in which heart rate, breathing, and brain activity are steady.

nonshared environmental influences Forces in the immediate environment (e.g., within a family) that make children different from one another.

norepinephrine A neurotransmitter that helps regulate the brain centres that allow people to experience pleasure; below-normal levels of norepinephrine may contribute to depression.

null hypothesis The hypothesis against which the experimental hypothesis is tested. The null hypothesis basically states that nothing the experimenter did has any effect.

O

object permanence The understanding, acquired in infancy, that objects exist independently of oneself.

observational learning Learning by observing; children learn a great deal from others simply by watching them.

observer bias A bias that occurs when the researcher performing observations tends to notice those behaviours that support the hypothesis and to discount those that do not, or interprets behaviours in such a way that they support the hypothesis.

observer influence A source of experimental error that occurs when the participants change their behaviour because they are being observed; the influence of the fact of observation.

one-to-one principle The counting principle that states that there must be one and only one number name for each object counted.

open adoption A form of adoption in which adopted children have contact with their birth families.

operant conditioning A view of learning, proposed by Skinner, that emphasizes reward and punishment.

organic mental retardation Mental retardation that can be traced to a specific biological or physical problem.

organization A memory strategy in which information that must be remembered is structured so that related information is placed together.

osteoporosis A disease, common among women over age 50, in which a person's bones become thin and brittle, and, as a consequence, sometimes break.

overextension When children define words more broadly than adults do.

over-regularization Children's application of rules to words that are exceptions to the rule; used as evidence that children master grammar by learning rules.

P

pain cry A cry that begins with a sudden, long burst, followed by a long pause and gasping.

parallel play When children play alone but are aware of and interested in what another child is doing; occurs soon after the first birthday.

passive grandparents Grandparents who are caught up in their grandchildren's development but without the intensity of influential or supportive grandparents; these grandparents do not assume parental roles.

period of the fetus The longest period of prenatal development, extending from the ninth week after conception until birth.

permissive parenting A style of parenting that offers warmth and caring but little parental control over children.

personal domain The domain of decisions concerning one's body (e.g., what to eat and wear) and choices of friends or activities.

personal fable The feeling of many adolescents that their feelings and experiences are unique and have never been experienced by anyone else before.

phenotype The physical, behavioural, and psychological features that are the result of the interaction between one's genes and the environment.

phonemes Unique speech sounds that can be used to create words.

phonological awareness The ability to hear the distinctive sounds associated with specific letters.

phonological memory The ability to briefly remember speech sounds.

phonology The sounds of a language.

pictorial cues Cues for depth that depend on the arrangement of objects in the environment, so called because these same cues are used by artists to convey depth in drawings and paintings.

pidgin A rudimentary language developed when groups of people from different linguistic backgrounds living in the same place need to communicate.

placenta The structure through which nutrients and wastes are exchanged between the mother and the developing child.

plasticity In the context of neural development, the extent to which brain organization is flexible.

polygenic inheritance When phenotypes are the result of the combined activity of many separate genes.

population A broad group of children who are the usual focus of research in child development.

positive correlation A relation between two variables in which larger values on one variable are associated with larger values on a second variable.

postconventional level The third level of reasoning in Kohlberg's theory, in which morality is based on a personal moral code.

postpartum depression A condition affecting 10 to 15 percent of new mothers in which irritability continues for months after the birth and is often accompanied by feelings of low self-worth, disturbed sleep, poor appetite, and apathy.

power assertion A discipline strategy in which a parent lays down the law with no explanation (e.g., "You'll do it because I said so").

practical ability In Robert Sternberg's theory of intelligence, the ability to know which solutions to problems are likely to work.

pragmatics How people use language to communicate effectively.

preconventional level The first level of reasoning in Kohlberg's theory, where moral reasoning is based on external forces.

prejudice A view of other people, usually negative, that is based on their membership in a specific group.

premature infant A baby born before the 38th week after conception.

premoral Having not yet developed moral sensibility.

preoccupied adults (attachment representation) A representation of parent—child relations in which adults describe childhood experiences emotionally and often express anger or confusion regarding relationships with their parents.

preoperational stage The second of Piaget's stages, from two to seven years of age, in which children first use symbols to represent objects and events.

primary circular reaction An action that occurs when an infant accidentally produces some pleasing event and then deliberately tries to recreate the event; for example, self-initiated thumb sucking.

primary sex characteristics Changes in bodily organs directly involved in reproduction (i.e., the ovaries, uterus, and vagina in girls, and the scrotum, testes, and penis in boys) that are signs of physical maturity.

private speech Ongoing commentary that children use that is not intended for others but rather to help children regulate their own behaviour.

propositions Ideas created during reading by combining words.

prosocial behaviour Any behaviour that benefits another person.

proximodistal Meaning "from in close to further out"; a development pattern of control over trunk of body first, then moving out toward the extremities.

psychodynamic theory A view first formulated by Sigmund Freud in which development is largely determined by how well people resolve the conflicts they face at different ages.

psychometrician A psychologist who specializes in the measurement of psychological characteristics such as intelligence and personality.

psychosocial theory A theory proposed by Erik Erikson in which personality development is the result of the interaction of maturation and societal demands.

puberty A collection of physical changes that marks the onset of adolescence, such as the growth spurt and the growth of breasts or testes.

punishment Applying an aversive stimulus (e.g., a spanking) or removing an attractive stimulus (e.g., TV viewing); an action that discourages the reoccurrence of the response that it follows.

Q

qualitative research Research in which there is in-depth study of individuals.

quantitative research Research that adds together many pieces of data.

quasi-experimental design An experimental design that includes groups that were not formed by random assignment; because participants are not assigned truly randomly, it is called a quasi-experiment.

R

rapid-eye-movement (REM) sleep (irregular sleep) Sleep during which an infant's eyes dart rapidly beneath the eyelids while the body is quite active.

reaction range The phenomenon that a particular genotype can interact with various environments to produce a range of phenotypes.

reactive aggression Aggression prompted by another child's behaviour.

recessive allele An allele whose instructions are ignored when it is combined with a dominant allele.

recursive thinking A child's ability to think about what others are thinking, particularly when another person's thoughts refer to the child (e.g., "He thinks that I think . . .").

referential style A style of language learning that describes children whose vocabularies are dominated by names of objects, persons, or actions.

reflexes Unlearned responses that are triggered by specific stimulation.

rehearsal A memory strategy that involves repeating information that is to be remembered.

reinforcement A consequence that increases the likelihood that a behaviour will be repeated in the future.

relational aggression A form of verbal aggression in which children try to hurt others by undermining social relationships.

relative size A perceptual cue to depth based on the fact that nearby objects look substantially larger than objects in the distance.

reliable research design An overall conceptual plan for research; the two most common designs are correlational and experimental designs.

resistant attachment A relationship in which, after a brief separation, infants want to be held but are difficult to console.

response bias The tendency for research participants to respond in ways that are socially more acceptable.

retinal disparity A perceptual cue to depth based on the fact that when a person views an object, the retinal images in the left and right eyes differ.

rough-and-tumble play A form of play common during the elementary school years in which children playfully chase, punch, kick, shove, fight, and wrestle with peers.

S

sample A group of children drawn from a population that participates in research.

savants Individuals with mental retardation who are quite talented in one domain.

scaffolding A teaching style in which adults adjust the amount of assistance that they offer based on the learner's needs.

schemas (or schemata) In Piaget's theory, active, continually changing, and developing mental structures that drive cognitive development.

school phobia An overwhelming fear of going to school and active resistance to attending school.

script The means by which people remember common events consisting of sequences of activities.

secondary circular reaction An action that occurs when an infant discovers repeated actions that involve an object; for example, hitting a mobile to cause it to move.

secondary sex characteristics Physical signs of maturity in body parts not linked directly to the reproductive organs (e.g., growth of breasts in girls, the appearance of facial hair in boys, the appearance of body hair in both boys and girls).

secular growth trends Changes in physical development from one generation to the next; for example, the fact that people in industrialized societies are larger and mature earlier than in previous generations.

secure adults (attachment representation) A representation of parent–child relations in which adults describe childhood experiences objectively and mention both positive and negative aspects of their parents.

secure attachment A relationship in which infants have come to trust and depend on their mothers.

self-concept Attitudes, behaviours, and values that a person believes make him or her a unique individual.

self-conscious emotions Emotions such as pride, guilt, or embarrassment that involve feelings of success when one's standards or expectations are met and feelings of failure when they aren't; emerge between 18 to 24 months of age.

self-control The ability to rise above immediate pressures and not give in to impulse.

self-efficacy The belief that one is capable of performing a certain task.

self-esteem A person's judgment and feelings about his or her own worth.

self-reports Children's answers to questions about specific topics.

semantic bootstrapping theory A view that children rely on their knowledge of word meanings to discover grammatical rules.

semantics The study of words and their meaning.

sensorimotor stage The first of Piaget's four stages of cognitive development, which lasts from birth to approximately two years of age, in which infants progress from responding reflexively to using symbols.

sensory and perceptual processes The means by which the nervous system receives, selects, modifies, and organizes stimulation from the world.

sensory memory A type of memory in which information is held in raw, unanalyzed form very briefly (no longer than a few seconds).

serotonin A neurotransmitter that helps regulate the brain centres that allow people to experience pleasure; below-normal levels of serotonin may contribute to depression.

sex chromosomes The 23rd pair of chromosomes, which determines the sex of the child.

sex-linked When a genetic disorder is linked to a gene carried by one of the sex chromosomes.

sickle-cell trait A disorder in which individuals show signs of mild anemia only when they are seriously deprived of oxygen; occurs in individuals who have one dominant allele for normal blood cells and one recessive sickle-cell allele.

size constancy The realization that an object's actual size remains the same despite changes in the size of its retinal image.

small-for-date infants Newborns who are substantially smaller than would be expected based on the length of time since their conception.

social cognitive theory A theory developed by Albert Bandura that stresses the use of cognition (thinking) in learning; children use reward, punishment, and imitation to try to understand what goes on in their world.

social conventions Arbitrary standards of behaviour agreed to by a cultural group to help coordinate interactions of individuals within the group.

social influence As applied to teen pregnancies, the view that when teenage girls give birth, a set of events are triggered that make it harder for these girls to provide a positive environment for their children's development.

social referencing A phenomenon in which infants in an unfamiliar or ambiguous environment look at their mother or father, as if searching for cues to help them interpret the situation.

social role A set of cultural guidelines about how one should behave, especially with other people.

social selection As applied to teen pregnancies, the view that some teenage girls are more likely than others to become pregnant, and these same factors put their children at risk.

social smiles Smiles that appear when infants see another human face, usually beginning at about two months of age.

socialized aggression Aggression that is expected within a situation, for example, a hockey fight.

sociocultural perspective The view that children's cognitive development is not only brought about by social interaction, but it is also inseparable from the sociocultural contexts in which they live.

spatial memory The ability to remember the position of objects in the environment.

specification The second phase in Super's theory of career development, in which adolescents learn more about specific lines of work and begin training.

spermarche The first spontaneous ejaculation of sperm-laden fluid; typically occurs around age 13.

spina bifida A disorder in which the embryo's neural tube does not close properly during the first month of pregnancy.

stable-order principle The counting principle that states that number names must always be counted in the same order.

stereotype threat The self-fulfilling prophecy in which knowledge of stereotypes leads to anxiety and reduced performance consistent with the original stereotype.

stranger wariness An infant's apparent concern or anxiety in the presence of an unfamiliar adult, typically observed at about six months of age.

stress A person's physical and psychological responses to threatening or challenging situations.

structured observation A method in which the researcher creates a setting to elicit the behaviour of interest.

sudden unexpected infant death (SUID) A disorder in which a healthy baby dies suddenly, for no apparent reason, typically occurring between two and four months of age.

superego According to Freud, the moral component of the personality that has incorporated adult standards of right and wrong.

supportive grandparents Grandparents who are very close to and involved with their grandchildren but do not take on parental roles.

surgency/extraversion A dimension of temperament that refers to the extent to which a child is generally happy, active, vocal, and seeks interesting stimulation.

swaddling A technique for calming a crying baby in which the baby is wrapped tightly in a blanket.

synapse The gap between one neuron and the next.

synaptic pruning Gradual loss of unused synapses, beginning in infancy and continuing into early adolescence.

syntax Rules that specify how words are combined to form sentences.

systematic desensitization A therapeutic technique that associates deep relaxation with progressively more anxiety-provoking situations.

systematic observation A method of observation in which investigators watch children and carefully record what they do or say.

T

telegraphic speech A style of speaking common in one-year-olds that includes only words directly relevant to meaning.

teleological explanation As applied to children's naïve theories of living things, the belief that living things and parts of living things exist for a purpose.

temperament A consistent style or pattern of behaviour.

teratogen An agent that causes abnormal prenatal development.

terminal buttons Small knobs at the end of an axon that release neurotransmitters.

tertiary circular reaction An action that occurs when an infant repeats old actions with new objects, as if he or she is trying to understand why different objects yield different outcomes.

texture gradient A perceptual cue to depth based on the fact that the texture of objects changes from coarse but distinct for nearby objects to finer and less distinct for distant objects.

theory An explanation of principles based on observation and reasoning; for example, an organized set of ideas that is designed to explain development.

theory of mind An intuitive understanding of the connections between thoughts, beliefs, intentions, and behaviour; develops rapidly in the preschool years.

time in Punishment that involves talking immediately with children who are misbehaving, to help them understand the situation and their own feelings.

time out Punishment that involves removing a child who is misbehaving to a quiet, unstimulating environment.

toddlers Young children who have just learned to walk.

U

ultrasound A prenatal diagnostic technique that involves bouncing sound waves off the fetus to generate an image of the fetus.

umbilical cord A structure containing veins and arteries that connects the developing fetus to the mother's placenta.

underextension When children define words more narrowly than adults do.

uninvolved parenting A style of parenting that provides neither warmth nor control and that minimizes the amount of time parents spend with children.

V

validity As applied to tests, the extent to which the test measures what it is supposed to measure.

variable Any factor subject to change.

vernix A thick, greasy substance that covers the fetus and protects it during prenatal development.

villi Finger-like projections from the umbilical blood vessels that are close to the mother's blood vessels and thus allow nutrients, oxygen, vitamins, and waste products to be exchanged between mother and embryo.

visual acuity Refers to the smallest pattern that one can distinguish reliably.

visual cliff A glass-covered platform that appears to have a "shallow" side and "deep" side; used to study infants' depth perception.

visual expansion A visual cue that provides information about the distance of an object: An object fills an ever greater proportion of the retina as it moves closer; for example, a thrown ball gets closer to the face.

W

word decoding The ability to identify individual words, either by retrieving them or sounding them out.

word recognition The process of identifying a unique pattern of letters.

working memory A type of memory in which a small number of items can be stored briefly.

Z

zone of proximal development The difference between what children can do with assistance and what they can do alone.

zygote The fertilized egg.

References

AAIDD Ad Hoc Committee on Terminology and Classification. (2010). *Intellectual disability* (11th ed.). Washington, DC: American Association on Intellectual and Developmental Disabilities.

Aboriginal Head Start (AHS). (2008). Aboriginal children: The healing power of cultural identity. Retrieved from http://www.phac-aspc.gc.ca/dca-dea/programs-mes/aboriginal-autochtones-eng.php

Aboud, F. E. (2003). The formation of in-group favoritism and out-group prejudice in young children: Are they distinct attitudes? *Developmental Psychology, 39,* 48–60.

Aboud, F.E., Mendelson, M.J., & Purdy, K.T. (2003). Cross-race peer relations and friendship quality. *International Journal of Behavioral Development, 27,* 165–173.

Aboud, F. E., Tredoux, C., Tropp, L. R., Brown, C. S., Niens, U., Noor, N. M. et al. (2012). Interventions to reduce prejudice and enhance inclusion and respect for ethnic differences in early childhood: A systematic review. *Developmental Review, 32,* 307–336.

Ackerman, B. P. (1993). Children's understanding of the speaker's meaning in referential communication. *Journal of Experimental Child Psychology, 55,* 56–86.

Ackerman, B. P., & Brown, E. D. (2006). Income poverty, poverty co-factors, and the adjustment of children in elementary school. In R. V. Kail (Ed.), *Advances in child development and behavior* (Vol. 34). Amsterdam, The Netherlands: Elsevier Academic Press.

Action Schools! BC. (n.d.). Retrieved from www.actionschoolsbc.ca

Active Healthy Kids Canada. (2012). *Physical Activity Levels.* Author. Retrieved from www.activehealthykids.ca

Adam, E. K. (2004). Beyond quality: Parental and residential stability and children's adjustment. *Current Directions in Psychological Science, 13,* 210–213.

Adam, E. K., & Chase-Lansdale, P. L. (2002). Home sweet home(s): Parental separations, residential moves, and adjustment problems in low-income adolescent girls. *Developmental Psychology, 38,* 792–805.

Adams, J. (1999). On neurodevelopmental disorders: Perspectives from neurobehavioral teratology. In H. Tager-Flusberg (Ed.), *Neurodevelopmental disorders* (pp. 451–468). Cambridge, MA: MIT Press.

Adams, M. J., Treiman, R., & Pressley, M. (1998). Reading, writing, and literacy. In W. Damon (Ed.), *Handbook of child psychology* (Vol. 4, pp. 275–355). New York, NY: Wiley.

Adams, R. E., Santo, J. B., & Bukowski, W. M. (2011). The presence of a best friend buffers the effects of negative experiences. *Developmental Psychology, 47,* 1786–1791.

Adams, R. J., & Courage, M. L. (1995). Development of chromatic discrimination in early infancy. *Behavioral Brain Research, 67,* 99–101.

Adler, R. (2007, 3 November). America's lost children. *New Scientist,* p. 22.

Administration for Children and Families. (2015). *Head Start program facts fiscal year 2015.* Washington DC: Author.

Adolph, K. E. (2000). Specificity of learning: Why infants fall over a veritable cliff. *Psychological Science, 11,* 290–295.

Adolph, K. (2002). Learning to keep balance. In R. V. Kail (Ed.), *Advances in child development and behavior* (Vol. 30, pp. 1–40). Orlando, FL: Academic Press.

Adolph, K. E., Cole, W. G., Komati, M., Garciaguirre, J. S., Badaly, D., Lingeman, J. M., et al. (2012). How do you learn to walk? Thousands of steps and dozens of falls per day. *Psychological Science, 23,* 1387–1394.

Adolph, K. E., & Robinson, S. R. (2013). The road to walking: What learning to walk tells us about development. In P. Zelazo (Ed.) *Oxford handbook of developmental psychology* (pp. 403–443). New York, NY: Oxford University Press.

Adolphus, K., Lawton, C. L., & Dye, L. (2013). The effects of breakfast on behavior and academic performance in children and adolescents. *Frontiers in Human Neuroscience, 7,* Article 425.

Adzick, N. S., Thom, E. A., Spong, C. Y., Brock, J. W., Burrows, P. K., Johnson, M. P. et al. (2011). A randomized trial of prenatal versus postnatal repair of myelomeningocele. *The New England Journal of Medicine, 364,* 993–1004.

Affi, T. O., Mota, N. P., Dasiewicz, P., MacMillan, H. L., & Sareen, J. (2012). Physical punishment and mental disorders: Results from a nationally representative US sample. *Pediatrics, 130*(2), 1–9.

Afifi, T. O., Enns, M. W., Cox, B. J., & Martens, P. J. (2005). Investigating health correlates of adolescent depression in Canada. *Canadian Journal of of Public Health, 96*(6), 427–431.

Ainsworth, M. D. S. (1978). The development of infant-mother attachment. In B. M. Caldwell & H. N. Ricciuti (Eds.), *Review of child development research* (Vol. 3, pp. 1–94). Chicago, IL: University of Chicago Press.

Ainsworth, M. S. (1993). Attachment as related to mother-infant interaction. *Advances in Infancy Research, 8,* 1–50.

Al-Sahab, B., Ardern, C. I., Hamadeh, M. J., & Tamim, H. (2010). Age at menarche in Canada: Results from the National Longitudinal Survey of Children and Youth. *BioMed Central Public Health, 10*:736. Retrieved from www.biomedcentral.com/1471-2458/10/736

Alatupa, S., Pulkki-Råback, L., Hintsanen, M., Elovainio, M., Mullola, S., & Keltikangas-Järvinen, L. (2013). Disruptive behavior in childhood and socioeconomic position in adulthood: A prospective study over 27 years. *International Journal of Public Health, 58,* 247–256.

Alphonso, C. (2013, April 18). Bullying expert turns her eye to Halifax board. *Globe and Mail,* p. A3.

Alberts, A. E. (2005). Neonatal behavioral assessment scale. In C. B. Fisher & R. M. Lerner (Eds.), *Encyclopedia of applied developmental science* (Vol. 1, pp. 111–115). Thousand Oaks, CA: Sage.

Aldridge, V., Dovey, T. M., & Halford, J. C. G. (2009). The role of familiarity in dietary development. *Developmental Review, 29,* 32–44.

Alexander, G. M., & Wilcox, T. (2012). Sex differences in early infancy. *Child Development Perspectives, 6,* 400–406.

Allen, J. P., Chango, J., Szwedo, D., Schad, M., & Marston, E. (2012). Predictors of susceptibility to peer influence regarding substance use in adolescence. *Child Development, 83,* 337–350.

Allen, L., Cipielewski, J., & Stanovich, K. E. (1992). Multiple indicators of children's reading habits and attitudes: Construct validity and cognitive correlates. *Journal of Educational Psychology, 84,* 489–503.

Alink, L. R. A., Cicchetti, D., Kim, J., & Rogosch, F. A. (2012). Longitudinal associations among child maltreatment, social functioning, and cortisol regulation. *Developmental Psychology, 48,* 224–236.

Almas, A. N., Degnan, K. A., Radulescu, A., Nelson, C. A., Zeanah, C. H., & Fox, N. A. (2012). Effects of early intervention and the moderating effects of brain activity on institutionalized children's social skills at age 8. *Proceedings of the National Academy of Sciences (PNAS), 109*(S.2), 17228–17231.

Alter, A. L., Aronson, J., Darley, J. M., Rodriguez, C., & Ruble, D. N. (2010). Rising to the threat: Reducing stereotype threat by reframing the threat as a challenge. *Journal of Experimental Social Psychology, 46,* 166–171.

Amato, P. R. (2001). Children of divorce in the 1990s: An update of the Amato and Keith (1991) meta-analysis. *Journal of Family Psychology, 15,* 355–370.

Amato, P. R. (2010). Research on divorce: Continuing trends and new developments. *Journal of Marriage and Family, 72,* 650–666.

Amato, P. R., & Fowler, F. (2002). Parenting practices, child adjustment, and family diversity. *Journal of Marriage and the Family, 64,* 703–716.

Amato, P. R., & Keith, B. (1991). Parental divorce and the well-being of children: A meta-analysis. *Psychological Bulletin, 110,* 26–46.

Amato, P. R., Kane, J. B., & James, S. (2011). Reconsidering the "good divorce." *Family Relations, 60,* 511–524.

American Academy of Pediatrics. (2008). *Feeding kids right isn't always easy: Tips for preventing food hassles.* Elk Grove Village, IL: Author.

American Academy of Pediatrics. (2011). *Caring for our children: National health and safety performance standards; guidelines for early child care and education programs* (3rd ed.). Elk Grove Village, IL: Author.

American College of Obstetricians and Gynecologists. (2011a). *Frequently asked questions: Pain relief during labor and delivery.* Washington DC: Author.

American College of Obstetricians and Gynecologists. (2011b). *Frequently asked questions: Cesarean birth.* Washington DC: Author.

American Lung Association. (2007). *State of lung disease in diverse communities: 2007.* New York, NY: Author.

American Psychiatric Association. (2004). *Diagnostic and statistical manual of mental disorders* (4th ed.). Washington, DC: Author.

American Psychological Association. (APA) (2010). *Publication Manual of the American Psychological Association.* Washington, DC: Author.

Amso, D., & Johnson, S. P. (2006). Learning by selection: Visual search and object perception in young infants. *Developmental Psychology, 42,* 1236–1245.

Amsterlaw, J., Lagattuta, K. H., & Meltzoff, A. N. (2009). Young children's reasoning about the effects of emotional and physiological states on academic performance. *Child Development, 80,* 115–133.

Anastasi, A. (1976). *Psychological testing* (4th ed.). New York, NY: MacMillan.

Anastasi, A. (1988). *Psychological testing* (6th ed.). New York, NY: Macmillan.

Anderson, C. A., Berkowitz, L., Donnerstein, E., Huessman, R., Johnson, J. D., Linz, D., et al. (2003). The influence of media violence on youth. *Psychological Science in the Public Interest, 4,* 81–106.

Anderson, D. R., Huston, A. C., Schmitt, K. L., Linebarger, D. L., & Wright, J. C. (2001). Early childhood television viewing and adolescent behavior. *Monographs of the Society for Research in Child Development, 66*(Serial No. 264).

Anderson, E. (2000). Exploring register knowledge: The value of "controlled improvisation." In L. Menn & N. B. Ratner (Eds.), *Methods for studying language production* (pp. 225–248). Mahwah, NJ: Erlbaum.

Anderson, S. W., Damasio, H., Tranel, D., & Damasio, A. R. (2001). Long-term sequelae of prefrontal cortex damage acquired in early childhood. *Developmental Neuropsychology, 18,* 281–296.

Ansari, D. (2008). Effects of development and enculturation on number representation in the brain. *Nature reviews – Neuroscience, 9*(4), 278–291. doi:10.1038/nrn2334

Ansari, D., Garcia, N. Luca, E., Hamon, K., & Dhital, B. (2005). Neural correlates of symbolic number processing in children and adults. *NeuroReport, 16*(7), 1769–1773.

Anzures, G., Quinn, P. C., Pascalis, O., Slater, A. M., Tanaka, J. W., & Lee, K. (2013). Developmental origins of the other-race effect. *Current Directions in Psychological Science, 22,* 173–178.

Anzures, G., Wheeler, A., Quinn, P. C., Pascalis, O., Slater, A. M., Heron-Delaney, M., et al. (2012). Brief daily exposures to Asian females reverses perceptual narrowing for Asian faces in Caucasian infants. *Journal of Experimental Child Psychology, 112,* 484–495.

Apfelbaum, E. P., Pauker, K., Ambady, N., Sommers, S. R., & Norton, M. I. (2008). Learning (not) to talk about race: When older children underperform in social categorization. *Developmental Psychology, 44,* 1513–1518.

Apgar, V. (1953). A proposal for a new method of evaluation of the newborn infant. *Current Researches in Anesthesia and Analgesia, 32,* 260–267.

Appleyard, K., Yang, C. M., & Runyan, D. K. (2010). Delineating the maladaptive pathways of child maltreatment: A mediated moderation analysis of the roles of self-perception and social support. *Development and Psychopathology, 22,* 337–352.

Arabi, M., Frongillo, E. A., Avula, R., & Mangasaryan, N. (2012). Infant and young child feeding in developing countries. *Child Development, 83,* 32–45.

Archer, J. (2004). Sex differences in aggression in real-world settings: A meta-analytic review. *Review of General Psychology, 8,* 291–322.

Archer, J. (2006). Testosterone and human aggression: An evaluation of the challenge hypothesis. *Neuroscience and Biobehavioral Reviews, 30,* 319–345.

Archer, J. (2013). Can evolutionary principles explain patterns of family violence? *Psychological Bulletin, 139,* 403–440.

Arctic Monitoring and Assessment Programme (AMAP). (2009). *Assessment 2009: Human health in the Arctic.* Oslo, Norway: Author.

Armstrong, L. L., & Manion, I. G. (2006). Suicidal ideation in young males living in rural communities: Distance from school as a risk factor, youth engagement as a protective factor. *Vulnerable Children and Youth Studies, 1,* 102–113.

Arndorfer, C. L., & Stormshak, E. A. (2008). Same-sex versus other-sex best friendship in early adolescence: Longitudinal predictors of antisocial behavior throughout adolescence. *Journal of Youth & Adolescence, 37,* 1059–1070.

Arseneault, L., Tremblay, R. E., Boulerice, B., & Saucier, J. F. (2002). Obstetrical complications and violent delinquency: Testing two developmental pathways. *Child Development, 73,* 496–508.

Arsenio, W. F., Gold, J., & Adams, E. (2006). Children's conceptions and displays of moral emotions. In M. Killen & J. G. Smetana (2006), *Handbook of moral development* (pp. 581–609). Mahwah, NJ: Erlbaum.

Arunachalam, S., Escovar, E., Hansen, M. A., & Waxman, S. R. (2013). Out of sight, but not out of mind: 21-month-olds use syntactic information to learn verbs even in the absence of a corresponding event. *Language and Cognitive Processes, 28,* 417–425.

Asbridge, M., Brubacher, J. R., & Chan, H. (2013). Cell phone use and traffic crash risk: A culpability analysis. *International Journal of Epidemiology, 42,* 259–267.

Asendorpf, J. B., Denissen, J. J. A., & van Aken, M. A. G. (2008). Inhibited and aggressive preschool children at 23 years of age: Personality and social transitions into adulthood. *Developmental Psychology, 44,* 997–1011.

Ashcraft, M. H. (1982). The development of mental arithmetic: A chronometric approach. *Developmental Review, 2,* 212–236.

Aslin, R. N. (1987). Visual and auditory discrimination in infancy. In J. D. Osofsky (Ed.), *Handbook of infant development* (2nd ed.). New York, NY: Wiley.

Aslin, R. N., Jusczyk, P. W., & Pisoni, D. B. (1998). Speech and auditory processing during infancy: Constraints on and precursors to language. In W. Damon (Ed.), *Handbook of child psychology* (Vol. 2). New York, NY: Wiley.

Aslin, R. N., & Newport, E. L. (2012). Statistical learning: From acquiring specific items to forming general rules. *Current Directions in Psychological Science, 21,* 170–176.

Associated Press. (July 15th, 2009). Oldest woman to give birth dies at 69, leaving twin three-year-old boys behind. Retrieved from www.mjtimes.sk.ca/Living/Health/2009-07-15/article-85046

Aspenlieder, L., Buchanan, C. M., McDougall, P., & Sippola, L. K. (2009). Gender nonconformity and peer victimization in pre- and early adolescence. *European Journal of Developmental Science, 3,* 3–16.

Astill, R. G., van der Heijden, K. B., van IJzendoorn, M. H., & van Someren, E. J. W. (2012). Sleep, cognition, and behavioral problems in school-age children: A century of research meta-analyzed. *Psychological Bulletin, 138,* 1109–1138.

Attar-Schwartz, S., Tan, J. P., Buchanan, A., Fluri, E., & Griggs, J. (2009). Grandparenting and adolescent adjustment in two-parent biological, lone-parent, and step families. *Journal of Family Psychology, 23,* 67–75.

Attaran, A., Caplan, A., Gaffney, C. & Igel, L. (2016). Open letter to Dr. Margaret Chan, Director-General, WHO. Retrieved from https://riooplympicslater.org/

Atwood, M. (1988). *Cat's eye.* Toronto, ON: McClelland & Stewart.

Au, T. K., & Glusman, M. (1990). The principle of mutual exclusivity in word learning: To honor or not to honor? *Child Development, 61,* 1474–1490.

Aunola, K., Stattin, H., & Nurmi, J. E. (2000). Parenting styles and adolescents' achievement strategies. *Journal of Adolescence, 23,* 205–222.

Autism Speaks Canada. (2016). About Autism: FAQs. Retrieved from www.autismspeaks.ca/about-autism/facts-and-faqs/

Avenevoli, S., & Steinberg, L. (2001). The continuity of depression across the adolescent transition. *Advances in Child Development & Behavior, 28,* 139–173

Averill, J. A. (1980). A constructivist view of emotion. In R. Plutchik & H. Kellerman (Eds.), *Emotion: Theory, research, and experience*: Vol. 1 Theories of emotion. New York, NY: Academic Press.

Awong, T., Grusec, J. E., & Sorenson, A. (2008). Respect-based control and anger as determinants of children's socio-emotional development. *Social Development, 17,* 941–959.

Azaiza, F. (2005). Parent-child relationships as perceived by Arab adolescents living in Israel. *International Journal of Social Welfare, 14,* 297–304.

Bachman, J. G., & Schulenberg, J. (1993). How part-time work intensity relates to drug use, problem behavior, time use, and satisfaction among high school seniors: Are these consequences or merely correlates? *Developmental Psychology, 29,* 229–230.

Bachman, J. G., Staff, J., O'Malley, P. M., & Freedman-Doan, P. (2013). Adolescent work intensity, school performance, and substance use: Links vary by race/ethnicity and socioeconomic status. *Developmental Psychology, 49,* 2125–2134.

Backscheider, A. G., Shatz, M., & Gelman, S. A. (1993). Preschoolers' ability to distinguish living kinds as a function of regrowth. *Child Development, 64*(4), 1242–1257.

Baddeley, A. (2012). Working memory: Theories, models, and controversies. *Annual Review of Psychology, 63,* 1–29.

Baenninger, M., & Newcombe, N. (1995). Environmental input to the development of sex-related differences in spatial and mathematical ability. *Learning and Individual Differences, 7,* 363–379.

Bagwell, C. L. (2004). Friendships, peer networks and antisocial behavior. In J. B. Kupersmidt & K. A. Dodge (Eds.), *Children's peer relations* (pp. 37–57). Washington, DC: American Psychological Association.

Bagwell, C. L., Newcomb, A. F., & Bukowski, W. M. (1998). Preadolescent friendship and peer rejection as predictors of adult adjustment. *Child Development, 69,* 140–153.

Bahrick, L. E., & Lickliter, R. (2002). Intersensory redundancy guides early perceptual and cognitive development. In R. V. Kail (Ed.), *Advances in child development and behavior* (Vol. 30, pp. 153–177). Orlando, FL: Academic Press.

Bahrick, L. E., & Lickliter, R. (2012). The role of intersensory redundancy in early perceptual, cognitive, and social development. In A. Bremner, D.J. Lewkowicz, & C. Spence (Eds.), *Multisensory development* (pp. 183–205). Oxford, UK: Oxford University Press.

Bailey, D. A., & Rasmussen, R. L. (1996). Sport and the child: Physiological and skeletal issues. In F. L. Smoll & R. E. Smith (Eds.), *Children and youth in sport: A biopsychological perspective* (pp. 187–199). Dubuque, IA: Brown & Benchmark.

Bailey, H. N., Redden, E., Pederson, D. R., & Moran, G. (2016). Parental disavowal of relationship difficulties fosters the development of insecure attachment. *Canadian Journal of Behavioural Science / Revue canadienne des sciences du comportement, 48*(1), 49–59.

Bailey, J. A., Hill, K. G., Oesterle, S., & Hawkins, J. D. (2009). Parenting practices and problem behavior across three generations: Monitoring, harsh discipline, and drug use in the intergenerational transmission of externalizing behavior. *Developmental Psychology, 45,* 1214–1226.

Bailey, J. M., Dunne, M. P., & Martin, N. G. (2000). Genetic and environmental influences on sexual orientation and its correlates in an Austrian twin sample. *Journal of Personality and Social Psychology, 78,* 524–436.

Baillargeon, R. (1987). Object permanence in 3½ and 4½-month-old infants. *Developmental Psychology, 23,* 655–664.

Baillargeon, R. (1994). How do infants learn about the physical world? *Current Directions in Psychological Science, 3,* 133–140.

Baillargeon, R. (2004). Infants' reasoning about hidden objects: Evidence for event-general and event-specific expectations. *Developmental Science, 7,* 391–424.

Baillargeon, R., Lie, J., Gertner, Y., & Wu, D. (2011). How do infants reason about physical events? In U. Goswami (Ed.), *The Wiley-Blackwell handbook of childhood cognitive development* (2nd ed., pp. 11–48). West Sussex, UK: Wiley-Blackwell.

Baillargeon, R. H., Zoccolillo, M., Keenan, K., Coté, S., Pérusse, D., Wu, H. X., et al. (2007). Gender differences in physical aggression: A prospective population-based survey of children before and after 2 years of age. *Developmental Psychology, 43*(1), 13–26.

Baker, L. (1994). Fostering metacognitive development. In H. W. Reese (Ed.), *Advances in child development and behavior* (Vol. 25). San Diego, CA: Academic Press.

Baker, L., & Brown, A. L. (1984). Metacognitive skills and reading. In P. D. Pearson (Ed.), *Handbook of reading research: Part 2.* New York, NY: Longman.

Bakermans-Kranenburg, M. J., & van IJzendoorn, M. H. (2009). The first 10,000 Adult Attachment Interviews: Distributions of adult attachment representations in clinical and non-clinical groups. *Attachment and Human Development, 11,* 223–263.

Bakermans-Kranenburg, M. J., & Van IJzendoorn, M. H. (2011). Differential susceptibility to rearing environment depending on dopamine-related genes: New evidence and a meta-analysis. *Development and Psychopathology, 23,* 39–52.

Bakermans-Kranenburg, M., van IJzendoorn, M. H., & Juffer, F. (2003). Less is more: Meta-analyses of sensitivity and attachment interventions in early childhood. *Psychological Bulletin, 129,* 195–215.

Bala, N., Paetsch, J. J., Bertrand, L. D., & Thomas, M. (2011). Testimonial support provisions for children and vulnerable adults (bill c-2): Case law review and perceptions of the judiciary. Canadian Research Institute for Law and the Family. Retrieved from www.justice.gc.ca/eng/pi/rs/rep-rap/2010/rr10_vic3/index.html

Bandura, A. (1977). *Social learning theory.* Englewood Cliffs, NJ: Prentice Hall.

Bandura, A. (1986). *Social foundations of thought and action: A social-cognitive theory*. Englewood Cliffs, NJ: Prentice Hall.

Bandura, A. (2006). Toward a psychology of human agency. *Perspectives on Psychological Science, 1*, 164–180.

Bandura, A. (2012). On the functional properties of self-efficacy revisited. *Journal of Management, 38*, 9–44.

Bandura, A., & Bussey, K. (2004). Social cognitive theory of gender development and functioning. In A. H. Eagly, A. E. Beall, & R. J. Sternberg (Eds.), *The psychology of gender* (2nd ed.). New York, NY: Guilford Press.

Bandura, A., Ross, D., & Ross, S. (1963). Imitation of film-mediated aggressive models. *Journal of Abnormal and Social Psychology, 66*(1), 3–11.

Banerjee, R., Watling, D., & Caputi, M. (2011). Peer relations and the understanding of faux pas: Longitudinal evidence for directional associations. *Child Development, 82*, 1887–1905.

Bannard, C., & Matthews, D. (2008). Stored word sequences in language learning: The effect of familiarity on children's repetition of four-word combinations. *Psychological Science, 19*, 241–248.

Banny, A. M., Heilbron, N., Ames, A., & Prinstein, M. (2011). Relational benefits of relational aggression: Adaptive and maladaptive associations with adolescent friendship quality. *Developmental Psychology, 47*, 1153–1166.

Banse, R., Gawronski, B., Rebetez, C., Gutt, H., & Morton, J. B. (2010). The development of spontaneous gender stereotyping in childhood: Relations to stereotype knowledge and stereotype flexibility. *Developmental Science, 13*, 298–306.

Baptista, M. (2005). New directions in pidgin and creole studies. *Annual Review of Anthropology, 34*, 33–42.

Barajas, R. G., Martin, A. Brooks-Gunn, J., & Hale, L. (2011). Mother-child bed-sharing in toddlerhood and cognitive and behavioral outcomes. *Pediatrics, 128*, e339–e347.

Barbaresi, W. J., Colligan, R. C., Weaver, A. L., Voigt, R. G., Killian, J. M., & Katusic, S. K. (2013). Mortality, ADHD, and psychosocial adversity in adults with childhood ADHD: A prospective study. *Pediatrics, 131*, 637–644.

Barca, L., Ellis, A. W., & Burani, C. (2007). Context-sensitive rules and word naming in Italian children. *Reading and Writing, 20*, 495–509.

Barkley, R. A. (2004). Adolescents with attention deficit/hyperactivity disorder: An overview of empirically based treatments. *Journal of Psychiatric Review, 10*, 39–56.

Barling, J., Zacharatos, A., & Hepburn, C. G. (1999). Parents' job insecurity affects children's academic performance through cognitive difficulties. *Journal of Applied Psychology, 84*, 437–444.

Barnett, M. A., Scaramella, L. V., Neppl, T. K., Ontai, L. L., & Conger, R. D. (2010). Grandmother involvement as a protective factor for early childhood social adjustment. *Journal of Family Psychology, 24*, 635–645.

Barnfield, A. M. C. (1999). Development of sex differences in spatial memory. *Perceptual and Motor Skills, 89*, 339–350.

Barnfield, A. M. C. (2003) Observational learning in the martial art studio: Instructors as models of positive behaviours. *Journal of Asian Martial Arts, 12*(3), 8–17.

Baron, A. S., & Banaji, M. R. (2006). The development of implicit attitudes: Evidence of race evaluations from ages 6 and 10 and adulthood. *Psychological Science, 17*, 53–58.

Baron, R., Manniën, J., de Jonge, A., Heymans, M.W., Klomp, T., Hutton, E. K., et al. (2013) Socio-demographic and lifestyle-related characteristics associated with self-reported any, daily and occasional smoking during pregnancy. *PLoS ONE, 8*(9), e74197.

Baron-Cohen, S. (2005). The Empathizing System: A revision of the 1994 model of the Mind Reading System. In B. J. Ellis & D. F. Bjorklund (Eds.), *Origins of the social mind: Evolutionary psychology and child development* (pp. 468–492). New York, NY: Guilford Press.

Barr, R. G., Barr, M., Fujiwara, T., Conway, J., Catherine, N., & Brant, R. (2009). Do educational materials change knowledge and behaviour about crying and shaken baby syndrome? A randomized controlled trial. *Canadian Medical Association Journal, 180*(7), 727–733.

Barrett, T. M., Davis, E. F., & Needham, A. (2007). Learning about tools in infancy. *Developmental Psychology, 43*, 352–368.

Bartik, T. J., Gormley, W., & Adelstein, S. (2012). Earning benefits of Tulsa's pre-K program for different income groups. *Economics of Education Review, 31*, 1143–1161.

Barton, M. E., & Tomasello, M. (1991). Joint attention and conversation in mother-infant-sibling triads. *Child Development, 62*, 517–529.

Bartsch, K., & Wellman, H. M. (1995). *Children talk about the mind*. New York, NY: Oxford University Press.

Baschat, A. A. (2007). From amniocentesis to selective laser coagulation. *Ob. Gyn. News, 42*(17), 17–18.

Bascoe, S. M., Davies, P. T., Sturge-Apple, M. L., & Cummings, E. M. (2009). Children's representations of family relationships, peer information processing, and school adjustment. *Developmental Psychology, 45*, 1740–1751.

Baskett, L. M. (1985). Sibling status effects: Adult expectations. *Developmental Psychology, 21*, 441–445.

Basso, K. H. (1970). *The Cibecue Apache*. New York, NY: Holt, Rinehart, and Winston.

Bates, E., Bretherton, I., & Snyder, L. (1988). *From first words to grammar: Individual differences and dissociable mechanisms*. New York, NY: Cambridge University Press.

Bates, J. E., Pettit, G. S., Dodge, K. A., & Ridge, B. (1998). Interaction of temperamental resistance to control and restrictive parenting in the development of externalizing behavior. *Developmental Psychology, 34*, 982–995.

Bauer, P. J. (2006). Event memory. In W. Damon & R. M. Lerner (Eds.), *Handbook of child psychology* (6th ed., Vol. 2). New York, NY: Wiley.

Bauer, P. J. & Larkina, M. (2014). Childhood amnesia in the making: Different distributions of autobiographical memories in children and adults. *Journal of Experimental Psychology: General, 143*(2), 597–611.

Bauer, P. J., & Leventon, J. S. (2013). Memory for one-time experiences in the second year of life: Implications for the status of episodic memory. *Infancy, 18*, 755–781.

Bauer, P. J., & Lukowski, A. F. (2010). The memory is in the details: Relations between memory for the specific features of events and long-term recall during infancy. *Journal of Experimental Child Psychology, 107*, 1–14.

Bauer, P. J., Larkina, M., & Deocampo, J. (2011). Early memory development. In U. Goswami (Ed.), *The Wiley-Blackwell handbook of cognitive development* (2nd ed., pp. 153–179). West Sussex UK: Wiley-Blackwell.

Bauer, P. J., San Souci, P., & Pathman, T. (2010). Infant memory. *WIREs Cognitive Science, 1*, 267–277.

Baumeister, R. F., Campbell, J. D., Krueger, J. I., & Vohs, K. D. (2003). Does high self-esteem cause better performance, interpersonal success, happiness, or healthier lifestyles? *Psychological Science in the Public Interest, 4*, 1–44.

Baumgartner, J. A., & Oakes, L. M. (2013). Investigating the relation between infants' manual activity with objects and their perception of dynamic events. *Infancy, 18*, 983–1006.

Baumrind, D. (1975). *Early socialization and the discipline controversy*. Morristown, NJ: General Learning Press.

Baumrind, D. (1991). Parenting styles and adolescent development. In R. M. Lerner, A. C. Petersen, & J. Brooks-Gunn (Eds.), *Encyclopedia of adolescence*. New York, NY: Garland.

Bauserman, R. (2002). Child adjustment in joint-custody versus sole-custody arrangements: A meta-analytic review. *Journal of Family Psychology, 16*, 91–102.

Bayley, N. (1970). Development of mental abilities. In P. H. Mussen (Ed.), *Carmichael's manual of child psychology*. New York, NY: Wiley.

Bayley, N. (1993). *Bayley scales of infant development: Birth to two years* (2nd ed.). San Antonio, TX: Psychological Corporation.

Bayley, N. (2006). *Bayley scales of infant and toddler development* (3rd ed.). San Antonio, TX: Harcourt Assessment.

Beal, C. R. (1996). The role of comprehension monitoring in children's revision. *Educational Psychology Review, 8*, 219–238.

Beal, C. R., & Belgrad, S. L. (1990). The development of message evaluation skills in young children. *Child Development, 61*, 705–712.

Beal, S. J., & Crockett, L. J. (2010). Adolescents' occupational and educational aspirations and expectations: Links to high school activities and educational attainment. *Developmental Psychology, 46*, 258–265.

Beauchamp, G. K., & Mennella, J. A. (2011). Flavor perception in human infants: Development and functional significance. *Digestion, 83*, 1–6.

Beck, E., Burnet, K. L., & Vosper, J. (2006). Birth-order effects on facets of extraversion. *Personality and Individual Differences, 40*, 953–959.

Becker, B. J. (1986). Influence again: An examination of reviews and studies of gender differences in social influence. In J. S. Hyde & M. C. Linn (Eds.), *The psychology of gender differences. Advances through meta-analysis* (pp. 178–209). Baltimore, MD: Johns Hopkins University Press.

Becker-Blease, K. A., Turner, H. A., & Finkelhor, D. (2010). Disasters, victimization, and children's mental health. *Child Development, 81*, 1040–1052.

Behnke, A. O., Plunkett, S. W., Sands, T., & Bámaca-Colbert, M. Y. (2011). The relationship between Latino adolescents' perceptions of discrimination, neighborhood risk, and parenting on self-esteem and depressive symptoms. *Journal of Cross-Cultural Psychology, 42*, 1179–1197.

Behnke, M., & Eyler, F. D. (1993). The consequences of prenatal substance use for the developing fetus, newborn, and young child. *International Journal of the Addictions, 28*, 1341–1391.

Beier, J. S., Over, H., & Carpenter, M. (2014). Young children help others to achieve their social goals. *Developmental Psychology, 50*, 934–940.

Bellagamba, F., Camaioni, L., & Colonnesi, C. (2006). Change in children's understanding of others' intentional actions. *Developmental Science, 9*, 182–188.

Bellugi, U., & Klima, E. (1978). Structural properties of American Sign Language. In L. S. Liben (Ed.), *Deaf children: Developmental perspectives* (pp. 43–68). New York, NY: Academic Press.

Belsky, J., & Pluess, M. (2013). Genetic moderation of early child-care effects on social functioning across childhood: A developmental analysis. *Child Development, 84*, 1209–1225.

Belsky, J., Bakermans-Kranenburg, M. J., & van IJzendoorn, M. H. (2007). For better and for worse: Differential susceptibility to environmental influences. *Current Directions in Psychological Science, 16*, 300–304.

Belsky, J., Houts, R. M., & Pasco Fearon, R. M. (2010). Infant attachment security and the timing of puberty: Testing an evolutionary hypothesis. *Psychological Science, 21*, 1195–1201.

Belsky, J., Jaffee, S. R., Sligo, J., Woodward, L., & Silva, P. A. (2005). Intergenerational transmission of warm-sensitive-stimulating parenting: A prospective study of mothers and fathers of 3-year-olds. *Child Development, 76*, 384–396.

Belsky, J., Steinberg, L., Houts, R. M., Halpern-Felsher, B., & NICHD Early Child Care Research Network. (2010). The development of reproductive strategy in females: Early maternal harshness → earlier menarche → increased sexual risk taking. *Developmental Psychology, 46*, 120–128.

Belsky, J., Woodworth, S., & Crnic, K. (1996) Troubled family interaction during toddlerhood. *Development and Psychopathology, 8*(3), 477–495.

Bem, D. J. (1996). Exotic becomes erotic: A developmental theory of sexual orientation. *Psychological Review, 103*, 320–335.

Benenson, J. F., & Christakos, A. (2003). The greater fragility of females' versus males' closest same-sex friendships. *Child Development, 74*, 1123–1129.

Bennett, D. S., Bendersky, M., & Lewis, M. (2008). Children's cognitive ability from 4 to 9 years old as a function of prenatal cocaine exposure, environmental risk, and maternal verbal intelligence. *Developmental Psychology, 44*, 919–928.

Benton, D. (2010). The influence of dietary status on the cognitive performance of children. *Molecular Nutrition and Food Research, 54*, 457–470.

Benton, S. L., Corkill, A. J., Sharp, J. M., Downey, R. G., & Khramtsova, I. (1995). Knowledge, interest, and narrative writing. *Journal of Educational Psychology, 87*, 66–79.

Bereiter, C., & Scardamalia, M. (1987). *The psychology of written composition*. Hillsdale, NJ: Erlbaum.

Berenbaum, S. A., Martin, C. L., Hanish, L. D., Briggs, P. T., & Fabes, R. A. (2008). Sex differences in children's play. In J. B. Becker, K. J. Berkley, N. Geary, E. Hampson, J. P. Herman, & E. A. Young (Eds.), *Sex differences in the brain* (pp. 275–290). New York, NY: Oxford University Press.

Bergen, D., & Mauer, D. (2000). Symbolic play, phonological awareness, and literacy skills at three age levels. In K. A. Roskos & J. F. Christie (Eds.), *Play and literacy in early childhood: Research from multiple perspectives* (pp. 45–62). Mahwah, NJ: Erlbaum.

Berger, C., & Dijkstra, J. K. (2013). Competition, envy, or snobbism? How popularity and friendships shape antipathy networks of adolescents. *Journal of Research on Adolescence, 23*, 586–595.

Berger, S. E., Adolph, K. E., & Lobo, S. A. (2005). Out of the toolbox: Toddlers differentiate wobbly and wooden handrails. *Child Development, 76*, 1294–1307.

Berk, L. E. (1992). Children's private speech: An overview of theory and the status of research. In R. M. Diaz & L. E. Berk (Eds.), *Private speech: From social interaction to self-regulation*. Hillsdale, NJ: Erlbaum.

Berk, L. E. (2003). Vygotsky, Lev. In L. Nadel (Ed.), *Encyclopedia of cognitive science* (Vol. 6). London, UK: Macmillan.

Berkman, E. T., Graham, A. M., & Fisher, P. A. (2012). Training self-control: A domain-general translational neuroscience approach. *Child Development Perspectives, 6*, 374–384.

Berko, J. (1958). The child's learning of English morphology. *Word, 14*, 150–177.

Berkowitz, M. W., Sherblom, S., Bier, M., & Battistich, V. (2006). Educating for positive youth development. In M. Killen & J. G. Smetana (2006), *Handbook of moral development* (pp. 683–702). Mahwah, NJ: Erlbaum.

Berlin, L. J., Appleyard, K., & Dodge, K. A. (2011). Intergenerational continuity in child maltreatment: Mediating mechanisms and implications for prevention. *Child Development, 82*, 162–176.

Berlin, L. J., Ispa, J. M., Fine, M. A., Malone, P. S., Brooks-Gunn, J., Brady-Smith, C., et al. (2009). Correlates and consequences of spanking and verbal punishment for low-income White, African American and Mexican American toddlers. *Child Development, 80*, 1403–1420.

Bernal, S., Dehaene-Lambertz, G., Millotte, S., & Christophe, A. (2010). Two-year-olds compute syntactic structure on-line. *Developmental Science, 13*, 69–76.

Berndt, T. J., & Perry, T. B. (1990). Distinctive features and effects of adolescent friendships. In R. Montemeyer, G. R. Adams, & T. P. Gullotta (Eds.), *From childhood to adolescence: A transition period?* London, UK: Sage.

Bernier, A., Carlson, S. M., & Whipple, N. (2010). From external regulation to self-regulation: Early parenting precursors of young children's executive functioning. *Child Development, 81*, 326–339.

Berry, J. W. & Bennett, J. A. (1992). Cree conceptions of cognitive competence. *International Journal of Psychology, 27*(1), 73–88.

Berry, J. W. & Hou, F. (2016). Immigrant acculturation and wellbeing in Canada. *Canadian Psychology/Psychologie canadienne, 57*(4), 254–264.

Berry, J. W., Phinney, J. S., Sam, D. L., & Vedder, P. (2006). Immigrant youth: Acculturation, identity, and adaptation. *Applied Psychology, 55*(3), 303–332.

Bertenthal, B. H., & Clifton, R. K. (1998). Perception and action. In W. Damon (Ed.), *Handbook of child psychology* (Vol. 2). New York, NY: Wiley.

Berthier, N. E. (1996). Learning to reach: A mathematical model. *Developmental Psychology, 32*, 811–823.

Berthier, N., & Carrico, R. L. (2010). Visual information and object size in infant reaching. *Infant Behavior and Development, 33*, 555–566.

Berton, P. (1977). *The Dionne years: A thirties melodrama*. Toronto, ON: McClelland & Stewart.

Best, C. T. (1995). Learning to perceive the sound pattern of English. In C. Rovee-Collier (Ed.), *Advances in infancy research*. Norwood, NJ: Ablex.

Best, J. R. (2010). Effects of physical activity on children's executive function: Contributions of experimental research on aerobic exercise. *Developmental Review, 30*, 331–351

Bettencourt, B. A., & Miller, N. (1996). Gender differences in aggression as a function of provocation: A meta-analysis. *Psychological Bulletin, 119*, 422–447.

Beuker, K. T., Rommelse, N. N. J., Donders, R., & Buitelaar, J. K. (2013). Development of early communication skills in the first two years of life. *Infant Behavior and Development, 36*, 71–83.

Bhutta, Z. A., Chopra, M., Axelson, H., Berman, P., Boerma, T., Bryce, J., et al. (2010). Countdown to 2015 decade report (2000–10): Taking stock of maternal, newborn, and child survival. *Lancet, 375*, 2032–2044.

Bialystok, E. (1988). Levels of bilingualism and levels of linguistic awareness. *Developmental Psychology, 24*, 560–567.

Bialystok, E. (1997). Effects of bilingualism and biliteracy on children's emerging concepts of print. *Developmental Psychology, 33*, 429–440.

Bialystok, E. (2011). Reshaping the mind: The benefits of bilingualism. *Canadian Journal of Experimental Psychology, 65*(4), 229–235.

Bialystok, E., & Martin, M. M. (2004). Attention and inhibition in bilingual children: Evidence from the dimensional change card sort task. *Developmental Science, 7*, 325–339.

Bialystok, E., & Viswanathan, M. (2009). Components of executive control with advantages for bilingual children in two cultures. *Cognition, 112*, 494–500.

Bialystok, E., Shenfield, T., & Codd, J. (2000). Languages, scripts, and the environment: Factors in developing concepts of print. *Developmental Psychology, 36*, 66–76.

Biblarz, T. J., & Stacey, J. (2010). How does the gender of parents matter? *Journal of Marriage and the Family, 72*, 3–22.

Bick, J., Zhu, T., Stamoulis, C., Fox, N. A., Zanah, C., & Nelson, C. A. (2015). Effect of early institutionalization and foster care on long-term white matter development. *Journal of the American Medical Association: Pediatrics.* doi: 10.1001/jamapediatrics.2014.3212

Bickerton, D. (1984). The language bioprogram hypothesis. *Behavioral and Brain Sciences, 7*, 173–221.

Bickerton, D. (1990). *Language and species*. Chicago, IL: University of Chicago Press.

Biddle, S. J. H., & Asare, M. (2011). Physical activity and mental health in children and adolescents: A review of reviews. *British Journal of Sports Medicine, 45*, 886–895

Biederman, J., Petty, C. R., Evans, M., Small, J., & Faraone, S. V. (2010). How persistent is ADHD? A controlled 10-year follow-up study of boys with ADHD. *Psychiatry Research, 177*, 299–304.

Bierman, K. L., Coie, J., Dodge, K., Greenberg, M., Lochman, J., McMohan, R., et al. (2013). School outcomes of aggressive-disruptive children: Prediction from kindergarten risk factors and impact of the Fast Track Prevention Program. *Aggressive Behavior, 39*, 114–130.

Big Brothers Big Sisters of Canada (n.d.). GoGirls! Retrieved from www.bigbrothersbigsisters.ca/en/Home/Programs/GoGirls.aspx

Bigler, R. S. (1995). The role of classification skill in moderating environmental influences on children's gender stereotyping: A study of the functional use of gender in the classroom. *Child Development, 66*, 1072–1087.

Bigler, R. S., & Liben L. S. (1990). The role of attitudes and interventions in gender-schematic processing. *Child Development, 61*, 1440–1452.

Bigler, R. S., & Liben, L. S. (1992). Cognitive mechanisms in children's gender stereotyping: Theoretical and educational implications of a cognitive-based intervention. *Child Development, 63*, 1351–1363.

Bigler, R. S., & Liben, L. S. (2007). Developmental intergroup theory: Explaining and reducing children's social stereotyping and prejudice. *Current Directions in Psychological Science, 16*, 162–166.

Bigler, R. S., Jones, L. C., & Lobliner, D. B. (1997). Social categorization and the formation of intergroup attitudes in children. *Child Development, 68*, 530–543.

bilaalrajan.com. (n.d.). *About Bilaal*. Retrieved from www.bilaalrajan.com/about_bilaal.html

Bingenheimer, J. B., Brennan, R. T., & Earls, F. J. (2005). Firearm violence exposure and serious violent behavior. *Science, 308*, 1323–1326.

Birch, S. A., Akmal, N., & Frampton, K. (2010). Two-year-olds are vigilant of others' non-verbal cues to credibility. *Developmental Science, 13*, 363–369.

Biro, S., & Leslie, A. M. (2007). Infants' perception of goal-directed actions: Development through cue-based bootstrapping. *Developmental Science, 8*, 36–43.

Bjerkedal, T., Kristensen, P., Skjeret, G. A., & Brevik, J. I. (2007). Intelligence test scores and birth order among young Norwegian men (conscripts) analyzed within and between families. *Intelligence, 35*, 503–514.

Bjorklund, D. F. (2005). *Children's thinking: Cognitive development and individual differences* (4th ed.). Belmont, CA: Wadsworth.

Bjorklund, D. F. (2012). *Children's thinking* (5th ed). Belmont, CA: Wadsworth.

Bjorklund, D. F., & Jordan, A. C. (2013). Human parenting from an evolutionary perspective. In W. B. Wilcox & K. K. Kline (Eds.), *Gender and parenthood: Biological and social scientific perspectives* (pp. 61–90). New York, NY: Columbia University Press.

Bjorklund, D. F., & Rosenblum, K. E. (2002). Context effects in children's selection and use of simple arithmetic strategies. *Journal of Cognition and Development, 3*, 225–242.

Bjorklund, D. F., Yunger, J. L., & Pellegrini, A. D. (2002). The evolution of parenting and evolutionary approaches to childrearing. In M. H. Bornstein (Ed.), *Handbook of parenting, Vol. 2: Biology and ecology of parenting* (pp. 3–30). Mahwah, NJ: Erlbaum.

Black-Gutman, D., & Hickson, F. (1996). The relationship between racial attitudes and social-cognitive development in children: An Australian study. *Developmental Psychology, 32*, 448–456.

Black, J. E. (2003). Environment and development of the nervous system. In I. B. Weiner, M. Gallagher, & R. J. Nelson (Eds.), *Handbook of psychology, Vol. 3: Biological psychology* (pp. 655–668). Hoboken, NJ: Wiley.

Blair, B. L., Perry, N. B., O'Brien, M., Calkins, S. D., Keane, S. P., & Shanahan, L. (2014). The indirect effects of maternal emotion socialization on friendship quality in middle childhood. *Developmental Psychology, 50*, 566–576.

Blakemore, J. E. O. (2003). Children's beliefs about violating gender norms: Boys shouldn't look like girls, and girls shouldn't act like boys. *Sex Roles, 48,* 411–419.

Blatt-Eisengart, I., Drabick, D. A. G., Monahan, K. C., & Steinberg, L. (2009). Sex differences in the longitudinal relations among family risk factors and childhood externalizing symptoms. *Developmental Psychology, 45,* 491–502.

Blaxall, J. (2008). Time-out or time-in? *Interaction, Fall,* 17–21.

Blennow, M., Ewald, U., Fritz, T., Holmgren, P. A., Jeppsson, A., Lindberg, E., Strömberg, B. (2009). One-year survival of extremely preterm infants after active perinatal care in Sweden. *Journal of the American Medical Association, 301*(21), 2225–2233.

Block, J. (1976). Debatable conclusions about sex differences. *Contemporary Psychology, 21,* 517–522.

Bloom, L. (1998). Language acquisition in its developmental context. In D. Kuhn & R. S. Siegler (Eds.), *Handbook of child psychology: Vol. 2. Cognition, perception, and language* (5th ed., pp. 309–370). New York, NY: Wiley.

Bloom, L., & Tinker, E. (2001). The intentionality model and language acquisition. *Monographs of the Society for Research in Child Development, 66*(Serial No. 267).

Bloom, L., Margulis, C., Tinker, E., & Fujita, N. (1996). Early conversations and word learning: Contributions from child and adult. *Child Development, 67,* 3154–3175.

Bloom, L., Rocissano, L., & Hood, L. (1976). Adult–child discourse: Developmental interaction between information processing and linguistic knowledge. *Cognitive Psychology, 8,* 521–552.

Boak, A., Hamilton, H. A., Adlaf, E. M., Henderson, J. L., & Mann, R. E. (2016). *The mental health and well-being of Ontario students, 1991–2015: Detailed OSDUS findings* (CAMH Research Document Series No. 43). Toronto, ON: Centre for Addiction and Mental Health.

Boden, J. M., Fergusson, D. M., & Horwood, L. J. (2008). Does adolescent self-esteem predict later life outcomes? A test of the causal role of self-esteem. *Development and Psychopathology, 20,* 319–339.

Bohn, A., & Berntsen, D. (2013). The future is bright and predictable: The development of prospective life stories across childhood and adolescence. *Developmental Psychology, 49,* 1232–1241.

Boiger, M., & Mesquita, B. (2012). The construction of emotion in interactions, relationships, and cultures. *Emotion Review, 4,* 221–229.

Boivin, M., Brendgen, M., Vitaro, F., Dionne, G., Girard, A., Pérusse, D., & Tremblay, R. E. (2013). Strong genetic contribution to peer relationship difficulties at school entry: Findings from a longitudinal twin study. *Child Development, 84,* 1098–1114.

Bonny, J. W., & Lourenco, S. F. (2013). The approximate number system and its relation to early math achievement: Evidence from the preschool years. *Journal of Experimental Child Psychology, 114,* 375–388.

Booth, J. L., & Siegler, R. S. (2006). Development and individual differences in pure numerical estimation. *Developmental Psychology, 42,* 189–201.

Bornstein, M. H., & Arterberry, M. E. (2003). Recognition, discrimination, and categorization of smiling by 5-month-old infants. *Developmental Science, 6,* 585–599.

Bornstein, M. H., Hahn, C-S., & Wolke, D. (2013). Systems and cascades in cognitive development and academic achievement. *Child Development, 84,* 154–162.

Bornstein, M. H., Putnick, D. L., Suwalsky, J. T., & Gini, M. (2006). Maternal chronological age, prenatal and perinatal history, social support, and parenting of infants. *Child Development, 77,* 875–892.

Bortfeld, H., & Morgan, J. L. (2010). Is early word-form processing stress-full? How natural variability supports recognition. *Cognitive Psychology, 60,* 241–266.

Bos, H., Goldberg, N., Van Gelderen, L., & Gartrell, N. (2010). Adolescents of the U.S. National Longitudinal Lesbian Family Study: Male role models, gender role traits, and psychological adjustment. *Gender and Society.* doi: 10.1177/0891243212445456

Bosco, F. M., Friedman, O., & Leslie, A. M. (2006). Recognition of pretend and real actions in play by 1- and 2-year-olds: Early success and why they fail. *Cognitive Development, 21,* 3–10.

Boseovski, J. J. (2010). Evidence for "rose-colored glasses": An examination of the positivity bias in young children's personality judgments. *Child Development Perspectives, 4,* 212–218.

Bosma, H. A., & Kunnen, E. S. (2001). Determinants and mechanisms in ego identity development: A review and synthesis. *Developmental Review, 21,* 39–66.

Bot, S. M., Engels, R. C. M. E., Knibbe, R. A., & Meeus, W. H. J. (2005). Friend's drinking behaviour and adolescent alcohol consumption: The moderating role of friendship characteristics. *Addictive Behaviors, 30,* 929–947.

Bouchard, T. J. (2004). Genetic influence on human psychological traits. *Current Directions in Psychological Science, 13,* 148–151.

Bouchard, T. J. (2009). Genetic influence on human intelligence (Spearman's g): How much? *Annals of Human Biology, 36,* 527–544.

Boudreau, F., Folman, M., & Konzak, B. (1995). Parental observations: Psychological and physical changes in school-age karate participants. *Journal of Asian Martial Arts, 4*(4), 50–69.

Bowker, A. (2006). The relationship between sports participation and self-esteem during early adolescence. *Canadian Journal of Behavioral Science, 38,* 214–229.

Bowlby, J. (1953). *Child care and the growth of love.* London, UK: Penguin.

Bowlby, J. (1969). Attachment and loss (Vol. 1). New York, NY: Basic Books.

Bowlby, J. (1991). Ethological light on psychoanalytic problems. In P. Bateson et al. (Eds.), *The development and integration of behaviour: Essays in honour of Robert Hinde.* Cambridge, UK: Cambridge University Press.

Boyce, T. W., Sokolowski, M. B., & Robinson, G. E. (2012). Toward a new biology of social adversity. *Proceedings of the National Academy of Sciences (PNAS), 109*(S. 2), 17143–17148.

Boyle, M. H., Georgiades, K., Racine, Y., & Mustard, C. (2007). Neighborhood and family influences on educational attainment: Results from the Ontario Child Health Study Follow-Up 2001. *Child Development, 78,* 168–189.

Bradley, L., & Bryant, P. E. (1983). Categorising sounds and learning to read—a causal connection. *Nature, 301,* 419–421.

Bradley, R. H., & Corwyn, R. F. (2007). Externalizing problems in fifth grade: Relations with productive activity, maternal sensitivity, and harsh parenting from infancy through middle childhood. *Developmental Psychology, 43,* 1390–1401.

Bradley, R. H., & Corwyn, R. F. (2002). Socioeconomic status and child development. *Annual Review of Psychology, 53,* 371–399.

Braine, M. D. S. (1992). What sort of innate structure is needed to "bootstrap" into syntax? *Cognition, 45,* 77–100.

Brainerd, C. J. (1996). Piaget: A centennial celebration. *Psychological Science, 7,* 191–203.

Brainerd, C. J., & Reyna, V. F. (2005). *The science of false memory.* New York, NY: Oxford University Press.

Brainerd, C. J., & Reyna, V. F. (2013). Dual processes in memory development: Fuzzy-trace theory. In P. J. Bauer & R. Fivush (Eds.), *Wiley-Blackwell handbook on the development of children's memory.* New York, NY: Wiley-Blackwell.

Brainerd, C. J., Holliday, R. E., Reyna, V. F., Yang, Y., & Toglia, M. P. (2010). Developmental reversals in false memory: Effects of emotional valence and arousal. *Journal of Experimental Child Psychology, 107,* 137–154.

Brainerd, C. J., Reyna, V. F., & Ceci, S. J. (2008). Developmental reversals in false memory: A review of data and theory. *Psychological Bulletin, 134,* 343–382.

Braungart-Rieker, J. M., Hill-Soderlund, A. L., & Karrass, J. (2010). Fear and anger reactivity trajectories from 4 to 16 months: The roles of temperament, regulation, and maternal sensitivity. *Developmental Psychology, 46,* 791–804.

Braza, P., Carreras, R., Muñoz, J. M., Braza, F., Azurmendi, A., Pascual-Sagastizábal, E., et al. (2014). Negative maternal and paternal parenting styles as predictors of children's behavioral problems: Moderating effects of the child's sex. *Journal of Child and Family Studies, 24,* 847–856. doi: 10.1007/s10826-013-9893-0

Brazelton, T. B., & Nugent, J. K. (1995). *Neonatal behavioral assessment scale* (3rd ed.). London, UK: MacKeith.

Brazelton, T. B., Nugent, J. K., & Lester, B. M. (1987). Neonatal behavioral assessment scale. In J. D. Osofsky (Ed.), *Handbook of infant development* (2nd ed.). New York, NY: Wiley.

Brechwald, W. A., & Prinstein, M. J. (2011). Beyond homophily: A decade of advances in understanding peer influence processes. *Journal of Research on Adolescence, 21,* 166–179.

Bredemeier, B. L., & Shields, D. L. (2006). Sports and character development. *President's Council on Physical Fitness and Sports–Research Digest, 7*(1), 1–8.

Brendgen, M. (2012). Genetics and peer relations: A review. *Journal of Research on Adolescence, 22*(3), 419–437.

Brendgen, M., Boivin, M., Dionne, G., Barker, E. D., Vitaro, F., Girard, A., et al. (2011). Gene-environment processes linking aggression, peer victimization, and the teacher-child relationship. *Child Development, 82,* 2021–2036.

Brendgen, M., Boivin, M., Vitaro, F., Bukowski, W. M., Dionne, G., Tremblay, R. E., et al. (2008). Linkages between chidren's and their friends' social and physical aggression: Evidence for a gene-environment interaction? *Child Development, 79,* 13–29.

Brendgen, M., Boivin, M., Vitaro, F., Girard, A., Dionne, G., & Pérusse, D. (2008). Gene-environment interaction between peer victimization and child aggression. *Development and Psychopathology, 20,* 455–471.

Brendgen, M., Lamarche, V., Wanner, B., & Vitaro, F. (2010). Links between friendship relations and early adolescents' trajectories of depressed mood. *Developmental Psychology, 46,* 491–501.

Brendgen, M., Vitaro, F., Boivin, M., Dionne, G., & Pérusse, D. (2006). Examining genetic and environmental effects on reactive versus proactive aggression. *Developmental Psychology, 42,* 1299–1312.

Brendtro, L. K. (2001). Worse than sticks and stones: Lessons from research on ridicule. *Reclaiming Children and Youth, 10*(1), 47–49, 53.

Brennan, P. A., Grekin, E. R., Mortensen, E. L., & Mednick, S. A. (2002). Relationship of maternal smoking during pregnancy with criminal arrest and hospitalization for substance abuse in male and female adult offspring. *American Journal of Psychiatry, 159,* 48–54.

Brennan, S. (2009). *Participation and activity limitation survey 2006: Facts on learning limitations.* Statistics Canada—Catalogue number 89-628-X 2009014. Retrieved from www.statcan.gc.ca/pub/89-628-x/89-628-x2009014-eng.htm

Brinkman, B. G., Jedinak, A., Rosen, L. A., & Zimmerman, T. S. (2011). Teaching children fairness: Decreasing gender prejudice among children. *Analyses of Social Issues and Social Policy, 11,* 61–81.

Brockington, I. (1996). *Motherhood and mental health.* Oxford, UK: Oxford University Press.

Brody, G. H. (1998). Sibling relationship quality: Its causes and consequences. *Annual Review of Psychology, 49,* 1–24.

Brody, G. H., & Ge, X. (2001). Linking parenting processes and self-regulation to psychological functioning and alcohol use during early adolescence. *Journal of Family Psychology, 15,* 82–94.

Brody, G. H., Kim, S., Murry, V. M., & Brown, A. C. (2003). Longitudinal direct and indirect pathways linking older sibling competence to the development of younger sibling competence. *Developmental Psychology, 39,* 618–628.

Brody, G. H., Stoneman, A., & McCoy, J. K. (1994). Forecasting sibling relationships in early adolescence from child temperaments and family processes in middle childhood. *Child Development, 65,* 771–784.

Brody, L. R., & Hall, J. A. (2008). Gender and emotion in context. In M. Lewis, J. M. Haviland-Jones, & L. F. Barrett (Eds.), *Handbook of emotions* (3rd ed., pp. 395–408). New York, NY: Guilford Press.

Brody, N. (1992). *Intelligence* (2nd ed.). San Diego, CA: Academic Press.

Brodzinsky, D. M., & Pinderhughes, E. (2002). Parenting and child development in adoptive families. In M. H. Bornstein (Ed.), *Handbook of parenting; Vol. 1. Children and parenting* (pp. 279–311). Mahwah, NJ: Erlbaum.

Bronfenbrenner, U. (1995). Developmental ecology through space and time: A future perspective. In P. Moen, G. H. Elder, Jr., & K. Luscher (Eds.), *Examining lives in context: Perspectives on the ecology of human development.* Washington, DC: American Psychological Association.

Bronfenbrenner, U., & Morris, P. (2006). The ecology of developmental processes. In W. Damon & R. M. Lerner (Eds.), *Handbook of child psychology* (6th ed., Vol. 1). New York, NY: Wiley.

Brooker, R. J., Buss, K. A., Lemery-Chalfant, K., Aksan, N., Davidson, R. J., & Goldsmith, H. H. (2013). The development of stranger fear in infancy and toddlerhood: Normative development, individual differences, antecedents, and outcomes. *Developmental Science, 16,* 864–878.

Brooks-Gunn, J., Klebanov, P. K., & Duncan, G. J. (1996). Ethnic differences in children's intelligence test scores: Role of economic deprivation, home environment, and maternal characteristics. *Child Development, 67,* 396–408.

Brotman, L. M., Calzada, E., Huang, K-Y., Kingston, S., Dawson-McClure, S., Kamboukos, D., et al. (2011). Promoting effective parenting practices and preventing child behavior problems in school among ethnically diverse families from underserved, urban communities. *Child Development, 82,* 258–276

Brown v. Board of Education of Topeka 347 U.S. 483. (1954). Retrieved from https://supreme.justia.com/cases/federal/us/347/483/case.html

Brown, B. B., & Bakken, J. P. (2011). Parenting and peer relationships: Reinvigorating research on family-peer linkages in adolescence. *Journal of Research on Adolescence, 21,* 153–165.

Brown, B. B., & Klute, C. (2003). Friendships, cliques, and crowds. In G. R. Adams & M. D. Berzonsky (Eds.), *Blackwell handbook of adolescence* (pp. 330–348). Malden, MA: Blackwell Publishing.

Brown, B. B., Herman, M., Hamm, J. V., & Heck, D. J. (2008). Ethnicity and image: Correlates of crowd affiliation among ethnic minority youth. *Child Development, 79,* 529–546.

Brown, B. B., Mounts, N., Lamborn, S. D., & Steinberg, L. (1993). Parenting practices and peer group affiliation in adolescence. *Developmental Psychology, 64,* 467–482.

Brown, J. R., & Dunn, J. (1992). Talk with your mother or your sibling? Developmental changes in early family conversations about feelings. *Child Development, 63,* 336–349.

Brown, J. R., & Dunn, J. (1996). Continuities in emotion understanding from three to six years. *Child Development, 67,* 789–802.

Brown, R. (1973). *A first language: The early stages.* Cambridge, MA: Harvard University Press.

Brown, R. P., Osterman, L. L., & Barnes, C. D. (2009). School violence and the culture of honor. *Psychological Science, 20,* 1400–1405.

Brown, R., Pressley, M., Van Meter, P., & Schuder, T. (1996). A quasi-experimental validation of transactional strategies instruction with low-achieving second-grade readers. *Journal of Educational Psychology, 88,* 18–37.

Brown, T. T., Kuperman, J. M., Chung, Y., Erhart, M., McCabe, C., Hagler, D. J. Jr., et al. (2012). Neuroanatomical Assessment of Biological Maturity. *Current Biology, 22,* 1–6, http://dx.doi.org/10.1016/j.cub.2012.07.002

Bruck, M., & Ceci, S. J. (1995). Amicus brief for the case of State of New Jersey vs. Michaels presented by Committee of Concerned Social Scientists. *Psychology, Public Policy, and Law, 1,* 272–322.

Brummelman, E., Thomaes, S., Orobio de Casto, B., Overbeek, G., & Bushman, B. J. (2014). "That's not just beautiful—that's incredibly beautiful!" The adverse impact of inflated praise on children with low self-esteem. *Psychological Science, 25,* 728–735.

Bryman, A., Teevan, J. J., & Bell (2012). *Social research methods* (3rd Canadian ed.). Don Mills, ON: Oxford University Press.

Buchanan, C. M., & Heiges, K. L. (2001). When conflict continues after the marriage ends: Effects of postdivorce conflict on children. In J. Grych & F. D. Fincham (Eds.), *Interparental conflict and child development* (pp. 337–362). New York, NY: Cambridge University Press.

Buckingham-Howes, S., Berger, S. S., Scaletti, L. A., & Black, M. M. (2013). Systematic review of prenatal cocaine exposure and adolescent development. *Pediatrics, 131,* e1917–d1936.

Bugental, D. B., & Happaney, K. (2004). Predicting infant maltreatment in low-income families: The interactive effects of maternal attributions and child status at birth. *Developmental Psychology, 40,* 234–243.

Bugental, D. B., & Schwartz, A. (2009). A cognitive approach to child maltreatment prevention among medically at-risk infants. *Developmental Psychology, 45,* 284–288.

Bukowski, W. M., Sippola, L. K., & Hoza, B. (1999). Same and other: Interdependency between participation in same- and other-sex friendships. *Journal of Youth and Adolescence, 28,* 439–459.

Bull, R., & Lee, K. (2014). Executive functioning and mathematics achievement. *Child Development Perspectives, 8,* 36–41.

Bullard, L., Wachlarowicz, M., DeLeeuw, J., Snyder, J., Low, S., Forgatch, M., et al. (2010). Effects of the Oregon model of Parent Management Training (PMTO) on marital adjustment in new stepfamilies: A randomized trial. *Journal of Family Psychology, 24,* 485–496.

Bullock, M., & Lütkenhaus, P. (1990). Who am I? The development of self-understanding in toddlers. *Merrill-Palmer Quarterly, 36,* 217–238.

Burack, J. A., Flanagan, T., Peled, T., Sutton, H. M., Zygmuntowicz, C., & Manly, J. T. (2006). Social perspective-taking skills in maltreated children and adolescents. *Developmental Psychology, 42,* 207–217.

Burk, W. J., & Laursen, B. (2005). Adolescent perceptions of friendship and their associations with individual adjustment. *International Journal of Behavioral Development, 29,* 156–164.

Burman, D. D., Minas, T., Bolger, D. J., & Booth, J. R. (2013). Age, sex, and verbal abilities affect location of linguistic connectivity in ventral visual pathway. *Brain & Language, 124,* 184–193.

Burnham, D., & Dodd, B. (2004). Auditory-visual speech integration by prelinguistic infants: Perception of an emergent consonant in the McGurk effect. *Developmental Psychobiology, 45,* 204–220.

Burns, T. C., Yoshida, K. A., Hill, K., & Werker, J. F. (2007). The development of phonetic representation in bilingual and monolingual infants. *Applied Psycholinguistics, 28,* 455–474.

Burton, C. M., Marshal, M. P., & Chisolm, D. J. (2014). School absenteeism and mental health among sexual minority youth and heterosexual youth. *Journal of School Psychology, 52,* 37–47.

Buss, K. A., & Goldsmith, H. H. (1998). Fear and anger regulation in infancy: Effects on the temporal dynamics of affective expression. *Child Development, 69,* 359–374.

Buttelmann, D., & Böhm, R. (2014). The ontogeny of the motivation that underlies in-group bias. *Psychological Science, 25,* 921–927.

Buttelmann, D., Zmyj, N., Daum, M., & Carpenter, M. (2013). Selective imitation of in-group over out-group members in 14-month-old infants. *Child Development, 84,* 422–428.

Byrnes, J. P., Miller, D. C., & Schafer, W. D. (1999). Gender differences in risk taking: A meta-analysis. *Psychological Bulletin, 125,* 367–383.

Cafri, G., van den Berg, P., & Thompson, J. K. (2006). Pursuit of muscularity in adolescent boys: Relations among biopsychosocial variables and clinical outcomes. *Journal of Clinical Child and Adolescent Psychology, 35*(2), 283–291.

Cai, H., Brown, J. D., Deng, C., & Oakes, M. A. (2007). Self-esteem and culture: Differences in cognitive self-evaluations or affective self-regard? *Asian Journal of Social Psychology, 10,* 162–170.

Cain, D. P., & Vanderwolf, C. H. (1990). A critique of Rushton on race, brain size and intelligence. *Personality and Individual Differences, 11*(8), 777–784.

Cain, K. (1999). Ways of reading: How knowledge and use of strategies are related to reading comprehension. *British Journal of Developmental Psychology, 17,* 293–312.

Caldwell, M. S., Rudolph, K. D., Troop-Gordon, W., & Kim, D. Y. (2004). Reciprocal influences among relational self-views, social disengagement, and peer stress during early adolescence. *Child Development, 75,* 1140–1154.

Callaghan, T., Moll, H., Rakoczy, H., Warneken, F., Liszkowski, U., Behne, T., et al. (2011). Early social cognition in three cultural contexts. *Monographs of the Society for Research in Child Development, 76*(Serial No. 299).

Callaghan, T., Rochat, P., Lillard, A., Claux, M. L., Odden, H., Itakura, S., et al. (2005). Synchrony in the onset of mental-state reasoning: Evidence from five cultures. *Psychological Science, 16,* 378–384.

Callahan, C. M. (2000). Intelligence and giftedness. In R. J. Sternberg (Ed.), *Handbook of intelligence* (pp. 159–175). Cambridge, UK: Cambridge University Press.

Calvert, S. L., & Valkenburg, P. M. (2013). The influence of television, video games, and the internet on children's creativity. In M. Taylor (Ed.), *The Oxford handbook of the development of imagination* (pp. 438–450). New York, NY: Oxford.

Cameron, L., Rutland, A., Brown, R., & Douch, R. (2006). Changing children's intergroup attitudes toward refugees: Testing different models of extended contact. *Child Development, 77,* 1208–1219.

Campaign 2000 (2009). *Report card on child and family poverty in Canada.* Author. Retrieved from www.campaign2000.ca/reportCards/national/2009English C2000NationalReportCard.pdf

Campaign 2000 (2012). *Needed: A federal action plan to eradicate child and family poverty in Canada – 2012 Report card on child and family poverty.* Author. Retrieved from www.campaign2000.ca/reportCards/national/C2000ReportCardNov2012.pdf

Campbell, F. A., Pungello, E. P., Burchinal, M., Kainz, K., Pan, Y., Wasik, B. H., et al. (2012). Adult outcomes as a function of an early childhood educational program: An Abecedarian Project follow-up. *Developmental Psychology, 48,* 1033–1043.

Campbell, R., & Sais, E. (1995). Accelerated metalinguistic (phonological) awareness in bilingual children. *British Journal of Developmental Psychology, 13,* 61–68.

Campos, J. J., Anderson, D. I., Barbu-Roth, M. A., Hubbard, E. M., Hertenstein, M. J., & Witherington, D. (2000). Travel broadens the mind. *Infancy, 1,* 149–219.

Campos, J. J., Hiatt, S., Ramsay, D., Henderson, C., & Svejda, M. (1978). The emergence of fear on the visual cliff. In M. Lewis & L. Rosenblum (Eds.), *The origins of affect*. New York, NY: Plenum.

Camras, L. A., & Fatani, S. S. (2008). The development of facial expressions: Current perspectives on infant emotions. In M. Lewis, J. M. Haviland-Jones, & L. F. Barrett (Eds.), *Handbook of emotions* (3rd ed., pp. 291–303). New York, NY: Guilford Press.

Camras, L. A., Chen, Y., Bakeman, R., Norris, K., & Cain, R. T. (2006). Culture, ethnicity, and children's facial expressions: A study of European American, Mainland Chinese, Chinese American, and adopted Chinese girls. *Emotion, 6*, 103–114.

Camras, L. A., Oster, H., Campos, J., Campos, R., Ujiie, T., Miyake, K., et al. (1998). Production of emotional facial expressions in European, American, Japanese, and Chinese infants. *Developmental Psychology, 34*, 616–628.

Canada Safety Council. (n.d.). *Preparation and communication the key for children home alone*. Retrieved from https://canadasafetycouncil.org/child-safety/preparation-and-communication-key-children-home-alone

Canadian Fertility and Andrology Society. (2013a). *Fertility FAQ*. Retrieved from www.cfas.ca/index.php?option=com_content&view=article&id=1126:fertilityfaq&catid=919:for-the-public&Itemid=692

Canadian Fertility and Andrology Society. (2013b). *Human assisted reproduction 2013: Live birth rates for Canada*. Retrieved from https://cfas.ca/?s=assisted+reproduction+live+birth+rate

Canadian Fitness and Lifestyle Research Institute. (CFLRI). (2011). *Physical activity levels of Canadian children and youth*. Ottawa, ON: Author. Retrieved from www.cflri.ca/media/node/972/files/CANPLAY%20Bulletin%202%20PA%20Levels%20EN.pdf

Canadian Institute for Health Information. (CIHI). (2004). *Giving birth in Canada: Providers of maternity and infant care*. Ottawa, ON: Author.

Canadian Institute for Health Information. (CIHI). (2012). *Highlights of 2010–2011. Selected indicators describing the birthing process in Canada*. Ottawa, ON: Author.

Canadian Institutes of Health Research. (CIHR). (2016). *Sex, gender and health research guide: A tool for CIHR applicants*. Retrieved from www.cihr-irsc.gc.ca/e/32019.html

Canadian Institute for Health Information. (CIHI). (2009). *Too early, too small: A profile of small babies across Canada*. Ottawa, ON: Author.

Canadian Institutes of Health Research, Natural Sciences and Engineering Research Council of Canada, Social Sciences and Humanities Research Council of Canada. (2014). *Tri-Council policy statement: Ethical conduct for research involving humans*. Ottawa, ON: Public Works and Government Services Canada.

Canadian Mental Health Association. (2016). *Fast facts about mental illness*. Retrieved from www.cmha.ca/media/fast-facts-about-mental-illness/#.WJJX3fK2EfQ

Canadian Paediatric Society (2005). News release: Keep firearms out of homes with children and teens, advise paediatricians. Retrieved from www.cps.ca/english/media/NewsReleases/2005/october19htm

Canadian Paediatric Society. (2012). Preventing playground injuries. Retrieved from www.cps.ca/documents/position/playground-injuries

Canadian Paediatric Society (2014/2017). *Nutrition for healthy term infants, six to 24 months: An overview*. Retrieved from www.cps.ca/en/documents/position/nutrition-healthy-term-infants-6-to-24-months

Canadian Red Cross (2013). *Facts and figures: Child drownings in Canada*. Retrieved from www.redcross.ca/crc/documents/What-We-Do/Swimming-Water-Safety/facts-and-figures-water-safety-week-2013.pdf

Canadian Red Cross (2014). *Water-related fatality facts at a glance: Canada 1991–2010*. Retrieved from www.redcross.ca/crc/documents/What-We-Do/Swimming-Water-Safety/water-related-fatality-facts-at-a-glance-canada-1991–2010.pdf

Canadian Society for Exercise Physiology (CSEP). (2011). *Candian Physical Activity Guidelines*. Retrieved from www.csep.ca/guidelines

Candel, I., Hayne, H., Strange, D., & Prevoo, E. (2009). The effect of suggestion on children's recognition memory for seen and unseen details. *Psychology, Crime, & Law, 15*, 29–39.

Canobi, K. H., Reeve, R. A., & Pattison, P. E. (2002). Young children's understanding of addition. *Educational Psychology, 22*, 513–532.

Cantrell, L., & Smith, L. B. (2013). Open questions and a proposal: A critical review of the evidence on infant numerical abilities. *Cognition, 128*, 331–352.

Capelli, C. A., Nakagawa, N., & Madden, C. M. (1990). How children understand sarcasm: The role of context and intonation. *Child Development, 61*, 1824–1841.

Caravolas, M., Lervåg, A., Mousikou, P., Efrim, C., Litavský, M., Onochie-Quintanilla, E., et al. (2012). Common patterns of prediction of literacy development in different alphabetic orthographies. *Psychological Science, 23*, 678–686.

Card, N. A. (2010). Antipathetic relationships in child and adolescent development: A meta-analytic review and recommendations for an emerging area of study. *Developmental Psychology, 46*, 516–529.

Card, N. A., & Hodges, E. V. (2006). Shared targets for aggression by early adolescent friends. *Developmental Psychology, 42*, 1327–1338.

Card, N. A., Stucky, B. D., Sawalani, G. M., & Little, T. D. (2008). Direct and indirect aggression during adolescence: A meta-analytic review of gender differences, intercorrelations, and relations to maladjustment. *Child Development, 79*, 1185–1229.

Carey, A. D., Murray, S. J., & Barnfield, A. M. C. (2013). The effects of therapeutic riding (TR) on children. *Scientific and Educational Journal of Therapeutic Riding, 2012/13*, 10–35.

Carlson, M. D., Mendle, J., & Harden, K. P. (2014). Early adverse environments and genetic influences on age at first sex: Evidence for gene × environment interaction. *Developmental Psychology, 50*, 1532–1554.

Carlson, S. M., & Meltzoff, A. N. (2008). Bilingual experience and executive functioning in young children. *Developmental Science, 11*, 282–298.

Carlson, S. M., Koenig, M. A., & Harms, M. B. (2013). Theory of mind. *WIREs Cognitive Science, 4*, 391–402.

Carlson Jones, D. (2004). Body image among adolescent girls and boys: A longitudinal study. *Developmental Psychology, 40*, 823–835.

Carpenter, P. A., & Daneman, M. (1981). Lexical retrieval and error recovery in reading: A model based on eye fixations. *Journal of Verbal Learning and Verbal Behavior, 20*, 137–160.

Carpenter, R., McGarvey, C., Mitchell, E. A., Tappin, D. M., Vennemann, M. M., Smuk, M., et al. (2013). Bedsharing when parents do not smoke: Is there a risk of SIDS? An individual level analysis of five major case-control studies. *British Medical Journal Open, 3*:e002299.

Carré, J. M., McCormick, C. M., & Hariri, A. R. (2011). The social neuroendocrinology of human aggression. *Psychoneuroendocrinology, 36*, 935–944.

Carrere, S., & Gottman, J. M. (1999). Predicting the future of marriages. In E. M. Hetherington (Ed.), *Coping with divorce, single parenting, and remarriage: A risk and resiliency perspective*. Mahwah, NJ: Erlbaum.

Carroll, D. W. (1999). *Psychology of language* (3rd ed.). Pacific Grove, CA: Books/Cole.

Carroll, J. B. (1993). *Human cognitive abilities: A survey of factor-analytic studies*. New York, NY: Cambridge University Press.

Carroll, J. B. (1996). A three-stratum theory of intelligence: Spearman's contribution. In I. Dennis & P. Tapsfield (Eds.), *Human abilities: Their nature and measurement*. Mahwah, NJ: Erlbaum.

Carroll, J. L., & Loughlin, G. M. (1994). Sudden infant death syndrome. In F. A. Oski, C. D. DeAngelis,

R. D. Feigin, J. A. McMillan, & J. B. Warshaw (Eds.), *Principles and practice of pediatrics*. Philadelphia, PA: Lippincott.

Carskadon, M. A. (2002). Factors influencing sleep patterns of adolescents. In M. A. Carskadon (Ed.), *Adolescent sleep patterns: Biological, social, and psychological influences* (pp. 4–26). New York, NY: Cambridge University Press.

Carter, C. S. (2014). Oxytocin pathways and the evolution of human behavior. *Annual Review of Psychology, 65*, 17–39.

Carver, K., Joyner, K., & Udry, J. R. (2003). National estimates of adolescent romantic relationships. In P. Florsheim (Ed.), *Adolescent romantic relations and sexual behavior: Theory, research, and practical implications* (pp. 23–56). Mahwah, NJ: Erlbaum.

Carver, P. R., Egan, S. K., & Perry, D. G. (2004). Children who question their heterosexuality. *Developmental Psychology, 40*, 43–53.

Casalin, S., Luyten, P., Vliegen, N., & Meurs, P. (2012). The structure and stability of temperament from infancy to toddlerhood: A one-year prospective study. *Infant Behavior and Development, 35*, 94–108.

Caselli, M. C., Rinaldi, P., Stefanini, S., & Volterra, V. (2012). Early action and gesture "vocabulary" and its relation with word comprehension and production. *Child Development, 83*, 526–542.

Casey, B. J., & Caudle, K. (2013). The teenage brain: Self control. *Current Directions in Psychological Science, 22*, 82–87.

Casey, B. J., Tottenham, N., Liston, C., & Durston, S. (2005). Imaging the developing brain: What have we learned about cognitive development? *Trends in Cognitive Sciences, 9*, 104–110.

Casiglia, A. C., Coco, A. L., & Zappulla, C. (1998). Aspects of social reputation and peer relationships in Italian children: A cross-cultural perspective. *Developmental Psychology, 34*, 723–730.

Casper, D. M., & Card, N. A. (2010). "We were best friends, but. . . ": Two studies of antipathetic relationships emerging from broken friendships. *Journal of Adolescent Research, 25*, 499–526.

Caspi, A., McClay, J., Moffitt, T. E., Mull, J., Martin, J., Craig, I. W., et al. (2002). Role of genotype in the cycle of violence in maltreated children. *Science, 297*, 851–854.

Caspi, A., Roberts, B. W., & Shiner, R. L. (2005). Personality development: Stability and change. *Annual Review of Psychology, 56*, 453–484.

Cassidy, J. (1994). Emotion regulation: Influences of attachment relationships. *Monographs of the Society for Research in Child Development, 59*(Serial No. 240), 228–283.

Castelli, L., Zogmaister, C., & Tomelleri, S. (2009). The transmission of racial attitudes within the family. *Developmental Psychology, 45*, 586–591.

Cattell, R. B. (1965). *The scientific analysis of personality*. Baltimore, MD: Penguin.

Cauvet, E., Limissuri, R., Millotte, S., Skoruppa, K., Cabrol, D., & Christophe, A. (2014). Function words constrain on-line recognition of verbs and nouns in French 18-month-olds. *Language Learning and Development, 10*, 1–18.

Ceci, S. J., & Bruck, M. (1995). *Jeopardy in the courtroom: A scientific analysis of children's testimony*. Washington, DC: American Psychological Association.

Ceci, S. J., & Bruck, M. (1998). Children's testimony: Applied and basic issues. In W. Damon (Ed.), *Handbook of child psychology* (Vol. 4). New York, NY: Wiley.

Center for Behavioral Health Statistics and Quality. (2012). *Depression triples between the ages of 12 and 15 among adolescent girls*. Rockville MD: Substance Abuse and Mental Health Services Administration.

Centers for Disease Control and Prevention. (2012). Youth risk behavior surveillance—United States, 2011. *Morbidity and Mortality Weekly Report, 61*. Atlanta GA: Author.

Centers for Disease Control and Prevention. (2013). *2011 Assisted Reproductive Technology Fertility Clinic Success Rates Report.* Atlanta, GA: Author.

Centers for Disease Control and Prevention. (2016a). *About SUID and SIDS.* Retrieved from www.cdc.gov/sids/aboutsuidandsids.htm

Centers for Disease Control and Prevention. (2016b). Autism Spectrum Disorder (ASD). Retrieved from www.cdc.gov/ncbddd/autism/data.html

Centre for Addiction and Mental Health. (2012). Male students in Ontario show declines in bullying, females show elevated rates of bullying and psychological distress. Retrieved from www.camh.en/hospital/about_camh/newsroom/.newsrelease

Cerella, J., & Hale, S. (1994). The rise and fall in information-processing rates over the life span. *Acta Psychologica, 86,* 109–197.

Champion, T. B. (2003). A "matter of vocabulary": Performance of low-income African-American Head Start children on the Peabody Picture Vocabulary Test. *Communication Disorders Quarterly, 24,* 121–127.

Chandler, M. J., & Carpendale, J. I. M. (1998). Inching toward a mature theory of mind. In M. D. Ferrari & R. J. Sternberg (Eds.), *Self-awareness: Its nature and development* (pp. 148–190). New York, NY: Guilford Press.

Chanquoy, L. (2001). How to make it easier for children to revise their writing: A study of text revision from 3rd to 5th grades. *British Journal of Educational Psychology, 71,* 15–41.

Chao, R. K. (2001). Extending research on the consequences of parenting style for Chinese Americans and European Americans. *Child Development, 72,* 1832–1843.

Chaplin, T. M., & Aldao, A. (2013). Gender differences in emotion expression in children: A meta-analytic review. *Psychological Bulletin, 139,* 735–765.

Chapman, P. D. (1988). *Schools as sorters: Lewis M. Terman, applied psychology, and the intelligence testing movement, 1890–1930.* New York, NY: New York University Press.

Chase-Lansdale, P. L., Cherlin, A., & Kiernan, K.E. (1995). The long-term effects of parental divorce on the mental health of young adults: A developmental perspective. *Child Development, 66,* 1614–1634.

Chavajay, P. (2008). Organizational patterns in problem solving among Mayan fathers and children. *Developmental Psychology, 44,* 882–888.

Chen, E., Cohen, S., & Miller, G. E. (2010). How low socioeconomic status affects 2-year-hormonal trajectories in children. *Psychological Science, 21,* 31–37.

Chen, J., & Gardner, H. (2005). Assessment based on multiple intelligences theory. In D. P. Flanagan & P. L. Harrison (Eds.), *Contemporary intellectual assessment: Theories, tests, and issues* (pp. 77–102). New York, NY: Guilford Press.

Chen, X., & French, D. C. (2008). Children's social competence in cultural context. *Annual review of Psychology, 59,* 591–616.

Chen, X., Rubin, K. H., Liu, M., Chen, H., Wang, L., Li, D., et al. (2003). Compliance in Chinese and Canadian toddlers: A cross-cultural study. *International Journal of Behavioural Development, 27*(5), 428–436.

Chen, X., Wang, L., & Cao, R. (2011). Shyness-sensitivity and unsociability in rural Chinese children: relations with social, school, and psychological adjustment. *Child Development, 82,* 1531–1543.

Chen, X., Wang, L., & DeSouza, A. (2006). Temperament, socioemotional functioning, and peer relationships in Chinese and North American children. In X. Chen, D. C. French, & B. H. Schneider (Eds.), *Peer relationships in cultural context* (pp. 123–147). New York, NY: Cambridge University Press.

Chen, Y., Norton, D. J., McBain, R., Gold, J., Frazier, J. A. & Coyle, J. T. (2012). Enhanced local processing of dynamic visual information in autism: Evidence from speed discrimination. *Neuropsychologia, 50,* 733–739.

Chen-Gaddini, M. (2012). Chinese mothers and adolescents' views of authority and autonomy: A study of parent-adolescent conflict in urban and rural China. *Child Development, 83,* 1846–1852.

Cheung, W. W., & Mao, P. (2012). Recent advances in obesity: Genetics and beyond. *ISRN Endocrinology,* Article ID 536905.

Chi, M. T. H. (1978). Knowledge structures and memory development. In R. Siegler (Ed.), *Children's thinking: What develops?* Hillsdale, NJ: Erlbaum.

Child Welfare Information Gateway. (2013). *Leaving your child home alone.* Washington DC: Children's Bureau.

Children's Defense Fund. (2010). *State of America's children: 2010.* Washington, DC: Author.

Choe, D. E., Olson, S. L., & Sameroff, A. J. (2013). The interplay of externalizing problems and physical and inductive discipline during childhood. *Developmental Psychology, 49,* 2029–2039.

Chomitz, V. R., Cheung, L. W. Y., & Lieberman, E. (1995). The role of lifestyle in preventing low birth weight. *The Future of Children, 5,* 121–138.

Chomsky, N. (1957). *Syntactic structures.* The Hague, The Netherlands: Mouton.

Chomsky, N. (1995). The minimalist program. Cambridge, MA: MIT Press.

Chorpita, B. F., & Barlow, D. H. (1998). The development of anxiety: The role of control in the early environment. *Psychological Bulletin, 124,* 3–21.

Chou, R. J. A. (2011). Filial piety by contract? The emergence, implementation, and implications of the "Family Support Agreement" in China. *Gerontologist, 51,* 3–16.

Chow, B. W., McBride-Chang, C., Cheung, H., & Chow, C. S. (2008). Dialogic reading and morphology training in Chinese children: Effects on language and literacy. *Developmental Psychology, 44,* 233–244.

Christensen, A., & Heavey, C. L. (1999). Intervention for couples. *Annual Review of Psychology, 50,* 165–190.

Chudley, A. E., Conry, J., Cook, J. L., Loock, C., Rosales, T., & LeBlanc, N. (2005). Fetal alcohol spectrum disorder: Canadian guidelines for diagnosis. *Canadian Medical Association Journal, 172*(5 suppl.), S1–S21.

Chung, H. L., & Steinberg, L. (2006). Relations between neighborhood factors, parenting behaviors, peer deviance, and delinquency among serious juvenile offenders. *Developmental Psychology, 42,* 319–331.

Chung-Hall, J., & Chen, X. (2010). Aggressive and prosocial peer group functioning: Effects on children's social, school, and psychological adjustment. *Social Development, 19,* 659–680.

Cicchetti, D., & Toth, S. L. (2006). Developmental psychopathology and preventive intervention. In W. Damon & R. M. Lerner (Eds.), *Handbook of child psychology* (Vol. 4). New York, NY: Wiley.

Citizenship and Immigration Canada. (2007). International adoption. Retrieved from www.cic.gc.ca/english//immigrate/adoption/index.asp#tphp%20idtphp

Clark, K. B. (1945). A brown girl in a speckled world. *Journal of Social Issues, 1,* 10–15.

Clark, K. B., & Clark, M. K. (1940). Skin color as a factor in racial identification of Negro preschool children. *Journal of Social Psychology, 11,* 159–169.

Clark, W. (2008). Kids' sports. *Canadian Social Trends, June 3, 2008,* 54–61. Statistics Canada. Retrieved from www.statcan.gc.ca/pub/11-008-x/2008001/article/10573-eng.pdf

Clarke, P. J., Snowling, M. J., Truelove, E., & Hulme, C. (2010). Ameliorating children's reading-comprehension difficulties: A randomized controlled trial. *Psychological Science, 21,* 1106–1116.

Clarke, P. J., Truelove, E., Hulme, C., & Snowling, M. J. (2014). *Developing reading comprehension.* Chichester, UK: Wiley.

Clarke-Stewart, K. A., & Bretano, C. (2005). *Till divorce do us part.* New Haven, CT: Yale University Press.

Clements, D. H. (1995). Teaching creativity with computers. *Educational Psychology Review, 7,* 141–161.

Cnattingius, S. (2004). The epidemiology of smoking during pregnancy: Smoking prevalence, maternal characteristics, and pregnancy outcomes. *Nicotine and Tobacco Research, 6,* S125–S140.

Coall, D. A., & Hertwig, R. (2011). Grandparent investment: A relic of the past or a resource for the future? *Current Directions in Psychological Science, 20,* 93–98

Coatsworth, J. D., & Conroy, D. E. (2009). The effects of autonomy-supporting coaching, need satisfaction, and self-perceptions on initiative and identity in youth swimmers. *Developmental Psychology, 45,* 320–328.

Cochlear War. (n.d.). Retrieved from www.cochlearwar.com/index.html

Coelho, J. S., Jansen, A., Roefs, A., & Nederkoom, C. (2009). Eating behavior in response to food-cue exposure: Examining the cue-reactivity and counteractive-control models. *Psychology of Addictive Behaviors, 23,* 131–139.

Cohen, G. L., Garcia, J., Apfel, N., & Master, A. (2006). Reducing the racial achievement gap: A social psychological intervention. *Science, 313,* 1307–1310.

Cohen, L. B., & Cashon, C. H. (2003). Infant perception and cognition. In R. M. Lerner, D. K. Freedheim, I. B. Weiner, M. A. Easterbrooks, & J. Mistry (Eds.), *Handbook of psychology: Developmental psychology.* Hoboken, NJ: Wiley.

Cohen, R. W., Martinez, M. E., & Ward, B. W. (2010). *Health insurance coverage: Early release of estimates from the National Health Interview Survey, 2009.* Hyattsville MD: National Center for Health Statistics.

Cohen, S., & Williamson, G. M. (1991). Stress and infectious disease in humans. *Psychological Bulletin, 109,* 5–24.

Cohen Kadosh, K., Johnson, M. H., Dick, F., Cohen Kadosh, R., & Blakemore, S-J. (2013). Effects of age, task performance, and structural brain development on face processing. *Cerebral Cortex, 23,* 1630–1642.

Coie, J. D., Dodge, K. A., Terry, R., & Wright, V. (1991). The role of aggression in peer relations: An analysis of aggression episodes in boys' play groups. *Child Development, 62,* 812–826.

Colby, A., Kohlberg, L., Gibbs, J. C., & Lieberman, M. (1983). A longitudinal study of moral development. *Monographs of the Society for Research in Child Development, 48*(Serial No. 200).

Cole, D. A. (1991). Change in self-perceived competence as a function of peer and teacher evaluation. *Developmental Psychology, 27,* 682–688.

Cole, M. (2006). Culture and cognitive development in phylogenetic, historical and ontogenetic perspective. In W. Damon & R. M. Lerner (Eds.), *Handbook of child psychology* (6th ed., Vol. 2). New York, NY: Wiley.

Cole, P. M., Tamang, B. L., & Shrestha, S. (2006). Cultural variations in the socialization of young children's anger and shame. *Child Development, 77,* 1237–1251.

Cole, T. J. (2000). Secular trends in growth. *Proceedings of the Nutrition Society, 59,* 317–324.

Collins, W. A. (2003). More than myth: The developmental significance of romantic relationships during adolescence. *Journal of Research on Adolescence, 13,* 1–24.

Collins, W. A., Welsh, D. P., & Furman, W. (2009). Adolescent romantic relationships. *Annual Review of Psychology, 60,* 631–652.

Committee on Genetics. (1996). Newborn screening fact sheet. *Pediatrics, 98,* 473–501.

Conboy, B. T., & Thal, D. J. (2006). Ties between the lexicon and grammar: Cross-sectional and longitudinal studies of bilingual toddlers. *Child Development, 77,* 712–735.

Condry, J. C., & Ross, D. F. (1985). Sex and aggression: The influence of gender label on the perception of aggression in children. *Child Development, 56,* 225–233.

Conduct Problems Prevention Research Group. (2011). The effects of the Fast Track Preventive Intervention on the development of conduct disorder across child-hood. *Child Development, 82,* 331–345.

Conger, R. D., & Elder, G. H. (1994). *Families in troubled times: Adapting to change in rural America.* New York, NY: Aldine De Gruyter.

Connolly, J., Craig, W., Goldberg, A., & Pepler, D. (2004). Mixed-gender groups, dating and romantic relationships in early adolescence. *Journal of Research on Adolescence, 14,* 185–207.

Conry-Murray, C., & Turiel, E. (2012). Jimmy's baby doll and Jenny's truck: Young children's reasoning about gender norms. *Child Development, 83,* 146–158.

Constantinescu, M., & Hines, M. (2012). Relating pre-natal testosterone exposure to postnatal behavior in typically developing children: Methods and findings. *Child Development Perspectives, 6,* 407–413.

Cook, E. C., Buehler, C., & Henson, R. (2009). Parents and peers as social influences to deter antiso-cial behavior. *Journal of Youth and Adolescence, 38,* 1204–1252.

Cooke, L. J., Chambers, L. C., Añez, E. V., Croker, H. A. Boniface, D., Yeomans, M. R., et al. (2011). Eating for pleasure or profit: The effects of incentives on children's enjoyment of vegetables. *Psychological Science, 22,* 190–196.

Cooper, H., Hedges, L. V., & Valentine, J. C. (Eds.). (2009). *The handbook of research synthesis and meta-analysis* (2nd ed.). New York, NY: Russell Sage Foundation.

Cooper, R. S., Kaufman, J. S., & Ward, R. (2003). Race and genomics. *New England Journal of Medicine, 384*(12), 1166–1170.

Coplan, R. J., & Armer, M. (2007). A "multitude" of solitude: A closer look at social withdrawal and nonsocial play in early childhood. *Child Development Perspectives, 1,* 26–32.

Coplan, R. J., & Ooi, L. (2014). The causes and consequences of "playing alone" in childhood. In R. J. Coplan & J. C. Bowker (Eds.), *The handbook of solitude: Psychological perspectives on social isolation, social withdrawal, and being alone* (pp. 111–128). Chichester, UK: Wiley.

Coplan, R. J., Gavinski-Molina, M. H., Lagace-Seguin, D. G., & Wichmann, C. (2001). When girls versus boys play alone: Nonsocial play and adjustment in kindergarten. *Developmental Psychology, 37,* 464–474.

Coplan, R. J., O'Neil, K., & Arbeau, K. A. (2005). Maternal anxiety during and after pregnancy and infant temperament at three months of age. *Journal of Prenatal and Perinatal Psychology and Health, 19*(3), 199–215.

Coplan, R. J., Rose-Krasnor, L., Weeks, M., Kingsbury, A., Kingsbury, M., & Bullock, A. (2013). Alone is a crowd: Social motivations, social withdrawal, and socioemotional functioning in later childhood. *Developmental Psychology, 49,* 861–875.

Copper, R. L., Goldenberg, R. L., Das, A., Elder, N., Swain, M., Norman, G., et al. (1996). The preterm prediction study: Maternal stress is associated with spontaneous preterm birth at less than thirty-five weeks' gestation. *American Journal of Obstetrics and Gynecology, 175,* 1286–1292.

Coppus, A. M. W. (2013). People with intellectual dis-ability: What do we know about adulthood and life expectancy. *Developmental Disabilities Research Reviews, 18,* 6–16.

Corballis, M. C., Badzakova-Trajkova, G., & Häberling, I. S. (2012). Right hand, left brain: Genetic and evolutionary assymetries for language and manual action. *WIREs Cognitive Science, 3,* 1–17.

Cordes, S., & Brannon, E. M. (2009). The relative salience of discrete and continuous quantity in young infants. *Developmental Science, 12,* 453–463.

Cornelius, M., Taylor, P., Geva, D., & Day, N. (1995). Prenatal tobacco exposure and marijuana use among adolescents: Effects on offspring gestational age, growth, and morphology. *Pediatrics, 95,* 738–743.

Corriveau, K. H., Kinzler, K. D., & Harris, P. L. (2013). Accuracy trumps accent in children's endorsement of object labels. *Developmental Psychology, 49,* 470–479.

Costa, P. T., & McRae, R. R. (2001). A theoretical con-text for adult temperament. In T. D. Wachs & G. A. Kohnstamm (Eds.), *Temperament in context* (pp. 1–21). Mahwah, NJ: Erlbaum.

Costigan, C. L., & Dokis, D. P. (2006). Relations between parent–child acculturation differences and adjustment within immigrant Chinese families. *Child Develop-ment, 77,* 1252–1267.

Costin, S. E., & Jones, D. C. (1992). Friendship as a facilitator of emotional responsiveness and prosocial interventions among young children. *Developmental Psychology, 28,* 941–947.

Coté, S., Tremblay, R. E., Nagin, D., Zoccolillo, M., & Vitaro, F. (2002a). The development of impulsivity, fearfulness, and helpfulness during childhood: Pat-terns of consistency and change in the trajectories of boys and girls. *Journal of Child Psychology and Psychia-try, 43*(5), 609–618.

Coté, S., Tremblay, R. E., Nagin, D., Zoccolillo, M., & Vitaro, F. (2002b). Childhood behavioural profiles leading to adolescent conduct disorder: Risk trajecto-ries for boys and girls. *Journal of the American Academy of Adolescent Psychiatry, 41*(9), 1086–1094.

Côté, S., Vaillancourt, T., Barker, E. D., Nagin, D., & Tremblay, R. E. (2007). The joint development of physical and indirect aggression: Predictors of conti-nuity and change during childhood. *Development and Psychopathology, 19,* 37–55.

Coté, S., Zoccolillo, M., Tremblay, R. E., Nagin, D., & Vitaro, F. (2001). Predicting girls' conduct disorder in adolescence from childhood trajectories of disruptive behaviours. *Journal of the American Academy of Child and Adolescent Psychiatry, 40*(6), 678–684.

Coulton, C. J., Crampton, D. S., Irwin, M., Spilsbury, J. C., & Korbin, J. E. (2007). How neighborhoods influence child maltreatment: A review of the lit-erature and alternative pathways. *Child Abuse and Neglect, 31,* 1117–1142.

Cousminer, D. L., Berry, D. J., Timpson, N. J., Ang, W., Thiering, E., Byrne, E. M., et al. (2013). Genome-wide association and longitudinal analyses reveal genetic loci linking pubertal height growth, pubertal timing, and childhood adiposity. *Human Molecular Genetics, 22,* 2735–2747.

Coutelle, C., Themis, M., Waddington, S. N., Buckley, S. M., Gregory, L. G., Nivsarkar, M. S., et al. (2005). Gene therapy progress and prospects: Fetal gene therapy—first proofs of concept—some adverse effects. *Gene Therapy, 12,* 1601–1607.

Coutts, M. (2007, February 5). Ethical concerns raised as woman, 60, gives birth to twins. *National Post.* Retrieved from www.nationalpost.com/m/story.html

Covell, K., & Howe, R. B. (2001). Moral education through the 3Rs: rights, respect and responsibility. *Journal of Moral Education, 30*(1), 29–40.

Covell, K., & Howe, R. B. (2009). *Rights and resilience: The long-term effects of RRR.* Report to Hampshire Education Authority. Cape Breton University Children's Rights Centre. Retrieved from www.childrensrightseducation .com/uploads/3/4/5/2/34521419/rrr_report_2009.pdf

Covell, K., & Howe, R. B. (2011). *Rights, respect and responsibility in Hampshire County: RRR and resilience report.* Cape Breton University Children's Rights Centre. Retrieved from www3.hants.gov.uk/rrr-in-hampshire-rrr-and-resilience-report.pdf

Covell, K., Howe, R. B., & McNeil, J. K. (2008). 'If there's a dead rat, don't leave it.' Young children's understanding of their citizenship rights and responsi-bilities. *Cambridge Journal of Education, 38*(3), 321–339.

Cox, M. J., & Paley, B. (2003). Understanding families as systems. *Current Directions in Psychological Science, 12,* 193–196.

Cox, M. J., Paley, B., & Harter, K. (2001). Interparental conflict and parent–child relationships. In J. H. Grych & F. D. Fincham (Eds.), *Interparental conflict*

and child development (pp. 249–272). New York, NY: Cambridge University Press.

Cox, R. H., Qui, Y., & Li, Z. (1993). Overview of sport psychology. In N. Singer, M. Murphy, & L. K. Tennant (Eds.), *Handbook of Research on Sports Psychology,* (pp. 3–31). New York, NY: MacMillan Publishing.

Cox, S. J., Mezulis, A. H., & Hyde, J. S. (2010). The influence of child gender role and maternal feedback to child stress on the emergence of the gender differ-ence in depressive rumination in adolescence. *Devel-opmental Psychology, 46,* 842–852.

Craig, A.P., & Beishuizen, J. J. (2002). Psychological test-ing in a multicultural society: Universal or particular competencies. *Intercultural Education, 13*(2), 201–213.

Craig, K. D., Whitfield, M. F, Grunau, R. V. E., Linton, J., & Hadjistavropoulos, H. D. (1993). Pain in the preterm neonate: Behavioural and physiological indi-ces. *Pain, 52,* 238–299.

Craig, W., Pepler, D., & Blais, J. (2007). Responding to bullying. *School Psychology International, 28*(4), 465–477.

Creusere, M. A. (1999). Theories of adults' understanding and use of irony and sarcasm: Applications to and evidence from research with children. *Developmental Review, 19,* 213–262.

Crick, N. R., & Dodge, K. A. (1994). A review and reformulation of social information-processing mech-anisms in children's social adjustment. *Psychological Bulletin, 115,* 74–101.

Crick, N. R., & Grotpeter, J. K. (1995). Relational aggression, gender, and social-psychological adjust-ment. *Child Development, 66,* 710–722.

Crick, N. R., & Werner, N. E. (1998). Response deci-sion processes in relational and overt aggression. *Child Development, 69,* 1630–1639.

Crick, N. R., Casas, J. F., & Nelson, D. A. (2002). Toward a more comprehensive understanding of peer maltreatment: Studies of relational victimization. *Current Directions in Psychological Science, 11,* 98–101.

Crick, N. R., Ostrov, J. M., Appleyard, K., Jansen, E. A., & Casas, J. F. (2004). Relational aggression in early childhood: "You can't come to my birthday party unless." In M. Puttalaz & K. L. Bierman (Eds.), *Aggression, antisocial behavior, and violence among girls* (pp. 71–89). New York, NY: Guilford Press.

Cristia, A. (2010). Phonetic enhancement of sibilants in infant-directed speech. *Journal of the Acoustical Society of America, 128,* 424–434.

Crocetti, E., Rubini, M., Luyckx, K., & Meeus, W. (2008). Identity formation in early and middle adolescence from various ethnic groups: From three dimensions to five statuses. *Journal of Youth and Ado-lescence, 37,* 983–996.

Crouter, A. C., & Bumpus, M. F. (2001). Linking parents' work stress to children's and adolescents' psychologi-cal adjustment. *Current Directions in Psychological Sci-ence, 10,* 156–159.

Crouter, A. C., Whiteman, S. D., McHale, S. M., & Osgood, D. (2007). Development of gender attitude traditionality across middle childhood and adoles-cence. *Child Development, 78,* 911–926.

Cruz, I., Quittner, A. L., Marker, C., DesJardin, J. L., & the DCaCI Investigative Team. (2013). Identification of effective strategies to promote language in deaf children with cochlear implants. *Child Development, 84,* 543–559.

Csizmadia, A., Brunsma, D. L., & Cooney, T. M. (2012). Racial identification and developmental outcomes among Black-White multiracial youth: A review from a life course perspective. *Advances in Life Course Research, 17,* 34–44.

Cuellar, I., Nyberg, B., Maldonado, R. E., & Roberts, R. E. (1997). Ethnic identity and acculturation in a young adult Mexican-origin population. *Journal of Community Psychology, 25,* 535–549.

Cummings, E. M., George, M. R. W., McCoy, K., P., & Davies, P. T. (2012). Interparental conflict in kindergarten and adolescent adjustment: Prospective investigation of emotional security as an explanatory mechanism. *Child Development, 83*, 1703–1715.

Cummings, E. M., Goeke-Morey, M. C., Merrilees, C. E., Taylor, L. K., & Shirlow, P. (2014). A social-ecological, process-oriented perspective on political violence and child development. *Child Development Perspectives, 8*, 82–89.

Cummings, E., Schermerhorn, A. C., Davies, P. T., Goeke-Morey, M. C., & Cummings, J. S. (2006). Interparental discord and child adjustment: Prospective investigations of emotional security as an explanatory mechanism. *Child Development, 77*, 132–152.

Cunningham, A. E., Perry, K. E., Stanovich, K. E., & Share, D. L. (2002). Orthographic learning during reading: Examining the role of self-teaching. *Journal of Experimental Child Psychology, 82*, 185–199.

Curtiss, S. (1989). The independence and task-specificity of language. In M. H. Bornstein & J. S. Bruner (Eds.), *Interaction in human development* (pp. 105–137). Hillsdale, NJ: Erlbaum.

Cvencek, D., Meltzoff, A. N., & Greenwald, A. G. (2011). Math-gender stereotypes in elementary school children. *Child Development, 82*, 766–779.

D'Onofrio, B. M., Goodnight, J. A., Van Hulle, C. A., Rodgers, J. L., Rathouz, P. J., Waldman, I. D., & Lahey, B. B. (2009). Maternal age at childbirth and offspring disruptive behaviors: Testing the causal hypothesis. *Journal of Child Psychology and Psychiatry, 50*, 1018–1028.

D'Onofrio, B. M., Singh, A. L., Iliadou, A., Lambe, M., Hultman, C. M., Neiderhiser, J. M., et al. (2010). A quasi-experimental study of maternal smoking during pregnancy and offspring academic achievement. *Child Development, 81*, 80–100.

Daniels, H. (2011). Vygotsky and psychology. In U. Goswami (Ed.), *The Wiley-Blackwell handbook of childhood cognitive development* (2nd ed., pp. 673–696). West Sussex, UK: Wiley-Blackwell.

Dannemiller, J. L. (1998). Color constancy and color vision during infancy: Methodological and empirical issues. In V. Walsh & J. Kulikowski (Eds.), *Perceptual constancy: Why things look as they do*. New York, NY: Cambridge University Press.

Dar-Nimrod, I., & Heine, S. J. (2006). Exposure to scientific theories affects women's math performance. *Science, 314*, 435.

Darling, H., Reeder, A. I., McGee, T., & Williams, S. (2006). Brief report: Disposable income, and spending on fast food, alcohol, cigarettes, and gambling by New Zealand secondary school students. *Journal of Adolescence, 29*, 837–843.

Darling, N., Cumsille, P., & Martinez, M. L. (2008). Individual differences in adolescents' beliefs about the legitimacy of parental authority and their own obligation to obey: A longitudinal investigation. *Child Development, 79*, 1103–1118.

Darwin, C. (1895). *On the origin of species by means of natural selection*. London, UK: Muray.

Dasgupta, N., & Asgari, S. (2004). Seeing is believing: Exposure to counterstereotypic women leaders and its effect on malleability of automatic gender stereotyping. *Journal of Experimental Social Psychology, 40*, 642–658.

David, A., & Rodeck, C. H. (2009). Fetal gene therapy. In C. H. Rodeck & M. J. Whittle (Eds.), *Fetal medicine: Basic science and clinical practice*. London, UK: Churchill Livingstone.

Davidov, M., Zahn-Waxler, C., Roth-Hanania, R., & Knafo, A. (2013). Concern for others in the first year of life: Theory, evidence, and avenues for research. *Child Development Perspectives, 7*, 126–131.

Davidson, F. H., & Davidson, M. M. (1994). *Changing childhood prejudice: The caring work of the schools*. Westport, CT: Bergin & Garvey/Greenwood.

Davies, P. T., & Cummings, E. M. (1998). Exploring children's emotional security as a mediator of the link between marital relations and child adjustment. *Child Development, 69*, 124–139.

Davies, P. T., Cicchetti, D., & Martin, M. J. (2012). Toward greater specificity in identifying associations among interparental aggression, child emotional reactivity to conflict, and child problems. *Child Development, 83*, 1789–1804.

Davila, J., & Sargent, E. (2003). The meaning of life (events) predicts changes in attachment security. *Personality and Social Psychology Bulletin, 29*(11), 1383–1395.

Davis, E. P., & Sandman, C. A. (2010). The timing of prenatal exposure to maternal cortisol and psychosocial stress is associated with human cognitive development. *Child Development, 81*, 131–148.

Davis, P. E., Meins, E., & Fernyhough, C. (2011). Self-knowledge in childhood: Relations with children's imaginary companions and understanding of mind. *British Journal of Developmental Psychology, 29*, 680–686.

De Beni, R., & Palladino, P. (2000). Intrusion errors in working memory tasks: Are they related to reading comprehension ability? *Learning and Individual Differences, 12*, 131–143.

De Brauwer, J., & Fias, W. (2009). A longitudinal study of children's performance on simple multiplication and division problems. *Developmental Psychology, 45*, 1480–1496.

De Guio, F., Mangin, J-F., Rivière, D., Perrot, M., Molteno, C. D., Jacobson, . . . & Jacobson, J. L. (2014). A study of cortical morphology in children with fetal alcohol spectrum disorders. *Human Brain Mapping, 35*, 2285–2296.

de Haan, M., Wyatt, J. S., Roth, S., Vargha-Khadem, F., Gadian, D., & Mishkin, M. (2006). Brain and cognitive-behavioral development after asphyxia at term birth. *Developmental Science, 9*, 441–442.

de Olivera-Szejnfeld, P. S., Levine, D., de Olivera Melo, A. S., Amorrim, M. M. R. S., Batista, A. G. M., Chimelli, L., … Tovar-Moll, F. (2016). Congenital brain abnormalities and Zika virus: What the radiologist can expect to see prenatally and postnatally. *Radiology, 281*(2), 1–16. doi: 10.1148/radiol.2016161584

De Wals, P., Tairou, F., Van Allen, M. I., Lowry, R. B., Evans, J. A., Van den Hof, M. C. et al. (2008). Spina bifida before and afer folic acid fortification in Canada. *Birth Defects Research (part A): Clinical and Molecular Teratology, 82*, 622–626.

De Wit, D. J., Lipman, E., Manzano-Munguia, M., Bisanz, J., Graham, K., Offord, D. R., et al. (2006). Feasibility of a randomized controlled trial for evaluating the effectiveness of the Big Brothers Big Sisters community match program at the national level. *Children and Youth Services Review, 29*, 383–404.

Deardorff, D. L. (2000). *Sports: A reference guide and critical commentary, 1980–1999*. Westport, CT: Greenwood Press.

Dearing, E., McCartney, K., & Taylor, B. A. (2009). Does higher quality early child care promote low-income children's math and reading achievement in middle childhood? *Child Development, 80*, 1329–1349.

Deary, I. (2012). Intelligence. *Annual Review of Psychology, 63*, 453–482.

Deater-Deckard, K., Lansford, J. E., Malone, P. S., Alampay, L. P. Sorbring, E., Bacchini, D., et al. (2011). The association between parental warmth and control in thirteen cultural groups. *Journal of Family Psychology, 25*, 790–794.

DeCasper, A. J., & Spence, M. J. (1986). Prenatal maternal speech influences newborns' perception of speech sounds. *Infant Behavior and Development, 9*, 133–150.

Declercq, E. (2012). The politics of home birth in the United States. *Birth, 39*, 281–285.

Degner, J., & Dalege, J. (2013). The apple does not fall far from the tree or does it? A meta-analysis of parent-child similarity in intergroup attitudes. *Psychological Bulletin, 139*, 1270–1304.

Dehaene, S., Izard, V., Pica, P., & Spelke, E. (2006). Core knowledge of geometry in an Amazonian indigene group. *Science, 311*, 381–384.

Dehaene-Lambertz, G., Dehaene, S., & Hertz-Pannier, L. (2002). Functional neuroimaging of speech perception in infants. *Science, 298*(6), 2013–2015.

Dekovic, M., & Janssens, J. M. (1992). Parents' child-rearing style and child's sociometric status. *Developmental Psychology, 28*, 925–932.

Del Giudice, M. (2011). Alone in the dark? Modeling the conditions for visual experience in human fetuses. *Developmental Psychobiology, 53*, 214–219.

Del Valle, J. F., Bravo, A., & Lopez, M. (2010). Parents and peers as providers of support in adolescents' social network: A developmental perspective. *Journal of Community Psychology, 38*, 16–27.

Delaney, C. (2000). Making babies in a Turkish village. In J. S. DeLoache & A. Gottlieb (Eds.), *A world of babies: Imagined child care guides for seven societies*. New York, NY: Cambridge University Press.

DeLoache, J. S. (1984). Oh where, oh where: Memory-based searching by very young children. In C. Sophian (Ed.), *Origins of cognitive skills*. Hillsdale, NJ: Erlbaum.

DeLoache, J. S. (1995). Early understanding and use of models: The modal model. *Current Directions in Psychological Science, 4*, 109–113.

DeLoache, J. S., Chiong, C., Sherman, K., Islam, N., Vanderborght, M., Troseth, G. L., et al. (2010). Do babies learn from baby media? *Psychological Science, 21*(11), 1570–1574. doi: 10.1177/0956797610384145

DeLoache, J. S., Miller, K. F., & Pierroutsakos, S. L. (1998). Reasoning and problem solving. In W. Damon (Ed.), *Handbook of child psychology* (5th ed., Vol. 2, pp. 801–850). New York, NY: Wiley.

DeLoache, J. S., Miller, K. F., & Rosengren, K. S. (1997). The credible shrinking room: Very young children's performance with symbolic and nonsymbolic relations. *Psychological Science, 8*, 308–313.

Demir, A., Levine, S. C., & Goldin-Meadow, S. (2010). Narrative skill in children with unilateral brain injury: A possible limit to functional plasticity. *Developmental Science, 13*, 636–647.

Denissen, J. J., Zarrett, N. R., & Eccles, J. S. (2007). I like to do it, I'm able, and I know I am: Longitudinal couplings between domain-specific achievement, self-concept, and interest. *Child Development, 78*, 430–447.

Desbiens, B. (2011). *Student testing: Why Ontario's on the right track*. EQAO. Retrieved from www.eqao.com/ Publications/ArticleReader.aspx?Lang=E&article= b11A005&section=

deVilliers, J. G., & deVilliers, P. A. (1985). The acquisition of English. In D. I. Slobin (Ed.), *The cross-linguistic study of language acquisition*. Hillsdale, NJ: Erlbaum.

Dewey, C., Fleming, P., Goldin, J., & the ALSPAC Study Team. (1998). Does the supine sleeping position have any adverse effects on the child? II. Development in the first 18 months. *Pediatrics, 101*, e5.

Dewey, K. G. (2001). Nutrition, growth, and complementary feeding of the breastfed infant. *Pediatric Clinics of North America, 48*, 87–104.

De Wolff, M. S., & van IJzendoorn, M. H. (1997). Sensitivity and attachment: A meta-analysis on parental antecedents of infant attachment. *Child Development, 68*, 571–591.

Dews, S., Winner, E., Kaplan, J., Rosenblatt, E., Hunt, M., Lim, K., et al. (1996). Children's understanding of the meaning and functions of verbal irony. *Child Development, 67*, 3071–3085.

Dhillon, C. & Young, M. G. (2010). Environmental racism and First Nations: A call for socially just public policy development. *Canadian Journal of Humanities and Social Sciences, 1*(1), 23–37.

Diamond, A. (2007). Interrelated and interdependent. *Developmental Science, 10*, 152–158.

Diamond, A. (2013). Executive functions. *Annual Review of Psychology, 64*, 135–168.

Diamond, A., & Lee, K. (2011). Interventions shown to aid executive function development in children 4 to 12 years old. *Science, 333*, 959–964.

Diamond, M., Johnson, R., Young, D., & Singh, S. (1983). Age-related morphologic differences in the rat cerebral cortex and hippocampus: Male-female; right-left. *Experimental Neurology, 81*, 1–13.

Dick-Read, G. (1959). *Childbirth without fear.* New York, NY: Harper and Brothers.

Dickens, W. T., & Flynn, J. R. (2006). Common ground and differences. *Psychological Science, 17,* 923–924.

DiDonato, M. D., & Berenbaum, S. A. (2011). The benefits and drawbacks of gender typing: How different dimensions are related to psychological adjustment. *Archives of Sexual Behavior, 40,* 457–463.

Diesendruck, G., Birnbaum, D., Deeb, I., & Segall, G. (2013). Learning what is essential: Relative and absolute changes in children's beliefs about the heritability of ethnicity. *Journal of Cognition and Development, 14,* 546–560.

Dietitians of Canada and Canadian Pediatric Society. (2010). *Promoting optimal monitoring of child growth in Canada: Using the new WHO growth charts.* Dietitians of Canada, Canadian Paediatric Society, The College of Family Physicians of Canada, Community Health Nurses of Canada. Retrieved from www.cps.ca/tools/growth-charts-statement-FULL.pdf

Digital Health Task Force. (2017). *Screen time and young children: Promoting health and development in a digital world.* Canadian Pediatric Society. Retrieved from www.cps.ca/en/documents/position/screen-time-and-young-children

Dijkstra, J. K., Cillessen, A. H. N., & Borch, C. (2013). Popularity and adolescent friendship networks: Selection and influence dynamics. *Developmental Psychology, 49,* 1242–1252.

Dionne, G., Dale, P. S., Boivin, M., & Plomin, R. (2003). Genetic evidence for bidirectional effects of early lexical and grammatical development. *Child Development, 74,* 394–412.

DiPietro, J. A. (2004). The role of prenatal maternal stress in child development. *Current Directions in Child Development, 13,* 71–74.

DiPietro, J. A., Bornstein, M. H., Hahn, C. S., Costigan, K., & Achy-Brou, A. (2007). Fetal heart rate and variability: Stability and prediction to developmental outcomes in early childhood. *Child Development, 78,* 1788–1798.

DiPietro, J. A., Caulfield, L., Costigan, K. A., Merialdi, M., Nguyen, R. H. N., Zavaleta, N., et al. (2004). Fetal neurobehavioral development: A tale of two cities. *Developmental Psychology, 40,* 445–456.

DiPietro, J. A., Hodgson, D. M., Costigan, K. A., & Hilton, S. C. (1996a). Fetal neurobehavioral development. *Child Development, 67,* 2553–2567.

DiPietro, J. A., Hodgson, D. M., Costigan, K. A., & Johnson, T. R. B. (1996b). Fetal antecedents of infant temperament. *Child Development, 67,* 2568–2583.

DiPietro, J. A., Novak, M. F., Costigan, K. A., Atella, L. D., & Reusing, S. P. (2006). Maternal psychological distress during pregnancy in relation to child development at age two. *Child Development, 77,* 573–587.

Dishion, T. J. (1990). The family ecology of boys' peer relations in middle childhood. *Child Development, 61,* 874–892.

Dishion, T. J., Poulin, F., & Burraston, B. (2001). Peer group dynamics associated with iatrogenic effects in group interventions with high-risk young adolescents. In D. W. Nangle & C. A. Erdley (Eds.), *The role of friendship in psychological adjustment* (pp. 79–92). San Francisco, CA: Jossey-Bass.

Divan, H. A., Kheifets, L., Obel, C., & Olsen, J. (2008). Prenatal and postnatal exposure to cell phone use and behavioral problems in children. *Epidemiology, 19*(4), 523–529.

Dixon, J. A., & Marchman, V. A. (2007). Grammar and the lexicon: Developmental ordering in language acquisition. *Child Development, 78,* 190–212.

Docherty, S. J., Davis, O. S. P., Kovas, Y., Meaburn, E. L., Dale P. S., Petrill, S. A., et al. (2010). A genome-wide association study identifies multiple loci associated with mathematics ability and disability. *Genes, Brain, and Behavior, 9,* 234–247.

Dodge, K. A., & Crick, N. R. (1990). Social information-processing bases of aggressive behavior in children. *Personality and Social Psychology Bulletin, 16,* 8–22.

Dodge, K. A., Bates, J. E., & Pettit, G. S. (1990). Mechanisms in the cycle of violence. *Science, 250,* 1678–1683.

Dodge, K. A., Coie, J. D., & Lynam, D. (2006). Aggression and antisocial behavior in youth. In N. Eisenberg (Ed.), *Handbook of child psychology: Vol. 3. Social, emotional, and personality development* (6th ed., pp. 719–788). New York, NY: Wiley.

Dodge, K. A., Coie, J., & Tremblay, R. E. (2006). Aggression. In W. Damon & R. M. Lerner (Eds.), *Handbook of child psychology, Vol. 3* (6th ed) New York, NY: Wiley.

Dodge, K. A., Godwin, J., & The Conduct Problems Prevention Research Group. (2013). Social-information-processing patterns mediate the impact of preventive intervention on adolescent antisocial behavior. *Psychological Science, 24,* 456–465.

Dodge, K. A., Greenberg, M. T., & Malone, P. S. (2008). Testing an idealized dynamic cascade model of the development of serious violence in adolescence. *Child Development, 79,* 1907–1927.

Dominé, F., Berchtold, A., Akré, C., Michaud, P-A., & Suris, J-C. (2009). Disordered eating beahviours: What about boys? *Journal of Adolescent Health, 44,* 111–117.

Donnellan, M. B., Trzesniewski, K. H., Robins, R. W., Moffitt, T. E., & Caspi, A. (2005). Low self-esteem is related to aggression, antisocial behavior, and delinquency. *Psychological Science, 16,* 328–335.

Donovan, W. L., Leavitt, L. A., & Walsh, R. O. (2000). Maternal illusory control predicts socialization strategies and toddler compliance. *Developmental Psychology, 36,* 402–411.

Dooley, M. & Stewart, J. (2007). Family income, parenting styles and child behavioural-emotional outcomes. *Health Economics 16*(2), 145–162.

Doornwaard, S. M., Branje, S., Meeus, W. H. J., & ter Bogt, T. F. M. (2012). Development of adolescents' peer crowd identification in relation to changes in problem behaviors. *Developmental Psychology, 48,* 1366–1380.

Dorn, L. D., Dahl, R. E., Woodward, H. R., & Biro, F. (2006). Defining the boundaries of early adolescence: A user's guide to assessing pubertal status and pubertal timing in research with adolescents. *Applied Developmental Science, 10,* 30–56.

Doumen, S., Smits, I., Luyckx, K., Duriez, B., Vanhalst, J., Verschueren, K., et al. (2012). Identity and perceived peer relationship quality in emerging adulthood: The mediating role of attachment-related emotions. *Journal of Adolescence, 35,* 1417–1425.

Doyle, J. M., & Kao, G. (2007). Are racial identities of multiracials stable? Change self-identification among single and multiple race individuals. *Social Psychology Quarterly, 70,* 405–423.

Doyle, R. A., Voyer, D., & Cherney, I. D. (2012). The relation between childhood spatial activities and spatial abilities in adulthood. *Journal of Applied Developmental Psychology, 33,* 112–120.

Dozier, M., Zeanah, C. H., & Bernard, K. (2013). Infants and toddlers in foster care. *Child Development Perspectives, 7,* 166–171.

Draghi-Lorenz, R., Reddy, V., & Costall, A. (2001). Rethinking the development of "nonbasic" emotions: A critical review of existing theories. *Developmental Review, 21,* 263–304.

Driscoll, A. K., Russell, S. T., & Crockett, L. J. (2008). Parenting styles and youth well-being across immigrant generations. *Journal of Family Issues, 29,* 185–209.

DuBois, D. L., Portillo, N., Rhodes, J. E., Silverthorn, N., & Valentine, J. C. (2011). How effective are mentoring programs for youth? A systematic assessment of the evidence. *Psychological Science in the Public Interest, 12,* 57–91.

Duckworth, A. L., & Carlson, S. M. (2013). Self-regulation and school success. In B.W. Sokol, F. M. E. Grouzet, & U. Müller (Eds.), *Self-regulation and autonomy: Social and developmental dimensions of human conduct* (pp. 208–230). New York, NY: Cambridge University Press.

Duerden, M. D., & Witt, P. A. (2010). An ecological systems theory perspective on youth programming. *Journal of Park and Recreational Administration, 28*(2), 108–120.

Duijts, L., Jaddoe, V. W. V., Hofman, A. and Moll, H. A. (2010). Prolonged and exclusive breastfeeding reduces the risk of infectious dieases in infancy. *Pediatrics, 126*(1), 18–25.

Duncan, D. T., & Hatzenbuehler, M. L. (2014). Lesbian, gay, bisexual, and transgender hate crimes and suicidality among a population-based sample of sexual-minority adolescents in Boston. *American Journal of Public Health, 104,* 272–278.

Duncan, G. J., & Brooks-Gunn, J. (2000). Family poverty, welfare reform, and child development. *Child Development, 71,* 188–196.

Duncan, G. J., & Magnuson, K. (2012). Socioeconomic status and cognitive functioning: Moving from correlation to causation. *WIREs Cognitive Science, 3,* 377–386.

Duncan, G. J., Dowsett, C. J., Claessens, A., Magnuson, K., Huston, A. C., Klebanov, P., et al. (2007). School readiness and later achievement. *Developmental Psychology, 43,* 1428–1446.

Duncan, R. M., & Pratt, M. W. (1997). Microgenetic change in the quality of preschooler's private speech. *International Journal of Behavioral Development, 20,* 367–383.

Dunham, P. J., Dunham, F., & Curwin, A. (1993). Joint-attentional states and lexical acquisition at 18 months. *Developmental Psychology, 29,* 827–831.

Dunham, Y., Baron, A. S., & Carey, S. (2011). Consequences of "minimal" group affiliations in children. *Child Development, 82,* 793–811.

Dunlop, W. L., Walker, L. J., & Matsuba, M. K. (2012). The distinctive moral personality of care exemplars. *The Journal of Positive Psychology, 7*(2), 131–143.

Dunn, J., & Brophy, M. (2005). Communication, relationships, and individual differences in children's understanding of mind. In J. W. Astington & J. A. Baird (Eds.), *Why language matters for theory of mind* (pp. 50–69). New York, NY: Oxford.

Dunn, J., & Davies, L. (2001). Sibling relationships and interpersonal conflict. In J. Grych & F. D. Fincham (Eds.), *Interparental conflict and child development* (pp. 273–290). New York, NY: Cambridge University Press.

Dunn, J., & Kendrick, C. (1981). Social behavior of young siblings in the family context: Differences between same-sex and different-sex dyads. *Child Development, 52,* 1265–1273.

Dunn, J., O'Connor, T. G., & Cheng, H. (2005). Children's responses to conflict between their different parents: Mothers, stepfathers, nonresident fathers, and nonresident stepmothers. *Journal of Clinical Child and Adolescent Psychology, 34,* 223–234.

Dunn, J., Slomkowski, C., & Beardsall, L. (1994). Sibling relationships from the preschool period through middle childhood and early adolescence. *Developmental Psychology, 30,* 315–324.

Dunson, D. B., Colombo, B., & Baird, D. D. (2002). Changes in age in the level and duration of fertility in the menstrual cycle. *Human Reproduction, 17,* 1399–1403.

Durik, A. M., Hyde, J. S., & Clark, R. (2000). Sequelae of cesarean and vaginal deliveries: Psychosocial outcomes for mothers and infants. *Developmental Psychology, 36,* 251–260.

Durrant, J. & Ensom, R. (2012). Physical punishment of children: Lessons from 20 years of research. *Canadian Medical Association Journal, 184*(12), 1373–1377.

Durrant, J. E. (2006). From mopping up the damage to preventing the flood: the role of social policy in preventing violence against children. *Social Policy Journal of New Zealand/Te Puna Whakaaro, 28,* 1–17.

Durston, S., Davidson, M. C., Tottenham, N., Galvan, A., Spicer, J., Fossella, J. A., et al. (2006). A shift from diffuse to focal cortical activity with development. *Developmental Science, 9,* 1–8.

Dwyer, T., & Ponsonby, A. L. (2009). Sudden Infant Death Syndrome and prone sleeping position. *Annals of Epidemiology, 19,* 245–249.

Dykas, M. J., & Cassidy, J. (2011). Attachment and the processing of social information across the life span: Theory and evidence. *Psychological Bulletin, 137,* 19–46.

Dzinas, K. (2000). Founding the Canadian Psychological Association: The perils of historiography. *Canadian Psychology, 41,* 205–212.

Eagly, A. H., & Wood, W. (2013). The nature-nurture debates: 25 years of challenges in understanding the psychology of gender. *Perspectives on Psychological Science, 8,* 340–357.

Eagly, A. H., Karau, S. J., & Makhijani, M. G. (1995). Gender and the effectiveness of leaders: A meta-analysis. *Psychological Bulletin, 117,* 125–145.

Eals, M., & Silverman, I. (1994). The hunter-gatherer theory of spatial sex differences: Proximate factors mediating the female advantage in recall of object arrays. *Ethology and Sociobiology, 15,* 95–105.

Easterbrook, M. A., Kisilevsky, B. S., Muir, D. W., & Laplante, D. P. (1999). Newborns discriminate schematic faces from scrambled faces. *Canadian Journal of Experimental Psychology, 53,* 231–241.

Eccles, J. S., & Harold, R. D. (1991). Gender differences in sport involvement: Applying the Eccles' expectancy-value model. *Journal of Applied Sports Psychology, 3,* 7–35.

Education Canada. (2016). *Self-regulation update: An interview with Stuart Shanker.* Retrieved from www.cea-ace.ca/education-canada/article/self-regulation-update

Education Quality and Accountability Office. (2013). *EQAO: Ontario's Provincial Assessment program its history and influence 1996–2012.* Toronto, ON: Author.

Edwards, C. A. (1994). Leadership in groups of school-age girls. *Developmental Psychology, 30,* 920–927.

Edwards, R. C., Thullen, M. J., Isarowong, N., Shiu, C-S., Henson, L., & Hans, S. L. (2012). Supportive relationships and the trajectory of depressive symptoms among young, African American mothers. *Journal of Family Psychology, 26,* 585–594.

Egan, S. K., & Perry, D. G. (1998). Does low self-regard invite victimization? *Developmental Psychology, 34,* 299–309.

Egan, S. K., Monson, T. C., & Perry, D. G. (1998). Social-cognitive influences on change in aggression over time. *Developmental Psychology, 34,* 996–1006.

Ehri, L. C., Nunes, S. R., Willows, D. M., Schuster, B. V., Yaghoub Zadeh, Z., & Shanahan, T. (2001). Phonemic awareness instruction helps children learn to read: Evidence from the National Reading Panel's meta-analysis. *Reading Research Quarterly, 36,* 250–287.

Ehrlich, K. B., Dykas, M. J., & Cassidy, J. (2012). Tipping points in adolescent adjustment: Predicting social functioning from adolescents' conflict with parents and friends. *Journal of Family Psychology, 26,* 776–783.

Eime, R. M., Young, J. A., Harvey, J. T., Charity, M. J., & Payne, W. R. (2013). A systematic review of the psychological and social benefits of participation in sport for children and adolescents: Informing development of a conceptual model of health through sport. *International Journal of Behavioral Nutrition and Physical Activity, 10,* 98.

Eisenberg, N. (2000). Emotion, regulation, and moral development. *Annual Review of Psychology, 51,* 665–697.

Eisenberg, N., & Fabes, R. A. (1998). Prosocial development. In W. Damon (Ed.), *Handbook of child psychology* (Vol. 3, pp. 701–778). New York, NY: Wiley.

Eisenberg, N., & Shell, R. (1986). Prosocial moral judgment and behavior in children: The mediating role of cost. *Personality and Social Psychology Bulletin, 12,* 426–433.

Eisenberg, N., Cumberland, A., Spinrad, T. L., Fabes, R. A., Shepard, S. A., Reiser, M., et al. (2001). The relations of regulation and emotionality to children's externalizing and internalizing problem behavior. *Child Development, 72,* 1112–1134.

Eisenberg, N., Duckwork, A. L., Spinrad, T. L., & Valiente, C. (2014). Conscientiousness: Origins in childhood? *Developmental psychology, 50*(5), 1331–1349.

Eisenberg, N., Fabes, R. A., & Spinrad, T. (2006). Prosocial development. In W. Damon & R. M. Lerner (Eds.), *Handbook of child psychology* (Vol. 3 6th ed.). New York, NY: Wiley.

Eisenberg, N., Hofer, C., Spinrad, T., Gershoff, E., Valiente, C., Losoya, S. L., et al. (2008). Understanding parent-adolescent conflict discussions: Concurrent and across-time prediction from youths' dispositions and parenting. *Monographs of the Society for Research in Child Development, 73*(Serial No. 290).

Eisenberg, N., Michalik, N., Spinrad, T. L., Hofer, C., Kupfer, A., Valiente, C., et al. (2007). The relations of effortful control and impulsivity to children's symptoms: A longitudinal study. *Cognitive Development, 22,* 544–567.

Eisenberg, N., Shepard, S. A., Fabes, R. A., Murphy, B. C., & Guthrie, I. K. (1998). Shyness and children's emotionality, regulation, and coping: Contemporaneous, longitudinal, and across-context relations. *Child Development, 69,* 767–790.

Eisenberg, N., Zhou, Q., & Koller, S. (2001). Brazilian adolescents' prosocial moral judgment and behavior: Relations to sympathy, perspective taking, gender-role orientation, and demographic characteristics. *Child Development, 72,* 518–534.

Eizenman, D. R., & Bertenthal, B. I. (1998). Infants' perception of object unity in translating and rotating displays. *Developmental Psychology, 34,* 426–434.

El Nokali, N. E., Bachman, H. J., & Votruba-Drzal, E. (2010). Parent involvement and children's academic and social development in elementary school. *Child Development, 81,* 988–1005.

El-Sheikh, M., Bub, K. L., Kelly, R. J., & Buckhalt, J. A. (2013). Children's sleep and adjustment: A residualized change analysis. *Developmental Psychology, 49,* 1591–1601.

Elbert, T., Pantev, C., Weinbruch, C., Rockstroh, B., & Taub, E. (1995). Increased cortical representation of the fingers of the left hand in strings players. *Science, 270,* 305–307.

Elgar, F. J., Craig, W., & Trites, S. J. (2013). Family dinners, communication, and mental health in Canadian adolescents. *Journal of Adolescent Health, 52,* 433–438. doi: 10.1016/j.jadohealth.2012.07.012

Eliot, L. (2013). Single-sex education and the brain. *Sex Roles, 69,* 363–381.

Elkind, D. (1978). *The child's reality: Three developmental themes.* Hillsdale, NJ: Erlbaum.

Elkind, D., & Bowen, R. (1979). Imaginary audience behavior in children and adolescents. *Developmental Psychology, 15,* 38–44.

Ellis, B. J. (2004). Timing of pubertal maturation in girls: An integrated life history approach. *Psychological Bulletin, 130,* 920–958.

Ellis, B. J., & Essex, M. J. (2007). Family environments, adrenarche, and sexual maturation: A longitudinal test of a life history model. *Child Development, 78,* 1799–1817.

Ellis, B. J., Bates, J. E., Dodge, K. A., Fergusson, D. M., Horwood, L. J., Pettit, G. S., & Woodward, L. (2003). Does father absence place daughters at special risk for early sexual activity and teenage pregnancy? *Child Development, 74*(3), 801–821.

Ellis, M. L., Weiss, B., & Lochman, J. E. (2009). Executive functions in children: Associations with aggressive behavior and appraisal processing. *Journal of Abnormal Child Psychology, 37,* 945–956.

Ellis, S., & Siegler, R. S. (1997). Planning and strategy choice, or why don't children plan when they should? In S. L. Friedman & E. K. Scholnick (Eds.), *The developmental psychology of planning: Why, how, and when do we plan?* (pp. 183–208). Hillsdale, NJ: Erlbaum.

Ellis, W. E., & Zarbatany, L. (2007). Explaining friendship formation and friendship stability: The role of children's and friend's aggression and victimization. *Merrill-Palmer Quarterly, 53*(1), 79–104.

Ellis, W. K., & Rusch, F. R. (1991). Supported employment: Current status and future directions. In J. L. Matson & J. A. Mulick (Eds.), *Handbook of mental retardation* (2nd ed.). New York, NY: Pergamon.

Else-Quest, N. M., Higgins, A., Allison, C., & Morton, L. C. (2012). Gender differences in self-conscious emotional experience: A meta-analysis. *Psychological Bulletin, 138,* 947–981.

Else-Quest, N. M., Hyde, J. S., & Linn, M. C. (2010). Cross-national patterns of gender differences in mathematics: A meta-analysis. *Psychological Bulletin, 136,* 103–127.

Else-Quest, N. M., Hyde, J. S., Goldsmith, H., & Van Hulle, C. A. (2006). Gender differences in temperament: A meta-analysis. *Psychological Bulletin, 132,* 33–72.

Emmorey, K. (2002). *Language, cognition and the brain: Insights from sign language research.* Mahwah, NJ: Erlbaum.

Engel, S. M., Berkowitz, G. S., Wolff, M. S., & Yehuda, R. (2005). Psychological trauma associated with the World Trade Center attacks and its effect on pregnancy outcome. *Paediatric and Perinatal Epidemiology, 19,* 334–341.

Engel, S. M., Zhu, C., Berkowitz, G. S., Calafat, A. M., Silva, M. J., Miodovnik, A. et al. (2009). Prenatal phthalate exposure and performance on the Neonatal Behavioral Assessment Scale in a multiethnic birth cohort. *Neurotoxicology, 30,* 522–528.

Engle, P., & Huffman, S. L. (2010). Growing children's bodies and minds: Maximizing child nutrition and development. *Food and Nutrition Bulletin, 31,* S186–S197.

English, A. (1992). Canadian psychologists and the aerodrome of democracy. *Canadian Psychology, 33*(4), 663–674.

Englund, M. M., Kuo, S. I., Puig, J., & Collins, W. A. (2011). Early roots of adult competence: The significance of close relationships from infancy to early adulthood. *International Journal of Behavioral Development, 35,* 490–496.

Ennemoser, M., & Schneider, W. (2007). Relations of television viewing and reading: Findings from a 4-year longitudinal study. *Journal of Educational Psychology, 99,* 349–368.

Erad, M. (2005, October 22). A language is born. *New Scientist,* 46–49.

Erikson, E. H. (1968). *Identity: Youth and crisis.* New York, NY: Norton.

Ernst, M., Moolchan, E. T., & Robinson, M. L. (2001). Behavioral and neural consequences of prenatal exposure to nicotine. *Journal of the American Academy of Child and Adolescent Psychiatry, 40,* 630–641.

Eskritt, M., & Lee, K. (2002). Remember when you last saw that card?: Children's production of external symbols as a memory aid. *Developmental Psychology, 38,* 254–266.

Eskritt, M., & McLeod, K. (2008). Children's note taking as a mnemonic tool. *Journal of Experimental Child Psychology, 101,* 52–74.

Espy, K. A., Fang, H., Johnson, C., Stopp, C., Wiebe, S. A., & Respass, J. (2011). Prenatal tobacco exposure: Developmental outcomes in the neonatal period. *Developmental Psychology, 47,* 153–169.

Eupopean Commission: EuroStat. (2011). *Fertility Statistics.* Retrieved from http://epp.eurostat.ec.europa.eu/statistics_explained/index.php/Fertility_statistics

Evans, G. W., & Kim, P. (2013). Childhood poverty, chronic stress, self-regulation, and coping. *Child Development Perspectives, 7,* 43–48.

Evans, G. W., Gonnella, C., Marcynyszyn, L. A., Gentile, L., & Salpekar, N. (2005). The role of chaos in poverty and children's socioemotional adjustment. *Psychological Science, 16*, 560–565.

Eyer, D. E. (1992). *Mother–infant bonding: A scientific fiction.* New Haven, CT: Yale University Press.

Fabes, R. A., Eisenberg, N., Jones, S., Smith, M., Guthrie, I., Poulin, R., et al. (1999). Regulation, emotionality, and preschoolers' socially competent peer interactions. *Child Development, 70*, 432–442.

Fabes, R. A., Eisenberg, N., Smith, M. C., & Murphy, B. C. (1996). Getting angry at peers: Associations with liking of the provocateur. *Child Development, 67*, 942–956.

Fabes, R. A., Martin, C. L., & Hanish, L. D. (2003). Young children's play qualities in same-, other-, and mixed-sex peer groups. *Child Development, 74*, 921–932.

Fabricius, W. V., & Luecken, L. J. (2007). Postdivorce living arrangements, parent conflict, and long-term physical health correlates for children of divorce. *Journal of Family Psychology, 21*, 195–205.

Falbo, T. (2012). Only children: An updated review. *Journal of Individual Psychology, 68*, 38–49.

Falbo, T., & Polit, E. F. (1986). Quantitative review of the only child literature: Research evidence and theory development. *Psychological Bulletin, 100*, 176–186.

Falbo, T., Poston, D. L., Triscari, R. S., & Zhang, X. (1997). Self-enhancing illusions among Chinese schoolchildren. *Journal of Cross-Cultural Psychology, 28*, 172–191.

Falk, D., & Bornstein, M. H. (2005). Infant reflexes. In C. B. Fisher & R. M. Lerner (Eds.), *Encyclopedia of applied developmental science* (Vol. 1, pp. 581–582). Thousand Oaks, CA: Sage.

Farh, C. I. C. C., Seo, M-G., & Tesluk, P. E. (2012). Emotional intelligence, teamwork effectiveness, and job performance: The moderating role of job context. *Journal of Applied Psychology, 97*, 890–900.

Farr, R. H., & Patterson, C. J. (2013). Coparenting among lesbian, gay, and heterosexual couples: Associations with adopted children's outcomes. *Child Development, 84*, 1226–1240.

Farr, R. H., Forssell, S. L., & Patterson, C. J. (2010). Parenting and child development in adoptive families: Does parental sexual orientation matter? *Applied Developmental Science, 14*, 164–178.

Farrant, B. M., Maybery, M. T., & Fletcher, J. (2012). Language, cognitive flexibility, and explicit false belief understanding: Longitudinal analysis in typical development and specific language impairment. *Child Development, 83*, 223–235.

Farrar, M. J., & Boyer-Pennington, M. (1999). Remembering specific episodes of a scripted event. *Journal of Experimental Child Psychology, 73*, 266–288.

Farver, J. M., & Shin, Y. L. (1997). Social pretend play in Korean- and Anglo-American preschoolers. *Child Development, 68*, 544–556.

Farver, J. M., Lonigan, C. J., & Eppe, S. (2009). Effective early literacy skill development for young Spanish-speaking English language learners: An experimental study of two methods. *Child Development, 80*, 703–719.

Fasig, L. (2002). Calling all researchers. *SRCD Developments, 45*, 3–5.

Faulkner, G., Goodman, J., Adlaf, E., Irving; H., Allison, K., & Dwyer, J. (2007). Participation in high school physical education—Ontario, Canada, 1999–2005. *Journal of the American Medical Association, 297*(8), 803–804.

Fazel, S., Bakiyeva, L., Cnattingius, S., Grann, M., Hultman, C. M., Litchtenstein, P., et al. (2012). Perinatal risk factors in offenders with severe personality disorder: A population-based investigation. *Journal of Personality Disorders, 26*, 737–750.

Feddes, A. R., Noack, P., & Rutland, A. (2009). Direct and extended friendship effects on minority and majority children's interethnic attitudes: A longitudinal study. *Child Development, 80*, 377–390.

Federal Interagency Forum on Child and Family Statistics. (2013). *America's children: Key national indicators of*

well-being, 2013. Washington, DC: U.S. Government Printing Office.

Feeney, B. C., Cassidy, J., & Ramos-Marcuse, F. (2008). The generalization of attachment representations to new social situations: Predicting behaviour during initial interactions with strangers. *Journal of Personality and Social Psychology, 95*(6), 1481–1498.

Feigenson, L., & Halberda, J. (2008). Conceptual knowledge increases infants' memory capacity. *Proceedings of the National Academy of Sciences (PNAS), 105*(29), 9926–9930. doi: 10.1073/pnas.0709884105

Feigenson, L., Carey, S., & Hauser, M. (2002). The representations underlying infants' choice of more: Object files versus analog magnitudes. *Psychological Science, 13*, 150–156.

Feigenson, L., Dehaene, S., & Spelke, E. S. (2004). Core systems of number. *Trends in Cognitive Sciences, 8*, 307–314.

Feinberg, M. E., McHale, S. M., Crouter, A. C., & Cumsille, P. (2003). Sibling differentiation: Sibling and parent relationships trajectories in adolescence. *Child Development, 74*, 1261–1274.

Feldman, R., & Klein, P. S. (2003). Toddlers' self-regulated compliance to mothers, caregivers, and fathers: Implications for theories of socialization. *Developmental Psychology, 39*, 680–692.

Feldman, S. S., & Wentzel, K. R. (1990). The relationship between parental styles, sons' self-restraint, and peer relations in early adolescence. *Journal of Early Adolescence, 10*, 439–454.

Feldman Farb, A., & Matjasko, J. L. (2012). Recent advances in research on school-based extracurricular activities and adolescent development. *Developmental Review, 32*, 1–48.

Fennell, C. T., Byers-Heinlein, K., & Werker, J. F. (2007). Using speech sounds to guide word learning: The case of bilingual infants. *Child Development, 78*, 1510–1525.

Fenson, L., Dale, P. S., Reznick, J. S., Bates, E., Thal, D. J., & Pethick, S. J. (1994). Variability in early communicative development. *Monographs of the Society for Research in Child Development, 59*(Whole No. 173).

Ferguson, G. G. (1992). Psychology in Canada 1939–1945. *Canadian Psychology, 33*(4), 697–704.

Fergusson, D. M., & Woodward, L. J. (2000). Teenage pregnancy and female educational underachievement: A prospective study of a New Zealand birth cohort. *Journal of Marriage and the Family, 62*, 147–161.

Fernyhough, C. (2010). Inner speech. In H. Pashler (Ed.), *Encyclopaedia of the mind.* Thousand Oaks, CA: Sage.

Ferreol-Barbey, M., Piolat, A., & Roussey, J. (2000). Text recomposition by eleven-year-old children: Effects of text length, level of reading comprehension, and mastery of prototypical schema. *Archives de Psychologie, 68*, 213–232.

Fidler, E. (2012). Sickle cell trait: A review and recommendations for training. *Strength and Conditioning Journal, 34*, 28–32.

Field, T. (2010). Postpartum depression effects on early interactions, parenting, and safety practices: A review. *Infant Behavior and Development, 33*, 1–6.

Field, T. M. (1990). *Infancy.* Cambridge, MA: Harvard University Press.

Field, T. M., & Widmayer, S. M. (1982). Motherhood. In B. J. Wolman (Ed.), *Handbook of developmental psychology.* Englewood Cliffs, NJ: Prentice Hall.

Field, T., & Diego, M. (2010). Preterm infant massage therapy research: A review. *Infant Behavior and Development, 33*, 115–124.

Field, T., Diego, M., & Hernandez-Reif, M. (2007). Massage therapy research. *Developmental Review, 27*, 75–89.

Fischer, K. W., & Immordino-Yang, M. H. (2008). The fundamental importance of the brain and learning for education. In *The Jossey-Bass reader on the brain and learning.* San Francisco, CA: Jossey-Bass.

FitzGerald, D. P., & White, K. J. (2003). Linking children's social worlds: Perspective-taking in parent-child

and peer contexts. *Social Behavior and Personality, 31*, 509–522.

Fitzgerald, J. (1987). Research on revision in writing. *Review of Educational Research, 57*, 481–506.

Fitzpatrick, E. M., Olds, J., Gaboury, I., McCrae, R., Schramm, D. & Durieux-Smith, A. (2012). Comparison of outcomes in children with hearing aids and cochlear implants. *Cochlear Implants International, 13*(1), 5–15. doi: 10.1179/146701011X12950038111611

Fivush, R., Brotman, M. A., Buckner, J. P., & Goodman, S. H. (2000). Gender differences in parent-child emotion narratives. *Sex Roles, 42*, 233–253.

Fivush, R., Reese, E., & Haden, C. A. (2006). Elaborating on elaborations: Role of maternal reminiscing style in cognitive and socioemotional development. *Child Development, 77*, 1568–1588.

Flavell, J. H. (1985). *Cognitive development* (2nd ed.). Englewood Cliffs, NJ: Prentice Hall.

Flavell, J. H. (1996). Piaget's legacy. *Psychological Science, 7*, 200–203.

Flavell, J. H. (2000). Development of children's knowledge about the mental world. *International Journal of Behavioral Development, 24*, 15–23.

Fletcher, J. (2012). Positive parenting, not physical punishment. *Canadian Medical Association Journal, 184*(12), 1339.

Flom, R., & Bahrick, L. E. (2007). The development of infant discrimination of affect in multimodal and uni-modal stimulation: The role of intersensory redundancy. *Developmental Psychology, 43*, 238–252.

Flook, L. (2011). Gender differences in adolescents' daily interpersonal events and well-being. *Child Development, 82*, 454–461.

Flores, E., Cicchetti, D., & Rogosch, F. A. (2005). Predictors of resilience in maltreated and nonmaltreated Latino children. *Developmental Psychology, 41*, 338–351.

Flynn, J. R. (1999). Searching for justice: The discovery of IQ gains over time. *American Psychologist, 54*, 5–20.

Flynn, J. R., & Weiss, L. G. (2007). American IQ gains from 1932 to 2002: The WISC subtests and educational progress. *International Journal of Testing, 7*, 209–224.

Fontaine, R. G. & Dodge, K. A. (2006). Real-time decision making and aggressive behavior in youth: A heuristic model of response evaluation and decision (RED). *Aggressive Behavior, 32*, 604–624.

Fontaine, R. G., Yang, C., Dodge, K. A., Pettit, G. S., & Bates, J. E. (2009). Development of response evaluation and decision (RED) and antisocial behavior in childhood and adolescence. *Developmental Psychology, 45*, 447–459.

Foster, E. M., & Watkins, S. (2010). The value of reanalysis: TV viewing and attention problems. *Child Development, 81*, 368–375.

Foster, S. H. (1986). Learning discourse topic management in the preschool years. *Journal of Child Language, 13*, 231–250.

Fox, S. E., Levitt, P., & Nelson, C. A. (2010). How the timing and quality of early experiences influence the development of brain architecture. *Child Development, 81*, 28–40.

Franklin, A., Pilling, M., & Davies, I. (2005). The nature of infant color categorization: Evidence from eye movements on a target detection task. *Journal of Experimental Child Psychology, 91*, 227–248.

Franquart-Declercq, C., & Gineste, M. (2001). Metaphor comprehension in children. *Annee Psychologique, 101*, 723–752.

Frazier, B. N., Gelman, S. A., Kaciroti, N., Russell, J. W., & Lumeng, J. C. (2012). I'll have what she's having: The impact of model characteristics on children's food choices. *Developmental Science, 15*, 87–98.

Fredricks, J. A., & Eccles, J. S. (2006). Is extracurricular participation associated with beneficial outcomes? Concurrent and longitudinal relations. *Developmental Psychology, 42*, 698–713.

Free the Children. (n.d.). Retrieved from www.freethechildren.com

French, S. E., Seidman, E., Allen, L., & Aber, J. (2006). The development of ethnic identity during adolescence. *Developmental Psychology, 42*, 1–10.

Frick, P. J., & Nigg, J. T. (2012). Current issues in the diagnosis of attention deficit hyperactivity disorder, oppositional defiant disorder, and conduct disorder. *Annual Review of Clinical Psychology, 8*, 77–107.

Fried, A. (2005). Depression in adolescence. In C. B. Fisher & R. M. Lerner (Eds.), *Encyclopedia of applied developmental science* (Vol. 1, pp. 332–334). Thousand Oaks, CA: Sage.

Fried, P. A. (2002). Conceptual issues in behavioral teratology and their application in determining long-term sequelae of prenatal marijuana exposure. *Journal of Child Psychology and Psychiatry, 43*(1), 81–102.

Fried, P. A., & Watkinson, B. (2001). Differential effects on facets of attention in adolescents prenatally exposed to cigarettes and marihuana. *Neurotoxicology and Teratology, 23*, 421–430.

Frye, D. (1993). Causes and precursors of children's theories of mind. In D. F. Hay & A. Angold (Eds.), *Precursors and causes in development and psychopathology.* Chichester, UK: Wiley.

Fu, G., Xu, F., Cameron, C. A., Herman, G., & Lee, K. (2007). Cross-cultural differences in children's choices, categorizations, and evaluations of truths and lies. *Developmental Psychology, 43*, 278–293.

Fuchs, L. S., Geary, D. C., Compton, D. L., Fuchs, D., Schatschneider, C., Hamlett, C. L., et al. (2013). Effects of first-grade number knowledge tutoring with contrasting forms of practice. *Journal of Educational Psychology, 105*, 58–77.

Fuhs, M. W., & McNeil, N. M. (2013). ANS acuity and mathematics ability in preschoolers from low-income homes: Contributions of inhibitory control. *Developmental Science, 16*, 136–148.

Fuld, G. L., Mulligan, D. A., Altmann, T. R., Brown, A., Christakis, D. A., Clarke-Pearson, K., et al. (2009). Policy statement—media violence. *Pediatrics, 124*, 1495–1503.

Fuligni, A. J., Kiang, L., Witkow, M. R., & Baldelomar, O. (2008). Stability and change in ethnic labeling among adolescents from Asian and Latin American immigrant families. *Child Development, 79*, 944–956.

Fuller-Thomson, E. (2005). Canadian First Nations grandparents raising grandchildren: A portrait in resilience. *International Journal of Aging and Human Development, 60*(4), 331–342.

Furlan, S., Agnoli, F., & Reyna, V. F. (2013). Children's competence or adults' incompetence: Different developmental trajectories in different tasks. *Developmental Psychology, 49*, 1466–1480.

Furman, W., & Lanthier, R. (2002). Parenting siblings. In M. Bornstein (Ed.), *Handbook of parenting: Practical issues in parenting* (Vol. 5, pp. 165–188). Mahwah, NJ: Erlbaum.

Furukawa, E., Tangney, J., & Higashibara, F. (2012). Cross-cultural continuities and discontinuities in shame, guilt, and pride: A study of children residing in Japan, Korea, and the USA. *Self and Identity, 11*, 90–133.

Gable, S., Krull, J. L., & Chang, Y. (2012). Boys' and girls' weight status and math performance from kindergarten entry through fifth grade: A mediated analysis. *Child Development, 83*, 1822–1839.

Gagliardi, A. (2005). Postpartum depression. In C. B. Fisher & R. M. Lerner (Eds.), *Encyclopedia of applied developmental science* (Vol. 2, pp. 867–870). Thousand Oaks, CA: Sage.

Gagne, J. R., & Saudino, K. J. (2010). Wait for it! A twin study of inhibitory control in early childhood. *Behavior Genetics, 40*, 327–337.

Gagné, J. R., Miller, M. M., & Goldsmith, H. H. (2013). Early—but modest—gender differences in focal aspects of childhood temperament. *Personality and Individual Differences, 55*, 95–100.

Galván, A. (2013). The teenage brain: Sensitivity to rewards. *Current Directions in Psychological Science, 22*, 88–93.

Garcia, M. M., Shaw, D. S., Winslow, E. B., & Yaggi, K. E. (2000). Destructive sibling conflict and the development of conduct problems in young boys. *Developmental Psychology, 36*, 44–53.

Gardner, H. (1983). *Frames of mind: The theory of multiple intelligences.* New York, NY: Basic Books.

Gardner, H. (1993). *Multiple intelligences: The theory in practice.* New York, NY: Basic Books.

Gardner, H. (1995). Reflections on multiple intelligences: Myths and messages. *Phi Delta Kappan, 77*, 200–203, 206–209.

Gardner, H. (1999). *Intelligence reframed: Multiple intelligences for the 21st century.* New York, NY: Basic Books.

Gardner, H. (2002). *MI millennium: Multiple intelligences for the new millennium* [video recording]. Los Angeles, CA: Into the Classroom Media.

Gardner, H. (2006). *Multiple Intelligences: New Horizons.* New York, NY: Basic Books.

Gardner, W., & Rogoff, B. (1990). Children's deliberateness of planning according to task circumstances. *Developmental Psychology, 26*, 480–487.

Gartrell, N. K., Bos, H. M. W., & Goldberg, N. G. (2011). Adolescents of the U. S. National Longitudinal Lesbian Family Study: Sexual orientation, sexual behavior, and sexual risk exposure. *Archives of Sexual Behavior, 40*, 1199–1209.

Gartstein, M. A., Putnam, S. P., & Rothbart, M. K. (2012). Etiology of preschool behavior problems: Contributions of temperament attributes in early childhood. *Infant Mental Health Journal, 33*, 197–211.

Gartstein, M. A., Slobodskaya, H. R., Zylicz, P. O., Gosztyla, D., & Nakagawa, A. (2010). A cross-cultural evaluation of temperament: Japan, USA, Poland, and Russia. *International Journal of Psychology and Psychological Therapy, 10*, 55–75.

Garvey, C., & Berninger, G. (1981). Timing and turn taking in children's conversations. *Discourse Processes, 4*, 27–59.

Gass, K., Jenkins, J., & Dunn, J. (2007). Are sibling relationships protective? A longitudinal study. *Journal of Child Psychology and Psychiatry, 48*, 167–175.

Gathercole, S. E., Willis, C. S., Emslie, H., & Baddeley, A. D. (1992). Phonological memory and vocabulary development during the early school years: A longitudinal study. *Developmental Psychology, 28*, 887–898.

Gaulin, S. J. C., & McBurney, D. H. (2001). *Psychology: An evolutionary approach.* Upper Saddle River, NJ: Prentice Hall.

Gauvain, M. (1998). Cognitive development in social and cultural context. *Current Directions in Psychological Science, 7*, 188–192.

Gauvain, M. (2001). *The social context of cognitive development.* New York, NY: Guilford Press.

Gauvain, M., & Munroe, R. L. (2009). Contributions of social modernity to cognitive development: A comparison of four cultures. *Child Development, 80*, 1628–1642.

Gauvain, M., & Munroe, R. L. (2012). Cultural change, human activity, and cognitive development. *Human Development, 55*, 205–228.

Ge, X., Brody, G. H., Conger, R. D., Simons, R. L., & Murry, V. M. (2002). Contextual amplification of pubertal transition effects on deviant peer affiliation and externalizing behavior in African American children. *Developmental Psychology, 38*, 45–54.

Geary, D. C. (2002). Sexual selection and human life history. In R. V. Kail (Ed.), *Advances in child development and behavior* (Vol. 30, pp. 41–102). San Diego, CA: Academic Press.

Geary, D. C. (2005). The origin of mind: Evolution of brain, cognition, and general intelligence. Washington, DC: American Psychological Association.

Geary, D. C. (2010). Mathematical learning disabilities. In P. Bauer (Ed.), *Advances in Child Development and Behavior* (Vol. 38, pp. 45–77). San Diego CA: Academic Press.

Geary, D. C. (2011). Cognitive predictors of achievement growth in mathematics: A 5-year longitudinal study. *Developmental Psychology, 47*, 1539–1552.

Geary, D. C. (2013). Early foundations for mathematics learning and their relations to learning disabilities. *Current Directions in Psychological Science, 22*, 23–27.

Geary, D. C., Byrd-Craven, J., Hoard, M. K., Vigil, J., & Numtee, C. (2003). Evolution and development of boys' social behavior. *Developmental Review, 23*, 444–470.

Geary, D. C., Hoard, M. K., Byrd-Craven, J., Nugent, L., & Numtee, C. (2007). Cognitive mechanisms underlying achievement deficits in children with mathematical learning disability. *Child Development, 78*, 1343–1359.

Geisel, T. (1960). *Green eggs and ham, by Dr. Seuss.* New York, NY: Beginner.

Gelman, R., & Meck, E. (1986). The notion of principle: The case of counting. In J. Hiebert (Ed.), *Conceptual and procedural knowledge: The case of mathematics.* Hillsdale, NJ: Erlbaum.

Gelman, S. A. (2003). *The essential child.* New York, NY: Oxford.

Gelman, S. A., & Gottfried, G. M. (1996). Children's casual explanations of animate and inanimate motion. *Child Development, 67*, 1970–1987.

Gelman, S. A., & Meyer, M. (2011). Child categorization. *WIREs Cognitive Science, 2*, 95–105.

Gelman, S. A., & Wellman, H. M. (1991). Insides and essences: Early understandings of the non-obvious. *Cognition, 38*, 213–244.

Gelman, S. A., Coley, J. D., Rosengren, K. S., Hartman, E., & Pappas, A. (1998). Beyond labeling: The role of maternal input in the acquisition of richly structured categories. *Monographs of the Society for Research in Child Development, 63*(Serial No. 253).

Gelman, S. A., Taylor, M. G., & Nguyen, S. P. (2004). Mother-child conversations about gender. *Monographs of the Society for Research in Child Development, 69*(Serial No. 275).

George, C., Kaplan, N., & Main, M. (1985). The adult attachment interview. Unpublished manuscript, University of California, Department of Psychology, Berkeley, CA.

George, J. B. F., & Franko, D. L. (2010). Cultural issues in eating pathology and body image among children and adolescents. *Journal of Pediatric Psychology, 35*, 231–242.

George, N. P. (2003) The rainbow/holistic approach to Aboriginal literacy. *Canadian Journal of Native Education, 27*(1), 29–40.

Gerry, D. W., Faux, A. L., & Trainor, L. J. (2010). Effects of Kindermusik training on infants' rhythmic enculturation. *Developmental Science, 13*, 545–551.

Gershkoff-Stowe, L., & Smith, L. B. (2004). Shape and the first hundred nouns. *Child Development, 75*, 1098–1114.

Gershoff, E. T. (2013). Spanking and child development: We know enough now to stop hitting our children. *Child Development Perspectives, 7*, 133–137.

Gershoff, E. T., & Bitensky, S. H. (2007). The case against corporal punishment of children: Converging evidence from social science research and international human rights law and implications for U.S. public policy. *Psychology, Public Policy, and the Law, 13*, 231–272.

Gershoff, E. T., Grogan-Kaylor, A., Lansford, J. E., Chang, L., Zelli, A., Deater-Deckard, K., et al. (2010). Parent discipline practices in an international sample: Associations with child behavior and moderation by perceived normativeness. *Child Development, 81*, 487–502.

Gertner, Y., Fisher, C., & Eisengart, J. (2006). Learning words and rules: Abstract knowledge of word order in early sentence comprehension. *Psychological Science, 17*, 684–691.

Ghavane, S., Murki, S., Subramanian, S., Gaddam, P., Kandraju, H., & Thumalla, S. (2012). Kangaroo mother care in kangaroo ward for improving the growth and breastfeeding outcomes when reaching term gestational age in very low birthweight infants. *Acta Paediatrica, 101,* 545–549.

Ghetti, S. (2008). Rejection of false events in childhood: A metamemory account. *Current Directions in Psychological Science, 17,* 16–20.

Ghetti, S., & Lee, J. (2011). Children's episodic memory. *WIREs Cognitive Science, 2,* 365–373.

Ghetti, S., Hembacher, E., & Coughlin, C. A. (2013). Feeling uncertain and acting on it during the preschool years: A metacognitive approach. *Child Development Perspectives, 7,* 160–165.

Gibbs, D. A., Martin, S. L., Kupper, L. L., & Johnson, R. E. (2007). Child maltreatment in enlisted soldiers' families during combat-related deployments. *Journal of the American Medical Association, 298,* 528–535.

Gibbs, J. C., Basinger, K. S., Grime, R. L., & Snarey, J. R. (2007). Moral judgment development across cultures: Revisiting Kohlberg's universality claims. *Developmental Review, 27,* 443–500.

Gibbs, J. C., Clark, P. M., Joseph, J. A., Green, J. L., Goodrick, T. S., & Makowski, D. (1986). Relations between moral judgment, moral courage, and field independence. *Child Development, 57,* 185–193.

Gibson, E. J., & Walk, R. D. (1960). The "visual cliff." *Scientific American, 202,* 64–71.

Giles, J. W., & Heyman, G. D. (2005). Young children's beliefs about the relationship between gender and aggressive behavior. *Child Development, 76*(1), 107–121.

Gillen-O'Neel, C., Huynh, V. W., & Fuligni, A. J. (2013). To study or to sleep? The academic costs of extra studying at the expense of sleep. *Child Development, 84,* 133–142.

Gilligan, C. (1982). *In a different voice: Psychological theory and women's development.* Cambridge, MA: Harvard University Press.

Gilligan, C., & Attanucci, J. (1988). Two moral orientations: Gender differences and similarities. *Merrill-Palmer Quarterly, 34,* 223–237.

Ginsburg-Block, M. D., Rohrbeck, C. A., & Fantuzzo, J. W. (2006). A meta-analytic review of social, self-concept, and behavioral outcomes of peer-assisted learning. *Journal of Educational Psychology, 98,* 732–749.

Giordano, G. (2005). *How testing came to dominate American schools: The history of educational assessment.* New York, NY: Peter Lang.

Gizer, I. R., & Waldman, I. D. (2012). Double dissociation between lab measures of inattention and impulsivity and the dopamine transporter gene (*DAT1*) and the dopamine D4 receptor gene (DRD4). *Journal of Abnormal Psychology, 121,* 1011–1023.

Gleason, T. R., & Hohmann, L. M. (2006). Concepts of real and imaginary friendships in early childhood. *Social Development, 15,* 128–144.

Glenwright, M., & Pexman, P. M. (2010). Development of children's ability to distinguish sarcasm and verbal irony. *Journal of Child Language, 37,* 429–451.

Glick, G. C., & Rose, A. J. (2011). Prospective associations between friendship adjustment and social strategies: Friendship as a context for building social skills. *Developmental Psychology, 47,* 1117–1132.

Global Initiative to End All Corporal Punishment of Children. (2011). States with full prohibition. Retrieved from www.endcorporalpunishment.org

Göbel, S. M., Watson, S. E., Lervåg, A. & Hulme, C. (2014). Children's arithmetic development: It is number knowledge, not the approximate number sense, that counts. *Psychological Science, 25,* 789–798.

Goeke-Morey, M. C., Cummings, E. M., Harold, G. T., & Shelton, K. H. (2003). Categories and continua of destructive and constructive conflict tactics from the perspective of U.S. and Welsh children. *Journal of Family Psychology, 17,* 327–338.

Goh, Y. I., & Koren, G. (2008). Folic acid in pregnancy and fetal outcomes. *Journal of Obstetrics and Gynecology, 28,* 3–13.

Goldfield, B. A., & Reznick, J. S. (1990). Early lexical acquisition: Rate, content, and the vocabulary spurt. *Journal of Child Language, 17,* 171–184.

Goldin-Meadow, S. (1999). The role of gesture in communication and thinking. *Trends in Cognitive Sciences, 3*(11), 419–429.

Goldin-Meadow, S., & Mylander, C. (1984). Gestural communication in deaf children: The effects and noneffects of parental input on early language development. *Monographs of the Society for Research in Child Development, 49*(3–4, Serial No. 207).

Goldin-Meadow, S., Mylander, C., & Franklin, A. (2007). How children make language out of gesture: Morphological structure in gesture systems developed by American and Chinese deaf children. *Cognitive Psychology, 55,* 87–135.

Goldsmith, H. H., Pollak, S. D., & Davidson, R. J. (2008). Developmental neuroscience perspectives on emotion regulation. *Child Development Perspectives, 2,* 132–140.

Goldstein, M. H., & Schwade, J. A. (2008). Social feedback to infants' babbling facilitates rapid phonological learning. *Psychological Science, 19,* 515–523.

Goldstein, S. (2011). Attention-deficit/hyperactivity disorder. In S. Goldstein and C. R. Reynolds (Eds.), *Handbook of neurodevelopmental and genetic disorders in children* (2nd ed., pp. 131–150). New York, NY: Guilford Press.

Goleman, D. (1995). *Emotional intelligence: Why it can matter more than IQ.* New York, NY: Bantam.

Goleman, D. (1998). *Working with emotional intelligence.* New York, NY: Bantam.

Goleman, D., Bayatzis, R., & McKee, A. (2002). *Primal leadership: Realizing the power of emotional intelligence.* Boston, MA: Harvard Business Press.

Golinkoff, R. M. (1993). When is communication a "meeting of minds"? *Journal of Child Language, 20,* 199–207.

Golombok, S. (2013). Families created by reproductive donation: Issues and research. *Child Development Perspectives, 7,* 61–65.

Golombok, S., Mellish, L., Jennings, S., Casey, P., Tasker, F., & Lamb, M. E. (2014). Adoptive gay father families: Parent-child relationships and children's psychological adjustment. *Child Development, 85,* 456–468.

Golombok, S., Perry, B., Burston, A., Murray, C., Mooney-Somers, J., Stevens, M., & Golding, J. (2003). Children with lesbian parents: A community study. *Developmental Psychology, 39,* 20–33.

Good, T. L., & Brophy, J. E. (1996). *Looking in classrooms* (7th ed.). New York, NY: Addison-Wesley.

Good, T. L., & Brophy, J. E. (2008). *Looking in classrooms.* Boston, MA: Pearson/Allyn and Bacon.

Goodman, S. H., Rouse, M. H., Connell, A. M., Broth, M. R., Hall, C. M., & Heyward, D. (2011). Maternal depression and child psychopathology: A meta-analytic review. *Clinical Child and Family Psychology Review, 14,* 1–27.

Goodnow, J. J. (1992). *Parental belief systems: The psychological consequences for children.* Hillsdale, NJ: Erlbaum.

Goodwyn, S. W., & Acredolo, L. P. (1993). Symbolic gesture versus word: Is there a modality advantage for onset of symbol use? *Child Development, 64,* 688–701.

Goossens, L. (2001). Global versus domain-specific statuses in identity research: A comparison of two self-report measures. *Journal of Adolescence, 24,* 681–699.

Gordon, B. N., Baker-Ward, L., & Ornstein, P. A. (2001). Children's testimony: a review of research on memory for past experiences. *Clinical Child and Family Psychology Review, 4*(2), 157-81.

Gordon, C. P. (1996). Adolescent decision making: A broadly based theory and its application to the prevention of early pregnancy. *Adolescence, 31,* 561–584.

Gordon, P. (2004). Numerical cognition without words: Evidence from Amazonia. *Science, 306,* 496–499.

Gordon, P. (2010). *Words and the mind: How words capture human experience.* New York, NY: Oxford University Press.

Gordon, R. A., Chase-Lansale, P. L., & Brooks-Gunn, J. (2004). Extended households and the life course of young mothers: Understanding the associations

using a sample of mothers with premature, low birth weight babies. *Child Development, 75,* 1013–1038.

Gormally, S., Barr, R. G., Wertheim, L., Alkawaf, R., Calinoiu, N., & Young, S. N. (2001). Contact and nutrient caregiving effects on newborn infant pain responses. *Developmental Medicine and Child Neurology, 43,* 28–38.

Gosso, Y., Morais, M. L. S., & Otta, E. (2007). Pretend play of Brazilian children: A window into different cultural worlds. *Journal of Cross-Cultural Psychology, 38,* 539–558.

Gottman, J. M. (1986). The world of coordinated play: Same- and cross-sex friendships in children. In J. M. Gottman & J. G. Parker (Eds.), *Conversations of friends.* New York, NY: Cambridge University Press.

Gottman, J. M., Katz, L. F., & Hooven, C. (1996). Parental meta-emotion philosophy and the emotional life of families: Theoretical models and preliminary data. *Journal of Family Psychology, 10,* 243–268.

Goubet, N., Clifton, R. K., & Shah, B. (2001). Learning about pain in preterm newborns. *Journal of Developmental and Behavioral Pediatrics, 22,* 418–424.

Gough, P. B., & Tunmer, W. E. (1986). Decoding, reading, and reading disability. *Remedial & Special Education, 7,* 6–10.

Gouws, J. (2003). Psychometric considerations in the assessment of non–North American cultural and language groups. *Psychology Ontario, 25*(1), 5–7.

Govier, E., & Salisbury, G. (2000). Age-related sex differences in performance on a side-naming spatial task. *Psychology, Evolution, and Gender, 2,* 209–222.

Govindshenoy, M., & Spencer, N. (2007). Abuse of the disabled child: A systematic review of population-based studies. *Child Care, Health, and Development, 33,* 552–558.

Grabe, S., Hyde, J. S., Ward, L. M. (2008). The role of the media in body image concerns among women: A meta-analysis of experimental and correlational studies. *Psychological Bulletin, 134,* 460–476.

Graber, J. A. (2013). Pubertal timing and the development of psychopathology in adolescence and beyond. *Hormones and Behavior, 64,* 262–269.

Graesser, A. C., Singer, M., & Trabasso, T. (1994). Constructing inferences during narrative text comprehension. *Psychological Review, 101,* 371–395.

Graham, S., & Perin, D. (2007). A meta-analysis of writing instruction for adolescent students. *Journal of Educational Psychology, 99,* 445–476.

Graham, S., Berninger, V. W., Abbott, R. D., Abbott, S. P., & Whitaker, D. (1997). Role of mechanics in composing of elementary school students: A new methodological approach. *Journal of Educational Psychology, 89,* 170–182.

Graham-Bermann, S. A., & Brescoll, V. (2000). Gender, power, and violence: Assessing the family stereotypes of the children of batterers. *Journal of Family Psychology, 14,* 600–612.

Grammer, J., Coffman, J. L., & Ornstein, P. (2013). The effect of teachers' memory-relevant language on children's strategy use and knowledge. *Child Development, 84,* 1989–2002.

Grammer, J. K., Purtell, K. M., Coffman, J. L., & Ornstein, P. A. (2011). Relations between children's metamemory and strategic performance: Time-varying covariates in early elementary school. *Journal of Experimental Child Psychology, 108,* 139–155.

Granie, M. A. (2009). Effects of gender, sex-stereotype conformity, age and internalization on risk-taking among adolescent pedestrians. *Safety Science, 47,* 1277–1283.

Granrud, C. E. (1986). Binocular vision and spatial perception in 4- and 5-month-old infants. *Journal of Experimental Psychology: Human Perception and Performance, 12,* 36–49.

Grantham-McGregor, S., Ani, C., & Gernald, L. (2001). The role of nutrition in intellectual development. In R. J. Sternberg & E. L. Grigorenko (Eds.), *Environmental effects on cognitive abilities* (pp. 119–155). Mahwah, NJ: Erlbaum.

Graves, R., & Landis, T. (1990). Asymmetry in mouth opening during different speech tasks. *International Journal of Psychology, 25,* 179–189.

Gray, S. W., & Klaus, R. A. (1965). An experimental preschool program for culturally deprived children. *Child Development, 36,* 887–898.

Gray-Little, B., & Hafdahl, A. R. (2000). Factors influencing racial comparisons of self-esteem: A quantitative review. Psychological Bulletin, 126, 26–54.

Graziano, P. A., Keane, S. P., & Calkins, S. D. (2007). Cardiac vagal regulation and early peer status. *Child Development, 78,* 264–278.

Green, C. R., Mihic, M., Brien, D. C., Armstrong, I. T., Nikkel, S. M., Stade, B. C., et al. (2009). Oculomotor control in children with fetal alcohol spectrum diorders assessed using a mobile eye-tracking laboratory. *Cognitive Neuroscience, 29,* 1302–1309.

Green, C. R., Munoz, D. P., & Reynolds, J. N. (2005). Saccadic eye movements: A novel diagnostic approach to fetal alcohol syndrome. Program No. 916.10. 2005 Abstract Viewer/Itinerary Planner. Washington, DC: Society for Neuroscience, 2005. Online. Retrieved from http://sfn.scholarone.com/itin2005/main.html

Greenberg, M. T., & Crnic, K. A. (1988). Longitudinal predictors of developmental status and social interaction in premature and full-term infants at age two. *Child Development, 59,* 554–570.

Greenberg, M. T., Lengua, L. J., Coie, J. D., Pinderhughes, E. E. & the Conduct Problems Prevention Research Group. (1999). Predicting developmental outcomes at school entry using a multiple-risk model: Four American communities. *Developmental Psychology, 35,* 403–417.

Greene, J. (2007). The secret joke of Kant's soul. In W. Sinnott-Armstrong (Ed.), *Moral psychology: The neuroscience of morality, emotion, brain disorders, and development* (pp. 35–80). Cambridge, MA: MIT.

Greenough, W. T., & Black, J. E. (1992). Induction of brain structure by experience: Substrates for cognitive development. In M. Gunnar & C. Nelson (Eds.), *Minnesota symposia on child psychology: Vol. 24: Developmental Behavioral Neuroscience* (pp. 155–200). Hillsdale, NJ: Erlbaum.

Gregory, A., Allen, J. P., Mikami, A. Y., Hafen, C. A., & Pianta, R. C. (2014). Effects of a professional development program on behavioral engagement of students in middle and high school. *Psychology in the Schools, 51,* 143–163.

Gregory, A. M., Light-Häusermann, J. H., Rijsdijk, F., & Eley, T. C. (2009). Behavioral genetic analyses of prosocial behavior in adolescents. *Developmental Science, 12,* 165–174.

Gregory, A. M., Rijsdijk, F., Lau, J. Y. F., Napolitano, M., McGuffin, P., & Eley, T. C. (2007). Genetic and environmental influences on interpersonal cognitions and associations with depressive symptoms in 8-year-old twins. *Journal of Abnormal Psychology, 116,* 762–775.

Greitemeyer, T., & McLatchie, N. (2011). Denying humanness to others: A newly discovered mechanism by which violent video games increase aggressive behavior. *Psychological Science, 22,* 659–665.

Grigorenko, E. L., Jarvin, L., & Sternberg, R. J. (2002). School-based tests of the triarchic theory of intelligence: Three settings, three samples, three syllabi. *Contemporary Educational Psychology, 27,* 167–208.

Grimshawe, G. M., Adlestein, A., Bryden, M. P., & McKinnon, E. (1995). First language acquisition in adolescence: A test of the critical period hypothesis. *Brain and Cognition, 28*(2), 190–191.

Gripshover, S. J., & Markman, E. M. (2013). Teaching young children a theory of nutrition: Conceptual change and the potential for increased vegetable consumption. *Psychological Science, 24,* 1541–1553.

Groen, G. J., & Resnick, L. B. (1977). Can preschool children invent addition algorithms? *Journal of Educational Psychology, 69,* 645–652.

Grosse, G., Scott-Phillips, T. C., & Tomasello, M. (2013). Three-year-olds hide their communicative intentions in appropriate contexts. *Developmental Psychology, 49,* 2095–2101.

Grotevant, H. D., & McDermott, J. M. (2014). Adoption: Biological and social processes linked to adaptation. *Annual Review of Psychology, 65,* 235–265.

Grotevant, H. D., McRoy, R. G., Wrobel, G. M., & Ayers-Lopez, S. (2013). Contact between adoptive and birth families: Perspectives from the Minnesota/Texas adoption research project. *Child Development Perspectives, 7,* 193–198.

Grusec, J. E. (2011). Socialization processes in the family: Social and emotional development. *Annual Review of Psychology, 62,* 243–269.

Grusec, J. E., & Goodnow, J. J. (1994). Impact of parental discipline methods on the child's internalization of values: A reconceptualization of current points of view. *Developmental Psychology, 30*(1), 4–19.

Grusec, J. E., Goodnow, J. J., & Cohen, L. (1996). Household work and the development of concern for others. *Developmental Psychology, 32,* 999–1007.

Grysman, A., & Hudson, J. A. (2013). Gender differences in autobiographical memory: Developmental and methodological considerations. *Developmental Review, 33,* 239–272.

Gucciardi, E., Pietrusiak, M. A., Reynolds, D. L., & Rouleau, J. (2002). Incidence of neural tube defects in Ontario, 1986–1999. *Canadian Medical Association Journal, 167*(3), 237–240.

Guerra, N. G., Williams, K. R., & Sadek, S. (2011). Understanding bullying and victimization during childhood and adolescence: A mixed methods study. *Child Development, 82,* 295–310.

Guhn, M., & Goelman, H. (2011). Bioecological theory, early childhood development and the validation of the population-level early development instrument. *Social Indicators Research, 103*(2), 193–217.

Gunderson, E. A., & Levine, S. C. (2011). Some types of parent number talk count more than others: relations between parents' input and children's cardinal-number knowledge. *Developmental Science, 14,* 1021–1032.

Güngör, D., & Bornstein, M. H. (2010). Culture-general and -specific associations of attachment avoidance and anxiety with perceived parental warmth and psychological control among Turk and Belgian adolescents. *Journal of Adolescence, 33,* 593–602.

Gunnar, M. R., Bruce, J., & Grotevant, H. D. (2000). International adoption of institutionally reared children: Research and policy. *Development and Psychopathology, 12,* 677–693.

Gurucharri, C., & Selman, F. L. (1982). The development of interpersonal understanding during childhood, preadolescence, and adolescence: A longitudinal follow-up study. *Child Development, 53,* 924–927.

Guttmacher Institute. (2013). *Facts on American teens' sexual and reproductive health.* New York, NY: Author.

Guxens, M., van Eijsden, M., Vermeulen, R., Loomans, E., Vrijkotte, T. G. M., Komhout, H., et al. (2013). Maternal cell phone and cordless phone use during pregnancy and behaviour problems in 5-year-old children. *Journal of Epidemiology and Community Health, 67,* 432–438.

Haeffel, G. J., Getchell, M., Koposov, R. A., Yrigollen, C. M., DeYoung, C. G., af Klinteberg, B., et al. (2008). Associations between polymorphisms in the dopamine transporter gene and depression: Evidence for a gene-environment interaction in a sample of juvenile detainees. *Psychological Science, 19,* 62–69.

Halford, G. S., & Andrews, G. (2011). Information-processing models of cognitive development. In U. Goswami (Ed.), *The Wiley-Blackwell handbook of childhood cognitive development* (2nd ed., pp. 697–722). Chichester, UK: Wiley-Blackwell.

Halgunseth, L. C., Ispa, J. M., & Rudy, D. (2006). Parental control in Latino families: An integrated review of the literature. *Child Development, 77,* 1282–1297.

Halim, M. L., Ruble, D. N., & Amodio, D. M. (2011). From pink frilly dresses to 'one of the boys': A social-cognitive analysis of gender identity development and gender bias. *Social and Personality Psychology Compass, 5,* 933–949.

Halim, M. L., Ruble, D., Tamis-Lemonda, C., & Shrout, P. E. (2013). Rigidity in gender-typed behaviors in early childhood. *Child Development, 84,* 1269–1284.

Hall, G. S. (1904). *Adolescence, 1.* New York, NY: Appleton.

Hallinan, M. T., & Teixeira, R. A. (1987). Opportunities and constraints: Black–white differences in the formation of interracial friendships. *Child Development, 58,* 1358–1371.

Halpern-Meekin, S., & Tach, L. (2008). Heterogeneity in two-parent families and adolescent well-being. *Journal of Marriage and Family, 70,* 435–451.

Halpern, D. F. (2000). *Sex differences in cognitive abilities* (3rd ed.). Mahwah, NJ: Erlbaum.

Halpern, D. F. (2005). A cognitive-process taxonomy for sex differences in cognitive abilities. *Current Directions in Psychological Science, 13*(4), 135–139.

Halpern, D. F. (2012). *Sex differences in cognitive abilities* (4th ed.). New York, NY: Psychology Press.

Halpern, D. F., Benbow, C. P., Geary, D. C., Gur, R. C., Hyde, J. S., & Gernsbacher, M. A. (2007). The science of sex differences in science and mathematics. *Psychological Science in the Public Interest, 8,* 1–51.

Halpern, L. F., MacLean, W. E., & Baumeister, A. A. (1995). Infant sleep-wake characteristics: Relation to neurological status and the prediction of developmental outcome. *Developmental Review, 15,* 255–291.

Hamamura, T., Heine, S. J., & Paulhus, D. L. (2008). Cultural differences in response styles: The role of dialectical thinking. *Personality and Individual Differences, 44,* 932–942.

Hamlin, J. K. (2013). Moral judgment and action in preverbal infants and toddlers: Evidence for an innate moral core. *Current Directions in Psychological Science, 22,* 186–193.

Hamlin, J. K. (2014). The origins of human morality: Complex socio-moral evaluations by preverbal infants. In J. Decety & Y. Christen (Eds.), *New frontiers in social neuroscience* (pp. 175–188). New York, NY: Springer.

Hamlin, J. K., Mahajan, N., Liberman, Z., & Wynn, K. (2013). Not like me! Bad: Infants prefer those who harm dissimilar others. *Psychological Science, 24,* 589–594.

Hamlin, J. K., Wynn, K., & Bloom, P. (2007). Social evaluation by preverbal infants. *Nature, 450,* 557–559.

Hamm, J. V. (2000). Do birds of a feather flock together? The variable bases for African American, Asian American, and European American adolescents' selection of similar friends. *Developmental Psychology, 36,* 209–219.

Hammen, C., & Rudolph, K. D. (2003). Childhood mood disorders. In E. J. Mash & R. A. Barkley (Eds.), *Child psychopathology* (2nd ed., pp. 233–278). New York, NY: Guilford Press.

Hane, A. A., & Fox, N. W. (2006). Ordinary variations in maternal caregiving influence human infants' stress reactivity. *Psychological Science, 17,* 550–556.

Hankin, B. L., Mermelstein, R., & Roesch, L. (2007). Sex differences in adolescent depression: Stress exposure and reactivity models. *Child Development, 78*(1), 279–295.

Hannon, E. E., & Trehub, S. E. (2005). Metrical categories in infancy and adulthood. *Psychological Science, 16,* 48–55.

Harden, K. P. (2014). Genetic influences on adolescent sexual behavior: Why genes matter for environmentally oriented researchers. *Psychological Bulletin, 140,* 434–465.

Harding, K. (2006, May 20). Bold strokes on language. *Globe and Mail,* pp. A1, A4.

Harkness, K. L., Lumley, M. N., & Truss, A. E. (2008). Stress generation in adolescent depression: The moderating role of child abuse and neglect. *Journal of Abnormal Child Psychology, 36,* 421–432.

Harlow, H. F., & Harlow, M. K. (1965). The affectional systems. In A. M. Schrier, H. F. Harlow, & F. Stollnitz (Eds.), *Behavior of nonhuman primates* (Vol. 2.). New York, NY: Academic Press.

Harre, N. (2007). Community service or activism as an identity project for youth. *Journal of Community Psychology, 35,* 711–724.

Harris, B. (1979). Whatever happened to Little Albert? *American Psychologist, 34,* 151–160.

Harris, K. C., Kuramoto, L. K., Schulzer, M., Retallack, J. E. (2009). Effect of school-based physical activity interventions on body mass index in children: A meta-analysis. *Canadian Medical Association Journal, 180*(7), 719–726.

Harris, L. J. (1985). James Mark Baldwin on the origins of right- and left-handedness: The story of an experiment that mattered. *Monographs of the Society for Research in Child Development, 50,* 44–64.

Harrison, K., Bost, K. K., McBride, B. A., Donovan, S. M., Grigsby-Toussaint, D. S., Kim, J., et al., (2011). Toward a developmental conceptualization of contributors to overweight and obesity in childhood: The Six-Cs model. *Child Development Perspectives, 5,* 50–58.

Harrist, A. W., Zaia, A. F., Bates, J. E., Dodge, K. A., & Pettit, G. S. (1997). Subtypes of social withdrawal in early childhood: Sociometric status and social-cognitive differences across four years. *Child Development, 68,* 278–294.

Harter, S. (1985). *Manual for the self-perception profile for children.* Denver, CO: University of Denver.

Harter, S. (1988). *Manual for the self-perception profile for adolescents.* Denver, CO: University of Denver.

Harter, S. (2005). Self-concepts and self-esteem, children and adolescents. In C. B. Fisher & R. M. Lerner (Eds.), *Encyclopedia of applied developmental science* (Vol. 2, pp. 972–977). Thousand Oaks, CA: Sage.

Harter, S. (2006). The self. In W. Damon & R. M. Lerner (Eds.), *Handbook of child psychology* (Vol. 3, 6th ed.). New York, NY: Wiley.

Harter, S. (2012). *The construction of the self: Developmental and sociocultural foundations* (2nd ed.). New York, NY: Guilford Press.

Harter, S., Waters, P., & Whitesell, N. R. (1998). Relational self-worth: Differences in perceived worth as a person across interpersonal contexts among adolescents. *Child Development, 69,* 756–766.

Harter, S., Whitesell, N. R., & Kowalski, P. S. (1992). Individual differences in the effects of educational transitions on young adolescents' perceptions of competence and motivational orientation. *American Educational Research Journal, 29*(4), 777–807.

Hartup, W. W. (1992). Friendships and their developmental significance. In H. McGurk (Ed.), *Contemporary issues in childhood social development.* London, UK: Routledge.

Hartup, W. W. (1983). Peer relations. In P. H. Mussen (Ed.), *Handbook of child psychology* (Vol. 4). New York, NY: Wiley.

Hartup, W. W., & Stevens, N. (1999). Friendships and adaptation across the life span. *Current Directions in Psychological Science, 8,* 76–79.

Hastings, P. D., & Rubin, K. H. (1999). Predicting mothers' beliefs about preschool-aged children's social behavior: Evidence for maternal attitudes moderating child effects. *Child Development, 70,* 722–741.

Hastings, P. D., McShane, K. E., Parker, R., & Ladha, F. (2007). Ready to make nice: Parental socialization of young sons' and daughters' prosocial beahviour with peers. *The Journal of Genetic Psychology, 168*(2), 177–200.

Hastings, P. D., Zahn-Waxler, C., & McShane, K. (2006). We are, by nature, moral creatures: Biological bases of concern for others. In M. Killen & J. G. Smetana (2006), *Handbook of moral development* (pp. 483–516). Mahwah, NJ: Erlbaum.

Hata, D., Dai, S-Y., & Marumo, G. (2010). Ultrasound for evaluation of fetal neurobehavioural development: From 2-D to 4-D ultrasound. *Infant and Child Development, 19,* 99–118.

Hawley, P. H. (1999). The ontogenesis of social dominance: A strategy-based evolutionary perspective. *Developmental Review, 19,* 7–132.

Haworth, C. M. A., Wright, M. J., Martin, N. W., Martine, N. G., Boomsma, D., Bartels, M., .et al. (2009). A twin study of the genetics of high cognitive ability selected from 11,000 twin pairs in six studies from four countries. *Behavioural Genetics, 39,* 359–370.

Hay, D., Pawlby, S. Waters, C. S., Perra, O., & Sharp, D. (2010). Mothers' antenatal depression and their children's antisocial outcomes. *Child Development, 81,* 149–165.

Hay, D. F. (2007). The gradual emergence of sex differences in aggression: Alternative hypotheses. *Psychological Medicine, 37,* 1527–1537.

Hay, D. F., Mundy, L., Roberts, S., Carta, R., Waters, C. S., Perra, O., et al. (2011). Known risk factors for violence predict 12-month-old infants' aggressiveness with peers. *Psychological Science, 22,* 1205–1211.

Hay, D. F., Waters, C. S., Perra, O., Swift, N., Kairis, V., Phillips, R., et al. (2014). Precursors to aggression are evident by 6 months of age. *Developmental Science, 17,* 471–480.

Hayes, D. P. (1988). Speaking and writing: Distinct patterns of word choice. *Journal of Memory and Language, 27,* 572–585.

Hayes, T. C., & Lee, M. R. (2005). The Southern culture of honor and violent attitudes. *Sociological Spectrum, 25,* 593–617.

Hayne, H., & Jack, F. (2011). Childhood amnesia. *WIREs Cognitive Science, 2,* 136–145.

Hazell, P. L. (2009). 8-year follow-up of the MTA sample. *Journal of the American Academy of Child and Adolescent Psychiatry, 48,* 461–462.

He, M., & Sutton, J. (2004). Using routine growth monitoring data in tracking overweight prevalence in young children. *Canadian Journal of Public Health, 95,* 419–423.

Health Canada. (2004, April 7). Minister Pettigrew announces a ban on baby walkers (news release). Retrieved from www.hc-sc.gc.ca/ahc-asc/media/nr-cp/2004/2004_15_e.html

Health Canada. (2006). It's your health: Fetal alcohol spectrum disorder. Retrieved from www.hc-sc.gc.ca/hl-vs/alt_formats/pacrb-dgapcr/pdf/iyh-vsv/diseases-maladies/fasd-etcaf-eng.pdf

Health Canada. (2010a). *Aboriginal Head Start on Reserve Program.* HC Pub.: 3571. Ottawa, ON: Author.

Health Canada. (2010b). Canadian gestational weight gain reccomendations. Retrieved from www.hc-sc.gc.ca/fn-an/nutrition/prenatal/qa-gest-gros-qr-eng.php

Health Canada. (2011a). *Aboriginal Head Start on Reserve – Backgrounder.* Retrieved from www.hc-sc.gc.ca/fniah-spnia/famil/develop/ahsor-bckgr-info-en

Health Canada. (2011b). *First Nations and Inuit health: Aboriginal Head Start on Reserve.* Retrieved from www.hc-sc.gc.ca/fniah-spnia/famil/develop/ahsor-papa_info-en.php

Health Canada. (2012). Healthy weight gain during pregnancy. Retrieved from www.hc-sc.gc.ca/fn-an/nutrition/prenatal/hwgdp-ppspg-eng.php

Health Canada. (2016). *Canada's food guide.* Retrieved from www.hc-sc.gc.ca/fn-an/food-guide-aliment/order-commander/index-eng.php

Hellekson, K. L. (2001). NIH consensus statement on phenylketonuria. *American Family Physician, 63,* 1430–1432.

Hemker, L., Granrud, C. E., Yonas, A., & Kavsek, M. (2010). Infant perception of surface texture and relative height as distance information: A preferential-reaching study. *Infancy, 15,* 6–27.

Henderson, C. E., Hayslip, B., Sanders, L. M., & Louden, L. (2009). Grandmother-grandchild relationship quality predicts psychological adjustment among youth from divorced families. *Journal of Family Issues, 30,* 1245–1264.

Henderson, L. M., Weighall, A. R., Brown, H., & Gaskell, M. G. (2012). Consolidation of vocabulary is associated with sleep in children. *Developmental Science, 15,* 674–687.

Henderson, N. D. (2010). Predicting long-term firefighter performance from cognitive and physical ability measures. *Personnel Psychology, 63,* 999–1039.

Henry, D. B., Schoeny, M. E., Deptula, D. P., & Slavick, J. T. (2007). Peer selection and socialization effects on adolescent intercourse without a condom and attitudes about the costs of sex. *Child Development, 78,* 825–838.

Hepach, R., Vaish, A., & Tomasello, M. (2012). Young children are intrinsically motivated to see others helped. *Psychological Science, 23,* 967–972.

Hepper, P. G., Wells, D. L., Dornan, J. C., & Lynch, C. (2013). Long-term flavor recognition in humans with prenatal garlic experience. *Developmental Psychobiology, 55,* 568–574.

Herlitz, A., & Lovén, J. (2013). Sex differences and the own-gender bias in face recognition: A meta-analytic review. *Visual Cognition, 21,* 1306–1336.

Herman, M. (2004). Forced to choose: Some determinants of racial identification in multiracial adolescents. *Child Development, 75,* 730–748.

Hernandez, D. J. (2004). Demographic change and the life circumstances of immigrant families. *Future of Children, 14,* 17–47.

Herrnstein, R. J., & Murray, C. (1994). *The bell curve: Intelligence and class structure in American life.* New York, NY: Free Press.

Hershkowitz, I., Lamb, M. E., Orbach, Y., Katz, C., & Horowitz, D. (2012). The development of communicative and narrative skills among preschoolers: Lessons from forensic interviews about child abuse. *Child Development, 83,* 611–622.

Hesketh, T., Zhou, X., & Wang, Y. (2015). The end of the one-child policy: Lasting implications for China. *Journal of the American Medical Association, 314*(24), 2619–2620. doi: 10.1001/jama.2015.16279

Hespos, S. J., Ferry, A. L., & Rips, L. J. (2009). Five-month-old infants have different expectations for solids and liquids. *Psychological Science, 20,* 603–611.

Hess, U., & Kirouac, G. (2000). Emotion expression in groups. In M. Lewis & J. Haviland-Jones (Eds.), *Handbook of emotions* (2nd ed., pp. 368–381). New York, NY: Guilford Press.

Hetherington, E. M., & Kelly, J. (2002). *For better or for worse: Divorce reconsidered.* New York, NY: W. W. Norton.

Hetherington, E. M., Bridges, M., & Insabella, G. M. (1998). What matters? What does not? Five perspectives on the association between marital transitions and children's adjustment. *American Psychologist, 53*(2), 167–184.

Heyman, G. D. (2009). Children's reasoning about traits. In P. Bauer (Ed.), *Advances in child development and behavior* (Vol. 37, pp. 105–143). London, UK: Elsevier.

Heyman, G. D., & Legare, C. H. (2004). Children's beliefs about gender differences in the academic and social domains. *Sex Roles, 50,* 227–239.

Hibbard, R., Barlow, J., MacMillan, H., & the Committee on Child Abuse and Neglect and American Academy of Child and Adolescent Psychiatry Child Maltreatment and Violence Committee (2012). Psychological maltreatment. *Pediatrics, 130*(2), 372–378.

Hill, A. J., & Oliver, S. (1992). Eating in the adult world: The rise of dieting in childhood and adolescence. *British Journal of Clinical Psychology, 31,* 95–105.

Hill, J. L., Brooks-Gunn, J., & Waldfogel, J. (2003). Sustained effects of high participation in an early intervention for low-birth-weight premature infants. *Developmental Psychology, 39,* 730–744.

Hill, S. E., & Flom, R. (2007). 18- and 24-month-olds' discrimination of gender-consistent and inconsistent activities. *Infant Behaviour and Development, 30,* 168–173.

Hillman, C. H., Buck, S. M., Themanson, J. R., Pontifex, M. B., & Castelli, D. M. (2009). Aerobic fitness and cognitive development: Event-related brain potential and task performance indices of executive control in preadolescent children. *Developmental Psychology, 45,* 114–129.

Hipwell, A. E., Keenan, K., Loeber, R., & Battista, D. (2010). Early predictors of sexually intimate behaviors in an urban sample of young girls. *Developmental Psychology, 46,* 366–378.

Hirsh-Pasek, K., & Golinkoff, R. M. (2008). King Solomon's take on word learning: An integrative account from the radical middle. In R. V. Kail (Ed.), *Advances in child development and behavior* (Vol. 36, pp. 1–29). San Diego, CA: Elsevier.

Hitlin, S., Brown, J., & Elder, G. H., Jr. (2006). Racial self-categorization in adolescence: Multiracial development and social pathways. *Child Development, 77,* 1298–1308.

Ho, C. S., & Fuson, K. C. (1998). Children's knowledge of teen quantities as tens and ones: Comparisons of Chinese, British, and American kindergartners. *Journal of Educational Psychology, 90,* 536–544.

Hodnett, E. D., Gates, S., Hofmeyr, G. J., & Sakala, C. (2012). Continuous support for women during childbirth. *Cochrane Database of Systematic Reviews,* Issue 10. Retrieved from www.cochranelibrary .com/cochrane-database-of-systematic-reviews/ table-of-contents/2012/Issue10/

Hofer, M. A. (2006). Psychobiological roots of early attachment. *Current Directions in Psychological Science, 15,* 84–88.

Hoff, E. (2006). How social contexts support and shape language development. *Development Review, 26,* 55–88.

Hoff, E. (2009). *Language development* (2nd ed.). Belmont, CA: Wadsworth Cengage Learning.

Hoff, E. L. (2014). *Language development* (5th ed.). Belmont, CA: Wadsworth, Cengage Learning.

Hoff, E., & Naigles, L. (2002). How children use input to acquire a lexicon. *Child Development, 73,* 418–433.

Hoff, E., Core, C., Rumiche, R., Señor, M., & Parra, M. (2012). Dual language exposure and early bilingual development. *Journal of Child Language, 39,* 1–27.

Hoff-Ginsberg, E., & Tardif, T. (1995). Socioeconomic status and parenting. In M. H. Bornstein (Ed.), *Handbook of parenting* (Vol. 2, pp. 161–188). Mahwah, NJ: Erlbaum.

Hoff, T. L. (1992). Psychology in Canada one hundred years ago: James Mark Baldwin at the University of Toronto. *Canadian Psychology, 33*(4), 638–694.

Hogan, A. M., de Haan, M., Datta, A., & Kirkham, F. J. (2006). Hypoxia: An acute, intermittent and chronic challenge to cognitive development. *Developmental Science, 9,* 335–337.

Hogge, W. A. (1990). Teratology. In I. R. Merkatz & J. E. Thompson (Eds.), *New perspectives on prenatal care.* New York, NY: Elsevier.

Holden, G. W., & Miller, P. C. (1999). Enduring and different: A meta-analysis of the similarity in parents' child rearing. *Psychological Bulletin, 125,* 223–254.

Hollich, G. J., Golinkoff, R. M., & Hirsh-Pasek, K. (2007). Young children associate novel words with complex objects rather than salient parts. *Developmental Psychology, 43,* 1051–1061.

Hollich, G. J., Hirsh-Pasek, K., & Golinkoff, R. M. (2000). Breaking the language barrier: An emergentist coalition model for the origins of word learning. *Monographs of the Society for Research in Child Development, 65*(Serial No. 262).

Hollon, S. D., Haman, K. I., & Brown, L. L. (2002). Cognitive-behavioral treatment of depression. In I. H. Gotlieb & C. L. Hammen (Eds.), *Handbook of depression* (pp. 383–403). New York, NY: Guilford Press.

Holowka, S., & Petitto, L. A. (2002). Left hemisphere cerebral specialization for babies while babbling. *Science, 297,* 1515.

Hood, B., Carey, S., & Prasada, S. (2000). Predicting the outcomes of physical events: Two-year-olds fail to reveal knowledge of solidity and support. *Child Development, 71,* 1540–1554.

Hopkins, B., & Westra, T. (1988). Maternal handling and motor development: An intercultural study. *Genetic, Social, and General Psychology Monographs, 14,* 377–420.

Horowitz, F. D., & O'Brien, M. (1986). Gifted and talented children: State of knowledge and directions for research. *American Psychologist, 41,* 1147–1152.

Hostinar, C. E., & Gunnar, M. R. (2013). The developmental effects of early life stress: An overview of current theoretical frameworks. *Current Directions in Psychological Science, 22,* 400–406.

Houston, D. M., & Jusczyk, P. W. (2003). Infants' long-term memory for the sound patterns of words and voices. *Journal of Experimental Psychology: Human Perception and Performance, 29,* 1143–1154.

Howe, M. L., & Courage, M. L. (1997). The emergence and early development of autobiographical memory. *Psychological Review, 104,* 499–523.

Howe, N., & Ross, H. S. (1990). Socialization perspective taking and the sibling relationship. *Developmental Psychology, 26,* 160–165.

Howell, K. K., Lynch, M. E., Platzman, K. A., Smith, G. H., & Coles, C. D. (2006). Prenatal alcohol exposure and ability, academic achievement, and school functioning in adolescence: A longitudinal follow-up. *Journal of Pediatric Psychology, 31,* 116–126.

Howell, S. R., Jankowicz, D., & Becker, S. (2005). A model of grounded language acquisition: Sensorimotor features improve lexical and grammatical learning. *Journal of Memory and Language, 53,* 258–276.

Howes, C., & Matheson, C. C. (1992). Sequences in the development of competent play with peers: Social and social pretend play. *Developmental Psychology, 28,* 961–974.

Howes, C., Unger, O., & Seidner, L. B. (1990). Social pretend play in toddlers: Parallels with social play and with solitary pretend. *Child Development, 60,* 77–84.

Hudson, J. A., Shapiro, L. R., & Sosa, B. B. (1995). Planning in the real world: Preschool children's scripts and plans for familiar events. *Child Development, 66,* 984–998.

Huesmann, L. R. (2007). The impact of media violence: Scientific theory and research. *Journal of Adolescent Health, 41,* S6–S13.

Huizink, A., Robles de Medina, P., Mulder, E., Visser, G., & Buitelaar, J. (2002). Psychological measures of prenatal stress as predictors of infant temperament. *Journal of the American Academy of Child and Adolescent Psychiatry, 41,* 1078–1085.

Hulit, L. M., & Howard, M. R. (2002). *Born to talk: An introduction to speech and language development* (3rd ed.). Boston, MA: Allyn and Bacon.

Hulme, C., & Snowling, M. J. (2009). *Developmental disorders of language learning and cognition.* Chichester, UK: Wiley-Blackwell.

Human Genome Project. (2003). *Genomics and its impact on science and society: A 2003 primer.* Washington, DC: U.S. Department of Energy.

Human Resources and Skills Development Canada. (2013). *Indicators of well-being in Canada: Family life – Age of mother at childbirth.* Retrieved from www4 .hrsdc.gc.ca/.3ndic.1t.4r@-eng.jsp?iid=75

Human Resources and Skills Development Canada. (n.d.). *Leave and benefits* (workplace programs, policies and practices). Retrieved from www.hrsdc.gc.ca/ en/lp/spila/wlb/wppp/02leave_benefits.shtml

Human Resources Development Canada. (2002). Knowledge matters: Skills and learning for Canadians. Retrieved from www.innovation.l/ino2/publications/ publications_kanada/knowledge.pdf

Hunt, E., & Carlson, J. (2007). Considerations relating to the study of group differences in intelligence. *Perspectives on Psychological Science, 2,* 194–213.

Hunt J. M. (1961). *Intelligence and experience.* New York, NY: Ronald.

Hurtado, N., Marchman, V. A., & Fernald, A. (2008). Does input influence uptake? Links between maternal talk, processing speed, and vocabulary size in Spanish-learning children. *Developmental Science, 11,* F31–F39.

Hurts, K. (2008). Building cognitive support for the learning of long division skills using progressive

schematization: Design and empirical validation. *Computers and Education, 50,* 1141–1156.

Huston, A. C. (2008). From research to policy and back. *Child Development, 79,* 1–12.

Huston, A. C., & Wright, J. C. (1998). Mass media and children's development. In W. Damon (Ed.), *Handbook of child psychology* (Vol. 4). New York, NY: Wiley.

Huston, A. C., Duncan, G. J., McLoyd, V. C., Crosby, D. A., Ripke, M. N., Weisner, T. S., et al. (2005). Impacts on children of a policy to promote employment and reduce poverty for low-income parents: New hope after 5 years. *Developmental Psychology, 41,* 902–918.

Hutchins, E. (1983). Understanding Micronesian navigation. In D. A. Gentner & A. Stevens (Eds.), *Mental models.* Hillsdale, NJ: Erlbaum.

Hutchinson, D. M., Rapee, R. M., & Taylor, A. (2010). Body dissatisfaction and eating disturbances in early adolescence: A structural modeling investigation examining negative affect and peer factors. *Journal of Early Adolescence, 30,* 489–517.

Huth-Bocks, A. C., Levendosky, A. A., Bogat, G. A., & von Eye, A. (2004). The impact of maternal characteristics and contextual variables on infant–mother attachment. *Child Development, 75,* 480–496.

Huttenlocher, J., Haight, W., Bryk, A., Seltzer, M., & Lyons, T. (1991). Early vocabulary growth: Relation to language input and gender. *Developmental Psychology, 27,* 236–248.

Huttenlocher, J., Waterfall, H., Vasilyeva, M., Vevea, J., & Hedges, L. V. (2010). Sources of variability in children's language growth. *Cognitive Psychology, 61,* 343–365.

Hyde, D. C., & Spelke, E. S. (2011). Neural signatures of number processing in human infants: Evidence for two core systems underlying numerical cognition. *Developmental Science, 14,* 360–371.

Hyde, J. S. (2014). Gender similarities and differences. *Annual Review of Psychology, 65,* 373–398

Hymel, S., Vaillancourt, T., McDougall, P., & Renshaw, P. D. (2004). Peer acceptance and rejection in childhood. In P. K. Smith & C. H. Hart (Eds.), *Blackwell handbook of childhood social development* (pp. 265–284). Malden, MA: Blackwell.

Iervolino, A. C., Hines, M., Golombok, S. E., Rust, J., & Plomin, R. (2005). Genetic and environmental influences on sex-typed behavior during the preschool years. *Child Development, 76,* 826–840.

Inhelder, B., & Piaget, J. (1958). *The growth of logical thinking from childhood to adolescence.* New York, NY: Basic Books.

Itard, J. M. G. (1962). *The wild boy of Aveyron* (G. Humphrey & M. Humphrey, Trans.). New York, NY: Appleton-Century-Crofts. (Original works published in 1801 & 1806.)

Iverson, J. M., & Goldin-Meadow, S. (2005). Gesture paves the way for language development. *Psychological Science, 16,* 367–371.

Izard, C. E. (2007). Basic emotions, natural kinds, emotion schemas, and a new paradigm. *Perspectives on Psychological Science, 2,* 260–280.

Izard, C. E., & Ackerman, B. P. (2000). Motivational, organizational, and regulatory functions of discrete emotions. In M. Lewis & J. Haviland-Jones (Eds.), *Handbook of emotions* (2nd ed., pp. 253–264). New York, NY: Guilford Press.

Izard, V., Dehaene-Lambertz, G., & Dehaene, S. (2008). Distinct cerebral pathways for object identity and number in human infants. *PLOS Biology, 6* (2):e11. doi: 10.1371/journal.pbio.0060011

Jack, F., MacDonald, S., Reese, E., & Hayne, H. (2009). Maternal reminiscing style during early childhood predicts the age of adolescents' earliest memories. *Child Development, 80,* 496–505.

Jacklin, C. N. (1989). Female and male: Issues of gender. *American Psychologist, 44,* 127–133.

Jacklin, C. N., & Maccoby, E. E. (1978). Social behavior at thirty-three months in same-sex and mixed-sex dyads. *Child Development, 49,* 557–569.

Jacobi, C., Hayward, C., de Zwaan, M., Kraemer, H. C., & Agras, W. S. (2004). Coming to terms with risk factors for eating disorders: Application of risk terminology and suggestions for a general taxonomy. *Psychological Bulletin, 130,* 19–65.

Jacobson, S. W., & Jacobson, J. L. (2000). Teratogenic insult and neurobehavioral function in infancy and childhood. In C. A. Nelson (Ed.), *The Minnesota Symposium on Child Psychology; Vol. 31. The effects of early adversity on neurobehavioral development* (pp. 61–112). Mahwah, NJ: Erlbaum.

Jaffee, S. R. (2003). Pathways to adversity in young adulthood among early childbearers. *Journal of Family Psychology, 16,* 38–49.

Jaffee, S., & Hyde, J. S. (2000). Gender differences in moral orientation: A meta-analysis. *Psychological Bulletin, 126,* 703–726.

Jahromi, L. B., Putnam, S. P., & Stifter, C. A. (2004). Maternal regulation of infant reactivity from 2 to 6 months. *Developmental Psychology, 40,* 477–487.

James, J., Ellis, B. J., Schlomer, G. L., & Garber, J. (2012). Sex-specific pathways to early puberty, sexual debut, and sexual risk taking: Tests of an integrated evolutionary-developmental model. *Developmental Psychology, 48,* 687–702.

James, W. (1981). The principles of psychology. F. Burkhardt & F. Bowers (Eds.), *The works of William James,* Vol. 3. Cambridge, MA: Harvard University Press. (Original work published 1890.)

Jamieson, J. P., & Harkins, S. G. (2007). Mere effort and stereotype threat performance effects. *Journal of Personality and Social Psychology, 93*(4), 544–564.

Jansen, J., de Weerth, C., & Riksen-Walraven, J. M. (2008). Breastfeeding and the mother-infant relationship—A review. *Developmental Review, 28,* 503–521.

Jahromi, L. B., Putnam, S. P., & Stifter, C. A. (2004). Maternal regulation of infant reactivity from 2 to 6 months. *Developmental Psychology, 40,* 477–487.

Jensen, L. A. (2012). Bridging universal and cultural perspectives: A vision for developmental psychology in a global world. *Child Development Perspectives, 6,* 98–104.

Jenson, J. (2004). Changing the paradigm: Family responsibility for investing in children. *Canadian Journal of Sociology, 29*(2), 169–192.

Jiao, Z. (1999, April). Which students keep old friends and which become new friends across a school transition? Paper presented at the 1999 meeting of the Society for Research in Child Development, Albuquerque, New Mexico.

Jiaojiao, R. (2005, March 17). When "little emperors" become parents. *China Daily,* n.p. Retrieved from www.chinadaily.com.cn/english/doc/2005-03/71/content_4259

Jipson, J. L., & Gelman, S. A. (2007). Robots and rodents: Children's inferences about living and nonliving kinds. *Child Development, 78,* 1675–1688.

John, O. P., & Gross, J. J. (2007). Individual differences in emotion regulation. In J. J. Gross (Ed.), *Handbook of emotion regulation* (pp. 351–372). New York, NY: Guilford Press.

Johnson, K. A., Robertson, I. H., Barry, E., Mulligan, A., Daibhis, A., Daly, M., et al. (2008). Impaired conflict resolution and alerting in children with ADHD: Evidence from the Attention Network Task (ANT). *Journal of Child Psychology and Psychiatry, 49,* 1339–1347.

Johnson, M. H., Grossman, T., & Cohen Kadosh, K. (2009). Mapping functional brain development: Building a social brain through interactive specialization. *Developmental Psychology, 45,* 151–159.

Johnson, O. (2012). A systematic review of neighborhood and institutional relationships related to education. *Education and Urban Society, 44*(4), 477–511.

Johnson, S. C., Dweck, C. S., Chen, F. S., Stern, H. L., Ok, S-J., & Barth, M. (2010). At the intersection of social and cognitive development: Internal working models of attachment in infancy. *Cognitive Science, 34,* 807–825.

Johnson, S. P. (2001). Visual development in human infants: Binding features, surfaces, and objects. *Visual Cognition, 8,* 565–578.

Johnston, C. C., Filion, F., Campbell-Yeo, M., Golet, C., Bell, L., McNaughton, K., et al. (2008). Kangaroo mother care diminishes pain from heel lance in very preterm neonates: A crossover trial. *BMC Pediatrics, 8*(13), 1–3.

Johnston, L. D., Delva, J., & O'Malley, P. M. (2007). Sports participation and physical education in American secondary schools: Current levels and racial/ethnic and socioeconomic disparities. *American Journal of Preventive Medicine, 33,* S195–S208.

Jokela, M. (2010). Characteristics of the first child predict the parents' probability of having another child. *Developmental Psychology, 46,* 915–926.

Jordan, N. C. (2007). The need for number sense. *Educational Leadership, 65,* 63–64.

Jordan, N. C., Kaplan, D., Ramineni, C., & Locuniak, M. N. (2009). Early math matters: Kindergarten number competence and later mathematics outcomes. *Developmental Psychology, 45,* 850–867.

Joseph, D. L., & Newman, D. A. (2010). Emotional intelligence: An integrative meta-analysis and cascading model. *Journal of Applied Psychology, 95,* 54–78.

Joseph, R. (2000). Fetal brain behavior and cognitive development. *Developmental Review, 20,* 81–98.

Joussemet, M., Vitaro, F., Barker, E. D., Côté, S., Nagin, D. S., Zoccollilo, M. & Tremblay, R. E. (2008). Controlling parenting and physical aggression during elementary school. *Child Development, 79*(2), 411–425.

Joyner, K., & Udry, J. R. (2000). You don't bring me anything but down: Adolescent romance and depression. *Journal of Health and Social Behavior, 41,* 369–391.

Juffer, F., & van IJzendoorn, M. H. (2007). Adoptees do not lack self-esteem: A meta-analysis of studies on self-esteem of transracial, international, and domestic adoptees. *Psychological Bulletin, 133,* 1067–1083.

Jusczyk, P. W. (1995). Language acquisition: Speech sounds and phonological development. In J. L. Miller & P. D. Eimas (Eds.), *Handbook of perception and cognition: Vol. 11. Speech, language, and communication.* Orlando, FL: Academic Press.

Jusczyk, P. W. (2002). How infants adapt speech-processing capacities to native-language structure. *Current Directions in Psychological Science, 11,* 15–18.

Justice Canada. (n.d.). Canadian Criminal Code Part I. Retrieved from www.laws.justice.gc.ca/eng/showdoc/cs/C-46/bo-ga:s_3_1//en#anchorbo-ga:s_3_1

Juvonen, J., & Graham, S. (2014). Bullying in schools: The power of bullies and the plight of victims. *Annual Review of Psychology, 65,* 159–185.

Kadir, R. A., & Economides, D. E. (2002). Neural tube defects and periconceptional folic acid. *Canadian Medical Association Journal, 167*(3), 255–256.

Kagan, J., Arcus, D., Snidman, N., Feng, W. Y., Hendler, J., & Greene, S. (1994). Reactivity in infants: A cross-national comparison. *Developmental Psychology, 30,* 342–345.

Kahn, P. H., Gary, H. E., & Shen, S. (2013). Children's social relationships with current and near-future robots. *Child Development Perspectives, 7,* 32–37.

Kaijura, H., Cowart B. J., & Beauchamp, G. K. (1992). Early developmental change in bitter taste responses in human infants. *Developmental Psychobiology, 25,* 375–386.

Kail, R. V. (2013). Influences of credibility of testimony and strength of statistical evidence on children's and adolescents' reasoning. *Journal of Experimental Child Psychology, 116,* 747–754.

Kail, R., & Hall, L. K. (1999). Sources of developmental change in children's word-problem performance. *Journal of Educational Psychology, 91,* 660–668.

Kail, R., & Zollner, T. (2005). *Children.* Toronto, ON: Pearson Education Canada.

Kail, R. V., McBride-Chang, C., Ferrer, E., Cho, J.-R., & Shu, H. (2013). Cultural differences in the development of processing speed. *Developmental Science, 16,* 476–483.

Kalil, A., & Ziol-Guest, K. M. (2005). Single mothers' employment dynamics and adolescent well-being. *Child Development, 76,* 196–211.

Kam, C.-M., Greenberg, M. T., Bierman, K. L., Coie, J. D., Dodge, K. A., Foster, M. E., et al. (2011). Maternal depressive symptoms and child social preference during the early school years: Mediation by maternal warmth and child emotion regulation. *Journal of Abnormal Child Psychology, 39,* 365–377.

Kamins, M. L., & Dweck, C. S. (1999). Person versus process praise and criticism: Implications for contingent self-worth and coping. *Developmental Psychology, 35*(3), 835–847.

Kaplan, H., & Dove, H. (1987). Infant development among the Ache of eastern Paraguay. *Developmental Psychology, 23,* 190–198.

Karasik, L. B., Tamis-LeMonda, C. S., & Adolph, K. E. (2011). Transition from crawling to walking and infants' actions with objects and people. *Child Development, 82,* 1199–1209.

Karevold, E., Røysamb, E., Ystrom, E., & Mathiesen, K. S. (2009). Predictors and pathways from infancy to symptoms of anxiety and depression in early adolescence. *Developmental Psychology, 45,* 1051–1060.

Kärnä, A., Voeten, M., Little, T. D., Alanen, E., Poskiparta, E., & Salmivalli, C. (2013). Effectiveness of the KiVa antibullying program: Grades 1–3 and 7–9. *Journal of Educational Psychology, 105,* 535–551.

Kärnä, A., Voeten, M., Little, T. D., Poskiparta, E., Kaljonen, A., & Salmivalli, C. (2011). A large-scale evaluation of the KiVa antibullying program: Grades 4–6. *Child Development, 82,* 311–330.

Karniol, R. (1989). The role of manual manipulative states in the infant's acquisition of perceived control over objects. *Developmental Review, 9,* 205–233.

Karraker, K. H., Vogel, D. A., & Lake, M. A. (1995). Parents' gender-stereotyped perceptions of newborns: The eye of the beholder revisited. *Sex Roles, 33,* 687–701.

Kärtner, J., Keller, H., Chaudhary, N., & Yovsi, R. D. (2012). The development of mirror self-recognition in different sociocultural contexts. *Monographs of the Society for Research in Child Development, 77*(Serial No. 307).

Katz, L. F., & Woodin, E. M. (2002). Hostility, hostile detachment, and conflict engagement in marriages: Effects on child and family functioning. *Child Development, 73,* 636–652.

Katz-Wise, S. L., Priess, H. A., & Hyde, J. S. (2010). Gender-role attitudes and behavior across the transition to parenthood. *Developmental Psychology, 46,* 18–28.

Kaufman, J., & Charney, D. (2003). The neurobiology of child and adolescent depression: Current knowledge and future directions. In D. Cicchetti & E. Walker (Eds.), *Neurodevelopmental mechanisms in psychopathology* (pp. 461–490). New York, NY: Cambridge University Press.

Kaufman, J., & Lichtenberger, E. O. (2002). *Assessing adolescent and adult intelligence* (2nd ed.). Boston, MA: Allyn and Bacon.

Kaufman, J. C., Kaufman, S. B., & Plucker, J. A. (2013). Contemporary theories of intelligence. In D. Reisberg (Ed.), *The Oxford handbook of cognitive psychology.* New York, NY: Oxford University Press.

Kavsek, M., & Bornstein, M. H. (2010). Visual habituation and dishabituation in preterm infants: A review and meta-analysis. *Research in Developmental Disabilities, 31,* 951–975.

Kawabata, Y., & Crick, N. R. (2011). The significance of cross-racial/ethnic friendships: Associations with peer victimization, peer support, sociometric status, and classroom diversity. *Developmental Psychology, 47,* 1763–1775.

Keane, S. P., Brown, K. P., & Crenshaw, T. M. (1990). Children's intention-cue detection as a function of maternal social behavior: Pathways to social rejection. *Developmental Psychology, 26,* 1004–1009.

Kearney, C. A. (2007). Forms and functions of school refusal behavior in youth: An empirical analysis of absenteeism severity. *Journal of Child Psychology and Psychiatry, 48*, 53–61.

Kearney, C. A., Haight, C., Gauger, M., & Schafer, R. (2011) School refusal behavior and absenteeism. In R. J. R. Levesque (Ed.), *Encyclopedia of adolescence* (pp. 2489–2492). New York, NY: Springer.

Keijsers, L., Loeber, R., Branje, S., & Meeus, W. (2011). Bidirectional links and concurrent development of parent-child relationships and boys' offending behavior. *Journal of Abnormal Psychology, 120*, 878–889.

Kelemen, D. (2003). British and American children's preferences for teleo-functional explanations of the natural world. *Cognition, 88*, 201–221.

Kelemen, D., & DiYanni, C. (2005). Intuitions about origins: Purpose and intelligent design in children's reasoning about nature. *Journal of Cognition and Development, 6*, 3–31.

Kell, H. J., Lubinski, D., & Benbow, C. P. (2013). Who rises to the top? Early indicators. *Psychological Science, 24*, 648–659.

Kellman, P. J., & Arterberry, M. E. (2006). Infant visual perception. In W. Damon & R. M. Lerner (Eds.), *Handbook of child psychology: Vol. 2. Cognition, perception, and language* (6th ed., pp. 109–160). Hoboken, NJ: Wiley.

Kellman, P. J., & Banks, M. S. (1998). Infant visual perception. In W. Damon (Ed.), *Handbook of child psychology* (Vol. 2). New York, NY: Wiley.

Kellman, P. J., & Spelke, E. S. (1983). Perception of partly occluded objects in infancy. *Cognitive Psychology, 15*, 483–524.

Kelly, P. (2011). Corporal punishment and child maltreatment in New Zealand. *Acta Paediatrica, 100*, 14–20.

Keltner, D., Kogan, A., Piff, P. K., & Saturn, S. R. (2014). The sociocultural appraisals, values, and emotions (SAVE) framework of prosociality: Core processes from gene to meme. *Annual Review of Psychology, 65*, 425–460.

Kerns, K. A., & Brumariu, L. E. (2014). Is insecure parent-child attachment a risk factor for the development of anxiety in childhood or adolescence? *Child Development Perspectives, 8*, 12–17.

Khalil, A., Syngelaki, A., Maiz, N., Zinevich, Y., & Nicolaides, K. H. (2013). Maternal age and adverse pregnancy outcomes: A cohort study. *Ultrasound in Obstetrics and Gynecology, 42*, 634–643.

Khashan, A. S., Baker, P. N., & Kenny, L. C. (2010). Preterm birth and reduced birthweight in first and second teenage pregnancies: A register-based cohort study. *BMC Pregnancy and Childbirth, 10*, 36.

Khoo, I. (2016, November 5). Oldest woman to give birth: 70-year-old welcomes first child. *Huffington Post*, n.p. Retrieved from www.huffingtonpost.ca/2016/05/11/oldest-woman-to-give-birth_n_9905080.html

Khurana, A., Romer, D., Betancourt, L. M., Brodsky, N. L., Giannetta, J. M., & Hurt, H. (2012). Early adolescent sexual debut: The mediating role of working memory ability, sensation seeking, and impulsivity. *Developmental Psychology, 48*, 1416–1428.

Kiang, L., Yip, T., Gonzales-Backen, M., Witkow, M., & Fuligni, A. J. (2006). Ethnic identity and the daily psychological well-being of adolescents from Mexican and Chinese backgrounds. *Child Development, 77*, 1338–1350.

Kidd, E. (2012). Implicit statistical learning is directly associated with the acquisition of syntax. *Developmental Psychology, 48*, 171–184.

Kidd, E., & Holler, J. (2009). Children's use of gesture to resolve lexical ambiguity. *Developmental Science, 12*, 903–913.

Kilgore, K., Snyder, J., & Lentz, C. (2000). The contribution of parental discipline, parental monitoring, and school risk to early-onset conduct problems in African American boys and girls. *Developmental Psychology, 36*, 835–845.

Killen, M., & McGlothlin, H. (2005). Prejudice in childhood. In C. B. Fisher & R. M. Lerner (Eds.), *Encyclopedia of applied developmental science* (Vol. 2, pp. 870–872). Thousand Oaks, CA: Sage.

Kim, J. Y., McHale, S. M., Crouter, A. C., & Osgood, D. (2007). Longitudinal linkages between sibling relationships and adjustment from middle childhood through adolescence. *Developmental Psychology, 43*, 960–973.

Kim, S.Y., Chen, Q., Wang, Y., Shen, Y. & Orozco-Lapray, D. (2013). Longitudinal linkages among parent–child acculturation discrepancy, parenting, parent-child sense of alienation, and adolescent adjustment in Chinese immigrant families. *Developmental Psychology, 49*, 900–912

Kim-Spoon, J., Cicchetti, D., & Rogosch, F. A. (2013). A longitudinal study of emotion regulation, emotion lability-negativity, and internalizing symptomatology in maltreated and nonmaltreated children. *Child Development, 84*, 512–527.

Kimball, M. M. (1986). Television and sex-role attitudes. In T. M. Williams (Ed.), *The impact of television* (pp. 265–301). New York, NY: Academic Press.

Kimura, D. (2004). Human sex differences in cognition, fact, not predicament. *Sexualities, Evolution and Gender, 6*, 45–53.

Kindermann, T. A. (2007). Effects of naturally existing peer groups on changes in academic engagement in a cohort of sixth graders. *Child Development, 78*, 1186–1203.

King, P. E., & Furrow, J. L. (2004). Religion as a resource for positive youth development: Religion, social capital, and moral outcomes. *Developmental Psychology, 40*, 703–713.

King, V. (2006). The antecedents and consequences of adolescents' relationships with stepfathers and non-resident fathers. *Journal of Marriage and the Family, 68*, 910–928.

Kirby, D. (2002). *Do abstinence-only programs delay the initiation of sex among young people and reduce teen pregnancy?* Washington, DC: National Campaign to Prevent Teen Pregnancy.

Kirby, D., & Laris, B. A. (2009). Effective curriculum-based sex and STD/HIV education programs for adolescents. *Child Development Perspectives, 3*, 21–29.

Kirkorian, H. L., Pempek, T. A., Murphy, L. A., Schmidt, M. E., & Anderson, D. R. (2009). The impact of background television on parent-child interaction. *Child Development, 80*, 1350–1359.

Kisilevsky, B. S., Hains, S. M. J., Brown, C. A., Lee, C. T., Cowperthwaite, B., Stutzman, S. S., et al. (2009). Fetal sensitivity to properties of maternal speech and language. *Infant Behavior and Development, 32*, 59–71.

Kithakye, M., Morris, A. S., Terranova, A. M., & Myers, S. (2010). The Kenyan political conflict and children's adjustment. *Child Development, 81*, 1114–1128.

Kjeldsen, A., Janson, H., Stoolmiller, M., Torgersen, L., & Mathiesen, K. S. (2014). Externalising behavior from infancy to mid-adolescence: Latent profiles and early predictors. *Journal of Applied Developmental Psychology, 35*, 25–34.

Klaczynski, P. A. (2004). A dual-process model of adolescent development: Implications for decision making, reasoning, and identity. In R. Kail (Ed.), *Advances in Child Development and Behavior* (Vol. 32, pp. 73–123). San Diego, CA: Elsevier.

Klahr, D. (1985). Solving problems with ambiguous subgoal ordering: Preschoolers' performance. *Child Development, 56*, 940–952.

Klahr, D., Zimmerman, C., & Jirout, J. (2011). Educational interventions to advance children's scientific thinking. *Science, 333*, 971–975.

Klaus, M., & Kennell, H. H. (1976). *Mother–infant bonding*. St. Louis, MO: Mosby.

Klemfuss, J. Z., & Ceci, S. J. (2012). Legal and psychological perspectives on children's competence to testify in court. *Developmental Review, 32*, 268–286.

Klimstra, T. A., Luyckx, K., Branje, S., Teppers, E., Goossens, L., & Meeus, W. H. J. (2013). Personality traits, interpersonal identity, and relationship stability: Longitudinal linkages in late adolescence and young adulthood. *Journal of Youth and Adolescence, 42*, 1661–1673.

Klump, K. L., & Culbert, K. M. (2007). Molecular genetic studies of eating disorders: Current status and future directions. *Current Directions in Psychological Science, 16*, 37–41.

Knight, G. P., & Carlo, G. (2012). Prosocial development among Mexican American youth. *Child Development Perspectives, 6*, 258–263.

Kochanska, G. (1997). Mutually responsive orientation between mothers and their young children: Implications for early socialization. *Child Development, 68*, 94–112.

Kochanska, G., Aksan, N., & Joy, M. E. (2007). Children's fearfulness as a moderator of parenting in early socialization: Two longitudinal studies. *Developmental Psychology, 43*, 222–237.

Kochanska, G., Coy, K. C., & Murray, K. T. (2001). The development of self-regulation in the first four years of life. *Child Development, 72*, 1091–1111.

Kochanska, G., Gross, J. N., Lin, M., & Nichols, K. E. (2002). Guilt in young children: Development, determinants, and relations with a broader system of standards. *Child Development, 73*, 461–482.

Kochenderfer-Ladd, B., & Wardrop, J. L. (2001). Chronicity and instability of children's peer victimization experiences as predictors of loneliness and social satisfaction trajectories. *Child Development, 72*, 134–151.

Koepke, S., & Denissen, J. A. (2012). Dynamics of identity development and separation-individuation in parent-child relationships during adolescence and emerging adulthood. *Developmental Review, 32*, 67–88.

Koh, J. B. K., & Wang, Q. (2012). Self-development. *WIREs Cognitive Science, 3*, 513–524.

Kohlberg, L. (1966). A cognitive-developmental analysis of children's sex-role concepts and attitudes. In E. E. Maccoby (Ed.), *The development of sex differences*. Stanford, CA: Stanford University Press.

Kohlberg, L. (1969). Stage and sequence: The cognitive-developmental approach to socialization. In D. Goslin (Ed.), *Handbook of socialization theory and research* (pp. 347–480). Chicago, IL: Rand McNally.

Kohlberg, L., & Ullian, D. Z. (1974). Stages in the development of psychosexual concepts and attitudes. In R. C. Friedman, R. M. Richart, & R. L. Van Wiele (Eds.), *Sex differences in behavior*. New York, NY: Wiley.

Kojima, Y. (2000). Maternal regulation of sibling interactions in the preschool years: Observational study in Japanese families. *Child Development, 71*, 1640–1647.

Kokai, M. (2003). School psychology: Assisting deaf and hard of hearing children with multicultural backgrounds. *Psychology Ontario, 25*(1), 8–11.

Kokis, J. V., Macpherson, R., Toplak, M. E., West, R. F., & Stanovich, K. E. (2002). Heuristic and analytic processing: Age trends and associations with cognitive ability and cognitive styles. *Journal of Experimental Child Psychology, 83*, 26–52.

Kokko, K., & Pulkkinen, L. (2000). Aggression in childhood and long-term unemployment in adulthood: A cycle of maladaptation and some protective factors. *Developmental Psychology, 36*, 463–472.

Kolb, B. (1989). Brain development, plasticity, and behavior. *American Psychologist, 44*, 1203–1212.

Kolb, B., & Teskey, G. C. (2012). Age, experience, injury, and the changing brain. *Developmental Psychobiology, 54*, 311–325.

Kolberg, K. J. S. (1999). Environmental influences on prenatal development and health. In T. L. Whitman & T. V. Merluzzi (Eds.), *Life-span perspectives on health and illness* (pp. 87–103). Mahwah, NJ: Erlbaum.

Kong, A., Frigge, M. L., Masson, G., Besenbacher, S., Sulem, P., Magnusson, G., et al. (2012). Rate of *de novo* mutations and the importance of father's age to disease risk. *Nature, 488,* 471–475.

Konijn, E. A., Nije Bijvank, M., & Bushman, B. J. (2007). I wish I were a warrior: The role of wishful identification in the effects of violent video games on aggression in adolescent boys. *Developmental Psychology, 43,* 1038–1044.

Kopp, C. B. (1997). Young children: Emotion management, instrumental control, and plans. In S. L. Friedman & E. K. Scholnick (Eds.), *The developmental psychology of planning: Why, how, and when do we plan?* (pp. 103–124). Mahwah, NJ: Erlbaum.

Kopp, C. B., & McCall, R. B. (1982). Predicting later mental performance for normal, at-risk, and handicapped infants. In P. B. Baltes & O. G. Brim (Eds.), *Life-span development and behavior* (Vol. 4). New York, NY: Academic Press.

Kornhaber, M., Fierros, E., & Veenema, S. (2004). *Multiple intelligences: Best ideas from research and practice.* Boston, MA: Allyn & Bacon.

Koss, K. J., George, M. R. W., Cummings, E. M., Davies, P. T., El-Sheikh, M., & Cicchetti, D. (2013). Asymmetry in children's salivary cortisol and alpha-amylase in the context of marital conflict: Links to children's emotional security and adjustment. *Developmental Psychobiology, 56,* 836–849.

Kotch, J. B., Lewis, T., Hussey, J. M., English, D., Thompson, R., Litrownik, A. L., et al. (2008). Importance of early childhood neglect for childhood aggression. *Pediatrics, 121*(4), 725–731.

Kowal, A., & Kramer, L. (1997). Children's understanding of parental differential treatment. *Child Development, 68,* 113–126.

Kramer, L. (2010). The essential ingredients of successful sibling relationships: An emerging framework for advancing theory and practice. *Child Development Perspectives, 4,* 80–86.

Krebs, D., & Gillmore, J. (1982). The relationship among the first stages of cognitive development, role-taking abilities, and moral development. *Child Development, 53,* 877–886.

Krebs, D. L., & Denton, K. (2005). Toward a more pragmatic approach to morality: A critical evaluation of Kohlberg's model. *Psychological Review, 113,* 672–675.

Kremarik, F. (2000). A family affair: Children's participation in sports. *Canadian Social Trends* (Autumn), 20–24. Ottawa, ON: Statistics Canada. Retrieved from http://www.statcan.gc.ca/pub/11-008-z/2000002/article/5166-eng.pc

Kreppner, J. M., Rutter, M., Beckett, C., Castle, J., Colvert, E., Groothues, C., et al. (2007). Normality and impairment following profound early institutional deprivation: A longitudinal follow-up into early adolescence. *Developmental Psychology, 43,* 931–946.

Kretch, K. S., & Adolph, K. E. (2013a). No bridge too high: Infants decide whether to cross based on the probability of falling not the severity of the potential fall. *Developmental Science, 16,* 336–351.

Kretch, K. S., & Adolph, K. E. (2013b). Cliff or step? Posture-specific learning at the edge of a drop-off. *Child Development, 84,* 226–240

Krispin, O., Sternberg, K. J., & Lamb, M. E. (1992). The dimensions of peer evaluation in Israel: A cross-cultural perspective. *International Journal of Behavioral Development, 15,* 299–314.

Kroger, J., & Green, K. E. (1996). Events associated with identity status change. *Journal of Adolescence, 19,* 477–490.

Kronenberg, M. E., Hansel, T. C., Brennan, A. M., Osofsky, H. J., Osofsky, J. D., & Lawrason, B. (2010). Children of Katrina: Lessons learned about postdisaster symptoms and recovery patterns. *Child Development, 81,* 1241–1259.

Kucirkova, N., & Tompkins, V. (2014). Personalization in mother-child emotion talk across three contexts. *Infant and Child Development, 23,* 153–169.

Kuehn, B. M. (2008). Infant mortality. *Journal of the American Medical Association, 300*(20), 2359.

Kuhl, P. K., Andruski, J. E., Chistovich, I. A., Chistovich, L. A., Kozhevnikova, E. V., Ryskina, V. L., et al. (1997). Cross-language analysis of phonetic units in language addressed to infants. *Science, 277,* 684–686.

Kuhl, P. K., Stevens, E., Hayashi, A., Deguchi, T., Kiritani, S., & Iverson, P. (2006). Infants show a facilitation effect for native language phonetic perception between 6 and 12 months. *Developmental Science, 9,* F13–F21.

Kuhn, D. (2011). What is scientific thinking and how does it develop? In U. Goswami (Ed.), *The Wiley-Blackwell handbook of cognitive development* (2nd ed., pp. 497–523). Chichester, UK: Wiley-Blackwell.

Kuhn, D. (2012). The development of causal reasoning. *WIREs Cognitive Science, 3,* 327–335.

Kuhn, D., Garcia-Mila, M., Zohar, A., & Andersen, C. (1995). Strategies of knowledge acquisition. *Monographs of the Society for Research in Child Development, 60*(Serial No. 245).

Kulkofsky, S., Wang, Q., & Koh, J. B. K. (2009). Functions of memory sharing and mother-child reminiscing behaviors: Individual and cultural variations. *Journal of Cognition and Development, 10,* 92–114.

Kumar, V., Abbas, A. K., Aster, J. C., & Fausto, N. (2010). *Robbins and Cotran pathologic basis of disease, professional edition* (8th ed.). Philadelphia, PA: W. B. Saunders.

Kuntsche, E., Pickett, W., Overpeck, M., Craig, W., Boyce, W., & Gaspar de Matos, M. (2006). Television viewing and forms of bullying among adolescents from eight countries. *Journal of Adolescent Health, 39,* 908–915.

Kuppens, S., Laurent, L., Heyvaert, M., & Onghena, P. (2013). Associations between parental psychological control and relational aggression in children and adolescents: A multilevel and sequential meta-analysis. *Developmental Psychology, 49,* 1697–1712.

Kuryluk, A., Cohen, R., & Audley-Piotrowski, S. (2011). The role of respect in the relation of aggression to popularity. *Social Development, 20,* 703–717.

Kwak, K., & Berry, J. W. (2006). Canada. In J. Gerogas, J. W. Berry, F. J. R. van de Vijiver, C. Ka¯gitçibas¸i, & Y. H. Poortinga (Eds.), *Families across cultures: A 30-nation psychological study* (pp. 284–292). Cambridge, UK: Cambridge University Press.

Lackner, C., Sabbagh, M. A., Hallinan, E., Liu, X., & Holden, J. J. A. (2012). Dopamine receptor D4 gene variation predicts preschoolers' developing theory of mind. *Developmental Science, 15,* 272–280.

Lacourse, E., Boivin, M., Brendgen, A., Petitclerc, A., Girard, A., Vitaro, F., et al. (2014). A longitudinal twin study of physical aggression during early childhood: evidence for a developmentally dynamic genome. *Psychological Medicine, 44,* 2617–2627.

Ladd, G. W. (1998). Peer relationships and social competence during early and middle childhood. *Annual Review of Psychology, 50,* 333–359.

Ladd, G. W. (2003). Probing the adaptive significance of children's behavior and relationships in the school context: A child by environment perspective. In R. V. Kail (Ed.), *Advances in child development and behavior* (Vol. 31). San Diego, CA: Academic Press.

Ladd, G. W. (2006). Peer rejection, aggressive or withdrawn behavior, and psychological maladjustment from ages 5 to 12: An examination of four predictive models. *Child Development, 77,* 822–846.

Ladd, G. W., & Ladd, B. K. (1998). Parenting behaviors and parent-child relationships: Correlates of peer victimization in kindergarten? *Developmental Psychology, 34,* 1450–1458.

Ladd, G. W., & Pettit, G. S. (2002). Parents and children's peer relationships. In M. Bornstein (Ed.), *Handbook of parenting: Vol. 4* (2nd ed., pp. 377–409). Hillsdale, NJ: Erlbaum.

Ladd, G. W., Herald-Brown, S. L., & Reiser, M. (2008). Does chronic classroom peer rejection predict the development of children's classroom participation during the grade school years? *Child Development, 79,* 1001–1015.

LaFreniere, P., & MacDonald, K. (2013). A post-genomic view of behavioral development and adaptation to the environment. *Developmental Review, 33,* 89–109.

LaFreniere, P., Strayer, F. F., & Gauthier, R. (1984). The emergence of same-sex affiliative preferences among preschool peers: A developmental/ethnological perspective. *Child Development, 55,* 1958–1965.

Lagattuta, K. (2014). Link past, present, and future: Children's ability to connect mental states and emotions across time. *Child Development Perspectives, 8,* 90–95.

Lagattuta, K. H., & Wellman, H. M. (2002). Differences in early parent–child conversations about negative versus positive emotions: Implications for the development of psychological understanding. *Developmental Psychology, 38,* 564–580.

Lagattuta, K. N., Nucci, L., & Bosacki, S. L. (2010). Bridging theory of mind and the personal domain: Children's reasoning about resistance to parental control. *Child Development, 81,* 616–635.

LaGreca, A. M. (1993). Social skills training with children: Where do we go from here? *Journal of Clinical Child Psychology, 22,* 288–298.

LaGreca, A. M., & Silverman, W. K. (2009). Treatment and prevention of posttraumatic stress reactions in children and adolescents to disasters and terrorism: What is the evidence? *Child Development Perspectives, 3,* 4–10.

Laible, D. J., & Carlo, G. (2004). The differential relations of maternal and paternal support and control to adolescent social competence, self-worth, and sympathy. *Journal of Adolescent Research, 19,* 759–782.

Lakes, K. D., & Hoyt, W. T. (2004). Promoting self-regulation through school-based martial arts training. *Journal of Applied Developmental Psychology, 25,* 283–302.

Lalumière, M. L., Blanchard, R., & Zucker, K. J. (2000). Sexual orientation and handedness in men and women: A meta-analysis. *Psychological Bulletin, 126,* 575–592.

Lamaze, F. (1958). *Painless childbirth.* London, UK: Burke.

Lamb, L. M., Bigler, R. S., Liben, L. S., & Green, V. A. (2009). Teaching children to confront peers' sexist remarks: Implications for theories of gender development and educational practice. *Sex Roles, 61,* 361–382.

Lamb, M. E. (1999). Nonparental child care. In M. E. Lamb (Ed.), *Parenting and child development in "nontraditional" families.* Mahwah, NJ: Erlbaum.

Lamb, M. E., & Lewis, C. (2010). The development and significance of father-child relationships in two-parent families. In M. E. Lamb (Ed.), *The role of the father in child development* (5th ed., pp. 94–153). Hoboken, NJ: Wiley.

Lamb, M. E., Sternberg, K. J., & Esplin, P. W. (2000). Effects of age and delay on the amount of information provided by alleged sex abuse victims in investigative interviews. *Child Development, 71,* 1586–1596.

Lambert, B. L., & Bauer, C. R. (2012). Developmental and behavioral consequences of prenatal cocaine exposure: A review. *Journal of Perinatology, 32,* 819–828.

Landerl, K., Fussenegger, B., Moll, K., & Willburger, E. (2009). Dyslexia and dyscalculia: Two learning disorders with different cognitive profiles. *Journal of Experimental Child Psychology, 103,* 309–324.

Lane, H., & Grodin, M. (1997). Ethical issues in cochlear implant surgery: An exploration into disease, disability, and the best interests of the child. *Kennedy Institute of Ethics Journal, 7*(3), 231–251.

Langille, D. B. (2007). Teenage pregnancy: Trends, contributing factors and the physician's role. *Canadian Medical Association Journal, 176*(11), 1601–1602.

Lansford, J. E. (2009). Parental divorce and children's adjustment. *Perspectives on Psychological Science, 4,* 140–152.

Lansford, J. E., Malone, P. S., Castellino, D. R., Dodge, K. A., Pettit, G. S., & Bates, J. E. (2006). Trajectories of internalizing, externalizing, and grades for children who have and have not experienced their parents' divorce or separation. *Journal of Family Psychology, 20,* 292–301.

Laplante, D. P., Barr, R. G., Brunet, A., Du Fort, G. G., Meaney, M. L., Saucier, J., et al. (2004). Stress during pregnancy affects general intellectual and language functioning in human toddlers. *Pediatric Research, 56,* 400–410.

Larroque, B., Ancel, P.-Y., Marchnad, L., André, M., Arnaud, C., Pierrat, V., et al. (2008). Neurodevelopmental disabilities and special care of 5-year-old children born before 33-weeks of gestation (the EPIPAGE study): A longitudinal cohort study. *The Lancet, 371,* 813–820.

Larsen, J. T., To, R. M., & Fireman, G. (2007). Children's understanding and experience of mixed emotions. *Psychological Science, 18,* 186–191.

Larson, R. W. (2001). How U.S. children and adolescents spend time: What it does (and doesn't) tell us about their development. *Current Directions in Psychological Science, 10,* 160–164.

Larson, R. W., Hansen, D. M., & Moneta, G. (2006). Differing profiles of developmental experiences across types of organized youth activities. *Developmental Psychology, 42,* 849–863.

Lau, J. Y. F., Belli, S. D., Gregory, A. M., Napolitano, M., & Eley, T. C. (2012). The role of children's negative attributions on depressive symptoms: An inherited characteristic or a product of the early environment? *Developmental Science, 15,* 569–578.

Lau, J. Y., Rijsdijk, F., Gregory, A. M., McGuffin, P., & Eley, T. C. (2007). Pathways to childhood depressive symptoms: The role of social, cognitive, and genetic risk factors. *Developmental Psychology, 43,* 1402–1414.

Laursen, B., & Collins, W. A. (1994). Interpersonal conflict during adolescence. *Psychological Bulletin, 115,* 197–209.

Laursen, B., Finkelstein, B. D., & Betts, N. T. (2001). A developmental meta-analysis of peer conflict resolution. *Developmental Review, 21,* 423–449.

Lazardis, M. (2013). The emergence of a temporally extended self and factors that contribute to its development: From theoretical and empirical perspectives. *Monographs of the Society for Research in Child Development, 78*(Serial No. 305).

Le Grand, R., Mondloch, C. J., Maurer, D., & Brent, H. P. (2001). Early visual experience and face processing. *Nature, 410,* 890.

Leaper, C., & Smith, T. E. (2004). A meta-analytic review of gender variations in children's language use: Talkativeness, affiliative speech, and assertive speech. *Developmental Psychology, 40,* 993–1027.

Leaper, C., Breed, L., Hoffman, L., & Perlman, C. A. (2002). Variations in the gender-stereotyped content of children's television cartoons across genres. *Journal of Applied Social Psychology, 32,* 1653–1662. doi: 10.1111/j.1559-1816.2002.tb02767.x

Lebel, C., Rasmussen, C., Wyper, K., Walker, L., Andrew, G., Yager, J., & Beaulieu, C. (2008). Brain diffusion abnormalities in children with fetal alcohol spectrum disorder. *Alcoholism: Clinical and Experimental Research, 32*(10), 1732–1740.

LeBlanc, J. E. (1996). *Straight talk about children and sport: Advice for parents, coaches, and teachers.* Oakville, ON: Canadian Association of Coaches.

Lecanuet, J. P., Granier-Deferre, C., & Busnel, M. C. (1995). Human fetal auditory perception. In J. P. Lecanuet, W. P. Fifer, N. A. Krasnegor, & W. P. Smotherman (Eds.), *Fetal development: A psychobiological perspective.* Hillsdale, NJ: Erlbaum.

Leclair, C., Nicholson, L., & Hartley, E. E. (2003). From the stories women tell: The Métis women's circle. In K. Anderson & B. Lawrence (Eds.), *Strong women stories* (pp. 55–69). Toronto, ON: Sumach Press.

Leclercq, A-L., & Majurus, S. (2010). Serial-order short-term memory predicts vocabulary development: Evidence from a longitudinal study. *Developmental Psychology, 46,* 417–427.

Ledebt, A. (2000). Changes in arm posture during the early acquisition of walking. *Infant Behavior and Development, 23,* 79–89.

Ledebt, A., van Wieringen, P. C. W., & Saveslsbergh, G. J. P. (2004). Functional significance of foot rotation in early walking. *Infant Behavior and Development, 27,* 163–172.

Lee, K. (2013). Little liars: Development of verbal deception in children. *Child Development Perspectives, 7,* 91–96.

Lee, M. J., Whitehead, J., Ntoumanis, N., & Hatzigeorgiadis, A. (2008). Relationships among values, achievement orientations, and attitudes in youth sport. *Journal of Sport and Exercise Psychology, 30,* 588–610.

Lee, P. C., Niew, W. I., Yang, H. J., Chen, V. C. H., & Lin, K. C. (2012). A meta-analysis of behavioral parent training for children with attention deficit hyperactivity disorder. *Research in Developmental Disabilities, 33,* 2040–2049.

Lee, S. J., Altschul, I., & Gershoff, E. T. (2013). Does warmth moderate longitudinal associations between spanking and child aggression in early childhood? *Developmental Psychology, 49,* 2017–2028.

Leekam, S. R., Prior, M. R., & Uljarevic, M. (2011). Restricted and repetitive behaviors in autism spectrum disorders: A review of research in the last decade. *Psychological Bulletin, 137,* 562–593.

Leerkes, E. M., Blankson, A. M., & O'Brien, M. (2009). Differential effects of maternal sensitivity to infant distress and nondistress on social-emotional functioning. *Child Development, 80,* 762–775.

Legare, C. H., Gelman, S. A., & Wellman, H. M. (2010). Inconsistency with prior knowledge triggers children's causal explanatory reasoning. *Child Development, 81,* 929–944.

Legare, C. H., Wellman, H. M., & Gelman, S. A. (2009). Evidence for an explanation advantage in naïve biological reasoning. *Cognitive Psychology, 58,* 177–194.

Leichtman, M. D., & Ceci, S. L. (1995). The effects of stereotypes and suggestions on preschoolers' reports. *Developmental Psychology, 31,* 568–578.

Leinaweaver, J. (2014). Informal kinship-based fostering around the world: Anthropological findings. *Child Development Perspectives, 8,* 131–136.

Lengua, L. J. (2006). Growth in temperament and parenting as predictors of adjustment during children's transition to adolescence. *Developmental Psychology, 42,* 819–832.

Lengua, L. J., Sandler, I. N., West, S. G., Wolchik, S. A., & Curran, P. J. (1999). Emotionality and self-regulation, threat appraisal, and coping in children of divorce. *Development and Psychopathology, 11,* 15–37.

Lenroot, R. K., & Giedd, J. N. (2010). Sex differences in the adolescent brain. *Brain and Cognition, 72,* 46–55.

Leon, K. (2003). Risk and protective factors in young children's adjustment to parental divorce: A review of the research. *Family Relations, 52,* 258–270.

Leppanen, J. M., Moulson, M. C., Vogel-Farley, V. K., & Nelson, C. A. (2007). An ERP study of emotional face processing in the adult and infant brain. *Child Development, 78,* 232–245.

Lerner, R. M., Fisher, C. B., & Giannino, L. (2006). Editorial: Constancy and change in the development of applied developmental science. *Applied Developmental Science, 10,* 172–173.

Lerner, R. M., Fisher, C. B., & Weinberg, R. A. (2000). Toward a science for and of the people: Promoting civil society through the application of developmental science. *Child Development, 71,* 11–20.

LeVasseur, V. M., Macaruso, P., & Shankweiler, D. (2008). Promoting gains in reading fluency: A comparison of three approaches. *Reading and Writing, 21,* 205–230.

Leventhal, T., & Brooks-Gunn, J. (2000). The neighborhood they live in: The effects of neighborhood residence on child and adolescent outcomes. *Psychological Bulletin, 126,* 309–337.

Leventhal, T., & Brooks-Gunn, J. (2003). Children and youth in neighborhood contexts. *Current Directions in Psychological Science, 12,* 27–31.

Levine, S. C., Ratliff, K. R., Huttenlocher, J., & Cannon, J. (2012). Early puzzle play: A predictor of preschoolers' spatial transformation skill. *Developmental Psychology, 48,* 530–542.

Levine, S. C., Vasilyeva, M., Lourenco, S. F., Newcombe, N. S., & Huttenlocher, J. (2005). Socioeconomic status modifies the sex difference in spatial skill. *Psychological Science, 16,* 841–845.

Levitt, A. G., & Utman, J. A. (1992). From babbling towards the sound systems of English and French: A longitudinal two-case study. *Journal of Child Language, 19,* 19–49.

Levitt, M. J., Guacci-Franco, N., & Levitt, J. L. (1993). Convoys of social support in childhood and early adolescence: Structure and function. *Developmental Psychology, 29,* 811–818.

Levy, B. A., Gong, Z., Hessels, S., Evans, M. A., & Jared, D. (2006). Understanding print: Early reading development and the contributions of home literacy experiences. *Journal of Experimental Child Psychology, 93,* 63–93.

Levy, G. D., Taylor, M. G., & Gelman, S. A. (1995). Traditional and evaluative aspects of flexibility in gender roles, social conventions, moral rules, and physical laws. *Child Development, 66,* 515–531.

Lewis, M. (1997). The self in self-conscious emotions. In J. G. Snodgrass & R. L. Thompson (Eds.), *The self across psychology: Self-awareness, self-recognition, and the self-concept* (pp. 119–142). New York, NY: New York Academy of Sciences.

Lewis, M. (2000). The emergence of human emotions. In M. Lewis & J. Haviland-Jones (Eds.), *Handbook of emotions* (2nd ed., pp. 265–280). New York, NY: Guilford Press.

Lewis, M. (2008). The emergence of human emotion. In M. Lewis, J. M. Haviland-Jones, & L. F. Barrett (Eds.), *Handbook of emotions* (3rd ed., pp. 304–319). New York, NY: Guilford Press.

Lewis, M., & Ramsay, D. (2004). Development of self-recognition, personal pronoun use, and pretend play during the second year. *Child Development, 75,* 1821–1831.

Lewis, M., Ramsay, D. S., & Kawakami, K. (1993). Differences between Japanese infants and Caucasian American infants in behavioral and cortisol response to inoculation. *Child Development, 64,* 1722–1731.

Lewis, M., Takai-Kawakami, K., Kawakami, K., & Sullivan, M. W. (2010). Cultural differences in emotional responses to success and failure. *International Journal of Behavioral Development, 34,* 53–61.

Lewis, M. D., Koroshegyi, C., Douglas, L., & Kampe, K. (1997). Age-specific associations between emotional responses to separation and cognitive performance in infancy. *Developmental Psychology, 33,* 32–42.

Lewkowicz, D. J. (2000a). The development of intersensory perception: An epigenetic systems/limitations view. *Psychological Bulletin, 126,* 281–308.

Lewkowicz, D. J. (2000b). Infants' perception of the audible, visible, and bimodal attributes of multimodal syllables. *Child Development, 71,* 1241–1257.

Lewontin, R. C. (1976). Race and intelligence. In N. J. Block & G. Dworkin (Eds.), *The IQ controversy* (pp. 78–92). New York, NY: Pantheon Books.

Li, Q. (2005). New bottle but old wine: A research of cyberbullying in schools. *Computers in Human Behaviour, 23,* 1777–1791.

Li, W., Farkas, G., Duncan, G. J., Burchinal, M. R., & Vandell, D. L. (2013). Timing of high-quality child care and cognitive, language, and preacademic development. *Developmental Psychology, 49,* 1440–1451.

Li, Y., Anderson, R. C., Nguyen-Jahiel, K., Dong, T., Archodidou, A., Kim, I.-H., et al. (2007). Emergent leadership in children's discussion groups. *Cognition and Instruction, 25,* 75–111.

Li-Grining, C. P. (2007). Effortful control among low-income preschoolers in three cities: Stability, change, and individual differences. *Developmental Psychology, 43,* 208–221.

Liben, L. S., & Bigler, R. S. (2002). The developmental course of gender differentiation. *Monographs of the Society for Research in Child Development, 67*(Serial No. 269).

Liben, L. S., Bigler, R. S., & Krogh, H. R. (2001). Pink and blue collar jobs: Children's judgments of job status and job aspirations in relation to sex of worker. *Journal of Experimental Child Psychology, 79*, 346–363.

Lidstone, J., Meins, E., & Fernyhough, C. (2011). Individual differences in children's private speech: Consistency across tasks, timepoints and contexts. *Cognitive Development, 26*, 203–213.

Liebal, K., Behne, T., Carpenter, M., & Tomasello, M. (2009). Infants use shared experience to interpret pointing gestures. *Developmental Science, 12*, 264–271.

Lieberman, A. M., Borovsky, A., Hatrak, M., & Mayberry, R. I. (2015). Real-time processing of ASL signs: Delayed first language acquisition affects organization of the mental lexicon. *Journal of Experimental Psychology: Learning, Memory, and Cognition, 41*(4), 1130–1139.

Lillard, A. S., Lerner, M. D., Hopkins, E. J., Dore, R. A., Smith, E. D., & Palmquist, C. M. (2013). The impact of pretend play on children's development: A review of the evidence. *Psychological Bulletin, 139*, 1–34.

Limpo, T., Alves, R. A., & Fidalgo. R. (2014). Children's high-level writing skills: Development of planning and revising and their contribution to writing quality. *British Journal of Educational Psychology, 84*, 177–193.

Lin, C. C., & Fu, V. R. (1990). A comparison of child-drearing practices among Chinese, immigrant Chinese, and Caucasian-American parents. *Child Development, 61*, 429–433.

Lindberg, S. M., Hyde, J. S., Petersen, J. L., & Linn, M. C. (2010). New trends in gender and mathematics performance: A meta-analysis. *Psychological Bulletin, 136*, 1123–1135.

Lindsay, C. (2008). *Are women spending more time on unpaid domestic work than men in Canada?* Statistics Canada Catalogue no. 89-630-X. Ottawa, ON: Minister of Industry.

Lindsey, E. W., & Colwell, M. J. (2003). Preschoolers' emotional competence: Links to pretend and physical play. *Child Study Journal, 33*, 39–52.

Lindsey, E. W., Cremeens, P. R., & Caldera, Y. M. (2010). Mother-child and father-child mutuality in two contexts: Consequences for young children's peer relationships. *Infant and Child Development, 19*, 142–160.

Linebarger, D. L., & Vaala, S. E. (2010). Screen media and language development in infants and toddlers: An ecological perspective. *Developmental Review, 30*, 176–202.

Lipman, E. L., Georgiades, K., & Boyle, M. H. (2011). Young adult outcomes of children born to teen mothers: Effects of being born during their teen or later years. *Journal of the American Academy of Child and Adolescent Psychiatry, 50*(3), 232–241.

Lipsitt, L. P. (2003). Crib death: A biobehavioral phenomenon. *Psychological Science, 12*, 164–170.

Liu, D., Gelman, S. A., & Wellman, H. M. (2007). Components of young children's trait understanding: Behavior-to-trait and trait-to-behavior predictions. *Child Development, 78*, 1543–1558.

Liu, D., Wellman, H. M., Tardif, T., & Sabbagh, M. A. (2008). Theory of mind development in Chinese children: A meta-analysis of false-belief understanding across cultures and languages. *Developmental Psychology, 44*, 523–531.

Liu, H. M., Kuhl, P. K., & Tsao, F. M. (2003). An association between mothers' speech clarity and infants' speech discrimination skills. *Developmental Science, 6*, F1–F10.

Liu, H. M., Tsao, F. M., & Kuhl, P. K. (2007). Acoustic analysis of lexical tone in Mandarin infant-directed speech. *Developmental Psychology, 43*, 912–917.

Liu, R. X., Lin, W., & Chen, Z. Y. (2010). School performance, peer association, psychological and behavioral adjustments: A comparison between Chinese

adolescents with and without siblings. *Journal of Adolescence, 33*, 411–417.

Livesley, W. J., & Bromley, D. B. (1973). *Person perception in childhood and adolescence*. New York, NY: Wiley.

Lloyd, B., & Howe, N. (2003). Solitary play and convergent and divergent thinking skills in preschool children. *Early Childhood Research Quarterly, 18*, 22–41.

Lobelo, F, Dowda, M., Pfeiffer, K. A., & Pate, R. R. (2009). Electronic media exposure and its association with activity-related outcomes in female adolescents: Cross-sectional and longitudinal analyses. *Journal of Physical Activity and Health, 6*, 137–143.

Lobo, M. A., & Galloway, J. C. (2012). Enhanced handling and positioning in early infancy advances development throughout the first year. *Child Development, 83*, 1290–1302.

LoBue, V., & DeLoache, J. S. (2010). Superior detection of threat-relevant stimuli in infancy. *Developmental Science, 13*, 221–228.

Lockl, K., & Schneider, W. (2007). Knowledge about the mind: Links between theory of mind and later metamemory. *Child Development, 78*, 148–167.

Logan, J. (2007, April 24). The how we live poll: The rules. *Globe and Mail*, p. L3.

Lollis, S., and Kuczynski, L. (1997). Beyond one hand clapping: Seeing bidirectionality in parent–child relations. *Journal of Social and Personal Relationships, 14*, 441–461.

London, K., Bruck, M., Poole, D. A., & Melnyk, L. (2011). The development of metasuggestibility in children. *Applied Cognitive Psychology, 25*, 146–155.

Loock, C., Conry, J., Cook, J. L., Chudley, A. E., & Rosales, T. (2005). Identifying fetal alcohol spectrum disorder in primary care. *Canadian Medical Association Journal, 172*, 628–630.

Lopez, A. B., Huynh, V. W., & Fuligni, A. J. (2011). A longitudinal study of religious identity and participation during adolescence. *Child Development, 82*, 1297–1309.

Lorch, R. F, Lorch, E. P., Calderhead, W. J., Dunlap, E. E., Hodell, E. C., & Freer, B. D. (2010). Learning the control of variables strategy in higher and lower achieving classrooms: Contributions of explicit instruction and experimentation. *Journal of Educational Psychology, 102*, 90–101.

Lowry, R., Wechsler, H., Kann, L., & Collins, J. L. (2001). Recent trends in participation in physical education among U.S. high school students. *Journal of School Health, 71*, 145–152.

Ludwig, J., & Phillips, D. (2007). The benefits and costs of Head Start. *SRCD Social Policy Report, 21*, 3–11, 16–18.

Luginaah, I., Smith, K., & Lockridge, A. (2010). Surrounded by Chemical Valley and 'living in a bubble': the case of the Aamjiwnaang First Nation, Ontario. *Journal of Environmental Planning and Management, 53*(3), 353–370.

Luke, N., & Banerjee, R. (2013). Differentiated associations between childhood maltreatment experiences and social understanding: A meta-analysis and systematic review. *Developmental Review, 33*, 1–28.

Lung, F-W., & Shu, B-C. (2011). Sleeping position and health status of children at six-, eighteen-, and thirty-six-month development. *Research in Developmental Disabilities, 32*, 713–718.

Luo, Y., Kaufman, L., & Baillargeon, R. (2009). Young infants' reasoning about physical events involving inert and self-propelled objects. *Cognitive Psychology, 58*, 441–486.

Lushington, K., Pamula, Y., Martin, J., & Kennedy, J. D. (2013). Developmental changes in sleep: Infancy and preschool years. In A. R. Wolfson and H. W. Montgomery-Downs (Eds.), *The Oxford handbook of infant, child, and adolescent sleep and behavior* (pp. 34–47). Oxford, UK: Oxford University Press.

Luthar, S. S., Shoum, K. A., & Brown, P. J. (2006). Extracurricular involvement among affluent youth: A scapegoat for "ubiquitous achievement pressures"? *Developmental Psychology, 42*, 583–597.

Luttikhuizen dos Santos, E. S., de Kieviet, J. F., Königs, M., van Elburg, R. M., & Oosterlaan, J. (2013). Predictive value of the Bayley Scales of Infant Development on development of very preterm/very low birth weight children: A meta-analysis. *Early Human Development, 89*, 487–496.

Luyckx, K., Klimstra, T. A., Duriez, B., Van Petegem, S., & Beyers, W. (2013). Personal identity processes through the late 20s: Age trends, functionality, and depressive symptoms. *Social Development, 22*, 701–721.

Lytton, H., & Romney, D. M. (1991). Parents' differential socialization of boys and girls: A meta-analysis. *Psychological Bulletin, 109*, 267–296.

Maccoby, E. E. (1984). Socialization and developmental change. *Child Development, 55*, 317–328.

Maccoby, E. E. (1990). Gender and relationships: A developmental account. *American Psychologist, 45*, 513–520.

Maccoby, E. E. (1998). *The two sexes: Growing up apart, coming together*. Cambridge, MA: Belknap Press.

Maccoby, E. E., & Jacklin, C. N. (1974). *The psychology of sex differences*. Stanford, CA: Stanford University Press.

Maccoby, E. E., & Jacklin, C. N. (1980). Sex differences in aggression: A rejoinder and reprise. *Child Development, 51*, 964–980.

MacDonald, N., Yanchar, N., & Hébert, P. C. (2007). What's killing and maiming Canada's youth? *Canadian Medical Association Journal, 176*(6), 737.

MacEvoy, J. P., & Asher, S. R. (2012). When friends disappoint: Boys' and girls' responses to transgressions of friendship expectations. *Child Development, 83*, 104–119.

Mackenzie, C. A., Lockridge, A., & Keith (2005). Declining sex ratio in a First Nation community. *Environmental Health Perspectives, 113*(10), 1295–1298.

MacKenzie, M. J., Nicklas, E., Waldfogel, J., & Brooks-Gunn, J. (2012). Corporal punishment and child behavioural and cognitive outcomes through 5 years of age: Evidence from a contemporary urban birth cohort study. *Infant and Child Development, 21*, 3–33.

MacKinnon, D. P., Goldberg, L., Cheong, J. W., Elliot, D., Clarke, G., & Moe, E. (2003). Male body esteem and physical measurements: Do leaner, or stronger, high school football players have a more positive body image? *Journal of Sport and Exercise Psychology, 25*, 307–322.

MacWhinney, B. (1998). Models of the emergence of language. *Annual Review of Psychology, 49*, 199–227.

Madigan, S., Atkinson, L., Laurin, K., & Benoit, D. (2013). Attachment and internalizing behavior in early childhood: A meta-analysis. *Developmental Psychology, 49*, 672–689.

Madore, O. (2007). The impact of economic instruments that promote healthy eating, encourage physical activity and combat obesity: Literature review. Ottawa, ON: Library of Parliament, PRB 06-34E, n.p. Retrieved from www.parl.gc.ca/information/library/PRBpubs/prb0634-e.htm

Magee, L., & Hale, L. (2012). Longitudinal associations between sleep duration and subsequent weight gain: A systematic review. *Sleep Medicine Reviews, 16*, 231–241.

Maggi, S., Ostry, A., Tansey, J., Dunn, J., Hershler, R., Chen, L., & Hertzman, C. (2008). Paternal psycho-social work conditions and mental health outcomes: A case-control study. *BMC Public Health, 8*, 104.

Magnuson, K., & Duncan, G. (2006). The role of family socioeconomic resources in black and white test score gaps among young children. *Developmental Review, 26*, 365–399.

Maguire, A. M., High, K. A., Auricchio, A., Wright, J. F, Pierce, E. A., Testa, F. et al. (2009). Age-dependent effects of RPE65 gene therapy for Leber's congenital amaurosis: A phase 1 dose-escalation trial. *Lancet, 374*, 1597–1605.

Maguire, E. A., Woollett, K., & Spiers, H. J. (2006). London taxi drivers and bus drivers: A structural

MRI and neuropsychological analysis. *Hippocampus, 16,* 1091–1101.

Mahoney, J. L., & Parente, M. E. (2009). Should we care about adolescents who care for themselves? What we have learned and what we need to know about youth in self-care. *Child Development Perspectives, 3,* 189–195.

Malenfant, E. C., Lebel, A., & Martel, L. (2010). *Projections of the diversity of the Canadian population: 2006 to 2031.* Ottawa, ON: Minister of Industry.

Malinosky-Rummell, R., & Hansen, D. J. (1993). Long-term consequences of childhood physical abuse. *Psychological Bulletin, 114,* 68–79.

Malti, T., & Krettenauer, T. (2013). The relation of moral emotion attributions to prosocial and antisocial behavior: A meta-analysis. *Child Development, 84,* 397–412.

Mandara, J., Gaylord-Harden, N. K., Richard, M. H., & Ragsdale, B. L. (2009). The effects of changes in racial identity and self-esteem on changes in African American adolescents' mental health. *Child Development, 80,* 1660–1675.

Mandel, D. R., Jusczyk, P. W., & Pisoni, D. B. (1995). Infants' recognition of the sound patterns of their own names. *Psychological Science, 6,* 314–317.

Mangelsdorf, S. C. (1992). Developmental changes in infant–stranger interaction. *Infant Behavior and Development, 15,* 191–208.

Mangelsdorf, S. C., Shapiro, J. R., & Marzolf, D. (1995). Developmental and temperamental differences in emotional regulation in infancy. *Child Development, 66,* 1817–1828.

Maracle, S. (2003). The eagle has landed: Native women, leadership and community development. In K. Anderson & B. Lawrence (Eds.), *Strong women stories* (pp. 70–80). Toronto, ON: Sumach Press.

Maratsos, M. (1998). The acquisition of grammar. In W. Damon (Ed.), *Handbook of child psychology* (Vol. 2). New York, NY: Wiley.

Maratsos, M. (2000). More overregularizations after all: New data and discussion on Marcus, Pinker, Ullman, Hollander, Rosen, and Xu. *Journal of Child Language, 27,* 183–212.

Marcia, J. E. (1980). Identity in adolescence. In J. Adelson (Ed.), *Handbook of adolescent psychology.* New York, NY: Wiley.

Marcia, J. E. (1983). Some directions for the investigation of ego development in early adolescence. *Journal of Early Adolescence, 3*(3), 215–223.

Marcia, J. E. (1991). Identity and self-development. In R. M. Lerner, A. C. Petersen, & J. Brooks-Gunn (Eds.), *Encyclopedia of adolescence* (Vol. 1). New York, NY: Garland.

Marcus, G. F., Pinker, S., Ullman, M., Hollander, M., Rosen, T. J., & Xu, F. (1992). Overregularization in language acquisition. *Monographs of the Society for Research in Child Development, 58*(4, Serial No. 228).

Mareschal, D., & Tan, S. H. (2007). Flexible and context-dependent categorization by eighteen-month-olds. *Child Development, 78,* 19–37.

Margett, T. E., & Witherington, D. C. (2011). The nature of preschoolers' concept of living and artificial objects. *Child Development, 82,* 2067–2082.

Markovits, H., Benenson, J., & Dolenszky, E. (2001). Evidence that children and adolescents have internal models of peer interactions that are gender differentiated. *Child Development, 72,* 879–886.

Marks, A. K., & Garcia Coll, C. (2007). Psychological and demographic correlates of early academic skill development among American Indian and Alaska Native youth: A growth modeling study. *Developmental Psychology, 43,* 663–674.

Marks, A. K., Patton, F., & García Coll, C. (2011). Being bicultural: A mixed-methods study of adolescents' implicitly and explicitly measured multiethnic identities. *Developmental Psychology, 47,* 270–288.

Marks, R. (1976). Providing for individual differences: A history of the intelligence testing movement in North America. *Interchange, 7*(3), 3–16.

Marschik, P. B., Einspieler, C., Strohmeier, A., Plienegger, J., Garzarolli, B., & Prechtl, H. F. R. (2008). From the reaching behavior at 5 months of age to hand preference at preschool age. *Developmental Psychobiology, 50,* 511–518.

Marsh, H. W. (1991). Employment during high school: Character building or a subversion of academic goals? *Sociology of Education, 64,* 172–189.

Marsh, H. W., & Craven, R. G. (2006). Reciprocal effects of self-concept and performance from a multidimensional perspective: Beyond seductive pleasure and unidimensional perspectives. *Perspectives on Psychological Science, 1,* 133–163.

Marsh, H. W., & Kleitman, S. (2005). Consequences of employment during high school: Character building, subversion of academic goals, or a threshold? *American Educational Research Journal, 42,* 331–369.

Marsh, H. W., & Yeung, A. S. (1997). Causal effects of academic self-concept on academic achievement: Structural equation models of longitudinal data. *Journal of Educational Psychology, 89,* 41–54.

Marsh, H. W., Ellis, L. A., & Craven, R. G. (2002). How do preschool children feel about themselves? Unraveling measurement and multidimensional self-concept structure. *Developmental Psychology, 38,* 376–393.

Marshall, K. (2012). *Paid and unpaid work over three generations.* Statistics Canada Catalogue no. 75-001-X Perspectives on Labour and Income. Ottawa, ON: Statistics Canada.

Martel, M. M. (2013). Sexual selection and sex differences in the prevalence of childhood externalizing and adolescent internalizing disorders. *Psychological Bulletin, 139,* 1221–1259.

Martel, M. M., & Nigg, J. T. (2006). Child ADHD and personality/temperament traits of reactive and effortful control, resiliency, and emotionality. *Journal of Child Psychology, 47,* 1175–1183.

Martin-Chang, S., Levy, B. A., & O'Neil, S. (2006). Word acquisition, retention, and transfer: Findings from contextual and isolated word training. *Journal of Experimental Child Psychology, 96,* 37–56.

Martin, C. L., & Fabes, R. A. (2001). The stability and consequences of young children's same-sex peer interactions. *Developmental Psychology, 37,* 431–446.

Martin, C. L., & Halverson, C. F. (1987). The roles of cognition in sex role acquisition. In D. B. Carter (Ed.), *Current conceptions of sex roles and sex typing: Theory and research.* New York, NY: Praeger.

Martin, C. L., & Ruble, D. (2004). Children's search for gender cues: Cognitive perspectives on gender development. *Current Directions in Psychological Science, 13*(2), 67–70.

Martin, C. L., Fabes, R. A., Evans, S. M., & Wyman, H. (1999). Social cognition on the playground: Children's beliefs about playing with girls versus boys and their relations to sex segregated play. *Journal of Social and Personal Relationships, 16,* 751–772.

Martin, C. L., Fabes, R. A., Hanish, L., Leonard, S., & Dinella, L. M. (2011). Experienced and expected similarity to same-gender peers: Moving toward a comprehensive model of gender segregation. *Sex Roles, 65,* 421–434.

Martin, C. L., Kornienko, O., Schaefer, D. R., Hanish, L. D., Fabes, R. A., & Goble, P. (2013). The role of sex of peers and gender-typed activities in young children's peer affiliative networks: A longitudinal analysis of selection and influence. *Child Development, 84,* 921–937.

Martin, C. L., & Dinella, L. M. (2012). Congruence between gender-stereotypes and activity preference in self-idntified tomboys and non-tomboys. *Archivbes of Sexual Behavior, 41*(3), 599–610.

Martin, J. A., Hamilton, B. E., Ventura, S. J., Osterman, M. J. K., & Mathews, T. J. (2013). Births: Final data for 2011. *National Vital Statistics Reports, 62,* no 1. Hyattsville, MD: National Center for Health Statistics.

Martin, J. L., & Ross, H. S. (2005). Sibling aggression: Sex differences and parents' reactions. *International Journal of Behavioural Development, 29*(2), 129–138.

Martin, R. P., Olejnik, S., & Gaddis, L. (1994). Is temperament an important contributor to schooling outcomes in elementary school? Modeling effects of temperament and scholastic ability on academic achievement. In W. B. Casey & S. C. McDevitt (Eds.), *Prevention and early intervention.* New York, NY: Brunner/Mazel.

Martin-Chang, S., Ouellette, G., & Madden, M. (2014). Does poor spelling equate to slow reading? The relationship between reading, spelling, and orthographic quality. *Reading and Writing, 27,* 1485–1505. doi: 10.1007/s11145-014-9502-7

Masten, A., Cutuli, J., Herbers, J., Hinz, E., Obradovic, J., & Wenzel, A. (2014). Academic risk and resilience in the context of homelessness. *Child Development Perspectives, 8,* 201–206.

Masten, A. S., & Narayan, A. J. (2012). Child development in the context of disaster, war, and terrorism: Pathways of risk and resilience. *Annual Review of Psychology, 63,* 227–257.

Masten, A. S., & Osofsky, J. D. (2010). Diasters and their impact on child development: Introduction to the special section. *Child Development, 81,* 1029–1039.

Masten, A. S., Roisman, G. I., Long, J. D., Burt, K. B., Obradovic, J., Riley, J. R., et al. (2005). Developmental cascades: Linking academic achievement and externalizing and internalizing symptoms over 20 years. *Developmental Psychology, 41,* 733–746.

Masur, E. F. (1995). Infants' early verbal imitation and their later lexical development. *Merrill-Palmer Quarterly, 41,* 286–306.

Matsuba, M. K., & Walker, L. J. (2004). Extraordinary commitment: Young adults involved in social organizations. *Journal of Personality, 72,* 413–436.

Matsuba, M. K., & Walker, L. J. (2005). Young adult moral exemplars: The making of self through stories. *Journal of Research on Adolescence, 15*(30), 275–297.

Mattys, S. L., & Jusczyk, P. W. (2001). Phonotactic cues for segmentation of fluent speech by infants. *Cognition, 78,* 91–121.

Matusov, E., Bell, N., & Rogoff, B. (2002). Schooling as cultural process: Working together and guidance by children from schools differing in collaborative practices. In R. V. Kail & H. W. Reese (Eds.), *Advances in child development and behavior* (Vol. 29, pp. 129–160). San Diego, CA: Academic Press.

Maximova, K., McGrath, J.J., Barnett, T., O'Loughlin, J., Paradis, G., & Lambert, M. (2008). Do you see what I see? Weight status misperception and exposure to obesity among children and adolescents. *International Journal of Obesity, 32,* 1008–1015.

May, P. A., Blankenship, J., Marais, A-S., Gossage, J. P., Kalberg, W. O., Joubert, B., et al. (2013). Maternal alcohol consumption producing fetal alcohol spectrum disorders (FASD): Quantity, frequency, and timing of drinking. *Drug and Alcohol Dependence, 133,* 502–512.

Mayberry, R. I., Lock, E., & Kazmi, H. (2002). Linguistic ability and early language exposure. *Nature, 417,* 38.

Mayer, J. D., Salovey, P., & Caruso, D. R. (2008). Emotional intelligence: New ability or eclectic traits? *American Psychologist, 63,* 503–517.

Maynard, A. E. (2002). Cultural teaching: The development of teaching skills in Maya sibling interactions. *Child Development, 73,* 969–982.

Mazur, E., Wolchik, S. A., Virdin, L., Sandler, I. N., & West, S. G. (1999). Cognitive moderators of children's adjustment to stressful divorce events: The role of negative cognitive errors and positive illusions. *Child Development, 70,* 231–245.

McAlister, A. R., & Peterson, C. C. (2013). Siblings, theory of mind, and executive functioning in children aged 3–6 years: New longitudinal evidence. *Child Development, 84,* 1442–1458.

McAloney, K., Stringer, M., & Mallett, J. (2013). The measurement of mistrust among religious group members in Northern Ireland. *Journal of Applied Social Psychology, 43*, E329-E338. doi: 10.1111/jasp.12029

McCall, R. B. (1993). Developmental functions for general mental performance. In D. K. Detterman (Ed.), *Current topics in human intelligence* (Vol. 3, pp. 3–29). Norwood, NJ: Ablex.

McCall, R. B., & Groark, C. J. (2000). The future of applied child development research and public policy. *Child Development, 71*, 197–204.

McCarthy, M. M. & Arnold, A. P. (2008). Sex differences in the brain: What's old and what's new? In: J. B. Becker, K. J. Berkley, N. Geary, E. Hampson, J. P. Herman, & E. A. Young (Eds.), *Sex differences in the brain: From genes to behavior* (pp. 15–33). New York, NY: Oxford University Press.

McCarty, M. E., & Ashmead, D. H. (1999). Visual control of reaching and grasping in infants. *Developmental Psychology, 35*, 620–631.

McClenahan, C., Irwing, P., Stringer, M., Giles, M., & Wilson, R. (2003). Educational differences in self-perceptions of adolescents in Northern Ireland. *International Journal of Behavioral Development, 27*(6), 513–518.

McClure, E. B. (2000). A meta-analytic review of sex differences in facial expression processing and their development in infants, children, and adolescents. *Psychological Bulletin, 126*, 424–453.

McConnell, A. R., Beilock, S. L., Jellison, W. A., Rydell, R. J., & Carr T. H. (2004). How do stereotypes threaten athletes? Exploring causal mechanisms of stereotype threat. NASPSPA Abstracts, 2004. *Journal of Sport and Exercise Psychology, 26*(Suppl.), S21.

McCormack, T. A. (2011). Planning in young children: A review and synthesis. *Developmental Review, 31*, 1–31.

McCormick, C. B. (2003). Metacognition and learning. In I. B. Weiner (Editor-in-Chief), W. M. Reynolds, & G. E. Miller (Eds.), *Handbook of psychology: Vol. 7. Educational Psychology* (pp. 79–102). New York, NY: Wiley.

McCrink, K., & Wynn, K. (2007). Ratio abstraction by 6-month-old infants. *Psychological Science, 18*, 740–745.

McCutchen, D., Covill, A., Hoyne, S. H., & Mildes, K. (1994). Individual differences in writing: Implications of translating fluency. *Journal of Educational Psychology, 86*, 256–266.

McCutchen, D., Francis, M., & Kerr, S. (1997). Revising for meaning: Effects of knowledge and strategy. *Journal of Educational Psychology, 89*, 667–676.

McDonald, K. L., Bowker, J. C., Rubin, K. H., Laursen, B., & Duchene, M. S. (2010). Interactions between rejection sensitivity and supportive relationships in the prediction of adolescents' internalizing difficulties. *Journal of Youth and Adolescence, 39*, 563–574.

McElwain, N. L., Booth-LaForce, C., & Wu, X. (2011). Infant-mother attachment and children's friendship quality: Maternal mental-state talk as an intervening mechanism. *Developmental Psychology, 47*, 1295–1311.

McFarlane, A. H., Bellissimo, A., Norman, G. R. (1995). Family structure, family functioning and adolescent well-being: The transcendent influence of parental style. *Child Psychology & Psychiatry & Allied Disciplines, 36*(5), 847–864.

McGee, L. M., & Richgels, D. J. (2004). *Literacy's beginnings* (4th ed.). Boston, MA: Allyn and Bacon.

McGraw, M. B. (1935). *Growth: A study of Johnny and Jimmy.* East Norwalk, CT: Appleton-Century-Crofts.

McGuire, S., & Shanahan, L. (2010). Sibling experiences in diverse family contexts. *Child Development Perspectives, 4*, 72–79.

McHale, J. P., Laurette, A., Talbot, J., & Pourquette, C. (2002). Retrospect and prospect in the psychological study of coparenting and family group process. In J. P. McHale & W. Grolnick (Eds.), *Retrospect and prospect in the psychological study of families* (pp. 127–165). Mahwah, NJ: Erlbaum.

McHale, S. M., Crouter, A. C., Kim, J. Y., Burton, L. M., Davis, K. D., Dotterer, A. M., et al. (2006). Mothers' and fathers' racial socialization in African American families: Implications for youth. *Child Development, 77*, 1387–1402.

McHale, S. M., Kim, J. Y., Whiteman, S., & Craster, A. C. (2004). Links between sex-typed time use in middle childhood and gender development in early adolescence. *Developmental Psychology, 40*(5), 868–881.

McHale, S. M., Updegraff, K. A., & Whiteman, S. D. (2013). Sibling relationships. In G. W. Peterson & K. R. Bush (Eds.), *Handbook of marriage and the family* (pp. 329–351). New York, NY: Springer Science+Business Media.

McKay, A. (2012). Trends in Canadian national and provincial/territorial teen pregnancy rates: 2001-2010. *The Canadian Journal of Human Sexuality, 21*(3–4), 161–175.

McKeough, A., Bird, S., Tourigny, E. Romaine, A., Graham, S., Ottmann, J., & Jeary, J. (2008). Storytelling as a foundation to literacy development for aboriginal children: Culturally and developmentally appropriate practices. *Canadian Psychology, 49*(2), 148–154.

McKeown, S., Stringer, M., & Cairns, E. (2016). Classroom segregation: Where do students sit and how is this related to group relations? *British Educational Research Journal, 42*(1), 40–55. doi: 10.1002/berj.3200

McKim, M. J., Cramer, K. M., Stuart, B., & O'Connor, D. L. (1999). Infant care decisions and attachment security: The Canadian Transition to Child Care Study. *Canadian Journal of Behavioural Science, 31*(2), 92–106.

McKusick, V. A. (1995). *Mendelian inheritance in man: Catalog of autosomal dominant, autosomal recessive, and X-linked phenotypes* (10th ed.). Baltimore, MD: Johns Hopkins University Press.

McLanahan, S. (1999). Father absence and the welfare of children. In E. M. Hetherington (Ed.), *Coping with divorce, single parenting, and remarriage: A risk and resilience perspective* (pp. 117–145). Mahwah, NJ: Erlbaum.

McLellan, J. A., & Youniss, J. (2003). Two systems of youth service: Determinants of voluntary and required youth community service. *Journal of Youth and Adolescence, 32*, 47–58.

McMurray, B. (2007). Defusing the childhood vocabulary explosion. *Science, 317*, 631.

McNeil, N. (2014). A "change-resistance" account of children's difficulties understanding mathematical equivalence. *Child Development Perspectives, 8*, 42–47.

McQuade, J. D., Murray-Close, D., Shoulberg, E. K., & Hoza, B. (2013). Working memory and social functioning in children. *Journal of Experimental Child Psychology, 115*, 422–435.

Meaney, M. J. (2010). Epigenetics and the biological definition of gene x environment interactions. *Child Development, 81*, 41–79.

Medland, S. E., Duffy, D. L., Wright, M. J., Geffen, G. M., Hay, D. A., Levy, F., et al., (2009). Genetic influences on handedness: Data from 25,732 Australian and Dutch twin families. *Neuropsychologia, 47*, 330–337.

Medwell, J., & Wray, D. (2014). Handwriting automaticity: The search for performance thresholds. *Language and Education, 28*, 34–51.

Meeker, J. D., & Benedict, M. D. (2013). Infertility, pregnancy loss and adverse birth outcomes in relation to maternal secondhand tobacco smoke exposure. *Current Women's Health Reviews, 9*, 41–49.

Meeus, W., van de Schoot, R., Keijsers, L., Schwartz, S. J., & Branje, S. (2010). On the progression and stability of adolescent identity formation: A five-wave longitudinal study in early-to-middle and middle-to-late adolescence. *Child Development, 81*, 1565–1581.

Mehta, C. M., & Strough, J. (2009). Sex segregation in friendships and normative contexts across the life span. *Developmental Review, 29*, 201–220.

Melby, J. N., Conger, R. D., Fang, S., Wickrama, K. A. S., & Conger, K. J. (2008). Adolescent family experiences and educational attainment during early adulthood. *Developmental Psychology, 44*, 1519–1536.

Melby-Lervåg, M., Lyster, S. H., & Hulme, C. (2012). Phonological skills and their role in learning to read: A meta-analytic review. *Psychological Bulletin, 138*, 322–352.

Melnyk, L., Crossman, A. M., & Scullin, M. H. (2007). The suggestibility of children's memory. In M. P. Toglia, J. D. Read, D. F. Ross, & R. C. L. Lindsay (Eds.), *Handbook of eyewitness psychology, Vol. I: Memory for events.* Mahwah, NJ: Erlbaum.

Meltzoff, A. N. (1995). Understanding the intentions of others: Re-enactment of intended acts by 18-month-old children. *Developmental Psychology, 31*, 838–850.

Mendle, J., & Ferrero, J. (2012). Detrimental psychological outcomes associated with pubertal timing in adolescent boys. *Developmental Review, 32*, 49–66.

Mendle, J., Turkheimer, E., & Emery, R. E. (2007). Detrimental psychological outcomes associated with early pubertal timing in adolescent girls. *Developmental Review, 27*, 151–171.

Mennella, J., & Beauchamp, G. K. (1997). The ontogeny of human flavor perception. In G. K. Beauchamp & L. Bartoshuk (Eds.), *Tasting and smelling. Handbook of perception and cognition.* San Diego, CA: Academic Press.

Mennella, J. A., & Beauchamp, G. K. (1996). The human infant's response to vanilla flavors in mother's milk and formula. *Infant Behavior and Development, 19*, 13–19.

Mennella, J. A., Jagnow, C. P., & Beauchamp, G. K. (2001). Prenatal and postnatal flavor learning by human infants. *Pediatrics, 107*, e88.

Metcalfe, J. S., McDowell, K., Chang, T.-Y., Chen, L.-C., Jeka, J. J., & Clark, J. E. (2005). Development of somatosensory-motor integration: An event-related analysis of infant posture in the first year of independent walking. *Developmental Psychobiology, 46*, 19–35.

Mezulis, A., Salk, R. H., Hyde, J. S., Priess-Groben, H. A., & Simonson, J. L., (2014). Affective, biological, and cognitive predictors of depressive symptom trajectories in adolescence. *Journal of Abnormal Child Psychology, 42*, 539–550.

Miceli, P. J., Whitman, T. L., Borkowsky, J. G., Braungart-Riekder, J., & Mitchell, D. W. (1998). Individual differences in infant information processing: The role of temperamental and maternal factors. *Infant Behavior and Development, 21*, 119–136.

Michaud, S. (2001). The national longitudinal survey of children and youth: Overview and changes after three cycles. *Canadian Studies in Population, 28*(2), 391–405.

Midgette, E., Haria, P., & MacArthur, C. (2008). The effects of content and audience awareness goals for revision on the persuasive essays of fifth- and eighth-grade students. *Reading and Writing, 21*, 131–151.

Miga, E. M., Gdula, J. A., & Allen, J. P. (2012). Fighting fair: Adaptive marital conflict strategies as predictors of future adolescent peer and romantic relationship quality. *Social Development, 21*, 443–460.

Milberger, S., Biederman, J., Faraone, S. V., Guite, J., & Tsuang, M. T. (1997). Pregnancy, delivery and infancy complication, and attention deficit hyperactivity disorder: Issues of gene–environment interaction. *Biological Psychiatry, 41*, 65–75.

Miles, S. B., & Stipek, D. (2006). Contemporaneous and longitudinal associations between social behavior and literacy achievement in a sample of low-income elementary school children. *Child Development, 77*, 103–117.

Miller, D. I., & Halpern, D. F. (2014). The new science of cognitive sex differences. *Trends in Cognitive Sciences, 18*, 37–45.

Miller, G. A. (1956). The magical number 7, plus or minus two: Some limits on our capacity for processing information. *Psychological Review, 63*, 81–97.

Miller, G. E., & Chen, E. (2010). Harsh family climate in early life presages the emergence of proinflammatory phenotype in adolescence. *Psychological Science, 21,* 848–856.

Miller, J. G., & Bersoff, D. M. (1992). Culture and moral judgment: How are conflicts between justice and interpersonal responsibilities resolved? *Journal of Personality and Social Psychology, 62,* 541–554.

Miller, K. F., Smith, C. M., Zhu, J., & Zhang, H. (1995). Preschool origins of cross-national differences in mathematical competence: The role of number-naming systems. *Psychological Science, 6,* 56–60.

Miller, P. H. (2011). Piaget's theory: Past, present, and future. In U. Goswami (Ed.), *The Wiley-Blackwell handbook of childhood cognitive development* (2nd ed., pp. 649–672). Chichester, UK: Wiley-Blackwell.

Miller, P. M., Danaher, D. L., & Forbes, D. (1986). Sex-related strategies of coping with interpersonal conflict in children aged five to seven. *Developmental Psychology, 22,* 543–548.

Miller, S. A. (2009). Children's understanding of second-order mental states. *Psychological Bulletin, 135,* 749–773.

Mills, C. M., & Keil, F. C. (2005). The development of cynicism. *Psychological Science, 16,* 385–390.

Mills-Koonce, W. R., Appleyard, K., Barnett, M., Deng, M., Putallaz, M., & Cox, M. (2011). Adult attachment style and stress as risk factors for early maternal sensitivity and negativity. *Infant Mental Health Journal, 32,* 277–285.

Milunsky, A. (2002). *Your genetic destiny: Know your genes, secure your health, and save your life.* Cambridge, MA: Perseus Publishing.

Minkler, M., & Fuller-Thomson, E. (2005). African American grandparents raising grandchildren: A national study using the Census 2000 American Community Survey. *Journals of Gerontology: Psychological Sciences and Social Sciences, 60B,* S82–S92.

Mischel, W. (1970). Sex-typing and socialization. In P. H. Mussen (Ed.), *Carmichaels' manual of child psychology* (Vol. 2). New York, NY: Wiley.

Mischel, W., & Ayduk, O. (2004). Willpower in a cognitive-affective processing system: The dynamics of delay of gratification. In R. F. Baumeister & K. D. Vohs (Eds.), *Handbook of self-regulation* (pp. 99–129). New York, NY: Guilford Press.

Mischel, W., & Ebbesen, E. (1970). Attention in delay of gratification. *Journal of Personality and Social Psychology, 16,* 329–337.

Mischel, W., Ayduk, O., Berman, M. G., Casey, B. J., Gotlib, I. H., Jonides, J., et al. (2011). "Willpower" over the life span: decomposing self-regulation. *Social Cognitive and Affective Neuroscience, 6,* 252–256.

Mix, K. S., Huttenlocher, J., & Levine, S. C. (2002). Multiple cues for quantification in infancy: Is number one of them? *Psychological Bulletin, 128,* 278–294.

Mize, J., & Ladd, G. W. (1990). A cognitive social-learning approach to social skill training with low-status preschool children. *Developmental Psychology, 26,* 388–397.

Mize, J., & Pettit, G. S. (1997). Mothers' social coaching, mother–child relationship style, and children's peer competence: Is the medium the message? *Child Development, 68,* 312–332.

Mize, J., Pettit, G. S., & Brown, E. G. (1995). Mothers' supervision of their children's peer play: Relations with beliefs, perceptions, and knowledge. *Developmental Psychology, 31,* 311–321.

Mizes, J., Scott, P., & Tonya, M. (1995). Eating disorders. In M. Hersen & R. T. Ammerman (Eds.), *Handbook of prevention and treatment with children and adolescents: Intervention in the real world context* (pp. 441–465). New York, NY: Wiley.

Moerk, E. L. (2000). *The guided acquisition of first language skills.* Westport, CT: Ablex.

Moffitt, T. E. (2005). The new look of behavioral genetics in developmental psychopathology: Gene-environment interplay in antisocial behaviors. *Psychological Bulletin, 131,* 533–554.

Moffitt, T. E., Arseneault, L., Belsky, D., Dickson, N., Hancox, R. J., Harrington, H., et al. (2011). A gradient of childhood self-control predicts health,

wealth, and public safety. *Proceedings of the National Academy of Sciences, 108,* 2693–2698.

Moffitt, T. E., Poulton, R., & Caspi, A. (2013). Lifelong impact of early self-control: Childhood self-discipline predicts adult quality of life. *American Scientist, 101,* 352–359.

Molfese, D. L., & Burger-Judisch, L. M. (1991). Dynamic temporal-spatial allocation of resources in the human brain: An alternative to the static view of hemisphere differences. In F. L. Ketterle (Ed.), *Cerebral laterality: Theory and research. The Toledo symposium.* Hillsdale, NJ: Erlbaum.

Molina, B. S. G., Hinshaw, S. P., Swanson, J. M., Arnold, L. E., Vitiello, B., Jensen, P. S., et al. (2009). The MTA at 8 years: Prospective follow-up of children treated for combined-type ADHD in a multisite study. *Journal of the American Academy of Child and Adolescent Psychiatry, 48,* 484–500.

Molloy, L. E., Gest, S. D., & Rulison, K. L. (2011). Peer influences on academic motivation: Exploring multiple methods of assessing youths' most "influential" peer relationships. *Journal of Early Adolescence, 31,* 13–40.

Monahan, K. C., Lee, J. M., & Steinberg, L. (2011). Revisiting the impact of part-time work on adolescent adjustment: Distinguishing between selection and socialization using propensity score matching. *Child Development, 82,* 96–112.

Monahan, K. C., Steinberg, L., & Cauffman, E. (2013). Age differences in the impact of employment on antisocial behavior. *Child Development, 84,* 791–801.

Mondloch, C. J., Lewis, T. L., Budreau, D. R., Maurer, D., Dannemiller, J. L., Stephens, B. R., et al. (1999). Face perception during early infancy. *Psychological Science, 10,* 419–422.

Money, J., & Ehrhardt, A. A. (1972). *Man and woman, boy and girl.* Baltimore, MD: Johns Hopkins University Press.

Monk, C., Fifer, W. P., Myers, M. M., Sloan, R. P., Trien, L., & Hurtado, A. (2000). Maternal stress responses and anxiety during pregnancy: Effects on fetal heart rate. *Developmental Psychobiology, 36,* 67–77.

Monk, C., Georgieff, M. K., & Osterholm, E. A. (2013). Research review: Maternal prenatal distress and poor nutrition—mutually influencing risk factors affecting infant neurocognitive development. *Journal of Child Psychology and Psychiatry, 54,* 115–130.

Monk, C., Spicer, J., & Champagne, F. A. (2012). Linking prenatal adversity to developmental outcomes in infants: The role of epigenetic pathways. *Development and Psychopathology, 24,* 1361–1376.

Montague, D. P., & Walker-Andrews, A. S. (2001). Peek-aboo: A new look at infants' perception of emotion expressions. *Developmental Psychology, 37,* 826–838.

Montgomery, D. L. (2006). Physiological profile of professional hockey players—a longitudinal comparison. *Applied Physiology and Nutritional Metabolism, 31,* 181–185.

Moore, C. F. (2003). *Silent scourge: Children, pollution, and why scientists disagree.* New York, NY: Oxford University Press.

Moore, K. L., Persaud, T. V. N., & Torchia, M. G. (2012). *Before we are born: Essentials of embryology and birth defects* (8th ed.). Philadelphia, PA: W. B. Saunders.

Moore, M. R., & Brooks-Gunn, J. (2002). Adolescent parenthood. In M. H. Bornstein (Ed.), *Handbook of parenting: Vol. 3: Being and becoming a parent* (2nd ed., pp. 173–214). Mahwah, NJ: Erlbaum.

Moreno, A. J., Klute, M. M., & Robinson, J. L. (2008). Relational and individual resources as predictors of empathy in early childhood. *Social Development, 17,* 613–637.

Morgan, B., & Gibson, K. R. (1991). Nutritional and environmental interactions in brain development. In K. R. Gibson & A. C. Peterson (Eds.), *Brain maturation and cognitive development: Comparative and cross-cultural perspectives.* New York, NY: Aldine De Gruyter.

Morgane, P. J., Austin-LaFrance, R., Bronzino, J. D., Tonkiss, J., Diaz-Cintra, S., et al. (1993). Prenatal

malnutrition and development of the brain. *Neuroscience and Biobehavioral Reviews, 17,* 91–128.

Morrissey, T. W. (2009). Multiple child-care arrangements and young children's behavioral outcomes. *Child Development, 80,* 59–76.

Morrongiello, B. A., & Schell, S. L. (2010). Child injury: The role of supervision. *American Journal of Lifestyle Medicine, 4,* 65–74.

Morrongiello, B. A., Klemencic, N., & Corbett, M. (2008). Interactions between child behavior patterns and parent supervision: Implications for children's risk of unintentional injury. *Child Development, 79,* 627–638.

Morrow, J. R., Martin, S. B., Welk, G. J., Zhu, W., & Meredith, M. D. (2010). Overview of the Texas Youth Fitness Study. *Research Quarterly for Exercise and Sport, 81,* S1–S5.

Mortimer, J. T., & Staff, J. (2004). Early work as a source of developmental discontinuity during the transition to adulthood. *Development and Psychopathology, 16,* 1047–1070.

Morton, J., & Johnson, M. H. (1991). CONSPEC and CONLERN: A two-process theory of infant face recognition. *Psychological Review, 98,* 164–181.

Moses, L. J., Baldwin, D. A., Rosicky, J. G., & Tidball, G. (2001). Evidence for referential understanding in the emotions domain at twelve and eighteen months. *Child Development, 72,* 718–735.

Moss, E., Cyr, C., Bureau, J.-F., Tarabulsy, G. M., & Dubois-Comtois, K. (2005). Stability of attachment during the preschool period. *Developmental Psychology, 41,* 773–783.

Moss, E., Smolla, N., Guerra, I., Mazzarello, T., Chayer, D., & Berthiaume, C. (2006). Attachement et problèmes de comportements intériorisés et extériorisés auto-rapportés á la période scolaire [Attachment and self-reported internalizing and externalizing behavior problems in school-age children]. *Canadian Journal of Behavioural Science, 38,* 142–157.

Mountain, J. L., & Risch, N. (2004). Assessing genetic contributions to phenotypic differences among "racial" and "ethnic" groups. *Nature Genetics, 36*(Suppl. 11), S48–S53.

Mounts, N. S. (2011). Parental management of peer relationships and early adolescents' social skills. *Journal of Youth and Adolescence, 40,* 416–427.

Mowatt, F. (1970/1973). *The Siberians.* Trowbridge, Wiltshire, UK: Redwood Press.

Mueller, C. M., & Dweck, C. S. (1998). Praise for intelligence can undermine children's motivation and performance. *Journal of Personality and Social Psychology, 75*(1), 33–52.

Mueller, M. M., & Elder, G. H. (2003). Family contingencies across the generations: Grandparent-grandchild relationships in holistic perspective. *Journal of Marriage and the Family, 65,* 404–417.

Mukherjee, R. A. S., Hollins, S., & Turk, J. (2006). Fetal alcohol spectrum disorder: An overview. *Journal of the Royal Society of Medicine, 99,* 298–302.

Murphy, N., & Messer, D. (2000). Differential benefits from scaffolding and children working alone. *Educational Psychology, 20,* 17–31.

Murray-Close, D., Hoza, B., Hinshaw, S. P., Arnold, L. E., Swanson, J., Jensen, P. S., et al. (2010). Developmental processes in peer problems of children with attention-deficit/hyperactivity disorder in the Multimodal Treatment Study of Children with ADHD: Developmental cascades and vicious cycles. *Development and Psychopathology, 22,* 785–802.

Mustanski, B. S., Viken, R. J., Kaprio, J., Pulkkinen, L., & Rose, R. J. (2004). Genetic and environmental influences on pubertal development: Longitudinal data from Finnish twins at ages 11 and 14. *Developmental Psychology, 40,* 1188–1198.

Muter, V., Hulme, C., Snowling, M. J., & Stevenson, J. (2004). Phonemes, rimes, vocabulary, and grammatical skills as foundations of early reading development: Evidence from a longitudinal study. *Developmental Psychology, 40,* 663–681.

Nadig, A. S., & Sedivy, J. C. (2002). Evidence of perspective-taking constraints in children's on-line reference resolution. *Psychological Science, 13*, 329–336.

Nahar, B., Hossain, M. I., Hamadani, J. D., Ahmed, T., Huda, S. N., Grantham-McGregor, S. M., et al. (2012). Effects of a community-based approach of food and psychosocial stimulation on growth and development of severely malnourished children in Bangladesh: A randomised trial. *European Journal of Clinical Nutrition, 66*, 701–709.

Naigles, L. G., & Gelman, S. A. (1995). Overextensions in comprehension and production revisited: Preferential-looking in a study of dog, cat, and cow. *Journal of Child Language, 22*, 19–46.

Nancekivell, S. E., Van de Vondervoort, J., & Friedman, O. (2013). Young children's understanding of ownership. *Child Development Perspectives, 7*, 243–247.

Nangle, D. W., Erdley, C. A., Zeff, K. R., Staunchfield, L. L., & Gold, J. A. (2004). Opposites do not attract: Social status and behavioral-style concordances and discordances among children and peers who like or dislike them. *Journal of Abnormal Child Psychology, 32*, 425–434.

Narayan, A. J., Englund, M. M., & Egeland, B. (2013). Developmental timing and continuity of exposure to interparental violence and externalizing behavior as prospective predictors of dating violence. *Development and Psychopathology, 25*, 973–990.

Nation, K., Adams, J. W., Bowyer-Crane, C. A., & Snowling, M. J. (1999). Working memory deficits in poor comprehenders reflect underlying language impairments. *Journal of Experimental Child Psychology, 73*, 139–158.

Nation, K., Cocksey, J., Taylor, J. S. H., & Bishop, D. V. M. (2010). A longitudinal investigation of early reading and language skills in children with poor reading comprehension. *Journal of Child Psychology and Psychiatry, 51*, 1031–1039.

National Aboriginal Health Organization. (2004). Midwifery and Aboriginal midwifery in Canada. Retrieved from www.naho.ca/english/pdf/aboriginal_midwifery.pdf

National Association for Sport and Physical Fitness. (2004). *Appropriate practices for high school physical education.* Reston, VA: Author.

National Cancer Institute. (2006). *DES: Questions and Answers.* Washington DC: Author.

National Institutes of Health (NIH). (n.d.). Biography: Dr. Frances Kathleen Oldham Kelsey. Retrieved from www.nlm.nih.gov/changingthefaceofmedicine/physicians/biography_182.html

National Science Foundation. (2008). *Science and engineering indicators 2008.* Retrieved from www.nsf.gov/statistics/seind08

Nebesio, T. D., & Hirsch Pescovitz, O. (2005). Historical perspectives: Endocrine disruptors and the timing of puberty. *Endocrinologist, 15*, 44–48.

Neblett, E. W., Rivas-Drake, D., & Umaña-Taylor, A. J. (2012). The promise of racial and ethnic protective factors in promoting ethnic minority youth development. *Child Development Perspectives, 6*, 295–303.

Neiss, M. B., Sedikides, C., & Stevenson, J. (2006). Genetic influences on level and stability of self-esteem. *Self and Identity, 5*, 247–266.

Nelson, E. A. S., Schiefenhoevel, W., & Haimerl, F. (2000). Child care practices in nonindustrialized societies. *Pediatrics, 105*, e75.

Nelson, E. L., Campbell, J. M., & Michel, G. F. (2013). Unimanual to bimanual: Tracking the development of handedness from 6 to 24 months. *Infant Behavior and Development, 36*, 181–188.

Nelson, F. (1999). Lesbian families: Achieving motherhood. *Journal of Gay and Lesbian Social Services, 10*, 27–46.

Nelson, G., Westhues, A., & MacLeod, J. (2003). A meta-analysis of longitudinal research on preschool prevention programs for children. *Prevention and Treatment, 6.* doi.org/10.1037/1522-3736.6.1.631a

Nelson, I. A., & Gastic, B. (2009). Street ball, swim team and the sour cream machine: A cluster analysis of out of school time participation portfolios. *Journal of Youth and Adolescence, 38*, 1172–1186.

Nelson, K. (1973). Structure and strategy in learning to talk. *Monographs of the Society for Research in Child Development, 38*(Serial No. 149).

Nelson, K. (1993). Explaining the emergence of autobiographical memory in early childhood. In A. F. Collins & S. E. Gathercole (Eds.), *Theories of memory.* Hove, UK: Erlbaum.

Nelson, K., & Fivush, R. (2004). The emergence of autobiographical memory: A social cultural developmental theory. *Psychological Review, 111*, 486–511.

Nesdale, D. (2001). The development of prejudice in children. In M. A. Augoustinos & K. J. Reynolds (Eds.), *Understanding prejudice, racism, and social conflict* (pp. 57–73). London, UK: Sage.

Nesdale, D., Maass, A., Durkin, K., & Griffiths, J. (2005). Group norms, threat, and children's ethnic racial prejudice. *Child Development, 76*, 652–663.

Nevid, J. S., Rathus, S. A., & Greene, B. (2003). *Abnormal psychology in a changing world* (5th ed.). Upper Saddle River, NJ: Prentice Hall.

Neville, H. J., Stevens, C., Pakulak, E., Bell, T. A., Fanning, J., Klein, S., et al. (2013). Family-based training program improves brain function, cognition, and behavior in lower socioeconomic status preschoolers. *PNAS, 110*, 12138–12143.

Newcomb, A. F., & Bagwell, C. L. (1995). Children's friendship relations: A meta-analytic review. *Psychological Bulletin, 117*, 306–347.

Newcombe, N. (2013). Cognitive development: Changing views of cognitive change. *WIREs Cognitive Science, 4*, 479–491.

Newcombe, N. S. (2002). The nativist-empiricist controversy in the context of recent research on spatial and quantitative development. *Psychological Science, 13*, 395–401.

Newkirk, D., Klima, E., Pedersen, C. C., & Bellugi, U. (1980). Linguistic evidence from slips of the hand. In V. Fromkin (Ed.), *Errors in linguistic performance: Slips of the tongue, ear, pen, and hand* (pp. 165–198). New York, NY: Academic Press.

Newman, G. E., & Keil, F. C. (2008). Where is the essence? Developmental shifts in children's beliefs about internal features. *Child Development, 79*, 1344–1356.

Newman, R., Ratner, N. B., Jusczyk, A. M., Jusczyk, P. W., & Dow, K. A. (2006). Infants' early ability to segment the conversational speech signal predicts later language development: A retrospective analysis. *Developmental Psychology, 42*, 643–655.

Newport, E. L. (1991). Contrasting conceptions of the critical period for language. In S. Carey & R. Gelman (Eds.), *The epigenesis of mind: Essays on biology and cognition* (pp. 111–130). Hillsdale, NJ: Erlbaum.

Ngon, C., Martin, A., Dupoux, E., Cabrol, D., Dutat, M., & Peperkamp, S. (2013). (Non)words, (non)words, (non)words: Evidence for a protolexicon during the first year of life. *Developmental Science, 16*, 24–34.

Nguyen, M. (2011). Closing the education gap: A case for Aboriginal early childhood education in Canada, a look at the Aboriginal Head Start program. *Canadian Journal of Education, 34*(3), 229–248.

Ni, Y., Chiu, M. M., & Cheng, Z-J. (2010). Chinese children learning mathematics: From home to school. In M. H. Bond (Ed.), *Oxford handbook of Chinese psychology* (pp. 143–154). New York, NY: Oxford University Press.

NICHD Early Child Care Research Network. (1997). The effects of infant child care on infant–mother attachment security: Results of the NICHD Study of Early Child Care. *Child Development, 68*, 860–879.

NICHD Early Child Care Research Network. (2001). Child-care and family predictors of preschool attachment and stability from infancy. *Developmental Psychology, 37*, 847–862.

NICHD Early Child Care Research Network. (2002). Child-care structure-process-outcome: Direct and indirect effects of child-care quality on young children's development. *Psychological Science, 13*, 199–206.

Nicoladis, E. (2006). Cross-linguistic transfer in adjective-noun strings by preschool bilingual children. *Bilingualism: Language and Cognition 9*(1), 15–32.

Nilsen, E. S., & Graham, S. A. (2012). The development of preschoolers' appreciation of communicative ambiguity. *Child Development, 83*, 1400–1415.

Nilsen, P. (2007). The how and why of community-based injury prevention: A conceptual and evaluation model. *Safety Science, 45*, 501–521.

NINDS. (2009). *Autism fact sheet* (NIH Publication No. 09-1877). Washington DC: Author.

Nisbett, R. E., Aronson, J., Clair, C., Dickens, W., Flynn, J., Halpern, D. F., et al. (2012). Intelligence: New findings and theoretical developments. *American Psychologist, 67*, 130–159.

Nishida, T. K., & Lillard, A. S. (2007). The informative value of emotional expressions: "Social referencing" in mother–child pretense. *Developmental Science, 10*, 205–212.

Nishina, A., & Juvonen, J. (2005). Daily reports of witnessing and experiencing peer harassment in middle school. *Child Development, 76*, 435–450.

Nolen, S. (2003, November 29). No rest for the wicked, no peace for the dead. *Globe and Mail*, pp. A1, A24.

Nolen, S. (2009, September 12). Land of the rising son. *Globe and Mail*, pp. F6–F7.

Nordine, J., Krajcik, J., & Fortus, D. (2011). Transforming energy instruction in middle school to support integrated understanding and future learning. *Science Education, 95*, 670–699.

Norlander, T., Erixon, A., & Archer, T. (2000). Psychological androgyny and creativity: Dynamics of gender-role and personality trait. *Social Behavior and Personality, 28*(5), 423–435.

Notaro, P. C., Gelman, S. A., & Zimmerman, M. A. (2001). Children's understanding of psychogenic bodily reactions. *Child Development, 72*, 444–459.

Novin, S., Rieffe, C., Banerjee, R., Miers, A. C., & Cheung, J. (2011). Anger response styles in Chinese and Dutch children: A socio-cultural perspective on anger regulation. *British Journal of Developmental Psychology, 29*, 806–822.

Nucci, L., & Gingo, M. (2011). The development of moral reasoning. In U. Goswami (Ed.), *The Wiley-Blackwell handbook of childhood cognitive development* (2nd ed., pp. 420–445). Chichester, UK: Wiley.

Nucci, L., & Weber, E. (1995). Social interactions in the home and the development of young children's conception of the personal. *Child Development, 66*, 1438–1452.

Nuñez, J., Sr. & Yonas, A. (1994). Effects of luminance and texture motion on infant defensive reactions to optical collision. *Infant Behavior and Development, 17*, 165–174.

Nunes, T., Bryant, P., & Barros, R. (2012). The development of word recognition and its significance for comprehension and fluency. *Journal of Educational Psychology, 104*, 959–973.

Nurmsoo, E., & Bloom, P. (2008). Preschoolers' perspective taking in word learning: Do they blindly follow eye gaze? *Psychological Science, 19*, 211–215.

Nyaradi, A., Li, J., Hickling, S., Foster, J., & Oddy, W. H. (2013). The role of nutrition in children's neurocognitive development, from pregnancy through childhood. *Frontiers in Human Neuroscience, 7*, Article 97.

O'Brien, T. (2013). Gene therapy for Type 1 diabetes moves a step closer to reality. *Diabetes, 62*, 1396–1397.

O'Conner, T., Heron, J., Golding, J., Beveridge, M., & Glover, V. (2002). Maternal antenatal anxiety and children's behavioural/emotional problems at 4 years. *British Journal of Psychiatry, 180*, 502–508.

O'Doherty, K., Troseth, G. L., Shimpi, P. M., Goldenberg, E., Akhtar, N., & Saylor, M. M. (2011). Third-party social interaction and word learning from video. *Child Development, 82*, 902–915.

O'Grady, K., Deussing, M-A., Scerbina, T., Fung, K., & Muhe, N. (2016). *Measuring up: Canadian Results of the OECD PISA Study.* Council of Ministers of Education - Canada, Toronto, ON, Author.

O'Hara, M. W. (2009). Postpartum depression: What we know. *Journal of Clinical Psychology, 65,* 1258–1269.

O'Hara, M. W., & McCabe, J. E. (2013). Postpartum depression: Current status and future directions. *Annual Review of Clinical Psychology, 9,* 379–407.

O'Neill, D. K. (1996). Two-year-old children's sensitivity to a parent's knowledge state when making requests. *Child Development, 67,* 659–677.

Oakhill, J. V., & Cain, K. (2012). The precursors of reading ability in young readers: Evidence from a four-year longitudinal study. *Scientific Studies of Reading, 16,* 91–121.

Oakhill, J. V., & Cain, K. E. (2004). The development of comprehension skills. In T. Nunes & P. E. Bryant (Eds.), *Handbook of children's literacy* (pp. 155–180). Dordrecht, The Netherlands: Kluwer Academic Publishers.

Oaten, M., Stevenson, R. J., & Case, T. I. (2009). Disgust as a disease-avoidance mechanism. *Psychological Bulletin, 135,* 303–321.

Odgers, C. L., Moffitt, T. E., Tach, L. M., Sampson, R. J., Taylor, A., Matthews, C. L., et al. (2009). The protective effects of neighborhood collective efficacy on British children growing up in deprivation: A developmental analysis. *Developmental Psychology, 45,* 942–957.

OECD - Social Policy Division - Directorate of Employment, Labour and Social Affairs (2013). *Family violence.* Retrieved from www.oecd.org/els/soc/SF3_4_Family_violence_Jan2013.pdf

Offer, D., Ostrov, E., Howard, K. I., & Atkinson, R. (1988). *The teenage world: Adolescents' self-image in ten countries.* New York, NY: Plenum.

Ojanen, T., & Perry, D. G. (2007). Relational schemas and the developing self: Perceptions of mother and of self as joint predictors of early adolescents' self-esteem. *Developmental Psychology, 43,* 1474–1483.

Okagaki, L., & Frensch, P. A. (1994). Effects of video game playing on measures of spatial performance: Gender effects in late adolescence. *Journal of Applied Developmental Psychology, 15,* 33–58.

Okami, P., Weisner, T., & Olmstead, R. (2002). Outcome correlates of parent–child bedsharing: An eighteen-year longitudinal study. *Developmental and Behavioral Pediatrics, 23,* 244–253.

Olineck, K. & Poulin-Dubois, D. (2009). Infants' understanding of intention from 10 to 14 months: Interrelations among visual attention and imitation tasks. *Infant Behavior and Development, 32,* 404–415.

Oliner, S. P., & Oliner, P. M. (1988). *The altruistic personality: Rescuers of Jews in Nazi Europe.* New York, NY: Free Press.

Olinghouse, N. G. (2008). Student- and instruction-level predictors of narrative writing in third-grade students. *Reading and Writing, 21,* 3–26.

Olson, S. L., Lopez-Duran, N., Lunkenheimer, E. S., Chang, H., & Sameroff, A. J. (2011). Individual differences in the development of early peer aggression: Integrating contributions of self-regulation, theory of mind, and parenting. *Development and Psychopathology, 23,* 253–266.

Olson, S. L., Sameroff, A. J., Kerr, D. C. R., Lopez, N. L., & Wellman, H. M. (2005). Developmental foundations of externalizing problems in young children: The role of effortful control. *Development and Psychopathology, 17,* 25–45.

Online Mendelian Inheritance in Man. (2013). Nathans Institute of Genetic Medicine, Johns Hopkins University (Baltimore, MD). Retrieved from http://omim.org/

Ontario Association of Children's Aid Societies. (2000). Court upholds the constitutionality of Section 43 of the Canadian Criminal Code. *OACAS Journal, 44,* 3–4.

Ontario Ministry of Children and Youth Services. (2016). *Can your baby hear?* Retrieved from www.children.gov.on.ca/htdocs/English/earlychildhood/hearing/brochure_hear.aspx

Ontario Ministry of Education. (2000). Individual education plans: Standards for development, program planning, and implementation 2000. Retrieved from www.edu.gov.on.ca/eng/general/elemsec/speced/iep/iep.html

Ontario Ministry of Education. (2004). The individual education plan (IEP): A resource guide. Retrieved from www.edu.gov.on.ca/eng/general/elemsec/speced/guide/resource/iepresguid.pdf

Ontario Ministry of Health and Long-Term Care. (2016). Fertility services: Ontario's fertility program. Retrieved from www.health.gov.on.ca/en/public/programs/ivf/

Ontario Ministry of Transportation. (2012). Safe & secure: Choosing the right car seat for your child. Retrieved from www.mto.gov.on.ca/english/safety/carseat/choose.shtml

Ontario Network of Women in Engineering (ONWiE). (2015). *Go Eng Girl/GÉNIales, les filles.* Retrieved from www.onwie.ca/programs/go-eng-girl

Opfer, J. E., & Gelman, S. A. (2011). Development of the animate-inanimate distinction. In U. Goswami (Ed.), *The Wiley-Blackwell handbook of childhood cognitive development* (2nd ed., pp. 213–238). Chichester, UK: Wiley-Blackwell.

Opfer, J. E., & Siegler, R. S. (2004). Revisiting preschoolers' living things concept: A microgenetic analysis of conceptual change in basic biology. *Cognitive Psychology, 49,* 301–332.

Opfer, J. E., & Siegler, R. S. (2007). Representational change and children's numerical estimation. *Cognitive Psychology, 55,* 169–195.

Opfer, J. E., & Siegler, R. S. (2012). Development of quantitative thinking. In K. Holyoak & R. Morrison (Eds.), *Oxford handbook of thinking and reasoning* (pp. 585–605). New York, NY: Oxford University Press.

Opler, M. G. A., & Susser, E. S. (2005). Fetal environment and schizophrenia. *Environmental Health Perspectives, 113*(9), 1239–1242.

Oppliger, P. A. (2007). Effects of gender stereotyping on socialization. In R. W. Preiss, B. M. Gayle, N. Burrell, M. Allen, & J. Bryant (Eds.), *Mass media effects research: Advances through meta-analysis* (pp. 199–214). Mahwah, NJ: Erlbaum.

Organisation for Economic Co-operation and Development. (OECD). (2010). PISA 2009 assessment framework—Key competencies in reading, mathematics and science. Paris: Author.

Organisation for Economic Co-operation and Development (OECD). (2016). *PISA 2015 Results in Focus* Paris: Author. Retrieved from www.oecd.org/pisa/pisa-2015-results-in-focus.pdf

Organisation for Economic Co-operation and Development. (2006). *Starting strong II: Early childhood education and care.* Paris: OECD Publishing.

Ornstein, P. A., Coffman, J., Grammer, J., San Souci, P., & McCall, L. (2010). Linking the classroom context and the development of children's memory skills. In J. L. Meece & J. S. Eccles (Eds.), *Handbook of research on schools, schooling, and human development* (pp. 42–59). New York, NY: Routledge.

Orth, U., Robins, R. W., Widaman, K. F., & Conger, R. D. (2014). Is low self-esteem a risk factor for depression? Findings from a longitudinal study of Mexican-origin youth. *Developmental Psychology, 50,* 622–633.

Ostrov, J. M., & Godleski, S. A. (2010). Toward an integrated gender-linked model of aggression subtypes in early and middle childhood. *Psychological Review, 117,* 233–242.

Oswald, F. L., & Hough, L. (2012). I-O 2.0 from Intelligence 1.5: Staying (just) behind the cutting edge of intelligence theories. *Industrial and Organizational Psychology: Perspectives on Science and Practice, 5,* 172–175.

Oude Luttikhuis, H., Baur, L., Jansen, H., Shrewsbury, V. A., O'Malley, C., Stolk, R. P., et al. (2009). Interventions for treating obesity in children. *Cochrane Database of Systematic Reviews, 3,* 1–57.

Ouellet-Morin, I., Wong, C. C. Y., Danese, A., Pariante, C. M., Papdopoulous, A. S., Mill, J. et al. (2013). Increased serotonin transport gene (SERT) DNA methylation is associated with bullying victimization and blunted cortisol response to stress in childhood: A longitudinal study of discordant monozygotic twins. *Psychological Medicine, 43,* 1813–1823.

Over, H., & Carpenter, M. (2009). Eighteen-month-old infants show increased helping following priming with affiliation. *Psychological Science, 20,* 1189–1193.

Owen-Kostelnik, J., Reppucci, N. D., & Meyer, J. R. (2006). Testimony and interrogation of minors: Assumptions about maturity and morality. *American Psychologist, 61,* 286–304.

Padilla, A. M., Lindholm, K. J., Chen, A., Duran, R., Hakuta, K., Lambert, W., et al. (1991). The English-only movement. Myths, reality, and implications for psychology. *American Psychologist, 46,* 120–130.

Pahlke, E., Bigler, R. S., & Martin, C. L. (2014). Can fostering children's ability to challenge sexism improve critical analysis, internalization, and enactment of inclusive, egalitarian peer relationships? *Journal of Social Issues, 70,* 115–133.

Paquette, D. (2004). Theorizing the father-child relationship: Mechanisms and developmental outcomes. *Human Development, 47,* 193–219.

Parault, S. J., & Schwanenflugel, P. J. (2000). The development of conceptual categories of attention during the elementary school years. *Journal of Experimental Child Psychology, 75,* 245–262.

Parcel, G. S., Simons-Morton, B. G., O'Hara, N. M., Baranowski, T., Kolbe, L. J., & Bee, D. E. (1989). School promotion of healthful diet and exercise behavior: An integration of organizational change and social learning theory interventions. *Journal of School Health, 57,* 150–156.

Park, G., Lubinski, D., & Benbow, C. P. (2008). Ability differences among people who have commensurate degrees matter for scientific creativity. *Psychological Science, 19,* 957–961.

Parke, R. D. (2002). Fathers and families. In M. H. Bornstein (Ed.), *Handbook of parenting; Vol. 3. Being and becoming a parent* (pp. 27–73). Mahwah, NJ: Erlbaum.

Parke, R. D. (2004). The Society for Research in Child Development at 70: Progress and promise. *Child Development, 75,* 1–24.

Parke, R. D., & Buriel, R. (1998). Socialization in the family: Ethnic and ecological perspectives. In W. Damon (Ed.), *Handbook of child psychology* (Vol. 3). New York, NY: Wiley.

Parke, R. D., & O'Neil, R. (2000). The influence of significant others on learning about relationships: From family to friends. In R. S. L. Mills & S. Duck (Eds.), *The developmental psychology of personal relationships* (pp. 15–47). New York, NY: Wiley.

Parker, J. G., Low, C. M., Walker, A. R., & Gamm, B. K. (2005). Friendship jealousy in young adolescents: Individual differences and links to sex, self-esteem, aggression, and social adjustment. *Developmental Psychology, 41,* 235–250.

Parker, J. D. A., Saklofske, D. H., Shaughnessy, P. A., Huang, S. H. S., Wood, L. M., & Eastabrook, J. M. (2005). Generalizability of the emotional intelligence construct: A cross-cultural study of North American Aboriginal youth. *Personality and Individual Differences, 39,* 215–227.

Parker, J. G., & Seal, J. (1996). Forming, losing, renewing, and replacing friendships: Applying temporal parameters to the assessment of children's friendship experiences. *Child Development, 67,* 2248–2268.

Parritz, R. H. (1996). A descriptive analysis of toddler coping in challenging circumstances. *Infant Behavior and Development, 19,* 171–180.

Partanen, E., Kujala, T., Naatanen, R., Liitola, A., Sambeth, A., & Houtilainen, M. (2013). Learning-induced neural plasticity of speech processing before birth. *Proceedings of the National Academy of Sciences (PNAS), 110,* 15145–15150.

Parten, M. (1932). Social participation among preschool children. *Journal of Abnormal and Social Psychology, 27,* 243–269.

Pascal, C. E. (2009). *With our best future in mind: Implementing early learning in Ontario.* Retrieved from https://dr6j45jk9xcmk.cloudfront.net/documents/89/earlylearningreporten.pdf

Pascalis, O., de Haan, M., & Nelson, C. A. (2002). Is face processing species-specific during the first year of life? *Science, 296,* 1321–1323.

Pascalis, O., Loevenbruck, H., Quinn, P., Kandel, S., Tanaka, J., & Lee, K. (2014). On the linkage between face processing, language processing, and narrowing during development. *Child Development Perspectives, 8,* 65–70.

Pascual, B., Aguardo, G., Sotillo, M., & Masdeu, J. C. (2008). Acquisition of mental state language in Spanish children: A longitudinal study of the relationship between the production of mental verbs and linguistic development. *Developmental Science, 11,* 454–466.

Pasterski, V. L., Geffner, M. E., Brain, C., Hindmarsh, P., Brook, C., & Hines, M. (2005). Prenatal hormones and postnatal socialization by parents as determinants of male-typical toy play in girls with congenital adrenal hyperplasia. *Child Development, 76,* 264–278.

Patterson, C. J. (2006). Children of lesbian and gay parents. *Current Directions in Psychological Science, 15,* 241–244.

Patterson, G. R. (1980). Mothers: The unacknowledged victims. *Monographs of the Society for Research in Child Development, 45*(5, Serial No. 186).

Patterson, G. R. (2008). A comparison of models for interstate wars and for individual violence. *Perspectives on Psychological Science, 3,* 203–223.

Patterson, M. M., & Bigler, R. S. (2006). Preschool children's attention to environmental messages about groups: Social categorization and the origins of intergroup bias. *Child Development, 77,* 847–860.

Pauker, K., Ambady, N., & Apfelbaum, E. P. (2010). Race salience and essentialist thinking in racial stereotype development. *Child Development, 81,* 1799–1813.

Pauletti, R. E., Menon, M., Menon, M., Tobin, D. D., & Perry, D. G. (2012). Narcissism and adjustment in preadolescence. *Child Development, 83,* 831–837.

Paulussen-Hoogeboom, M. C., Stams, G. J. J., Hermanns, J. M., & Peetsma, T. T. (2007). Child negative emotionality and parenting from infancy to preschool: A meta-analytic review. *Developmental Psychology, 43,* 438–453.

Paus, T. (2010). Growth of white matter in the adolescent brain: Myelin or axon? *Brain and Cognition, 72,* 26–35.

Peake, P. K., Hebl, M., & Mischel, W. (2002). Strategic attention deployment for delay of gratification in working and waiting situations. *Developmental Psychology, 38,* 313–326.

Pears, K. C., Kim, H. K., Fisher, P. A., & Yoerger, K. (2013). Early school engagement and late elementary outcomes for maltreated children in foster care. *Developmental Psychology, 49,* 2201–2211.

Pearson, J., & Wilkinson, L. (2013). Family relationships and adolescent well-being: Are families equally protective for same-sex attracted youth? *Journal of Youth and Adolescence, 42,* 376–393.

Pederson, D. R., Gleason, K. E., Moran, G., & Bento, S. (1998). Maternal attachment representations, maternal sensitivity, and the infant–mother attachment relationship. *Developmental Psychology, 34,* 925–933.

Pellicano, E. (2013). Testing the predictive power of cognitive atypicalities in autistic children: Evidence from a 3-year follow-up study. *Autism Research, 6,* 258–267

Pellis, S. M., & Pellis, V. C. (2007). Rough-and-tumble play and the development of the social brain. *Current Directions in Psychological Science, 16,* 95–98.

Peltola, M. J., Leppänen, J. M., Palokangas, T., & Hietanen, J. K. (2008). Fearful faces modulate looking duration and attention disengagement in 7-month-old infants. *Developmental Science, 11,* 60–68.

Pennisi, E. (2005). Why do humans have so few genes? *Science, 309,* 80.

Pepler, D. J., Craig, W. M., Connolly, J. A., Yuile, A., McMaster, L., & Jiang, D. (2006). A developmental perspective on bullying. *Aggressive Behavior, 32,* 376–384.

Pepler, D. J., Craig, W., & Roberts, W. L. (1998). Observations of aggressive and nonaggressive children on the school playground. *Merrill-Palmer Quarterly, 44,* 55–76.

Peritz, I. (2015, July 1). Medical heroine gets her due. *Globe and Mail,* pp. A1, A4.

Perkins, D. F., Jacobs, J. E., Barber, B. L., & Eccles, J. S. (2004). Childhood and adolescent sports participation as predictors of participation in sports and physical fitness activities during young adulthood. *Youth and Society, 35,* 495–520.

Peterson, C. (2012). Children's autobiographical memories across the years: Forensic implications of childhood amnesia and eyewitness memory for stressful events. *Developmental Review, 32,* 287–306.

Peterson, C. C., Wellman, H. M., & Slaughter, V. (2012). The mind behind the message: Advancing theory-of-mind scales for typically developing children, and those with deafness, autism, or Aspberger syndrome. *Child Development, 83,* 469–485.

Peterson, C., & Rideout, R. (1998). Memory for medical emergencies experienced by 1- and 2-year-olds. *Developmental Psychology, 34,* 1059–1072.

Peterson, L. (1983). Role of donor competence, donor age, and peer presence on helping in an emergency. *Developmental Psychology, 19,* 873–880.

Petrass, L. A., & Blitvich, J. D. (2013). Unobtrusive observation of caregiver-child pairs at public pools and playgrounds: Implications for child unintentional injury risk. *International Journal of Aquatic Research and Education, 7,* 204–213.

Pettit, G. S., Bates, J. E., & Dodge, K. A. (1997). Supportive parenting, ecological context, and children's adjustment: A seven-year longitudinal study. *Child Development, 68,* 908–923.

Pettito, L., Holowka, S., Sergio, L. E., Levy, B., & Ostry, D. J. (2004). Baby hands that move to the rhythm of language: Hearing babies acquiring sign languages babble silently on the hands. *Cognition, 93,* 43–73.

Pettito, L. A., Katerelos, M., Levy, B. G., Gauna, K., Tetreault, K., et al. (2001). Bilingual signed and spoken language acquisition from birth: Implications for the mechanisms underlying early bilingual language acquisition. *Journal of Child Language, 28,* 453–496.

Pettoni, A. N. (2011). Fetal alcohol effects. In S. Goldstein & J. A. Naglieri (Eds.), *Encyclopedia of child behavior and development* (pp. 649–650). New York, NY: Springer Science+Business Media.

Phinney, J. S. (2005). Ethnic identity development in minority adolescents. In C. B. Fisher & R. M. Lerner (Eds.), *Encyclopedia of applied developmental science* (Vol. 1, pp. 420–423). Thousand Oaks, CA: Sage.

Phipps, M. G., Rosengard, C., Weitzen, S., Meers, A., & Billinkoff, Z. (2008). Age group differences among pregnant adolescents: Sexual behavior, health habits, and contraceptive use. *Journal of Pediatric and Adolescent Gynecology, 21,* 9–15.

Piaget, J. (1929). *The child's conception of the world.* New York, NY: Harcourt, Brace.

Piaget, J. (1952/1963). *The origins of intelligence in children* (M. Cook, Trans.). New York, NY: Norton.

Piaget, J. (1962). *The moral judgement of the child.* New York, NY: Collier Books.

Piaget, J., & Inhelder, B. (1956). *The child's conception of space.* Boston, MA: Routledge & Kegan Paul.

Piaget, J., & Inhelder, B. (1969). *The psychology of the child* (H. Weaver, Trans.). New York, NY: Basic Books.

Pianta, R. C. (2007). Developmental science and education: The NICHD Study of Early Child Care and Youth Development findings from elementary school. In R. V. Kail (Ed.), *Advances in child development and*

behavior, *Vol. 35* (pp. 254–296). Amsterdam, The Netherlands: Elsevier.

Piasta, S. B., Justice, L. M., McGinty, A. S., & Kaderavek, J. N. (2012). Increasing young children's contact with print during shared reading: Longitudinal effects on literacy achievement. *Child Development, 83,* 810–820.

Picard, A. (2012, November 4). Where is Canada's apology? *Globe and Mail,* p. L6.

Piehler, T. F., & Dishion, T. J. (2007). Interpersonal dynamics within adolescent friendships: Dyadic mutuality, deviant talk, and patterns of antisocial behavior. *Child Development, 78,* 1611–1624.

Pina, A. A., Zerr, A. A., Gonzales, N. A., & Ortiz, C. D. (2009). Psychosocial interventions for school refusal behavior in children and adolescents. *Child Development Perspectives, 3,* 11–20.

Pinker, S. (1989). *Learnability and cognition: The acquisition of argument structure.* Cambridge, MA: MIT Press.

Plante, I., de la Sablonnière, R., Aronson, J. M., & Théorêt, M. (2013). Gender stereotype endorsement and achievement-related outcomes: The role of competence beliefs and task values. *Contemporary Educational Psychology, 38,* 225–235.

Plomin, R. (2013). Child development and molecular genetics: 14 years later. *Child Development, 84,* 104–120.

Plomin, R., & Petrill, S. A. (1997). Genetics and intelligence: What's new? *Intelligence, 24,* 53–77.

Plomin, R., & Spinath, F. (2004). Intelligence: Genes, genetics, and genomics. *Journal of Personality and Social Psychology, 86,* 112–129.

Plomin, R., DeFries, J. C., McClearn, G. E., & McGuffin, P. (2001). *Behavioral genetics* (4th ed.). New York, NY: Freeman.

Poehlmann, J., Schwichtenberg, A. J., Bolt, D. M., Hane, A., Burnson, C., & Winters, J. (2011). Infant physiological regulation and maternal risks as predictors of dyadic interaction trajectories in families with a preterm infant. *Developmental Psychology, 47,* 91–105.

Pollett, T. V., Nettle, D., & Nelissen, M. (2007). Maternal grandmothers do go the extra mile: Factoring distance and lineage into differential contact with grandchildren. *Evolutionary Psychology, 5,* 832–843.

Polman, J. L. (2004). Dialogic activity structures for project-based learning environment. *Cognition and Instruction, 22,* 431–466.

Pols, H. (2002). Between the laboratory and life: Child development research in Toronto, 1919–1956. *History of Psychology, 5,* 135–162.

Pomerantz, E. M., Ng, F. F., Cheung, C. S., & Qu, Y. (2014). Raising happy children who succeed in school: Lessons from China and the United States. *Child Development Perpsectives, 8,* 71–76.

Poole, D. A., & Bruck, M. (2012). Divining testimony? The impact of interviewing props on children's reports of touching. *Developmental Review, 32,* 165–180.

Poole, D. A., & Lindsay, D. S. (1995). Interviewing preschoolers: Effects of nonsuggestive techniques, parental coaching, and leading questions on reports of nonexperienced events. *Journal of Experimental Child Psychology, 60,* 129–154.

Popliger, M., Talwar, V., & Crossman, A. (2011). Predictors of children's prosocial lie-telling: Motivation, socialization variables, and moral understanding. *Journal of Experimental Child Psychology, 110,* 373–392.

Popp, D., Laursen, B., Kerr, M., Stattin, H., & Burk, W. K. (2008). Modeling homophily over time with an actor-partner interdependence model. *Developmental Psychology, 44,* 1028–1039.

Porath, A. J., & Fried, P. A. (2005). Effects of prenatal cigarette and marijuana exposure on drug use among offspring. *Neurotoxicity and Tertology, 27*(2), 267–277.

Porter, R. H. & Winberg, J. (1999). Unique salience of maternal breast odors for newborn infants. *Neuroscience & Biobehavioral Reviews, 23,* 439–449.

Posner, M. I., & Rothbart, M. K. (2007). Research on attention networks as a model for the integration of psychological science. *Annual Review of Psychology, 58,* 1–23.

Posner, M. I., Rothbart, M. K., Sheese, B. E., & Voelker, P. (2012). Control networks and neuromodulators of early development. *Developmental Psychology, 48,* 827–835.

Postman, N. (1982). *The Disappearance of Childhood.* New York, NY: Delacorte Press.

Poulin, F., & Boivin, M. (2000). The role of proactive and reactive aggression in the formation and development of boys' friendships. *Developmental Psychology, 36,* 233–240.

Poulin, F., & Chan, A. (2010). Friendship stability and change in childhood and adolescence. *Developmental Review, 30,* 257–272.

Poulin, F., & Pedersen, S. (2007). Developmental changes in gender composition of friendship networks in adolescent girls and boys. *Developmental Psychology, 43,* 1484–1496.

Poulin-Dubois, D., Serbin, L. A., Eichstedt, J. A., Sen, M. A., Beissel, C. F. (2002). Men don't put on make-up: Toddlers' knowledge of the gender stereotyping of household activities. *Social Development, 11*(2), 166–181.

Poulson, C. L., Kymissis, E., Reeve, K. F., Andreatos, M., & Reeve, L. (1991). Generalized vocal imitation in infants. *Journal of Experimental Child Psychology, 51,* 267–279.

Powers, C. J., Bierman, K. L., & The Conduct Problems Prevention Research Group (2013). The multifaceted impact of peer relations on aggressive-disruptive behavior in early elementary school. *Developmental Psychology, 49,* 1174–1186.

Powlishta, K., Serbin, L. A., Doyle, A., & White, D. R. (1994). Gender, ethnic, and body type biases: The generality of prejudice in childhood. *Developmental Psychology, 30,* 526–536.

Pratt, M. W., Hunsberger, B., Pancer, S. M., & Alisat, S. (2003). A longitudinal analysis of personal values socialization: Correlates of a moral self-ideal in late adolescence. *Social Development, 12,* 563–585. doi: 10.1111/1467-9507.00249

Prencipe, A., & Helwig, C. C. (2002). The development of reasoning about the teaching of values in school and family contexts. *Child Development, 73,* 841–856.

Pressley, M. (2002). *Reading instruction that works: The case for balanced teaching* (2nd ed.). New York, NY: Guilford Press.

Pressley, M., & Hilden, K. (2006). Cognitive strategies. In D. Kuhn & R. S. Siegler (Eds.), *Handbook of child psychology* (6th ed., Vol., 2., pp. 511–556). Hoboken, NJ: Wiley.

Price, T. S., Grosser, T., Plomin, R., & Jaffee, S. R. (2010). Fetal genotype for the xenobiotic metabolizing enzyme NQO1 influences intrauterine growth among infants whose mothers smoked during pregnancy. *Child Development, 81,* 101–114.

Priel, B., & deSchonen, S. (1986). Self-recognition: A study of a population without mirrors. *Journal of Experimental Child Psychology, 41,* 237–250.

Principe, G. F., & Ceci, S. J. (2002). I saw it with my own ears: The effects of peer conversations on preschoolers' reports of nonexperienced events. *Journal of Experimental Child Psychology, 83,* 1–25.

Principe, G. F., & Schindewolf, E. (2012). Natural conversations as a source of false memories in children: Implications for the testimony of young witnesses. *Developmental Review, 32,* 205–223.

Prinstein, M. J., & Cillessen, A. H. N. (2003). Forms and functions of adolescent peer aggression associated with high levels of peer status. *Merrill-Palmer Quarterly, 49,* 310–342.

Prinstein, M. J., & La Greca, A. M. (2004). Childhood peer rejection and aggression as predictors of adolescent girls' externalizing and health risk behaviors: A 6-year longitudinal study. *Journal of Consulting and Clinical Psychology, 72,* 103–112.

Protzko, J., Aronson, J., & Blair, C. (2013). How to make a young child smarter: Evidence from the Database of Raising Intelligence. *Perspectives on Psychological Science, 8,* 25–40.

Provins, K. A. (1997). Handedness and speech: A critical reappraisal of the role of genetic and environmental factors in the cerebral lateralization of function. *Psychological Review, 104,* 554–571.

Public Health Agency of Canada. (2010). *Canadian incidence study of reported child abuse and neglect– 2008: Major Findings.* Ottawa: Author. Retrieved from www.phac-aspc.gc.ca

Public Health Agency of Canada. (2015). *Data blog: Osteoporosis – the bone thief.* Retrieved from http://infobase.phac-aspc.gc.ca/datalab/osteo-blog-en.html-osteoporose/index-eng.php

Puhl, R. M., & Brownell, K. D. (2005). Bulimia nervosa. In C. B. Fisher & R. M. Lerner (Eds.), *Encyclopedia of applied developmental science* (Vol. 1, pp. 192–195). Thousand Oaks, CA: Sage.

Puhl, R. M., & Latner, J. D. (2007). Stigma, obesity, and the health of the nation's children. *Psychological Bulletin, 133,* 557–580.

Qin, L., Pomerantz, E. M., & Wang, Q. (2009). Are gains in decision-making autonomy during early adolescence beneficial for emotional functioning? The case of the United States and China. *Child Development, 80,* 1705–1721.

Quas, J. A., Goodman, G. S., Bidrose, S., Pipe, M., Craw, S., & Ablin, D. S. (1999). Emotion and memory: Children's long-term remembering, forgetting, and suggestibility. *Journal of Experimental Child Psychology, 72,* 235–270.

Quillian, L., & Campbell, M. E. (2003). Beyond black and white: The present and future of multiracial friendship segregation. *American Sociological Review, 68,* 540–566.

Quinn, P. H. (2004). Development of subordinate-level categorization in 3- to 7-month-old infants. *Child Development, 75,* 886–899.

Quinn, P. H. (2011). Born to categorize. In U. Goswami (Ed.), *The Wiley-Blackwell handbook of childhood cognitive development* (2nd ed., pp. 129–152). Chichester, UK: Wiley-Blackwell.

Raabe, T., & Beelmann, A. (2011). Development of ethnic, racial, and national prejudice in childhood and adolescence: A multinational meta-analysis of age differences. *Child Development, 82,* 1715–1737.

Racz, S. J., & McMahon, R. J. (2011). The relationship between parental knowledge and monitoring and child and adolescent conduct problems: A 10-year update. *Clinical Child and Family Psychology Review, 14,* 377–398.

Raedeke, T. D., & Smith, A. L. (2004). Coping resources and athlete burnout: An examination of stress mediated and moderation hypotheses. *Journal of Sport & Exercise Psychology, 26,* 525–541.

Rakic, P. (1995). Corticogenesis in human and nonhuman primates. In M. S. Gazzaniga (Ed.), *The cognitive neurosciences.* Cambridge, MA: MIT Press.

Rakison, D. H., & Hahn, E. R. (2004). The mechanisms of early categorization and induction: Smart or dumb infants? *Advances in Child Development and Behavior, 32,* 281–322.

Rakison, D. H., & Yermolayeva, Y. (2010). Infant categorization. *WIREs Cognitive Science, 1,* 894–905.

Rakoczy, H. (2008). Taking fiction seriously: Young children understand the normative structure of joint pretence games. *Developmental Psychology, 44,* 1195–1201.

Ralph, L. J., & Brindis, C. D. (2010). Access to reproductive healthcare for adolescents: Establishing healthy behaviors at a critical juncture in the lifecourse. *Current Opinion in Obstetrics and Gynecology, 22,* 369–374.

Ram, A., & Ross, H. S. (2001). Problem solving, contention, and struggle: How siblings resolve a conflict of interests. *Child Development, 72,* 1710–1722.

Ram, B., & Hou, F. (2005). Sex differences in the effects of family structure on children's aggressive behaviour. *Journal of Comparative Family Studies, 36*(2), 329–341.

Raman, L., & Gelman, S. A. (2005). Children's understanding of the transmission of genetic disorders and contagious illnesses. *Developmental Psychology, 41,* 171–182.

Ramey, C. T., & Landesman-Ramey, S. (2000). Intelligence and public policy. In R. J. Sternberg (Ed.), *Handbook of intelligence.* New York, NY: Cambridge University Press.

Rancourt, D., Conway, C. C., Burk, W. J., & Prinstein, M. J. (2013). Gender composition of preadolescents' friendship groups moderates peers socialization of body change behaviors. *Health Psychology, 32,* 283–292.

Ransjoe-Arvidson, A. B., Matthiesen, A. S., Lilja, G., Nissen, E., Widstroem, A. M., & Uvnaes-Moberg, K. (2001). Maternal analgesia during labor disturbs newborn behavior: Effects on breastfeeding, temperature, and crying. *Birth-Issues in Perinatal Care, 28,* 5–12.

Raskauskas, J., & Stoltz, A. D. (2007). Involvement in traditional and electronic bullying among adolescents. *Developmental Psychology, 43,* 564–575.

Rasmussen, C., & Bisanz, J. (2005). Representation and working memory in early arithmetic. *Journal of Experimental Child Psychology, 91,* 137–157.

Raudenbush, B., & Meyer, B. (2003). Muscular dissatisfaction and supplement use among male intercollegiate athletes. *Journal of Sport and Exercise Psychology, 25,* 161–170.

Rayner, K., Foorman, B. R., Perfetti, C. A., Pesetsky, D., & Seidenberg, M. S. (2001). How psychological science informs the teaching of reading. *Psychological Science in the Public Interest, 2,* 31–75.

Rayner, K., Foorman, B. R., Perfetti, C. A., Pesetsky, D., & Seidenberg, M. S. (2002). How should reading be taught? *Scientific American, 286,* 85–91.

Ready, D. D., & Wright, D. L. (2011). Accuracy and inaccuracy in teachers' perceptions of young children's cognitive abilities: The role of child background and classroom context. *American Educational Research Journal, 48,* 335–360.

Reese, E., & Cox, A. (1999). Quality of adult book reading affects children's emergent literacy. *Developmental Psychology, 35,* 20–28.

Reich, P. A. (1986). *Language development.* Englewood Cliffs, NJ: Prentice Hall.

Reichenberg, A., Gross, R., Weiser, M., Bresnahan, M., Silverman, J., Harlap, S., et al. (2006). Advancing paternal age and autism. *Archives of General Psychiatry, 63,* 1026–1032.

Reid, D. H., Wilson, P. G., & Faw, G. D. (1991). Teaching self-help skills. In J. L. Matson & J. A. Mulick (Eds.), *Handbook of mental retardation* (2nd ed.). New York, NY: Pergamon.

Reimer, M. S. (1996). "Sinking into the ground": The development and consequences of shame in adolescence. *Developmental Review, 16,* 321–363.

Reiter, B. A. (2004). The application of a WISC-III short form for screening gifted elementary students in Canada. *Canadian Journal of School Psychology, 19*(1/2), 191–203.

Repacholi, B. M. (1998). Infants' use of attentional cues to identify the referent of another person's emotional expression. *Developmental Psychology, 34,* 1017–1025.

Repacholi, B. M., & Meltzoff, A. N. (2007). Emotional eavesdropping: Infants selectively respond to indirect emotional signals. *Child Development, 78,* 503–521.

Repacholi, B. M., Meltzoff, A. N., & Olsen, B. (2008). Infants' understanding of the link between visual perception and emotion: "If she can't see me doing it, she won't get angry." *Developmental Psychology, 44,* 561–574.

Reuters. (2007, January 28). Oldest women to give birth deceived clinic, paper says. Retrieved from www.reuters.com/article/idUSL281649320070129

Reynolds, A. J., & Robertson, D. L. (2003). School-based early intervention and later child maltreatment in the Chicago Longitudinal Study. *Child Development, 74,* 3–26.

Reynolds, A. J., Temple, J. A., White, B. A. B., Ou, S., & Robertson, D. L. (2011). Age 26 cost-benefit analysis of the child-parent center early education program. *Child Development, 82,* 379–404.

Rhoades, K. A. (2008). Children's responses to inter-parental conflict: A meta-analysis of their associations with child adjustment. *Child Development, 79,* 1942–1956.

Ricciardelli, L. A., & McCabe, M. P. (2004). A biopsychosocial model of disordered eating and the pursuit of muscularity in adolescent boys. *Psychological Bulletin, 130,* 179–205.

Richland, L. E., & Burchinal, M. R. (2013). Early executive function predicts reasoning development. *Psychological Science, 24,* 87–92.

Richters, J. E., Arnold, L. E., Jensen, P. S., Abikoff, H., Conners, C. K., Greenhill, L. L., et al. (1995). NIMH collaborative multisite multimodal treatment study of children with ADHD: I. Background and rationale. *Journal of the American Academy of Child and Adolescent Psychiatry, 34,* 987–1000.

Rindermann, H., & Thompson, J. (2013). Ability rise in NAEP and narrowing ethnic gaps? *Intelligence, 41,* 821–831.

Rivas-Drake, D., Seaton, E. K., Markstrom, C., Quintana, S., Syed, M., Lee, R. M., et al. (2014). Ethnic and racial identity in adolescence: Implications for psychosocial, academic, and health outcomes. *Child Development, 85,* 40–57.

Roben, C. K. P., Cole, P. M., & Armstrong, L. M. (2013). Longitudinal relations among language skills, anger expression, and regulatory strategies in early childhood. *Child Development, 84,* 891–905.

Roberts, J. E., Burchinal, M., & Durham, M. (1999). Parents' report of vocabulary and grammatical development of African American preschoolers: Child and environmental associations. *Child Development, 70,* 91–106.

Roberts, K. C., Shields, M., de Groh, M., Aziz, A., & Gilbert, J-A. (2012). Overweight and obesity in children and adolescents: Results from the 2009 to 2011 Canadian Health Measures Survey. *Statistics Canada Health Reports, 23*(3), 3–7. Retrieved from www.statcan.gc.ca/pub/82-003-x/2012003/article/11706-eng.pdf

Robinson, E. J., Champion, H., & Mitchell, P. (1999). Children's ability to infer utterance veracity from speaker informedness. *Developmental Psychology, 35,* 535–546.

Roby, A. C., & Kidd, E. (2008). The referential communication skills of children with imaginary companions. *Developmental Science, 11,* 531–540.

Roche, A. F. (1979). Secular trends in stature, weight, and maturation. *Monographs of the Society for Research in Child Development, 44*(3/4), 3–27.

Rodeck, C. H., & Whittle, M. J. (Eds.). (2009). *Fetal medicine: Basic science and clinical practice.* London, UK: Churchill Livingstone.

Roffwarg, H. P., Muzio, J. N., & Dement, W. C. (1966). Ontogenetic development of the human sleep-dream cycle. *Science, 152,* 604–619.

Rogers, L. A., & Graham, S. (2008). A meta-analysis of single subject design writing intervention research. *Journal of Educational Psychology, 100,* 879–906.

Rogoff, B. (1998). Cognition as a collaborative process. In W. Damon (Ed.), *Handbook of child psychology* (5th ed., Vol. 2, pp. 679–744). New York, NY: Wiley.

Rogoff, B. (2003). *The cultural nature of human development.* New York, NY: Oxford University Press.

Rogoff, B., Mistry, J., Goncu, A., & Mosier, C. (1993). Guided participation in cultural activity by toddlers and caregivers. *Monographs of the Society for Research in Child Development, 58*(Serial No. 236).

Rohrbeck, C. A., Ginsburg-Block, M. D., Fantuzzo, J. W., & Miller, T. R. (2003). Peer-assisted learning interventions with elementary school students: A meta-analytic review. *Journal of Educational Psychology, 95,* 240–257.

Rood, L., Roelofs, J., Bögels, S. M., Nolen-Hoeksema, S., & Schouten, E. (2009). The influence of emotion-focused rumination and distraction in depressive symptoms in non-clinical youth: A meta-analytic review. *Clinical Psychology Review, 29,* 607–616.

Roschelle, J. M., Pea, R. D., Hoadley, C. M., Gordin, D. N., & Means, B. M. (2000). Changing how and what children learn in school with computer-based technologies. *Future of Children, 10,* 76–101.

Rose, A. J., & Asher, S. R. (1999). Children's goals and strategies in response to conflicts within a friendship. *Developmental Psychology, 35,* 69–79.

Rose, A. J., & Rudolph, K. D. (2006). A review of sex differences in peer relationship processes: Potential trade-offs for the emotional and behavioral development of girls and boys. *Psychological Bulletin, 132,* 98–131.

Rose, S. A., Feldman, J. F., Jankowski, J. J., & Van Rossem, R. (2012). Information processing from infancy to 11 years: Continuities and prediction of IQ. *Intelligence, 40,* 445–457.

Rosengren, K. S., Gelman, S. A., Kalish, C., & McCormick, M. (1991). As time goes by: Children's early understanding of growth in animals. *Child Development, 62,* 1302–1320.

Ross, M., & Wang, Q. (2010). Why we remember and what we remember: Culture and autobiographical memory. *Perspectives on Psychological Science, 5,* 401–409.

Rotenberg, K. J., & Mayer, E. V. (1990). Delay of gratification in native and white children: A cross-cultural comparison. *International Journal of Behavioral Development, 13,* 23–30.

Rothbart, M. K. (2011). *Becoming who we are: Temperament and personality in development.* New York, NY: Guilford Press.

Rothbart, M. K., & Rueda, M. R. (2005). The development of effortful control. In U. Mayr, E. Awh, & S. W. Keele (Eds.), *Developing individuality in the human brain: A tribute to Michael I. Posner* (pp. 167–188). Washington, DC: American Psychological Association.

Rothbart, M. K., & Sheese, B. E. (2007). Temperament and emotion regulation. In J. J. Gross (Ed.), *Handbook of emotion regulation* (pp. 331–350). New York, NY: Guilford Press.

Rothbaum, F., Weisz, J., Pott, M., Miyake, K., & Morelli, G. (2000). Attachment and culture: Security in the United States and Japan. *American Psychologist, 55,* 1093–1104.

Rotherman-Borus, M. J., & Langabeer, K. A. (2001). Developmental trajectories of gay, lesbian, and bisexual youths. In A. R. D'Augelli & C. Patterson (Eds.), *Lesbian, gay, and bisexual identities among youth: Psychological perspectives* (pp. 97–128). New York, NY: Oxford University Press.

Rothman, L., McArthur, C., To, T., Builung, R., & Howard, A. (2014). Motor vehicle-pedestrian collisions and walking to school: The role of the built environment. *Pediatrics, 133,* 776–784.

Rovee-Collier, C. (1997). Dissociations in infant memory: Rethinking the development of implicit and explicit memory. *Psychological Review, 104,* 467–498.

Rovee-Collier, C. (1999). The development of infant memory. *Current Directions in Psychological Science, 8,* 80–85.

Rovee-Collier, C., & Barr, R. (2010). Infant learning and memory. In T. D. Wachs & G. Bremner (Eds.), *Blackwell handbook of infant development* (2nd ed.). Oxford, UK: Blackwell.

Rowe, M. L. (2012). A longitudinal investigation of the role of quantity and quality of child-directed speech in vocabulary development. *Child Development, 83,* 1762–1774.

Rowe, M. L., Raudenbush, S. W., & Goldin-Meadow, S. (2012). The pace of vocabulary growth helps predict later vocabulary skill. *Child Development, 83,* 508–525.

Rowland, C. F., Pine, J. M., Lieven, E. V. M., & Theakston, A. L. (2005). The incidence of error in young children's wh-questions. *Journal of Speech, Language, and Hearing Research, 48,* 384–404.

Rubin, C. M. (2012, September 17). The global search for education: It takes a community. *HuffPost Education.* Retrieved from www.huffingtonpost.com

Rubin, K., Bukowski, W., & Parker, J. (2006). Peer interaction and social competence. In W. Damon & R. M. Lerner (Eds.), *Handbook of child psychology* (6th ed., Vol. 3.). New York, NY: Wiley.

Rubin, K. H., Coplan, R. J., & Bowker, J. C. (2009). Social withdrawal in childhood. *Annual Review of Psychology, 60,* 141–171.

Rubinstein, O., Henik, A., Berger, A., & Shahar-Shalev, S. (2002). The development of internal representations of magnitude and their association with Arabic numerals. *Journal of Experimental Child Psychology, 81,* 74–92.

Ruble, D., Martin, C. L., & Berenbaum, S. A. (2006). Gender development. In N. Eisenberg, W. Damon, & R. Lerner, (Eds.), *Handbook of child psychology: Vol. 3, Social, emotional, and personality development* (6th ed., pp. 858–932). Hoboken, NJ: John Wiley & Sons.

Ruble, D. N., & Martin, C. L. (1998). Gender development. In W. Damon (Ed.), *Handbook of child psychology: Vol. 3. Social, emotional, and personality development* (5th ed., pp. 933–1016). New York, NY: Wiley.

Ruble, D. N., Boggiano, A. D., Feldman, N. S., & Loebl, N. H. (1980). Developmental analysis of the role of social comparison in self-evaluation. *Developmental Psychology, 16,* 105–115.

Rudolph, K. D., Ladd, G., & Dinella, L. (2007). Gender differences in the interpersonal consequences of early-onset depressive symptoms. *Merrill-Palmer Quarterly, 53,* 461–488.

Rudolph, K. D., Troop-Gordon, W., & Flynn, M. (2009). Relational victimization predicts children's social-cognitive and self-regulatory responses in a challenging peer context. *Developmental Psychology, 45,* 1444–1454.

Ruff, H. A., & Capozzoli, M. C. (2003). Development of attention and distractibility in the first 4 years of life. *Developmental Psychology, 39,* 877–890.

Rushton, J. P., & Bonds, T. A. (2005). Mate choice and friendship in twins. *Psychological Science, 16,* 555–559.

Rushton, J. P., & Jensen, A. R. (2006). The totality of available evidence shows the race IQ gap still remains. *Psychological Science, 17,* 921–922.

Russell, A., & Finnie, V. (1990). Preschool children's social status and maternal instructions to assist group entry. *Developmental Psychology, 26,* 603–611.

Rutland, A., Killen, M., & Abrams, D. (2010). A new social-cognitive developmental perspective on prejudice: The interplay between morality and group identity. *Perspectives on Psychological Science, 5,* 279–291.

Rutter, M. (2002). Nature, nurture, and development: From evangelism through science toward policy and practice. *Child Development, 73,* 1–21.

Rutter, M., Sonuga-Barke, E. J., Beckett, C., Castle, J., Kreppner, J., Kumsta, R. et al. (2010). Deprivation-specific psychological patterns: Effects of institutional deprivation. *Monographs of the Society for Research in Child Development,, 75*(1, Serial No. 295).

Ryan, R. M., & Claessens, A. (2013). Associations between family structure changes and children's behavior problems: The moderating effects of timing and marital birth. *Developmental Psychology, 49,* 1219–1231.

Rymer, R. (1993). *Genie.* New York, NY: Harper Collins.

Sabbagh, M. A. (2004). Understanding orbitofrontal contributions to theory-of-mind reasoning: Implications for autism. *Brain and Cognition, 55,* 209-219.

Sabbagh, M. A. & Seamans, E.L. (2008). Intergenerational transmission of theory-of-mind. *Developmental Science, 11*(3), 354–360.

Saewyc, E. M. (2011). Research on adolescent sexual orientation: Development, health disparities, stigma, and resilience. *Journal of Research on Adolescence, 21,* 256–272.

Saffran, J. R., Aslin, R. N., & Newport, E. L. (1996). Statistical learning by 8-month-old infants. *Science, 274,* 1926–1928.

Saffran, J. R., Werker, J. F., & Werner, L. A. (2006). The infant's auditory world: Hearing, speech, and the beginnings of language. In W. Damon & R. M. Lerner (Eds.),

Handbook of child psychology: Vol. 2. Cognition, perception, and language (6th ed., pp. 58–108). Hoboken, NJ: Wiley.

Sagi, A., Koren-Karie, N., Gini, M., Ziv, Y., & Joels, T. (2002). Shedding further light on the effects of various types and quality of early child care on infant-mother attachment relationship: The Haifa study of early child care. *Child Development, 73,* 1166–1186.

Sahni, R., Fifer, W. P., & Myers, M. M. (2007). Identifying infants at risk for sudden infant death syndrome. *Current Opinion in Pediatrics, 19,* 145–149.

Saigal, S., Stoskopf, B., Streiner, D., Boyle, M., Pinelli, J., Panath, N., & Goddeeris, J. (2006). Transition of extremely low-birth-weight infants from adolescence to young adulthood: Comparison with normal birth-weight controls. *Journal of the American Medical Association, 295*(6), 667–675.

Salmivalli, C., & Isaacs, J. (2005). Prospective relations among victimization, rejection, friendlessness, and children's self- and peer-perceptions. *Child Development, 76,* 1161–1171.

Salovey, P., & Grewal, D. (2005). The science of emotional intelligence. *Current Directions in Psychological Science, 14,* 281–285.

Sameroff, A. (2010). A unified theory of development: A dialectic integration of nature and nurture. *Child Development, 81,* 6–22.

Sanders, M. & Kirby, J. N. (2014). A public health approach to improving parenting and promoting children's well being. *Child Development Perspectives, 8*(8), 250–257. doi: 10.1111/cdep.12086

Sandler, I. N., Tein, J. Y., Mehta, P., Wolchik, S., & Ayers, T. (2000). Coping efficacy and psychological problems of children of divorce. *Child Development, 71,* 1099–1118.

Sangrigoli, S., Pallier, C., Argenti, A.-M., Ventureyra, V. A. G., & de Schonen, S. (2005). Reversibility of the other-race effect in face recognition during childhood. *Psychological Science, 16,* 440–444.

Sann, C., & Streri, A. (2007). Perception of object shape and texture in human newborns: Evidence from cross-modal transfer tasks. *Developmental Science, 10,* 399–410.

Sapolski, R. M. & Share, L. J. (2004) A pacific culture among wild baboons: Its emergence and transmission, "Summary." *PLoS Biology, 2*(4), 534–541.

Saudino, K. J. (2009). Do different measures tap the same genetic influences? A multi-method study of activity level in young twins. *Developmental Science, 12,* 626–633.

Saudino, K. J. (2012). Sources of continuity and change in activity level in early childhood. *Child Development, 83,* 266–281.

Saudino, K. J., & Wang, M. (2012). Quantitative and molecular genetic studies of temperament. In M. Zentner & R. L. Shiner (Eds.), *Handbook of temperament* (pp. 315–346). New York, NY: Guilford Press.

Saxe, G. B. (1988). Candy selling and math learning. *Educational Researcher, 17,* 14–21.

Scarr, S. (1992). Developmental theories for the 1990s: Development and individual differences. *Child Development, 63,* 1–19.

Scarr, S., & McCartney, K. (1983). How people make their own environments: A theory of genotype-environment effects. *Child Development, 54,* 424–435.

Schaal, B., Soussignan, R., & Marlier, L. (2002). Olfactory cognition at the start of life: The perinatal shaping of selective odor responsiveness. In C. Rouby et al., (Eds.), *Olfaction, taste, and cognition* (pp. 421–440). Cambridge, UK: Cambridge University Press.

Scharfe, E., & Cole, V. (2006). Stability and change of attachment representations during emerging adulthood: An examination of mediators and moderators of change. *Personal Relationships, 13,* 363–374.

Schauble, L. (1996). The development of scientific reasoning in knowledge-rich contexts. *Developmental Psychology, 32,* 102–119.

Schelleman-Offermans, K., Knibbe, R. A., & Kuntsche, E. (2013). Are the effects of early pubertal timing on the initiation of weekly alcohol use mediated by peers and/or parents? A longitudinal study. *Developmental Psychology, 49,* 1277–1285.

Scherf, K. S., Behrmann, M., Humphreys, K., & Luna, B. (2007). Visual category-selectivity for faces, places and objects emerges along different developmental trajectories. *Developmental Science, 10,* F15–F30.

Schermerhorn, A. C., & Cummings, E. M. (2008). Transactional family dynamics: A new framework for conceptualizing family influence processes. In R. V. Kail (Ed.), *Advances in child development and behavior* (Vol. 36, pp. 187–250). Amsterdam, The Netherlands: Academic Press.

Schermerhorn, A. C., Chow, S., & Cummings, E. M. (2010). Developmental family processes and interparental conflict: Patterns of microlevel influences. *Developmental Psychology, 46,* 869–885.

Schlam, T. R., Wilson, N. L., Shoda, Y., Mischel, W., & Ayduk, O. (2013). Preschoolers' delay of gratification predicts their body mass 30 years later. *The Journal of Pediatrics, 162,* 90–93.

Schmidt, F. L., & Hunter, J. (2004). General mental ability in the world of work: Occupational attainment and job performance. *Journal of Personality and Social Psychology, 86,* 162–173.

Schmidt, M. E., & Vandewater, E. A. (2008). Media and attention, cognition, and school achievement. *Future of Children, 18,* 63–85.

Schneider, B. H., Dixon, K., & Udvari, S. (2007). Closeness and competition in the inter-ethnic and co-ethnic friendships of early adolescents in Toronto and Montreal. *Journal of Early Adolescence, 27,* 115–138.

Schneider, W. (2011). Memory development in childhood. In U. Goswami (Ed.), *The Wiley-Blackwell handbook of cognitive development* (2nd ed., pp. 347–376). Chichester, UK: Wiley-Blackwell.

Schneider, W., & Bjorklund, D. F. (1998). Memory. In W. Damon (Ed.), *Handbook of child psychology* (Vol. 2). New York, NY: Wiley.

Schneiders, J., Nicolson, N. A., Berkhof, J., Feron, F. J., van Os., J., & deVries, M. W. (2006). Mood reactivity to daily negative events in early adolescence: Relationship to risk for psychopathology. *Developmental Psychology, 42,* 543–554.

Schoemaker, K., Mulder, H., Dekovic, M., & Matthys, W. (2013). Executive functions in preschool children with externalizing behavior problems: A meta-analysis. *Journal of Abnormal Child Psychology, 41,* 457–471.

Schofield, T. J., Parke, R. D., Kim, Y., & Coltrane, S. (2008). Bridging the acculturation gap: Parent-child relationship quality as a moderator in Mexican American families. *Developmental Psychology, 44,* 1190–1194.

Schröder, L., Keller, H., Kärtner, J., Kleis, A., Abels, M., Yovsi, R. D. et al. (2013). Early reminiscing in cultural contexts: Cultural models, maternal reminiscing styles, and children's memories. *Journal of Cognition and Development, 14,* 10–34.

Schuetze, P., Molnar, D. S., & Eiden, R. D. (2012). Profiles of reactivity in cocaine-exposed children. *Journal of Applied Developmental Psychology, 33,* 282–293.

Schug, M. G., Shusterman, A., Barth, H., & Patalano, A. L. (2013). Minimal-group membership influences children's responses to novel experience with group members. *Developmental Science, 16,* 47–55.

Schum, N., Jovanovic, B., & Schwarzer, G. (2011). Ten- and twelve-month-olds' visual anticipation of orientation and size during grasping. *Journal of Experimental Child Psychology, 109,* 218–231.

Schwartz, C., Issanchou, S., & Nicklaus, S. (2009). Developmental changes in the acceptance of the five basic tastes in the first year of life. *British Journal of Nutrition, 102,* 1375–1385.

Schwartz, C. E., Wright, C. I., Shin, L. M., Kagan, J., & Rauch, S. L. (2003). Inhibited and uninhibited infants "grown up": Adult amygdalar response to novelty. *Science, 300,* 1952–1953.

Schwartz, D., Chang, L., & Farver, J. M. (2001). Correlates of victimization in Chinese children's peer groups. *Developmental Psychology, 37,* 520–532.

Schwartz, D., Dodge, K. A., Pettit, G. S., Bates, J. E., & The Conduct Problems Prevention Research Group. (2000). Friendship as a moderating factor in the pathway between early harsh home environment and later victimization in the peer group. *Developmental Psychology, 36,* 646–662.

Schwartz, O. S., Dudgeon, P., Sheeber, L. B., Yap, M. B. H., Simmons, J. G., & Allen, N. B. (2012). Parental behaviors during family interactions predict changes in depression and anxiety symptoms during adolescence. *Journal of Abnormal Child Psychology, 40,* 59–71.

Schwartz, P. D., Maynard, A. M., & Uzelac, S. M. (2008). Adolescent egocentrism: A contemporary view. *Adolescence, 43,* 441–448.

Schwartz-Mette, R. A., & Rose, A. J. (2012). Co-rumination mediates contagion of internalizing symptoms within youths' friendships. *Developmental Psychology, 48,* 1355–1365.

Schwarzer, G., Freitag, C., Buckel, R., & Lofruthe, A. (2013). Crawling is associated with mental rotation ability by 9-month-old infants. *Infancy, 18,* 432–441.

Schwebel, D. C., Davis, A. L., & O'Neal, E. E. (2012). Child pedestrian injury: A review of behavioral risks and preventive strategies. *American Journal of Lifestyle Medicine, 6,* 292–302.

Schweitzer, M. M. (Ed.). (1999). *American Indian grandmothers: Traditions and transitions.* Albuquerque, NM: University of New Mexico Press.

Schwenck, C., Bjorklund, D. F., & Schneider, W. (2009). Developmental and individual differences in young children's use and maintenance of a selective memory strategy. *Developmental Psychology, 45,* 1034–1050.

Scott, L. S., Pascalis, O., & Nelson, C. A. (2007). A domain-general theory of the development of perceptual discrimination. *Current Directions in Psychological Science, 16,* 197–201.

Scott, W. A., Scott, R., & McCabe, M. (1991). Family relationships and children's personality: A cross-cultural, cross-source comparison. *British Journal of Social Psychology, 30,* 1–20.

Scrimgeour, M. B., Blandon, A. Y., Stifter, C. A., & Buss, K. A. (2013). Cooperative coparenting moderates the association between parenting practices and children's prosocial behavior. *Journal of Family Psychology, 27,* 506–511.

Scrimsher, S., & Tudge, J. (2003). The teaching/learning relationship in the first years of school: School revolutionary implications of Vygotsky's theory. *Early Education and Development, 14,* 293–312.

Sears, H. A., Graham, J., & Campbell, A. (2009). Adolescent boys' intentions of seeking help from male friends and female friends. *Journal of Applied Developmental Psychology, 30,* 738–748.

Sears, R. R. (1975). Your ancients revisited: A history of child development. In E. M. Hetherington (Ed.), *Review of child development research* (Vol. 5, pp. 1–73). Chicago, IL: University of Chicago Press.

Seaton, E. K., Yip, T., Morgan-Lopez, A., & Sellers, R. M. (2012). Racial discrimination and racial socialization as predictors of African Americans adolescents' racial identity development using latent transition analysis. *Developmental Psychology, 48,* 448–458.

Secada, W. G., Fennema, E., & Adajian, L. B. (Eds.). (1995). *New directions for equity in mathematics education.* New York, NY: Cambridge University Press.

Sedgh, G., Finer, L. B., Bankole, A., Eilers, M. A., & Singh, S. (2015). Adolescent pregnancy, birth, and abortion rates across countries: Levels and trends. *Journal of Adolescent Health, 56,* 223–230. doi: 10.1016/j.jadohealth.2014.09.007

Segrin, C., Taylor, M. E., & Altman, J. (2005). Social cognitive mediators and relational outcomes associated with parental divorce. *Journal of Social and Personal Relationships, 22,* 361–377.

Seidl, A., & Johnson, E. L. (2006). Infant word segmentation revisited: Edge alignment facilitates target extraction. *Developmental Science, 9,* 565–573.

Selman, R. L. (1980). *The growth of interpersonal understanding: Developmental and clinical analyses.* New York, NY: Academic Press.

Selman, R. L. (1981). The child as a friendship philosopher: A case study in the growth of interpersonal understanding. In S. R. Asher & J. M. Gottman (Eds.), *The development of children's friendships.* Cambridge, UK: Cambridge University Press.

Sénéchal, M., & LeFevre, J. (2002). Parental involvement in the development of children's reading skill: A five-year longitudinal study. *Child Development, 73,* 445–460.

Sénéchal, M., Thomas, E., & Monker, J. (1995). Individual differences in 4-year-old children's acquisition of vocabulary during storybook reading. *Journal of Educational Psychology, 87,* 218–229.

Senghas, A., & Coppola, M. (2001). Children creating language: How Nicaraguan sign language acquired a spatial grammar. *Psychological Science, 12*(4), 323–328.

Senghas, A., Kita, S., & Özyürek, A. (2004, September 17). Children creating core properties of language: Evidence from an emerging sign language in Nicaragua. *Science, 305,* 1779–1782.

Serbin, L. A., Poulin-Dubois, D., Colburne, K. A., Sen, M. G., & Eichstedt, J. A. (2001). Gender stereotyping in infancy: Visual preferences for and knowledge of gender-stereotyped toys in the second year. *International Journal of Behavioral Development, 25,* 7–15.

Serbin, L. A., Powlishta, K. K., & Gulko, J. (1993). The development of sex typing in middle childhood. *Monographs of the Society for Research in Child Development, 58*(Serial No. 232).

Serpell, R. (2000). Intelligence and culture. In R. J. Sternberg (Ed.), *Handbook of intelligence.* New York, NY: Cambridge University Press.

Setliff, A. E., & Courage, M. L. (2011). Background television and infants' allocation of their attention during toy play. *Infancy, 16,* 611–639.

Shanahan, L., McHale, S. M., Crouter, A. C., & Osgood, D. (2007). Warmth with mothers and fathers from middle childhood to late adolescence: Within- and between-families comparisons. *Developmental Psychology, 43,* 551–563.

Shanahan, M. J., Elder, G. H., Burchinal, M., & Conger, R. D. (1996a). Adolescent earnings and relationships with parents: The work-family nexus in urban and rural ecologies. In J. T. Mortimer & M. D. Finch (Eds.), *Adolescents, work, and family: An intergenerational developmental analysis.* Thousand Oaks, CA: Sage.

Shanahan, M. J., Elder, G. H., Burchinal, M., & Conger, R. D. (1996b). Adolescent paid labor and relationships with parents: Early work-family linkages. *Child Development, 67,* 2183–2200.

Shanker, S. (2014). *Self-regulation: Calm, alert, and learning.* Retrieved from www.cea-ace.ca/education-canada/article/self-regulation-calm-alert-and-learning

Shapka, J. D., & Keating, D. P. (2005). Structure and change in self-concept during adolescence. *Canadian Journal of Behavioural Sciences, 37,* 83–96.

Share, D. L. (2008). Orthographic learning, phonological recoding, and self-teaching. In R. V. Kail (Ed.), *Advances in child development and behavior* (Vol. 36, pp. 31–84). San Diego, CA: Elsevier.

Shariff, A. F., & Tracy, J. L. (2011). What are emotion expressions for? *Current Directions in Psychological Science, 20,* 395–399.

Shatz, M. (1983). Communication. In P. H. Mussen (Ed.), *Handbook of child psychology* (Vol. 3). New York, NY: Wiley.

Shatz, M., & Gelman, R. (1973). The development of communication skills: Modifications in the speech of young children as a function of listener. *Monographs of the Society for Research in Child Development, 38* (5, Serial No. 152).

Shaughnessy, J. J., Zechmeister, E. B., & Zechmeister, J. S. (2009). *Research methods in psychology* (8th ed.). New York, NY: McGraw-Hill.

Shaw, D. S., & Shelleby, E. C. (2014). Early-starting conduct problems: Intersection of conduct problems and poverty. *Annual Review of Clinical Psychology, 10,* 503–528.

Shaw, D. S., Winslow, E. B., & Flanagan, C. (1999). A prospective study of the effects of marital status and family relations on young children's adjustment among African American and European American families. *Child Development, 70,* 742–755.

Sheridan, M. A., Fox, N.A., Zeanah, C. H., McLaughlin, K. A, & Nelson, C. A. (2012). Variations in neural development as a result of exposure to institutionalization early in childhood. *Proceedings of the National Academy of Sciences (PNAS), 109*(S. 2). Retrieved from www.pnas.org/cgi/doi/10.1073/pnas.1200041109

Sherman, D. K., Hartson, K. A., Binning, K. R., Purdie-Vaughns, V., Garcia, J., Taborsky-Barba, S., et al. (2013). Deflecting the trajectory and changing the narrative: How self-affirmation affects academic performance and motivation under identity threat. *Journal of Personality and Social Psychology, 104,* 591–618.

Sherrod, K. B., O'Connor, S., Vietze, P. M., & Altemeier, W. A., III (1984). Child health and maltreatment. *Child Development, 55,* 1174–1183.

Shi, R. (2014). Functional morphemes and early language acquisition. *Child Development Perspectives, 8,* 6–11.

Shi, R., & Werker, J. F. (2001). Six-month old infants' preference for lexical words. *Psychological Science, 12,* 70–75.

Shiner, R. L., & Caspi, A. (2012). Temperament and the development of personality traits, adaptations, and narratives. In M. Zentner & R. L. Shiner (Eds.), *Handbook of temperament* (pp. 497–516). New York, NY: Guilford Press.

Shneidman, L. A., & Goldin-Meadow, S. (2012). Language input and acquisition in a Mayan village: How important is directed speech? *Developmental Science, 15,* 659–673.

Shoemaker, L. B., & Furman, W. (2009). Interpersonal influences on late adolescent girls' and boys' disordered eating. *Eating Behaviors, 10,* 97–106.

Shonkoff, J. P. & Bales, S. N. (2011). Science does not speak for itself: Translating child development research for the public and its policymakers. *Child Development, 82,* 17–32.

Shulman, S., & Kipnis, O. (2001). Adolescent romantic relationships: A look from the future. *Journal of Adolescence, 24,* 337–351.

Shusterman, A., Lee, S. A., & Spelke, E. W. (2008). Young children's spontaneous use of geometry in maps. *Developmental Science, 11,* F1–F7.

Shutts, K., Banaji, M. R., & Spelke, E. S. (2010). Social categories guide young children's preferences for novel objects. *Developmental Science, 13,* 599–610.

Siddiqui, A. (1995). Object size as a determinant of grasping in infancy. *Journal of Genetic Psychology, 156,* 345–358.

Sidebotham, P., Heron, J., & the ALSPAC Study Team. (2003). Child maltreatment in the "children of the nineties": The role of the child. *Child Abuse and Neglect, 27,* 337–352.

Siegler, R. S. (1981). Developmental sequences within and between concepts. *Monographs of the Society for Research in Child Development, 46*(Serial No. 189).

Siegler, R. S. (1986). Unities in strategy choices across domains. In M. Perlmutter (Ed.), *Minnesota symposia on child development* (Vol. 19). Hillsdale, NJ: Erlbaum.

Siegler, R. S. (1996). *Emerging minds: The process of change in children's thinking.* New York, NY: Oxford University Press.

Siegler, R. S. (2000). The rebirth of children's learning. *Child Development, 71,* 26–35.

Siegler, R. S. (2007). Cognitive variability. *Developmental Science, 18,* 303–307.

Siegler, R. S., & Alibali, M. W. (2005). *Children's thinking* (4th ed.). Upper Saddle River, NJ: Prentice Hall.

Siegler, R. S., & Ellis, S. (1996). Piaget on childhood. *Psychological Science, 7,* 211–215.

Siegler, R. S., & Jenkins, E. (1989). *How children discover new strategies.* Hillsdale, NJ: Erlbaum.

Siegler, R. S., & Mu, Y. (2008). Chinese children excel on novel mathematics problems even before elementary school. *Psychological Science, 19,* 759–763.

Siegler, R. S., & Robinson, M. (1982). The development of numerical understandings. In H. W. Reese & L. P. Lipsitt (Eds.), *Advances in child development and behavior* (Vol. 16). New York, NY: Academic Press.

Siegler, R. S., & Shrager, J. (1984). Strategy choices in addition and subtraction: How do children know what to do? In C. Sophian (Ed.), *Origins of cognitive skills.* Hillsdale, NJ: Erlbaum.

Siegler, R. S., Duncan, G. J., Davis-Kean, P. E., Duckworth, K., Claessens, A., Engel, M. et al. (2012). Early predictors of high school mathematics achievement. *Psychological Science, 23,* 691–697.

Signorielli, N., & Lears, M. (1992). Children, television, and conceptions about chores: Attitudes and behaviors. *Sex Roles, 27,* 157–170.

Sikora, J. & Pokropek, A. (2012). Gender segregation of adolescent science career plans in 50 countries. *Science education, 96*(2), 234–264. doi: 10.1002/sce.20479

Silk, J. S., Morris, A. S., Kanaya, T., & Steinberg, L. D. (2003). Psychological control and autonomy granting: Opposite ends of a continuum or distinct constructs? *Journal of Research on Adolescence, 13,* 113–128.

Silva, K. G., Correa-Chávez, M., & Rogoff, B. (2010). Mexican-heritage children's attention and learning from interactions directed to others. *Child Development, 81,* 898–912.

Silverman, I., & Choi, J. (2006). Non-Euclidian navigational strategies of women: Compensatory response or evolved dimorphism? *Evolutionary Psychology, 4,* 75–84.

Silverman, I., & Eals, M. (1992). Sex differences in spatial abilities: Evolutionary theory and data. In J. H. Barkow, L. Kosmides, & J. Tooby (Eds.), *The adapted mind* (pp. 533–549). New York, NY: Oxford.

Silverman, I., Choi, J., & Peters, M. (2007). The hunter-gatherer theory of sex differences in spatial abilities: Data from 40 countries. *Archives of Sexual Behavior, 36*(2), 261–268.

Silverman, W. K., La Greca, A. M., & Wasserstein, S. (1995). What do children worry about? Worries and their relations to anxiety. *Child Development, 66,* 671–686.

Simcock, G., & Hayne, H. (2002). Breaking the barrier? Children fail to translate their preverbal memories into language. *Psychological Science, 13,* 225–231.

Simons, D. J., & Keil, F. C. (1995). An abstract to concrete shift in the development of biological thought: The insides story. *Cognition, 56,* 129–163.

Simons, L. G., & Conger, R. D. (2007). Linking mother-father differences in parenting to a typology of family parenting styles and adolescent outcomes. *Journal of Family Issues, 28,* 212–241.

Simpson, E. L. (1974). Moral development research: A case study of scientific cultural bias. *Human Development, 17,* 81–106.

Simpson, J. M. (2001). Infant stress and sleep deprivation as an aetiological basis for the sudden infant death syndrome. *Early Human Development, 61,* 1–43.

Sinha, M. (2014). *Spotlight on Canadians—results from the general social survey: Child care in Canada.* Statistics Canada. Retrieved from www.statcan.gc.ca/pub/89-652-x/89-652-x2014005-eng.pdf

Skinner, B. F. (1957). *Verbal behavior.* New York, NY: Appleton-Century-Crofts.

Skinner, E. A. (1985). Determinants of mother-sensitive and contingent-responsive behavior: The role of childbearing beliefs and socioeconomic status. In I. E. Sigel (Ed.), *Parental belief systems: The psychological consequences for children* (pp. 51–82). Hillsdale, NJ: Erlbaum.

Skolnick Weisberg, D., & Bloom, P. (2009). Young children separate multiple pretend worlds. *Developmental Science, 12,* 699–705.

Slater, A., Bremner, G., Johnson, S. P., Sherwood, P., Hayes, R., & Brown, E. (2000). Newborn infants' preference for attractive faces: The role of internal and external facial features. *Infancy, 1,* 265–274.

Slater, A. M., Riddell, P., Quinn, P. C., Pascalis, O., Lee, K., & Kelly, D. J. (2010). Visual perception. In T. D. Wachs & G. Bremner (Eds.), *Blackwell handbook of infant development* (2nd ed.). Oxford, UK: Blackwell.

Sleddens, E. F. C., Kremers, S. P. J., Candel, M. J. J. M., De Vries, N. N. K., & Thijs, C. (2011). Validating the Children's Behavior Questionnaire structure in Dutch children: Psychometric properties and a cross-cultural comparison of factor structures. *Psychological Assessment, 23,* 417–426.

Sloane, S., Baillargeon, R., & Premack, D. (2012). Do infants have a sense of fairness? *Psychological Science, 23,* 196–204.

Slobin, D. I. (1985). Cross-linguistic evidence for the language-making capacity. In D. I. Slobin (Ed.), *The cross-linguistic study of language acquisition: Vol. 2. Theoretical issues.* Hillsdale, NJ: Erlbaum.

Slutske, W. S., Moffitt, T. E., Poulton, R., & Caspi, A. (2012). Undercontrolled temperament at age 3 predicts disordered gambling at age 32: A longitudinal study of a complete birth cohort. *Psychological Science, 23,* 510–516.

Smetana, J. G. (2002). Culture, autonomy, and personal jurisdiction in adolescent-parent relationships. *Advances in Child Development & Behavior, 29,* 52–87.

Smetana, J. G. (2006). Social-cognitive domain theory: Consistencies and variations in children's moral and social judgments. In M. Killen & J. G. Smetana (2006). *Handbook of moral development* (pp. 119–153). Mahwah, NJ: Erlbaum.

Smetana, J. G. (2011). Parenting beliefs, parenting, and parent-adolescent communication in African American families. In N. E. Hill, T. Mann, & H. E. Fitzgerald (Eds.), *African-American children's mental health: Vol. 1. Development and context* (pp. 173–197). Santa Barbara, CA: Praeger.

Smetana, J. G., Rote, W. M., Jambon, M., Tasopoulos-Chan, M., Villalobos, M., & Comer, J. (2012). Developmental changes and individual differences in young children's moral judgments. *Child Development, 83,* 683–696.

Smith, A., & Schneider, B. H. (2000). The inter-ethnic friendships of adolescent students: A Canadian study. *International Journal of Intercultural Relations, 24,* 247–258.

Smith, E. R., & Mackie, D. M. (2000). *Social psychology* (2nd ed.). Philadelphia, PA: Psychology Press.

Smith, J., & Ross, H. (2007). Training parents to mediate sibling disputes affects children's negotiation and conflict understanding. *Child Development, 78,* 790–805.

Smith, L. B. (2000). How to learn words: An associative crane. In R. Golinkoff & K. Hirsch-Pasek (Eds.), *Breaking the word learning barrier* (pp. 51–80). Oxford, UK: Oxford University Press.

Smith, L. B. (2009). From fragments to geometric shape: Changes in visual object recognition between 18 and 24 months. *Current Directions in Psychological Science, 18,* 290–294.

Smith, L. B., Jones, S. S., Landau, B., Gershkoff-Stowe, L., & Samuelson, L. (2002). Object name learning provides on-the-job training for attention. *Psychological Science, 13,* 13–19.

Smith, L. B., Quittner, A. L., Osberger, M. J., & Miyamoto, R. (1998). Audition and visual attention: The developmental trajectory in deaf and hearing populations. *Developmental Psychology, 34,* 840–850.

Smith, P. K., & Drew, L. M. (2002). Grandparenthood. In M. H. Bornstein (Ed.), *Handbook of parenting: Vol. 3. Status and social conditions of parenting* (2nd ed., pp. 141–172). Mahwah, NJ: Erlbaum.

Smith, R., Paul, J., Maiti, K., Tolosa, J., & Gemma, M. (2012). Recent advances in understanding the endocrinology of human birth. *Trends in Endocrinology and Metabolism, 23,* 516–523.

Smith, R. E., & Smoll, F. L. (1996). The coach as the focus of research and intervention in youth sports. In F. L. Smoll & R. E. Smith (Eds.), *Children and youth in sport: A biopsychological perspective* (pp. 125–141). Dubuque, IA: Brown & Benchmark.

Smith, R. E., & Smoll, F. L. (1997). Coaching the coaches: Youth sports as a scientific and applied behavioral setting. *Current Directions in Psychological Science, 6,* 16–21.

Smith, S. L., Choueiti, M., Prescott, A., & Pieper, K. (2012). *Gender roles and occupations: A look at character attributes and job-related aspirations in film and television.* Los Angeles, CA: Geena Davis Institute on Gender in Media.

Smits, I., Soenens, B., Vansteenkiste, M., Luyckx, K., & Goossens, L. (2010). Why do adolescents gather information or stick to parental norms? Examining autonomous and controlled motives behind adolescents' identity style. *Journal of Youth and Adolescence, 39,* 1343–1356.

Smock, T. K. (1999). *Physiological psychology: A neuroscience approach.* Upper Saddle River, NJ: Prentice Hall.

Smoll, F. L., & Schutz, R. W. (1990). Quantifying gender differences in physical performance: A developmental perspective. *Developmental Psychology, 26,* 360–369.

Snedeker, B. (1982). *Hard knocks: Preparing youth for work.* Baltimore, MD: Johns Hopkins University Press.

Snedeker, J., Geren, J., & Shafto, C. L. (2007). Starting over: International adoption as a natural experiment in language development. *Psychological Science, 18,* 79–87.

Snell, E. K., Adam, E. K., & Duncan, G. J. (2007). Sleep and the body mass index and overweight status of children and adolescents. *Child Development, 78,* 309–323.

Snow, C. W. (1998). *Infant development* (2nd ed.). Upper Saddle River, NJ: Prentice Hall.

Snow, D. (2006). Regression and reorganization of intonation between 6 and 23 months. *Child Development, 77,* 281–296.

Snow, M. E., Jacklin, C. N., & Maccoby, E. E. (1983). Sex-of-child differences in father–child interaction at one year of age. *Child Development, 54,* 227–232.

Snowling, M. J., & Hulme, C. (2012). Annual research review: The nature and classification of reading disorders—a commentary on proposals for DSM-5. *Journal of Child Psychology and Psychiatry, 53,* 593–607.

Sobol, M. P., & Daly, K. J. (1994). Canadian adoption statistics: 1981–1990. *Journal of Marriage and the Family, 56,* 493–499.

Sodian, B., Zaitchik, D., & Carey, S. (1991). Young children's differentiation of hypothetical beliefs from evidence. *Child Development, 62,* 753–766.

Sokol, R. J., Delaney-Black, V., & Nordstrom, B. (2003). Fetal alcohol spectrum disorder. *Journal of the American Medical Association, 290,* 2996–2999.

Solantaus, T., Leinonen, J., & Punamäki, R. L. (2004). Children's mental health in times of economic recession: Replication and extension of the family economic stress model in Finland. *Developmental Psychology, 40,* 412–429.

Solomon, G. E. A., & Zaitchik, D. (2012). Folkbiology. *WIREs Cognitive Science, 3,* 105–115.

Somerville, L. H., & Casey, B. J. (2010). Developmental neurobiology of cognitive control and motivational systems. *Current Opinion in Neurobiology 20,* 236–241.

Somerville, M. (2012, September 29). The preposterous politics of female feticide. *Globe and Mail,* p. F9.

Sommerville, J. A., & Woodward, A. L. (2005). Pulling out the intentional structure of action: The relation between action processing and action production in infancy. *Cognition, 95,* 1–30.

Song, L., Tamis-LeMonda, C. S., Yoshikawa, H., Kahana-Kalman, R., & Wu, I. (2012). Language experiences and vocabulary development in Dominican and Mexican infants across the first 2 years. *Developmental Psychology, 48,* 1106–1123.

Southgate, V., & Csibra, G. (2009). Inferring the outcome of an ongoing novel action at 13 months. *Developmental Psychology, 45,* 1794–1798.

Southgate, V., Johnson, M. H., El Karoui, I., & Csibra, G. (2010). Motor system activation reveals infants' on-line prediction of others' goals. *Psychological Science, 21,* 355–359.

Sowislo, J. F., & Orth, U. (2013). Does low self-esteem predict depression and anxiety? A meta-analysis of longitudinal studies. *Psychological Bulletin, 139,* 213–240.

Spearman, C. (1904). "General intelligence" objectively determined and measured. *American Journal of Psychology, 15,* 201–293.

Spector, F., & Maurer, D. (2009). Synesthesia: A new approach to understanding the development of perception. *Developmental Psychology, 45,* 175–189.

Spelke, E. S., & Kinzler, K. D. (2007). Core knowledge. *Developmental Science, 10,* 89–96.

Spelke, E. S., Gilmore, C. K., & McCarthy, S. (2011). Kindergarten children's sensitivity to geometry in maps. *Developmental Science, 14,* 809–821.

Spencer, J. P., Perone, S., & Buss, A. T. (2011). Twenty years and going strong: A dynamic systems revolution in motor and cognitive development. *Child Development Perspectives, 5,* 260–266.

Spitz, R. A. (1965). *The first year of life.* New York, NY: International Universities Press.

Springer, K., & Keil, F. C. (1991). Early differentiation of causal mechanisms appropriate to biological and non-biological kinds. *Child Development, 62,* 767–781.

St. George, I. M., Williams, S., & Silva, P. A. (1994). Body size and the menarche: The Dunedin study. *Journal of Adolescent Health, 15,* 573–576.

St. James-Roberts, I. (2007). Helping parents to manage infant crying and sleeping: A review of the evidence and its implications for services. *Child Abuse Review, 16,* 47–69.

St. James-Roberts, I., & Plewis, I. (1996). Individual differences, daily fluctuations, and developmental changes in amounts of infant waking, fussing, crying, feeding, and sleeping. *Child Development, 67,* 2527–2540.

Staff, J., & Schulenberg, J. E. (2010). Millenials and the world of work: Experiences in paid work during adolescence. *Journal of Business and Psychology, 25,* 247–255.

Staiano, A. E., & Calvert, S. L. (2011). Exergames for physical education courses: Physical, social, and cognitive benefits. *Child Development Perspectives, 5,* 93–98.

Stairs, A., Bernhard, J. K., with Aboriginal Colleagues & Indigenous Feedback. (2002). Considerations for evaluating "good care" in Canadian Aboriginal early childhood settings. *McGill Journal of Education 37,* 309–330.

Stanik, C. E., Riina, E. M., & McHale, S. M. (2013). Parent-adolescent relationship qualities and adolescent adjustment in two-parent African American families. *Family Relations, 62,* 597–608.

Stanovich, K. E., Toplak, M. E., & West, R. F. (2008). The development of rational thought: A taxonomy of heuristics and biases. In R. V. Kail (Ed.), *Advances in child development and behavior* (Vol. 36, pp. 251–285). San Diego, CA: Elsevier.

Starky, S. (2005). *The Obesity Epidemic in Canada.* Ottawa, ON: Library of Parliament, Government of Canada.

Statistics Canada. (2003). Ethnic Diversity Survey. Retrieved from www.statcan.ca/Daily/English030929/d030929a .htm

Statistics Canada. (2004, June 15). Canadian community health survey: First information on sexual orientation. The Daily. Retrieved from www.statcan.ca/Daily/English/040615/d040615bb.htm

Statistics Canada (2004). The gap in achievement between boys and girls. Statistics Canada Education Matters. Retrieved from www.statcan.ca/english/freepub/81-004-XIE/200410mafe.htm

Statistics Canada. (2005). A brief review of research on neighbourhoods in Canada. Statistics Canada, Research and Analysis Division. Retrieved from www.infrastructure.gc.ca/research-recherche/result/notes/rn05_e.shtml

Statistics Canada. (2009). Divorces by province and territory. Retrieved from www40.statcan.gc.ca/l01/cst01/famil02-eng.htm

Statistics Canada. (2011a). Retrieved from www12.statcan.gc.ca/nhs-enm/2011/as-sa/99-010-x/99-010-x2011001-eng.cfm

Statistics Canada. (2011b). Gay pride - by the numbers. Retrieved from www42.statcan.gc.ca/smr08/2011/smr08_158_2011-eng.htm

Statistics Canada. (2012a). Family characteristics, by family type, family composition and characteristics of parents. Retrieved from www5.statcan.gc.ca/cansim/pick-choisir?lang=eng&p2=33&id=1110011

Statistics Canada. (2012b). Fifty years of families in Canada: 1961–2011. Retrieved from www12.statcan.ca/census-recensement/2011as-sa/98-312-x/98

Statistics Canada. (2012c). Portrait of families and living arrangements in Canada. Retrieved from www12.statcan.ca/census-recensement/2011as-sa/98-312-x/98

Statistics Canada. (2012d). Full-time and part-time employment by sex and age group. Retrieved from www.statcan.gc.ca/tables-tableaux/sum-som/l01/cst01/labor12-eng.htm

Statistics Canada. (2012e). Leading causes of death, infants. Retrieved from www5.statcan.gc.ca/cansim/pick-choisir?lang=eng&p2=33&id=1020562

Statistics Canada. (2012f). Visual Census. 2011 Census. Ottawa. Released October 24, 2012. Retrieved from www12.statcan.gc.ca/census-recensement/2011/dp-pd/vc-rv/index.cfm?Lang=ENG&TOPIC_ID=4&GEOCODE=01

Statistics Canada. (2012g). Linguistic characteristics of Canadians: Language, 2011 Census of Population. Ottawa, ON: Minister of Industry.

Statistics Canada. (2015a). Time spent on upaid care of a child in the household, by working arrangement and age of youngest child, Canada, 2010. Retrieved from www.statcan.gc.ca/pub/89-503-x/2010001/article/11546/tbl/tbl006-eng.htm

Statistics Canada. (2015b). Sexual behaviour and condom use of 15- to 24-year-olds in 2003 and 2009/2010. Retrieved from www.statcan.gc.ca/pub/82-003-x/2012001/article/11632/summary-sommaire-eng.htm

Statistics Canada. (2016a) Divorce. Retrieved from www.statcan.gc.ca/eng/help/bb/info/divorce

Statistics Canada (2016b). International adoptions. Retrieved from www.statcan.gc.ca/pub/11-402-x/2012000/chap/c-e/c-e02-eng.htm

Statistics Canada. (2016c). Leading causes of death, infants, by sex, Canada. Retrieved from www5.statcan.gc.ca/cansim/a26?lang=eng&retrLang=eng&id=1020562&pattern=sudden+infant+death&tabMode=dataTable&srchLan=-1&p1=1&p2=1

Statistics Canada. (2016d) Mean age of mother at time of delivery (live births), Canada, provinces and territories - annual (years). Retrieved from www5.statcan.gc.ca/cansim/a26?lang=eng&id=1024504

Stattin, H., Kerr, M., & Skoog, T. (2011). Early pubertal timing and girls' problem behavior: Integrating two hypotheses. Journal of Youth and Adolescence, 40, 1271–1278.

Steeger, C. M., & Gondoli, D. M. (2013). Mother-adolescent conflict as a mediator between adolescent problem behaviors and maternal psychological control. Developmental Psychology, 49, 804–814.

Steelandt, S., Thierry, B., Broihanne, M-H., & Dufour, V. (2012). The ability of children to delay gratification in an exchange task. Cognition, 122, 416–425.

Steele, C. M. (1997). A threat in the air: How stereotypes shape intellectual identity and performance. American Psychologist, 52, 613–629.

Steele, C. M., & Aronson, J. (1995). Stereotype threat and the intellectual test performance of African Americans. Journal of Personality and Social Psychology, 69, 797–811.

Steelman, J. D. (1994). Revision strategies employed by middle level students using computers. Journal of Educational Computing Research, 11, 141–152.

Steinberg, L. (2001). We know some things: Parent-adolescent relationships in retrospect and prospect. Journal of Research on Adolescence, 11, 1–19.

Steinberg, L., & Dornbusch, S. M. (1991). Negative correlates of part-time employment during adolescence: Replication and elaboration. Developmental Psychology, 27, 304–313.

Steinberg, L., & Monahan, K. C. (2007). Age differences in resistance to peer influence. Developmental Psychology, 43, 1531–1543.

Steinberg, L., & Silk, J. (2002). Parenting adolescents. In M. Bornstein (Ed.), Handbook of parenting (Vol. 1, 2nd ed., pp. 103–133). Hillsdale, NJ: Erlbaum.

Steinberg, L., Graham, S., O'Brien, L., Woolard, J., Cauffman, E., & Banich, M. (2009). Age differences in future orientation and delay discounting. Child Development, 80, 28–44.

Steinberg, L., Graham, S., O'Brien, L., Woolard, J., Cauffman, E., & Banich, M. (2009). Age differences in future orientation and delay discounting. Child Development, 80, 28–44.

Steinberg, L. D. (1999). Adolescence (5th ed.). Boston, MA: McGraw-Hill.

Stenberg, G. (2012). Why do infants look at and use positive information from some informants rather than others in ambiguous situations? Infancy, 17, 642–671.

Stephens, B. E., Tucker, R., & Vohr, B. R. (2010). Special health care needs of infants born at the limits of viability. Pediatrics, 125(6), 1152–1158.

Sternberg, R. J. (1999). The theory of successful intelligence. Review of General Psychology, 3, 292–316.

Sternberg, R. J., & Grigorenko, E. L. (2002). Dynamic testing: The nature and measurement of learning potential. New York, NY: Cambridge University Press.

Sternberg, R. J., & Kaufman J. C. (1998). Human abilities. Annual Review of Psychology, 49, 479–502.

Sternberg, R. J., Grigorenko, E. L., & Kidd, K. K. (2005). Intelligence, race, and genetics. American Psychologist, 60, 46–59.

Stevens, E., Plumert, J. M., Cremer, J. F., & Kearney, J. K. (2013). Preadolescent temperament and risky behavior: Bicycling across traffic-filled intersections in a virtual environment. Journal of Pediatric Psychology, 38, 285–295.

Stevens, J., & Ward-Estes, J. (2006). Attention-deficit/hyperactivity disorder. In M. Hersen & J. C. Thomas (Series Ed.), & R. T. Ammerman (Eds.), Comprehensive handbook of personality and psychopathology, Vol. 3: Child psychopathology (pp. 316–329). Hoboken, NJ: Wiley.

Stevenson, H. W., & Lee, S. (1990). Contexts of achievement. Monographs of the Society for Research in Child Development, 55(Serial No. 221).

Stevenson, H. W., & Stigler, J. W. (1992). The learning gap. New York, NY: Summit Books.

Stevenson, R. J., Oaten, M. J., Case, T. I., Repacholi, B. M., & Wagland, P. (2010). Children's response to adult disgust elicitors: Development and acquisition. Developmental Psychology, 46, 165–177.

Stewart, L., & Pascual-Leone, J. (1992). Mental capacity constraints and the development of moral reasoning. Journal of Experimental Child Psychology, 54, 251–287.

Stice, E., & Shaw, H. (2004). Eating disorder prevention programs: A meta-analytic review. Psychological Bulletin, 130, 206–227.

Stice, E., Shaw, H., Bohon, C., Martin, C. N., & Rohde, P. (2009). A meta-analytic review of depression prevention programs for children and adolescents: Factors that predict magnitude of intervention effects. Journal of Consulting and Clinical Psychology, 77, 486–503.

Stice, E., South, K., & Shaw, H. (2012). Future directions in etiologic, prevention, and treatment research for eating disorders. Journal of Clinical Child and Adolescent Psychology, 41, 845–855

Stifter, C. A., Cipriano, E., Conway, A., & Kelleher, R. (2009). Temperament and the development of conscience: The moderating role of effortful control. Social Development, 18, 353–374.

Stigler, J. W., Gallimore, R., & Hiebert, J. (2000). Using video surveys to compare classrooms and teaching across cultures: Examples and lessons from the TIMSS video studies. Educational Psychologist, 35, 87–100.

Stiles, J., Reilly, J., Paul, B., & Moses, P. (2005). Cognitive development following early brain injury: Evidence for neural adaptation. Trends in Cognitive Sciences, 9, 136–143.

Stipek, D., & Miles, S. (2008). Effects of aggression on achievement: Does conflict with the teacher make it worse? Child Development, 79, 1721–1735.

Stjernqvist, K. (2009). Predicting development for extremely low birthweight infants: Sweden. In K. Nugent, B. J. Petrauskas, & T. B. Brazelton (Eds.), The newborn as a person: Enabling healthy infant development worldwide. Hoboken, NJ: Wiley.

Stobart, G. (2005). Fairness in multicultural assessment systems. Assessment in Education, 12(3), 275–287.

Straus, M. A. (2000). Corporal punishment and primary prevention of physical abuse. Child Abuse and Neglect, 9, 1109–1114.

Strayer, D. L., Drews, F. A., & Crouch, D. J. (2006). A comparison of the cell phone driver and the drunk driver. Human Factors, 48, 381–391.

Strayer, J., & Roberts, W. (2004). Children's anger, emotional expressiveness, and empathy: Relations with parents' empathy, emotional expressiveness, and parenting practices. Social Development, 13, 229–254.

Striano, T., Tomasello, M., & Rochat, P. (2001). Social and object support for early symbolic play. Developmental Science, 4, 442–455.

Stright, A. D., Gallagher, K. C., & Kelley, K. (2008). Infant temperament moderates relations between maternal parenting in early childhood and children's adjustment in first grade. Child Development, 79, 186–200.

Strough, J., & Berg, C. A. (2000). Goals as a mediator of gender differences in high-affiliation dyadic conversations. Developmental Psychology, 36, 117–125.

Sturaro, C., van Lier, P. A. C., Cuijpers, P., & Koot, H. M. (2011). The role of peer relationships in the development of early school-age externalizing problems. Child Development, 82, 758–765.

Sturge-Apple, M. L., Davies, P. T., & Cummings, E. M. (2010). Typologies of family functioning and children's adjustment during the early school years. Child Development, 81, 1320–1335.

Subotnik, R. F., Olszewski-Kubilius, P., & Worrell, F. C. (2011). Rethinking giftedness and gifted education: A proposed direction forward based on psychological science. Psychological Science in the Public Interest, 12, 3–54.

Sullivan, M. W., & Lewis, M. (2003). Contextual determinants of anger and other negative expressions in young infants. Developmental Psychology, 39, 693–705.

Super, C. M. (1981). Cross-cultural research on infancy. In H. C. Triandis & A. Heron (Eds.), Handbook of cross-cultural psychology: Vol. 4. Developmental psychology. Boston, MA: Allyn & Bacon.

Super, C. M., Herrera, M. G., & Mora, J. O. (1990). Long-term effects of food supplementation and psychosocial intervention on the physical growth of Colombian infants at risk of malnutrition. Child Development, 61, 29–49.

Susser, E., Hoek, H. W., & Brown, A. (1998). Neurodevelopmental disorders after prenatal famine: The story of the Dutch Famine Study. American Journal of Epidemiology, 147(3), 213–216.

Sussman, S., Pokhrel, P., Ashmore, R. D., & Brown, B. B. (2007). Adolescent peer group identification and characteristics: A review of the literature. Addictive Behaviors, 32, 1602–1627.

Suzuki, L., & Aronson, J. (2005). The cultural malleability of intelligence and its impact on the racial/ethnic hierarchy. Psychology, Public Policy, and Law, 11, 320–327.

Svirsky, M. A., Robbins, A. M., Kirk, K. I., Pisoni, D. B., & Miyamoto, R. T. (2000). Language development in profoundly deaf children with cochlear implants. *Psychological Science, 11,* 153–158.

Sweeney, M. M. (2010). Remarriage and stepfamilies: Strategic sites for family scholarship in the 21st century. *Journal of Marriage and Family, 72,* 667–684.

Sylvan, L. J., & Christodoulou, J. A. (2010). Understanding the role of neuroscience in brain based products: A guide for educators and consumers. *Mind, Brain, and Education, 4,* 1–7.

Symonds, W. C., Schwartz, R. B., & Ferguson, R. (2011). *Pathways to prosperity: Meeting the challenge of preparing young Americans for the 21st century.* Cambridge, MA: Harvard Graduate School of Education.

Szücks, D., & Goswami, U. (2007). Educational neuroscience: Defining a new discipline for the study of mental representations. *Mind, Brain, and Education, 1,* 114–127.

Tager-Flusberg, H. (1993). Putting words together: Morphology and syntax in the preschool years. In J. Berko Gleason (Ed.), *The development of language* (3rd ed.). New York, NY: Macmillan.

Tager-Flusberg, H. (2007). Evaluating the theory-of-mind hypothesis of autism. *Current Directions in Psychological Science, 16,* 311–315.

Tahiroglu, D., Mannering, A. M., & Taylor, M. (2011). Visual and auditory imagery associated with children's imaginary companions. *Imagination, Cognition, and Personality, 31,* 99–112.

Tamis-LeMonda, C. S., & Bornstein, M. H. (1996). Variation in children's exploratory, nonsymbolic, and symbolic play: An explanatory multidimensional framework. In C. Rovee-Collier & L. P. Lipsitt (Eds.), *Advances in infancy research* (Vol. 10). Norwood, NJ: Ablex.

Tamis-LeMonda, C. S., & Bornstein, M. H. (2002). Maternal responsiveness and early language acquisition. In R. V. Kail & H. W. Reese (Eds.), *Advances in child development and behavior* (Vol. 29, pp. 90–127). San Diego, CA: Academic Press.

Tamis-LeMonda, C. S., Adolph, K. E., Lobo, S. A., Karasik, L. B., Ishak, S., & Dimitropoulou, K. A. (2008). When infants take mothers' advice: 18-month-olds integrate perceptual and social information to guide motor action. *Developmental Psychology, 44,* 734–746.

Tan, K. L. (2009). Bed sharing among mother-infant pairs in Kiang District, Peninsular Malaysia, and its relationship to breast-feeding. *Journal of Developmental & Behavioral Pediatrics, 30,* 420–425.

Tandon, S. L., & Sharma, R. (2006). Female foeticide and infanticide in India: An analysis of crimes against girl children. *International Journal of Criminal Justice Sciences, 1*(1), n.p. Retrieved from www.sascv.org/ijcjs/Snehlata.html

Tanner, J. M. (1970). Physical growth. In P. H. Mussen (Ed.), *Carmichael's manual of child psychology* (3rd ed.). New York, NY: Wiley.

Tanner, J. M. (1990). *Fetus into man: Physical growth from conception to maturity* (2nd ed.). Cambridge, MA: Harvard University Press.

Tarabulsy, G. M., Bernier, A., Provost, M. A., Maranda, J., Larose, S., Moss, E., et al. (2005). Another look inside the gap: Ecological contributions to the transmission of attachment in a simple of adolescent mother–infant dyads. *Developmental Psychology, 41,* 212–224.

Tarantino, N., Tully, E. C., Garcia, S. E., South, S., Iacono, W. G., & McGue, M. (2014). Genetic and environmental influences on affiliation with deviant peers during adolescence and early adulthood. *Developmental Psychology, 50,* 663–673.

Tardif, T., So, C. W-C., & Kaciroti, N. (2007). Language and false belief: Evidence for general, not specific, effects in Cantonese-speaking preschoolers. *Developmental Psychology, 43,* 318–340.

Tardif, T., Fletcher, P., Liang, W., Zhang, Z., Kaciroti, N., & Marchman, V. A. (2008). Baby's first 10 words. *Developmental Psychology, 44*(4), 929–938.

Taylor, J., & Schatschneider, C. (2010). Genetic influence on literacy constructs in kindergarten and first grade: Evidence from a diverse twin sample. *Behavior Genetics, 40,* 591–602.

Taylor, M., Carlson, S. M., Maring, B. L., Gerow, L., & Charley, C. M. (2004). The characteristics and correlates of fantasy in school-age children: Imaginary companions, impersonation, and social understanding. *Developmental Psychology, 40,* 1173–1187.

Taylor, M., Hulette, A. C., & Dishion, T. J. (2010). Longitudinal outcomes of young high-risk adolescents with imaginary companions. *Developmental Psychology, 46,* 632–1636.

Taylor, M. G., Rhodes, M., & Gelman, S. A. (2009). Boys will be boys; cows will be cows: Children's essentialist reasoning about gender categories and animal species. *Child Development, 80,* 461–481.

Teachman, J. (2008). Complex life course patterns and the risk of divorce in second marriages. *Journal of Marriage and Family, 70,* 294–305.

Tegethoff, M., Greene, N., Olsen, J., Meyer, A. H., & Meinlschmidt, G. (2010). Maternal psychosocial adversity is associated with length of gestation and offspring size at birth: Evidence from a population-based cohort study. *Psychosomatic Medicine, 72,* 419–426.

Teichman, Y. (2001). The development of Israeli children's images of Jews and Arabs and their expression in human figure drawings. *Developmental Psychology, 37,* 749–761.

Teilmann, G., Pedersen, C. B., Skakkeback, N. E., & Jensen, T. K. (2006). Increased risk of precocious puberty in internationally adopted children in Denmark. *Pediatrics, 118,* 391–399.

Tenenbaum, H. R., & Leaper, C. (2002). Are parents' gender schemas related to their children's gender-related cognitions? A meta-analysis. *Developmental Psychology, 38*(4), 615–630.

Terlecki, M. S., & Newcombe, N. S. (2005). How important is the digital divide? The relations of computer and videogame usage to gender differences in mental rotation ability. *Sex Roles, 53,* 433–441.

Thelen, E., & Ulrich, B. D. (1991). Hidden skills. *Monographs of the Society for Research in Child Development, 56*(Serial No. 223).

Thelen, E., Ulrich, B. D., & Jensen, J. L. (1989). The developmental origins of locomotion. In M. H. Woollacott & A. Shumway-Cook (Eds.), *Development of posture and gait across the life span.* Columbia, SC: University of South Carolina Press.

Thiele, A. T., & Leier, B. (2010). Towards an ethical policy for the prevention of fetal sex selection in Canada. *Journal of Obstetrics and Gynaecology Canada, 32*(1), 54–57.

Thiessen, E. D., & Saffran, J. R. (2003). When cues collide: Use of stress and statistical cues to word boundaries by 7- to 9-month-old infants. *Developmental Psychology, 39,* 706–716.

Thiessen, E. D., Hill, E., & Saffran, J. R. (2005). Infant-directed speech facilitates word segmentation. *Infancy, 7,* 53–71.

ThinkFirst Foundation of Canada. (n.d.). Playing smart soccer. Retrieved from www.thinkfirst.ca/documents/ThinkFirst-Soccer-English.pdf

Thomaes, S., Brummelman, E., Reijntjes, A., & Bushman, B. (2013). When Narcissus was a boy: Origins, nature, and consequences of childhood narcissism. *Child Development Perspectives, 7,* 22–26.

Thomas, A., & Chess, S. (1977). *Temperament and development.* New York, NY: Brunner/Mazel.

Thomas, A., Chess, S., & Birch, H. G. (1968). *Temperament and behavior disorders in children.* New York, NY: New York University Press.

Thomas, J. R., & French, K. E. (1985). Gender differences across age in motor performance: A meta-analysis. *Psychological Bulletin, 98,* 260–282.

Thomas, J. R., Alderson, J. A., Thomas, K. T., Campbell, A. C., & Elliot, B. C. (2010). Developmental gender differences for overhand throwing in Aboriginal Australian children. *Research Quarterly for Exercise and Sport, 81,* 432–441.

Thomas, R., & Zimmer-Gembeck, M. J. (2011). Accumulating evidence for parent-child interaction therapy in the prevention of child maltreatment. *Child Development, 82,* 177–192.

Thomas, R., & Zimmer-Gembeck, M. J. (2012). Parent-Child Interaction Therapy: An evidence-based treatment for child maltreatment. *Child Maltreatment, 17,* 253–266.

Thomas, S., Reijntjes, A., Orobio de Castro, B., Bushman, B. J., Poorthuis, A., & Telch, M. J. (2010). I like me if you like me: On the interpersonal modulation and regulation of preadolescents' state self-esteem. *Child Development, 81,* 811–825.

Thompson, A. E., & Voyer, D. (2014). Sex differences in the ability to recognise non-verbal displays of emotion: A meta-analysis. *Cognition and Emotion, 28,* 1164–1195.

Thompson, G. E., Cameron, R. E., & Fuller-Thomson, E. (2013) Walking the red road: The role of First Nations grandparents in promoting cultural wellbeing. *International Journal of Aging and Human Development, 76*(1), 55–78.

Thompson, G. G. (1952). *Child psychology.* Boston, MA: Houghton Mifflin.

Thompson, R. (2007). *What is albinism?* East Hampstead, NH: National Organization for Albinism and Hypopigmentation.

Thompson, R. A. (2000). The legacy of early attachments. *Child Development, 71,* 145–152.

Thompson, R. A. (2006). The development of the person: Social understanding, relationships, conscience, self. In N. Eisenberg (Ed.), *Handbook of child psychology: Vol. 3. Social, emotional, and personality development* (6th ed.). Hoboken, NJ: Wiley.

Thompson, R. A., & Limber, S. (1991). "Social anxiety" in infancy: Stranger wariness and separation distress. In H. Leitenberg (Ed.), *Handbook of social and evaluation anxiety.* New York, NY: Plenum.

Thompson, R. A., Laible, D. J., & Ontai, L. L. (2003). Early understandings of emotion, morality, and self: Developing a working model. *Advances in Child Development and Behavior, 31,* 137–172.

Thompson, R. A., Lewis, M. D., & Calkins, S. D. (2008). Reassessing emotion regulation. *Child Development Perspectives, 2,* 124–131.

Thornberry, T. P., Krohn, M. D., Lizotte, A. J., Smith, C. A., & Tobin, K. (2003). *Gangs and delinquency in developmental perspective.* New York, NY: Cambridge University Press.

Thorne, B. (1993). *Gender play: Girls and boys in school.* New Brunswick, NJ: Rutgers University Press.

Thurstone, L. L., & Thurstone, T. G. (1941). Factorial studies of intelligence. *Psychometric Monograph, No. 2.*

Tincoff, R., & Jusczyk, P. W. (1999). Some beginnings of word comprehension in 6-month-olds. *Psychological Science, 10,* 172–175.

Tisak, M. (1993). Preschool children's judgements of moral and personal events involving physical harm and property damage. *Merrill-Palmer Quarterly, 39,* 375–390.

Tither, J. M., & Ellis, B. J. (2008). Impact of fathers on daughters' age at menarche: A genetically and environmentally controlled sibling study. *Developmental Psychology, 44,* 1409–1420.

Todd, R. M., Evans, J. W., Morris, D., Lewis, M. D., & Taylor, M. J. (2011). The changing face of emotion: Age-related patterns of amygdala activation to salient faces. *SCAN, 6,* 12–23. doi: 10.1093/scan/nsq007

Tomasello, M., & Vaish, A. (2013). Origins of human cooperation and morality. *Annual Review of Psychology, 64,* 231–255.

Tomasello, M., Carpenter, M., & Liszkowski, U. (2007). A new look at infant pointing. *Child Development, 78,* 705–722.

Tomlinson, M., Cooper, P., & Murray, L. (2005). The mother–infant relationship and infant attachment in a South African peri-urban settlement. *Child Development, 76,* 1044–1054.

Tomson, L. M., Pangrazi, R. P., Friedman, G., & Hutchison, H. (2003). Childhood depressive symptoms, physical activity and health related fitness. *Journal of Sport Psychology, 25,* 419–439.

Tooby, J., & Cosmides, L. (2008). The evolutionary psychology of emotions and their relationship to internal regulatory variables. In M. Lewis, J. M. Haviland-Jones, & L. F. Barrett (Eds.), *Handbook of emotions* (3rd ed., pp. 114–137). New York, NY: Guilford Press.

Torgesen, J. K. (2004). Learning disabilities: A historical and conceptual overview. In B. Y. L. Wong (Ed.), *Learning about learning disabilities* (3rd ed., pp. 3–40). San Diego, CA: Elsevier.

Tracy, B., Reid, R., & Graham, S. (2009). Teaching young students strategies for planning and drafting stories. The impact of self-regulated strategy development. *Journal of Educational Research, 102,* 323–331.

Traffic Injury Research Foundation. (2005). *Youth and road crashes.* Retrieved from www.aim-digest.com/ gateway/pages/drive/articles/canada.htm

Traffic Injury Research Foundation. (TIRF). (2015). *Alcohol and drug use among fatally injured teen drivers.* Retrieved from www.tirf.ca/publications/ publications_show.php?pub_id=327

Trainor, L. J., & Heinmiller, B. M. (1998). The development of evaluative responses to music: Infants prefer to listen to consonance over dissonance. *Infant Behavior and Development, 21,* 77–88.

Trainor, L. J., Austin, C. M., & Desjardins, R. N. (2000). Is infant-directed speech prosody a result of the vocal expression of emotion? *Psychological Science, 11,* 188–195.

Tran, H., & Weinraub, M. (2006). Child care effects in context: Quality, stability, and multiplicity in non-maternal child care arrangements during the first 15 months of life. *Developmental Psychology, 42,* 566–582.

Treiman, R., & Kessler, B. (2003). The role of letter names in the acquisition of literacy. *Advances in Child Development and Behavior, 31,* 105–135.

Tremblay, M. S., LeBlanc, A. G., Kho, M. E., Saunders, T. J., Larouche, R., Colley, R. C., et al. (2011). Systematic review of sedentary behaviour and health indicators in school-aged children and youth. *International Journal of Behavioral Nutrition and Physical Activity, 8,* Article 98

Tremblay, S., Morrison, R., & Tremblay, M. (2006). Estimating child BMI growth curves for Canada. Statistics Canada International Symposium Series – Proceedings. Ottawa, ON: Statistics Canada.

Troseth, G. L., Pierroutsakos, S. L., & DeLoache, J. S. (2004). From the innocent to the intelligent eye: The early development of pictorial competence. In R. V. Kail (Ed.), *Advances in child development and behavior* (Vol. 32, pp. 1–35). San Diego, CA: Elsevier.

Trzesniewski, K. H., Donnellan, M. B., Caspi, A., Moffitt, T. E., Robins, R. W., & Poultin, R. (2006). Adolescent low self-esteem is a risk factor for adult poor health, criminal behavior, and limited economic prospects. *Developmental Psychology, 42,* 381–390.

Tse, J. (2006). Research on day treatment programs for preschoolers with disruptive behaviour disorders. *Psychiatric Services, 57*(4), 477–486. Retrieved from www.ps.psychiatryonline.org

Tsubota, Y., & Chen, Z. (2012). How do young children's spatio-symbolic skills change over short time scales? *Journal of Experimental Child Psychology, 111,* 1–21.

Tucker, M. S. (2011). *Surpassing Shanghai: An agenda for American education built on the world's leading systems.* Cambridge, MA: Harvard Education Press.

Tucker-Drob, E. M., Briley, D. A., & Harden, K. P. (2013). Genetic and environmental influences on cognition across development and context. *Current Directions in Psychological Science, 22,* 349–355.

Tudge, J. R. H., Winterhoff, P. A., & Hogan, D. M. (1996). The cognitive consequences of collaborative problem solving with and without feedback. *Child Development, 67,* 2892–2909.

Turiel, E. (1998). The development of morality. In W. Damon (Ed.), *Handbook of child psychology, Vol. 3: Social, emotional, and personality development* (pp. 863–932). New York, NY: Wiley.

Turiel, E. (2006). The development of morality. In W. Damon & R. M. Lerner (Eds.), *Handbook of child psychology, Vol. 3* (6th ed). New York, NY: Wiley.

Twells, L. K., Gregory, D. M., Reddigan, J., & Midodzi, W. K. (2014). Current and predicted prevalence of obesity in Canada: A trend analysis. *Canadian Medical Association Open.* doi: 10.9778/cmajo.20130016.

Twemlow, Stuart W., Biggs, B. K., Nelson, T .D., Vernberg, E. M., Fonagy, P., & Twemlow, Stephen W. (2008). Effects of participation in a martial arts-based antibullying program in elementary schools. *Psychology in the Schools, 45*(10), 947–959.

Twenge, J. M., & Campbell, W. K. (2001). Age and birth cohort differences in self-esteem: A cross-temporal meta-analysis. *Personality and Social Psychology Review, 5,* 321–344.

Twenge, J. M., & Crocker, J. (2002). Race and self-esteem: Meta-analysis comparing Whites, Blacks, Hispanics, and American Indians and comment on Gray-Little and Hafdahl (2000). *Psychological Bulletin, 128,* 371–408.

Tynes, B. M. (2007). Role taking in online "classrooms": What adolescents are learning about race and ethnicity. *Developmental Psychology, 43,* 1312–1320.

Tynes, B. M., Umaña-Taylor, A. J., Rose, C. A., Lin, J., & Anderson, C. J. (2012). Online racial discrimination and the protective function of ethnic identity and self-esteem for African American adolescents. *Developmental Psychology, 48,* 343–355.

Tzuriel, D. (2013). Dynamic assessment of learning potential. In M. M. C. Mok (Ed.), *Self-directed learning oriented assessments in the Asia-Pacific* (pp. 235–235). Heidelberg, Germany: Springer Dordrecht.

Tzuriel, D., & Egozi, G. (2010). Gender differnces in spatial ability of young children: The effects of training and processing strategies. *Child Development, 81,* 1417–1430.

U.S. Centers for Disease Control. (2012). *Breastfeeding report card—United States, 2012.* Atlanta GA: Author.

U.S. Department of Health and Human Services. (2010). *The Surgeon General's vision for a healthy and fit nation.* Rockville, MD: Author.

Uberlacker, S. (2017, July 26). In-utero surgery gives baby Sebastian good heart-start in life. *National Post.* Retrieved from http://nationalpost.com/pmn/ news-pmn/canada-news-pmn/in-utero-surgery-gives-baby-sebastian-good-heart-start-in-life/ wcm/8603e838-8ac0-4a20-b0b6-85a58ae857f4

Uchiyama, I., Anderson, D. I., Campos, J. J., Witherington, D., Frankel, C. B., Lejeune, L. et al. (2008). Locomotor experience affects self and emotion. *Developmental Psychology, 44,* 1225–1231.

Ullman, M. T., Miranda, R. A., & Travers, M. L. (2008). Sex differences in the neurocognition of language. In J. B. Becker, K. J. Berkley, N. Geary, E. Hampson, J. P. Herman, & E. A. Young (Eds.), *Sex Differences in the Brain* (pp. 291–309). New York, NY: Oxford University Press.

Umaña-Taylor, A., Diversi, M., & Fine, M. (2002). Ethnic identity and self-esteem among Latino adolescents: Distinctions among Latino populations. *Journal of Adolescent Research, 17,* 303–327.

Umaña-Taylor, A. J., & Guimond, A. B. (2010). A longitudinal examination of parenting behaviors and perceived discrimination predicting Latino adolescents' ethnic identity. *Developmental Psychology, 46,* 636–650.

Umbel, V. M., Pearson, B. Z., Fernandez, M. C., & Oller, D. K. (1992). Measuring bilingual children's receptive vocabularies. *Child Development, 63,* 1012–1020.

United Nations Children's Fund (UNICEF). (2004). *The state of the world's children 2005.* New York, NY: Author.

UNICEF. (2007). The state of the world's children 2008: Child survival. New York, NY: Author. Retrieved from www.unicef.org/publications/index_42623 .html

UNICEF. (2010). *Facts for life* (4th ed.). New York, NY: Author.

UNICEF, WHO, & The World Bank. (2012). *UNICEF-WHO-World Bank joint malnutrition estimates.* New York, NY: Author.

UNICEF, WHO, World Bank, & UN-DESA Population Division. (2015). Levels and trends in child mortality: Report 2015. Estimates developed by the UN Inter-agency Group for Child Mortality.Retrieved from www.who.int/maternal_child_adolescent/ documents/levels_trends_child_mortality_2015/en/

United Nations, Department of Economic and Social Affairs, Population Division. (2015). World population prospects: The 2015 revision, key findings and advance tables. Working Paper No. ESA/P/WP.241. Retrieved from https://esa.un.org/unpd/wpp/ publications/files/key_findings_wpp_2015.pdf

Updegraff, K. A., Thayer, S. M., Whiteman, S. D., Denning D. J., & McHale, S. M. (2005). Aggression in adolescents' sibling relationships: Links to sibling and parent–adolescent relationship quality. *Family Relations: Interdisciplinary Journal of Applied Family Studies, 54,* 373–385.

Usher, E. L., & Pajares, F. (2009). Sources of self-efficacy in mathematics: A validation study. *Contemporary Educational Psychology, 34,* 89–101.

Uskul, A. (2004). Women's menarche stories from a multicultural sample. *Social Sciences and Medicine, 59,* 667–679.

Uttal, D. H., Meadow, N. G., Tipton, E., Hand, L. L., Alden, A. R., Warren, C., et al. (2013). The malleability of spatial skills: A meta-analysis of training studies. *Psychological Bulletin, 139,* 352–402.

Vail, S. (2002). *Family values: Choosing a "made in Canada" family policy,* (338-02 Report). Ottawa, ON: The Conference Board of Canada.

Vaillancourt, T., Brittain, H. L., McDougall, P., & Duku, E. (2013). Longitudinal links between childhood peer victimization, internalizing and externalizing problems, and academic functioning: Developmental cascades. *Journal of Abnormal Child Psychology, 41,* 1203–1215.

Vaillant-Molina, M., Bahrick, L. E., & Flom, R. (2013). Young infants match facial and vocal emotional expressions of other infants. *Infancy, 18*(S1), E97–E111.

Vaish, A., Carpenter, M., & Tomasello, M. (2009). Sympathy through affective perspective taking and its relation to prosocial behavior in toddlers. *Developmental Psychology, 45,* 534–543.

Vaish, A., Woodward, A., & Grossmann, T. (2008). Not all emotions are created equal: The negativity bias in social-emotional development. *Psychological Bulletin, 134,* 383–403.

Valenza, E., & Bulf, H. (2011). Early development of object unity: Evidence for perceptual completion in newborns. *Developmental Science, 14,* 799–808.

van der Mark, I. L., van IJzendoorn, M. H., & Bakermans-Kranenburg, M. J. (2002). Development of empathy in girls during the second year of life: Associations with parenting, attachment, and temperament. *Social Development, 11,* 451–468.

Van Duijvenvoorde, A. C. K., Huizenga, H. M., & Jansen, B. R. J. (2014). What is and what could have been: Experiencing regret and relief across childhood. *Cognition and Emotion, 28,* 926–935.

van Goozen, S. H., Fairchild, G., Snoek, H., & Harold, G. T. (2007). The evidence for a neurobiological model of childhood antisocial behavior. *Psychological Bulletin, 133,* 149–182.

Van Hof, P., van der Kamp, J., & Savelsbergh, G. J. P. (2002). The relation of unimanual and bimanual reaching to crossing the midline. *Child Development, 73,* 1352–1362.

Van IJzendoorn, M. H., & Bakermans-Kranenburg, M. J. (2012). Integrating temperament and attachment: The different susceptibility paradigm. In M. Zentner & R. L. Shiner (Eds.), *Handbook of temperament* (pp. 403–424). New York, NY: Guilford Press.

Van IJzendoorn, M. H., & Sagi-Schwartz, A. (2008). Cross-cultural patterns of attachment: Universal and contextual dimensions. In J. Cassidy & P. R. Shaver (Eds.), *Handbook of attachment: Theory, research, and clinical applications* (pp. 713–734). New York, NY: Guilford Press.

Van IJzendoorn, M. H., Bakermans-Kranenburg, M. J., & Ebstein, R. P. (2011). Methylation matters in child development: Toward developmental behavioral epigenetics. *Child Development Perspectives, 5,* 305–310.

van IJzendoorn, M. H., Schuengel, C., & Bakermans-Kranenburg, M. J. (1999). Disorganized attachment in early childhood: Meta-analysis of precursors, concomitants, and sequelae. *Development and Psychopathology, 11,* 225–249.

van IJzendoorn, M. H., Vereijken, C. M. J. L., Bakermans-Kranenburg, M. J., & Riksen-Walraven, J. (2004). Assessing attachment security with the Attachment Q Sort: Meta-analytic evidence for the validity of the observer AQS. *Child Development, 75,* 1188–1213.

van Lier, P. A. C., Vitaro, F., Barker, E. D., Brendgen, M., Tremblay, R. E., & Boivin, M. (2012). Peer victimization, poor academic achievement, and the link between childhood externalizing and internalizing problems. *Child Development, 83,* 1775–1788.

Van Tuijl, L. A., de Jong, P. J., Sportel, B. E., de Hullu, E., & Nauta, M. H. (2014). Implicit and explicit self-esteem and their reciprocal relationship with symptoms of depression and social anxiety: A longitudinal study in adolescents. *Journal of Behavior Therapy and Experimental Psychiatry, 45,* 113–121.

Van Zalk, M., Herman, W., Kerr, M., Branje, S. J. T., Stattin, H., & Meeus, W. H. J. (2010). It takes three: Selection, influence, and de-selection processes of depression in adolescent friendship networks. *Developmental Psychology, 46,* 927–938.

Vandell, D. L., Pierce, K., & Dadisman, K. (2005). Out-of-school settings as a developmental context for children and youth. In R. V. Kail (Ed.), *Advances in child development and behavior* (Vol. 33, pp. 43–77). Amsterdam, The Netherlands: Elsevier Academic Press.

Vander Wal, J. S., & Thelen, M. H. (2000). Eating and body image concerns among obese and average-weight children. *Addictive Behaviors, 25,* 775–778.

Vazsonyi, A. T., & Huang, L. (2010). Where self-control comes from: On the development of self-control and its relationship to deviance over time. *Developmental Psychology, 46,* 245–257.

Vazsonyi, A. T., & Snider, J. B. (2008). Mentoring, competencies, and adjustment in adolescents: American part-time employment and European apprenticeships. *International Journal of Behavioral Development, 32,* 46–55.

Vazsonyi, A. T., Hibbert, J. R., & Snider, J. B. (2003). Exotic enterprise no more? Adolescent reports of family and parenting practices from youth in four countries. *Journal of Research on Adolescence, 13,* 129–160.

Veenstra, R., Lindberg, S., Oldenhinkel, A. J., De Winter, A. F., Verhulst, F. C., & Ormel, J. (2005). Bullying and victimization in elementary schools: A comparison of bullies, victims, bully/victims, and uninvolved preadolescents. *Developmental Psychology, 41,* 672–682.

Véronneau, M-H., Vitaro, F., Brendgen, M., Dishion, T. J., & Tremblay, R. E. (2010). Transactional analysis of the reciprocal links between peer experiences and academic achievement from middle childhood to early adolescence. *Developmental Psychology 46*(4), 773–790.

Verschaeve, L. (2009). Genetic damage in subjects exposed to radiofrequency radiation. *Mutation Research—Reviews in Mutation Research, 681,* 259–270.

Victora, C. G., Adam, T., Bruce, J., & Evans, D. B. (2006). Integrated management of the sick child. In

D. T. Jamison et al. (Eds.), *Disease control priorities in developing countries* (2nd ed., pp. 1172–1192). New York, NY: Oxford University Press.

Vieno, A., Nation, M., Pastore, M., & Santinello, M. (2009). Parenting and antisocial behavior: A model of the relationship between adolescent self-discosure, parental closeness, parental control, and adolescent antisocial behavior. *Developmental Psychology, 45,* 1509–1519.

Vijayalaxmi & Prihoda, T. J. (2012). Genetic damage in human cells exposed to non-ionizing radiofrequency fields: A meta-analysis of the data from 88 publications (1990–2011). *Mutation Research/Genetic Toxicology and Environmental Mutagenesis, 749,* 1–16.

Visher, E. B., Visher, J. S., & Pasley, K. (2003). Remarriage families and stepparenting. In F. Walsh (Ed.), *Normal family processes* (pp. 153–175). New York, NY: Guilford Press.

Vitiello, B., & Swedo, S. (2004). Antidepressant medications in children. *New England Journal of Medicine, 350,* 1489–1491.

Volling, B. L. (2012). Family transitions following the birth of a sibling: An empirical review of changes in the firstborn's adjustment. *Psychological Bulletin, 138,* 497–528.

Vorhees, C. V., & Mollnow, E. (1987). Behavior teratogenesis: Long-term influences on behavior. In J. D. Osofsky (Ed.), *Handbook of infant development* (2nd ed.). New York, NY: Wiley.

Vouloumanos, A., & Werker, J. F. (2004). Tuned to the signal: The privileged status of speech for young infants. *Developmental Science, 7*(3), 270–276.

Vouloumanos, A., Hauser, M. D., Werker, J. F., & Martin, A. (2010). The tuning of human neonates' preference for speech. *Child Development, 81,* 517–527.

Voyer, D., & Saunders, K. (2004). Gender differences on the mental rotations test: A factor analysis. *Acta Psychologica, 117,* 79–94.

Voyer, D., Postma, A., Brake, B., & Imperato-McGinley, J. (2007). Gender differences in object location memory: A meta-analysis. *Psychonomic Bulletin & Review, 14,* 23–38.

Voyer, D., Voyer, S., & Bryden, M. P. (1995). Magnitude of sex differences in spatial abilities: A meta-analysis and consideration of critical variables. *Psychological Bulletin, 117,* 250–270.

Vraneković, J., Božović, I. B., Grubić, Z., Wagner, J., Pavlinić, D., Dahoun, S., et al. (2012). Down syndrome: Parental origin, recombination, and maternal age. *Genetic Testing and Molecular Biomarkers, 16,* 70–73.

Vygotsky, L. S. (1978). *Mind in society: The development of higher psychological processes* (M. Cole, V. John-Steiner, S. Scribner, & E. Soubermen, Eds.). Cambridge, MA: Harvard University Press.

Wachs, T. D., & Bates, J. E. (2001). Temperament. In G. Bremner & A. Fogel (Eds.), *Blackwell handbook of infant development* (pp. 465–501). Malden, MA: Blackwell.

Wagner, K., & Dobkins, K. R. (2011). Synaesthetic associations decrease during infancy. *Psychological Science, 22,* 1067–1072.

Wainwright, J. L., & Patterson, C. J. (2008). Peer relations among adolescents with female same-sex parents. *Developmental Psychology, 44,* 117–126.

Wainwright, J. L., Russell, S. T., & Patterson, C. J. (2004). Psychosocial adjustment, school outcomes, and romantic relationships of adolescents with same-sex parents. *Child Development, 75,* 1886–1898.

Wakschlag, L. S., Leventhal, B. L., Pine, D. S., Pickett, K. E., & Carter, A. S. (2006). Elucidating early mechanisms of developmental psychopathology: The case of prenatal smoking and disruptive behavior. *Child Development, 77,* 893–906.

Walberg, H. J. (1995). General practices. In G. Cawelti (Ed.), *Handbook of research on improving student achievement*. Arlington, VA: Educational Research Service.

Walden, T., Kim, G., McCoy, C., & Karrass, J. (2007). Do you believe in magic? Infants' social looking during violation of expectations. *Developmental Science, 10,* 654–663.

Walker, L. J. (1980). Cognitive and perspective-taking prerequisites for moral development. *Child Development, 51,* 131–139.

Walker, L. J. & Taylor, J. H. (1991). Family interactions and the development of moral reasoning. *Child Development, 62,* 264–283.

Walker, L. J., Hennig, K. H., & Krettenauer, T. (2000). Parent and peer contexts for children's moral reasoning development. *Child Development, 71,* 1033–1048.

Walker, P., Bremner, J. G., Mason, U., Spring, J., Mattock, K., Slater, A., et al. (2010). Preverbal infants' sensitivity to synaesthetic cross-modality correspondences. *Psychological Science, 21,* 21–25.

Wallentin, M. (2009). Putative sex differences in verbal abilities and language cortex: A critical review. *Brain & Language, 108,* 175–183.

Wang, Q. (2006). Culture and the development of self-knowledge. *Current Directions in Psychological Science, 15,* 182–187.

Wang, Q., Pomerantz, E. M., & Chen, H. (2007). The role of parents' control in early adolescents' psychological functioning: A longitudinal investigation in the United States and China. *Child Development, 78,* 1592–1610.

Wang, S. & Baillargeon, R. (2005). Inducing infants to detect a physical violation in a single trial. *Psychological Science, 16,* 542–549.

Wang, S. S., & Brownell, K. D. (2005). Anorexia nervosa. In C. B. Fisher & R. M. Lerner (Eds.), *Encyclopedia of applied developmental science* (Vol. 1, pp. 83–85). Thousand Oaks, CA: Sage.

Wansink, B., & Sobal, J. (2007). Mindless eating: The 200 daily food decisions we overlook. *Environment and Behavior, 39,* 106–123.

Warneken, F., & Tomasello, M. (2006). Altruistic helping in human infants and young chimpanzees. *Science, 311,* 1301–1303.

Warner, B., Altimier, L., & Crombleholme, T. M. (2007). Fetal surgery. *Newborn and Infant Nursing Reviews, 7,* 181–188.

Warnock, F., & Sandrin, D. (2004). Comprehensive description of newborn distress behavior in response to acute pain (newborn male circumcision). *Pain, 107,* 242–255.

Warren, A. R., & McCloskey, L. A. (1993). Pragmatics: Language in social contexts. In J. Berko Gleason (Ed.), *The development of language* (3rd. ed., pp. 195–238). New York, NY: Macmillan.

Warren-Leubecker, A. & Bohannon, J. N. (1989). Pragmatics: Language in social contexts. In J. Berko Gleason (Ed.), *The development of language* (2nd ed., pp. 327–368). Columbus, OH: Merrill.

Waterhouse, L. (2006). Multiple intelligences, the Mozart effect, and emotional intelligence: A critical review. *Educational Psychologist, 41,* 207–225.

Waters, E., & Cummings, E. M. (2000). A secure base from which to explore close relationships. *Child Development, 71,* 164–172.

Waters, H. F. (1993, July 12). Networks under the gun. *Newsweek,* 64–66.

Waters, H. S. (1980). "Class news": A single-subject longitudinal study of prose production and schema formation during childhood. *Journal of Verbal Learning and Verbal Behavior, 19,* 152–167.

Waters, S. F., West, T. V., & Mendes, W. B. (2014). Stress contagion: Physiological covariation between mothers and infants. *Psychological Science, 25,* 934–942.

Watson, J. B. (1925). *Behaviorism.* New York, NY: Norton.

Watt, H. M. G., Shapka, J. D., Morris, Z. A., Durik, A. M., Keating, D. P., Eccles, J. S. (2012). Gendered motivational processes affecting high school mathematics participation, educational aspirations, and career plans: A comparison of samples from Australia, Canada, and the United States. *Developmental Psychology, 48*(6), 1594–1611. doi: 10.1037/a0027838

Watts, J. (2007, August 31). Chinese province has 165 boys per 100 girls. *Guardian Weekly,* p. 11.

Wax, J. R., Pinette, M. G., & Cartin, A. (2010). Home versus hospital birth: Process and outcome. *Obstetrical & Gynecological Survey, 65,* 132–140.

Waxman, S., Medin, D., & Ross, N. (2007). Folkbiological reasoning from a cross-cultural developmental perspective: Early essentialist notions are shaped by cultural beliefs. *Developmental Psychology, 43,* 294–308.

Webb, S. J., Monk, C. S., & Nelson, C. A. (2001). Mechanisms of postnatal neurobiological development: Implications for human development. Developmental Neuropsychology, 19, 147–171.

Webster-Stratton, C. H., Reid, M. J., & Beauchaine, T. (2011). Combining parent and child training for young children with ADHD. *Journal of Clinical Child and Adolescent Psychology, 40,* 191–203.

Weichold, K. & Silbereisen, R. K. (2005). Puberty. In C. B. Fisher & R. M. Lerner (Eds.), *Encyclopedia of applied developmental science* (Vol. 2, pp. 893–898). Thousand Oaks, CA: Sage.

Weinert, F. E., & Hany, E. A. (2003). The stability of individual differences in intellectual development: Empirical evidence, theoretical problems, and new research questions. In R. J. Sternberg, J. Lautrey, & T. I. Lubart (Eds.), *Models of intelligence: International perspectives* (pp. 169–181). Washington, DC: American Psychological Association.

Weisgram, E. S., Bigler, R. S., & Liben, L. S. (2010). Gender, values, and occupational interests among children, adolescents, and adults. *Child Development, 81,* 778–796.

Weisleder, A., & Fernald, A. (2013). Talking to children matters: Early language experience strengthens processing and builds vocabulary. *Psychological Science, 24,* 2143–2152.

Weisner, T. S. & Wilson-Mitchell, J. E. (1990). Nonconventional family lifestyles and sex typing in six-year-olds. *Child Development, 61,* 1915–1933.

Weisner, T. S., Garnier, H., & Loucky, J. (1994). Domestic tasks, gender egalitarian values and children's gender typing in conventional and nonconventional families. *Sex Roles, 30,* 23–54.

Weiss, M. R., & Smith, A. L. (2002). Moral development in sport and physical activity: Theory, research, and intervention. In T. S. Horn (Ed.), *Advances in sport psychology* (2nd ed., pp. 243–279). Champaign, IL: Human Kinetics.

Weissman, M. D. & Kalish, C. W. (1999). The inheritance of desired characteristics: Children's view of the role of intention in parent-offspring resemblance. *Journal of Experimental Child Psychology, 73,* 245–265.

Weisz, J. R., McCarty, C. A., & Valeri, S. M. (2006). Effects of psychotherapy for depression in children and adolescents: A meta-analysis. *Psychological Bulletin, 132,* 132–149.

Weizman, Z. O., & Snow, C. E. (2001). Lexical output as related to children's vocabulary acquisition: Effects of sophisticated exposure and support for meaning. *Developmental Psychology, 37,* 265–279.

Welder, A. N. (2000). Sexual abuse victimization and the child witness in Canada: Legal, ethical, and professional issues for psychologists. *Canadian Psychology/Psychologie canadienne, 41*(3), 160–173.

Wellman, H. M. (2002). Understanding the psychological world: Developing a theory of mind. In U. Goswami (Ed.), *Blackwell handbook of childhood cognitive development* (pp. 167–187). Malden, MA: Blackwell.

Wellman, H. M. (2011). Developing a theory of mind. In U. Goswami (Ed.), *The Wiley-Blackwell handbook of childhood cognitive development* (2nd ed., pp. 258–284). Chichester, UK: Wiley-Blackwell.

Wellman, H. M. (2012). Theory of mind: Better methods, clearer findings, more development. *European Journal of Developmental Psychology, 9,* 313–330.

Wellman, H. M. & Gelman, S. A. (1998). Knowledge acquisition in foundational domains. In W. Damon (Ed.), *Handbook of child psychology* (Vol. 2). New York, NY: Wiley.

Wentworth, N., Benson, J. B., & Haith, M. M. (2000). The development of infants' reaches for stationary and moving targets. *Child Development, 71,* 576–601.

Wentzel, K. R., Filisetti, L., & Looney, L. (2007). Adolescent prosocial behavior: The role of self-processes and contextual cues. *Child Development, 78,* 895–910.

Werker, J. (1989). Becoming a native listener. *American Scientist, 77,* 54–59.

Werker, J. F., Pons, F., Dietrich, C., Kajikawa, S., Fais, L., & Amano, S. (2007). Infant-directed speech supports phonetic category learning in English and Japanese. *Cognition, 103,* 147–162.

Werker, J. F., Yeung, H. H., & Yoshida, K. A. (2012). How do infants become experts at native-speech perception? *Current Directions in Psychological Science, 21,* 221–226.

Werner, E. E., & Smith, R. S. (2001). *Journeys from childhood to midlife: Risk, resilience, and recovery.* Ithaca, NY: Cornell University Press.

Werner, H. (1948). *Comparative psychology of mental development.* Chicago, IL: Follet.

Werner, N. E., Eaton, A. D., Lyle, K., Tseng, H., & Holst, B. (2014). Maternal social coaching quality interrupts the development of relational aggression during early childhood. *Social Development, 23,* 470–486.

Wertsch, J. V., & Tulviste, P. (1992). L. S. Vygotsky and contemporary developmental psychology. *Developmental Psychology, 28,* 548–557.

West, F., Sanders, M. R., Cleghorn, G. J., & Davies, P. S. W. (2010). Randomised clinical trial of a family-based lifestyle intervention for childhood obesity involving parents as the exclusive agents of change. *Behaviour Research and Therapy, 48,* 1170–1179.

West, S. G., Biesanz, J. C., & Pitts, S. C. (2000). Causal inference and generalization in field settings: Experimental and quasi-experimental designs. In H. T. Reis & C. M. Judd (Eds.), *Handbook of research methods in social and personality psychology* (pp. 40–84). New York, NY: Cambridge University Press.

Whitaker, K. J., Vértes, P. E., Romero-Garcia, R., Váša, F., Moutoussis, M., Preabhu, G., Weiskopf, N., Callaghan, M. F., …, Bullmore, E. T. (2016). Adolescence is associated with genomically patterned consolidation of the hubs of the human brain connectome. *Proceedings of the National Academy of Sciences (PNAS), 113*(32), 9105–9110.

Whitaker, R. C., Wright, J. A., Pepe, M. S., Seidel, K. D., & Dietz, W. H. (1997). Predicting obesity in young adulthood from childhood and parental obesity. *New England Journal of Medicine, 337,* 869–873.

White, F. A., Abu-Rayya, H. M., & Weitzel, C. (2014). Achieving twelve-months of intergroup bias reduction: The dual identity-electronic contact (DIEC) experiment. *International Journal of Intercultural Relations, 38,* 158–163.

White, L. & Gilbreth, J. G. (2001). When children have two fathers: Effects of relationships with stepfathers and noncustodial fathers on adolescent outcomes. *Journal of Marriage and the Family, 63,* 155–167.

White, S. H. (1996). The relationships of developmental psychology to social policy. In E. F. Zigler, S. L. Kagan, & N. W. Hall (Eds.), *Children, families, and government: Preparing for the twenty-first century.* New York, NY: Cambridge University Press.

Whitehurst, G. J., & Vasta, R. (1975). Is language acquired through imitation? *Journal of Psycholinguistic Research, 4,* 37–59.

Whiting, J. W. M., & Child, I. L. (1953). *Child training and personality: A cross-cultural study.* New Haven, CT: Yale University Press.

Wicks-Nelson, R., & Israel, A. C. (2006). *Behavior disorders of childhood* (6th ed.). Upper Saddle River, NJ: Pearson.

Widen, S. C., & Russell, J. A. (2013). Children's recognition of disgust in others. *Psychological Bulletin, 139,* 271–299.

Wie, O. B., Falkenberg, E.-S., Tvete, O., & Tomblin, B. (2007). Children with a cochlear implant: Characteristics and determinants of speech recognition, speech-recognition growth rate, and speech production. *International Journal of Audiology, 46,* 232–243.

Wiegers, T. A., van der Zee, J., & Keirse, M. J. (1998). Maternity care in the Netherlands: The changing home birth rate. *Birth, 25,* 190–197.

Willatts, P. (1999). Development of means–end behavior in young infants: Pulling a support to retrieve a distant object? *Developmental Psychology, 35,* 651–667.

Williams, J. E., & Best, D. L. (1990). *Measuring sex stereotypes: A thirty-nation study* (rev. ed.). Newbury Park, CA: Sage.

Williams, S. T., Conger, K. J., & Blozis, S. A. (2007). The development of interpersonal aggression during adolescence: The importance of parents, siblings, and family economics. *Child Development, 78,* 1526–1542.

Williams, T. L., & Davidson, D. (2009). Interracial and intra-racial stereotypes and constructive memory in 7- and 9-year-old African-American children. *Journal of Applied Developmental Psychology, 30,* 366–377.

Willoughby, T., Adachi, P. J. C., & Good, M. (2012). A longitudinal study of the association between violent video game play and aggression among adolescents. *Developmental Psychology, 48,* 1044–1057.

Willoughby, T., Porter, L., Belsito, L, & Yearsley, T. (1999). Use of elaboration strategies by students in grades two, four, and six. *The Elementary School Journal, 99*(3), 221–232.

Wills, T. A., Sandy, J. M., Yaeger, A., & Shinar, O. (2001). Family risk factors and adolescent substance use: Moderation effects for temperament dimensions. *Developmental Psychology, 37,* 283–297.

Wilson, B. J., Smith, S. L., Potter, W. J., Kunkel, D., Linz, D., Colvin, C. M., & Donnerstein, E. (2002). Violence in children's television programming: Assessing the risks. *Journal of Communication, 52,* 5–35.

Wilson, E. O. (2000). *Sociobiology: The new synthesis, 25th Anniversary Edition.* Cambridge, MA: Harvard University Press.

Wilson, G. T., Heffernan, K., & Black, C. M. D. (1996). Eating disorders. In E. J. Marsh & R. A. Barkley (Eds.), *Child psychopathology.* New York, NY: Guilford Press.

Wilson, R. D. (2000). Amniocentesis and chorionic villus sampling. *Current Opinion in Obstetrics and Gynecology, 12,* 81–86.

Winner, E. (2000). Giftedness: Current theory and research. *Current Directions in Psychological Science, 9,* 153–156.

Witherspoon, D., Schotland, M., Way, N., & Hughes, D. (2009). Connecting the dots: How connectedness to multiple contexts influences the psychological and academic adjustment of urban youth. *Applied Developmental Science, 13,* 199–216.

Wolfe, C. D., & Bell, M. A. (2007). Sources of variability in working memory in early childhood: A consideration of age, temperament, language, and brain electrical activity. *Cognitive Development, 22,* 431–455.

Wolfe, D. A. (1985). Child-abusive parents: An empirical review and analysis. *Psychological Bulletin, 97,* 462–482.

Wolff, P. H. (1987). *The development of behavioral states and the expression of emotions in early infancy.* Chicago, IL: University of Chicago Press.

Wolke, D., Copeland, W. E., Angold, A., & Costello, E. J. (2013). Impact of bullying on adult health, wealth, crime, and social outcomes. *Psychological Science, 24,* 1958–1970.

Wolke, D., Woods, S., & Samara, M. (2009). Who escapes or remains a victim of bullying? *British Journal of Developmental Psychology, 27,* 835–851.

Wolpe, D., Johnson, S., Jaekel, J., & Gilmore, C. (n.d.). The impact of premature birth on maths achievement and schooling. Nuffield Foundation. Retrieved from www.nuffieldfoundation.org/impact-premature-birth-maths-achievement-and-schooling

Wolraich, M. L., Lindgren, S. D., Stumbo, P. J., Stegink, L. D., Appelbaum, M. I., & Kiritsy, M. C. (1994). Effects of diets high in sucrose or aspartame on the behavior and cognitive performance of children. *New England Journal of Medicine, 330,* 301–307.

Women's Hospital Manitoba. (n.d.). Kangaroo Care: The human incubator for the premature infant. Retrieved from www.umanitoba.ca/womens_health/kangaroo.htm

Wong-Fillmore, L., Ammon, P., McLaughlin, B., & Ammon, M. S. (1985). *Learning English through bilingual instruction*. Rosslyn, VA: National Clearinghouse for Bilingual Education.

Woodward, A. L. (2009). Infants' grasp of others' intention. *Current Directions in Psychological Science, 18,* 53–57.

Woodward, A. L., & Markman, E. M. (1998). Early word learning. In W. Damon (Ed.), *Handbook of child psychology* (Vol. 2). New York, NY: Wiley.

World Health Organization (WHO). (2004). *The analytic review of the integrated management of childhood illness strategy*. Geneva, Switzerland: Author.

World Health Organization (WHO). (2005). Report on the Regional consultation towards the development of a strategy for optimizing fetal growth and development. Retrieved from www.who.int/nutrition/publications/FinalReportRegCons.pdf

World Health Organization (WHO). (2012). *Recommendations for management of common childhood conditions*. Geneva, Switzerland: Author.

World Health Organization (WHO). (2013a). *Growth reference 5–19 years: WHO 2007*. Retrieved from www.who.int/growthref/en/

World Health Organization (WHO). (2013b). *World health statistics 2013*. Geneva, Switzerland: Author. Retrieved from www.who.int/gho/publications/world_health_statistics/2013/en

World Health Organization (WHO). (2015). Global health trends: Infant mortality. Retrieved from www.who.int/gho/child_health/mortality/neonatal_infant_text/en/

World Health Organization (WHO). (2017). *Maternal, newborn, child and adolescent health: Breastfeeding*. Retrieved from www.who.int/maternal_child_adolescent/topics/newborn/nutrition/breastfeeding/en/

Worobey, J. (2005). Effects of malnutrition. In C. B. Fisher & R. M. Lerner (Eds.), *Encyclopedia of applied developmental science* (Vol. 2, pp. 673–676). Thousand Oaks, CA: Sage.

Worthman, C. M., & Brown, R. A. (2007). Companionable sleep: Social regulation of sleep and cosleeping in Egyptian families. *Journal of Family Psychology, 21,* 124–135.

Wray-Lake, L., Crouter, A. C., & McHale, S. M. (2010). Developmental patterns in decision-making autonomy across middle childhood and adolescence: European American parents' perspectives. *Child Development, 81,* 636–651.

Wright, J. C., Huston, A. C., Murphy, K. C., St. Peters, M., Piñon, M., Scantlin, R., et al. (2001). The relations of early television viewing to school readiness and vocabulary of children from low-income families: The Early Window Project. *Child Development, 72,* 1347–1366.

Wright, M. J. (1983). *Compensatory education in the preschool*. Ypsilanti, MI: High/Scope Press.

Wright, M. J. (1992). Women ground-breakers in Canadian psychology: World War II and its aftermath. *Canadian Psychology, 33*(4), 675–682.

Wynn, K. (1992). Addition and subtraction by human infants. *Nature, 358,* 749–750.

Wynn, K. (1996). Infants' individuation and enumeration of actions. *Psychological Science, 7,* 164–169.

Xie, H., Li, Y., Boucher, S. M., Hutchins, B. C., & Cairns, B. D. (2006). What makes a girl (or a boy) popular (or unpopular)? African American children's perceptions and developmental differences. *Developmental Psychology, 42,* 599–612.

Xu, Y., Farver, J. A., & Zhang, Z. (2009). Temperament, harsh and indulgent parenting, and Chinese children's proactive and reactive aggression. *Child Development, 80,* 244–258.

Yap, M. B. H., Allen, N. B., & Ladouceur, C. D. (2008). Maternal socialization of positive affect: The impact of invalidation on adolescent emotion regulation and depressive symptomatology. *Child Development, 79,* 1415–1431.

Yau, J., Smetana, J. G., & Metzger, A. (2009). Young Chinese children's authority concepts. *Social Development, 18,* 210–229.

Yoshida, K. A., Pons, F., Maye, J., 7 Werker, J. F. (2010). Distributional phonetic learning at 10 months of age. *Infancy, 15*(4), 420–433.

Young, S. K., Fox, N. A., & Zahn-Waxler, C. (1999). The relations between temperament and empathy in 2-year-olds. *Developmental Psychology, 35,* 1189–1197.

Youniss, J., McLellan, J. A., & Yates, M. (1999). Religion, community service, and identity in American youth. *Journal of Adolescence, 22,* 243–253.

Yuan, S., & Fisher, C. (2009). "Really? She blicked the baby?": Two-year-olds learn combinatorial facts about verbs by listening. *Psychological Science, 20,* 619–626.

Yumoto, C., Jacobson, S. W., & Jacobson, J. L. (2008). Fetal substance exposure and cumulative environmental risk in an African American cohort. *Child Development, 79,* 1761–1776.

Zahn-Waxler, C., Radke-Yarrow, M., Wagner, E., & Chapman, M. (1992). Development of concern for others. *Developmental Psychology, 28,* 126–136.

Zalewski, M., Lengua, L. J., Wilson, A. C., Trancik, A., & Bazinet, A. (2011). Emotion regulation profiles, temperament, and adjustment problems in preadolescents. *Child Development, 82,* 951–966.

Zarbatany, L., Hartmann, D. P., & Rankin, D. B. (1990). The psychological functions of preadolescent peer activities. *Child Development, 61,* 1067–1080.

Zelazo, P. D., & Cunningham, W. A. (2007). Executive function: Mechanisms underlying emotion regulation. In J. J. Gross (Ed.), *Handbook of emotion regulation* (pp. 135–158). New York, NY: Guilford Press.

Zelazo, P. D., Anderson, J. E., Richler, J., Wallner-Allen, K., Beaumont, J. L., & Weintraub, S. (2013). NIH Toolbox Cognition Battery (CB): Measuring executive function and attention. In P. D. Zelazo and P. J. Bauer (Eds.), National Institutes of Health Toolbox Cognition Battery (NIH Toolbox CB): Validation for children between 3 and 15 years. *Monographs of the Society for Research in Child Development, 78*(Serial No. 309), 16–33.

Zemach, I., Chang, S., & Teller, D. (2007). Infant color vision: Prediction of infants' spontaneous color preferences. *Vision Research, 47,* 1368–1381.

Zeman, J., & Garber, J. (1996). Display rules for anger, sadness, and pain: It depends on who is watching. *Child Development, 67,* 957–973.

Zeman, J., & Shipman, K. (1997). Social-contextual influences on expectancies for managing anger and sadness: The transition from middle childhood to adolescence. *Developmental Psychology, 33,* 917–924.

Zhang, B., Cartmill, C., & Ferrence, R. (2008). The role of spending money and drinking alcohol in adolescent smoking. *Addiction, 103,* 310–319.

Zhang, F., & Liu, S. (2012). Kangaroo mother care may help oral growth and development in premature infants. *Fetal and Pediatric Pathology, 31,* 191–194.

Zhou, Q., Eisenberg, N., Losoya, S. H., Fabes, R. A., Reiser, M., Guthrie, I. K., et al. (2002). The relations of parental warmth and positive expressiveness to children's empathy-related responding and social functioning: A longitudinal study. *Child Development, 73,* 893–915.

Zhou, Q., Lengua, L., & Wang, Y. (2009). The relations of temperament reactivity and effortful control to children's adjustment problems in China and the United States. *Developmental Psychology, 45,* 724–739.

Zhou, Q., Wang, Y., Eisenberg, N., Wolchik, S., Tein, J-W., & Deng, X. (2008). Relations of parenting and temperament to Chinese children's experience of negative life events, coping efficacy, and externalizing problems. *Child Development, 79,* 493–513.

Zhu, J. L., Madsen, K. M., Vestergaard, M., Olesen, A. V., Basso, O., & Olsen, J. (2005). Paternal age and congenital malformations. *Human Reproduction, 20*(11), 3173–3177.

Ziegler, J. C., Bertrand, D., Tóth, D., Csépe, V., Reis, A., Faísca, L., et al. (2010). Orthographic depth and its impact on universal predictors of reading: A cross-language investigation. *Psychological Science, 21,* 551–559.

Zigler, E. (1998). A place of value for applied and policy studies. *Child Development, 69,* 532–542.

Zigler, E. F., & Muenchow, S. (1992). *Head Start: Inside story of America's most successful educational experiment*. New York, NY: Basic Books.

Zigler, E., & Finn-Stevenson, M. (1992). Applied developmental psychology. In M. H. Bornstein & M. E. Lamb (Eds.), *Developmental psychology: An advanced textbook*. Hillsdale, NJ: Erlbaum.

Zimiles, H., & Lee, V. E. (1991). Adolescent family structure and educational progress. *Developmental Psychology, 27,* 314–320.

Zimmer-Gembeck, M. J., & Helfand, M. (2008). Ten years of longitudinal research on U.S. adolescent sexual behavior: Developmental correlates of sexual intercourse, and the importance of age, gender and ethnic background. *Developmental Review, 28,* 153–224.

Zimmer-Gembeck, M. J. & Skinner, E. A. (2011). The development of coping across childhood and adolescence: An integrative review and critique of research. *International Journal of Behavioral Development, 35,* 1–17.

Zimmer-Gembeck, M. J., Seibenbruner, J., & Collins, W. A. (2001). Diverse aspects of dating: Associations with psychosocial functioning from early to middle adolescence. *Journal of Adolescence, 24,* 313–336.

Zimmerman, B. J. (2001). Theories of self-regulated learning and academic achievement: An overview and analysis. In B. J. Zimmerman & D. H. Schunk (Eds.), *Self-regulated learning and academic achievement: Theoretical perspectives* (2nd ed., pp. 1–37). Mahwah, NJ: Erlbaum.

Zimmerman, C. (2007). The development of scientific thinking skills in elementary and middle school. *Developmental Review, 27,* 172–223.

Zinar, S. (2000). The relative contributions of word identification skill and comprehension-monitoring behavior to reading comprehension ability. *Contemporary Educational Psychology, 25,* 363–377.

Zivin, G., Hassan, N. R., DePaula, G. F., Monti, D. A., Harlan, C., Hossein, K. D., & Patterson, K. (2001). An effective approach to violence prevention: Traditional martial arts in middle school. *Adolescence, 36*(143), 443–459.

Zohsel, K., Buchmann, A. F., Blomeyer, D., Hohm, E., Schmidt, M. H., Esser, G., et al. (2014). Mothers' prenatal stress and their children's antisocial outcomes: A moderating role for the dopamine receptor D4 (DRD4) gene. *Journal of Child Psychology and Psychiatry, 55,* 69–76.

Zosuls, K. M., Ruble, D. N., & Tamis-Lemonda, C. S. (2014). Self-socialization of gender in African American, Dominican immigrant, and Mexican immigrant toddlers. *Child Development, 85,* 2202–2217. doi: 10.1111/cdev.12261

Zosuls, K. M., Ruble, D. N., Tamis-LeMonda, C. S., Shrout, P. E., Bornstein, M. H., & Greulich, F. K. (2009). The acquisition of gender labels in infancy: Implications for gender-typed play. *Developmental Psychology, 45,* 688–701.

Zucker, R. A., Heitzeg, M. M., & Nigg, J. T. (2011). Parsing the undercontrol-disinhibition pathway to substance use disorders: A multilevel developmental problem. *Child Development Perspectives, 5,* 248–255.

Zuckerman, M. & Brody, N. (1988). Oysters, rabbits and people: A critique of "Race differences in behaviour" by J. P. Rushton. *Personality and Individual Differences, 9*(6), 1025–1033.

Zukow-Goldring, P. (2002). Sibling caregiving. In M. H. Bornstein (Ed.), *Handbook of parenting: Vol. 3. Status and social conditions of parenting* (2nd ed., pp. 253–286). Mahwah, NJ: Erlbaum.

Name Index

Abbas, A. K., 49
Abbott, R. D., 255
Abbott, S. P., 255
Abels, M., 235
Aber, J., 381
Abikoff, H., 174
Ablin, D. S., 235
Aboud, F. E., 396, 398
Abrams, D., 397
Abu-Rayya, H. M., 399
Achy-Brou, A., 77
Ackerman, B. P., 336, 346, 526
Acredolo, L. P., 312
Adachi, P. J. C., 430
Adajian, L. B., 455
Adam, E. K., 17, 125, 488
Adam, T., 141
Adams, E., 417
Adams, J. W., 94, 253
Adams, M. J., 254
Adams, R. E., 512
Adams, R. J., 162
Adelstein, S., 288
Adlaf, E. M., 140, 427, 436
Adler, R., 108
Adlestein, A., 340
Adolph, K. E., 167, 177, 178, 179, 180
Adolphus, K., 137
Adzick, N. S., 98
af Klinteberg, B., 385
Afifi, T. O., 458, 500
Agnoli, F., 245
Agras, W. S., 137
Aguardo, G., 221
Ahmed, T., 136
Ainsworth, M. D. S., 364
Akhtar, N., 320
Akmal, N., 313
Akré, C., 138
Aksan, N., 347, 358
Al-Sahab, B., 130
Alampay, L. P., 480
Alanen, E., 438
Alatupa, S., 427
Alberts, A. E., 110
Aldao, A., 457
Alden, A. R., 453
Alderson, J. A., 391, 448
Aldridge, V., 127

Alexander, G. M., 448, 450, 457
Alibali, M. W., 198, 206, 246, 252
Alink, L. R. A., 499
Alisat, S., 479
Alkawaf, R., 159
Allen, J. P., 484, 518, 530
Allen, L., 318, 381
Allen, N. B., 385
Allison, C., 457
Allison, K., 140
Almas, A. N., 151
Alphonso, C., 437
Alter, A. L., 291
Altemeier, W. A., 502
Altimier, L., 98
Altman, J., 487
Altmann, T. R., 430
Altschul, I., 428
Alves, R. A., 255
Amano, S., 308
Amato, P. R., 479, 487, 488
Ambady, N., 397
Ames, A., 430
Ammon, M. S., 322
Ammon, P., 322
Amodio, D. M., 467
Amorrim, M. M. R. S., 87
Amso, D., 166
Amsterlaw, J., 351
Anastasi, A., 289, 290
Ancel, P-Y., 106
Anderson, C. A., 247, 430
Anderson, C. J., 381
Anderson, D. I., 169, 179
Anderson, D. R., 266
Anderson, E., 335
Anderson, J. E., 172
Anderson, S. W., 146
André, M., 106
Andreatos, M., 310
Andrew, G., 89
Andrews, G., 206
Andruski, J. E., 308
Añez, E. V., 127
Ang, W., 132
Angold, A., 437
Ani, C., 137
Ansari, D., 258
Anzures, G., 170
Apfel, N., 291

Apfelbaum, E. P., 397
Apgar, V., 110
Appelbaum, M. I., 73
Appleyard, K., 368, 426, 499, 501
Arabi, M., 126
Arbeau, K. A., 82
Archer, J., 456, 457, 502
Archer, T., 469
Arcus, D., 357
Ardern, C. I., 130
Argenti, A.-M., 170
Armer, M., 508
Armstrong, I. T., 90
Armstrong, L. L., 183
Armstrong, L. M., 352
Arnaud, C., 106
Arndorfer, C. L., 511
Arnold, A. P., 468
Arnold, L. E., 173, 174
Aronson, J. M., 286, 287, 288, 289, 290, 291, 449, 450
Arseneault, L., 105, 359
Arsenio, W. F., 417
Arterberry, M. E., 161, 162, 166, 168, 350
Arunachalam, S., 314
Asare, M., 182
Asbridge, M., 91
Asendorpf, J. B., 427
Asgari, S., 455
Ashcraft, M. H., 260
Asher, S. R., 511, 512
Ashmead, D. H., 180
Ashmore, R. D., 516
Aslin, R. N., 166, 305, 306, 307
Aspenlieder, L., 462
Aster, J. C., 49
Astill, R. G., 125
Atella, L. D., 83
Atkinson, L., 366
Atkinson, R., 384
Attanucci, J., 414
Attar-Schwartz, S., 491
Attaran, A., 87
Atwood, M., 436
Au, T. K., 313
Audley-Piotrowski, S., 519
Aunola, K., 479
Auricchio, A., 99

Austin, C. M., 308
Austin-LaFrance, R., 136
Averill, J. A., 345
Avula, R., 126
Awong, T., 391
Axelson, H., 141
Ayduk, O., 406, 408
Ayers, T., 489
Ayers-Lopez, S., 496
Azaiza, F., 384
Aziz, A., 138
Azurmendi, A., 479

Bacchini, D., 480
Bachman, H. J., 530
Bachman, J. G., 524
Backscheider, A. G., 215
Badaly, D., 178
Baddeley, A. D., 206, 317
Badzakova-Trajkova, G., 181
Baenninger, M., 453
Bagwell, C. L., 512, 513
Bahrick, L. E., 163, 164, 350
Bailey, D. A., 184
Bailey, H. N., 368
Bailey, J. A., 481
Bailey, J. M., 516
Baillargeon, R. H., 212, 213, 416, 456
Baird, D. D., 85
Bakeman, R., 349
Baker, L., 253, 255
Baker, P. N., 83
Bakermans-Kranenburg, M. J., 66, 356, 365, 367, 368, 421
Bakiyeva, L., 105
Bakken, J. P., 509
Bala, N., 240
Baldwin, D. A., 350
Bales, S. N., 6
Bámaca-Colbert, M. Y., 390
Banaji, M. R., 397, 467
Bandura, A., 13, 461
Banerjee, R., 351, 396, 499
Banich, M., 377
Bankole, A., 515
Banks, M. S., 165
Bannard, C., 330
Banny, A. M., 430
Banse, R., 446
Baptista, M., 329

Subject Index

Aamjiwnaang people, 91–92
Aboriginal Head Start (AHS) program, 287–288
Aboriginal Head Start in Reserve (AHSOR) program, 287
Aboriginal peoples. *See* First Nations peoples
abstract principles, 412
abuse. *See* maltreatment
academic skills
   educational implications of cross-cultural findings, 264–265
   low academic self-esteem, 391–392
   numbers, 255–265
   reading, 248–253
   scholastic competence, 387, 400
   writing, 253–255
accidents, 141–142
accommodation, 190
acculturation, 382–383
the Ache of Paraguay, 179
achievement, 379
Action Schools! BC program, 140
Active Healthy Kids Canada, 140
active-passive child issue, 21, 222, 268, 370
adaptation to environment, 191–192
adaptive emotions, 346
addition, 256–257, 257*f*, 259–260
adolescent egocentrism, 378
adolescents
   adolescent egocentrism, 378
   depression, 385, 458
   emotional regulation, 352
   ethnic identity, 380–383
   friendship, 510–514
   growth spurt, 128–135
   identity, search for, 378–385
   identity crisis, 379
   illusion of invulnerability, 379
   imaginary audience, 378
   immigrant youth, identity and acculturation of, 382–383
   interpersonal norms, 412
   leading cause of death, 142
   and life stressors, 360
   menarche, 130, 132
   moral reasoning and behaviour, 419
   parents, influence of, 380
   part-time employment, 523–525
   peer relations, 510
   personal fable, 378–379
   prejudice, 399
   problem solving, 242, 244–245
   psychological impact of puberty, 134–135
   puberty, 128–135
   and religion, 419
   rites of passage, 131
   romantic relationships, 514–516
   self-concept, 377
   self-esteem, 387–388
   sexual behaviour, 514–515
   sexual maturation, 128, 130
   sexual orientation, 515–516
   sleep problems, 125
   spermarche, 130
   storm and stress, 384–385
   teenage pregnancy, 83–85, 515
adopted children, 496
adoption studies, 63–64, 63*t*, 64*t*
affluence, 524
Afghanistan, 107
Africa
   average physical growth in, 124
   childhood deaths in, 140
   cultural practices and motor skill, 178, 179, 179*f*
   Efe parents, 15
gestures used to communicate, 338
African American English, 335
African Americans, 142
   ethnic identity, 381, 389
   segregated schooling, 399–400
   self-affirmation, 291
   self-esteem, 389
   stereotype threat, 291–292
African Canadians
   sickle-cell disease, 54
   socioeconomic status, 288
   stereotype threat, 290–291
African American English, 335
after school activities, 521–523
age, and parenting, 485
Age of Enlightenment, 4
age of viability, 77*f*, 78
aggression, 426
   biological contributions, 428
   change and stability, 426–427
   cognitive processes, 431–433
   community, influence of, 429–431
   cultural influences, 429–431
   culture of violence, 431
   defined, 426
   family, impact of, 428–429
   and friendship, 513
   gender differences, 456
   hostile aggression, 426
   instrumental aggression, 426
   multiple, cascading risks, 434
   peers, influence of, 430
   and poverty, 431
   reactive aggression, 426
   relational aggression, 426–427
   roots of aggressive behaviour, 427–434
   and school failure, 430–431
   sibling aggression, 456
   social-information-processing theory, 432–433
   socialized aggression, 434
   stability over time, 427
   television and video games, 429–430
   victims of aggression, 436–438
aggressive behaviour. *See* aggression
AIDS, 87, 87*t*
albinism, 55*t*
alcohol, 89–90
alcohol-related neurodevelopmental disorder (ARND), 90
alert inactivity, 111
alleles, 53, 53*f*
allophones, 322
altruism, 420, 422
   see also prosocial behaviour
American Academy of Pediatrics (AAP), 114, 499
American Association for the Advancement of Science (AAAS), 6
American Psychological Association (APA), 5, 40, 41
American Sign Language (ASL), 303, 322, 338–339, 340
amniocentesis, 96, 97–98, 97*f*, 98*t*
amniotic fluid, 76, 77, 97, 100
amniotic sac, 76, 81, 97
amodal, 163
amodal information, 163
analytic ability, 277
androgens, 130, 131, 456, 468
androgynous, 469–470
anger, 346–347, 349, 351, 352, 358
Angola, 107
animism, 193